GENDERED LIVES: INTERSECTIONAL PERSPECTIVES

SEVENTH EDITION

GWYN KIRK AND MARGO OKAZAWA-REY

NEW YORK   OXFORD

OXFORD UNIVERSITY PRESS

Oxford University Press is a department of the University of Oxford.
It furthers the University's objective of excellence in research, scholarship,
and education by publishing worldwide. Oxford is a registered trade mark of
Oxford University Press in the UK and certain other countries.

Published in the United States of America by Oxford University Press
198 Madison Avenue, New York, NY 10016, United States of America.

Library of Congress Cataloging-in-Publication Data

Names: Kirk, Gwyn, author. | Okazawa-Rey, Margo, author.
Title: Gendered lives : intersectional perspectives / Gwyn Kirk and Margo
  Okazawa-Rey.
Other titles: Women's lives
Description: Seventh edition. | New York : Oxford University Press, [2020]
Identifiers: LCCN 2019017536 | ISBN 9780190928285 (pbk.)
Subjects: LCSH: Women—United States—Social conditions. |
Women—United States—Economic conditions. | Feminism—United States.
Classification: LCC HQ1421 .K573 2020 | DDC 305.420973—dc23 LC record available at
https://lccn.loc.gov/2019017536

Printing number: 9 8 7 6 5 4 3 2 1
Printed by Sheridian Books, Inc., United States of America

To those who connect us to the past,
women who birthed us, raised us,
taught us, inspired us, held us to high standards, and loved us
Edwina Davies, Kazuko Okazawa, Willa Mae Wells, and Yoko Lee.
We also honor Eiko Matsuoka, our extraordinary Bay Area mother,
and the late Maha Abu-Dayyeh, visionary feminist and human rights
defender, who dedicated her life to the liberation of Palestine and
Palestinian women.

To those who connect us to the future
Jeju Daisy Ahn Miles
Charlotte Elizabeth Andrews-Briscoe
Irys Philippa Ewuraba Casey
Zion Neil Akyedzi Casey
Gabrielle Raya Clancy-Humphrey
Jesse Simon Cool
Mitchell Stephen Davies-Munden
William Marshall Davies-Munden
Dominica Rose Edwards (Devecka-Rinear Smiley)
Issac Kana Fukumura-White
Akani Kazuo Ai Lee James
Ayize Kimani Ming Lee James
Hansoo Lim
Maple Elenore McIntire
Uma Talpade Mohanty
Ali Nakhleh, Yasmin Nakhleh, Zaina Nakhleh, Tala Nakhleh,
Ingrid Elisabet Pansini-Jokela
Sara Refai, Adam Refai, Rita Refai
Maven Jude Riding In
May Maha Shamas
Alma Shawa, Hani Shawa
Keziah Sade Story
Camille Celestina Stovall-Ceja
Aya Sato Venet

BRIEF CONTENTS

CONTENTS

PART II   **OUR BODIES, OURSELVES**   *137*

PART III   HOME AND WORK IN A GLOBALIZING WORLD   289

CHAPTER 7   Making a Home, Making a Living   290

CHAPTER 10   Gender, Militarism, War, and Peace   437

PREFACE

An introductory course is perhaps the most challenging women's and gender studies (WGS) course to conceptualize and teach. Depending on their overall goals for the course, instructors must make difficult choices about what to include and what to leave out. Students come into the course for a variety of reasons and with a range of expectations and prior knowledge, and most will not major in WGS. The course may fulfill a distribution requirement for them, or it may be a way of taking one course during their undergraduate education out of a personal interest in gender. For majors and minors, the course plays a very different role, offering a foundation for their area of study.

This text started out as two separate readers that we used in our classes at Antioch College (Gwyn Kirk) and San Francisco State University (Margo Okazawa-Rey) in the mid-1990s. Since then, we have learned a lot about teaching an introductory course, and the book has grown and developed as understandings of gender—and the wider political climate—have changed.

Women's and gender studies programs continue to build their reputations in terms of academic rigor and scholarly standards. WGS scholarship is on the cutting edge of many disciplines and interdisciplinary fields, especially in the arts, humanities, and social sciences. At the same time, it occupies a marginal position within academia, challenging male-dominated knowledge and pedagogy, with all the pressures that entails. WGS faculty and allies live with these tensions personally and professionally. Outside the academy, government policies and economic changes have made many people's lives more difficult. This includes the loss of factory and office work as jobs continue to be moved overseas or become automated; government failure to introduce and support adequate health care and child care systems; cuts in various social-service programs and funding for education; hostility toward and greater restriction of government support, when available, to immigrants and their families; large numbers of people incarcerated; and vast expenditures on war and preparations for war.

In the past decade, the political climate for WGS on campuses and in the wider society has become more challenging as conservative viewpoints have gained ground through political rhetoric and the narrow range of public discourse. In addition, a slow erosion of academic freedom on campuses has made many teachers' lives more difficult. Increasingly, faculty may face challenges to their teaching methods and course content; their work may be written off as "biased," unscholarly, or politically motivated (Nisenson 2017). Also, academic institutions have become increasingly beholden to corporate funding and values. Budget cuts, department mergers, and the fact that more than two-thirds of faculty are on part-time or temporary contracts these days all affect the organization and viability of interdisciplinary programs like WGS.

The current Federal administration's destruction of already inadequate "safety nets," contempt for the natural environment, support for overtly racist, sexist, trans- and homophobic attacks, and the daily circulation of distortions, half-truths, and out-right lies all challenge us profoundly. This is not new, especially for indigenous people on this continent, for other communities of color, and for those in subjugated nations, but it has become starker, more clear-cut, and increasingly affects many of us with rela-tive access and privilege. What to think? Where to focus? How to respond to one crisis after another? As students, how to support your friends, peers, and families as they ex-perience direct and indirect impacts? As faculty, how to support students trying to find their footing in this maelstrom?

We believe that our job as feminist scholars and teachers is to think big, to help provide spaces where students can think clearly and face current challenges. The strong tradition of organizing for social justice in the United States needs to be much better known, as well as the many efforts underway today. They provide lessons, models, and inspiration. We cannot afford to despair or to nurture despair in others. We must remember the gains made in the past and continue to work for and hold out the pos-sibility of progressive change even as past gains are being attacked and unraveled. A silver lining in this turbulent time is that even as some political spaces are being closed down, new social movements are opening up others.

WHAT WE WANT IN AN INTRODUCTORY WOMEN'S AND GENDER STUDIES BOOK

As teachers, we want to present a broad range of gendered experiences to students in terms of class, race, culture, national origin, dis/ability, age, sexuality, and gender iden-tity and expression. We want teaching materials that do justice to the diversity of US women's lives—whether queer, femme, lesbian, gender nonconforming, or trans, as well as heterosexual and cisgender women. We also want materials that address the lo-cation of the United States in a globalizing world. We include some discussion of theory because a basic understanding of theoretical frameworks is a powerful tool, not only for WGS courses but also for other courses students take. We also emphasize activism. There are many women's and LGBTQI activist and advocacy projects across the United States, but students may not know about them. Much of the information that students learn in WGS may be discouraging, but knowing what people are doing to support each other and to promote feminist values and concerns can be empowering, even in the face of sometimes daunting realities. This knowledge reinforces the idea that current inequalities and problems are not fixed but have the potential to be changed.

LINKING INDIVIDUAL EXPERIENCES TO NATIONAL AND TRANSNATIONAL TRENDS AND ISSUES

We are both trained in sociology, and we have noted that students coming into our classes are much more familiar with psychological explanations for behaviors and ex-periences than they are with structural explanations. People in the United States tend to see inequality and injustice in terms of low self-esteem, poor identity development, learned helplessness, or the work of a few "bad apples" that spoil the barrel. Students invariably enjoy first-person accounts of life experiences, but a series of stories—even wonderfully insightful stories—are not enough to understand the circumstances and forces that shape people's lives. Accordingly, we provide a broader context for the selected readings in the overview essays that open each chapter.

We recognize that many women in the United States—especially white, cisgendered women in higher socioeconomic groups—have greater opportunities for self-expression, for earning a living, and for engagement in the wider world compared with in the past. However, humankind faces serious challenges in the twenty-first century: challenges regarding work and livelihood, personal and family relationships, violence on many levels, and the mounting pressures on the fragile natural environment. These issues raise major questions about personal and societal values and the distribution of resources. How is our society going to provide for people in the years to come? What are the effects of the increasing polarization between rich and poor in the United States and between richer and poorer nations? These themes of security and sustainability provide the wider framework for this book.

As teachers, we are concerned with students' knowledge and understanding and, beyond that, with their aspirations, hopes, and values, as well as their fears. One of our goals for this book is to provide a series of lenses that will help students understand their own lives and the lives of others. A second goal is that through this understanding, students will be able to participate, in some way, in the creation of a genuinely secure and sustainable future.

NEW TO THE SEVENTH EDITION

This seventh edition of what was formerly *Women's Lives: Multicultural Perspectives*, now renamed *Gendered Lives: Intersectional Perspectives*, has undergone a major revision. We rely on the analyses, principles, and style of earlier editions, but with substantial changes to take account of recent scholarship and events. Specific changes include:

- A greater emphasis on gender identity and gender variance to show how trans activists and scholars have challenged, unsettled, and transformed previous understandings of gender.
- An expanded chapter, "Creating Knowledge," that includes greater discussion of media representations and the role of mass media in the creation of knowledge. In other chapters, we include several articles about media representations to further this discussion.
- Greater emphasis on the insights of dis/ability activists and scholarship, following new developments in this field in recent years.
- Inclusion of materials on Web-based information technologies, especially their impacts on sexualized violence, transnational surrogacy, and feminist organizing.
- Greater emphasis on the transnational and global levels of analysis, including attention to the impact of extractivism in the Global South, barriers to immigration in Europe and the United States, and effects of environmental destruction, war, and militarism worldwide.

- Updated statistics throughout, as well as updated information on activist organizations.
- In our overview essays, reference clusters on particular topics, often spanning years of feminist scholarship. As well as supporting the arguments we make, these also serve as suggestions for further reading.
- A revised and updated, password-protected Instructor's Manual—including alternative Tables of Contents for flexible use of the book—available on our companion website (www.oup.com/us/kirk-okazawa-rey).

A number of considerations, sometimes competing or contradictory, have influenced the decisions we made to ensure this edition meets our goals. Since the beginning, we have been committed to including the work of established scholars and lesser-known writers from a range of backgrounds. As in previous editions, we have looked for writers who integrate several levels of analysis (micro, meso, macro, and global) in their work. Students we have talked with, including those in our own classes, love first-person accounts, and such narratives help to draw them into more theoretical discussions. In our experience, teachers invariably want more theory, more history, and more research-based pieces.

As we searched for materials, we found much more theoretical work by white women in the US than by women of color. We assume this is because there are fewer women of color in the academy, because white scholars and writers have greater access to publishers, and because prevailing ideas about what theory is and what form it should take tend to exclude cross-genre work by women of color. This can give the misleading impression that aside from a few notable exceptions, women of color are not theorists. We have tried not to reproduce this bias in our selection, but we note this issue here to make this aspect of our process visible. We include personal essays and narratives that make theoretical points, what scholar and writer Gloria Anzaldúa (2002) called "autohistoriateoria"—a genre of writing about one's personal and collective history that may use fictive elements and that also theorizes. In a similar vein, people living in the United States have limited access to writings by and about women and gender nonconforming people from the Global South, whether personal accounts, academic research, journalists' reports, policy recommendations, or critiques of policies imposed by countries of the North. Relatively few scholars and fiction writers not working in English are published widely. Again, structural limitations of the politics of knowledge affect who has access to book publishers or websites and whose work may be translated for English-language readers.

This new edition represents our best effort to balance these considerations as we sought to provide information, analysis, and inspiration concerning the myriad daily experiences, opportunities, limitations, oppressions and fears, hopes, joys, and satisfactions that make up gendered lives.

ACKNOWLEDGMENTS

Many people—especially our students, teachers, colleagues, and friends—made it possible for us to complete the first edition of this book over twenty years ago. We acknowledge everyone at Mayfield Publishing who worked on our original manuscript: Franklin Graham, our editor, whose confidence in our ideas never wavered and whose light hand on the steering wheel and clear sense of direction got us into print; also Julianna Scott Fein, production editor; the production team; and Jamie Fuller, copyeditor extraordinaire. For the second edition, we were fortunate to have the support of colleagues and librarians at Hamilton College as well as the Mayfield production team led by editor Serina Beauparlant and assisted by Margaret Moore, another wonderful copyeditor.

McGraw-Hill published editions two through six. We worked with several production teams—too many to name here. Also, for the third edition we benefited from the support of the Women's Leadership Institute at Mills College and the Data Center, an Oakland-based nonprofit that provided research and training to grassroots social justice organizations across the country.

For this seventh edition, we are deeply indebted to Sherith Pankratz of Oxford University Press for the chance to revise and update this work. We are honored to work with her and acknowledge her encouragement, enthusiasm, skills, and deep commitment to publishing. Many thanks to Grace Li, Wesley Morrison, and Brad Rau for their production and copyediting work and to Lynn Mayo, Hamilton College librarian. Thanks also to those who reviewed the manuscript for this seventh edition: Padmini Banerjee, Delaware State University; Laura Brunell, Gonzaga University; Sara Diaz, Gonzaga University; Molly Ferguson, Ball State University; Meredith Heller, Northern Arizona University; Alison Kibler, Franklin and Marshall College; Rachel Lewis, George Mason University; Stella Oh, Loyola Marymount University; Harleen Singh, Brandeis University; Barbi Smyser-Fauble, Butler University; Katy Strzepek, St. Ambrose University; Deborah Wickering, Aquinas College; Tessa Ong Winkelmann, University of Nevada, Las Vegas; and two anonymous reviewers. We greatly appreciate their insights and suggestions.

As before, this new edition builds on the accumulated work, help, and support of many people. Thank you to Leslie Campos, Jonathan Grove, Deborah Lee, Loan Tran, and Mariko Uechi for writing new pieces for this edition. Thanks also to Judith

Arcana, Joyce Barry, Sarah Bird, Anita Bowen, Charlene Carruthers, SuzyJane Edwards, Aimee Germain, Priya Kandaswamy, Robin D. G. Kelley, Anne Lacsamana, Miyé Oka Lamprière, Martha Matsuoka, Anuja Mendiratta, Albie Miles, Aurora Levins Morales, Jose Plascencia, Catherine Pyun, Elizabeth Reis, Sonya Rifkin, Meredith Staples, Louisa Stone, Sé Sullivan, Pavitra Sundar, Loan Tran, Ash-Lee Woodard Henderson, and Kathleen Yep for providing new information and insights. We acknowledge the feminist scholars, organizations, and activists whose work we have reprinted and all those whose research and writing have informed our understandings of gendered lives and shaped the field of WGS. We are grateful for the independent bookstores and small presses that keep going thanks to dedicated staff and loyal readers. We also rely on other feminist "institutions": scholarly journals, the *Women's Review of Books*, *Ms.*, and WMST-L. We have benefited enormously from discussions on the WMST-L list and suggestions for readings and classroom activities generously shared by teachers. We are grateful to the undergraduate WGS students in our courses at various institutions across the country. Their experiences have shown us what has changed in this society and what has not, what has been gained and what has been lost. Most of all, they have taught us the importance of seeing them on their own terms as we engage them with new ideas and encourage them to see beyond themselves and the current sociopolitical moment.

The world continues to gain brilliant young feminist writers, teachers, organizers, and artists—some of whose work is included here. We also acknowledge the ground-breaking contributions made by an older generation of writers and scholars who have passed on: especially Gloria Anzaldúa, Grace Lee Boggs, Lorraine Hansberry, June Jordan, Melanie Kaye/Kantrovitz, Yuri Kochiyama, Audre Lorde, Grace Paley, Adrienne Rich, and Ntozake Shange.

Lastly, we acknowledge our friendship over twenty-five years, which has provided a deep foundation for our work together. We continue to be inspired by national treasures, Sweet Honey in the Rock, and the "sociological imagination"—C. Wright Mills' touchstone concept—that draws on the need for complex social analysis in order to make change.

To everyone, very many thanks.

— Gwyn Kirk and Margo Okazawa-Rey

We have chosen each other
and the edge of each other's battles
the war is the same
if we lose
someday women's blood will congeal
upon a dead planet
if we win
there is no telling
we seek beyond history
for a new and more possible meeting.

—Audre Lorde

Women's and Gender Studies

Knowing and Understanding

CHAPTER 1

Untangling the "F"-word

Feminist Movements and Frameworks
The Focus of Women's and Gender Studies
Collective Action for a Sustainable Future
The Scope of This Book
    Questions for Reflection
    Finding Out More on the Web
    Taking Action
Readings

Keywords: capitalism, discrimination, feminism, genealogy, gender binary, heteronormativity, ideology, imperialism, intersectionality, liberalism, patriarchy, prejudice, socialism, transgender

Whether or not you consider yourself a feminist as a matter of personal identity, political perspective, or both, in women's and gender studies courses you will study feminist perspectives because these seek to understand and explain inequalities based on gender. Fundamentally, feminism is about liberation from gender discrimination and other forms of **oppression**. For some people, this means securing equal rights within marriage, education, waged work, politics, law, or the military. For others, it means changing these institutions to create a secure and sustainable future for all. Still others focus on deconstructing or transforming the **gender binary**, the assumption that everyone fits neatly into one of two categories labeled male or female. Sociologist Judith Lorber (1991) argued that "the long-term goal of feminism must be . . . the eradication of gender as an organizing principle of . . . society" (p. 355) (see the box feature "Gender: What's in a Name?").

For many people, feminist thinking offers compelling ways to understand their lives, and feminist projects and campaigns have mobilized millions of people in the United States for over a century. Although serious gender inequalities remain, feminist theorizing and activism have achieved significant gains. Women in the United States have won the right to speak out on public issues, to vote, to own property in our own names, to divorce, and to have custody of our children. Women have been

Gender: What's in a Name?

In recent years, **transgender** individuals and activists have challenged, unsettled, and transformed understandings of gender together with others who identify as gender variant, nonbinary, or gender nonconforming. They have opened up the possibility of gender fluidity as a site of experimentation or a source of personal authenticity. As a result, increasing numbers of people are not interested in identifying with what they see as rigid gender categories.

At an institutional level, gender is more fixed, though this is changing to some extent with the legalization of same-sex marriage, for example, and some states are issuing gender-neutral ID cards. However, most people in the USA live according to a male/female binary, some adamantly so. Others may not pay much attention to this issue unless gender markers are missing or ambiguous.

We note that people are using the language of sex and gender very differently and mean different things by these terms. In this book, we straddle and bridge various gender paradigms and perspectives. We use *LGBTQI* (lesbian, gay, bi, trans, queer, and intersex) as a shorthand term for the range of people who question or repudiate heteronormativity, which we discuss more fully in Chapters 3 and 4. We use *woman* and *women* to include anyone who identifies as or is identified as female. This may include those who identify as queer, femme, butch, lesbian, gender nonconforming, and trans, as well as heterosexual and **cisgender** women (those whose **gender identity** is the same as they were assigned at birth). Please keep these definitions in mind as you read on and understand that definitions currently in use –both in this book and in the wider society– may change or be discarded in favor of new terminology. Definitions are always being contested and challenged as people's thinking and practices develop.

able to attend college, become professionals, and learn skilled trades. Developments in birth control and reproductive technologies mean that women are freer to decide if and when to have a child. Also, changing social expectations mean that we can choose whether to marry and how to express our gender and sexuality. Gender-based violence, though still widespread, is now discussed openly. In 2017 and 2018, Hollywood celebrities, Congressional staffers, media workers, farmworkers, students, fashion models, and athletes spoke out about long-standing patterns of sexual harassment as part of the #MeToo and #TimesUp movements, which reverberated around the world (see Reading 59). *Time* magazine named these "silence breakers" as its 2017 Person of the Year. Some of the high-profile men named have faced real consequences: they have been forced to resign, fired, or prosecuted for these crimes.

These feminist movements illustrate shifts in public opinion and what is considered appropriate for women—in all our diversity—and for men or people who are male-identified. However, the term *feminism* carries a lot of baggage. For some, it is positive and empowering. For others, it conjures up negative images of females who do not shave their legs or are considered ugly according to dominant US standards of beauty. Some assume that feminists are white women, or lesbians, or man-haters, or all of the above. Feminist ideas and goals have been consistently distorted, trivialized, and mocked by detractors. In the nineteenth century, suffragists who campaigned for legal rights for women, including the right to vote, were caricatured as "mannish," "castrators," and "home-wreckers." Over a century later, *Time* magazine published no fewer than 119 negative articles on feminism between the early 1970s and the mid-1990s (Jong 1998).

Antifeminist ideas continue to be a staple of right-wing talk shows and social media sites. In a well-known example, Rush Limbaugh maintained that "[f]eminism was established to allow unattractive women easier access to the mainstream of pop culture" (Media Matters 2015). Feminists are ridiculed and written off as complaining, angry, and humorless. When women speak of gender-based violence—battering, rape, sexual assault, and child sexual abuse—or of racism, living in poverty, or aging without health care, detractors describe them as whining critics who are out to destroy men and the male establishment. In our society, most women are socialized to care for men and to spare their feelings, but acknowledging institutional inequalities between females and men as a group is very different from "man-bashing." Many women are pushing back by critiquing antifeminist social media and calling out antifeminist perspectives (see, e.g., Cohn 2018; Lawrence and Ringrose 2018).

The claim that we are now living in a postfeminist era is part of the opposition to feminism. It involves a complex maneuver that recognizes the need for feminism in the past but declares that this is now over because it has been successful. Media critic Susan Douglas (2010) argued that even though "women's achievements, or their desire for achievement, are simply part of the cultural landscape" (p. 9), many contemporary media images of women are

> images of imagined power that mask, even erase, how much still remains to be done for girls and women, images that make sexism seem fine, even fun, and insist that feminism is now utterly pointless—even bad for you. (p. 6)

In this chapter, we introduce feminist ideas from different historical periods to highlight the diversity, breadth, and richness of feminist thinking in the United States. We hope this will help you to think about how you define feminism and what it means to you.

FEMINIST MOVEMENTS AND FRAMEWORKS

Many historians and commentators have divided US feminist movements into distinctive periods, described as waves. In this formulation, **"first wave feminism"** denotes efforts to gain legal rights for women, including the right to vote, dating from the 1840s to 1920. **"Second wave feminism"** refers to the feminist theorizing and organizing that flourished in the 1960s and 1970s. The next generation, in the 1990s, described themselves as **"third wave" feminists**. Some rejected what they knew of the feminism associated with their mothers' generation; others emphasized continuities with earlier feminist work (see, e.g., Dicker and Piepmeier 2003; Findlen 1995; Labaton and Martin 2004).

Defining historical periods is highly selective, focusing attention on certain events or perspectives and downplaying or erasing others. The wave metaphor suggests both continuity and discontinuity with the past as feminists have shaped and reshaped theoretical understandings for their generation, circumstances, and time in history. Also, this approach makes complex movements seem much neater and more static than they really are. Historians Kathleen Laughlin and colleagues (2010) noted: "The waves metaphor entrenches the perception of a 'singular' feminism in which gender is the predominate category of analysis" (p. 77). It leaves out large areas of women's activism, such as nineteenth-century movements of women workers in the New

England textile mills, or Black[1] women's opposition to slavery and lynching, and their struggles for economic improvement. As well as focusing on gender discrimination, women have campaigned for labor rights, civil rights, welfare rights, and immigrant rights, where gender is "tied to racial, class, religious, sexual, and other identities" (Boris 2010, p. 93).

Native American Antecedents

Among many possible pathways into US feminist thought, we chose Paula Gunn Allen's article about the "red roots of white feminism" (Reading 1). She discusses centuries-old practices that gave Native American women policy-making power in the Iroquois Confederation, especially the power to decide matters of peace and war. She lists various Native American principles that overlap with feminist and other progressive ideals: respect for women and their importance in society, respect for elders, an egalitarian distribution of goods and **power**, diverse ideas about beauty, cooperation among peoples, and respect for the earth. She emphasizes the importance in her community of knowing your ancestry and argues that all "feminists must be aware of our history on this continent"—a history that varies for different social and racial groups.

Legal Equality for Women

In the mid-nineteenth century, white middle-class women involved in the antislavery movement began to articulate parallels between systems of inequality based on race and gender. In 1840, Lucretia Mott and Elizabeth Cady Stanton met at the World Anti-Slavery Convention in London. Both were passionately opposed to slavery and were shocked to find that women delegates were not allowed to speak at the convention (Schneir 1994). The irony of working against the system that enslaved people of African descent while experiencing discrimination as women prompted them to work for women's rights. In 1848, they called a Women's Rights Convention at Seneca Falls, New York, where Stanton lived. Stanton drafted the Declaration of Sentiments (Reading 2), modeled after the nation's foundational Declaration of Independence. This document, which was read and adopted at the convention, rallied women and men to the cause of legal equality for US women, and this issue was fiercely debated in newspapers, at public meetings, among churchgoers, in women's organizations, and at dinner tables nationwide.

Following the Civil War, three constitutional amendments—the Thirteenth, Fourteenth, and Fifteenth Amendments—granted all men the right to vote but still allowed states to deny the vote to women. Suffragists split over whether to support the Fifteenth Amendment that enfranchised Black men. The American Woman Suffrage Association supported it and decided to campaign for women's suffrage state by state. Wyoming was the first territory to allow women the right to vote in 1869. Elizabeth Cady Stanton and Susan B. Anthony did not support it. Rather, they formed the National Woman

---

[1] When referring to people, we use *Black* rather than *black*. Black is an identity forged in the context of struggles for self-respect. It replaced *Negro* in a particular moment of self-assertion and carries that history with it. Capitalized, it's a proper noun, a name; lowercase, it's just an adjective. *White* does not carry the same connotations, except in the case of White racist organizations. So, because of the history of racism and race relations in the United States, white and black are not equivalent.

Suffrage Association and worked for a constitutional amendment granting votes for women. In 1920, seventy-two years after the Seneca Falls convention, the Nineteenth Amendment to the US Constitution stopped states from denying women the right to vote. This success had taken enormous effort, focus, and dedication. It spanned the lives of generations of leaders and activists and included public education campaigns, lobbying, mass demonstrations, civil disobedience actions, arrests, and hunger strikes (see, e.g., Free 2015; McConnaughy 2013; Weiss 2018).

This dogged campaign for legal equality grew out of **liberalism**, a theory of individual rights and freedom with roots in seventeenth-century European ideas, especially the writings of political philosopher John Locke. Liberalism has been central to US political thinking since the founding of the nation, although political and legal rights were originally limited to white men who owned land and property. Achieving greater equality among people in the United States has been a long, uneven process marked by hard work, gains, and setbacks—and a process that is far from complete. (Some key events are detailed in the box feature "Milestones in US History: Institutionalizing and Challenging Social Inequalities.")

Milestones in US History: Institutionalizing and Challenging Social Inequalities

1565 Spanish settlers established the first European colony in what is now the state of Florida and called it St. Augustine.

1584 Walter Raleigh founded Virginia, an English colony, at Roanoke Island.

1605 A Spanish settlement was established at what is now Santa Fe, New Mexico.

1607 Captain Christopher Newport of the London Company established an English colony at Jamestown, Virginia.

1619 A Dutch "man of war" sailed into Jamestown harbor with twenty Africans on board; the captain sold his human cargo to the colonists.

1691 The first legal ban on interracial marriages was passed in Virginia. Subsequently, other states prohibited whites from marrying Blacks; marriages between whites and Native Americans, Filipinos, and Asians, were also forbidden.

1776 The Second Continental Congress adopted the Declaration of Independence, written mostly by Thomas Jefferson and asserting that "all men are created equal."

1787 In order to ratify the Constitution of the United States, the 13 states negotiated a compromise. Southern states were allowed to count three out of every five enslaved people in determining the number of representatives to Congress, even though they were excluded from the electorate.

In a second compromise, the agreement that created the Senate gave less populous states more power than they would have had otherwise. These agreements enabled Southern senators to use their power to preserve slavery before the Civil War and Jim Crow during and after Reconstruction. Indian people were not counted for the purpose of Congressional representation because the US government designated the tribes as nation-like entities with whom they had to negotiate, as with foreign powers.

1820 Missouri entered the Union as the twelfth slave state "balanced" by Maine as the twelfth free state. Slavery was banned in the Louisiana Territory (purchased from France in 1803 for approximately $15 million).

1830 Congress passed, the Indian Removal Act, which moved all Indian tribes from the southeastern United States to land west of the Mississippi River and granted them rights to these new lands "in perpetuity."

1834 The Department of Indian Affairs was established within the War Department to monitor the creation of reservations for Indian tribes. The Department was later transferred to the Department of the Interior as the Bureau of Indian Affairs.

1848 The Treaty of Guadalupe Hidalgo ended the Mexican-American War (begun in 1846). It established the Rio Grande as the international boundary; ceded Texas to the United States together with Arizona, California, Nevada, and New Mexico; and guaranteed existing residents their land, language, culture, and US citizenship.

The first Women's Rights Convention was held in Seneca Falls, New York. Delegates issued a Declaration of Sentiments, listing inequities faced by women and urging that women be given the right to vote (see Reading 2).

1857 In *Dred Scott v. Sandford*, the Supreme Court argued that as an enslaved man, Dred Scott was not a citizen and therefore had no standing to sue his master for his freedom even though he had been living in free territory for four years. To grant Scott's petition, the Court argued, would deprive his owner of property without compensation, violating the Fifth Amendment. This invalidated states' rights to determine whether slavery should be banned.

1863 Abraham Lincoln issued the Emancipation Proclamation freeing slaves in Alabama, Arkansas, Florida, Georgia, Louisiana, Mississippi, North Carolina, South Carolina, Tennessee, Texas, and Virginia.

1864 US military forces terrorized Indian nations. Navajo people endured the "long walk" to imprisonment at Fort Sumner (New Mexico Territory). US troops massacred Cheyenne warriors (supported by Kiowa, Apache, Comanche, and Arapahoe warriors) at Sand Creek.

1865 Following the assassination of Abraham Lincoln, the Civil War was ended after four years. Congress established the Freedmen's Bureau, responsible for relief to former slaves and those made destitute by the war. The Thirteenth Amendment to the Constitution officially ended slavery and involuntary servitude.

1869 The first transcontinental railroad was completed. Chinese workers, allowed into the country to work on the railroad, experienced increased discrimination and "anti-Oriental" hysteria.

1870 Congress ratified the Fifteenth Amendment, which enfranchised Black men but permitted states to deny the vote to all women.

Julia Ward Howe issued a Mother's Day Proclamation for peace.

1877 Ordered off their land in Oregon, the Nez Percé tribe attempted to flee to Canada, a trek of 1,600 miles, to avoid war with US troops. They were forced to surrender 40 miles short of the border and sent to Oklahoma, where many died.

1887 Congress passed the Dawes Act, providing for the dissolution of Indian tribes and division of tribal holdings among the members. Over the next fifty years, white settlers took nearly two-thirds of Indian land holdings by deceit and intimidation.

1896 In *Plessy v. Ferguson*, the Supreme Court validated a Louisiana law requiring Blacks and whites to ride in separate railroad cars. The law had been challenged as a violation of the Fourteenth Amendment's right of equal protection, but the majority opinion held that "separate but equal" satisfied the constitutional requirement. This decision led to a spate of segregation laws in southern states. From 1870 to 1900, twenty-two Black men served in Congress, but with the introduction of literacy tests, poll taxes, grandfather clauses, and white primaries, none were left by 1901.

1898 The United States declared war on Spain and acquired former Spanish colonial territories: the Philippines, Guam, Puerto Rico, and Cuba. Congress also approved US annexation of the Hawaiian Islands.

1919 Suffragists were arrested in Washington, DC for blocking sidewalks during a demonstration in support of women's right to vote.

Fifteen thousand Black people marched silently down New York's Fifth Avenue, protesting lynching and discrimination against Blacks.

The Jones Act granted full US citizenship to Puerto Ricans and the right to travel freely to the continental United States.

1920 The Women's Suffrage Amendment (Nineteenth Amendment) barred states from denying women the right to vote.

1924 The Indian Citizenship Act extended citizenship to Native Americans, previously defined as wards of the US government. As late as 1952, some states still denied Indians voting rights.

1935 The National Labor Relations Act protected the right of workers to organize into unions.

The Social Security Act established entitlements to government assistance in the form of pensions and health benefit programs.

1941 Congress declared war on Japan, Italy, and Germany.

1942 President Roosevelt issued Executive Order 9066, permitting military authorities to evacuate 110,000 people of Japanese ancestry (mostly US citizens) from West Coast states and incarcerate them in isolated locations.

 The Bracero Program permitted Mexican citizens to work in agricultural areas in the United States on a temporary basis and at lower wages than US workers.

1945 World War II ended after the United States dropped atomic bombs on the Japanese cities of Hiroshima and Nagasaki.

1954 In *Brown v. Board of Education*, the Supreme Court reversed its *Plessy v. Ferguson* decision and declared that segregated schools were inherently unequal. In 1955, the Court ordered the desegregation of schools "with all deliberate speed."

1963 The Equal Pay Act mandated that men and women doing the same work must receive the same pay.

 To gain public support for a comprehensive civil rights law, 250,000 people participated in a March on Washington.

1964 Congress passed the most comprehensive Civil Rights Act in the history of the nation. Under Title VII, employment discrimination was prohibited on the basis of race, color, religion, sex, or national origin.

1965 The Voting Rights Act ended the use of literacy tests as a prerequisite for voting.

1972 Congress passed the Equal Rights Amendment and sent it to the states for ratification. It had been introduced in every session since 1923.

1973 The Rehabilitation Act (Section 504) prohibited discrimination against people with disabilities in programs that receive federal financial assistance.

1975 The Individuals with Disabilities Education Act guaranteed children with disabilities a free, appropriate public education.

1982 The Equal Rights Amendment failed, being ratified by thirty-five rather than the required minimum of thirty-eight states. Subsequent efforts to revive this campaign have not been successful.

1990 The Americans with Disabilities Act prohibited discrimination on the basis of disability by employers, public accommodations, state and local governments, public and private transportation, and in telecommunications.

1994 The Violent Crime Control and Law Enforcement Act legislated mandatory life imprisonment for persons convicted in federal court of a "serious violent felony" and who had two or more prior convictions in federal or state courts, at least one of which was a "serious violent felony" (the "three strikes" law). The other prior offense may be a "serious drug offense." States adopted similar laws.

1996 The Personal Responsibility and Work Opportunity Reconciliation Act replaced families' entitlement to government assistance with Temporary Assistance for Needy Families, a time-limited work-based program.

 The Defense of Marriage Act forbade the federal government from recognizing same-sex or polygamous marriages under any circumstances and stipulated that no state, city, or county is required to recognize a marriage between persons of the same sex even if the marriage is recognized in another state.

2001 The Uniting and Strengthening America by Providing Appropriate Tools Required to Intercept and Obstruct Terrorism Act (USA Patriot Act) greatly increased law enforcement agencies' powers of detention, search, and surveillance. It permitted expanded use of secret searches and allowed financial institutions to monitor daily transactions and academic institutions to share information about students.

2015 A Supreme Court ruling allowed same-sex marriage in all 50 states.

2017 President Trump signed executive orders that restricted entry of refugees to the United States and citizens of various Muslim-majority countries, including Iran, Iraq, Libya, Somalia, Sudan, Syria, and Yemen.

2018 New immigration guidelines separated children from parents or other adults at the US-Mexico border. This included families applying for asylum. Due to immense public pressure, these guidelines were suspended after more than 2,300 children had been separated from their parents (see Reading 44).

Primary source: A. Hernandez (1975, 2002). Also see the box feature "A Timeline of Key U.S. Immigration Law and Policy" in Chapter 3.

Liberal feminism is part of this liberal tradition and explains the oppression of women in terms of unequal access to political, economic, and social institutions (see, e.g., Eisenstein 1981; Friedan 1963; Steinem 1983). Much feminist organizing in the United States—including campaigns for women's rights to vote, to divorce, to enter universities and professions, to run for political office, and to train for combat—has been and continues to be based on this view. You may hold liberal feminist opinions even though you may not realize it. Despite the disclaimer "I'm not a feminist . . . ," the comment "but I *do* believe in equal pay" is a liberal feminist position. Liberal feminism may be criticized because it accepts existing institutions as they are, only seeking equal access for women within them. However, as the decades-long campaign for women's legal rights shows, this goal should not be underestimated given the strength of **patriarchy**, or male dominance, as a system of power.

Resisting Interlocking Systems of Oppression

The Combahee River Collective, a group of young Black feminists active in the Boston area in the 1970s, offered a very different view of feminism generated by their experiences of interlocking systems of oppression based on race, class, gender, and sexuality (Reading 3). As Black feminists and lesbians, Collective members found many white feminists too focused on male domination at the expense of oppressions based on race and class. Group members did not advocate equal rights for women within current institutions but argued for the transformation of the political and economic system as essential for women's liberation. They defined themselves as **socialists** and believed that "work must be organized for the collective benefit of those who do the work and create the products, and not for the profit of the bosses," as argued by German philosophers Frederick Engels and Karl Marx during the 1840s (shortly before the Seneca Falls convention). Collective members offered a strong critique of **capitalism** and **imperialism** and stood in solidarity with liberation struggles then being waged in colonized nations of Africa and Asia. Such transnational feminist thinking is both relevant and necessary today to understand the impacts of the global economic system, a point we take up in later chapters.

Socialist feminism views the oppression of women in terms of two interconnected and reinforcing systems: patriarchy and capitalism (see, e.g., Federici 2012; Hennessy and Ingraham 1997; Radical Women 2001; S. Smith 2005). The post–World War II rivalry between the West and the Soviet Union led to the discrediting of socialist thinking in the United States, although interest in it is reviving as more people experience the inequalities and insecurities generated by capitalism.

Theoretical perspectives that integrate gender with other systems of inequality have become known by the shorthand term **intersectionality**. For African American women, this has a long history. From the 1830s onward, Black speakers and writers like Frances E. W. Harper, Maria Stewart, and Sojourner Truth explicitly linked oppressions based on race and gender (Guy-Sheftall 1995). More recently, organizer and writer Linda Burnham (2001) noted that

> Black women's experience as women is indivisible from their experiences as African Americans. They are always "both/and," so analyses that claim to examine gender while neglecting a critical stance towards race and class inevitably do so at the expense of African American women's experiences. (p. 1)

An emphasis on intersectionality is not solely the prerogative of women of color. Since the writings of Aphra Behn in the early 1600s, some white women have been concerned with race and class as well as gender. White feminists worked against slavery in the nineteenth century; they organized against lynching and the activities of the Ku Klux Klan in the 1920s and 1930s; and they participated in labor movements, the welfare rights movement, and the civil rights movement of the 1950s and 1960s (see, e.g., Bush 2004; Frankenberg 1993; Pratt 1984; Rich 1986c; Segrest 1994). An intersectional approach is central to women's and gender studies, as exemplified by the readings in this book and in our overview essays.

Many media accounts of "second wave" feminism have ignored or erased alliances among women across lines of race and class. They have focused on the thinking and organizing of white middle-class feminists who were in the media spotlight, like Betty Friedan (1963) and Gloria Steinem (1983). This distorted view still circulates among antifeminist commentators even though more nuanced histories show the limitations of those skewed accounts (see, e.g., Baxandall and Gordon 2000; Laughlin et al. 2010; Moraga and Anzaldúa 1981; Roth 2003; Springer 2005; B. Thompson 2002). Unfortunately, students and activists who do not know this history also repeat inaccurate versions of feminism as the province of white middle-class women and erase the feminist thinking and organizing by a whole generation of women of color. Mathangi Subramanian, whose parents immigrated to the United States from India, had assumed that feminism was a white, Western thing, incompatible with her South Asian American identity, and wondered, "What does feminism have to do with *me*?" (Reading 4). She was excited to discover the intersectional writings of South Asian feminists like Chandra Talpade Mohanty (2003b; also see Alcoff 2013) that focused on "families and religion and food and history" and found that "[t]his feminism fit."

Queer and Trans Feminisms

Like members of the Combahee River Collective, many feminist writers and activists of the 1970s and 1980s were lesbians who rejected what Adrienne Rich (1986a) called "compulsory heterosexuality." Literary critic Michael Warner (1999) introduced a related term—**heteronormativity**—the belief that heterosexuality is the normal and natural way to express sexuality. Lesbians and gay men challenged this view, as did those who reclaimed the word *queer*, which had been used as a hateful term to oppress lesbians and gay men. This revamped notion of *queer* emphasized fluidity, experimentation, and playfulness, and it generated new political movements like ACT UP and Queer Nation (see, e.g., Gage, Richards, and Wilmot 2002; Nestle, Howell, and Wilchins 2002; Rodríguez 2003). The development of gay and lesbian studies and queer theory has influenced women's and gender studies over the past twenty years, especially in analyzing heteronormativity. Also, trans individuals and activists have challenged, unsettled, and transformed understandings of gender.

Loan Tran questions whether gender still matters and, if so, what it means these days when "technological, linguistic, and cultural shifts are allowing us to think about gender in a way that was unimaginable just a few decades ago" (Reading 5). They (Loan Tran's preferred pronoun) see that the way "gender is embodied indicates a tremendous blossoming of human possibility" and argue for a trans feminism that is both broad and based in daily material realities. For Tran, this means that feminists must be concerned with the lives of trans people as well as capitalism, white supremacy, displacement, and war.

THE FOCUS OF WOMEN'S AND GENDER STUDIES

Women's studies programs in United States date from the early 1970s and grew out of the vibrant women's liberation movements of those times. Early courses had titles like "Women's Liberation," "The Power of Patriarchy," and "Sexist Oppression and Women's Empowerment." Texts often included mimeographed articles from newsletters and pamphlets because there was so little material available in books. Over the years, scholars and activists have generated new understandings about gender with extensive bodies of literature and hundreds of programs in the United States and around the world, including Master's and PhD programs. Some departments have shifted their emphasis to women's and gender studies, or to women's, gender, and sexuality studies. Interdisciplinary fields like gay and lesbian studies, queer studies, ethnic studies, masculinity studies, cultural studies, and media studies have all shaped and benefitted from gender scholarship, as have older disciplines like literature, history, and sociology. As authors and editors, we draw on a wide range of sources to illustrate the breadth and vitality of women's and gender studies today.

The readings in this chapter provide a tiny sampling of the richness and diversity of US feminist thought. Over the generations, feminist writers and activists have drawn on their life experiences and beliefs in human liberation, evolving new perspectives that were often shocking at the time. Some arguments put forward by earlier generations might seem self-evident these days, but it is important to consider them in context. Earlier feminist thought provides foundations for current thinking and practice, which will also develop and change as others make their contributions to this ongoing endeavor.

These introductory readings are also in dialogue with those in the rest of this book. A key issue that links feminist thinking and movements internationally is violence against women in its many forms. This includes the #MeToo movement (Reading 59), Mexican women's protests against the killing of young women in the border region (Reading 30), West African women's efforts to heal from the turmoil and sexual violence of war (Reading 49), and those working to support Syrian refugees (Reading 47). Another theme concerns environmental justice: women in South India campaigning to stop Coca-Cola from plundering local water supplies (Reading 55); indigenous women in Latin America opposing mining, logging, and big dams that destroy their lands and livelihoods (Reading 39); and international organizations that are developing feminist principles for a just economy (Reading 60).

For students, women's and gender studies courses provide perspectives on individual experience and on other college courses in ways that are often life-changing. Many students report that these courses are both informative and empowering. Critical reading and integrative thinking, which are emphasized in women's and gender studies, are important academic and workplace skills. Graduates go on to work in business, community organizing, education, electoral politics, feminist advocacy projects, filmmaking, health, international policy, journalism, law, library work, publishing, social and human services, and more (see, e.g., Berger and Radeloff 2011; Luebke and Reilly 1995; Stewart 2007).

Women's and gender studies started as a critique of scholarship that ignored gender or treated women in stereotypical ways. It sought to provide missing information, new theoretical perspectives, and new ways of teaching. This kind of study can evoke strong emotions because you may be deeply affected by topics under discussion. Readings and class discussions may make you angry at the many forms of gender oppression, at other students' ignorance or lack of concern, or at being female in a male-dominated world. You may be challenged to rethink some of your assumptions and experiences as well as your views on various issues.

Most feminist teachers do not use what Brazilian educator Paulo Freire (1970) called the "banking method" of education, common in many fields, where students are like banks and teachers deposit information—historical facts, dates, definitions, formulae—and withdraw it in quizzes and exams. Regardless of its relevance for other subjects, this method is not appropriate for women's and gender studies, where students come into class with life experience and views on many of the topics discussed. As students, you are familiar with opinions circulating in social media, for example, or how your spiritual community views matters you care about. In women's and gender studies classes, you are encouraged to reflect on your experiences and to relate the readings and class discussions to your own life. At the end of each chapter, we raise questions and suggest activities to help do this. We believe that you should understand how your experiences are connected to wider social and historical contexts so that you are part of your own system of knowledge.

Although not always explicit, education has always been a political matter: who has been allowed to learn, and what kinds of learning (basic literacy, skilled trades, or abstract thinking) are deemed appropriate for different groups. For several generations, important goals in US women's education concerned equality: to study alongside men, to have access to the same curriculum, and to be admitted to male-dominated professions. Beyond this, feminist thinking has called into question the gendered nature of knowledge itself, with its focus on white, male, elite perspectives that are deemed to be universal, as we discuss in Chapter 2. As women's and gender studies programs continue to build their scholarly work and academic rigor, they occupy a contradictory position within academia, challenging male-dominated knowledge. Many myths and misunderstandings about feminism and women's and gender studies circulate on campuses and in the wider society. We consider three of these myths here, and then look at the related topic of men in women's and gender studies.

Myth 1: Women's and Gender Studies Is Ideological

Some people assume that women's and gender studies is feminist propaganda, not "real" scholarship. They may believe that such courses are too "touchy-feely" or constitute extended gripe sessions against men. Feminist inquiry, analysis, and activism have arisen from women's life experiences and from well-researched inequalities and discrimination. One example is the fact that, on average, US women's wages for full-time, year-round work are 77 percent to 80 percent of what men earn on average, meaning that women earn between 77 and 80 cents (depending on age) for every dollar earned by men. For African American women, this is 63 cents—and for Latinas, 54 cents—compared to white men (AAUW 2018). Knowledge is never neutral, and in women's and gender studies, this is made explicit.

Given its movement origins, the field has valued scholarly work that is relevant to activist concerns. Women's and gender studies courses seek to link intellectual, experiential, and emotional forms of knowing with the goal of improving everyone's lives. This is a rigorous endeavor, but it differs from much traditional scholarship, which values abstract knowledge, narrowly defined, as discussed in Chapter 2. By contrast, women's and gender studies scholarship places a high value on breadth and connectedness. This kind of rigor requires broad understandings grounded in diverse experiences and the ability to make connections between insights from different perspectives.

To some people, feminism is more than an area of study. It is a cause to believe in because it provides cogent ways to understand the world, which may be personally empowering. In the face of egregious gender-based discrimination, it may be tempting to blame everything on "the patriarchy" or "rich white men" without taking the trouble to read or think critically. Students who do this are being anti-intellectual; they limit their own understanding and inadvertently reinforce the notion that women's and gender studies is anti-intellectual.

Myth 2: Women's and Gender Studies Is Narrow

Women's and gender studies seeks to understand and explain the significance of intersecting inequalities based on gender, race, class, dis/ability, sexuality, age, national origin, and so on. Feminist analyses provide a series of lenses to examine many topics and contribute to a long list of academic disciplines, from anthropology to ethnic studies, history, law, literature, psychology, and more. Feminist scholarship is on the cutting edge of many fields and raises crucial questions about teaching and learning, research design and methodologies, and theories of knowledge. Thus, far from being narrow, women's and gender studies is concerned with thinking critically about the world in all its complexity, as illustrated in this book.

Myth 3: Women's and Gender Studies Is a White, Middle-Class, Western Thing

Many notable scholars, writers, and activists of color identify as feminists. Among them are Julia Alvarez, Gloria Anzaldúa, Patricia Hill Collins, bell hooks, Aurora Levins Morales, Nadine Naber, Loan Tran, and others whose work is included in this anthology. They link analyses of gender with race, class, and other systems of power and inequality, as do homegrown feminist movements in Africa, Asia, Latin America, and the Caribbean (see, e.g., Basu 2016; Moghadam 2005; Naples and Desai 2002). As African American writer and cultural critic bell hooks (2000) argued: "there should be billboards; ads in magazines; ads on buses, subways, trains; television commercials spreading the word, letting the world know more about feminism" because "feminism is for everybody" (p. x).

Men Doing Feminism

Women's and gender studies classes include a growing number of men, and courses increasingly include scholarly work on masculinities. There is a long history of men's support for women's rights in the United States (see, e.g., Digby 1998; Kaufman and Kimmel 2011; Tarrant 2007; also see Reading 29). Indeed, the changes we discuss in this book cannot be achieved without men's full participation—whether as sons, brothers, fathers, partners, lovers, friends, classmates, coworkers, supervisors, labor organizers, spiritual leaders, teachers, doctors, lawyers, police officers, judges, legislators, and more. Women's and gender studies courses provide a strong grounding for this. Moreover, the #MeToo and #TimesUp movements have prompted discussions of manliness and masculinities, which hopefully will continue.

Because masculinities are socially constructed and highly constrained in this society, as in others, we assume that there is something for men in feminism beyond being allies to women (see, e.g., A. Johnson 2005; Tarrant 2007). People in dominant positions on any social dimension (gender, race, class, ability, nation, and so forth) have obvious benefits, and those with **privilege** may be afraid of losing it. At the same time, such structures of power and inequality are limiting for everyone. Privilege separates people and makes those of us in dominant positions ignorant of important truths. To be able to look others fully in the eye, we have to work to end systems of inequality. This repudiation of privilege is not a sacrifice, we believe, but rather the possibility of entering into genuine community where we can all be more truly human.

COLLECTIVE ACTION FOR A SUSTAINABLE FUTURE

In the past forty years or so, there has been a proliferation of popular and scholarly books, journals, magazines, websites, and blog posts on gender issues. When opinion polls, academic studies, government data, public debates, grassroots research, and personal narratives are added, it is easy to be swamped with information and varying perspectives. In making our selections as writers and editors, we have filtered this wealth of material according to four main principles—our particular road map, which provides the framework for this book.

1.   A Matrix of Oppression, Privilege, and Resistance

Underlying our analysis is the concept of oppression, which we see as a group phenomenon even though individuals in specific groups many not think they are oppressed or want to be in positions of dominance. Every form of oppression—such as **sexism, racism, classism, heterosexism, anti-Arabism, anti-Semitism,** and **able-bodyism**—is rooted in social institutions like the family, education, religion, government, law, and media. Those who are dominant in this society, as in others, use their relative power and privilege to rule, control, and exploit other groups—those who are subordinate—for the benefit of the dominant group.

Oppression works through systems of power and inequality, including the dominance of certain values, beliefs, and assumptions about people and how society should be organized. Members of dominant groups generally have built-in economic, political, and cultural power and benefits regardless of whether they are aware of, or even want, these advantages. This process of accruing benefits is often referred to as privilege. Those most privileged may be least able to recognize it. Men, as a group, are advantaged by sexism, whereas women, as a group, are disadvantaged, though there are significant differences within these groups based on race, class, dis/ability, sexuality or gender expression.

Oppression involves **prejudice**, which we define as unreasonable, unfair, and hostile *attitudes* and *judgments* toward people, and **discrimination**, or differential *treatment* favoring those who are in positions of dominance. But oppression reaches beyond individual behavior. It is promoted by every social institution and cannot be fully changed without fundamental changes in institutional practices and **ideologies**—the ideas, attitudes, and values that institutions embody and perpetuate. Our definition of oppression assumes that everyone learns to participate in oppressive practices, thus helping to maintain them. People may be involved as perpetrators or passive beneficiaries, or they may direct **internalized oppression** at members of their own group. Oppression results in appropriation and the loss—both voluntary and involuntary—of voice, identity, and agency of oppressed peoples. What examples can you think of to illustrate this?

It is important to think about oppression as a system, at times blatantly obvious and at others subtly nuanced, rather than as an either/or dichotomy of privileged/disadvantaged or oppressor/oppressed. People may be privileged in some respects (e.g., in terms of race or gender) and disadvantaged in others (e.g., class or sexual expression). We use the phrase **matrix of oppression, privilege, and resistance** to describe the interrelatedness of various forms of oppression, the fact that people may be privileged on certain dimensions and disadvantaged on others, and to recognize both oppression and privilege as potentially powerful sources of resistance and change. We note that people of different groups learn what is considered appropriate behavior for them in their families, in school, or from media representations and popular culture. As a result, people may internalize dominant ideas so that we "police" ourselves without the need for overt oppression from outside.

2.   From the Personal to the Global

Throughout this book, we make connections between people's personal experiences and wider social systems that we are part of. We use the analytical terms **micro level** (personal or individual), **meso level** (community, neighborhood, or school), **macro level** (national or institutional), and **global level** to make these links. To understand people's experiences or the complexity of a particular issue, it is necessary to look at all of these levels and how they interconnect. Take a personal relationship, for instance. This operates on a micro level. However, both partners bring all of themselves to the relationship. So in addition to individual factors like being funny, generous, or "hot," there are meso-level aspects—like where you live and what high school you went to, which are affected by economic inequalities and segregation in housing—and macro-level factors—like the obvious or hidden ways in which men or white people are privileged in this society. As editors, we make connections between these levels of analysis in our overview essays and have chosen readings that also make these links.

Given the diversity and complexity of US society, we have chosen to focus on the United States in this book. However, we also discuss the preeminence of the United States in the world. This is evident through the dominance of the English language and the widespread distribution of US movies, news media, TV shows, music, books, and websites. It manifests through the power of the dollar as an international currency and the impact of US-based corporations abroad, especially in poorer countries of the Global South. Dominance is also apparent in the broad reach of US foreign and military policy. Students who have lived in other parts of the world often know this from their own experience. We see "nation" as an analytical category like race or gender, and in some places, we refer to gender issues and feminist thinking and activism in other nations. A global level of analysis recognizes that patriarchy, heteronormativity, and militarism are global phenomena, although with differences in practice from nation to nation.

3.   Linking the Head, Heart, and Hands

Humankind faces serious challenges if we are to sustain ourselves, our children, *their* children, and the environment that supports all life. Although some women in the United

States have benefited from greater opportunities for education and wage earning, many are now working harder or longer hours than their mothers did, and are under pressure to keep a job and to juggle waged work with caring for a family. Over the past forty years, economic changes and government policies have made many people's lives more diffi- cult. Examples include a loss of factory and office jobs as work has been moved overseas or become automated, government failure to introduce an adequate system of child care or a health care system that benefits everyone, cuts in welfare programs, restrictions of government support to immigrants and their families, and a dramatic increase in the number of people who are incarcerated. Government spending illustrates these priori- ties. Some states spend more on incarceration than on higher education, for example. A massive 47 percent of the federal discretionary budget is earmarked for military spend- ing, a total of $717 billion for fiscal year 2019 (US Department of Defense 2018). At the same time, thousands of people are homeless, many urban schools lack basic resources, and funding for services from preschool programs to the Veterans Administration has been cut back. Individuals are affected by such policies as they negotiate intimate rela- tionships, raise children, and make a living for themselves and their families.

In the face of these negative economic and political trends, we mention many in- spiring projects and organizations to showcase activist work that is often not recog- nized in the mainstream media. We urge you to find out more about such projects on the Web and to take action yourself. We see collective action for progressive social change as a major goal of scholarly work, especially in a field like women's and gender studies. Doing something about an issue requires us to have an explanation about it, to have ideas for a different way of doing things, followed by action—linking the head, heart, and hands (a theme we will return to later).

4.   A Secure and Sustainable Future

Security and sustainability are central issues for the twenty-first century. This includes the personal security of knowing who we are as individuals; having sturdy relation- ships with family and friends; living free from threats, violence, or coercion; having adequate income or livelihood; and enjoying health and well-being. It also involves security for communities, nations, and our overburdened planet. We see structural inequalities based on race, class, gender, and nation as a major threat to long-term se- curity worldwide because they create literal and metaphorical walls, gates, and fences that separate people and maintain hierarchies among us. We argue that creating a more sustainable future means rethinking materialism and consumerism and finding fairer ways to distribute wealth so that everyone may thrive.

Throughout our discussion, we emphasize the diversity of women's experiences. We assume no easy "sisterhood" across lines of race, class, nation, age, ability, sexual- ity, or gender expression, but we do believe that alliances built on the recognition and understanding of such differences can make effective collective action possible.

THE SCOPE OF THIS BOOK

This book is concerned with the conditions facing people of all genders and the long- term work of transforming those conditions. In Part I (Chapters 1–3), we introduce ex- amples of feminist thought from the United States; we argue for a theoretical framework that allows students to understand the significance of gender, race, class, sexuality, dis/ability, nation, and more; and we discuss the role of identity and social location as standpoints for creating knowledge and understanding. Part II (Chapters 4–6) explores women's experiences of their bodies, sexuality, health, and sexualized violence. In Part III (Chapters 7 and 8), we look at what is involved in making a home and making a living, and how opportunities in the United States and abroad are shaped by global factors. In Part IV (Chapters 9–11), we continue to explore concepts of security and sustainability by looking at crime and criminalization, militarization, and the impacts of environmental destruction. Finally, in Part V (Chapter 12), we examine the importance of theories, visions, and actions for creating change, using the head, heart, and hands together.

Throughout the book, we draw on personal narratives, journalists' accounts, government data, scholarly papers, and the work of nonprofit research and advocacy organizations. Our overview essays provide some historical and contemporary context for the readings, which amplify key points. Our overall argument is that improving people's lives in the United States also means directing ourselves, our communities, this society, and the wider world toward a more sustainable future.

QUESTIONS FOR REFLECTION

As you read and discuss this chapter, think about these questions:

1. What is your ancestry—biologically, culturally, and intellectually? How would you answer Paula Gunn Allen's question: Who is your mother?
2. How can you learn more about the history of feminist movements? Who will be your teachers? What sources will you use?
3. What does feminism mean to you? Keep your answer, and return to this question at the end of the course.

FINDING OUT MORE ON THE WEB

1. In Reading 1, Paula Gunn Allen mentions Lysistrata. Who was she?
2. In Reading 3, the writers mention Dr. Kenneth Edelin, Joan Little, and Inéz Garcia. Who were these people? Why were they significant?
3. How many Black men held seats in the US Congress in 2000 compared to 1900?
4. Look at how blogs such as Feministing (http://feministing.com) or Quirky Black Girls (http://quirkyblackgirls.blogspot.com) discuss current feminist issues.

TAKING ACTION

1. Find quotes or slogans about feminism that resonate for you.
2. Find a feminist blog you like, and read it regularly.
3. Ask older people in your family or community about their involvement in a social movement.
4. Interview your professors or the staff of your campus women's center to learn about the beginnings of women's and gender studies at your college or university.
5. Join an organization or support a campaign on a feminist issue you care about.

PAULA GUNN ALLEN

1 WHO IS YOUR MOTHER? RED ROOTS OF WHITE FEMINISM (1986)

Paula Gunn Allen (1939–2008) was a poet, novelist, essayist, and literary critic of Laguna, Sioux, Lebanese, and Scottish ancestry who grew up on the Laguna Pueblo (New Mexico). Among many awards, she received a Pulitzer Prize nomination for *Pocahontas: Medicine Woman, Spy, Entrepreneur, Diplomat* (2004), a Lifetime Achievement Award from the Native Writer's Circle of the Americas (2001), and the American Book Award from the Before Columbus Foundation for *Spider Woman's Granddaughters: Traditional Tales and Contemporary Writing* (1990).

At Laguna Pueblo in New Mexico, "Who is your mother?" is an important question. At Laguna, one of several of the ancient Keres gynocratic societies of the region, your mother's identity is the key to your own identity. Among the Keres, every individual has a place within the universe—human and nonhuman—and that place is defined by clan membership. In turn, clan membership is dependent on matrilineal descent. Of course, your mother is not only that woman whose womb formed and released you—the term refers in every individual case to an entire generation of women whose psychic, and consequently physical, "shape" made the psychic existence of the following generation possible. But naming your own mother (or her equivalent) enables people to place you precisely within the universal web of your life, in each of its dimensions: cultural, spiritual, personal, and historical.

Among the Keres, "context" and "matrix" are equivalent terms, and both refer to approximately the same thing as knowing your derivation and place. Failure to know your mother, that is, your position and its attendant traditions, history, and place in the scheme of things, is failure to remember your significance, your reality, your right relationship to earth and society. It is the same as being lost—isolated, abandoned, self-estranged, and alienated from your own life. This importance of tradition in the life of every member of the community is not confined to Keres Indians; all American Indian Nations place great value on traditionalism.

The Native American sense of the importance of continuity with one's cultural origins runs counter to contemporary American ideas: in many instances, the immigrants to America have been eager to cast off cultural ties, often seeing their antecedents as backward, restrictive, even shameful. Rejection of tradition constitutes one of the major features of American life, an attitude that reaches far back into American colonial history and that now is validated by virtually every cultural institution in the country. . . .

The American idea that the best and the brightest should willingly reject and repudiate their origins leads to an allied idea—that history, like everything in the past, is of little value and should be forgotten as quickly as possible. This all too often causes us to reinvent the wheel continually. We find ourselves discovering our collective pasts over and over, having to retake ground already covered by women in the preceding decades and centuries. The Native American view, which highly values maintenance of traditional customs, values, and perspectives, might result in slower societal change and in quite a bit less social upheaval, but it has the advantage of providing a solid sense of identity and lowered levels of psychological and interpersonal conflict.

Source: Republished with permission of Beacon Press, from Paula Gunn Allen, *The Sacred Hoop* (Boston, MA. Beacon Press, 1986); permission conveyed through Copyright Clearance Center, Inc.

Contemporary Indian communities value individual members who are deeply connected to the traditional ways of their people, even after centuries of concerted and brutal effort on the part of the American government, the churches, and the corporate system to break the connections between individuals and their tribal world. In fact, in the view of the traditionals, rejection of one's culture—one's traditions, language, people—is the result of colonial oppression and is hardly to be applauded. They believe that the roots of oppression are to be found in the loss of tradition and memory because that loss is always accompanied by a loss of a positive sense of self. In short, Indians think it is important to remember, while Americans believe it is important to forget....

Re-membering Connections and Histories

The belief that rejection of tradition and of history is a useful response to life is reflected in America's amazing loss of memory concerning its origins in the matrix and context of Native America. America does not seem to remember that it derived its wealth, its values, its food, much of its medicine, and a large part of its "dream" from Native America.... Hardly anyone in America speculates that the constitutional system of government might be as much a product of American Indian ideas and practices as of colonial American and Anglo-European revolutionary fervor.

Even though Indians are officially and informally ignored as intellectual movers and shapers in the United States, Britain, and Europe, they are peoples with ancient tenure on this soil. During the ages when tribal societies existed in the Americas largely untouched by patriarchal oppression, they developed elaborate systems of thought that included science, philosophy, and government based on a belief in the central importance of female energies, autonomy of individuals, cooperation, human dignity, human freedom, and egalitarian distribution of status, goods, and services. Respect for others, reverence for life and, as a by-product, pacifism as a way of life; importance of kinship ties in the customary ordering of social interaction; a

sense of the sacredness and mystery of existence; balance and harmony in relationships both sacred and secular were all features of life among the tribal confederacies and nations. And in those that lived by the largest number of these principles, gynarchy [government by women] was the norm rather than the exception. Those systems are as yet unmatched in any contemporary industrial, agrarian, or postindustrial society on earth.

... Femaleness was highly valued, both respected and feared, and all social institutions reflected this attitude. Even modern sayings, such as the Cheyenne statement that a people is not conquered until the hearts of the women are on the ground, express the Indians' understanding that without the power of woman the people will not live, but with it, they will endure and prosper.

Indians did not confine this belief in the central importance of female energy to matters of worship. Among many of the tribes (perhaps as many as 70 percent of them in North America alone), this belief was reflected in all of their social institutions. The Iroquois Constitution or White Roots of Peace, also called the Great Law of the Iroquois, codified the Matrons' decision-making and economic power:

The lineal descent of the people of the Five Fires [the Iroquois Nations] shall run in the female line. Women shall be considered the progenitors of the Nation. They shall own the land and the soil. Men and women shall follow the status of their mothers. (Article 44)

The women heirs of the chieftainship titles of the League shall be called Oiner or Otinner [Noble] for all time to come. (Article 45)

If a disobedient chief persists in his disobedience after three warnings [by his female relatives, by his male relatives, and by one of his fellow council members, in that order], the matter shall go to the council of War Chiefs. The Chiefs shall then take away the title of the erring chief *by order of the women in whom the title is vested.* When the chief is deposed, the women shall notify the chiefs of the League ... and the chiefs of the League shall sanction the act. The women will then select another of their sons as a candidate and the chiefs shall elect him. (Article 19) (Emphasis mine)[1]

The Matrons held so much policy-making power traditionally that once, when their position was threatened they demanded its return, and consequently the power of women was fundamental in shaping the Iroquois Confederation sometime in the sixteenth or early seventeenth century. It was women

who fought what may have been the first successful feminist rebellion in the New World. The year was 1600, or thereabouts, when these tribal feminists decided that they had had enough of unregulated warfare by their men. Lysistratas among the Indian women proclaimed a boycott on lovemaking and childbearing. Until the men conceded to them the power to decide upon war and peace, there would be no more warriors. Since the men believed that the women alone knew the secret of childbirth, the rebellion was instantly successful.

In the Constitution of Deganawidah the founder of the Iroquois Confederation of Nations had said: "He caused the body of our mother, the woman, to be of great worth and honor. He purposed that she shall be endowed and entrusted with the birth and upbringing of men, and that she shall have the care of all that is planted by which life is sustained and supported and the power to breathe is fortified: *and moreover that the warriors shall be her assistants.*"

The footnote of history was curiously supplied when Susan B. Anthony began her "Votes for Women" movement two and a half centuries later. Unknowingly the feminists chose to hold their founding convention of latter-day suffragettes in the town of Seneca [Falls], New York. The site was just a stone's throw from the old council house where the Iroquois women had plotted their feminist rebellion. (Emphasis mine)[2]

Beliefs, attitudes, and laws such as these became part of the vision of American feminists and of other human liberation movements around the world. Yet feminists too often believe that no one has ever experienced the kind of society that empowered women and made that empowerment the basis of its rules of civilization. The price the feminist community must pay because it is not aware of the recent presence of gynarchical societies on this continent is unnecessary confusion, division, and much lost time.

The Root of Oppression Is Loss of Memory

. . . As I write this . . . I am keenly aware of the lack of image Americans have about our continent's recent past. I am intensely conscious of popular notions of Indian women as beasts of burden, squaws, traitors, or, at best, vanished denizens of a long-lost wilderness. How odd, then, must my contention seem that the gynocratic tribes of the American continent provided the basis for all the dreams of liberation that characterize the modem world.

We as feminists must be aware of our history on this continent. We need to recognize that the same forces that devastated the gynarchies of Britain and the Continent also devastated the ancient African civilizations, and we must know that those same materialistic, antispiritual forces are presently engaged in wiping out the same gynarchical values, along with the peoples who adhere to them, in Latin America. I am convinced that those wars were and continue to be about the imposition of patriarchal civilization over the holistic, pacifist, and spirit-based gynarchies they supplant. To that end the wars of imperial conquest have not been solely or even mostly waged over the land and its resources, but they have been fought within the bodies, minds, and hearts of the people of the earth for dominion over them. I think this is the reason traditionals say we must remember our origins, our cultures, our histories, our mothers and grandmothers, for without that memory, which implies continuance rather than nostalgia, we are doomed to engulfment by a paradigm that is fundamentally inimical to the vitality, autonomy, and self-empowerment essential for satisfying, high-quality life.

The vision that impels feminists to action was the vision of the Grandmothers' society, the society that was captured in the words of the sixteenth-century explorer Peter Martyr nearly five hundred years ago. . . . That vision as Martyr told it is of a country where there are "no soldiers, no gendarmes or police, no nobles, kings, regents, prefects, or judges, no prisons, no lawsuits . . . All are equal and free," or so Friedrich Engels recounts Martyr's words.[3]

Columbus wrote:

> Nor have I been able to learn whether they [the inhabitants of the islands he visited on his first journey to the New World] held personal property, for it seemed to me that whatever one had, they all took shares of . . . They are so ingenuous and free with all they have, that no one would believe it who has not seen it; of anything that they possess, if it be asked of them, they never say no; on the contrary, they invite you to share it and show as much love as if their hearts went with it.[4]

At least that's how the Native Caribbean people acted when the whites first came among them; American Indians are the despair of social workers, bosses, and missionaries even now because of their deeply ingrained tendency to spend all they have, mostly on others. In any case, as the historian William Brandon notes,

> the Indian *seemed* free, to European eyes, gloriously free, to the European soul shaped by centuries of toil and tyranny, and this impression operated profoundly on the process of history and the development of America. Something in the peculiar character of the Indian world gave an impression of classlessness, of propertylessness, and that in turn led to an impression, as H. H. Bancroft put it, of "humanity unrestrained . . . in the exercise of liberty absolute."[5]

A Feminist Heroine

Early in the women's suffrage movement, Eva Emery Dye, an Oregon suffragette, went looking for a heroine to embody her vision of feminism. . . . She found Sacagawea (or Sacajawea) buried in the journals of Lewis and Clark. The Shoshoni teenager had traveled with the Lewis and Clark expedition, carrying her infant son, and on a small number of occasions acted as translator.[6]

Dye declared that Sacagawea, whose name is thought to mean Bird Woman, had been the guide to the historic expedition, and through Dye's work Sacagawea became enshrined in American memory as a moving force and friend of the whites, leading them in the settlement of western North America.[7]

But Native American roots of white feminism reach back beyond Sacagawea. The earliest white women on this continent were well acquainted with tribal women. They were neighbors to a number of tribes and often shared food, information, child care, and health care. Of course little is made of these encounters in official histories of colonial America, the period from the Revolution to the Civil War, or on the ever-moving frontier. Nor, to my knowledge, has either the significance or incidence of intermarriage between Indian and white or between Indian and Black been explored. By and large, the study of Indian-white relations has been focused on government and treaty relations, warfare, missionization, and education. It has been almost entirely documented in terms of formal white Christian patriarchal impacts and assaults on Native Americans, though they are not often characterized as assaults but as "civilizing the savages." Particularly in organs of popular culture and miseducation, the focus has been on what whites imagine to be degradation of Indian women ("squaws"), their equally imagined love of white government and white conquest ("princesses"), and the horrifyingly misleading, fanciful tales of "bloodthirsty, backward primitives" assaulting white Christian settlers who were looking for life, liberty, and happiness in their chosen land.

But, regardless of official versions of relations between Indians and whites or other segments of the American population, the fact remains that great numbers of apparently "white" or "Black" Americans carry notable degrees of Indian blood. With that blood has come the culture of the Indian, informing the lifestyles, attitudes, and values of their descendants. . . . Among these must be included "permissive" child-rearing practices, for . . . imprisoning, torturing, caning, strapping, starving, or verbally abusing children was considered outrageous behavior. Native Americans did not believe that physical or psychological abuse of children would result in their edification. They did not believe that children are born in sin, are congenitally predisposed to evil, or that a good parent who wishes the child to gain salvation, achieve success, or earn the respect of her or his fellows can be helped to those ends by physical or emotional torture.

The early Americans saw the strongly protective attitude of the Indian people as a mark of their "savagery"—as they saw the Indian's habit of bathing frequently, their sexual openness, their liking for scant clothing, their raucous laughter at most things, their suspicion and derision of authoritarian structures, their quick pride, their genuine courtesy, their willingness to share what they had with others less fortunate than they, their egalitarianism, their ability to act as if various lifestyles were a normal part of living, and their granting that women were of equal or, in individual cases, of greater value than men.

Yet the very qualities that marked Indian life in the sixteenth century have, over the centuries since contact between the two worlds occurred, come to mark much of contemporary American life. . . .

Contemporary Americans find themselves more and more likely to adopt a "live and let live" attitude in matters of personal sexual and social styles. Two-thirds of their diet and a large share of their medications and medical treatments mirror or are directly derived from Native American sources. Indianization is not a simple concept, to be sure, and it is one that Americans often find themselves resisting; but it is a process that has taken place, regardless of American resistance to recognizing the source of many if not most of American's vaunted freedoms in our personal, family, social, and political arenas.

This is not to say that Americans have become Indian in every attitude, value, or social institution. Unfortunately, Americans have a way to go in learning how to live in the world in ways that improve the quality of life for each individual while doing minimal damage to the biota, but they have adapted certain basic qualities of perception and certain attitudes that are moving them in that direction.

An Indian-Focused Version of American History

American colonial ideas of self-government came as much from the colonists' observations of tribal governments as from their Protestant or Greco-Roman heritage. Neither Greece nor Rome had the kind of pluralistic democracy as that concept has been understood in the United States since Andrew Jackson, but the tribes, particularly the gynarchical tribal confederacies, did. It is true that the *oligarchic* form of government that colonial Americans established was originally based on Greco-Roman systems in a number of important ways, such as its restriction of citizenship to propertied white males over twenty-one years of age, but it was never a form that Americans as a whole have been entirely comfortable with. Politics and government in the United States during the Federalist period also reflected the English common law system as it had evolved under patriarchal feudalism and monarchy—hence the United States' retention of slavery and restriction of citizenship to propertied white males.

The Federalists did make one notable change in the feudal system from which their political system derived on its Anglo side. They rejected blooded aristocracy and monarchy. This idea came from the Protestant Revolt to be sure, but it was at least reinforced by colonial America's proximity to American Indian nonfeudal confederacies and their concourse with those confederacies over the two hundred years of the colonial era. . . .

The Iroquois federal system, like that of several in the vicinity of the American colonies, is remarkably similar to the organization of the federal system of the United States. It was made up of local, "state," and federal bodies composed of executive, legislative, and judicial branches. The Council of Matrons was the executive: it instituted and determined general policy. The village, tribal (several villages), and Confederate councils determined and implemented policies when they did not conflict with the broader Council's decisions or with theological precepts that ultimately determined policy at all levels. The judicial was composed of the men's councils and the Matron's council, who sat together to make decisions. Because the matrons were the ceremonial center of the system, they were also the prime policymakers.

Obviously, there are major differences between the structure of the contemporary American government and that of the Iroquois. . . . The Iroquois system is spirit-based, while that of the United States is secular, and the Iroquois Clan Matrons formed the executive. The female executive function was directly tied to the ritual nature of the Iroquois politic, for the executive was lodged in the hands of the Matrons of particular clans across village, tribe, and national lines. The executive office was hereditary, and only sons of eligible clans could serve, at the behest of the Matrons of their clans, on the councils at the three levels. Certain daughters inherited the office of Clan Matron through their clan affiliations. No one could impeach or disempower a Matron, though her violation of certain laws could result in her ineligibility for the Matron's council. For example, a woman who married *and took her husband's name* could not hold the title Matron.

American ideas of social justice came into sharp focus through the commentaries of Iroquois observers who traveled in France in the colonial period. These observers expressed horror at the great gap between the lifestyles of the wealthy and the poor, remarking to the French philosopher Montaigne, who would heavily influence the radical communities of Europe, England, and America, that "they had noticed that in Europe there seemed to be two moities, consisting of the rich 'full gorged' with wealth, and the poor, starving 'and bare with need and povertie.' The Indian tourists not only marveled at the division, but marveled that the poor endured 'such an injustice, and that they took not the others by the throte, or set fire on their house.'"[8] It must be noted that the urban poor eventually did just that in the French Revolution. . . .

The feminist idea of power . . . stems from tribal sources. The central importance of the Clan Matrons in the formulation and determination of domestic and foreign policy as well as in their primary role in the ritual and ceremonial life of their respective Nations was the single most important attribute of the Iroquois, as of the Cherokee and Muskogee, who traditionally inhabited the southern Atlantic region. The latter peoples were removed to what is now Oklahoma during the Jackson administration, but prior to the American Revolution they had regular and frequent communication with and impact on both the British colonizers and later the American people, including the African peoples brought here as slaves.

Ethnographer Lewis Henry Morgan wrote an account of Iroquoian matriarchal culture, published in 1877,[9] that heavily influenced Marx and the development of communism, particularly lending it the idea of the liberation of women from patriarchal dominance. The early socialists in Europe, especially in Russia, saw women's liberation as a central aspect of the socialist revolution. Indeed, the basic ideas of socialism, the egalitarian distribution of goods and power, the peaceful ordering of society, and the right of every member of society to participate in the work and benefits of that society, are ideas that pervade American Indian political thought and action. . . .

When Eva Emery Dye discovered Sacagawea and honored her as the guiding spirit of American womanhood, she may have been wrong in bare historical fact, but she was quite accurate in terms of deeper truth. The statues that have been erected depicting Sacagawea as a Matron in her prime signify an understanding in the American mind, however unconscious, that the source of just government, of right ordering of social relationships, the dream of "liberty and justice for all" can be gained only by following the Indian Matrons' guidance.

NOTES

1. The White Roots of Peace, cited in *The Third Woman: Minority Women Writers of the United States*, ed. Dexter Fisher (Boston: Houghton Mifflin, 1980), p. 577.
2. Stan Steiner, *The New Indians* (New York: Dell, 1968), pp. 219–220.
3. William Brandon, *The Last Americans: The Indian in American Culture* (New York: McGraw-Hill, 1974), p. 294.
4. Brandon, *Last Americans*, p. 6.
5. Brandon, *Last Americans*, pp. 7–8. The entire chapter "American Indians and American History" (pp. 1–23) is pertinent to the discussion.
6. Ella E. Clark and Margot Evans, *Sacagawea of the Lewis and Clark Expedition* (Berkeley: University of California Press, 1979), pp. 93–98.
7. The implications of this maneuver did not go unnoticed by either whites or Indians, for the statues of the idealized Shoshoni woman, the Native American matron Sacagawea, suggest that American tenure on American land—indeed, the right to

be on this land—is given to whites by her. While that implication is not overt, it certainly is suggested in the image of her that the sculptor chose: a tall, heavy woman, standing erect, nobly pointing the way westward with upraised hand. The impression is furthered by the habit of media and scholars of referring to her as "the guide." Largely because of the popularization of the circumstances of Sacagawea's participation in the famed Lewis and Clark expedition, Indian people have viewed her as a traitor to her people, likening her to Malinalli (La Malinche, who acted as interpreter for Cortes and bore him a son) and Pocahontas, that unhappy girl who married John Rolfe (not John Smith) and died in England after bearing him a son. Actually none of these women engaged in traitorous behavior. Sacagawea led a long life, was called Porivo (Chief Woman) by the Commanches, among whom she lived for more than twenty years, and in her old age engaged her considerable skill at speaking and manipulating white bureaucracy to help in assuring her Shoshoni people decent reservation holdings.

8. Brandon, *Last Americans*, p. 6.

9. Lewis Henry Morgan, *Ancient Society or Researches in the Lines of Human Progress from Savagery Through Barbarism to Civilization* (New York: Henry Holt and Company, 1877).

2 DECLARATION OF SENTIMENTS (1848)

The Seneca Falls Declaration of Sentiments and Resolutions was adopted at a founding convention of nineteenth-century suffragists, called to consider the "social, civil, and religious conditions and rights of woman," held at the Wesleyan Chapel, Seneca Falls, New York, on July 19, 1848 (Schneir 1994, p. 76). **Elizabeth Cady Stanton** drafted this document, using the Declaration of Independence as a model.

When, in the course of human events, it becomes necessary for one portion of the family of man to assume among the people of the earth a position different from that which they have hitherto occupied, but one to which the laws of nature and of nature's God entitle them, a decent respect to the opinions of mankind requires that they should declare the causes that impel them to such a course.

We hold these truths to be self-evident: that all men and women are created equal; that they are endowed by their Creator with certain inalienable rights; that among these are life, liberty, and the pursuit of happiness; that to secure these rights governments are instituted, deriving their just powers from the consent of the governed. Whenever any form of government becomes destructive of these ends, it is the right of those who suffer from it to refuse allegiance to it, and to insist upon the institution of a new government, laying its foundation on such principles, and organizing its powers in such form, as to them shall seem most likely to effect their safety and happiness. Prudence, indeed, will dictate that governments long established should not be changed for light and transient causes; and accordingly all experience hath shown that mankind are more disposed to suffer, while evils are sufferable, than to right themselves by abolishing the forms to which they were accustomed. But when a long train of abuses and usurpations, pursuing invariably the same object evinces a design to reduce them under absolute despotism, it is their duty to throw off such government, and to provide new guards for their future security. Such has been the patient sufferance of the women under this government, and such is now the necessity which constrains them to demand the equal station to which they are entitled.

The history of mankind is a history of repeated injuries and usurpations on the part of man toward woman, having in direct object the establishment of an absolute tyranny over her. To prove this, let facts be submitted to a candid world.

He has never permitted her to exercise her inalienable right to the elective franchise.

He has compelled her to submit to laws, in the formation of which she had no voice.

He has withheld from her rights which are given to the most ignorant and degraded men—both natives and foreigners.

Having deprived her of this first right of a citizen, the elective franchise, thereby leaving her without representation in the halls of legislation, he has oppressed her on all sides.

He has made her, if married, in the eye of the law, civilly dead.

He has taken from her all right in property, even to the wages she earns.

He has made her, morally, an irresponsible being, as she can commit many crimes with impunity, provided they be done in the presence of her husband. In the covenant of marriage, she is compelled to

---

Source: Primary source from the Seneca Falls Convention, the first US women's rights convention, July 1848.

promise obedience to her husband, he becoming, to all intents and purposes, her master—the law giving him power to deprive her of her liberty, and to administer chastisement.

He has so framed the laws of divorce, as to what shall be the proper causes, and in case of separation, to whom the guardianship of the children shall be given, as to be wholly regardless of the happiness of women—the law, in all cases, going upon a false supposition of the supremacy of man, and giving all power into his hands.

After depriving her of all rights as a married woman, if single, and the owner of property, he has taxed her to support a government which recognizes her only when her property can be made profitable to it.

He has monopolized nearly all the profitable employments, and from those she is permitted to follow, she receives but a scanty remuneration. He closes against her all the avenues to wealth and distinction which he considers most honorable to himself. As a teacher of theology, medicine, or law, she is not known.

He has denied her the facilities for obtaining a thorough education, all colleges being closed against her.

He allows her in Church, as well as State, but a subordinate position, claiming Apostolic authority for her exclusion from the ministry, and, with some exceptions, from any public participation in the affairs of the Church.

He has created a false public sentiment by giving to the world a different code of morals for men and women, by which moral delinquencies which exclude women from society, are not only tolerated, but deemed of little account in man.

He has usurped the prerogative of Jehovah himself, claiming it as his right to assign for her a sphere of action, when that belongs to her conscience and to her God.

He has endeavored, in every way that he could, to destroy her confidence in her own powers, to lessen her self-respect, and to make her willing to lead a dependent and abject life.

Now, in view of this entire disfranchisement of one-half the people of this country, their social and religious degradation—in view of the unjust laws above mentioned, and because women do feel themselves aggrieved, oppressed, and fraudulently deprived of their most sacred rights, we insist that they have immediate admission to all the rights and privileges which belong to them as citizens of the United States.

In entering upon the great work before us, we anticipate no small amount of misconception, misrepresentation, and ridicule; but we shall use every instrumentality within our power to effect our object. We shall employ agents, circulate tracts, petition the State and National legislatures, and endeavor to enlist the pulpit and the press in our behalf. We hope this Convention will be followed by a series of Conventions embracing every part of the country.

Resolutions

WHEREAS, The great precept of nature is conceded to be, that "man shall pursue his own true and substantial happiness." Blackstone in his Commentaries remarks, that this law of Nature being coeval with mankind, and dictated by God himself, is of course superior in obligation to any other. It is binding over all the globe, in all countries and at all times; no human laws are of any validity if contrary to this, and such of them as are valid, derive all their force, and all their validity, and all their authority, mediately and immediately, from this original; therefore,

Resolved, That such laws as conflict, in any way, with the true and substantial happiness of woman, are contrary to the great precept of nature and of no validity, for this is "superior in obligation to any other."

Resolved, That all laws which prevent woman from occupying such a station in society as her conscience shall dictate, or which place her in a position inferior to that of man, are contrary to the great precept of nature, and therefore of no force or authority.

Resolved, That woman is man's equal—was intended to be so by the Creator, and the highest good of the race demands that she should be recognized as such.

Resolved, That the women of this country ought to be enlightened in regard to the laws under which they live, that they may no longer publish their degradation by declaring themselves satisfied with their present position, nor their ignorance, by asserting that they have all the rights they want.

Resolved, That inasmuch as man, while claiming for himself intellectual superiority, does accord to woman moral superiority, it is pre-eminently his duty to encourage her to speak and teach, as she has an opportunity, in all religious assemblies.

Resolved, That the same amount of virtue, delicacy, and refinement of behavior that is required of woman in the social state, should also be required of man, and the same transgressions should be visited with equal severity on both man and woman.

Resolved, That the objection of indelicacy and impropriety, which is so often brought against woman when she addresses a public audience, comes with a very ill-grace from those who encourage, by their attendance, her appearance on the stage, in the concert, or in feats of the circus.

Resolved, That woman has too long rested satisfied in the circumscribed limits which corrupt customs and a perverted application of the Scriptures have marked out for her, and that it is time she should move in the enlarged sphere which her great Creator has assigned her.

Resolved, That it is the duty of the women of this country to secure to themselves their sacred right to the elective franchise.

Resolved, That the equality of human rights results necessarily from the fact of the identity of the race in capabilities and responsibilities.

Resolved, therefore, That, being invested by the Creator with the same capabilities, and the same consciousness of responsibility for their exercise, it is demonstrably the right and duty of woman, equally with man, to promote every righteous cause by every righteous means; and especially in regard to the great subjects of morals and religion, it is self-evidently her right to participate with her brother in teaching them, both in private and in public, by writing and by speaking, by any instrumentalities proper to be used, and in any assemblies proper to be held; and this being a self-evident truth growing out of the divinely implanted principles of human nature, any custom or authority adverse to it, whether modern or wearing the hoary sanction of antiquity, is to be regarded as a self-evident falsehood, and at war with mankind.

[At the last session Lucretia Mott offered and spoke to the following resolution:]

Resolved, That the speedy success of our cause depends upon the zealous and untiring efforts of both men and women, for the overthrow of the monopoly of the pulpit, and for the securing to woman an equal participation with men in the various trades, professions, and commerce.

3 A BLACK FEMINIST STATEMENT (1977)

Active in the mid to late 1970s, the **Combahee River Collective** was a group of Black feminists in Boston who took their name from the guerrilla action led by Harriet Tubman that freed more than 750 slaves and is the only military campaign in US history to have been planned and led by a woman.

We are a collective of Black feminists who have been meeting together since 1974. During that time we have been involved in the process of defining and clarifying our politics, while at the same time doing political work within our own group and in coalition with other progressive organizations and movements. The most general statement of our politics at the present time would be that we are actively committed to struggling against racial, sexual, heterosexual, and class oppression and see as our particular task the development of integrated analysis and practice based upon the fact that the major systems of oppression are interlocking. The synthesis of these oppressions creates the conditions of our lives. As Black women we see Black feminism as the logical political movement to combat the manifold and simultaneous oppressions that all women of color face.

We will discuss four major topics in the paper that follows: (1) the genesis of contemporary Black feminism; (2) what we believe, i.e., the specific province of our politics; (3) the problems in organizing Black feminists, including a brief herstory of our collective; and (4) Black feminist issues and practice.

1. The Genesis of Contemporary Black Feminism

Before looking at the recent development of Black feminism we would like to affirm that we find our origins in the historical reality of Afro-American women's continuous life-and-death struggle for survival and liberation. Black women's extremely negative relationship to the American political system (a system of white male rule) has always been determined by our membership in two oppressed racial and sexual castes. As Angela Davis points out in "Reflections on the Black Woman's Role in the Community of Slaves," Black women have always embodied, if only in their physical manifestation, an adversary stance to white male rule and have actively resisted its inroads upon them and their communities in both dramatic and subtle ways. There have always been Black women activists—some known, like Sojourner Truth, Harriet Tubman, Frances E. W. Harper, Ida B. Wells Barnett, and Mary Church Terrell, and thousands upon thousands unknown—who had a shared awareness of how their sexual identity combined with their racial identity to make their whole life situation and the focus of their political struggles unique. Contemporary Black feminism is the outgrowth of countless generations of personal sacrifice, militancy, and work by our mothers and sisters.

A Black feminist presence has evolved most obviously in connection with the second wave of the American women's movement beginning in the late 1960s. Black, other Third World, and working women have been involved in the feminist movement from its start, but both outside reactionary forces and racism and elitism within the movement itself have served to obscure our participation. In 1973 Black feminists, primarily located in New York, felt the necessity of forming a separate Black feminist group. This became the National Black Feminist Organization (NBFO).

Source: Republished with permission of The Monthly Review Press from Zillah Eisenstein, *Capitalist Patriarchy and the Case for Socialist Feminism* (New York: Monthly Review Press, 1979); permission conveyed through Copyright Clearance Center, Inc.

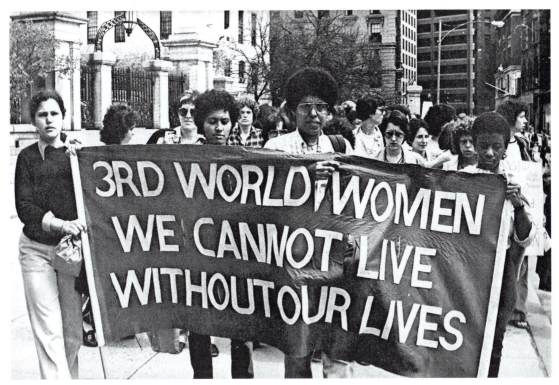

© *Tia Cross*

Black feminist politics also have an obvious connection to movements for Black liberation, particularly those of the 1960s and 1970s. Many of us were active in those movements (civil rights, Black nationalism, the Black Panthers), and all of our lives were greatly affected and changed by their ideology, their goals, and the tactics used to achieve their goals. It was our experience and disillusionment within these liberation movements, as well as experience on the periphery of the white male left, that led to the need to develop a politics that was antiracist, unlike those of white women, and antisexist, unlike those of Black and white men.

There is also undeniably a personal genesis for Black feminism, that is, the political realization that comes from the seemingly personal experiences of individual Black women's lives. Black feminists and many more Black women who do not define themselves as feminists have all experienced sexual oppression as a constant factor in our day-to-day existence. As children we realized that we were different from boys and that we were treated differently. For example, we were told in the same breath to be quiet both for the sake of being "lady-like" and to make us less objectionable in the eyes of white people. As we grew older we became aware of the threat of physical and sexual abuse by men. However, we had no way of conceptualizing what was so apparent to us, what we *knew* was really happening.

Black feminists often talk about their feelings of craziness before becoming conscious of the concepts of sexual politics, patriarchal rule, and most importantly, feminism, the political analysis and practice that we women use to struggle against our oppression. The fact that racial politics and indeed racism are pervasive factors in our lives did not allow us, and still does not allow most Black women, to look more deeply into our own experiences and, from that sharing and growing consciousness, to build a politics that will change our lives and inevitably end our oppression. Our development must also be tied to the contemporary economic and political position of Black people. The post–World War II generation of Black youth was the first to be able to minimally partake of certain educational and employment options, previously closed completely to Black people. Although our economic position is still at the very bottom of the American capitalistic economy, a handful of us have been able to gain certain tools as a result of tokenism in education and employment which potentially enable us to more effectively fight our oppression.

A combined antiracist and antisexist position drew us together initially, and as we developed politically we addressed ourselves to heterosexism and economic oppression under capitalism.

2.   What We Believe

Above all else, our politics initially sprang from the shared belief that Black women are inherently valuable, that our liberation is a necessity not as an adjunct to somebody else's but because of our need as human persons for autonomy. This may seem so obvious as to sound simplistic, but it is apparent that no other ostensibly progressive movement has ever considered our specific oppression as a priority or worked seriously for the ending of that oppression. Merely naming the pejorative stereotypes attributed to Black women (e.g., mammy, matriarch, Sapphire, whore, bulldagger), let alone cataloguing the cruel, often murderous, treatment we receive, indicates how little value has been placed upon our lives during four centuries of bondage in the Western Hemisphere. We realize that the only people who care enough about us to work consistently for our liberation are us. Our politics evolve from a healthy love for ourselves, our sisters and our community which allows us to continue our struggle and work.

This focusing upon our own oppression is embodied in the concept of identity politics. We believe that the most profound and potentially the most radical politics come directly out of our own identity, as opposed to working to end somebody else's oppression. In the case of Black women this is a particularly repugnant, dangerous, threatening, and therefore revolutionary concept because it is obvious from looking at all the political movements that have preceded us that anyone is more worthy of liberation than ourselves. We reject pedestals, queenhood, and walking ten paces behind. To be recognized as human, levelly human, is enough.

We believe that sexual politics under patriarchy is as pervasive in Black women's lives as are the politics of class and race. We also often find it difficult to separate race from class from sex oppression because in our lives they are most often experienced simultaneously. We know that there is such a thing as racial-sexual oppression which is neither solely racial nor solely sexual, e.g., the history of rape of Black women by white men as a weapon of political repression.

Although we are feminists and lesbians, we feel solidarity with progressive Black men and do not advocate the fractionalization that white women who are separatists demand. Our situation as Black people necessitates that we have solidarity around the fact of race, which white women of course do not need to have with white men, unless it is their negative solidarity as racial oppressors. We struggle together with Black men against racism, while we also struggle with Black men about sexism.

We realize that the liberation of all oppressed peoples necessitates the destruction of the political-economic systems of capitalism and imperialism as well as patriarchy. We are socialists because we believe the work must be organized for the collective benefit of those who do the work and create the products, and not for the profit of the bosses. Material resources must be equally distributed among those who create these resources. We are not convinced, however, that a socialist revolution that is not also a feminist and antiracist revolution will guarantee our liberation. We have arrived at the necessity for developing an understanding of class relationships that takes into account the specific class position of Black women who are generally marginal in the labor force, while at this particular time some of us are temporarily viewed as doubly desirable tokens at white-collar and professional levels. We need to articulate the real class situation of persons who are not merely raceless, sexless workers, but for whom racial and sexual oppression are significant determinants in their working/economic lives. . . .

A political contribution which we feel we have already made is the expansion of the feminist principle that the personal is political. In our consciousness-raising sessions, for example, we have in many ways gone beyond white women's revelations because we are dealing with the implications of race and class as well as sex. Even our Black women's style of talking/testifying in Black language about what we have experienced has a resonance that is both cultural and political. We have spent a great deal of energy delving into the cultural and experiential nature of our oppression out of necessity because none of these matters has ever been looked at before. No one before has ever examined the multilayered texture of Black women's lives. An example of this kind of revelation/conceptualization occurred at a meeting as we discussed the ways in which our early intellectual interests had been attacked by our peers, particularly Black males. We discovered that all of us, because we were "smart" had also been considered "ugly," i.e., "smart-ugly." "Smart-ugly" crystallized the way in which most of us had been forced to develop our intellects at great cost to our "social" lives. The sanctions in the Black and white communities against Black women thinkers are comparatively much higher than for white women, particularly ones from the educated middle and upper classes.

As we have already stated, we reject the stance of lesbian separatism because it is not a viable political analysis or strategy for us. It leaves out far too much and far too many people, particularly Black men, women, and children. We have a great deal of criticism and loathing for what men have been socialized to be in this society: what they support, how they act, and how they oppress. But we do not have the misguided notion that it is their maleness, per se—i.e., their biological maleness—that makes them what they are. As Black women we find any type of biological determinism a particularly dangerous and reactionary basis upon which to build a politic. We must also question whether lesbian separatism is an adequate and progressive political analysis and strategy, even for those who practice it, since it so completely denies any but the sexual sources of women's oppression, negating the facts of class and race.

3. Problems in Organizing Black Feminists

During our years together as a Black feminist collective we have experienced success and defeat, joy and pain, victory and failure. We have found that it is very difficult to organize around Black feminist issues, difficult even to announce in certain contexts that we *are* Black feminists. We have tried to think about the reasons for our difficulties, particularly since the white women's movement continues to be strong and to grow in many directions. In this section we will discuss some of the general reasons for the organizing problems we face and also talk specifically about the stages in organizing our own collective.

The major source of difficulty in our political work is that we are not just trying to fight oppression on one front or even two, but instead to address a whole range of oppressions. We do not have racial, sexual, heterosexual, or class privilege to rely upon, nor do we have even the minimal access to resources and power that groups who possess any one of these types of privilege have.

The psychological toll of being a Black woman and the difficulties this presents in reaching political consciousness and doing political work can never be underestimated. There is a very low value placed upon Black women's psyches in this society, which is both racist and sexist. As an early group member once said, "We are all damaged people merely by virtue of being Black women." We are dispossessed psychologically and on every other level, and yet we feel the necessity to struggle to change the condition of all Black women. In "A Black Feminist's Search for Sisterhood," Michele Wallace arrives at this conclusion:

> We exist as women who are Black who are feminists, each stranded for the moment, working independently because there is not yet an environment in this society remotely congenial to our struggle—because, being on the bottom, we would have to do what no one else has done: we would have to fight the world.[1]

Wallace is pessimistic but realistic in her assessment of Black feminists' position, particularly in her allusion to the nearly classic isolation most of us face. We might use our position at the bottom, however, to make a clear leap into revolutionary action. If Black women were free, it would mean that everyone else would have to be free since our freedom would necessitate the destruction of all the systems of oppression.

Feminism is, nevertheless, very threatening to the majority of Black people because it calls into question some of the most basic assumptions about our existence, i.e., that sex should be a determinant of power relationships. Here is the way male and female voices were defined in a Black nationalist pamphlet from the early 1970s:

> We understand that it is and has been traditional that the man is the head of the house. He is the leader of the house/nation because his knowledge of the world is broader, his awareness is greater, his understanding is fuller and his application of this information is wiser . . . After all, it is only reasonable that the man be the head of the house because he is able to defend and protect the development of his home . . . Women cannot do the same things as men—they are made by nature to function differently. Equality of men and women is something that cannot happen even in the abstract world. Men are not equal to other men, i.e., ability, experience or even understanding. The value of men and women can be seen as in the value of gold and silver—they are not equal but both have great value. We must realize that men and women are a complement to each other because there is no house/family without a man and his wife. Both are essential to the development of any life.[2]

The material conditions of most Black women would hardly lead them to upset both economic and sexual arrangements that seem to represent some stability in their lives. Many Black women have a good understanding of both sexism and racism, but because of the everyday constrictions of their lives cannot risk struggling against them both.

The reaction of Black men to feminism has been notoriously negative. They are, of course, even more threatened than Black women by the possibility that Black feminists might organize around our own needs. They realize that they might not only lose valuable and hard-working allies in their struggles but that they might also be forced to change their habitually sexist ways of interacting with and oppressing Black women. Accusations that Black feminism divides the Black struggle are powerful deterrents to the growth of an autonomous Black women's movement.

Still, hundreds of women have been active at different times during the three-year existence of our group. And every Black woman who came, came out of a strongly-felt need for some level of possibility that did not previously exist in her life.

When we first started meeting early in 1974 after the NBFO first eastern regional conference, we did not have a strategy for organizing, or even a focus. We just wanted to see what we had. After a period of months of not meeting, we began to meet again late in the year and started doing an intense variety of consciousness-raising. The overwhelming feeling that we had is that after years and years we had finally found each other. Although we were not doing political work as a group, individuals continued their involvement in Lesbian politics, sterilization abuse and abortion rights work, Third World Women's International Women's Day activities, and support activity for the trials of Dr. Kenneth Edelin, Joan Little, and Inéz García. During our first summer, when membership had dropped off considerably, those of us remaining devoted serious discussion to the possibility of opening a refuge for battered women in a Black community. (There was no refuge in Boston at that time.) We also decided around that time to become an independent collective since we had serious disagreements with NBFO's bourgeois-feminist stance and their lack of a clear political focus.

We also were contacted at that time by socialist feminists, with whom we had worked on abortion rights activities, who wanted to encourage us to attend the National Socialist Feminist Conference in Yellow Springs. One of our members did attend and despite the narrowness of the ideology that was promoted at that particular conference, we became more aware of the need for us to understand our own economic situation and to make our own economic analysis.

In the fall, when some members returned, we experienced several months of comparative inactivity and internal disagreements which were first conceptualized as a Lesbian-straight split but which were also the result of class and political differences. During the summer those of us who were still meeting had determined the need to do political work and to move beyond consciousness-raising and serving exclusively as an emotional support group. At the beginning of 1976, when some of the women who had not wanted to do political work and who also had voiced disagreements stopped attending of their own accord, we again looked for a focus. We decided at that time, with the addition of new members, to become a study group. We had always shared our reading with each other, and some of us had written papers on Black feminism for group discussion a few months before this decision was made. We began functioning as a study group and also began discussing the possibility of starting a Black feminist publication. We had a retreat in the late spring which provided a time for both political discussion and working out interpersonal issues. Currently we are planning to gather together a collection of Black feminist writing. We feel that it is absolutely essential to demonstrate the reality of our politics to other Black women and believe that we can do this through writing and distributing our work. The fact that individual Black feminists are living in isolation all over the country, that our own numbers are small, and that we have some skills in writing, printing, and publishing makes us want to carry out these kinds of projects as a means of organizing Black feminists as we continue to do political work in coalition with other groups.

4. Black Feminist Issues and Projects

During our time together we have identified and worked on many issues of particular relevance to Black women. The inclusiveness of our politics makes us concerned with any situation that impinges upon the lives of women, Third World and working people. We are of course particularly committed to working on those struggles in which race, sex, and class are simultaneous factors in oppression. We might, for example, become involved in workplace organizing at a factory that employs Third World women or picket a hospital that is cutting back on already inadequate health care to a Third World community, or set up a rape crisis center in a Black neighborhood. Organizing around welfare and daycare concerns might also be a focus. The work to be done and the countless issues that this work represents merely reflect the pervasiveness of our oppression.

Issues and projects that collective members have already worked on are sterilization abuse, abortion rights, battered women, rape and health care. We have also done many workshops and educationals on Black feminism on college campuses, at women's conferences, and most recently for high school women.

One issue that is of major concern to us and that we have begun to publicly address is racism in the white women's movement. As Black feminists we are made constantly and painfully aware of how little effort white women have made to understand and combat their racism, which requires among other things that they have a more than superficial comprehension of race, color, and Black history and culture. Eliminating racism in the white women's movement is by definition work for white women to do, but we will continue to speak to and demand accountability on this issue.

In the practice of our politics we do not believe that the end always justifies the means. Many reactionary and destructive acts have been done in the name of achieving "correct" political goals. As feminists we do not want to mess over people in the name of politics. We believe in collective process and a nonhierarchical distribution of power within our own group and in our vision of a revolutionary society. We are committed to a continual examination of our politics as they develop through criticism and self-criticism as an essential aspect of our practice. . . .

As Black feminists and Lesbians we know that we have a very definite revolutionary task to perform and we are ready for the lifetime of work and struggle before us.

NOTES

1. Michele Wallace, "A Black Feminist's Search for Sisterhood," *The Village Voice*, July 28, 1975, pp. 6–7.

2. Mumininas of Committee for Unified Newark, *Mwanamke Mwananchi* [*The Nationalist Woman*] (Newark, NJ: Mumininas of CFUN, 1971), pp. 4–5.

4 THE BROWN GIRL'S GUIDE TO LABELS (2010)

Mathangi Subramanian is an Indian American writer and educator. She is a senior policy analyst with New York City Council, where she covers education and social service issues. She has published scholarly work in PENN GSE *Perspectives on Urban Education*, *Current Issues in Comparative Education*, and the *Encyclopedia of Women and Islamic Cultures*. Her children's fiction has appeared in *Kahani* magazine.

1998

When they heard that I had been accepted at Brown University, friends from my suburban high school filled my yearbook with dire warnings and heartfelt advice about the cosmetic consequences of my potential liberalization.

"Don't forget to shave your armpits," was a popular one.

"Don't let me see you burning your bra on CNN next year," was another.

When I got to Brown, I was told that getting a degree was important, but that the real reason we were in college was to find ourselves.

I soon discovered that the most common way to find oneself was to adopt a label. Among my white girlfriends, the most popular of these labels was *feminist*.

"I'm not saying that men and women shouldn't be different," they told me. "I'm just saying they should be equal."

This sounded about right to me, so I decided to investigate. In between my highly practical science classes, I listened in on spirited conversations about the need to move away from the image of bra-burning, pierced harridans with hairy armpits (this sounded familiar) and toward embracing and celebrating our desire to wear lipstick and short skirts without judgment. Other than a modicum of knowledge I had gained in seventh grade, which is the year I spent wearing foundation and designer skirts in a desperate attempt to cover up my acne

and naiveté, I didn't know much about fashion. Then there was the whole battle to reclaim the word *sexy*, a battle I couldn't join simply because I couldn't bring myself to invest in reclaiming a word I had never claimed in the first place, and probably never would. White girls were sexy. Bespectacled Indian girls who took AP physics and ran for president of the debate team were not.

Of course, the whole Indian thing presented another option: Released from the white-washed suburbs, I discovered a contingent of South Asian Americans who embraced their ethnic identities by labeling themselves either as *desi* or *brown*. I occasionally ate lunch with them before lab or spent late nights with them working on problem sets. The girls ironed their hair, wore huge earrings, and lusted after South Asian boys who shortened their names to "Jay" or "Ace" and wore too much cologne.

"Oh my god, did you hear Deepti likes Jay?" went a typical conversation.

"Seriously. You know she's just trying to snag a husband," it continued.

"Um, gross. Wait, I totally saw the perfect wedding sari online yesterday, wanna see?" it usually ended.

Well, clearly this wasn't going to work. It wasn't until years later that I discovered that these girls were the minority, and that there was a whole subset of desi women who fantasized about political activism and artistic fame, rather than elaborate

Source: From *Click: When We Knew We Were Feminists*, edited by Courtney E. Martin and J. Courtney Sullivan (Emeryville: Seal Press, 2010): pp. 181-190. Reprinted with permission of Mathangi Subramanian.

weddings. At the time, though, I thought that brown was not the label for me.

By the end of my freshman year, I had picked out several potential majors, and no potential labels.

1999

The summer I turned nineteen, I went to India for the second time in my life and hated every minute. I spent half the time sitting silently on display before a parade of relatives who discussed me in Tamil as if I weren't there. The other half I spent cursing my weak stomach: If I wasn't throwing up, I was popping Pepto-Bismol.

One morning, while I was sitting on the balcony attempting to catch the weak excuse for a breeze, my mother came out and patted my sweaty hair.

"How you doing?" she asked, flopping into a chair next to me.

"Ugh," I said, wiping the sweat pooled around my temples.

My mother's mother wandered out onto the balcony, wiping her brow with her sari. My *patthi* is impossibly intelligent, able to rattle off everything from the symptoms associated with rare diseases to the color of the heroine's sari in every Tamil movie ever made. In later years, when I visited, we would watch Tamil serials together, and she would provide a running commentary that confirmed my theory that facility with sarcasm is a genetic trait. That summer, though, we did not yet know how much we had in common. To me, she was still a quirky, vacant woman prone to non sequiturs.

"Mathangi, when are you getting married?" she asked me in Tamil.

"Amma!" my mom yelled. "She's only nineteen. Leave her alone."

"She should start thinking now," my grandmother said. "She must get married before she's too old."

"She doesn't have to get married at all," my mom said, stroking my hair, but staring defiantly at my grandmother. "I've always told her and her brother that they should be independent. There's no reason for her to get married if she's not in love."

"Not for love," my grandmother said, unexpectedly switching into her choppy Indian English. "Just to have someone to take care of you."

"She can take care of herself," my mother said firmly, her hands raking through my hair with increasingly violent strokes.

I wandered inside and found my brother huddled beneath the ceiling fan, reading the paper.

"What are you doing?" I asked him.

"Finding you a husband," he said without looking up.

"Seriously?" I said.

"Yeah," he said, pushing his glasses up on his nose. "But you're doomed." He said *doomed* the way my family always said that word to each other: with a thick Indian accent, rolling our tongues around the d's. "Basically, they all want someone to cook them curry."

"What?" I said. "I make damn good curry."

"It's not about how good the curry is," he said. "It's about focusing your skill set. As in, only being able to make curry. In this market, autonomy and independent thought seem to be discouraged. But hey, if you drop out of college, you might still make the cut. If you finish, you'll be overqualified."

My grandmother slid up beside me and placed her gnarled hand on my shoulder. Her wrinkled brown skin always reminded me of walnuts.

"Mathangi," she said, "men are useless. Your mother is right. Don't get married."

"Oh," I said. "Okay. Um, thanks."

"Good," she said. She nodded, adjusted the *pallu* of her sari, and walked resolutely into the kitchen.

My brother tapped the paper excitedly. "Hey, this guy wants someone with a master's degree. I bet he'd settle for someone with a bachelor's," he said. "This is it! This is your man!"

"Be still my beating heart," I said.

2002

After I graduated from college, I prepared to move to the border of Mexico, where I had landed my first job: teaching chemistry at a public high school. My family was pleased, but my girlfriends were not.

"But don't you want to go to India?" they asked. "I mean, women there are *so* oppressed. Don't you want to help people where you're from?"

I didn't want to go to India and suffer through a year or two of mosquito bites the size of quarters and frequent trips to pit toilets in the middle of nowhere. I wanted to live in the United States and eat whatever I chose and sleep without a mosquito net and cross the street without fear of death-by-autorickshaw. And if it came down to where I was from, I was from America. American girls were failing out of school and living in poverty and raising babies when they were still in their teens. It seemed like I could really make a difference here, at home.

Besides, I wasn't sure what feminism had to do with it. It's not like any Indian women I knew wore makeup, other than a little bit of eyeliner now and then, and why wear a short skirt when you could wear a sari?

2003

"*Mmmff*, hello?"

"Honey? Did I wake you?"

I forced myself to sit up, blinking in the South Texas sunlight that seeped through the slats of the blinds on my windows.

"Mom, is that you?" I asked, fumbling for my glasses. "What time is it?"

"It's eight o'clock," she said. "Do you want me to call back? Were you sleeping in?"

"No, no," I said, yawning. "Is everything okay?"

"I have big news," she said. I could hear the rhythm of a knife on a cutting board in the background, and I knew that, as she often did, she was cooking as she spoke to me.

"Oh?" I said, getting out of bed and padding across the carpet into my own kitchen, fully stocked with small Tupperware containers of spices my mother gave me when I left home.

"I told you I read that book you gave me, the book about men and makeup?" she said.

"*The Beauty Myth*," I said. She had stopped buying makeup after she read it.

"Yes, that one! Well, I just read that other book you got me. *Sex and Power*?"

"Right," I said. I hadn't read it at the time, but my mom had just gotten a hard-won promotion, so I thought it was appropriate.

"I related to every single page!" she said. "It was like reading my life. There were all these stories about women taking care of their family and working full-time, and how they can't put in the same hours as men because they have to go home and cook dinner, which, you know, I used to do." My mom had taught my father to cook when she went back to school for her associate's degree in computer science and couldn't work, study, and run the house by herself anymore. "And then there was a whole part about how women get passed over for promotions," she continued. What she didn't mention is that, when she figured out her boss had passed her over the last time for yet another white male, she had marched into his office and declared loudly with the door open, "I can be a lot of things, but I can't be white!" *She* got the promotion two weeks later.

"So then I realized something," she said. I could hear the crackle of mustard seeds in hot oil, and my stomach began to rumble.

"Tell me," I said, pushing aside a stack of my students' ungraded chemistry tests to make room on the counter for a box of cereal.

"I'm a feminist!" she said, exhaling all at once.

"Wow, Mom, that's great," I said, weakly.

"Isn't that wonderful? I have been all this time, and we just didn't have a word for it," she said. I heard a splatter and she said, "Oh, hold on, I'm just adding some potatoes to the oil. Just a second."

As I chewed on my cereal, I wondered how everyone in the world seemed to be okay with the label feminist when I wasn't. Lately, I had been working my way through the collection of books about India in the local public library, particularly the ones about Indian women, which I noticed seemed to be mostly written by non-Indian women. If these books were to be believed then Indian women were submissive, abused, mouse-like creatures draped in bright colors and regrets. No matter where I looked, the message was clear: You could be Indian, and you could be a feminist, but you couldn't be both.

And yet, here was my mother, who grew up in a village in the South of India, declaring herself a feminist. If she was a feminist, was I?

2006

During my second semester of graduate school, it was time, yet again, to pick a label.

"Don't forget that one of the key parts of writing the methodology section of any ethnography is to discuss your positionality," my professor said. "You should also describe what kind of researcher you are. You might be postmodern for example, or a positivist, or a feminist."

Groan, that word again.

"I'm passing out a couple of articles that may help you decide what you are," she said, passing out a thick packet of reading.

I began reading the packet on the subway the next day. I flipped through the essays and scanned the titles and the authors' names. Then, suddenly, I stopped.

"Chandra Mohanty?" I said out loud, feeling the familiar taste of an Indian name on my tongue. I began to read. And read. And read. And I missed my stop and ended up in Brooklyn. I got out of the train, crossed the platform, and began to read again.

Mohanty called herself a third world feminist. She talked about how Western feminists fought for the right to work, while third world feminists acknowledged that women did most of the world's work, and were therefore fighting for the right to rest. She talked about how third world women fought their battles in the home, defying their family's rules about gender roles. She celebrated daily acts of defiance, like rejecting the necessity of marriage or insisting that men contribute to household chores, and said they required just as much sacrifice and courage as attending any rally in the streets. The stories she told were those of my aunts and my mother and my grandmothers, and, of course, myself.

Now this feminism fit. I wrapped it around me and snuggled in it, the yards of words like the soft fabric of my grandmother's saris.

2008

One morning, before the SAT class I started teaching at a community center in Queens, one of my Indian American students came to class with delicate swirls of henna all over her hands.

"What's with the *mendhi*?" I asked her. "Did someone get married?"

"It's Karwa Chauth," she said, holding out her hands so I could admire them. "Wives are supposed to fast for their husband's health. Are you fasting, miss?"

"No," I said, touching the tips of her fingers approvingly. "I don't have a husband, and I hate fasting. Did your mom do it?"

"Yes," she said. "And so do I."

"Who do you fast for?" I asked.

"My husband," she said. Then, seeing the look on my face, she added, "I mean, my future husband."

"Why?" I asked. "You have plenty of time to worry about being married! Worry about your career and your education now, not your marriage. Besides, it's not like your future husband is fasting for you."

"Actually," she said, "my boyfriend did fast for me."

"Really?" I asked. "Is that common?"

"Well, no," she said. "And especially not him. He's Bangladeshi and Muslim. But I told him I was doing it, and so we agreed that it was only fair if he did it, too. So he is."

"Wow," I said, truly impressed. I was about to tell her that she was quite the young feminist, but I stopped myself. I had dropped the word on the center before, and the girls usually rolled their eyes and told me, "That word's for white ladies."

How could I correct them? Two years before, I had agreed with them. I suppose I could've explained how after reading Chandra Mohanty, I had discovered Uma Narayan and Kumari Jayawardena. I could describe how I had read essay after essay about families and religion and food and history, and how I had discovered a strand of feminism that resonated with me and didn't require me to compromise myself or my past or my future. I could share my realization that every Indian woman I have ever met is a feminist, and every Bangladeshi and Sri Lankan and Pakistani woman, too, because the only place I have ever met submissive desi women is between the pages of books written by women who do not live in our community.

But what was the point? Labeled or unlabeled, brown women everywhere are struggling for each other. No matter what people call them—or, I should say, no matter what people call us—what matters the most is what we call ourselves.

5 DOES GENDER MATTER? NOTES TOWARD GENDER LIBERATION (2018)

Loan Tran is a socialist, queer, gender nonconforming Vietnamese writer and organizer based in the US South. They* have been organizing for over a decade across various struggles for liberation. Loan believes that through revolutionary solidarity and compassion we can create a world that prioritizes human needs over profit.

Activists, writers, theorists, and students have questioned, wrestled with, and problematized the concept of gender for decades, if not centuries. Different definitions have shown up in our theoretical debates, in the policies that dictate our lives, in the practices held private in our homes, in the standards we follow in public.

Gender still matters, but perhaps in different ways than it did at any other point in history. Our world is entering a new period where the understanding, practicing, and performances of gender are constantly changing. Technological, linguistic, and cultural shifts are allowing us to think about gender in a way that was unimaginable just a few decades ago. And, now, the way gender is embodied indicates a tremendous blossoming of human possibility. What do we do with all of this? How do we make sense of these changes and evolutions?

If gender still matters, how do we decide which version of it we subscribe to? The evolutions in how we understand and express gender does not make history irrelevant. That would only be the case if we understand gender unidimensionally and want to live in a stagnant world. In order for us to take up the task of undoing patriarchy and recreating a world where all of us, regardless of and in respect to our genders, can be free, we should seek to understand human change and development as dialectical, not linear. This means examining human change from as many perspectives and experiences as possible. In doing so we have the opportunity to see our histories fully, with their contradictions, trials, and errors.

We build towards a gender-liberated future that takes history into account and pays homage to those ancestors who came before us and forged a path so that we can act and speak the truth of our bodies. We also build towards this future recognizing the many pitfalls and challenges of a colonial gender binary, the structural core to patriarchy that has wedded gender to white supremacy and the logics of white supremacist violence and individualism. The colonial gender binary presupposes that being cisgender, i.e., not transgender, is the norm, and that it is acceptable to apply this norm to all gender-oppressed people in our society. Or more detrimental, the colonial gender binary can make our efforts to dismantle patriarchy reinforce cisgender as the norm if we only understand patriarchy as an issue impacting cisgender people.

Many of us alive today have the opportunity to express our most authentic selves because a "woman" or a "drag king," a "lesbian" or a "fag," a "transsexual" or a "gender deviant" person survived. Those who came before us probably did not have many of these words to describe themselves, nor were they warmly accepted. Some of these words might be outdated today. But it is still important to recognize this history, as part of the material basis for understanding gender; the material basis of being who we are, what we have access to, and how we see ourselves as informed by our relationships to each other, and to society through the social, political, and economic structures that shape our lives.

Source: Loan Tran, written for this volume.
*They is used here as the author's preferred pronoun.

Everyone is impacted by patriarchy so what we demand, under the banner of feminism, must not cause harm to anyone. In 1851, Sojourner Truth delivered the speech "Ain't I A Woman?" in an unapologetic attempt to raise the question of Black women's struggles in the broader suffrage movement. Speaking before an audience in Akron, Ohio, she asked, "If my cup won't hold but a pint, and yours holds a quart, wouldn't you be mean not to let me have my little half measure full?" In 1992, Leslie Feinberg, a transgender revolutionary, came out with a pamphlet titled "Transgender Liberation: A Movement Whose Time Has Come." Ze wrote this pamphlet to tell about the lives of transgender people who have existed throughout history and who had been both cogs and lynchpins in social, political, and economic systems. At the Women's March in 2017 in Washington, DC, Angela Davis proclaimed, "Women's rights are human rights all over the planet and that is why we say freedom and justice for Palestine. We celebrate the impending release of Chelsea Manning. And Oscar López Rivera. But we also say free Leonard Peltier. Free Mumia Abu-Jamal. Free Assata Shakur."

The common thread tying together the tremendous contributions of these revolutionaries is their ability to imagine something different, and push the boundaries of what is possible. The struggle for gender liberation is not a "women's issue" alone; it intersects with every aspect of our world. Still, we uplift the gains that have been made under the banner of women's rights, under the banner of a feminism that at times has wrongly excluded Black women, poor women, Third World women, migrant women. There is something to learn from feminism that has excluded trans people, trans women, and gender nonconforming people in particular. Namely, we are pushed to examine biological essentialism—the reduction of women's lives and experiences to mere biology (a tactic also commonly used by active proponents of patriarchy)—and how it impacts what we are able to imagine for gender liberation. Trans-exclusionary feminism has shown us that we still have much work to do to better understand how patriarchy functions and how it can evolve in order to remain relevant.

However, we cannot continue on this trajectory if we believe in a world without patriarchy. If feminists are to be concerned with women's issues, we must be concerned with trans people; if we are concerned about war, about displacement, about capitalism, about white supremacy, we must be concerned with trans people. If feminists are to be concerned with gender liberation, we must be concerned with understanding gender and gender oppression in an expansive, responsive, and materialist way—not separated from its many contradictions, tensions, and relationships to other systems of oppression and ways of being.

A Trans Feminism

In many ways, the contributions and lived experiences of transgender (trans) and gender nonconforming (GNC) communities are at the helm of advancing our understanding of gender, despite the many efforts of a white supremacist, capitalist, and patriarchal society to pathologize us. Trans and GNC people embody a fundamental reality of life: that being determines consciousness. That those who are actively transcending the colonial gender binary are living in different worlds all at once: the one which currently embraces patriarchy, the one which strives to be free of patriarchy, and the one which is free of patriarchy.

This living is complex and does not automatically create a more progressive consciousness. We should reject gender essentialism; that means we should not assume that every trans or GNC person is inherently feminist or revolutionary. The active choice to move between these worlds, identity aside, is a practice of feminism: a trans feminism that centers an analysis of the materialist politics of anti-capitalism and anti-imperialism, and embodies the values of nuance, compassion, and change.

One does not have to be trans to practice a trans feminism. On a fundamental level, gender liberation removes all pretenses about what it means to be gendered in a patriarchal society and opens up space for people to determine their own lives, bodies, and identities. There are numerous myths and false stories told about the lives of gender-oppressed people. Historical and modern-day women's movements have done significant work to undo some of the most fundamental rigidities tied to a woman's identity: the taken-for-granted notions of marriage, childrearing, or being visible but never heard.

Trans and GNC communities face similar rigidities and are not only gendered, but are gendered incorrectly. These rigidities seek to trap trans and GNC people within genders assigned at birth. This means that if a person were assigned "girl" at birth, the expectations that she be heterosexual, childrearing, and docile are suffocating. If a person were assigned "boy" at birth, the expectations are that he is heterosexual, strong, aggressive, emotionless. Often times, even when a person realizes that they are not cisgender, they are not given room to create their own path. They are expected to aspire to whatever is opposite their assigned gender. This set of contradictions can be intimidating for many cisgender people in the feminist movement who are conditioned to believe in the colonial gender binary. Some subscribe to the idea that trans people, by choosing to determine their own genders, are attempting to placate or accommodate to patriarchy's standards; that trans and GNC people are trans because there is something useful or appealing about the existing patriarchal world. Instead, feminists should recognize the self-determination of trans people as a positive contribution to feminist efforts: the struggle to allow the full breadth of human possibility to exist, even with patriarchal violence.

The experiences of trans and GNC people are not identical to those of cisgender women. But we share a common fight. The system of patriarchy is fundamentally interested in the oppression of anyone who is not a cisgender man, understanding that there are also different relationships cisgender men have to patriarchy as a result of their sexuality, migration status, race, etc. Patriarchy may offer some benefit and relief to cisgender women, especially those who are complicit in white supremacy, and who align themselves with, and thus ostensibly benefit from, heterosexist relations, and transphobia. But we all bear the ultimate cost, including cisgender women. Trans and GNC people's resistance to patriarchy's colonial binary and the performance of any adherence to the standards set for cisgender

people poses a threat to patriarchy. As feminists of all genders, oppressed by patriarchy or not, we should understand the potential for revolutionary change under the banner of trans feminism.

Trans feminism, in its best expression, is a demand that patriarchy oppresses no one; that it does not favor those who can conform while preventing the freedom of other gender-oppressed people. And more, it offers the basis for understanding the various systems that all of us are part of: white supremacy, capitalism, imperialism, classism, heterosexism and homophobia.

White Supremacy, Capitalism, and Imperialism

A materialist understanding of gender oppression benefits from understanding the intimate relationship between white supremacy, capitalism, and imperialism. In the United States we can trace a history of gender development that reveals the role white supremacy and colonialism have played in constructing a transphobic, gender binary, patriarchal society. Starting with the genocide of many Indigenous communities and the enslavement and captivity of Africans, patriarchy has worked hand-in-hand with capitalism to create the gender molds and roles that are only fit for profiteering, not for human development. This includes the erasure of Indigenous people through violence, boarding schools, and Christianization, and the subjugation of the Black body through coerced reproduction, family separation, and forced migration, which has had an undeniable impact on how this nation and the world constructs and understands gender.

Also, it is important to recognize that this construction of gender has enabled the creation of white women's identities as pillars of support for white supremacy and capitalism. It has allowed white middle- and upper-class women to benefit from racist and colonial violence, even at the cost of being defined as fragile victims, whose lives have been narrowed as a result of their complicity in the interlocking violence of white supremacy, capitalism, and patriarchy.

The silver lining is that Indigenous people have not been disappeared, that Black communities have survived for several centuries in this country, and that oppressed peoples around the globe continue to live in the traditions and spirit of their ancestry, even while imperialism attempts to undermine this. And despite the lures of capitalism and violence, many women have found that there is more power in demanding what is just, rather than succumbing to the pressures of profit making.

White supremacy, capitalism, and imperialism are thriving today, in spite of the tireless organizing led by communities of color, women, LGBTQ people, and working-class people globally to resist and to transform their lives. In the United States, it is no coincidence that young people of color are targeted as recruits for the military. It is no coincidence that Black trans women are murdered at an alarming rate. It is no coincidence that justifications for war include the infantilization of Muslim women in the Middle East. It is no coincidence that queer people are expected to be content with the legalization of gay marriage. These are the living legacies of colonization, where the intersections of gender and class, of gender and race, of gender and sexuality blare out like foghorns. The very same systems that have historically oppressed people on the basis of nation, sexualities, and genders, have a vested interest in morphing to co-opt the question of gender liberation. The ultimate goal is to make patriarchy invisible and to fragment feminist movements under the false notion that we must fight each other over the changing nature of gender and gender oppression, versus uniting to understand its many different and sometimes new manifestations.

It is in the tension of what people have lost or been harmed by and what many people have maintained, protected, and preserved, that allows us to see some of the most beautiful advances in gender expression and identity. Those advances have been made possible by the resilience, theoretical contributions, and revolutionary spirit of women, gender nonconforming people, Two-Spirit people, transgender people, and others who fight to live in defiance of colonial gender structures.

Identity as a Site of Solidarity

In an increasingly capitalistic and individualistic world, mostly we are exposed to an understanding of gender and identity as hyper-personal. While our identities are expressions of how we understand ourselves, there are so many opportunities for our identities to allow us to connect to each other. Communities built around shared identities have existed for a long time. These communities, which often exist on the margins, create sub- and countercultures that allow people to exist as their truest selves in the world, as much as this is possible.

We know that this is especially true for GNC and transgender communities, whose experiences are not a part of the dominant narrative. Trans and GNC people forge relationships over shared sadness about loved ones and families who are not accepting; through the shared reality of job or employment discrimination; in the shared fear of isolation and dehumanization. Trans and GNC people also forge bonds through the intimate processes of self-actualization, of existing in the face of many odds, of becoming and changing in a world opposed to change.

And this is also true for all gender-oppressed communities; for the networks and connections that are built outside of and in spite of patriarchal relations. Gender oppressed people have created communities of care in defiance of traditional kinds of relationships. We are not simply connected through marriage, through subservience or domestic work, or through the subjection of our images and bodies. We have acted selflessly to make our world more collective.

In short, identity matters. What we can do with our identities, beyond lenses through which we experience in the world, is even more exciting. Imagine if we saw our identities as sites of solidarity, that prioritize who are and can be together, versus who we are not. Even though it is important to acknowledge that the experiences of cisgender and trans people are different, this recognition should also carry an understanding of our shared positionality in relationship to patriarchy.

What would it be like for cisgender women to recognize the internalized patriarchy that makes women compete against each other? What is being defended here and why does it matter? What if feminist spaces offered a different possibility, one that unapologetically claims gender and womanhood to be also about anti-capitalist and anti-imperialist values, versus the notion that these spaces support some women's freedom while trans and GNC people are oppressed? What if a feminist movement in the twenty-first century sought to embrace change and acknowledge that change means another world is possible, even though most of us are led to believe that the way things are is inevitable?

This is how we can use our identities as opportunities for solidarity. As feminists we should seek understanding; to identify patterns and locate a shared vision. We work out our identities on the way to that vision, not the other way around. Around the globe, people are organizing to re-create the world. This includes attempts to be our fullest selves, with what we have and where we are. Our solidarity is what will make that possible and allow the quantitative change—how often we hear about trans and GNC people, for example—to become qualitative change—a world without patriarchy, capitalism, or imperialism.

Towards a Gender-Liberated Future

If we understand identities as sites of solidarity—our genders, sexualities, nationalities, class positions, and more—our connections can generate a blueprint toward a gender-liberated future, meaning a liberated future for all of us. What could this look like? In a gender-liberated future gender-oppressed people will not be CEOs and billionaires.

Women will not play the role of warmonger; trans and GNC people will not serve in imperialist wars. Also, this is definitely not a future where the existing power structures are inverted; where gender oppressed people are positioned to oppress others. This gender-liberated future would be a world without capitalism, without imperialism, and without the many manifestations of a society in decay: war, homelessness, poverty, unemployment, student debt, and more.

A gender-liberated future may not be entirely free of patriarchy, transphobia, or homophobia but it will affirm that biology is not destiny, and that destiny is not what we inherit or what we are told. Destiny is what we craft in the safety and security of our connections to each other, where self-determination is not an individualistic concept but the basis for our shared freedom.

This gender-liberated future will provide infinite opportunities to stop competing with each other, to stop warring with one another. We will have access to what we need to enable us to be who we need to be. We exist at a terrifying and exciting time in human evolution. We have witnessed oppressed communities change and progress in spite of dehumanization. Let the gender-liberated future be another space for limitless imagination of what is possible for humanity. And let us unite, in as many ways as possible, to make it a reality.

CHAPTER 2

Creating Knowledge:

Integrative Frameworks for Understanding

Keywords: epistemology, essentialism, media literacy, objectivity, Orientalism, relativism, standpoint, subjectivity, subjugated knowledge

People have sought to understand themselves, their home environments, and the world around them since the beginning of time. Through observation, reasoning, and trial-and-error experimentation, women developed knowledge about the breeding of wild grains; the domestication of animals; the care of infants and children; the production of materials for clothing, household items, and building; the medicinal properties of plants; and theories of health and well-being. With greater literacy, women observed and analyzed their social worlds in poetry, songs, novels, and essays that conveyed their understandings, feelings, and beliefs. These forms of expression have been powerful ways for all whose voices have been silenced or misrepresented by those in dominant positions.

Some have asked what we now think of as feminist questions: Why are women and gender nonconforming people considered less valuable than cisgender men? Why is gender-based violence a global issue? What does sexuality mean? Why is rape used as a weapon of war? Why are girls in the United States generally better at creative writing than at math? Why don't US girls do as well in math and science as their international peers? Why do so many children in the world go to bed hungry?

In this chapter, we examine theory and theory making and continue the discussion of feminist frameworks started in Chapter 1. As preparation for understanding the material presented in the rest of the book, we look at how knowledge is created and validated. People often say that facts speak for themselves. On the contrary, we argue that facts are open to interpretation and are influenced by one's perspective and beliefs. In short, how you think about people's situations and experiences affects what you see and what you understand by what you see.

Theory making takes work. As teachers, we want you to stretch yourselves intellectually as you engage with the material in this book. Also, we want you to critically assess other sources of information, whether mainstream news reporting, social media, talk shows, popular culture, or blogs. In the past twenty years or so, the climate of opinion in the United States has become more challenging for women's and gender studies as **misogyny**, racism, and **xenophobia** have gained ground in official rhetoric, legislation, policy, and the narrowing of public discourse. We urge you to take yourselves seriously as thinkers, as intellectuals, who do not settle for simplistic explanations.

WHAT IS A THEORY?

Think about the following assertion regarding poverty that many people in our society make: poor people are poor because they are lazy.

1. What is the purpose of this statement?
2. What are the underlying assumptions on which it is based?
3. Who came up with this idea, under what circumstances, and when?
4. How did this idea become popular?
5. If this statement were true, what would it imply about action that should be taken? If the statement were not true, what ideological purpose might it serve?
6. What would you need to know in order to decide whether this statement is really true?

The preceding statement is a **theory**; it is one explanation of poverty. Built on a set of assumptions, or certain factors taken for granted, this theory assumes there are well-paying jobs for all who want to work and that everyone has the necessary requirements for those jobs, such as education, skills, or a means of providing for child care. This explanation of poverty takes a moral perspective. A psychological explanation might contend that people are poor because they have low self-esteem, lack self-confidence, or take on self-defeating behaviors. A sociological explanation might conclude that structures in our society, such as the educational and economic systems, are organized to exclude certain groups from being able to live above the poverty line. Each theory explicitly or implicitly suggests how to address the issue, which can then lead to appropriate action. If the problem is defined in terms of laziness, a step to ending poverty might be to punish people who are poor; if it is defined in psychological terms, assertiveness training or counseling might be suggested; and if it is defined in terms of structural inequality, ending discrimination or creating more jobs would be the answer.

Theories may also have ideological purposes. The term **ideology** refers to an organized collection of ideas applied to public issues. America is a Christian nation, for example. Heterosexuality is normal, for another. Prisons are necessary to safeguard society, yet another. Dominant ideologies—the ideas that represent the foundational values of a particular society—often appear neutral, whereas alternative ideologies seem radical, regardless of their content. Putting forward particular ideologies is fundamental to political activity, including the roles of branches of government, political parties, lobbyists, and news reporters. **Social institutions** like education, mass media, law, and criminal justice help to support and perpetuate dominant ideologies. People in both advantaged groups and disadvantaged groups may accept dominant ideologies even though these may not be in their best interests. Can you think of examples of this?

CREATING KNOWLEDGE: EPISTEMOLOGIES, VALUES, AND METHODS

Feminist philosopher Sandra Harding (1987) identified three elements that are basic to the process of creating knowledge:

1. *Epistemology*—a theory about knowledge, who can know, and under what circumstances.
2. *Methodology*—the researcher's values and choices about how to carry out research. Researchers can pose questions, collect evidence, and analyze information in different ways based on assumptions about what knowledge is and how best to create it.
3. *Method*—the techniques for gathering and analyzing information, whether from direct observation, listening to personal stories, conducting interviews, reading documents, undertaking media analysis, statistical analysis, and so on.

Virtually everyone thinks up explanations for their experiences; that is, they create theory. For instance, we may analyze sexual abuse in our communities or the impact of unemployment on our state. Theories generated by ordinary people, however, are usually not regarded as worthy of consideration beyond their immediate circle of friends, classmates, or coworkers. Historically, white, Western, university-educated men from the upper classes and their theories, which are supported by societal institutions such as education and government, have had the greatest impact on how human beings and social phenomena are explained and understood. In the following sections, we discuss how certain kinds of theories have been legitimized in this society and suggest another way of developing knowledge. (For questions to ask in attempting to understand any theoretical perspective, see the box feature "Understanding Theoretical Perspectives.")

Dominant Perspectives

From the perspective of the **dominant culture**—the values, symbols, language, and interests of the people in power in this society—only certain types of theories have authority. Generally, the authoritativeness of a theory about human beings and society is evaluated along two dimensions. One is how closely its development followed a particular way of theorizing, the scientific method. The second is the scope and the assumed generalizability of the theory.

Most of us learned the basics of the scientific method in high school science classes. Although there are several variations, key elements must be present for a theory to fit in this category. The scientific method, originally devised by natural scientists, rests on the presumption of **objectivity**, "an attitude, philosophy, or claim . . . independent of the individual mind" (Kohl 1992, p. 84). Objectivity is seen as both a place to begin the process of theorizing and the outcome of that process. Theories developed using the scientific method are held out as value-free and neutral. The method is also empirical. That is, for something to be a fact, it must be physically observable, countable, or measurable. This proposition is extended to include the notion that something is either true or not true, fact or not fact. Last, the experimental method, commonly used in science, "attempts to understand a whole by examining its parts, asking how something works rather than why it works, and derives abstract formulas to predict future results" (Duff 1993, p. 51). These elements add up to research methods that generally

> require a distancing of the researcher from her or his subjects of study; . . . absence of emotions from the research process; ethics and values are deemed inappropriate in the research process, either as the reason for scientific inquiry or as part of the research process itself; . . . adversarial debates, whether written or oral, become the preferred method of ascertaining truth: the arguments that can withstand the greatest assault and survive intact become the strongest truth. (P. H. Collins 1990, p. 205)

Scholars in the social sciences adopted the scientific method as a way to validate and legitimate social scientific knowledge beginning in the late nineteenth century, as disciplines such as psychology and sociology were being developed. Since then, fields like education, nursing, and social work have also adopted the scientific method as the primary way to develop new knowledge, furthering the dominance of this approach.

The second dimension for evaluating and judging a theory concerns its scope and generality. The range is from the most specific explanation with the narrowest scope to the other end of the continuum, the general theory, which is the most abstract and is assumed to have the most general application. Many general theories have been promoted and accepted as universally applicable. One of them, **biological determinism**, holds that human behavior is determined by people's genes, brain size, or other biological factors like the ability to bear children. This is in contrast to the theory that human behavior—like **gender roles**, for example—is socially constructed and learned through childhood **gender socialization** and everyday experience. Most social scientists and feminist theorists argue that variations in gender roles within a society or from one society to another provide strong evidence that gender is a **social construction** (Lorber and Farrell 1991). The implication of this argument is that gender arrangements are not fixed or inevitable but can be changed. More recently, scientific researchers have come to see that ideas of biological sex, too, are constructed, as discussed by Anne Fausto-Sterling in Reading 6.

Critiques of Dominant Perspectives

Feminist theorists exposed fallacies, biases, and harmful outcomes of the scientific method as a way of creating knowledge (see, e.g., Bleier 1984; P. H. Collins 1990; Duran 1998; Shiva 1988). The primary criticisms are that knowledge created in this way is not value-free, neutral, or generalizable to the extent it is claimed to be. Science, as with other academic disciplines, is "a cultural institution and as such is structured by the political, social, and economic values of the culture within which it is practiced" (Tuana 1989, p. xi). Rather than being neutral, knowledge reflects and serves the interests of the culture that produced it. The problem is not that theories are value-laden but that the values and biases of many theories are hidden under the cloak of "scientific objectivity." Moreover, scholars, policy makers, and commentators apply many theories developed in the United States to the rest of the world, often without acknowledging that they primarily serve the interests of the dominant group in this country. An example can be found in theories of modernization, which assume that the economic development of Western Europe and North America is the path that all other nations should and will follow. This has generated a language to differentiate "developed" and "underdeveloped" nations, with the assumption that countries becoming more industrialized can be called "developing" countries, a point we return to in Chapter 8.

In Reading 6, feminist biologist Anne Fausto-Sterling provides an example of how knowledge reflects and serves the interests of the culture that produces it, and also how scientists may be pushed to rethink their perspectives as the wider society changes. Intersex activists confronted doctors who used their knowledge and authority to insist that intersex infants and children needed "corrective" surgeries to make them "fit" the male/female binary, often with horrendous consequences (Pagonis 2015). Fausto-Sterling explains that in defining biological sex, experts distinguish several levels: the genetic and cellular level, the hormonal level, and the anatomical level. She accepts criticism of her own earlier work as overly focused on genitals, the anatomical level. She came to see that these different levels make many mixes and permutations of maleness and femaleness possible, not just two, or even five—as she had proposed. "A chromosomal, hormonal and genital male (or female) may emerge with a female (or male) gender identity. Or a chromosomal female with male fetal hormones and masculinized genitalia—but with female pubertal hormones—may develop a female gender identity (Fausto-Sterling 2000, p. 22). She comments that medical and scientific communities "have yet to adopt a language that is capable of describing such diversity" (p. 22), and recognizes that "the evolving discussion about how to treat children with ambiguous genitalia is the tip of a biocultural iceberg . . . that continues to rock both medicine and our culture at large" (p. 19).

Creating knowledge is a political project, regardless of whether this is acknowledged. Social theories that explain the behavior of human beings and society support the existing social order or challenge it. For those, like feminists, who are interested in progressive social change, it is important to generate knowledge that explains everyone's experiences (particularly those whose lives and experiences have been dismissed), that provides satisfactory solutions to their difficulties, or that helps lead to their liberation.

The Role of Values

Charlotte Bunch, former director of the Center for Women's Global Leadership at Rutgers University, recommended a four-step model for theory making: describe what exists, analyze why that reality exists, determine what should exist, and hypothesize how to change what is to what should be (Bunch 1987).

Determining what should exist—the third step—is a matter of values and beliefs. It involves being able to envision (if only vaguely) another way of organizing society, free from oppression. By definition, feminism is concerned with values in its quest for liberation from intersecting discriminations based on gender, race, class, sexuality, dis/ability, nationality, and so on. Values do not emerge from facts or from the analysis of a situation but rather from people's beliefs in fairness, equality, or justice. We may learn such principles from our families, in school, or through faith-based traditions (as discussed by Deborah Lee in Reading 57). Whatever the source, feminist theorizing and projects invariably involve values, whether stated explicitly or implied. Notice the value positions in the readings included in this book—and in this book itself.

SOCIALLY LIVED THEORIZING

Theorizing is not only for elites. Feminist legal scholar Catharine MacKinnon (1991) wrote about the importance of "articulating the theory of women's practice—resistance, visions, consciousness, injuries, notions of community, experiences of inequality. By practic[e], I mean socially lived" (p. 20).

In the 1960s and 1970s, US feminists popularized the slogan "the personal is political" to validate individual women's experiences in recognizing and understanding gender-based discrimination. This promoted the practice of "starting from one's own experience" as a legitimate way to create new knowledge. This practice also counteracted the dominant view of theorizing that personal experience, along with emotions and values, contaminates the "purity" of the scientific method.

We argue that a **theoretical framework** should allow people to see the diversity of our lives and the structures of power, inequality, and opportunity that shape our experiences. Sociologist Jackie Stacey (1993) noted that the concept of **patriarchy**, meaning "the systematic organization of male supremacy" (p. 53), is central to feminist theorizing. In Reading 7, Allan G. Johnson argues that patriarchy is not just a collection of individuals but rather a system whose core values are control and domination. Everyone is involved and implicated in this system, but we can choose how we participate. This emphasis on a wider system is crucial. Without it, as Johnson suggests, our thinking is reduced to the personal or micro level, and discussion easily becomes bogged down in accusations, defensiveness, and hurt feelings.

First-person stories are compelling ways to learn about others. In this book, we include several articles by writers who reflect on their experience in order to examine social processes and institutions—that is, to open a window onto a wider world. In Reading 9, Nadine Naber discusses her upbringing in an Arab Christian family in the San Francisco Bay Area. Growing up, she was surprised to learn that her US Arab community "had more socially conservative understandings of religion, family, gender, and sexuality than their counterparts in Jordan" and asked why the stakes of family respectability were so high in America. She explains this by referring to **Orientalism,** a concept introduced by Palestinian American scholar Edward Said (1979), who argued that Western notions of Eastern or Oriental people have been "defined in terms of cultural or religious essences that are invulnerable to historical change." This generated rigid, binary, categories: Arabs or Westerners. Naber shows that as a way of retaining their culture in this country, her parents' generation "simply reversed Orientalism and used its binary categories . . . for different purposes," often valuing Arab over American culture. As a scholar-activist, she has sought to create a third place to stand: to speak frankly about the complexities of Arab American women's experiences without "Arab bashing" or Orientalism.

Standpoint Theory

Naber's work provides an example of **standpoint theory**. Sandra Harding (1998) identified four elements that contribute to constructing a standpoint as a place to generate knowledge:

1. *Physical location*—including geographical location, bodily experiences, gendered activities, and the effects of race/ethnicity, class, and nation that "place" people differently.
2. *Interests*—different locations generate different interests.
3. *Access to discourses*—provides tools for making sense of specific experiences.
4. *Social organization of knowledge production*—being situated in a university, working for a nonprofit organization, or talking informally with friends and coworkers all facilitate the creation of some kinds of knowledge and obstruct others.

By definition, standpoints are grounded and limited. We chose to open this book with Paula Gunn Allen's essay on the "red roots of white feminism" rather than with feminist writings generated in Western Europe. Allen's standpoint opens up a different perspective, grounded in the history of this nation-state, the USA, as well as a more critical view of first-wave US feminism. Our discussion of intersectionality in Chapter 1 provides another example. Many academics cite a groundbreaking paper by critical legal scholar Kimberlé Crenshaw (1993) as the source of this concept. In Chapter 1, we saw that Black women in the Combahee River Collective used this idea in the 1970s. Moreover, Beverley Guy-Sheftall (1995), a scholar dedicated to African American women's issues and writings, has pointed out that Black women in the United States were talking publicly about the intersection of race and gender as early as the 1830s, though they did not use this term back then. Each of these formulations draws on a different context or standpoint to make sense of the intertwining of race and gender in the lives of African American women—indeed, all women and men, whether heterosexual, queer, gender -nonconforming, or trans.

For Patricia Hill Collins, standpoint is not about individual experience or point of view but "historically shared, group-based experiences" (1997, p. 375). As a university professor who was raised in an African American community, she draws on these two very different standpoints in her discussion of Black feminist thought (see Reading 8). She argues that traditional creators of Black feminist thought were not recognized as theorists by university-based Eurocentric masculinist **epistemologies**, or theories of knowledge. Such thinkers included "blues singers, poets, autobiographers, storytellers, and orators validated by everyday Black women as experts on a Black woman's standpoint." As African American women have gained advanced degrees and academic positions, some have chosen to "make creative use of their outsider-within status" in resisting the dominant nature of white male patterns of thinking. Because Black women's standpoint exists in a context of domination, Collins refers to Black women's thought as **subjugated knowledge,** a term introduced by French philosopher and historian Michel Foucault (1980). Moreover, she notes that the suppression of Black women's ideas motivated them "to create knowledge that empowers people to resist domination."

Challenges to Situated Knowledge and Standpoint Theory

Critiques of **situated knowledge** and **standpoint theory** emphasize the self-centeredness of **subjectivity**, "in which knowledge and meaning [are] lodged in oneself" (Maher and Tétreault 1994, p. 94). This leads to comments such as "I can only know my own experience," "I can only speak for myself," or "What does all this have to do with *me?*"

Historian Joan Scott (1993) examined the authority of personal experience in creating theory. She acknowledged the value of theorizing from experience, especially if this has been ignored, denied, or silenced in dominant systems of knowledge production. However, she argued that experience should not be "the origin of our explanation, but that which we want to explain" (p. 412). And she warned that assuming experience to be an authoritative source of knowledge precludes questions about the constructed nature of experience. Poet and writer Minnie Bruce Pratt (1984) provided an example of this. As a white woman becoming aware of inequalities based on race, she re-thought her assumptions about herself and the world. Her new understandings meant that she learned

> a way of looking at the world that is more accurate, complex, multilayered, multidi-
> mensioned, more truthful. . . . I've learned that what is presented to me as an accurate
> view of the world is frequently a lie. . . . So I gain truth when I expand my constricted
> eye, an eye that has only let in what I have been taught to see. (p. 17)

A second critique of situated knowledge involves **relativism**. Situated knowledge is taken as authoritative because it is some group's real experience. From a relativist perspective, each group's thought is considered equally valid. Thus, the white supremacist views of neo-Nazi members are as valid as those held by antiracist activists. As a result, others may think they have no basis on which to question or challenge racism and no right to do so.

Patricia Hill Collins provided a solution to this problem. She argued that Black feminist thought offers a specific and partial perspective on domination that "allows African American women to bring a Black women's standpoint to larger epistemological dialogues" concerning the nature of domination. Thus, the ideas that are validated by other oppressed groups, based on distinctive but overlapping standpoints, become the broadest truths. This methodology requires spaces and settings—classrooms, community centers, social media, or public discussions—for sharing knowledge and for conscientious listening. Similarly, Chandra Talpade Mohanty (2003a) called for ethical and caring "non-colonized" dialogue across differences, divisions, and conflicts. These conversations are one aspect in creating **transnational feminisms**. They should be anchored in equality and respect to avoid reproducing power dynamics and inequalities among feminists that parallel those in the wider world.

In practice, such conversations may be challenging. Most of us have had few opportunities to engage in honest dialogue with others—both people like ourselves, and those from different backgrounds—about contentious issues. However, thoughtful dialogue and critical questions move us beyond excessive subjectivity because this process offers a basis for evaluating facts and experiences. It compels us to see and understand many different sides of an issue, and it allows appropriate action in a given situation. Such conversations provide a framework for deciding where to draw the line on cultural relativism.

For students of women's and gender studies, it is important to take a position on complex issues after thinking carefully about them and drawing on diverse standpoints. This is not the same as universalizing from one's own perspective or telling people what to think or what to do. Many people's experiences and agency have been excluded or erased by dominant theoretical approaches, and we do not want to replicate that way of knowing.

Purposes of Socially Lived Theorizing

We believe that knowledge should be useful for helping to transform structures of power and inequality into a sustainable world for all. As Catharine MacKinnon (1991) remarked many years ago, "It is common to say that something is good in theory but not in practice. I always want to say, then it is not such a good theory, is it?" (p. 1).

In writing about the Holocaust—the mass murder primarily of Jewish people but also of Roma, people with disabilities, and gay people in Europe before and during World War II—philosopher Alan Rosenberg (1988) made an important distinction between knowing and understanding. According to Rosenberg, knowing is having the facts about a particular event or condition. We know the Holocaust happened. The Nazis, under the leadership of Adolf Hitler, were the perpetrators. Some people inside and outside Germany tried to resist these atrocities; others, including the United States initially, were unable or refused to help. The result was the slaughter of some eight million people including six million Jews. Traditional educational practices, epitomized by the scientific method, teach us primarily to know. For Rosenberg, knowing is the first step toward understanding, a much deeper process that, in the case of the Holocaust, involves not only comprehending its significance and long-term effects but also trying to discover how to prevent similar injustices in the future:

> Knowing . . . refers to factual information or the process by which it is gathered. Understanding refers to systematically grasping the significance of an event in such a way that it becomes integrated into one's moral and intellectual life. Facts can be

absorbed without their having any impact on the way we understand ourselves or the world we live in; facts in themselves do not make a difference. It is the understanding of them that makes a difference. (Rosenberg 1988, p. 382)

Many assume that the scientific method involves authoritativeness and rigor. We maintain that the socially lived theorizing described here is also rigorous in that it requires thinking systematically and critically and talking about differences honestly. This approach obligates us to consider the implications and consequences of our theories. Knowledge created in this way helps us to grasp "the significance of an event in such a way that it becomes integrated into [our] moral and intellectual life," as Rosenberg argued.

MEDIA REPRESENTATIONS AND THE CREATION OF KNOWLEDGE

Media representations provide another avenue for disseminating information and shaping opinion. It is a truism to say that we live in a media-saturated culture with TV and radio stations broadcasting 24/7, weekly magazines, new movie releases, and constant access to the Internet. Social media platforms have expanded media access enormously, with a plethora of online publications and discussion forums.

The Stories Behind the Headlines

Mainstream media reporters, editors, and corporate sponsors are in powerful positions in terms of producing knowledge. They employ their own theories of what issues are important and who is a credible "authority." Their methodologies are shaped by their values and assumptions regarding what constitutes a "good story" and what they believe "the public wants to know." Thus, media outlets have their own standpoints: their physical and social locations, interests, and access to particular discourses. Patricia Hill Collins' view that all standpoints represent a partial perspective helps to see the limits of much media reporting, although it is often passed off as being generally relevant.

The shift from print to electronic formats means that journalists are under greater pressure to produce reports for the 24-hour news cycle. Fewer reporters have time for intensive research compared to in the past. Media scholars, critics, and some leading journalists are increasingly concerned about the "unasked" as well as "unanswered" questions in much contemporary journalism. Further, the mainstream media are owned and controlled by corporate conglomerates like Disney/ABC and Time Warner/Turner. These US media also have an international reach as shows are marketed globally. One of the media's main functions is to round up an audience for advertisers, and advertisers influence media content, especially in television. From time to time, they may threaten to pull advertising if they think a show's content will "turn off" their intended audience, and editors and directors are expected to toe the line.

Proliferating web-based media, with their various sub-audiences, undercut the assumed authoritativeness of older media outlets. However, social media platforms like Facebook, YouTube, Twitter, Pinterest, and Instagram are also corporate ventures dominated by advertising (Shepherd 2014). As a condition of our using such sites, these companies have unprecedented access to our personal information in order to direct specific advertising our way. Moreover, online business models that seek to maximize "clicks" as a way to earn advertising revenue encourage the posting of information that is "click-worthy" regardless of whether it is accurate. Indeed, fake news has become a worldwide phenomenon in recent years. This occurs when someone posts inaccurate material that is then "picked up by dozens of other blogs, retransmitted by hundreds of websites, cross-posted over thousands of social media accounts and read by hundreds of thousands" of people (Bounegru et al. 2017). This may be done deliberately or inadvertently, but always has the effect of misleading readers about the facts of an issue. This is especially significant as 62 percent of US adults get news from social media (Gottfried and Shearer 2016, p. 2). (Note: this is very different from President Trump's use of the term *fake news* to refer to accurate news stories that he does not like.)

Whose Knowledge?

Women are marginalized in US news media, as are men of color and white working-class men. Although a few notable female media personalities like Rachel Maddow and Oprah Winfrey host TV news and talk shows, most women on television appear in the context of entertainment, home, and personal relationships. Much media representation serves to reinforce ideological notions of women's roles, bodies, and sexuality. Women are more likely to be included in "lifestyle" pieces as opposed to "hard" news, business, or sports. Women are least likely to be quoted in stories about foreign affairs, giving the impression that there are no women with expertise in this area. Moreover, faculty and administrators "who run the nation's journalism and mass communication schools are overwhelmingly white, and two-thirds of them are male," even though about two-thirds of their students are women (University of Maryland 2007).

A similar pattern is seen internationally. Compiling data from 114 countries, the Global Media Monitoring Project found that women were a minority of people in the news and a minority of reporters and presenters; also, most news reports had little or no serious gender perspective (Macharia 2015). In Reading 40, Mark Graham and Anasuya Sengupta note that Wikipedia, the go-to resource for information, written by volunteers, is slanted by geography and by gender. In 2017, the majority of the world's population had online access, yet "web content remains heavily skewed toward rich, Western countries." Further, information studies researcher Safiya Umoja Noble (2018) shows how search engines use algorithms based on assumptions that reinforce racist stereotypes.

Alternative media provide important sources of news (e.g., www.womensenews.org, www.alternet.org, and www.dollarsandsense.org) and feminist perspectives (e.g., https://www.bitchmedia.org and http://feministing.com/). International women's organizations use websites, newsletters, radio shows, and community theater to share their perspectives. Examples include Asia Pacific Forum on Women, Law, and Development; Development Alternatives with Women for a New Era (DAWN); Federation of African Media Women; FEMPRESS (Chile); International Women's Media Foundation; ISIS International Manila; Women's Feature Service (India); and the projects and organizations cited in other chapters throughout this book.

Reading Media Texts

Media texts are often layered and complex. TV shows take up serious issues; US news reports focus on the flip, titillating, and controversial; social media offer a range of information and opinion; and popular culture provides enjoyment as well as ways to think about salient social issues.

As media consumers, people develop sophisticated skills in "reading" media texts, whether they are ads, blogs, sitcoms, news reports, feature films, or documentaries (see the box feature "Principles of Media Literacy"). Media audiences and Internet users bring our standpoints to what we watch, read, and hear, just as students bring their communities' standpoints into the classroom. The more we know about particular people, the more we are able to judge the accuracy of media representations and to notice whether they reproduce myths and stereotypes, romanticize or exoticize people, or open up the possibility of new—even transgressive—readings. Reading "with the grain" involves reading a text as the author or filmmaker likely intended it to be understood. In reading "against the grain," we analyze beliefs or assumptions that typically go unexamined in a text, "drawing attention to gaps, silences, and contradictions" (Teaching Tolerance 2018). Whitney Pow provides an example of this in her critique of media representations of Asian Americans in Reading 10. Asian Americans constitute a very diverse group, with connections to the United States reaching back generations. Asian American women and men topped the US earnings charts in 2017 and many young Asian Americans are in college, yet mainstream media still portray Asian Americans in stereotypical ways.

Many scholars, commentators, and policy-makers argue that consumers must develop media literacy. The United Nations Educational Scientific and Cultural Organization (UNESCO) contends that

> Media and [i]nformation [l]iteracy . . . lies at the core of freedom of expression and information—since it empowers citizens to understand the functions of media and other information providers, to critically evaluate their content, and to make informed decisions as users and producers of information and media. (UNESCO 2018)

While accepting the value of this, media researcher Rosalind Gill observes that an emphasis on media literacy "forces the work of deconstructing media back on to individuals" (2014, p. 595). Writing about sexism in media representations she asks:

> When did engaging with sexist media seem to call out for an ever more sophisticated and literate media user rather than a campaign to stamp out sexism? (p. 596)

In other chapters we include several articles about media representations that further this discussion (see Readings 17, 18, 21, 22, 28, and 59).

To summarize, in this chapter we argue that facts are always open to interpretation and that everyone makes theory in trying to understand their experiences. Feminist theories involve analyses of gender and patriarchy. They are based on clear value positions and constitute a critique of the dominant view that sees theory as "objective" or "value-free." Socially lived theorizing requires collective dialogue, careful listening to other people's views, and sophisticated skills in "reading" media texts so that we do not incorporate stereotypical notions of others into our theory making.

This chapter may seem abstract at first, and you may want to return to it as you work with the later material in this book. It is also a good idea to review it at the end of your course. Or, you can study this chapter after you have read some of the thematic chapters that follow.

Principles of Media Literacy

1. **All media messages are "constructed."** Media messages involve many decisions about what to include or exclude and how to present "reality." Knowing this enables readers to challenge the power of media to present transparent messages. Semiotics, the science of signs and how meanings are socially produced, has contributed greatly to media literacy. It aims to challenge the apparent naturalness of a message, the "what goes without saying."
   Question: Who created this message?

2. **Media messages are constructed using a creative language with its own rules.** Students of media literacy analyze the dual meanings of signs: the *signifier*, the more literal reference to content, and the *signified*, the more subjective significations of a message. As you watch a film or TV show, try to separate what you see or hear from what you think or feel.
   Question: What creative techniques are being used to attract my attention?

3. **Different people experience the same media messages differently.** Cultural studies professor Stuart Hall (1980) distinguished between the encoding of media texts by producers and the decoding by consumers. This distinction highlights the ability of audiences to produce their own readings and meanings and to decode texts in "deviant" or oppositional ways, as well as "preferred" ways in line with the dominant ideology. Differences of gender, race, class, sexuality, dis/ability, or national origin may allow people to produce different readings.
   Question: How might different people understand this message differently?

4. **Media have embedded values and points of view.** Analyzing the content of media messages is a key approach in cultural studies in order to question and expose ideology, bias, and the connotations explicit and implicit in media representations. Commenting on the TV series *Buffy, the Vampire Slayer*, Kellner and Share (2005) noted that the monsters "can be read as signifying the dangers of drugs, rampant sexuality, or gangs producing destructive violence. Content is often highly symbolic and thus requires a wide range of theoretical approaches to grasp the multi-dimensional social, political, moral, and sometimes philosophical meanings of a cultural text" (p. 376).
   Question: What values, lifestyles, and points of view are represented in, or omitted from, this message?

5. **Most media messages are organized to gain profit or power.** Mainstream media messages are generated in an industry dominated by a handful of mega-corporations. Their purpose is not simply to entertain or inform. Knowing which corporation owns a particular news outlet or what system of production dominates given media forms will help in interpreting the viewpoints embedded in media texts.
   Questions: Why is this message being sent? Why is it being sent at this time?

Sources: Kellner and Share (2005); also see Center for Media Literacy (www.medialit.org).

QUESTIONS FOR REFLECTION

As you read and discuss this chapter, think about these questions:

1. How do *you* explain poverty? In the United States? Worldwide? Are these linked? If so, how?
2. How do you explain inequalities based on gender and race in the United States?
3. What does it take for a member of a dominant group (e.g., a white man or cis-woman) to learn from and value the experiences of someone from another group (e.g., a Native American woman or a trans person)?
4. What standpoints help to give full and cogent explanations of issues such as fat shaming or global warming?
5. Consider people and events that have affected the development of your thinking. How did this happen? Who—or what—influenced you?
6. What do you value, and how did you learn this?
7. How do you know what you know? How is this connected to your standpoint?

FINDING OUT MORE ON THE WEB

1. Explore the website of a feminist organization. What can you learn about the organization's theoretical framework? How does this inform its activities? Here are some examples to get you started:

    Development Alternatives with Women for a New Era (DAWN): www.dawnnet.org
    Fund for a Feminist Majority: http://feminist.org
    Global Fund for Women: https://www.globalfundforwomen.org
    Global Women's Strike: www.globalwomenstrike.net
    International Community of Women Living with HIV/AIDS: http://www.icwglobal.
    org/our-organization/today
    National Organization for Women: www.now.org
    Revolutionary Association for Women in Afghanistan: www.rawa.org
    Women Living Under Muslim Laws: http://www.wluml.org/

2. Compare editorial perspectives and news coverage of an issue you care about in progressive magazines, foreign newspapers online, or feminist blogs with those of mainstream US media reporting. Examples of feminist blogs include:

    http://feministing.com
    http://msmagazine.com/blog/
    http://quirkyblackgirls.blogspot.com
    https://blog.feedspot.com/feminist_blogs/
    https://ladyeconomistdotcom.wordpress.com
    https://www.msafropolitan.com/

3. Find out about the work of international women's media organizations cited in this chapter, as well as the work of the following:
    Global Media Monitoring Project: http://whomakesthenews.org/
    International Women's Media Foundation: https://www.iwmf.org/
    Whose Knowledge? https://whoseknowledge.org/

TAKING ACTION

1. Analyze what happens when you get into an argument with a friend, classmate, or teacher about an issue. Are you both using the same assumptions? Do you understand the other person's point of view? Could you explain your position more clearly, or do you need to rethink it? How might you convince someone who is skeptical of your views? Use what you have learned from this chapter to express your opinions.
2. Incorporate the ideas from this chapter into your "reading" of popular culture and social media.
3. Look critically at media representations of people like you and people in other groups. How are they portrayed? Is anything left out of these representations? If they reinforce stereotypes how do they do it?
4. Read a novel like Gerd Brantenberg's *Egalia's Daughters* (2004) that redefines gender roles and stereotypes. What do you learn about your assumptions?

ANNE FAUSTO-STERLING

6 THE FIVE SEXES, REVISITED (2000)

Anne Fausto-Sterling is Brown University Professor Emerita and fellow of the American Association for the Advancement of Science. She is a leading expert in biology and gender development. Her books include *Myths of Gender: Biological Theories about Women and Men* (1992), *Sexing the Body: Gender Politics and the Construction of Sexuality* (2000), and *Sex/Gender: Biology in a Social World* (2012).

As Cheryl Chase stepped to the front of the packed meeting room in the Sheraton Boston Hotel, nervous coughs made the tension audible. Chase, an activist for intersexual rights, had been invited to address the May 2000 meeting of the Lawson Wilkins Pediatric Endocrine Society (LWPES), the largest organization in the United States for specialists in children's hormones. Her talk would be the grand finale to a four-hour symposium on the treatment of genital ambiguity in newborns, infants born with a mixture of both male and female anatomy, or genitals that appear to differ from their chromosomal sex. The topic was hardly a novel one to the assembled physicians.

Yet Chase's appearance before the group was remarkable. Three and a half years earlier, the American Academy of Pediatrics had refused her request for a chance to present the patients' viewpoint on the treatment of genital ambiguity, dismissing Chase and her supporters as "zealots." About two dozen intersex people had responded by throwing up a picket line. The Intersex Society of North America (ISNA) even issued a press release: "Hermaphrodites Target Kiddie Docs."

It had done my 1960s street-activist heart good. In the short run, I said to Chase at the time, the picketing would make people angry. But eventually, I assured her, the doors then closed would open. Now, as Chase began to address the physicians at their own convention, that prediction was coming true. Her talk, titled "Sexual Ambiguity:

The Patient-Centered Approach," was a measured critique of the near-universal practice of performing immediate, "corrective" surgery on thousands of infants born each year with ambiguous genitalia. Chase herself lives with the consequences of such surgery. Yet her audience, the very endocrinologists and surgeons Chase was accusing of reacting with "surgery and shame," received her with respect. Even more remarkably, many of the speakers who preceded her at the session had already spoken of the need to scrap current practices in favor of treatments more centered on psychological counseling.

What led to such a dramatic reversal of fortune? Certainly, Chase's talk at the LWPES symposium was a vindication of her persistence in seeking attention for her cause. But her invitation to speak was also a watershed in the evolving discussion about how to treat children with ambiguous genitalia. And that discussion, in turn, is the tip of a biocultural iceberg—the gender iceberg—that continues to rock both medicine and our culture at large.

Chase made her first national appearance in 1993, in these very pages, announcing the formation of ISNA in a letter responding to an essay I had written for *The Sciences*, titled "The Five Sexes" [March/April 1993]. In that article I argued that the two-sex system embedded in our society is not adequate to encompass the full spectrum of human sexuality. In its place, I suggested a five-sex system. In addition to males and females, I included "herms" (named after true hermaphrodites, people born with both a testis and an ovary); "merms" (male

Source: Anne Fausto Sterling, "The Five Sexes, Revisited" *The Sciences*, July/August 2000, pp. 19-23. Reprinted with permission of John Wiley & Sons; permissions conveyed through Copyright Clearance Center, Inc.

pseudohermaphrodites, who are born with testes and some aspect of female genitalia); and "ferms" (female pseudohermaphrodites, who have ovaries combined with some aspect of male genitalia).

I had intended to be provocative, but I had also written with tongue firmly in cheek. So I was surprised by the extent of the controversy the article unleashed. Right-wing Christians were outraged, and connected my idea of five sexes with the United Nations–sponsored Fourth World Conference on Women, held in Beijing in September 1995. At the same time, the article delighted others who felt constrained by the current sex and gender system.

Clearly, I had struck a nerve. The fact that so many people could get riled up by my proposal to revamp our sex and gender system suggested that change— as well as resistance to it—might be in the offing. Indeed, a lot has changed since 1993, and I like to think that my article was an important stimulus. As if from nowhere, intersexuals are materializing before our very eyes. Like Chase, many have become political organizers, who lobby physicians and politicians to change current treatment practices. But more generally, though perhaps no less provocatively, the boundaries separating masculine and feminine seem harder than ever to define.

Some find the changes underway deeply disturbing. Others find them liberating.

Who is an intersexual—and how many intersexuals are there? The concept of intersexuality is rooted in the very ideas of male and female. In the idealized, Platonic, biological world, human beings are divided into two kinds: a perfectly dimorphic species. Males have an X and a Y chromosome, testes, a penis and all of the appropriate internal plumbing for delivering urine and semen to the outside world. They also have well-known secondary sexual characteristics, including a muscular build and facial hair. Women have two X chromosomes, ovaries, all of the internal plumbing to transport urine and ova to the outside world, a system to support pregnancy and fetal development, as well as a variety of recognizable secondary sexual characteristics.

That idealized story papers over many obvious caveats: some women have facial hair, some men have none; some women speak with deep voices, some men veritably squeak. Less well known is the fact that, on close inspection, absolute dimorphism disintegrates even at the level of basic biology. Chromosomes, hormones, the internal sex structures, the gonads and the external genitalia all vary more than most people realize. Those born outside of the Platonic dimorphic mold are called intersexuals.

In "The Five Sexes" I reported an estimate by a psychologist expert in the treatment of intersexuals, suggesting that some 4 percent of all live births are intersexual. Then, together with a group of Brown University undergraduates, I set out to conduct the first systematic assessment of the available data on intersexual birthrates. We scoured the medical literature for estimates of the frequency of various categories of intersexuality, from additional chromosomes to mixed gonads, hormones and genitalia. For some conditions we could find only anecdotal evidence; for most, however, numbers exist. On the basis of that evidence, we calculated that for every 1,000 children born, seventeen are intersexual in some form. That number—1.7 percent—is a ballpark estimate, not a precise count, though we believe it is more accurate than the 4 percent I reported.

Our figure represents all chromosomal, anatomical and hormonal exceptions to the dimorphic ideal; the number of intersexuals who might, potentially, be subject to surgery as infants is smaller—probably between one in 1,000 and one in 2,000 live births. Furthermore, because some populations possess the relevant genes at high frequency, the intersexual birthrate is not uniform throughout the world.

Consider, for instance, the gene for congenital adrenal hyperplasia (CAH). When the CAH gene is inherited from both parents, it leads to a baby with masculinized external genitalia who possesses two X chromosomes and the internal reproductive organs of a potentially fertile woman. The frequency of the gene varies widely around the world: in New Zealand it occurs in only forty-three children per million; among the Yupik Eskimo of southwestern Alaska, its frequency is 3,500 per million.

Intersexuality has always been to some extent a matter of definition. And in the past century physicians have been the ones who defined children as intersexual—and provided the remedies. When only the chromosomes are unusual, but the external genitalia and gonads clearly indicate either a male or a female, physicians do not advocate intervention. Indeed, it is not clear what kind of intervention could be advocated in such cases. But the story is quite different when infants are born with mixed genitalia, or with external genitals that seem at odds with the baby's gonads.

Most clinics now specializing in the treatment of intersex babies rely on case-management principles developed in the 1950s by the psychologist John Money and the psychiatrists Joan G. Hampson and John L. Hampson, all of Johns Hopkins University in Baltimore, Maryland. Money believed that gender identity is completely malleable for about eighteen months after birth. Thus, he argued, when a treatment team is presented with an infant who has ambiguous genitalia, the team could make a gender assignment solely on the basis of what made the best surgical sense. The physicians could then simply encourage the parents to raise the child according to the surgically assigned gender. Following that course, most physicians maintained, would eliminate psychological distress for both the patient and the parents. Indeed, treatment teams were never to use such words as "intersex" or "hermaphrodite"; instead, they were to tell parents that nature intended the baby to be the boy or the girl that the physicians had determined it was. Through surgery, the physicians were merely completing nature's intention.

Although Money and the Hampsons published detailed case studies of intersex children who they said had adjusted well to their gender assignments, Money thought one case in particular proved his theory. It was a dramatic example, inasmuch as it did not involve intersexuality at all: one of a pair of identical twin boys lost his penis as a result of a circumcision accident. Money recommended that "John" (as he came to be known in a later case study) be surgically turned into "Joan" and raised as a girl. In time, Joan grew to love wearing dresses and having her hair done. Money proudly proclaimed the sex reassignment a success.

But as recently chronicled by John Colapinto, in his book *As Nature Made Him*, Joan—now known to be an adult male named David Reimer—eventually rejected his female assignment. Even without a functioning penis and testes (which had been removed as part of the reassignment) John/Joan sought masculinizing medication, and married a woman with children (whom he adopted).

Since the full conclusion to the John/Joan story came to light, other individuals who were reassigned as males or females shortly after birth but who later rejected their early assignments have come forward. So, too, have cases in which the reassignment has worked—at least into the subject's mid-twenties. But even then the aftermath of the surgery can be problematic. Genital surgery often leaves scars that reduce sexual sensitivity. Chase herself had a complete clitoridectomy, a procedure that is less frequently performed on intersexuals today. But the newer surgeries, which reduce the size of the clitoral shaft, still greatly reduce sensitivity.

The revelation of cases of failed reassignments and the emergence of intersex activism have led an increasing number of pediatric endocrinologists, urologists and psychologists to reexamine the wisdom of early genital surgery. For example, in a talk that preceded Chase's at the LWPES meeting, the medical ethicist Laurence B. McCullough of the Center for Medical Ethics and Health Policy at Baylor College of Medicine in Houston, Texas, introduced an ethical framework for the treatment of children with ambiguous genitalia. Because sex phenotype (the manifestation of genetically and embryologically determined sexual characteristics) and gender presentation (the sex role projected by the individual in society) are highly variable, McCullough argues, the various forms of intersexuality should be defined as normal. All of them fall within the statistically expected variability of sex and gender. Furthermore, though certain disease states may accompany some forms of intersexuality, and may require medical intervention, intersexual conditions are not themselves diseases.

McCullough also contends that in the process of assigning gender, physicians should minimize what he calls irreversible assignments: taking steps such as the surgical removal or modification of gonads or genitalia that the patient may one day want to have reversed. Finally, McCullough urges physicians to abandon their practice of treating the birth of a child with genital ambiguity as a medical or social emergency. Instead, they should take the time to perform a thorough medical workup and should disclose everything to the parents, including the uncertainties about the final outcome. The treatment mantra, in other words, should be therapy, not surgery.

I believe a new treatment protocol for intersex infants, similar to the one outlined by McCullough, is close at hand. Treatment should combine some basic medical and ethical principles with a practical but less drastic approach to the birth of a mixed-sex child. As a first step, surgery on infants should be performed only to save the child's life or to substantially improve the child's physical well-being. Physicians may assign a sex—male or female—to an intersex infant on the basis of the probability that the child's particular condition will lead to the formation of a particular gender identity. At the same time, though, practitioners ought to be humble enough to recognize that as the child grows, he or she may reject the assignment—and they should be wise enough to listen to what the child has to say. Most important, parents should have access to the full range of information and options available to them.

Sex assignments made shortly after birth are only the beginning of a long journey. Consider, for instance, the life of Max Beck: Born intersexual, Max was surgically assigned as a female and consistently raised as such. Had her medical team followed her into her early twenties, they would have deemed her assignment a success because she was married to a man. (It should be noted that success in gender assignment has traditionally been defined as living in that gender as a heterosexual.) Within a few years, however, Beck had come out as a butch lesbian; now in her mid-thirties, Beck has become a man and married his lesbian partner, who (through the miracles of modern reproductive technology) recently gave birth to a girl.

Transsexuals, people who have an emotional gender at odds with their physical sex, once described themselves in terms of dimorphic absolutes—males trapped in female bodies, or vice versa. As such, they sought psychological relief through surgery. Although many still do, some so-called transgendered people today are content to inhabit a more ambiguous zone. A male-to-female transsexual, for instance, may come out as a lesbian. Jane, born a physiological male, is now in her late thirties and living with her wife, whom she married when her name was still John. Jane takes hormones to feminize herself, but they have not yet interfered with her ability to engage in intercourse as a man. In her mind Jane has a lesbian relationship with her wife, though she views their intimate moments as a cross between lesbian and heterosexual sex.

It might seem natural to regard intersexuals and transgendered people as living midway between the poles of male and female. But male and female, masculine and feminine, cannot be parsed as some kind of continuum. Rather, sex and gender are best conceptualized as points in a multidimensional space. For some time, experts on gender development have distinguished between sex at the genetic level and at the cellular level (sex-specific gene expression, X and Y chromosomes); at the hormonal level (in the fetus, during childhood and after puberty); and at the anatomical level (genitals and secondary sexual characteristics). Gender identity presumably emerges from all of those corporeal aspects via some poorly understood interaction with environment and experience. What has become increasingly clear is that one can find levels of masculinity and femininity in almost every possible permutation. A chromosomal, hormonal and genital male (or female) may emerge with a female (or male) gender identity. Or a chromosomal female with male fetal hormones and masculinized genitalia—but with female pubertal hormones—may develop a female gender identity.

The medical and scientific communities have yet to adopt a language that is capable of describing such diversity. In her book *Hermaphrodites and the Medical Invention of Sex*, the historian and medical ethicist Alice Domurat Dreger of Michigan State University in East Lansing documents the emergence of current medical systems for classifying gender ambiguity. The current usage remains rooted in the Victorian approach to sex. The logical structure of the commonly used terms "true hermaphrodite," "male pseudohermaphrodite" and "female pseudohermaphrodite" indicates that only the so-called true hermaphrodite is a genuine mix of male and female. The others, no matter how confusing their body parts, are really hidden males or females. Because true hermaphrodites are rare—possibly only one in 100,000—such a classification system supports the idea that human beings are an absolutely dimorphic species.

At the dawn of the twenty-first century, when the variability of gender seems so visible, such a position is hard to maintain. And here, too, the old medical consensus has begun to crumble. Last fall the pediatric urologist Ian A. Aaronson of the Medical University of South Carolina in Charleston organized the North American Task Force on Intersexuality (NATFI) to review the clinical responses to genital ambiguity in infants. Key medical associations, such as the American Academy of Pediatrics, have endorsed NATFI. Specialists in surgery, endocrinology, psychology, ethics, psychiatry, genetics and public health, as well as intersex patient-advocate groups, have joined its ranks.

One of the goals of NATFI is to establish a new sex nomenclature. One proposal under consideration replaces the current system with emotionally neutral terminology that emphasizes developmental processes rather than preconceived gender categories. For example, Type I intersexes develop out of anomalous virilizing influences; Type II result from some interruption of virilization; and in Type III intersexes the gonads themselves may not have developed in the expected fashion.

What is clear is that since 1993, modern society has moved beyond five sexes to a recognition that gender variation is normal and, for some people, an arena for playful exploration. Discussing my "five sexes" proposal in her book *Lessons from the Intersexed*, the psychologist Suzanne J. Kessler of the State University of New York at Purchase drives this point home with great effect:

> The limitation with Fausto-Sterling's proposal is that . . . [it] still gives genitals . . . primary signifying status and ignores the fact that in the everyday world gender attributions are made without access to genital inspection. . . . What has primacy in everyday life is the gender that is performed, regardless of the flesh's configuration under the clothes.

I now agree with Kessler's assessment. It would be better for intersexuals and their supporters to turn everyone's focus away from genitals. Instead, as she suggests, one should acknowledge that people come in an even wider assortment of sexual identities and characteristics than mere genitals can distinguish. Some women may have "large clitorises or fused labia," whereas some men may have "small penises or misshapen scrota," as Kessler puts it, "phenotypes with no particular clinical or identity meaning."

As clearheaded as Kessler's program is—and despite the progress made in the 1990s—our society is still far from that ideal. The intersexual or transgendered person who projects a social gender—what Kessler calls "cultural genitals"—that conflicts with his or her physical genitals still may die for the transgression. Hence legal protection for people whose cultural and physical genitals do not match is needed during the current transition to a more gender-diverse world. One easy step would be to eliminate the category of "gender" from official documents, such as driver's licenses and passports. Surely attributes both more visible (such as height, build and eye color) and less visible (fingerprints and genetic profiles) would be more expedient.

A more far-ranging agenda is presented in the International Bill of Gender Rights, adopted in 1995 at the fourth annual International Conference on Transgender Law and Employment Policy in Houston, Texas. It lists ten "gender rights," including the right to define one's own gender, the right to change one's physical gender if one so chooses and the right to marry whomever one wishes. . . .

No one could have foreseen such changes in 1993. And the idea that I played some role, however small, in reducing the pressure—from the medical community as well as from society at large—to flatten the diversity of human sexes into two diametrically opposed camps gives me pleasure.

Sometimes people suggest to me, with not a little horror, that I am arguing for a pastel world in which androgyny reigns and men and women are boringly the same. In my vision, however, strong colors coexist with pastels. There are and will continue to be highly masculine people out there; it's just that some of them are women. And some of the most feminine people I know happen to be men.

ALLAN G. JOHNSON

7 PATRIARCHY, THE SYSTEM: AN IT, NOT A HE, A THEM, OR AN US (1997)

Allan G. Johnson (1946–2017) was a sociologist, author, and public speaker with thirty years of teaching experience exploring issues of privilege, oppression, and social inequality. His books include *The Forest and the Trees: Sociology as Life, Practice, and Promise* (1997), and *The Gender Knot: Unraveling Our Patriarchal Legacy* (1997).

"When you say patriarchy," a man complained from the rear of the audience, "I know what you *really* mean—me!" A lot of people hear "men" whenever someone says "patriarchy," so that criticism of male privilege and the oppression of women is taken to mean that all men—each and every one of them—are oppressive people. It's enough to prompt many men to take it personally, bristling at what they often see as a way to make them feel guilty. And some women feel free to blame individual men for patriarchy simply because they're men. Some of the time, men feel defensive because they identify with patriarchy and its values and don't want to face the consequences these produce or the prospect of giving up male privilege. But defensiveness can also reflect a common confusion about the difference between patriarchy as a kind of society and the people who participate in it. If we're ever going to work toward real change, it's a confusion we'll have to clear up.

To do this, we have to realize that we're stuck in a model of social life that views everything as beginning and ending with individuals. Looking at things in this way, the tendency is to think that if bad things happen in the world, it's only because there are bad people who have entered into some kind of conspiracy. Racism exists, then, because white people are racist bigots who hate members of racial and ethnic minorities and want to do them harm. The oppression of women happens because men want and like to dominate women and act out hostility toward them. There is poverty and class oppression because people in the upper classes are greedy, heartless, and cruel. The flip side of this individualistic model of guilt and blame is that race, gender, and class oppression are actually not oppression at all, but merely the sum of individual failings on the part of Blacks, women, and the poor, who lack the right stuff to compete successfully with whites, men, and others who know how to make something of themselves.

What this kind of thinking ignores is that we are all participating in something larger than ourselves or any collection of us. On some level, most people are familiar with the idea that social life involves us in something larger than ourselves, but few seem to know what to do with that idea. Blaming everything on "the system" strikes a deep chord in many people. But it also touches on a basic misunderstanding of social life, because blaming "the system" (presumably society) for our problems, doesn't take the next step to understanding what that might mean. What exactly *is* a system, for example, and how could it run our lives? Do *we* have anything to do with shaping *it*, and if so, how? How, for example, do we participate in patriarchy, and how does that link us to the consequences? How is what we think of as "normal" life related to male privilege, women's oppression, and the hierarchical, control-obsessed world in which everyone's lives are embedded? . . .

If we see patriarchy as nothing more than men's and women's individual personalities, motivations, and behavior, for example, then it probably won't even occur to us to ask about larger contexts—such as institutions like the family, religion, and the economy—and how people's lives are shaped in relation to them. From this kind of individualistic perspective, we might ask why a particular man raped, harassed, or beat a woman. We wouldn't ask, however, what kind of society would promote persistent *patterns* of such behavior in everyday life, from wife-beating jokes to the routine inclusion of sexual coercion and violence in mainstream movies. We'd be quick to explain rape and battery as the acts of sick or angry men, but we'd rarely take seriously the question of what kind of society would produce so much male anger and pathology or direct it toward sexual violence rather than something else. We'd rarely ask how gender violence might serve other more "normalized" ends such as male control and domination. We might ask why a man would like pornography that objectifies, exploits, and promotes violence against women, or debate whether the Constitution protects an individual's right to produce and distribute it. But it'd be hard to stir up interest in asking what kind of society would give violent and degrading visions of women's bodies and human sexuality such a prominent and pervasive place in its culture to begin with.

. . . We need to see and deal with the social roots that generate and nurture the social problems that are reflected in and manifested through the behavior of individuals. We can't do this without realizing that we all participate in something larger than ourselves, something we didn't create but that we have the power to affect through the choices we make about *how* to participate.

Some readers have objected to "participate" as a way to describe women's relation to patriarchy. This is based on the idea that participation is something voluntary, freely chosen, entered into as equals, and it therefore makes little sense to suggest that women can participate in their own oppression. But that is not my meaning here, nor is it a necessary interpretation of the word. To *participate* is simply to have a *part* in what goes on, to do something (or *not*) and to have the choice affect the consequences, regardless of whether it is conscious or unconscious, coerced or not. Of course, the *terms* of women's participation differ dramatically from those that shape men's, but it is participation, nonetheless.

This concept is similar to the participation of workers in the system of capitalism. They do not participate as equals to the capitalists who employ them or on terms they would choose if they could. Nevertheless, without them, capitalism cannot function as a system that oppresses them.

The importance of participation can be seen in the great variety of ways that women and working-class people respond to oppression—all the forms that fighting back or giving in can take. To argue that women or workers do not participate is to render them powerless and irrelevant to patriarchy's and capitalism's past and future, for it is only as participants that people can affect anything. . . .

The something larger we all participate in is patriarchy, which is more than a collection of individuals (such as "men"). It is a system, which means it can't be reduced to the people who participate in it. If you go to work in a corporation, for example, you know the minute you walk in the door that you've entered "something" that shapes your experience and behavior, something that isn't just you and the other people you work with. You can feel yourself stepping into a set of relationships and shared understandings about who's who and what's supposed to happen and why, and all of this limits you in many ways. And when you leave at the end of the day you can feel yourself released from the constraints imposed by your participation in that system. You can feel the expectations drop away and your focus shift to other systems such as family or a neighborhood bar that shape your experience in different ways.

To understand a system like a corporation, we have to look at more than people like you, because all of you aren't the corporation, even though you make it run. If the corporation were just a collection of people, then whatever happened to the corporation would by definition also happen to them, and vice versa. But clearly this isn't so. A corporation can go bankrupt or cease to exist altogether without any of the people who work there going bankrupt or disappearing. Or everyone who works for a corporation could quit, but that wouldn't necessarily mean the end of the corporation, only the arrival of a new set of participants. We can't understand a system, then, just by looking at the people who participate in it, for it is something larger and has to be understood as such.

Even more so, we cannot understand the world and our lives in it without looking at the dynamic relationship between individual people and social systems. Nor can we understand the countless details—from sexual violence to patterns of conversation to unequal distributions of power—that make up the reality of male privilege and the oppression of women.

As the accompanying figure shows, this relationship has two parts. The arrow on the right side represents the idea that as we participate in social systems, we are shaped as individuals. Through the process of *socialization*, we learn how to participate in social life—from families, schools, religion, and the mass media, through the examples set by parents, peers, coaches, teachers, and public figures—a continuing stream of ideas and images of people and the world and who we are in relation to them.

Through all of this, we develop a sense of personal identity—including gender—and how this positions us in relation to other people, especially in terms of inequalities of power. As I grew up watching movies and television, for example, the message was clear that men are the most important people on the planet because they're the ones who supposedly do the most important things as defined by patriarchal culture. They're the strong ones who build, the heroes who fight the good fight, the geniuses, writers and artists, the bold leaders, and even the evil—but always interesting—villains. Even God is gendered male.

Among the many consequences of such messages is to encourage in men a sense of entitlement in relation to women—to be tended to and taken care of, deferred to and supported no matter how badly they behave. In the typical episode of the television sitcom *Everybody Loves Raymond*, for example, Ray Barone routinely behaves toward his wife, Debra, in ways that are insensitive, sexist, adolescent, and downright stupid, but by the end of each half hour we always find out why she puts up with it year after year—for some reason that's never made clear, she just loves the guy. This sends the message that it's reasonable for a heterosexual man to expect to "have" an intelligent and beautiful woman who will love him and stay with him in spite of his behaving badly toward her a great deal of the time.

Invariably, some of what we learn through socialization turns out not to be true and then we may have to deal with that. I say "may" because powerful forces encourage us to keep ourselves in a state of denial, to rationalize what we've learned in order to keep it safe from scrutiny, if only to protect our sense of who we are and ensure our being accepted by other people, including family and friends. In the end, the default is to adopt the dominant version of reality and act as though it's the only one there is.

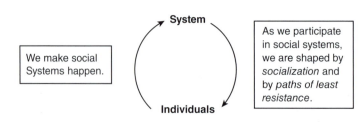

In addition to socialization, participation in social systems shapes our behavior through *paths of least resistance*, a concept that refers to the conscious and unconscious choices we make from one moment to the next. When a man hears other men tell sexist jokes, for example, there are many things he *could* do, but they vary in how much social resistance they're likely to provoke. He could laugh along with them, for example, or remain silent or ignore them or object. And, of course, there are millions of other things he could do—sing, dance, go to sleep, scratch his nose, and so on. Most of these possibilities won't even occur to him, which is one of the ways that social systems limit our options. But of those that do occur to him, usually one will risk less resistance than all the rest. The path of least resistance is to go along, and unless he's willing to deal with greater resistance, that's the choice he's most likely to make.

Our daily lives consist of an endless stream of such choices as we navigate among various possibilities in relation to the path of least resistance in each social situation. Most of the time, we make choices unconsciously without realizing what we're doing. It's just what seems most comfortable to us, most familiar, and safest. The more aware we are of what's going on, however, the more likely it is that we can make conscious, informed choices, and therein lies our potential to make a difference.

This brings us to the arrow on the left side of the figure, which represents the fact that human beings are the ones who make social systems happen. . . . Because people make systems happen, then people can also make systems happen differently. And when systems happen differently, the consequences are different as well. In other words, when people step off the path of least resistance, they have the potential not simply to change other people, but to alter the way the system itself happens. Given that systems shape people's behavior, this kind of change has enormous potential. When a man objects to a sexist joke, for example, it can shake other men's perception of what's socially acceptable and what's not so that the next time they're in this kind of situation, their perception of the social environment itself—not just of other people as individuals,

whom they may or may not know personally—may shift in a new direction that makes old paths (such as telling sexist jokes) more difficult to choose because of the increased risk of social resistance.

The model in the figure represents a basic sociological view of the world at every level of human experience, from the global capitalist economy to sexual relationships. Patriarchy fits this model as a social system in which women and men participate. As such, it is more than a collection of women and men and can't be understood simply by understanding *them*. We are not patriarchy, no more than people who believe in Allah *are* Islam or Canadians *are* Canada. Patriarchy is a kind of society organized around certain kinds of social relationships and ideas that shape paths of least resistance. As individuals, we participate in it. Paradoxically, our participation both shapes our lives and gives us the opportunity to be part of changing or perpetuating it. But *we are not it*, which means patriarchy can exist without men having "oppressive personalities" or actively conspiring with one another to defend male privilege.

To demonstrate that gender privilege and oppression exist, we don't have to show that men are villains, that women are good-hearted victims, that women don't participate in their own oppression, or that men never oppose it. If a society is oppressive, then people who grow up and live in it will tend to accept, identify with, and participate in it as "normal" and unremarkable life. That's the path of least resistance in any system. It's hard not to follow it, given how we depend on society and its rewards and punishments that hinge on going along with the status quo. When privilege and oppression are woven into the fabric of everyday life, we don't need to go out of our way to be overtly oppressive for a system of privilege to produce oppressive consequences, for, as Edmund Burke tells us, evil requires only that good people do nothing.

"The System"

. . . The crucial thing to understand about patriarchy or any other social system is that it's something people participate in. It's an arrangement of shared understandings and relationships that connect people to one another and something larger than themselves. In some ways, we're like players who participate in a game. Monopoly, for example, consists of a set of ideas about things such as the meaning of property and rent, the value of competition and accumulating wealth, and various rules about rolling dice, moving around a board, buying, selling, and developing property, collecting rents, winning, and losing. It has positions—player, banker, and so on—that people occupy. It has material elements such as the board, houses and hotels, dice, property deeds, money, and "pieces" that represent each player's movements on the board. As such, the game is something we can think of as a social system whose elements cohere with a unity and wholeness that distinguish it from other games and from nongames.[1] Most important, we can describe it as a system without ever talking about the personal characteristics or motivations of the individual people who actually play it at any given moment.

If we watch people play Monopoly, we notice certain routine patterns of feeling and behavior that reflect paths of least resistance inherent in the game itself. If someone lands on a property I own, for example, I collect the rent (if I happen to notice); and if they can't pay, I take their assets and force them from the game. The game encourages me to feel good about this, not necessarily because *I'm* greedy and merciless, but because the game is about winning, and this is what winning consists of in Monopoly. Since everyone else is also trying to win by driving me out of the game, each step I take toward winning protects me and alleviates some anxiety about landing on a property whose rent *I* can't pay.

Because these patterns are shaped by the game far more than by the individual players, we can find ourselves behaving in ways that might seem disturbing in other situations. When I'm not playing Monopoly, I behave quite differently, even though I'm still the same person. This is why I don't play Monopoly anymore—I don't like the way it encourages me to feel and behave in the name of "fun," especially toward people I care about. The reason we behave differently outside the game doesn't

lie in our personalities but in the *game's* paths of least resistance, which define certain behavior and values as appropriate and expected. When we see ourselves as Monopoly players, we feel limited by the rules and goals the game defines, and experience it as something external to us and beyond our control.

It's important to note how rarely it occurs to people to simply change the rules. The relationships, terms, and goals that organize the game aren't presented to us as ours to judge or alter. The more attached we feel to the game and the more closely we identify ourselves as players, the more likely we are to feel helpless in relation to it. If you're about to drive someone into bankruptcy, you can excuse yourself by saying, "I've got to take your money, those are the rules," but only if you ignore the fact that you could choose not to play or could suggest a change in the rules. Then again, if you can't imagine life without the game, you won't see many alternatives to doing what's expected.

If we try to explain patterns of social behavior only in terms of individual people's personalities and motives—people do greedy things, for example, because they *are* greedy—then we ignore how behavior is shaped by paths of least resistance found in the systems people participate in. The "profit motive" associated with capitalism, for example, is typically seen as a psychological motive that explains capitalism as a system: Capitalism exists because there are people who want to make a profit. But this puts the cart before the horse by avoiding the question of where wanting to make a profit comes from in the first place. We need to ask what kind of world makes such wants possible and encourages people to organize their lives around them, for although we may pursue profit as we play Monopoly or participate in real-world capitalism, the psychological profit motive doesn't originate with us. We aren't born with it. It doesn't exist in many cultures and was unknown for most of human history. The profit motive is a historically developed aspect of market systems in general and capitalism in particular that shapes the values, behavior, and personal motives of those who participate in it.

To argue that managers lay off workers, for example, simply because managers are heartless or cruel ignores the fact that success under capitalism often depends on this kind of competitive, profit-maximizing, "heartless" behavior. Most managers probably know in their hearts that the practice of routinely discarding people in the name of profit and expedience is hurtful and unfair. This is why they feel so bad about having to be the ones to carry it out, and protect their feelings by inventing euphemisms such as "downsizing" and "outplacement." And yet they participate in a system that produces these cruel results anyway, not because of cruel personalities or malice toward workers, but because a capitalist system makes this a path of least resistance and exacts real costs from those who stray from it. . . .

In spite of all the good reasons to not use individual models to explain social life, doing so constitutes a path of least resistance because personal experience and motivation are what we know best. As a result, we tend to see something like patriarchy as the result of poor socialization through which men learn to act dominant and masculine and women learn to act subordinate and feminine. While there is certainly some truth to this, it doesn't work as an explanation of patterns like privilege and oppression. It's no better than trying to explain war as simply the result of training men to be warlike, without looking at economic systems that equip armies at huge profits and political systems that organize and hurl armies at one another. It's like trying to understand what happens during Monopoly games without ever talking about the game itself and the kind of society in which it would exist. Of course, soldiers and Monopoly players do what they do because they've learned the rules, but this doesn't tell us much about the rules themselves and why they exist to be learned in the first place. Socialization is merely a process, a mechanism for training people to participate in social systems. Although it tells us how people learn to participate, it doesn't illuminate the systems themselves. As such, it can tell us something about the *how* of a system like patriarchy, but very little about the *what* and the *why*. . . .

We can't find a way out of patriarchy or imagine something different without a clear sense of what patriarchy is and what it's got to do with us. . . .

We need to see more clearly what patriarchy is about as a system. This includes cultural ideas about men and women, the web of relationships that structure social life, and the unequal distribution of power, rewards and resources that underlies privilege and oppression. We need to see new ways to participate by forging alternative paths of least resistance; for the system doesn't simply "run us" like hapless puppets. It may be larger than us, it may not *be* us, but it doesn't happen except *through* us. And that's where we have power to do something about it and about ourselves in relation to it.

Patriarchy

. . . Patriarchy's defining elements are its male-dominated, male-identified, male-centered, and control-obsessed character, but this is just the beginning. . . . Patriarchal culture includes ideas about the nature of things, including women, men, and humanity, with manhood and masculinity most closely associated with being human and womanhood and femininity relegated to the marginal position of "other." . . . It's about standards of feminine beauty and masculine toughness, images of feminine vulnerability and masculine protectiveness, of older men coupled with younger women, of elderly women alone. It's about defining women and men as opposites, about the "naturalness" of male aggression, competition, and dominance and of female caring, cooperation, and subordination. It's about the valuing of masculinity and maleness and the devaluing of femininity and femaleness. It's about the primary importance of a husband's career and the secondary status of a wife's, about child care as a priority in women's lives and its secondary importance in men's. It's about the social acceptability of anger, rage, and toughness in men but not in women, and of caring, tenderness, and vulnerability in women but not in men.

Above all, patriarchal culture is about the core value of control and domination in almost every area of human existence. From the expression of emotion to economics to the natural environment, gaining and exercising control is a continuing goal. Because of this, the concept of power takes on a narrow definition in terms of "power over"—the ability to control others, events, resources, or one's self in spite of resistance—rather than alternatives such as the ability to cooperate, to give freely of oneself, or to feel and act in harmony with nature. To have power over and to be prepared to use it are culturally defined as good and desirable (and characteristically "masculine"), and to lack such power or to be reluctant to use it is seen as weak if not contemptible (and characteristically "feminine"). This is a major reason that patriarchies with the means to do so are often so quick to go to war. Studies of the (mostly) men who formulate US military strategy, for example, show that it is almost impossible to lose standing by advocating an excessive use of force in international relations (such as the US response to terrorism and the 2003 invasion of Iraq). But anyone—especially a man—who advocates restraint in the use of force, runs the serious risk of being perceived as less than manly and, therefore, lacking credibility.

The main use of any culture is to provide symbols and ideas out of which to construct a sense of what is real. As such, language mirrors social reality in sometimes startling ways. In contemporary usage, for example, the words *crone, witch, bitch*, and *virgin* describe women as threatening, evil, or heterosexually inexperienced and thus incomplete. In prepatriarchal times, however, these words evoked far different images. The crone was the old woman whose life experience gave her insight, wisdom, respect, and the power to enrich people's lives. The witch was the wise-woman healer, the knower of herbs, the midwife, the link joining body, spirit, and Earth. The bitch was Artemis-Diana, goddess of the hunt, most often associated with the dogs who accompanied her. And the virgin was merely a woman who was unattached, unclaimed, and unowned by any man and therefore independent and autonomous. Notice how each word has been transformed from a positive cultural image of female power, independence, and dignity to an insult or a shadow of its former self so that few words remain to identify women in ways both positive and powerful.

Going deeper into patriarchal culture, we find a complex web of ideas that define reality and what's considered good and desirable. To see the world through patriarchal eyes is to believe that women and men are profoundly different in their basic natures, that hierarchy is the only alternative to chaos, and that men were made in the image of a masculine God with whom they enjoy a special relationship. It is to take as obvious the idea that there are two and only two distinct genders; that patriarchal heterosexuality is "natural" and same-sex attraction is not; that because men neither bear nor breast-feed children, they cannot feel a compelling bodily connection to them; that on some level every woman, whether heterosexual or lesbian, wants a "real man" who knows how to "take charge of things," including her; that females can't be trusted, especially when they're menstruating or accusing men of sexual abuse. In spite of all the media hype to the contrary, to embrace patriarchy still is to believe that . . . women are weak and men are strong, that women and children need men to support and protect them, all in spite of the fact that in many ways men are not the physically stronger sex, that women perform a huge share of hard physical labor in many societies (often larger than men's), that women's physical endurance tends to be greater than men's over the long haul, that women tend to be more capable of enduring pain and emotional stress. . . .

To live in a patriarchal culture is to learn what's expected of men and women—to learn the rules that regulate punishment and reward based on how individuals behave and appear. These rules range from laws that require men to fight in wars not of their own choosing to customary expectations that mothers will provide child care. Or that when a woman shows sexual interest in a man or merely smiles or acts friendly, she gives up her right to say no and to control her own body. And to live under patriarchy is to take into ourselves ways of feeling—the hostile contempt for femaleness that forms the core of misogyny and presumptions of male superiority, the ridicule men direct at other men who show signs of vulnerability or weakness, or the fear and insecurity that every woman must deal with when she exercises the right to move freely in the world, especially at night and by herself in public places.

Such ideas make up the symbolic sea we swim in and the air we breathe. . . . As such, they provide a taken-for-granted everyday reality, the setting for our interactions with other people that continually fashion and refashion a sense of what the world is about and who we are in relation to it. This doesn't mean that the ideas underlying patriarchy determine what we think, feel, and do, but it does mean they define what we'll have to deal with as we participate in it.

The prominent place of misogyny in patriarchal culture, for example, doesn't mean that every man and woman consciously hates all things female. But it does mean that to the extent that we don't feel such hatred, it's *in spite of* paths of least resistance contained in our culture. Complete freedom from such feelings and judgments is all but impossible. It is certainly possible for heterosexual men to love women without mentally fragmenting them into breasts, buttocks, genitals, and other variously desirable parts. It is possible for women to feel good about their bodies, to not judge themselves as being too fat, to not abuse themselves to one degree or another in pursuit of impossible male-identified standards of beauty and sexual attractiveness. All of this is possible, but to live in patriarchy is to breathe in misogynist images of women as objectified sexual property valued primarily for their usefulness to men. This finds its way into everyone who grows up breathing and swimming in it, and once inside of us it remains, however unaware of it we may be. So, when we hear or express sexist jokes and other forms of misogyny, we may not recognize it, and even if we do, we may say nothing rather than risk other people thinking we're "too sensitive" or, especially in the case of men, "not one of the guys." In either case, we are involved, if only by our silence.

The symbols and ideas that make up patriarchal culture are important to understand because they have such powerful effects on the structure of social life. By *structure*, I mean the ways privilege and oppression are organized through social relationships and unequal distributions of power, rewards, opportunities, and resources. This appears in countless patterns of everyday life in family and work, religion and politics, community and education. It is found in family divisions of labor that exempt fathers from most domestic work even when both parents work outside the home and in the concentration of women in lower-level pink-collar jobs and male predominance almost everywhere else. It is in the unequal distribution of income and all that goes with it, from access to health care to the availability of leisure time. It is in patterns of male violence and harassment that can turn a simple walk in the park or a typical day at work or a lovers' quarrel into a life-threatening nightmare. More than anything, the structure of patriarchy is found in the unequal distribution of power that makes male privilege possible, in patterns of male dominance in every facet of human life, from everyday conversation to global politics. By its nature, patriarchy puts issues of power, dominance, and control at the center of human existence, not only in relationships between men and women, but among men as they compete and struggle to gain status, maintain control, and protect themselves from what other men might do to them. . . .

The System in Us in the System

One way to see how people connect with systems is to think of us as occupying social positions that locate us in relation to people in other positions. We connect to families, for example, through positions such as "mother," "daughter," and "cousin"; to economic systems through positions such as "vice president," "secretary," or "unemployed"; to political systems through positions such as "citizen," "registered voter," and "mayor"; to religious systems through positions such as "believer" and "clergy." How we perceive the people who occupy such positions and what we expect of them depend on cultural ideas—such as the belief that mothers are naturally better than fathers at child care. Such ideas are powerful because we use them to construct a sense of who we and other people are. . . .

From this perspective, *who* we and other people think we are has a lot to do with *where* we are in relation to social systems and all the positions we occupy in them. We wouldn't exist as social beings if it weren't for our participation in one social system or another. . . . Take away language and all that it allows us to imagine and think, starting with our names. Take away all the positions that we occupy and the roles that go with them—from daughter and son to occupation and nationality—and with these all the complex ways our lives are connected to other people. Not much would be left over that we'd recognize as ourselves.

We can think of a society as a network of inter-connected systems within systems, each made up of social positions and their relations to one another. To say, then, that I'm white, male, college educated, nondisabled, and a writer, sociologist, US citizen, heterosexual, middle-aged, husband, father, grandfather, brother, and son identifies me in re-lation to positions which are themselves related to positions in various social systems, from the entire world to the family of my birth. In another sense, the day-to-day reality of a society only exists through what people actually do as they partici-pate in it. Patriarchal culture, for example, places a high value on control and maleness. By them-selves, these are just abstractions. But when men and women actually talk and men interrupt women more than women interrupt men, or men ignore topics introduced by women in favor of their own or in other ways control conversation, or when men use their authority to harass women in the work-place, then the reality of patriarchy as a kind of soci-ety and people's sense of themselves as female and male within it actually happen in a concrete way.

In this sense, like all social systems, patriarchy exists only through people's lives. . . . This has two important implications for how we understand pa-triarchy. First, to some extent people experience patriarchy as external to them. But this doesn't mean that it's a distinct and separate thing, like a house in which we live. Instead, by participating in patriarchy we are *of* patriarchy and it is *of* us. Both exist *through* the other and neither can exist without the other. Second, patriarchy isn't static. It's an ongoing *process* that's continuously shaped and reshaped. Since the thing we're participating in is patriarchal, we tend to behave in ways that create a patriarchal world from one moment to the next. But we have some freedom to break the rules and construct everyday life in different ways, which means that the paths we choose to follow can do as much to change patriarchy as they can to perpetuate it.

We're involved in patriarchy and its consequences because we occupy social positions in it, which is all it takes. Because patriarchy is, by definition, a system of inequality organized around gender categories, we can no more avoid being involved in it than we can avoid being female or male. *All* men and *all* women are therefore involved in this oppressive system, and none us can control *whether* we participate, only *how*. As Harry Brod argues, this is especially important in relation to men and male privilege:

> We need to be clear that there is no such thing as giving up one's privilege to be "outside" the system. One is always in the system. The only question is whether one is part of the system in a way which challenges or strengthens the status quo. Privilege is not something I take and which I therefore have the option of not taking. It is something that soci-ety gives me, and unless I change the institutions which give it to me, they will continue to give it, and I will continue to have it, however noble and egalitarian my intentions.[2]

NOTES

1. Although the game analogy is useful, social systems are quite unlike a game in important ways. The rules and other understandings on which social life is based are far more complex, ambiguous, and con-tradictory than those of a typical game and much more open to negotiation and "making it up" as we go along.
2. Harry Brod, "Work Clothes and Leisure Suits: The Class Basis and Bias of the Men's Movement," in *Men's Lives*, ed. Michael S. Kimmel and Michael A. Messner (New York: Macmillan, 1989), 280.

PATRICIA HILL COLLINS

8 EXCERPT FROM "BLACK FEMINIST THOUGHT: KNOWLEDGE, CONSCIOUSNESS, AND THE POLITICS OF EMPOWERMENT" (1990)

Patricia Hill Collins is an award-winning writer and social theorist. Her books include *Black Feminist Thought: Knowledge, Consciousness and the Politics of Empowerment* (1990); *Black Sexual Politics: African Americans, Gender, and the New Racism* (2004); and *From Black Power to Hip Hop: Racism, Nationalism, and Feminism* (2006). She is Distinguished University Professor of Sociology at the University of Maryland–College Park and former president of the American Sociological Association Council.

Black feminist thought demonstrates Black women's emerging power as agents of knowledge. By portraying African American women as self-defined, self-reliant individuals confronting race, gender, and class oppression, Afrocentric feminist thought speaks to the importance that knowledge plays in empowering oppressed people. One distinguishing feature of Black feminist thought is its insistence that both the changed consciousness of individuals and the social transformation of political and economic institutions constitute essential ingredients for social change. New knowledge is important for both dimensions of change. . . .

Epistemological Shifts: Dialogue, Empathy, and Truth

Black Women as Agents of Knowledge

Living life as an African American woman is a necessary prerequisite for producing Black feminist thought because within Black women's communities thought is validated and produced with reference to a particular set of historical, material, and epistemological conditions. African American women who adhere to the idea that claims about Black women must be substantiated by Black women's sense of our own experiences and who anchor our knowledge claims in an Afrocentric epistemology have produced a rich tradition of Black feminist thought.

Traditionally such women were blues singers, poets, autobiographers, storytellers, and orators validated by everyday Black women as experts on a Black women's standpoint. Only a few unusual African-American feminist scholars have been able to defy Eurocentric masculinist epistemologies and explicitly embrace an Afrocentric feminist epistemology. Consider Alice Walker's description of Zora Neale Hurston:

> In my mind, Zora Neale Hurston, Billie Holiday, and Bessie Smith form a sort of unholy trinity. Zora *belongs* in the tradition of black women singers, rather than among "the literati." . . . Like Billie and Bessie she followed her own road, believed in her own gods, pursued her own dreams, and refused to separate herself from "common" people. (Walker 1977, xvii–xviii)

Zora Neale Hurston is an exception for prior to 1950, few African American women earned advanced degrees and most of those who did complied with Eurocentric masculinist epistemologies. Although these women worked on behalf of Black women, they did so within the confines of pervasive race and gender oppression. Black women scholars were in a position to see the exclusion of African American women from scholarly discourse, and the thematic content of their work often reflected their interest in examining a Black women's standpoint. However, their tenuous status in academic institutions led them to adhere to Eurocentric masculinist epistemologies so that their work would be accepted as scholarly. As a result, while they produced Black feminist thought, those African American women most likely to gain academic credentials were often least likely to produce Black feminist thought that used an Afrocentric feminist epistemology.

An ongoing tension exists for Black women as agents of knowledge, a tension rooted in the sometimes conflicting demands of Afrocentricity and feminism. Those Black women who are feminists are critical of how Black culture and many of its traditions oppress women. For example, the strong pronatal beliefs in African American communities that foster early motherhood among adolescent girls, the lack of self-actualization that can accompany the double-day of paid employment and work in the home, and the emotional and physical abuse that many Black women experience from their fathers, lovers, and husbands all reflect practices opposed by African American women who are feminists. But these same women may have a parallel desire as members of an oppressed racial group to affirm the value of that same culture and traditions. . . . Thus strong Black mothers appear in Black women's literature, Black women's economic contributions to families is lauded, and a curious silence exists concerning domestic abuse.

As more African American women earn advanced degrees, the range of Black feminist scholarship is expanding. Increasing numbers of African American women scholars are explicitly choosing to ground their work in Black women's experiences, and, by doing so, they implicitly adhere to an Afrocentric feminist epistemology. Rather than being restrained by their both/and status of marginality, these women make creative use of their outsider-within status and produce innovative Afrocentric feminist thought. . . .

In establishing the legitimacy of their knowledge claims, Black women scholars who want to develop Afrocentric feminist thought may encounter the often conflicting standards of three key groups. First, Black feminist thought must be validated by ordinary African American women who, in the words of Hannah Nelson, grow to womanhood "in a world where the saner you are, the madder you are made to appear" (Gwaltney 1980, p. 7). To be credible in the eyes of this group, scholars must be personal advocates for their material, be accountable for the consequences of their work, have lived or experienced their material in some fashion, and be willing to engage in dialogues about their findings with ordinary, everyday people. Second, Black feminist thought also must be accepted by the community of Black women scholars. These scholars place varying amounts of importance on rearticulating a Black women's standpoint using an Afrocentric feminist epistemology. Third, Afrocentric feminist thought within academia must be prepared to confront Eurocentric masculinist political and epistemological requirements.

The dilemma facing Black women scholars engaged in creating Black feminist thought is that a knowledge claim that meets the criteria of adequacy for one group . . . may not be translatable into the terms of a different group. Using the example of Black English, June Jordan illustrates the difficulty of moving among epistemologies:

> You cannot "translate" instances of Standard English preoccupied with abstraction or with nothing/nobody evidently alive into Black English. That would warp the language into uses antithetical to the guiding perspective of its community of users. Rather you must first change those Standard English sentences, themselves, into ideas consistent with the person-centered assumptions of Black English. (Jordan 1985, 130)

Although both worldviews share a common vocabulary, the ideas themselves defy direct translation.

For Black women who are agents of knowledge, the marginality that accompanies outsider-within status can be the source of both frustration and creativity. In an attempt to minimize the differences between the cultural context of African American communities and the expectations of social institutions, some women dichotomize their behavior and become two different people. Over time, the strain of doing this can be enormous. Others reject their cultural context and work against their own best interests by enforcing the dominant group's specialized thought. Still others manage to inhabit both contexts but do so critically, using their outsider-within perspectives as a source of insights and ideas. But while outsiders within can make substantial contributions as agents of knowledge, they rarely do so without substantial personal cost. "Eventually it comes to you," observes Lorraine Hansberry, "the thing that makes you exceptional, if you are at all, is inevitably that which must also make you lonely" (1969, 148).

Once Black feminist scholars face the notion that, on certain dimensions of a Black women's standpoint, it may be fruitless to try and translate ideas from an Afrocentric feminist epistemology into a Eurocentric masculinist framework, then other choices emerge. Rather than trying to uncover universal knowledge claims that can withstand the translation from one epistemology to another (initially, at least), Black women intellectuals might find efforts to rearticulate a Black women's standpoint especially fruitful. Rearticulating a Black women's standpoint refashions the concrete and reveals the more universal human dimensions of Black women's everyday lives. "I date all my work," notes Nikki Giovanni, "because I think poetry, or any writing, is but a reflection of the moment. The universal comes from the particular" (1988, 57). bell hooks maintains, "my goal as a feminist thinker and theorist is to take that abstraction and articulate it in a language that renders it accessible—not less complex or rigorous—but simply more accessible" (1989, 39). The complexity exists; interpreting it remains the unfulfilled challenge for Black women intellectuals.

Situated Knowledge, Subjugated Knowledge, and Partial Perspectives

"My life seems to be an increasing revelation of the intimate face of universal struggle," claims June Jordan:

> You begin with your family and the kids on the block, and next you open your eyes to what you call your people and that leads you into land reform into Black English into Angola leads you back to your own bed where you lie by yourself, wondering if you deserve to be peaceful, or trusted or desired or left to the freedom of your own unfaltering heart. And the scale shrinks to the size of a skull: your own interior cage. (Jordan 1981, p. xi)

Lorraine Hansberry expresses a similar idea: "I believe that one of the most sound ideas in dramatic writing is that in order to create the universal, you must pay very great attention to the specific. Universality, I think, emerges from the truthful identity of what is" (1969, 128). Jordan and Hansberry's insights that universal struggle and truth may wear a particularistic, intimate face suggest a new epistemological stance concerning how we negotiate competing knowledge claims and identify "truth."

The context in which African American women's ideas are nurtured or suppressed matters. Understanding the content and epistemology of Black women's ideas as specialized knowledge requires attending to the context from which those ideas emerge. While produced by individuals, Black feminist thought as situated knowledge is embedded in the communities in which African American women find ourselves (Haraway 1988).

A Black women's standpoint and those of other oppressed groups is not only embedded in a context but exists in a situation characterized by domination. Because Black women's ideas have been suppressed, this suppression has stimulated African American women to create knowledge that empowers people to resist domination. Thus Afrocentric feminist thought represents a subjugated knowledge (Foucault 1980). A Black women's standpoint may provide a preferred stance from which to view the matrix of domination because, in principle, Black feminist thought as specialized thought is less likely than the specialized knowledge produced by dominant groups to deny the connection between ideas and the vested interests of their creators. However, Black feminist thought as subjugated knowledge is not exempt from critical analysis, because subjugation is not grounds for an epistemology (Haraway 1988).

Despite African American women's potential power to reveal new insights about the matrix of domination, a Black women's standpoint is only one angle of vision. Thus Black feminist thought represents a partial perspective. The overarching matrix of domination houses multiple groups, each with varying experiences with penalty and privilege that produce corresponding partial perspectives, situated knowledges, and, for clearly identifiable subordinate groups, subjugated knowledges. No one group has a clear angle of vision. No one group possesses the theory or methodology that allows it to discover the absolute "truth" or, worse yet, proclaim its theories and methodologies as the universal norm evaluating other groups' experiences. Given that groups are unequal in power in making themselves heard, dominant groups have a vested interest in suppressing the knowledge produced by subordinate groups. Given the existence of multiple and competing knowledge claims to "truth" produced by groups with partial perspectives, what epistemological approach offers the most promise?

Dialogue and Empathy

Western social and political thought contains two alternative approaches to ascertaining "truth." The first, reflected in positivist science, has long claimed that absolute truths exist and that the task of scholarship is to develop objective, unbiased tools of science to measure these truths. But Afrocentric, feminist, and other bodies of critical theory have unmasked the concepts and epistemology of this version of science as representing the vested interests of elite white men and therefore as being less valid when applied to experiences of other groups and, more recently, to white male recounting of their own exploits. Earlier versions of standpoint theories, themselves rooted in a Marxist positivism, essentially reversed positivist science's assumptions

concerning whose truth would prevail. These approaches suggest that the oppressed allegedly have a clearer view of "truth" than their oppressors because they lack the blinders created by the dominant group's ideology. But this version of standpoint theory basically duplicates the positivist belief in one "true" interpretation of reality and, like positivist science, comes with its own set of problems.

Relativism, the second approach, has been forwarded as the antithesis of and inevitable outcome of rejecting a positivist science. From a relativist perspective all groups produce specialized thought and each group's thought is equally valid. No group can claim to have a better interpretation of the "truth" than another. In a sense, relativism represents the opposite of scientific ideologies of objectivity. As epistemological stances, both positivist science and relativism minimize the importance of specific location in influencing a group's knowledge claims, the power inequities among groups that produce subjugated knowledges, and the strengths and limitations of partial perspective (Haraway 1988).

The existence of Black feminist thought suggests another alternative to the ostensibly objective norms of science and to relativism's claims that groups with competing knowledge claims are equal. In this volume I placed Black women's subjectivity in the center of analysis and examined the interdependence of the everyday, taken-for-granted knowledge shared by African American women as a group, the more specialized knowledge produced by Black women intellectuals, and the social conditions shaping both types of thought. This approach allowed me to describe the creative tension linking how sociological conditions influenced a Black women's standpoint and how the power of the ideas themselves gave many African American women the strength to shape those same sociological conditions. I approached Afrocentric feminist thought as situated in a context of domination and not as a system of ideas divorced from political and economic reality. Moreover, I presented Black feminist thought as subjugated knowledge in that African American women have long struggled to find alternative locations and techniques for articulating our own standpoint. . . .

This approach to Afrocentric feminist thought allows African American women to bring a Black women's standpoint to larger epistemological dialogues concerning the nature of . . . domination. Eventually such dialogues may get us to a point at which, claims Elsa Barkley Brown, "all people can learn to center in another experience, validate it, and judge it by its own standards without need of comparison or need to adopt that framework as their own" (1989, 922). In such dialogues, "one has no need to 'decenter' anyone in order to center someone else; one has only to constantly, appropriately, 'pivot the center'" (p. 922).

Those ideas that are validated as true by African American women, African American men, Latina lesbians, Asian American women, Puerto Rican men, and other groups with distinctive standpoints, with each group using the epistemological approaches growing from its unique standpoint, thus become the most "objective" truths. Each group speaks from its own standpoint and shares its own partial, situated knowledge. But because each group perceives its own truth as partial, its knowledge is unfinished. Each group becomes better able to consider other groups' standpoints without relinquishing the uniqueness of its own standpoint or suppressing other groups' partial perspectives. "What is always needed in the appreciation of art, or life," maintains Alice Walker, "is the larger perspective. Connections made, or at least attempted, where none existed before, the straining to encompass in one's glance at the varied world the common thread, the unifying theme through immense diversity" (1983, 5). Partiality and not universality is the condition of being heard; individuals and groups forwarding knowledge claims without owning their position are deemed less credible than those who do.

Dialogue is critical to the success of this epistemological approach, the type of dialogue long extant in the Afrocentric call-and-response tradition whereby power dynamics are fluid, everyone has a voice, but everyone must listen and respond to other voices in order to be allowed to remain in the community. Sharing a common cause fosters dialogue and encourages groups to transcend their differences.

Existing power inequities among groups must be addressed before an alternative epistemology such as that described by Elsa Barkley Brown or Alice Walker can be utilized. The presence of subjugated knowledges means that groups are not equal in making their standpoints known to themselves and others. "Decentering" the dominant group is essential, and relinquishing privilege of this magnitude is unlikely to occur without struggle. But still the vision exists, one encompassing "coming to believe in the possibility of a variety of experiences, a variety of ways of understanding the world, a variety of frameworks of operation, without imposing consciously or unconsciously a notion of the norm" (Brown 1989, 921).

REFERENCES

Brown, Elsa Barkely. 1989. "African-American Women's Quilting: A Framework for Conceptualizing and Teaching African-American Women's History." *Signs* 14(4): 921–29.

Foucault, Michel. 1980. *Power/Knowledge: Selected Interviews and Other Writings 1972–1977*, edited by Colin Gordon. New York: Pantheon.

Giovanni, Nikki. 1988. *Sacred Cows . . . and Other Edibles*. New York: Quill/William Morrow.

Gwaltney, John Langston. 1980. *Drylongso, A Self-Portrait of Black America*. New York: Vintage.

Hansberry, Lorraine. 1969. *To Be Young, Gifted and Black*. New York: Signet.

Haraway, Donna. 1988. "Situated Knowledges: The Science Question in Feminism and the Privilege of Partial Perspective." *Feminist Studies* 14(3): 575–99.

hooks, bell. 1989. *Talking Back: Thinking Feminist, Thinking Black*. Boston: South End Press.

Jordan, June. 1981. *Civil Wars*. Boston: Beacon Press.

Walker, Alice. 1977. "Zora Neale Hurston: A Cautionary Tale and a Partisan View." Foreword to Zora *Neale Hurston: A Literary Biography*, by Robert Hemenway, xi–xviii. Urbana: University of Illinois Press.

_____. 1983. *In Search of Our Mothers' Gardens*. New York: Harcourt Brace Jovanovich.

NADINE NABER

9 DECOLONIZING CULTURE: BEYOND ORIENTALIST AND ANTI-ORIENTALIST FEMINISMS (2010)

Nadine Naber is Associate Professor of Gender and Women's Studies at the University of Illinois, Chicago, where she is also part of the Asian American Studies program. Her research interests focus on the racialization of Arab and Muslim Americans within the contexts of empire and diaspora. Her books include *Arab America: Gender, Cultural Politics, and Activism* (2012); *Arab and Arab American Feminisms: Gender, Violence, and Belonging* (2011) (co-editor); and *Race and Arab Americans Before and After 9/11* (2008) (co-editor).

I was born in San Francisco, three years after my parents arrived from Al Salt, Jordan. Over the next twenty years, my parents moved a dozen times across the Bay Area, creating for me a childhood and a sense of community that was both rigidly structured and ever changing. Throughout my childhood, "culture" was a tool, an abstract, ephemeral notion of what we do and what we believe, of who belongs and who does not. Culture was the way that my parents exercised their control over me and my siblings. The same fight, I knew from my aggrieved conversations with friends and relatives, was playing out in the homes of countless other Arab families. The typical generational war—about whether we teenagers could stay out late at night, or whether we could spend the night at our friends' slumber parties—was amplified into a grand cultural struggle. The banalities of adolescent rebellion became a battle between two stereotypes, between rigid versions of "Arab" and "American" values. To discipline us, our parents' generation invoked the royal "we," as in: "No, you can't go to the school dance because we don't do that." Here, "we" meant "Arabs."

I hated these words. I hated these declarations of what "we" did and didn't do. Yet, they worked. Sort of. Sometimes, I actually listened. Or, more often as time went on, I simply tried to hide these parts of my life from my parents. Because even worse than disobeying my parents was the threat—always tangible in my house and in our community centers—that I might be disobeying *my people*—a term that signified anyone from the Naber family, to everyone in Jordan, to all Arab Christians, to *al Arab*. Transgressing my parents' rules was not merely adolescent rebellion, but was a form of cultural loss, of cultural betrayal. And even worse, each moment of transgression meant the loss of Arab culture to *al Amerikan*, that awesome and awful world that encompassed everything from the American people to the American government to the American way of life (at least as my parents seemed to imagine it).

Our Arab community, like so many immigrant networks, was wildly diverse, comprising Muslim and Christian, Jordanian, Lebanese, Palestinian, and Syrian families. Yet we all seemed to have a remarkably similar idea of what "American" and "Arab" meant. We seemed to share a tacit knowledge that *al Amerika* was the trash culture, degenerate, morally bankrupt, and sexually depraved. In contrast, *al Arab* (Arabs) were morally respectable— we valued marriage, family, and close relationships.

Source: Nadine Naber, "Decolonizing Culture" from *Arab and Arab American Feminisms: Gender, Violence and Belonging*, edited by Rabab Abdulhadi, Evelyn Alsultany, and Nadine Naber (Syracuse: Syracuse University Press, 2011). Reprinted with permission of the publishers.

It was not only our parents who put this pressure on us. What we learned at school and from the US media reinforced this dichotomy.

As with all products of human belief, there were caveats, and shades of gray, and matters of proportion. Our immigrant parents' generation disproportionately pressured girls to uphold idealized demands of Arab culture. Girls' behavior seemed to symbolize the respectability of our fathers and our families, as well as . . . the continuation of Arab culture in America. Particularly as my girlfriends, cousins, and I hit puberty, the pressure seemed to intensify. I couldn't wear my trendy jeans with the tear down the side for fear that my relatives and parents' friends would curse my sloppy clothes and my bare skin. By the time my friends and I graduated from college, young women's bodies and behaviors seemed to be the key signifiers in the stereotyped distinction between Arabs and Americans.

Compounding matters, our parents raised us in predominantly white suburbs and encouraged us—in certain ways—to assimilate. They encouraged us to befriend the "American kids" and dress up for colonial days at school. And many of us watched our fathers change their names from Yacoub, Mohammed, and Bishara to Jack, Mo, and Bob when they arrived at their grocery and convenience stores as the sun rose. It was only later that I came to understand that many men of my parents' generation changed their names after being called "dirty Arab" or "Palestinian terrorist," or after customers refused to shop at their stores.

Despite this, and despite the fact that our parents were encouraging us to adopt the values of middle-class America, the fundamental message in our family and community remained: *we* were Arab and *they* were American. It felt like we were living between two worlds, one within the confines of our modest suburban homes and the Arabic church, the other at the mall and in the unfettered streets of San Francisco. With each passing year, it seemed more and more impossible to live in such a bifurcated way. I fought with my parents all the time, and because I started to doubt which "side" of me was really me, the demands from both sides just made me want to rebel against everything.[1]

Even as I yelled at them, I knew that my parents wanted only the best for me. Because of my adolescent myopia, I had only the faintest sense of the difficulties of their lives and the concurrent struggle of their immigrant generation to simultaneously foster cultural continuity and be Arab in America. Just like I was with my ripped jeans, they too were trying to articulate who they were. It would be years before I grasped how each day they confronted not only the pressures of assimilation but also the realities of an expanding US imperialist war in the Arab region and intensifying anti-Arab Orientalist and racist discourses in their new home.

More than thirty years ago, Edward Said argued that "Orientalism" is a European fabrication of "the East," that "the Orient" is shaped by European imperialist attitudes and assumes that Eastern or Oriental people can be defined in terms of cultural or religious essences that are invulnerable to historical change. Orientalism, he explained, configures the "East" in irreducible attributes such as religiosity or femininity. This political vision, he contended, has promoted the idea of insurmountable differences between the familiar (Europe, West, "us") and the strange (the Orient, the East, "them"). Like Said, critics of Orientalism have long argued that essentialist representations of Islam are crucial to Orientalist thought. In Orientalist thought, Muslims, Arabs, and other "Orientals" are hopelessly mired in a host of social ills, the cause of which is an unchanging tradition that exists outside of history and is incompatible with civilization.[2] Feminist scholars such as Rabab Abdulhadi have in turn argued that this strand of Orientalist thought has constructed our contemporary visions of Arab and Muslim societies as either completely decadent, immoral, and permissive or strict and oppressive to women.[3] This new Orientalism relies on representations of culture (Arab) and religion (Islam) as a justification for post–Cold War imperial expansion in the Middle East and the targeting of people perceived to fit the racial profile of a potential terrorist living in the United States—Arabs, Middle Easterners, Muslims.[4] New Orientalist discourses have birthed a variety of widely accepted ideas: of Arab and Muslim queers oppressed by a homophobic culture and religion, of hyperoppressed shrouded Arab and Muslim women who need to be saved by American heroes, of a culture of Arab Muslim sexual savagery that needs to be disciplined—and in the process, modernized—through US military violence.[5]

The impact of Orientalism, I began to see, was everywhere. Our Arab community had a plethora of cultural and political organizations to put on music concerts, festivals, and banquets and a range of political organizations that focused on civil rights issues and homeland politics. Yet there were no resources for dealing with the difficult issues within our families. As in many immigrant families, ours opted to avoid bringing attention to personal matters, particularly in public space and particularly among other Arabs. Throughout high school especially, many of my Arab American peers were devastated by the conflicting feelings of love, pain, and guilt toward our parents and the ideas about Arab culture that we learned from our parents and US society. We joked about fleeing our community altogether. We swore to each other that we would never marry an Arab. It was clear that these problems were pushing Arabs away from each other. In addition, on my trips to Jordan to visit relatives, I learned that many of my neighbors in the Bay Area had more socially conservative understandings of religion, family, gender, and sexuality than their counterparts in Jordan. I was baffled: why were the stakes of family respectability so high in America?

Articulating Arabness

After I survived the dual gauntlet of high school and my parents' expectations, and after I moved out of their home, I began listening more carefully to the stories of our immigrant parents. I began asking why they came to the United States, what they experienced when they arrived, and what they dreamed of and worked for in America. Not surprisingly, our parents' commitments to cultural continuity were much more complicated than what I had understood them to be. . . . I worked with community-based organizations and did ethnographic research with eighty-six men and women, ages eighteen to twenty-eight, whose families had immigrated to the United States, primarily from Jordan, Lebanon, Palestine, and Syria. I interviewed fifteen immigrants from their parents' generation, immigrants who came to the Bay Area between the 1950s and 1970s, an era characterized by increased Arab migration to the United States, the expansion of American empire in the Arab region, and the intensification of racism and xenophobia in California.[6] . . .

For several years, as I conducted in-depth interviews with teens and twentysomethings, we shared stories about the norms and expectations of our immigrant communities. Orientalism was at the heart of this struggle. The dominant middle-class Arab immigrants' articulation of Arabness through rigid, binary categories . . . was based on a similar framework that guided Orientalist discourses about Arabs. My parents and their peers simply reversed Orientalism and used its binary categories (liberated Americans versus oppressed Arab women, bad Arabs versus good Americans) differently and for different purposes. Articulating immigrant cultural identity through rigid binaries is not an unfamiliar resolution to immigrant and people of color's struggles in a society structured by a pressure for assimilation and racism.[7] As Vijay Prashad argues, this dynamic, while a reaction to political and historical conditions, is an attempt to depoliticize the immigrant experience where culture is articulated not as living, changing social relations but a set of timeless traits.[8] . . .

The uninterrogated naturalization of a dichotomy between Arab and American culture among Arab Americans—usually associated as it is with essentialist understandings of religion, family, gender, and sexuality among Arab communities—allows Orientalist thought to be left intact and activated. Consigned to the "cultural," aspects of dynamic, lived experience come to be seen as frozen in time—essentialist Arab traditions that exist outside of history—which is the same conceptualization that operates as the basis for the demonization of Arab communities in the discourses of US empire.

Within the dominant middle-class Arab immigrant discourse that circulated in my interlocutors' homes and community networks, gender and sexuality were among the most powerful symbols consolidating an imagined difference between "Arabs" and "Americans." . . .

> JUMANA: My parents thought that being American was spending the night at a friend's house, wearing shorts, the guy-girl thing, wearing makeup, reading teen magazines, having pictures of guys in my room. My parents used to tell me, "If you go to an American's house, they're smoking, drinking . . . they offer you this and that. But if you go to an Arab house, you don't see as much of that. *Bi hafiu ala al banat* [They watch over their daughters]."

> TONY: There was a pressure to marry an Arab woman because the idea was that "She will stand by her family, she will cook and clean, and have no career. She'll have kids, raise kids, and take care of her kids, night and day. She will do anything for her husband." My mom always says, "You're not going to find an American woman who stands by her family like that. . . . American women leave their families."

In the quotes above . . . [i]dealized concepts of femininity are connected to idealized notions of family and an idealized concept of heterosexual marriage. These ideals underpin a generalized pressure for monogamy—and more specifically, for no sex before marriage—and for compulsory heterosexuality. Some interlocutors recalled their parents' reaction to what they perceived to be signs of homosexuality. Here is how Ramsy said his Palestinian mother reacted to photographs of him in drag: "My mom took one look at the pictures and said, 'My God! What are we doing in this country! Oh, look what this country did to us!' They definitely see it as an American thing. They don't know that there are a lot of gay people back home." Among the middle-class Arab immigrant communities I worked with, dominant articulations of Arabness were structured by a strict division between an inner Arab domain and an outer American domain, a division that is built upon the figure of the woman as the upholder of values and an ideal of family, heterosexuality, and, most important, heterosexual marriage.

This jumble of ideals about Arabness and Americanness . . . created a fundamental split

between a gendered and sexualized notion of an inner-familial-communal (Arab) domain and an external-public (American) domain . . . This split was terribly familiar to me and, at the same time, largely undiscussed both in my own life and in the larger Arab American community. . . .

As my research progressed, I began interpreting the predicament of growing up in new ways. Both my parents and the parents of my interlocutors constantly referred to Arab culture—as the thing that rooted us, and often, it seemed, ruled us. This amorphous entity shaped our calendar and our thoughts, what our goals were and who our friends were. But the more I searched, the harder it became to find this culture. All I could find, instead, was an amalgam of influences. . . . Concepts of Arabness among my parents' generation, and through them my peers' and my interlocutors', have ultimately been shaped not by a ceaseless and unchanging Arab tradition but by a collision of historically contingent realities and varying modes of diasporic living in the American empire—of running a grocery store, of traveling to the Arab world, of the travel of news and stories through the Internet and satellite television, by past and present Arab responses to European colonialism and US empire, and by the words of the corporate media.

By interrogating the process by which middle-class Arab diasporas come to herald particular ideals as markers of an authentic, essential, true, or real Arab culture, I have learned that these ideals are best understood as cultural sensibilities that have permeated the Arab region for centuries and have become entangled in concepts of Arabness and Americanness that circulate in the United States. Even with regards to the Arab region, essentialist cultural frameworks cannot explain concepts and practices of family, marriage, gender, and sexuality, as these are very much entangled in European and US discourses and are constantly changing in light of socioeconomic transformations.[9] Consider, for instance, that modernist nationalist concepts of gender and sexuality became dominant in the Arab region as European involvement in the region introduced certain new ideas about gender and sexuality.[10] These new European-influenced concepts replaced a much more varied structure of gender and ambiguous, fluid sexual attitudes that were common during centuries of Islamic rule.[11]

To a certain extent, I interpret dominant middle-class Arab American concepts of "Arab culture" as an immigrant survival strategy for replacing US colonialist and Orientalist discourses about Arabs, Muslims, and the Middle East with seemingly positive or empowering concepts of cultural identity, a strategy that reverses the binary structure of bad, misogynist Arabs versus good, modern Americans and instead advances good Arab girls versus bad American(ized) girls. . . . Yet I also contend that this dominant middle-class Arab American discourse is shaped by the liberal logic of US multiculturalism, a logic for imagining and performing cultural identity that becomes available to Arab diasporas upon their arrival in the United States. Liberal US multiculturalism requires immigrants, people of color, and indigenous people to craft concepts of culture that are depoliticized and ahistorical. . . . Furthermore, while the dominant middle-class Arab American discourse idealizes family and heterosexual marriage as *Arab*, and not American, in fact, patriarchy and idealized concepts of "family values" and compulsory heterosexuality are fundamental to the demands of white US middle-class acceptability. This small sampling from my research calls for a broader analysis of sensationalized issues such as "Arab" and "Muslim" patriarchy and homophobia. At the least, it points to an urgent need to transcend essentialist frameworks that explain structures of patriarchy among Arab families and communities as simply "cultural" matters. I believe that a diasporic Arab feminist theory, a theory that locates "Arab" patriarchy and homophobia at the interplay among long-standing cultural sensibilities, Orientalism and imperial formations, and the pressures of immigration and assimilation, opens up such possibilities.

Social Movements and "Arab Culture"

Working within various Arab and Arab American activist movements, I learned that it was not only conventional middle-class Arab American discourses that conceptualized family, gender, and sexuality as characteristics of an inner-communal-"cultural" domain. . . . In leftist Arab American political movements focused on Palestine and Iraq, for instance, many Arab and Arab American feminists have been working to liberate issues of gender and sexuality from a seemingly internal-cultural domain. In nearly every Arab and Arab American organization where I have worked, political actions were focused externally—on ending war and racism, on raising awareness about the links between sexual violence and US and Israeli militarism, and on liberating Arab land from colonization. In 2002, I participated in a community-based organization that led a campaign to end US sanctions on Iraq and launched a divest-from-Israel movement modeled after the South African anti-Apartheid movement. This leftist Arab movement operated according to a collective consciousness that Israel was killing and displacing Palestinians en masse, that the US war in Iraq was looking more and more like genocide, and that US tax dollars were paying for it. Mobilized by daily images circulating in alternative media sources of dead Palestinian and Iraqi children, activists operated as a community in crisis.

Crisis mode meant that certain issues were privileged over others. This point was most clearly evident in moments when people raised critiques of sexism or homophobia within our movement. These critiques were met with an official movement logic that contended that the issue of sexism was secondary to the fact that "our people are dying back home." Alternately, it positioned discussions of homophobia as entirely irrelevant or outside the boundaries of acceptability. . . .

Not only were gender and sexuality barely discussed, but the official movement discourse insisted that discussing these internal issues in public could actually endanger the goals activists were fighting for. Many members of this movement shared the belief that US Orientalist representations of Arabs and Muslims, specifically images of hyperoppressed Arab and Muslim women and Arab Muslim sexual savagery, were among the most common images Americans saw—especially from the news media and Hollywood. In their analysis,

Orientalist representations were a key reason so many Americans supported US military interventions in the Middle East and why many Americans, particularly liberals, expressed profound empathy for Arab and Muslim women—perceived to be victims of their culture and religion—but little concern over the impact of U.S. policies on Arab and Muslim communities.[12] . . .

The fear of washing our dirty laundry in public has haunted my own experiences working on various Arab and Arab American feminist issues in the United States. Since 1993, I have been involved in a range of projects that presented various Arab and Arab American feminist perspectives . . . All of these projects were anchored in a sort of anti-Orientalist feminism that disregarded issues internal to our communities because we were either cautious about the ways such issues could be used against us or because we felt that other matters such as war and occupation were the more pressing issues of our times. These efforts focused on deconstructing the proliferation of Orientalist US discourses that represent Arab culture through images of oppressed Arab women, explaining the magnitude of these discourses to the legitimization of US and Israeli militarism and war, and calling liberal US feminists to task for reinforcing Orientalist feminisms and ignoring critiques of US empire and its gendered and sexualized underpinnings.

In 2002, I joined the Arab Movement of Women Arising for Justice (AMWAJ), a new group of Arab and Arab American feminists, some of whom had been active in the previous projects but were tired of the privileging of "external" problems of racism and war among Arab feminist activists in the United States. Many of us were also tired of the silence surrounding forms of sexism and homophobia that take place among our families and communities. Yet we recognized that there were few spaces to talk about "internal" issues—particularly since we felt that most US feminist spaces, as well as some Arab American feminist spaces—were dominated by Orientalist perspectives about Arab women. . . . A shared desire for a space to discuss the range of issues that impact our lives—including the issues that we confront among

our families and Arab communities—inspired us to organize a gathering for Arab women, queer, and transgender people living in the United States in Chicago in 2005. . . . We were very clear that the project of addressing "internal" Arab community-based matters was fraught in the United States, but we were committed to going beyond Orientalism and anti-Orientalism. We strategically used the idea of "internal" and "external" domains for organizing our initial gathering. We began by fostering a space where people could speak openly about "internal" matters—since many of us rarely had this opportunity beforehand—beyond the intimate spaces of friendship and loved ones. . . .

AMWAJ activists modeled our gathering after the "I Am Your Sister" conference honoring Audre Lorde. Harnessing the wisdom of other "third-world" and women-of-color feminist collectives that have come before them, AMWAJ activists created new possibilities for transcending dominant masculinist and colonialist concepts of what can and what cannot be discussed or fought for. We were contributing to the emergence of a diasporic Arab feminist politics, a multi-issued, feminist politics that seeks to dismantle sexism, homophobia, imperialism, and racism and refuses to be silent on the ways these power structures operate within Arab families and communities. Yet while we maintained these commitments, we could not escape the predicament that has circumscribed antiracist, anti-imperialist Arab feminisms: how can we speak frankly about our experiences in ways that neither reinscribe Arab bashing nor engage in Orientalism?

Decolonizing Arabness

Collective projects such as AMWAJ have fostered new visions for social justice that are aiming to transcend bifurcated and simplistic options represented by the "cultural" self and the "political" self that force activists to choose between speaking about internal issues or working on externally focused causes such as war and racism. The overt ways that anti-Arab racism operates—with and through the themes of family, gender, and sexuality—elucidate that these categories of oppression are linked and cannot be dismantled separately. During the Israeli siege on Gaza in January 2009, I heard a guest on National Public Radio claim that Israel will continue to have the right to attack Palestinians as long as "Arabs love their guns more than they love their children." While this statement is loaded with assumptions about Palestinian culture and Palestinian mothers, it also reflects a dominant US and Israeli discourse that justifies violence and occupation. A fuller analysis of empire takes seriously the gendered and sexualized logics through which empire works. . . . I believe we need to broaden our analysis of the empire. How are Arab diasporas, for instance, articulating who they are, determining their community boundaries and who is included and excluded against the invasive and shifting relations of power central to US imperial formations? I believe we need to struggle beyond crisis mode, create alternatives to the sense that the external attacks are so profound that "we can't take anything else on right now." What are the historical conditions and power structures through which anti-imperialist social movements determine what constitutes violence or what forms of violence are worth ending? How

will we define the fragility of life and what forms of life are worth fighting for? Arab diasporas live life on multiple tracks—our days are built upon the divide between the internal and the external, "the communal" and "the political." Sometimes these tracks seem to exist side by side, and sometimes the gulf between the two seems impossible to bridge. Navigating the multiplicity can be maddening, yet, I believe, it can also be liberating. By unlocking the rigid back-and-forth between Orientalism and anti-Orientalism, we can respond to imperialism and Orientalism and we can also transcend the reliance upon the figure of the "woman" or compulsory heterosexuality to determine the survival of "Arabs" in "America."

This essay is an excerpt from my book, *Articulating Arabness: Gender and Cultural Identity in the Diaspora*. I am grateful to Rabab Abdulhadi, Evelyn Alsultany, Lara Deeb, and Andrea Smith for their invaluable feedback on this essay. My deepest appreciation goes to all of the people who participated in my research. There are not enough words to thank them for their contribution.

NOTES

1. To some extent, working-class Arab kids we knew from church or school faced similar struggles. Yet the stakes seemed to be different among middle-class immigrant families, as the reputation of one's father's family name was very much tied up in socioeconomic class status.

2. Anouar Majid, *Unveiling Traditions: Postcolonial Islam in a Polycentric World* (Durham: Duke University Press, 2000), 7; Minoo Moallem, *Between Warrior Brother and Veiled Sister: Islamic Fundamentalism and the Politics of Patriarchy in Iran* (Berkeley and Los Angeles: University of California Press, 2005); Ella Shohat and Robert Stam, *Unthinking Eurocentrism: Multiculturalism and the Media* (New York: Routledge, 1994).

3. Rabab Abdulhadi, "Sexualities and the Social Order in Arab and Muslim Communities," in *Islam and Homosexuality*, ed. Samar Habib (Santa Barbara: Praeger, 2010), 470.

4. This also includes South Asians and others perceived to be any of these categories: Sunaina

Maira, *Missing: Youth, Citizenship, and Empire after 9/11* (Durham: Duke University Press, 2009).

5. Jasbir K. Puar, *Terrorist Assemblages: Homonationalism in Queer Times* (Durham: Duke University Press, 2007); Lila Abu-Lughod, "Do Muslim Women Really Need Saving? Anthropological Reflections on Cultural Relativism and Its Others," *American Anthropologist*, 104, no. 3 (2002). . . .

6. For analyses of intensified xenophobia and racism in California, see Jewelle Taylor Gibbs and Teiahsha Bankhead, *Preserving Privilege: California Politics, Propositions, and People of Color* (Westport, Conn.: Praeger, 2001); and Tomas Almaguer, *Racial Fault Lines: The Historical Origins of White Supremacy in California* (Berkeley and Los Angeles: University of California Press, 1994). Engseng Ho ("Empire Through Diasporic Eyes: A View from the Other Boat," *Comparative Studies in Society and History* 46, no. 2 [2004]: 210–46) provides a useful analysis of the United States as an empire. He argues that U.S. empire is a mode of imperial domination that has

global reach and disavows administration on the ground.. . . . Yet at the same time, the United States has a devastating mode of domination that forces local governments to make appalling choices. Generally, . . . US empire works through covert and overt mechanisms and through economic, military, and cultural hegemony. . . .

7. Vijay Prashad, *The Karma of Brown Folk* (Minneapolis: University of Minnesota Press, 2000); Yen Le Espiritu, *Home Bound: Filipino American Lives Across Cultures, Communities, and Countries* (Berkeley: University of California Press, 2003); Cathy J. Cohen, *The Boundaries of Blackness: AIDS and the Breakdown of Black Politics* (Chicago: University of Chicago Press, 1999); Kevin Gaines, *Uplifting the Race: Black Leadership, Politics, and Culture in the Twentieth Century* (Chapel Hill: University of North Carolina Press, 1996).

8. Prashad, 150.

9. Lila Abu-Lughod, "The Marriage of Feminism and Islamism in Egypt: Selective Repudiation as a Dynamic of Postcolonial Cultural Politics," in *Remaking Women: Feminism and Modernity in the Middle East*, ed. Lila Abu-Lughod (Princeton: Princeton University Press, 1998), 243–69; Homa Hoodfar, *Between Marriage and the Market: Intimate Politics and Survival in Cairo*, Comparative Studies on Muslim Societies, vol. 24 (Berkeley: University of California Press, 1997).

10. Afsaneh Najmabadi, *Women with Mustaches and Men Without Beards: Gender and Sexual Anxieties of Iranian Modernity* (Berkeley: University of California Press, 2005); Abdulhadi, "Sexualities and Social Order"; Leila Ahmed, *Women and Gender in Islam: Historical Roots of a Modern Debate* (New Haven: Yale University Press, 1992).

11. Abdulhadi, "Sexualities and Social Order"; Joseph Andoni Massad, *Desiring Arabs* (Chicago: University of Chicago Press, 2007); Najmabadi; Samar Habib, ed., *Islam and Homosexuality* (Santa Barbara: Praeger, 2010).

12. For further analysis of the deployment of images of women in discourses of war, see Amira Jarmakani, *Imagining Arab Womanhood: The Cultural Mythology of Veils, Harems, and Belly Dancers in the U.S.* (New York: Palgrave Macmillan, 2008); Abu-Lughod, "Do Muslim Women Really Need Saving?"; and Sherene H. Razack, "Geopolitics, Culture Clash, and Gender after September 11," *Social Justice* 32, no. 4 (2005).

WHITNEY POW

10 THAT'S NOT WHO I AM: CALLING OUT AND CHALLENGING STEREOTYPES OF ASIAN AMERICANS (2012)

Based in Chicago, **Whitney Pow** is a PhD candidate at Northwestern University and also the lead artist and graphic designer at ARRiBot Game Design, an educational board game company. Pow writes about queer games, about queer and transgender histories of software and computing, and has worked with several organizations, including Asian American Writers Workshop, Autostraddle, The Feminist Press, and Literary Death Match. Her scholarly work has appeared in *The Velvet Light Trap* and *In Media Res*.

Asian America: land of the immigrants, the ninjas, the kung-fu masters, laundromat owners, Eastern mystics, Chinese restaurant waiters and people who can't pronounce their Ls and Rs properly. It's a land of slanted eyes and incorrect grammar. It's a land of the yellow menace taking America's money. It's a land of stereotypes—at least, according to television and film.

Asian stereotypes are everywhere, and oftentimes they go unnoticed and unquestioned. More often than not, if you see an Asian/American depicted on the screen, you'll also see an Asian stereotype. From the character Han Lee in *2 Broke Girls*[1] to Long Duk Dong in *Sixteen Candles*[2] . . . these stereotypes are unrealistic and offensive. Unfortunately, these stereotypes too often fall under the popular radar and aren't discussed or acknowledged as much as they should be.

I want to get the discussion started. I'd like to examine three of the most pervasive Asian stereotypes—the Media Action Network for Asian Americans' website, MANAA.org,[3] has an amazing breakdown of the negative Asian stereotypes[4] we see so often in mainstream media. I've taken three of the points from MANAA's list and I'll be building upon them in this article. This is an invitation to find, look at, and think about the uncomfortable

portrayals of Asian/Americans you see in the media—and start your own discussions.

1. "Asian Americans as foreigners who cannot be assimilated."

"Because [Asian/Americans] are racially and culturally distinctive from the American mainstream, Asian people have been widely seen as unable to be absorbed into American society. According to this view, anything Asian is thus inherently 'alien' to America."

If I had an ARGH for every time I've seen or experienced this stereotype, I would be ARGH-ing all day. The few portrayals of Asian/Americans in mainstream TV and film are often characterized by "unassimilated" or "exotic" stereotypes, like Asian accents, martial arts ability, unusual appearance (like traditional clothing), foreign birthplace and language of origin, and a propensity for eating exotic or culturally unacceptable things like dogs or cats. The problem in my lived experience is that these few portrayals end up being what people expect of me, and other Asian/Americans, too, and they create a kind of cultural

Source: Reprinted with permission of Whitney Pow. This article originally appeared on Autostraddle.com

identity erasure. When people look at me, they expect something that I am not—they expect an exotic other that doesn't "belong here" (that is, in the United States).

These stereotypes are so pervasive that they leave no space in the cultural landscape for an Asian/American who speaks English with a North American accent (like I do), an Asian/American who does not speak an Asian language with fluency (like I do) and an Asian/American who was born in the United States (like I was). Instead, I'm approached by people who assume that I'm either an immigrant restaurant worker (we'll get to stereotypical Asian occupations in a bit) or an international student at the local university—two things that place an immigrant or foreign identity on me, even though I'm an American citizen and have been living in the US my entire life. My elementary school classmates all thought I could do kung-fu. I've been told that I speak English "remarkably well" (that is, without an Asian accent). And acquaintances are often shocked when they hear I've never been to China. . . .

The stereotype of Asian/Americans as foreign or "other" creates a divide between who I am and how I am perceived—it's like my US citizenship status is dictated by my appearance and my ethnic background. People who look Asian, the assumption goes, are somehow unable to be American— we can see this demonstrated in the racist Chinese restaurant scene in *A Christmas Story*,[5] when the all-American family has its Christmas dinner in a Chinese restaurant. The otherness of the Chinese people in the restaurant is demonstrated by horrible ethnic caricatures: Traditional dress, lack of understanding of American customs and most glaringly, what I'd like to call "fa ra ra ra bullshit"— the racist stereotype that Asian/Americans swap the Ls and Rs in their speech interchangeably. I've never, ever heard any Chinese or Asian non-native English speaker sound the way the singers sound in *A Christmas Story*. Ever. Period. And the supposed humor in the scene comes from the irony of it all— the all-American family having an all-American Christmas meal at a Chinese restaurant, which, as

it's played in the film, is the most un-American experience anyone could ever have.

These stereotypes are embedded in our culture and pass by unnoticed, especially since *A Christmas Story* is a culturally beloved film that almost everyone has seen. . . . I was shocked when I first saw the film. The lack of discussion about this scene sends the message that this racism against Asian/Americans is still acceptable (or even funny)—that making fun of Asian/Americans through unrealistic Asian accents and an inability to speak English "correctly" (and highlighting this by titling the YouTube clips of the scene things like "Fa Ra Ra") is A-OK.

The cultural identity of Asian/Americans is deeply affected by racist scenes like this, especially when these racist tropes are not talked about or discussed—without acknowledging how other-izing and racist these scenes are, this "unassimilated" and "unassimilate-able" identity of Asian/Americans becomes the norm, and it becomes what's expected from people who look like me. From people greeting me with phrases like "konichiwa" to people saying things like "herro" to me (which is supposed to be "hello" with a racist affect), my identity as an Asian American becomes invisible . . . people see a stereotype of non-English-speaking immigrant when they look at me rather than an Asian American individual who's a citizen of the United States.

2. "Asian cultures as inherently predatory."

> "For decades, Americans have viewed Asian immigrants as 'taking' from this country without giving anything back. This perception was reinforced by early laws making it difficult for Asians to immigrate and impossible for them to become naturalized citizens. Although these laws have since been repealed, the image of the Asian as alien predator still infuses popular media."

In 1982, Vincent Chin was beaten to death in Detroit, Michigan. Chin had been in a bar celebrating his soon-to-be wedding. Two white men, Ronald Ebens and Michael Nitz, approached Chin and said to him, "Because of you motherfuckers, we're out of work." According to Helen Zia, a journalist and race activist . . . who covered the murder in Detroit:

> Vincent replied, "Don't call me a fucker," and a scuffle ensued. . . . Both groups were ejected from the bar. Ebins and Nitz hunted for Chin and the other Chinese man in his group . . . They drove through the area for a half hour with a neighborhood man whom they paid to help them "get the Chinese." Finally they spotted Vincent and his friend in front of a crowded McDonald's on Woodward Avenue, Detroit's main central thoroughfare. Creeping up behind the Chinese Americans, Nitz held Vincent Chin down while his stepfather [Ebins] swung his Louisville Slugger baseball bat into Vincent's skull four times, "as if he were going for a home run." Two off-duty cops who were moonlighting as security guards witnessed the attack. . . . Mortally wounded, Vincent died four days later. His four hundred wedding guests attended his funeral instead."[6]

According to Roland Hwang, an attorney with the Michigan Department of Attorney General,[7] Ebins and Nitz got away with committing a racially motivated murder *in front of two cops* virtually scot-free. For second-degree murder, each man was sentenced to "three years probation and a fine of $3,000."[8]

How does this happen? When any group of people is racially coded as "outside" of American culture, we start to think of them as inhuman, and they become an easy target for frustrations and resentments. In the early 1980s, the automotive industry in Detroit was failing, and fuel- and cost-efficient Japanese cars were on the rise. The blame for the failing economy was placed on Japan, and as a result, Detroit suffered from a great deal of racism and racial anxiety against Asian Americans, regardless of ethnicity. Chin wasn't Japanese—he was a Chinese American man who worked in Detroit, just like Ebins and Nitz. But because of his "outsider" status coded by his race, he became a target, and a symbol of a hated "other" or "outsider" that was supposedly taking American money. Chin became an American scapegoat for a symbolic, race-based hatred. . . .

3. "Asian Americans restricted to clichéd occupations."

> "Asians and Asian Americans make their living in a wide array of professions, but too often, Asian American professionals are depicted in a limited and predictable range of jobs: restaurant workers, Korean grocers, Japanese businessmen, Indian cab drivers, TV anchorwomen, martial artists, gangsters, faith healers, laundry workers, and prostitutes."

My grandfather owned a dry cleaner in Manhattan, and he worked day shifts as a waiter in a Chinese restaurant. My grandmother was a seamstress. These occupations were part of—but not the entirety of—my grandparents' contributions to America.

My grandfather also fought for the US in World War II in the Flying Tigers as an airplane mechanic and gunman. Victoria Moy writes about this experience beautifully in her Huffington Post article, titled "You Must Remember This"[9]:

> When I asked my grandpa, "what was the happiest moment of your life?" I thought he'd surprise me with a romantic story about how he met my grandmother, but he didn't. "My happiest days?" he said, "it was with the boys, in the army."
>
> "When did you first feel like a real American?" I asked.
>
> "In the Army. I was an airplane mechanic for the Flying Tigers. There were over 1,000 of us, Chinese Americans, with the 14th Air Force. We traveled through the Himalayas, India, and Africa to China."
>
> Grandpa sang me army songs, and taught me to march like a soldier; his pride in being American was intense. It made me wonder if nationality would ever imprint itself onto my identity so strongly. At 13, I asked him to tell me his story one more time. He died that year.

Moy's descriptions of her grandfather fit my grandfather to a T: Our grandfathers both speak Toisanese (a village dialect of Cantonese) and English, watch American films religiously, worked in Laundromats and dry cleaners, were paper sons,[10] fought for America in WWII, and, most of all, are American. It's a picture of the Asian America of half a century ago that I've never seen acknowledged in mainstream media—Asian Americans as patriotic, hard working, and resourceful. These men, who are part of my family and 1,000 other Asian American families, fought in a war and risked their lives for this country—a story that gets overlooked too often.

When the few Asian Americans in the media are relegated to shop owners (Han Lee in *2 Broke Girls* and Mrs. Kim in *Gilmore Girls*) and other service positions, we miss out on the larger picture: The value of the work Asian Americans do, the sacrifices we've made for this country and our patriotic ties to our communities. Overlooking the contributions of Asian Americans has a long history, though—take, for instance, the thousands of Asian Americans who worked on the Transcontinental railroad and were excluded from the celebratory ceremonies,[11] and most notably, the railroad's completion photo,[12] in favor of their white counterparts. Or the official US Air Force films from WWII, which depict the Flying Tigers as white servicemen[13] rescuing the hapless Chinese — without a mention of the Chinese Americans who fought on America's side, too.

These stereotypical jobs focus on just the economic ties that Asian Americans have with America, ignoring the other contributions we have made. They present Asian Americans as "predators" who benefit from America and are just waiting to go back to "where they came from" with American money, without offering anything in return. In the popular imagination, the "American" part of Asian America is flimsily attached to our identities and is fundamentally insecure. The limited set of occupations available to Asian Americans on TV and in the movies reinforces the belief that Asian Americans don't belong here, and aren't really helping America, either.

The representation of Asian Americans is slowly expanding—we now have doctors, played by Sandra Oh in *Grey's Anatomy* and Charlyne Yi in *House*; there are dancers and singers played by Jenna Ushkowitz and Harry Shum Jr. in *Glee*; the ensemble cast of Community includes Asian American students Danny Pudi and Ken Jeong. Still,

you only need two hands to count the number of Asian Americans currently on network TV. The lack of varied and two-dimensional Asian American (main) characters in mainstream media is staggering, especially to those who are looking to see themselves in the media, like I am. The times I have felt kinship or identification with a character or person on TV and film are few and far between— and these representations can be more easily found in independent media rather than the mainstream.

The first time I felt like a film was really talking about me and to me was in late college; the film was Renee Tajima-Peña's *My America . . . or Honk if You Love Buddha*,[14] a documentary that looked at Asian America, stereotypes of Asian Americans, and even interviewed Asian American families that have been in America for over eight generations. It's an amazing film, and I haven't connected to any film or show the same way since, except for Pearl Girls Productions' queer Asian American web series *That's What She Said*.[15] The representations of Asian/Americans in mainstream TV and film don't seem to speak about Asian Americans from a place of knowing or understanding, or even trying to know or understand; instead, I've seen a lot of racial tropes being repeated over and over again. Why? Maybe it's an unquestioned convention? Maybe we need more people of color in charge of media representation? I'm not sure. But the cycle continues: Asian/American stereotypes are used; these stereotypes are not corrected or talked about or thought about; rinse and repeat. How do we fix these things? We become more aware. We think about the representations of race and gender we see. We talk about them. We maybe even yell about them. We acknowledge how these representations make us feel uncomfortable about ourselves, or, in the best cases, proud to be who we are. As a person of color, I feel out of control when I think of the way the media has historically portrayed people like me—the eternal immigrant, the restaurant worker, the money-sucking Chinese threat; the accented, L-and-R-swapped comic relief. It's painful to see how few times I felt I could identify with people like me. It's been difficult just trying to wrest enough authority over my own identity to be able to stand up and say something as simple as "I'm Asian American" without feeling ashamed. No one should have to go through this, but we do.

As queer people and as women, trans and non-binary people, activists and people of color, we are people fighting for who we are in all of our nuanced selfhood. We are fighting for the right to our own identities and who we are. And by examining these representations of ourselves and how people see us, and how we see ourselves, there is power in creating agency over our own identities. It's an ongoing process: Think, talk, yell, fight. Rinse. Repeat.

NOTES

1. Tim Goodman, "The Sorry State of '2 Broke Girls': Racism and Lame Sex Jokes," *The Hollywood Reporter*, October 24, 2011, http://www.hollywoodreporter.com/bastard-machine/sorry-state-2-broke-girls-252579

2. Alison MacAdam, "Long Duk Dong: Last of the Hollywood Stereotypes," *NPR.org*, March 24, 2008, http://www.npr.org/templates/story/story.php?storyId=88591800

3. http://www.manaa.org/

4. http://www.manaa.org/asian_stereotypes.html

5. http://www.youtube.com/watch?v=xTq20prt0K8

6. Helen Zia, *Asian American Dreams: The Emergence of an American People* (New York: Farrar Straus & Giroux, 2000).

7. http://www.michbar.org/journal/pdf/pdf4article1505.pdf

8. Zia, *Asian American Dreams*.

9. Victoria Moy, "You Must Remember This," *Huffington Post*, May 25, 2011, http://www.huffingtonpost.com/victoria-moy/you-must-remember-this_b_593748.html

10. "Chinese Exclusion Act," *Wikipedia*, https://en.wikipedia.org/wiki/Chinese_Exclusion_Act

11. Zak Keith, "Anti-Chinese USA: Racism and Discrimination from the Onset," *Keith Productions*, 2009, http://www.zakkeith.com/articles,blogs,forums/anti-Chinese-persecution-in-the-USA-history-timeline.htm

12. See http://cprr.org/Museum/Locomotives/I_ACCEPT_the_User_Agreement/images/russell_promontory_uprr.html

13. https://www.youtube.com/watch?v=Tq0ivpKAvn4

14. http://www.speakoutnow.org/userdata_display.php?modin=52&uid=4778

15. Whitney Pow, "'That's What She Said' Is Queer Asian American in Your Face," *Autostraddle*, August 9, 2011, https://www.autostraddle.com/thats-what-she-said-interview-103177/

Identities and Social Locations

Keywords: categorization, cisgender, cultural appropriation, identity, identity formation, levels of analysis, marginality, queer, social location, symbolic identity

Discovering and claiming our unique identity is a process of growth throughout a person's lifetime. Although one's identity may seem tangible and fixed at any given point, over the life span it is likely to be more fluid. For example, an able-bodied woman who suddenly finds herself needing to use a wheelchair after a car accident, an assimilated Jewish woman who begins to recover her cultural heritage, an immigrant woman from Guatemala "coming out" as queer in the United States, a queer student wanting to identify as transgender, or a suburban middle-class college student becoming politicized by an environmental justice organization on campus, will probably find themselves redefining who they are, what they value, and what "home" and "community" mean to them.

Identity formation is the result of the interplay among a range of factors: individual decisions and choices, specific life events, community recognition and expectations, societal categorization, socialization, and national or international events. It is an ongoing process that involves several key questions:

Who am I? Who do I want to be?
Who do others think I am and want me to be?

How do societal and community institutions, such as schools, religious institutions, health care organizations, and the law, categorize me and tell me who and what I am?

Where/what/who are my "home" and "community"?

Which social group(s) do I want to affiliate with? Why these groups?

Who decides the answers to these questions, and on what basis?

The *American Heritage Dictionary* (1982) defines *identity* as

the collective aspect of the set of characteristics by which a thing is definitely recognizable or known;

a set of behavioral or personal characteristics by which an individual is recognizable as a member of a group;

the distinct personality of an individual regarded as a persisting entity; individuality. (p. 639)

The same dictionary defines *to identify* as "to associate or affiliate (oneself) closely with a person or group; to establish an identification with another or others" (p. 639).

These definitions point to the connections between us as individuals and how we are perceived by other people and classified by the wider society. Gender, race, ethnicity, class, nationality, sexuality, age, religion, dis/ability, culture, and language are all significant social categories by which we recognize people. Indeed, on the basis of these categories, others may think they know who we are and how we should behave. Personal decisions about our affiliations, culture, and loyalties to specific groups are also shaped by these categories. For example, in communities of color and immigrant communities, women may struggle over the question of race versus gender. Is race a more important factor than gender in shaping their lives? If Latinx people speak out about oppression against trans people, are they betraying women and men in their community? This separation of categories sets up false dichotomies in which people may feel that they have to choose one aspect of their identity over another. It also presents particular difficulties for mixed-race, bisexual, or trans people who bridge or transcend singular categories and reinforces the need for an intersectional framework, as argued in Chapter 1.

Using social categories is not the same as being "labeled," which is usually done to name people in a pejorative way and perhaps to neutralize and undermine their political perspectives, especially those that counter prevailing views. Students may say "I don't want to be labeled a feminist" even though they support demands for gender justice. Being labeled by others is not the same as claiming an identity for yourself, though people sometimes use these terms interchangeably (see Reading 4).

In order to understand the complexity and richness of a person's experiences, we examine them from the micro, meso, macro, and global levels of social relations and institutional arrangements (see Fig. 3.1). Each level involves the standards—beliefs, behaviors, customs, and worldview—that people value. But it is important to emphasize that in a society marked by serious social and economic inequality, such as the United States, people in subordinate positions rarely see their values reflected in the dominant culture. Indeed, this absence is an important aspect of their oppression.

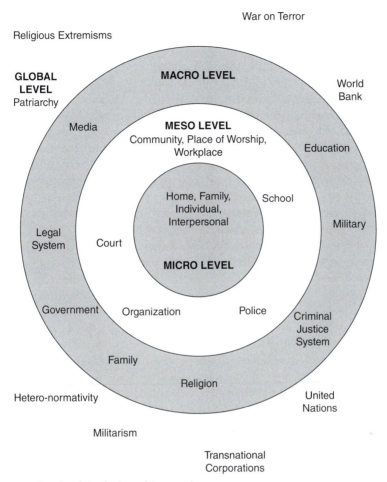

FIGURE 3.1   Levels of Analysis and Interaction

For example, writing about her family, whom she describes as "the ungrateful poor," Dorothy Allison in Reading 11 states: "My family's lives were not on television, not in books, not even comic books. There was a myth of the poor in this country; but it did not include us, no matter how hard I tried to squeeze us in." In this essay, Allison struggles with feelings of loyalty to her family. At times she distances herself from them, at times she despises herself, but she comes to accept her relatives, and to understand inequalities based on class.

Analyzing identity at all levels allows us to see that it is much more than an individual decision or choice about who we are in the world, but rather a set of complex and often contradictory and conflicting psychological, physical, geographical, political, cultural, historical, and spiritual factors. Identities are always political—involving interpersonal and institutional relations of power—irrespective of whether, as individuals, we think of them that way.

BEING MYSELF: THE MICRO LEVEL

At the micro level, we define ourselves and structure our daily activities according to our needs and preferences. At this level, we feel and experience the process of identity formation, which includes naming specific forces and contexts that shape our identities. Also at this level, we seem to have more control of the process, although there are always interconnections between events and experiences at this level and the others.

Critical life events may serve as catalysts for a shift in how we think about ourselves. A five-year-old Haitian American child of immigrant parents may experience the first challenge to her sense of identity when her kindergarten teacher admonishes her to speak only in English. A white, middle-class, professional woman who thinks of herself as a "competent attorney" may give more weight to the significance of gender if she witnesses younger, less experienced male colleagues in her law office passing her by in terms of promotions. A woman who has been raped and attends a meeting of a campus support group may experience a new sense of connection with other rape survivors. An African American lesbian feminist woman who transitions to a trans man may still identify as an African American lesbian feminist. An eighty-year-old woman, whose partner of fifty years has just died, must face the loss of her lifetime companion, friend, and lover. Such experiences shape each person's ongoing formulation of self, whether or not the process is conscious, deliberate, reflective, or even voluntary.

Thus, identity formation is a lifelong venture that may include discovery of the new; recovery of the old, forgotten, or appropriated; and syntheses of new and old, as illustrated by the writers in this chapter. Experiences in our families, communities, and schools, as well as our readings of media representations and popular culture, all contribute to identity formation and changes in our unfolding sense of self. At important junctures, individuals may mark an identity change in tangible ways, as with established rituals like weddings and funerals. An African American woman may decide to change her name from the anglicized Susan to Aisha, with roots in Islamic and African cultures. A Chinese immigrant woman, by contrast, may adopt an anglicized name, exchanging Nu Lu for Yvonne Lu as part of becoming a US citizen. Another way of marking and effecting a shift in identity is by altering your physical appearance: changing your wardrobe or makeup; cutting your hair very short, wearing it natural rather than permed or pressed, dyeing it purple, or letting the gray show after years of using hair coloring. More permanent changes might include tattoos, piercings, a facelift or tummy tuck, or for Asian American women, eyelid surgery. Individuals may change sex or **gender expression** through some combination of surgery, hormone therapy, and the ways they dress, talk, and move through the world. Other markers of a change in identity include setting up home for the first time, or relocating to another neighborhood, another city, or even another part of the world in search of a new home.

For many people, home is where we grow up until we become independent, such as by going to college, moving in with friends or a partner, or getting married; where our parents, siblings, and maybe grandparents are; where our needs for safety, security, and belonging are sought and often met. In reality, however, what we think of as home may be complicated and contradictory. Some things we need may be present but others not. Some people's homes are comfortable in a material sense yet are also places of emotional or physical violence. Some children grow up in homes that provide emotional safety but that may become a source of discomfort, even alienation, as they grow older, especially if their values diverge from those of their parents. Children adopted across lines of class, race, culture, and nation may never feel fully comfortable in their adoptive homes. An important step in integrating the different parts of their identities may be to find their birth mothers, trace their biological ancestry, or gain the support and friendship of other adoptees.

Regardless of such experiences, or perhaps because of them, most people continue to seek places of belonging. Home may be a geographical, social, emotional, and spiritual space where we hope to find comfort, familiarity, acceptance, love, and understanding, and where we can feel and be our best, whole selves. Home may be in several places at once or in different places at different times of our lives. Finally, this process of naming or finding a home may involve searching outside ourselves and piecing together the scattered parts of our identities, an inward as well as an outward journey.

COMMUNITY RECOGNITION AND EXPECTATIONS: THE MESO LEVEL

It is at the meso level—at school, in the workplace, in the neighborhood, or on the street—that people most frequently ask "Who are you?" or "Where are you from?" in an attempt to categorize us and determine their relationship to us. The single most visible signifier of identity is physical appearance. How we look to others affects their perceptions, judgments, and treatment of us. Questions like "Where do you come from?" and questioning behaviors, such as feeling the texture of your hair or asking if you speak a particular language, are commonly used to interrogate someone whose physical appearance or behavior does not match assumptions about established categories. At root, we are being asked "Are you one of us or not?" Mariko Uechi, a mixed-race woman who can "pass" as white, discusses this in Reading 14 as she works out what home and community mean to her. She links her personal experiences to her family's story and, beyond that, to the geopolitical context of their lives.

As a trans woman, Julia Serano (2007) states, "I am often confronted by people who insist that I am not, nor can I ever be, a 'real woman'" (p. 35). She argues that media depictions often focus on trans women in the act of "putting on" their feminine exteriors—"lipstick, dresses, and high heels, thereby making it clear to the audience that the trans woman's femaleness is an artificial mask" (p. 41). In Reading 13, Eli Clare, who identifies as a genderqueer crip, offers three lessons from the disability rights movement that are valuable for trans experience: the importance of naming, disclosure, and "living in our familiar, ordinary bodies" (2013, p. 264), "even as we're treated as curious, exotic, unbelievable, deceptive, sick, threatening from the outside" (2013, p. 265). He concludes:

> I'm reaching toward a disability politics of transness, not one of simple analogy but one . . . that questions the idea of normal and the notion of cure, that values self-determination, that resists shame and the medicalization of identity—a politics that will help all of us to come home to our bodies. (p. 265)

As Clare suggests, home and community may be physical, geographical, emotional, or all three, and they provide ways for people to express group affiliations. Community might be an organized group like Alcoholics Anonymous, a faith-based group, or the environmental group 350.org. Community may be cultural or religious, as discussed by Nadine Naber in Reading 9, Melanie Kaye/Kantrowitz in Reading 12, and Julia Alvarez in Reading 15, or something more abstract, as in "the queer community" or "the disability rights community." In these examples, there is an assumption of shared values, interests, culture, or language that is considered essential for group membership and belonging. Increasingly, these may be virtual communities as the Internet links people worldwide.

At the community level, individual identities and needs confront group standards, expectations, obligations, responsibilities, and demands. You compare yourself with others and are subtly compared. Others size up your clothing, accent, personal style, and knowledge of the group's history and culture. You may be challenged directly: "You say you're Latinx. What does that mean? Do you speak Spanish?" Or: "You're working class? What are you doing in a professional job?" These experiences may affirm our identities and also create or highlight inconsistencies and contradictions in who we believe we are, how we are viewed by others, our role and status in the community, and our sense of belonging. In Reading 15, writer Julia Alvarez examines the significance of the quinceañera coming-of-age ceremony as a way of affirming and remaking Latinx cultural identities and traditions in the United States. This formerly upper-class celebration has become a rite of passage for US-born daughters of immigrant families, including those with very modest incomes. It incorporates traditions from Mexico, Central America, and the Caribbean, enlarged by US consumerism. Also, these North American ways of celebrating the quinceañera, Alvarez notes, are being exported "back home."

Some individuals move in two or more worlds and are accepted as insiders in both, at least in part. Examples include people who identify as bi, trans, or mixed race, who all live in at least two cultures. For instance, Tracy, a white, working-class woman, leaves her friends behind after high school graduation as she goes off to an elite university. Though excited and eager to be in this new setting, she often feels alienated at college because her culture, upbringing, and level of economic security differ from those of upper-middle-class and upper-class students. During the winter break, she goes back to her hometown, where she discovers a gulf between herself and her old friends who stayed at home and took jobs or attended community college. She notices that she is now speaking a slightly different language from them and that her interests and preoccupations are different from theirs. Tracy experiences **marginality**, with a foot in both worlds. She has become sufficiently acculturated at college to begin to know that community as an insider and has retained her old friendships at home, but she is not entirely at ease or wholly accepted by either group. Her identity is complex, composed of several parts, some of which may conflict.

In Reading 11, Dorothy Allison describes her experience of marginality in high school and college. First-generation immigrants invariably experience marginality, as described by Julia Alvarez in Reading 15, Nadine Naber in Reading 9, and by Mariko Uechi in Reading 14. The positive side of this is a wider range of vision than that of people who are embedded in only one context. This gives bicultural people a broader standpoint and helps them to be cultural interpreters and bridge builders, especially at the micro and meso levels.

SOCIAL CATEGORIES AND STRUCTURAL INEQUALITIES: MACRO AND GLOBAL LEVELS

Social categories such as gender, race, class, and sexuality are used to establish and maintain a particular kind of social order; therefore, they are political as well as social. These classifications and their specific features, meanings, and significance are constructed through history, politics, and culture. They have been used to justify the conquest, colonization, domination, and exploitation of entire groups of people. Although the specifics may have changed over time, this system of categorizing and classifying continues and is internalized, wholly or in part, by specific groups. In Reading 11, Dorothy Allison points out that a "horror of class stratification, racism, and prejudice is that some people begin to believe that the security of their families and community depends on the oppression of others, that for some to have good lives others must have lives that are mean and horrible."

In the writings of early colonizers on this continent, Native American people were considered brutal, uncivilized, and ungovernable savages. This justified the near-genocide of indigenous people by white settlers, national and local public officials, and US troops, as well as the breaking of treaties between the US government and Native American nations. Today, Native Americans are less likely to be called savages, but they are often thought of as a dying group or a nonexistent people already wiped out, thereby rationalizing their neglect by the dominant culture and erasing their long-standing and continuing resistance. Native American writers and activists speak to the oppression of Native American people, as well as to their success in retaining traditional values and the cultural revival they have undertaken (see Readings 1 and 27; Daly 1994; Deer 2015; Dunbar-Ortiz 2014). In Reading 58, Patricia St. Onge describes how Native Americans and African Americans have been pitted against each other. She reflects on the different and also similar histories of these two groups, whose people have found ways to resist their dehumanization.

Those in dominant positions are deemed superior and legitimate, and those relegated—whether explicitly or implicitly—to subordinate positions are deemed inferior and illegitimate. Of course, individuals do not simply occupy dominant or subordinate positions. A college-educated, Arab American, heterosexual, cisgender man has privilege in terms of gender, class, and sexuality but is considered subordinate in terms of race and culture. Depending on specific contexts, these aspects of his identity will contribute to his experiences of privilege or disadvantage. Self-awareness involves recognizing and understanding the significance of our identities at the macro level. For white people who are descended from European immigrants to the United States, the advantages of being white are not always fully recognized or acknowledged. Psychologist Mary C. Waters (1996) showed how this country's racial hierarchy benefits European Americans who may choose to claim an ethnic identity as, for example, Irish American or Italian American. She sees this kind of symbolic identity as individualistic and without serious costs for the individual compared with racial and ethnic identities of people of color in the United States. As a result, white people tend to think of identities as equal: "I'm Italian American, you're Polish American. I'm Irish American, you're African American." This assumed equivalence ignores significant differences between a symbolic identity and an identity rooted in oppression attached to a socially imposed and enforced category such as race.

African Americans, for instance, have been categorized as Black, even if their parentage includes people of Native American, Asian, or European ancestry. A 1662 Virginia law maintained that people with only "one drop" of Black blood had to identify as Black. This rule was "upheld as recently as 1985, when a Louisiana court ruled that a woman with a black great-great-great-great-grandmother could not identify herself as 'white' on her passport" (Bradt 2010).

Note, too, that all Europeans were not considered equal when they came to the United States in the nineteenth and early twentieth centuries. German, English, Scottish, Irish, French, Italian, Polish, and Russian Jewish people were differentiated in a hierarchy based on skin color, culture, language, and their histories in Europe. In Reading 12, Melanie Kaye/Kantrowitz considers how Jews in the United States fit into established categories of race, class, religion, and national origin. She notes the diversity and complexity of Jewish people's experiences, with histories of severe oppression and times of relative calm. In the United States, Jews may be considered white, though this is not consistent across the country. To the extent that it happens, assimilation into the dominant culture has involved a loss of knowledge and familiarity with Jewish history, culture, and language. Moreover, this process of assimilation, Kaye/Kantrowitz recognizes, has relied on racism, especially against African Americans.

Defining Gender Identities

Gender is one of the major ways that people "read" each other and organize their lives. As sociologist Judith Lorber (1991) noted, many people may not pay much attention to how they react to signs of gender unless these are missing or ambiguous. Gender regimes are fundamental to patriarchal societies, though they may define gender differently. A society may have more than two gender categories or include socially recognized fluid gender roles (see, e.g., Reichard 2015a; Schmidt 2016).

The United States has a clear gender binary. Language is gendered, especially pronouns, as well as clothing, children's games, and most public bathrooms, to cite a few obvious examples. Parenting is also gendered, although more men care for children these days, especially middle-class men whose economic position insulates them from being considered less manly if they undertake tasks associated with women. In families, schools, and community settings, children are taught gender conformity despite some tolerance for tomboyish girls and young boys playing with dolls and makeup. A daily barrage of media images illustrates appropriate gender behavior and looks. A gendered division of labor means that women do most care work, whether paid or unpaid (see Chapter 7). Feelings of unhappiness or distress about one's gender identity are defined as a mental illness—gender identity disorder—included in the *Diagnostic and Statistical Manual of Mental Disorders*. However, as more people identify as gender neutral or gender nonconforming, some states have changed their policies regarding ID cards and drivers' licenses. Several US states now issue non-binary documents, with an X option for those who do not identify as M or F (Wong 2018). In 2018, airline trade organizations approved changes for making plane reservations to include non-binary gender options. United Airlines became the first to adopt this new standard in March 2019 (Wilson 2019).

Philosopher and queer theorist Judith Butler (1990) considered the gender binary to be a "regulatory fiction" that consolidates and naturalizes the power of masculine and heterosexist oppression (p. 33). Her much-cited conception of gender as performative makes gender a verb: doing gender. It allows and requires us to think of gender more fluidly than two rigid categories permit. This opens up the possibility that people could have a wider repertoire of gender expressions and behaviors than most currently do. At the same time, Butler noted that people "who fail to do their gender right" by standards held to be appropriate in specific contexts, may be punished for it, through name calling, discrimination, hate, outright violence, even murder (p. 140). Moreover, although most feminists argue that gender is socially constructed, some have used categories like "woman-born woman" to limit trans women's access to women-only spaces, as Loan Tran mentions in Reading 5 (also see Serano 2007, 2013).

People who adopt nonconforming gender expressions challenge the gender binary on a daily basis. Leslie Feinberg (1998) listed "masculine females and feminine males, cross-dressers, transsexual men and women, intersexuals born on the anatomical sweep between female and male, gender-blenders, many other sex and gender-variant people, and our significant others" (p. 5) which zie called "transgender warriors" (1996). Trans people often see gender discrimination in new ways after transitioning. Trans men, for example, talk about suddenly being listened to and considered important, an experience they did not have as females; trans women may be shocked to experience everyday sexism. The fact that sex reassignment surgery is more available these days and that trans communities are more visible, especially in larger US cities, means that more people may define themselves as trans or consider having surgery or taking hormones (Stryker 2008). Further, there is much more conversation about the limitations of rigid gender categories and greater reluctance by young people, including children, to embrace strict gender definitions and behaviors (Risman 2018). In October 2018, a US Department of Health and Human Services' memo argued that government agencies should adopt a fixed binary definition of gender "determined by the genitals that a person is born with" in an effort to roll back recognition and protections for transgender people under federal civil rights law (Green, Benner, and Pear 2018; Reis 2018).

Currently, the vast majority of people in the United States do not identify as trans and may be referred to as cisgender (*cis* derives from Latin, meaning "on this side of"), where their gender identity is aligned with the sex they were assigned at birth. So a cis woman is someone who was defined as female at birth and continues to identify as female. However, this term may not incorporate the experiences of intersex people; it groups together lesbian, gay, bi, queer, and asexual people with those who identify as heterosexual; and it says nothing about people's relationships to power in society.

Maintaining Systems of Structural Inequality

Public discourse, media representations, laws, public policy, and bureaucratic practices are all part of maintaining macro-level systems of inequality and require ongoing **objectification** and dehumanization of subordinated peoples. Appropriating their identities is a particularly effective method of doing this for it defines who the subordinated person or group is or ought to be. This can happen in several ways:

Using the values, characteristics, and features of the dominant group as the supposedly neutral standard against which all others are judged and treated. Men of a particular racial/ethnic group are generally physically larger and stronger than women of that group. Many of the clinical trials for new pharmaceutical drugs have been conducted using men's bodies and activities as the standard. The results, however, have been applied to both men and women. Women are often prescribed the same dosage of a medication as men even though their physical makeup is not the same. Thus, women, as a distinct group, do not exist in this type of research.

Using terms that distinguish the subordinate from the dominant group. Terms such as "non-white" and "minority" connote a relationship to another group: white or majority, respectively. A non-white person is the negative of the white person; a minority person is less than a majority person. Neither have an identity in their own right.

Stereotyping. This involves making a generalization about a group and claiming or assuming that all members of the group conform to it. Stereotypes are behavioral and psychological attributes: they are commonly held beliefs about groups rather than individual beliefs about individuals, and they persist in spite of contradictory evidence. For example, lesbians hate men. Or, people with physical disabilities are asexual. Or, welfare mothers are lazy. As philosopher Judith Andre asserted, "A 'stereotype' is pejorative; there is always something objectionable in the beliefs and images to which the word refers" (1988, p. 260; see Reading 10).

Exoticizing and romanticizing. These two forms of appropriation are particularly insidious because, on the surface, they seem to be appreciative. For example, Asian American women may be described as "pearls of the Orient," Native American women as "earth mothers," and Black women as "towers of strength." In all three cases, seemingly positive traits and cultural practices are admired, yet, like negative stereotyping, this prevents others from seeing the truth and complexity of who these women are.

Romanticization of "others" may include **cultural appropriation**, where, for instance, white people wear "dreadlocks," have their hands decorated with henna, or claim to have been Native American in a former life. Many consumers do not think about the culture or history of the people who created the designs that are commodified and sold in the global marketplace. Thus, objects and styles are extracted from their original contexts and become "cool new stuff" for others to buy. Joanna Kadi (1996) argued that cultural appropriation reinforces imperialist attitudes and constitutes a form of cultural genocide. She urged people to think carefully about their right to wear "exotic" clothing or to play musical instruments from other cultures. Our intentions, our knowledge of those cultures, and authentic connections with people from those groups are all part of moving from cultural appropriation to what Kadi called "ethical cultural connections."

These processes of identity appropriation are used to create demeaning media images. How are various groups typically depicted—in ads, movies, TV shows, and online images? Countering negative images through independent media produced by people who present the truths about their own lives is a powerful way of resisting this dehumanization, as mentioned in Chapter 2.

In the face of structural inequalities, the issue of identity and representation can be a matter of life and death, literally and metaphorically, for members of subordinated groups. They are reduced to the position of the "other"—that is, fundamentally unlike "us"—made invisible, misunderstood, misrepresented, sometimes demonized, and often feared. Examples in contemporary US society include trans people, Black boys and men, as well as Arab Americans and Muslims (see Readings 32 and 43). Designating a group as "other" justifies its exploitation, its exclusion from whatever benefits the society may offer, and the violence and, in extreme cases, even genocide committed against it. At the macro and global levels, then, identity is a matter of collective well-being and survival. Those in dominant positions typically judge individual members of subordinate groups according to negative stereotypes. If a young African American woman is a poor single mother, she reinforces the stereotype held by the dominant group. When young African American women earn college degrees and are economically well off, those in dominant positions think of them as exceptional rather than revising their assumptions about race, gender, and class.

Given the significance of identity appropriation as an aspect of oppression, many groups have sought to change their identities and take control of positive identity formation and representation as part of their liberation struggles. One aspect of this is to get rid of pejorative labels in favor of names that express who people are in their own terms. As with individual identity, naming ourselves collectively is an important act of empowerment. One example is the way trans people have repudiated earlier medical terminology developed by doctors and psychologists that implied pathology and abnormality. Another approach is to reclaim a formerly negative term and redefine it as a positive, so that disability activists now use *crip* (from *cripple*). According to Sunaura Taylor (2017), "to crip something" is to "invest it with disability history, politics, and pride while . . . questioning paradigms of independence, normalcy, and medicalization" (p. 12). Similarly, LGBTQIA people reclaimed the derogatory term *queer*—the "Q" in LGBTQIA (lesbian, gay, bi, trans, queer, intersex, asexual). This acronym is changing, with several terms currently in use: LGBTQ2SIA includes two-spirited people, an English-language term for Native Americans who constitute a third gender; LGBT-STGNC includes lesbian, gay, bisexual, two-spirit, trans, and gender nonconforming people (Audre Lorde Project 2017). The evolution of names that African Americans have used to identify themselves, from Colored to Negro to Black to Afro-American, and African American, provides another example. Among the very diverse peoples connected historically, culturally, and linguistically to Spain, Portugal, and their former colonies (in the United States, Mexico, the Caribbean, and Central and South America), some use specific names like Puerto Rican, Nicaraguan, Chilean, or Cuban; others prefer broader terms such as Hispanic, Latino/a, or Latinx—a gender-neutral term. This relatively new term has both proponents and detractors (see, e.g., Hernandez 2017; A. P. Lopez 2018; Ramirez and Blay 2016; Reichard 2015b). In 2018, it was added to the *Merriam-Webster* dictionary, a sign that it is becoming more generally accepted.

Colonization, Immigration, and the US Landscape of Race and Class

Macro- and global-level factors affecting people's identities include colonization and immigration. Popular folklore has it that the United States has welcomed "the tired, huddled masses yearning to breathe free." This idea that the United States is "a land of immigrants" obscures important factors excluded from much mainstream debate about immigration. Native American peoples and Mexicans were already living on this continent. The former experienced near-genocide, and the latter became part of the United States after the Mexican-American War (1846–1848), in effect made foreigners in their own land. Not all Americans came to this country voluntarily, either. African peoples were captured, enslaved, imported here, and forced to labor and bear children. They were brutally exploited and violated—physically, emotionally, culturally, and spiritually—to serve the interests of those in power. These groups' experiences in the United States are fundamentally different from those who chose to immigrate here, even though the latter may have faced severe personal risks and hardships.

Robert Blauner (1972) made a useful distinction between "colonized minorities," all of them people of color whose original presence in this nation was involuntary, and "immigrant minorities," whose presence was voluntary. Colonized minorities have faced insurmountable structural inequalities, based primarily on race, that have prevented their full participation in social, economic, political, and cultural arenas of US life. Historically, the Naturalization Law of 1790 (only repealed in 1952) prohibited peoples of color from becoming US citizens, and Slave Codes restricted every aspect of life for enslaved African peoples. Such laws and policies made race into an indelible line that separated "insiders" from "outsiders." White people were designated insiders and granted many privileges, while all others were confined to systematic disadvantage

FIGURE 3.2   Latinas at a Rally for Immigration Rights

© *Rick Reinhard 1996*

A Timeline of Key US Immigration Laws and Policies

US immigration laws and policies seek to balance a concern for national security with the fact that immigrants contribute greatly to the country's economy. Tens of millions of newcomers have made their way to the United States throughout the nation's history, and the USA has resettled more refugees on a permanent basis than any other industrialized country. Immigration law changes in response to economic shifts, political concerns, and perceived threats to national security.

1790 The Naturalization Law of 1790, which was not repealed until 1952, limited naturalization to "free white persons" who had resided in the United States for at least two years. Slave Codes restricted every aspect of life for enslaved African peoples.

1875 The Immigration Act of 1875 denied admission to individuals considered "undesirable," including revolutionaries, prostitutes, and those carrying "loathsome or dangerous contagious diseases."

1882 The Chinese Exclusion Act, one of the most racist immigration laws in US history, was adopted; variations were enforced until 1943. The act was a response to fear of the large numbers of Chinese laborers brought to the United States to lay railroads and work in mines.

1917 Congress banned immigration from Asia except Japan and the Philippines.

1921 The Immigration Act of 1921 set an overall cap on the number of immigrants admitted each year and established a nationalities quota system that strongly favored northern Europeans at the expense of immigrants from southern and eastern Europe and Asia.

1924 The Immigration Act of 1924 based immigration quotas on the ethnic composition of the US population in 1920; it also prohibited Japanese immigration.

1945 President Truman issued a directive after World War II allowing for the admission of 40,000 refugees.

1946 The War Brides Act permitted 120,000 foreign wives and children to join their husbands in the United States.

1948 The Displaced Persons Act of 1948 permitted entry to an additional 400,000 refugees and displaced persons as a result of World War II.

1952 The Immigration and Nationality Act of 1952 was a response to fear of communism and barred the admission of anyone who might engage in acts "prejudicial to the public interest, or that endanger the welfare or safety of the United States." It allowed immigration for all nationalities, however, and established family connections as a criterion for immigrant eligibility.

1953 The Refugee Relief Act of 1953 admitted 200,000 people, including Hungarians fleeing communism and Chinese emigrating after the Chinese revolution.

1965 The Immigration Act of 1965 established an annual quota of 120,000 immigrants from the Eastern Hemisphere, which increased the number of Asian immigrants, especially middle-class and upper-middle-class people.

1980 The Refugee Act of 1980 codified into US law the 1951 United Nations Convention Relating to the Status of Refugees and its 1967 Protocol; it defines a refugee as a person outside her or his country of citizenship who has a well-founded fear of persecution on account of race, religion, nationality, political opinion, or membership in a particular ethnic or social group.

1986 The Immigration Reform and Control Act of 1986 was intended to control the growth of illegal immigrants through an "amnesty" program to legalize undocumented people resident in the United States before January 1, 1982, and the imposition of sanctions against employers who knowingly employ undocumented workers.

1990 The Immigration Act of 1990 affirmed family reunification as the basis for most immigration cases; redefined employment-based immigration; created a new system to diversify the nationalities immigrating to the United States, ostensibly to compensate for the domination of Asian and Latin American immigration since 1965; and created new mechanisms to provide refuge to those fleeing civil strife, environmental disasters, or political upheaval in their homelands.

1996 The Illegal Immigration Reform and Immigrant Responsibility Act provided for increased border controls and penalties for document fraud, changes in employer sanctions, restrictions on immigrant eligibility for public benefits, and drastic streamlining of the asylum system.

continued

A Timeline of Key US Immigration Laws and Policies   *continued*

The Personal Responsibility and Work Opportunity Reconciliation Act mainly dealt with changes in the welfare system and made legal immigrants ineligible for various kinds of federal assistance. In 1997, Congress restored benefits for some immigrants already in the country when this law took effect.

2001   The Uniting and Strengthening America by Providing Appropriate Tools Required to Obstruct Terrorism Act (USA Patriot Act) was signed into law following the attacks on the World Trade Center and the Pentagon on September 11th. It significantly enhances the government's powers of detention, search, and surveillance. (See "Milestones in U.S. History" in Chapter 1).

2001–2012 Various bills were introduced into Congress to benefit children of undocumented immigrants who came to this country with their parents, but none passed into law. In 2012, President Obama issued a policy directive, effective for two years, that allows some 800,000 children of undocumented immigrants to stay without fear of deportation.

Airport security has been tightened nationwide. The US-Mexico border has become increasingly militarized. Immigration and Customs Enforcement (ICE) has stepped up raids on homes, schools, and workplaces in many towns and cities (see Reading 44). At the same time, immigrant communities have asserted their presence by taking to the streets in huge demonstrations.

The "pull" factors drawing immigrants to the United States include the possibility of better-paying jobs, better education (especially for children), and greater personal freedom. "Push" factors include poverty, wars, political upheaval, authoritarian regimes, and fewer personal freedoms in the countries they have left. Immigration will continue to be a thorny issue in the United States as the goals of global economic restructuring, filling the country's need for workers, and providing opportunities for family members to live together are set against the fears of those who see continued immigration as a threat to the country's prosperity and security and to the dominance of European Americans.

Thanks to Wendy A. Young for providing material.

(See the box feature "A Timeline of Key US Immigration Laws and Policies") The stories that European Americans learn of how their grandparents and great-grandparents triumphed in the United States usually focus on individual effort, determination, and hard work. The role of labor unions, community organizations, political parties, and government policies that allowed settlers to take ownership of Native American land, as well as racism, are often left out of these accounts. When white people consider our relationships to the United States, we need to incorporate these macro-level factors into our awareness of who we are, how our ancestors came here, how we present ourselves, and how others view us.

Studies of US immigration show the unequal positioning of different ethnic groups, challenging the myth of equal opportunity for all. According to political scientist Lawrence Fuchs (1990), "Freedom and opportunity for poor immigrant whites in the seventeenth and eighteenth centuries were connected fundamentally with the spread of slavery" (p. 294). It was then that diverse groups of European immigrants, such as Irish, Polish, and Italian people, ranked lower according to a European hierarchy, began to learn to be white (Roediger 1991). Whiteness was constructed in relation to Blackness. Acclaimed writer James Baldwin (1984) commented: "no one was white before he/she came to America" and "it took generations, and a vast amount of coercion, before this became a white country" (p. 90). Thus, the common belief among descendants of European immigrants that the successful **assimilation** of their ancestors is evidence that anyone can "pull themselves up by the bootstraps" if they work hard enough does not take into account the racialization of immigration that favored white people. Also, in her discussion of Jewish assimilation in the United States in Reading 12, Melanie Kaye/Kantrowitz notes that despite its benefits, this process has been accompanied by great cultural loss—of language, history, literature, music, cultural diversity, and experience of rich Jewish traditions.

This emphasis on race tends to mask differences based on class, an important distinction among immigrant groups. For example, Chinese and Japanese people—mainly men—who were allowed to come to the United States in the nineteenth and early twentieth centuries to work on plantations in Hawai'i, as loggers in Oregon, or building roads and railroads in several western states were from rural areas of China and Japan. The immigration law of 1965 made way for a "second wave" of Asian immigration (Takaki 1987). It set preferences for professionals, highly skilled workers, and members of the middle and upper middle classes. Vietnamese immigrants who came to this country between the mid-1970s and 1980 were from the middle and upper classes and were tied to the political side supported by the US government. By contrast, the second wave of Vietnamese immigrants was composed of poor and rural people. The class backgrounds of immigrants affect their sense of themselves, their coping skills, and their expectations. People who have no literacy skills in their own language will have a harder time learning to become literate in English compared with those who had formal schooling in their home country that may have included basic English. Some immigrants retain strong ties to their country of origin and may travel back and forth regularly, maintaining family and community in more than one place (see Reading 15 and Chapter 8).

MULTIPLE IDENTITIES AND SOCIAL LOCATIONS

People's experiences of our complex identities may be both enriching and contradictory, and these experiences may push us to face questions about our loyalties to individuals and groups. As this chapter shows, a person's identity incorporates individual, community, societal, and global factors. Taken together, these elements constitute our **social location**. This concept places us in relationship to others, to the dominant culture of the United States, and to the rest of the world. It shapes the kinds of power and privilege we have access to and can exercise, as well as situations in which we are disadvantaged. As we consider our own identities, how do we accept and appreciate who we are, recognize who others are, and meet the challenges of a multicultural world?

Some people may feel that this emphasis on the complexities of identity is divisive. However, we believe that everyone needs an honest understanding of who they are in relation to others, how past inequalities operate and are reinforced today, and how we negotiate inequalities of power and privilege. We see this as vital for creating friendships, partnerships, and political alliances with others across lines of gender, race, class, and so on, a topic we return to in Chapter 12.

An ability to reflect on one's social location contributes to the generation of knowledge. This overlaps with three concepts we mentioned in Chapter 2: intersectionality, standpoint, and subjugated knowledge. Paula Gunn Allen in Reading 1 and Melanie Kaye/Kantrowitz in Reading 12 both assert the importance of knowing one's genealogy, which they define broadly to include family, culture, and history. One's standpoint, as described by Patricia Hill Collins concerns "historically shared, group-based experiences" (1997, p. 375), the meso- and macro-level parts of identity and category.

In the readings that follow, writers describe key aspects of who they are. Some mention difficulties in coming to terms with their identities and the complexities of contradictory positions. An emphasis on the micro level helps us to understand other people, to empathize with them, and to see their humanity—an important corrective to distorted media representations and our personal prejudices. Also crucial, these articles go beyond the micro level to include insights regarding the author's community and the macro-level factors that shape their experiences and group history. They also write about the empowerment gained from deepening understandings that enable them to claim their place in the world.

QUESTIONS FOR REFLECTION

As you read and discuss this chapter, think about these questions:

1. Who are you? How do you figure out your identity? Has your identity changed? If so, when and how?
2. Are there parts of your identity that you emphasize or downplay? Why? How does a particular context shape your identity?
3. Who are your people? What do home and community mean to you?
4. How many generations have your family members been in the United States? Under what conditions did they become a part of this country?
5. What do you know of your family's culture and history before it became a part of the United States?
6. How do you define your social location?
7. Which of the social dimensions of your identity provide power and privilege? Which provide disadvantage?
8. How do people with privilege contribute to eliminating the systems that benefit them? Why might they want to do this?

FINDING OUT MORE ON THE WEB

1. Find out about people who are very different from you (in terms of culture, class, race/ethnicity, gender expression, sexuality, nationality, or religion) and how they think about their identities.
2. Research identity-based organizations. Why did they form? Who are their members? What are their purposes and goals?
3. Research how social categories were constructed early in the history of the United States. Who constructed them and through what process(es)? How have the categories changed, if at all, and why?

TAKING ACTION

1. Take some action to affirm an aspect of your identity.
2. Talk to your parents or grandparents about your family history. How have they constructed their cultural and racial/ethnic identities?
3. Create a trusting space for a conversation among friends or classmates about gender categories and identities, and think about these historically and intersectionally.

11 A QUESTION OF CLASS (1993)

Dorothy Allison authored the critically acclaimed novel *Bastard Out of Carolina* (1992), a finalist for the 1992 National Book Award, which became an award-winning movie. Other titles include *Trash* (1988); *Skin: Talking About Sex, Class and Literature* (1994); *Two or Three Things I Know for Sure* (1995); and *Cavedweller* (1998). She has won many awards, including the 2007 Robert Penn Warren Award for Fiction. She describes herself as a feminist, a working-class story-teller, a Southern expatriate, a sometime poet, and a happily born-again Californian.

. . . My people were not remarkable. We were ordinary, but even so we were mythical. We were the *they* everyone talks about, the ungrateful poor. I grew up trying to run away from the fate that destroyed so many of the people I loved, and having learned the habit of hiding, I found that I also had learned to hide from myself. I did not know who I was, only that I did not want to be *they*, the ones who are destroyed or dismissed to make the real people, the important people, feel safer. By the time I understood that I was queer, that habit of hiding was deeply set in me, so deeply that it was not a choice but an instinct. Hide, hide to survive, I thought, knowing that if I told the truth about my life, my family, my sexual desire, my real history, then I would move over into that unknown territory, the land of *they*, would never have the chance to name my own life, to understand it or claim it.

Why are you so afraid? my lovers and friends have asked me the many times when I have suddenly seemed to become a stranger, someone who would not speak to them, would not do the things they believed I should do, simple things like applying for a job, or a grant, or some award they were sure I could acquire easily. Entitlement, I have told them, is a matter of feeling like *we*, not *they*. But it has been hard for me to explain, to make them understand. You think you have a right to things, a place in the world, I try to say. You have a sense of entitlement I don't have, a sense of your own importance. I have explained what I know over and

over again, in every possible way I can, but I have never been able to make clear the degree of my fear, the extent to which I feel myself denied, not only that I am queer in a world that hates queers but that I was born poor into a world that despises the poor. The need to explain is part of why I write fiction. I know that some things must be felt to be understood, that despair can never be adequately analyzed; it must be lived. . . .

I have known I was a lesbian since I was a teenager, and I have spent a good twenty years making peace with the effects of incest and physical abuse. But what may be the central fact of my life is that I was born in 1949 in Greenville, South Carolina, the bastard daughter of a poor white woman from a desperately poor family, a girl who had left the seventh grade the year before, who worked as a waitress and was just a month past fifteen when she had me. That fact, the inescapable impact of being born in a condition of poverty that this society finds shameful, contemptible, and somehow deserved, has dominated me to such an extent that I have spent my life trying to overcome or deny it. I have learned with great difficulty that the vast majority of people pretend that poverty is a voluntary condition, that the poor are different, less than fully human, or at least less sensitive to hopelessness, despair, and suffering.

The first time I read [Jewish writer] Melanie Kaye/Kantrowitz's poems, I experienced a frisson of recognition. It was not that my people had been "burned off the map" or murdered as hers had. No, we had been erased, encouraged to destroy ourselves, made invisible because we did not fit the myths of the middle class. Even now, past forty and stubbornly proud of my family, I feel the draw of that mythology, that romanticized, edited version of the poor. I find myself looking back and wondering what was real, what true. Within my family, so much was lied about, joked about, denied or told with deliberate indirection, an undercurrent of humiliation, or a brief pursed grimace that belies everything that has been said—everything, the very nature of truth and lies, reality and myth. What was real? The poverty depicted in books and movies was romantic, a kind of backdrop for the story of how it was escaped. The reality of self-hatred and violence was either absent or caricatured. The poverty I knew was dreary, deadening, shameful. My family was ashamed of being poor, of feeling hopeless. What was there to work for, to save money for, to fight for or struggle against? We had generations before us to teach us that nothing ever changed, and that those who did try to escape failed.

My mama had eleven brothers and sisters, of whom I can name only six. No one is left alive to tell me the names of the others. It was my grandmother who told me about my real daddy, a shiftless pretty man who was supposed to have married, had six children, and sold cut-rate life insurance to colored people out in the country. My mama married when I was a year old, but her husband died just after my little sister was born a year later. When I was five, Mama married the man she lived with until she died. Within the first year of their marriage Mama miscarried, and while we waited out in the hospital parking lot, my stepfather molested me for the first time, something he continued to do until I was past thirteen. When I was eight or so, Mama took us away to a motel after my stepfather beat me so badly it caused a family scandal, but we returned after two weeks. Mama told me that she really had no choice; she could not support us alone. When I was eleven I told one of my cousins that my stepfather was molesting me. Mama packed up my sisters and me and took us away for a few days, but again, my stepfather swore he would stop, and again we

went back after a few weeks. I stopped talking for a while, and I have only vague memories of the next two years.

My stepfather worked as a route salesman, my mama as a waitress, laundry worker, cook, or fruit packer. I could never understand how, since they both worked so hard and such long hours, we never had enough money, but it was a fact that was true also of my mama's brothers and sisters, who worked in the mills or the furnace industry. In fact, my parents did better than anyone else in the family, but eventually my stepfather was fired and we hit bottom—nightmarish months of marshals at the door, repossessed furniture, and rubber checks. My parents worked out a scheme so that it appeared my stepfather had abandoned us, but instead he went down to Florida, got a new job, and rented us a house. In the dead of night, he returned with a U-Haul trailer, packed us up, and moved us south.

The night we left South Carolina for Florida, my mama leaned over the back seat of her old Pontiac and promised us girls, "It'll be better there." I don't know if we believed her, but I remember crossing Georgia in the early morning, watching the red clay hills and swaying gray blankets of moss recede through the back window. I kept looking back at the trailer behind us, ridiculously small to contain everything we owned. Mama had, after all, packed nothing that wasn't fully paid off, which meant she had only two things of worth, her washing and sewing machines, both of them tied securely to the trailer walls. Through the whole trip, I fantasized an accident that would burst that trailer, scattering old clothes and cracked dishes on the tarmac.

I was only thirteen. I wanted us to start over completely, to begin again as new people with nothing of the past left over. I wanted to run away completely from who we had been seen to be, who we had been. That desire is one I have seen in other members of my family, to run away. It is the first thing I think of when trouble comes, the geographic solution. Change your name, leave town, disappear, and make yourself over. What hides behind that solution is the conviction that the life you have lived, the person you are, are valueless, better off abandoned, that running away is easier than trying to change anything, that change itself is not possible, that death is easier than this life. Sometimes I think it is that conviction—more seductive than alcoholism or violence and more subtle than sexual hatred or gender injustice—that has dominated my life, and made real change so painful and difficult.

Moving to central Florida did not fix our lives. It did not stop my stepfather's violence, heal my shame, or make my mother happy. Once there our lives became dominated by my mother's illness and medical bills. She had a hysterectomy when I was about eight and endured a series of hospitalizations for ulcers and a chronic back problem. Through most of my adolescence she superstitiously refused to allow anyone to mention the word cancer. (Years later when she called me to tell me that she was recovering from an emergency mastectomy, there was bitter fatalism in her voice. The second mastectomy followed five years after the first, and five years after that there was a brief bout with cancer of the lymph system which went into remission after prolonged chemotherapy. She died at the age of fifty-six with liver, lung, and brain cancer.) When she was not sick, Mama, and my stepfather, went on working, struggling to pay off what seemed an insurmountable load of debts.

By the time I was fourteen, my sisters and I had found ways to discourage most of our stepfather's sexual advances. We were not close but we united against our stepfather. Our efforts were helped along when he was referred to a psychotherapist after losing his temper at work, and was prescribed psychotropic drugs that made him sullen but less violent. We were growing up quickly, my sisters moving toward dropping out of school, while I got good grades and took every scholarship exam I could find. I was the first person in my family to graduate from high school, and the fact that I went on to college was nothing short of astonishing.

Everyone imagines her life is normal, and I did not know my life was not everyone's. It was not until I was an adolescent in central Florida that I began to realize just how different we were. The people we met there had not been shaped by the rigid class structure that dominated the South Carolina Piedmont. The first time I looked around my junior high classroom and realized that I did not know who those people were—not only as individuals but as categories, who their people were and how they saw themselves—I realized also that they did not know me. In Greenville, everyone knew my family, knew we were trash, and that meant we were supposed to be poor, supposed to have grim low-paid jobs, have babies in our teens, and never finish school. But central Florida in the 1960s was full of runaways and immigrants, and our mostly white working-class suburban school sorted us out, not by income and family background, but by intelligence and aptitude tests. Suddenly I was boosted into the college-bound track, and while there was plenty of contempt for my inept social skills, pitiful wardrobe, and slow drawling accent, there was also something I had never experienced before, a protective anonymity, and a kind of grudging respect and curiosity about who I might become. Because they did not see poverty and hopelessness as a foregone conclusion for my life, I could begin to imagine other futures for myself.

Moving into that new world and meeting those new people meant that I began to see my family from a new vantage point. I also experienced a new level of fear, a fear of losing what before had never been imaginable. My family's lives were not on television, not in books, not even comic books. There was a myth of the poor in this country, but it did not include us, no matter how hard I tried to squeeze us in. There was an idea of the good poor—hard-working, ragged but clean, and intrinsically noble. I understood that we were the bad poor, the ungrateful: men who drank and couldn't keep a job; women, invariably pregnant before marriage, who quickly became worn, fat, and old from working too many hours and bearing too many children; and children with runny noses, watery eyes, and bad attitudes. My cousins quit school, stole cars, used drugs, and took dead-end jobs pumping gas or waiting tables. We were not noble, not grateful, not even hopeful. We knew ourselves despised.

But in that new country, we were unknown. The myth settled over us and glamorized us. I saw it in the eyes of my teachers, the Lions' Club representative who paid for my new glasses, and the lady from the Junior League who told me about the scholarship I had won. Better, far better, to be one of the mythical poor than to be part of the *they* I had known before. *Don't let me lose this chance*, I prayed, and lived in fear that I might suddenly be seen again as what I knew I really was.

As an adolescent, I thought that the way my family escaped South Carolina was like a bad movie. We fled like runaway serfs and the sheriff who would have arrested my stepfather seemed like a border guard. Even now, I am certain that if we had remained in South Carolina, I would have been trapped by my family's heritage of poverty, jail, and illegitimate children—that even being smart, stubborn, and a lesbian would have made no difference. My grandmother died when I was twenty, and after Mama went home for the funeral, I had a series of dreams in which we still lived up in Greenville, just down the road from where Granny had died. In the dreams I had two children and only one eye, lived in a trailer, and worked at the textile mill. Most of my time was taken up with deciding when I would finally kill my children and myself. The dreams were so vivid, I became convinced they were about the life I was meant to have had, and I began to work even harder to put as much distance as I could between my family and me. I copied the dress, mannerisms, attitudes, and ambitions of the girls I met in college, changing or hiding my own tastes, interests, and desires. I kept my lesbianism a secret, forming a relationship with an effeminate male friend that served to shelter and disguise us both. I explained to friends that I went home so rarely because my stepfather and I fought too much for me to be comfortable in his house. But that was only part of the reason I avoided home, the easiest reason. The truth was that I feared the person I might become in my mama's house.

It is hard to explain how deliberately and thoroughly I ran away from my own life. I did not forget where I came from, but I gritted my teeth and hid it. When I could not get enough scholarship money to pay for graduate school, I spent a year of blind rage working as a salad girl, substitute teacher, and maid. I finally managed to get a job by agreeing to take any city assignment where the Social Security Administration needed a clerk. Once I had a job and my own place far away from anyone in my family, I became sexually and politically active, joining the Women's Center support staff and falling in love with a series of middle-class women who thought my accent and stories thoroughly charming. The stories I told about my family, about South Carolina, about being poor itself, were all lies, carefully edited to seem droll or funny. I knew damn well that no one would want to hear the truth about poverty, the hopelessness and fear, the feeling that nothing you do will make any difference, and the raging resentment that burns beneath the jokes. Even when my lovers and I formed an alternative lesbian family, sharing all our resources, I kept the truth about my background and who I knew myself to be a carefully obscured mystery. I worked as hard as I could to make myself a new person, an emotionally healthy radical lesbian activist, and I believed completely that by remaking myself I was helping to remake the world.

For a decade, I did not go home for more than a few days at a time.

It is sometimes hard to make clear how much I have loved my family, that every impulse to hold them in contempt has sparked in me a countersurge of stubborn pride . . . I have had to fight broad generalizations from every possible theoretical viewpoint. Traditional feminist theory has had a limited understanding of class differences or of how sexuality and self are shaped by both desire and denial. The ideology implies that we are all sisters who should turn our anger and suspicion only on the world outside the lesbian community. It is so simple to say the patriarchy did it, that poverty and social contempt are products of the world of the fathers. How often I felt a need to collapse my sexual history into what I was willing to share of my class background, to pretend that both my life as a lesbian and my life as a working-class escapee were constructed by the patriarchy. The difficulty is that I can't ascribe everything that has been problematic or difficult about my life simply and easily to the patriarchy, or even to the invisible and much-denied class structure of our society. . . .

One of the things I am trying to understand is how we internalize the myths of our society even as we hate and resist them. Perhaps this will be more understandable if I discuss specifically how some of these myths have shaped my life and how I have been able to talk about and change my own understanding of my family. I have felt a powerful temptation to write about my family as a kind of moral tale with us as the heroes and the middle and upper classes as the villains. It would be within the romantic myth, for example, to pretend that we were the kind of noble Southern whites portrayed in the movies, mill workers for generations until driven out of the mills by alcoholism and a family propensity to rebellion and union talk. But that would be a lie. The truth is that no one in my family ever joined a union. Taken as far as it can go, the myth of the poor would make my family over into union organizers or people broken by the failure of the unions. The reality of my family is far more complicated and lacks the cardboard nobility of the myth.

As far as my family was concerned, union organizers, like preachers, were of a different class, suspect and hated as much as they might be admired for what they were supposed to be trying to achieve. Serious belief in anything—any political ideology, any religious system, or any theory of life's meaning and purpose—was seen as unrealistic. It was an attitude that bothered me a lot when I started reading the socially conscious novels I found in the paperback racks when I was eleven or so. I particularly loved Sinclair Lewis's novels and wanted to imagine my own family as part of the working man's struggle. But it didn't seem to be that simple.

"We were not joiners," my Aunt Dot told me with a grin when I asked her about the union. My cousin Butch laughed at that, told me the union charged dues and said, "Hell, we can't even be persuaded to toss money in the collection plate. Ain't gonna give it to no fat union man." It shamed me that the only thing my family wholeheartedly believed in was luck, and the waywardness of fate. They held the dogged conviction that the admirable and wise thing to do was to try and keep a sense of humor, not to whine or cower, and to trust that luck might someday turn as good as it had been bad—and with just as much reason. Becoming a political activist with an almost religious fervor was the thing I did that most outraged my family and the Southern working-class community they were part of.

Similarly, it was not my sexuality, my lesbianism, that was seen by my family as most rebellious; for most of my life, no one but my mama took my sexual preference very seriously. It was the way I thought about work, ambition, and self-respect that seemed incomprehensible to my aunts and cousins. They were waitresses, laundry workers, and counter girls. I was the one who went to work as a maid, something I never told any of them. They would have been angry if they had known, though the fact that some work was contemptible was itself a difficult notion. They believed that work was just work, necessary, that you did what you had to do to survive. They did not believe so much in taking pride in doing your job as they did in stubbornly enduring hard work and hard times when you really didn't have much choice about what work you did. But at the same time they did believe that there were some forms of work, including maid's work, that were only for black people, not white, and while I did not share that belief, I knew how intrinsic it was to how my family saw the world. Sometimes I felt as if I straddled cultures and belonged on neither side. I would grind my teeth at what I knew was my family's unquestioning racism but still take pride in their pragmatic endurance, but more and more as I grew older what I truly felt was a deep estrangement from the way they saw the world, and gradually a sense of shame that would have been completely incomprehensible to them.

"Long as there's lunch counters, you can always find work," I was told by both my mother and my aunts, and they'd add, "I can always get me a little extra with a smile." It was obvious that there was supposed to be nothing shameful about it, that needy smile across a lunch counter, that rueful grin when you didn't have rent, or the half-provocative, half-begging way my mama could cajole the man at the store to give her a little credit. But I hated it, hated the need for it and the shame that would follow every time I did it myself. It was begging as far as I was concerned, a quasi-prostitution that I despised even while I continued to use it (after all, I needed the money). But my mother, aunts, and cousins had not been ashamed, and my shame and resentment pushed me even further away from them.

"Just use that smile," my girl cousins used to joke, and I hated what I knew they meant. After college, when I began to support myself and study feminist theory, I did not become more understanding of the women of my family but more contemptuous. I told myself that prostitution is a skilled profession and my cousins were never more than amateurs. There was a certain truth in this, though like all cruel judgments made from the outside, it ignored the conditions that made it true. The women in my family, my mother included, had sugar daddies, not Johns, men who slipped them money because they needed it so badly. From their point of view they were nice to those men because the men were nice to them, and it was never so direct or crass an arrangement that they would set a price on their favors. They would never have described what they did as prostitution, and nothing made them angrier than the suggestion that the men who helped them out did it just for their favors. They worked for a living, they swore, but this was different.

I always wondered if my mother had hated her sugar daddy, or if not *him* then her need for what he offered her, but it did not seem to me in memory that she had. Her sugar daddy had been an old man, half-crippled, hesitant and needy, and he treated my mama with enormous consideration and, yes, respect. The relationship between them was painful because it was based on the fact that she and my stepfather could not make enough money to support the family. Mama could not refuse her sugar daddy's money, but at the same time he made no assumptions about that money buying anything she was not already offering. The truth was, I think, that she genuinely liked him, and only partly because he treated her so well.

Even now, I am not sure whether or not there was a sexual exchange between them. Mama was a pretty woman and she was kind to him, a kindness he obviously did not get from anyone else in his life, and he took extreme care not to cause her any problems with my stepfather. As a teenager with an adolescent's contempt for moral failings and sexual complexity of any kind, I had been convinced that Mama's relationship with that old man was contemptible and also that I would never do such a thing. The first time a lover of mine gave me money, and I took it, everything in my head shifted. The amount she gave me was not much to her, but it was a lot to me and I needed it. I could not refuse it, but I hated myself for taking it and I hated her for giving it to me. Worse, she had much less grace about my need than my mama's sugar daddy had displayed toward her. All that bitter contempt I had felt for my needy cousins and aunts raged through me and burned out the love I had felt. I ended the relationship quickly, unable to forgive myself for *selling* what I believed should only be offered freely—not sex but love itself.

When the women in my family talked about how hard they worked, the men would spit to the side and shake their heads. Men took real jobs—hard, dangerous, physically daunting work. They went to jail, not just the hard-eyed, careless boys who scared me with their brutal hands and cold eyes, but their gentler, softer brothers. It was another family thing, what people expected of my mama's family, my people. "His daddy's that one was sent off to jail in Georgia, and his uncle's another. Like as not, he's just the same," you'd hear people say of boys so young they still had their milk teeth. We were always driving down to the county farm to see somebody, some uncle, cousin, or nameless male relation. Shaven-headed, sullen, and stunned, they wept on Mama's shoulder or begged my aunts to help. "I didn't do nothing, Mama," they'd say and it might have been true, but if even we didn't believe them, who would? No one told the truth, not even about how their lives were destroyed. . . .

By 1975, I was earning a meager living as a photographer's assistant in Tallahassee, Florida, but the real work of my life was my lesbian feminist activism, the work I did with the local Women's Center and the committee to found a Feminist Studies Department at Florida State University. Part of my role as I saw it was to be a kind of evangelical lesbian feminist, and to help develop a political analysis of this woman-hating society. I did not talk about class, more than by giving lip service to how we all needed to think about it, the same way I thought we all needed to think about racism. I was a serious and determined person, living in a lesbian collective, studying each new book that purported to address feminist issues and completely driven by what I saw as a need to revolutionize the world. . . .

The idea of writing fiction or essays seemed frivolous when there was so much work to be done, but everything changed when I found myself confronting emotions and ideas that could not be explained away or postponed for a feminist holiday. The way it happened was simple and completely unexpected. One week I was asked to speak to two completely divergent groups: an Episcopalian Sunday School class and a juvenile detention center. The Episcopalians were all white, well-dressed, highly articulate, nominally polite, and obsessed with getting me to tell them (without their having to ask directly) just what it was that two women did together in bed. The delinquents were all women, eighty percent black and Hispanic, dressed in green uniform dresses or blue jeans and work shirts, profane, rude, fearless, witty, and just as determined to get me to talk about what it was that two women did together in bed.

I tried to have fun with the Episcopalians, teasing them about their fears and insecurities, and being as bluntly honest as I could about my sexual practices. The Sunday School teacher, a man who had assured me of his liberal inclinations, kept blushing and stammering as the questions about my growing up and coming out became more detailed. When the meeting was over, I stepped out into the sunshine angry at the contemptuous attitude implied by all their questions, and though I did not know why, also so deeply depressed that I couldn't even cry. The delinquents were different. Shameless, they had me blushing within the first few minutes, yelling out questions that were partly curious and partly a way of boasting about what they already knew.

"You butch or femme?" "You ever fuck boys?" "You ever want to?" "You want to have children?" "What's your girlfriend like?" I finally broke up when one very tall confident girl leaned way over and called out, "Hey girlfriend! I'm getting out of here next weekend. What you doing that night?" I laughed so hard I almost choked. I laughed until we were all howling and giggling together. Even getting frisked as I left didn't ruin my mood. I was still grinning when I climbed into the waterbed with my lover that night, grinning right up to the moment when she wrapped her arms around me and I burst into tears.

It is hard to describe the way I felt that night, the shock of recognition and the painful way my thoughts turned. That night I understood suddenly everything that happened to my cousins and me, understood it from a wholly new and agonizing perspective, one that made clear how brutal I had been to both my family and myself. I understood all over again how we had been robbed and dismissed, and why I had worked so hard not to think about it. I had learned as a child that what could not be changed had to go unspoken, and worse, that those who cannot change their own lives have every reason to be ashamed of that fact and to hide it. I had accepted that shame and believed in it, but why? What had I or my cousins really done to deserve the contempt directed at us? Why had I always believed us contemptible by nature? I wanted to talk to someone about all the things I was thinking that night, but I could not. Among the women I knew there was no one who would have understood what I was thinking, no other working-class women in the women's collective where I was living. I began to suspect that we shared no common language to speak those bitter truths.

In the days after that I found myself . . . thrown back into my childhood, into all the fears and convictions I had tried to escape. Once again I felt myself at the mercy of the important people who knew how to dress and talk, and would always be given the benefit of the doubt while I and my family would not.

I felt as if I was at the mercy of an outrage so old I could not have traced all the ways it shaped my life. I understood again that some are given no quarter, no chance, that all their courage, humor, and love for each other is just a joke to the ones who make the rules, and I hated the rule makers. Finally I also realized that part of my grief came from the fact that I no longer knew who I was or where I belonged. I had run away from my family, refused to go home to visit, and tried in every way to make myself a new person. How could I be working-class with a college degree? As a lesbian activist? I thought about the guards at the detention center, and the way they had looked at me. They had not stared at me with the same picture-window empti-ness they turned on the girls who came to hear me, girls who were closer to the life I had been meant to live than I could bear to examine. The contempt in their eyes was contempt for me as a lesbian, differ-ent and the same, but still contempt. . . .

In the late 1970s, the compartmentalized life I had created burst open. It began when I started to write and work out what I really thought about my family. . . . I went home again. I went home to my mother and my sisters, to visit, talk, argue, and begin to understand.

Once home I saw that, as far as my family was concerned, lesbians were lesbians whether they wore suitcoats or leather jackets. Moreover, in all that time when I had not made peace with myself, my family had managed to make a kind of peace with me. My girlfriends were treated like slightly odd versions of my sisters' husbands, while I was simply the daugh-ter who had always been difficult but was still a part of their lives. The result was that I started trying to confront what had made me unable to really talk to my sisters for so many years. I discovered that they no longer knew who I was either, and it took time and lots of listening to each other to rediscover my sense of family, and my love for them.

It is only as the child of my class and my unique family background that I have been able to put together what is for me a meaningful politics, gained a sense of why I believe in activism, why self-revelation is so important for lesbians, reex-amining the way we are seen and the way we see ourselves. There is no all-purpose feminist analy-sis that explains away all the complicated ways our sexuality and core identity are shaped, the way we see ourselves as parts of both our birth families and the extended family of friends and lovers we invari-ably create within the lesbian community. For me the bottom line has simply become the need to resist that omnipresent fear, that urge to hide and

disappear, to disguise my life, my desires, and the truth about how little any of us understand—even as we try to make the world a more just and human place for us all. Most of all I have tried to under-stand the politics of *they*, why human beings fear and stigmatize the different while secretly dreading that they might be one of the different themselves. Class, race, sexuality, gender, all the categories by which we categorize and dismiss each other need to be examined from the inside.

The horror of class stratification, racism, and prejudice is that some people begin to believe that the security of their families and community de-pends on the oppression of others, that for some to have good lives others must have lives that are mean and horrible. It is a belief that dominates this culture; it is what made the poor whites of the South so determinedly racist and the middle class so contemptuous of the poor. It is a myth that allows some to imagine that they build their lives on the ruin of others, a secret core of shame for the middle class, a goad and a spur to the marginal working class, and cause enough for the homeless and poor to feel no constraints on hatred or vio-lence. The power of the myth is made even more apparent when we examine how within the lesbian and feminist communities, where so much atten-tion has been paid to the politics of marginaliza-tion, there is still so much exclusion and fear, so many of us who do not feel safe even within our chosen communities.

I grew up poor, hated, the victim of physical, emotional, and sexual violence, and I know that suffering does not ennoble. It destroys. To resist destruction, self-hatred, or lifelong hopelessness, we have to throw off the conditioning of being de-spised, the fear of becoming that *they* that is talked about so dismissively, to refuse lying myths and easy moralities, to see ourselves as human, flawed and extraordinary. All of us—extraordinary.

12 JEWS, CLASS, COLOR, AND THE COST OF WHITENESS (1992)

Melanie Kaye/Kantrowitz (1945-2018) has taught literature, Women's Studies, and Jewish Studies. She was also a long-time activist for social justice, was founding director of Jews for Economic and Racial Justice, and former Director of Queens College/CUNY Worker Education Extension Center. Her published work includes *The Issue Is Power: Essays on Women, Jews, Violence, and Resistance* (1992) and *The Colors of Jews: Racial Politics and Radical Diasporism* (2007). After her father's death, she reclaimed her Jewish name, Kantrowitz, which "pressured by the exigencies of being a Jew in the forties" he had changed to Kaye.

. . . Last night on Broadway I saw the man who had asked me and Helena for money, and I ran across the street against the light and dangerously close to traffic to get away. He scares me. A couple of weeks ago we were walking home, we were almost on my block, 106th between Amsterdam and Columbus, where no one ever asks for money because no one assumes anyone east of Amsterdam has any money. We told him, sorry, not today. I had just given money to two different people, and Helena had three dollars to her name.

By the time we reached the end of the block he'd circled back, stood in front of us, asking again. *You know, I don't want to rob or anything but I just might have to,* he says.

I'm not about to respond, but he keeps talking. *I don't want to be like this, asking for money on the street, but you know I need money, and I don't want to rob or anything. . . .* Finally Helena gives him a dollar.

It seems that he came back to us, rather than the dozen other people on the street, because he (a black man) assumes we have money (we're white) and will be afraid (we're women). The truth is, we are neither moneyed nor afraid, and we give (Helena) or not (me) for our own reasons. The truth also is, he's desperate and we're not.

The next night I'm walking home by myself, late, and there he is, practically in front of my building. He approaches, extends his hand. *I'm sorry about last night,* he says. We shake hands, smile. Then he says, *but I need some money again, could you give me some?*

Late and dark. I don't want to stand there going through my pockets and especially taking out my wallet. Most of all I'm disturbed that he knows me. . . . I don't want to be responsible for him. I don't want him to expect anything from me. . . .

. . . I say, *I can't give you money today*—and now I am stuck with my lie. I could give something. But I want to keep moving, get home.

He demands, *I need money.*

I can't . . .

I need . . .

I can't . . .

I need . . .

until finally I say, *hey man, I dig it but do you hear me?*

He nods. We both know I'm lying, that I'm the one who gets to say yes or no. We say goodnight, smile.

Let me walk you around my [New York City] neighborhood. On 106th Street at Broadway, people of all colors and ages shopping, walking, sitting at street cafes, waiting for buses, heading for the subway, wheeling children in strollers. But notice the people, and there are many, stretched out asleep on the benches and even on the sidewalks—winter is harsh here and still they're in the street, sometimes without shoes—the people shaking cups, asking,

Source: Excerpted from The Issue is Power © 1992 by Melanie Kaye/Kantrowitz. Reprinted by permission of Aunt Lute Books. www.auntlute.com.

can you spare some change, saying, *I'm very hungry, can you give me something, even a quarter.* They're almost all African American men, a few women, also African American. Look at the taxi drivers. Step into one of the hundreds of small shops, restaurants, groceries, stationery shops that line Broadway. I see owners and often their families, and hired clerks: Asian, Indian, Arab, Latino, Greek, Jewish, sometimes Caribbean Black. Rarely are they African American. Practically all of them speak English wrapped in the vowels and consonants of their mother tongue, which is not English; except their kids, teenagers who help out after school and Saturdays, as I used to help out in my parents' store, are fluently bilingual, perfect English, as well as rapid-fire Chinese, Korean, Spanish . . . They will go to college, their kids will probably lose their language, their culture. This is the American dream.

South of 96th Street the balance of color shifts from brown to white, Latino to yuppie. Gentrified, white graduates of elite colleges live in buildings with swimming pools and elaborate doormen, views of the George Washington bridge—men and women in their twenties whose parents, or trust funds, bought them apartments costing maybe a million dollars.

There are lots of old Jews, surviving still in their rent-controlled apartments that will probably turn co-op when they die. Lots of harried thirty-somethings and forty-something Jewish women and men, their Jewishness visible only to those familiar with the intricacies and codes of New York Jews. They had their kids late, they split economically between upper middle and middle, and politically between liberals and radicals. Some are insistent about sending their kids to public schools, and some have given up on the public schools, refusing, in their words, to sacrifice their kids to a principle. They are professionals who live on schedules so tight that any unforeseen disruption is a minor disaster. To cope with the stress of life by the clock, and because they were raised to, or have taught themselves to, expect some joy and fulfillment in life, they see therapists, acupuncturists, chiropractors, and belong to health clubs where they work out and stay in shape. On the

Upper West Side (and all over New York City) class shows in well-developed calves and trim forms. Fat is sloppy. Fat is poor. I am sure that the average weight in my immediate neighborhood among the women is 15 pounds higher than 15 blocks south.

One more thing: in my immediate neighborhood, when you see women with children, they tend to be the same color, brown to black. A few blocks west or south, when I see a woman and child of the same color, I'm almost surprised; the norm is women of color caring for white children, what I've come to think of as the underbelly of feminism. Most of the women are immigrants. Some of the children are Jews.

Let me adjust the lens, for accuracy. Not all Jews are professionals (45 percent are working class or poor); not all African Americans are homeless or poor, generation after generation (though a full third live below the poverty line). Not all whites are yuppies, New York is not the nation, and the Upper West Side is not even all of New York.

For example, I recently visited Seattle; at the Asian community health clinic, the brochures come in ten different languages for clients from Hong Kong and the hills of Laos (imagine in the early part of this century, a "European" clinic had to serve Irish, Poles, Italians, Slavs, Greeks, Jews, and Swedes, from farms and *shtetlekh,* from Sicily, Dublin, Paris and Prague). In Seattle the homeless are white men, and antiracist coalitions include Jews as a matter of course, because skinheads and other white supremacist groups . . . target Jews and people of color. Or in New Mexico, where I used to live and where I still return as often as I can, the poor are Native American and after them, Chicano/a; Anglos buy up the beautiful old adobes; the issues are development and ecology, water table first and foremost. In Maine and Vermont, where I also have lived, and which share with New Mexico and Mississippi the honor of being the poorest states in the union, the poor are mostly white, nationally invisible because small-town and rural and the only news that counts happens in the big cities, where media thrive. For rural and small-town residents, the issues are not street violence; there are few streets and hardly anyone is anonymous, though women and children endure and resist violence in their homes. Rural issues are development and agriculture; the question is whether all food production will rest in the hands of a few multinational corporations.

But whatever is coming apart in the nation is doing so to some extent in New York first. When the public schools are essentially abandoned; when thousands upon thousands of people have no place to live, and everyone who does carries key rings heavy with metal, for the two to five locks required to simply get in one's apartment; when the threat of rape and other street violence against women controls our every decision about where to go, how long to stay, how much it will cost, and how much anxiety we can tolerate; when hate crimes of all kinds are on the rise, this is the future of our nation if something doesn't change. A recent survey found that even in rural areas, nearly half the people encounter on a daily basis people with no place to live. This is the human cost of our nation's priorities.

In the early and mid-eighties, I was working out some thoughts on racism and anti-Semitism, heavily influenced by these places I'd lived, and by my friends, many of whom were women of color, from both poor/working- and middle-class families, and white poor and working-class women. The way the debate was being framed as Black-Jewish or even Black-white obscured, I felt, the issue of class and the complexity of race. I wrote about the ways racism played out very differently against the various peoples of color—Chinese, Japanese, Arab, Native American. . . . I wrote about why I saw anti-Semitism as a form of racism, meaning racist ideology. This last seemed like a truism to me; the camps of Europe were revealed three months before I was born. And in New Mexico, Maine, Vermont, I was certainly an alien. And I said then, the difficulty some people have in grasping anti-Semitism as a serious concern and as a form of racism is that it hasn't kept Jews poor. (In fact, anti-Semitism often claims that all Jews are rich.) I also saw what was getting called Black-Jewish conflict as a mutual scapegoating—Jews were getting blamed for white

racism and Blacks for christian anti-Semitism—as well as obscured class conflict.[1]

But I have come to believe that this analysis needs to be pushed further. I am troubled, for example, by analogies between Asians and Jews, between Arabs and Jews, not because these analogies are not valid—with the difference that Asians almost always look Asian, while Jews and Arabs may often pass. What troubles me is this: while class and general principles of race-hate are illuminated by these analogies, something else gets obscured: the intransigence and virulence of oppression of African Americans . . . and something else.

The structure of apartheid is useful to contemplate here, not because things in the US are so fixed and clear; they're not. But let me pursue the analogy. South Africa has not two racial categories, but three: white, black and colored. It's the particular buffer zone of colored that I want to examine. Colored are those who will never be white but at least aren't black. Colored are those who have more access to higher status and all that implies—better housing, jobs, education, health, leisure, safety, respect. I want to suggest that in many places in the US, Japanese, Korean, and some Chinese, Indians and Pakistanis, Arabs and lighter-skinned or wealthier Latinos get to be colored. Sometimes Caribbean Blacks, by virtue of their accent, their education, the strength of growing up as the majority, also get to be colored. And African Americans, I want to suggest, are not the only "blacks," though they are the most visible. Many Latinos are black—dark in color—and also those most Indian of Chicanos, tracked in the lowest social and economic status. Immigrants from Southeast Asia hold some of the hardest, worst-paying jobs in the nation. And in the Southwest and sometimes Northwest, where there are few African Americans, Native Americans are kept the lowest of the low, and every cruel stereotype of inferiority shows up in local racist culture.

As I've said, these categories are not totally fixed. There is a certain permeability that characterizes the class-race system in the US, a certain amount of passing—literally, for those with skin light enough, who shed their accents, language, culture; and approximately, for those who, laboring under the heavy burden of racism, through luck and extraordinary heroism and sometimes through hardness against their own people, still squeak through. Clarence Thomas rises up from poverty to hobnob with the white male club called the Senate precisely by abandoning his people's concerns.

The point of this white/colored/black classification is not to violate the hope of solidarity among people of color by dividing them, but to recognize divisions that exist and must be named in order to bridge them. The Iraqi-Black conflicts in Detroit; Korean-Black in Flatbush and LA; Cuban-Black in Miami. Conflicts which a generation ago often were Jewish-Black because they are in part the inevitable result of who owns what in whose community, and who is poor, and who is accessible.

You could say, as my sister did when I was sharing these thoughts with her, aren't you talking about class? Yes and no. I'm talking about *caste as access to class*, as representing the probability either of moving up or standing still. . . .

Let me meander for a moment in the swamp of class. Top down, billionaires, millionaires: control and power; wealth so beyond the needs of one person, one family, it staggers the mind; here we find unlimited access to health care, comfort, resources; mostly WASP. Seventy percent of Congress comes from this class. While most white people aren't in it, most people in it are white, some Jews.

Middle class includes low-level managers, social workers, small shop-keepers, and teachers—K-12, secondary school, junior college, university—as well as business people, doctors, lawyers, and other professionals with incomes of $200,000 a year and more . . . When a class category includes both those piling up assets and those applying for food stamps, we should recognize an obsolete term and come up with something else. Here is where we find over half the Jews in the US, spread throughout the category, and a fair number of people of color, mostly represented at the lower end of the class.

Working class is also problematic as an economic category. The non-unionized women in the chicken factories, Black in the South, white in Maine; Asians and Latinas in the endlessly transforming, infinitely stable New York City sweatshops once worked by Italian and Jewish women: these are working-class, and, as we see, part of the problem with the category is gender. Working class also includes the racially diverse members of the UAW, the men whose sons used to be guaranteed the best paid laboring jobs in the US—but today Michigan, heart of the auto industry, endures 35 percent unemployment. Working class excludes the endemic poor, the poor without a prayer of breaking out of it, not those who perform backbreaking work of past generations of immigrants but those who can find no work at all, or can only find work that pays so badly that, for example, women with children can't afford to give up welfare to earn money that will all get swallowed by child care costs. They are African American, Latino, Native American, Asian. As for the rural white poor, because there are no jobs, their children leave for the cities, become essentially immigrants, and in the cities their white skin serves them in finding work—but, like other immigrants, they lose their culture. Working class spans well-paid unionized fields, many of which are now threatened because of automation, and because successful unionization has challenged owners' greed and sent manufacturing jobs abroad to pay workers less and maximize profits. . . . The two fields of labor still growing in the US, the hardest to organize and the worst paid, are office work and the service industry, including maids and restaurant workers.

Who does this office and service work? Women. People of color, especially immigrants, a replenishing, flexible pool of cheap labor, thankful to work hideously long hours for little money, because it is more than they had, and because they came here, often, not for their own betterment but for their children's. And so they groom their kids to escape the parents' lives, to assimilate, much as I, raised passionately pro-union, was groomed to escape the working class, and even the lower-middle-class shopkeeping existence at which my parents had succeeded.

It is precisely this access to better-paid working-class jobs or lower-middle-class small business opportunities, along with access to education for the next generation, that characterizes the experience of "colored" in the US. It is precisely this lack of better working-class jobs and small business opportunities, along with sytematic disadvantaging and exclusion by the educational system, that characterizes the experience of "blacks" in the US. Sherry Gorelick's *City College and the Jewish Poor*[2] describes how City College was created as a path to upward mobility to distract the radical Jewish poor from the revolutionary class struggle predicted by Marx; the path of higher education was taken by thousands and thousands of poor and working-class Jews. But college was free for us, and there was room, if not at the top, then certainly in the middle. Where are the free colleges now? . . . And where is room in the middle, when even the middle is suffering?

This shared economic disaster could and should unite most people across lines of color. But the illusory protection of "whiteness" offers a partial escape route toward which anyone who can scrambles. This desire to identify with whiteness, as well as bigotry and fear, blocks solidarity.

In this white-colored-black scheme, where are the Jews?

Of the groups I've named as targeted by a general hate I'll call race-hate, Jews are the closest to white. Many would say we are white, and indeed a common-sense visual response suggests that many of us are.

But listen to the prophet James Baldwin: "No one was white before he/she came to America," Baldwin wrote in the mid-eighties. "It took generations, and a vast amount of coercion, before this became a white country . . .

It is probable that it is the Jewish community—or more accurately, perhaps, its remnants—that in America has paid the highest and most extraordinary price for becoming white. For the Jews came here from countries where they were not white, and they came here in part because they were not white; and incontestably—in the eyes of the Black American (and not only in those eyes) American Jews have opted to become white. . . . [3]

Now, the point is not for us, Jews, to escape the category "white," to evade confronting our own racism, nor is it to insert ourselves artificially into a category of oppression, as sometimes happens in our movements where oppression in some puny

paradoxical way confers privilege. It is to recognize a continuum where we are the closest of the coloreds to white, or the closest of the whites to colored.

This is hardest to see in New York City, where Jews can hardly be called a minority. If there is the diaspora and Eretz Yisroel, I have come to think of New York as a third category, somewhere between the two. . . . Jews in New York City, except for select neighborhoods, experience the luxury of normality. To assume christianity in New York is to be hopelessly provincial. In New York one finds Jewish culture on a broad spectrum: orthodox, secular, lesbian and gay, Sephardic, Yiddishist, feminist. . . . The paradoxical result is a majority of Jews who operate without consciousness of their Jewishness. It's not an issue. Anti-Semitism is occasional, focused, and historical, and in recent years, for New Yorkers, has been associated mostly with African Americans. Quite the opposite from what's going on in the farm belt, the Northwest, and the South, where alliances between Jews and people of color are obvious to everyone.

Yet I'm suggesting that progressive Jews recognize our position in between colored and white, a source of tension but also of possibility. . . . The challenge is to build progressive coalitions not only among the coloreds but between the coloreds and the blacks, and between these and the economically struggling whites—and then to expand still further. The issue of hate crimes, for example, can unite Jews with people of color, and with lesbians and gays; and we should insist on the legal—and moral—classification of violence against women as a hate crime. That will be a powerful coalition indeed.

What I want to focus on is this: in James Baldwin's phrase, "the extraordinary price of becoming white."

Many of us chose, or had chosen for us, a white path. A path of assimilation, of passing, often accompanied by extreme cultural loss. How many of us speak or read Yiddish or Ladino or Judeo-Arabic? What do we know of our own histories, our literature, our music, our cultural diversity, our rich traditions? What do we know beyond or besides the now-usual sources of American Jewish identity, which are, in a nutshell, religion, Israel, and the Holocaust. Nothing wrong with these sources—but as the sum total of Jewish identity, this is limited. Where does this restricted focus leave secularists or confirmed diasporists? What happens when we disagree, as we do, about solutions to the Israeli-Palestinian conflict? How does this restricted focus help us create and strengthen an authentic Jewish American identity? How does it enable us to see the Holocaust in a context of Jewish history, the tragedy of which was not only the destruction of millions of lives—as though that were not tragedy enough—but also the destruction of a rich and varied culture.

It's called assimilation. We, like others who pass or partly pass, can choose where to direct our allegiance: upward and whitening, restricting our Jewishness to that which assimilation increasingly demands, *a Jew at home, a "man" in the streets,*[4] white people who go to Jewish church, i.e., synagogue; or we can deepen both our identity and our affiliation, with the other "others," the outsiders: the coloreds and the blacks.

Think about shedding whiteness. I don't mean to pretend that Jews who are white endure the same visual vulnerability as people of color; though we should recognize that many Jews, especially outside the US, simply *are* people of color, that the definition of Jews as automatically "European" is incorrect. In addition, many Sephardi and also many Ashkenazi Jews are sufficiently dark to be readily perceived, at least in the South and in the heartland, as people of color. Think also about the Hasids; think about wearing a Jewish star, or other item that identifies you as a Jew; think about never taking it off. Think about driving through Mississippi.

So: is fighting anti-Semitism a diversion from fighting racism? Do we think we can fight anti-Semitism without fighting racism? Do we think Jews can be safe within a white supremacist society?

I do not. I believe, along with a great many other Jews, that a color/class barrier means injustice, and our culture teaches us to pursue justice. I also believe that a color/class barrier threatens Jews, in two ways:

1) Because race-hate will never exclude us. As long as the world is divided into us and them, minorities are vulnerable. Fascism is on the rise. . . . [C]an we be naive about the danger?

2) Because the particular nature of anti-Semitism, which defines Jews as money, as powermongers—especially marks us as scapegoats for the abuses of capitalism, and we are living through a time of rampant abuse. . . .

The rich get richer. And who does the dominant culture blame? Jews; Asians, especially Japanese; Arabs; foreigners; let's face it, "the colored" get blamed for various contributions to economic disaster; for controlling the economy, or making money on the backs of the poor; for raising the price of oil; for stealing or eliminating jobs (by importing goods or exporting production). African Americans, Latinos, Native Americans, "the blacks," get blamed for urban violence and chaos, for drugs, for the skyrocketing costs and failures of social programs. That is, coloreds get blamed for capitalism's crimes; blacks for capitalism's fallout. Do I need to point out who escapes all blame?

When we are scapegoated we are most conscious of how we feel humiliated, alienated, and endangered. But the other function of scapegoating is at least as pernicious. Scapegoating protects the source of the problem we are being scapegoated for, the vicious system of profit and exploitation, of plenty and scarcity existing side by side. . . .

I want to make one last point about Jews and class, and this is about privilege and power. Hatred, chauvinism, oppression always function to keep people from their power, to mute their strength. Because they're laboring under heavier odds. Because they're taught to feel bad about themselves.

Anti-Semitism has a peculiar edge because the myth is that we're too powerful, too rich, and much too pushy. . . . Any particle of this that we absorb makes us afraid of our strength, loath to use our power, embarrassed by the relative economic and social success of Jews as a people, afraid it will be used against us (and it will).

Jewish progressives often buy into this scheme of contempt for "most Jews," assumed to be uniformly well off, or they experience a nostalgic longing for the time when Jews were authentically the right class, that is, poor and working class.

I think we need to look critically at this attitude. First, because it erases working-class Jews and poor Jews. Second, because it writes off the political energy and concerns that exist sometimes apart from class, the ripe possibilities for coalition of feminist Jews, of lesbian and gay Jews, of Jewish educators and cultural workers, of Jewish seniors, and on and on, not to mention Jews who see anti-Semitism for what it is, a form of race-hate which must be fought along with other forms of race-hate, and those who are simply hungry for economic and social justice. Who do not wish to spend our lives deciding whether or not to give quarters or dollars to other human beings who need more than we can possibly give; who do not wish to abandon the cities with their fabulous human variety because of the stresses of economic inequality, alienation, and violence; who still believe a better way is possible.

Third, because this attitude of contempt for Jews who are not poor, which is, after all, a form of internalized anti-Semitism, ignores the fact that education, choice, comfort are all valuable. One cannot walk the streets of any of our cities, see people living in cardboard boxes or wrapped in torn blankets, and not appreciate the material basis for human existence. The problem is not relative Jewish success. The problem is a severe class system that distributes success so unequally.

Used well, education, choice, even comfort, can strengthen people, individually and collectively. As for money—let me say the dirty word—nothing gets done without it. The question is, what do we do with our education, our choice, privilege, skills, experience, passion for justice: our power. Don't racism and anti-Semitism make you sick? Doesn't hatred scare you? Don't you feel at least a little desperate about the way things are going unless something intervenes?

I think Jews need to gather our power, make it visible, and use it right. I'm sick of the more conservative wing of the Jewish community speaking for all of us. Everyone knows that Jews are all over progressive movements, what I've come to think of as the political diaspora. Maybe our task is to ingather the Jews, just a little, into a new civil and human rights coalition, in which we are present and visible as Jews. It means being proud of our collective strength, confident that we can use it right. Someone will always call us pushy. Isn't it time to really push?

NOTES

An earlier version of this essay was given as a talk at the New Jewish Agenda National Conference, Carrying It On: Organizing Against Anti-Semitism and Racism, in Philadelphia, 1991.

1. See Melanie Kaye/Kantrowitz, "To Be a Radical Jew in the Late Twentieth Century," in *The Issue is Power: Essays on women, Jews, violence and resistance* (San Francisco: Aunt Lute Books 1992), pp. 92-115, and "Class, Feminism, and 'the Black-Jewish Question'" in *The Issue is Power: Essays on women, Jews, violence and resistance* (San Francisco: Aunt Lute Books 1992), pp. 116--130, Also see "*In gerangl*/In struggle," exercises in *The Tribe of Dina: A Jewish Women's Anthology,* by myself and Irena Klepfisz, with Bernice Mennis (Boston: Beacon Press, 1989).

2. Sherry Gorelick, *City College and the Jewish Poor* (NJ: Rutgers University Press, 1981).

3. James Baldwin, "On Being 'White' and Other Lies" *Essence* (April 1984), pp. 90-92.

4. The phrase was used to characterize the "modern" Jew of the European Enlightenment.

ELI CLARE

13 BODY SHAME, BODY PRIDE: LESSONS FROM THE DISABILITY RIGHTS MOVEMENT (2013)

Eli Clare is a writer and activist who lives at the intersection of trans, genderqueer, disability, peace, and antiracist movements for social justice. He is a sought-after speaker and award-winning writer. His books include *Exile and Pride* (1999), *The Marrow's Telling: Words in Motion* (2007), and *Brilliant Imperfection: Grappling with Cure* (2017).

Introduction

I wrote the following first as a keynote speech for a FTM [female-to-male] conference in Milwaukee, Wisconsin, in 2007. Imagine a hotel ballroom full of trans people—mostly on the FTM spectrum, but not exclusively—and our friends, family, lovers, spouses, and allies. We've spent the last two days attending workshops and talking politics, dancing and flirting, sitting in community, and listening to stories. From the podium as I look over the jam of people, I see more genders than I can count. I feel a tremendous responsibility to all the overlapping communities gathered in this corporate hotel. What follows is a revised version of what I read that night.

All my life as a genderqueer crip, I have puzzled my way through bodily difference, struggling with my own shame and love, other people's pity and hatred. Tonight as I stand here in this ballroom overflowing with people, I'm reminded of the incredible importance of community, how bodily difference means one thing in isolation and quite another when we come together, finding ourselves reflected in each other's stories.

My first experience of queerness—of bodily difference—centered, not upon sexuality or gender, but upon disability. Early on I understood that my body was irrevocably different from my neighbors, classmates, playmates, siblings: shaky, off balance, speech hard to understand, a body that moved slow, wrists cocked at odd angles, muscles knotted with tremors. But really, I am telling a kind of lie, a

half-truth. Irrevocably different would have meant one thing. Bad, wrong, broken, in need of repair meant quite another. I heard these every day as my classmates called *retard, monkey, defect*; as nearly everyone I met gawked at me, as my parents grew impatient with my clumsiness. Irrevocably different would have been easy compared to this. I stored the taunting, gawking, isolation in my bones; they became the marrow, my first experience of bodily difference.

Because of that, I always come to community hungry, seeking reflection, wanting dialogue, hoping for a bridge. I know I'm not the only one. Tonight I want to continue my puzzling through bodily difference, spanning the distance between disability politics and trans experience. Of course I could start with the substantial presence of disabled folks in trans communities, and by disability I mean chronic illness and intellectual, cognitive, learning, sensory, and psych disability, as well as physical disability. Or I could start with the truisms about bringing experiences of multiple oppressions and identities to our work. Or start with the long overdue need for accessible spaces, the importance of integrating ableism— that is disability-based oppression—into our understanding of oppression.

But really I want to delve beyond the rhetoric we often don't pay attention to, delve into the myriad of lived bodily differences here in this room tonight and think hard about three lessons I've learned from the disability rights movement. The first is about naming; the second, about coming out and disclosure; the third, about living in our familiar, ordinary bodies.

First, naming: I often hear trans people—most frequently folks who are using, or want to use, medical technology to reshape their bodies—name their transness a disability, a birth defect. They say, "I should have easy access to good, respectful health care, just as other disabled people do. I simply need a cure." The word *defect* always takes my breath away; it's a punch in the stomach. But before I get to that, I need to say the whole equation makes me incredulous, even as I work to respect the people who frame their transness this way. Do they *really* believe disability ensures decent—much less good and respectful—health care? I could tell you a litany of stories, cite you pages of statistics, confirming that exactly the opposite is true. Disabled people routinely deal with doctors who trivialize and patronize us, who believe some of the worst ableist stereotypes, and who sometimes even think we'd be better off dead. I could rant for hours about ableism in medical contexts. But my frustration doesn't stop here.

To couple disability with the need for cure accepts wholesale some of the exact bigotry that I and other disabled people struggle against every day. It takes for granted that disability is an individual medical problem curable, or at least treatable, by doctors. It runs counter to the work of disability activists who frame disability as an issue of social justice, not of medical condition: disability lodged not in paralysis, but rather in stairs without an accompanying ramp; not in depression or anxiety, but rather in a whole host of stereotypes; not in dyslexia, but in teaching methods unwilling to flex. It ignores the reality that many of us aren't looking for cures, but for civil rights.

I've been asked more than once whether I'd take the hypothetical cure pill, always asked in ways that make it clear there's only one real answer: "Why, of course, in a heartbeat." But that's not my answer. For me, having cerebral palsy is like having blue eyes and red hair. I simply don't know my body any other way. Thank you very much, but no: no to the New Age folks who have offered crystals and vitamins, no to the preachers who have prayed over me, no to the doctors who have suggested an

array of drugs and possible surgery, all with uncertain outcomes.

All of this gets complicated when I turn back to trans community, to those of us who seek to reshape our gendered and sexed bodies. But really it's not our desire or need for bodily change that I'm challenging here. Rather, it's how we name those desires and needs, because to claim our bodies as defective, and to pair defect with cure, not only disregards the experiences of many disabled people, it also leaves us as trans people wide open to shame.

Of course there's another important strand of naming at work in our communities—a strand that declares transness not a disease, gender nonconformity not a pathology, and bodily uniqueness not an illness—a strand that turns the word *dysphoria* inside out, claiming that we are not the ones dysphoric about our genders, but rather dysphoria lives in the world's response to us. This naming acts as a necessary counterbalance. But I have to ask: what about those of us who do in truth deal with deep, persistent body dissonance, discomfort, dysphoria? A social justice politics by itself will never be enough to resist shame.

And now let me move close to the word *defect* because it keeps ringing in my ears. It's an intense word, loaded in this culture with pity and hatred, a word that has tracked me all my life and brought nothing but shame. The bullies have circled round, calling, *defect, monkey, retard, hey defect*, leaving me no escape. Complete strangers on the street have asked, *What's your defect?*, curiosity and rudeness splaying my skin. Doctors have filled my chart with the phrase "birth defect," observed my gait, checked my reflexes, measured my muscle tone. That word is certainly a punch in the stomach.

And so when folks name their transness a birth defect, invoking some horrible bodily wrongness and appealing to cure as a means to end that wrongness, I find myself asking a disbelieving why. Why would anyone freely choose that word for themselves? But the question really needs to be: what leads us to the belief that our bodies are defective in the first place? The answer has to include shame, which medical technology alone will never cure.

Don't get me wrong: I'm not dismissing medical transition as caving into the gender binary or into shame itself. In truth, hormones and surgery can be powerful tools along the way for those of us who have the money or health insurance necessary to access health care in the USA. And just as powerful are the choices to live in all kinds of gendered and sexed bodies—as a man with breasts, as a woman with a penis, as some third, fourth, fifth gender, the possibilities way too many to name. All I mean is that medical technology will never be the whole answer for any of us.

Rather than resorting to some naïve and stereotyped notion of disability, we need to grapple with the complex twine of gender dysphoria and body shame. What are the specifics of our shame? How do we move through hatred, disgust, numbness, toward comfort and love, all the while acknowledging body dissonance as a real, sometimes overwhelming, force? Let's lean towards places where we name our bodily differences, even through our ambivalence, grief, and longing, in ways that don't invite and encourage shame.

That's naming, and now let me move on to a second lesson I've learned from the disability rights movement, a lesson about disclosure and coming out. In trans communities we talk a lot about disclosure, but so often that talk is full of misunderstanding and accusation. Folks who choose to be "stealth" are accused of shame, and folks who choose to be "out" are told they'll regret it later. In these community controversies, we lose all the nuance—the layers of history, fear, protection, exhaustion, resistance, pride, and pure practicality—that come with being out or not. I want us to nurture the most complex conversations possible about how we disclose our bodies and identities to strangers, friends, co-workers, lovers, tricks, doctors, family. I want to honor all the losses and gains contained in each decision about outness. At the same time, I want to challenge the argument I hear sometimes that being trans is simply a private bodily and medical matter, no one's business beyond our closest intimates.

The ability to keep bodily matters private is a privilege that some of us don't have. Just ask a poor person on welfare, a fat person, a visibly disabled person, a pregnant woman. Ask a person of color whose ethnic heritage isn't seemingly apparent.

Ask an African American man who's been pulled over by the cops for "driving while black." Just ask a seriously ill person, a gender ambiguous person, a nonpassing trans man or trans woman. All these people experience public scrutiny, in one way or another, of their bodies. In this culture bodily difference attracts public attention. For many of us, privacy is simply not an option.

Certainly as a disabled person, I never get a choice about privacy. Sometimes I can choose how to deal with gawking, how to correct the stereotypes and lies, how to live with my particular bodily history. But I don't get to choose privacy, much less *medical* privacy. The first thing people want to know is what's wrong with me. Sometimes they ask carefully about my *disability*, other times demand loudly about my *defect*. But either way they're asking for a medical diagnosis. And if I choose not to tell, they'll just pick one for me anyway and in the picking probably make a heap of offensive assumptions. The lack of privacy faced by poor people, fat people, disabled people, people of color, and visibly queer and gender nonconforming people has many consequences connected to a variety of systems of oppression. I'm not saying that bodies should be public, just that many people don't have access to bodily privacy.

And so when I hear the argument that being trans is a private matter, I want to ask: do you know that bodily privacy is a privilege regulated by systems of power and control? And if you have that privilege, how are you using it, even when it's laced with ambivalence and stress? In asking these questions, I'm not suggesting that all trans people need to come out all the time, nor that those of us who choose to be "stealth" are suspect. As a genderqueer who lives in the world as a white guy, I certainly understand the challenges and risks of disclosure on a daily basis. In a transphobic world all the available options are fraught. And it goes without saying that nonconsensual disclosure is just plain wrong, and in some cases, deadly. Yet if we are to make a sustaining community that profoundly challenges shame and nurtures pride, we need to acknowledge the political implications that trail our personal, individual decisions and question the value some trans people place on privacy.

In contrast, the disability rights movement values self-determination. Who gets to make which choices about our bodies—where we sleep, what we eat, who we socialize with? A popular disability slogan declares, "Nothing about us without us." For peoples who have long histories of institutionalization in nursing homes, group homes, psych wards, state-run hospitals, and rehab centers, self-determination is a radical and liberating politics. We get to determine how and when to explain ourselves, bodies not reduced to medical histories and issues but rather belonging fully to us, doctors playing only small, bit roles. A politics of self-determination declares that only we—not doctors, psychiatrists, physical therapists, case workers, social workers, the folks ruling on our SSI [Supplemental Security Income] and food stamp applications—have authority over our bodies, know what works for us and what doesn't, can say who we are and what we want. It discards the notion that our bodies are medical curiosities, scientific theories, social burdens and perversities. It is a simple, matter-of-fact, and entirely profound politics. By valuing self-determination, we invite many different kinds of bodies to the table. We reach toward liberation rather than privilege.

Turning back to trans disclosure, I remember what intimate and risky work it is, so full of conflicting urges and emotions—exhaustion, frustration, necessity, fear, desire. What would disclosure look like if trans communities shaped a politics around self-determination, rather than privacy?

Naming, disclosure, and now I'll turn to a third lesson I've learned from the disability rights movement, a lesson about living in our familiar, ordinary bodies. I watch marginalized people in a variety of communities yearn towards—or make declarations of—normality. So many FTMs aspire to be normal men, MTFs [male-to-females] to be normal women. There are trans folks who don't want to be queer in any way, and others who embrace their queerness loudly and with pride. Personally I'd like to completely discard the idea of normality. I don't mean that everyone ought to be queer; it's just that the very idea of normal means

comparing ourselves to some external, and largely mythical, standard. But being normal or being queer aren't the only choices.

All too often in trans communities we buy into the wholesale medicalization of our bodies and lose what is simply ordinary and familiar about them. I think of the long-standing argument that trans activists are embroiled in about the DSM [*Diagnostic and Statistical Manual of Mental Disorders*] and Gender Identity Disorder. Does the diagnosis that trans people use to access medical technology belong in the DSM; is transness a *psychiatric* disorder; where does it belong if not in the DSM? This conversation has been, and continues to be, long and fraught. The details are important, and I find myself agreeing with parts of both arguments. But in the end, I think we're asking the wrong questions.

These debates have highlighted the need for a diagnosis for transsexuality, underscored the differences between a psychiatric and a medical framework, and articulated the trouble with the word *disorder*. Still we haven't questioned the fundamental relationship between trans people and the very idea of diagnosis. Many of us are still invested in the ways we're medicalized. How often have you heard trans people come out by saying, "I have Gender Identity Disorder," explain and defend their choices by referencing that diagnosis? We praise our doctors, rail against their quirks, measure our transitions in medical terms. Even trans folks who have no interest in medical transition are assumed to be in relationship to it. How many female-assigned genderqueer people are sick of the question, "When are you going to start testosterone?"

In counterpoint, the disability rights movement fiercely resists the medicalization of bodies. Certainly disabled people sometimes need medical technology to sustain our very life's breath, but that doesn't transform our bodies into mere medical conditions. We have become practiced at defining ourselves from the inside out, stepping away from the shadow called normal, understanding what doctors can offer and what they can't, knowing our disabled bodies as familiar and ordinary. If trans people took up this disability rights lesson and defined ourselves on our own terms rather than through the lens of medicine, we'd still care about finding good doctors and getting good medical treatment, but our bodily truths wouldn't ultimately be medical truths. From this place of power, the question of psychiatric versus medical diagnosis would become less pressing.

At the same time, issues surrounding psychiatric diagnosis are often about life and death for many folks trapped inside the mental health system. As we talk about the DSM, let's not act as if trans people don't belong in the DSM because we aren't *really* "crazy," unlike the "crazies" over there—folks labeled with depression, bipolar disorder, dissociative behavior, schizophrenia, and so on. Let's work from the knowledge that the DSM wields incredible power and causes tremendous trouble for so many different people. Let's remember the gender nonconforming youth who endure psychiatric abuse, the transsexuals who need drug treatment programs but can't find placements because their transness is seen as psychiatric illness.

With a disability politics, we could learn to use diagnosis without being defined by it, all the while resisting the institutions that hold power over us. Simply changing where Gender Identity Disorder lives without changing our relationship to the idea of diagnosis isn't nearly enough. Rather than being attached to diagnosis, we could understand our lives and histories as *ordinary* from the inside, even as we're treated as curious, exotic, unbelievable, deceptive, sick, threatening from the outside. We could frame bodily difference as neither good nor bad, but as profoundly *familiar*.

In the end I'm reaching toward a disability politics of transness, not one of simple analogy, but one that delves into the lived experiences of our bodies, that questions the idea of normal and the notion of cure, that values self-determination, that resists shame and the medicalization of identity—a politics that will help all of us come home to our bodies.

14 BETWEEN BELONGING: A CULTURE OF HOME (2018)

Mariko Uechi is finishing her last year at Clark University, studying History with a concentration in Comparative Race and Ethnic Relations. Her interest in history began as a high school student, when she noticed that her textbooks inaccurately described the incarceration of Japanese Americans during World War II. Inspired by unjust representations of similarly marginalized groups in the United States, Mariko will be attending graduate school at John Hopkins University and hopes to pursue a career in secondary education.

Family and Belonging

If you relied on stereotypes and assumptions you would not see my people, my family, or my home. When my parents met in the summer of 1984, my mother's parents had been Christian missionaries for almost twenty years on Ishigaki Island, one of the Ryukyu Islands, now the Okinawa Prefecture of Japan. Her people came from small town Pennsylvania and a dairy farm in Wisconsin but she was born a *gaijin* in Japan. Later she attended a boarding school in South Carolina as an English-as-a-second-language student. My father is Okinawan. He was a kite-surfer instructor with big dreams of owning a computer and moving to America. He was invited by my grandmother for a summer feast, and smooth-talked my mother into accepting a date. At the end of the summer, he left the sandy beaches of Ishigaki-shi and followed her to frigid Minnesota where she was enrolled in a nursing program.

I have one older brother, Ryo—charismatic, handsome, generous, with infectious positivity. He looks more typically Okinawan than me. As an infant, he had a seizure that affected his frontal lobe, the center for decision-making and impulse control. Teachers branded Ryo a hyper-child, a problem child, the child who would likely end up in prison. Perhaps it was that mentality that allowed them to turn their backs on him. Everyone who was responsible for supporting him, emotionally and academically, failed him. As a teenager, he became a distant stranger in our home. We did not share his laughter the way we once did, his joy faded. I wonder if he felt as isolated and alone as I did, although for different reasons.

My father suffered as he watched the American education system fail his first-born. He'd come to the United States believing that he would become a homeowner, that his children would go to university and become successful doctors and lawyers. As time passed, my father became bitter and disappointed with the failure of the so-called American Dream. He was physically present, but with each technical job he obtained then quickly lost, he began to disconnect from us as a family. He came home from work, *tadaima!* We would respond, *okaeri!* This was the extent of our conversations. He would watch his *Nihongo no terebi* at night before falling asleep on the couch. Our mother worked the night shift as a nurse. Most nights she would do what she could to feed my brother and me before she left for work. If we needed homework help, we went to our family friend's house. But Ryo and I rarely went for help. We didn't want to elicit questions about our family dynamics that we had no way of answering. We didn't want pity or handouts. Perhaps we inherited our father's pride.

After years of searching for decent work, it seemed that nobody would hire my father without a college degree. My parents decided that it would help him to be around his own people, that he might find a more lucrative position in Okinawa. Ryo was already in elementary school but I was not. They decided that my father would take me with him to Okinawa where I could learn the language and customs.

So when I was three years old I lived on Ishigaki Island for a year and went to an Okinawan preschool. My Japanese became so fluent that I lost my

Source: Mariko Uechi, written for this volume.

command of English. I felt Okinawan in my core. I saw myself in the people I was surrounded by. I've always identified with my Okinawan side more than my American side. My thought-processes, my mannerisms, values, palate, and deep love for the ocean all resemble Okinawan culture. However, the legitimacy of my Okinawan self feels like it is always under fire. I feel in a consistent state of invalidity, divided into parts: one part Okinawan, one part American, one-part "other" and one-part white, colonized and colonizer. This status is reinforced every time I check "other" on the US census, school papers, and job applications. *Haafu, hambun, hapa,* Amerasian, Eurasian, all terms signifying half-ness, mixed-blood. Despite my parents' good qualities, the names they had for me never felt right.

My parents had their own racial experiences but they could never understand mine. As a child, my American teachers sent letters home about my inability to express my emotions in what they called a healthy way, but noted that I was always sensitive to my peers. The school asked my parents to send me to therapy to help with my "emotional expression". Therapy was very white, too. Therapists often blamed my parents for being absent, but I do not believe this is true. My parents did their best for us given the difficult circumstances they faced as an immigrant family, but my white therapists did not understand the sacrificial work ethic that many immigrant families know. I often left those sessions feeling more isolated, alienated, and alone.

Silent Struggling

I am a very reserved person but I pay attention. I began to question and challenge the values and ways of US society. First, I noticed how the same teachers treated Ryo and me differently. They praised me for my calmness; they told me that I was a much better student, and that I would be successful. These comments implied Ryo's deficits—not calm, not a good student, will not succeed. Although subtly conveyed, I knew what my teachers meant when they said those things.

Although teachers saw my strengths, my social life was different. When I brought my *obento* box

lunch to school, my peers would ask who passed gas because they thought my lunch smelt terrible. When I brought lunches like the white students had, I was invited into their group. In the shopping mall, I noticed that people would engage in conversation as they attempted to sell items to my white mother. However, when I was with my Okinawan father they wouldn't talk to him. If they did, they raised their voices and slowed down their speech as if he couldn't understand their English. The more inequalities I witnessed around me, the less I wanted to be Okinawan, and the more I played up my whiteness. I asked to quit *Nihongo no hiyouko-shiyo* on Saturdays after years of Japanese language classes because I did not want to be close to Japanese culture anymore. I lied and told my mom it was because I wanted to play soccer. I hated soccer practice too.

My ability to "pass" grants me access to powers and privileges across racial definitions and boundaries. However, it is a source of shame and confusion. I ask myself, why was I born white passing while my brother was not? I question how people would treat me if I looked a little more like my brother, my father, or my Okinawan grandparents? If I went by Mariko, the name my parents called me at home, rather than Emily. Would they be as friendly and complimentary?

Internally I juggle these complex identities and classifications. My white looks allow me to pick and choose when to turn on behaviors that mimic white America. Usually people assume that I am white and treat me as such. The elders in my community comment on how respectful, polite, and "sweet" I am, sometimes insisting that other young people are not this way. Perhaps this reflects how I was socialized to follow gender roles across the Okinawan diaspora. To some people of color, my oppression is minute and insignificant. Depending on my environment, I am simply a white woman. To others, I am erotically exotic, a guessing game as in "Let's-Guess-Her-Ethnicity," starting with the irritatingly common question: Where are you from? Note: this is not a fun game for biracial and multiracial people. This game subsumes complex individuals into whatever simplistic categories other people recognize and makes them feel comfortable. They may feel proud of themselves if they guess somewhere close to my father's homeland. Then there are those who challenge me over how legitimate my Okinawan heritage is by asking me to "prove it." These games come with a heaviness of never feeling like I belong in the United States or Japan. I feel as though I have to try to assimilate in order to fit into a rigid racial order.

When I step outside of the United States into Okinawa, I am viewed as *haafu*: half-Okinawan and half-American. My racial hybridity puts into question my allegiance and cultural competence as a Japanese citizen. During a visit to Okinawa when I was seven years old, I was enrolled in the local school. I remember spending a lot of time alone as the kids would not play with me. They taunted me with invitations to play but then told me I was stupid to believe them. They always called me *ainoko* or *haafu*. I did not know it then but they were calling me an "illegitimate" child of war, a "half-breed" human. Now I am an adult, native Japanese people become silent when I reveal my racial mixture and stop asking questions about me. I never know what they think of me, whether they accept me or not. I am a constant reminder to my Okinawan relatives of the influx of US citizens living on Okinawan land, many of them US military personnel. In Okinawa, there is a culture of locating oneself through family ties and long lineage. Neither my father, his siblings, nor I ever learned the full truth about what my ancestors experienced before, during, and after World War II. However, their lives and unspoken memories are what motivate me to learn about history, searching for purpose and belonging in what public information I do have access to.

War Trauma and Memories

It is very difficult to understand my experience without knowing Okinawan history and the relationship between the United States, Japan, and Okinawa. In 1879, Japan annexed or colonized the Ryukyu kingdom, as Okinawans called their nation then. Japan forced people to eradicate traditional Ryukyu culture, including their native language, religion, and other cultural practices.

Public schools had to use standard Japanese only, and teachers shamed and punished students who spoke their native tongue, similar to what my settler-colonial ancestors did to indigenous people in the States. Many Okinawan people responded to Japan's tyranny and oppression with deep and long-standing hostility. My family still refuses to identify as Japanese. They never were and never will be.

In 1945, the Battle of Okinawa, the final and bloodiest battle of the Pacific War, took the lives of nearly 300,000 people, including an estimated 150,000 Okinawan civilians. Some Okinawan casualties included people forced to obey an order of the Japanese Imperial Army to commit "mass suicide."[1] My family hid in the mountains of Miyakojima to escape being caught in the crossfire between Japanese and US armies. Their allegiance lay with neither side. Similar to my own racial identity, Okinawan people belonged neither to Japan nor the US. They were a colonized people, dominated by both these nations.[2]

My Okinawan family never spoke the names of family members and friends who died during the Battle of Okinawa. Nor did they talk about their personal wartime experiences, but their distrust of the United States has always been transparent. When my parents were married, it took Ryo's birth for *Obaasan* to accept that her eldest son had left Okinawa for America, for a white woman whose blue eyes reminded her of US military men. My upbringing has been heavily influenced by my grandparents' wartime trauma, of their rape, of their suffering; more importantly, my existence, my determination and perseverance are due to their sacrifices and unyielding desire for survival. My father was raised with an awareness of total war and the significance of historical colonization. He made it very clear that this particular history was an extension of my own existence. Without my ancestors' will to survive, I would not be here.

Awakening Understanding

I did not always understand my identity in the way I do now. I was saved from mixed feelings and internalized self-hatred after I became friends with girls from the Black Student Union in high school and witnessed their sisterhood and pride in who they are. I became more interested in decolonization and liberation because of them. They eagerly invited me into their group *because* I am Okinawan American. True, the oppression I face as a white-passing woman of color is different from theirs. Yet, as I began to decolonize my mind, I saw the whole world as "us" versus "them." I began to critique my mother's politics, my teachers, and even life-long friends. In my newborn vigilance, I found myself even more isolated in my identity consciousness than before.

In addressing and unlearning my own internalized prejudices, self-loathing, and blame, I felt less shame in my multiethnic identity. I no longer blamed myself for not being able to fit in, or feel a sense of home. I discovered Asian American and multiethnic histories that I had never learned before. In my tenth-grade oral history project, I'd interviewed people about Japanese incarceration camps during WWII, and healing from that trauma. My last interview question was: If there is anything you want us young people to carry on in memory of racism and relocation, what would you want it to be? My friend Howie, an elder from the Japanese American church I grew up in, answered this in two words: Stay Vigilant. Those words have never left me as I continue my quest for self-discovery, curiosity for learning, and ultimately, liberation.

It was not until college when I took a course about violence in Black communities that I found a connection between healing and history and could trace the ways in which identity and history are intertwined. In studying the histories of communities of color, in women and gender studies, and queer studies I learned about healing as part of collective struggle and how people strive for justice. I began to channel my feelings of isolation and anger into social justice work and education around identity and belonging. My struggles became very public. I allowed myself to talk about my experience. In vocalizing my struggles, I found healing. I discovered that other biracial and multiracial people related to me. Finding people working against oppression—from white supremacy, sexism, and racism among many other isms—gave me a space of belonging. In vigilance, I found love amongst anger. I found joy in kinship. I found home.

NOTES

1. Masaaki, Aniya. 2008. "Compulsory Mass Suicide, the Battle of Okinawa, and Japan's Textbook Controversy," *The Asia Pacific Journal*, 6 (1).
2. Many critics of the current geopolitical relationship between Japan, Okinawa, and the US maintain that Okinawa continues to be a colony, given that it is the poorest prefecture and that it bears the burden of the massive presence of US military bases and personnel.

15   EXCEPT FROM "ONCE UPON A QUINCEAÑERA: COMING OF AGE IN THE USA" (2007)

Born in New York City and raised in the Dominican Republic, **Julia Alvarez** has published essays, collections of poetry, books for children, and five books of fiction, including *How the García Girls Lost Their Accents* (1991). Her work has earned numerous awards, including a 2013 National Medal of Arts. She is one of the founders of Border of Lights, a movement to promote peace and collaboration between Haiti and the Dominican Republic. She lives in Vermont.

You are dressed in a long, pale pink gown, not sleek and diva-ish, but princessy, with a puffy skirt of tulle and lace that makes you look like you're floating on air when you appear at the top of the stairs. Your court of fourteen couples has preceded you, and now they line up on the dance floor, forming a walkway through which you will pass to sit on a swing with garlanded ropes, cradling your last doll in your arms. Your mami will crown you with a tiara recessed in a cascade of curls the hairstylist spent most of the afternoon sculpting on your head. Then your papi will replace the flats you are wearing with a pair of silver heels and lead you out to the dance floor, where you will dance a waltz together.

No, you are not Miss America or a princess or an actress playing Cinderella in a Disney movie. In fact, you are not exceptionally beautiful or svelte and tall, model material. Your name is María or Xiomara or Maritza or Chantal, and your grandparents came from Mexico or Nicaragua or Cuba or the Dominican Republic. Your family is probably not rich; in fact, your mami and papi have been saving since you were a little girl or they've mortgaged the house or lined up forty godparents to help sponsor this celebration, as big as a wedding. If challenged about spending upward of five thousand dollars—the average budget—on a one-night celebration instead of investing in your college education or putting aside the money for their own mortgage payments, your parents will shake their heads knowingly because you do not understand: this happens only once.

What is going on?

You are having your quinceañera . . .

A "quinceañera" (the term is used interchangeably for the girl and her party) celebrates a girl's passage into womanhood with an elaborate, ritualized fiesta on her fifteenth birthday. (*Quince años*, thus *quinceañera*, pronounced: *keen-seah-gneer-ah*.) In the old countries, this was a marker birthday: after she turned fifteen, a girl could attend adult parties; she was allowed to tweeze her eyebrows, use makeup, shave her legs, wear jewelry and heels. In short, she was ready for marriage. . . . Even humble families marked a girl's fifteenth birthday as special, perhaps with a cake, certainly with a gathering of family and friends at which the quinceañera could now socialize and dance with young men. Upperclass families, of course, threw more elaborate parties at which girls dressed up in long, formal gowns and danced waltzes with their fathers.

Somewhere along the way these fancier parties became highly ritualized. In one or another of our Latin American countries, the quinceañera was crowned with a tiara; her flat shoes were changed by her father to heels; she was accompanied by a court of fourteen damas escorted by fourteen chambelanes, who represented her first fourteen years; she received a last doll, marking both the end of childhood and her symbolic readiness to bear her own child. And because our countries were at least nominally Catholic, the actual party was often preceded by a Mass or a blessing in church or, at the very least, a priest was invited to give spiritual heft to the fiesta. These celebrations were covered in the newspapers, lavish spreads of photos I remember poring over as a little girl in the Dominican Republic, reassured by this proof that the desire to be a princess did not have to be shed at the beginning of adulthood, but could in fact be played out happily to the tune of hundreds upon thousands of Papi's pesos.

In the late sixties, when many of our poor headed to el Norte's land of opportunity, they brought this tradition along, and with growing economic power, the no-longer-so-poor could emulate the rich back home. The spin-offs grew (quinceañera cruises, quinceañera resort packages, quinceañera videos and photo shoots); . . . further elaborations were added . . . and in our Pan-Hispanic mixing stateside, the US quinceañera adopted all the little touches of specific countries to become a much more elaborate (and expensive) ceremony, exported back to our home countries. But rock-bottom, the US quinceañera is powered by that age-old immigrant dream of giving the children what their parents had never been able to afford back where they came from.

In fact, . . . many of us older, first-generation Latinas never had a quinceañera. There was no money back when we were fifteen, or we had recently arrived in the United States and didn't want anything that would make us stand out as other than all-American. Or we looked down our noses at such girly-girl fuss and said we didn't want a quince because we didn't understand that this was not just about us.

These cultural celebrations are also about building community in a new land. Lifted out of the context of our home cultures, traditions like the quinceañera become malleable; they mix with the traditions of other cultures that we encounter here; they become exquisite performances of our ethnicities within the larger host culture while at the same time reaffirming that we are not "them" by connecting us if only in spirit to our root cultures. In other words, this tradition tells a larger story of our transformation into Latinos, a Pan-Hispanic group made in the USA, now being touted as the "new Americans."

It's that story which intrigues me. Why, when I was invited by an editor to write a book about quinceañeras, I welcomed the opportunity to follow the tradition wherever it might lead me. . . .

. . . I traveled to various Latino communities in the United States: Dominican Americans in Lawrence, Massachusetts, and Queens, New York; Cuban Americans in Miami; Mexican Americans in San Antonio and Los Angeles. . . .

I also spoke with dozens of girls and their families and members of their courts, with events providers and photographers, with parish priests and youth ministers and choreographers. I talked to Latinas my age and older, Latinas in academia and in businesses catering to the quinceañera market, who observed that the quinceañera has become an even bigger deal stateside than it had ever been back home.

With that elaboration and expense, a certain entitlement has set in. Many of the Latina girls I interviewed who responded in writing often termed the celebration "my right of passage." Given that spell-check would not have picked up this transposition, this was an understandable orthographical mistake, but it also seemed an apt description of what happens to traditions in the United States. Rites become rights. New generations feel entitled to what older first generations struggled to obtain for them.

By the same token, this entitlement ethic does not seem to shield our young Latina population from failure. As I read the research, I was alarmed by how our teen Latinas are topping the charts for all sorts of at-risk behaviors: from teen pregnancy to substance abuse to dropping out of high school. What is going on? We are crowning them princesses, and meanwhile the statistics are showing a large number of our young girls headed for poverty and failure. Are these the same girls, I wonder?

So, what began as the study of a tradition became a journey of exploration rife with questions and misgivings. I admit that the disjunction between this grand Latina debut and the reality of their lives, the enormous cost of the celebration to struggling families, made me initially skeptical about the tradition. And yet, time and time again as I attended these celebrations I felt deeply moved by something at the heart of the tradition, a desire to empower our young women, a need to ritually mark their passage into adulthood, remind them of their community and its past, and by doing so give them and ourselves hope. Who could argue with that?

. . . Our exported tradiciones mix and combine with those of other Latin American and Caribbean countries stateside and become more elaborate, more expensive, more traditional than they ever were back home.

In fact, to have a full-blown traditional quinceañera in our Pan-Hispanic United States is to have adopted every other Latino group's little traditions and then some. So that now, Cuban quinceañeras in Miami are hiring Mexican mariachis to sing the traditional "Las Mañanitas." The full court of fourteen damas and chambelanes, "each couple representing a year of the quinceañera's life," a mostly Mexican practice, is now a . . . must. As is the changing of the shoes to heels, which seems to originally have been a Puerto Rican embellishment. From the Puerto Ricans as well, though some say from the Mexicans, came the tradition of la última muñeca, a "last doll" dressed exactly like the quinceañera, which the girl cradles to symbolize the "end of her childhood" or "the child that she herself will be having in the not-too-distant future" (both explanations given to me by different events planners). The quinceañera might keep this last doll as a keepsake or give it away to a younger member of the family. In one celebration, perhaps inspired by the wedding bouquet, the quinceañera threw her last doll over her shoulder to be caught by a screaming group of little girls, anticipating their own future quinceañeras.

This symbol of bygone childhood is also mirrored in a Central American or Puerto Rican custom (I've heard both) of having a very little girl dress up in a minuscule version of the quinceañera's dress and be "the symbol of innocence." Sometimes she is accompanied by a young escort, though the tradition has now been further elaborated so that "the symbol of innocence" (a toddler) as well as a slightly older little prince and princess—three total—are part of a full traditional court.

There is also always some sort of photo session to commemorate the event . . . there are whole albums of the young lady in different outfits, in different locations, a practice that seems to have started with the Cuban community in Miami, where girls sometimes just have the photo shoot and forego the party. Many girls also have videos made, recounting their lives since birth, with still shots and footage of themselves at different ages and credits rolling as if this were a real movie with the quinceañera playing the lead and her parents starring as "padre" and "madre" and Julio Iglesias's "De Niña a Mujer" as the score, of course. . . .

The tradition of crowning the young girl is often ascribed to the Mexicans, who seem to be the group that has most ritualized the ceremony. But here in America, every quinceañera gets her tiara. The bouquet the quinceañera carries to put at the Virgin Mary's statue at the Mass is also part of the Mexican and Central American tradition, as is the Mass, which our more hedonistic Caribbean party-cultures dispensed with back home. But now the Mass and the Virgin's bouquet have become part of our Dominican and Puerto Rican and Cuban "tradition" in the United States. . . .

"Today, it's all about supersizing," Nina Diaz, the executive producer of *My Super Sweet 16*, told *U.S. News & World Report*. (The price tag for a recent quince party featured in one of the episodes was $180,000.) One quince site I happened upon in cruising the Web for Q-lore—just Google "quinceañera" and you will get 8,230,000 hits (if you put the tilde over the "n") or 4,220,000 hits (if you dispense with the tilde)—urged providers to register with their site. "The Hispanic population's buying power is expected to reach $300 billion by 2006. Timing is prime to begin your Sweet 16 and Quinceanera advertising campaign. The demand for more vendors that cater to Latinos is of epic proportions." . . .

At Disneyland, Denny Nicholas, manager of corporate and wedding sales, says he has seen anything from a modest $5,000 to $50,000 for a quinceañera, the average nowadays being about $12,000 to $15,000. When I ask Denny if he doesn't find this *average* shocking given that the poverty threshold for a family of three is $15,277, he laughs. "By the time families come to me, they've already made the decision that this is what they want. All I do is provide the elements they need to make their dreams come to life." . . .

Trying to track down the origins of the quinceañera tradition is a little like playing that old party game, telephone. A whispers some news in B's ear, B then recounts the news to C, all the way around the circle. By the time the news has come back to A, and is pronounced out loud, it has morphed into a skewed version of whatever it was that A claims to have originally said.

Many books, articles, and websites state that the roots of the quinceañera tradition lie in an ancient Aztec rite. Sometimes the origin is given as Mayan as well as Aztec, and sometimes more generally described as "indigenous." I don't know if it's because the phrase "an ancient Aztec tradition" has a phony ring to it—an alliterative angling for authenticity in ancientness. But when I repeatedly read this claim in too many articles, I begin to search the bibliographies (in the few cases where one is provided) to see what I can find.

Most folks quote as their source Michele Salcedo's *Quinceañera!*, an informative, well-written guide, the best in its genre. Through a series of e-mails, I finally track down Michele Salcedo at the *South Florida Sun-Sentinel*, where she is assistant city editor. She tells me how about a decade ago, she took a year off from her reporting job to study the quinceañera tradition and write a planner-slash-background book. She is gracious and generous with her time but understandably cannot cite chapter and verse for the source of a detail in a book she wrote more than fifteen years ago. She does recall getting some of her material on origins from "a nun's book." This has to be one of Sister Angela's many manuals where I, too, have read about this ancient Aztec and Mayan tradition.

And so I e-mail Sister Angela trying not to sound like the doubting Thomas I am, and she sends me to some books—Sylvanus Morley's *The Ancient Maya* and Victor Von Hagen's *Los Aztecas: Hombre y Tribu*. I end up inside the compendious *Florentine Codex*, which was assembled back in the 1560s by a Spanish priest, Fray Bernardino de Sahagún, from testimonies given forty years earlier to a mission of Franciscan monks by twelve high priests of the Aztec empire about their traditions. (Think again of the telephone game: a conquered nation as understood by Catholic priests interviewed four decades later by another Franciscan.) Whatever "facts" we know about the Aztecs are several critical removes from a true and living practice.

But Sister Angela is absolutely right that our indigenous American ancestors did indeed acknowledge the passage of young girls into womanhood. What is uncertain is the age at which the ritual took place. We do know that the Aztec maiden was ready for marriage at the age of fifteen. Presumably at an earlier juncture there was a ceremony of some sort. The *Codex* cites long ceremonial speeches in which fathers and mothers publicly admonished their daughters, probably as part of some ritual. The speeches themselves are quite moving to read. The tenderness is palpable. The father describes his daughter's coming-of-age in heart-tugging words:

> It is as if thou wert an herb, a plant which hath propagated, sprouted, blossomed. It is also as if thou hadst been asleep and hadst awakened.

Meanwhile, the mother warns "my dove, my little one, my child, my daughter" that life is dangerous and she must be careful. (So my own mami's dire warnings were not so off the mark. It seems a traditional task of mothers to terrify their daughters into good behavior.) "Behold the road thou art to follow," the mother advises:

> On earth we live, we travel along a mountain peak. Over here there is an abyss, over there is an abyss. If thou goest over here, or if thou goest over there, thou wilt fall in. Only in the middle doth one go, doth one live. Place this word, my daughter, dove, little one, well within the chambers of thy heart. Guard it well.

This is a far cry from Mami crowning her daughter with a rhinestone tiara or Papi dancing with her as Julio Iglesias sings "De Niña a Mujer." But in both cases there is a transmission going on, an acknowledgment that womanhood is upon her and a life of perils and possibilities is about to begin.

Mayans, too, celebrated the onset of puberty with an elaborate ceremony. Again, the age given by sources varies. Part of the female ceremony involved the mother cutting off a red shell that had been tied around her daughter's waist as a child. Presumably the girl was now considered ripe for marriage and childbearing. We can, of course, stretch the comparison and find in the cutting off of the red shell of virginity a parallel to the casting off of the last doll of childhood. But why belabor the point? Down through the generations the human family has celebrated passages in our mortal lives with rites that use the symbols and signs of our moment in time. We don't have to prove the legitimacy of these rites. They are what they are, part of our human legacy.

This push to legitimize the quinceañera by connecting it with an indigenous past is a fairly recent thing. Back in our home countries in the fifties, elite families would have blanched at any suggestion that their presentation parties had any connection at all to an "Indian" rite. "Indigenous heritage was played down in favor of European and North American culture," writes Valentina Napolitano in *Migration, Mujercitas, and Medicine Men*. Instead, "the fifteenth-birthday celebration used the symbology of European culture (for example, waltzes, performances of classical music, maids of honor, and pages)." It was only with the democratizing of the tradition stateside that the supposed Aztec connection began to be talked about. The desire for native credentials demonstrates both a yearning to reconnect with something forever lost as well as what Renato Rosaldo calls . . . "imperialist nostalgia," a nostalgia for a culture you have dominated, a people you have destroyed.

More traceable are the courtly elements of the quinceañera tradition. "The first elaborate quinceañeras were balls staged by families of means who liked to pride themselves on their Spanish ancestry and manners," writes Maricel Presilla in an article in the *Miami Herald*. . . . The Empress Carlotta of Mexico . . . "invited the daughters of members of her court to be presented as young ladies eligible for marriage." Interestingly, . . . the quinceañera has changed from a celebration for daughters of the elite to a fiesta for all classes. "When I was your age, only rich girls had quinceañeras," Estrella's mother tells her in *Estrella's Quinceañera*, one of the young adult novels . . . that centers on this tradition.

Most historians trace this shift to the 1960s and the beginning of vast migrations to el Norte's land of opportunity; the tradition soon became an option for middle and lower classes, both here in the USA and back home. Cross-fertilization knows no borders, and influences travel without visa or green card. In fact, even in present-day Cuba, the quinceañera is seeing a revival, as Cuban girls dream of parties like their Cuban American cousins enjoy in Miami. Many stateside families send their old quinceañera gowns and tiaras along with dollars and medicines to their needy relatives.

Certainly the quinceañera found welcome soil in the American consumer culture, where businesses stood to gain from the expensive elaborations of the ceremony. In fact, when the Los Angeles archdiocese issued guidelines back in January 1990 to try to curtail the growing commercialization and expense of quinceañeras, the outcry came not from the parishioners but from Grupo Latino Por Nuestras Tradiciones, which despite its name was made up of many small-business owners. The group's president, Luis Yanez, declared that "for the church, quinceañeras are not important, but for us they are one of the few traditions we have left," and in the same breath he complained that his shop, which supplies everything from the dresses to the headpieces and artificial bouquets and monogrammed cups, had seen a drastic decline from fifty quinceañeras to five since the guidelines were issued.

And so, while the quinceañera is touted as a marker of ethnicity, it is in many ways an ethnicity with a label that reads MADE IN THE USA (or "Remade in the USA," if you will). Even as the younger generations assimilate in every other way to a mainstream culture, they are holding on to this old-country tradition, which is actually being created here. Odd. Or is it?

In fact, this creation of a past that never was turns out to be a common enough social phenomenon. In his book *The Invention of Tradition*, Eric Hobsbawm coins the term "invented traditions" to describe both traditions actually invented from whole cloth (Kwanzaa, the Bat Mitzvah, just to mention a couple) as well as traditions that "emerge in a less easily traceable manner within a brief and datable period, establishing themselves with great rapidity." These invented traditions are likely to appear when a group is undergoing transformation, and they serve as a way to legitimize and galvanize its members by establishing continuity with a past that may be largely fictitious.

This is not to dismiss them as bogus, Hobsbawm is quick to point out. Instead, they are interesting hot spots in a group's evolution where adaptation and self-creation and legitimization are in progress, as well as moving testimonies toward cohesion just as the winds of dispersal are blowing us hither and yon. . . .

And so, it makes perfect sense for Mr. Ramos to want his daughter to hold on to her roots by doing something that comes to him from a past that never was—at least not for his working-class family prior to 1960. As his daughters grow up in the USA, speaking spotty Spanish . . . this is the one thing he can give them that might remind them of who they are. . . . A last Latin spin with his little girl because who knows where she'll end up?

"It used to be that you could give your daughter a wedding. But you don't know anymore if she's going to get married or if she's going to live with her boyfriend first like they do here, or if she's going to get divorced and get remarried several times," Mr. Ramos explained to me, a sentiment echoed by many parents. . . .

Twenty-five-year-old Maurice Mompoint, . . . based in Miami, represents a younger generation of quinceañera business entrepreneurs. His website, yourquinces.com, is allied with his mother's Happy Holidays Travel Agency, which does a large volume of the crucero business.

. . . "I give it ten years," he says cryptically, and for a moment I think he's talking about how long

he can last at his job. But he says that in ten years, quinces will be a thing of the past. "The next generation growing up, their parents will all have been born and raised here. A lot of them won't even speak Spanish that well. There isn't going to be that grandparent or parent from the old country pushing for the quinceañera." Is he worried about this? Not really. "In ten years, a lot of these girls are going to be getting married. I've been building my database, and with a couple of switches, I can turn yourquinces.com into a wedding site."

I wondered about Maurice's prognosis. Are quinceañeras on a culturally endangered list? Higinio Muñoz, who is part of the Muñoz dynasty of photographers that for three generations has been snapping quinces in Cuba and now in south Florida, does not think so at all. "For the last forty years of this business, you think, oh, the tradition is going to end with the next generation, but I've now got second- and third-generation girls, and the tradition is not waning. In fact, it's growing. I have Haitian quinceañeras and African American quinceañeras and American girls wanting quinceañeras." He has a point. At www.quinceañera.us.com, where you can register your quinceañera, there are mothers registering little girls who will be turning fifteen in 2015!

But history would seem to be on Maurice's side. After all, generations of immigrants have trod the assimilation path in America, shedding most of their ethnic past, with maybe only a parade left to commemorate those roots, a green cardigan on St. Patrick's Day, a polka night at the Polish American club . . .

On the other hand, America is now seeing a new kind of immigrant whose ties to a homeland are never completely severed. In his rousing and passionate book *Living in Spanglish: The Search for Latino Identity in America*, Ed Morales explains that the old idea of "Americanization" involved the loss of contact with people from the old country. "But the continuing migration of Latinos to the north has the effect of reinforcing the Latin culture that we would otherwise have lost."

And the travel is not just north but back and forth. In fact, the whole concept of nation-states with set borders you cross and leave behind is not the way the world really works anymore, according to Michael Dear, head of the Geography Department at the University of Southern California. In "Postborder Cities/Postborder World?" he notes how people, money, communication, and culture are all moving in new currents and combinations. Globalization is creating a new kind of mobile and mutating world citizenry. . . .

Quinces definitely have the potential of introducing a new story into the imagination of the next generation, one that might indeed help them live happier, more productive lives.

Why else would companies like Maggi and Kern's Nectar choose the quinceañera as the target tradition at which to aim their public relations campaigns? They know a powerful cultural icon when they see one.

But others are drawn to the tradition not as an advertising tool but as an opportunity to truly empower young people to believe that their dreams for their lives can come true.

Enter the fairy godmothers.

Isabella Martínez Wall. . . dispensing advice from her website, bellaquinceañera.com, and committed to making each girl feel like the queen of her life; Priscilla Mora, organizing expos to educate Latinas on financially responsible and culturally meaningful quinceañeras; Sister Angela, using the tradition as a teachable moment for Catholic youth, boys and girls, Latino or not. . . . Ana Maria Schachtell, founded the Stay-in-School Quinceañera Program, which could well become a model for such programs elsewhere.

In Idaho, of all places. . . .

. . . "We start in January, twice a week, one school night and then one Saturday, thirty to forty fourteen-year-old girls and boys," Ana Maria explains. . . . "Most of them have just started high school or are going to start in the fall." She figures she has a small window in which to make a difference about how their lives are going to go. "Most of these kids come from poor migrant families. Their parents haven't had much education. . . . So, we bring in teachers from the high school to talk about what to expect there. We bring in community leaders to encourage them to think about their future and make them proud of their past, their roots, their traditions. Judge Gutierrez, our only Hispanic

judge in Idaho, has come to talk to them, and this last year we brought in Loretta Sanchez!" This is obviously a big fish, and I'm embarrassed not to know who she is. Later I Google her and find out she is a congresswoman from California. . . .

According to Ana Maria, the kids have a lot of fun—"or they wouldn't keep coming back, week after week." Much of that fun comes from doing things that affirm their sense of pride in their culture. "They learn old cerámica techniques. We brought in an eighty-nine-year-old woman to teach the girls how to make their traditional coronas out of wax flowers, a Mexican handiwork that is being lost because of the cheap plastic crowns around. And for the boys, we bring in a charro, that's the original American cowboy. A lot of people don't know that. The charro tradition represents the best of machismo, how to be a real hombre, responsible to your familia and community. The boys eat it up."

I bet they do. How could they not, with Ana Maria cheering them on? The whole program culminates in a gala night, a fundraiser for the Hispanic Cultural Center. The center has a stock of thirty gowns for the girls, and it rents tuxedos for the boys. The governor comes, the senators, the mayor. (The Hispanic population of the state is growing at four times the rate of the non-Hispanic population. No doubt, these elected officials have done the numbers.)

What is inspiring about Ana Maria's program, which is now in its eighth year, is that it takes the tradition of the quinceañera, acknowledging its power as a coming-of-age ceremony, but recasts it with new content, including a strong emphasis on education. What does it mean to be a man, un hombre, un charro, in this new country? What does it mean to be una mujer who knows her tradiciones, can make the old-country wax flowers for a corona but can also run for Congress? In other words, the Stay-in-School program takes the occasion of the quinceañera to revise the limited narrative the rite has traditionally endorsed. . . .

But the fact that these old restrictive narratives about womanhood persist in our young Latina girls speaks to the need for retooling. And the quinceañera tradition—as a number of fairy godmothers have discovered—can provide that amazing learning opportunity. . . .

Our Bodies, Ourselves

Sexuality

Keywords: asexuality, consent, erotic, heteronormativity, heteropatriarchy, polyamory

This chapter focuses on sexuality, which we regard as both personal and political. We consider the micro-, meso-, and macro-level forces that shape people's sexual experiences, the patriarchal state's promotion of heterosexism, as well as the power of the erotic.

WHAT DOES SEXUALITY MEAN TO YOU?

Sexual attitudes and behaviors vary from society to society and across historical time periods (Caplan 1987; Lancaster and di Leonardo 1997; Weeks 2010). Sexuality is partly instinctive and also taught. In this society, we learn about sexuality from our families, our peers, sex education in school, media representations and popular culture, discussions with partners, and by listening to our own bodies. In Reading 16, writer Daisy Hernández describes her family's attitudes to intimacy and her experiences with boyfriends and girlfriends as she developed a sense of her sexuality and sexual orientation.

Feminist sex educator Shere Hite (1994) pioneered extensive surveys of women's sexual experiences and preferences. One of her surveys included the following questions, which we invite you to reflect on:

Is sex important to you? What part does it play in your life?

Who sets the pace and style of sex—you or your partner or both? Who decides when it's over?

If you are sexually active, do you ever fake orgasms? If so, why?

What are your best sex experiences? What would you like to try that you never have?

What is it about sex that gives you the greatest pleasure? Displeasure?

Have you chosen to be celibate at any point? What was/is that like for you?

In the best of all possible worlds, what would sexuality be like for you?

Do you know as much as you'd like to know about your own body? Orgasm? Conception and pregnancy? Safe sex?

Do your partners know about your sexual desires and your body? If not, do you ask for it or act yourself to get it? (Hite 1994, pp. 17–22)

About 1 percent of people in the United States consider themselves to be asexual; they are interested in friendship but not in sexual relationships. Sexuality is one of the few recognized ways in our society for people to make intimate connections. These may be temporary or longer term, with a single partner or more, in person or online. Historian Jeffrey Weeks remarked that the Internet has opened up spaces for "erotic excitement, enticement and entanglement at the click of a button" with sex chat rooms, news groups, bulletin boards, social networks, virtual sex, and more (2010, p. 107).

For many teens, sex is a "rite of passage," an important part of growing up. Some young people pledge virginity before marriage but do not necessarily rule out sex play. On the basis of research into the sexual lives of nearly 100 young women over a ten-year period, psychologist Lisa Diamond (2008) came to see women's sexuality as dynamic and characterized by fluidity, openness to variation, and a capacity to act on varying attractions and desires. Some people are attracted to polyamory, or being involved with more than one person, typically with consent and openness among all involved, which is described as ethical and responsible non-monogamy. Over the course of our lives, sexuality may take different forms and take on different degrees of significance. The important thing is that people seek to live according to their own sexual expressions and desires, and that sex should be consensual and pleasurable for all participants (Stryker 2017).

HETEROPATRIARCHY PUSHES HETEROSEX . . .

Sex, this most personal of experiences, is also shaped by meso- and macro-level factors. The system of patriarchy is structured to promote and maintain male dominance, as discussed by Allan G. Johnson in Reading 7. Heterosexuality is a central institution in patriarchal societies, and many aspects of daily life—marriage, family arrangements, work, income, and law—are organized along heteropatriarchal lines (Ingraham 2004). Over the years, feminists have engaged in heated arguments about female sexuality and the possibility of genuine sexual agency in patriarchal cultures. Medical anthropologist Carole Vance (1984) emphasized these contradictions:

> Sexuality is simultaneously a domain of restriction, repression, and danger as well as a domain of exploration, pleasure, and agency. To focus only on pleasure and gratification ignores the patriarchal structure in which women act, yet to speak only of sexual violence and oppression ignores women's experience with sexual agency and choice. (p. 1)

As with other systems of power, such as whiteness, wealth, and masculinity, the dominant category, in this case heterosexuality, has been much less scrutinized than the subordinated category, homosexuality. According to historian Jonathan Katz (1995), the word *heterosexuality* was first used in the 1890s as an obscure medical term applied to non-procreative sex—that is, sex for pleasure. At the time, this was considered deviant and to show an "abnormal or perverted appetite toward the opposite sex" (p. 86). Webster's dictionary did not include the word until 1934, and it gradually came into common usage in the United States as a "stable sign of normal sex" (p. 40).

Writer Roxane Gay (2014) points out the role of fairy tales in inculcating basic heterosexual lessons: there's a man (Prince Charming) and a woman who have to overcome an obstacle of some kind to reach the happy ending. Disney versions include *Cinderella*, *Snow White*, *The Little Mermaid*, and *Beauty and the Beast*. Typically, a woman pays a price to find her prince. Gay discusses a contemporary version found in E. L. James' popular trilogy—*Fifty Shades of Grey*, *Fifty Shades Darker*, and *Fifty Shades Freed*—where Ana, the female protagonist, accommodates herself to the "magnetism" of Christian Grey, a "predatory tycoon" (Flood 2017). Gay argues that Ana "consistently clarifies her overall disinterest in serving as Christian's submissive." She "has very reasonable expectations and boundaries," but Christian "willfully ignores" them "and she allows him to" (2014, p. 240). Gay concludes that "[w]hen considering the overwhelming popularity of this trilogy, we cannot simply dismiss the flaws because the books are fun and the sex is hot," (p. 241). She argues that this modern fairy tale "reinforces pervasive cultural messages women are already swallowing about what they should tolerate in romantic relationships . . . to be loved by their Prince Charming" (p. 241). *Fifty Shades of Grey* topped best-seller lists around the world, was translated into fifty-two languages, and sold 125 million copies in the first three years. Are women reading this as fantasy? As encouragement to be "more adventurous" sexually? Do readers buy the patriarchal message that eroticizes inequality?

In her now-classic essay, poet and writer Adrienne Rich (1986a) discussed how social institutions like law, religion, official kinship, and popular culture support what she termed "compulsory heterosexuality." Moreover, patriarchy demands heterosexuality in order to keep women serving masculinist interests. For Rich, it was important to explain not why women might identify as lesbians but rather how and why so many women are heterosexual, when typically we first experience emotional intimacy and physical nurturance with women: our mothers or other female caregivers. In many cultural settings, women and girls spend time together, care for and depend on one another, and enjoy each other's friendship—often passionately. Rich asks: Why would women redirect that focus? She argues that **heteropatriarchy**, like other structures of dominance, has to be constantly re-created through the imposition of cultural norms, beliefs, expectations, and social institutions.

. . . and Racist, Ageist, Ableist Stereotypes

In advertising images and much popular culture, sexuality is the prerogative of those who are young, slender, and able-bodied. Many images portray white women. Melba Wilson (1993) noted that racism and sexism converge in stereotypes of women of color as "exotic creatures of passion" (p. 66). Asian and Asian American women have been stereotyped as "exotic flowers," overly promiscuous and at the same time sexually accommodating and intent on serving men. A widely popular 1957 novel, *The World of Suzie Wong*, adapted for stage, film, and ballet, is a staple of this genre. It drew on and reinforced racist and sexist stereotypes of Asian women in its portrayal of a "bar girl" working in a Hong Kong hotel that catered to British and US sailors. Suzie Wong also personified another stereotype: the hooker with a heart of gold. Asian women, especially Filipinas, continue to work in bars and clubs near US bases in South Korea, for example, and in ports in Thailand and the Philippines used by the US navy for "rest and recreation." Cynthia Enloe (1990, 1993) emphasized male officials' shared assumptions about soldiers' predatory sexuality. Racist and sexist assumptions about Asian women—as exotic and sexually compliant—are an integral part of this system and are held both by individual soldiers and at the institutional level. T-shirts on sale near US bases in the Philippines in the 1980s and 1990s referred to women working in neighborhood bars and clubs as "Little Brown Fucking Machines Powered With Rice" (Santos 1992).

Sociologist Patricia Hill Collins (2004) argued that "ideas about hot-blooded Latinas, exotic Suzy Wongs, wanton jezebels" (p. 30) were used in contrast to notions of pure white womanhood, adopted in Europe and the United States. She continued:

> Civilized nation-states required uncivilized and backward colonies for their national identity to have meaning, and the status of women in both places was central to this endeavor. In this context, Black women became icons of hypersexuality.

More recently, Brittney Cooper (2017) has argued that Black women are defined as "always already sexually free, insatiable, ready to go, freaky, dirty, and by consequence unrapeable" (p. 54). In Reading 17, Ariane Cruz discusses a more nuanced rendering of Black female sexuality in *The Misadventures of Awkward Black Girl* by Issa Rae, which premiered on YouTube in 2011. The central character, J, a young Black woman living in Los Angeles, "channels her frustration over her dead-end job, irksome co-workers, profound social awkwardness, and difficult love life by writing and rhyming ferocious, profane raps" (Cruz 2015, p. 74). In this way, Cruz argues, the show challenges "dominant codes of Black female sexuality anchored in a foundation of pathology and policed by the politics of respectability, silence, and patriarchal heternormativity" (p. 73). Cruz situates her discussion in a wide historical and cultural context, which makes for a detailed and multilayered analysis of this show.

By contrast, older women of all racial groups and women with disabilities are stereotyped as sexless (see, e.g., Kaufman, Silverberg, and Odette 2003; Wilkerson 2011). Journalist Emily Yates (2016) notes the dearth of information about sexuality for young women with disabilities when she was growing up, as well as the lack of videos with subtitles, easy-to-read information, or images of bodies that reflected disability of any kind. She turned to the Internet searching for information on sexual positions that "would be possible without causing a great amount of pain" and now works with "The Love Lounge", an online site, where she generates the kinds of material she wishes she could have found when she was younger. She writes, "I'm much more than a girl in a wheelchair. I have the same tatts, tinted hair and love of fashion as many women my age, and I hope that others see that as well as the wheelchair."

Cultural limitations on women's sexuality and sexual expression can divide women across generations. In Reading 9, Nadine Naber describes the impact this had in her immigrant community where people of her parents' generation shared

> a tacit knowledge that *al Amerika* was the trash culture, degenerate, morally bankrupt, and sexually depraved. In contrast, *al Arab* (Arabs) were morally respectable—we valued marriage, family, and close relationships.

These tensions played out in struggles over young women's behavior, where women's bodies were key signifiers in a stereotyped distinction between Arabs and Americans. Psychologist Shamita das Dasgupta and pediatrician Sayantani DasGupta (1996), who are mother and daughter, describe the policing role expected of mothers in immigrant South Asian families:

> As Asian women of two different generations, we attest to the politically divisive and psychologically unbearable situation in which we have been placed. As daughters, we are faced with the choice of rejecting our community and culture or destroying our sexual selves. As mothers, we can be exiled as destroyers of community culture or be our daughters' prison guards. (p. 240)

Like Naber, these writers understand South Asian communities' control of young women's sexuality as an attempt to resist cultural erasure in the United States, and as a response both to the racism of this society and to patriarchal control within their own communities. They endorse Indian women's activism (against gender-based violence and for LGBTQ rights) as a way of creating a progressive South Asian space to "define our private selves as public and discover our collective power" (p. 241).

Objectification and Double Standards

As sex objects in advertising or popular culture, feminine-looking women are commonly portrayed as child-like or doll-like playthings, or as waiting for male heroes to notice them. These images flow from and reinforce patriarchal constructions of gender and sexuality that assume: heterosexuality is natural for women and men; men are the initiators in heterosexual encounters; and male sexuality is forceful and assertive. Traditionally, a woman has been expected to remain a virgin until marriage, untouched except by her husband, and this attitude is still strong in some communities in the United States and around the world. By contrast, men's sexual activity is assumed and accepted; after all, "boys will be boys."

This double standard—promoting men's sexuality and expecting women to be chaste—has resulted in the construction of "good" and "bad" women: virgins and whores. Literature professor Gloria Wade-Gayles (1993) learned this double standard growing up, but women in her Memphis neighborhood also divided men into two groups: good men who cared for their wives and families, and "dogs" (p. 84), who only "want one thing from a woman" (p. 85). This latter group included white men who cruised the neighborhood "in search of Black women who, they assumed, were naturally sensuous, sexually superior, and easy" (p. 84). Growing up in a Mexican American community, Sandra Cisneros (1996) wrote that *la Virgen de Guadalupe* was the model held up for girls. The boys "were fornicating like rabbits . . . while the Church . . . pointed us women toward our destiny—marriage and motherhood. The other alternative was *putahood*," being defined a whore (p. 48).

Girls may easily get a "bad reputation" and be condemned as "sluts" or "hos" espe-

© Rina Piccolo

cially in the age of the Internet (Tanenbaum 2015). Writers Leora Tanenbaum (2000) and Emily White (2002) found several reasons that US girls are labeled this way: they may be early developers, victims of rape, outsiders to the community, or targets of revenge. Some may be sexually active, but many are not. In response to this double standard, some women have sought to reclaim "slut" as a positive identification that emphasizes independence and sexual agency. SlutWalks are a public example, originating in Canada in reply to a Toronto police officer's comment that women should stop dressing like sluts to avoid being raped (Cooper 2017; Currans 2017). As the media zoomed in on angry, young, (mostly) white women, some of whom marched in their underwear, many feminists decried this action as playing into sexist stereotypes, as a display of white privilege, or because they believe the term *slut* cannot be reclaimed. Nevertheless, SlutWalks spread to Brazil, Costa Rica, India, Israel, Singapore, South Korea, Switzerland, and the United States, and they generated conversation and debate about victim-blaming and slut-shaming. Feminist writer Alice Walker commented:

> I've always understood the word "slut" to mean a woman who freely enjoys her own sexuality in any way she wants to, undisturbed by other people's wishes for her behavior. Sexual desire originates in her and is directed by her. In that sense it is a word well worth retaining. (quoted in Cooper 2017, p. 53)

Brittney Cooper (2017) remarked that since white women have been shamed and their sexuality disciplined by being called sluts, this dramatic response was necessary and powerful. She commented that as a Black woman, this particular put-down does not resonate for her, and noted the many names that a Black woman "who freely enjoys her own sexuality" has been called: "bitch," "jezebel," "hoochie," "ho," and more.

As well as the virgin/whore bind for females, trans woman Julia Serano (2008) notes a double bind for males: "assholes" who fulfill the sexual aggressor stereotype as opposed to "nice guys" who refuse it. She asks why women are attracted to the bad-boy stereotype and why "nice guys" are seen as desexualized and unmanly—nice enough as friends but not as boyfriends. Serano argues for a "movement that refuses to render invisible and desexualize men who are not predators" (p. 239). Similarly, bell hooks (1994) urged women to stop being seduced by men who are disrespectful, even violent.

Media Representations

Filmmakers and TV producers promote ideas of sexuality and may reproduce clichés and stereotypes that reinforce patriarchal norms, the objectification of women, sexual double standards, and the hypersexualization of women of color, especially African Americans. Popular culture provides a powerful forum for learning about sex and sexuality in the circulation of sexualized images, scenarios, and scripts. Some shows pushed the boundaries of what was then considered acceptable, such as MTV's *Spring Break*, Comedy Central's *The Man Show*, or the video series *Girls Gone Wild*, which featured young women on spring break in vacation resorts or nightclubs who agreed to show their bodies on camera in exchange for *Girls Gone Wild*–branded paraphernalia. Also, starting in the early 2000s, TV shows featuring LGBTQ people, such as *Will and Grace*, *Queer as Folk*, *The L Word*, and *Queer Eye for the Straight Guy*, attracted significant audiences. Diane Raymond (2003), a professor of philosophy and women's studies, argued that there are many ways to "read" these shows depending on viewers' own perspectives, as mentioned in Chapter 2.

Sociologist Gail Markle (2008) analyzed "sexual scripts" embedded in the comedy series *Sex and the City*, which debuted in 1998 and became an instant hit internationally. As successful thirty-something single women in Manhattan, the four main characters wanted to have sexual encounters like men, characterized as "without feeling, for pleasure only, and with no commitment" (p. 46). The show broke new ground in its explicit discussion of heterosexual women's sexuality, and it contributed to the cultural messages in circulation about female desire and sexual experiences. Twenty years after its debut, Jennifer Keishin Armstrong revisited *Sex and the City* to assess how it holds up in the #MeToo era (Reading 18). She argues that the show's "classic girl-talk scenes" modeled open talk about sex positions and relationships, which allowed viewers to think about their own likes and dislikes, as well as how to set clear boundaries "in the heat of a moment, or during the shock and confusion of a nonconsensual encounter." Although *Sex and the City* did not address issues of sexual assault and harassment, Armstrong sees it as a stepping-stone toward current understandings.

QUEERING SEXUALITY

People who identify as LGBTQI have long challenged the "normalcy" of heterosexuality, and researchers have dug back into history to show that same-sex relationships are nothing new (see, e.g., P. G. Allen 1986; Boswell 1994; Cavin 1985; Duberman, Vicinus, and Chauncey 1989; Faderman 1981; Feinberg 1996; Grahn 1984; History Project 1998). In Canada and the United States, two-spirit people—an English-language

iStock.com/Rawpixel Ltd

term for Native Americans who constitute a third gender—have been recognized for centuries and revered as medicine men, parental figures, ambassadors in negotiations with white colonists, and as holding important roles in ceremony (Deerinwater 2018; Feinberg 1996, ch. 3).

During the 1980s and 1990s, younger gays and lesbians reclaimed the word *queer*, which had been used as a hateful and oppressive term against lesbians and gay men (Bernstein and Silberman 1996). This is a broad term in current usage, with an emphasis on fluidity, experimentation, and playfulness, and it can include all who challenge **heteronormativity** and sexual binaries (see, e.g., Gage, Richards, and Wilmot 2002; Nestle, Howell, and Wilchins 2002; Rodríguez 2003). Nicholas Teich (2012), a trans-identified social worker, maintained that "[e]ven allies to the queer community can also identify on the queer spectrum" (p. 18).

What was defined forty years ago as a gay/lesbian movement has grown in size, complexity, and visibility. Currently, several terms include a range of gender and sexual identities. One is LGBTQQIA (lesbian, gay, bi, trans, queer, questioning, intersex, asexual). LGBTQ2SIA includes two-spirited people; LGBTSTGNC includes two-spirit and gender nonconforming people (Audre Lorde Project 2017). These growing lists seek to recognize the many ways people are defining themselves in terms of gender as it intersects with sexual orientation. Kim Katrin Milan comments, "I think about our acronym: LGBTQ2SIA. A seemingly endless evolution of self and . . . community, but also this really deep desire not to leave anyone behind" (Milan and Milan 2016). As understanding and practice continues to develop, new groups may be added.

"Queer" as a Catch-All?

Nicholas Teich (2012) made the point that "[q]ueer is an easy 'catch-all' word for those who are gay, lesbian, bisexual, transgender, questioning their sexuality or otherwise do not fit into the heterosexual or male/female binary worlds" (p. 16). Although they do not have a common base of experience, these groups all repudiate heteronormativity. Moreover, LGBTQI is an identity that seeks to bring sexually variant and nonconforming people together as a political community.

In practice, there are points of identification and agreement as well as areas of difference among the diverse group who might be called or call themselves queer. Some of these categories are more clearly based on gender. We see trans and intersex in this way. Trans and intersex people may choose any sexual orientation, including identifying as heterosexual. Other identifications are more directly related to sexual identity, sexual attraction, and sexual orientation. Many published accounts describe specific experiences of "coming out" as LGBTQI or of transitioning among genders or sexual orientations—experiences that are also inflected by class, race/ethnicity, age, dis/ability, national origin, and so on (see, e.g., Anzaldúa 1987; Boylan 2003; Eng and Hom 1998; Feinberg 1998; Halberstam 1998; R. Leong 1996; Rodríguez 2003; Serano 2013; B. Smith 1998; A. Stein 2018; Trujillo 1991).

The broad LGBTQI movement encompasses a range of goals and perspectives, including same-sex marriage, the rights of LGBTQI people to serve in the military, and the right for everyone to freedom of expression and self-definition. Different groups within this broad movement are not always allies. Lesbians—who may define themselves as high femme, butch, or gender nonconforming—may not relate to the term *queer* because it minimizes or erases their experience. Political science professor Sheila Jeffreys (2003) argued that within a mixed queer culture, "masculinity became the highest value," with lesbian feminism seen as "boring and unsexy" (pp. 30–31; also see Walters 1996). Queer politics incorporates critiques of heterosexuality but may not focus on patriarchy to the same extent. This raises the question of whether theoretical understandings developed by one group—in this case lesbian feminists—are insightful or even relevant for other groups, and of what is needed in order to create effective alliances (see Chapter 12 for more on this issue).

Queering Economies and Nation-States

Historian John D'Emilio (1984) pointed to the importance of various economic and social trends, as well as individual desires, in his analysis of US gay and lesbian communities in the 1980s. These factors included industrial development that boosted the growth of cities, technological advances like the contraceptive pill and other reproductive technologies, and decreasing family size. Together, he argued, these macro- and global-level forces created conditions "that allow some men and women to organize a personal life around their erotic/emotional attraction to their own sex" (p. 104). D'Emilio accepted that there have been same-sex partnerships for generations. However, he differentiated homosexual *behavior* from homosexual *identity* and argued that only under certain conditions are homosexual identity and community possible. Clare Hemmings (2002) also noted that cities with strong LGBTQI communities like Northampton, Massachusetts, and San Francisco, California, have provided supportive locations for such communities to take root and flourish. Other major US cities, and European cities like Amsterdam and London, all have neighborhoods that perform this same role.

Judith Halberstam (2005) pointed out that much queer theorizing has been centered on metropolitan areas like New York and San Francisco, and warned against simplistic urban assumptions of small towns as intolerant. Halberstam examined the life of Brandon Teena (Figure 4.1), a young white trans man who was killed while living in Falls City, Nebraska. Two films about his death—a documentary, *The Brandon Teena Story*, and a feature film, *Boys Don't Cry*— both implicated rural homophobia and **transphobia** in his killing though his girlfriends described him as a "dream guy."

Expanding this discussion in Reading 19, international relations scholar V. Spike Peterson reviews a broad swath of historical material to show how modern states have constituted and normalized binary sex/gender differences and heteropatriarchal kinship relations. The patri-

FIGURE 4-1   Hilary Swank plays Brandon Teena in *Boys Don't Cry* (1999).

Moviestore collection Ltd / Alamy Stock Photo

archal family/household has been the basic socioeconomic unit, regulating women's biological reproduction and policing sexual activities more generally. Thus, the family is the cornerstone of the nation, a claim made today by political theorists as well as politicians of many stripes. Peterson's goal is not to present an exhaustive history but to use available data to tell a different story that shows the centrality of sex/gender and sexualities in constituting and reproducing structural inequalities. Heteronormativity is political, she argues, both because it oppresses people who identify as nonheterosexual and also because state-making produces hierarchical sex/gender and related inequalities that are used to justify the domination of all who are stigmatized as feminine: women, "effeminate men," and "others."

DEFINING SEXUAL FREEDOM

Over the past twenty-five years, there has been increasing discussion of women's sexual needs and desires in books, blogs, and magazines (see, e.g., Boston Women's Health Book Collective 2011; Cox 1999; Ensler 1998; M. L. Johnson 2002; Muscio 1999; Queen and Rednour 2015; Rose 2003). Feminist debates about sexuality and power have focused on issues such as prostitution/sex work and pornography and whether women can experience these forms of sexuality as liberating (see, e.g., Chateauvert 2013; Dines 2010; Dworkin 1993; Feminist Anti-Censorship Task Force 1992; Kempadoo and Doezema 1998; Nagel 1997; Whisnant and Stark 2004).

What counts as sexual freedom varies among individuals and groups, and it may take different encounters and relationships for people to define it for themselves, as described by Daisy Hernández in Reading 16. Tiq Milan and Kim Katrin Milan (2016) talk about their "vision of love and marriage" as queer and trans people who are part of a community "living their authentic selves along the gender spectrum." The late June Jordan (1992), poet, essayist, and scholar, urged bisexuality and sexual freedom as part of a wider struggle for freedom and justice:

> If you are free, you are not predictable and you are not controllable. To my mind, that is the keenly positive, politicizing significance of bisexual affirmation: . . . to insist upon the equal validity of all the components of social/sexual complexity. (p. 193)

Currently, the Bisexual Resource Center (2019) explains bisexuality in more inclusive, less-binary terms:

> We use "bi" and "bi+" as inclusive terms for those who are non-monosexual/non-monoromantic and can include those who identify as bisexual, pansexual, omnisexual, fluid, queer, and asexual, among other free identifiers, including those who do not wish to use a label.

Radical Heterosexuality

Feminist thinkers have long argued that controlling sexuality is a key element in women's liberation. In 1873, Victoria Woodhull advocated "absolute and entire freedom" of sexuality for women (quoted in Kolmar and Bartowski, 2010, p. 88). Margaret Sanger (1920) urged women to take responsibility for birth control as a way to personal freedom. Anne Koedt (1973) dismissed Sigmund Freud's contention that vaginal orgasm is inherently superior and more mature than clitoral orgasm and noted: "The clitoris has no other function than that of sexual pleasure" (quoted in Kolmar and Bartowski, 2010, p. 187). Writer Naomi Wolf (2009) advocated what she called "radical heterosexuality," recognizing that for this to be possible women would need financial independence, marriage would have to be very different, and women and men would need to give up their "gender benefits." Sociologist Pepper Schwartz (1994) commented that in US culture, "male leadership and control is often assumed to be inherently erotic" (p. 70). By contrast, she advocated for more egalitarian sexual relationships. Shere Hite (1994) saw women as "revolutionary agents of change" in heterosexual relationships, working with men to renegotiate this intimate part of their lives.

For philosopher Marilyn Frye (1992), sexual freedom meant being "her own person." She remarked that

> the word *virgin* did not originally mean a woman whose vagina was untouched by any penis, but a free woman, one not betrothed, not married, not bound to, not possessed by any man. It meant a female who is sexually and hence socially her own person. (p. 133)

Lesbian feminists create ways of living this kind of virginity, and Frye questioned whether it is possible for heterosexual women unless they are willing to be wild and undomesticated—sexually, socially, and politically. As she put it, "Can you fuck without losing your virginity?" (p. 136).

Certainly, some heterosexual women repudiate a "nice girl" persona, perhaps by wearing skimpy outfits, T-shirts with a Playboy Bunny logo or PORN STAR across the chest, lap dancing, pole dancing, "stripper aerobics," or going to strip clubs and commercial sex parties (Levy 2005). The women interviewed by journalist Ariel Levy described these activities as fun, tongue-in-cheek, sexy, and empowering. Film producers, magazine editors, club owners and managers argued that "raunch culture" showed that feminist goals had been met, and that "it was time for us to join the frat party of popular culture where men had been enjoying themselves all along" (p. 4), though Levy questioned whether "equal opportunity" sexual freedom in a misogynist society is liberating for women.

This leads to wider questions about individual agency and the social structures we are part of. What space is there, given that we live in patriarchal and racist systems, for people of all genders and sexual orientations to pursue sexual pleasure free of dominant assumptions and practices? What kinds of contexts would facilitate and support this? To what extent is our thinking and behavior constrained by wider structures?

Eroticizing Consent

Many "women, queers, femmes, and female-identified people" are claiming the right to "express desire, to explore pleasure, to seek intimacy and adventure" on their own terms (Penny 2017, pp. viii–ix). And they are doing so despite the distortions, contradictions, double standards, and sexual violence of patriarchal cultures.

Whatever sexual practices people enjoy and engage in, many would agree that sexual freedom involves the notion of consent. "Yes" is only "Yes" when there is the option and agency for a meaningful "No" (Friedman and Valenti 2008). This might sound straightforward, but it is worth asking what considerations women weigh, if only fleetingly, as part of their "Yes." Is this "Yes" about maintaining a relationship they depend on materially or emotionally? Is it affected by peer pressure? Is it part of a person's self-image as loving, sexy, or liberated? Can a sexual relationship be consensual if there is a power differential between those involved? Writer and mental health advocate Joellen Notte (2017) argued that "going with the flow" is not consent. "Trying to be unobtrusive is not consent. Being afraid to bother anyone with your problem is not consent. . . . Hiding yourself to make someone else's life easier is not consent" (p. 13). Writer and poet Porscha Coleman (2017) noted that when people rely on the idea that sex "just happens" or "one thing leads to another," then "conversations about consent can range from blurry to nonexistent" (p. 26).

The #MeToo and #TimesUp movements have sparked new conversations on consent and sexual coercion (see Reading 59). Some men question how they are supposed to date, or even flirt, in the post-#MeToo era. One hundred prominent French women published a letter in *Le Monde*, a national daily, decrying #MeToo as threatening sexual freedom, valuing a culture of victimhood, and "absurdly puritanical" (Breeden and Peltier 2018). The letter included the comment:

> Bordering on ridiculous, in Sweden a bill was presented that calls for explicit consent before any sexual relations! Next we'll have a smartphone app that adults who want to sleep together will have to use to check precisely which sex acts the other does or does not accept. (*Le Monde* 2018)

Indeed, in the 1990s, Antioch College in Ohio introduced a policy that expected students to talk through a sexual encounter, giving verbal consent at each step (Gold and Villari 2000), and in 2014, the state of California enacted its own Affirmative Consent Law. In an anthology focused on creating a consent culture at home, in schools, at work, as well as in bed, Porscha Coleman (2017) cites a way of talking about and understanding consent that she attributes to Planned Parenthood. This is the FRIES model, where consent is Freely given, Reversible (anyone can change their mind at any time), Informed (you know what you are consenting to), Enthusiastic (YES!!! not just ummm), and Specific (you are consenting to this but not that) (p. 30).

The Erotic as Power

Black lesbian poet, teacher, and activist Audre Lorde discusses the power of the erotic in the broadest way in her now classic essay (Reading 20). She described the erotic as "our most profoundly creative source"—passion, energy, and aliveness that is physical, intellectual, emotional, and spiritual. She maintained that women have been "taught to separate the erotic . . . from most vital areas of our lives other than sex." By contrast, she wrote:

> When I speak of the erotic . . . I speak of it as an assertion of the life force of women: of that creative energy empowered, the knowledge and use of which we are now reclaiming in our language, our history, our dancing, our loving, our work, our lives.

Lorde saw the distortion and suppression of the erotic as a way that patriarchal cultures and institutions oppress women, and she concluded: "Recognizing the power of the erotic in our lives can give us the energy to pursue genuine change within our world . . ."

As Audre Lorde argued, dominant US culture takes a much more limited view of the erotic, reducing it to sexuality—and restricted or distorted notions of sexuality at that. Lorde was 50 years old when she wrote this essay. She was writing to women and used a binary conceptualization that many feminists would not use today. Nonetheless, this article shows a scholar trying to give language to ideas that were and are very different from mainstream views on this subject. Like much feminist theorizing of that era, this piece has been foundational to feminist ideas and politics since then. Thinking through this piece now, what does the erotic mean for LGBTQI people today, for heterosexual women and men, and for anyone who is male identified?

It is important to note that many females, as well as males, experience sexual coercion and abuse—in childhood, as adults, or both (see Chapter 6). Some people struggle for years with the devastating effects of sexual abuse on their self-confidence, ability to trust, and sense of sexuality. In Reading 26, Aurora Levins Morales refers to her childhood experience of sexual abuse and her path toward reclaiming what she calls "the wounded erotic." At the core of that process, she writes, is "blazing and untarnished aliveness."

Finally, a number of online educational and activist organizations provide information for young people about sexuality and health (e.g., Go Ask Alice, Scarleteen, Teenwire, and Youth Resource). The Asexual Visibility and Education Network (AVEN) provides information and connections for people who identify as asexual or are interested in learning about asexuality. Other groups and projects address issues of sexuality for LGBTQI people. Some provide information and social connections. Others run on-line publications; support political candidates for local, state, or national office; or oppose city and state ordinances designed to limit LGBTQI rights. Examples include BiNet USA (Arlington, VA); Old Lesbians Organizing for Change (Woodstock, NY); Trikone: Lesbian, Gay, Bisexual, and Transgendered South Asians (San Francisco); New York Association for Gender Rights Advocacy; the National Center for Transgender Equality (Washington, DC); the National LGBTQ Taskforce (Washington, DC); Unid@s: The National Latino/a LGBT Human Rights Organization (Washington, DC); and Outright International-LGBTIQ Human Rights (New York).

QUESTIONS FOR REFLECTION

As you read and discuss this chapter, think about these questions:

1. Do Shere Hite's questions, listed on page 139, help you to think about what sexuality means to you? What other questions do you have about sex?
2. How do you recognize if you are truly consenting? Under what circumstances are your "Yes" and "No" genuine and unconstrained?
3. What advice would you give to high school students about sexuality? Why?
4. How do you recognize the power of the erotic as described by Audre Lorde? Have you ever experienced that power? If so, under what circumstances? If not, why not?

FINDING OUT MORE ON THE WEB

1. Review the information about sexuality provided by organizations mentioned in this chapter.
2. The Web is a significant tool in the **commodification** of women through sexuality. Type "Philippine women" or "Asian women" into your search engine and see what comes up.
3. Research an organization mentioned in this chapter. What are its goals, strategies, and activities?
4. Analyze one or more UN human rights conventions and declarations for content on sexuality and sexual rights. If you were to write a UN declaration on sexual rights, what would you want to include and why?

TAKING ACTION

1. Write in your journal or have a candid conversation with a friend about your ideas and desires regarding sexuality and the erotic.
2. Examine the way female sexuality is represented in popular culture and public discourse, and analyze how these representations are gendered, raced, and classed.
3. Use the following hashtags developed by people with disabilities who are challenging negative assumptions about sexuality to claim your own sexuality as a person with a disability, a person in solidarity with the disability community, or both: #hotpersoninawheelchair, #babewithamobiltyaid, and #disabledandcute.

4. However you define your sexuality, participate in campus or community events to commemorate National Coming-Out Day (usually in October), Gay Pride (usually in June), and International Transgender Visibility Day (March 31).
5. Gather your friends and classmates to organize an educational event or day of action on your campus or in the community related to an aspect of sexuality that you and your co-organizers believe are important for others to know about.

16 EVEN IF I KISS A WOMAN (2014)

Daisy Hernández is the author of the award-winning memoir *A Cup of Water Under My Bed* (2014) and co-editor of *Colonize This! Young Women of Color on Today's Feminism* (2002). The former editor of *ColorLines* magazine, she has reported for *The Atlantic*, The *New York Times*, and *Slate*, published essays and fiction, and is a contributing editor for the Buddhist magazine *Tricycle*. She is an assistant professor in the Creative Writing Program at Miami University, Ohio.

My mother and tías warn me about dating Colombian men: *"Esos no sirven."* They say the same thing about the 1970s television set in our kitchen. "That TV *no sirve para nada.*" It doesn't work.

As a child, I think being married to a Colombian man will be like fighting with our old television. It only gets three channels, but we make it work because it is the one we have. We switch between channels by turning the knob with a wrench. Then we spin the antennas in circles, and when one points at the sink and the other out the window—past the clothesline with Tía Chuchi's three-dollar pants—we find it does work, and we have the telenovela *Simplemente María.*

Although my five uncles are in Colombia, phone calls between New Jersey and Bogotá bring stories of my charming, whiskey-drinking tíos and all the evidence for why Colombian men don't work. From the kitchen, my mother and aunties dictate warnings that over the years come to sound like twisted nursery rhymes.

> Colombian men get drunk, beat their women,
> cheat on their wives, and never earn enough
> money.
> They keep mistresses, have bastard children,
> and never come home on time.
> They steal, lie, sneak around, and come home
> to die,
> cradled in the arms of bitter wives.

The same could perhaps have been said about men in other countries, but it's easier to believe the worst about the people you know best.

At sixteen then, I know to stay away from Colombian men. I know that Julio is Colombian. But he works the grill at the McDonald's where I have my first after-school job and he winks at me. While I know the dangers of Colombian men, I have also been reading Harlequin romance novels since fifth grade, and I have been waiting for a man to wink at me. Men do this with beautiful women, and those women are always happy. They do not work at fast-food places. They get to go to college. They speak English perfectly and French as well.

Julio talks to me in Spanish. *Querida, mi amor, mi cielo.* In Spanish, there are so many words to love a woman—words I have never heard before. When things are slow in the kitchen, Julio stands behind me at the register and helps me with the orders. *"Ya mi amor, I got that for you. Get the next customer."*

I give him my phone number, which is to the say the number at my mother's house.

Most women stick to their own kind. They base love and their marriages on the lines drawn between countries. My high school friends have mothers from Chile, Perú, Ecuador, and Argentina, and these mothers have married men from their homelands. Some wed there and migrated together. Others met their husbands here in Jersey among friends, at a house party, a work place. Coming

Source: Republished with permission of Beacon Press, from Daisy Hernández, *A Cup of Water Under My Bed: A Memoir* (Boston, MA. Beacon Press, 2014); permission conveyed through Copyright Clearance Center, Inc.

from the same country was the start of connection, the entry point to love.

The women in my family do not believe in such intimacies.

My mother married my Cuban father, Tía Rosa settled with a Puerto Rican, and Tía Dora a Peruvian. They married men with dark eyes and *papeles*, men whose wallets had Social Security cards. Tía Chuchi never bothered with any man since everyone knows that God is the only man who truly works.

The women in my family then teach me a complicated formula of what works with men. My father's alcoholism is better than womanizing or, worse, a man who can't hold down a job. My Peruvian uncle is snobbish at times, but he drives a Chevrolet and takes us to Great Adventure, Action Park, and Niagara Falls. My Puerto Rican uncle is fat and has kids from a first marriage, but he reads tarot cards and cooks a good *arroz con pollo* for Thanksgiving. Finally, God does nothing to stop the war in Colombia, but he is reason enough for Tía Chuchi to wake up early every morning and have someone to think about other than the *violencia* over there and the unemployment lines here.

My mother and aunties advise me on what to look for in love:

> A man with a college degree is best, but choose white over black because no one sees the diploma on the street, in churches, and at the *supermercados*.
>
> Forget Caribbean men. They want sex all the time, speak Spanish with missing syllables, and if they are not black, their grandmothers might be.
>
> Forget Central Americans. They want sex all the time, do not grow any taller, and if they are not *indios*, their grandmothers might be.
>
> Consider Argentineans. They want sex all the time, but most are white, have law degrees, and if they are not Italian, their grandmothers might be.
>
> Remember to ask if he grew up in the *capital* or some no-name *campo*. It is the difference between marrying the Bronx and Fort Lee.

When Julio begins calling, I get under the bedcovers with the telephone receiver. My mother and aunties roll their eyes, sure that it is a passing interest. They are certain I will marry American. Anything made in America works. The cars, the washing machines, the light bulbs, even the men.

Of course, they hear the same accusation, "*Esos no sirven*," hurled at Americans. They even know a woman who left her husband and children for an Americano. Months later, the gringo dumped her.

"No better than a Colombian," declares Tía Dora, tucking a stray hair behind her ear. "He wanted her for you know what *y nada más*."

But it is the Colombian men that my mother and aunties knew best. In our kitchen, they are the guiltiest.

Julio is a paradox for my family. He has hazel eyes and pale skin and looks more American than the Italians who run my mother's factory. He calls my mother Doña and returns from fishing trips with trout for my father. My mother is suspicious; my father delighted about the free seafood.

Six months later, my tías and mother don't know what to say. The last time a woman in our family dated a Colombian was almost two decades earlier in a country where that was the only choice. My mother gives me an accusatory look that calls to mind the writings of Achy Obejas: "We came all the way from Colombia so you could date this guy?"

I continue dating Julio, however, because I am confident in the love of the women in my family. Despite their dictates about men, my mother and aunties teach me that our primary ties are to each other as women. The four of them rely on each other for the cleaning, the shopping, the respite of a good *chisme*. It's a woman who will fry you a good salty *bistec*, and it's a woman, a sister, who has now pulled out the sofa bed in the living room, because Tía Rosa's husband left and a commuter van hit her on Kennedy Boulevard, leaving my auntie in the middle of the street like a mashed-up bird. She's been released from the hospital and has come to live with us.

In a home run by women, I hold high court. The three aunties have no children of their own, and as the first born to my mother, I am *la consentida* and also their American brat. National identity can carry many meanings; in our home, it is a get-out-of-jail-free card that extends to dating a Colombian man. Everyone—my mother, my tías, and even me—we blame my transgressions on my American side.

My own concerns, though, have to do with another border. I am a virgin, and Julio has said he will wait until I am ready. I expect to be ready soon.

The women in my family do not talk to me about sex, and women's magazines do not mention poverty or race. My mother and tías tell me that men either work for you or they do not. Romance happens between seven and nine in the evening on Spanish soap operas. Sex comes later.

But at the library, I read the truth about multiple orgasms in *Cosmo*. I rely on a library copy of Judy Blume's novel *Forever* to tell me I can have sex with a boy and not marry him. Something can happen between a broken hymen and baby showers. College and a career, of course, but mostly it will be a lot of sex. My best friend and I spend our teenage summers reading Judith Krantz novels and watching porn videos from her father's collection. We see that women can have sex in swimming pools and hotel rooms and even on a spaceship. They can do it with different men and with each other. I observe this, analyze it, and come to my final conclusion: sex is good.

By the time I watch women have sex with each other on my friend's nineteen-inch TV set, I have already heard about women like them.

I am ten years old and sitting at the kitchen table when a friend of my mother's tells her and the tías the latest *chisme*: a woman they all know from the neighborhood has left her husband and children to be with another woman. Gasps make their way around the kitchen table where *café con leche* is being served.

"Can you believe it?"

"She's that way?"

"I never would have thought it!"

Everyone is shocked that a woman was so moved by love that it flung her into the arms of another woman. I, for one, find it terribly romantic. It's like a Harlequin romance novel but without the stoic, rich guy, or like *Romeo and Juliet* but without the suicides. Two women in love confirms for me

that there is a love that can push you beyond what everyone else says is possible.

I am also not sure why the women in my family are so startled about a woman going off with another *mujer*. Besides discussing how Colombian men don't work, all we ever do at home is talk about women.

There are two types of women in this world. The telenovela one is a fair-skin lovely who works as a maid, suffers public humiliations, and marries her well-to-do man in the last episode. Then, there is Iris Chacón.

On Saturdays, my family gathers to watch a variety show on Spanish-language television, where Iris Chacón is all sequined thong and big brown ass, and salsa is a side note. She is a curve of glitter on the screen, an exaggeration turned into art of what it means to be a woman, and we are very much in love with her. Or at least, my father and I are.

My mother and tías talk endlessly about Iris Chacón.

"Look at her *tetas*!"

"*Qué grandes, no?*"

"And her backside!"

"*Cómo lo mueve!*"

They discuss other dancers and performers, debating who has silicone implants and fake behinds. I stare at the screen, wondering how real Iris Chacón is.

"She might as well wear nothing!" my mother declares, as if to chastise us for looking.

My father and I nod but keep our eyes on the screen, grateful that the reception is good on the old television set.

After a year of dating, I am very much in love with Julio, his old white Camaro with its black doors, and the tender way he kisses me. He takes me down the shore at night when the world is flooded with stars and the sound of crashing waves, and life feels so much bigger than what I ever imagined. I am seventeen and in love.

I am also beginning to resent my mother and tías for finding any fault in a man who takes me to the movies, the mall, and upscale versions of McDonald's, like Houlihans. The more they raise their dark eyebrows and ask if Julio ever plans to attend college and amount to anything more than a fast-food job, the more I call him and tell him I will love him forever.

Sex is a different matter.

Growing up in a small town where love easily means nine months of *gordura* and no high school graduation, I am determined not to become a teenage mother. I tell Julio that sex between us shall happen after my high school graduation, when I am on my way to college with a four-year scholarship.

I then go about sex like the overachiever from a working-class home I truly am. First, I start taking the pill. Then, I drag Julio to the local clinic to be tested for HIV. There, I carefully read the pamphlets on STDs and abortions. I pepper the counselor with questions. I check the expiration dates on the condoms and examine the rubbers for visible signs of tears. Finally, I am ready.

Sex with a man is like what I have read in books and *Glamour*. There is suspense and need, an aching and much throbbing. There is *el* spot, and when Julio touches it, I understand immediately that this is the reason women cheat on their men, risk their corporate jobs, and abandon their children. And that Judy Blume was right, too. Something else could happen.

By the time I start wearing a fake gold chain that proclaims "Julio [heart] Daisy 2-14-91," my mother and aunties refuse to speak to him. It only makes me want him more. At nineteen, I move in with him, setting up our home in a basement apartment while commuting to college and working two part-time jobs. I love Julio against all odds, but mostly against the wishes of my mother and tías.

When we break up a year later, Julio says my mother was right. He feared what she desired: that I would leave him for the guy with more money and a better car. Guilt-ridden, I tell him he's wrong. The other guy understands me better. He's also in college and a writer.

But Julio is right. The other guy does have a better car. He didn't emigrate from Colombia and he has the money to attend college. He's not Italian, but his grandmother is.

How did I end up heeding my mother's warnings? Were the romance novels wrong? Does love follow the lines of race and class?

To the degree that I am disturbed, my mother and tías are delighted. Finally, I am listening to them. I am in college, living back home, working part-time at a newspaper, and dating a gringo.

The sign in the student center at William Paterson College reads "Workshop on Sexuality for Women * Hosted by the Feminist Collective."

I would like to say now that the afternoon, which changed my life, was cinematic. But it wasn't. One night, I was in the arms of my new boyfriend; the next afternoon, I was sitting in a carpeted room with other college girls, giggling, fully clothed, drawing portraits of our vulvas.

The facilitator, a woman from Planned Parenthood, is genuinely cheerful and unfazed by our work. "That's it everyone! You're doing great!" she calls out. "Fanny, that's beautiful! I love the colors. Keep going! We've got crayons for everyone! Don't be shy."

I glance up and down the table. All the women are drawing vulvas in startling shapes and colors and spending time on the size and details of their clitorises. So engrossed in staring, I almost don't hear the Latina sitting next to me when she starts talking.

Fanny is the president of the Feminist Collective and she's encouraging me to attend the group's weekly lunch meetings. I nod politely, but I'm too preoccupied with the portrait of another woman's vulva, which looks like strawberries that have been plucked, washed, and pried opened.

Fanny introduces me to the white woman sitting next to her, saying, "This is my girlfriend."

Maybe it's the rich colors of all those vulvas in one room or the slow and purposeful way she says "girlfriend," but I understand her immediately. And as I nod at Girlfriend, I think, "I have never met one." A lesbian.

Lesbians happen on television like Iris Chacón. They belong to another country. The idea of actually kissing a girl has never occurred to me. As Fanny and Girlfriend peck each other ever so lightly on the lips, I feel so embarrassed and enthralled that I frantically look around for a place to put my eyes.

Finding nothing, I stare down at the crayon drawings of their vulvas.

What is wrong with me? *Qué me pasa?* Why had it never occurred to me? A girl. I love kissing boys, but a girl. I could kiss a girl. The facilitator passes by, murmuring, "Daisy, why don't you add some colors, open it up."

I look down and it's there for the whole world to see: my vulva. I have drawn a small brown mound, a little hill speckled with black ants for curls.

Not sure of where to meet a girl I can kiss, I head for the weekly meetings of the Feminist Collective. I dress in what I think are my best plaid shirts, but instead of meeting a girl, I find myself immersed in women's rights. We talk about sexual abuse, organize our school's Take Back the Night, and analyze the importance of lube. The women's studies professor gives us impromptu talks about the fluidity of gender identity and desire, and it is all I can do to sit still next to the girl who looks like a boy.

It is the mid-nineties and multicultural everything is in. I have the books, the teachers, and the new friends to teach me that being queer is about as normal as me being a Latina at a predominantly white college. Sure, Latinas and queers are outnumbered, but now the laws are on our side, and we have a small but visible community.

The more I listen to Fanny talk about her life with a woman, the more comfortable I also feel. She knows about Audre Lorde and *arroz con frijoles*, and she throws a Spanish word into the conversation every now and then. She is close enough to remind me of home, the equivalent of my mother and aunties in one woman, with the lesbian and feminist parts added.

The worst part about trying to date women is that I don't have my mother's warnings. There is no indicator if I am doing it right or wrong. And so, my queer friends and the spoken-word artists in New York are my teachers, and they know the formula.

Sleep with your friend, sleep with her friend.
Break up and get back together again.
Write her a poem, show her the piers, pretend
    you want less than you do.

One-night stands, one-night nothing.
You'll see her at Henrietta's again and again.

My friend is Dominican, and she reminds me of Iris Chacón. When we make love, I can't tell what's more exciting: her large, naked breasts against my own B-cup–sized ones or the inversion afterwards of gender roles. I am now the one buying dinner, picking up the flowers, driving us upstate. Every time she mixes Spanish and English in the same sentence, a part of myself collapses into what I am sure is eternal love.

Within months, however, the relationship sours. So, I try dating another friend. She e-mails that she isn't interested.

I go out with a Puerto Rican butch, who drinks about as many Coronas as my father. My mother and aunties would be horrified. I am too, after two months.

I meet another Dominican femme, but this one drives an SUV, has her hair straightened once a week, and keeps a butch lover in the Bronx. After three times in bed, I get tired of being on top.

Dating a transgender man, I get tired of being on the bottom.

I go back to what I know and try dating a Colombian woman. But she lives across the Hudson River and doesn't have a phone with long distance.

I persevere though—drinking flat Diet Coke at lesbian bars and giving women my phone number—because I do not believe my mother. I have read the romance novels, seen the movies, and heard the songs. Love will work no matter what job I have, what nationality I claim, or what street I want to live on. It will work even if I kiss a woman.

And it does.

For a few months, I fall in love with a dark-haired woman who has a way of tilting her bony hip that gives her ownership of the room. Men hit on Lisette and she snaps, "I don't think my girlfriend would appreciate that." She is the most feminine woman I have dated (hours are spent dabbing eye shadow in multiple directions), but also the most masculine. She carries my bags, buys me overpriced jeans, leans in to kiss me. She talks to me about the films she will make one day and the books I will write. She follows me into the dressing room at Express and whispers that she wants to go down on me right there. "I like it when you scream," she tells me in bed. "I need you to do it like this morning. Scratch my back when I'm fucking you."

I had heard those lines before from men and from women, but it's different this time. I am sure I will never date anyone else ever again.

When she breaks up with me (yes, by e-mail), I don't know if I am crying over her or because I can't talk about it with Mami and Tía Chuchi and Tía Dora and Tía Rosa, the first women I loved. Instead, I tell them it is the rigors of graduate school that now make me sob in my mother's arms in the middle of a Tuesday afternoon.

After another night of crying about lost love, I call my mother into my bedroom. Unsure of where to begin, I choose the logical. "Mami," I begin in Spanish, "it's been a long time since I've had a boyfriend."

She nods and gives me a small smile.

I look at the pink wall of the bedroom I have in my parent's home, the writing awards, the Ani DiFranco CDs, the books. "*Estoy saliendo con mujeres.*" I'm dating women.

Her mouth opens, but no sound comes out. She covers her heart with her right hand in a pose similar to the one of the Virgin Mary that hangs over the bed she shares with my father.

"Mami, are you ok?"

"*Ay, Dios mío.*"

When she doesn't say anything else, I fill the silence between us with a concise history of the LGBT, feminist, and civil right movements, which combined have opened the door to higher education, better laws, and supportive communities of what would be otherwise marginalized people. "It's because of how hard you worked to put me through school that I am fortunate enough to be so happy and make such good decisions for myself."

By this time, my mother is hyperventilating and fanning herself with her other hand. She stammers, "I've never heard of this. This doesn't happen in Colombia."

"You haven't been in Colombia in twenty-seven years."

"But I never saw anything like this there."

In the days that follow, Tía Chuchi accuses me of trying to kill my mother.

We're on the phone. She's at Tía Dora's apartment. As if it's not enough that I am murdering my mother, Tía Chuchi adds with grim self-satisfaction: "It's not going to work, *sabes*? You need a man for the equipment."

For this, I am ready. I am not being sassy. I really do believe she doesn't know and that I can inform her. "Tía, you can buy the equipment."

She breaks out into a Hail Mary and hangs up the phone.

My mother develops a minor depression and a vague but persistent headache. She is not well, the tías snap at me.

"Don't say anything to her!" barks Tía Dora over the phone. "The way this woman has suffered I will never know."

But she wants me to know.

Tía Dora stops talking to me. She throws away a gift from me because she can see that the present (a book on indigenous religions in Mexico) is my way of trying to convert her to loving women. Tía Chuchi begins walking into the other room when I arrive home. Tía Rosa alludes to the vicious rumors the other two aunties have started about me. "It's terrible," she says, and then: "*Siéntate, siéntate.* I made you *buñuelos* just the way you like. Are you hungry?"

Tía Rosa still complains about the back pains from the accident of years before, but she is living in her own apartment again. In her sixties now, she is a short, robust woman with thick eyeglasses and hair the color of black ash. Her husband is long gone, and since the bed is half empty, Tía Rosa has covered the mattress with prayer cards. Every night, she lies down on that blanket made of white faces, gold crosses, and pink-rose lips.

That my romantic choices could upset my mother and tías had been a given since high school. A lot can be said about a woman who dates the wrong man. But dating the same sex or dating both sexes has no explanation.

My mother now is hurt. More than anything, she is bruised, and she wonders what she did wrong. "This isn't what we expected," she says quietly one day as we walk toward Bergenline Avenue to catch the bus.

I keep thinking that if only I could tell my mother how it works with women, she would understand. The problem is I don't know.

The closest I have to an explanation is a Frida Kahlo painting titled *The Two Fridas*, where the artist is sitting next to her twin who holds her heart, an artery, and a pair of scissors. That is how I feel about loving women. They can dig into you and hold the insides of you, all bloodied and smelly, in their hands. They know you like that. But this is nothing I can say to my mother.

I miss the conversations now. More than anything, I long for the days when I came home to report that Julio had given me flowers or promised to take me to Wildwood. We have, my family and me, including my father (who demanded to know if Julio was gay the whole time), settled into a region called "Don't Ask, Don't Tell." And it is hard, I imagine, for people who have not experienced this to understand the weight of that silence and how the absence of language can feel like a death.

Often when my mother tells me about those early days in her relationship with my father, she mentions the *postres*.

"He would bring pastries from the bakery," she recalls, smiling and then adding with a warning, "That's how they get you."

Kristina does it with *dulce de leche*.

Our first date is a month after September 11. The city is struggling to be normal. The subways are running and the *New York Times* is publishing its "Portraits of Grief." Kristina and I eat burritos on Christopher Street and walk to the piers. In the summers, brown butches and black divas light up the area, their bodies pretzeled around their loves and friends and strangers, but tonight the piers are empty, muted, *solitos*. With the bone skeleton of lower Manhattan near us and Jersey's lights across the river, Kristina and I kiss for the first time.

She's mixed: white, Chicana, Californian, New Mexican. She reminds me of the women in my family, the shape of their bodies, *ni gorda ni flaca*. It's how quick she lights up when I say, "I've got *chisme*," and the way she talks to her mother on the phone and then laughs and says to me: "I'm on hold. Walter Mercado's on."

This is our routine: I take a bus from Jersey, then switch to the 1 train. She meets me at the stop near her apartment in the Bronx. We make love. Afterwards, Kristina rolls over on her side and asks, "You want some ice cream?"

She dresses and crosses the street to the deli for small cups of *dulce de leche*. I eat the cold caramel on her sofa, my head on her shoulder, crying into the *helado*, because Halle Berry has won the Oscar.

My mother would like Kristina. She would probably like her more than she likes me. Kristina believes in diplomacy. Like my mother, she doesn't see why I need to write about sexuality. She values privacy. My mother would appreciate that.

When Kristina and I break up, almost five years after we first ate *dulce de leche* together, I call Tía Chuchi to deliver the news. "We've ended," I say in Spanish. "For good this time."

I don't know what to expect from my auntie, but I'm figuring she will say something along the lines of good riddance. Instead, she exclaims, "That's why you're taking the martial arts class!"

"What?"

"That's why you're taking martial arts. I knew this woman who rented a room once from a lady and it turned out the lady was, *tu sabes*, gay." The lesbian had terrible fights with her partner. "It was horrible," my auntie recalls, as if she had been in the room when the arguments exploded. "They threw pots and pans at each other and fought with their fists." Tía sighs. "It's good you're taking the martial arts classes to defend yourself."

I start laughing and crying, because my ex-girlfriend couldn't face a kitchen mouse let alone strike another woman, because I loved her so much and walked away, because I glimpse in my tía's words some deeper emotion, some love that struggles to be steady even when it hurts.

ARIANE CRUZ

17 (MIS)PLAYING BLACKNESS: RENDERING BLACK FEMALE SEXUALITY IN *THE MISADVENTURES OF AWKWARD BLACK GIRL* (2015)

Ariane Cruz is Associate Professor of Women's, Gender, and Sexuality Studies at Pennsylvania State University. She teaches classes on feminist visual culture, racialized sexuality, and representations of race, gender, and sexuality. Her publications include articles on black female sexuality in *Camera Obscura*, *The Feminist Porn Book*, *Hypatia*, and *Women & Performance*. Her first book is *The Color of Kink: Black Women, BDSM, and Pornography* (2016).

The *Misadventures of Awkward Black Girl (ABG)*, which premiered on YouTube on February 3, 2011, is a comedy web series that chronicles the life and times of J, a young Black woman living in Los Angeles played by actor/producer/director/writer Issa Rae. Two seasons and twenty-five episodes later, *ABG* has transformed from a self-funded "guerrilla style" project into an award-winning web series with a sizable and devoted fan following, a professional staff, significant media coverage, and financial investors (both public and private).[1] *ABG* has come a long way from its humble grassroots origins and has projected Rae beyond the realm of web celebrity status. . . . She has been the focus of media attention on blogs and websites, as well as CNN, NBC, NPR, the *New York Times*, the Associated Press, *BET, Vibe* magazine, *Essence* magazine, *Jet*, the *Huffington Post, Rolling Stone*, and *Forbes*.[2] In addition to establishing Rae as a web series guru and a veritable force in American popular entertainment, *ABG* has transformed the web series into "legitimate entertainment" and has profoundly challenged prevailing representations (and lack thereof) of Black women in American popular culture.[3]

ABG is a dynamic example of Black women's use of new media to challenge dominant codes of Black female sexuality anchored in a foundation of pathology and policed by the politics of respectability, silence, and patriarchal heteronormativity. The show paints a complex and contradictory portrait of Black female sexuality that is simultaneously unwieldy and easily consumed, hyper-racialized and deracialized, unique and universal, aggressive and diffident. . . .

When the character J first started spinning around in Rae's head two years before she created the show, she consciously set out to challenge hegemonic and trite paradigms of Black womanhood. Twenty-seven-year-old Senegalese American Rae—who graduated from Stanford with a BA in African American Studies and Political Science and studied filmmaking at NYU—aimed to challenge the "pop cultural idea [*or better yet ideal*] of Blackness" and fill a void in the televisual rendering of Black womanhood.[4] This gap is primarily addressed through the main character, J, a young Black woman living in Los Angeles, who channels her frustration over her dead-end job, irksome co-workers, profound social awkwardness, and difficult love life by writing and rhyming ferocious, profane raps. J's failed sexual relationships are the core of this romantic comedy. The "awkward" in the show's title is performed via moments of sexual liaison: getting dumped, sleeping with a co-worker, choosing between two suitors (one white and the other Black), and experiencing difficulty consummating a new relationship. It is the fractured, bipolar composition of timorous, gawky proletarian and aggressive, outspoken "ratchet" MC that makes J such a magnetic character and enables Rae to both recite and rebuff prevailing stereotypes of Black female sexuality, while simultaneously adhering to politics of respectability and bucking these conventions.[5] Indeed, what is most fascinating about the character J is her ambivalence: her simultaneous perpetuation and contestation of stereotypes and representations of blackness within the dominant socio-cultural imagination all within the span of an episode. Moreover, J effects an urgent self-representation, an "exaggerated" version of Rae and her experiences: "it was more for me, for representation of me," Rae notes, "because it . . . filled a void that I just didn't see in media."[6] Rae imagines J as "the Black Liz Lemon," a similarly socially maladroit female character in the highly acclaimed NBC sitcom *30 Rock*.[7] Rae "relate[s] to Jerry Seinfeld's pet peeves or Liz Lemon's insecurities, but it bothers [her] that there aren't people of color in those roles."[8] In the tradition of Black female racial sexual alterity and its performance on screen by an enduring though evolving set of stereotypes—mammies, sapphires, jezebels, matriarchs, tragic mulattas—this awkwardness is a different kind of difference. J's awkwardness, that is, represents a different enactment of exclusion, deviance, nonbelonging, otherness, outsiderness, and marginalization than previously seen in the tradition of Black women's representation.

The Power of Awkwardness

Rae relies on universality, as she consistently deracializes the character J and, through her, the show itself. In various interviews she posits this universality through the trope of awkwardness. . . . In . . . interviews Rae confirms the racial dilution of awkwardness, stating that "even though J is Black, the things she goes through are universal" and that "awkwardness doesn't have a race."[9] This deracialization is significant for many reasons. First, it is contradictory. In many interviews, Rae is outspoken about having created J in response to a dearth of Black female characters in mainstream television and *ABG* as a political project of Black (self) representation and reinvention. It conflicts with

the title and much of the plot, which chronicles the quotidian happenings of an awkward Black girl, not just an awkward girl. This quasi-colorblind notion of universality defies the unique events J experiences as a Black woman. For example, she must field racist questions about her hair from her (white) boss, Boss Lady, and has to throw up her "nigga shield." Part of this colorblindness comes, I contend, from Rae's desire to market the show in a way that appeals to wide and diverse audiences. We could read this universalizing tendency as a sort of sales technique. A similar impetus of deracialization resounds in Black female screenwriter/director/producer Shonda Rhimes's description of her Black female protagonist Olivia Pope, played by actress Kerry Washington on the hit ABC drama *Scandal*. Rhimes describes this first African American female lead on a major network television show in thirty-eight years as "any human being . . . who happened to be born female and Black."[10] Like Rae, Rhimes wrote her Black female lead into being with the hope of changing both prevailing images and the collective imaginings of Black women.[11] . . . [N]otions of colorblindness that Rhimes and Rae articulate are not necessarily evidence of either a modernist racial ideology or postracial politics in contemporary American television; rather, it represents an urgent, if even veiled, campaigning for recognition of Black women's humanity.[12]

This universalizing tendency signals both the limits of our collective imagination in envisioning Black women and the enduring legacy of oppressive images of Black women in popular entertainment. Where are the boundaries of our vision when it comes to conceiving Black womanhood? What does it mean for Blackness, Black femininity, and Black female sexuality to be universal? What kind of Black womanhood is not universal? I am especially interested in these questions, the identity politics that animate such inquiries, and how awkwardness mediates performances of Black female racial and sexual authenticity on *ABG*. If awkward is something that Black people are not or should not be—as another web series, *Black Folk Don't* (which also comically explores Blackness, authenticity, and the notion that "Black folk don't do awkward"), suggests—J's awkwardness seems to dis-authenticate her Blackness. Yet, Black womanhood remains ultimately legible through its non-belonging however comic.[13] I read J's awkwardness, what Rae calls "the idea of being a social misfit," as being both prompted by her Blackness and instantiating it. If we understand Blackness to be a state of nonbelonging, abjection, and marginalization, then we might read J's awkwardness as a characteristic of her Blackness and not as a quality that somehow nullifies it.

The first episode of season 1, "The Stop Sign," depicts an important sequence of events, the first of which is J's reading of the stop sign itself. She states, "The stop sign: to any ordinary person, it's a simple sign of direction, but for me it's the epitome of social misdirection, because I am awkward." More than cueing J's signature style of self-depreciating self-analysis via the voice-over as a primary narrative mode, which evidences Spike Lee's influence on her work (Rae produced and staged two theatrical adaptations of Lee's films while at Stanford), this confession asserts her awkwardness as a misplay while establishing *ABG* as a deliberate project on the nature of belonging that, in turn, makes evident its investment in the ontology of Black women. It is a critical moment of legibility: not just how we read J but also of how she reads broadly. The second event is J's introduction of herself, a performative declarative utterance of Blackness and awkwardness executed through her statement "My name is J and I'm awkward . . . and Black. Someone once told me those were the two worst things anyone could be." . . . This proclamation is a critical moment of Black female subject constitution and self-narration. As such, J's performative declaration resonates with what Henry Louis Gates Jr. identifies as the Black American's urgent need to write himself (herself) into "the human condition" in and through the genre of the slave narrative as a testament of Black female humanity.[14] Echoing the slave narrative's characteristic opening statement, "I was born," J's narrative is one of both self-definition and self-constitution.[15] But what do we not hear in this critical J's assertion? While the title *Awkward Black Girl* explicitly announces a specific gender, J's affirmation, her introduction of self, lacks any assertion of or reference to gender. If being Black and awkward are "the two worst things anyone [can] be," we are left with the oft-cited words of Janie's grandmother in Hurston's *Their Eyes Were Watching God* ringing in our ears: "De Nigger woman is de mule uh de world so fur as Ah can see."[16] What happens when female is added to the mix?[17] Hearing how Rae echoes the voices of her African American literary ancestors allows us to not only place *ABG* in a vibrant lineage of African American cultural production and critical artistic self-authorship, it also inspires us to take pop culture and new media seriously in this continuing project of Black reinvention. . . .

Against Ratchets: New Kind of Single Lady?

Pharrell Williams is one of Rae's most enthusiastic fans and one with the deepest pockets. The three-time Grammy award–winning rapper, singer, composer, producer, and fashion designer is now a media empire potentate and the executive producer of *ABG*. Williams says, "When I saw the show I didn't see . . . this Black woman catering to that annoying characterization that you see on every television show, . . . you saw someone that was incredibly honest."[18] . . . Williams's comment highlights two themes that recur in critical reviews of the show: stereotypes and authenticity. The common view is that *ABG* projects less stereotypical (less galling) images of Black women and that these new representations are somehow less trite and more real because of their non-recital of such stereotypes. Although J is a critical intervention in the popular stereotype of the single lady that permeates the televisual topography of Black female representation, she challenges, through her ratchet alter ego, prevailing paradigms of Black female sexuality as pathological.

As the phrase "single ladies," the title of both Beyoncé's 2008 quadruple platinum hit song and a VH1 sitcom suggests, Black women's solitary romantic status is a hot issue in American popular culture. The low marriage rates of Black women, especially those who are financially successful and highly educated, has recently received attention in the media and academia.[19] . . . Despite studies that suggest that Black women prioritize their educational development and standard of living, other sources posit that Black women are at fault for their single status. Televisual performances of single Black womanhood, in "reality" TV in particular, represent Black women as complicit in their own loneliness, thereby condemning them as unsuitable, idealistic, and impossible (unloving and unlovable) partners.

The character J is distinct in a reality television landscape that is dominated by shows such as *Basketball Wives*, *Single Ladies*, *Love & Hip Hop* (all on VH1), and *The Real Housewives of Atlanta* (Bravo), wherein romantic relationship drama reigns, animosity prevails between Black women and their (Black) men, and Black women's sexual labor eclipses their actual labor. J challenges these prevalent characterizations of single ladies on multiple fronts. Her awkwardness mediates her Blackness as a kind of performance of racial authenticity. Moreover, J also challenges stereotypes about class, physicality, and sexuality. She is definitively working class, and her work is an important element of the show's narrative, much of which revolves around J's nine-to-five job as a telephone salesperson at Gut Buster, a company that sells weight-loss products.

She looks nothing like most single ladies we see in the visual media (she wears very little makeup and has no weave, no cocktail dresses, no Louboutins, no implants, and no bling). With her darker skin and short natural hair, she may be seen as resisting Western ideals of beauty, body, and skin color. Mistaken for a butch lesbian in season 2, episode 1 ("The Sleepover"), she asks, "Is there a non-homophobic way to tell someone you're not gay?" This reveals that J often reads as if not queer, then queer-allied, and while she resists popular stereotypes of Black female sexuality, she succumbs to sexual hierarchies. Indeed, her fervent denial of lesbianism through statements such as "no lesbo" and "pussy tastes like fish, fish, fish . . . no homo" represents more than just a reassertion of her heterosexuality; it is a reinstatement of institutional heteronormativity.

Unlike her wanton single-lady sisters, J presents a reserved, inexperienced, and, yes, incredibly awkward approach to sex and sexuality. *ABG* works

against the prevailing image of Black women perpetrated by reality television as not just unlucky in love but unlovable because of their bellicosity and aggression. In a domain where Black womanhood is characterized as physically and verbally hostile . . . , J embodies a kind of self-antagonism. The wars she wages are staged in the psychic battleground of her exceedingly active imagination, not in physical fisticuffs with others. While she is not the pugnacious drama queen we are accustomed to seeing, J enacts the prevailing single-lady construct through her "bad bitch" pantomime. In what J identifies as her "ratchet alter ego," the brazen, lascivious, MC ying to her meek, sexually awkward, nine-to-fiver yang, she conjures a flashy single-lady sisters-on-television persona.[20]

The Black female ratchet is rampant in contemporary American pop culture, particularly in the arenas of hip-hop and reality television. An amalgamated offspring of the jezebel, matriarch, mammy, and welfare mother figures, she is a modern "controlling image," to evoke Patricia Hill Collins's terminology, of black female sexuality.[21] Like the mechanical device it is named after, the term "ratchet"—also defined as "a situation or process that is perceived to be deteriorating or changing steadily in a series of irreversible steps"—is an equivocal tool used to debase black women.[22] The foundation of this evolving stereotype, which evokes shame, pride, fear, laughter, and desire, is rooted in a history that denigrates and pathologizes black women's eroticism. If the ratchet is both revered and reviled in contemporary American pop culture and represents, the ambivalent figuration of black female sexuality, J's enactment of ratchetness is also deeply ambiguous. Unlike the purportedly authentic televisual ratchet performances she mimics from reality shows, J's ratchet soliloquies, as mostly privatized, highly dramatized alter-egos, illuminate the performed nature of such a stereotype. Private in the show yet open for public consumption, J's ratchet outbursts perpetuate, nonetheless, a recital of the stereotype that remains problematic, even beyond its reliance on black female sexual pathology as comedic fodder. In many episodes, she enacts this alternate ratchet persona, often using hip-hop as her medium to communicate her malapropos thoughts and sexual desires. Through this ratchet personality, Rae plays with stereotypes while simultaneously resisting the politics of respectability that can script performances of Black female sexuality. In the season 2 trailer, J raps "I am not a basketball wife," but has she escaped "the Black girl curse"?

Continuing to gain currency in popular culture and scholarly arenas, "the Black girl curse" was dubbed the term for this highly problematic Black single-lady phenomenon in 2009 when *ABC News Nightline* journalist Linsey Davis interviewed four single professional Black women in Atlanta about being single in their thirties. One of the participants said, "We have a saying called the 'black girl curse.' A lot of our white friends are married by 25, happily married with kids by 27, and we're like, 'What's the deal with the BGs?'—and that's black girls."[23] By problematic I am referring to the ways this trend has been discursively deliberated and theorized. Davis's interviewees offered an etiology of this so-called curse that, on the one hand, blames Black women for having standards that are "too high" and unreasonable or for having unrealistic expectations for a life partner; on the other hand, it suggests that the pool of eligible Black male bachelors is small ("slim pickings") in ways that exonerate Black women. In either case, Black women are considered accountable for their own single status. Books such as Jimi Izrael's *The Denzel Principle: Why Black Women Can't Find Good Men* (2009) and Eric Culpeper's *The Black Girl Curse* (2009) have blazed the trail of Black women's culpability, suggesting that Black women are on a futile search for a mythical Black man and need to lower their utopian standards to secure a "good" brother. Such rhetoric refashions the prevailing oppressive notions of Black women as accountable for the failure of the heteronormative Black family unit that was cemented into our national consciousness in March 1965 with the publication of Senator Patrick Moynihan's contentious report *The Negro Family: The Case for National Action*. The "Black girl curse," much like the Moynihan Report, perpetuates the idea that the "tangle of pathology" that Black women find themselves ensnared in is inevitably of their own making.[24]

So what are the J-like single Black ladies of the world to do? Black male "comedian-turned-relationship guru Steve Harvey," whom *Nightline* solicited to evaluate this "serious dilemma," suggests that Black women need to "compromise": they need to stop trying to find Black men who match their own education level, corporate status, and income.[25] Ralph Richard Banks, the author of *Is Marriage for White People?* (2011), asserts that, according to recent statistics, Black women are reluctant to date outside their race and should do so; and, indeed, the character J does just that. Black women are the least likely racial group to do this. Only 5.5 percent of married Black women in the United States have husbands of different races.[26] While J's relationship with her beau White J reinforces the heteronormative mandate of mainstream television's representation of Black romance, we may read her interracial romance as contesting the order of Black-on-Black love often endorsed by the single ladies we see on television. Still J's relationship illustrates the always already political, "always extraordinary" nature of Black-and-white interracial intimacy in American culture. As historian Kevin Mumford reminds us, "Because of History—slavery, racism, gender relations, sexual repression, power politics—sex across the color line always represents more than just sex."[27] It also compounds the problem of J's racial sexual authenticity. Her comments such as, "What do white people listen to when they have sex? Taylor Swift? Michael Bolton? Eminem?" communicate the vexed nature of enactments of cross-racial intimacy on the show. Couched in a signature *ABG* brand of racially charged humor, these statements reveal profound anxieties about race, racial difference, and racial anxiety while mining (for comedic currency) the tensions not between Black and white but rather surrounding race that is at once performed and essential. Such statements speak to the show's investment in contesting, albeit sardonically, assumptions of essentialized racial authenticity, both Black and white. . . .

Sisters in Cyberspace?

ABG is a dynamic example of Black women's use of new media to rewrite dominant codes of Black female sexuality. It is also part of the contemporary landscape of Black female cybersexualitites. In this section, I explore how the Internet facilitates alternative performances of racialized sexualities and how cyberspace catalyzes technologically inspired rearticulations of popular Black female sexuality in Black web series and pornography.[28] Since the invention of the printing press in the fifteenth century, pornography has maintained a critical relationship with technology. It has pioneered and used ever-evolving visual technologies to reinvent itself. Pornographers have consistently been among the first to exploit new publishing and visual reproduction technologies. I engage and consider pornography here not only because of such technological manipulation but also because of the ways it has enabled and empowered Black women, long before the web series, to command their own sexualities. In mapping the landscape of black female cybersexualities through web pornography, we can better understand the critical field of black female cybersexualities as an arena for showcasing novel, nonhegemonic paradigms of Black female sexualities.

In her conception of the Internet as a critical medium in rewriting codes of Black womanhood, Rae resembles many of today's Black female pornographers who use it as a mode of self-representation to create images that counter prevailing representations of marginalized Black female sexuality and maintain control over the projection of these images. The web series, Rae asserts, "is going to be the opportunity for people of color, not just African Americans but others. . . . I think that this is the space for niche communities to find content and for niche creators to find their audiences."[29] According to Rae, unlike Hollywood, the fact that the Internet lacks gatekeepers means that it offers "way more opportunities" to people of color.[30] This "frontier" "allows you to express yourself more creatively and more freely" and provides an audience for this expression. . . . Recognizing the autonomy and audience potential of the Web, Rae is among a new generation of contemporary Black female media producers who use new media to create alternative schemas of Black female sexuality and desire.

For example, Black lesbian filmmaker Shine Louise Houston uses digital technology, particularly cyberspace, as her primary architectonic instrument to transform queer pornography. Resisting mainstream representations of so-called normative Black female sexuality in porn, she asserts that "there is power in creating images, and for a woman of color and a queer to take that power. . . . I don't find it exploitative; I think it's necessary."[31] Houston's "hardcore indie feminist dyke porn" exhibits stunning cinematography, incredibly diverse performers, and fresh diegeses, critically queering renditions of Black female sexuality, while presenting paradigms of pleasure outside the dominant, heteronormative portrayals of Black womanhood in porn.[32] Like Rae, Houston's production was motivated by the need for alternative images of black womanhood: "There needs to be more voices. I believe in my politics. If you don't like it, do what I did. I didn't like what was going on in the porn industry in terms of representation of gay, lesbian, queer, and trans folk, so I made my own stuff."[33] . . . Rae's use of the Internet as a platform for reinventing Black female sexuality occurs in a similar context wherein cyberspace serves as a laboratory for the projection of new paradigms of Black female sexuality. . . .

. . . The Internet is increasingly becoming an extension of our physical selves, a sphere where we project, present, and represent our material bodies; and as fantasies of cyber-disembodiment, transcendent identities, and postraciality dwindle, questions of authenticity reanimate in new ways. *ABG* reveals a profound investment in the question of authenticity: J's Blackness mediates her awkwardness, she misplays the "real" single ladies who dominate the televisual landscape, and she pursues interracial romance. . . . Like most fans, I harbor mixed feelings about the show's rumored transition from the Internet to cable television. Part of me feels that it is a type of selling out and another part of me fears the kind of watering down that Rae herself initially expressed about the show's content—its autonomy, radicalism, and innovation—as a result of being on the Web.[34] Nevertheless, I look forward to more diverse representations of Black womanhood in the televisual landscape—something that will provide some stiff competition to the current trope of single ladies in the media.

NOTES

A portion of this essay draws from a section of Ariane Cruz, "Gettin' *Down Home with the Neelys*: Gastro-Porn & Televisual Performances of Gender, Race & Sexuality," *Women and Performance* 23, no. 3 (2013): 1–27.

1. . . . See Antia McCollough, "The Awkward Black Girl Lands ABC Show," *Amsterdam News*, October 22, 2012, http://www.amsterdamnews.com/testing/the-awkward-Black-girl-lands-abc-show/article_efd08824–1c65–11e2–8bde-0019bb2963f4.html, accessed October 31, 2012. The show raised over $50,000 through kickstarter.com, an online fundraising platform for creative projects. . . .

2. In early October, Shondaland, Shonda Rhimes's production company, sold a half-hour comedy written by Rae entitled *I Hate LA Dudes* to ABC. Rae will write and co-executive produce the show.

3. Rae has created four other web series, *FLY GUYS Present "The 'F' Word," Dorm Diaries, Ratchetpiece Theatre,* and *Roomieloverfriends* (a collaboration with Blackandsexytv.com). . . .

4. Issa Rae, "Black Folk Don't Like to Be Told They're Not Black," *Huffington Post*, August 4, 2011, http://www.huffingtonpost.com/issa-rae/Black-folk-dont-movie_b_912660.html, accessed August 13, 2012.

5. I discuss what I call J's *ratchet alter ego* in more depth later in the essay; however, I use the term "ratchet," a contradictory and problematic often-used contemporary colloquialism in African American vernacular and pop culture, specifically hip-hop, to generally refer to a stereotype of wild, degenerate, "ghettoized" black womanhood. Simultaneously adored and abhorred, desired and disparaged, the term "ratchet" reifies historical myths of black womanhood signifying black women's supposed physical and sexual aggressiveness, madness, irrationality, excess, and utter lasciviousness. Yet it is simultaneously a trope of black female agency.

6. . . . Lily Rothman, "Issa Rae of *Awkward Black Girl* on the Future of the Web Series," *Time*, July 10, 2012, http://entertainment.time.com/2012/07/10/issa-rae-of-awkward-Black-girl-on-the-future-of-the-web-series/, accessed August 13, 2012.

7. Such characters have proved to be comedic gold. Highly lauded and in its seventh season, *30 Rock* has garnered seventy-seven Emmy nominations and fourteen wins and numerous other awards. For more, see "About the Show," http://www.nbc.com/30-rock/about/.

8. Clover Hope, "That Awkward Moment When . . . 'Awkward Black Girl' Blows Up," *Vibe*, April 17, 2012, http://www.vibe.com/article/awkward-moment-when-awkward-Black-girl-blows, accessed July 22, 2012.

9. See Hope, "That Awkward Moment When"; see also "'Awkward Black Girl' Web Hit," *CNN*, October 8, 2011, http://www.cnn.com/video/#/video/living/2011/10/08/whitfield-issa-rae-interview.cnn, accessed July 22, 2012.

10. According to Nielsen, an average of 7.3 million people watched *Scandal*'s finale, of which 1.8 million were African American. See Sarah Springer, "'Scandal' Updates Image of Black Women on Network Television," *CNN*, March 25, 2012, http://inamerica.blogs.cnn.com/2012/05/25/scandal-updates-image-of-Black-women-on-network-television/, accessed June 8, 2012. . . .

11. Rhimes states, "I hope that Olivia Pope being a lead of a television series and being smart and vulnerable and the most desirable woman in any room that she walks into changes something for someone in the way they perceive women of color." See Springer, "'Scandal' Updates Image of Black Women on Network Television."

12. Analyzing race through the lens of US miscegenation laws, Peggy Pascoe argues that the Supreme Court adopted a modernist racial ideology . . . , the "powerfully pervasive belief that the eradication of racism depends on the deliberate nonrecognition of race." See Pascoe, "Miscegenation Law, Court Cases, and Ideologies of 'Race' in Twentieth-Century America," *Journal of American History* 88, no. 1 (1996): 48. . . .

13. *Black Folk Don't*, a web series . . . is a satire about Black authenticity. For more, see http://Blackfolkdont.com/pages/about/. Another contemporary Black web series, *Dear White People*, similarly satirically explores racial authenticity; see http://dear-white-people.tumblr.com/.

14. Henry Louis Gates Jr., *The Signifying Monkey: A Theory of African-American Literary Criticism* (Oxford: Oxford University Press, 1989), 163.

15. James Olney notes that the phrase "I was born" occurs in the first few sentences of many slave narratives, corroborating the humanity of the slave author. See Olney, "'I Was Born': Slave Narratives, Their Status as Autobiography and as Literature," *Callaloo* 20 (Winter 1984): 50.

16. Zora Neale Hurston, *Their Eyes Were Watching God* (New York: Harper Collins, 1937), 14.

17. Legal scholar Toni Lester's question resounds here, "What does it mean to have a multiple, marginalized, identity in a world that tends to frame all identities through the lens of the white, heterosexual majority culture?" See Lester, "Race, Sexuality and the Question of Multiple, Marginalized Identities in U.S. and European Discrimination Law," in *Gender Nonconformity, Race, and Sexuality: Charting the Connections*, ed. Toni Lester (Madison: University of Wisconsin Press, 2003), 84.

18. "Issa Rae and Pharrell at the Awkward Black Girl Screening," YouTube video, posted by iamOTHER, August 16, 2012, http://www.youtube.com/watch?v=TXh3XNJ5Utg&feature=g-all-u, accessed August 22, 2012.

19. See Brian Alexander, "Marriage Eludes High-Achieving Black Women," *MSNBC*, August 13, 2009, http://www.msnbc.msn.com/id/32379727/ns/health-sexual_health/t/marriage-eludes-high-achieving-Black-women/, accessed November 4, 2009; Joy Jones, "Marriage Is for White People," *Washington Post*, March 26, 2006, http://www.washingtonpost.com/wp-dyn/content/article/2006/03/25/AR2006032500029.html, accessed November 4, 2009; and Eric Johnson, "Nightline Face-Off: Why Can't a Successful Black Woman Find a Man?," *ABC News*, April 21, 2010, http://abcnews.go.com/Nightline/FaceOff/nightline-Black-women-single-marriage/story?id=10424979, accessed May 7, 2010.

20. In another of Rae's web series, *Ratchetpiece Theatre*, Rae concedes that while she can't provide a "dictionary definition," ratchet "is like if ghetto and hot shitty mess had a baby, and that baby had no father and became a stripper, then made a sex tape with an athlete and became a reality star." See "[Ep. 1] RATCHETPIECE Theatre | Rasheeda (Love & Hip-Hop: Atlanta)," uploaded by Issa Rae, July 20, 2012, http://www.youtube.com/watch?v=JtJOaBer5kk, accessed May 19, 2014.

21. Though the ratchet is a cross-racial stereotype, the specific ways it is commonly racialized, sexualized, classed, and gendered within the dominant sociocultural imagination relies heavily on the bodies of black women. Black feminist scholar Patricia Hill Collins identifies four controlling images, jezebel, mammy, matriarch, and welfare mother, arguing that these images function to provide the ideological basis for oppression of Black women on the basis of race, gender, class, and sex. For more, see Patricia Hill Collins, *Black Feminist Thought: Knowledge, Consciousness, and the Politics of Empowerment* (London: Routledge, 1990).

22. *Oxford Dictionaries*, s.v. "ratchet," http://oxforddictionaries.com/us/definition/american_english/ratchet, accessed March 5, 2013.

23. Chato Waters quoted in "Single, Black, Female—And Plenty of Company," *ABC News*, December 22, 2009, http://abcnews.go.com/Nightline/single-black-females/story?id=9395275, accessed June 2, 2014.

24. Chapter 4, entitled "The Tangle of Pathology," analyzes Black matriarchy, "the reversed roles of husband and wife," as the root cause of the failure of the Black family, which, according to Moynihan, includes high rates of poverty, delinquency, and crime and the educational deficiency of Black youth. See Daniel Patrick Moynihan, *The Negro Family: The Case for National Action* (Washington, DC: Office of Policy Planning and Research, US Department of Labor, 1965), http://www.dol.gov/oasam/programs/history/webid-meynihan.htm.

25. In addition to being an entertainer, Harvey's qualifications to evaluate this "crisis" in Black female sexuality includes his authoring of the book *Act Like a Lady, Think Like a Man: What Men Really Think about Love, Relationships, Intimacy, and Commitment* (New York: Harper Collins, 2009).

26. This figure refers to Black women's rate of interracial marriage in 2008. For more, see Jeffrey S. Passel, Wendy Wang, and Paul Taylor, "Marrying Out: One-in-Seven New U.S. Marriages Is Interracial or Interethnic," *Pew Research & Social Demographic Trends*, June 4, 2010, http://pewresearch.org/pubs/1616/american-marriage-interracial-interethnic, accessed July 3, 2012. The report finds that "some 22 percent of all Black male newlyweds in 2008 married outside their race, compared with just 9 percent of Black female newlyweds."

27. See Kevin J. Mumford, *Interzones: Black/White Sex Districts in Chicago and New York in the Early Twentieth Century* (New York: Columbia University Press, 1997), xi.

28. The Internet, which some have imagined as a democratized space, has proven itself a site for narratives by and about others. Examples of web series focusing on Black women include: *Chick, In(HER) view: A Conversation with Black Women, Blind Date, Afrocity, Celeste Bright, Buppies, Got2Be Real, Diary of a Single Mom*, and *Kindred*. For more about Black web series, see Joshua R. Weaver, "7 Must-Watch

Black Web Series," *The Root*, August 9, 2012, http://www.theroot.com/articles/culture/2012/08/best_black_web_series_the_roots_favorites.html, accessed September 1, 2012; and Aymar Jean Christian, "Black Web Series," Televisual, February2012,http://tvisual.org/Black-web-series/, accessed May 19, 2014. . . .

29. Rothman, "Issa Rae of *Awkward Black Girl* on the Future of the Web Series."

30. Ibid.

31. "Shine Louise Houston," CrashPadSeries.com, http://crashpadseries.com/queer-porn/shine-louise-houston/, accessed May 19, 2014.

32. "Preview: The Crash Pad: Director's Cut," http://crashpadseries.com/queer-porn/?feature=the-crash-pad-directors-cut, accessed May 7, 2012.

33. Jillian Eugenios, "Chatting up Shine Louise Houston," *Curve*, September 20, 2011, http://www.curvemag.com/Curve-Magazine/Web-Articles-2011/Chatting-up-Shine-Louise-Houston/, accessed March 5, 2012.

34. Sarah Springer and Sarah Edwards, "'Awkward Black Girl' Creator Issa Rae Responds to Racism," *CNN*, April 24, 2012, http://inamerica.blogs.cnn.com/2012/04/24/awkward-Black-girl-creator-issa-rae-responds-to-racism, accessed July 22, 2012.

JENNIFER KEISHIN ARMSTRONG

18 HOW *SEX AND THE CITY* HOLDS UP IN THE #METOO ERA (2018)

Jennifer Keishin Armstrong is a writer who spent a decade on staff at *Entertainment Weekly*. Since then, her work has appeared in *BBC Culture*, *The New York Times Book Review*, *Vice*, *New York Magazine*, and *Billboard*. She is the author of *Seinfeldia: How the Show About Nothing Changed Everything* (2016); a history of *The Mary Tyler Moore Show*, *Mary and Lou and Rhoda and Ted*:(2013); and *Sex and the City and Us: How Four Single Women Changed the Way We Think, Live, and Love*.(2018)

Sex and the City premiered on HBO [more than] 20 years ago . . . staking its claim to a bold thesis: maybe women want sex as much as men do, and maybe they don't need men for much else. This represented a huge shift at the end of the millennium, a time when sex was on everyone's mind and newscast: Independent Counsel Ken Starr's investigation into President Bill Clinton had just taken a prurient turn by focusing on Clinton's sexual relationship with White House intern Monica Lewinsky, and the nation was hanging on the intimate details. But the dominant narrative was still the tale of a powerful man taking advantage of a much younger woman.

Sex and the City had a different story about sex to tell. Over six seasons, the series presented its case for Carrie, Charlotte, Miranda, and Samantha as the models of a new kind of womanhood: they supported themselves, they made their friends their family, and they had lots of sex. Some of it was good, some of it wasn't, but all of it was central to *Sex and the City*'s vision of female freedom.

But the show's landmark portrayal of women's sexual freedom is exactly what can make it feel anachronistic now, in the age of #MeToo. Amid the four main characters' many encounters with men, very few involve danger, nonconsensual sex, or even harassment. Such incidents that do occur are played off as jokes, "bad sex," or occasions warranting no more than an eyeroll.

Sex and the City had a good reason to favor the fun and frivolous side of sex: it was meant to portray a glittery, glamorous version of the single woman. Before the show, single women in media were spinsters, cat ladies, and "Cathy" comic strips; if they were lucky, they were Mary on the 1970s's *Mary Tyler Moore Show* (required to be perfect in exchange for her freedom), or Ally on *Ally McBeal* (unhinged, baby-crazy . . .), which ran from 1997 to 2002. The last thing single women needed at the time of *Sex and the City* was another *Looking for Mr. Goodbar* (indiscriminate sex results in brutal death, 1977) or *Fatal Attraction* (desperate single women are coming to steal your husband and boil your bunny, 1987). *Sex and the City*'s unrealistically positive depiction of women's sexual freedom was one of its most revolutionary qualities.

In an era that has seen the rise of such shows as *Girls*, *Broad City*, and *The Bold Type*, it's easy to forget just how groundbreaking *Sex and the City* was when it came to HBO on June 6, 1998. An adaptation of Candace Bushnell's newspaper column-turned-book, the show followed a fashionable, Bushnell-like character named Carrie Bradshaw and her three best friends: romantic Charlotte, success-driven Miranda, and libertine Samantha. The formula sounds familiar, right down to the core foursome of distinct personalities. But this wasn't just a younger version of *The Golden Girls*. It included some of the most graphic sex talk ever featured in a prime-time television show targeted at the masses. Its spot on premium cable allowed this, of course, but what made it even more radical was that the sex talk happened among women who were presented as the norm, not some fringe exception.

The sex scenes themselves reflected the female gaze. The women looked great during their bedroom romps, but they weren't objectified. The scenes were played more for humor, insight, and character development than for eroticism. Sex, the show told us, was hardly ever perfect, but it was often fun and/or funny. As show-runner Michael Patrick King told me in an interview for my book, *Sex and the City and Us: How Four Single Women Changed the Way We Think, Live, and Love*, "Sex, up until *Sex and the City*, was sort of dipped in black, and it was dark and dirty and oily. After us, sex was seen differently. We made it pink. And fizzy. We took it into the light and made it something empowering, but also funny."

At the time, it seemed impossible to pull sex out of the dark depths and into the pink and fizzy—while still addressing its more dangerous side. So there is very little #MeToo in *Sex and the City* sex. This was of a piece with the many bargains *Sex and the City* seemed to strike, intentionally or not, as a show that raised hackles. It was sex-positive but apolitical, and in one episode, even anti-political. When Carrie dates a politician . . . she reveals that she's not even registered to vote. The message seemed to be: *Don't worry, guys. We're only exercising our newfound power in the bedroom; we're not coming for your public sphere, too*. The show demonstrated women's financial independence, but mainly through extravagant fashion and lifestyle spending. *Don't worry, guys. We'll just be over here shopping.*

This approach worked: *Sex and the City* became not just a hit, but a worldwide phenomenon. It made rabbit vibrators, Manolo Blahniks, nameplate necklaces, cosmopolitans, and cupcakes trends across the globe. It was nominated for 54 Emmy awards and won seven. It spawned two movies that broke box-office records, even though they were widely regarded as less than great.

Countless people have watched the show in reruns, streaming, and on DVD since. It has become a rite of passage for women and gay men in particular.

Of course, as younger generations have watched, and even as older generations have re-watched, our modern eyes can spot a few stray *Sex and the City* moments worthy of #MeToo reflection. There are some passing instances that didn't register with most of us at the time—like when the "modelizer" films his sex with models and uses it as art without concern for consent, or when Charlotte wonders if an older artist is considering a show at her gallery only because he finds her "charming." Carrie asks if he wants her to "hold his paintbrush." Miranda: "If he so much as suggests what she's suggesting, you give me a call and we'll sue the hell out of him. That's the only proper way to trade sex for power." . . .

The most classic #MeToo encounter happens in the sanctity of the fashion closet at *Vogue*, where Carrie is freelancing. There, an editor who has taken a liking to her . . . drops his pants after plying her with martinis and rare shoes. She rejects him and runs . . .

In another, murkier situation, Carrie puts up with physically punishing—but consensual—sex with Charlotte's husband Harry's best man. Carrie shows up at the wedding hunched over with a "sex sprain" and dismisses the experience as "jackrabbit sex." She declines a second round with the perpetrator and incurs his wrath: "If I'd known you were just using me," he says, "I wouldn't have made love to you like that." Let's just say a *lot* of us have been there, and it's exactly the kind of problem that would be solved by more affirmative and enthusiastic consent practices.[1]

All of these are perfect examples of typical incidents in many women's lives, the kinds of things we've always assumed are just normal—because they have been. The show models exactly this: it doesn't imply that these guys are right, but it shows how women have long dealt with such situations. You complain about it to your girlfriends, then move on. The #MeToo movement is liberating because it allows us all to verbalize such experiences in public—to not explain them away or joke about them, to acknowledge that they chipped away at us.

Sex and the City did give us one great tool for more empowered sex lives, whether we're seeking better experiences in bed or trying to process how sex has been used against us in the past: brunch. The show's classic girl-talk scenes were its most revolutionary and lasting contribution to women's culture. They modeled open and honest talk about sex positions, kinks, and relationships, and—critically—they allowed each of the characters to debate and clearly verbalize her own likes and dislikes.

This allowed them to create a conversational version of what's known as a yes/no/maybe list[2]—a lengthy menu of sexual options that you can peruse alone or with a partner to determine what you're into. If you're with a partner, it allows for the clearest enthusiastic consent possible. If you're alone, you're setting boundaries for yourself so you're clearer about them in the heat of a moment, or during the shock and confusion of a nonconsensual encounter. If you're with your friends at brunch, it serves the same purposes, along with extra bonuses like learning others' boundaries and alleviating shame and guilt.

Carrie Bradshaw may not have been as enlightened about sexual harassment and assault as we are in 2018. But her couldn't-help-but-wonder attitude did help us get here. . . .

NOTES

1. Samantha Cooney, "The Aziz Ansari Allegation Has People Talking About 'Affirmative Consent." What's That?" *Time*, January 17, 2018, http://time.com/5104010/aziz-ansari-affirmative-consent/

2. "Our Favorite Yes/No/Maybe Lists Available Online," Self Serve: Your Sexuality Research Center, n.d., http://selfservetoys.com/resourcecenter/favorite-yesnomaybe-lists-available-online/

V. SPIKE PETERSON

<table>
<tr><td>19</td><td>

THE INTENDED AND UNINTENDED QUEERING OF STATES/NATIONS (2013)

</td></tr>
</table>

V. Spike Peterson is Professor of International Relations at the University of Arizona, with courtesy appointments in the Department of Gender and Women's Studies and Institute for LGBT Studies. She is the author of *A Critical Rewriting of Global Political Economy: Reproductive, Productive and Virtual Economies* (2003) and co-author, with Anne Sisson Runyan, of *Global Gender Issues in the New Millennium* (2010).

> The appeal to the "natural" is one of the most powerful aspects of common-sense thinking, but it is a way of understanding social relations which denies history.
>
> (WEEDON 1987:3)

To characterize something as "natural" both denies its history and erases its politics. As a contribution to queering states/nations, I consider in this essay the history—hence politics—of "sex," "sexuality," and states. Reading early state formation—the "rise of civilization"—as constituting and normalizing binary sex/gender difference and heteropatriarchal kinship relations, I argue that "making states is making sex." Making both involves multiple, interactive transformations: in self/subject and collective identities, symbolic systems of meaning, institutional arrangements, and regulatory, coercive, and juridical forms of power. Once states are successfully "made," to ensure intergenerational continuity they monitor biological and social reproduction. This has historically featured instituting a heteropatriarchal family/household as the basic socioeconomic unit, regulating women's biological reproduction, and policing sexual activities more generally. . . .[1]

I argue that the normalization of heteropatriarchal relations in early states instituted—via birthright transmission of membership/citizenship and property ownership claims—intergenerational reproduction of inequalities within and between polities. On this view, retaining nation-states and existing birthright citizenship and inheritance patterns in effect sustains heteronormativity and its problematic politics (Peterson 1999; Stevens 1999, 2004, 2010). The latter includes dramatic and increasing inequalities of resource distribution—exacerbated by neoliberal policies—and the global insecurities these entail (Peterson 2010b). Yet at the same time, neoliberal globalization alters the autonomy and arrangements of states, and feminist/queer movements challenge the "givens" of heteropatriarchy. Hence, at this historical juncture queer theory is a crucial, arguably imperative, component of critically analyzing "politics" writ large. It offers not only the most telling and informed critique of heteronormativity and its political effects, but also, potentially, the most transformative analysis of power inequalities—across individual, interpersonal, group, national, and global levels.

The objective of this essay then is to denaturalize identities, ideologies, and institutional practices that were stabilized through early state formation, largely taken-for-granted in the transition to (European) modernity, and continue to discipline our being, thinking, and doing in—and in response to—contemporary local, national, and global politics. The point is less to offer a definitive history

Source: Republished with permission of John Wiley and Sons from V. Spike Peterson, "The Intended and Unintended Queering of States/Nations" *Studies in Ethnicity and Nationalism* 13:1, 2013, pp. 57-68; permission conveyed through Copyright Clearance Center, Inc.

than to tell a different story—one that illuminates the centrality of sex/gender and sexualities in constituting and reproducing structural inequalities.

Early States and Sex/Gender Politics

> States have been the world's largest and most powerful organizations for more than 5,000 years.
>
> (TILLY 1990:1)

While clouded by the mists of time, social relations of prehistory are not entirely opaque. We have a variety of sources from which to speculate about the prehistory of early human relations and social formations. The conventional story of "human evolution" took shape in the modern era, authorized by Europeans becoming more aware of and producing knowledge claims about their "own" history and its relation to that of temporally and spatially separate "Others." The power relations operating in this historical context inevitably shaped which questions were asked, by whom, and to what purpose. . . . The foundational narrative that was stabilized—especially its presuppositions regarding sex difference, patriarchal structures, social hierarchies, and "progress through a Western lens"—has become, for many, common sense. But that story too is being rewritten as advances in research (technologies, methods, new evidence) take place in the context of increasingly prominent critical, feminist, queer, poststructuralist, and postcolonial interventions. What matters here is a growing awareness of the long duration, hence viability, of small, cooperative groups preceding agricultural settlements, and of the variation, complexity, and multidimensional aspects of social relations—past and present. The emerging scholarship especially challenges "common-sense" assumptions regarding sex, gender, human nature, and (adversarial) intergroup relations.[2]

Consider that accumulation processes were irrelevant for most of human history (at least 40,000, arguably 100,000 years), as groups subsisted on a tremendous variety of gathering, hunting, and fishing practices. With respect to sex and gender, while

early humans were presumably aware of anatomical and biological (reproductive) sex differences, it is unclear what this implied for gender or sexuality. Dobres (2004: 213) observes that

> archeologists cannot say with any confidence or agreement . . . how many different genders may have existed in any given time or place, much less what were their particularly associated roles, values, and so forth. . . . [I]t is probable that different cultures practiced different sorts of gender configurations. . . Nor is there any evidence to indicate compulsory heterosexuality. The possibility of third, fourth, or even fifth genders is quite likely. . . . Fathers, brothers, uncles . . . probably shared in the caring of children, for this was likely considered a highly valued and culturally important task, as it is with modern hunting and gathering cultures.

The idea of "private property" and processes of accumulation attend the gradual spread of agriculture and settled communities, followed in some places by early state formation. The latter entailed effective centralization of accumulation processes, political authority, and military exploits; centralized regulation of social relations through formal laws (in contrast to customary practices); institutionalization of stratifying divisions of labor and heteropatriarchal household formations; reconfiguration of individual and collective identities; and ideological legitimation of these transformations, stabilized through the "written word" that endured through time and space. All of these had profound implications for social relations, as civilizations institutionalized structural inequalities.

These dramatic transformations were by no means inevitable: they were widely resisted—perhaps for millennia (Bolger 2010; Mann 1986)—and their realization depended on historically contingent forms of coercion and consent.[3] Kinship-based groups varied, and some engaged in sporadic raiding and feuding that emphasized male-dominated endeavors. But state formations engaged in organized militarism as a relatively continual aspect of sustaining centralized rule, expanding territorial control, and enhancing accumulation in the form of both material goods (war booty) and human labor (concubines, slaves)—all in support of nonproductive elites and state projects (construction, military).

The multifaceted, cross-cutting, and nuanced social relations typical of larger kin networks afforded women (and men) various claims to respect, authority, and resources. Effective centralization required a reconfiguration of social arrangements, which typically involved states establishing relatively independent heteropatriarchal "family"/ households as the basic socio-economic unit; the latter facilitated resource extraction, military conscription, regulation of property (including women), and centralized control more generally.[4] This shift eroded the authority and power of lineage networks (some of which were matrilineal), and as one effect, emphasized women's sexual/ reproductive role, at the expense of other previously valued dimensions of their identities and activities. To ensure a numerically adequate population, establish (inheritable) claims to property and membership, and promote "in-group" allegiance, states regulated sexual relations. Typically, this involved restrictive expectations as well as legal codes disciplining women's sexual activities and establishing a norm of (biologically reproductive) heterosexuality (without presuming modernist understandings of "homosexual" identity or proscriptions against homoerotic behaviors). That females faced greater restrictions than males alludes to deepening sex/ gender asymmetries.

In these processes, states abstracted and centralized authority in a "political (public) sphere" that was thus distinguished from, while being dependent upon, a "household (private) sphere" focused on subsistence and social reproduction. Men—especially those with inherited claims to property—acquired status, authority, and resources as patriarchal heads-of-households, and some gained additional status through identification with military activities or religious or political authority. Women typically lost status, authority, and resource claims that they variously enjoyed in kinship communities; in the transition to patriarchy they became transmitters of property and—in norms regarding adultery—property of "their" men. Relatively isolated in individual households,

women became more dependent upon fathers and husbands, losing access to the countervailing support of extended kin networks. These altered arrangements amplified male–female distinctions and presumably cultivated gender-differentiated "identities" (subjectivities).

In the Western tradition (flowing from Greek city-states), centralization involved "normalizing" foundational dichotomies (public–private, reason–affect, mind–body, culture–nature, civilized–barbarian, masculine–feminine) both materially (divisions of authority, power, labor, and resources) as well as conceptually (justificatory ideologies, collective belief systems). Not least because state-making involved the invention of writing, these systemic transformations were codified, and that codification (in Western philosophy, political theory, classical and religious texts) profoundly shaped subsequent theory/practice.

Early states are important then, for the patterns and institutions they stabilized: sex/gender asymmetries (divisions of labor and status; women as property; heteropatriarchal households), masculinism (male right to rule; patriarchal transmission of property and membership claims), and inequalities of status, resources, and power (elite rule; public over private; "productive" or specialized over reproductive or menial labor; citizens over "Others"). Given the salience of inherited claims to property and membership status, (women's) adultery was severely punished, but nonreproductive sexual behaviors—that did not threaten heteropatriarchal structures—drew far less attention.

Modern European States/Nations and Heteronormative Politics

[T]o understand the forces that . . . make up the "us" and "them" comprising the affinities and enmities of enduring interstate inequality and systemically violent conflict, then we must move . . . towards a deeper understanding of the rules that hold together the state as a membership organization.

(STEVENS 2006:755)

While patriarchal dominance and gendered ideology were contested and only eventually took shape in early state formation, they were largely taken for granted in European state-making processes and their colonizing practices. In the intervening centuries, patriarchal authority was routinized in monotheistic belief systems and patriarchal kinship reproduced and extended (unequal) divisions of authority, power, labor, and resources. The modern era's celebration of rationalist/objectivist science did complicate how authority was legitimated, but not how it was gendered masculine.

By definition, European state-making replicated earlier processes: centralization of resources and authority, organization of military capacity, and ideological consolidation under elite control. But state-making in the modern era was shaped by both the legacy of earlier states and the emergence of new techniques, modalities, and operations of power. . . .

Modern states required far more knowledge about their subjects. Hence, their interest in and cultivation of the social and human "life" sciences (to provide "expertise") and development of "biopolitical" strategies (censuses, statistics, programs to enhance the health, education, etc. of expanding populations)—all in support of producing "civilized" subjects who will govern and care for themselves and "exercise their citizenship responsibly" (Rose 1996:45). In complex and varying ways, the emerging "art of government" (re)configured categories and relations of sex/gender, sexuality, and ethnicity/race.[5] But while there are many critiques of sexism, of heteronormativity, and of nationalism, how these overlap and interact has only recently become a focus of inquiry (e.g. Morgensen 2010; Puar 2007). I turn then to briefly consider how pervasively nationalism presumes and tends to reproduce sexist and heteronormative assumptions and practices.[6]

First, nationalist policies involve regulating under what conditions, when, how many, and whose children women will bear. The forms taken are historically specific—shaped by socio-religious norms, technological developments, economic pressures, and political priorities. But states often seek to increase—or replenish—their numbers, and in the context of pronatalist policies, nonreproductive sexual activities are deemed threatening to national interests. States may restrict access to contraception, criminalize abortion, reward childbearing, demonize homosexuality, and/or represent the primary purpose of "family life" as sexual reproduction. In general, potentially reproductive women will be encouraged (pressured?) to bear children "for the nation" while nonreproductive sexual activities will be discouraged (punished?) for undermining national objectives.

Second, states have an interest in whether children are "appropriately" socialized, and therefore in the constitution of families/households as primary sites of social reproduction. In particular, states sustain sexist and heteronormative principles through legislation regarding marriage, child adoption and custody, and transmission of property and citizenship claims. Exclusively heteropatriarchal family life ensures that heterosexual coupling and gendered divisions of labor/power/authority are the only apparent options, which reproduces sexist and heteronormative expectations. Worldwide, male parenting and care-giving take many forms, but "homosexual" families/households are rare and nowhere are men expected to parent and care for dependents to the same extent and in the same way that women are. Hence, some men who want to parent are denied this option, and most men who have the option do not engage it fully. Of course this leaves women over-burdened, but it has other important effects. Men's systemic exclusion from primary parenting and care-giving surely affects their subjectivities and worldviews—for instance, by constraining their emotional experience and circumscribing forms of bonding available to them. Finally, heteropatriarchal marriage and citizenship rules exclude nonheterosexuals from a variety of benefits, rights, and privileges, not least with respect to immigration options.

Third, the symbolic coding of the nation carries gender as well as sexuality. The metaphors of nation-as-woman and woman-as-nation suggest how women—as bodies and cultural repositories—become the battleground of group struggles. *Nation-as-woman* expresses a spatial, embodied femaleness: the land's fecundity must be protected against invasion and violation. It is also a temporal metaphor: the rape of the body/nation not only violates frontiers but disrupts—by planting alien seed or destroying reproductive viability—the maintenance of the community through time. Rape has been practiced in countless wars and has become a metaphor of national humiliation. But consider two assumptions in place before rape can "make sense" as a nationalist strategy: that men are willing (eager?) to violate women/the feminine in this way, and that the "target" is a (heterosexually) fertile woman/body. Imagining the "beloved country" as a female child, a lesbian, a prostitute, or a postmenopausal wise woman generates quite different pictures and suggests quite different understandings of community.

Woman-as-nation marks the boundaries of (insider) group identity, and as symbols of cultural authenticity women face a variety of pressures to conform to idealized models of behavior. This suggests the political significance often attached to women's outward attire and/or public behavior, as women—but not men—are held "responsible for the transmission of culture" and at the same time presumed "those most vulnerable to [heterosexual] abuse, violation or seduction by 'other' men" (Pettman 1992:5–6). This heterosexist ideology features powerfully in nationalist projects—exemplified when European colonizers used notions of bourgeois "respectability" (read: heteronormative, well-bred) to legitimate their domination of "Others" (whose sexual practices were deemed "backward"), and when any state power justifies foreign interventions as "rescue/civilizing missions," ostensibly to "save" women from oppression by their "own" men.[7]

Fourth, these points suggest the historical—and continuing—fusion of nationalism, militarism, and (heterosexist) masculinism (e.g. Puar 2007). Recall that state-making in Europe was spurred primarily by military objectives: political conditions propelled centralizing processes of accumulation to pay for men and equipment to fight ongoing wars, and one effect of state centralization was political-economic imperialist expansion that required a reliable supply of males willing to secure (as soldiers) and administer (as civil/public servants) local and colonial governments. Male bonding within and

allegiance to the "fraternal" state/nation became crucial. And while masculinist privilege is not homogeneously shared, in theory all men (compared to women) can identify with the cultural valorization of men and (hegemonic) masculinity and men's favored access to public sphere activities, authority, and power. And in practice, militarization as a male-dominated activity encourages men to bond politically and militarily as they play out the "us vs. them" script of protecting "their own" women and violating the enemy's men/women. In effect, modern states cultivate male homosocial politics celebrating masculinity's cultural valorization and (abstract) male bonding across (actual) differences—while decisively proscribing homosexual practices.[8]

Indeed, in modern states—and in most countries today—"homosexuals" (and women) were excluded from military service. Recent challenges to this exclusion expose how deeply heterosexist premises underpin hegemonic masculinity. As a site of celebrated (because nonsexual) homosocial bonding, the military affords men a relatively unique opportunity to experience intimacy and interdependence, especially with men, in ways that heterosexist identities and divisions of labor otherwise constrain. Cohn (1998:145) argues that for many, the military is effectively a guarantee of heterosexual masculinity, affording a rare situation where

> men are allowed to experience erotic, sexual, and emotional impulses that they would otherwise have to censor . . . for fear of being seen . . . as homosexual and therefore not real men. They are not only escaping a negative—imputations of homosexuality—but gaining a positive, the ability to be with other men in ways that transcend the limitations on male relationships that most men live under in civilian life.

Finally, the heterosexist state/nation denies homosexual bonding to both men and women. But whereas men are expected to bond politically (homosocially) with other men of the state/nation, the dichotomy of public and private spheres denies women's homosocial bonding as well. Rather, as an effect of heteropatriarchal households and inheritance rules, women are linked to the state through their fathers/husbands and are expected to bond only through and with "their men."[9]

Women then are not merely symbols or victims within nationalist struggles. They are also agents: supporting their men/nation, participating in militarization, and increasingly, taking up arms. To be effective, however, in hyper-masculinized arenas, women are pressured to appear and reinforce heteronormative/masculinist strategies, including the cultural devalorization and physical destruction of "Others."

The Queering of States/Nations

Heterosexuality is at once necessary to the state's ability to constitute and imagine itself, while simultaneously marking a site of its own instability.

(ALEXANDER 1997:65, citing Hart 1994:8)

I have argued that the hierarchical binaries of embodied male–female sex difference and cultural masculine–feminine gender differentiation were constitutive of early state-making, and taken for granted in modern (nationalist) state-making and its colonizing projects. Gradually, most people/nations have been incorporated into a world system that presumes heteronormative sex/gender/sexuality and heteropatriarchal transmission of property and citizenship claims. From a critical perspective, these arrangements tend to (re)produce intergenerational inequalities not only of sex/gender and sexuality but also of class, ethnicity/race, and nationality. Yet these arrangements are also being transformed by feminist challenges to sex/gender relations, queer disruptions of heteronormative premises, and neoliberal erosions of state-based political power.

These contradictory developments reveal the instability of heterosexual and state-centric arrangements. For present purposes, I suggest they reveal a queering of states/nations: intentionally by critics of heteronormativity and unintentionally by advocates of neoliberal policies that alter state-based formations. More generally, these points illuminate the centrality of sex/gender, sexualities, and kinship rules in constituting and reproducing structural inequalities. Heteronormativity is political then not only because it oppresses those who

identify as nonheterosexual but also because (in state-making processes) it is produced by and (re)produces hierarchical sex/gender and the corollary asymmetric valorization that "legitimates" domination of all—women, "effeminate men," "Others"—who are stigmatized as feminine.

I draw two related conclusions. In fundamental ways (e.g. polarized gender identities, heteropatriarchal family/household forms, masculinist/militarist/nationalist ideology), heterosexist polities achieve group coherence and continuity through hierarchical (sex/gender) relations within the group. As the binary and corollary inequality that is most naturalized (read: whose history is lost and politics erased), sex/gender difference is at the same time invoked to justify hierarchical (adversarial) relations between groups. On this view, the sex/gender/heterosexist hierarchy of masculine over feminine and the nationalist domination of insiders over outsiders are doubly linked. First, (state-based) nationalism reproduces gendered/heterosexist privilege and oppression within the group—at the expense of women and feminized (nonheterosexual, racialized, "under-class," etc.) males—regardless of the group's "identity" differentiation (based on political ideology, ethnicity/race, religion, etc.) from other groups. Second, nationalism is sexed/gendered/heterosexist in terms of how the justification of adversarial relations between groups (through devalorization of feminized "Others") invokes and reproduces the "foundational" binary of sex difference and (depoliticized) masculine dominance. Sex/gender and heteronormative sexuality are thus "naturalized" and their histories—and politics—erased. In this important sense, feminist and queer critiques of heteronormativity are central to all critiques of structural inequalities/hierarchies, including the problematic politics of (heteropatriarchal) nation-states.

In the final analysis the social movement that will be the vanguard of a revolution against all forms of state boundaries, that could organize on behalf of the unhindered movement and full-fledged development of capacities regardless of one's birthplace or parentage, is a movement that will be queer.

(Stevens 2004:225)

NOTES

1. Briefly here: Heteropatriarchy combines the twin processes of heterosexualization and patriarchy (Alexander 1997:65); masculinism refers to the system/structure of masculine privilege and/or the ideological codes that normalize gender hierarchy; gender operates intersectionally; and while masculinity is generally privileged over femininity, context-specific masculinities may be devalorized relative to hegemonic masculinities. I understand feminism as theoretical/practical efforts to transform all structural hierarchies (e.g. racism, heterosexism, imperialist geopolitics) intertwined and naturalized by feminizing (devalorizing) the "Other" (e.g. Peterson 2005; Peterson and Runyan 2010).

2. As Cameron (1997:21) notes, Hobbes' depiction of "life in the state of nature as 'nasty, brutish and short' was pure speculation." Critiques of Eurocentric and masculinist bias in archaeological research include Bolger (2006, 2010); Conkey (2003); Dobres (2004); Joyce (2008); Nelson (1997, 2006); Nelson and Rosen-Ayalon (2002); and Pyburn (2004).

3. There was resistance to initial centralization as well as cycles of resistance after some stabilization of state formation (Feinman and Marcus 1998); and of course, nonstate formations continued to exist both during and beyond the period of early state formation. My account draws especially from Cameron (1997); Dobres (2004); Frader (2006); Lerner (1986); and Stearns (2006). This short essay cannot address complexities and debates but summarizes from extensive research and reflects well-developed arguments in the relevant bodies of scholarship. For references in support of the claims and argumentation presented here—and my own attempts to complicate them—see, e.g., Peterson (1988, 1992, 1997, 2010a).

4. Terms referenced here (family, household, public, private) carry multiple meanings and typically overstate the formalization of such "categories" in early social formations. They appear here for brevity and to highlight the significant contrast between kinship networks (without rigid divisions) and states (with their structural divisions and new "household" base).

5. On developing gender and race hierarchies and ideologies, see, e.g., Federici (2004); Hartman (2004); Landes (1998); McClintock (1995); Mosse (1985, 1996); Pateman (1988, 1989); Stoler (1995).

6. For elaboration and extensive references, see Peterson (1999), from which the following section draws.

7. On justifying colonial wars and obscuring their racist, economic, and heteronormative dynamics, see Chatterjee (1986); McClintock (1995); Said (1979, 1993); Spivak (1987); Stoler (1991). Marginalized (read: feminized) men more generally are subject to this crusading "logic": in colonial wars to "modernize" gender relations, nationalist wars to promote idealized (heteronormative) families, wars on poverty that demoralize the (racialized) underclass, and battles against HIV/AIDS that demonize gay men.

8. As Parker et al. (1991:6) note: "Typically represented as a passionate brotherhood, the nation finds itself compelled to distinguish its 'proper' homosociality from more explicitly sexualized male–male relations, a compulsion that requires the identification, isolation, and containment of male homosexuality." See also Sedgwick (1985, 1990).

9. In Alexander's (1997:64) words, "women's sexual agency . . . and erotic autonomy have always been troublesome for the state . . . pos[ing] a challenge to the ideological anchor of an originary nuclear family, . . . which perpetuates the fiction that the family is the cornerstone of society. Erotic autonomy signals danger to the heterosexual family and to the nation."

REFERENCES

Alexander, M. Jacqui. 1997. "Erotic Autonomy as a Politics of Decolonization: An Anatomy of Feminist and State Practice in the Bahamas Tourist Economy." In *Feminist Genealogies, Colonial Legacies, Democratic Futures*, ed. M. Jacqui Alexander and Chandra Talpade Mohanty. New York: Routledge.

Bolger, Diane L. 2006. "Gender and Human Evolution." In *Handbook of Gender in Archaeology*, ed. Sarah Milledge Nelson. Lanham, MD: AltaMira.

Bolger, Diane L. 2010. "The Dynamics of Gender in Early Agricultural Societies of the Near East." *Signs: Journal of Women in Culture and Society* 35 (2): 503–31.

Cameron, Rondo. 1997. *A Concise Economic History of the World: From Paleolithic Times to the Present*. 3rd ed. New York: Oxford University Press.

Chatterjee, Partha. 1986. *Nationalist Thought and the Colonial World: A Derivative Discourse?* London: Zed.

Cohn, Carol. 1998. "Gays in the Military: Texts and Subtexts." In *The "Man Question" in International Relations*, ed. Marysia Zalewski and Jane Parpart. Boulder, CO: Westview.

Conkey, Margaret W. 2003. "Has Feminism Changed Archaeology?" *Signs: Journal of Women in Culture and Society* 28 (3): 867–80.

Dobres, Marcia-Anne. 2004. "Gender in the Formation of the Earliest Human Societies." In *A Companion to Gender History*, ed. Teresa A. Meade and Merry E. Wiesner-Hanks. Oxford: Blackwell.

Federici, Silvia. 2004. *Caliban and the Witch: Women, the Body and Primitive Accumulation*. New York: Autonomedia Pluto.

Feinman, Gary M. and Joyce Marcus, eds. 1998. *Archaic States*. Santa Fe, NM: School of American Research Press.

Foucault, Michel. 1980. *Power/Knowledge: Selected Interviews and Other Writings, 1972–1977*, ed. and trans. Colin Gordon. New York: Pantheon.

Frader, Laura Levine. 2006. "Gender and Labor in World History." In *A Companion to Gender History*, ed. Teresa A. Meade and Merry E. Wiesner-Hanks. Oxford: Blackwell.

Giddens, Anthony. 1987. *The Nation-State and Violence: Volume Two of a Contemporary Critique of Historical Materialism*. Berkeley: University of California Press.

Hart, Lynda. 1994. *Fatal Women: Lesbian Sexuality and the Mark of Aggression*. Princeton, NJ: Princeton University Press.

Hartman, Mary S. 2004. *The Household and the Making of History: A Subversive View of The Western Past*. Cambridge: Cambridge University Press.

Joyce, Rosemary A. 2008. *Ancient Bodies, Ancient Lives: Sex, Gender, and Archaeology*. London: Thames & Hudson.

Landes, Joan B. 1998. *Feminism, the Public and the Private*. Oxford: Oxford University Press.

Lerner, Gerda. 1986. *The Creation of Patriarchy*. New York: Oxford University Press.

Mann, Michael. 1984. "The Autonomous Power of the State." *Archives Europeenes Sociologiques* XXV: 185–213.

Mann, Michael. 1986. *The Sources of Social Power*. Vol. 1. Cambridge: Cambridge University Press.

McClintock, Anne. 1995. *Imperial Leather: Race, Gender and Sexuality in the Colonial Contest*. New York: Routledge.

Morgensen, Scott Lauria. 2010. "Settler Homonationalism: Theorizing Settler Colonialism within Queer Modernities." *GLQ* 16 (1–2): 105–31.

Mosse, George L. 1985. *Nationalism and Sexuality: Respectability and Abnormal Sexuality in Modern Europe*. New York: H. Fertig.

Mosse, George L. 1996. *The Image of Man: The Creation of Modern Masculinity*. New York: Oxford University Press.

Nelson, Sarah Milledge. 1997. *Gender in Archaeology: Analyzing Power and Prestige*. Walnut Creek, CA: AltaMira.

Nelson, Sarah Milledge, ed. 2006. *Handbook of Gender in Archaeology*. Lanham, MD: AltaMira.

Nelson, Sarah Milledge and Myriam Rosen-Ayalon, eds. 2002. *In Pursuit of Gender: Worldwide Archaeological Approaches*. Walnut Creek, CA: AltaMira.

Parker, Andrew, Mary Russo, Doris Sommer, and Patricia Yaeger, eds. 1991. *Nationalisms and Sexualities*. New York: Routledge.

Pateman, Carole. 1988. *The Sexual Contract*. Stanford, CA: Stanford University Press.

Pateman, Carole. 1989. *The Disorder of Women: Democracy, Feminism, and Political Theory*. Stanford, CA: Stanford University Press.

Peterson, V. Spike. 1988. "An Archeology of Domination: Historicizing Gender and Class in Early Western State Formation." Ph.D. diss., The American University.

Peterson, V. Spike, ed. 1992. *Gendered States: (Re)Visions of International Relations Theory*. Boulder, CO: Lynne Rienner.

Peterson, V. Spike. 1997. "Whose Crisis? Early and Postmodern Masculinism." In *Innovation and Transformation in International Studies*, ed. Stephen Gill and James H. Mittelman. Cambridge: Cambridge University Press.

Peterson, V. Spike. 1999. "Sexing Political Identities/Nationalism as Heterosexism." *International Feminist Journal of Politics* 1 (1): 34–65.

Peterson, V. Spike. 2005. "How (the Meaning of) Gender Matters in Political Economy." *New Political Economy* 10 (4): 499–521.

Peterson, V. Spike. 2010a. "A Long View of Globalization and Crisis." *Globalizations* 7 (1–2): 187–202.

Peterson, V. Spike. 2010b. "Informalization, Inequalities and Global Insecurities." *International Studies Review* 12: 244–70.

Peterson, V. Spike and Anne Sisson Runyan. 2010. *Global Gender Issues in the New Millennium*. 3rd ed. Boulder, CO: Westview.

Pettman, Jan Jindy. 1992. "Women, Nationalism and the State: Towards an International Feminist Perspective." Occasional Paper 4 in Gender and

Development Studies, Asian Institute of Technology. Bangkok.

Puar, Jasbir K. 2007. *Terrorist Assemblages: Homonationalism in Queer Times*. Durham, NC: Duke University Press.

Pyburn, K. Anne, ed. 2004. *Ungendering Civilization*. New York: Routledge.

Rose, Nikolas. 1996. "Governing 'Advanced' Liberal Democracies.". In *Foucault and Political Reason: Liberalism, Neo-liberalism and Rationalities of Government*, ed. Andrew Barry, Thomas Osborne, and Nikolas Rose. Chicago, IL: University of Chicago Press.

Said, Edward. 1979. *Orientalism*. New York: Vintage.

Said, Edward. 1993. *Culture and Imperialism*. New York: Knopf.

Sedgwick, Eve Kosofsky. 1985. *Between Men: English Literature and Male Homosocial Desire*. New York: Columbia University Press.

Sedgwick, Eve Kosofsky. 1990. *Epistemology of the Closet*. Berkeley, CA: University of California Press.

Spivak, Gayatri Chakravorty. 1987. *In Other Worlds: Essays in Cultural Politics*. London: Methuen.

Stearns, Peter N. 2006. *Gender in World History*. 2nd ed. New York: Routledge.

Stevens, Jacqueline. 1999. *Reproducing the State*. Princeton, NJ: Princeton University Press.

Stevens, Jacqueline. 2004. "The Politics of LGBTQ Scholarship." *GLQ* 10 (2): 220–26.

Stevens, Jacqueline. 2006. "Recreating the State." *Third World Quarterly* 27 (5): 755–66.

Stevens, Jacqueline. 2010. *States without Nations: Citizenship for Mortals*. New York: Columbia University Press.

Stoler, Ann Laura. 1991. "Carnal Knowledge and Imperial Power." In *Gender at the Crossroads*, ed. Micaela di Leonardo. Berkeley, CA: University of California Press.

Stoler, Ann Laura. 1995. *Race and the Education of Desire: Foucault's History of Sexuality and the Colonial Order of Things*. Durham, NC: Duke University Press.

Tilly, Charles. 1990. *Coercion, Capital, and European States, AD 990–1990*. Cambridge: Basil Blackwell.

Weedon, Chris. 1987. *Feminist Practice and Poststructuralist Theory*. Oxford: Basil Blackwell.

AUDRE LORDE

20 USES OF THE EROTIC: THE EROTIC AS POWER (1984)

Audre Lorde (1934–1992) was an acclaimed writer and educator whose books included *Sister Outsider* (1984), *The Cancer Journals* (1980), *and Zami: A New Spelling of My Name* (1982). She held many teaching positions and toured the world as a lecturer, founding Sisterhood in Support of Sisters (SISA) in South Africa and the St. Croix Women's Coalition. She published ten volumes of poetry, numerous essays, and won awards and honors, including being named New York State's Poet Laureate. She co-founded Kitchen Table: Women of Color Press.

There are many kinds of power, used and unused, acknowledged or otherwise. The erotic is a resource within each of us that lies in a deeply female and spiritual plane, firmly rooted in the power of our unexpressed or unrecognized feeling. In order to perpetuate itself, every oppression must corrupt or distort those various sources of power within the culture of the oppressed that can provide energy for change. For women, this has meant a suppression of the erotic as a considered source of power and information within our lives.

We have been taught to suspect this resource, vilified, abused, and devalued within Western society. On the one hand, the superficially erotic has been encouraged as a sign of female inferiority; on the other hand, women have been made to suffer and to feel both contemptible and suspect by virtue of its existence.

It is a short step from there to the false belief that only by the suppression of the erotic within our lives and consciousness can women be truly strong. But that strength is illusory, for it is fashioned within the context of male models of power.

As women, we have come to distrust that power which rises from our deepest and nonrational knowledge. We have been warned against it all our lives by the male world, which values this depth of feeling enough to keep women around in order to exercise it in the service of men, but which fears this same depth too much to examine the possibilities of it within themselves. So women are maintained at a distant/inferior position to be psychically milked, much the same way ants maintain colonies of aphids to provide a life-giving substance for their masters.

But the erotic offers a well of replenishing and provocative force to the woman who does not fear its revelation, nor succumb to the belief that sensation is enough.

The erotic has often been misnamed by men and used against women. It has been made into the confused, the trivial, the psychotic, the plasticized sensation. For this reason, we have often turned away from the exploration and consideration of the erotic as a source of power and information, confusing it with its opposite, the pornographic. But pornography is a direct denial of the power of the erotic, for it represents the suppression of true feeling. Pornography emphasizes sensation without feeling.

The erotic is a measure between the beginnings of our sense of self and the chaos of our strongest feelings. It is an internal sense of satisfaction to which, once we have experienced it, we know we can aspire. For having experienced the fullness of this depth of feeling and recognizing its power, in honor and self-respect we can require no less of ourselves. . . .

This internal requirement toward excellence which we learn from the erotic must not be misconstrued as demanding the impossible from ourselves nor from others. Such a demand incapacitates everyone in the process. For the erotic is not a question only of what we do; it is a question of how acutely and fully we can feel in the doing. Once we know the extent to which we are capable of feeling that sense of satisfaction and completion, we can then observe which of our various life endeavors bring us closest to that fullness.

The aim of each thing that we do is to make our lives and the lives of our children richer and more possible. Within the celebration of the erotic in all our endeavors, my work becomes a conscious decision—a longed-for bed, which I enter gratefully and from which I rise up empowered.

Of course, women so empowered are dangerous. So we are taught to separate the erotic demand from most vital areas of our lives other than sex. And the lack of concern for the erotic root and satisfactions of our work is felt in our disaffection from so much of what we do. For instance, how often do we truly love our work even at its most difficult?

The principal horror of any system that defines the good in terms of profit rather than in terms of human need or that defines human need to the exclusion of the psychic and emotional components of that need—the principal horror of such a system is that it robs our work of its erotic value, its erotic power and life appeal and fulfillment. Such a system reduces work to a travesty of necessities, a duty by which we earn bread or oblivion for ourselves and those we love. . . .

As women, we need to examine the ways in which our world can be truly different. I am speaking here of the necessity for reassessing the quality of all the aspects of our lives and of our work and of how we move toward and through them.

The very word *erotic* comes from the Greek word *eros*, the personification of love in all its aspects— born of Chaos and personifying creative power and harmony. When I speak of the erotic, then, I speak of it as an assertion of the life force of women, of that creative energy empowered, the knowledge and use of which we are now reclaiming in our language, our history, our dancing, our loving, our work, our lives.

There are frequent attempts to equate pornography and eroticism, two diametrically opposed uses of the sexual. Because of these attempts, it has become fashionable to separate the spiritual (psychic and emotional) from the political, to see them

as contradictory or antithetical. . . . In the same way, we have attempted to separate the spiritual and the erotic, thereby reducing the spiritual to a world of flattened affect, a world of the ascetic who aspires to feel nothing. But nothing is farther from the truth. For the ascetic position is one of the highest fear, the gravest immobility. The severe abstinence of the ascetic becomes the ruling obsession. And it is one not of self-discipline but of self-abnegation.

The dichotomy between the spiritual and the political is also false, resulting from an incomplete attention to our erotic knowledge. For the bridge which connects them is formed by the erotic—the sensual—those physical, emotional, and psychic expressions of what is deepest and strongest and richest within each of us, being shared: the passions of love in its deepest meanings.

Beyond the superficial, the considered phrase, "It feels right to me," acknowledges the strength of the erotic into a true knowledge, for what that means is the first and most powerful guiding light toward any understanding. And understanding is a handmaiden, which can only wait upon, or clarify, that knowledge, deeply born. The erotic is the nurturer or nursemaid of all our deepest knowledge.

The erotic functions for me in several ways, and the first is in providing the power that comes from sharing deeply any pursuit with another person. The sharing of joy, whether physical, emotional, psychic, or intellectual, forms a bridge between the sharers, which can be the basis for understanding much of what is not shared between them and lessens the threat of their difference.

Another important way in which the erotic connection functions is the open and fearless underlining of my capacity for joy. In the way my body stretches to music and opens into response, hearkening to its deepest rhythms, so every level upon which I sense also opens to the erotically satisfying experience, whether it is dancing, building a bookcase, writing a poem, examining an idea.

That self-connection shared is a measure of the joy that I know myself to be capable of feeling, a reminder of my capacity for feeling. And that deep and irreplaceable knowledge of my capacity for joy comes to demand from all of my life that it be lived within the knowledge that such satisfaction is possible and does not have to be called *marriage*, nor *god*, nor *an afterlife*.

This is one reason why the erotic is so feared and so often relegated to the bedroom alone when it is recognized at all. For once we begin to feel deeply all the aspects of our lives, we begin to demand from ourselves and from our life-pursuits that they feel in accordance with that joy that we know ourselves to be capable of. Our erotic knowledge empowers us, becomes a lens through which we scrutinize all aspects of our existence, forcing us to evaluate those aspects honestly in terms of their relative meaning within our lives. And this is a grave responsibility, projected from within each of us, not to settle for the convenient, the shoddy, the conventionally expected, nor the merely safe.

During World War II, we bought sealed plastic packets of white, uncolored margarine, with a tiny, intense pellet of yellow coloring perched like a topaz just inside the clear skin of the bag. We would leave the margarine out for a while to soften, and then we would pinch the little pellet to break it inside the bag, releasing the rich yellowness into the soft pale mass of margarine. Then taking it carefully between our fingers, we would knead it gently back and forth, over and over, until the color had spread throughout the whole pound bag of margarine, thoroughly coloring it.

I find the erotic such a kernel within myself. When released from its intense and constrained pellet, it flows through and colors my life with a kind of energy that heightens and sensitizes and strengthens all my experience.

We have been raised to fear the *yes* within ourselves, our deepest cravings. But, once recognized, those which do not enhance our future lose their power and can be altered. The fear of our desires keeps them suspect and indiscriminately powerful, for to suppress any truth is to give it strength beyond endurance. The fear that we cannot grow beyond whatever distortions we may find within ourselves keeps us docile and loyal and obedient, externally defined, and leads us to accept many facets of our oppression as women.

When we live outside ourselves, and by that I mean on external directives only rather than from our internal knowledge and needs, when we live

away from those erotic guides from within ourselves, then our lives are limited by external and alien forms, and we conform to the needs of a structure that is not based on human need, let alone an individual's. But when we begin to live from within outward, in touch with the power of the erotic within ourselves, and allowing that power to inform and illuminate our actions upon the world around us, then we begin to be responsible to ourselves in the deepest sense. For as we begin to recognize our deepest feelings, we begin to give up, of necessity, being satisfied with suffering and self-negation and with the numbness which so often seems like their only alternative in our society. Our acts against oppression become integral with self, motivated and empowered from within.

In touch with the erotic, I become less willing to accept powerlessness or those other supplied states of being which are not native to me, such as resignation, despair, self-effacement, depression, self-denial.

And yes, there is a hierarchy. There is a difference between painting a back fence and writing a poem, but only one of quantity. And there is, for me, no difference between writing a good poem and moving into sunlight against the body of a woman I love.

This brings me to the last consideration of the erotic. To share the power of each other's feelings is different from using another's feelings as we would use a kleenex. When we look the other way from our experience, erotic or otherwise, we use rather than share the feelings of those others who participate in the experience with us. And use without consent of the used is abuse.

In order to be utilized, our erotic feelings must be recognized. The need for sharing deep feeling is a human need. But within the European American tradition, this need is satisfied by certain proscribed erotic comings-together. These occasions are almost always characterized by a simultaneous looking away, a pretense of calling them something else, whether a religion, a fit, mob violence, or even playing doctor. And this misnaming of the need and the deed gives rise to that distortion which results in pornography and obscenity—the abuse of feeling.

When we look away from the importance of the erotic in the development and sustenance of our power, or when we look away from ourselves as we satisfy our erotic needs in concert with others, we use each other as objects of satisfaction rather than share our joy in the satisfying, rather than make connection with our similarities and our differences. To refuse to be conscious of what we are feeling at any time, however comfortable that might seem, is to deny a large part of the experience and to allow ourselves to be reduced to the pornographic, the abused, and the absurd.

The erotic cannot be felt secondhand. As a Black lesbian feminist, I have a particular feeling, knowledge, and understanding for those sisters with whom I have danced hard, played, or even fought. This deep participation has often been the forerunner for joint concerted actions not possible before.

But this erotic charge is not easily shared by women who continue to operate under an exclusively European American male tradition. I know it was not available to me when I was trying to adapt my consciousness to this mode of living and sensation.

Only now, I find more and more women-identified women brave enough to risk sharing the erotic's electrical charge without having to look away and without distorting the enormously powerful and creative nature of that exchange. Recognizing the power of the erotic within our lives can give us the energy to pursue genuine change within our world rather than merely settling for a shift of characters in the same weary drama.

For not only do we touch our most profoundly creative source, but we do that which is female and self-affirming in the face of a racist, patriarchal, and anti-erotic society.

Bodies, Health, and Wellness

Keywords: contraception, cultural capital, eugenics, fat shaming, fertility, health disparities, infant mortality, reproductive justice

Our bodies grow and develop from the first moments of life. Through them, we experience sensation, sexuality, pain, and healing. We develop strength and flexibility through exercise, dance, sports, or yoga. We may have an awareness of our bodily rhythms throughout the day or the menstrual cycle—the ups and downs of physical and mental energy, tiredness, stiffness, and cramps. Pregnancy and childbirth provide intense understandings of women's bodies' elasticity and stamina, and the wonder of being able to sustain another body growing inside us. Trans people also experience specific physical changes as part of their transition process, though their identities are not dependent on their physicality or medical procedures.

This chapter discusses human embodiment, beauty ideals and standards, reproductive justice, mental and emotional health, as well as health disparities related to age, race, class, gender expression, and dis/ability. We assume that health is a complex mix of "physical, mental, and social well-being and not merely the absence of disease or infirmity," as defined by the World Health Organization (1946).

Photo by David Sherman/NBAE via Getty Images

HUMAN EMBODIMENT

Human bodies vary in looks and capabilities. US society holds strict norms and ideals for what counts as a "proper" body, though reality is much more complicated. Let's start with biology. Biologist Anne Fausto-Sterling discusses developments in scientific and medical understandings of human bodies, as mentioned in Chapter 2. In explaining biological sex, for example, experts now distinguish several levels:

- The genetic and cellular level (sex-specific gene expression, X and Y chromosomes).
- The hormonal level (in the fetus, during childhood and after puberty).
- The anatomical level (genitals and secondary sexual characteristics).

This makes many mixes and permutations of maleness and femaleness possible. "A chromosomal, hormonal and genital male (or female) may emerge with a female (or male) gender identity. Or a chromosomal female with male fetal hormones and masculinized genitalia—but with female pubertal hormones—may develop a female gender identity" (Fausto-Sterling 2000, p. 22). Fausto-Sterling argues that medical and scientific communities "have yet to adopt a language that is capable of describing such diversity" and suggests that rather than a male-female continuum, sex and gender variations constitute "points in multidimensional space" (p. 22).

As Fausto-Sterling notes, however, body variability is constrained by dominant cultural and medical assumptions of a gender binary. Intersex activists have challenged doctors' beliefs that "corrective" surgery to reduce anatomical ambiguities was necessary for them to lead so-called normal lives. For example, Pidgeon Pagonis (2015), who identifies as nonbinary and intersex, and who uses the pronouns they/them, argues that such surgeries affected their life profoundly as they were growing up. Pagonis accepts that their parents consented to surgical interventions because doctors argued that this was good for their child, but Pagonis condemns the doctors for lying and arrogantly assuming that they knew best.

The area of competitive sports provides another example, as with the controversy over Caster Semenya, a South African athlete who was raised female and is apparently intersex. She won the women's 800-meter race at the World Championships in 2009 but was subjected to "highly publicized gender verification testing" and withdrawn from competition until the International Association of Athletics Federations (IAAF) cleared her to compete as a woman (K. Hall 2011, p. 2). She went on to win Olympic gold medals in 2012 and 2016, as well as the 2017 World Championships. Arguments about fairness and discrimination still surround her success, with the IAAF now requiring such "hyper-androgenous" women athletes to take medication that will lower their natural testosterone levels.

Ynestra King (1993) emphasized the contingent nature of bodily experience due to illness, injury, or aging:

> The common ground for the person—the human body—is a place of shifting sand that can fail us at any time. It can change shape and properties without warning; this is an essential truth of embodied existence. Of all the ways of becoming "other" in our society, disability is the only one that can happen to anyone in an instant, transforming that person's life and identity forever. (p. 75)

Further, disability scholar Rosemarie Garland-Thomson (2002) argued that

> disability is a pervasive cultural system that stigmatizes certain kinds of bodily varia-
> tions. . . . The informing premise of feminist disability theory is that disability, like fe-
> maleness, is not a natural state of corporeal inferiority, inadequacy, excess, or a stroke
> of misfortune. Rather, disability is a culturally fabricated narrative of the body, similar
> to what we understand as the fictions of race and gender. (p. 5)

Sunaura Taylor (2017) distinguishes a medical model of disability that "locates a
disabled person's struggles solely within their own body" (p. 13) and a social justice
model that focuses on how society is organized. This includes buildings that do
not accommodate people with disabilities, the isolation of living in institutions,
violence committed by caregivers, and other limitations of social and economic
systems that constitute barriers to people with disabilities. Moreover, ideologies of
disability reinforce ableist assumptions that "markers of disability, such as vulnerability, weakness, physical and mental abnormality, and dependency are undesirable" (p. 17). Everyday language—such as "lame," "dumb," "retarded," "crippled,"
or "paralyzed"—reinforces stereotypes of disability as broken, incapable, or defective. In Reading 14, Eli Clare, who identifies as a genderqueer crip, emphasizes the
importance of "living in our familiar, ordinary bodies . . . even as we're treated as
curious, exotic, unbelievable, deceptive, sick, threatening from the outside" (2013,
pp. 264–265; also see, e.g., Clare 2009, 2017; K. Hall 2011; Kafer 2013; Smith and
Hutchison 2004).

Body Ideals and Beauty Standards

People's physical attributes, cultural assumptions, beliefs, and preferences shape our
day-to-day decisions about our "presentations of self" in terms of appearance and
gender expression—clothes, makeup, hairstyles, tattoos, piercings, Botox injections,
facelifts, tummy tucks, hormone therapies—as well as the meanings we ascribe to
these decisions and the way they are read by others. In Reading 21, Asian American
studies professor Linda Trinh Võ analyzes Asian and Asian American women's use of
circle contact lenses that retailers claim will make the wearer's eyes appear "gorgeous,
luminous, bigger, sexier, and more alluring." Young women promote these lenses
online by posting how-to videos, dispensing beauty advice, and garnering commercial
endorsements. Võ sees such transnational online circuits as repositioning young Asian
American women in setting beauty trends, in contrast to how corporate America positions them as outside societal beauty norms.

Body ideals and beauty standards are cultural constructs and vary among different
societies, though white Western beauty ideals circulate worldwide. US feminist scholars have analyzed ads and media representations that target women and girls with
an ideal of beauty defined as thin, lean, toned, tall, young, white, and heterosexual,
with flawless skin and well-groomed hair. Where women of color are used in ads, they
are often light-skinned and conform to this same body type. This beauty standard is
backed by a multi-billion-dollar industry that sees women's bodies as a series of problems in need of correction (see, e.g., Bordo 1993; Bryant 2013; Brumberg 1997; Molina-
Guzmán 2010; Riley 2002; Wolf 2009).

The aim is to promote insecurity, self-hatred, and distorted perceptions of size, appetite, and attractiveness so that we will consume the countless products, diet plans, and cosmetic surgeries marketed to remedy our alleged deficiencies. Reality TV shows like *Extreme Makeover* and *America's Next Top Model* normalize this goal. Much research, commentary, and concern have focused on obsessive dieting, which mainly affects young, white, middle-class women, exemplified by Abra Fortune Chernik, who describes her ordeal with anorexia in Reading 56. In terms of looks, the extreme thinness or "heroin chic" promoted by the fashion industry may also be associated with malnutrition, drug addiction, or illnesses such as cancer or AIDS, which eat away the body from the inside. To the extent that women or female-identified people internalize ideal beauty standards, we set ourselves up to pursue a goal that is largely unattainable. Even the elite corps of full-time fashion models have their photos airbrushed and digitally enhanced (L. Collins 2008; Reaves et al. 2004).

Writer Courtney Martin (2007) discussed what she called the "frightening new normalcy of hating your body." Jean Kilbourne (1999; *Killing Us Softly 4; Slim Hopes*) focuses on the toxic cultural environment of advertising images that can severely undermine girls' self-confidence and sense of agency. Social media, especially Instagram and Snapchat, have ramped up this trend, with apps available so that young women can retouch their photos before they post them. Kilbourne notes the objectification and commodification of women's bodies as things, especially in advertising. We learn to see ourselves as disconnected parts—thighs, hips, bottoms, breasts, noses, and chins—all in need of improvement. Sociologist Barbara Omolade (1983) described an egregious historical example of the objectification of enslaved African women, whose body parts were divided up and commodified for the white plantation economy:

> Her back and muscle were pressed into field labor where she was forced to work with men and work like men. Her hands were demanded to nurse and nurture the white man and his family. . . . Her vagina, used for his sexual pleasure, was the gateway to the womb, which was his place of capital investment—the capital investment being the sex act and the resulting child the accumulated surplus, worth money on the slave market. (p. 354)

Body Acceptance

There are many ways of looking female, from feminine femmes to sturdy butches. Queer, trans, nonbinary, and other gender nonconforming people broaden the range of bodily appearance. A fundamental argument of this chapter is for everyone to accept and appreciate their bodies, to love their capabilities and vitality (the physical grounding of life), and to value health and wellness over externally imposed standards based on looks. Noting that mainstream culture equates beauty and power for women, Silva Tenenbein (1998) reversed the beauty-power equation for lesbians:

> For dykes it's not beauty which makes us powerful but power that makes us beautiful . . . our passion, our strength, and our courage to choose to be the "other" . . . our adamant refusal to be deflected from what we want. (pp. 159–160)

Large women of all racial and ethnic groups challenge mainstream assumptions and stereotypes that they are sloppy, irresponsible, undisciplined, depressed, sexless, unwanted, or unhealthy (see, e.g., Lamm 1995; Rothblum and Solovay 2009). Judith Ortiz Cofer (1993) noted that "a fuller figure" was admired in her Puerto Rican community. Many African American women say, "I don't want to be no skinny minny!" Queen T'isha wrote:

> Racism and sexism as practiced in America includes body hostilities. I didn't grow up with the belief that fat women were to be despised. The women in my family were fat, smart, sexy, employed, wanted, married, and the rulers of their households. (Quoted in Edison and Notkin 1994, p. 106)

Also noteworthy is the American Jewish word *zaftig*, a positive term for women who are fleshy, voluptuous, and thought to embody strength, sexiness, comfort, and nurturance (St. Paige 1999).

In Reading 22, Margitte Kristjansson sees corpulence as a subversive cultural practice and argues that fat bodies **queer** ideas of consumption, as fat fashionistas develop "their own ways to engage with fashion when the industry refuses to recognize them as viable customers" (2014a, p. 134). She refers to the "male gaze," a concept introduced by film theorist and filmmaker Laura Mulvey (1975) to suggest a sexualized way of looking that empowers heterosexual males and objectifies females—though fat women are not included in this sexualized representation. Also, Kristjansson draws on the concept of **cultural capital**—where an attribute that society values, like thinness, can be cultivated for social profit and exchanged for other forms of power. In this society, thin bodies are seen not only as more beautiful but also as more controlled and refined, whereas fat bodies are associated with undisciplined overconsumption. Yet, Kristjansson reported, over 50 percent of US women wear at least some item of clothing in a size 16, and more wear dresses in size 16 than sizes 0, 2, and 4 combined (Kristjansson 2014b).

A transnational movement of fat fashion bloggers has sparked media attention and body-positive activism online. Many feminists have welcomed the notion of "fat acceptance" and see the concept of "overweight" as a social construction. Organizations working to counter fat oppression include the Council on Size and Weight Discrimination and the National Association to Advance Fat Acceptance. Photographers have also undertaken "full body" projects that celebrate women of all shapes and sizes (see, e.g., Nimoy 2007; R. Olson 2008).

By contrast, public health researchers Antronette Yancey, Joanne Leslie, and Emily Abel (2006) argue that feminist teachers and scholars have tended to downplay the "accumulating data about the health consequences" of what they call "the obesity epidemic," which they found "surprising and troubling" (p. 425). They view obesity as caused by social and economic factors that contribute to an "obesity-causing environment" that particularly affects low-income people of color (see the box feature "Maintaining Health: Social and Economic Factors"). They advocate prevention policies and programs that address underlying causes as being much more effective than simply urging individuals to lose weight. These writers endorsed government definitions of overweight as having a body mass index of 25 to 29.9 and obesity as an index of 30

Maintaining Health: Social and Economic Factors

Magazine articles and websites focus on individual lifestyle factors—diet, cigarette smoking, weight, exercise, and a positive attitude to coping with stress—and urge people to take more personal responsibility for their health. Although this is valuable advice, lifestyle is only part of the story.

- *Access to nutritious food.* Eating well takes greater effort in low-income neighborhoods, which tend to have more liquor and convenience stores rather than full-service supermarkets that carry fresh fruits and vegetables. Fast-food restaurants are more prevalent in poorer neighborhoods than in middle-class areas, and fast food is offered at lower prices relative to more healthy options (see, e.g., Agyeman and Alkon 2011; Azuma 2007; Gottlieb and Joshi 2010; Guthman 2011).
- *Costs for foods.* Prices for foods such as milk, eggs, vegetables, chicken, and beef have risen, mainly related to oil prices and the growing demand for alternative fuels like ethanol and biodiesel based on food crops such as corn and soybeans. Industrialized food processing has made "energy-dense" snacks and desserts—with a high proportion of fat and sugar—extremely inexpensive (Brownell and Horgen 2004).

- *Time.* Responsibilities of waged-work and caring for families may mean that women have little time or energy to shop for food, cook meals from scratch, or exercise.
- *Exercise.* Most people in the United States lead sedentary lives. Fewer girls than boys take up sports, and many adult women have no regular exercise practice. Larger women may feel self-conscious in gyms. Also, women do not want to walk—or allow their children to play—in unsafe neighborhoods.
- *Self-care.* Many women have been socialized to take care of others in their families and communities rather than themselves. They may pay for clothes, hair care, and nails rather than exercise programs or fitness classes.
- *Overeating.* Eating can be a source of comfort and pleasure. Women may eat as a way to cope with frustration, anger, anxiety, and sadness; physical, emotional, or sexual abuse; and the daily pain of sexism, racism, classism, and heterosexism (see, e.g., Gold 2011; Morrone 2009; Skover 2012).
- *Sexualized violence.* This type of violence affects physical and mental health, as discussed in Chapter 6.

or more. On this standard, 32 percent of US adults are overweight, and a further 38 percent are obese (see Table 1 in Fryar, Carroll, and Ogden 2016). In terms of race and ethnicity, 57 percent of Black women were estimated to be obese, compared with 47 percent of Latinas, 38 percent of white women, and 12 percent of Asian American women (see Table 3 in Fryar, Carroll, and Ogden 2016). Medical professionals and health advocates have underlined the links between weight and illness, especially heart disease, diabetes, stroke, and joint problems. Fat acceptance activists, however, challenge or downplay these claims.

REPRODUCTIVE HEALTH, REPRODUCTIVE JUSTICE

Pregnancy and having a baby are profound experiences. A woman may become pregnant because she wants a child, wants to experience pregnancy and childbirth, wants to be recognized as a grown woman, or all of the above. She may believe it will make her a "real" woman, or she may hope that it will keep her relationship together or make her partner happy. Some women plan to become pregnant, others get pregnant by accident, and still others as a result of being raped. This deeply personal experience is also a public issue. Especially for teens, LGBTQI women, women with disabilities, and mothers receiving welfare, there may be a serious tension between the personal event of pregnancy and societal attitudes to it.

Non Sequitur © 2003 Wiley Ink, Inc.. Dist. By Andrews Mcmeel Syndication.

Focusing on Fertility

Women's reproductive years span half our lifetimes or more, from our teens to our forties. Many women in the United States want to control their fertility: to limit the number of children they have, to postpone pregnancy until they are older, to avoid pregnancy with a particular partner, or to avoid it altogether. For others—especially for women of color and women with disabilities—the emphasis is on having children, and we return to this point below.

Sex Education and Teen Pregnancy

Decisions about sex education are made at the state and local levels. Some states emphasize abstinence-only-until-marriage, though there is no firm evidence that this stops—or even delays—teen sex. According to the Centers for Disease Control and Prevention (2015), fewer than half of US high schools and only 20 percent of middle schools teach about sexually transmitted infections, HIV, and pregnancy, though this varies from state to state. Mexican American and Puerto Rican girls interviewed by sociologist Lorena Garcia (2012) were dissatisfied with the sex education they received in school, in which teachers and guest speakers emphasized that they should be "good girls," discouraged their questions, assumed that their risk for pregnancy was linked to "Latino culture," and sometimes cancelled sex ed to allow more time to prepare for standardized tests.

Babies born to teens present a tremendous responsibility for young mothers and their families. Government and community organizations have made major efforts to reduce the number of teen births from an all-time high in 1991 of 62 births per 1,000 girls aged 15 to 19. This rate continues to fall, with a new low in 2016 of 20 births per 1,000 girls, 74 percent of them to young women aged 18 or 19 (US Department of Health and Human Services 2016). Research suggests that this is due to increased use of contraceptives by young people, though the United States continues to have the highest rate of teen pregnancy among industrialized nations (Guttmacher Institute 2018a). In terms of race and ethnicity, US teen birth rates are highest for Latinx and African American teens compared to white girls and highest in southern states (see Figures 1 and 2 in US Department of Health and Human Services 2016).

Sexually Transmitted Infections

The term *sexually transmitted infection*, or STI, refers to more than twenty-five diseases, including herpes, genital warts, pubic lice ("crabs"), chlamydia, gonorrhea, and syphilis. The prevalence of all STIs is increasing at an alarming rate, with about 2.3 million new cases of chlamydia, gonorrhea, and syphilis diagnosed in 2017, almost half of them to people aged 15 to 24 (Centers for Disease Control and Prevention 2018c). Chlamydia, gonorrhea, and syphilis are curable with antibiotics, but most cases are undiagnosed and untreated. For women, STIs may not be noticeable or may be difficult to diagnose, as women often do not have any symptoms or, if they do, the symptoms are mistaken for something else. If untreated, STIs can lead to pelvic inflammatory disease, infertility, or stillborn infants. Knowing about safer-sex practices is important in reducing the risk of STIs as well as HIV/AIDS. A benefit of condoms as a method of birth control is that they also give some protection against STIs, though women are not always able to influence male partners to use condoms.

Birth Control

Barrier methods like condoms and diaphragms have been used for many years. Condoms are available over the counter, but a doctor must fit a diaphragm. In the 1960s, the intrauterine device, or IUD, often called the coil, was introduced, as was "the pill"—the most popular form of contraception today for women under 30 and the first chemical contraceptive to be taken every day. The pill affects the whole body continuously, as do newer injectable contraceptives or those implanted under the skin. Low-income African American, Native American, and Latinx women are more likely than white women to be encouraged to use these long-acting methods. Official policy seeks to limit their pregnancies and assumes that they will be unreliable in using other methods. The Black Women's Health Network, the National Latina Health Organization, and other women's health advocates have shown that many women using implants had difficulty getting them removed. In addition, these methods may compound health problems that affect low-income women of color, like hypertension and diabetes.

Emergency contraception that prevents fertilization is available over the counter to people 17 years and over, under the trade names Plan B One-Step or Next Choice. These can be used in the event of unprotected (hetero)sex or if another form of contraception fails. This is a chemical method that involves taking oral contraceptives up to five days after unprotected sex, the sooner the better.

Abortion

Attitudes toward abortion as a way to limit fertility have varied greatly over time and from one society to another. Women in pre-industrial societies sometimes used herbal remedies to "bring on a period." Historically, the Catholic Church held the view that the soul did not enter the fetus for at least forty days after conception and allowed abortion up to that point. Until the mid-nineteenth century, US women were allowed to seek an abortion in the early part of pregnancy before they felt the fetus moving, a subjectively determined time referred to as the quickening. After the Civil War, more restrictive abortion laws were passed, partly to increase births and also to shift authority over women's reproductive lives to the developing medical profession. Also, in 1869, Pope Pius IX declared that life begins at conception, and thus all abortion became murder in the eyes of the Catholic Church. By 1900, the only legal ground for an abortion in the United States was to save the life of the mother. Many women were forced to bring unwanted pregnancies to term. Thousands died trying to conduct an abortion themselves or at the hands of "backstreet" abortionists. Some upper- and middle-class women found doctors to perform safe abortions for a price, and some doctors did abortions for poor women. The women and the doctors risked prosecution if found out (Solinger 2000). Those with knowledge of herbs, massage, or medicine helped others. Between 1969 and 1973, women in the Chicago area, nicknamed the Janes, operated a clandestine abortion service that provided some 11,000 safe abortions on a pay-what-you-can basis (see, e.g., Arcana 2005; Boynton 2018; Kamen 2000).

In 1973, the US Supreme Court ruled 7–2 in the case of *Roe v. Wade* that a right to privacy under the Constitution extended to a woman's decision to have an abortion, but that this must be balanced against the state's interest in regulating abortions, protecting women's health, and the potentiality of human life. In disallowing many state and federal restrictions on abortion then in place, *Roe v. Wade* generated a national debate that continues to polarize the country to this day. This provision was contested from the beginning, and the 1977 Hyde Amendment withdrew state funding for abortion for poor women. Subsequently, states have imposed hundreds of restrictions, including mandatory waiting periods, parental consent for teens, bans on late-term abortions, and being required to hear about risks and alternatives as a condition of getting an abortion. Although two generations of women have grown up taking abortion rights for granted, this issue is highly politicized, with a wide and growing gap between legality and access.

For over forty years, well-funded anti-abortion groups have worked to undermine and overturn the right to abortion. Some have bombed clinics, harassed patients, and killed doctors known to perform abortions as part of their practice (see, e.g., Jefferis 2011; A. Robb 2010). Abortion opponents have elected anti-choice political candidates at state and congressional levels. Republicans in Congress and state legislatures have introduced bills to whittle away the legality of abortion and elevate the unborn child, even as a "nonviable fetus," to the status of "personhood," with rights equal to or greater than those of the mother. In response, women's health advocates have struggled to keep clinics open, but legal restrictions and severe harassment have reduced the number of abortion providers. In 2014, 90 percent of US counties had no abortion provider; 39 percent of women lived in one of those counties (Guttmacher Institute 2014).

The number of women who seek abortion is falling. In 2014, the abortion rate was 14.6 out of every 1,000 women aged 15 to 44, the lowest since 1975, and 31 percent of all abortions were medication abortions, which the Food and Drug Administration approved in 2000 (Jones and Jerman 2017). This drop in abortions is due to increased use of contraception, reduced access to abortion, and fewer apparently unintended pregnancies. Most women who had an abortion in 2014 were in their twenties, white, and unmarried; 66 percent of the procedures were done in the first eight weeks of pregnancy, and 89 percent in the first twelve weeks (Guttmacher Institute 2018b). Proportionate to their numbers in the overall population, Black and Latinx women were more likely to have an abortion than white women. When interviewed, women gave the following reasons for terminating an unwanted pregnancy: their responsibilities for other people (74 percent); they could not afford a baby (73 percent); a baby would interfere with their schooling, job, or caring for other dependents (69 percent); and not wanting to be a single parent (48 percent).

Judith Arcana (1994) has argued that abortion is a decision a woman makes because she believes it is the best for herself and her baby. Pro-choice activists have tended to downplay the profound responsibility of choosing to end a life as they focused on keeping abortion legal. Arcana calls a fetus a baby, and argues that the semantics of "*fetus* or *embryo*" used by pro-choice organizers skirts the central moral issue. It has conceded the space for anti-choice activists to excoriate women who have abortions as heartless and irresponsible (see, e.g., Arcana 2005; Jacob 2002). If the Supreme Court overturns *Roe v. Wade*, legal jurisdiction will revert to the states, many of them poised to ban abortion or to re-criminalize it. Recognizing that this issue is critical to women's ability to control our lives, health advocates are developing in-person and online ways to support safe, self-managed abortions (Donovan 2018; Rios 2018).

Reproductive Technologies

Technologies such as in vitro fertilization, or IVF, constitute an important development, mainly marketed to middle- and upper-middle-class women as a way of widening individual choice. A woman's eggs are fertilized outside her body, and the fertilized embryo implanted into her womb. This pushes the **medicalization** of pregnancy and childbirth a step further and holds out the hope that infertile couples, postmenopausal women, or trans people can have a baby. Also, young women may bear a child as a surrogate mother under contract to an infertile couple, with promises of compensation ranging from $30,000 to $50,000 plus expenses and medical coverage. Ads specify attributes sought in the birth mothers, including race, skin color, age, IQ, etc. Fertility clinics also need ovum "donors"—more accurately, sellers—and harvest the eggs of young, college-educated women from a range of specified racial and ethnic groups (Reis 2011). Infertility treatments are expensive, involve heavy doses of hormones, and have a notably low success rate. Infertility may be caused by STIs, the effects of IUDs, delayed childbearing, and environmental factors. Infertility rates have dropped compared to previous decades, but this issue has a higher profile nowadays because of technological developments. International surrogacy is organized by businesses in various countries of the Global South at lower costs than in the United States (see Reading 38).

These reproductive technologies open up an array of moral, legal, and economic questions (see, e.g., Danna 2015; D. Davis 2009; M. Davis 2017; Ragone and Twine 2000; Teays and Purdy 2001). Are they liberating for women? If so, for which women? And at what costs? Who pays the price, and in what ways? In her now classic text, radical feminist Shulamith Firestone (1970) argued that women's liberation required freedom from biological reproduction and looked forward to developments in reproductive technology that would make it possible for a fetus to develop outside the womb. This is in stark contrast to sociologist Barbara Katz Rothman (1986) and myriad women who claim that if women lose our ability to bear a child, we lose a "quintessential female experience" (p. 111). Other feminist critics of reproductive technologies have emphasized their invasiveness and consumers' lack of power over and knowledge about these methods, as compared with medical experts (see, e.g., Deech and Smajdor 2007; Klein 2017; Lublin 1998).

Reproductive Justice: An Intersectional Framework

White feminists have made abortion the centerpiece of reproductive rights activism. Advocates originally campaigned for women's *right* to abortion but then moved to a "softer" pro-choice framework. Rights apply to everyone; choice is only meaningful for those with resources. Women of color health advocates have developed the broader concept of **reproductive justice** that links reproductive rights to social and economic justice, as explained by Loretta Ross in Reading 23 (also see Reading 52; Gurr 2015; Piepmeier 2013; Silliman et al. 2004; A. Smith 2005a). This approach emphasizes the way successive governments have limited motherhood, especially for women of color, and emphasizes the need for resistance to reproductive oppression, including sterilization abuse and infant mortality.

Sterilization

Sterilization, without women's full knowledge or under duress, has been a common practice in the United States for poor Puerto Rican, African American, and Native American women. By the early 1980s, 24 percent of African American women, 35 percent of Puerto Rican women, and 42 percent of Native American women had been sterilized, compared with 15 percent of white women (Black Women's Health Project 1995). Currently, sterilization is federally funded under the Medicaid program and is free on demand to low-income women.

African American women have consistently tried to be self-determining in their reproductive lives despite having been used as breeders by slaveholders and subjected to state interventions to control their fertility (see, e.g., P. H. Collins 2004; L. J. Ross 1993; Silliman et al. 2004). These interventions include sterilization programs and long-acting chemical contraceptives, which legal scholar Dorothy Roberts (1997) described as "killing the black body." This continues the long connection between birth control and **eugenics**, or selective breeding linked to racism and ableism. Historically, eugenics has been justified as a benefit to society on the grounds that it creates healthier and more intelligent people, lessens human suffering, and saves resources that would otherwise be required to care for people with disabilities. Women with disabilities fight for the right to have children in the face of dominant assumptions that they are nonsexual beings or that they could not cope with motherhood (see, e.g., Finger 1990; Prilleltensky 2003; Saxton 1995; Wilkerson 2011). In Reading 24, Alison Kafer contributes to this discourse by discussing the experience of a deaf lesbian couple who chose to conceive and raise a deaf child and the public reactions to their decision.

Pregnancy and Childbirth

Before there were male gynecologists, midwives helped women through pregnancy and childbirth (Ehrenreich and English 2010). As medicine became professionalized in the nineteenth century, gynecology and obstetrics developed as an area of medical specialization. Doctors eroded the position of midwives and ignored or scorned their knowledge as "old wives' tales." Largely for the convenience of the doctor, women began to give birth lying on their backs, perhaps the hardest position in which to deliver a baby. From the 1950s onward, cesarean sections (C-sections) became more common, often for the doctors' convenience or from fear of malpractice suits. In 2015, 32 percent of births in the United States were C-sections, though health researchers argue that many of these were not medically necessary (Thielking 2015). The past forty years have seen an extension of this medicalization process as doctors monitor pregnancy with procedures like amniocentesis, sonograms, and ultrasound. Although this technology allows practitioners—and through them, pregnant women—to know details about the health and condition of the fetus, it also changes women's experiences of pregnancy and childbirth and may undermine their knowledge of and confidence in their bodily processes. Writers and researchers involved in Black Women Birthing Justice emphasize the importance of maternal health and care during pregnancy and childbirth, as well as sterilization abuse and high death rates among Black mothers and infants (Oparah and Bonaparte 2015; Oparah et al. 2017).

Infant Mortality

This refers to babies who die before their first birthday. Although rates of infant mortality have steadily decreased in the United States, Black infants continue to die at more than twice the rate of white infants. For babies born in 2016, Asian babies had the lowest infant mortality rate (at 3.6 deaths per 1,000 births), followed by white (4.9 deaths), Hispanic (5.0 deaths), Native Hawaiian and Pacific Islander (7.4 deaths), American Indian or Native Alaskan (9.4 deaths), and African American babies (11.4 deaths per 1,000 births) (Centers for Disease Control and Prevention 2018b). Infant mortality is linked to individual factors such as smoking during pregnancy and macro-level factors like poverty. Mortality rates were higher for infants whose mothers did not have prenatal care in the first trimester, and more common among Native American, Mexican American, and African American women, compared with Asian American and white women as these data show.

HEALTH AND WELLNESS

Everyone needs nourishing food, clean water, adequate exercise, and freedom from stress in order to maintain health and vitality. Wellness is partly linked to genetics, physical environment, and socio-economic factors such as race, class, dis/ability, gender expression, and aging. In Box 5.2 we present data from the World Health Organization to show that, worldwide, the deadliest disease is poverty.

Health Disparities

Disparities in health among different groups are due to a mix of overlapping causes, including income level, educational attainment, occupation, access to health services, and environmental conditions—factors linked to race, class, dis/ability, and gender expression. People with disabilities and trans people may have difficulty in finding doctors who are sensitive to their bodies and their health needs, and they may have limited medical insurance to cover their care. Taken as a whole, the health of white women and Asian American women is significantly better than that of African American, Latinx, and Native American women.[1] We note a few examples here.

---

1 Most US government data are analyzed according to race/ethnicity in three categories: white, Black, and Hispanic—which includes Puerto Ricans, Cubans, Mexican Americans, and people from Central and South America. Some reports give details for Native Americans and Native Alaskans, or for Asians and Pacific Islanders—another very heterogeneous group. Data on social issues are rarely analyzed according to socioeconomic class. Bear this in mind during this discussion of health disparities, which suffers from limitations of the data available.

The World's Deadliest Disease Is Poverty

- In 2017, worldwide, 5.4 million children died before their fifth birthday, mainly from malnutrition, malaria, acute respiratory infections, diarrhea, and prenatal complications. Nearly half of these deaths were newborns.
- Children in sub-Saharan Africa are over 15 times more likely to die before their fifth birthday than are those in high-income countries.
- Most of these conditions can be prevented or cured with improvements in sanitation, clean water supplies, better housing, adequate food, and general hygiene. The majority of deaths from infectious diseases can be prevented with existing, cost-effective measures, including childhood vaccinations, bed nets and other malaria-prevention treatments, oral rehydration therapy, and antibiotics.

- Poor nutrition and being underweight puts children under age five at increased risk for infections like diarrhea and pneumonia. Being underweight remains a pervasive problem in countries of the Global South, where poverty causes household food insecurity, mothers' inadequate nutrition, unhealthy environments, and poor health care.
- The Sustainable Development Goals adopted by the United Nations in 2015 were developed to promote well-being for all children. Goal 3 is to end preventable deaths of newborns and children under age five by 2030. Accelerated progress is needed to achieve this, especially in sub-Saharan Africa and South East Asia.

Source: World Health Organization (2018).

Tuberculosis, an infectious disease associated with poor living conditions, was all but eradicated in the United States during the twentieth century. Compared with the rest of the population, Native Americans are four times as likely to have tuberculosis. Hypertension, a major risk factor for heart disease and stroke, is much more prevalent among African American women than among white women. Public health researchers have attributed this difference, in part, to stress related to racism and poverty (American Psychological Association 2016).

Women with HIV/AIDS have not been diagnosed as early as men because their symptoms are not so clear-cut and doctors were less likely to look for HIV/AIDS in women. Also, negative stereotypes of HIV-positive women (as drug users and people with multiple sex partners) have affected their visibility and care. Far more women than men contract HIV through heterosexual contact. Of women in the United States who were living with HIV/AIDS in 2016, 59 percent were Black, 19 percent were Latinx, and 17 percent were white (Centers for Disease Control and Prevention 2018a).

Toxic workplaces are a health hazard, especially for low-income women. Some companies have kept women out of the most hazardous work—which is often the highest paid work as well—or required that they be sterilized first, to avoid being sued if these workers later give birth to babies with disabilities. Women working in computer manufacturing, housecleaning, chicken processing, and the dairy industry are all exposed to chemicals on the job, as are nail salon workers and farm workers.

After skin cancer, breast cancer is the most common cancer for women. It affects one woman in eight nationwide, though there are higher incidences in certain geographical areas. The likelihood of being diagnosed with breast cancer increases with age. Middle-class women are more likely than low-income women to have insurance to cover mammograms to detect breast cancer. Late diagnosis is directly related to higher mortality rates. For women under 45, breast cancer is more common in African American women than white women, and African American women are more likely to die of breast cancer. Asian, Hispanic, and Native American women have a lower risk of developing and dying from breast cancer (Breastcancer.org 2018).

Mental and Emotional Health

In various ways, historically oppressed and marginalized people have been stereotyped and characterized as somehow less emotionally and mentally healthy than those in the dominant group. Philosopher Denise Russell (1995) traced definitions of madness from medieval Europe, where it was thought of as a combination of error and sin. During the seventeenth century, economic crises and rising unemployment prompted local officials to build "houses of confinement" for beggars, drunks, vagabonds, petty criminals, and those considered mad. Later, as psychiatry developed, doctors headed asylums in Europe and the United States and theorized that much mental distress experienced by women was due to their sexuality and reproductive capacities.

Hysteria, thought to be due to a disturbance of the womb, became a catch-all category to describe women's mental illness. The English word *hysterical* comes from the Greek *hysterikos*, meaning "of the womb." Writer and literary critic Elaine Showalter (1987) and psychotherapist Phyllis Chesler (1972) showed how definitions of madness were used to suppress women's creativity, education, and political involvement. Nineteenth-century white upper- and middle-class women who wanted to write, paint, travel, or speak out on issues of the day were often assumed by their husbands—and by psychiatrists—to be insane. Charlotte Perkins Gilman's powerful fictional work, *The Yellow Wallpaper* (2000), describes this experience from having lived through it. More recently, "depression" and "premenstrual syndrome" (or "PMS") have replaced "hysteria" as catch-all terms used in describing mental illness in women.

In 1973, the American Psychiatric Association removed homosexuality from its *Diagnostic and Statistical Manual of Mental Disorders* (DSM). Currently, they include gender dysphoria in the most recent edition, the DSM-5 (American Psychiatric Association 2013). The American Psychiatric Association's website (2018) describes this as "a conflict between a person's physical or assigned gender and the gender with which he/she/they identify," which leads to "significant distress and/or problems functioning". Although careful to include societal factors and to separate gender dysphoria from gender nonconformity in discussing "challenges and complications" associated with the condition, this language and the fact of being included in the DSM reinforce a medicalized and stigmatizing approach.

Alongside the negative attitudes described above, there are serious mental health concerns among marginalized peoples, and studies have shown the relationship between oppression and mental distress (see, e.g., Fernando 2010). For instance, many more women are diagnosed as having some sort of mental illness, especially depression, compared to men. Adult African Americans are 20 percent more likely to report serious psychological distress than white people. People who identify as transgender experience mental health issues at a higher rate than cisgender women or men (Schreiber 2016). Seeking and getting help is another aspect of the issue. Seeking help is shaped by cultural attitudes to mental health treatment, while getting help is linked to one's ability to pay and finding a suitable therapist or other mental health provider. It is more socially acceptable for women as a group to seek help for mental health concerns compared to men. However, not everyone who "seeks help" does so voluntarily. Sometimes seeing a counselor or therapist is required by a social service agency or is a condition of probation. Patients in mental hospitals represent a relatively small proportion of those who are suffering mentally and emotionally. In general, women are admitted to mental hospitals as inpatients in roughly the same numbers as men.

Denise Russell (1995) pointed to many external factors affecting women's mental health, including sexual abuse, rape, intimate partner violence, restricted educational or economic opportunities, racism, and pressure to look beautiful, to be thin, and to be compliant wives and long-suffering mothers—any of which, she argued, could reasonably make women depressed or "crazy." Hopelessness and anger at such circumstances are not irrational reactions. Women's symptoms may seem vague to doctors; even when understood, such traumas and problems are not easy to alleviate.

Women have written powerful fictional and autobiographical accounts of mental illness (see, e.g., Danquah 1998; Kaysen 1994; Millet 1990; Plath 1971; Shannonhouse 2003; Slater 1998). In Reading 25, cultural critic bell hooks refers to the severe long-term effects of racism and internalized oppression on African Americans' mental and emotional health. She notes that slave narratives often emphasized the importance of Black people's capacity to repress feelings as a key to their survival, and that this habit has been passed on through family experiences. As a result, "many black females have learned to deny our inner needs while we develop our capacity to cope and confront in public life." Sociologist Tamara Beauboeuf-Lafontant (2007, 2009) argued that "being strong" is often taken as a sign of emotional health for white women. However, "being strong" is a "culturally specific expectation placed on Black women," which "normalizes struggle, selflessness, and internalization strategies" that compromise Black women's health (2007, p. 46; also see Evans, Bell and Burton 2017; Parks 2010).

According to a report published in *Psychology Today*, the high rate of "distress and impairment, considered essential characteristics of mental disorders" among transgender individuals is linked primarily to the discrimination, stigma, non-acceptance, and physical and psychological abuse they face regularly and consistently as a social group (Schreiber 2016). This finding is consistent with studies over the past decades, which show that

> for many adults, dealing with discrimination results in a state of heightened vigilance and changes in behavior, which in itself can trigger stress responses—that is, even the anticipation of discrimination is sufficient to cause people to become stressed. (American Psychological Association 2016, p. 8)

Moreover, other studies have suggested similar experiences among refugees and asylum seekers, also due to the stress of marginalization and discrimination (see, e.g., Kastrup 2016; Volkan 2017).

People of all classes and racial groups may attempt to deal with the pain and difficulty of their lives through drugs and alcohol. In the United States, drug addiction has been considered a crime rather than a health issue. In recent years, highly addictive medications prescribed for chronic pain have been responsible for an increasing number of deaths, especially among white people. There are far fewer drug-treatment programs than required, and fewer for women and transgender people than for men.

Aging and Health

The health of women in middle age and later life is partly linked to how healthy they were when they were younger. The effects of poor nutrition, smoking, stress, or lack of exercise build up over time. Many older women have felt pressure to conform to dominant beauty ideals and gender expectations of caretaking others throughout their adult lives. As they age, they have to face their changing looks, physical limitations, and loss of independence and loved ones, which calls for patience, courage, optimism, and religious faith. Shevy Healey (1997) argued that confronting **ageism** in society as well as one's own negative feelings about aging is a must for mental health. Feminist researchers Margaret Morganroth Gullette (2004, 2011), Margaret Cruickshank (2013), and Ashton Applewhite (2016) all emphasize the social construction of aging. Cruickshank (2003) critiqued the field of gerontology for accepting a medical model of aging and proposed an approach that emphasizes longevity, embraces life changes and older women's needs, and includes research conducted by older women. Calasanti and Slevin (2006) countered the cultural insistence on "successful aging" (p. 3) and the ways "the anti-aging industry operates to reinscribe gendered, ageist stereotypes onto the body" (quoted in Winterich 2007, p. 784). In general, women live longer than men in all racial groups, but white and Asian American women live longer than Latinx or Black women. To live well in older age, women need financial security, family and friends, and support for conditions like arthritis, Alzheimer's, diabetes, deafness, broken bones, digestive conditions, and osteoporosis that typically affect women and worsen with age.

Feminists have organized health projects since the early 1970s. Examples include college courses in women's health; informal self-health groups like the Bloomington Women's Health Collective (Bloomington, IN); women's health centers (e.g., Equality Health Center in Concord, NH); campaigns for reproductive rights (e.g., NARAL Pro-Choice America and regional affiliates) or for breast cancer research and treatment (e.g., Women's Community Cancer Project, Cambridge, MA); community health campaigns for LGBTQ people (e.g., FORGE, Milwaukee, WI; Gender Diversity, Seattle, WA; GLBT Health Access Project, MA); and national organizations like Black Women's Health Imperative (Washington, DC),, the National Latina Health Organization (Oakland, CA), the National Women's Health Network (Washington, DC), and the Native American Women's Health and Education Resource Center (Lake Andes, SD). The Boston Women's Health Book Collective's groundbreaking book *Our Bodies, Ourselves*, which inspired the title for Part II of this book, first started as mimeographed notes for a course in women's health and was later developed for publication. It has gone through many editions and is an essential resource on women's health and sexuality, translated and adapted for use in many countries (K. Davis 2007).

QUESTIONS FOR REFLECTION

As you read and discuss this chapter, think about these questions:

1. How do you feel about your own body? What makes you feel good about your body? How do you know when you're healthy? Sick?
2. What are the main body and health issues for women in your family or on your campus?
3. If you are transgender or a gender nonconforming person, what specific health and wellness concerns do you face?

4. How do you and your family cover the costs of health care?
5. What do you understand about the difference between reproductive rights and reproductive justice? What do you see as the advantages and limitations of these approaches?
6. How much did you eat while reading this section? How much exercise did you do?

FINDING OUT MORE ON THE WEB

1. Several governments, including those of Australia, Britain, France, Italy, and Spain, have introduced regulations that ban very thin models from participating in fashion shows and companies from using overly photoshopped advertising images. Use your search engine to find out about the effects of such initiatives, and examine your own beliefs about them.
2. Find out about the history of *Roe v. Wade*. How and why did this initiative gain support? What was the cultural and historical context? Who were some of the key players who helped to make it happen? What is its status now?
3. Research organizations that support trans people's health and wellness throughout the life course.

TAKING ACTION

1. Make it your daily practice to affirm your body. List all the steps you take to care for yourself and any additional ones you want to take.
2. Find out more about what your family and community consider effective self-care practices. Where can women and gender nonconforming or trans people go to keep healthy or to get quality health care in your community?
3. Organize an activity on your campus or in your home community to draw attention to body issues and to challenge common stereotypes.

LINDA TRINH VÕ

21 TRANSNATIONAL BEAUTY CIRCUITS: ASIAN AMERICAN WOMEN, TECHNOLOGY, AND CIRCLE CONTACT LENSES (2016)

Linda Trinh Võ is a professor of Asian American Studies at University of California, Irvine. She authored *Mobilizing an Asian American Community* (2004), co-authored *Vietnamese in Orange County* (2015), and co-edited *Contemporary Asian American Communities: Intersections and Divergences* (2002); *Asian American Women: The "Frontiers" Reader* (2004); and *Labor Versus Empire: Race, Gender, and Migration* (2004); as well as *Keywords for Asian American Studies* (2015). She is Series Editor Emeritus for the Asian American Culture and History series published by Temple University Press, which includes over seventy books.

In the early 1990s, controversy surrounded the Olympic figure skater, Kristi Yamaguchi, a fourth-generation Japanese American, because of the lack of endorsement contracts she received compared to other gold medalists of her stature. Although publicly she was reluctant to attribute any discrimination to corporate America, critics noted that after Yamaguchi won the gold medal, she received few commercial mega-multi-million-dollar endorsements compared to the Anglo American bronze medalist Nancy Kerrigan, who received numerous offers, including a lucrative advertising contract as the face of Revlon, an established cosmetics company. Wholesome and telegenic, Yamaguchi was popular and relatively well liked by the public, but racially she did not quite fit the "all-American" image, so she was perceived as less marketable to American consumers.[1]

Moreover, the racial controversy was heightened when Yamaguchi accepted an offer to become the spokesperson for a prescription color contact lenses company. She appeared in print ads for DuraSoft Colors contact lenses with copy that read, *"When I want a little change I go green, violet, or gray,"* so one can change their eye color "even if you don't need visual correction." At a promotional event in New York in 1992 . . . , Yamaguchi stated, "I change my eye color to match my clothes, or sometimes just to match my mood." Questions were raised about altering a physical characteristic as one would change clothing, but the debates had a layered racial component given Yamaguchi's ethnic background. She was criticized for opting to endorse a product that muted her ethnicity by wearing color contacts that match Caucasian eye colors. Others defended her right to promote beauty products that were intended to enhance facial appearance, thereby downplaying any racial overtones with wearing color contacts. . . .

These controversies highlight the reoccurring theme of women of color positioned outside the societal norms of beauty by corporate America and point to how transformations of their physical characteristics can become racialized. Bodily features such as eye color or skin color are often politicized, since racial ideologies are attached to them, so biological characteristics are imbued with societal values and meaning. Similar to the ways that hair has become a contentious racial identifier for African Americans, eyes and noses have become visible and magnified racial markers for Asian Americans. They are used as tangible demarcations of racial difference, in which certain characteristics are desirable or undesirable; in this case, Asian "flat

Source: Reprinted with permission of NYU Press from *Global Asian American Popular Cultures*, edited by Shilpa Davé, Leilani Nishime, and Tasha Oren. (New York: New York University Press, 2016); permission conveyed through Copyright Clearance Center, Inc.

noses and slanted eyes" are perceived as racially defining characteristics that are inferior to Caucasian "bigger noses and rounder eyes." There is often a conflation of aesthetic and moral judgments associated with altering the appearance of the eyes. Some critics, including Yamaguchi's, regard any alteration to the Asian eyes as artificial or unnatural and marred by psychological afflictions of internalized racism or an inferiority complex, labeling such acts as white emulation or condemning them as an enslavement to Eurocentric standards of beauty.

Although the Yamaguchi case has faded from the American imagination, the issues it raises resurfaced with the emergence of a contemporary and global case involving circle contact lenses. . . .

The Circulation of Circle Contact Lenses

Larger than regular color lenses, circle contact lenses are color tinted or patterned, not only in areas that cover the iris of the eye but also in an extra-wide outer rim that covers some of the white part of the eye, resulting in the illusion of a larger iris and making the eye appear larger. They are 14–17 mm in diameter, which is at least 2 mm larger than the average iris diameter. These decorative lenses are part of the makeup routines that can be used along with mascara, eyeliner, eye shadow, and fake eyelashes to give the impression of rounder, larger eyes. Part of the global multi-billion-dollar beauty and fashion industries, circle contact lenses, or big eye contact lenses, are popular with fashion-conscious girls and young women, and sometimes with males as well. Trendy in China, Japan, Malaysia, the Philippines, Singapore, South Korea, Taiwan, and Thailand, they have made their way to Australia, Europe, the Middle East, and North America.

For the most part, over-the-counter sales of circle contact lenses, prescription and nonprescription, are technically illegal in the United States, but online sales of this product [are] difficult to regulate.[2] Medical experts from the United States and overseas warn about the dangers of infections and

© iStock/ RyanKing999

vision impairment, but this has not deterred young female consumers from purchasing the lenses. A host of manufacturers, vendors, bloggers, and consumers counter the negative media reports about the lenses by praising their beautification benefits, touting the cost savings, and minimizing or equating the dangers to those of wearing regular contacts.

Circle contact lenses increased in popularity partly because of their lower price point compared to regularly obtained prescription contact lenses, the variety of appealing designs, and availability through the Internet . . . Customers can purchase them directly from online sellers and can choose the strength of their lenses as well as the color, pattern, and size, so the variety of choices and immediate access is part of their appeal. They can be bought online for $20–$30 a pair directly from overseas producers such as GEO or sellers such as Eyecandy's or Korea Bigeyes. Given their relative affordability and the constant unveiling of new designs, consumers are encouraged to purchase multiple lenses. They come in shades such as black, blue, brown, green, gray, and pink with a range of geometric or artistic patterns with catchy names such as Angel, Bella, Diamond, Flower, Nudy, Princess Mimi, Shimmer, Trend, Twilight, and Wing. While some of these lenses are prescription-strength corrective lenses, others are merely decorative. Some online distributors do not openly list their business locations, others such as Tokyo Wink, based in Hong Kong, Candylens, based in Malaysia, Contactlens Xchange, based in Singapore/Malaysia, and Angel Contacts, based in Canada name their locale. . . .

Although these lenses are sold in different continents, it is striking that the online companies promote their products with prominent images of Asian female models. Generated by the producers of circle contact lenses, these online advertising images are used by distributors to market them, so the same images are duplicated on multiple sites. Notably, the advertisements feature Asian models who emulate "Caucasian" beauty standards with their starkly angular faces, dyed blondish hair, very light skin, and sharp noses, features that in some cases appear to be surgically enhanced.

Online stores, retailers, and distributors market big eye contact lenses as a novel beauty enhancement tool that will make the wearer's eyes appear "gorgeous, luminous, bigger, sexier, and more alluring." One of the more popular sites remarks on their popularity that, "in fact, here in Asia, they are so widespread that girls consider them as makeup staples like eyeshadow or false eyelashes!"[3] These evocative advertising slogans promote a "normalized" beauty standard that speciously treats physical traits as if they are as interchangeable as clothing. They recommend adding that "pop of color to your eye" to match your natural eye color, skin tone, eye shadow, or outfit, reminiscent of the Yamaguchi advertising campaign for DuraSoft. . . .

Beyond just improving appearances, these advertisements make claims about emotional and personal enhancement. The *Pinky Paradise* website states, "Circle lenses are more than colored contact lens, but they are also [a] fashion trend, confidence booster, and a new way to present yourself. Make a change and make a different [*sic*] today!"[4] These messages focus on beauty enhancement for the younger generation who has leisure time and wants to make a fashion statement. The companies also concentrate on delivering psychological messages emblematic of the cosmetic industry around improving self-confidence and boosting popularity. Slogans for self-empowerment and self-confidence are interwoven in these ads. . . .

The Trajectories of Gyaru and Ulzzang Style

The circle contact lens fad in Japan is part of the gyaru, or kogyaru, subculture, which started in the early 1990s and has attracted imitators in other nations. "Gyaru" is a Japanese word that translates into the English word "gal," . . . The style has a number of variants and has mutated over the years but is characterized by girly-glam style, with fans favoring dyed-blonde or reddish hair, sexy clothing, and bedazzling colors. A staple has been fake, decorated nails and big eyes achieved by using eyelid glue or tape (and sometimes plastic surgery), dark eyeliner, fake eyelashes, and circle contact lenses. . . .

The adoption of the gyaru style has been noted for contesting cultural ideals of Japanese womanhood as well as traditional social protocol or decorum and is regarded as a sign of youthful rebellion. Japanese and overseas media have featured sensationalized stories of the younger generation's provocative fashion choices and liberated lifestyles, especially their sexualized and promiscuous behavior. Social critics have denounced the youth for promoting excessive materialism and superficiality as well as immoral decadence, blaming them for a decline in national character. In contrast, as Marx notes, "Radical voices and feminists saw the young women as cleverly negotiating their own position in a male patriarchal world."[5] . . .

As gyaru style dominated consumer culture with its innovation and followers, these fashionable youth caught the attention of marketers. Shibuya, the modern center for youth in the center of Tokyo, became the main attraction for those desiring gyaru accessories, especially the Shibuya 109 multi-story shopping mall. By the late 1990s, as gyaru fashion became widespread, kogyaru girls were hired as sales clerks at 109 shops and became the "authoritative power" on fashion branding and styles, influencing customer preferences, and these in-store transactions with customers created fans and followers. These trendsetters became a valuable business asset for moving merchandise, essential for the commercialization and commodification of gyaru style, displacing the power entrusted formerly only to big-brand stylists or magazine editors.[6]

Once shunned or accused of being rule breakers, the "gals" were being courted "for their spending power, their adventurous mindset and even as a cultural export."[7] Mihoko Nishii, of Japan's largest advertising group Dentsu, says that studies show that about 12 percent of women between eighteen and thirty-four are devoted gyaru "gals," but over half of the women surveyed share similar fashion tastes: . . . One of the most popular gyaru models is Tsubasa Masuwaka, who has her own brand of makeup called "Candy Doll," a line of false eyelashes called "Dolly Wink," and a series of circle contact lenses called "Bambi" in Japanese markets and "Princess Mimi" overseas. . . .

Influenced by Japanese gyaru fashion, the ulzzang style was popularized in South Korea, and these transnational cultural influences on style have spread to other countries, such as China, Japan, the Philippines, Singapore, Thailand, Vietnam, and North America through visual images easily found on the Internet.[8] The rise of ulzzang style extends gyaru fashion and parallels the popularity of Korean popular culture, or the K-Pop phenomenon, which is exporting a global celebrity fashion that includes circle contact lenses and its accoutrements through movies, television series, and the entertainment industry. "Ulzzang," or "uljjang," roughly translates to "best face" or "good-looking" in Korean. Through Internet portal communities, girls compete for the ulzzang title through contests in which girls post their headshots and are judged by the global online community. For example, the *Ulzzangasia* website created what it refers to as a "netizen community" online that allows individuals to post photos and invites peers to vote for those they consider most attractive, with some winners achieving ulzzang celebrity status and garnering fans from global subscribers.[9]

As gyaru style dispersed across national borders through the Internet, it was adapted to local cultural forms; for example, while the visual imagery in Japan is highly sexualized, in South Korea the emphasis is on a childlike innocence and the style is less flamboyant. Although ulzzang subculture is about fashion that includes hair and clothing, its emphasis on facial features helped to popularize circle contact lenses. As one report describes the ulzzang style: "Huge, delicate bambi-like eyes with double lids and a tiny, delicate nose with a high bridge are a prerequisite. Smooth, pale snow-white skin, and rosebud lips are also a must. So is a small and sharp chin to achieve the perfect "*V-line*" face, which should ideally be no bigger than the size of your palm."[10] . . . Talk shows, YouTube tutorials, and websites feature makeup techniques, showing followers how to attain this look, which is likened to Japanese anime. Dissimilar to the gyaru that emphasizes the artificial style, the ulzzang rendition emphasizes "innocent," "natural," or "pure" beauty, even though the ethereal appearance is actually achieved through unnatural means such as circle contact lenses and plastic surgery or skin-whitening products, as well as retouched or edited photos. Young Asian female youth fueled the popularity of circle contact lenses through gyaru fashion in Japan and ulzzang style in South Korea, so what originated in Asia spread though the Internet to Asian American youth, who followed a similar trajectory to become style makers and influential figures in popularizing circle contacts lenses to US consumers as well as redirecting cultural flows.

Lady Gaga, Michelle Phan, and Internet Beauty Gurus

Online culture, as an accelerated form of communication and an expansive form of social networking, has been instrumental in circulating consumer trends across national borders and popularizing circle contact lenses among Asian American young women in the United States. An informal overview indicates that a high percentage of bloggers and users that post photos of themselves wearing circle contact lenses, and many of their fans posting comments, are Asian or Asian American females. . . . These makeup artists, both amateur and professionally trained, are referred to as "beauty gurus." Many use English as a medium; however, language is peripheral in the tutorials, since they rely heavily on visual images to reveal how to apply makeup and which products to use. Geography and location is inconsequential, since amateur fashionistas with basic computer equipment can film themselves in their bedrooms or bathrooms demonstrating beauty techniques and discussing style secrets that can easily be uploaded on YouTube, which gains them instantaneous popularity. They have generated additional fans and consumers of the circle contact lenses worldwide, who then promote it further through their online networks.

What once might have originated as a hobby to create how-to videos simply to share their knowledge or to garner attention has become for some a full-time entrepreneurial enterprise that has gained these "beauty gurus" notoriety. It is reported that "viewers watch more than 120 million how-to and beauty videos every day on YouTube" and "makeup videos are now the most frequently searched how-to content on the platform," so marketers began recognizing its potential.[11] Companies, domestic and international, have sought these style makers out for endorsements, product placements, and sponsorships as well as requesting their expertise on predicting fashion trends or surveying them to test out new products. The beauty gurus promote circle contact lenses products by showing the brands prominently in their videos, evaluating and recommending them and listing them in the description of their videos. In turn, companies offer bloggers and YouTube beauty gurus sponsorship opportunities, inviting them to contact the company and to send links to their websites or blogs. The promotional placements can be direct advertisements or appear in subtle forms on the fashion guru sites, with the young females wearing circle contact lenses while they feature accessories, clothes, hair, nails, shoes, or other style tips. Company websites prominently feature YouTube reviews and how-to videos by the beauty gurus that show purchasers how to open vials and how to wear and wash the lenses as well as rating their comfort level and displaying the latest designs. On the beauty guru sites, companies offer the viewers discounts through codes that can be used to buy the lenses or provide them with a free gift with their purchase.

Asian American young women have created their own cultural niche and launched their careers by providing makeup instructions tailored to Asian facial features, including their skin tones, the shape of their eyes, or their cheekbones. Through the Internet, Asian American fans are finding tips on how to wear clothes that fit their physique or how to style their hair. The Internet provides alternative avenues for Asian Americans to purchase cosmetic products, shifting from the importance of traditional malls, department stores, drugstores, and cosmetic or beauty shops that ignored ethnic consumers. Similarly, US beauty and fashion magazines have rarely included advertisements, fashion spreads, or advice columns that cater to those with Asian facial features. Using social network media and video-sharing platforms, Asian American young women use their innovation and expertise to influence consumers, generate demand, and promote trends.

Michelle Phan, one of the most popular and successful of the beauty gurus, and other Asian

American beauty gurus have created their own fashion venues and found their own consumer base. Phan, who is in her early twenties, is a Los Angeles–based self-taught makeup artist who debuted her first how-to makeup videos in 2006 using her laptop. Raised by her mother, a Vietnamese refugee who worked as a manicurist, Phan grew up in her mother's beauty salon in Florida. In 2010, with over 160 videos that had been viewed over 479 million times and with over 1 million subscribers, she became the number-one most subscribed female on YouTube.[12] Increasing her subscribership to 5 million worldwide, and with her first video logging over 10 million views, Phan has been instrumental in using these online videos to spread beauty trends, including the use of circle contact lenses. . . .

. . . Phan has popularized other "Caucasian" fashion looks, often using circle contact lenses with her wide-eyed "Barbie Transformation," "Lady Gaga Poker Face," and Disney princess characters such as her "Snow White" tutorials. Phan's tutorials often pop up on websites for circle contact lens companies globally that also feature still images of Asian models wearing their products, so presumably they are marketing to an Asian or Asian American consumer base. Some that are repeatedly featured are her "Brighter Larger Looking Eyes," "Aurora Eyes," "Avatar Inspired Look," and "Metallic Knight Look," makeup tutorials in which she wears color contact or circle contact lenses.

Phan seems aware of the damaging racial messages that women of color receive about beauty ideals, and in some respects, she has used her personal experiences to attract attention to Asian and Asian American women's beauty culture; however, she has been criticized for simultaneously reinforcing racial hierarchies through her visual tutorials. She reflected in an interview how growing up in a racialized environment affected her perception of beauty: "Western beauty is considered the dominant beauty in the world. . . . Tall, blond, blue eyes. I always felt a little self-conscious because I wanted to be more Caucasian. I tried to get bigger eyes. . . . I would dress preppy."[13] It seems her largest and most-dedicated fan base is in Asia, especially in Japan, where she ranks at the top for YouTube viewers, and she sources online information for makeup trends in China, Japan, Korea, Vietnam, and other parts of Asia, . . . In this way, racial aesthetics are reappropriated and recirculated across national borders in a circuitous fashion. Given her racial background, she attracted an Asian American viewership, some of whom are critical of the racial overtones in her makeup tutorials, such as online commentaries of her being "fake" or "wanting to look white with her color contacts" rather than embracing her Asian features, which is similar to the Yamaguchi controversy. . . .

The popularity of Phan's online tutorials gained her a contract in 2010 to be the first-ever video makeup artist representing Lancôme cosmetics, a subsidiary of the L'Oréal corporation, and they also supported the launch of her own makeup line, EM Cosmetics, which can be shipped all over the world. She is also featured in a Diet Dr. Pepper television commercial, which played during prime-time programming, showing her in front of her laptop filming herself putting on makeup and highlighting a montage of images from her beauty videos, . . . The commercial casts her as a waitress, her real-life former job, in an all-American diner serving the diet soda, saying at the end, "I'm Michelle Phan, and I'm one of a kind." She is one of the rare beauty gurus who has been able to transfer her Internet status to gain entrée into the mainstream beauty industry, as well as leveraging it to gain contracts to endorse other products and business ventures. In 2014, she reached a milestone of 1 billion views on YouTube and released a book, *Make Up: Your Life Guide to Beauty, Style and Success—Online and Off.*[14] As fashion trendsetters who employ the latest technology, young Asian and Asian American women have found pathways to becoming pivotal figures of attention and influence, while concurrently being co-opted and marketed by global capital; thus the operations of cultural transmission is multi-faceted and multi-directional.

Manga, Anime, and Transnational Cultural Circuits

Circle contact lenses extend color and patterns beyond the iris, providing an innocent doe-eyed or doll-like look that has been popularized by the gyaru or ulzzang style, which cultural commenters remark is reminiscent of Japanese manga (graphic novels) or anime (animation).[15] Michelle Phan is also aware of the transnational connections and references Asian popular cultural forms, remarking that, "in Asia, it's all about the eyes in makeup. . . . They like the whole innocent doll-like look, almost like anime."[16] . . . In their Facebook pages, fans of circle contact lenses in Asia and the United States merge global cultural forms as well, often listing in the "Like" section of their "About" pages the names of companies that produce circle lenses as well as links to anime, manga, and Michelle Phan. The media has picked up on these linkages in reporting the anime connection to circle lenses, with one editorial warning in its title that "Unapproved Contacts to Emulate Japanese Anime Look Not Worth Risk to Vision."[17]

These contemporary linkages to anime have historical roots that reveal transnational cultural interconnections. With the post–World War II defeat of Japan and the subsequent American Occupation, Western cultural forms were introduced to Japan, which reshaped contemporary Japanese traditional and national aesthetics as it remade itself into a global economic power. Disproportionately large eyes are considered a staple of manga and anime styles popular in Japan; however, there are distinct US influences that shaped what is considered a Japanese cultural form that has been transplanted to the United States. In the early 1950s one of the most influential founding fathers of anime, Osamu Tezuka, was inspired by the enormous eyes of the famous US cartoon character Betty Boop, along with Walt Disney's Mickey Mouse and Bambi animation characters.[18] These animal and human images have been noted for influencing his most famous creation, Astroboy/Astro Boy, who has large, round eyes. Betty Boop originally appeared as a dog-like cabaret singer in the Max Fleischer short animation *Dizzy Dishes* in 1930 and was eventually transformed into a humanized female who was portrayed as a sexualized and "glamorous international icon" with her big, round eyes and long eyelashes.[19] . . .

Other Japanese artists emulated Tezuka's style, which morphed into characters who are identified as "Japanese" but have exaggerated eyes that

can be blue or green.[20] The cultural intermixing is reflected in Japanese manga comic and anime characters which are drawn with large, round, eyes and blond, brown, orange, or red hair.[21] For more than two decades, US television networks have imported Japanese anime, such as Robotech, Voltron, Sailor Moon, Hamtaro, Pokémon, Naruto, and Yu-Gi-Oh, and these shows are popular with American children. In the United States, the "big eyes" look is associated with Japanese manga and anime and, by extension, Japanese popular culture. Hayao Miyazaki's animated Japanese feature films, *Princess Mononoke* (1997), *Spirited Away* (2001), *Howl's Moving Castle* (2004), and *Ponyo* (2008), which were successfully distributed in the United States, also created more anime fans. . . .

While some bloggers and fans counter the criticism that these characters with their large orbs privilege whiteness, others argue they are "raceless" and that the eyes merely depict traits such as innocence and allow them to be more expressive. Defenders regard the intermingling and intersecting of Western and Japanese aesthetics and the fantasy spaces they create as representative of a transnational or stateless culture, characterized by a global hybridity that is a merging of global and local cultures that is neither purely Western or Japanese. Rejecting the idea of American domination of mass culture in which Japanese culture is subsumed into a hegemonic global culture, others regard the popularity of Japanese anime and manga as forms of cultural resistance to the dominance of Western culture.[22]

The repeated ways in which anime and manga characters with large orbs are displayed is instrumental in creating an acceptable aesthetic for circle contact lenses in Japan and abroad. Producers and distributors of circle contacts lenses have capitalized on the popularity of manga and anime to their predominantly female consumers. Noticeable is that, in these fantasy or science fiction theme narratives, there are female superheroes or cyborgs who are shown as independent and powerful, while sometimes simultaneously depicted with sexualized or cute features. This imagery counters the prevalent stereotypes of submissive females and the constraining gender roles imposed upon women in modern Japanese society, somewhat reflective of the ways in which the gyaru fashion intermixes sexuality and independence.[23] . . .

The imaginary spaces of manga and anime are transmuting idealized standards of beauty, notably influencing the desire for racialized reconfigurations of the body. Anime and manga, which are based on narratives of science fiction or fantasy, have generated avid global devotees who are imitating the anime look. Even white women are emulating Japanese anime characters, or similarly transforming themselves to resemble living dolls, and are further popularizing circle contact lenses, which engenders public fascination and, sometimes, repulsion.[24] This complicates a merely straightforward mimicry of whiteness and analysis shows the malleability of new technologies and possibilities for cultural interventions. Undeniably savvy in employing new technologies, Asian American women resist their disenfranchisement on the peripheries and attempt to democratize the marketplace and redistribute technological resources through online consumption and the dispensation of beauty cultures to dictate what is fashionable. Online technologies allocate more control to consumers who can redirect the capitalist economy and dictate trends in the marketplace. Producers and vendors are able to communicate directly with their buyers and receive instantaneous feedback on products as well as promote and sell directly to buyers across transnational borders. While Asian American young women are neglected in mainstream marketing, these transnational circuits have repositioned their economic spheres of influence, increased their clout in setting trends, and allowed them a space to redefine women's beauty culture that is more racially inclusive. Nonetheless, there are limitations to this analysis of inclusive communities and repositioning, since it is also driven by self-interest and economic profit. These young girls and women are still confined by the limiting dictates of a global beauty culture that caters to making them appealing to the opposite sex, places primacy on superficial or frivolous aesthetics of self-enhancement, and emphasizes the homogenization of beauty standards.

Circle contact lenses emerged at a time when technological advances via the Internet allowed young consumers to converse directly with one another globally and fostered the creation of virtual communities. These lenses are a fashion fad that will be replaced by the next obsession with bodily and facial modification; however, even as a temporal product, it is suggestive of the ways in which transnational cultural markets and emerging technologies can evolve to bring new possibilities for intervention, once unimaginable, by Asian and Asian American cultural producers and innovators. It also illuminates the complexities of how racialization figures into these questions of transnational consumption and cultural production in a digital age.

NOTES

1. Elena Tajima Creef, *Imaging Japanese America: The Visual Construction of Citizenship, Nation, and the Body* (New York: NYU Press, 2004), 167–171; Thomas S. Mulligan, "Yamaguchi's Endorsement Deals Prove Good as Gold," *Los Angeles Times*, March 17, 1992, http://articles.latimes.com/1992–03–17/business/fi-4044_1_endorsement-deals, accessed March 27, 2014; Glen Macnow, "Different Shade of Gold—Racism Could Prevent Yamaguchi from Cashing In," *Seattle-Times*, March 8, 1992, http://community.seattletimes.nwsource.com/archive/?date=19920308&slug=1479888, accessed March 4, 2011; Laura Zinn, "To Marketers, Kristi Yamaguchi Isn't as Good as Gold," *Business Week*, March 8, 1992, http://www.bloomberg.com/bw/stories/1992–03–08/to-marketers-kristi-yamaguchi-isnt-as-good-as-gold, accessed April 27, 2014. . . .

2. Juju Chang, Chris Strathmann, and Sabrina Parise, "Eye-Popping New Fashion Trend Could Carry Dangers, Docs Say," *ABC News*, July 6, 2010, http://abcnews.go.com/GMA/ConsumerNews/circle-lenses-dangerous-docs/story?id=11093873, accessed January 22, 2013.

3. "Which Color Suits Me?" *Eyecandy's*, http://www.eyecandys.com/which-color-suits-me, accessed January 20, 2012.

4. "Wear and Care Guide for Beginners," *Pinky Paradise*, video, http://www.pinkyparadise.com/Video_s/1893.htm, accessed January 22, 2013.

5. W. David Marx, "The History of the Gyaru—Part Two," *Néojaponisme*, May 8, 2012, http://neojaponisme.com/2012/05/08/the-history-of-the-gyaru-part-two, accessed April 15, 2013.

6. Ibid.

7. Mariko Oi, "Japan Harnesses Fashion Power of Gals," *BBC News-Tokyo*, August 29, 2012, http://www.bbc.co.uk/news/world-asia-19332694, accessed January 23, 2013.

8. Julieann de Lacy, "Ulzzang!" *Scene Project Online Magazine*, n.d., http://sceneprojectonlinemag.weebly.com/fashion-ulzzang.html, accessed January 23, 2013.

9. "About," *Ulzzangasia*, http://www.ulzzangasia.com/about, accessed January 23, 2013.

10. Elizabeth Soh, "Korean 'Ulzzang' Beauty Mania Comes to Singapore," *Singapore Showbiz, Yahoo! Entertainment*, October 29, 2012, http://sg.entertainment.yahoo.com/blogs/singapore-showbiz/korean-ulzzang-beauty-mania-comes-singapore-072253957.html, accessed February 23, 2013.

11. Stephanie Buck, "Michelle Phan: Behind the Makeup of YouTube's Fairy Godmother," *Mashable*, August 23, 2014, http://mashable.com/2013/08/23/michelle-phan, accessed June 7, 2014.

12. "About," Michelle Phan website, http://www.michellephan.com/about, accessed March 30, 2012.

13. Stephanie Hayes, "Michelle Phan, a YouTube Sensation for Her Makeup Tutorials, Has Transformed Her Life," *Tampa Bay Times*, August 23, 2009, http://www.tampabay.com/features/humaninterest/michelle-phan-a-youtube-sensation-for-her-makeup-tutorials-has-transformed/1029747, accessed October 16, 2015.

14. Michelle Phan, *Make Up: Your Life Guide to Beauty, Style and Success—Online and Off* (New York: Harmony Books, 2014).

15. "Unapproved Contacts to Emulate Japanese Anime Look Not Worth Risk to Vision," *Seattle Times*, July 9, 2010, http://www.seattletimes.com/opinion/unapproved-contacts-to-emulate-japanese-anime-look-not-worth-risk-to-vision, accessed January 23, 2013.

16. Catherine Saint Louis, "What Big Eyes You Have, *Dear*, but Are Those Contacts Risky?" *New York Times*, July 4, 2010, A1, http://www.nytimes.com/2010/07/04/fasion/04lenses.html, accessed October 16, 2015.

17. See "Unapproved Contacts."

18. Art Young, "Why Circle Contact Lenses Are So Popular," *Helium*, July 7, 2010, http://www.helium.com/items/1883360-why-circle-contact-lenses-are-so-popular, accessed January 23, 2013.

19. Fleischer Studios, "Part One: Betty's Rise to Fame," http://www.fleischerstudios.com/betty1.html, accessed November 2, 2015.

20. Rachael Rainwater-McClure, Weslynn Reed, and Eric Mark Kramer, "A World of Cookie-Cutter Faces," in *The Emerging Monoculture: Assimilation and the "Model Minority,"* ed. by Eric Mark Kramer (Westport, CT: Praeger, 2003), 221–233.

21. Andrew Lam, "Are Asians Increasingly Undergoing Plastic Surgery to Look White?" *New America Media* at *Alternet*, March 31, 2007, http://www.alternet.org/story/49894, accessed March 5, 2011.

22. Susan J. Napier, *Anime from Akira to Howl's Moving Castle: Experiencing Contemporary Japanese Animation* (New York: Palgrave MacMillan, 2005), 9.

23. Ibid., 31–33.

24. Ingrid Schmidt, "Top 10 Beauty Videos on YouTube," *Los Angeles Times*, January 2, 2013, http://www.latimes.com/features/image/alltherage/la-ar-top-10-beauty-videos-on-youtube-20130102,0,3361513.story, accessed January 23, 2013.

22 FASHION'S "FORGOTTEN WOMAN": HOW FAT BODIES QUEER FASHION AND CONSUMPTION (2014)

Margitte Kristjansson is a feminist activist, writer, and filmmaker whose work on beauty and body image is published in anthologies and blogs, including Bitch Media and the Good Men Project. She has toured campuses nationwide with her documentary, *The Fat Body (In)Visible* (2011). She is Assistant Communications Director at United Domestic Workers of America. She blogs at http://www.thegoodandplenty.com.

. . . Fat people, so the cultural logic goes, are consumers who *over*-consume: the material evidence of their corpulence is "proof" of this. Fat women in particular experience a double-bind in this regard: while their fatness represents an inability to exercise proper consumptive control, their status as *women* renders their desire for consumption taboo and potentially dangerous. In *Unbearable Weight* (1993), Susan Bordo asserts that for women, the desire to eat—voraciously or otherwise—is conflated with inappropriate sexual desire. The consuming woman as metaphor, she argues, is about the fear that women will literally "consume the body and soul of the male" and thus their appetites "must be curtailed and controlled" (117). . . . Fat people more generally, with their out-of-control bodies and apparent inability to resist the temptations of consumer culture, are not commonly understood as particularly sophisticated consumers. As a result, fat-specific consumption practices are currently under-theorized. What is there to study, after all, if the fat consumer will eat or buy anything?

Through an analysis of fat fashion, I will attempt to explore some of the ways that the fat female body both exposes the cultural dimensions of fat consumption practices and is also capable of queering those consumption practices. I use "queering" here to point to an intentional subversion of cultural norms about consumption—that is who is allowed to consume and how much and in what ways . . . An article published in *The New York Times* in 1969—"The Forgotten Woman in the 'Skinny Revolution'" [Klemesrud 1969]—is an example of early explorations into fat consumption practices and operates as a catalyst here to consider the ways in which fat women have consumed fashion since the 1960s. This chapter is buoyed by historical examples, but also uses work on fat female subjectivity by Michael Moon and Eve Sedgwick, Kathleen LeBesco, Samantha Murray, and others to situate this discussion at the intersections of issues about race, gender, class and sexuality *as well as* size in order to explore the consumption of fat fashion as an act that queers what we believe to be true about fat bodies and possibly consumption itself.

Taste, Cultural Capital, and the Fat Consumer

In his extensive scholarship on consumption practices and social class, Pierre Bourdieu emphasizes the importance of cultural capital, "anything that a society recognises as meaningful, valuable, or estimable [that] can be cultivated for social profit, exchanged for other forms of power, and subject to the range of strategies commonly associated with economic maneuvering" (Gerber and Quinn

2008: 5). That is, while economic capital remains the central mode of power in society, a recognition of the influence of *cultural* capital is necessary to any understanding of how power is negotiated in and through society. Bourdieu argues that taste— that is, stylized and valorized preferences within consumption practices—operates as a mechanism for distinguishing between those with varying amounts and types of cultural capital. These "manifested preferences" are "the practical affirmation of an inevitable difference . . . asserted purely negatively, by the refusal of other tastes" (Bourdieu 1984: 56). In other words, one of the ways in which we distinguish ourselves from cultural and social "others" is through our taste as well as through *dis*taste, disgust, and aesthetic intolerance. Similarly, Deborah Lupton further examines how taste is used to mask cultural privilege. According to Lupton, "taste is both an aesthetic and a moral category . . . a way of subtly identifying and separating 'refined' individuals from the lower, 'vulgar' classes. Good taste is something that is *acquired through acculturation* into a certain subculture rather than being explicitly taught" (1996: 95, emphasis added). Similarly, Gerber and Quinn argue that preferences in consumption make the effects of social and cultural privilege "appear to be the result of individual refinement rather than social structure and the different kinds of power which animate it" (2008: 5).

As fat studies scholars have maintained, fat bodies are particularly disadvantaged in terms of cultural capital (Gerber and Quinn 2008, LeBesco 2004). In a culture that values slimness over corpulence as not only more beautiful or desirable but also more moral and good, fatness has a negative effect on one's cultural capital and, subsequently, one's ability to acquire other types of capital. Importantly, Bourdieu argues that one of the most significant aspects of cultural capital is its embeddedness within the body . . . While "one's taste might be expressed through the relatively transitory choices made in commodity consumption— how one dresses, the style in which one's house is decorated—[it] is represented and reproduced in a far more permanent way through embodiment"

(Lupton 1996: 95). The thin body is read as moral/ good/controlled/refined. This is because, in part, the thin body is never regarded as a "natural" body. As Bourdieu asserts, "the legitimate use of the body is spontaneously perceived as an index of moral uprightness, so that its opposite, a 'natural' body, is seen as an index of *laisser-aller* ('letting oneself go') . . . " (1984: 193). The thin body, for most people, is only attainable through rigorous effort, requiring time and money. . . .

Read any number of news pieces on the "obesity epidemic" and it is clear that fat people have become a scapegoat of sorts for a lot of the Western world's worst qualities. More often than not, they are imagined as one large homogenous group that exemplify all that is "wrong" with Western culture: they drive around in gas-guzzling SUVs, watch endless hours of TV on expensive plasma screens, and eat mindlessly out of fast-food containers, all while remaining miraculously ignorant of basic health principles and the environmental impact of their selfish consumption practices. As a culture, we seem to be unable to disconnect the metaphor of fatness from its reality. Fat folks, just like their thin or "average" sized counterparts, consume food (healthy and unhealthy), buy cars (hybrids and gas-guzzlers alike), purchase homes, and consume many other necessary (and not-so-necessary) products. On the other hand, as cultural outsiders with sometimes-limited access to the capital required to engage in normative consumption practices, many fat people are required to consume differently. Importantly, this point is especially true with regard to the consumption of fashion. . . .

The late nineteenth and early twentieth centuries in the United States saw the birth of the department store and the growth of the "ready-to-wear" fashion industry. A history of ready-to-wear fashion in America made specifically for fat women can be traced to Lithuanian immigrant Lena Bryant, who, in the 1920s, turned her maternity-wear line into a clothing company for "stout" women, the first of its kind (Clifford 2010). Today, Lane Bryant is one of the most prominent and prolific plus-size retailers in the country. The plus-size market has seen growth above and beyond the fashion industry at large, and events such as Full Figured Fashion Week in New York City are gaining in popularity. Online, a transnational movement of fat fashion bloggers has sparked a mini-frenzy of media attention and body-positive activism (Cochran 2010). "If the personal is political," writes social commentator Erin Keating, "then being able to find clothes that fit and make you feel good is a political plus" (quoted in LeBesco 2004: 72). In an industry where the fat fashionista has been called the "forgotten woman"—a plus-size store with this name existed in New York in the 1980s—the possibilities for her today seem much improved. However, as many fat fashion bloggers are quick to point out, the physical and economic accessibility of fashionable clothing for fat women is still a major issue, and it continues to bring many young and dissatisfied people into the fold of fat- and body-positive activism. Fat fashion, asserts fat studies scholar Kathleen LeBesco, has the capacity to be "revolutionary": when fat women "disdain 'blending in' in favor of cobbling together a look from the scattered resources available and becoming more brave about appearing in ways that defy the 'tasteful' intentions of the commodities of corpulence[,]" they subvert cultural norms about what it means to be fat (2004: 73). Unequal access to fat-sized fashion is a well-documented and long-term phenomenon (Klemesrud 1969, Riggs 1983, Feuer 1999, Adam 2001, LeBesco 2004, Kinzel 2012). Even now, after several decades of fat-positive activism and consumer interest fuelling the creation of more fat fashion, clothing in larger sizes is not nearly as accessible as "straight-sized" clothing, in terms of quantity as well as quality. As such, today's fa(t)shionistas have developed their own ways to engage with fashion when the industry refuses to recognize them as viable customers. This has manifested itself in hundreds of fatshion blogs, community-building events such as fat-only clothing swaps, online fatshion-centered communities and forums, independent fat-positive fashion shows, and the creation of zines and even documentaries cataloguing the efforts of fat women to render their bodies visible via the fashion that they consume. And while today's fatshion scene is very focused on the present, I would like to point to an important historical moment, while fat-positive

activism was still in its infancy, to highlight and analyze the ways in which fat bodies not only queer normative consumption of fashion, but are, in and of themselves, queer.

The "Forgotten Woman" in 1969

"The Forgotten Woman in the 'Skinny Revolution'" appeared in the "Food Fashions Family Furnishings" section on page 58 of *The New York Times* on Monday, December 1, 1969. It occupies just under half the page, and underneath it are articles about a curmudgeonly English chef and his large, American-style New York City banquet, a profile on Broadway actress-turned-marine biologist Sylvia Short and her family, and the grand opening of a specialty chocolate shop at Bloomingdale's. On the bottom left hand corner is an advertisement for Faberge Cologne . . . also exclusive to Bloomingdale's. To the contemporary reader, the placement of a story about fat fashion and issues of accessibility might seem odd nestled atop fluff pieces about gourmet chocolate and socialite banquets. The piece on Sylvia Short, a woman who left show business to pursue her doctorate, also seems out of place here. However, when it is revealed that Short chose to quit her career as an actress because daycare costs became too expensive (her husband, also an actor, chose to stay on Broadway and later won a Tony for his efforts), the organization of these articles and their placement under the decidedly feminine catchall "Food Fashions Family Furnishings" become a little clearer.

Klemesrud covered a myriad of topics in her 19 years at the paper, including articles about the accessibility of jobs in the fashion industry for African Americans, the women's liberation movement and its various influences on everyday life, and a small handful of articles about the intersections of fashion, fat, and food. In one such article from 1975 titled "The Woman Who Isn't Slim Desires High Fashion, Too[,]" Klemesrud quotes a fat woman who suspects that, "because of women's lib, we're going to have a lot more big women": "women are tired of the façade and the false eyelashes, and finally we're saying 'we're just going to be ourselves'" (45). . . .

. . . "The Forgotten Woman" tells the stories of eight fat women—all wealthy, many of them famous—and their various difficulties finding clothes that fit well and are fashionable. Klemesrud blames the "skinny revolution"—ostensibly a trend in fashion attributed to famously slender supermodel Twiggy—for these difficulties. "I think it's the worst thing that's ever happened to heavy women. There is hardly a dress made over size 14," laments Totie Fields, the unapologetically fat comedian. Along with Fields, the women profiled by Klemesrud are New York restaurateur Elaine Kaufman, opera singer Eileen Farrell, Cass Elliot of popular vocal group The Mamas and the Papas, President of the UN General Assembly Angie Brooks of Liberia, owner of the New York Mets Mrs. Charles Shipman Payson, the New Jersey governor's wife Mrs. Richard J. Hughes, and popular singer Kate Smith. For almost every woman featured, the solution to the problem of accessibility is to have her clothes made for her, or, in the case of Angie Brooks, to make them herself. Fields is quoted as saying she spends as much as $100,000 a year (over $500,000 in 2012 dollars) on her entirely custom-made wardrobe. This is of course only an option, Klemesrud admits, for "women of means" such as those listed above.

An interesting pattern appears as Klemesrud continues her story: "Miss Fields, whose weakness is rye bread" is followed by "Miss Smith, who has gone from 255 pounds to 185 pounds[,]" which is followed by "Mrs. Charles Shipman, known for her fondness for hot dogs, peanuts, ice cream, chocolate bars, and Cokes[,]" which is followed by "Mrs. Hughes, who received nationwide publicity when she dieted and went from 230 to 150 pounds. (She has since gained back 23 of them)." Although the topic at hand is clothing, the things Klemesrud finds worth noting about these women are inextricably linked to culturally ingrained assumptions about fat women (that they overeat) and their habits (that they are trying to lose weight). Many of the women offered up this information on their own: "eight years ago I quit smoking and gained 30 pounds. But that's no excuse," confesses Shipman, "I've always been big." Most of these women, Klemesrud concludes, fall under

one of two categories: those who celebrate their size by wearing loud and/or revealing clothing, and those who use clothing to hide or minimize their corpulence. The opera diva Eileen Farrell is pictured . . . , wearing a no-nonsense dark suit and helping herself to what looks like pasta. The caption reads, "Eileen Farrell, the soprano, who frequently goes on diets, prefers to wear dark-colored fashions." Kate Smith, likewise, "always wear[s] sleeves" to hide her "ham"-like upper arms. Elaine Kauffman, on the other hand, chooses loud prints while Cass Elliot and Mrs. Richard J. Hughes dare to wear pants, apparently a fashion don't for fat women in the late 60s. Totie Fields "break[s] all the rules": "ruffles, ostrich feathers, fox coats. You look fat in fox anyway, so if you start fat, you only look a little bit fatter."

It seems easy, then, to assume that Klemesrud is correct in her assertion about these two types of fat women, but a closer reading of the text troubles this simple conception of fat female identities as either celebratory and self accepting or unhappy and self-hating.

Totie Fields, who for all intents and purposes embodies the ultimate "if you've got it, flaunt it" fat woman, explains her desire to create a plus-size fashion line inspired by her own striking style. The sizes, she says, would be marked "in the tiny sizes of 3, 5 and 7" (typically plus sizes today are sizes 14+). "Mentally, it will make us feel better," she says. Perhaps in the article it is assumed that the experience of being fat is universally negative, but this statement, made without any comment by Klemesrud, seems to betray the conception of Fields as a revolutionary who loves her body. Similarly, the restaurateur Elaine Kaufman, who says of her fashion sense "the bolder the better," admits to an ambivalence about her body that isn't fully drawn out by Klemesrud: "I never quite think of myself as 'big' but I know I must be because my dresses take up a lot of fabric." And then, when telling the story of how a "very beautiful—but very unhappy" fashion model asked her why she refused to lose weight, Kaufman retorts, "I am involved in the mind, and that's all that matters." For all the work these women seem to be doing to advance some sort of ideology of "body acceptance" or celebration of the fat female form, they don't seem particularly happy with their size (Fields) or even aware of themselves as being *connected* to their fat bodies (Kaufman).

Consumption and Fat Female Subjectivity

The inclusion of only wealthy—and almost entirely white—women in this article is not incredibly surprising, but is still worth noting. On the one hand, wealthy fat women have access to personal tailors and clothes custom-made by designers and costumers to a much larger degree than women who do not have the same economic and cultural capital. On the other hand, as LeBesco points out, fat bodies in America are threatening inasmuch as they suggest not only "downward mobility" but "provoke racial anxieties in the West because of their imagined resemblance to those of maligned ethnic and racial Others; fatness haunts as the specter of disintegrating physical privilege" (2004: 56). More recently, Amy Erdman Farrell has elaborated on the links between colonialist discourses around nonwhite bodies, contemporary racism, and the cultural distaste for fat (2011). Presenting the fat woman as a worthy consumer of fashion is then more "palatable" if the woman we are confronted with is as un-Other as possible. A woman who, although fat, has the taste and distinction of one who possesses great social and cultural capital. . . . After all, how threatening to the status quo can "Mrs. Charles Shipman" be, as a wealthy white woman with a husband to boot? In other words, the subversive potential of the article is tempered by its focus on subjects who, beyond their desire to disrupt fashion norms, have a vested interest in maintaining the status quo. The inclusion of the more body-positive and feminist-leaning Fields, along with Angie Brooks, a black woman and Liberian political leader, is perhaps reflective of the influence of the civil rights and women's liberation movements of the 1960s.

It could be argued that a relatively positive article about fat women, appearing in such a widely read and well-regarded paper, is reflective of a cultural shift perhaps inspired by women's lib. Of course there are tensions when naming the move to demand increased access to fashionable clothing as "liberatory" or even "feminist." Danae Clark, in

her 1991 essay "Commodity Lesbianism," warns of the kind of commodification that looks like acceptance or even empowerment but is actually about a business's bottom line: the capitalist is happy to welcome queer folk as "consuming subjects" but remains unwilling to acknowledge them as "social subjects" (192). Similar arguments can be made for the fat consumer. As LeBesco explains, the demand for increased access to fashionable clothing for fat women often requires insisting that fat women want to be beautiful, too, and reinforces a particular kind of female subjectivity that, in a capitalist society, can only be accessed through consumption. In this way, "the objectification against which feminists have been fighting for decades becomes the new dream state of the fat woman consumer" (2004: 68). In 1969, when women's lib found many thin women choosing to buck fashion trends and the cultural imperatives to present themselves in traditionally "beautiful" ways, the fat woman was fighting to be recognized as someone worthy of these things in the first place. This is problematic, yes, but not a simple reproduction of patriarchy and other cultural norms as some might argue, a point I will return to later. Nevertheless, the "fat woman in a clothing store," Sedgwick asserts, "lights up a pinball machine of economic, gender, and racial meanings" (2001: 294) and offers interesting ways to think about female subjectivity through consumption. The fat woman shopping is plagued by a "primal denial," . . . the mostly unspoken sentence . . . "there's nothing here for you to spend your money on" (ibid.). . . .

In their musings on the "glass closet," Michael Moon and Eve Sedgwick [2001] draw parallels between non-normative (queer?) bodies and non-normative (queer) sexualities. "Closet of sexuality. Closet of size. . . . What kind of secret can the body of a fat woman keep?" asks Moon (305). After all, he asserts, everyone who sees a fat woman believes "they know something about her that she doesn't herself know" much in the way that gay people have reported coming out to friends and family members who, instead of being surprised, respond with relief that they can publicly acknowledge what they already believed to be true (ibid.). But, Sedgwick adds, there is more to the "closet" as it functions in a fat woman's life, whether literally as a container for clothes that do not exist or as a place to keep a secret that everyone already knows:

> There *is* a process of *coming out as a fat woman*. [It] involves . . . risk [and] making clear to the people around one that their cultural meanings will be, and will be heard as, assaultive and diminishing to the degree that they are not fat-affirmative. [It] is a way of speaking one's claim to insist on, and participate actively in, a renegotiation of *the representational contract* between one's body and one's world. (306)

In her chapter on "The Queerness of Fat," LeBesco explores the many parallels between fatness and queerness, including the above-mentioned concern with "coming out," early scientific understandings of fat and queer bodies as the product of either environmental factors or genetics . . . and an understanding of both fat and queer sexuality as deviant (2001: 85–88). In fact, fat and queer author Hanne Blank maintains that "because fat people are not supposed to be sexy or sexual, any sex involving a fat person is by definition 'queer,' no matter what the genders of any of the partners involved" (quoted in LeBesco 2001: 89).

. . . Just nine months after "The Forgotten Woman," *The New York Times* published "There Are a Lot of People Willing to Believe Fat Is Beautiful[,]," an article by Klemesrud about the emergence of NAAFA (then the National Association to Aid Fat Americans, today the National Association to Advance Fat Acceptance). William Fabrey, the founder, is here positioned as a fat admirer, a thin person who prefers fat women as sexual partners. It is not coincidental that then, as is often the case today, a fat woman's worth is asserted based on her ability to appeal to heterosexual men as an object of desire. Even the article itself is couched in a way that problematically ties the fat woman's subjectivity with the male gaze's objectification of her body. However, . . . Jane Feuer argues that "we need to distinguish among issues involving the male gaze, those involving norms of beauty culture at a given time, and those involving body size per se . . . It is only by approximating other norms of beauty culture and thus evoking a male gaze that fat women today can gain access to representation in a form that does

not code them as repellent" (1999, 185). In a world where fat women experience what Feuer terms "visual oppression"—a complete lack of positive representation in visual media—"representation as objects of visual pleasure is progressive" (198). This is especially true, she adds, when the images are being consumed by a female/lesbian spectator.

Still, it could be argued that the subversive potential of fat women's participation in fashion is necessarily mitigated by heteronormative expectations of femininity. How is a woman wearing a fancy dress, for example, non-normative in any way? However, the fat woman is always already figured as *outside of* these expectations—so when she chooses to dress "femme," she is faced with entirely different readings of her femininity (and thus, her status as an object of desire) by others. "The fat woman is a masquerade of femininity," Feuer asserts, "as the figure of Divine well parodies" (186). Rather than painstakingly attempting to reproduce femininity, many fat women are "playing at" the feminine in ways that feel empowering to them *outside of* patriarchal beauty norms. This understanding of fat femme as subversive performance must, of course, be attentive to intentionality. Even still, heteronormative expectations of femininity are such that fat women can *never fully meet them*—whether now or in 1969—thus rendering the fat woman's participation in fashion necessarily different.

While it is clear that Klemesrud's "Forgotten Woman" has many desires, her sexuality is generally avoided in favor of highlighting a lust for fashion and, problematically, food. Only one woman, Mrs. Hughes, is represented as a sexual subject, and this characterization is itself a bit of a stretch: "my mother told me I looked terrible in pants, but my husband said I looked great[,]" she says. The reason she is comfortable breaking this fashion "rule," at least according to her, is because of the validation provided by her husband that she is attractive and thus desirable. This is the only mention of fat women and sexuality, and yet the article is littered with language that is often used when describing sexual desire: Totie Fields is rendered "weak," some of the women "flaunt" what they've "got." Mrs. Charles Shipman has a "fondness," and Cass Elliot is caught "mooning over." These words do not describe the desire these women have for *other bodies*, but for food they should not be eating, and rule-breaking outfits they should not be wearing. . . . Bordo's assertion, that we conflate a woman's desire to eat with sexual desire, and that the slender body represents proper restraint with regard to both sex and food, is . . . salient here (1993). Moon and Sedgwick find similar parallels in the films of John Waters and his muse, fat drag queen Divine. Klemesrud's "Forgotten Woman" lives a life of excess: too much food, too much fabric, and a body that takes up too much space. Obscuring her sexual subjectivity in food talk could be read as an attempt to render the subversive excessiveness of her body "safe." Dieting is the only "proof" a fat woman has that she is at least trying to take "control" of her body (and thus her sexuality): it is not surprising, then, that Klemesrud focuses so much attention on the eating patterns of these women.

Body "Language"

Language, as a tool that can be used to reinforce or reinscribe power relations, is especially important when we consider the body and how we talk about it. Many social justice movements have taken to "reclaiming" the words that have been used to disempower marginalized groups in the past: similarly, the fat-positive movement from the very beginning has privileged "fat" over other words to describe fat bodies. Despite this, euphemisms for fat continue to be used more often than not. In "The Forgotten Woman," Klemesrud (or the fat women themselves) use the following descriptors: "larger women," "heavy women," "her 'football player figure,'" "stout women," "big," and "sizeable." Notably, the only woman who calls herself fat is Totie Fields, and the only other occurrence of the word is used by Klemesrud to describe Fields's line of clothing for "fat women"; it is certainly possible that Klemesrud was either asked by Fields to word it this way, or only felt comfortable using the word after Fields herself used it.

These euphemisms are used to make fat women feel better, so as not to risk offending them by using a word that has often been used to belittle or hurt them. But the choice certainly seems puzzling: like the glass closet, what does calling a fat woman "heavy" or "stout" *really* do? It certainly cannot hide the fact that she is fat. But the pervasive use of euphemisms for fat bodies sheds some light on why many fat women, like Sedgwick, feel the need to "come out as fat"; not only is it a declaration of one's commitment to the resignification of the fat body, but it is the refusal to metaphorically hide one's body behind words like "voluptuous" or "sizeable." Interestingly, in her 1975 article "The Woman Who Isn't Slim Desires High Fashion, Too," Klemesrud uses "fat" exclusively, unless she is directly quoting someone else.

While language certainly plays a pivotal role in the resignification of the fat female body, it would not be unwarranted to question just how much reclaiming "fat" can do when the fat body is already imbued with so much meaning, when the fat woman is "outed" before she can "out" herself: "bodies speak, without necessarily talking because they become coded with and as signs . . . " (Elizabeth Grosz quoted in LeBesco 2004: 6–7). We are taught to understand fat bodies not only as indicators of poor health, but as lazy, having poor hygiene and slow intellect, and lacking willpower (Blaine and McElroy 2002: 351). As fat studies scholar Samantha Murray (2008) maintains, . . . the fat body always already confesses to these "sins" "and thus an interior 'truth' is supposedly assigned to the 'fat' subject, for them to then admit and confirm" (75) . . . It is not surprising then, how much of "The Forgotten Woman" is focused on the fat women themselves "confessing": what and how much they eat, failed attempts at dieting, and the admission by Mrs. Charles Shipman that she has "no excuse" for being fat: "I've always been this big." This perhaps begs the question: how is this type of (fat-negative) confession different than the seemingly liberatory and fat-positive "coming out" posed by Sedgwick?

Queer Bodies Queering Fashion

In 1971, *Time Magazine* reported on fat Las Vegas performer Nancy Austin's new line of plus-size clothing "Pudgy Playmates." The article, about the surprising success the independent designer was seeing, marvels at the fact that Austin sold "size 52 hot pants" along with "gold lame pantsuits, gaucho pants, knickers, and patio dresses" ("Modern Living: Big Business"). While *Time* seems to laud Austin's audacity and her belief that these clothes "make fat women feel happier," the unnamed author concludes that "dieting would be a better solution," because the overall "effect" of happy fat women in hot pants is "grotesque" (ibid.). This perfectly echoes LeBesco's claim that most people will perceive fat-positive identification as "grotesque perversion" (2001: 83) and find fat bodies to be "revolting" (75). However, she argues, "if we think of *revolting* in terms of overthrowing authority, rebelling, protesting, and rejecting, then corpulence carries a whole new weight as a subversive cultural practice" (ibid.); corpulence, in other words, has the power to *queer* how we think about bodies. The "Pudgy Play-mates" line of clothing is perhaps a better example of this potential than are Klemesrud's "forgotten women"—in fact, the line sounds remarkably similar to the contemporary lines put out by independent and queer fat fashion designers. . . .

The various ways in which fat folks queer fashion and its consumption are even clearer today. Perhaps one of the best examples of this is provided by Charlotte Cooper (2008) in her explanation of The Big Fat Flea (originally Fat Girl Flea) in New York City. The annual fashion event/rummage sale, held at the LGBT Community Center and benefiting NOLOSE, a fat-positive and queer-centered nonprofit, attracts over 500 visitors:

> It builds community and autonomous fat culture across social boundaries, and participants are encouraged to share stories and clothes. It also exposes an archaeology of fat fashion, digging through the stacks of clothes gives a clear picture of what the fashion industry has decided is appropriate garb for fat bodies. Yet at the Flea these rules are subverted, people squeeze into clothes of the "wrong" size, they make things their own, and play dressing-up for the fun of it. This empowers an underclass of people with a pernicious heritage of self-hatred to experiment with kinder and more affirming ways of experiencing our bodies through playing with clothes in a supportive atmosphere. The Flea addresses American consumerism and suggests more environmentally-friendly alternatives. Profits go towards making NOLOSE conferences accessible to people who could not normally attend. (15–16)

In 1969, it was literally *newsworthy* that a fat woman like Mama Cass wore pants, or that Totie Fields allowed herself luxuries only afforded to wealthy thin women, such as fur. Today, while the exact rules have changed (fat women are now allowed to wear pants, but are still encouraged to wear darker "slimming" colors and avoid horizontal stripes and stretchy fabric), the cultural impetus to follow them remains the same. Fat people who dare to "squeeze into clothes of the 'wrong' size" and "make things their own, play[ing] dress-up for the fun of it" continue to subvert oppressive fashion norms and—through alternative consumption events like The Flea and the creation of fashion lines by queer fat designers—potentially queer the industry itself.

When fat women wear clothing that renders them visible in unexpected ways, when they break the "rules" and "defy 'tasteful' conventions," fashion can be used as a tool to "stymie fat oppression" (LeBesco 2004: 73). The very fact of a fat woman performing a kind of "traditional" beauty ("nice" clothes, makeup, and so on.) that she is not supposed to have access to, forces us to rethink culturally-embedded ideas about beauty and even femininity in the first place. Although it is important to be critical of the problematic ways Klemesrud's "Forgotten Woman" plays into dominant discourses about race, gender, class, sexuality and bodies, it is still possible to understand her as—at least in part—committing truly subversive, even "revolutionary" acts through her clothing. A far cry from current cultural conceptions of fat consumers, the fa(t)shionista—both in 1969 and today—allows us to analyze fat embodiment, consumption practices, and style in complex and exciting ways.

REFERENCES

Adam, A. 2001. Big girls' blouses: Learning to live with polyester, in *Through the Wardrobe: Women's Relationships with Their Clothes*, edited by A. Guy and E. Green. Oxford: Berg, 39–53.

Blaine, B. and McElroy, J. 2002. Selling stereotypes: Weight loss infomercials, sexism, and weightism. *Sex Roles*, 46, 351–7.

Bordo, S. 1993. *Unbearable Weight*. Berkeley: University of California Press.

Bourdieu, P. 1984. *Distinction: A Social Critique of the Judgment of Taste.* Cambridge: Harvard University Press.

Clark, D. 1991. Commodity lesbianism. *Camera Obscura*, 9(1–2 25–26), 181–201.

Clifford, S. 2010. Plus-size revelation: Bigger women have cash, too. *The New York Times.* [Online, 18 June] Available at: http://www.nytimes.com/2010/06/19/business/19plus.html [accessed 12 October 2011].

Cochrane, K. 2010. Young, fat, and fabulous. *The Guardian*, [Online, 30 January] Available at: http://www.guardian.co.uk/theguardian/2010/jan/30/fat-fashion-blogs [accessed 12 October 2011].

Cooper, C. 2008. What's fat activism? (Working paper WP2008–02). Available at University of Limerick Department of Sociology Working Paper Series website: http://www3.ul.ie/sociology/docstore/working-papers/wp2008-02.pdf [accessed 3 November 2012].

Farrell, A. E. 2011. *Fat Shame: Stigma and the Fat Body in American Culture.* New York: New York University Press.

Feuer, J. 1999. Averting the male gaze: Visual pleasure and images of fat women, in *Television, History, and American Culture: Feminist Critical Essays*, edited by M. Haralovich and L. Rabinowitz. Durham: Duke University Press, 181–199.

Gerber, L. and Quinn, S. 2008. Blue chip bodies, fat phobia and the cultural economy of body size, in *Bodily Inscriptions: Interdisciplinary Explorations into Embodiment*, edited by L. D. Kelly. Newcastle: Cambridge Scholars, 1–27.

Kinzel, L. 2012. *Two Whole Cakes.* New York: Feminist Press at the City University of New York.

Klemesrud, J. 1969. The forgotten woman in the "skinny revolution." *The New York Times*, 1 December, p. 52, accessed 9 June 2011 from ProQuest Historical Newspapers Database (Document ID: 89387415).

Klemesrud, J. 1970. There are a lot of people willing to believe fat is beautiful . . . *The New York Times*, 18 August, p. 38, accessed 9 June 2011 from ProQuest Historical Newspapers Database (Document ID: 78803213).

Klemesrud, J. 1975. The woman who isn't slim desires high fashion, too. *The New York Times*, 10 April, p. 45, accessed 9 June 2011 from ProQuest Historical Newspapers Database (Document ID: 76552603).

LeBesco, K. 2001. Queering fat bodies/politics, in *Bodies Out of Bounds: Fatness and Transgression*, edited by J. E. Braziel and K. LeBesco. Berkeley: University of California Press, 74–87.

LeBesco, K. 2004. *Revolting Bodies? The Struggle to Redefine Fat Identity.* Amherst, MA: University of Massachusetts Press.

Lupton, D. 1996. *Food, the Body, and the Self.* London: Sage Publications.

Modern living: Big business, *Time Magazine*, November 29, 1971. Available at: http://www.time.com/time/magazine/article/0.9171.877469.00.html [accessed 9 June 2001].

Moon, M. and Sedgwick, E. K. 2001. Divinity: A dossier, a performance piece, a little-understood emotion, in *Bodies Out of Bounds: Fatness and Transgression*, edited by J. E. Braziel and K. LeBesco. Berkeley: University of California Press, 292–328.

Murray, S. 2008. *The "Fat" Female Body.* New York: Palgrave Macmillan.

Riggs, C. 1983. Fat women and clothing, an interview with Judy Freespirit, in *Shadow on a Tightrope: Writings by Women on Fat Oppression*, edited by L. Schoenfielder and B. Weiser. Iowa City: Aunt Lute Press, 139–143.

LORETTA J. ROSS

23 UNDERSTANDING REPRODUCTIVE JUSTICE (2011)

Loretta J. Ross was a co-founder and the National Coordinator of the SisterSong Women of Color Reproductive Justice Collective (2005–2012). She is a co-author of *Undivided Rights: Women of Color Organize for Reproductive Justice* (2004); *Reproductive Justice: An Introduction* (2017), co-authored with Rickie Solinger; and co-editor of the anthology, *Radical Reproductive Justice: Foundations, Theory, Practice, and Critique* (2017). Recipient of many awards for her lifelong activism, Loretta Ross was Visiting Associate Professor at Arizona State University for the 2018–2019 academic year and serves as a consultant for Smith College, collecting oral histories of feminists of color for the Sophia Smith Collection, which also contains her personal archives.

Since SisterSong nationally debuted the term "Reproductive Justice" at our first national conference in November 2003, the term has blossomed in the consciousness of the reproductive rights movement, including activists, funders, researchers, academics, and advocates. Many individuals, groups and organizations find the term helpful in moving beyond the singular focus on abortion that dominates the pro-choice movement. People in other social justice movements find it useful in incorporating an understanding of reproductive health issues in organizations not primarily concerned with women's rights. It also provides a way to link groups concerned about sexual rights and gender identity issues with those working on reproductive issues. A Google search in November 2006 on the term produced 76,000 hits, proving the wide acceptance and usefulness for a term coined in 1994 by African American women before the International Conference on Population and Development in Cairo, Egypt. According to Marlene Fried of the Civil Liberties and Public Policy Program at Hampshire College, reproductive justice provides a political home for a set of ideas, aspirations and visions in language that encompasses all the social justice and human rights issues.

Because of the popularity and viability of the term "Reproductive Justice," or RJ as we call it, SisterSong is concerned that people who use the term with our free and open permission understand what we mean by this language, because it is not merely a substitute for the terms "pro-choice," "reproductive rights," or even "sexual rights." While we are encouraged at how quickly the term was adopted and adapted by so many allies in our movements, we hope that those who use the term fully appreciate its breadth, depth and strength.

Reproductive Justice is, in fact, a paradigm shift beyond demanding gender equality or attaching abortion rights to a broader reproductive health agenda. All of these concepts are . . . encompassed by the Reproductive Justice framework. RJ is an expansion of the theory of intersectionality developed by women of color and the practice of self-help from the Black women's health movement to the reproductive rights movement, based on the application of the human rights framework to the United States. Reproductive justice is in essence an intersectional theory emerging from the experiences of women of color whose multiple communities experience a complex set of reproductive oppressions. It is based on the understanding that the impacts of race, class, gender and gender identity oppressions are not additive but integrative, producing this paradigm of intersectionality. For each individual and each community, the effects will be different, but they share some of the basic characteristics of intersectionality—universality, simultaneity and interdependence.

Reproductive Justice is a positive approach that links sexuality, health, and human rights to social justice movements by placing abortion and reproductive health issues in the larger context of the well-being and health of women, families and communities because reproductive justice seamlessly integrates those individual and group human rights particularly important to marginalized communities. We believe that the ability of any woman to determine her own reproductive destiny is directly linked to the conditions in her community and these conditions are not just a matter of individual choice and access. For example, a woman cannot make an individual decision about her body if she is part of a community whose human rights as a group are violated, such as through environmental dangers or insufficient quality health care. Reproductive justice addresses issues of population control, bodily self-determination, white supremacy, immigrants' rights, economic and environmental justice, sovereignty, and militarism and criminal injustices that limit individual human rights because of group or community oppressions.

Reproductive justice does not replace other language used by our movement, but invites us to examine reproductive issues through the women's human rights framework. Reproductive justice is simultaneously a new theory, a new practice and a new strategy that has quickly proven effective in providing a common language and broader unity in our movement. For this progress to continue, we believe that our movement must share a deepened understanding of the potential power of this framework for moving beyond the congealed debates on abortion in reproductive politics.

The theory of reproductive justice was created because women of color were looking for a way to articulate the needs of our communities. Sister-Song's three core reproductive justice principles developed since our founding in 1997 reflect the theory and practice we collectively learned and shared. We believe that every woman has the human right to:

- Decide if and when she will have a baby and the conditions under which she will give birth
- Decide if she will not have a baby and her options for preventing or ending a pregnancy

- Parent the children she already has with the necessary social supports in safe environments and healthy communities, and without fear of violence from individuals or the government . . .

The Core Problem Is Reproductive Oppression

Reproductive oppression is the control and exploitation of women, girls, and individuals through our bodies, sexuality, labor, and reproduction. The regulation of women and individuals thus becomes a powerful strategic pathway to controlling entire communities. It involves systems of oppression that are based on race, ability, class, gender, sexuality, age and immigration status.

—ASIAN COMMUNITIES FOR REPRODUCTIVE JUSTICE (ACRJ)

Women of color have historically and are now still experiencing "reproductive punishment" described by Dorothy Roberts, or "reproductive oppression" defined by ACRJ. Both terms summarize the way that the state and others refuse to support us with quality services and resources, but at the same time interfere in our lives and decisions. Reproductive oppression is implemented, for example, through discriminatory foster care enforcement, criminalizing pregnancy, immigration restrictions, preventing LGBTQ individuals from parenting, and forced abortions for incarcerated women. As stated above, reproductive oppression is a means of selectively controlling the destiny of entire communities through the bodies of women and individuals, a newer and subtler form of negative eugenics. In fact, according to the United Nations' Convention on the Prevention and Punishment of the Crime of Genocide, reproductive oppression meets genocidal standards because it can be characterized as: "Imposing measures intended to prevent births within the group, and forcibly transferring children of the group to another group." As a society, we can endlessly argue intent versus outcome, but the facts remain that women of color—and our children—experience oppressive reproductive politics leading to harmful outcomes by state and non-state actors.

It is equally important to understand how the US system of white supremacy facilitates reproductive oppression, an aspect understated by the mainstream movement. The concept of reproductive justice works similarly for white women as well because their individual decisions are directly tied to their communities—in particular, racist fears triggered by the decreasing percentage of white children born in the United States. Many of the restrictions on abortion, contraception, scientifically accurate sex education, and stem cell research are directly related to an unsubtle campaign of positive eugenics to force heterosexual white women to have more babies. In contrast, children of color are often deemed unwanted, excessive and perceived as a threat to the body politic of the United States by being described as a "youth bulge" creating a dysfunctional education system, economic chaos, environmental degradation, and a criminal underclass.

The isolation of abortion from other social justice issues that concern all our communities contributes to, rather than counters, reproductive oppression. Abortion isolated from other social justice/human rights issues neglects issues of economic justice, the environment, criminal justice, immigrants' rights, militarism, discrimination based on race and gender identity, and a host of other concerns directly affecting an individual woman's decision-making process. Of equal concern, support for abortion rights is even frequently isolated from other reproductive health issues because abortion is deeply stigmatized by both sides of the debate rather than being seen as part of the continuum of women's lived reproductive health experiences and part of their human rights entitlements.

We must end the separation of abortion rights from other social justice, reproductive rights and human rights issues because it is difficult—if not impossible—to mobilize communities in defense of abortion rights if abortion is taken out of the context of empowering women, creating healthier families, and promoting sustainable communities.

By shifting the definition of the problem to one of reproductive oppression rather than a singular focus on protecting the legal right to abortion, SisterSong offers a more inclusive and catalytic vision of how to move forward in building a new movement for women's human rights.

In order to better understand the way that SisterSong intends the reproductive justice analysis to be used in conjunction with the human rights framework, it is important to review the current eight categories of human rights to get a sense of their relevance to everyone's lives. These categories have developed and expanded since the writing of the Universal Declaration of Human Rights in 1948.

8 Categories of Human Rights

Civil Rights—Non-Discrimination, Equality

Political Rights—Voting, Speech, Assembly

Economic Rights—Living Wage, Workers' Rights

Social Rights—Health Care, Food, Shelter, Education

Cultural Rights—Religion, Language, Dress

Environmental Rights—Clean Air, Water, and Land; No Toxic Neighborhoods

Developmental Rights—Control Own Natural Resources

Sexual Rights—Right to Have or Not Have Children, Right to Marry & When, Same-Sex Rights, Transgender Rights, Right to Birth Control and Abortion, Right to Sexual Pleasure and Define Families

It is important to understand that . . . spurious claims of "human rights for the unborn" (in actuality a violation of the Universal Declaration of Human Rights [UDHR]) are used by those who manipulate the framework rather than uphold it. This strategy seeks to deny all of our human rights to privacy, bodily self-determination, and justice, but especially the rights of women. In fact, the first article of the UDHR states that, "All human beings *are born* free and equal in dignity and rights. . . . " The UDHR does not confer human rights to those who are not here yet, but does demand that the rights of people already born be respected and protected. Human rights are not negotiable—they are inalienable. Human rights are our birthright as human beings. To achieve our human rights, we seek reproductive justice for ourselves, our families, and our communities.

Three Frameworks for Our Activism

> Reproductive Justice is the complete physical, mental, spiritual, political, social, and economic well-being of women and girls, based on the full achievement and protection of women's human rights.
>
> —ACRJ

In its 2005 discussion paper, Asian Communities for Reproductive Justice expanded on the original SisterSong analysis by evaluating the three main frameworks for fighting reproductive oppression: 1) Reproductive Health which deals with service delivery, 2) Reproductive Rights which address the legal regime, and 3) Reproductive Justice which focuses on movement building. (See *A New Vision for Reproductive Justice* by ACRJ at www.reproductivejustice.org.) These three frameworks provide a complimentary and comprehensive response to reproductive oppression, as well as a proactive vision articulating what we are fighting for and how to build a new movement to advance women's human rights.

Reproductive Health is a service delivery model, which addresses the reproductive health needs of women. It focuses on lack of health care, services, information, as well as research and health data. The goals are to improve and expand services, research and access, particularly in prevention, and provide culturally competent care for communities of color.

Reproductive Rights is a legal and advocacy-based model that serves to protect an individual woman's legal right to reproductive health care services. It addresses the lack of legal protection or enforcement of laws implemented to protect an individual woman's legal right to reproductive health care services. The goal is to have universal legal protection for all individuals and claim these protections as constitutional rights.

Reproductive Justice is a movement-building framework that identifies how reproductive oppression is the result of the intersections of multiple oppressions and is inherently connected to the struggle for social justice and human rights. A woman's societal institutions, environment, economics and culture affect her reproductive life.

Each of these frameworks has strengths and limitations, but together they form the matrix of reproductive activism in our movement. Reproductive justice calls for an integrated analysis, a holistic vision and comprehensive strategies that push against the structural and societal conditions that control our communities by regulating our bodies, sexuality, labor and reproduction. It demands that we work across social justice movements to build a united struggle for universal human rights. It allows us to pursue a vision that will protect and determine our complete physical, mental, spiritual, political, economic, and social well-being. In order to turn reproductive justice into action, we must develop new leaders, organize our youth, and educate our community leaders.

> Reproductive Justice is achieved when women, girls and individuals have the social, economic, and political power and resources to make healthy decisions about our bodies, sexuality and reproduction for ourselves, our families and our communities.
>
> —ACRJ

Why Do We Need a New Framework?

Reproductive Justice also speaks to the shortcomings of the "choice" movement. There are . . . eight inadequacies with the choice framework countered by the reproductive justice framework, according to Marlene Fried [mentioned above]:

- Choice does not speak to the complexities of women's lives. It excludes the lack of access women face and the depth of women's experiences. No woman seeking an abortion ever has just one human rights issue confronting her.
- Choice leaves out opposition to population control. Reproductive choice in the United States only speaks to the right not to have a child, but it doesn't address a woman's right to have as many children as she wants.

- Choice is a politically conservative concept. In order to fight conservative politics in the 1970s, the movement made "choice" a libertarian anti-government concept that would appeal to larger segments of the population, which de-emphasized women's rights, sex rights and sexual pleasure, and failed to support women as moral decision-makers.
- Choice is a consumerist or marketplace concept. Abortion is a reproductive right that is only available to those who can afford it. The marketplace privatizes the governmental obligation not only to protect choice but to ensure that choices are achievable for all.
- Choice is an individual concept that does not address the social problems that prohibit women from exercising their rights. Unplanned pregnancies and poverty are not an individual woman's problems.
- Choice primarily resonates with those who feel they can make choices in other areas of their lives, those whose human rights are less likely to be violated.
- Choice is not a sufficiently powerful moral argument, especially when you have to challenge the "life" framework of those opposed to women's rights.
- Choice is not a compelling vision. It's not the vision needed to mobilize the kind of movement capable of winning clear and consistent victories. . . .

The Future of our Reproductive Justice Movement

SisterSong believes that our Reproductive Justice analysis offers a compelling and more defensible framework for empowering women and individuals to create healthier families, and sustainable communities. This is a clear and consistent message for the movement. We believe we collectively have the potential to motivate an admittedly disheartened pro-choice movement by bringing in new voices to expand our base, reframe our vision, and connect to other social justice movements. The Reproductive Justice analysis helps reposition the public debate on reproductive health from one dominated by abortion to broader issues of reproductive health, rights and justice. Using this analysis, we can integrate multiple issues and bring together constituencies that are multi-racial, multi-generational, and multi-class in order to build a more powerful and relevant grassroots movement that can create systemic social change.

As an example of the reproductive justice framework in action, more than 1.15 million people participated in the April 25, 2004 March for Women's Lives, making it the largest protest march in US history. "The March for Women's Lives was a perfect example of using reproductive justice to create a bigger movement," according to Kathy Spillar, Vice President of the Feminist Majority Foundation, one of the principal organizations that first called and provided some of the resources, staff and office space for the March. Spillar spoke at a Funders' Briefing on Reproductive Justice that SisterSong sponsored in October 2005. March organizers linked the domestic assault on abortion with the global gag rule, the spread of HIV/AIDS through faulty abstinence-only education, the debt crisis that impoverishes developing countries, the war against Iraq, the undermining of privacy and citizenship rights, the attacks on gay marriage, the contempt for international mechanisms like the United Nations and human rights treaties, and the corruption of our political system that selects rather than elects presidents while denying direct democracy to all of us. The success of the March was a testament to the power of human rights to mobilize and unite diverse sectors of the social justice movement to support women's human rights in the United States and abroad. . . .

We stand at a critical time in which to consider the pro-choice movement's future direction. The implications for women's lives are increasingly acute in light of the extreme political conservatism sweeping the nation from all quarters and affecting reproductive and sexual health policies on all levels—ranging from the US President and the Supreme Court, to state legislatures and local school boards and foreign policies. Moreover, assaults upon the civil and human rights of communities of color and other disenfranchised members of our society continue to rise within our nation's policies and the rapidly changing political climate. As such, we believe it is essential to utilize the reproductive justice frame as a means to unite women and their communities, be relevant to communities of color, and link to advocates from the nation's capital to the grassroots in order to develop proactive strategies to protect and preserve our lives.

It is beyond the scope of this article to fully discuss SisterSong's use of self-help techniques in our practice of applying the Reproductive Justice framework to our movement and building unity among our Collective. Self-help is described in detail in *Undivided Rights: Women of Color Organize for Reproductive Justice* published in 2004 by South End Press. It is vital, however, to mention that reproductive justice demands a process by which differences among women and individuals can be transcended in order to build a united movement for reproductive justice. Self-help addresses issues of internalized oppression and empowerment that are critical to confront when working across divisions of race, class, age, ethnicity, religion, sexual identity, gender identity, disabilities, and immigration status. Multi-issue and multi-sectoral work is extremely difficult without a proven process for

maintaining unity while addressing complex, intersectional oppressions. The Reproductive Justice framework is incomplete and only partially understood without incorporating the principles and practices of self-help pioneered by the National Black Women's Health Project and the National Latina Health Organization in the 1980s.

SisterSong provides Reproductive Justice 101 trainings for organizations, groups and individuals who wish to explore the reproductive justice framework in more depth, learning more about its component parts of intersectionality, human rights, self-help and empowerment.

SisterSong offers these trainings so that we can help ensure that the meaning of Reproductive Justice is not compromised or limited as people embrace and adjust the framework to fit their own needs. While we cannot and do not wish to prohibit anyone from using this language because we recognize its enormous appeal, we hope that the theoretical origins and its concomitant movement building practices originating in the experiences of women of color will be respected with the same integrity and generosity with which we offer our perspectives.

ALISON KAFER

24 DEBATING FEMINIST FUTURES: SLIPPERY SLOPES, CULTURAL ANXIETY, AND THE CASE OF THE DEAF LESBIANS (2013)

Alison Kafer is a professor of feminist studies at Southwestern University, where she teaches courses on disability studies, reproductive justice, animal studies, and feminist and queer theory. She is co-editor of *Deaf and Disability Studies: Interdisciplinary Perspectives* (2010) and author of *Feminist, Queer, Crip* (2013), which examines the possibilities of cross-movement theories and politics to create more just and accessible futures.

The pervasiveness of prenatal testing, and especially its acceptance as part of the standard of care for pregnant women, casts women as responsible for their future children's able-bodiedness/able-mindedness; prospective parents are urged to take advantage of these services so as to avoid burdening their future children with any disabilities.[1] This notion of "burdening" children finds an echo in the debate over same-sex marriage, with LGBT couples cast as selfish parents, placing their own desires over the physical and mental health of their children . . . The possibility that same-sex parents might produce queer children is one of the most common reasons given for opposing such families, a reasoning that takes for granted the homophobic worldview that queerness must be avoided at all costs.

It is in the literature of reproductive technologies and their "proper" use that heterocentrism and homophobia intersect powerfully with ableism and stereotypes about disability. These stories reveal profound anxieties about reproducing the family as a normative unit, with all of its members able-bodied/able-minded and heterosexual. At sites where disability, queerness, and reproductive technologies converge, parents and prospective parents are often criticized and condemned for their alleged misuse of technology. Assistive reproductive technologies are to be used only to deselect or prevent disability; doing otherwise—such as selecting for disability—means failing to properly reproduce the family.

In this chapter, I explore one such story in which ableism and heterocentrism combine, a situation in which parents were widely condemned for failing to protect their children from both disability and queerness. Sharon Duchesneau and Candace McCullough, a deaf lesbian couple in Maryland, attracted publicity and controversy for their 2001 decision to use a deaf sperm donor in conceiving their son. What most interests me about their story, and what I focus on here, is the consistency with which cultural critics and commentators took for granted the idea that a better future is one without disability and deafness. In order to illustrate this dimension of the story, I frame their account with an analysis of Marge Piercy's influential utopia, *Woman on the Edge of Time*. In that novel, as in the responses to McCullough and Duchesneau, "common sense" dictates that disabled minds/bodies have no place in the future, and that such decisions merit neither discussion nor dissent. Both stories, in other words, center around the proper use of assistive reproductive technology and the future of children.

This is What the Future Looks Like: Reproduction and Debate in *Woman on the Edge of Time*

In 2001, I served as a teaching assistant in an introduction to women's studies course at a liberal arts college . . . One of the assigned texts was Marge Piercy's novel *Woman on the Edge of Time*

Source: Alison Kafer, *Feminist, Queer, Crip* (Bloomington: Indiana University Press, 2013). Copyright © 2013 by Alison Kafer. Reprinted with permission of Indiana University Press.

(1976), chosen by the professor in order to spark discussion about feminist futures . . . Published over three decades ago, the novel continues to be popular among feminists for its representation of an egalitarian society. Students responded enthusiastically to Piercy's book, finding its imagined utopia hopeful, enviable, and desirable. As a disability studies scholar, however, I found the novel troubling for its erasure of disability and disabled bodies, an erasure that is never debated or discussed in the novel. With the marked exception of mental illness, an exception to which I will return, *Woman on the Edge of Time* simply assumes that a feminist future is, by definition, one without disability and disabled bodies.

Woman on the Edge of Time . . . chronicles the experiences of Connie Ramos, a poor Chicana woman who has been involuntarily institutionalized in a New York mental ward. The novel moves back and forth among three settings: mental institutions and Connie's neighborhoods in 1970s New York; Mattapoisett, a utopian village in 2137; and a future, dystopic New York City inhabited by cyborgs and machines in which all humans have been genetically engineered to fulfill certain social roles. While incarcerated in the violent ward of a mental institution in 1976, Connie develops the ability to travel mentally into the future, interacting with a woman named Luciente who lives in the utopian Mattapoisett community. During one attempt at mental travel, Connie's attention is diverted and she finds herself in the dystopic future Manhattan, but the rest of her time travels involve Mattapoisett.

Piercy lovingly describes Mattapoisett. She has clearly thought a great deal about difference in constructing this world, trying to envision a thoroughly feminist, antiracist, socially just, and multicultural community. All sexual orientations and identities are present and respected in her vision of Mattapoisett, everyone possesses equal wealth and resources, and all have access to education according to their interests. People in Mattapoisett have developed harvesting and consumption patterns intended to redress the global imbalance of wealth, resources, and consumption wrought during Connie's era. The world is viewed holistically, with Mattapoisett's inhabitants aware of how their actions affect others both within the borders of their community and beyond.

Luciente explains to Connie that Mattapoisett's communal harmony has been achieved through radical changes in the system of reproduction. All babies are born in the "brooder," a machine that mixes the genes from all the population's members, so that children are not genetically bound to any two people. Three adults co-mother each child, a task that is undertaken equally by men and women. Through hormone treatments, both men and women are able to breast-feed, exemplifying the community's belief that equality between the sexes can be engineered through technological intervention and innovation. By breaking the traditional gendered nature of reproduction, explains Luciente, the brooder has eliminated fixed gender roles and sexism within the community. It has also eradicated racism by mixing the genes from all "races," thereby rendering everyone mixed-race and making notions of "racial purity" impossible to maintain. Cultural histories and traditions have been preserved, but have been separated from the concept of "race." Luciente's friend Bee tells Connie that the community has recently decided to create more "darker-skinned" babies in order to counteract the historical devaluation of people of color, resulting in a village inhabited by people of all skin tones: "[W]e don't want the melting pot where everybody ends up with thin gruel. We want diversity, for strangeness breeds richness."[2]

All decisions concerning the community are publicly debated during open meetings. Decisions are made on the basis of consensus, and every community member is allowed and expected to participate. People volunteer to serve as representatives to intercommunity meetings at which decisions affecting a larger population are debated. No decisions are made for other people by other people. Every person has the right to speak out on issues that affect him or her.

To illustrate the way this participatory democracy works, Piercy gradually introduces Connie, and the reader, to a conflict currently being played out in Mattapoisett. The "Mixers" and the "Shapers" are involved in a heated disagreement about the next direction the brooder should take . . . The Mixers would prefer to maintain the status quo: the brooder currently screens out genes linked to birth defects and disease susceptibility, thereby preventing "negative" characteristics from being passed down to children. The Shapers, however, want to program the brooder to select for "positive" traits as well, ensuring that children will have the traits most desired by the community. Luciente and her friends are on the side of the Mixers, arguing that it is impossible to know which traits will be necessary or valued in the future. Piercy makes it clear that Luciente's perspective mirrors her own; the genetically engineered inhabitants of her dystopian New York suggest the logical, and undesirable, result of a Shaper victory. Piercy refuses, however, to simply impose a Mixer victory on Mattapoisett; she depicts a continuing process of respectful dialogue and public debate between the two groups, creating a vision of a feminist community in which all people participate equally in the decisions that affect them. The Mixers-Shapers debate is never resolved in the novel, illustrating Piercy's notion of the importance of open-ended dialogue and group process.

It is this description of democratic decision-making, of a community debating publicly how it wants technology to develop in the future, that has made *Woman on the Edge* such an attractive text to feminist scholars of science studies and political theory. Decades after its initial publication, the novel continues to inspire feminist thinkers with its image of an egalitarian future in which all people's voices are heard, respected, and addressed. . . .

Similarly, several feminist political theorists and science studies scholars cast the book as a vital exploration of political and technological processes influenced by feminist principles. José van Dijck, for example, praises Piercy for depicting science as "a political and democratic process in which all participants participate," a depiction that recognizes genetics "as a political, rather than a purely scientific," practice. Political theorist Josephine Carubia Glorie shares van Dijck's assessment, noting that Piercy's novel features a society in which all community members are able to engage in social critique. Even those who disagree with Piercy's

pro–genetic engineering and pro–assisted reproduction stance, such as ecofeminists Cathleen McGuire and Colleen McGuire, find *Woman on the Edge of Time* to be a compelling vision of a world without social inequalities.[3] As these comments suggest, over thirty years after its initial publication, *Woman on the Edge of Time* remains a powerful, productive text for feminist theorists concerned with the role of technology in the lives of women and committed to envisioning an egalitarian, just world. Piercy's articulation of the "Mixers vs. Shapers" debate—should we breed children for desired traits?—seems prescient in the early twenty-first century as bioethicists and geneticists debate the morality and feasibility of allowing prospective parents to create or select embryos on the basis of such traits as sex, hair color, or height.[4]

What has gone unnoticed in these praises of Piercy's novel, however, is the place of disability, and specifically disabled bodies, in her imagined utopia. In a world very carefully constructed to contain people of every skin tone and sexual orientation, where people of all genders and ages are equally valued, disabled people are absent. This absence cannot simply be attributed to oversight or neglect; it is not that Piercy forgot to include disability and disabled people among her cast of characters and life experiences. On the contrary, the place, or rather the absence, of disability in Piercy's utopia is at the heart of the Mixers-Shapers debate: both the Shapers and the Mixers agree on the necessity of screening the gene pool for "defective genes" and "predispositions" for illness and "suffering." It is taken for granted by both sides—and by Piercy and (presumably) her audience—that everyone knows and agrees which genes and characteristics are negative and therefore which ones should be eliminated; questions about so-called negative traits are apparently not worth discussing. Thus, disabled people are not accidentally missing from Piercy's utopia; they have intentionally and explicitly been written out of it. . . .

At first glance, mental disability seems to be an exception to this absence. Not only is the novel highly critical of the institutionalization of people with mental disability, it also casts "crazy" as a diagnosis more likely to be attached to poor women of color and to those who refuse to adhere to cultural norms. Unlike the stigma and forced institutionalization Connie faced in 1970s New York, the inhabitants of Mattapoisett recognize mental disability as part of a normal course of life, with people "dropping out" of their communities as needed to tend to their mental and emotional needs. But this requirement to drop out, to separate oneself from the community until one's functioning returns to "normal," enacts another version of this erasure of disability. . . .

Neither Piercy, writing in the mid-1970s, nor theorists such as van Dijck and Glorie, writing in the late 1990s, seem to have noticed that the entire Mixers-Shapers debate rests on profound assumptions about whose bodies matter. . . . Never once do the nondisabled members of Mattapoisett debate the decision to eliminate ostensibly defective genes, never do they question how one determines which genes are labeled "defective" or what "defective" means. Van Dijck highlights Piercy's recognition that genetics is political—contested and contestable, subject to debate and disagreement—but fails to realize that screening the gene pool for allegedly negative traits is also political. In both the novel and interpretation of the novel, it is assumed that disability has no place in feminist visions of the future, and that such an assumption is so natural, so given, that it does not merit public debate. . . .

I suggest that Piercy's depiction and, more importantly, feminist theorists' praise of it mean that disability in the United States is often viewed as an unredeemable difference. Disability and the disabled body are problems that must be solved technologically, and there is allegedly so much cultural agreement on this point that it need not be discussed or debated. Disability, then, plays a huge, but seemingly uncontested, role in how contemporary Americans envision the future. Utopian visions are founded on the elimination of disability, while dystopic, negative visions of the future are based on its proliferation; as we will see below, both depictions are deeply tied to cultural understandings and anxieties about the proper use of technology.

I turn now to one particular case of the alleged misuse of technology . . . The story of Sharon Duchesneau and Candace McCullough, a deaf lesbian couple who selected a deaf sperm donor for their pregnancies, has been presented to the public almost exclusively in terms of what the future can, should, and will include. . . . I am less interested in arguing for or against these women's decision than in detailing how critics of the couple utilize dystopic rhetoric in their condemnations, presenting deafness and disability as traits that obviously should be avoided. As with *Woman on the Edge of Time*, a world free of impairment is portrayed as a goal shared by all, a goal that is beyond question or analysis, a goal that is natural rather than political.

Deaf/Disabled: A Terminological Interlude

For most hearing people, to describe deafness as a disability is to state the obvious: deaf people lack the ability to hear, and therefore they are disabled. For some people, however, deaf and hearing alike, it is neither obvious nor accurate to characterize deafness as a disability and deaf people as disabled. Rather, Deaf people are more appropriately described as members of a distinct linguistic and cultural minority, more akin to Spanish speakers in a predominantly English-language country than to people in wheelchairs or people who are blind.[5] Spanish speakers are not considered disabled simply because they cannot communicate in English without the aid of an interpreter, and, according to this model, neither should Deaf people, who rely on interpreters in order to communicate with those who cannot sign, be considered disabled. Drawing parallels between Deaf people and members of other cultural groups, supporters of the linguistic-cultural model of deafness note the existence of a vibrant Deaf culture, one that includes its own language (in the United States, American Sign Language [ASL]), cultural productions (e.g., ASL poetry and performance), residential schools, and social networks, as well as high rates of intermarriage.[6] . . . This linguistic-cultural model of deafness shares a key assumption of the social model of disability—namely, that it is society's interpretations of and responses to bodily and sensory variations that are the problem, not the variations themselves.

Everyone Here Spoke Sign Language, Nora Groce's study of hereditary deafness on Martha's Vineyard from the early eighteenth century to the mid-twentieth century, provides an example of this perspective. Groce argues that genetic deafness and deaf people were so interwoven into the population that almost every person on the island had a deaf relative or neighbor.[7] As a result, "everyone [there] spoke sign language," a situation that proves it is possible for hearing people to share the responsibility of communication rather than simply expecting deaf people to lip-read and speak orally or alleviate their hearing loss with surgeries and hearing aids.[8] Groce's study challenges the idea that deafness precludes full participation in society, suggesting that the barriers deaf people face are due more to societal attitudes and practices than to one's audiological conditions. . . .

Although some Deaf people are averse to the label "disabled," either because of their immersion in Deaf culture or because of an internalized ableist impulse to distance themselves from disabled people, others are more willing to explore the label politically. This kind of exploration is based on making a distinction between being labeled as "disabled" by others, especially medical or audiological professionals and the hearing world in general, and choosing to self-identify as disabled. Many Deaf people who choose to take up the label of disability do so for strategic reasons. For some, the decision stems from a desire to ally themselves with other disabled people. They recognize that people with disabilities and Deaf people share a history of oppression, discrimination, and stigmatization because of their differences from a perceived "normal" body. As a group, Deaf and disabled people can work together to fight discrimination, and they have done so since the birth of the modern disability rights movement in the late 1960s. Thus, while some Deaf people may be opposed to (or at the very least ambivalent about) seeing deafness as a disability, they may simultaneously be willing to identify themselves as disabled or to ally themselves with disabled people in order to work toward social changes and legal protections that would benefit both populations.[9]

Recognizing this affinity between disability and deafness is particularly important in an analysis of cure narratives and utopian discourse, because it is precisely the image of deafness as disability that animates these narratives. What makes the actions of parents who express a preference for a deaf baby—the case under consideration here—so abhorrent to the larger culture is the refusal to eradicate disability from the lives of their children.

Reproducing Cultural Anxiety: The Case of the Deaf Lesbians

In November 2001, the same year that I taught Piercy's novel, Sharon Duchesneau and Candace (Candy) McCullough, a white lesbian couple living in Maryland, had a baby boy named Gauvin, who was conceived by assisted insemination. Both Duchesneau, the birth mother, and McCullough, the adoptive mother, are deaf, as is their first child, Jehanne. Jehanne and her new brother Gauvin were conceived with sperm donated by a family friend, a friend who also is deaf. Duchesneau and McCullough had originally intended to use a sperm bank for the pregnancies, but their desire for a deaf donor eliminated that option: men with congenital deafness are precluded from becoming sperm donors; reminiscent of the eugenic concern with the "fitness" of potential parents, deafness is one of the conditions that sperm banks and fertility clinics routinely screen out of the donor pool.[10] Several months after he was born, Gauvin underwent an extensive audiology test to determine if he shared his parents' deafness.[11] To the delight of Duchesneau and McCullough, the diagnosis was clear: Gauvin had "a profound hearing loss" in one ear, and "at least a severe hearing loss" in the other.[12] Duchesneau noted that they would have accepted and loved a hearing child, but a deaf child was clearly their preference. "A hearing baby would be a blessing," Duchesneau explained, "a Deaf baby would be a special blessing."[13]

Liza Mundy covered Duchesneau and McCullough's story for the *Washington Post Magazine* in March of 2002, and her essay provided a detailed explanation of these women's reproductive choices. Although the piece acknowledged the criticisms lodged against Duchesneau and McCullough, it was largely sympathetic; Mundy took care to explain the women's understanding of Deaf identity and to situate them within a larger understanding of Deaf culture and community. She also, of necessity, mentioned the women's lesbian relationship, but it was not a central component of the piece. For Mundy, it was the women's deafness, and their decision to have deaf children within a larger Deaf community, that made their story newsworthy.

The piece made quite a splash, and the story of the Deaf lesbian couple was picked up by other newspapers and wire services. Papers across the United States and England ran versions of and responses to the story, and cultural critics from across the ideological spectrum began to weigh in. The Family Research Council, a Washington-based organization that "champions marriage and family as the foundation of civilization," issued a press release with comments from Ken Connor, the group's president at the time. Describing Duchesneau and McCullough as "incredibly selfish," Connor berated the pair for imposing on their children not only the "disadvantages that come as a result of being raised in a homosexual household" but also the "burden" of disability. Connor linked disability and homosexuality, casting both as hardships that these two women "intentionally" handed their children. The Family Research Council's press release closed with a quote from Connor . . . "One can only hope that this practice of intentionally manufacturing disabled children in order to fit the lifestyles of the parents will not progress any further. The places this slippery slope could lead to are frightening."[14] The use of the term "lifestyles"—a word frequently used to refer derisively to queers and our sexual/relational practices—effectively blurs deafness and queerness, suggesting that both characteristics are allegedly leading "us" down the road to ruin. . . .

The Family Research Council was not alone in discussing these women's desire for a Deaf baby in the context of their sexuality. Indeed, even some queer commentators found something troubling, and ultimately dystopic, about the idea. Queer novelist Jeanette Winterson seemed to suggest that it was precisely these women's queerness that made their decision so anathema:

If either of the Deaf Lesbians in the United States had been in a relationship with a man, Deaf or hearing, and if they had decided to have a baby, there is absolutely no certainty that the baby would have been Deaf. You take a chance with love; you take a chance with nature, but it is those chances and the unexpected possibilities they bring, that give life its beauty.[15] . . .

Winterson condemned Duchesneau and McCullough for removing the element of "chance" from their pregnancy and guaranteeing themselves a deaf baby, a guarantee that could not happen "with nature."[16] However, her remarks obscure the fact that the women's use of a deaf donor provided no such guarantee, a fact made clear in Mundy's article. Duchesneau, McCullough, and their deaf donor; Winterson's hypothetical deaf heterosexual couple: both groups would have exactly the same odds of having a deaf child, yet Winterson found no fault with the imagined heterosexual conception. . . . an odd position for a queer writer to take and one that has certainly been influenced by dominant ableist culture.

Winterson clearly took for granted that "everyone" views these women's behavior as reprehensible; for her, it was a "simple fact" that life as a deaf person is inferior to life as a hearing person. . . . Winterson echoed Connor's "slippery slope" rhetoric when she suggested that these women's actions will lead to other, allegedly even more troubling futures. "How would any of us feel," she asked, "if the women had both been blind and claimed the right to a blind baby?" The tone and content of Winterson's essay answers this question for her readers, making clear that "we" would feel justifiably outraged. It is perhaps no accident that Winterson referred to "blind women" rather than "blind people," again implying that it might be "natural" for a heterosexual blind couple to reproduce, but not a lesbian one. She even drew on this image for the title of her essay, "How Would We Feel if Blind Women Claimed the Right to a Blind Baby?"

This rhetorical move—shifting from an actual case involving deafness to a hypothetical situation involving a different disability—is a popular strategy to convince a disabled person that her decision to choose for disability, either by having a disabled child or by refusing technological fixes, is misguided, illogical, and extreme. By decontextualizing the situation, removing it from a Deaf person's own sphere of reference, it is assumed that the Deaf person will be able to recognize her error in judgment. This practice suggests that some disabilities are worse than others, that eventually one can substitute a particular disability that is so "obviously" undesirable that the disabled person will change her mind. Cross-disability alliances are presumed to be nonexistent; it is assumed that all Deaf people believe it would be best to eliminate the birth of "blind babies" or people with X disability.

This story is complicated by the fact that Winterson's stance is not without basis. In the *Washington Post* story, McCullough does express a preference for a sighted child. According to Mundy,

> If they themselves—valuing sight—were to have a blind child, well then, Candy acknowledges, they would probably try to have it fixed, if they could, like hearing parents who attempt to restore their child's hearing with cochlear implants. "I want to be the same as my child," says Candy. "I want the baby to enjoy what we enjoy."[17]

McCullough and Duchesneau's position that Deaf babies are "special blessings" does not mean that they are not also simultaneously implicated in the ableism of the larger culture; their desire for deafness does not necessarily extend to a desire for any and all disabilities. Deaf and disabled people are not immune to the ableist—or homophobic—ideologies of the larger culture. (It is worth noting in this context, however, that McCullough does not express a desire for genetic testing and selective abortion.)

Indeed, even some disabled queers mirrored the blend of heterocentrism and ableism circulating through mainstream responses to Duchesneau and McCullough's reproductive choices. A participant on the QueerDisability listserv, for example, found the couple's decision to choose a Deaf donor troubling, partly because of the hardships and social barriers their children would face, partly because of the alleged financial burden their children would place on the state. Echoing Winterson, the listserv

member drew a distinction between the "naturally" Deaf children who result from heterosexual relationships and the "unnaturally," and therefore inappropriately, Deaf children who result from queer relationships.[18] . . . Her comments lead me to believe that she would, like Winterson, find less fault with the imagined heterosexual couple than with the real homosexual one: either deafness or homosexuality in isolation would be permissible, but the combination is too abnormal, too disruptive, too queer, even for some gays and lesbians and people with disabilities.

These kinds of responses to the use of assisted insemination by Deaf queers support Sarah Franklin's argument that, while reproductive technology "might have been (or is to a limited extent) a disruption of the so-called 'natural' basis for the nuclear family and heterosexual marriage, [it] *has instead provided the occasion for reconsolidating them.*"[19] With few exceptions, Franklin explains, the state has taken little action to guarantee queers and/or single parents equal access to assisted reproductive technologies, and prominent people in the field of reproductive medicine have been outspoken in their belief that these technologies should not be available to same-sex couples or single parents.[20] As sociologist Laura Mamo points out, "[A]ccess to reproductive technologies in the United States is from the outset a class-based and sexuality-based phenomenon, and the institutional organization of these services enacts the reproduction of class and sexuality hierarchies by assuring the survival and ongoing proportionality of middle-class (usually white) heterosexual families."[21]

Mamo details the ways in which lesbians and (single heterosexual women) are disadvantaged within the medical system. Insurance policies, for example, require a diagnosis of infertility before they agree to cover assistive technologies, yet such a diagnosis is difficult to make in the absence of heterosexual sex. Many lesbians want to use sperm donated by a friend or family member, yet some clinics forbid the use of sperm from a known donor unless the woman is married to the donor.[22] Dorothy Roberts and Elizabeth Weil note that many fertility clinics require proof of a "stable" marriage before initiating treatment, an open-ended requirement that has been used to block the treatment of queers, women of color, and poor people.[23] . . .

Dorothy Roberts notes that racism also plays a role in access to assisted reproductive technologies, as doctors are far less likely to recommend fertility treatments for black women than for whites.[24] Although clinics cannot legally discriminate against potential patients on the basis of race, they can neglect to inform people of color about all possible treatments.[25] Ableist attitudes pose similar barriers to disabled people's use of assisted reproductive technologies. Many disabled women report being discouraged by their doctors and families from having children, a fact that suggests that they might not receive all the fertility assistance they need. The policing of these technologies serves to reinforce the dominant vision of a world without impairment and to perpetuate the stigmatization of the queer, disabled, nonwhite body. . . .

None of the articles tracing the reproductive choices of Sharon Duchesneau and Colleen McCullough questioned the assumption that a future without disability and deafness is superior to one with them. As in Piercy's fictional debate between the Mixers and the Shapers, no one recognized the screening out of deaf sperm donors as a political decision; indeed, it was not recognized as a decision at all because no other possibility was even conceivable. The vast majority of public reactions to these women's choices tell a story about the appropriate place of disability/deafness in the future; it is assumed that everyone, both hearing and Deaf, disabled and nondisabled, will and should prefer a nondisabled, hearing child. Thus the future allegedly invoked by the couple's actions is dangerous because it advocates an improper use of technology; technology can and should be used only to *eliminate* disability, not to *proliferate* it. Such a goal is *natural*, not *political*, and therefore neither requires nor deserves public debate.

Open to Debate? Disability and Difference in a Feminist Future

. . . As illustrated by *Woman on the Edge of Time*, and as manifested in the furor surrounding McCullough and Duchesneau's reproductive choices,

disability is often seen as a difference that has no place in the future. Disability is a problem that must be eliminated, a hindrance to one's future opportunities, a drag on one's quality of life. Speaking directly about the Duchesneau and McCullough case, bioethicist Alta Charo argues, "The question is whether the parents have violated the sacred duty of parenthood, which is to maximize to some reasonable degree the advantages available to their children. I'm loath to say it, but I think it's a shame to set limits on a child's potential."[26] Similar claims are made in opposition to same-sex parenting; critics argue that children raised in queer households will have a lower quality of life than children raised in heterosexual ones. However, in both of these situations, it is assumed not only that disability and queerness inherently and irreversibly lower one's quality of life but also that there is only one possible understanding of "quality of life" and that everyone knows what "it" is without discussion or elaboration.

In *The Trouble with Normal*, Michael Warner condemns the use of "quality of life" rhetoric, arguing that this terminology masks dissent by taking for granted the kinds of experiences the term includes. Although he is challenging the use of "quality of life" arguments in public debates about pornography and public sex, Warner's argument resonates with cultural constructions of disability, as becomes clear when we substitute "disability" for "porn":

> The rhetoric of "quality of life" tries to isolate [disability] from political culture by pretending that there are no differences of value or opinion in it, that it therefore does not belong in the public sphere of critical exchange and opinion formation. When [people] speak of quality of life, [they] never acknowledge that different people might want different qualities in their lives, let alone that [disability] might be one of them.[27]

Susan Wendell suggests that living with disability or illness "creates valuable *ways of being* that give valuable perspectives on life and the world," ways of being that would be lost through the elimination of illness and disability.[28] She notes, for example, that adults who require assistance in the activities of daily life, such as eating, bathing, toileting, and dressing, have opportunities to think through cultural ideals of independence and self-sufficiency; these experiences can potentially lead to productive insights about intimacy, relationship, and interdependence. "If one looks at disabilities as forms of difference and takes seriously the possibility that they may be valuable," argues Wendell,

> it becomes obvious that people with disabilities have experiences, by virtue of their disabilities, which nondisabled people do not have, and which are [or can be] sources of knowledge that is not directly accessible to nondisabled people. Some of this knowledge, for example, how to live with a suffering body, would be of enormous practical help to most people. . . . Much of it would enrich and expand our culture, and some of it has the potential to change our thinking and our ways of life profoundly.[29]

To eliminate disability is to eliminate the possibility of discovering alternative ways of being in the world, to foreclose the possibility of recognizing and valuing our interdependence.

. . . [T]he proliferation of prenatal testing and the increasing availability of pre-implantation genetic diagnosis certainly send a message about the proper and expected approach to disability. Public discussions of these technologies have lagged far behind their use and development, and they rarely include the perspectives of disabled people. As H-Dirksen L. Bauman argues, "Presumptions about the horrors of deafness are usually made by those not living Deaf lives."[30] The Prenatally and Postnatally Diagnosed Conditions Awareness Act (2008) is a step in the right direction, mandating that women receive comprehensive information about disability prior to making decisions about their pregnancies, but it remains unclear how well this policy will be funded or enforced. Moreover, as the debate surrounding Duchesneau and McCullough's reproductive choices makes clear, selecting for disability remains a highly controversial position, and hypothetical disabled children continue to be used to justify genetic research and selective abortion. . . .

I want to suggest that stories of Deaf lesbians intentionally striving for Deaf babies be read as counternarratives to mainstream stories about the necessity of a cure for deafness and disability, about the dangers of nonnormative queer parents having children. Their stories challenge the feasibility of technological promises of an "amazing future" in which impairment is cured through genetic and medical intervention, thereby resisting a compulsory able-bodied/able-minded heterosexuality that insists upon normal minds/bodies. It is precisely this challenge that has animated the hostile responses these families have received. Their choice to choose deafness suggests that reproductive technology can be used as more than a means to screen out alleged defects, that disability cannot ever fully disappear, that not everyone craves an able-bodied/able-minded future, that there might be a place for bodies with limited, odd, or queer movements and orientations, and that disability and queerness can indeed be desirable both in the future as well as now.

The story of the Deaf lesbians, Candace McCullough and Sharon Duchesneau, is only one among many. An ever-increasing number of memoirs, essays, and poems about life with a disability, as well as theoretical analyses of disability and able-bodiedness, tell other stories about disability, providing alternatives to the narratives of eradication and cure offered by Marge Piercy in *Woman on the Edge of Time*. There are stories of people embracing their bodies, proudly proclaiming disability as sexy, powerful, and worthy; tales of disabled parents and parents with disabled children refusing to accept that a bright future for our children precludes disability and asserting the right to bear and keep children with disabilities; and narratives of families refusing to accept the normalization of their bodies through surgical interventions and the normalization of their desires through heterocentric laws and homophobic condemnations. These stories deserve telling, and the issues they raise demand debate and dissent.

It is not that these tales are any less partial or contested than the others in public circulation; they, too, can be used to serve multiple and contradictory positions. Indeed, Lennard Davis argues that we need to question whether these kinds of reproductive decisions—choosing deafness and disability—are "radical ways of fighting against oppression" or "technological fixes in the service of a conservative, essentialist agenda."[31] I would only add that the two are not mutually exclusive; the same choice can serve both agendas. Just as selecting for girls can be as problematic as selecting for boys, with both choices potentially reliant on narrow gender norms and expectations, selecting for disability has the potential to reify categories of able-bodiedness as much as deselecting disability does. What is needed then are examinations of how particular choices function in particular contexts; what does it mean for lesbian parents to choose deafness in this context, or a single mother to refuse to terminate a pregnancy after receiving a Down diagnosis in that context? Such explorations are impossible as long as selecting for disability remains largely inconceivable, as long as we all assume—or are assumed to assume—that disability cannot belong in feminist visions of the future and that its absence merits no debate.

NOTES

1. A wide range of feminist studies and disability studies scholars have addressed the issue of prenatal testing and selective abortion, analyzing the impact these practices have on women and disabled people and deconstructing the assumptions about gender, pregnancy, and disability that underlie them. For examples of this work, see, among others. Adrienne Asch, "A Disability Equality Critique of Routine Testing and Embryo or Fetus Elimination Based on Disabling Traits," *Political Environments* 11 (2007): 43–47, 78; Dena S. Davis, *Genetic Dilemmas: Reproductive Technology, Parental Choices, and Children's Futures* (New York: Routledge, 2001); Anne Finger, *Past Due: A Story of Disability, Pregnancy, and Birth* (Seattle: Seal Press, 1990); Erik Parens and Adrienne Asch, eds., *Prenatal Testing and Disability Rights* (Washington, DC: Georgetown University Press, 2000); Rayna Rapp, *Testing Women, Testing the Fetus: The Social Impact of Amniocentesis in America* (New York: Routledge, 1999); Janelle Taylor, *The Public Life of the Fetal Sonogram: Technology, Consumption, and the Politics of Reproduction* (New Brunswick, NJ: Rutgers University Press, 2008); Karen H. Rothenberg and Elizabeth J. Thomson, eds., *Women and Prenatal Testing: Facing the Challenges of Genetic Technology* (Columbus: Ohio State University Press, 1994); Marsha Saxton, "Disability Rights and Selective Abortion," in *Abortion Wars: A Half-Century of Struggle: 1950–2000*, ed. Rickie Solinger (Berkeley: University of California Press, 1998), 374–93; and Tom Shakespeare, "Arguing about Genetics and Disability," *Interaction* 13, no. 3 (2000): 11–14. See also Generations Ahead, *Bridging the Divide: Disability Rights and Reproductive Rights and Justice Advocates Discussing Genetic Technologies*, July 2009; and Generations Ahead, *A Disability Rights Analysis of Genetic Technologies: Report on a Convening of Disability Rights Leaders*, March 2010, http://www.generations-ahead.org/resources.

2. Marge Piercy, *Woman on the Edge of Time* (New York: Fawcett Crest, 1976), 96.

3. José van Dijck, *Imagenation: Popular Images of Genetics* (New York: New York University Press, 1998), 86, 87; Josephine Carubia Glorie, "Feminist Utopian Fiction and the Possibility of Social Critique," in *Political Science Fiction*, ed. Donald M. Hassler and Clyde Wilcox (Columbia: University of South Carolina Press, 1997), 156; Cathleen McGuire and Colleen McGuire, "Grass-roots Ecofeminism: Activating Utopia," in *Ecofeminist Literary Criticism: Theory, Interpretation, Pedagogy*, ed. Greta Gaard and Patrick D. Murphy (Urbana: University of Illinois Press, 1998). . . .

4. For discussion of these issues, see, among others, Lori B. Andrews, *Future Perfect: Confronting Decisions about Genetics* (New York: Columbia University Press, 2001); Glenn McGee, *The Perfect Baby: Parenthood in the New World of Cloning and Genetics* (Lanham, MD: Rowman and Littlefield, 2000); and Dena S. Davis, *Genetic Dilemmas: Reproductive Technology, Parental Choices, and Children's Futures* (New York: Routledge, 2001). . . .

5. The use of "Deaf," with a capital "D," emerged in the late twentieth century as a way to signal pride in one's identity and in the cultural practices and historical traditions of deaf people. Deaf with a capital letter is thus a way to draw attention to a cultural deaf identity, whereas Deaf with a small "d" simply connotes being unable to hear or hard-of-hearing. This use is not universally accepted, however, with some deaf people and deaf studies scholars moving away from the "big D/little d" convention. For . . . discussion about the limitations of American discourses of deaf identity, see Susan Burch and Alison Kafer, eds., *Deaf and Disability Studies: Interdisciplinary Perspectives* (Washington, DC: Gallaudet University Press, 2010).

6. Carol Padden and Tom Humphries, *Deaf in America: Voices from a Culture* (Cambridge, MA: Harvard University Press, 1988); John Vickrey Van Cleve and Barry Crouch, *A Place of Their Own: Creating the Deaf Community in America* (Washington, DC: Gallaudet University Press, 1989).

7. Nora Ellen Groce, *Everyone Here Spoke Sign Language: Hereditary Deafness on Martha's Vineyard* (Cambridge, MA: Harvard University Press, 1985). For a more recent discussion of deafness on Martha's Vineyard, see Annelies Kusters, "Deaf Utopias? Reviewing the Sociocultural Literature on the World's 'Martha's Vineyard Situations,'" *Journal of Deaf Studies and Deaf Education* 15, no. 1 (2010): 3–16.

8. Unfortunately, there is an extensive history of requiring Deaf people to do precisely that: to learn to lip-read, speak orally, and abandon signing, and to undergo painful surgeries and medical treatments in order to "correct" their hearing loss. Scholars of Deaf studies have documented histories of Deaf people being punished, often brutally, for engaging in sign language, and of the campaigns waged against residential schools and Deaf communities. In spite of such treatment, the Deaf community continued to use and fight for sign language. Robert M. Buchanan, *Illusions of Equality: Deaf Americans in School and Factory, 1850–1950* (Washington, DC: Gallaudet University Press, 1999); Susan Burch, *Signs of Resistance: American Deaf Cultural History, 1900 to World War II* (New York: New York University Press, 2002).

9. For one example of these kinds of coalitions, see Corbett Joan O'Toole, "Dale Dahl and Judy Heumann: Deaf Man, Disabled Woman—Allies in 1970s Berkeley," in *Deaf and Disability Studies: Interdisciplinary Perspectives*, ed. Susan Burch and Alison Kafer (Washington, DC: Gallaudet University Press, 2010): 162–87. . . .

10. Sperm banks [also] exclude male donors who have family histories of cystic fibrosis, Tay-Sachs, alcoholism, and other conditions deemed problematic or undesirable. Under guidelines established by the FDA, most sperm banks forbid gay men and men who have had sex with men in the last five years from donating. For discussion of the politics of sperm banks and sperm donation, see Cynthia Daniels, *Exposing Men: The Science and Politics of Male Reproduction* (New York: Oxford University Press, 2006); and Laura Mamo, *Queering Reproduction: Achieving Pregnancy in the Age of Technoscience* (Durham, NC: Duke University Press, 2007).

11. Indeed, Gauvin's deafness was not a given. There are many different genetic combinations that result in deafness, but the trait is recessive; two congenitally deaf parents will not automatically or necessarily produce deaf children.

12. Liza Mundy, "A World of their Own," *Washington Post Magazine*, March 31, 2002, www.washingtonpost.com. Sadly, Gauvin died suddenly and unexpectedly from an inherited condition (unrelated to his deafness). In sharp contrast to his birth, his passing was met with very little news coverage or public reaction.

13. [Ibid.]

14. Family Research Council, "*Washington Post* Profiles Lesbian Couple Seeking to Manufacture a Deaf Child," PR Newswire Association, April 1, 2002. . . .

15. Jeanette Winterson, "How Would We Feel if Blind Women Claimed the Right to a Blind Baby?" *Guardian* (UK), April 9, 2002.

16. For feminist and queer deconstructions of nature rhetoric, particularly uses of "nature" to proscribe gender and sexuality identities and practices, see, for example, Catriona Mortimer-Sandilands and Bruce Erickson, eds. *Queer Ecologies: Sex, Nature, Politics, Desire* (Bloomington: Indiana University Press, 2010); and Noël Sturgeon, *Environmentalism in Popular Culture: Gender, Race, Sexuality, and the Politics of the Natural* (Tucson: University of Arizona Press, 2009).

17. Mundy, "A World of Their Own."

18. These comments were not left unaddressed by other members on the listserv, however. Participants questioned the assumptions about the "burdens" caused by disability and about the inappropriateness of Deaf women choosing a donor that reflected their own lives, a choice nondisabled couples make regularly. They also challenged the contention that Deaf children pose a financial strain on the state, arguing that economic arguments about the "strain" caused by people with disabilities have often been used to justify coerced and forced sterilization, institutionalization, and coerced abortion.

19. Sarah Franklin, "Essentialism, Which Essentialism? Some Implications of Reproductive and Genetic Technoscience," in *If You Seduce a Straight Person, Can You Make Them Gay? Issues in Biological Essentialism versus Social Constructionism in Gay and Lesbian Identities*, ed. John P. DeCecco and John P. Elia (Binghamton, NY: Harrington Park, 1993), 30; italics in original.

20. Patrick Steptoe, known as the "father of in vitro fertilization," remarked that "it would be unthinkable to willingly create a child to be born into an unnatural situation such as a gay or lesbian relationship." Quoted in Franklin, "Essentialism, Which Essentialism?" 31.

21. Mamo, *Queering Reproduction*, 72.

22. Ibid., 134.

23. Dorothy Roberts, *Killing the Black Body: Race, Reproduction, and the Meaning of Liberty* (New York: Vintage, 1998); Elizabeth Weil, "Breeder Reaction," *Mother Jones* 31, no. 4 (2006): 33–37.

24. Roberts, *Killing the Black Body*, 254. . . . Roberts notes that fertility clinics are increasingly including *elite* women of color in their campaigns; even as these technologies become available to a wider range of women, their availability mirrors the unequal distribution of health care in this country. See, for example, Dorothy Roberts, "Race, Gender, and Genetic Technologies: A New Reproductive Dystopia?" *Signs: Journal of Women in Culture and Society* 34, no. 4 (2009): 783–804.

25. This trend is only the latest in a long history of marginalization, discrimination, and abuse; disabled, African American, Latina, and Native American women have undergone forced and coerced sterilization, medical experimentation, and coerced abortion at the hands of medical professionals and government employees who deemed them unfit. See, for example, Elena R. Gutiérrez, *Fertile Matters: The Politics of Mexican-Origin Women's Reproduction* (Austin: University of Texas Press, 2008); Jennifer Nelson, *Women of Color and the Reproductive Rights Movement* (New York: New York University Press, 2003); Nancy Ordover, *American Eugenics: Race, Queer Anatomy, and the Science of Nationalism* (Minneapolis: University of Minnesota Press, 2003); and Roberts, *Killing the Black Body*.

26. Quoted in David Teather, "Lesbian Couple Have Deaf Baby by Choice," *Guardian* (UK), April 8, 2002, http://www.guardian.co.uk/world/2002/apr/08/davidteather.

27. Michael Warner, *The Trouble with Normal: Sex, Politics, and the Ethics of Queer Life* (New York: Free Press, 1999), 183. . . .

28. Susan Wendell, "Unhealthy Disabled: Treating Chronic Illnesses as Disabilities," *Hypatia: A Journal of Feminist Philosophy* 16, no. 4 (2001), 31; emphasis in original.

29. Susan Wendell, *The Rejected Body: Feminist philosophical reflections on disability* (New York: Routledge, 1996), 69.

30. H-Dirksen L. Bauman, "Designing Deaf Babies and the Question of Disability," *Journal of Deaf Studies and Deaf Education* 10, no. 3 (2005): 313.

31. Lennard J. Davis, "Postdeafness," in *Open Your Eyes: Deaf Studies Talking*, ed. H-Dirksen Bauman (Minneapolis: University of Minnesota Press, 2008), 319.

25 LIVING TO LOVE (1993)

bell hooks describes herself as a "black woman intellectual" and "revolutionary activist." She is an educator and popular public speaker whose work focuses on gender, race, culture, and media representations. A prolific writer, she has published over thirty books and numerous articles for scholarly and popular audiences.

Love heals. We recover ourselves in the act and art of loving. A favorite passage from the biblical Gospel of John that touches my spirit declares: "Anyone who does not love is still in death."

Many black women feel that we live lives in which there is little or no love. This is one of our private truths that is rarely a subject for public discussion. To name this reality evokes such intense pain that black women can rarely talk about it fully with one another.

It has not been simple for black people living in this culture to know love. Defining love in *The Road Less Traveled* as "the will to extend one's self for the purpose of nurturing one's own or another's personal growth," M. Scott Peck shares the prophetic insight that love is both an "intention and an action." We show love via the union of feeling and action. Using this definition of love, and applying it to black experience, it is easy to see how many black folks historically could only experience themselves as frustrated lovers, since the conditions of slavery and racial apartheid made it extremely difficult to nurture one's own or another's spiritual growth. Notice, that I say, difficult, not impossible. Yet, it does need to be acknowledged that oppression and exploitation pervert, distort, and impede our ability to love.

Given the politics of black life in this white-supremacist society, it makes sense that internalized racism and self-hate stand in the way of love. Systems of domination exploit folks best when they deprive us of our capacity to experience our own agency and alter our ability to care and to love ourselves and others. Black folks have been deeply and profoundly "hurt," as we used to say down home, "hurt to our hearts," and the deep psychological pain we have endured and still endure affects our capacity to feel and therefore our capacity to love. We are a wounded people. Wounded in that part of ourselves that would know love, that would be loving. The choice to love has always been a gesture of resistance for African Americans. And many of us have made that choice only to find ourselves unable to give or to receive love.

Slavery's Impact on Love

Our collective difficulties with the art and act of loving began in the context of slavery. It should not shock us that a people who were forced to witness their young being sold away; their loved ones, companions, and comrades beaten beyond all recognition; a people who knew unrelenting poverty, deprivation, loss, unending grief, and the forced separation of family and kin; would emerge from the context of slavery wary of this thing called love. They knew firsthand that the conditions of slavery distorted and perverted the possibility that they would know love or be able to sustain such knowing.

Though black folks may have emerged from slavery eager to experience intimacy, commitment, and passion outside the realm of bondage, they must also have been in many ways psychologically unprepared to practice fully the art of loving. No wonder then that many black folks established domestic households that mirrored the brutal arrangements they had known in slavery. Using a hierarchical model of family life, they created domestic spaces where there were tensions around power, tensions that often led black men

Source: bell hooks, "Living to Love" (1993).

to severely whip black women, to punish them for perceived wrongdoing, that led adults to beat children to assert domination and control. In both cases, black people were using the same harsh and brutal methods against one another that had been used by white slave owners against them when they were enslaved. . . . We know that slavery's end did not mean that black people who were suddenly free to love now knew the way to love one another well.

Slave narratives often emphasize time and time again that black people's survival was often determined by their capacity to repress feelings. In his 1845 narrative, Frederick Douglass recalled that he had been unable to experience grief when hearing of his mother's death since they had been denied sustained contact. Slavery socialized black people to contain and repress a range of emotions. Witnessing one another being daily subjected to all manner of physical abuse, the pain of over-work, the pain of brutal punishment, the pain of near-starvation, enslaved black people could rarely show sympathy or solidarity with one another just at that moment when sympathy and solace was most needed. They rightly feared reprisal. It was only in carefully cultivated spaces of social resistance, that slaves could give vent to repressed feelings. Hence, they learned to check the impulse to give care when it was most needed and learned to wait for a "safe" moment when feelings could be expressed. What form could love take in such a context, in a world where black folks never knew how long they might be together? Practicing love in the slave context could make one vulnerable to unbearable emotional pain. It was often easier for slaves to care for one another while being very mindful of the transitory nature of their intimacies. The social world of slavery encouraged black people to develop notions of intimacy connected to expedient practical reality. A slave who could not repress and contain emotion might not survive.

Repressed Emotions: A Key to Survival

The practice of repressing feelings as a survival strategy continued to be an aspect of black life long after slavery ended. Since white supremacy and racism did not end with the Emancipation Proclamation, black folks felt it was still necessary to keep certain emotional barriers intact. And, in the world-view of many black people, it became a positive attribute to be able to . . . mask, hide, and contain feelings. . . . To show one's emotions was seen as foolish. Traditionally in Southern black homes, children were often taught at an early age that it was important to repress feelings. Often, when children were severely whipped, we were told not to cry. Showing one's emotions could lead to further punishment. Parents would say in the midst of painful punishments: "Don't even let me see a tear." Or if one dared to cry, they threatened further punishment by saying: "If you don't stop that crying, I'll give you something to cry about."

How was this behavior any different from that of the slave owner whipping the slave by denying access to comfort and consolation, denying even a space to express pain? And if many black folks were taught at an early age not only to repress emotions but to see giving expression to feeling as a sign of weakness, then how would they learn to be fully open to love? Many black folks have passed down from generation to generation the assumption that to let one's self go, to fully surrender emotionally, endangers survival. They feel that to love weakens one's capacity to develop a stoic and strong character.

"Did You Ever Love Us?"

When I was growing up, it was apparent to me that outside the context of religion and romance, love was viewed by grown-ups as a luxury. Struggling to survive, to make ends meet, was more important than loving. In that context, the folks who seemed most devoted to the art and act of loving were the old ones, our grandmothers and great grandmothers, our granddaddys and great granddaddys, the Papas and Big Mamas. They gave us acceptance, unconditional care, attention and, most importantly, they affirmed our need to experience pleasure and joy. They were affectionate. They were physically demonstrative. Our parents and their struggling-to-get-ahead generation often behaved as though love was a waste of time, a feeling or an action that got in the way of them dealing with the more meaningful issues of life.

When teaching Toni Morrison's novel *Sula*, I am never surprised to see black female students nodding their heads in recognition when reading a passage where Hannah, a grown black woman, asks her mother, Eva: "Did you ever love us?" Eva responds with hostility and says: "You settin' here with your healthy-ass self and ax me did I love you? Them big old eyes in your head would a been two holes of maggots if I hadn't." Hannah is not satisfied with this answer for she knows that Eva has responded fully to her children's material needs. She wants to know if there was another level of affection, of feeling and action. She says to Eva: "Did you ever, you know, play with us?" Again Eva responds by acting as though the question is completely ridiculous:

> Play? Wasn't nobody playin' in 1895. Just 'cause you got it good now you think it was always this good? 1895 was a killer girl. Things was bad. Niggers was dying like flies. . . . What would I look like leapin' round that little old room playin' with youngins with three beets to my name?

Eva's responses suggest that finding the means for material survival was not only the most important gesture of care, but that it precluded all other gestures. This is a way of thinking that many black people share. It makes care for material well-being synonymous with the practice of loving. The reality is, of course, that even in a context of material privilege, love may be absent. Concurrently, within the context of poverty, where one must struggle to make ends meet, one might keep a spirit of love alive by making a space for playful engagement, the expression of creativity, for individuals to receive care and attention in relation to their emotional well-being, a kind of care that attends to hearts and minds as well as stomachs. As contemporary black people commit ourselves to collective recovery, we must recognize that attending to our emotional well-being is just as important as taking care of our material needs.

It seems appropriate that this dialogue on love in *Sula* takes place between two black women, between mother and daughter, for their interchange symbolizes a legacy that will be passed on through the generations. In fact, Eva does not nurture Hannah's spiritual growth, and Hannah does not nurture the spiritual growth of her daughter, Sula. Yet, Eva does

embody a certain model of "strong" black womanhood that is practically deified in black life. It is precisely her capacity to repress emotions and do whatever is needed for the continuation of material life that is depicted as the source of her strength. . . .

If We Would Know Love

Love needs to be present in every black female's life, in all of our houses. It is the absence of love that has made it so difficult for us to . . . live fully. When we love ourselves we want to live fully. Whenever people talk about black women's lives, the emphasis is rarely on transforming society so that we can live fully, it is almost always about applauding how well we have "survived" despite harsh circumstances or how we can survive in the future. When we love ourselves, we know that we must do more than survive. We must have the means to live fully. To live fully, black women can no longer deny our need to know love.

If we would know love, we must first learn how to respond to inner emotional needs. This may mean undoing years of socialization where we have been taught that such needs are unimportant. Let me give an example. In . . . *The Habit of Surviving: Black Women's Strategies for Life*, Kesho Scott opens the book sharing an incident from her life that she feels taught her important survival skills:

> Thirteen years tall, I stood in the living room doorway. My clothes were wet. My hair was mangled. I was in tears, in shock, and in need of my mother's warm arms. Slowly, she looked me up and down, stood up from the couch and walked towards me, her body clenched in criticism. Putting her hands on her hips and planting herself, her shadow falling over my face, she asked in a voice of barely suppressed rage, "What happened?" I flinched as if struck by the unexpected anger and answered, "They put my head in the toilet. They say I can't swim with them." "They" were eight white girls at my high school. I reached out to hold her, but she roughly brushed my hands aside and said, "Like hell! Get your coat. Let's go."

. . . [Kesho] asserts: "My mother taught me a powerful and enduring lesson that day. She taught me that I would have to fight back against racial and sexual injustice." Obviously, this is an important survival strategy for black women. But Kesho was also learning an unhealthy message at the same time. She was made to feel that she did not deserve comfort after a traumatic painful experience, that indeed she was "out-of-line" to even be seeking emotional solace, and that her individual needs were not as important as the collective struggle to resist racism and sexism. Imagine how different this story would read if we were told that as soon as Kesho walked into the room, obviously suffering distress, her mother had comforted her, helped repair the damage to her appearance, and then shared with her the necessity of confronting (maybe not just then, it would depend on her psychological state whether she could emotionally handle a confrontation) the racist white students who had assaulted her. Then Kesho would have known, at age thirteen, that her emotional well-being was just as important as the collective struggle to end racism and sexism—that indeed these two experiences were linked.

Many black females have learned to deny our inner needs while we develop our capacity to cope and confront in public life. This is why we can often appear to be functioning well on jobs but be utterly dysfunctional in private. . . . I see this chaos and disorder as a reflection of the inner psyche, of the absence of well-being. Yet until black females believe, and hopefully learn when we are little girls, that our emotional well-being matters, we cannot attend to our needs. Often we replace recognition of inner emotional needs with the longing to control. When we deny our real needs, we tend to feel fragile, vulnerable, emotionally unstable and untogether. Black females often work hard to cover up these conditions.

Let us return to the mother in Kesho's story. What if the sight of her wounded and hurt daughter called to mind the mother's deep unaddressed inner wounds? What if she was critical, harsh, or just downright mean, because she did not want to break down, cry, and stop being the "strong black woman"? And yet, if she cried, her daughter might have felt her pain was shared, that it was fine to name that you are in pain, that we do not have to keep the hurt bottled up inside us. What the

mother did was what many of us have witnessed our mothers doing in similar circumstances—she took control. She was domineering, even her physical posture dominated. Clearly, this mother wanted her black female presence to have more "power" than that of the white girls.

A fictional model of black mothering that shows us a mother able to respond fully to her daughters when they are in pain is depicted in Ntozake Shange's novel *Sassafrass, Cypress and Indigo*. Throughout this novel, Shange's black female characters are strengthened in their capacity to self-actualize by a loving mother. Even though she does not always agree with their choices she respects them and offers them solace. Here is part of a letter she writes to Sassafrass who is "in trouble" and wants to come home. The letter begins with the exclamation: "Of course you can come home! What do you think you could do to yourself that I wouldn't love my girl?" First giving love and acceptance, Hilda later chastises, then expresses love again:

> You and Cypress like to drive me crazy with all this experimental living. You girls need to stop chasing the coon by his tail. And I know you know what I'm talking about . . . Mark my words. You just come on home and we'll straighten out whatever it is that's crooked in your thinking. There's lots to do to keep busy. And nobody around to talk foolish talk or experiment with. Something can't happen every day. You get up. You eat, go to work, come back, eat again, enjoy some leisure, and go back to bed. Now, that's plenty for most folks. I keep asking myself where did I go wrong? Yet I know in my heart I'm not wrong. I'm right. The world's going crazy and trying to take my children with it. Okay. Now I'm through with all that. I love you very much. But you're getting to be a grown woman and I know that too. You come back to Charleston and find the rest of yourself. Love, Mama.

Loving What We See

The art and practice of loving begins with our capacity to recognize and affirm ourselves. That is why so many self-help books encourage us to look at ourselves in the mirror and talk to the image we see there. Recently, I noticed that what I do with the image I see in the mirror is very unloving. I inspect it. From the moment I get out of bed and look at myself in the mirror, I am evaluating. The point of the evaluation is not to provide self-affirmation but to critique. Now this was a common practice in our household. When the six of us girls made our way downstairs to the world inhabited by father, mother, and brother, we entered the world of "critique." We were looked over and told all that was wrong. Rarely did one hear a positive evaluation.

Replacing negative critique with positive recognition has made me feel more empowered as I go about my day. Affirming ourselves is the first step in the direction of cultivating the practice of being inwardly loving. I choose to use the phrase "inwardly loving" over self-love, because the very notion of "self" is so inextricably bound up with how we are seen by and in relation to others. Within a racist/sexist society, the larger culture will not socialize black women to know and acknowledge that our inner lives are important. Decolonized black women must name that reality in accord with others among us who understand as well that it is vital to nurture the inner life. As we examine our inner life, we get in touch with the world of emotions and feelings. Allowing ourselves to feel, we affirm our right to be inwardly loving. Once I know what I feel, I can also get in touch with those needs I can satisfy or name those needs that can only be satisfied in communion or contact with others.

Where is the love when a black woman looks at herself and says: "I see inside me somebody who is ugly, too dark, too fat, too afraid—somebody nobody would love, 'cause I don't even like what I see"; or maybe: "I see inside me somebody who is so hurt, who is just like a ball of pain and I don't want to look at her 'cause I can't do nothing about that pain." The love is absent. To make it present, the individual has to first choose to see herself, to just look at that inner self without blame or censure. And once she names what she sees, she might think about whether that inner self deserves or needs love.

I have never heard a black woman suggest during confessional moments in a support group that she does not need love. She may be in denial about that need but it doesn't take much self-interrogation to break through this denial. If you ask most black women straight-up if they need love—the answer is likely to be yes. To give love to our inner selves we must first give attention, recognition and acceptance. Having let ourselves know that we will not be punished for acknowledging who we are or what we feel can name the problems we see. I find it helpful to interview myself, and I encourage my sisters to do the same. Sometimes it's hard for me to get immediately in touch with what I feel, but if I ask myself a question, an answer usually emerges.

Sometimes when we look at ourselves, and see our inner turmoil and pain, we do not know how to address it. That's when we need to seek help. I call loved ones sometimes and say, "I have these feelings that I don't understand or know how to address, can you help me?" There are many black females who cannot imagine asking for help, who see this as a sign of weakness. This is another negative debilitating worldview we should unlearn. It is a sign of personal power to be able to ask for help when you need it. And we find that asking for what we need when we need it is an experience that enhances rather than diminishes personal power. Try it and see. Often we wait until a crisis situation has happened when we are compelled by circumstances to seek the help of others. Yet, crisis can often be avoided if we seek help when we recognize that we are no longer able to function well in a given situation. For black women who are addicted to being controlling, asking for help can be a loving practice of surrender, reminding us that we do not always have to be in charge. Practicing being inwardly loving, we learn not only what our souls need but we begin to understand better the needs of everyone around us as well.

Black women who are *choosing* for the first time (note the emphasis on choosing) to practice the art and act of loving should devote time and energy showing love to other black people, both people we know and strangers. Within white-supremacist capitalist patriarchy, black people do not get enough love. And it's always exciting for those of us who are undergoing a process of decolonization to see other black people in our midst respond to loving care. Just the other day T. told me that she makes a point of going into a local store and saying warm greetings to an older black man who works there. Recently, he wanted to know her name and then thanked her for the care that she gives to him. A few years ago when she was mired in self-hate, she would not have had the "will" to give him care. Now, she extends to him the level of care that she longs to receive from other black people when she is out in the world.

When I was growing up, I received "unconditional love" from black women who showed me by their actions that love did not have to be earned. They let me know that I deserved love; their care nurtured my spiritual growth.

Many black people, and black women in particular, have become so accustomed to not being loved that we protect ourselves from having to acknowledge the pain such deprivation brings by acting like only white folks or other silly people sit around wanting to be loved. When I told a group of black women that I wanted there to be a world where I can feel love, feel myself giving and receiving love, every time I walk outside my house, they laughed. For such a world to exist, racism and all other forms of domination need to change. To the extent that I commit my life to working to end domination, I help transform the world so that it is that loving place I want it to be.

Love Heals

Nikki Giovanni's "Woman Poem" has always meant a lot to me because it was one of the first pieces of writing that called out black women's self-hatred. Published in the anthology, *The Black Woman*, edited by Toni Cade Bambara, this poem ends with the lines: "face me whose whole life is tied up to unhappiness cause it's the only for real thing i know." Giovanni not only names in this poem that black women are socialized to be caretakers, to deny our inner needs, she also names the extent to which self-hate can make us turn against those who are caring toward us. The black female narrator says: "how dare you care about me—you ain't got no good sense—cause i ain't shit you must be lower than that to care." This poem was written in 1968. Here we are, decades later, and black women are still struggling to break through denial to name the hurt in our lives and find ways to heal. Learning how to love is a way to heal.

I am empowered by the idea of love as the will to extend oneself to nurture one's own or another's spiritual growth because it affirms that love is an action, that it is akin to work. For black people it's an important definition because the focus is not on material well-being. And while we know that material needs must be met, collectively we need to focus our attention on emotional needs as well. There is that lovely biblical passage in "Proverbs" that reminds us: "Better a dinner of herbs, where love is, than a stalled ox and hatred therewith."

When we as black women experience fully the transformative power of love in our lives, we will bear witness publicly in a way that will fundamentally challenge existing social structures. We will be more fully empowered to address the genocide that daily takes the lives of black people—men, women and children. When we know what love is, when we love, we are able to search our memories and see the past with new eyes; we are able to transform the present and dream the future. Such is love's power. Love heals.

Sexualized Violence

Keywords: child sexual abuse, feminicide, hate crime, intimate partner violence, rape, sexual harassment, state violence, transphobia

This chapter focuses on sexualized violence—including battery, rape, child sexual abuse, stalking, sexual harassment at school or work, online bullying and intimidation, and state violence. We see sexualized violence as a means of patriarchal control of women, LGBTQI, and gender nonconforming people, whether committed by individuals or the **state**, and also as a tool of racism and colonialism.

We recognize that this is a tough issue for many people. It may bring up memories or push you to rethink your experiences and opinions. We urge you to support yourself as needed by talking to a friend, a professor, members of student-centered groups (e.g., a women's center, multicultural center, or antirape group), or go to your counseling center. Seeking support from staff or faculty may mean dealing with your college or university's institutional reporting requirements, which may be frustrating but could secure help and also help others who find themselves in a situation similar to yours.

Note that different writers and researchers use varied terms in discussing this topic. Many use the term gender-based violence, though older sources refer to violence against women. Both phrases imply that incidents of sexualized violence are between males and females, whereas this also happens in same-sex relationships, where one party may seek to dominate the other through physical, emotional, sexual abuse, or all of these. Thus, there is some inevitable unevenness in this discussion as we bridge different sources and perspectives.

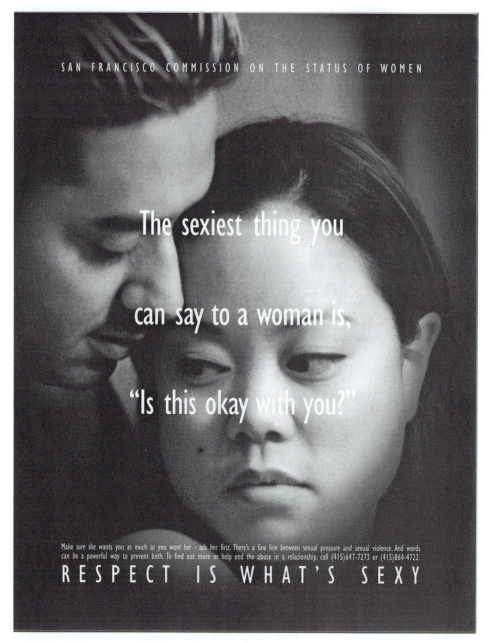

Reprinted with permission. All rights reserved.

WHAT COUNTS AS SEXUALIZED VIOLENCE?

The World Health Organization (2017) reports that violence against women, especially intimate partner violence, is a "major public health problem and a violation of women's human rights" worldwide.

For many US women—gender nonconforming, trans, heterosexual, queer, or lesbian—gendered violence is a part of daily life. We are hassled on the street, in parks, on public transit, or in cafés and bars. We are subjected to online abuse and threats (discussed in Reading 28) as misogyny has morphed to adapt to new technologies (Mantilla 2015, chap. 5). We may put up with sexist or homophobic comments from bosses or coworkers in order to keep a job. We sometimes make compromises as part of maintaining intimate relationships, including going along when we do not really want to have sex. We may define some of these experiences as violence and others not, and individuals may differ in how they define violence.

The landmark United Nations Declaration on Violence Against Women (General Assembly resolution 48/104) of December 20, 1993, defined violence against women as

> any act of gender-based violence that results in, or is likely to result in, physical, sexual or psychological harm or suffering to women, including threats of such acts, coercion or arbitrary deprivation of liberty whether occurring in public or private life. (quoted in Heise, Pitanguy, and Germain 1994, p. 46)

The resolution recognized that in patriarchal societies, males as a group have power over females as a group—the women they are close to and those they encounter at work or in public places, now also including the Internet. Women may be physically smaller or weaker; they may be economically dependent on their partner of whatever gender; they may need their boss' support to keep their jobs or to get a promotion or a pay raise. Journalist Bernice Yeung (2018) interviewed night-shift janitors, farmworkers, domestic workers, and hotel workers who were all vulnerable to sexual harassment at work, in part due to the isolated nature of their jobs. Thus, macro-level inequalities are present in threats or acts of violence at the micro level.

Women or gender nonconforming people may be violent. Some are abusers in same-sex or nonbinary relationships. Some abuse children, other family members, or people who work for them. Women may contribute to the dynamic of a violent relationship by provoking an argument or hitting their partner first (see Fig. 6.1). Occasionally, women kill abusive partners, as a way out of situations in which they believe they would be killed if they did not defend themselves.

THE INCIDENCE OF SEXUALIZED VIOLENCE

Intimate partner violence, rape, sexual harassment, and child sexual abuse are crimes in the United States. However, the incidence of such crimes is notoriously difficult to estimate accurately because of discrepancies in definition and terminology, limited research, and underreporting, so available data must be used with caution.

Intimate Partner Violence

The idealized family is assumed to provide a secure home for its members, what historian Christopher Lasch (1977) called a "haven in a heartless world." For some, this is generally true. For others, however, home is not a safe place but one where they experience emotional or physical violence. For purposes of this discussion, intimate partners include current and former spouses, whatever their gender expression or sexual orientation. The narrower term *domestic violence*, used for many years, still appears in some government reports, news items, and academic studies.

FIGURE 6.1 The Dynamics of Domestic Violence: Power and Control Wheel.

Developed by the Domestic Abuse Intervention Programs in Duluth, MN. Adapted by the Asian Women's Shelter, San Francisco.

According to the Centers for Disease Control and Prevention (2017), nearly one in four US women reported that they had experienced violence by a current or former spouse or boyfriend at some point in their lives. Abuse-related injuries range from bruises, cuts, and burns, to concussion, broken bones, knife wounds, miscarriages, partial loss of hearing or vision, and physical disfigurement. There are also serious mental health effects of isolation, humiliation, and ongoing threats of violence. Many researchers and commentators emphasize specific physical acts that can be measured rather than emotional violence and the fear of threats, which cannot be quantified. Also, the legal system demands demonstrable damage in order to bring charges of violence. The problem with this kind of quantification is that one cannot see the interpersonal dynamics or the structural power relationships within which intimate partner violence occurs.

Writing in an anthology of short stories about battering and resistance, Barbara Harman (1996) described how a woman in an abusive relationship is always second-guessing and responding to her partner in her attempts to avoid further violence:

> Don't raise your voice. Don't talk back. Don't say no to sex. Like whatever he does. Don't ask him to do anything he has not already done. Get up when he gets up. Go to bed when he goes to bed. Wait. Do what he wants to do. Never contradict him. Laugh at what he thinks is funny. Never ask for his time, attention, his money. Have your own money, but give it to him if he wants it. Never go out alone but do not expect him to go with you. If he is angry in the car, walk home. Be his friend except when he needs an enemy. Defend his family except when he hates them. Understand everything. (p. 287)

The Centers for Disease Control (2017) reported that approximately 23 percent of teen women have experienced physical, emotional, or verbal abuse from a dating partner before the age of 18. Young males may use criticism, intimidation, threats, or force to establish and maintain control over their girlfriends. Widespread use of cell phones and social media has greatly increased the ease of informal "surveillance" by individuals, and this may be exacerbated by a wider culture of abuse. Young women are vulnerable to abuse because they may feel that involvement in an intimate relationship is necessary to fit in. They may be flattered by having a partner who demands their time and attention, and they lack experience in negotiating affection and sexual behavior.

Rape and Sexual Assault

Rape is defined as forced sexual intercourse—vaginal, anal, or oral penetration. The legal definition turns on force and non-consent. Consent may be defined as a "Yes" that is freely given when the option of "No" is present and viable (Friedman and Valenti 2008). Consent is not meaningful if given under the influence of alcohol, drugs, or prescription medication. Consent may not be meaningful in situations defined by power differentials, as with film directors and actors, bosses and workers, teachers and students, politicians and aides, or priests and congregants. Sexual assault includes attacks involving unwanted sexual contact; it may involve force and include grabbing or fondling, as well as sexual comments and verbal threats. According to the Centers for Disease Control (2017), approximately one in three US women and nearly one in six US men have experienced sexual assault at some point in their lives. Those most at risk for both rape and sexual assault are 18- to 24-year-olds (Sinozich and Langton 2014). The psychological effects of these violations can be traumatic and long-lasting and include feelings of humiliation, helplessness, anger, self-doubt, and self-hate. Survivors may become depressed and withdrawn, sleep badly, feel scared and on edge, lose their ability to concentrate, and turn to alcohol or drugs as a way to cope. Women survivors are more likely than men to need medical care, to need to move from

© Jacky Fleming

where they were living, and to miss a day or more of school and work (Centers for Disease Control 2017).

In contrast to popular ideas about rape committed by a stranger in a dark alley, most survivors who reported that they had been raped or physically assaulted said that their assailant was someone they knew, such as a partner, former partner, date, or acquaintance. On college campuses, sexual assault has been described as "pervasive" and includes a small percentage of men (Peterson's 2018). The incidence of rape or sexual assault, whether through physical force or incapacitation due to alcohol or drugs, is highest among undergraduate women and students who identify as transgender, genderqueer, nonconforming, and questioning (Cantor et al. 2015).

Survivors who report rapes have often been blamed for putting themselves in compromising situations, especially if they have been drinking. In many cases, college men accused of rape or sexual misconduct have been protected and punished lightly if at all, especially if they are university athletes. Some administrators have been concerned about the effects of alcohol and drug use and the role of fraternity parties in campus rapes. Others seem more concerned to downplay or ignore accusations of sexual violence to protect their college's reputation. Campus educational materials and workshops on date rape for incoming students emphasize girls' and boys' different socialization and attitudes toward dating. Antioch College's sexual offense policy, developed in the 1990s, expects students to talk through a sexual encounter step by step, giving verbal consent at each step (Gold and Villari 2000), as discussed in reference to building a consent culture in Chapter 4 (Stryker 2017).

Female students are most at risk of acquaintance rape during the first few weeks of their first year in college. They often do not report a rape due to confusion, guilt, or fear, or because they feel betrayed. They may be ashamed to tell friends, parents, or college counselors, and they may not identify the experience as rape. Under the 1990 Jeanne Clery Disclosure of Campus Security Policy and Campus Crime Statistics Act, all colleges and universities that receive federal funding must spell out rape victims' rights and publish information on prevention programs.

Effects of Gender Expression, Race, Class, Nation, Sexuality, and Disability

Females in all socioeconomic classes and all racial/ethnic groups may experience sexualized violence. However, race, class, sexuality, age, immigration status, and disability compound vulnerabilities based on gender. Psychologist Rebecca Stotzer (2009) found that trans people are at risk for multiple types and incidences of violence throughout their lives. The Human Rights Campaign, Transgender Law Center, and Trans People of Color Coalition have reported that violence against transgender people is rising (Astor 2017). This may be defined as a **hate crime** if the act is based on the perpetrator's bias against the victim's actual or perceived sexual orientation, gender identity, disability, or gender.

In 2017, the Human Rights Campaign tracked 28 deaths of transgender people, killed by acquaintances, partners, and strangers. Such killings disproportionately affected transgender women of color, who live at the intersection of racism, sexism, homophobia, and transphobia (Human Rights Campaign 2018b).

Immigrant women who are dependent on an abusive partner for their legal status may fear repercussions from ICE (Immigration and Customs Enforcement) if they report violence. Elderly women may not report acts of violence committed by spouses, adult children, caregivers, relatives, or neighbors because they fear losing their caregiver, their home, or independent access to money. Worldwide, women and girls with physical and mental disabilities are particularly vulnerable to physical, emotional, and sexual abuse from partners, caregivers, and service providers. Recognizing this, the United Nations attached the Optional Protocol on the Situation of Women and Girls with Disabilities to the Convention on the Rights of Persons with Disabilities (United Nations 2015). The few studies that exist suggest that women with disabilities are between four and ten times as likely to be sexually assaulted as other women (S. Taylor 2017).

Also noteworthy, 84 percent of Native American and Alaska Native women have experienced violence during their lifetime, with 56 percent of them facing sexual violence. In the vast majority (90 percent) of cases of sexual violence, the perpetrators were white men, not tribal members (Gilpin 2016; Rosay 2016). In recent years, expansion of the oil and gas industries—in North Dakota, for example—has attracted an influx of male workers who live in "man camps," temporary housing facilities located near indigenous communities. Reports show a direct correlation between these encampments and violence against women (Secwepcul'ecw Assembly 2017). In Reading 27, Alleen Brown discusses murdered and missing indigenous women in the United States and Canada who often disappeared in suspicious circumstances.

Whether or not people report incidents of violence often depends on their communities' experiences with the police. In the case of women of color, poor women, prostituted women, and trans women, this is often negative. Women of color may decide not to report violence to avoid bringing more trouble on husbands, partners, friends, and acquaintances who already face discrimination based on race. Also, their community may expect them not to reinforce racist assumptions on the part of outsiders by "airing dirty laundry in public." Similarly, some women and men have been reluctant to speak about abuse in gay, lesbian, queer, gender nonconforming, or transgender relationships, not wanting to feed negative stereotypes circulating in the wider society about their communities.

Gender-Based State Violence

A key factor in being recognized as an independent sovereign state is having a monopoly on force and violence. **State violence** "focuses on the direct use of coercive, and frequently lethal, force in the context of law enforcement and military operations" (Center on Institutions and Governance n.d.). US law enforcement officials often victimize vulnerable people, such as people of color, trans people, and sex workers,. Those surviving under precarious conditions, including being undocumented, living with mental illness, or being homeless, are also disproportionately affected.

In 2015, Associated Press researchers found nearly 1,000 US police officers whose licenses to work in law enforcement had been revoked in a six-year period for committing acts of sexual violence, including rape, sodomy, soliciting sex from community members, and possessing child pornography (Sedensky 2015). According to the Cato Institute, in 2010 sexual assault was the second most common form of police brutality after excessive use of force, and it was primarily reported by women of color (cited in Carpenter 2014). Sexual assault is underreported, as mentioned earlier, and this is exacerbated when perpetrators are state agents, including police officers, Border

Patrol, and prison guards, with power and authority to inflict further violence on victims, such as arrest, incarceration, deportation, and other forms of retaliation. Those in authority may tolerate or actively perpetrate cultures of law enforcement that ignore, condone, justify, or encourage these practices. They may refuse to believe survivors' testimony, close down public discussion, and cover up evidence. Culprits may be promoted, protected, or let off with a slap on the wrist. Later in this chapter, we consider the contradictions involved in seeking state support to end gender-based violence. Several readings in this and other chapters address aspects of state violence and extend this discussion (see Readings 19, 30, 43, 44, and 49).

EXPLAINING SEXUALIZED VIOLENCE

Intimate partner violence, rape, and child sexual abuse are sometimes chalked up to an individual mental health problem, innate sexual craving, an "unhealthy" relationship, or a personal dysfunction on the part of the perpetrator or the victim/survivor. In individual cases, these explanations may carry some weight, but they cannot account for such a universal and systemic phenomenon. It is essential to consider macro-level explanations to understand this issue fully. Various explanations focus on gender or on other systemic inequalities that intersect with gender-based oppression.

Explanations Focused on Gender

Explanations focused on gender emphasize the cultural legitimation of male violence and the economic, political, and legal systems that marginalize, discriminate against, and disempower women—all part of patriarchal societies, as argued by Allan G. Johnson in Reading 7. At the same time, it is important to remember that all men do not participate in gender-based violence, and that some are actively working to stop it.

The Cultural Legitimation of Male Violence

This includes cultural beliefs in male superiority and male control of women's behavior and of the family, which are supported by social institutions, such as education, law, and religion. In some communities, cultural attitudes and religious beliefs support domestic violence as a husband's prerogative to "discipline" his wife. Historically, wives, as part of their marriage contract, were assumed to agree to sex whenever their husbands wanted it. Early US rape laws included an exemption for marriage. In response to pressure from advocacy groups, marital rape has been defined as a crime in all fifty states, though it continues to be underreported and difficult to prosecute.

The cultural legitimation of male superiority involves patterns of socialization in the family and in schools. Competitive games, aggressive sports, war toys, and violence on TV, in video games, and during movies are integral to children's socialization, especially for boys. A related factor is the social construction of masculinity and male sexuality (Kimmel 2000, chap. 11; Kimmel and Messner 1998). Julia Serano (2008) describes a predator/prey mindset in which men are viewed as sexual aggressors and women as sexual objects. She notes a double bind for men: "assholes" who fulfill the sexual aggressor stereotype and "nice guys" who refuse it. She argues that some men become "assholes" to get attention from women and asks why women are attracted to "bad boys" and why "nice guys" are seen as desexualized and unmanly.

Popular culture, news media, and advertising images reinforce these attitudes and contribute to the objectification and commodification of women. The music business, MTV, TV shows, and feature films include gender-based violence in their lyrics, story lines, and representations. A further example of male control is street harassment, where women may be "touched, harassed, commented upon in a stream of constant small-scale assaults" (Benard and Schlaffer 1997, p. 395). Public space is defined as male where women without male escorts may be considered "fair game."

Economic Systems that Disempower Women

As a group, US women earn less than men, and women of color are worse off in this regard than white women. A woman may not be able to leave a violent marriage or relationship if she is financially dependent on her partner, especially if she has children. In the workplace, a woman may find it difficult to speak up about sexual harassment whether she is a farmworker or a Hollywood actor.

Legal and Political Systems that Discriminate Against Women

As a result of ongoing pressure by women's advocates, the United States has introduced laws regarding intimate partner violence. Also, rape laws have been strengthened. There is no longer a need for witnesses to corroborate a victim's testimony; women are no longer required to have resisted their attackers; and the sexual histories of rape victims are no longer a subject for cross-examination unless they are shown to be relevant. However, insensitive treatment of women by police and the courts continues. The "statute of limitations," a limit on the time period allowed to bring a lawsuit for damages or criminal charges against a perpetrator, stops some women from using the law for redress in cases of rape or childhood sexual abuse. In the latter case, they may be in their twenties—and years past the time limit—before they even recognize that they were abused as children and gain the personal strength to confront the perpetrator publicly.

Compared to male voters, more women are concerned about gender-based violence. More women also favor gun control, believing that this would increase their security and the safety of their communities. These issues are often not taken seriously by many legislators or are blocked, as is the case with gun control.

These explanations are rooted in a heteropatriarchal framework, which is appropriate to many situations and assumed by government policies. To explain same-sex abuse requires a broader framework based on the use of power by one person to control or exploit another.

Sexualized Violence Is Not Only About Gender

Factors such as heterosexism, racism, difficult working conditions, unemployment, poverty, or loss of status and cultural roots that may accompany immigration are all external pressures that affect personal and family relationships from the outside. This is not to excuse those who abuse their partners or children but rather to provide a wider context for understanding stressors that may contribute to acts of violence.

Andy Smith, co-founder of Incite! Women of Color Against Violence, has shown how sexualized violence was integral to European colonization of North America, with sickening examples of the rape and mutilation of Native American women by white settlers and soldiers, a dimension of US history that is rarely taught in schools (Smith 2005b) and part of what historian Roxanne Dunbar-Ortiz (2014) called the "culture of conquest" that "drill[s] to the core of US history, to the very source of the country's existence" (p. xiii). Thus, as well as being a means of patriarchal control, rape is also a tool of colonialism and racism (Deer 2015).

During slavery times, the rape of Black women in the United States was commonplace. Enslaved women were chattel, the legal property of their masters. As such they could not be violated as they were not considered fully human. Currently, negative stereotypes about women of color, poor white women, prostituted women, lesbians, as well as gender nonconforming, queer, and transgender women all perpetuate the idea, in the wider society, that they are not worthy of respect. They are less likely to be taken seriously if they report acts of violence. Also, there is "a marked disparity" in conviction rates according to the race of the rape victim (Tetlow 2009, p. 90).

In her history of rape in the United States, historian Estelle Freedman (2013) argues that after the Civil War, the lynching of Black men in southern states was partly justified in terms of defending "white southern womanhood against the sexual threat of black men" (p. 8). Although most lynchings had nothing to do with this, accusations of rape were central to the political strategy of disenfranchising Black men and maintaining white dominance. Later, these racist assumptions followed African American men who moved to northern cities. In the 1950s, for example, African American men in Chicago "were over five times more likely than white men to be prosecuted for rape; when convicted they received longer sentences" (p. 272).

African American feminist scholars have discussed how the dehumanization of racism distorts and limits ideas of manhood and womanhood in African American communities (Cole and Guy-Sheftall 2003; P. H. Collins 2004). Discussing gender-based violence in Black communities, bell hooks (1994) commented:

> Black males, utterly disenfranchised in almost every arena of life in the United States, often find that the assertion of sexist domination is their only expressive access to the patriarchal power they are told all men should possess as their gendered birthright. (p. 110)

Sexualized violence is learned behavior, perhaps through media representations, personal experience, or both. Perpetrators may have witnessed acts of violence in childhood or have been abused themselves by family members, caretakers, coaches, or priests. Tens of thousands of Native American children were taken from their families and forced into government-run boarding schools as part of a strategy of attempted assimilation. They were not allowed to speak their languages or wear traditional clothes. Boys were forced to cut their hair. Many remember humiliation and abuse—physical and sexual. The legacies of these experiences continue to impact Native American communities to this day (Dunbar-Ortiz 2014; L. White 2016).

ENDING SEXUALIZED VIOLENCE

In the late nineteenth century, feminists challenged wife beating as part of anti-drinking campaigns, and again during the 1930s in campaigns for child custody and welfare for single mothers so that they could leave abusive men (Gordon 1988, 1997). In the 1960s and 1970s, women reframed and politicized the issue of rape, arguing that it is about power and control, not sex (see, e.g., Brownmiller 1975; Griffin 1971; D. E. H. Russell 1975). In 2017, US women from many walks of life—Hollywood celebrities, Congressional staffers, media reporters, film industry workers, farmworkers, and athletes—spoke out about sexual harassment in the workplace as part of the #MeToo and #TimesUp movements. #MeToo went viral almost overnight, with participants from eighty-five countries who showed the global scale of this issue and sparked unprecedented national and transnational conversations about it (see Reading 59; also see, e.g., Fox and Diehm 2017; Mahdavi 2018).

Providing Support for Victims/Survivors

Feminist theorizing about the systemic nature of gender-based violence under patriarchy led to concerted efforts to provide supports and safe places for those who experience such violence, to educate the wider society on the issue, and to change public policy.

The first shelter for battered women in the United States opened in 1974. Now there are nearly 3,000 shelters and service programs nationwide, all stretched to capacity. More shelters are needed to cope with the demand for them, and those that exist need to be more accessible—physically and culturally—to women with disabilities, women of color, immigrant women, lesbians, queer, and trans women. Organizations that emphasize culturally relevant perspectives and services include the Alianza National de Campesinas (Oxnard, CA); Asian Women's Shelter (San Francisco); Ayuda-Hermanas Unidas (Washington, DC); Baitul Salaam (Atlanta); Black, Indian, Hispanic, and Asian Women in Action—BIHA (Minneapolis); Casa Myrna (Boston); the Korean American Family Service Center (Flushing, NY); Minnesota Indian Women's Resource Center (Minneapolis), Sakhi for South Asian Women (New York), White Buffalo Calf Women's Society (Mission, SD), and Wingspan Domestic Violence Project (Tucson, AZ). Organizations that work with LGBTQI clients include Community United Against Violence (San Francisco) and Forge (Milwaukee), a national transgender anti-violence organization that serves transgender, gender nonconforming, and gender nonbinary survivors of sexual assault.

Similarly, rape crisis centers operate in many cities throughout the country. Volunteers and paid staff answer emergency calls to crisis hotlines, offer information and support, and refer women who have been raped to counseling, medical, and legal services. They may accompany a woman to the police or a doctor, or advocate for her in court proceedings. Rape crisis centers often conduct public education and self-defense training for women, and many have peer counselors who are rape survivors.

Years of work on the part of anti-violence advocates helped to pass the Violence Against Women Act (VAWA), signed into federal law as part of the Violent Crime and Law Enforcement Act of 1994. It authorized funds for battered women's shelters and community initiatives, training for judges and court personnel, improvements in arrest policies, and legal advocacy programs for victims. In 2013, the reauthorized VAWA included new provisions for LGBTQI communities, Native American women, immigrant women, and victims/survivors of human trafficking.

Public and Professional Education

Compared with a generation ago, there is now much more public information and awareness about gender-based violence, including public service announcements, bumper stickers, and ads on billboards, buses, and TV. Increasingly, employers and labor unions recognize that intimate partner violence can interfere with a person's ability to get, perform, or keep a job. Some corporations and labor unions have developed education and training programs on this issue for managers and workers; others contribute financially to shelters.

Professional knowledge and awareness has also expanded. Police officers, judges, doctors, nurses, emergency room staff and other health care providers, as well as social workers and teachers may undergo professional training in order to recognize and address instances of gendered violence, although much more still needs to be done in this regard.

National-level organizations like Alianza National Latino/Alliance for the Elimination of Domestic Violence (Espaniola, NM), Incite!, the National Coalition Against Domestic Violence (Denver, CO), National Domestic Violence Hotline (Austin, TX), the National Resource Center on Domestic Violence (Harrisburg, PA), the Network for Battered Lesbians and Bisexual Women (Boston), Rape Abuse and Incest National Network (Washington, DC), and V-Day (New York) provide visibility, public education, research, and expertise to local organizations, news reporters, and policy-makers. Finally, an organization supporting survivors of child sexual abuse is Generation Five (Oakland, CA), which has the goal of eliminating this devastating problem within five generations. In Reading 26, Aurora Levins Morales describes her journey to reclaim her sexuality and sense of integrity after experiencing sexual abuse as a child.

The Importance of a Political Movement

Judith Herman, MD, argued that changing public consciousness about gender-based violence takes a concerted political movement. In her groundbreaking study of trauma and recovery connected to violence, Herman (1992) wrote that perpetrators "ask bystanders to do nothing, simply to ignore the atrocity," whereas "victims demand action, engagement, and remembering" (pp. 7–8).

Nowadays, in order to emphasize women's agency, feminist writers, advocates, and workers in shelters and rape crisis projects often use the term *survivor* to refer to those who are coping with acts of violence. Although Herman's use of the term *victim* is somewhat dated, her comments on the ways that perpetrators attempt to avoid responsibility for acts of violence are very insightful:

> In order to escape accountability for his crimes, the perpetrator does everything in his power to promote forgetting. Secrecy and silence are the perpetrator's first line of defense. If secrecy fails, the perpetrator attacks the credibility of his victim. If he cannot silence her absolutely, he tries to make sure that no one listens. To this end, he marshals an impressive array of arguments, from the most blatant denial to the most sophisticated . . . rationalization. After every atrocity one can expect to hear the same predictable apologies: it never happened; the victim lies; the victim exaggerates; the victim brought it upon herself; and in any case it is time to forget the past and move on. The more powerful the perpetrator, the greater is his prerogative to name and define reality, and the more completely his arguments prevail. (p. 8)

Herman argued that to cut through the power of the perpetrators' arguments "requires a social context that affirms and protects the victim and that joins victim and witness in a common alliance" (p. 9). For the individual victim/survivor of violence, relationships with family and friends create this context. For the wider society, "the social context is created by political movements that give voice to the disempowered" (p. 9).

The organizations and projects mentioned in this chapter are all part of creating this context. Students and women's groups organize "Take Back the Night" marches and rallies on campuses and in their neighborhoods where women and men speak out about their experiences of sexual violence, some of them for the first time in a public setting. Students, staff, and faculty from hundreds of US colleges and universities have performed Eve Ensler's script, *The Vagina Monologues*, as part of the V-Day College Initiative, a nationwide project to celebrate women and to oppose sexual violence. Some campus or community groups have adapted the script for their cultural contexts and to reflect current understandings of gender and gender fluidity. More recently, the Women's Marches and the #MeToo and #TimesUp movements have all contributed to public discussion and shaping public opinion.

Men's projects that work on gender-based violence are essential in creating change on this issue. Examples include the National Organization for Men Against Sexism (Denver, CO), Emerge (Cambridge, MA), Men Can Stop Rape (Washington, DC), and Men Stopping Violence (Decatur, GA). Campus groups offer educational programs in men-only settings, show films, bring speakers to campus, and participate in campus or community events. Examples include Haverford Men Against Sexism and Rape (Haverford, PA), Men Educating Men on the Prevention of Sexual Assault (Bowling Green, OH), Tulane One in Four (New Orleans, LA), Unite Against Sexual Assault Yale (New Haven, CT), and the Men's Project at Pacific Lutheran University (Tacoma, WA) discussed by Jonathan Grove in Reading 29.

Contradictions in Seeking State Support to End Gender-Based Violence

An increase in government funding has provided for the expansion of services, organizations, and professional training, as already mentioned. At the same time, however, shelters and rape crisis centers have come under closer official scrutiny. Many leadership positions now require a Master's degree in social work (MSW) or a counseling qualification. Over a decade ago, long-time activist Mimi Kim (2006) warned that increased federal funding for anti-violence organizations under VAWA often requires greater collaboration with the police and the promotion of pro-arrest policies, negatively impacting low-income communities of color and specifically men of color given the racism and classism of the US criminal justice system.

At the first Color of Violence conference, held at the University of California, Santa Cruz, in April 2000, activist, writer, and scholar Angela Davis (2000) highlighted a core contradiction in anti-violence work that looks to the government—the state—for solutions:

> Given the racist and patriarchal patterns of the state, it is difficult to envision the state as the holder of solutions to the problem of violence against women. However, as the anti-violence movement has been institutionalized and professionalized, the state plays an increasingly dominant role in the way we conceptualize and create strategies to minimize violence against women. One of the major tasks of this conference, and of the anti-violence movement as a whole, is to address this contradiction, especially as it presents itself to poor communities of color. (p. 13)

Increasingly advocates are creating community-based approaches that seek to address violence against women without increasing state violence against men (see, e.g., Casselman 2016; M. Kim 2006; A. Smith 1999). Also, similar efforts are being made in LGBTQI communities.

SEXUALIZED VIOLENCE AND HUMAN RIGHTS

Gender-based violence occurs in all societies across the life cycle, and has engaged the attention, anger, and activist efforts of scholars, policy makers, and organizers around the world (see the box feature "Gender Violence Worldwide, Throughout the Life Cycle). In December 1979, the United Nations adopted the Convention on the Elimination of All Forms of Discrimination Against Women (CEDAW), which includes gender-based violence. One hundred eighty-nine countries have ratified CEDAW and adopted it as national policy, though often with many reservations so that implementation has been much more limited. Forty years later, US women's organizations are still lobbying for the United States to ratify this Convention.

Defining gender-based violence in terms of human rights has been a successful way to get this issue onto the international agenda (see, e.g., Agosín 2001; Beasley and Thomas 1994; Bunch and Carillo 1991; Kerr 1993). In June 1993, women from many countries organized the Global Tribunal on Violations of Women's Human Rights to coincide with the Non-Governmental Organization Forum of the UN World Conference on Human Rights, held in Vienna (Bunch 2018; Bunch and Reilly 1994). A year later, the UN Commission on Human Rights created a new position—the Special Rapporteur on Violence Against Women, Its Causes and Consequences—based in Geneva, Switzerland. The Center for Women's Global Leadership (Rutgers University) sponsors an annual 16 Days of Activism Against Gender-Based Violence from November 25th, International Day for the Elimination of Violence Against Women, to December 10th, International Human Rights Day. Initiated by activists from the Global North and South, these campaigns emphasize that all forms of gender-based violence, whether in the public or private sphere and irrespective of a particular gender, are a violation of human rights.

Gender Violence Worldwide, Throughout the Life Cycle

PHASE	TYPE OF VIOLENCE
Prebirth	Inadequate prenatal care due to poverty; battering during pregnancy; coerced pregnancy (for example, mass rape in war); sex-selective abortion.
Infancy	Emotional and physical abuse; differential access to food and medical care for girl infants; female infanticide.
Girlhood	Sexual abuse by family members and strangers; differential access to food and medical care; child prostitution; child marriage; genital mutilation.
Adolescence	Dating and courtship violence; economically coerced sex; sexual abuse in the workplace; rape; sexual harassment; forced prostitution and trafficking.
Reproductive age	Abuse of women by intimate male partners; marital rape; partner homicide; psychological abuse; sexual abuse in the workplace; sexual harassment; rape; abuse of women with disabilities; dowry abuse and murders.
Elderly	Abuse of widows; elder abuse (in the United States, for example, this affects mostly women).

Source: Heise, Pitanguy, and Germain (1994), p. 5.

An example of systematic gendered violence can be found in the US-Mexico border area, centered on Ciudad Juárez, where hundreds of women and girls have been murdered, tortured, and subjected to sexual violence since the early 1990s. In Reading 30, Brazilian anthropologist Rita Laura Segato attempts to understand the economic, political, and cultural factors that may explain why these killings have been carried out, and why the authorities have done so little to identify the perpetrators despite outrage and protest from family members, Mexican women's groups, and international human rights organizations. Mexican Congresswoman Marcela Lagarde y de los Ríos (2010, p. xiv) emphasized that "disinformation, uncertainty, and anxiety have held sway, fostering the exaggeration or downplaying of the facts."

Rather than using the term *femicide* (*femicidio* in Spanish, which means the homicide of women), feminist policy-makers, lawyers, and organizers have introduced the term *feminicide* (*feminicidio*) to emphasize the collective nature of these violent crimes as genocide against women (Fregoso and Bejarano 2010). Some frame *feminicidio* as a state crime, pointing to "the state's role in fomenting a climate of impunity for the most heinous violations of women's rights," and arguing that "a state's failure to guarantee women's rights to live a life free from violence is itself a human rights violation" (Fregoso and Bejarano 2010, p. 19). Segato's research and theorizing contribute to a broader transnational feminist discourse on this issue that is both analytical and deeply engaged at an activist level. This article repays careful reading to understand her analysis and methodology. Ultimately, she sees these acts of violence as a callous form of communication where the perpetrators confront the state with their power.

As this chapter makes clear, there is an urgent need for many changes at the micro, meso, macro, and global levels for women in all our diversity to be secure from violence. These changes include:

- The socialization and education of children and young people to respect and value each other.
- Changes in social constructions of gender and the abolition of cultural attitudes and systems of inequality that support male superiority.
- An end to the objectification and commodification of women.
- Respect for queer, gender-nonconforming, and trans people.
- Changes in women's work and wages, and support for community-based economic development to give women economic security and independence.
- Changes in laws, court decisions, police practices, and political systems focused on human rights.
- Continued collaboration among all who are working to end violence, and challenges to those who are not.

Writer and cultural critic bell hooks (1984b) argued against "hierarchical rule and coercive authority that is the root cause of violence against women, of adult violence against children, of all violence between those who dominate and those who are dominated" (p. 118). Feminists need to oppose all forms of coercive domination—including racism, imperialism, sexism, and heterosexism—in order to address gender-based violence fully.

QUESTIONS FOR REFLECTION

In reading and discussing this chapter, think about these questions:

1. What beliefs about rape are really myths? How would your life be different if rape and the threat of rape did not exist?
2. How do boys in your community learn to respect women? To disrespect women?
3. How has abuse or violence affected your life? Your family? Your community?
4. What kinds of manhood and womanhood would help to create personal security for women and for men?
5. What are men's roles and responsibilities in ending gender-based violence?
6. How do race, class, nation, sexuality, and other systems of inequality affect sexualized violence?

FINDING OUT MORE ON THE WEB

1. Research US and international organizations mentioned in this chapter that are working to end physical and sexual violence against women, queer, gender-nonconforming, and trans people. What are their goals, strategies, and activities? What theoretical frameworks shape their work? Additional organizations to consider:

   Green Dot: www.livethegreendot.com
   National Coalition against Domestic Violence: https://www.ncadv.org
   The NW Network of Bi, Trans, Lesbian and Gay Survivors of Abuse: https://www.nwnetwork.org/
   Women Against Violence Europe: https://www.wave-network.org/
   Women Living Under Muslim Laws: http://www.wluml.org/

2. Review the cartoon about consent at https://www.youtube.com/watch?v=JjPMsjph CUU. Do you find this cartoon effective? Is there anything that you would change or add to a cartoon like this?

3. Find out about ways to counter gender trolling and online violence. The following sites provide some starting places:
   http://www.pewinternet.org/2017/07/11/online-harassment-2017/
   http://www.crashoverridenetwork.com/
   https://weaponizedsocial.aspirationtech.org/Main_Page
   https://tallpoppy.io/resources/

TAKING ACTION

1. Talk about the issue of sexualized violence with classmates and friends, and join in discussions or events on your campus or in your community.
2. Find out about your college's policy on sexual assault and how well it is enforced. Find out about rape crisis centers, shelters, and support groups in your area so that you can offer this information to someone who is coping with sexual assault or rape.
3. Volunteer with a rape crisis project on campus or at a shelter for domestic violence survivors. Male students: work with other men on this issue.

26 RADICAL PLEASURE: SEX AND THE END OF VICTIMHOOD (1998)

Aurora Levins Morales is a Puerto Rican Ashkenazi Jewish feminist writer and activist. She is the author of six books, including *Medicine Stories: Essays for Radicals* (1998), *Kindling: Writings on the Body* (2013), and *Remedios: Stories of Earth and Iron from the History of Puertorriqueñas* (1998). She produces the podcast Letters from Earth and blogs at www.patreon.com/auroralevinsmorales.

1

I am a person who was sexually abused and tortured as a child. I no longer define myself in terms of my survival of this experience, but what I learned from surviving it is central to my political and spiritual practice. The people who abused me consciously and deliberately manipulated me in an attempt to break down my sense of integrity so they could make me into an accomplice to my own torture and that of others. They deliberately and consciously interfered with my sexuality as one method of accomplishing this. We are so vulnerable in our pleasures and desires. The fact they could induce physical pleasure in me against my will allowed them to shame me. It allowed them to persuade me that my sexuality was untrustworthy and belonged to others. It allowed them to persuade me that my desires were dangerous and were one of the causes of my having been abused. My sexuality has stuttered ever since, flaring and subsiding in ways I have not known how to manage, ricocheting from intense excitement to absolute numbness, from reckless trust to impenetrable guardedness. This place of wounded eroticism is one that is honored in survivor culture, evidence of blows inflicted and then denied by our abusers. When the skeptical ask us "Where are your scars?" we can point to the unsteady rhythms of fascination and disgust, obsession and revulsion through which we experience sex as evidence of what we know to be true.

2

"So why choose to reclaim sex?" This is the final question in a five-hour interview of me by my friend Staci Haines. We have been talking about the seductiveness of the victim role; about the thin satisfactions that come from a permanent attitude of outrage. About how having to resist too much, too young, locks us into rigid stances of resistance that interfere with intimacy, which ultimately requires vulnerability and surrender. About the seductiveness of an identity built on righteous indignation, and how close that stance actually lies to rampant self-pity. So when she asks me "Why reclaim sex?" I answer in layers.

Of course because it is part of aliveness. But among the many topics we've ranged over in our hours of conversation, the one that grabs me now is the need and obligation to leave victimhood behind. Staci and I share a somewhat taboo belief that as survivors we have an obligation to think about the healing of the perpetrators who are, after all, our kin—victims who survived in body but were unable to remain spiritually intact. So what comes to mind is the high price we pay when we settle for being wronged. Victimhood absolves us from having to decide to have good lives. It allows us to stay small and wounded instead of spacious, powerful and whole. We don't have to face up to our own responsibility for taking charge of things, for changing the world and ourselves. We can place our choices about being vulnerable and intimate and effective in the hands of our abusers. We can stay powerless and send them the bill.

But deciding not to heal fully, not to reclaim that place of intimate harm and make it flourish, is also unjust. By making the damage done to us permanent and irreversible, we lock both ourselves and the perpetrators away from any hope of healing. We saddle them with an even bigger spiritual debt than they have already incurred, and sometimes the reason is revenge, as if our full recovery would let them off the hook and we must punish them by seeing to it that our victimhood is never diminished or challenged. But when we refuse healing for the sake of that rage, we are remaking ourselves in the image of those who hurt us, becoming the embodiment of the wound, forsaking both ourselves and the abandoned children who grew up to torment us.

3

The path of reclaiming the wounded erotic is neither placid nor boring. It is full of dizzying precipices, heady moments of release, crushing assaults of shame. But at its core is the real fire we are all after, that blazing and untarnished aliveness that lies within everything of value and spirit that we do. Right here in our bodies, in our defense of our right to experience joy, in the refusal to abandon the place where we have been most completely invaded and colonized, in our determination to make the bombed and defoliated lands flower again and bear fruit, here where we have been most shamed is one of the most radical and sacred places from which to transform the world. To shamelessly insist that our bodies are for our own delight and connection with others clearly defies the predatory appropriations of incestuous relatives and rapists; but it also defies the poisoning of our food and water and air with chemicals that give us cancer and enrich the already obscenely wealthy, the theft of our lives in harsh labor, our bodies used up to fill bank accounts already bloated, the massive abduction of our young people to be hurled at each other as weapons for the defense and expansion of those bank accounts—all the ways in which our deep pleasure in living has been cut off so as not to interfere with the profitability of our bodies. Because the closer I come to that bright, hot center of pleasure and trust, the less I can tolerate its captivity, and the less afraid I am to be powerful, in a world that is in desperate need of unrepentant joy.

ALLEEN BROWN

27 INDIGENOUS WOMEN HAVE BEEN DISAPPEARING FOR GENERATIONS: POLITICIANS ARE FINALLY STARTING TO NOTICE (2018)

Alleen Brown is New York–based reporter for *The Intercept*, focused on environmental justice issues. Before joining *The Intercept*, she was an education reporter in Minnesota. Her work has been published in *The Nation*, *In These Times*, *YES! Magazine*, and several Twin Cities publications.

Women on the Yakama Indian Reservation in Washington state didn't have any particular term for the way the violent deaths and sudden disappearances of their sisters, mothers, friends, and neighbors had become woven into everyday life.

"I didn't know, like many, that there was a title, that there was a word for it," said Roxanne White, who is Yakama and Nez Percé and grew up on the reservation. White has become a leader in the movement to address the disproportionate rates of homicide and missing persons cases among American Indian women, but the first time she heard the term "missing and murdered Indigenous women" was less than two years ago, at a Dakota Access pipeline resistance camp at Standing Rock. There, she met women who had traveled from Canada to speak about disappearances in First Nations to the north, where Prime Minister Justin Trudeau's administration launched a historic national inquiry into the issue in 2016.

"I knew exactly what they were talking about," White said. "I had survived all of this and witnessed all of this." White's aunt was murdered in 1996, and there were plenty of others in her orbit who had disappeared or died violently.

In the mid-2000s, the FBI re-examined 16 deaths in the vicinity of the Yakama reservation, mostly Native American women whose remains were found between 1980 and 1992—so many deaths in such quick succession that many were convinced it must have been the work of a serial killer. As the mysterious deaths went unsolved, community members also became convinced[1] of the FBI's indifference.

In 2009, the agency released[2] its findings; investigators had discovered no serial killer or any one culprit. Ten of the deaths were believed by the FBI to be homicides—women who had been shot, stabbed, beaten, or run over. Two of the deaths were classified as accidental drownings, one woman died of hypothermia, and in three cases, the cause of death was unknown. Media attention moved on after the anticlimactic results, although women on the reservation continued[3] to disappear[4] and die under suspicious circumstances.

Nearly 10 years later, a new law[5] set to take effect in June will require the Washington State Patrol to determine just how many American Indian women have gone missing in the state. Working with tribes and the Department of Justice, the agency will use the data as part of a study to determine how to report and identify missing women.

The law's sponsor was state Republican Rep. Gina Mosbrucker, whose district includes Yakama—Mosbrucker is a fifth-generation resident of Klickitat County, which includes the southern edge of the reservation. But Mosbrucker was compelled to act on the issue of missing and murdered Indigenous women not in the wake of the murders on the reservation near her home, but after seeing the 2017 film *Wind River*,[6] a fictional account of the murder of a young woman found frozen in the snow on a reservation in Wyoming. "The more I looked into it, and the more I spoke to tribal members living in Washington, I realized this isn't just some Hollywood storyline," Mosbrucker said.[7]

"There's a little bit of justice in the acknowledgement that there's an injustice," said Carolyn DeFord, whose mother, Leona LeClair Kinsey, a member of the Puyallup Tribe, disappeared 18 years ago. "It's a slow boat to turn around, because it's a 500-year-old problem."

For the first time, the US government is taking steps toward addressing a problem that until recently went unnamed. The Washington law is among a handful of recent legislative efforts, including proposed legislation in Minnesota and a federal bill known as Savanna's Act, that seek to ramp up data collection around missing Indigenous persons and improve protocols for investigations of crimes on reservation land.

But if Canada provides any clues, the road ahead will be steep for organizers and families who are pushing for an end to the violence and neglect. There, many families have rescinded their support for the inquiry launched by Trudeau, arguing that it has been mismanaged and re-traumatizing for families and has followed a colonial model that excludes the grassroots.

Organizers argue that any chances of success lie in the government's willingness to follow the lead of communities most impacted. As Annita Lucchesi, a Southern Cheyenne cartographer who is building a database of missing and murdered Indigenous women, put it, "I don't think you can fix problems that have been created by poor legislation with more legislation rooted in the same way of knowing and in the same culture."

Data Reveals Indifference

Lucchesi's database includes cases in the US and Canada going back to 1900, relying on news reports, law enforcement data, government missing persons databases, and information shared by Indigenous families and community members. So far, her data set includes[8] 2,501 cases, and it's far from complete.

Behind the vanishing women is an array of causes—domestic violence and sex trafficking, as well as police indifference, racism, lack of resources allocated to tribal governments, and complex jurisdictional issues between tribal, federal, and local law enforcement that slow down investigations in their crucial first days and make it easier for non-Indigenous people to get away with violent crime. For most criminal cases, tribal courts lack the ability to prosecute perpetrators who are not tribal members. Although the 2013 Violence Against Women Reauthorization Act allowed tribal courts to pursue domestic violence cases committed by non-Native people, not all tribes exercise[9] that jurisdiction, and many other types of physical and sexual violence are not covered by the exception.

Lucchesi is building her database because no government entity has undertaken such an effort. As demonstrated in an investigative series[10] by Reveal, data collection on missing persons is terrible in the US—the central repository for information, the National Missing and Unidentified Persons System, or NamUs, contains data that's submitted only voluntarily by law enforcement and is thus incomplete. When it comes to Indigenous women, the problem is exacerbated by confusing jurisdictional issues on reservation land, where it's often unclear which agencies have responsibility to look for a missing person or submit their information to the database.

Data about those who have been murdered is also sparse—it's been less than a priority for US police to track homicide rates of Indigenous women, if the convoluted responses to Lucchesi's requests for historical data are any indication.

But the data that does exist provides a window into the scope of the violence and its impact on Indigenous women's lives. According to the results[11] of the 2010 National Intimate Partner and Sexual Violence Survey, 84 percent of Indigenous women interviewed had experienced violence in their life; 56 percent had experienced sexual violence. According to data collected[12] between 1992 and 2001, American Indians were twice[13] as likely as any other racial group to be raped or sexually assaulted. A study[14] of American Indian causes of death between 1999 and 2009 found Indigenous women had a homicide rate three times that of white women. And an analysis[15] of data collected between 1994 and 1998 showed that some counties had murder rates of American Indian women that were more than 10 times the national average. Much of this data is limited by the willingness of individuals to report violence to police and of law enforcement to designate deaths as homicide.

Improving the data is a key objective of the proposed laws. The most significant piece of legislation so far is Savanna's Act,[16] introduced in October 2017 by US Sen. Heidi Heitkamp, a Democrat from North Dakota. The act is named for Savanna LaFontaine-Greywind, a 22-year-old member of the Spirit Lake Tribe who was eight months pregnant when she disappeared from her home in Fargo in August 2017. Her body was found a week later in the Red River. She had been murdered[17] by neighbors who kidnapped her newborn.

The law would see tribal affiliation added to federal databases, including NamUS; the National Crime Information Center (the FBI's primary data collection system); and other databases that aggregate fingerprints and DNA. It would force the US attorney general to develop a plan for making those databases more accessible to tribal governments and require the Department of Justice to develop a standard protocol for investigating cases of missing and murdered Indigenous people. The government would also be required to submit an annual report with statistics about missing and murdered Indigenous women and recommendations for improving the data. . . .

Additional federal legislation would provide grants[18] for victims services in tribal communities, collect better data[19] on American Indian human trafficking victims, and improve access[20] to the AMBER alert system in Indian country.

In Minnesota, legislation[21] to create a task force on missing and murdered Indigenous women was introduced on March 1. The bill asks the task force to uncover the "underlying historical, social, economic, institutional, and cultural factors" behind the violence and provide recommendations on how to better track missing Indigenous women, prevent violence against them, and support healing from trauma.

The legislation was pushed[22] forward by two Indigenous lawmakers. One of them, state Rep. Jamie Becker-Finn, who grew up on the Leech Lake Reservation, has described[23] how her great-grandmother disappeared back in 1931. Although her body was later discovered, how she died has never been determined.

Everybody Knows Somebody

After her mother disappeared, Carolyn DeFord, who was raising her three young children paycheck to paycheck at the time, found a void of support and information. Her mom lived in the small town of La Grande, Oregon, and had struggled with addiction for a couple of years. DeFord felt that police didn't move quickly to find her because they knew her history. DeFord recalled an officer with the La Grande Police Department reminding her that it was not illegal for an adult to disappear—it was implied that her mother might be out partying. But DeFord knew her mother would never have left her beloved dog locked in the house; something severe had happened. Nearly two decades later, DeFord's mother has not reappeared.

As time went on, DeFord began reaching out to other women whose family members had gone missing. She manages a Facebook[24] page that features photos of missing persons and the details of their cases. When she travels, she brings a stack of posters "of somebody who's in my mind that day. I don't necessarily pick or choose. Whoever I'm feeling, I put out there," she said. The stories she's heard from others are familiar: investigations delayed because of assumptions about the lifestyle of the missing person—or about Indigenous people more broadly; lack of clarity around which agency should be searching; little support for families grappling with trauma; and an overwhelming sense of erasure.

The growing movement around missing and murdered Indigenous women didn't arise out of data—it came from the fact that so many Indigenous women know someone who has died violently or disappeared. One of the hallmarks of the movement is that it does not center around how the woman was murdered or who killed her. It identifies the generations-long elimination of thousands of women from Indigenous communities as a direct result of government attempts to eliminate Indigenous cultures.

Recent legislative efforts at addressing the complex matrix of issues behind the violence only begin to acknowledge that long history. Already, Lucchesi and other advocates say the new legislation in Washington overlooks some of the root causes of the unsolved disappearances. In particular, Lucchesi points to the fact that it is the Washington State Patrol that will conduct the state's study.

"They're probably not the best agency to do it," she said. "That's already a fraught relationship there." The Yakama Nation Tribal Council, for example, recently passed a resolution[25] declaring a public safety crisis on the reservation, noting that the crisis can be traced in part to the state patrol's "refusal to actively patrol" Washington's public rights of way that fall within reservation boundaries.

"That's an unfortunate replication of the [Canadian] inquiry—to rely on Western legal framework," said Lucchesi. "There's quite a few families who don't feel comfortable talking to law enforcement, that would feel more comfortable coming forward and sharing these stories if it was someone from their own community."

Canada's Inquiry Leaves Families Disillusioned

When Maggie Cywink was grappling with the 1994 murder of her sister Sonya Nadine, women were only beginning to hold marches in Canada to draw attention to their disappeared friends and relatives.

Cywink shared her story with Amnesty International, which published a groundbreaking report[26] in 2004, titled "Stolen Sisters: A Human Rights Response to Discrimination and Violence Against Indigenous Women in Canada." Three years later, serial killer Robert Pickton was sentenced to life imprisonment after the remains of 33 women—including a number of Indigenous women and sex workers—were found on his pig farm. An inquiry[27] carried out between 2010 and 2012 found that because of who the women were, "police investigations into the missing and murdered women were blatant failures." Meanwhile, organizing around the issue was intensifying—the Indigenous Idle No More[28] movement made missing and murdered Indigenous women a central issue in its high-profile actions that began in 2012.

Momentum only continued to build. In 2014, the Royal Canadian Mounted Police released its estimate[29] of Canada's missing and murdered Indigenous women: 1,181 between 1980 and 2012, which some have argued is a significant undercount.[30] Then, in 2015, Canada's Truth and Reconciliation Commission[31] released its findings. The commission was the result of a class-action lawsuit brought by survivors of Canada's residential schools, which were rife with abuse and served as a key part of the country's assimilation attempts, tearing children from their families and cultures. One of the commission's recommendations was that a missing and murdered Indigenous women inquiry should be launched.

"Then the Liberal government made the national inquiry a campaign promise," said Cywink. "It went from something that was personal, that was grassroots, that was family, to something that became a political thing."

As prime minister, Trudeau has promised a "total renewal"[32] of relations with Indigenous Canadians and announced the launch of the National Inquiry into Missing and Murdered Indigenous Women and Girls,[33] which also includes transgender, two-spirit, and nonbinary people as part of its mandate.

"We all felt a sense of relief. We all felt a sense of validation, that thank god this government is actually paying attention—helping us carry this burden we've been carrying all these generations. Maybe a little bit of our guard was let down," said Sheila North Wilson, grand chief of Manitoba's Keewatinowi Okimakanak organization.

Many families and advocates quickly became disillusioned, as commissioners were chosen with little input from long-time organizers. "We are deeply concerned and confused as to why so many of the most renowned family leaders, advocates, activists, and grassroots (in short, those known and respected across the country with a deep subject matter expertise), have not been asked to help," wrote Cywink and more than 50 other advocates and family members in a letter[34] to Chief Commissioner Marion Buller in May 2017.

Soon afterward, a commissioner and multiple staffers quit—the inquiry seemed to be in disarray.

In another letter[35] addressed to Trudeau, more than 140 signatories called for a "hard reset" of the inquiry, including the replacement of Buller, a member of the Mistawasis First Nation and British Columbia's first Indigenous Provincial Court judge, who was described in the letter as sidelining family members rather than including their voices as central to the process.

But the inquiry continued, with commissioners touring the nation, offering families space to publicly share their missing or murdered relatives' stories. Cywink was disturbed by the lack of trauma care offered by the commission, and she didn't think it was clear what the stories would even be used for. She decided not to submit the story of her sister.

When the commissioners finished their tour last month, they requested an additional two years to complete their ambitious goal: to build a foundation from which Indigenous women could reclaim their power and place and ultimately end cycles of violence rooted in Canada's foundations as a nation. Some critics[36] of the inquiry, such as the Native Women's Association of Canada, have come out in support[37] of an extension (which so far has not been granted).

But Cywink and other organizers felt that the commission's time was up. "You've had testimony from over 1,000 people. That should be plenty," Cywink explained in an interview with *The Intercept*. "Write your report and be done with it. Then we'll take all the recommendations that you give us, plus the thousands that we've already got, and we'll ask the government for more money, then we'll start to implement them."

"The national inquiry has bulldozed through our communities and with an extension will continue to exacerbate the emotional and psychological burden on the very people it is intended to solace," Cywink, North Wilson, and around 200 families and leaders wrote in another letter[38] on April 11. "A recurring narrative from communities has emerged: They came, they took stories, they left."

"Caught between the inquiry's dysfunction and government inaction, Canadians remain immobilized voyeurs and consumers of horrific stories of missing and murdered Indigenous women, girls, trans and two spirit people."

After decades, the signatories were ready to be done proving the issue exists.

"We Have to Be the Ones to Demand Justice"

Amanda Takes War Bonnet, a public education specialist for the Native Women's Society of the Great Plains, pointed out that what happened in Canada is unlikely to happen the same way in the US—at least not anytime soon. She works in South Dakota, where legislators passed a law[39] in 2010 meant to prevent Native communities from holding the churches that ran American Indian boarding schools accountable for sexual assault.

For now, in a country where so little has been done to account for 500 years of colonization and genocide, she takes heart from legislative efforts by politicians like Heitkamp—even if they've missed some of the root causes of the issue. She acknowledged that Heitkamp's support for the oil industry in some ways conflicts with her work on human trafficking and missing and murdered Indigenous women. (The Trudeau administration, too, has been blasted by leaders of Canadian First Nations for agreeing this week to purchase the highly controversial Trans Mountain Pipeline for $4.5 billion, after pipeline owner Kinder Morgan threatened to drop the project. Several First Nations have been fighting in court to stop the project and leaders have called[40] the purchase a betrayal of the reconciliation process.)

Heitkamp played a key role[41] in ending the crude oil export ban, opening up the Bakken oil region to new markets overseas. On Heitkamp's press releases[42] about Savanna's Law, she noted her previous efforts to address violence against Indigenous women, including pushing for the opening of an FBI field office on tribal land after the oil boom brought[43] an influx of drugs, sex trafficking, and other crime.

"She's a politician, so you've got to ride the fence, and you've got to do both things," said Takes War Bonnet. She feels the federal legislation is a crucial first step for the US government. "It's really important work that she's doing, because it helps set precedent."

On May 5, communities across the US held gatherings in acknowledgement of a newly designated

National Day of Awareness for Missing and Murdered Native Women and Girls. Roxanne White led a march of tribal members dressed in red through the Yakama reservation town of Toppenish, Washington. She asked marchers for the names of women and men who were gone. "I had so many people telling me this name, this name, all at once," White said. White estimates she called out 30 names.

"We're the only ones that are going to speak for them. It's not going to be the president or the governor," White said. "We have to be the ones to come out and demand justice, demand the police, when somebody goes missing, to do their damn job, hold them accountable."

NOTES

1. Timothy Egan, "13 Unsolved Deaths Feed Indian Mistrust of F.B.I.," *New York Times*, April 18, 1993, https://www.nytimes.com/1993/04/18/us/13-unsolved-deaths-feed-indian-mistrust-of-fbi.html

2. Federal Bureau of Investigation, Seattle Division, "Results of FBI Analysis of Reservation Deaths Announced," May 6, 2009, https://archives.fbi.gov/archives/seattle/press-releases/2009/se050609-1.htm

3. Associated Press, "Authorities Investigating Death of Yakama Tribal Member," *KIMA*, January 5, 2018, http://kimatv.com/news/local/authorities-investigating-death-of-yakama-tribal-member

4. Ariella Toren, "FBI Identifies Remains Found on Yakama Nation Reservation as Missing Harrah Woman," *KIMA*, June 27, 2017, http://kimatv.com/news/local/fbi-identifies-remains-found-on-yakama-nation-reservation-as-missing-harrah-woman

5. See http://lawfilesext.leg.wa.gov/biennium/2017-18/Pdf/Bills/Session%20Laws/House/2951-S.SL.pdf

6. See https://www.imdb.com/title/tt5362988/

7. "New Law Aims to Shed Light on Missing and Murdered Indigenous Women," *Tribal Tribune*, April 6, 2018, http://www.tribaltribune.com/news/article_c797c802-39ad-11e8-9c5d-e33133bc6574.html

8. See https://www.sovereign-bodies.org/mmiw-database

9. "VAWA 2013's Special Domestic Violence Criminal Jurisdiction Five-Year Report," March 20, 2018, http://www.niwrc.org/resources/vawa-2013%E2%80%99s-special-domestic-violence-criminal-jurisdiction-five-year-report

10. "Left for Dead: Inside America's Coldest Cases," *Reveal*, https://www.revealnews.org/topic/left-for-dead/page/3/?0&1

11. André B. Rosay, "Violence Against American Indian and Native Alaskan Women and Men," National Institute of Justice Research Report, May 2016, https://www.ncjrs.gov/pdffiles1/nij/249736.pdf

12. Bureau of Justice Statistics, "American Indians and Crime," December 2004, https://www.bjs.gov/content/pub/pdf/aic02.pdf

13. "Victims of Sexual Violence," *RAINN.org*, https://www.rainn.org/statistics/victims-sexual-violence

14. David K. Espey et al., "Leading Causes of Death and All-Cause Mortality in American Indians and Alaska Natives," *American Journal of Public Health* 104(suppl 3), https://www.ncbi.nlm.nih.gov/pmc/articles/PMC4035872/

15. Ronet Bachman et al., "Violence Against American Indian and Alaska Native Women and the Criminal Justice Response: What Is Known," National Institute of Justice, August 2008, https://www.ncjrs.gov/pdffiles1/nij/grants/223691.pdf

16. See https://www.congress.gov/bill/115th-congress/senate-bill/1942/text

17. John Reinan, "Pregnant Fargo Woman Was Alive when Baby Was Cut from Her Woman, Prosecutors Say," *Star-Tribune*, February 2, 2018, http://www.startribune.com/pregnant-fargo-woman-was-alive-when-baby-was-cut-from-her-womb-prosecutors-say/472388733/

18. See https://www.congress.gov/bill/115th-congress/senate-bill/1870

19. US Senate Committee on Indian Affairs, "Hoeven Bill to Reauthorize, Enhance Tribal Law and Order Act Clears Committee," February 15, 2018, https://www.indian.senate.gov/news/press-release/hoeven-bill-reauthorize-enhance-tribal-law-and-order-act-clears-committee-0

20. See https://judiciary.house.gov/press-release/house-passes-amber-alert-indian-country-act/

21. See https://www.revisor.mn.gov/bills/text.php?number=SF2768&version=latest&session=ls90&session_year=2018&session_number=0

22. Vincent Shilling, "Native Legislators in Minnesota Call for Task Force to Stop Violence," *Indian Country Today*, March 2, 2018, https://indiancountrymedianetwork.com/news/politics/mn-violence-indigenous-women/

23. Briana Bierschbach, "Legislature Proposes Finding Out Why a Staggering Number of Native American Women in Minnesota Are Murdered or Go

Missing," *MinnPost.com*, April 12, 2018, https://www.minnpost.com/politics-policy/2018/04/legislature-proposes-finding-out-why-staggering-number-native-american-women

24. See https://www.facebook.com/MMNAWM/?ref=profile_intro_card

25. See http://www.yakamanation-nsn.gov/resolution_t_057_18.pdf

26. Amnesty International, "Stolen Sisters," October 2004, https://www.amnesty.ca/sites/amnesty/files/amr200032004enstolensisters.pdf

27. See http://www.missingwomeninquiry.ca/obtain-report/

28. See http://www.idlenomore.ca/vision

29. See http://www.rcmp-grc.gc.ca/en/missing-and-murdered-aboriginal-women-national-operational-overview#sec3

30. Nash Jenkins, "Missing and Murdered Indigenous Women in Canada 'Far Higher' than Estimates," *Time*, February 17, 2016, http://time.com/4226951/native-women-canada-inquiry/

31. See http://www.trc.ca/websites/trcinstitution/index.php?p=3

32. See https://pm.gc.ca/eng/news/2015/12/15/statement-prime-minister-release-final-report-truth-and-reconciliation-commission

33. See http://www.mmiwg-ffada.ca/

34. See http://christibelcourt.com/open-letter-to-chief-commissioner-marion-buller-national-inquiry-on-missing-and-murdered-indigenous-women-and-girls/s

35. "Open Letter," August 28, 2017, https://www.scribd.com/document/355809527/Open-Letter-to-PM-Trudeau-August-8

36. Native Women's Association of Canada, "NWAC Report Card: May 2017–March 2018," https://www.nwac.ca/wp-content/uploads/2018/05/NWAC-MMIWG-Report-Card-3-May17-Mar18.pdf

37. Native Women's Association of Canada, "NWAC Supports MMIWG Inquiry's Request for Extension," March 6, 2018, https://www.nwac.ca/wp-content/uploads/2018/03/NWAC-SUPPORTS-MMIWG-INQUIRY%E2%80%99S-REQUEST-FOR-EXTENSION.pdf

38. See http://www.manitoulin.ca/2018/04/11/an-open-letter-calling-for-the-refusal-of-the-mmiwg-inquiry-extension-request/

39. Stephanie Woodard, "South Dakota Legislature Quashes New Childhood sexual-Abuse Bill," *Indian Country Today*, February 9, 2012, https://indiancountrymedianetwork.com/news/south-dakota-legislature-quashes-new-childhood-sexual-abuse-bill/

40. Jorge Barrera, "Buying and Expanding Trans-Mountain Pipeline Not a Violation of Indigenous Rights, Says Minister," *CBC*, May 29, 2018, http://www.cbc.ca/news/indigenous/trans-mountain-pipeline-bc-first-nations-1.4682395

41. Niels Lesniewski, "How Heitkamp Kept Crude Oil from Being 'Keystoned,'" *Roll Call*, December 17, 2015, https://www.rollcall.com/news/how-heitkamp-kept-crude-oil-from-being-keystoned

42. See https://www.heitkamp.senate.gov/public/index.cfm/2017/10/heitkamp-introduces-savanna-s-act-to-help-address-crisis-of-missing-and-murdered-native-american-women

43. "Oil and Crime in Indian Country," *FBI.gov*, June 7, 2016, https://www.fbi.gov/news/stories/fbi-director-visits-reservation-in-north-dakota-to-discuss-rising-threat

NICOLA HENRY AND ANASTASIA POWELL

28 TECHNOLOGY-FACILITATED SEXUAL VIOLENCE (2018)

Nicola Henry is senior lecturer in crime, justice, and legal studies at La Trobe University (Melbourne, Australia). Her research focuses on justice responses to sexual violence in international and domestic spaces. Her books include *War and Rape: Law, Memory and Justice* (2011); *Preventing Sexual Violence: Interdisciplinary Approaches to Overcoming a Rape Culture*, co-edited with Anastasia Powell (2014); *Rape Justice: Beyond the Criminal Law*, co-edited with Anastasia Powell and Asher Flynn (2015); and *Sexual Violence in a Digital* Age, co-authored with Anastasia Powell (2017).

Anastasia Powell is senior lecturer in justice and legal studies at RMIT University (Melbourne, Australia). Her research specializes in policy and prevention concerning violence against women. Her books include *Sex, Power and Consent: Youth Culture and the Unwritten Rules* (2010); *Preventing Sexual Violence: Interdisciplinary Approaches to Overcoming a Rape Culture*, co-edited with Nicola Henry (2014); *Rape Justice: Beyond the Criminal Law*, co-edited with Nicola Henry and Asher Flynn (2015); and *Sexual Violence in a Digital Age*, co-authored with Nicola Henry (2017).

Digital technologies have unequivocally transformed contemporary social life, with profound effects on information exchange and access, social interaction, democratic participation, and even emancipatory social change. Despite the seemingly endless possibilities offered by rapidly developing digital technologies, the Internet serves as a "breeding ground" for trolls, hackers, and underground criminal enterprises looking for new ways to extort, humiliate, and abuse victims. Perpetrators of domestic and sexual violence are no different and will use whatever tools are on hand to exert power and control over their victims. But how are digital technologies being used to facilitate sexual violence and harassment? And can technology play a role in preventing or addressing these harms?

To date, scholarly investigations of online predatory or abusive behaviors have largely been focused on child sexual exploitation (e.g., Kloess, Beech, & Harkins, 2014), cyberbullying (e.g., Kowalski, Limber, Limber, & Agatston, 2012), cyberfraud, and property-based offenses (e.g., Yar, 2013). Less attention has been paid to the phenomenon of technology-facilitated sexual violence, where mobile and online technologies are used to perpetrate sexual violence, sexual harassment, and/or domestic violence using blackmail, manipulation, coercion, or humiliation. Research suggests that there is a gendered dimension to these emerging abusive digital behaviors (Henry & Powell, 2015a; Powell & Henry 2017). Recent studies, for instance, suggest that young women, and women in general, are the main targets of online sexual harassment (e.g., Powell & Henry, 2016; Pew Research Center, 2014; Staude-Müller, Hansen, & Voss, 2012), intimate partner cyberstalking (e.g., Burke, Wallen, Vail-Smith, & Knox, 2011; Woodlock, 2016), and online gender-based hate speech (e.g., Ballard & Welch, 2015; Powell & Henry, 2017). In our 2015 study, we found that 20% (*N* = 563) of Australian respondents and 16.6% (*N* = 471) of UK respondents reported having experienced digital "sexual harassment" in their lifetime, with young women aged 18–24 years being significantly more likely to have experienced these harms (Powell & Henry, 2016).

A number of studies have also documented the ways in which perpetrators use digital technologies as part of their battering tactics in domestic violence contexts (NNEDV, 2014; Southworth, Finn, Dawson, Fraser, & Tucker, 2007; Woodlock, 2016) or in relation to online bullying against nonheterosexual individuals on the basis of their gender and sexuality (Green, Bobrowicz, & Ang, 2015; Walker, 2015). Despite the growing awareness of and attention to these varied forms of technology-facilitated violence, overall, little empirical research to date has investigated the phenomenon of technology-facilitated sexual violence.

The different behaviors that we discuss shortly can be viewed on a continuum of sexual violence (Kelly, 1998), allowing comparisons to be made between contact and noncontact offenses, as well as the impacts and the responses to them. This also enables the recognition of structural gender inequality and unequal power dynamics as key factors underlying the perpetration of digital forms of sexual violence (Henry & Powell, 2014; Powell & Henry, 2017). In conceptualizing technology-facilitated sexual violence, we find it useful to consider three main overlapping categories.

The first category refers to technology-enabled sexual assault and rape threats, as well as the online harassment of victim-survivors of sexual violence. Behaviors include the distribution of rape jokes, rape memes, and the promotion of rape-supportive attitudes; threats of sexual violence, including publicly posting the names and addresses of women who "deserve to be raped"; simulated sexual violence, also known as *virtual rape*; and the use of online-dating and other sites or mobile-phone apps to facilitate a contact sexual offense.

The second category refers to the nonconsensual creation or distribution (including the threat of distribution) of sexually explicit or intimate images of another person, also known as *revenge pornography, nonconsensual pornography,* or *sextortion* (Citron & Franks, 2014; Henry & Powell, 2015a; Powell & Henry, 2017). This includes images originally produced or obtained with or without the consent of the victim (including photoshopped images of a victim's face onto a pornographic image); images of a sexual assault; images obtained from the use of hidden devices to record another person engaged in a sexual act; stolen images from a person's computer or other device; and images obtained consensually or otherwise in the context of an intimate relationship. In cases where sexual assaults are recorded and then distributed via mobile phones or uploaded onto social-media websites, digital technologies provide a new medium for the continuation of the harm well beyond the original sexual assault. In the high-profile 2012 Steubenville, Ohio, case, for example, numerous individuals filmed and photographed the sexual assault of an incapacitated 16-year-old girl by two high school footballers and then proceeded to distribute the images via mobile phone and social-media sites. Such examples demonstrate not only the involvement or complicity of multiple offenders but also the significant and unique impacts on victims of these offensive acts.

The third and final category is online sexual harassment, which includes sexual solicitation (e.g., repeated requests for sex), image-based harassment (e.g., *dick pics*), and gender-based hate speech. Social-media sites, online games, mobile phones, and other devices, for example, are being used to make sexual remarks or repeated requests for sex. Offenders may use technologies to impersonate, harass, or humiliate victims, using sexual nicknames or images, or will bombard victims with erotic or pornographic images via text, e-mail, or online posts (Barak, 2005). Women gamers are often vilified on the basis of their sex. While online attacks against women may be relatively random, there are many examples of sustained campaigns that have included *doxing* (publicly revealing a person's personal details), e-mail hacking, and threats of rape and death by mobs of anonymous trolls (Chess & Shaw, 2015; Citron, 2014; Mantilla, 2013). Although many Internet service providers have acknowledged the problem of hate speech and have put in place policies and practices in an attempt to address this problem, some freedom-of-speech advocates claim that such vitriol is a form of crude or ironic humor or even a form of counterhegemony or resistance (see Jane, 2014) and that any attempt to curtail offensive speech is a violation of freedom of speech. Such arguments, however, fail to take into account the significant and damaging impacts that abusive online behaviors have on victims and on populations collectively.

These three categories are not intended to signal discrete types of sexual violence but, rather, can and often do overlap with each other, as well as with more "traditional" forms of sexual and domestic violence. Nonetheless, we argue that it is important to explicitly identify, describe, and understand these various categories and their associated behaviors since there are some differences that emerge, in particular with respect to varying levels of acknowledgment and justice responses in legal contexts and across jurisdictions.

Furthermore, while digital forms of abuse and harassment may simply resemble more conventional forms of violence, and as such, digital technologies may be no more than "tools" of abuse, it is important not to overlook the unique harms experienced by victims of digitally based harms. Such harms are "embodied" and "real" for victims (Henry & Powell, 2015b; Powell & Henry, 2017), with resonance and social implications *specifically* for women and other marginalized "others." These impacts are compounded by the fact that digital technologies act as a "force multiplier" (Yar, 2013). For instance, nude or sexually explicit images can be distributed to potentially millions of Internet users, and it may be difficult, if not impossible, to remove such images from the Internet or personal devices. Major difficulties also arise in identifying individuals who remain anonymous or immune from detection or prosecution. These unique and significant impacts mean that the strategies and interventions that are designed to address abusive behaviors must be tailored to enhance, rather than limit, the continued participation of victims in social and political life. As such, directing victims to simply "turn off their devices" or "walk away" when targeted by abusers not only fails to recognize the deep and sometimes long-lasting impacts that such behaviors can have (e.g., leaving victims feeling they are being watched or monitored 24/7) but also fails to appreciate the increasing importance or centrality of digital technology in our social and intimate lives. Moreover, the spotlight on victims only serves to further attach responsibility and blame to victims while leaving the perpetrators of these harms beyond both scrutiny and response (Henry & Powell, 2014).

It is therefore important to note the role that technology might play in . . . prevention of domestic and sexual violence. Evidence of technology-facilitated sexual violence can be preserved for prosecuting or suing offenders in criminal cases or civil litigation (Powell, 2015a). Victim-survivors have much greater access to helpful information about violence (and what they can do) through accessible online sites. Social-marketing campaigns that seek to prompt bystander intervention are further examples of the ways in which support for victims, and challenges to systemic attitudes condoning gender-based violence, can be harnessed. Social-networking and user content generation platforms also enable diverse voices and participation in renewed feminist movements across the globe, with many heralding the emergence of digital feminisms . . . (Powell, 2015b).

REFERENCES

Ballard, M. E., & Welch, K. M. (2015). Virtual warfare: Cyberbullying and cyber-victimization in MMOG play (online before print). *Games and Culture*. doi: 10.1177/1555412015592473

Barak, A. (2005). Sexual harassment on the Internet. *Social Science Computer Review, 23*(1), 77–92.

Burke, S. C., Wallen, M., Vail-Smith, K., & Knox, D. (2011). Using technology to control intimate partners: An exploratory study of college undergraduates. *Computers in Human Behavior, 27*(3), 1162–1167.

Chess, S., & Shaw, A. (2015). A conspiracy of fishes, or, how we learned to stop worrying about #GamerGate and embrace hegemonic masculinity. *Journal of Broadcasting & Electronic Media, 59*(1), 208–220.

Citron, D. K. (2014). *Hate crimes in cyberspace*. Cambridge, MA: Harvard University Press.

Citron, D. K., & Franks, M.A. (2014). Criminalizing revenge porn. *Wake Forest Law Review, 49*, 345–391.

Green, M., Bobrowicz, A., & Ang, C. S. (2015). The lesbian, gay, bisexual and transgender community online: Discussions of bullying and self-disclosure in YouTube videos. *Behaviour & Information Technology, 34*, 704–712.

Henry, N., & Powell, A. (2014). The dark side of the virtual world: Towards a digital sexual ethics. In N. Henry & A. Powell (Eds.), *Preventing sexual violence: Interdisciplinary approaches to overcoming a rape culture* (pp. 84–104). Basingstoke, UK: Palgrave Macmillan.

Henry, N., & Powell, A. (2015a). Beyond the "sext": Technology-facilitated sexual violence and harassment against adult women. *Australian & New Zealand Journal of Criminology, 48*(1), 104–118.

Henry, N., & Powell, A. (2015b). Embodied harms: Gender, shame, and technology-facilitated sexual violence. *Violence Against Women, 21*, 758–779.

Jane, E. (2014). Flaming? What flaming? The pitfalls and potentials of researching online hostility. *Ethics and Information Technology, 17*(1), 65–87.

Kelly, L. (1998). *Surviving sexual violence*. Cambridge, UK: Polity.

Kloess, J. A., Beech, A. R., & Harkins, L. (2014). Online child sexual exploitation: Prevalence, process, and offender characteristics. *Trauma, Violence, & Abuse, 15*(2), 126–139.

Kowalski, R. M., Limber, S., Limber, S. P., & Agatston, P.W. (2012). *Cyberbullying: Bullying in the digital age*. Hoboken, NJ: John Wiley & Sons.

Mantilla, K. (2013). Gendertrolling: Misogyny adapts to new media. *Feminist Studies, 39*(2), 563–570.

National Network to End Domestic Violence. (2014). A glimpse from the field: How abusers are misusing technology. Retrieved from http://staticl.square-space.com/static/51dc541ce4b03ebab8c5c88c/t/ 54e3d1b6e4b08500fcb455a0/1424216502058/ NNEDV_Glimpse+From+the+Field+-+2014.pdf

Pew Research Center. (2014, October). Online harassment. Retrieved from http://www.pewinternet.org/ files/2014/10/P1_OnlineHarassment_102214_pdfl. pdf

Powell, A. (2015a). Seeking rape justice: Formal and informal responses to sexual violence through technosocial counter-publics. *Theoretical Criminology, 19*, 571–588.

Powell, A. (2015b). Young women, activism and the "politics of (sexual) choice": Are Australian youth cultures post-feminist? In S. Baker, B. Robards, & B. Buttigie (Eds.), *Youth cultures and subcultures: Australian perspectives*. Farnham, Surrey, UK: Ashgate.

Powell, A., & Henry, N. (2016). Technology-facilitated sexual violence victimization: Results from an online survey of Australian adults (online before print). *Journal of Interpersonal Violence.* doi:10.1177/0886260516672055

Powell, A., & Henry, N. (2017). *Sexual violence in a digital age*. Basingstoke, UK: Palgrave Macmillan.

Southworth, C., Finn, J., Dawson, S., Fraser, C., & Tucker, S. (2007). Intimate partner violence, technology, and stalking. *Violence Against Women, 13*, 842–856.

Staude-Müller, F., Hansen, B., & Voss, M (2012). How stressful is online victimization? Effects of victim's personality and properties of the incident. *European Journal of Developmental Psychology, 9*(2), 260–274.

Walker, C. (2015). An analysis of cyberbullying among sexual minority university students. *Journal of Higher Education Theory and Practice, 15*(7), 44–50.

Woodlock, D. (2016). The abuse of technology in domestic violence and stalking (Online before print). *Violence Against Women.* doi:10.1177/1077801216646277

Yar, M. (2013). *Cybercrime and society* (2nd ed.). Thousand Oaks, CA: Sage.

JONATHAN GROVE

29 ENGAGING MEN AGAINST VIOLENCE (2018)

A student organizer at George Mason University, **Jonathan Grove** later served as the Men Against Violence Program Coordinator at Pacific Lutheran University's Women's Center (2006–2014). He works as a writer and consultant on "engaging men" with universities, local government, and the military alongside his primary role: raising two beautiful boys. His writing can be found at https://tacoma-washington.academia.edu/JonathanGrove

> Fighting against the world that we don't want is a critical first step, but fighting for the world that we do want is where liberation truly begins.
>
> —COURTNEY MARTIN

Engaging men in violence prevention has received increasing attention in recent years. As entire communities must be involved for effective prevention, the involvement of large numbers of men in efforts to end violence against women and children is needed. However, women have driven many of these efforts to date; men's participation is long overdue.

This article explores why men have largely been absent from anti-violence efforts and offers strategies to engage men in this work. I contextualize my approach through my own experience. I believe that our lives are the greatest resource we have for understanding each other. Further, our stories offer a point of connection for others to hear us in a profoundly human way.

What you should know about me is that my writing this article is an accident. My goal upon enrolling in college was to find a way out of financial insecurity by becoming an FBI agent. A badge and gun would secure my masculinity and class standing, *and* allow me to believe I would be helping people. What I did not realize then was that it was I who needed the "helping." Indeed, coming to terms with my experience of both privilege and trauma within systems of domination will be lifelong.

Men benefit from patriarchy in a multitude of ways and we do not often think of the price we pay for this power. I felt that any attack on the status quo was an attack on me personally, rather than on a male-dominant system. Traditional masculinity values traits like being tough, unemotional, successful, and dominant, though it is impossible for a human being to always be unemotional or successful. Men inevitably fail to perfectly embody the version of masculinity that is socially valued. As a result, many men experience tremendous insecurity because of this supposed failure. This is important, given that men exhibit hyper-masculinity in direct proportion to their feelings of insecurity about their male identity. Since gender (binary or not) is foundational to our sense of self, this insecurity is particularly profound. Given this, men unconsciously perceive attacks on the system as an attack on their source of personal value. Rather than challenge the patriarchal system that keeps us from loving ourselves, we re-double our efforts to use sexism and heterosexism to deny the value of others. What I had not realized was that my insecurity about my masculinity had caused me to hurt people. Equally, I had yet to learn to love myself regardless of how well I fit someone else's definition of who I should be. I had to stop striving to be a "man" and accept my complicated humanness. Like my whiteness, ability, or heterosexuality, I had to realize that my full humanity is only possible outside the hierarchies that deny full humanity to others.

Luckily, I had mentors who helped me to value my humanity above my masculinity. The first, an insightful professor, challenged me to consider violence *and* gender—specifically my own. She

Source: Jonathan Grove, written for *Women's Lives: Multicultural Perspectives*, 6/e and updated for this volume.

connected me with our campus Women's Center but it took two weeks for this "tough guy" to find the courage to walk in there! The center's director helped me begin to understand how others may experience parts of me in ways that parallel my own experiences of marginalization. Then another Women's Center director offered me an opportunity to both teach and continue to learn about gender, violence and privilege. These women built upon the foundation my parents created in my childhood: that boys and men can also be human.

Through this process I came to understand how patriarchy harms everyone, though in different ways. As bell hooks (1984, 2004) noted, some suffer less than others but patriarchy has the potential to make us all comrades in struggle. Drawing on this insight and my own experience, my approach to working with men has been based on three related ideas:

- *Rates of gender-based violence are high*

Although only a small percentage of men are perpetrators, levels of assault are high: 1 in 4 college women (Krebs et al. 2007) or 1 in 6 boys (Dube et al. 2005). Many men feel guilty by association. We often excuse the perpetrator by blaming the victims, or we compromise our integrity by remaining silent. Our silence effectively condones the harm done to those we love, as well as those we may never meet. While we are taught to protect patriarchy with a battle-cry of "bros before hoes," this is inconsistent with our love for the women in our lives. Men must end our collective silence about the abuse of those we love at the hands of other men.

- *Restricted ideas of masculinity limit everyone*

The homophobia, transphobia, and sexism used to narrowly define what is considered manly (or not) in our culture hurts everyone, including heterosexual cis-men (Kaufmann 1999). This hurts everyone, including heterosexual men, by creating an impossible standard of masculinity that can never be fully achieved. Dominant ideas of manhood deny us meaningful connection to ourselves and to other men. Masculinity is vaguely defined as "not female," which creates huge opportunities for insecurity for men. Lastly, all men are familiar with other men's violence from a young age. Constant competition to

not be seen as "queer" or "weak" produces the threat and experience of bullying and physical assault to ensure that men both learn to negotiate violence at a young age and accept it as normal.

- *Self-interest motivates us most effectively*

While this may sound cynical, it offers great hope in understanding what will help people change their behavior. The previous two points provide powerful motivations for men to become critical of patriarchy.

To date, relatively few men have chosen to participate in anti-violence projects and to consciously challenge hegemonic masculinity. Generally, those who do this have some pre-existing analysis of oppression and violence, often gained through their own experience around gender, sexuality, race, class, or another subordinated identity. They take Women's Studies classes, attend events like Take Back the Night, or volunteer at a shelter. Though these men certainly are familiar with dominant ideas of masculinity they do not often represent the "Average Joe." The assumption that these men will bring others into this work is false because they have little social capital in the traditional male hierarchy. Given the high cost of gendered violence, there is an immediate need for everyone to help change the culture of violence that affects us all. The overall goal is to engage the majority of men who are needed if we are to do this.

Speaking to the Majority of Men

Men cannot challenge violence rooted in sexism and heterosexism without challenging hegemonic masculinity because gender-based violence is woven into the very fabric of that identity. Men who are trapped in a hyper-masculine identity are often unable or unwilling to address violence against women and children. Doing so would require them to defy the sexism that defines what is "manly." Understanding how men might come to perceive and challenge the very thing that causes their dominance and their insecurity is critical to their involvement.

I have used two theoretical tools in my work: the "Framework for Engaging Men" (Fig. R29.1), and the work of Dr. Keith Edwards (2006), which

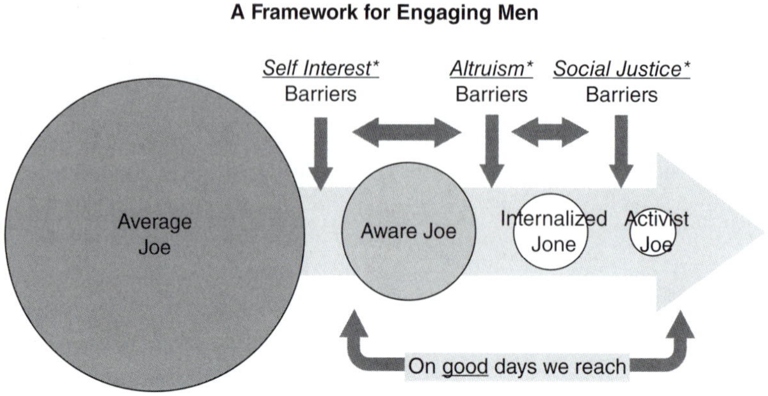

A Framework for Engaging Men

FIGURE R29.1   A Framework for Engaging Men

help us to think about how men become allies in the work against violence against women. Edwards' research provides insight into how some men move from believing that they should respond to gender violence only when it impacts someone they love, to becoming involved to protect women in general, to involvement for the sake of everyone's liberation (see Fig. R29.2). Although each man is unique, he is expected to conform to the hegemonic male norm, as mentioned earlier, which provides a commonality of experience among men. The Framework is designed to work with men as a group by speaking to that norm.

The Framework lays out a continuum showing how men in our culture might move from the understandings of an "Average Joe" to become "Activist Joes." Most men have given little thought to gender-based violence and may resist conversations about it. As they realize that some of their friends and loved ones are impacted by it (an "Aware Joe") this results in a desire to protect those they love. This may prompt a man to become concerned for women who are impacted by violence, male privilege, and his own participation in sexism (an "Internalized Joe"). Some may get stuck in a chivalrous approach to anti-violence work. Although this can provide a starting point, it is rooted in the sexism that violence against women supports. "Saving the women" does not address the central problem.

Gradually, Joe may come to understand that everyone is harmed by sexism, and begin to understand his participation in this system as both oppressor and repressed.[1] He becomes an "Activist Joe" and begins the hard work necessary for personal and societal change. For male allies on this journey, there must be a community where men can learn, share their struggles, be challenged, get feedback, and refine their views with others engaged in a similar process. If men get involved without wrestling with the costs of patriarchy to themselves—and the generally higher price that others pay within this system—they may inadvertently act from a place of paternalism that can negate their best intentions.

Although untrue, it is easy to believe that the "Average Joe" is somehow unreachable. Examining ourselves, the ways we reproduce gender norms, and the messages we received in the past, are critical steps to engaging the majority of men. Assumptions about what other men care about may be incorrect and may keep us from asking them to join our efforts. Initially, I bought into the stereotype that football players on our campus did not care about preventing sexual violence. For example, even as a former football player myself, at first I accepted the stereotype that our university's football team did not care about sexual violence when I should have known better!

The Messages Men Hear

A major initial barrier to men's involvement is the belief that gender-based violence is a "women's issue." Men hear messages based in women's

Aspiring Ally Identity Development

(Partial Summary)   Dr Keith Edwards

Aspiring Ally for:	Self-Interest	Altruism	Social Justice
Motivation	Selfish – for people I know and love	Other - I do this for them	Combined Selfishness and Altruism – we do this for us
Ally to...	A person	target group	an issue
Relationship to system	Not interested in systems – just stopping the bad people	An exception from the system, yet ultimately perpetuates it	Seeks to escape, amend, and/ or redefine the system
Privilege	Doesn't see privilege – but wants to maintain status quo	Feels guilty about privilege and tries to distance self from privilege	Sees illumination of privilege as liberating
Power	I'm powerful - protective	Empower them — they need our help	Empower us all
Admitting Mistakes	I don't make mistakes – I'm good, and perpetrators are just bad people	Difficult– struggles with critique or own issues – highly defensive about behavior	Seeks critique and admits mistakes – has accepted own isms and seeks help
Focus of the work	Perpetrators	Other members of the dominant group	My people – doesn't separate self from other agents

FIGURE R29.2   Aspiring Ally Identity Development

Dr. Keith Edwards

experience of rape culture. These often sound like: "Don't Rape." This message is based in an assumption that all men have the potential to rape (and beat, stalk etc.) if not told otherwise. This makes sense from a potential victim's perspective in which self-protection dictates that any man is a potential perpetrator. However, men's experience of this perpetrator-or-victim message is that *all* men— whose gender role not incidentally requires domination, never victimization—are rapists. Since men know this is untrue of themselves (and men they respect), and since no one wants to be called a bad person, it is not surprising that men respond very defensively to the topic when presented like this. Because this perspective does not define any helping role for them, it reinforces the idea that male violence is a women's problem.

Since men's experience of patriarchy is different from women's, effective messages must

acknowledge this. While we maintain that male experience is privileged, we must also understand and validate a man's experiences of frustration and struggle with gender roles. This provides an opportunity for him to help, to critique patriarchy, and launch a powerful conversation about how women experience his privilege. The basis for his involvement is who he is, what he values, and how that conflicts with the version of manhood he has been sold.

This focus on how men can help create change (for themselves and others) is critical to creating the space for Average Joe to minimize his defensiveness and to become an ally. Discussing masculinity produces insecurity because, while it is easy to list negative "manly" characteristics (being violent, emotion-less, controlling etc.), it is much more difficult to note positive attributes. Therefore, it is easy for men to only hear negative things about their gender. Since they may have little evidence to challenge these stereotypes, they can feel powerless and defensive in their insecurity. By focusing on men as helpers with a personal stake in change, we offer security and avoid defensiveness.

Similarly, when men model positive masculinity for boys by engaging in prevention activities, they offer an example for others to emulate. This empowers the men to continue redefining masculinity in ways that promote their identity, and shows others that it can be done. Language, practical examples, and discussions of *positive* masculinity are very rare among men. I believe we hunger for them, and the sense of security they bring. This approach validates men's own problematic experiences of patriarchy and frees them to critique a culture that sanctions rape, the de-humanization of women, queer-identified people, and men as well. By addressing self-interest, men can be allies from the start.

What Does This *Look* Like?

There are a growing number of examples of all this in practice. Events for "Average Joe" should sound like and reflect the worldview of high-status "Joes," so the discussion is relevant. One is the *Walk A Mile In Her Shoes* fundraising event, in which men raise money for anti-violence projects by walking a mile in high-heeled shoes. Although there is legitimate concern about the potential for reinforcing homophobia or transphobia, having men participate in large numbers provides an opportunity to start a conversation about these topics. Other examples are *Mentors in Violence Prevention*,[2] *Green Dot*,[3] and Men Can Stop Rape's *Where Do You Stand?*[4] that build skills and knowledge to prepare whole communities to prevent violence. These bystander engagement models offer a useful first step because they are intentional about creating a space for men to help.

During my time on the Pacific Lutheran University campus, male leaders from every corner of campus—Diversity Center, Residential Life, Campus Ministry, ROTC, Health Center, men's basketball, football and the Women's Center to name a few—were partners in our Men's Project (see Fig. R29.3). This unique collaboration allowed us to connect with the whole campus while maintaining accountability to women leaders. Additionally, the name suggested that these are men's issues without requiring guys to take a stance simply by talking with us.

This project had three central goals:

1. Collaboratively develop ideas and language for positive, healthy, responsible and equitable masculinities, as men often lack terminology to discuss their humanity in positive ways. What does it look like to be an emotionally present, courageous, and nurturing man? If you cannot describe it, living that way is far more difficult.

2. To share this language with others. This not only passes along language developed in privileged spaces, but also requires the "teacher" to fully understand and practice what he claims. Further, grounded in the belief that each person has important truths to share, it opens up a conversation in which the "teacher" may also be the learner.

3. To act out this masculinity for our communities. Many have few positive examples of what it means to be a man who is fully connected to his humanity. Providing such examples can present a powerful opportunity for hope and change. Our goal was to do projects that responded to various social justice issues and that were relevant and educational for a diverse group of men.

An example of these three goals in practice is a Men's Retreat that explores hegemonic masculinity and the costs of patriarchy in men's lives. Male leaders representing a wide range of groups and experiences help provide real-life examples of multiple masculinities and challenge male norms. Following the retreat, participants then host an event for boys with fun activities where they also share their own stories. Hearing men talk about struggling to define themselves in ways authentic to who they are, rather than accepting society's version of masculinity is a novel and potentially life changing experience for everyone involved. Moreover, legitimizing multiple versions of maleness offers permission and a pathway toward healthier manhood.

FIGURE R29.3   A basketball player supports Men As Partners Promoting Equality (MAPPE) at a Pacific Lutheran University home game.

Photo by Jonathan Grove.

Other Men's Project events include men making and serving a Mother's Day Brunch for women in a domestic violence shelter, while others did activities with their sons that discussed healthy relationships and positive expressions of masculinity. Another example is a Celebration of Children put on for kids in the community who may not get much affirmation, or who may have had few positive experiences with men. Specific examples must meet individual community needs, but the three core goals remain the same.

In all these cases, the event supports violence prevention by challenging sexism and heterosexism, while offering "Average Joe" a point of entry that supports their male identity. What is most important is providing men a welcoming and supportive environment to voice their concerns and struggles in fitting the masculine stereotype they have been taught to project. Without these conversations men are highly unlikely to engage in antiviolence efforts as they remain unable to engage with what has been labeled a "women's issue." Further, if men do get involved without wrestling with the costs to themselves and the generally higher price others pay within patriarchy, the un-checked paternalism that may come with their help may negate their efforts.

While men must maintain accountability to women's leadership in these efforts, this does not mean that we should wait for women to do our work for us. It is imperative that men who are involved in anti-oppression work take a more active role. Feminism's promise of gender equity and intrinsic human value is something men desperately want. Given the high cost in human lives, none of us can allow our fears to stand in the way.

NOTES

1. I use *repressed* here to denote that men's experience under patriarchy is not directly comparable to that of women and gender queer individuals; men retain benefits that others do not.
2. See www.jacksonkatz.com/aboutmvp.html
3. See www.livethegreendot.com
4. See www.mencanstoprape.org

REFERENCES

Dube, S. R. et al. 2005. Long-term consequences of childhood sexual abuse by gender of victim. *American Journal of Preventive Medicine* 28: 430–438.

Edwards, K. E. 2006. Aspiring social justice ally identity development. *NASPA Journal,* 43(4), 39–60.

hooks, bell. 1984. *Feminist Theory: From Margin to Center.* Cambridge, Mass.: South End Press.

_____. 2004. *The will to change: Men, masculinity and love.* New York: Washington Square Press.

Kaufman, M. 1999. Men, feminism, and men's contradictory experiences of power. In J. A. Kuypers (ed.), Men and power (pp. 59–83). Halifax: Fernwood Books.

Krebs, C.P. et al. 2007. *The campus sexual assault study final report,* National Criminal Justice Reference Service (xiii, 5-5). Oct. 2007, available at http://www.ncjrs.gov/pdffiles1/nij/grants/221153.pdf

RITA LAURA SEGATO

30 TERRITORY, SOVEREIGNTY, AND CRIMES OF THE SECOND STATE: THE WRITING ON THE BODY OF MURDERED WOMEN (2010)

Rita Laura Segato is a professor of anthropology at the Universidad de Brasilia (Brazil), where she holds the UNESCO Chair of Anthropology and Bioethics. She is also a senior researcher at the Brazilian National Council for Scientific and Technological Development. A specialist in gender-based violence and human rights, she is the author of many publications on structures of violence. In 2016, Segato was an expert witness in a case involving senior Guatemalan military officers convicted of crimes against humanity for holding fourteen women in sexual and domestic slavery.

. . . I was invited to go to Ciudad Juárez in July 2004 because in the preceding year two women from the Mexican organizations Epikeia and Nuestras Hijas de Regreso a Casa (Bring Our Daughters Home) had heard me lay out what seemed to me the only plausible hypothesis for the enigmatic crimes that haunted the city: the deaths of women of a similar physical type, which were perpetrated with an excess of cruelty, exhibited evidence of gang rape and torture, and being disproportionately numerous and continuing for more than eleven years, seemed unintelligible. . . .

. . . [I]n Ciudad Juárez, it appears that there are no coincidences. As I will try to argue, everything works as part of one complex communication machine whose messages are intelligible only to those who, for one reason or another, are able to break the code. Thus, the first problem that the hideous crimes of Ciudad Juárez pose for foreigners and distant audiences is that of intelligibility. And it is precisely in their unintelligibility that the murderers take refuge. . . . To give only one example of this . . . I turn to one of the journalist Graciela Atencio's articles on the murdered women of Ciudad Juárez. In it she questions whether it was mere coincidence that precisely on August 16, 2003, when her newspaper, the daily La Jornada of Mexico City, first published

the news of a Federal Bureau of Investigation (FBI) report "describing a possible *modus operandi* in the kidnapping and disappearance of young women" that problems with the mail prevented its distribution in Ciudad Juárez (Atencio 2003).

Unfortunately, this was not the only apparently significant coincidence during my time in the city. On Monday, July 26, after having given my first talk and halfway through our forum—and exactly four months after the discovery of the last corpse—the dead body of the maquiladora worker Alma Brisa Molina Baca appeared. I will spare you the description of the many irregularities committed by investigators and the local press regarding Alma Brisa's remains. . . . But I will note that the body was found in the same empty lot in the center of the city where another victim had been found the year before. That other victim was the murdered daughter, still a child, of the mother who we had in fact interviewed just the evening before, on July 25, in the bleak neighborhood of Lomas de Poleo, in the barren desert that crosses the border between Chihuahua and the US State of New Mexico.[1] General comments also pointed to the fact that the year before another body had been found during the federal intervention in the Mexican State of Chihuahua ordered by then President Vicente Fox.

The cards were on the table. This sinister "dialogue" seemed to confirm that we were inside the code and that the traces we were following led to a destination.

This is the interpretative path I will trace here. . . . It is a path that describes the relationship between the deaths, the illicit results of the ferocious neoliberalism globalized across the borders of the "Great Frontier" after the North America Free Trade Agreement, and the unregulated accumulation that was concentrated in the hands of certain families of Ciudad Juárez. Indeed, what stands out the most when you take the pulse of Ciudad Juárez is the vehemence with which public opinion rejects the names that law enforcement presents as the presumed culprits. It gives the impression that people want to look in another direction and are waiting for the police to direct their suspicions to the other side—to the city's rich neighborhoods.[2] The illegal traffic to the other side is of every possible type: It includes the commodities produced from the work extorted from the maquiladora workers and the surplus that the value extracted from that work adds, as well as drugs and bodies—in short, all of the considerable capital that these businesses generate south of paradise. . . .

Two things can be said of Ciudad Juárez without risk. They are, in fact, said by everybody: the police, the attorney general, the special prosecutor, the human rights commissioner, the press, and the activists. One is that "the *narcos* (drug traffickers) are responsible for the crimes," sending us to a subject that looks like a thug and reaffirming our fear of the margins of social life. The other is that "these are sexually motivated crimes." On the day after Alma Brisa's body was discovered, the newspaper repeated that this was "yet another sexually motivated crime," and the special prosecutor emphasized, "It is very difficult to reduce the number of sexual crimes"—confusing the evidence yet again and sending the public down what I believe is the wrong path. This is how, while pretending to speak in favor of the law and rights, opinion makers and the authorities foster an indiscriminate perception of the misogynist crimes occurring in Ciudad Juárez, as well as in other parts of Mexico, Central America, and the world: crimes of passion, domestic violence, sexual abuse, rape by serial aggressors, crimes related to drug debts, trafficking of women, cyber-pornography crimes, trafficking of organs, and so on. . . .

It is as if concentric circles formed by various forms of aggression are hiding in their center a particular type of crime (not necessarily the most numerous but the most enigmatic, given its precise. . . characteristics): the kidnapping of young women of a distinct physical type, most of them workers or students, who are held captive for several days and tortured, gang raped . . . , mutilated, and murdered. This is followed by the mixing or loss of clues and evidence by law enforcement, threats and attacks by lawyers and journalists, deliberate pressure by authorities to blame scapegoats who are clearly innocent—and, ultimately, the continuation of these crimes, uninterrupted, from 1993 to the present. The impunity over all these years is terrifying and can be described by three characteristics: (1) the absence of indicted perpetrators who are credible in public opinion; (2) the absence of consistent lines of inquiry; and (3) an endless repetitive cycle of this sort of crime as a consequence.

Two brave investigative journalists—Diana Washington Valdez, the author of *Cosecha de mujeres* (*Harvest of Women*; 2005), and Sergio González Rodríguez, the author of *Huesos en el desierto* (*Bones in the Desert*; 2002)—gathered numerous details that the police had set aside over the years and came up with a long list of places and people that, in one way or another, are linked to the disappearances and murders of women.[3]

I spoke with Diana Washington on two occasions . . . and I read Sergio González's book. What emerges is that people from "good" families—large landholders—are connected to the murders. But a crucial link is missing: What drives these respected, financially successful heads of prestigious families to become involved in gruesome and, as all signs indicate, collectively committed crimes? What could be the plausible link between these men and the kidnappings and gang rapes that would allow them to be identified and formally accused? A reason seems missing. It is precisely here, in the search for this reason, that the overused idea of "sexual motives" is insufficient. New classifications, legal

AP Photo/Marco Ugarte

categories, and clearer definitions are needed to be able to understand the specificity of a limited number of deaths in Ciudad Juárez. It is particularly necessary to state what appears obvious: that no crime committed by common outcasts would remain in complete impunity for this long, and no serious police force would speak so lightly of criminal motives, which generally are determined after lengthy investigation. . . .

. . . I tend not to understand the feminicides of Ciudad Juárez as crimes in which hatred toward the victim is the dominant factor (Radford and Russell 1992). I do not doubt that misogyny, in the strict sense of intense hatred of women, is common in the environment in which the crimes take place and constitute a precondition for their occurrence. Yet I am convinced that the victim is the waste product of the process, a discardable piece, and that extreme conditions and requirements for

being accepted into a group of peers are behind the enigma of Ciudad Juárez. Those who give meaning to the scene are other men, not the victim . . . The privileged interlocutors in this scene are the peers: the members of this mafia fraternity, to guarantee and seal their covenant; its opponents, to exhibit power before their business competitors, local authorities, federal authorities, activists, scholars, and journalists who dare to get mixed up in their sacred domain; or the victims' fathers, brothers, or male friends. . . .

The Feminicides of Ciudad Juárez: A Criminological Proposal

I present here a list of several ideas that together paint a possible picture of the feminicides' setting, motives, ends, meanings, and occasions and the conditions that make them possible. My problem is that the analysis can be rendered only in the form of a list. Nevertheless, the issues outlined together paint a picture that makes sense. It is not a linear list of successive items but a meaningful whole: the world of Ciudad Juárez. . . . To speak of causes and effects does not seem adequate to me; to speak of a universe of intertwined meanings and intelligible motivations does.

The Place: The Great Border

As a frontier between excess and lack, North and South, Mars and the Earth, Ciudad Juárez is not a cheerful place. . . .

It is the frontier that money has to cross, virtually and materially, to reach the firm land where capital finds itself finally safe and gives its rewards in prestige, security, comfort and health. It is the frontier beyond which capital gets moralized and reaches worthwhile, sound banks.

It is the frontier to the most patrolled country in the world, with its almost infallible tracking and close-range surveillance. Here, around this line in the desert more than anywhere else, illicit actions must be carried out in the utmost stealth and secrecy by the most cohesive clandestine organization. A rigorous pact of silence is its requisite.

This is the frontier where the great entrepreneurs "work" on one side and live on the other. It is the frontier of the great expansion and fast valorization, where terrain is literally stolen from the desert each day, each time nearer the Río Bravo.

It is the frontier of the world's most lucrative traffic—in drugs; in bodies.

It is the frontier that separates one of the most expensive labor forces from one of the cheapest.

This frontier is the background of the longest-lasting series of attacks on women's bodies with similar modus operandi known in so-called peacetime.

The Purposes

The evidence that the justice system had an extremely long period of inertia around these crimes immediately points our attention to their persistent subtext: The crimes speak of impunity . . . and as such impunity is the way into deciphering them. Although the environment I have just described, characterized by a concentration of economic and

political power and, therefore, high levels of privilege and protection for some groups, is the ideal cauldron for brewing the murders, it occurs to me that we are mistaken when we see impunity exclusively as a causal factor.

I propose that the feminicides of Ciudad Juárez can be better understood if we stop thinking of them as a consequence of impunity and imagine them as producers and reproducers of impunity. This was my first hypothesis, and it is also possible that it was the first purpose of perpetrators: to seal, with collectively shared complicity in the hideous torturing and killing of captive and defenseless women, a vow of silence able to guarantee the unbreakable loyalty to mafia brotherhoods operating across the most patrolled border in the world. The feminicides also serve as proof of the capacity for cruelty and power of death required for conducting extremely dangerous business. The sacrificial ritual, violent and macabre, unites the members of the mafia and makes their bond unbreakable. The sacrificial victim, part of a dominated territory, is forced to hand over the tribute of her body for the cohesion and vitality of the group. The stain of her blood defines the assassins' esoteric belonging to the group. In other words, more than a cause, impunity can be understood as a product, as the result, of these crimes, and the crimes can be seen as a means for producing and reproducing impunity: a blood pact sealed with the victims' blood. There is also another dimension: to give proof of the capacity for the extreme cruelty and unwavering death power that highly dangerous and illicit businesses require.

In this sense, we can point to a fundamental difference between this sort of crime and the gender crimes perpetrated in the intimacy of domestic space against daughters, stepdaughters, nieces, wives, and other victims who belong to the circle of the abuser. If in the shelter of domestic space a man abuses the women who depend on him because he can—that is, because they are part of the territory that he controls—the aggressor who takes possession of the female body in an open, public space does so because he must prove that he can. The first case is a matter of affirming an existing domination; the latter is the exhibition of a capacity for domination that must be restaged with certain regularity and can be associated with the ritual gestures that renew vows of virility. Power here is conditioned on a regularly dramatized public exhibition of a predatory action against a woman's body. . . . The classic strategy that sovereign power uses to reproduce itself . . . is to broadcast and even spectacularize the fact that it is above the law. . . . We can also understand the crimes of Ciudad Juárez in this way and suggest that they also fulfill the *exemplary function* by means of which sovereign power lets slip the crude reality of its presence in everyday life together with its underworld vitality as a ruling *second state* that is acting and shaping society from beneath the law.

This is so because, in the capacity to kidnap, torture, and kill repeatedly and with impunity, the subject/author of these crimes displays, beyond any doubt, the cohesion, vitality, and territorial control of the corporatist web that he commands and the code of norms at work in it. It is evident that the continuity of this sort of crime over eleven years requires considerable human and material resources, including the command of an extensive web of loyal associates; access to detention and torture sites; vehicles for transporting victims; and access to, influence over, or power to blackmail or intimidate representatives of public order at every level, including the federal level. What is important to note is that, as this powerful network of allies is set in motion for cover-up by those who command the corporatist crimes of Ciudad Juárez, the existence of the web is exhibited in an ostentatious display of a totalitarian domination over the area.

The Meanings

It is precisely when this last function is accomplished that the crimes begin to behave as a communication system. If we listen carefully to the messages that circulate there, we can see the face of the subject speaking through them. Only when we understand what he says, to whom and with what ends, will we be able to locate the position from which he speaks. This is why we must insist that each time the sexual-motive explanation is repeated lightly, before analyzing minutely what is being "said" in these dialogic acts, we lose a chance to follow the trail of he who hides behind the bloody text.

In other words, the feminicides are messages sent by a subject/author who can be identified, located, and profiled only by rigorously "listening" to these crimes as communicative acts. . . .

If the violent act is understood as a message, and the crimes are seen as orchestrated in a clear call-and-response style, we find ourselves in a scene where the acts of violence communicate efficiently with those who "know" the code, the well informed, those who speak the language, *even when they are not taking part directly in the enunciative action*. This is why once a communication system with a violent alphabet is installed it is very difficult to de-install and eliminate it. Violence, constituted and crystallized within a communication system, is transformed into a stable language and comes to behave in the nearly automatic fashion of any language.

To ask in these cases why there are killings in a certain place is similar to asking why a certain language is spoken there—Italian in Italy, Portuguese in Brazil. At some point, each one of these languages was established through historical processes, be they conquest, colonization, migration, or the unification of territories under one national state. In this sense, the reason we speak a certain language is arbitrary and cannot be explained by logic. The processes by which a language is wiped out, eradicated from a territory, are also historical. The problem of violence as a language is even worse if we consider that there are certain languages that, in particular historical conditions, tend to become the lingua franca and spread across the ethnic or national borders that defined their original niche.

And so we ask: Who is speaking here? To whom? What is being said? When? What is the language of feminicide? My bet is that the author of these crimes is a subject who values profit and control of territory above all else, even above his own personal happiness; a subject with an entourage of vassals who in this way makes it absolutely clear that Ciudad Juárez has landlords and that these landlords kill women precisely to show themselves as such. . . .

He, the sovereign, addresses himself to all men in the domain: to those who should have been responsible for the victim and all of the others like her in the domestic space and to those responsible for their protection as representatives of the state. He also speaks to the men of the other, either friendly or hostile fraternities to show the array of resources he has at his disposal and the strength of his support network. To his allies and business partners he confirms that the group communion and loyalty continue unaltered. He tells them that his control over the territory is total; that his web of alliances is cohesive and trustworthy; and that his resources and contacts are unlimited.

He pronounces himself in this way during the consolidation of a brotherhood; when planning a dangerous, illicit business transaction on this patrolled border; when the doors are opened to a new member; when another mafia group challenges his control of the territory; or when there are external inspections, intrusions on his total control of the area.

The language of feminicide uses women's bodies to indicate what can be sacrificed for a higher good, a collective good, such as the constitution of a mafia brotherhood. The woman's body is the supreme index of the position of she who renders tribute, of the victim whose sacrifice and consumption will be most easily absorbed and naturalized by the community. Part of this process of digestion is the usual double victimization of she who is already victim, as well as the double and triple victimization of her family, usually represented by a mourning mother. . . .

Just as it is usual for the convicted to blame their victims for their own fate and loss of freedom, in the same way the community is ever more engulfed in a misogynist cycle that, lacking appropriate support for dealing with the discomfort, leads it to blame the victim herself for the cruelty she faced. We easily choose to reduce our own suffering when confronted with testimony of intolerable injustices, alleging that "there must be a reason." In this way, the women murdered in Ciudad Juárez quickly are transformed into prostitutes, liars, partygoers, drug addicts, and all that which can inoculate us from the responsibility and bitterness of facing the injustice of their fate. . . .

Gang rape, as in pacts of blood, is the mixing of body substances of all those who take part in it; the act of sharing intimacy in its most ferocious aspect, of exposing what is kept under the greatest of zeal—sex itself, as the leak of the most intimate of all secretions. As the willing cut from where blood flows, rape is the making public of the fantasy, the transgression of a limit, a radically compromising gesture.

In the language of feminicide, the female body also signifies territory, . . . It has been constitutive of the language of wars, tribal and modern, that the woman's body is annexed as part of the nation that is conquered. The sexuality poured over it expresses the taming act, the taking possession of, when inseminating the woman's body territory. This is how the mark of territorial control by the lords of Ciudad Juárez can be inscribed on the body of the city's women as part of or as an extension of the domain they declare as their own. Rape as sexual domination implies, in conjunction, not only physical control over the victim, but also moral reduction of the victim and its associates. Moral reduction is a requisite for domination to be consummated. . . .

What, then, does *feminicide* mean in the sense that Ciudad Juárez gives to the term? It is the murder of a generic woman, of a type of woman, simply for being a woman and being of this type, in the same way genocide is a generic and lethal attack on all who belong to the same ethnic, racial, linguistic, religious, or ideological group. Both crimes are directed at a category, not a specific subject. Indeed, this subject is depersonalized as a subject, for the category it belongs to is more relevant than its individual biographical or personality traits.

But it seems to me that there is a difference between these two kinds of crimes that should be further examined and discussed. If in genocide the rhetorical construction of hate toward the other leads to the act of his or her elimination, in feminicide the misogyny that lies behind the act is a feeling more like that of hunters for their trophy: a contempt for that life or the conviction that the only value of that life lies in its availability for appropriation. . . .

The Conditions of Possibility: Asymmetry and Siege

The extreme asymmetry that results from local elites' unregulated extraction of wealth is essential to establishing a context of impunity. When the inequality is as extreme as it is in an unrestricted neoliberal regime, there is no real chance to separate legal from illicit business. Inequality becomes so extreme that it allows for absolute territorial control at a sub-state level by certain groups and their webs of support and alliance. These webs establish a true provincial totalitarianism and come to mark and express, without a doubt, the regime of control in force in the region. The torturing and murdering of women in Ciudad Juárez seem to me to be a way to signify this territorial control.

One thing that strongly characterizes totalitarian regimes is enclosure—that is, the representation of totalitarian space as a universe with no outside, encapsulated and self-sufficient, where the siege strategy of the elites hinders inhabitants' access to a different, external, alternative perception of reality. . . .

Like national totalitarianism, one of the principal strategies of regional totalitarianism is to turn the collective away from any discourse that might be called non-native, not issued and sealed by the commitment to an internal loyalty. "Foreigner" and "outsider in town" are transformed into accusations, and the possibility of speaking "from the outside" is barred. Therefore, the rhetoric is one of a cultural heritage that must be defended above all else and of a loyalty to territory that predominates and excludes other loyalties—for example, those of abiding by the law, of struggling to expand rights, and of activism and international mediation to protect human rights. . . . The idea of "us" becomes defensive, entrenched, patriotic, and anyone who infringes it is accused of treason. In this kind of patriotism the first victims are the others inside the nation, the region, the locale—always the women, the black people, the First Nations/indigenous people, and the dissidents. These inside others are coerced to sacrifice, and postpone their complaints and the argument of their differences in the name of the sacralized and essentialized unity of the collective.

It is by articulating in public discourse these "patriotic" values . . . that the media of Ciudad Juárez disqualify, one by one, foreign views of the local cruel practices on women. When we "listen" to the subtext of the discourse of the news media, when we read between the lines, we hear: "Better a local murderer, no matter how cruel, than a foreign avenger, even if he is in the right." This well-known basic propaganda strategy builds up, every day, the totalitarian wall around Ciudad Juárez and has contributed over all these years to holding back the truth from the people and the neutralization of the law, from the municipal to the federal level. . . .

The feminicides of Ciudad Juárez's are not ordinary gender crimes. They are corporative crimes and, more specifically, crimes of . . . a parallel state. As a phenomenon, they are more like the rituals cementing the unity of secret societies and totalitarian regimes. They share an idiosyncratic characteristic of the abuses of political power: They appear to be crimes without a personalized subject carried out against victims who are also not personalized: A secret force abducts a certain type of woman, victimizing her, to reaffirm and renew its capacity for control. Therefore, they are more like state crimes, crimes against humanity, where the parallel state that produces them cannot be classified for lack of efficient legal categories and procedures.

This is why it would take the creation of new juridical categories to make these crimes legally intelligible, classifiable. . . .

Epilogue

. . . [T]he theoretical, ethical, and legal issue of the feminicides is similar to the great issue of the Holocaust and its dilemmas. Both crimes are a heritage and a lesson that belong to all of humanity. Its perpetrators are not beyond the limits of our common humanity; nor are its victims gifted with an idiosyncratic and essential quality that distinguishes them from all other peoples massacred across history. Historical conditions that can transform us into monsters or the accomplices of monsters threaten us all, and the menace of becoming monsters hangs over us all, without exception, as does the threat of becoming victims. All it takes is the creation of a strict and exact frontier between an "us" and a "them" for the process to begin. . . .

But this is not the only reason I say we are facing a problem that concerns us all. As I have argued, in the particular case of the feminicides of Ciudad Juárez, I understand these to be crimes perpetrated against us, addressed to us and for us, the law-abiding citizens. What puts us into dialogue with the perpetrators is deliberate and intentional. I am saying this not in general but in the strict sense that I am convinced that these crimes are directed at us, thrown our way as a declaration of that sovereign power acting in partnership with the state persists and continues in force underneath the statutory surface. . . . These murders are aimed at exhibiting *for us* an intense capacity to produce death, an expertise in cruelty, and a sovereign domain over a territory to tell us that this is a matter of an occupied jurisdiction in which we cannot interfere. It is precisely because we disagree with this, because we think that Ciudad Juárez is neither outside Mexico nor outside the world—that we have to resist the submissive position where the murders prevent us from engaging in an active opposition to the regime they impose on us.

What to Do?

. . . I my heart of hearts I wonder whether, and am afraid that, the tragic nature of human destiny may be the pattern structuring personal lives and histories. If tragedy has one characteristic, among many, it is that it does not shelter the possibility of justice without distorting its nature. What if justice is not possible, but some occasional degree of peace is? Would any peace be enough? Could we resign ourselves to the women's murders of Ciudad Juárez simply stopping one day and slowly transforming into a thing of the past, without justice ever being done?

I ask these questions seriously, honestly. I ask them first of all of myself, in deepest privacy. If we were told that the only way out is an armistice,

would I, would you, be able to accept it? And would we be able not to accept it? I am still perplexed by this question . . . . A decade of impunity indicates that the crimes of Ciudad Juárez are crimes of power, and therefore it may be that we can only negotiate their decrease and cessation.

NOTES

Translated by Sara Koopman.

1. Alma Brisa's remains were found amid sunflowers on the same plot of land in the center of the city where the body of Brenda Berenice, daughter of Juanita, one of the main collaborators of the Epikeia project, was found.
2. For example, in November 2004 in the main plaza of the neighborhood of Coyoacán, in Mexico City, I witnessed a protest of mothers and relatives of the victims who demanded both an end to impunity for the real murderers of women and the liberation of "el cerillo," a youngster jailed and, according to them, falsely accused of the crimes. The attorney Irene Blanco, whose child suffered an attack, is also well known for her work defending Latif Sharif, who was falsely accused of the crimes, as is the work of the mothers against the jailing of the Los Rebeldes (Rebels) gang, for the same reason.
3. Also published in Spanish in Mexico and Spain, *Harvest of Women* compiles Washington's column for the *El Paso Times* newspaper. González Rodríguez was beaten and left for dead on a street in Mexico City in 2000 while he researched his book. He was hospitalized for a month and lost all his teeth.

REFERENCES

Atencio, Graciela. 2003. "El circuito de la muerte." *Triple Jornada* (monthly feminist supplement to *La Jornada*) September, 61.

Radford, J., and E. H. Diana, eds. 1992. *Femicide: The politics of woman killing*. New York: Twayne

Home and Work in a Globalizing World

Making a Home, Making a Living

Keywords: comparable worth, daddy track, feminization of poverty, gender roles, gendered division of labor, glass ceiling, living wage, mommy track, mommy tax, second shift, solidarity economy

Asking for support from family and friends, falling in love, moving in with a room-mate or partner, holding your newborn baby for the first time, breaking up with a lover, struggling to understand a teenage son or daughter, or helping your mother die in peace are commonplace events that define the very texture of our lives. This chapter explores US women's experiences of home, family, and making a living. We argue that personal and economic security is fundamental to our well-being and to the security and resilience of our families and communities.

RELATIONSHIPS, HOME, AND FAMILY

Personal and family relationships are central to individual development from baby-hood onwards, as noted in Chapter 3. In the family, we learn about socially defined **gender roles**: what it means to be a daughter, brother, wife, or father, and what is expected of us. We learn about our family's cultural heritage, ideas of right and wrong, practical aspects of life, and how to negotiate the world outside the home. As an example of this, Sara Lomax-Reese, a Black mother of three sons, asks, "how do I em-power and encourage my sons to walk tall and fearlessly in the world, but arm them with the reality that in America Black men are often considered criminals at first sight rather than students, sons, fathers" (Reading 32). Family resources, including material possessions, emotional ties, cultural connections, language, and status in the wider community, all contribute to our identity and sense of belonging.

Partnership and Marriage

How parents and siblings treat us during childhood and our observation of adult relationships provide the early foundation for our own intimate relationships. Friends and family, magazine features, advice columns, self-help books, and blog posts all coach us on how to catch a partner and how to keep them happy once we have.

Marriage is often thought to be an essential part of a woman's life, and a stigma is still attached to being single in some cultural groups. At the micro and meso levels, marriage provides recognition, validation, and status. It is the respected way of publicly affirming commitment to a partner and being supported in this by family and friends as well as societal institutions. Also, there are material benefits in terms of taxes, health insurance, pension rights, ease of inheritance, and immigration status. In 2003, the US General Accountability Office (GAO) found no fewer than 1,138 federal laws in which benefits, rights, and privileges depend on marital status (GAO 2004).

The ideal of a committed partnership seems to hold across gender and sexual identities—with women, men, trans, and gender nonconforming people looking for love—although fewer heterosexual women in the United States are marrying these days and those who do are marrying later (Traister 2016). Many women appear to be less interested in—and perhaps have less need for—what sociologist Judith Stacey (1996) called "the patriarchal bargain." Jaclyn Geller (2001) detailed the history of marriage as the institutionalization of inequalities between women and men. She viewed marriage as *the* institution that makes heterosexuality appear natural and normal, and as a heterosexual woman, she vehemently opposed it. In Reading 17, Ariane Cruz notes Black women's low marriage rates compared to white women.

Demands for marriage equality in the interest of equal treatment for LGBTQI and heterosexual couples offer an interesting counterweight to feminist critiques of marriage as inherently patriarchal. Advocates maintain that discriminatory marriage laws have denied same-sex couples the many legal, economic, and social benefits that privilege heterosexual marriages. The Netherlands was the first nation to allow gay marriage in 2001. By 2011, Argentina, Belgium, Canada, Iceland, Norway, Portugal, South Africa, Spain, and Sweden had done the same. Massachusetts was the first US state to allow same-sex marriage in 2004. In response to growing pressure for same-sex marriage, 26 states passed laws or constitutional amendments restricting marriage to a union between a man and a woman. However, as a result of lawsuits and determined political campaigning, the US Supreme Court struck down state bans on same-sex marriage in 2015 and legalized it in all fifty states. Many queer couples joyfully "tied the knot."

Others within LGBTQI communities oppose the assimilationist goals of same-sex marriage and argue that LGBTQI liberation must be much broader than the right to marry. Political science professor Mary Shanley (2004) proposed various arrangements that would support committed relationships—queer or not—such as civil unions, universal caregiving partnerships, "non-conjugal relationships of economic and emotional interdependency" (p. 112), and polyamorous relationships.

The Ideal Nuclear Family

In much public debate, the nuclear family is touted as the centerpiece of American life and invoked by conservative politicians in their rhetoric on "traditional family values." This idealized family consists of a heterosexual couple, married for life, with two or three children. The father is the provider, while the wife/mother runs the home, even if she has paid work outside. Although such families are a minority of US families today, this ideal has strong ideological impact. This family is portrayed in ads for food, cars, cleaning products, life insurance, and elder care, for example, which rely on our recognizing—if not identifying with—this symbol of togetherness. The ideal family, with its rigid, gender-based division of labor, always applied more to white families than to families of color, and to middle-class families of all racial/ethnic groups. Most women of color and working-class white women have had to work outside the home. Commonplace images of the nuclear family give no hint of family violence or the challenges inherent in juggling paid work and raising children; also, they serve to mask and delegitimize the diversity of family forms in the United States (see, e.g., Moniz 2016; Moniz and Smith 2011).

Eleanor Palo Stoller and Rose Campbell Gibson (1994) noted that "when children are orphaned, when parents are ill or at work, or biological mothers are too young to care for their children alone, other women take on child care, sometimes temporarily, sometimes permanently" (p. 162). Sociologist Barbara Omolade (1986) described

strong, female-centered networks linking African American families, which include mothers, aunties, grandmothers, and "other mothers" in the community. She opposed official characterization of these families as "dysfunctional" and showed how single mothers support one another in creating stable homes for their children. Anthropologist Leith Mullings (1997) noted that women-headed households are an international phenomenon, affected by the movement of jobs from former industrialized nations to countries of the Global South, the destruction of traditional forms of livelihood, and the dislocations caused by conflict and war. Also, an increasing number of families are split between countries, as we discuss in Chapter 8.

Queer people have established intimate partnerships and networks of friends who function as families (see, e.g., Brettschneider 2006; Howey and Samuels 2000; Moraga 1997). The Family Equality

Gina Kelly / Alamy Stock Photo

Council (2011) estimated that LGBTQI parents are raising some two million children nationally, as birth parents or adoptive parents. Same-sex couples of color are more likely to be raising children than same-sex white couples.

GENDER AND WORK

All women in the world work, whether paid or not. They are farmers, artists, craft workers, factory workers, businesswomen, maids, nannies, engineers, secretaries, soldiers, teachers, nurses, sex workers, administrators, journalists, bus drivers, lawyers, therapists, waitpersons, prison guards, doctors, cashiers, airline pilots, executives, sales staff, professors, carpenters, dishwashers, filmmakers, mail carriers, dancers, homemakers, mothers, and wives. Anthropologist Leith Mullings (1997) distinguished four kinds of women's work in her research into Black women's lives: paid work in the formal sector; reproductive work, including housework and raising children, as well as paid work taking care of children, elderly people, or those who are sick; work in the informal sector, which may be paid under the table or in favors returned; and transformational work, such as volunteering in community organizations and professional groups.

According to dictionary definitions, the English word *economy* comes from two Greek words: *oikos*, meaning "house," and *nemo*, meaning "to manage." Thus, economy can be understood as managing the affairs of the household and, beyond that, the wider society. Modern-day economists make a distinction between "productive" and "unproductive" work, which is not implied in this original definition. So-called productive work is done for money; unpaid work is considered unproductive to the economy. In this analysis, someone who makes family meals, does the laundry, finds schoolbooks and football shoes, packs school lunches, cleans the kitchen floor, waits in for the TV repair person, takes a toddler to the playground, walks the dog, meets children after school, helps with homework, soothes sick children, goes to the doctor's office with their mother, plans a birthday party for their mother-in-law, makes calls for an upcoming Parent-Teacher Association meeting, changes the cat litter, or pays household bills is not involved in the **productive economy** (Waring 1988). In most families, women have mainly done this unpaid sustenance work, without which society could not function. Even when women are employed outside the home, they still carry major responsibilities for housework and raising children, a point we return to later.

One effect of this **gendered division of labor** in the home has been a similar distinction in waged work. Although some women have broken into professions and blue-collar jobs that were once male preserves (see Figure 7.1), most women in the United States work in day care centers, elder care facilities, garment factories, food processing, retail stores, restaurants, laundries, and other women's homes. Even professional work is gendered: elementary school teachers, social workers, nurses, and health care workers tend to be female. There is an emphasis on caring for and serving others in many women's jobs; some may also require being on display and meeting dominant beauty standards.

Gendered patterns of work and assumptions about women's roles and capabilities permeate habits of thinking in the workplace. Supervisors and coworkers often apply double standards in judging women and men as workers. Journalist Lisa Belkin (2007) commented that women senior executives are often advised: take charge, but

FIGURE 7-1   Debby Tewa, solar electrician for the Hopi Foundation.

Photo: Sandia National Laboratories

don't get angry; be nice, but not too nice; speak up, but don't talk too much. She reported that women who focus on working relationships and express concern for other people's perspectives may be considered less competent than men. Women in managerial and leadership positions navigate these contradictory beliefs and assumptions as part of the job. However, if they behave in ways that are seen as more "male"—such as acting assertively, focusing on the task, or displaying ambition—they may be seen as "too tough" and "unfeminine." Awareness of such bias is an essential step toward reframing perceptions and evaluations of women's work and working styles.

BALANCING HOME AND WORK

Given the rising cost of rents and housing payments, medical insurance, and college tuition, it has become much harder for many US families to make ends meet. Much manufacturing, such as car assembly work, which was relatively well paid and mainly done by men, has been automated or moved to other countries. As a result, US men's wages have fallen on average, sometimes drastically. In response, more women have entered the paid workforce, with 60 percent of US women in waged work in 1999, a figure that grew steadily from the 1960s. The Great Recession of 2008 caused many people to lose their jobs. Economic recovery has been patchy, and slower for women, so that by 2015, 57 percent of US women were in paid work (Toossi and Morisi 2017, p. 2).

Juggling the conflicting demands of employment and family responsibilities is a defining life experience for many women. Feminist writer Adrienne Rich (1986b) argued that it is not motherhood that is oppressive but the way our society constructs motherhood. In Reading 31, journalist Claire Cain Miller echoes this point and argues that motherhood has become more demanding. She points to the fact that many parents now spend more time and money on child care, and that they feel more pressure to do enriching activities with their children and to supervise them.

Adrienne Rich advocated thinking of pregnancy and childbirth, a short-term condition, separately from childrearing, a much longer-term responsibility and one that can be shared. Feminist psychologists Nancy Chodorow (1978) and Dorothy Dinnerstein (1976) both argued that shared parenting is essential in undermining gender roles that cut off many men, practically and emotionally, from the organic and emotional needs of children, and thus disconnect them from fundamental life processes. A contemporary image of a young mother with immaculate hair and makeup, wearing a chic business suit, laptop in one hand and toddler in the other, may define an ideal for some young people. But it also sets a standard that is virtually unattainable without causing the mother to come apart at the seams, especially if she does not have a generous budget for prepared foods, work clothes, dry cleaning, hairdressing, and child care—or a partner who takes major responsibility for running the home and caring for children.

Despite contradictions and challenges, many women find great joy and affirmation in motherhood. In the early 1990s, writer and editor Ariel Gore started the upbeat zine *Hip Mama* as her senior project in college. Highlights from the first ten years provide hilarious and heart-wrenching essays "from the cutting edge of parenting" (Gore 2004; also see, e.g., Kinser 2010; A. O'Reilly 2006, 2010; Sarah 2006). Since then, young mothers have created blogs to share their satisfactions and frustrations with parenting and to seek support in this from others (see, e.g., www.blogher.com).

The Second Shift

Sociologist Arlie Hochschild (1989) introduced the term **second shift** to refer to the work of maintaining the home in addition to paid work. She researched the expectations and negotiations among married couples concerning the division of household work. Undoubtedly, this pattern varies among partners, and perhaps at different stages in their lives as well as whether they are in a same-sex relationship. Nevertheless, gendered expectations still obtain in many households, even with so many women in the paid workforce. Men may "help out" or "pitch in," but generally, they do not take the same responsibility as women. For all women and men, including those without children, only 19 percent of men on an average day in 2017 did housework—such as cleaning or laundry—compared with 49 percent of women; 46 percent of men did food preparation or cleanup, compared with 69 percent of women, a rise from 35 percent for men in 2003 (Bureau of Labor Statistics 2018a, Table 1). As a way to reduce the second shift, families rely more on take-out meals and do less cleaning than in the past. Affluent and middle-class households hire other women as cleaners, nannies, maids, and caregivers for elderly parents, which helps to free wealthier women from the stress and time crunch of balancing home and work (see Reading 33; also see Boris and Klein 2012; Duffy 2011; Poo 2015; C. Stacey 2011).

Caring for Children

In 2017, 65 percent of US mothers with children under 6 years old, and 75 percent of those whose youngest child was between 6 and 17 years old, were in full-time work (Bureau of Labor Statistics 2018b, Table 4). Mother-only families made up nearly one quarter (24 percent) of families with children (Women's Bureau 2016, p. 1). In 2014, 74 percent of Black mothers with at least one child under age 18 were the primary or only earner in their household, compared with 43 percent of Latinx families, 38 percent of white families, and 31 percent of Asian families (Women's Bureau 2016, p. 9). However, sociologist Aasha Abdill (2018) warns against the stereotype of Black men as absent "deadbeat dads." Despite race-based factors such as disproportionate unemployment and incarceration, many Black men are finding ways to be involved in their children's lives, she argues, even though they may not live in the same household.

In Reading 31, Claire Cain Miller reports that many women appear to have underestimated the demands and financial costs of motherhood, especially women with college degrees or who delayed having a baby until they were older. Child care is a major expense for many parents. Federal and state governments, employers, and labor unions offer some assistance in the form of tax credits to parents, grants to child care programs, on-site care at some workplaces, provisions for child care as part of a benefits package, flextime, leave for family emergencies, and the possibility of working from home. Taken overall, these provisions are woefully inadequate. Many parents have to piece together child care, especially before and after school and during school vacations. Politicians and policy-makers regularly declare that children are the nation's future and greatest resource, yet parents are given little practical help in raising them. The editors of *Mothering* magazine pulled no punches when they asked:

> Why is the United States the only industrial democracy in the world that provides no universal pre- or postnatal care, no universal health coverage; . . . has no national standards for child care; makes no provision to encourage at-home care in the early years of life; . . . has no explicit family policies such as child allowances and housing subsidies for all families? (Quoted in Brennan, Winklepleck, and MacNee 1994, p. 424)

Baby Blues © 2003 by Blues Partnership, Dist. By King Features Syndicate, Inc.

Twenty-five years later, this question still stands. Most European countries have instituted integrated family policies. In the United States, the few policies that support families, like tax relief, parental leave, unemployment assistance, and welfare, are uncoordinated and inadequate.

Although many parents struggle to afford child care, child care workers are poorly paid, and many have no health insurance or retirement benefits, as reported by Linda Burnham and Nik Theodore in Reading 33. On average, child care workers earn less than dog walkers, parking lot attendants, or garbage collectors. Several scholars point to a "crisis of care" in wealthy nations. In the United States, women of color and women from countries of the Global South like the Dominican Republic, El Salvador, and the Philippines are working as nannies, nursing home aides, and home health care workers, a trend that has been a growing focus of feminist research (see, e.g., Brown 2011; Flores-González et al. 2013; Folbre 2012; Hondagneu-Sotelo 2001; Macdonald 2010; Parreñas 2015).

Flextime, Part-Time, and Home Working

Despite the fact that around 70 percent of US mothers are in paid work, the labor market is still structured so that the best positions are reserved "for those adults who have someone on call to handle the life needs of an always-available worker" (Withorn 1999, p. 9). Many parents—often mothers—need flexible work schedules if they are to care for children or aging parents. This may mean working jobs that allow some flextime, seeking part-time work, or working from home. Ann Withorn (1999), a professor of social policy, noted that part-time work is often a "devil's bargain," with low wages and no benefits. Telecommuting is touted for professional and corporate workers as a means to greater personal freedom and no stressful commuting, but it also has raised expectations of workers being available and accessible for more hours than before. For some parents it may be a way to manage paid work and child care. But note that the majority of home workers are low-paid women: garment workers and child care providers.

In the 1980s, some firms adopted a "mommy track." Professional women who wanted career advancement comparable to that of men either would not have children or would be prepared to work long hours, attend out-of-town meetings, take little vacation time, and do whatever the job demanded. Otherwise, they could "opt" for the mommy track and be recompensed accordingly. Law professor and legal scholar Joan Williams (2000) argued that professional women knew full well that this would mean being marginalized in their careers, and all but a few avoid the mommy track. Some decide, reluctantly, to leave paid work in order to focus on parenting, as noted in Reading 31. Journalist and writer Ann Crittenden (2001) left a well-paid job at the *New York Times* for this reason and later calculated what this cost her in lost earnings. This discriminatory "mommy tax," as she called it, was "between $600,000 and $700,000, not counting the loss of a pension" (p. 89). In 2018, *Working Mother* magazine published a calculator to show how much money women lose when they stay at home with their kids (Kingo 2018). Anthropologist Riché Daniel Barnes (2016) interviewed Black professional women who decided to leave their careers to focus on parenting, at least while their children were young. She saw this in terms of "strategic mothering" and argued that "Black mothers continuously navigate and redefine their relationship with work to best fit the needs of their families and their communities" (p. 2). Some larger companies are providing paid parental leave for fathers. Gradually, more men are taking this, but they also worry that it will affect their career advancement.

GENDER AND ECONOMIC SECURITY

The best-paid positions in the United States are as lawyers, physicians, computer software engineers, and managers in many fields. Some women are working these jobs, but many earn the minimum wage or not much more. According to the US Census Bureau (2018, p. 1), on average women who worked full-time year-round earned 82 cents for every dollar that men earned in 2017. This was 63 cents for African American women and 54 cents for Latinas compared to white men (AAUW 2018). This gap has slowly narrowed since passage of the Equal Pay Act in 1963, when women workers earned 59 cents for men's dollar. This is partly because women's wages have improved but more because men's wages have fallen. Looking at weekly wage data by race and ethnicity, Asian American women and men had the highest earnings for the first time in 2017, compared to other groups:

	Weekly Earnings ($)	Wage Ratio
All women	770	
White women	795	88
Asian women	903	100
Black women	657	73
Latinas	603	67
All men	941	
White men	971	80
Asian men	1,207	100
Black men	710	59
Latinos	690	57

Source: US Census Bureau (2018), Table 1.

Education and Job Opportunities

Levels of education tend to correlate with earnings. Women have made steady gains in educational attainment across all racial and ethnic groups; nowadays more women than men enroll in undergraduate and graduate programs. In 2017, however, only 10 percent of women in professional occupations were employed in high-paying computer and engineering fields, compared with 46 percent of men in professional occupations (US Census Bureau 2018, Table 2). Sixty-seven percent of professional women worked in lower-paying fields, such as education and health care (US Census Bureau 2018, Table 2). Although women make up half the college-educated workforce they are only 29 percent of the science and engineering workforce and tend to specialize in social sciences and environmental sciences, which pay less well. Programs to get girls more interested in STEM (science, tech, engineering, and math) fields seek to change these numbers in the future. At the same time, high-tech employers are facing complaints that they discriminate against women workers and men of color (Levin 2017).

For many women in low-paid work, a lack of education is a key obstacle, particularly for those on welfare who need greater educational opportunity to get jobs that pay sustainable wages. Women receiving welfare used to be able to attend college and move out of poverty, including Congresswoman Barbara Lee, who graduated from Mills College (Oakland, CA). The 1996 Personal Responsibility and Work Opportunity Reconciliation Act only allows short-term vocational training or "job readiness education" as a work activity, not preparation for professional work. Scholars and activists have advocated for changes in this policy and for more academic institutions, community agencies, and foundations to provide the academic, financial, and social backing necessary for poor women to succeed (see, e.g., Adair 2004; Adair and Dahlberg 2003; Martinson and Strawn 2003; Marx 2002).

Women with disabilities generally have lower educational attainment than non-disabled women. They may have missed a lot of school as children or may not have received relevant education. Vocational schools and rehabilitation programs tend to channel women with disabilities into low-paying "women's work" or dependent roles within the family. Those who work and live independently report great satisfaction in this, but also the challenges they face: the need to make special arrangements for transportation or home care, the cost of these supports, their frustration with having to prove they can do the job, and the prejudices and ignorance of employers and co-workers (see, e.g., Mason 2004; Rousso 2013). Researcher Mary Grimely Mason (2004) found that women with a disability are likely to work part-time and have lower earnings than disabled men and nondisabled women. Lisa Schur (2004), a professor of labor studies, recommended that high schools and colleges assist women with disabilities in making the transition from school to work, that advocates and self-help organizations offer employment counseling to help them find jobs, and that these women be actively involved in developing programs to improve their job prospects. Although such meso-level changes would be helpful, more fundamental macro-level changes are also needed to eliminate the barriers to economic security for women with disabilities.

Even with a college education, however, and with equivalent work experience and skills, women are far less likely than men to get to the top of their professions or corporations. They are halted by unseen structural barriers, such as men's negative attitudes regarding senior women, negative perceptions of their leadership abilities, and skepticism about their motivation, training, and judgment. The image of a **glass ceiling** has been used to describe these obstacles. Senior women can see what the top positions in their company look like, but few women reach them, especially women of color. In Reading 34, Linda Steiner discusses journalism's "glassy architecture," with its glass doors and ceilings, pink ghettos, and velvet niches, that impedes women's advancement. Sheryl Sandberg (2013), Chief Operating Officer at Facebook, urged women to "lean in,"—to work hard, dream big, and want leadership enough—, as if such individual efforts are enough for women to reach the top. In 2018, white women held nearly a third (32.5 percent) of management positions, far more than Latinas (4.1 percent), Black women (3.8 percent), or Asian American women (2.4 percent) (Bureau of Labor

Statistics 2018c, Table 11). Women were 5 percent of CEOs and 11 percent of the top earners at Fortune 500 companies (Catalyst 2018). A related term, **sticky floor**, describes the structural limitations that affect women employed in low-paid, low-status jobs who cannot move up.

Sociologist Andrew Cutler-Seeber (2018) reported particular employment challenges for trans people. This includes discrimination in hiring, harassment from co-workers, and limited job options available. People who were able to continue in the same job before and after their transition were often better off than those who had to find new employment. Employers' expectations about career history are another factor. Trans men who worked in a female-dominated field like elementary school teaching or social work would be expected to have a career path where they rose through the ranks as if on a "glass escalator" that transports men in such fields up the organizational hierarchy. An overly "female" résumé without rapid promotion could make potential employers question their competence and hesitate to hire them (pp. 123–124).

Organized Labor and Collective Action

Members of labor unions usually make significant gains in pay and working conditions compared to non-union workers. In 2017, women union members in full-time work earned 30 percent more than non-union women. Analysis by race/ethnicity showed that Asian American women union members earned 14 percent more than Asian American women who were not union members. For Black women, the difference was 23 percent; for white women, 32 percent; and for Latinas, 36 percent (Patrick and Heydermann 2018). Also, union workers are more likely to have health and pension benefits. Currently, women—many of them women of color—are joining unions at a faster rate than men, particularly hotel workers (HERE), service employees (SEIU), garment workers (UNITE), public employees (AFSCME), and communication workers (CWA).

The majority of women in the US workforce are not union members. This is partly due to the decline of unions nationally in recent decades and partly due to the fact that many women work in jobs that are hard to unionize, such as retailing or the fast-food business, where they are scattered at separate locations. Further, the nation's largest employer, Walmart, is strongly anti-union. Walmart's stringent cost-cutting—of prices, wages, and operating costs—has redefined corporate practice, summed up in the phrase: the "Walmart-ing" of the economy.

Instead of the standardized minimum wage, some labor organizers campaign for a "living wage" that reflects regional variations in the cost of living. Others use a "self-sufficiency standard" that "provides a measure of income needed to live at a basic level" (Women's Foundation 2002). The "Fight For $15," now a national movement backed by the Service Employees International Union (SEIU), started in 2013 when fast-food workers walked off the job in New York City. This campaign has gained increases in the minimum wage in several cities over the past few years, with demands for $15 an hour.

Over two million women—domestic workers, nannies, housekeepers, and caregivers—take care of families and homes in the United States, as mentioned earlier (also see Reading 33). Mostly women of color or immigrants, these workers are particularly vulnerable due to the isolated nature of their work, which takes place behind closed doors and out of the public eye. Domestic work was specifically excluded from the 1935 National Labor Relations Act. In 2007, the National Domestic

Workers Alliance and affiliated groups started organizing for recognition and fair labor standards. In 2010, the state of New York introduced the first Domestic Workers Bill of Rights, bringing domestic workers into line with workers in other industries. Since then, seven other states have done the same, meaning that domestic workers in these states are entitled to minimum wage or more, overtime pay, and meal breaks, regardless of their citizenship or immigration status. This campaign continues with the goal of eliminating discrimination against domestic workers nationwide.

Working and Poor

In public debate, poor people are often assumed to be on welfare, masking the reality of life for many low-income people, some of whom are working two or even three minimum-wage jobs. Others work part-time or seasonally. They may be involved in the informal economy as babysitters or gardeners, for example, or doing home work for the garment trade, fixing cars, carrying and selling small amounts of drugs, getting money for sex, or selling roses at off-ramps. In Reading 35, Emir Estrada and Pierrette Hondagneu-Sotelo report on their research with Latina teens who work three shifts: schoolwork, housework, and selling food in street markets as part of a family business. The authors comment on the way childhood for middle-class children has been constructed to mean school and play rather than being economically productive. By contrast, these street-vending girls take on adult-like responsibilities and work alongside their parents to help their families make ends meet.

More women than men live in poverty worldwide, which led feminist researchers to use the term **feminization of poverty** (see, e.g., Abramovitz 1996; Dujon and Withorn 1996; Sidel 1996). The two poorest groups in the United States are women raising children alone and women over 65 years living alone. Women of color are more than twice as likely to be poor compared with white women. *Poverty* is a complex term, with economic, emotional, and cultural dimensions. One may be materially well off but emotionally impoverished, for example, and vice versa. Poverty also needs to be thought about in the context of costs and responsibilities—for housing, food, transportation, health care, child care, and clothes needed for work—hence the importance of a self-sufficiency standard. Poverty is also linked to social expectations. For example, many poor children in the United States bug their families for expensive name-brand clothing in response to high-pressure advertising.

Women with disabilities are another low-income group. Policy researchers Peiyun She and Gina A. Livermore (2006) found that a majority of those in the working-age population who experience long-term poverty have a disability. As noted earlier, many employers are reluctant to hire people with disabilities. But more than that, the employment system discriminates against them as it is organized in inflexible ways that cannot accommodate many people with disabilities.

Pensions, Disability Payments, and Welfare

For women who cannot work because of illness, age, or disability, and for those who are made redundant or who cannot leave their children, there is a complex patchwork of income-support measures and means-tested allowances provided by federal and state governments and private pension plans. Pensions are based on wage levels while the person was working and on the number of years in paid work. Women's pensions are significantly lower than those paid to men because, on average, women earn less than men, they are more likely to work part time, and they may move in and out of the workforce to care for children. Fifty-five percent of women over 65 years of age rely on Social Security for 50 percent of their income or more (Tucker and Matsui 2018). For older Black women and Latinas, Social Security is the most common source of income (Institute for Women's Policy Research 2011).

Social Security and Social Security Disability Insurance allow individuals who are considered to be "deserving" to draw from an insurance fund to which they have contributed during their working lives. By contrast, welfare payments are based on the concept of public assistance. In 1996, the federal government ended entitlement to assistance, which dated back to the 1935 Social Security Act, and replaced those earlier entitlements with Temporary Assistance for Needy Families (TANF). TANF is a work-based program with lifetime limits and an emphasis on marriage incentive programs. Women are required to spend up to 40 hours a week in "work experience." For employers, TANF has the advantage that—in place of wages—it is paid out of state funds.

Myths about welfare recipients abound in public discourse, stigmatizing those who need to rely on assistance because their family caregiving work is not paid. Typically, TANF rates are too low to live on, which means that recipients have to supplement their welfare checks in some way. Not reporting additional income to the welfare office may make women liable for criminal charges for perjury or fraud. No one who is wanted by law enforcement officials for a felony or for violating the terms of parole or probation—which may be something as little as missing a meeting—can receive any government benefits. Anyone found guilty of a drug-related felony is banned from receiving benefits for life. States can require drug tests, fingerprints, and photographs from applicants for benefits. Women who give birth to a child while on welfare are denied a financial increase despite the fact that they have another child to care for. Law professor Kaaryn Gustafson (2005) argued that poor families are penalized in several ways: through "completely inadequate levels of support, . . . public shaming, and . . . intrusive administrative forays into their personal lives that none but the truly needy would tolerate" (p. 2). She has researched government surveillance of people on welfare and the investigation of alleged welfare fraud, which she describes as "the criminalization of poverty" (Gustafson 2011). Several welfare-rights organizations have sought to redefine welfare as caregivers' income, including Every Mother Is a Working Mother Network (Los Angeles, CA and Philadelphia, PA) and Welfare Warriors (Milwaukee, WI) (see, e.g., Nadasen 2005; Orleck 2005; Reese 2005). Currently, government supports for poor or older people, from food stamps (Supplemental Nutrition Assistance Program [SNAP]) to Social Security, are being cut or are under threat, which particularly affects low-income women.

It is important to note that many people in this society receive some kind of government support. This includes income-tax deductions for homeowners, medical benefits for those who have served in the military, tax breaks to corporations, agricultural subsidies to farmers, government bailouts to banks, or government funding for high-tech, military-related research conducted by universities and private firms. This is often not mentioned in discussions of welfare, but it should be.

Understanding Class Inequalities

Class is a key concept in any discussion of economic security. For Marxist theorists, a person's class is defined in relation to economic production—whether they must work for a living. The vast majority of people in the United States are workers, but most describe themselves as *middle class*, a loose term that includes a wide range of incomes, occupations, life situations, and levels of personal and economic security. In much public debate, class is more of a psychological concept than an economic one. Poverty is often explained as resulting from low self-esteem, laziness, or dysfunctional families, as pointed out in Chapter 2. In Reading 11, Dorothy Allison notes the power of class stratification, racism, and prejudice whereby

> some people begin to believe that the security of their families and community depends on the oppression of others. . . . It is a belief that dominates this culture; it is what made the poor whites of the South so determinedly racist and the middle class so contemptuous of the poor.

Class differences among US women are enormous. Calls for educated women to break into top-echelon positions in business and politics do nothing to change the fact that women make up two-thirds of low-wage workers, almost half of them women of color.

As mentioned in Chapter 5, government studies and census data are analyzed for racial differences, which gives the impression that race is more significant than class. Intersectional analysis makes class one facet, among others, of a person's or group's social location. In practice, race and class overlap. More attention to economic inequality may provide a basis for alliances between people of color and white people along class lines (see the box feature "Economic Inequalities"). In this society, work is an

---

Economic Inequalities

- America's top 25 billionaires together hold $1 trillion in wealth: real estate, bank deposits, stocks and bonds, life insurance, pension plans, mutual funds, equity in businesses, and trust funds. These 25 billionaires have as much wealth as 56 percent of the population, a total of 178 million people or 70 million households (Collins and Hoxie 2017).

- In 1980, 11.5 million children lived in poverty in this country; in 2016, this had increased to 13.2 million. Eighteen percent of children are poor; Black, Latinx, and Native American children are more than twice as likely to be poor as white children (Children's Defense Fund 2017, p. 1).

- One in five US children do not have enough to eat (Edmond 2017).

- In 2018, a federal minimum-wage job paying $7.25 an hour for a full-time, year-round worker with two children provided a family income of $15,080. In

that year the federal poverty level for a three-person family was $20,780 (DHHS 2018).

- In 2016, US CEOs in the largest firms made 271 times the annual average pay of a typical worker, up from a ratio of 59:1 in 1989 and 20:1 in 1965 (Mishel and Schieder 2017).

- The United States leads the world in Gross Domestic Product (GDP) (Statista 2017), military expenditures, and military exports (McCarthy 2017) but ranks high among industrialized nations in child poverty (Edmond 2017).

- Citizens in several US cities are using GoFundMe campaigns for families who cannot pay for school meals (Quart 2018).

- In 2018, 42 people in the world held as much wealth as the 3.7 billion who made up the poorest half of the world's population (Elliott 2018).

economic necessity, and the "work ethic" carries strong moral overtones. Note that this principle is not applied to those among the very rich who live on unearned income from corporate profits, investments, trust funds, or rents.

RESILIENCE AND SUSTAINABILITY

Given the gender wage gap, and the struggle many women face in balancing home and paid work, feminist scholars, policy-makers, and activists have argued for good-quality child care subsidized by government and employers, shared parental responsibility for children, regular payment of child support, and redrawing the terms of divorce so that both postdivorce households have the same standard of living. Also, many local projects help women to start small businesses as an alternative to working low-waged jobs.

Feminist advocates have encouraged women to return to school to improve their educational qualifications and have opposed sexual harassment at work. Researchers and policy analysts have challenged inequities in pay between women and men. These disparities may be partly explained by differences in education, qualifications, and work experience, but part of this wage gap is simply attributable to gender. This insight led to analysis of the **comparable worth** of women's jobs when examined alongside men's jobs. Advocates have argued that wage rates should be based on the knowledge and skills needed to perform a job, the mental demands or decision-making involved, accountability or the degree of supervision, and specific working conditions, such as how physically demanding and dangerous a job is. Such analysis has revealed discrepancies in pay between women's work and men's work and some re-evaluation of wage rates.

Organizations focused on improving women's workplace conditions include the Institute for Women's Policy Research (Washington, DC), the National Organization for Women (Washington, DC), and 9 to 5 (Milwaukee, WI). Several groups have created opportunities for women to enter well-paying trades like carpentry and construction, including Hard Hatted Women (Cleveland, OH), Massachusetts Tradeswomen Association, Sisters in the Building Trades (St. Paul, MN), and Vermont Works for Women (Winooski, VT).

Low educational attainment, low wages, having children, and divorce all undermine women's economic security. Also, the nature of this economic system, with its booms and slumps, impacts wages rates and the availability of work. The Great Recession of 2008 was a severe setback for many people who lost jobs or homes, or who saw the value of their home or pension drop dramatically (Hayes and Hartmann 2011). Employers downsized jobs and replaced full-time workers with part-timers at lower wages and without benefits. Unemployment, poverty, and hunger increased. For some people, this was a temporary crisis; for others, it has been more permanent.

If technological trends continue—with increased automation, robotics, and use of artificial intelligence—many people in the United States, especially young people of color, will never be in regular, full-time employment in their lives. Such changes force us to confront fundamental contradictions that affect how we think about and organize work in this society and globally:

What should count as work?

Does the distinction between "productive" and "unproductive" work make sense?

How should work be rewarded?

How should those without paid work be supported?

How can inequalities between haves and have-nots be justified?

Is the work ethic useful?

Is materialism the mark of success?

In response to such questions, various feminist thinkers are calling for a new economy (see, e.g., Allard, Davidson, and Matthei 2007; Boggs 2011; Folbre 2006). Riane Eisler (2012), a lawyer and social scientist, contends that a change in the economic system will require "reexamining underlying cultural beliefs about what is valuable or not valuable" (p. 67). She emphasizes the fact that economic systems are human creations and argues for much greater investment of resources in caring for people and for nature. Eisler advocates a partnership model centered on egalitarian and democratic relationships in the family and the state. Similarly, Vandana Shiva (2005), a researcher and advocate concerned with sustainable development, has argued that a sustainable economy means putting people and nature, rather than the market system, at the center. She notes that nature's economy, which is primary to human survival, depends on ecological processes, such as the water cycle, oxygen cycle, and nitrogen cycle that sustain forests, wetlands, and all forms of life. Second, the sustenance economy must be valued, including everything people provide to maintain their lives: biological reproduction, creating a home, socializing and educating children, training workers, and caring for all members of society.

Some have used the term **solidarity economy** to refer to these ideas and related projects like worker cooperatives that are democratically controlled, local currencies and bartering schemes, and sustainable food projects. Examples include the Women's Bean Project (Denver, CO), Tierra Wools (Los Ojos, NM), Four Winds Weavers (Winslow, AZ), White Earth Land Recovery Project (Callaway, MN), and the Dudley Street Neighborhood Initiative (Boston, MA). We need more thinking and organizing to link these inspiring but often isolated projects into a more sustainable system. In Reading 60, several international women's organizations have articulated feminist principles for a just economy that contribute to this discussion.

QUESTIONS FOR REFLECTION

As you read and discuss this chapter, think about these questions:

1. What do you hope for in an intimate relationship?
2. How do you define family? Whom do you consider your family?
3. What changes are necessary to involve more men in parenting? Look at the micro, meso, macro, and global levels of analysis.
4. What have you learned through working? About yourself? About other people's lives? About the wider society? How did you learn it? Who were your teachers?
5. Is there anything you have wanted to change in your work situations? What would it take to make these changes? What recourse do you have as a worker to improve your conditions of work?
6. How do you justify differences in pay?

FINDING OUT MORE ON THE WEB

1. Find out about family policies in Western European countries (especially Denmark, France, Germany, the Netherlands, and Sweden). Why do you think these countries provide better supports for families than the United States?

2. Delve deeper into these issues by exploring organizational websites such as:
   9 to 5 National Association of Working Women: www.9to5.org
   Children's Defense Fund: www.childrensdefense.org
   Coalition of Labor Union Women: www.cluw.org
   Institute for Women's Policy Research: www.iwpr.org
   Moms Rising: www.momsrising.org
   National Jobs for All Coalition: www.njfac.org

3. Find out how much the government spends on welfare compared with other federal expenditures:
   National Priorities Project: www.nationalpriorities.org
   War Resisters League: www.warresisters.org/federalpiechart

TAKING ACTION

1. Talk with your peers about your non-negotiables in a personal relationship. What are you willing to compromise on, if anything? Why? Under what circumstances?

2. Draw up a detailed budget of your needs, expenses, income, and savings. What did you learn by doing this?

3. Talk with your mother or grandmother (or women of their ages) about their experiences of marriage, parenting, family, and work. What opportunities did they have? What choices did they make? What similarities and differences do you notice between your own life and theirs at the same age?

4. Look critically at how magazines, ads, movies, and TV shows portray women in relationships and the family, and as workers. What is being promoted through these media?

CLAIRE CAIN MILLER

31 THE COSTS OF MOTHERHOOD ARE RISING, AND CATCHING WOMEN OFF GUARD (2018)

Claire Cain Miller is a correspondent for *The New York Times*. She writes about gender, families, and the future of work for *The Upshot*, a *Times* site for analysis of policy and economics. She was part of a team that won a Pulitzer Prize in 2018 for public service for reporting on workplace sexual harassment issues. Before joining the *Times* in 2008, Ms. Miller covered the tech industry for *Business Day*.

An economic mystery of the last few decades has been why more women aren't working. A new paper offers one answer: Most plan to, but are increasingly caught off guard by the time and effort it takes to raise children.

The share of women in the United States labor force has leveled off since the 1990s,[1] after steadily climbing for half a century. Today, the share of women age 25 to 54 who work is about the same[2] as it was in 1995, even though in the intervening decades, women have been earning more college degrees than men, entering jobs previously closed to them and delaying marriage and childbirth.

The new analysis[3] suggests something else also began happening during the 1990s: Motherhood became more demanding. Parents now spend more time[4] and money[5] on child care. They feel more pressure[6] to breast-feed,[7] to do enriching activities[8] with their children and to provide close supervision.[9]

A result is that women underestimate the costs of motherhood. The mismatch is biggest for those with college degrees, who invest in an education and expect to maintain a career, wrote the authors, Ilyana Kuziemko and Jenny Shen of Princeton, Jessica Pan of the National University of Singapore and Ebonya Washington of Yale.

The study—a working paper, meaning it has not yet been published in a peer-reviewed journal—tries to quantify what many parents feel as they struggle with the stress[10] of long, inflexible work hours[11] combined with the demands of STEM classes, screen time rules, college prep, family dinners and children's sick days.

The researchers documented a sharp decline in employment for women after their first children were born, in both the United States and Britain, even though about 90 percent of women worked before having children. They used data from the Labor Department's National Longitudinal Surveys, the University of Michigan's Panel Study of Income Dynamics and the British Household Panel Survey. Each covers several decades, but the study focused mostly on women born between 1965 and 1975, who were in their 30s in the 2000s.

For many women, the researchers show, stopping work was unplanned. Since about 1985, no more than 2 percent of female high school seniors said they planned to be "homemakers" at age 30, even though most planned to be mothers. The surveys also found no decline in overall job satisfaction post-baby. Yet consistently, between 15 percent and 18 percent of women have stayed home.

One key to understanding why women have diverged from their plans, the economists found, is that their beliefs about gender roles change after their first baby. The surveys ask questions like whether work inhibits a woman's ability to be a good mother and whether both parents should contribute financially to a family. Women tend to give more traditional answers after becoming mothers.

The people most surprised by the demands of motherhood were those the researchers least expected: women with college degrees, or those who had babies later, those who had working mothers and those who had assumed they would have careers. Even though highly educated mothers were less likely to quit working than less educated mothers, they were more likely to express anti-work beliefs, and to say that being a parent was harder than they expected.

Though the study did not analyze fathers' role in depth, it found that their beliefs did not change significantly before and after having a baby. They were less likely than women to say that parenthood was harder than they expected. (Women still do the bulk of child care, even in two-earner families.)

Women got it so wrong, the researchers argue, because it has become harder to work and have children.

The cost of motherhood fell[12] for most of the 20th century because of inventions like dishwashers, formula and the birth control pill. But that's no longer the case, according to data cited in the paper. The cost of child care has increased by 65 percent since the early 1980s. Eighty percent of women breast-feed, up from about half. The number of hours that parents spend on child care has risen, especially for college-educated parents, for whom it has doubled.

Overall, women have had great success in entering the labor force. Seventy percent[13] of mothers with children under 18 work. Women are more likely to work[14] than previous generations at almost every age,[15] found Claudia Goldin, a Harvard economist. They're slightly more likely to stop in their late 30s and early 40s, around the time many are taking care of young children—but they usually return to the labor force, particularly if they have degrees.

Still, the new paper raises questions about why the work-family juggle seems to be getting harder. "It is deeply puzzling that at a moment when women are more prepared than ever for long careers in the labor market, norms would change in a manner that encourages them to spend more time at home," the researchers wrote.

One possible reason is that increasingly, people who work long, inflexible hours are paid disproportionately more, Ms. Goldin's research has found.[16] More women with degrees and these kinds of demanding jobs are having children, and they're likely to be married to men with similar jobs, as Marianne Bertrand, an economist at the University of Chicago, has described.[17] A result is that dual-earning couples may feel the best choice is for one member, usually the mother, to step back from work so the other parent can maximize the family's earnings.

To try to set their children on the best path amid increased competition for college admission, parents, especially college-educated ones, invest significantly more time than they used to in child care, found Valerie Ramey and Garey Ramey, economists at the University of California, San Diego. They described it as the "rug rat race"[18] for top colleges.

The lack of family-friendly policies in the United States—such as paid family leave and subsidized child care—most likely plays a role,[19] too. Although policies have improved somewhat since the early 1990s, women's labor force participation in countries that have more generous policies has continued to increase, unlike in the United States.[20]

As women do more paid work, men have not increased their child care and housekeeping tasks to the same extent[21]—another surprise for young women who, research[22] has shown, expected more egalitarian partnerships.

Generations of girls have been told they can achieve anything they aspire to, including having both a career and children—and many women have done so. But at the same time, both work and parenting have become more demanding. The result is that women's expectations seem to be outpacing the realities of public policy, workplace culture and family life.

NOTES

1. Federal Reserve Bank of St. Louis, "Labor Force Participation Rate: Women," https://fred.stlouisfed.org/series/LNS11300002

2. Federal Reserve Bank of St. Louis, "Employment Rate: Aged 25–54: Females for the United States," https://fred.stlouisfed.org/series/LREM25FEUSM156S

3. Ilyana Kuziemko, Jessica Pan, Jenny Shen, and Ebonya Washington, "The Mommy Effect: Do Women Anticipate the Employment Effets of Motherhood?" NBER Working Paper 24740, June 2018, http://www.nber.org/papers/w24740

4. Suzanne M. Bianchi, John P. Robinson, and Melissa A. Milkie, *Changing Rhythms of American Family Life* (New York: Russell Sage Foundation, 2007).

5. Care.com Editorial Staff, "This Is How Much Child Care Costs in 2018," *Care.com*, July 17, 2018, https://www.care.com/c/stories/2423/how-much-does-child-care-cost/

6. Claire Howorth, "Motherhood Is Hard to Get Wrong," *Time*, October 19, 2017, http://time.com/4989068/motherhood-is-hard-to-get-wrong/

7. Lori Gottlieb, "'Lactivism, by Courtney Junt," New York Times, December 14, 2015, https://www.nytimes.com/2015/12/20/books/review/lactivism-by-courtney-jung.html

8. Claire Cain Miller, "Class Differences in Child-Rearing Are on the Rise," *New York Times*, December 17, 2015, https://www.nytimes.com/2015/12/18/upshot/rich-children-and-poor-ones-are-raised-very-differently.html

9. Kim Brooks, "Motherhood in the Age of Fear," *New York Times*, July 27, 2018, https://www.nytimes.com/2018/07/27/opinion/sunday/motherhood-in-the-age-of-fear.html

10. Claire Cain Miller, "Stressed, Tired, Rushed: A Portrait of the Modern Family," *New York Times*, November 4, 2015, https://www.nytimes.com/2015/11/05/upshot/stressed-tired-rushed-a-portrait-of-the-modern-family.html

11. Claire Cain Miller, "The 24/7 Work Culture's Toll on Families and Gender Equality," *New York Times*, May 28, 2015, https://www.nytimes.com/2015/05/31/upshot/the-24-7-work-cultures-toll-on-families-and-gender-equality.html

12. Claudia Goldin, "The Quiet Revolution that Transformed Women's Employment, Education, and Family," *AEA Papers and Proceedings* (May 2006): 1–21, https://scholar.harvard.edu/goldin/publications/quiet-revolution-transformed-womens-employment-education-and-family

13. Mark DeWolf, "12 States about Working Women," US Department of Labor Blog, March 1, 2017, https://blog.dol.gov/2017/03/01/12-stats-about-working-women

14. Claire Cain Miller, "More Women in Their 60s and 70s Are Having 'Way Too Much Fun' to Retire," *New York Times*, February 11, 2017, https://www.nytimes.com/2017/02/11/upshot/more-women-in-their-60s-and-70s-are-having-way-too-much-fun-to-retire.html

15. Claudia Goldin and Joshua Mitchell, "The New Life Cycle of Women's Employment: Disappearing Humps, Expanding Middles, Sagging Tops," *Journal of Economic Perspectives* 31(Winter 2017), 161–1852, https://pubs.aeaweb.org/doi/pdfplus/10.1257/jep.31.1.161

16. Claudia Goldin, "Hours Flexibility and the Gender Gapin Pay," Center for American Progress, April 2015, https://scholar.harvard.edu/files/goldin/files/goldin_equalpay-cap.pdf

17. Marianne Bertrand, "Coase Lecture—The Glass Ceiling," *Economia* 85(April 2018), 205–231, https://onlinelibrary.wiley.com/doi/abs/10.1111/ecca.12264

18. Gary Ramey and Valerie A. Ramey, "The Rug Rat Race," NBER Working Paper 152 84, August 2009, http://www.nber.org/papers/w15284

19. Francine D. Blau, and Lawrence M. Kahn, "Female Labor Supply: Why Is the US Falling Behind?" NBER Working Paper 18702, January 2013, http://www.nber.org/papers/w18702

20. Claire Cain Miller and Liz Alderman, "Why US Women Are Leaving Jobs Behind," *New York Times*, December 12, 2014, https://www.nytimes.com/2014/12/14/upshot/us-employment-women-not-working.html

21. Claire Cain Miller, "Men Do More at Home, but Not as Much as They Think," *New York Times*, November 12, 2015, https://www.nytimes.com/2015/11/12/upshot/men-do-more-at-home-but-not-as-much-as-they-think-they-do.html

22. Claire Cain Miller, "Millenials Aren't the Dads They Thought They'd Be," *New York Times*, July 30, 2015, https://www.nytimes.com/2015/07/31/upshot/millennial-men-find-work-and-family-hard-to-balance.html

32   BLACK MOTHER/SONS (2016)

Sara Lomax-Reese is the President and CEO of WURD Radio, Pennsylvania's only African American–owned talk radio station, which works on air, online, and in the community. Prior to her work with WURD, she cofounded *HealthQuest: Total Wellness for Body, Mind & Spirit*, the first nationally circulated African American health magazine. She has won numerous awards and was recognized as one of the "100 People to Watch" by *Philadelphia Magazine* and selected for the "Women of Distinction" award by the *Philadelphia Business Journal*.

I will not allow this twoness to fracture my mind, body, and spirit. W. E. B. DuBois nailed it back in 1903 when he wrote: "It is a peculiar sensation, this double-consciousness, this sense of always looking at one's self through the eyes of others, of measuring one's soul by the tape of a world that looks on in amused contempt and pity. One ever feels his twoness, an American, a Negro; two souls, two thoughts, two unreconciled strivings; two warring ideals in one dark body, whose dogged strength alone keeps it from being torn asunder."[1]

One hundred and thirteen years later, DuBois's words ring with a truth and clarity that haunts me as the mother of three Black sons. I am utterly confounded when I confront this timeless struggle that Black mothers have wrestled with for hundreds of years: how do I empower and encourage my sons to walk tall and fearlessly in the world, but arm them with the reality that in America Black men are often considered criminals at first sight rather than students, sons, fathers, men—full human beings?

Any illusion that, with the election of our first Black president, America has evolved beyond its racist roots was shattered in a quiet neighborhood in Sanford, Florida, in 2012 when Trayvon Martin was stalked, shot, and killed by George Zimmerman. My knee-jerk reaction was to try and find something about this boy that separated his experience from my three sons, two of them close to his age. But at the end of the day, what was so completely terrifying was the reality that Trayvon Martin could have been any Black teen, including my son: the jaunt to the local convenience store for some junk food (check), the hoodie (check), the cell phone conversation chronicling his every move (check). He was a young kid doing what young kids do and ended up gunned down, dead.

Listening to my then fourteen-year-old son and his friends trying to make sense out of this one was absolutely heartbreaking. "Glad I don't live in Florida," said one. "I'm not wearing any more hoodies," said another. And when I asked my son Elijah what would he do in a situation similar to Trayvon's, he said he would confront the person stalking him. "No, no, no," I said, "that's what got Trayvon killed. The goal is for you to get home alive." But the twisted reality is that there is no credible plan to give your child in this kind of situation.

I recently had the opportunity to attend an interview between Tracy Martin, Trayvon's father, and Philadelphia journalist and WURD Radio talk show host, Solomon Jones. With a quiet, calm dignity, Martin shared the intimate details of his son's birth. He told of being the first person to hold baby Trayvon in his arms; the boundless love that engulfed him; the personal commitment to be his mentor, guide, protector, friend throughout his lifetime. He talked of their close relationship, even though he was separated from Trayvon's mother—weekends at the local basketball court, telephone conversations that always ended with "I love you." He was a committed, loving father, fully engaged in his son's life. Eventually, the inevitable came when he shared the heart-breaking story of the night Trayvon was murdered. Unlike me, sniffling with tears dripping down my face, Tracy Martin spoke plainly, with strength and determination, of the utter horror that shattered his family's life. I left that event in a fog of sadness and confusion. How could this man survive what surely would have killed me? Not only did he have to endure the absurdity of George Zimmerman's murderous fear, he had to confront a criminal justice system that did everything to justify his son's killing. The slander included: Trayvon had used drugs; he wasn't a great student; he had been suspended from school—anything to confine this young man to the box of "Black male criminality." And, therefore, the theory goes, he deserved what he got. In fact, George Zimmerman was just protecting his neighborhood from a "menacing thug."

But Trayvon was just the beginning. Over the past four years, the death toll kept rising: Jordan Davis, also in Florida; Eric Garner in Long Island; Michael Brown in Ferguson; Tamir Rice in Cleveland. And the unfathomable reality is that even when caught on video or with eyewitnesses, in most of these cases, the killers, often police officers, were exonerated.

As the mother of Black sons, the harsh truth is that there is no sane answer for the insanity of racism. The weight of this brutal reality, while insisting that my sons can achieve anything, reach for their dreams, have boundless success, is at the heart of DuBois's twoness. It can really make you crazy—or depressed—or resilient.

Perhaps this twoness is at the heart of our creative genius. Throughout time, Black people have been innovative, creating brilliance out of chaos. From Negro Spirituals to Ragtime, Jazz to Hip Hop, we have figured out a way to transform pain into power. This is the message I try to marry with the inexplicable in an effort to empower my children.

I also want my children to believe in the innate kindness that exists in most people—another dimension of the twoness. Despite the realities of racism, discrimination, and injustice, I still have a deep and abiding belief in human decency. One day, my then ten-year-old son Julian asked me: "Is there any place in America where Black people are equal to white people?" Once again I was stumped. While I hemmed and hawed, trying to find an

optimistic answer for my youngest child, I sadly concluded, no. This blunt answer, however, had some caveats. I asked him if he felt discriminated against in his day-to-day life. At that time he was a fourth grader at Germantown Friends, a Quaker school in Philadelphia. As he thought about it, he concluded that his friends and teachers treat him with respect and kindness. So my more nuanced answer was that people are generally kind and decent on a one-on-one basis. However, there are deep structural policies rooted in this country's historic avoidance of its racist past and present that have created institutional racism and inequality.

This was seen with profound clarity on March 4, 2015, when the Justice Department released its findings on the widespread corruption in the Ferguson, Missouri, police department and court system. It proved irrefutably that Black people were being over-policed, picked up on minor or manufactured charges that carried jail time and large fines, which were then used to fund the city. What better example of Michelle Alexander's theory that we're living in the "New Jim Crow"?[2]

Black people have always been an economic engine of the American economy. From chattel slavery, when America prospered on the backs of 250 years of free labor, to the Ferguson findings, our exploitation is a part of America's capitalist system. Our current reality is the natural extension of a nation built on DuBois's "twoness." Even as the phrase "all men are created equal" was being penned in the Declaration of Independence, white men were conspiring to institutionalize the permanent dehumanization of Black men and women. That chasm between lofty democratic ideals and the daily practice of buying and selling human beings is the cancer that has metastasized into our current reality. Today, the promise of America still rings hollow for many Black Americans who disproportionately live in communities with the highest poverty rates, underfunded and low-performing public schools, and an often hostile police presence.

I think about my parents, who left West Philadelphia in 1968 to raise six children—three boys and three girls—in Bucks County, at that time, an almost all-white rural community about an hour north of Philadelphia. While I wasn't conscious of it then, my siblings and I were part of the "integration generation." When I look back and realize how there were just a few short years between the widespread, state-sanctioned terror of the pre-1960s and my arrival at an all-white elementary school in Perkasie, Pennsylvania in 1974, I am inspired by the general kindness that I received from teachers, students, and parents. Even still, while I don't have tales of cross burnings or beat downs, there was a palpable undercurrent of being "other." While seemingly accidental, the N-word made regular appearances. This was way before Black music, style, and culture was synonymous with cool. I am proud of the eight-year-old me that was able to navigate my personal twoness—a home that was defiantly Black, with conversations about race and racism discussed regularly, and a school life that was so deeply invested in whiteness that anything associated with the color Black was synonymous with wholesale inferiority.

My parents provided me with a powerful roadmap for raising children, especially Black boys, in a society firmly grounded in presumptive white privilege. While they undoubtedly feared for the well-being of their children, they gave us incredible freedom and independence to travel our own paths. As my mother used to say, "I'm going to surround you with the light." Essentially she was saying, "I can't control what happens to you once you go out into the world. It is in God's hands, the ancestors, and the power of the Divine." It was a way of surrendering to the unknown, a way to make peace with your worst fears. As I look at it now, as a parent, I think it was about mental survival.

Their weapon for arming us against the macro and micro aggressions we faced in our daily lives was Black art, culture, family, and history. Our home was filled with vibrant paintings, soulful music, and heated conversation that reflected the complexity, genius, and diversity of the Black community. My parents were intent upon exposing us to the brilliance of Blackness through classic stage plays like *Purlie*, *The Wiz*, and *Black Nativity*. They would pack all six of us into the car to go see Stevie Wonder or The Temptations or the Edward Hawkins Singers. Annual trips to Jamaica exposed us to life in a Black nation where Blackness was the norm, not the exception. Weekly jaunts to West Philly for Sunday dinner at our grandmother's house provided psychological, spiritual, and physical soul food. A deep exhale. These moments allowed us to shed armor we didn't even know we were carrying.

My hope is that my husband and I are sowing similar seeds of pride and possibility in our sons, creating a wellspring of consciousness embedded deep inside their minds, bodies, and spirits, ready to be tapped when needed. This is our attempt at unifying the negative aspects of our double consciousness—the twoness—that for centuries has sought to fracture the souls of Black folks.

NOTES

1. Du Bois, W. E. B. 1903. *The Souls of Black Folk*. New York: Dover Publications.

2. Alexander, M. 2010. *The New Jim Crow: Mass Incarceration in the Age of Colorblindness*. New York: The New Press.

LINDA BURNHAM AND NIK THEODORE

33 | EXCERPT FROM "HOME ECONOMICS: THE INVISIBLE AND UNREGULATED WORLD OF DOMESTIC WORK" (2012)

Linda Burnham is Research Director of the National Domestic Workers Alliance. She is co-founder and former Executive Director of the Women of Color Resource Center and has published numerous articles on African American women, African American politics, and feminist theory.

Nik Theodore is Associate Professor in the Department of Urban Planning and Policy at the University of Illinois at Chicago and former Director of the Center for Urban Economic Development. He has published widely on economic development, labor markets, and urban policy.

Domestic workers are critical to the US economy. They help families meet many of the most basic physical, emotional, and social needs of the young and the old. They help to raise those who are learning to be fully contributing members of our society. They provide care and company for those whose working days are done, and who deserve ease and comfort in their older years. While their contributions may go unnoticed and uncalculated by measures of productivity, domestic workers free the time and attention of millions of other workers, allowing them to engage in the widest range of socially productive pursuits with undistracted focus and commitment. The lives of these workers would be infinitely more complex and burdened absent the labor of the domestic workers who enter their homes each day. Household labor, paid and unpaid, is indeed the work that makes all other work possible.

Despite their central role in the economy, domestic workers are often employed in substandard jobs. Working behind closed doors, beyond the reach of personnel policies, and often without employment contracts, they are subject to the whims of their employers. Some employers are terrific, generous, and understanding. Others, unfortunately, are demanding, exploitative, and abusive. Domestic workers often face issues in their work environment alone, without the benefit of co-workers who could lend a sympathetic ear.

The social isolation of domestic work is compounded by limited federal and state labor protections for this workforce. Many of the laws and policies that govern pay and conditions in the workplace simply do not apply to domestic workers. And even when domestic workers are protected by law, they have little power to assert their rights.

Domestic workers' vulnerability to exploitation and abuse is deeply rooted in historical, social, and economic trends. Domestic work is largely women's work. It carries the long legacy of the devaluation of women's labor in the household. Domestic work in the US also carries the legacy of slavery with its divisions of labor along lines of both race and gender. The women who perform domestic work today are, in substantial measure, immigrant workers, many of whom are undocumented, and women of racial and ethnic minorities. These workers enter the labor force bearing multiple disadvantages.

Home Economics: The Invisible and Unregulated World of Domestic Work presents the results of the first national survey of domestic workers in the US. It breaks new ground by providing an empirically based and representative picture of domestic employment in

Source: Reprinted with permission of the authors and the National Domestic Workers Alliance.

twenty-first century America. We asked a sample of domestic workers a standardized set of questions focusing on four aspects of the industry:

- pay rates, benefits, and their impact on the lives of workers and their families;
- employment arrangements and employers' compliance with employment agreements;
- workplace conditions, on-the-job injuries, and access to health care;
- abuse at work and the ability to remedy substandard conditions.

We surveyed 2,086 nannies, caregivers, and house-cleaners in 14 metropolitan areas. The survey was conducted in nine languages. Domestic workers from 71 countries were interviewed. The study employed a participatory methodology in which 190 domestic workers and organizers from 34 community organizations collaborated in survey design, the fielding of the survey, and the preliminary analysis of the data.

Summary of Findings

The survey revealed that substandard working conditions are pervasive in the domestic work industry. Wage rates are low, the work is often hazardous, and workers rarely have effective recourse to improve substandard conditions.

- Low pay is a systemic problem in the domestic work industry.
  - 23 percent of workers surveyed are paid below the state minimum wage.
  - 70 percent are paid less than $13 an hour.
  - 67 percent of live-in workers are paid below the state minimum wage, and the median hourly wage of these workers is $6.15.
  - Using a conservative measure of income adequacy, 48 percent of workers are paid an hourly wage in their primary job that is below the level needed to adequately support a family.
- Domestic workers rarely receive employment benefits.
  - Less than 2 percent receive retirement or pension benefits from their primary employer.
  - Less than 9 percent work for employers who pay into Social Security.

- 65 percent do not have health insurance, and only 4 percent receive employer-provided insurance.
- Domestic workers experience acute financial hardships. Many indicate that their most basic needs go unmet.
- 60 percent spend more than half of their income on rent or mortgage payments.
- 37 percent of workers paid their rent or mortgage late during the year prior to being interviewed.
- 40 percent paid some of their other essential bills late during the same time period.
- 20 percent report that there were times in the previous month when there was no food to eat in their homes because there was no money to buy any.
- Domestic workers have little control over their working conditions. Employment is usually arranged without the benefit of a formal contract.
  - Key provisions in standard employment agreements are often absent for domestic workers.
  - 35 percent of domestic workers report that they worked long hours without breaks in the prior 12 months.
  - 25 percent of live-in workers had responsibilities that prevented them from getting at least five hours of uninterrupted sleep at night during the week prior to being interviewed.
  - 30 percent of workers who have a written contract or other agreement report that their employers disregarded at least one of the provisions in the prior 12 months.
  - Among workers who are fired from a domestic work job, 23 percent are fired for complaining about working conditions, and 18 percent are fired for protesting violations of their contract or agreement.
- Domestic work can be hazardous. Workers risk long-term exposure to toxic chemicals and a range of workplace injuries.
  - 38 percent of workers suffered from work-related wrist, shoulder, elbow, or hip pain in the past 12 months.
  - 31 percent suffered from other soreness and pain in the same period.

- 29 percent of housecleaners suffered from skin irritation, and 20 percent had trouble breathing in the prior 12 months.
- 36 percent of nannies contracted an illness while at work in the prior 12 months.
- 29 percent of caregivers suffered a back injury in the prior 12 months.
- Domestic workers experience disrespect and abuse on the job.
  - Interviews with domestic workers reveal that they often endure verbal, psychological, and physical abuse on the job—without recourse. Domestic workers, who are unprotected by contracts and laws available to other workers, fear employer retaliation.
  - 91 percent of workers who encountered problems with their working conditions in the prior 12 months did not complain because they were afraid they would lose their job.
  - 85 percent of undocumented immigrants who encountered problems with their working conditions in the prior 12 months did not complain because they feared their immigration status would be used against them.

Summary of Recommendations

The report offers a set of recommendations that could transform the working conditions of domestic workers. Action is required on several fronts:

- We must enact and enforce policies that rectify the exclusion of domestic workers from employment and labor laws. Among these protections are the right to organize, earn the minimum wage, get paid for overtime, take regular rest and meal periods, claim workers' compensation and unemployment insurance, have healthy and safe work environments, and have effective remedies for discrimination, abuse, and harassment. In addition, policies are required to assure benefits, such as paid vacation and holidays or notice of termination, that are difficult for domestic workers to negotiate with their employers. Policies are needed to address issues particular to live-in workers, such as standard hours of uninterrupted sleep.

- Employers can be a significant part of the solution if they educate themselves about workers' rights and hold themselves accountable to fair labor standards. Employers should be prepared to provide domestic workers with a contractual agreement, fair wages including overtime pay and regular pay raises, access to affordable medical care, secure retirement income, paid leave, and a safe and healthy work environment. Practicing respectful communications and keeping accurate records of hours worked can go a long way toward improving the quality of the employment relationship.

- We must create a more equitable economic environment for all low-wage workers. It is difficult to advocate for the rights of domestic workers in an economic and political environment in which the rights of low-wage workers more broadly are so badly frayed. An increase in the federal minimum wage, a strengthened safety net, paid sick and family leave, access to affordable medical care, and opportunities for career advancement for the low-wage workforce would be major steps toward improving job quality and quality of life for domestic workers. The immigrant workforce would benefit dramatically from a pathway to citizenship. Public policies that raise standards across the low-wage labor market will positively influence the lives of domestic workers.

- We also need to offer social support to families with caregiving responsibilities. Families scramble to craft individual solutions to manage the competing priorities of home, work, and family. Meeting the challenges of intergenerational care will require policy commitments to make high-quality child care affordable and widely available, to assist families that care for elders in their homes, and to support women who struggle to balance their work and family obligations. Bold solutions will be needed to address the changing generational demographics underway, especially an increased need for home-based, long-term care for the aged.

Domestic workers are an essential part of the solution. Domestic work, though conducted in private homes, contributes substantially to the public good. Household labor is a lynchpin connecting the economics of the home and the economics of the workplace. By committing to improving domestic workers' conditions of work, policy makers and employers—and indeed society as a whole—commit to building an economy based on dignity and care.

We have the opportunity to improve, materially and substantially, the conditions of a critical and especially vulnerable sector of our labor force. Both in the US and globally, a domestic workers' movement for rights and respect has been steadily gaining strength. Domestic workers, through their organizing, are pointing the way forward. It is past time for both employers and policy makers to take heed.

LINDA STEINER

34 GLASSY ARCHITECTURES IN JOURNALISM (2014)

Linda Steiner is Professor of Journalism at the University of Maryland and editor-in-chief of the journal *Journalism and Communication Monographs*. Her research focuses on alternative media, gendered media employment, women and technology, and ethics. She has won awards for feminist scholarship and has published widely, including the co-edited books *Critical Readings: Media and Gender* (2004) and the *Routledge Companion to Media and Gender* (2014).

Many theories have been proposed to explain why more women are not news media executives and why, as either journalists or leaders of news organizations, women have not had more impact on journalism. Using data about US news media, this chapter considers several concepts used to explain (none convincingly) why women and men should behave differently, but seemingly do not, when producing news content or running newsrooms. For several decades, when any single newsroom had only one or two women reporters, the leading theory was that when women are present only as tokens they cannot challenge prevailing practices [and] so cannot achieve significant organizational change. Meanwhile, the assumption was that media representations have major impact, that representations reflect their makers, and that when women could, they would want to produce different kinds of content. Now that women are at least one-third of newsroom staffs, the paucity of women at the upper echelons of media industry organizations is a popular explanation for newsrooms' resistance to new ways of doing journalism. It's more complicated, however.

Gender in the Newsroom: The Statistics

A progressive nonprofit that works to make women visible and powerful in media, the Women's Media Center, amassed statistics from several sources with regard to roles of women in US media in 2012 (Klos 2013):

- . . . At newspapers, women were 18 percent of publishers and held 34.2 percent of supervisory positions. Women held 37 percent of all job categories; women of color are 6 percent of newsroom staffs.
- Men were far more likely than women to be quoted (across news platforms), including with respect to abortion, birth control, and women's rights.
- At both legacy and online news sites, women are often relegated to "pink topics"—food, family, furniture, and fashion.
- On Sunday TV talk shows, women were 25–29 percent of roundtable guests.
- Seven of 100 honorees on the Daily Beast's Digital Power Index were women.
- Women were 30 percent of television news directors.
- Women directed 39 percent of documentaries shown at major festivals.
- Women were 20 percent of radio news directors. One woman—the conservative Laura Ingraham—was among the ten most important radio talk show hosts.

The Historic Glass Door

At least before the second-wave women's movement took hold, the widely perceived problem for women was that media organizations had a "glass door" (Hassink and Russo 2010): Women stood on the outside looking in, but could not get inside. If they were hired, to continue the

Source: *The Routledge Companion to Media and Gender*, edited by Cynthia Carter, Linda Steiner, and Lisa McLaughlin (New York: Routledge, 2014). Reproduced by permission of Taylor & Francis Books UK.

architectural metaphors, they remained on a sticky floor; at best they climbed a frustrating pink ladder essentially leading them nowhere. The writer Nora Ephron (2010) described working, in 1962, at *Newsweek*: "If you were a college graduate (like me) who had worked on your college newspaper (like me) and you were a girl (like me), they hired you as a mail girl. If you were a boy (unlike me) with exactly the same qualifications, they hired you as a reporter and sent you to a bureau." Ephron moved from mail girl to clipper to fact-checker, without noticing *Newsweek's* "brilliantly institutionalized" sexism, before getting a job at the *New York Post*.

Women rarely still celebrate the pink ladder. The Pink Ladders website collects stories about women ascending pink ladders while integrating personal and work life "into a fully blended experience" (http://pinkladders.com). More typically, even women who have found satisfaction in the media's pink ghetto, or climbed to the top of the women's pages, have resented the constraints. Some women have overtly resisted. In 1970, forty-six *Newsweek* women filed the first class-action sex-discrimination lawsuit; their action against the magazine's "caste system" (Povich 2012: 3) came, ironically, the same day as *Newsweek's* cover story on the feminist movement. Sex- and race-based discrimination suits soon followed elsewhere, first at Time Inc. magazines, and then at the *Washington Post*, *Newsday*, the *Detroit News*, and the *Baltimore Sun*. In 1977 *Reader's Digest* agreed to pay $1.5 million to 2,600 women employees. The *New York Times* promised $200,000 to 550 women and a new affirmative-action plan (and probably retains the best record of hiring women). Lynn Povich became *Newsweek's* first woman senior editor in 1975. Yet, women still encounter significant sexism. As Povich says, cultural transformation is harder than legal reform.

The Notion of Critical Mass

Finding that isolation prohibited women from offering new visions or implementing new management methods, Rosabeth Moss Kanter (1977) proposed that once (but not before) women were about one-third of an organization women could form alliances, support one another, and affect group culture. This notion of critical mass, which nuclear physicists use to refer to the quantity needed to start a chain reaction, became hugely popular among feminists and underwrote their optimism. Once women reached "critical mass" in a work environment, activists thought, they would change their institutions. Media and journalism scholars likewise argued that women should be hired because, once hired in sufficient numbers (again, this was usually estimated to be around 30 percent), they would redefine news and reform news organizations. Once women reporters reached this irreversible turning point, they would produce, and women would get, more, and more accurate, news coverage. Meanwhile, lack of critical mass was often referenced to explain why women's work was not (yet) more different from men's. One woman columnist said: "You have to have 'the rule of three' functioning before there will consistently be impact. If there is just one woman in a story conference or editorial page meeting, you have to blend in. If there are two, you compete for attention. When there are three women, you reach a critical mass" (quoted in Mills 1997: 45).

Once women journalists approached or surpassed 30 percent of newsrooms, the search began in earnest for evidence of the difference they made. For example, data suggest (summarized in Steiner 2012) that women are more likely to use a greater diversity of sources, going beyond officials and political and social elites to cite nonelites and nongovernmental or unofficial figures, including women. The evidence is not overwhelming, however; large-scale surveys do not show significant gender differences, including in ethics (see, e.g., Weaver et al. 2007). Whether this is a matter of organization-specific factors, socialization of women into prevailing definitions of newsworthiness originated by men, or dictates from the top, women do not overturn newsroom conventions or volunteer a distinctly woman's perspective.

. . . In any case, since most stories are both assigned and edited, differences in topics and approach perhaps say more about assignment and editorial processes than individual choice.

Ironically, achieving critical mass briefly provoked hysteria that journalism was becoming a pink ghetto (Beasley and Theus 1988). This claim that women's successful incursion into journalism inevitably would undermine journalism, including by lowering salaries and thereby pushing out men, borrowed from findings about other pink ghetto or pink collar jobs such as child care, nursing, and secretarial work. Since jobs typically associated with women tend to be lower in status and pay than those of men, when a domain shifts from male to female dominated its pay and prestige fall in a vicious circle, thus facilitating the entry of more women. Notably, only slightly better are the velvet ghettos, that is, spheres employing mainly women, who in this case are high profile (implying affirmative action, diversity, and progressiveness), albeit essentially powerless. Indeed, in the mid-1980s public relations "slid" into a velvet ghetto, dominated by women, as men left for higher-status, higher-pay jobs. Meanwhile, having hired many women in their public relations divisions, corporations were less pressured to hire women in more influential jobs. For some years, two-thirds or more of PR practitioners in the US have been women (Toth et al. 1998). Other research similarly indicates that, generally, managers earn less when their subordinates, peers, or supervisors are largely women (and younger), at least once women hit a 50 percent threshold; women in women-dominated industries and workplaces also suffer pay inequities (Pollard 2006).

As it turns out, the decrease in journalism's pay and status should be connected to interrelated changes in technology, a general de-skilling of journalism, and the emergence of online and citizen projects, and a corresponding (if not resulting) decline in newspapers. Journalism has become neither a pink nor a velvet ghetto. In any case, theories regarding the pink ghetto and critical mass are conceptually and empirically weak. At best these endorse a kind of double bind for women, whatever the domain—politics, business, or journalism— requiring women to bring something distinctive to the table and to be an advocate for an agenda, but simultaneously to uphold journalism's professional ideology and value system. Women journalists appear to have opted for the latter.

The Glass Ceiling in Leadership

In the 1980s, attention shifted to women's difficulties getting into high-level, high-status, and high-paying jobs. That is, the issue became the glass ceiling, an invisible barrier to promotion to leadership positions, such that, in the US, white and African American women can see elite positions but cannot attain them. Among Fortune 500 companies, women constituted only 3.6 percent of the chief executive officers, 6 percent of the highest-paying positions, 16 percent of the corporate officers, and 16.6 percent of the board members (Catalyst 2012). More specifically, in 2012 the CEOs of the top 15 media corporations (a mix of print, online, television, and radio) were all men; only 17 percent of their board members are women. Global news media research found glass ceilings for women in twenty of fifty-nine nations studied, with women holding 27 percent of the top management jobs (Byerly 2011).

The Federal Glass Ceiling Commission's (1995) report identified several barriers in businesses that could be relevant to news organizations, including recruiting practices that fail to seek out women and minorities, a prevailing white male culture, unfair performance and evaluation standards, sexist treatment, stereotyping and harassment by colleagues, lack of family-friendly policies, and lack of role models. Highlighting the problem for women of a long, slow track to promotion, the Commission also highlighted "pipeline" barriers—lack of mentoring and of management training, clustering women in staff positions that don't lead to the top. While some say not enough women are in the pipeline, others contend that credentialed, trained women are being unjustly held back from advancement by unacknowledged "leaks" or "blockages" in the pipes. The Commission's report in 1995, when 97 percent of the senior managers of the largest 1,000 companies were white men, noted that underlying all of these barriers may be the fear of many white men that they were losing control of their advancement opportunities.

Usually, the term "glass ceiling" is attributed to Gay Bryant, a magazine editor (*Family Circle* and *Working Woman*), who first used the term during a 1984 interview. Later Bryant expanded on the related problem of getting stuck in middle management, called a "sticky ladder":

> Women may already be in middle management, but the steps from there up to the senior hierarchy are likely to be slow and painstakingly small. Partly because corporations are structured as pyramids, with many middle managers trying to move up into the few available spots, and partly because of continuing, though more subtle, discrimination, a lot of women are hitting a "glass ceiling" and finding they can rise no further. (Bryant 1985: 19)

The intersection of the glass ceiling with critical mass, then, suggests women are artificially and wrongly prevented from moving into decision-making positions where they would, and could, buck male norms. The "topping-out factor" suggests that what matters most is having women at the very top, with three remaining the magic number. One study of corporate boards found that "a critical mass of three or more women can cause a fundamental change in the boardroom and enhance corporate governance" (Kramer et al. 2006). The Thirty Percent Coalition, a US advocacy organization of business leaders and women's groups, insists that corporate boards with a "critical mass" of at least three women have richer discussions, better decision-making, more collaborative management, and stronger organization (http://www.30percentcoalition.org/). The Supreme Court is similarly offered as a perfect example: One woman Justice is newsworthy as a "first"; two is better but still an exception; and once three women sit on the Court, they stop being unusual (White House Project 2009).

Applied to journalism leadership, the idea was that only when women attained high-level management and executive positions in critical mass could they undo the newsroom's macho culture and encourage news serving women. The paucity of women executives and editors and publishers would explain why women were not bringing about significant changes, despite their presence as reporters. This was consistent with David Manning White's (1950) study of a single wire editor whose personal and even idiosyncratic beliefs of newsworthiness shaped the news. The Glass Ceiling Commission said something similar in 1995: lack of ownership of media outlets by minorities and women negatively impacts news reporting; greater diversity at the top could reduce stereotyping.

The glass ceiling is not absolutely impenetrable.[1] But women attempting to breach the organizational and/or cultural barriers risk serious injury from the broken glass; women close to the glass ceiling experience the greatest pay gap. As it turns out, some research connects overall wage gaps not so much to the gender gap at top levels, but rather to a "glass escalator" that quickly and smoothly transports white men through the organizational ranks (Smith 2012). As a result, white men retain a wage, benefits, and promotion advantage at each level of authority, such that wage gaps are wider between white men and other groups even for employees who report to women and minorities. Other group differences are important, too. For example, women journalists, especially executives, are significantly less likely than men to live with a partner or have children, just as, among US executives, 90 percent of men but 65 percent of women have children; and women are twice as likely as men to delay having children (Pollard 2005; Robinson 2005).

Notably, as with the issue of women journalists, rhetoric about women's leadership has shifted from fairness and equality to women's superiority. A research institute says Fortune 500 companies with high percentages of women officers are generally more profitable because appointing women to the board signals that the company is already doing well; moreover, women bring new skills to the mix (Curtis 2012). Women leaders were rated by peers, bosses, and other associates as better overall leaders than their male counterparts, but scored especially higher than men on integrity and "nurturing" competencies such as building relationships (Zenger and Folkman 2012).

Such celebrations of women's profound impact as executives notwithstanding, newsroom gatekeeping did not change with "Ms. Gates," nor do women newsroom executives generally promote other women. One so-called Ms. Gates selected few stories dealing with women's issues or featuring women as the main subject or main source and she denied that gender regularly influenced her decision-making (Bleske 1991). Women and men editors and television news directors seem to make similar decisions (Burks and Stone 1993). Likewise finding no significant gender differences among managers regarding coverage of political figures' private lives, Splichal and Garrison (2000) concluded that managers are rewarded for conformity and adapting to newsroom culture. Somewhat later studies also found that editor gender made little difference to which topics were covered, although women-headed newspapers tended to focus on positive stories and to treat reporters with gender equity slightly more often than newspapers headed by men (Craft and Wanta 2004). At a March 27, 2013 panel on "Diversity in a Digital Age" held at the University of Maryland, Mary Bryne, managing editor for sports at *USA Today*, bragged that she had personally selected for publication the cheesecake photographs of a coach's wife. Photographs of the bikini-clad former model would bring "clicks" from the audience, Bryne said, "and I need clicks."

One explanation for this failure to find gender difference is simply that running a major news organization—and earning profits when profits are rare—requires the same logic of women and men. One might also argue that women and men who make it to the top have learned the same professional ideology and values. Alternatively, women leaders' difficulties in counteracting a male-dominated culture have been said to reflect lack of critical mass at the top. Yet, even when women held the top four leadership positions at the Sarasota (FL) *Herald-Tribune*—more than meeting the standard for critical mass—its news content did not differ much from newspapers led by men, although it placed a high value on teamwork, collaboration, and family–work balance (Everbach 2006). That said, Gallagher correctly ridicules fears that women are already invading and feminizing journalism's upper echelons:

It is as if one woman at the top is as much as the system can absorb without being thrown into a paroxysm of professional anguish about the potential effects on status, salaries, self-esteem of "feminization." . . . The "one at a time" mentality vis-à-vis women in senior editorial management precludes the possibility of women building up the kind of power base necessary for real change either in terms of journalistic output or in the way the institutions of journalism are organized. (Gallagher 2001)

The Glass Cliff

Michelle Ryan and Alex Haslam (2007) analyze the "glass cliff." The glass ceiling's obverse, this predicts that leadership positions awarded to women carry greater risks of failure. Women do not always fail as executives, of course; but they seem more often to be asked to accept difficult jobs before getting enough information and tools, or where no one is likely to succeed. Moreover, when women fail, their poor performance is attributed to their sex/gender. Even when performing exactly the same leadership roles as men, women managers are often under greater scrutiny and criticism and tend to be evaluated less favorably. In contrast, men are more likely to advise men friends and colleagues to stay away from doomed projects. In part as a result, men are more likely to turn down overly risky jobs; they win safer and more secure jobs. When men fail in those top jobs, their masculinity is not treated as causal. Eagly and Karau (2002) speculate that the incongruity between two qualities—seeming womanly and managerial—causes less favorable evaluations of both women's leadership potential and women leaders' actual behaviors, putting women leaders in a lose–lose situation. If their behavior confirms stereotypes about women, they do not seem to be proper leaders; if their behavior is consistent with leadership stereotypes, they are not thought of as proper women.

According to Ryan and Haslam, women are overrepresented in precarious leadership positions not because of hostile sexism or a desire to see women fail, but because employers regard traditionally feminine traits such as sympathy, understanding, and intuition as particularly important for struggling companies. Sexists and nonsexists (and women and men) are equally likely to put women on glass cliffs. Perhaps it is a combination of benign sexism—the notion of doing women a favor, which also protects the power brokers from charges of overt discrimination—as well as the notion that women are more expendable (easier to get rid of) and have greater scapegoat potential (easier to blame for problems they may not have directly caused). This tendency to "think crisis— think female" would surely seem to apply to news organizations. Indeed, the . . . appointment of Marissa Mayer as CEO of the troubled Yahoo may exemplify the glass cliff.[2]

Conclusion: New Spins on Old Debates

Public opinion data indicated that most—overall, 89 percent of those polled—US women and men express readiness to see women take the highest leadership positions across all ten sectors studied, from academia and business to media (White House Project 2009).[3] Indeed, 96 percent were confident women could succeed as heads of film and television studios and as newspaper editors.

Ironically, this expressed comfort level was accompanied by the misperception that women are already widely enjoying leadership roles across major employment sectors, equally with men. But if the public opinion exaggerates the extent of women's leadership, women *are* working across media fields—just as women have entered other public spheres, including in elite positions in business, government, nonprofits, and politics. This is true even of the journalism beats once nearly monopolized by men, such as science, technology, economics, and even sports and war reporting. Arguably news content has changed over the last several decades. Perhaps this represents the cumulative effect of feminists pushing for changes, major economic, societal, and political transformations, including in gender relations, and in journalism itself. Van Zoonen (1998) properly emphasizes how news organizations "feminized" in order to attract new markets, such as working women. Whether this continues to change reporting—and whether the same gender differences will persist in the twenty-first century—is a different question.

Women do not enjoy statistical parity in terms of their journalistic employment across all genres, beats, and platforms. Among the many issues is the continuing marginalization of women's work (including the journalistic beats associated with women) as "soft" and unimportant. This circular and self-fulfilling problem, both real and perceptual, undermines what could otherwise be faster improvements in women journalists' pay, status, and leadership opportunities.

Moreover, women reporters also still confront significant sexism, including crude and repugnant sexist behavior, although they rarely complain of it. A very quickly growing Tumblr site (http://saidtoladyjournos.tumblr.com/) collects sexist, patronizing, and boorish remarks made to women journalists; these comments reveal how sources and colleagues treat women journalists as either brainless and dainty or, more often, sexual partners. . . .

Moreover, while women are now about 37 percent of all US journalists, they are half of the rookies, and less likely than men to be married and have children, suggesting that they leave in greater numbers—apparently when they are interested in having children (Robinson 2005). "This career is not conducive to having a family," one woman reporter said (Weaver et al. 2007: 122). US women who quit journalism blamed low salaries, the daily grind, lack of mentoring, and especially ability to spend time with their families (Everbach and Flournoy 2007). Indeed, compared to men, women journalists experience more stress—more exhaustion and work pressures interfering with personal lives—although lower levels of professional efficacy and burnout (Reinardy 2009).

Of course, the crucial challenge of juggling work and family is not specific to high-level journalism jobs or even to media jobs more generally. Recent years have seen yet another eruption of furious controversy and ferment over women and work. Explaining why she quit the State Department, Anne-Marie Slaughter (2012) asserted that women "still can't have it all." Slaughter vigorously refuted what she called the feminist mythology that women could juggle high-level work with family and parenting responsibilities if they were sufficiently committed, married the right person (she noted that an actively helpful, supportive mate is necessary but not sufficient), and correctly sequenced things. Meanwhile, criticizing those who would discourage women from trying to reach the top, Sheryl Sandberg (2013), Facebook's chief operating officer and its first woman board member, calls on women to "lean in" to their careers. At the other extreme, journalist Hannah Rosin (2012) argues that "traditionally" feminine attributes, like empathy, patience, and flexibility, make women perfect for the new global economy. According to her, that women around the world still don't get equal pay for equal work, much less achieve leadership positions, is merely the last artifact of a vanishing age. Finally, Warren Farrell (2005) says women choose to give up pay in exchange for overall greater happiness and personal growth, safety, flexibility, shorter hours, and proximity to home. These advantages lead to more competition for these jobs and thus lower pay. In contrast, he says, men's trade-offs include working more hours; taking more hazardous assignments; agreeing to move to undesirable locations; and training for more technical jobs and higher-pay jobs.

In my view, binary understandings of gender are problematic on several fronts. First, they ignore how sexism and discrimination can still prevent women from getting good jobs—ones that provide for a sense of satisfaction, with fair pay, and flexibility. Changing journalism's hard-driving, intense work culture could allow for more flexible hours, working from home, and a reevaluation of family responsibilities, which would benefit both women and men across the pay/status hierarchy. . . .

Static ideas of gender, even ones that ostensibly acknowledge the social constructedness of gender, not only presume but demand implausible distinctions between men and women, ignoring politics, sexuality, race, culture, and geography. Responding to complaints by *New York Times* staff about executive editor Jill Abramson (as uncaring, absent/disengaged, or impatient), her managing editor Dean Baquet defended Abramson by vigorously criticizing the "really easy caricature . . . of the bitchy woman" versus the calmer guy (Byers 2013). This seems reasonable: The *Times*'s top person is neither saintly nor bitchy. In making the issue gender instead of equity, the dichotomy in topics does not serve women reporters, who are uncomfortably and even unfairly expected to cover (and to want to cover) women's interests, which are at best vaguely defined, and to do so in some distinctively but universalized womanly way. Meanwhile, to simultaneously uphold journalism principles and reform them. Journalists and news audiences—in their very real diversity—are better served when a rich variety of approaches are developed to give serious consideration to a range of topics, from human rights to consumer finance, from war to parenthood.

NOTES

1. The "glass ceiling" generated related concepts. Similar to the "sticky floor," "glass walls" are barriers blocking lateral movement from low-paying domains to ones with opportunity for advancement. The "concrete wall" and "concrete ceiling" represent the compounding barriers facing many minority women. The "glass closet" invokes the exclusion of gay men and lesbians, while "celluloid ceiling" denotes a paucity of women in creative positions in Hollywood. "Bamboo ceilings" block East Asian Americans, while "gray ceilings" denote the problem for Generation Xers unable to advance given the numbers of baby boomers ahead of them. No wonder a website for women executives is called "The Glass Hammer" (http://www.theglasshammer.com/).

2. If anyone doubted the company was troubled, it became explicit when Mayer, as one of her early decisions, ended telecommuting for employees, at least until the "crisis" passes.

3. The lowest ranking was in the military: 70 percent expressed comfort with women as generals.

REFERENCES

Beasley, M. and K. T. Theus (1988) *The New Majority: A Look at What the Preponderance of Women in Journalism Education Means to the Schools and to the Profession.* Lanham, MD: University Press of America.

Bleske, G. L. (1991) "Ms. Gates Takes Over: An Updated Version of a 1949 Case Study," *Newspaper Research Journal* 12: 88–97.

Bryant, G. (1985) *The Working Woman Report,* New York: Simon & Schuster.

Burks, K. K. and V. A. Stone (1993) "Career-Related Characteristics of Male and Female News Directors," *Journalism Quarterly* 70: 542–9.

Byerly, C. (2011) "Global Report on Women in the News Media. International Women's Media Foundation." http://iwmf.org/pdfs/IWMF-Global-Report-Summary.pdf

Byers, D. (2013) "Turbulence at *The Times*," *Politico*. April 23. http://www.politico.com/story/2013/04/new-york-times-turbulence-90544_Page2.html

Catalyst (2012) "US Women in Business: Pyramids." http://www.catalyst.org/publication/132/us-women-in-business

Craft, S. and W. Wanta (2004) "Women in the Newsroom: Influences of Female Editors and Reporters on the News Agenda," *Journalism & Mass Communication Quarterly* 81: 124–38.

Curtis, M. (2012) "Does Gender Diversity Improve Performance?" July 31. https://infocus.credit-suisse.com/app/article/index.cfm?fuseaction=OpenArticle&aoid=360157&lang=EN

Eagly, A. H. and S. J. Karau (2002) "Role Congruity Theory of Prejudice toward Female Leaders," *Psychological Review* 109: 573–98.

Ephron, N. (2010) "The Graduate," *Elle, November* 10. http://www.elle.com/pop-culture/reviews/the-graduate-nora-ephron

Everbach, T. (2006) "The Culture of a Women-Led Newspaper: An Ethnographic Study of the *Sarasota Herald-Tribune*." *Journalism & Mass Communication Quarterly* 83: 477–93.

Everbach, T. and C. Flournoy (2007) "For Better Pay, Work Conditions," *Newspaper Research Journal* 28(3): 52–63.

Farrell, W. (2005) *Why Men Earn More*, New York: American Management Association.

Federal Glass Ceiling Commission (1995) *Good for Business: Making Full Use of the Nation's Capital*, Washington. DC: Federal Glass Ceiling Commission.

Gallagher, M. (2001) "Reporting on Gender in Journalism: Why Do So Few Women Reach the Top?" *Nieman Reports*, Winter. http://www.nieman.harvard.edu/reportsitem.aspx?id=101542

Hassink, W. H. J. and G. Russo (2010) "The Glass Door: The Gender Composition of Newly-Hired Workers across Hierarchical Job Levels," Tjalling C. Koopmans Research Institute #4858. http://forumonpublicpolicy.com/archive07/pollard.pdf

Kanter, R. M. (1977) *Men and Women of the Corporation*, New York: Basic Books.

Klos, D. M. (2013) "The Status of Women in the U.S. Media 2013," The Women's Media Center. http://www.womensmediacenter.com/

Kramer, V. W., A. M. Konrad, and S. Erkut (2006) "Critical Mass on Corporate Boards: Why Three or More Women Enhance Governance," WCW 11, Wellesley Centers for Women.

Mills, K. (1997) "What Difference Do Women Journalists Make?" in P. Norris (ed.) *Women, Media, and Politics*, New York: Oxford University Press, pp. 41–55.

Pollard, P. L. (2005) "A Critical Analysis of the Glass Ceiling Phenomenon." http://wfnetwork.bc.edu/encyclopedia_template.php?id=871

——. (2006) "A Critical Analysis of Gender Based Workplace Challenges Facing Women: Gender and Compensation," *Forum on Public Policy*. http://forumonpublicpolicy.com/archive07/pollard.pdf

Povich, L. (2012) *The Good Girls Revolt: How the Women of* Newsweek *Sued Their Bosses and Changed the Workplace*, New York: Public Affairs.

Reinardy, S. (2009) "Female Journalists More Likely to Leave Newspapers," *Newspaper Research Journal* 30(3): 42–57.

Robinson, G. J. (2005) *Gender, Journalism and Equity: Canadian, US and European Experiences*, Cresskill, NJ: Hampton Press.

Rosin, H. (2012) *The End of Men and the Rise of Women*, New York: Riverhead Books.

Ryan, M. K. and S. A. Haslam (2007) "The Glass Cliff: Exploring the Dynamics Surrounding Women's Appointment to Precarious Leadership Positions," *Academy of Management Review* 32: 549–72.

Sandberg, S. (2013) *Lean In: Women, Work, and the Will to Lead*, New York: Knopf.

Slaughter, A.-M. (2012) "Why Women Still Can't Have It All," *The Atlantic*, July/August. http://www.theatlantic.com/magazine/archive/2012/07/why-women-still-cant-have-it-all/309020/

Smith, R. A. (2012) "Money, Benefits, and Power: A Test of the Glass Ceiling and Glass Escalator Hypotheses," *Annals of the American Academy of Political and Social Science* 639: 149–72.

Splichal, S. and B. Garrison (2000) "Covering Public Officials: Gender and Privacy Issue Differences," *Journal of Mass Media Ethics* 15: 167–79.

Steiner, L. (2012) "Failed Theories: Explaining Gender Difference in Journalism," *Review of Communication* 12: 201–23.

Toth, E. L., S. A. Serini, D. K. Wright, and A. Emig (1998) "Trends in Public Relations Roles: 1990–95," *Public Relations Review* 24: 145–63.

van Zoonen, L. (1998) "One of the Girls?: The Changing Gender of Journalism," in C. Carter, G. Branston, and S. Allan (eds.) *News, Gender and Power*, New York: Routledge, pp. 33–46.

Weaver, D. H., R. A. Beam, B. J. Brownlee, P. S. Voakes, and G. C. Wilhoit (2007) *The American Journalist in the 21st Century: U.S. News People at the Dawn of a New Millennium*, Mahwah, NJ: Erlbaum.

White, D. M. (1950) "The 'Gate Keeper': A Case Study in the Selection of News," *Journalism Quarterly* 27: 383–91.

White House Project (2009) "Benchmarking Women's Leadership." http://www.in.gov/icw/files/benchmark_wom_leadership.pdf

Zenger, J. and J Folkman (2012) "Are Women Better Leaders than Men? *Harvard Business Review*, March 15. https://hbr.org/2012/03/a-study-in-leadership-women-do

EMIR ESTRADA AND PIERRETTE HONDAGNEU-SOTELO

35 | LIVING THE THIRD SHIFT: LATINA ADOLESCENT STREET VENDORS IN LOS ANGELES (2013)

Emir Estrada is an assistant professor in the School of Human Evolution and Social Change at Arizona State University. Her research focuses on international migration from Mexico and Central America, work in the informal sector, and family work relations. Her first book is *Kids at Work: Latinx Families Selling Food on the Streets of Los Angeles* (2019).

Pierrette Hondagneu-Sotelo is a professor of sociology at the University of Southern California. An award-winning teacher and mentor, her books include *Paradise Transplanted: Migration and the Making of California Gardens* (2014), *God's Heart Has No Borders: Religious Activism for Immigrant Rights* (2008), and the co-edited volumes *Nation and Migration* (2009) and *Domestica: Immigrant Workers Cleaning and Caring in the Shadows of Affluence* (2007).

Adriana is a thirteen-year-old middle school student in East Los Angeles. During the day, she attends school, but on selected weeknights and on weekends, Adriana and her parents sell food at La Cumbrita, a small street in East Los Angeles where other street-vending families congregate to sell food from their home country, such as pupusas, tamales, atole, and tacos. Adriana has been street vending with her parents since they came from Puebla, Mexico, when she was five years old. . . .

Second-wave feminist scholarship taught us to see the invisible private sphere of household work (Oakley 1985) and alerted us to the "second-shift" work obligations faced by many employed women (Hochschild 1989). The ideal family type now includes breadwinner but "involved" dads, working moms, and children who are supported by adults. Children and teens in postindustrial societies are . . . shielded from the public sphere of work by their parents, although it is generally thought appropriate and desirable for children to have "chores" or household tasks that teach them responsibility (Zelizer 2002). While middle-class children are indulged and provided with consumer items (Pugh 2009), their public lives have shrunk, leading to what Barrie Thorne (2004) calls "the privatization of childhood." . . .

The daily practices of street-vending daughters of Central American and Mexican immigrant parents call into question current ideas about childhood and adolescence in the United States in the early twenty-first century as well as about the lives of working-class Latina girls. Not only do these daughters of Latino immigrant workers attend to their school work, but they are saddled with significant household-work responsibilities—cleaning, cooking, laundering, and looking after younger siblings. In addition, they dedicate time to income-generating street-vending work. In other words, these Latina girls negotiate a triple shift—street vending, household work, and schoolwork.

This paper extends the feminist literature on intersectionality by exploring the world of Latina/o teenage street vendors from a perspective that takes into account gendered expectations resulting not only from the familiar intersecting relations of race and class but also from the age as well as the inequality of nations that gives rise to particular patterns of international labor migration. . . .

As Mexican and Central American immigrants make their way in subordinated and saturated Los Angeles labor markets, many of them find that their best economic options are to utilize the possible labor from all family members (Dyrness 2001). Yet curiously, among the street-vending families in this study, the girls are preferred over boys. Based on nine months of ethnographic observations and twenty in-depth interviews with adolescent street vendors (sixteen girls and four boys), we address three research questions: (1) Why do more girls than boys do street vending with their families? (2) How do the girls experience this activity? and (3) Do the girls see this "third shift" as a burden or as a source of empowerment?

First Shift: School

For many children today, school is like work. Children and teens, especially in the middle class and affluent social classes, are highly scheduled, monitored, and subjected to what Annette Lareau (2003) calls the practice of "concerted cultivation." Parents want to reproduce their familial class status or seek mobility for their kids and do so by attempting to structure their children's high achievement in education and extracurricular activities (music lessons, sports, tutoring, enrichment programs, and so forth).

This intensive focus on educational achievement is not only class based but also a comparatively recent historical construction. . . . Sociologist Viviana Zelizer (1985) analyzes the transformation of notions of childhood that took place in the United States between 1870 and 1930, using the term *useful child* to refer to the nineteenth-century child who actively contributed to the family's economic survival through labor. In the twentieth century, she notes the emergence of the productively "useless" yet emotionally "priceless" child. Philip Ariès (1962), Zelizer (1985), and others have noted that this ideal of the sacred, sentimentalized child emerged in the context of industrialization, urbanization, and the concomitant rise of compulsory schooling, prevalent first among the middle class and later spreading to working-class and immigrant families. . . . These notions of childhood—that children must be educated, "developed," and

"raised"—today prevail in most Western, postindustrial nations (Thorne 2004). . . .

Many children of Latino immigrants grow up in working-class circumstances but also face strong parental expectations to do well in school. They do not have access to tutors, prep schools, or, in many cases, even a quiet desk at which to do their homework, but they are expected to achieve educationally. Parents often underscore their own migration sacrifices and hard work at low-paying jobs as reasons the children must study. Some scholars have referred to this as part of the "immigrant bargain" that second-generation US-born children must make with their parents (Smith 2006; Suarez-Orozco and Suarez-Orozco 1995). The idea is that parental sacrifice will be redeemed by the children's American success story.

Yet many low-income immigrant families depend on the economic contributions of all family members (Dyrness 2001) and thus are unable to maintain the level of normative child-rearing practices where children are indulged in the private sphere of home and dedicate effort only to school. Does this mean that the immigrant parents support the neglect of children's education? Our answer, based on the research for this paper, is no. Yet a good deal of the literature on children and informal-sector street vending remains predicated on the idea that work detracts from children's appropriate focus, education (Basu 1999).

Second Shift: Household Work

Household work has for centuries been identified as women's domain. This is true across all social classes, but women with money can outsource or buy out of some of the gender oppression by paying poor, racialized women to do housework (Ehrenreich and Hochschild 2005; Hondagneu-Sotelo 2001; Torres Sarmiento 2002). What happens when Latina immigrant women go into the public sphere for paid work? How do they manage their cleaning, cooking, and caregiving? Since they lack the resources to hire help for their household work, they turn to family members, typically female kin, including their daughters.

These gendered transitions reinforce the gender division of household work among Latino children.

Many studies in Mexico show this pattern, with girls expected to assume more household responsibilities than boys. . . . These household burdens on female children seem to increase with migration. Ethnographic observations by Orellana (2001) in Central American immigrant households showed that girls as young as seven do numerous household chores (for example, unpacking groceries, bathing and dressing a younger sibling, and cleaning) without being asked to do so by their parents. This demand for young girls to help out in the home increases not only when their mothers go to work but also "when families are detached from the support networks of extended kin" (Thorne et al. 2003, 252).

Third Shift: Working the Streets of Los Angeles

. . . The notion of children working is often seen as backward and anachronistic, and as a Third World child-labor practice rejected by developed nations such as the United States (Edmonds and Pavcnik 2008; Song 1999; Zelizer 1985). However, the reality is that children in the United States today do engage in paid-work activities and that such activities are not restricted only to immigrant children of color. Zelizer (2002, 2005) has noted that some jobs are seen as desirable for children and teens in particular contexts (for example, household chores and babysitting). Ong and Terriquez (2008) have found that white middle-class youth engage in paid economic activities more than do black, Asian, and Hispanic youth, a finding the authors attribute to the resources available to white middle-class kids, such as access to better transportation (including owning a car to take them to and from work) and the ubiquity of appropriate jobs near their places of residence. Inner cities, such as in Los Angeles, conversely, have very few jobs available for the youth.

. . . However, ethnic business enclaves have historically provided employment opportunities for children of color who must juggle school, home, and work responsibilities, not for résumé building or "experience," but to keep their family's business afloat. These family arrangements are often gendered, with daughters experiencing unequal divisions of labor. . . .

. . . [I]n a US study, Lisa Sun-Hee Park (2005, 73) has observed that Korean entrepreneurs employ family members, including children, in their restaurants, liquor stores, laundries, dry cleaners, and more. Park notes that respondents were "conscious of their gender division of labor." Girls started working at younger ages than their male siblings and were usually relegated to "mother's helper" positions. The work that girls performed with their mothers was seen as appropriate and natural, in large part because "immigrant work has historically been gendered as 'female'" (98). In contrast, boys who worked with their parents were demasculinized. Working with their parents caused children, boys in particular, to experience a prolonged childification (104).

Some street-vending businesses, like other ethnic businesses, rely on the work of children, but street vending complicates the work kids do because the practice is illegal in Los Angeles (Cross and Morales 2007; Hamilton and Chinchilla 2001; Muñoz 2008) and is performed in open visible spaces. Unlike the children who work in formal-sector family ethnic enclave businesses, such as Korean dry cleaners or Chinese restaurants, the Latina street-vending kids lack safety, protection, and respect from the larger society and government authorities. Not only the appropriateness of the work comes into play but also the appropriateness of the place where this work is performed: the street.

The work that girls do as street vendors both perpetuates and challenges gendered expectations. On the one hand, they are performing a type of work that has been gendered as feminine (preparation of food); on the other, they are doing this gendered work on the street, a space that has been gendered as masculine and inappropriate for *señoritas* (virginal women). Thus, an analysis of gender in this type of ethnic business allows us to see how gendered beliefs are not only enforced by societal norms but also internalized, reinforced, challenged, and adjusted by family members to meet the needs of the family business while still providing protection for their daughters.

Methods

This study is based on nine months of ethnographic fieldwork at various sites in the Los Angeles area and on twenty in-depth interviews with adolescents who sell items on the street with at least one parent. . . .

Our sample was not equally distributed by gender. Sixteen of the respondents were girls, and four were boys. We had originally planned to interview ten boys and ten girls, but our time in the field showed that more girls were engaged in this activity. Respondents were not able to recommend boys for our study, echoing our observations that this was a predominantly female activity. Twelve of the kids did not receive regular monetary remuneration for their work; the others received between five and thirty dollars per day. Four girls and one boy sold merchandise alone while their family members did street vending at other sites, while the others sold alongside their parents, though they were left alone at times while their parents ran errands. Thirteen of the respondents were second-generation, US-born citizens, an important characteristic because previous literature on street vendors has focused on first-generation immigrants from Mexico and Central America (Dohan 2003; Hamilton and Chinchilla 2001), Nineteen of the respondents were attending school, and three attended private Catholic schools.

Most of the ethnographic fieldwork took place at a street we call La Cumbrita, a small side street just off a main avenue in the heart of East Los Angeles. By day, it is an isolated strip. Two large parking lots take up most of the space. One parking lot belongs to a supermarket; across the street is a parking lot for Bank of America customers. By night, both parking lots are filled with hungry customers who seek "authentic" Mexican and Central American food. As soon as the sun sets, this street transforms into a lively open market where predominantly Mexican, Guatemalan, and El Salvadoran families sell prepared food from their home country— tamales, pupusas, champurrado, tacos, pozole, and platanos fritos. They also sell candies, gelatins, pirated DVDs and CDs, toys, clothes, cosmetics, and much more. The families at La Cumbrita typically sell from 7:00 to 11:00 every Friday, Saturday, and Sunday evening. However, our observations took place as early as 6:00 P.M. and as late as 12:30 A.M., allowing the researchers to witness interactions among street vendors, family members, customers, and gang members in a more informal setting. The street vendors gabbed about fights, the police, gang intervention, children's education, and an alliance that was forming to settle street-vending disputes with the city. . . .

None of the respondents and their families received payment for their interviews. In exchange for the children's time, Estrada offered educational support, such as filling out applications for financial aid and college, and helped them write résumés.

The Gendered Division of Labor in the Household and the Street

Boys Slack Off: Household Responsibilities

. . . Almost all of the girls listed household responsibilities that included a combination of cleaning, cooking, and taking care of their younger siblings. Twelve-year-old Esmeralda, who had two younger sisters and three younger brothers, said, "I do the beds, I do the dishes, and sometimes I [clean] the balcony with my other sisters. [My brothers] just stay there and watch TV and do *tiradero* [a mess] and everything, and [my sisters and I] have to sometimes pick it up." Gloria, a fourteen-year-old who sold tacos with her parents, similarly reported, "I go wash with my mom at the Laundromat. . . . I have to help her because it's my clothes also. My [ten-year-old] sister sometimes goes too, and then my [twelve-year-old] brother, he doesn't go. He stays with my dad. But it is usually me, [my mother], and my grandma."

Ten of the sixteen girls in our sample also had some type of responsibility for caring for their siblings or extended family members. According to Mariana, a sixteen-year-old who sold fruit with her parents, "*Pos yo entro a las siete y salgo como a las dos. . . . Mi hermana los cuida [a mis hermanos] cuando yo estoy en la escuela y luego yo llego de la escuela y los cuido yo. . . .* [I start school at seven, and I get out at around two. . . . My sister takes care of [my siblings] when I am in school, and then when I get home from school, I take care of them]." . . . These responsibilities shift as the children grow. Eighteen-year-old Carmen, for example, is no longer required to take care of her eight-year-old brother, though she did so when he was younger . . . Carmen still bore the brunt of household cleaning responsibilities, however: "*Mis hermanos nomás se paran y bueno trabajan pues y yo no, yo tengo quehacer—tender las camas, barrer, y bueno muchas cosas* [My brothers just get up, and well, they work and all. But me, I have household work—make the beds, sweep the floor, and well, many things]."

Some of the girls in this study cooked for their entire families or prepared food for family businesses. Street vendors who sell prepared food spend a good deal of time purchasing ingredients and making the food at home. Monica, an eighteen-year-old who sold tamales with her parents, reported, "My responsibilities [were] to get home from school and help my mom do the tamales . . . help around the house and then clean everything in the house."

By contrast, both the boys in this study and the brothers of the girls in this study relied on sisters, mothers, or sisters-in-law to do household domestic work. Eric, an eighteen-year-old boy who sold raspados on his own, lived with his three older brothers and his sister-in-law: In their household, cleaning and cooking was his sister-in-law's job. Other boys in this study simply looked puzzled when asked if they had any household responsibilities. For example, Juan, a ten-year-old boy who sells homemade jewelry with his father, responded "No" to this question, but his sister, just a few years older and also involved in selling jewelry with her father and two brothers, was in charge of cleaning the house. She laughed at the idea that her brothers would clean the house. But when she was asked how she felt about having to do more household work than her brothers, she answered in an annoyed way, "Well, not good, because they don't do anything. They slack off." Many of the girls we interviewed echoed the idea that boys avoid doing household work, consistently reporting that their brothers were expected to do very little if any household work. . . .

Boys Can Also Slack Off on Street Vending

The boys' ability to avoid work extended to the sphere of public street vending. Even boys who did not have sisters at home to pick up the household workload had light responsibilities. Edgar, a thirteen-year-old who sells *tejuino* (a corn-based Mexican drink) with his mother, is an only child. Edgar reported that when he was not selling *tejuino*, he worked out at a local gym with his friend. . . .

Many girls faced a different situation. Katia, age twenty-one, sold fruit with her older brother and mother when she was younger. She recalled that her brother "was more wild. He used to go help [my mother] and then go home. He was not like us. [My cousin and I were] stuck to my mom." Katia did not resent the fact that her brother went home while she had to work with her mother, attributing such arrangements to "natural" gender differences: "[I am] a girl, he is a guy. I guess he ha[d] a girlfriend already? *Él se iba más temprano* [He would leave much earlier] with his friends. *Le ayudaba un ratito [a mi mamá] y se iba con sus* [He would help my mom for a while and then he would take off with his] friends. *Y yo me tenía que quedar ahí* [I had to stay there] because I was a girl. I was with my mom. And he is a guy. Guys, they just leave with their friends."

Other girls sang a similar refrain. They were typically brought to the street-vending site by their parents or by an older sibling. Once there, they were allowed to return home only when escorted by a family member at the end of the day. This strategy was predicated on the belief that girls required family protection to maintain their virginity and family honor, a belief that is widely shared in Mexican Catholic culture (González-López 2003, 2005) as well as in Filipino society (Espiritu 2001). This strategy yielded an added family economic benefit, as the girls were required to put in many hours of work. Yet the parents were then faced with the dilemma of protecting the girls while they were working in the streets.

Strategies for Protection

Some street-vending girls worked alongside family members, but others were unaccompanied as they sold food. In these cases, the families and the girls employed other protection strategies. One strategy was to have the girls stationed in public parks where a familial environment prevailed—for example, at a playground. In another family, the daughter sold cut-up fruit alone at a park. While these girls sold at relatively safe parks or busy street corners on their own, their parents often sold at more dangerous spots and/or sold merchandise that was considered more dangerous than food (pirated DVDs, for example). While Adriana was selling fruit by herself at a popular park in East Los Angeles, her mother sold fruit and flowers by a freeway entrance, a location perceived as more dangerous for a young girl, and her father sold pirated CDs and DVDs. Even though Adriana lacked a permit, selling fruit inside a park was perceived as safer than being near the free-way or selling products that would merit jail time if police chose to intervene. . . . Similarly, Lolita, a sixteen-year-old who sold corn on the cob, mangos, and churros at a park south of Los Angeles, was dropped off by her father early every Saturday and Sunday. Her father then would sell the same items, but he did so while walking down the street, a practice that made him more visible and vulnerable to police harassment. Lolita, however, sold in a more controlled environment where many Mexican immigrant families went to spend their weekend days.

Another parental strategy was to monitor the girls via cell phone. The girls were instructed to use the phone in case of an emergency, and they received instructions from their parents via telephone. During one of the fieldwork observations, Estrada accompanied Lolita's seventeen-year-old sister, Martha, who sold corn on the cob, churros, and raspados . . . Martha used her phone to obtain business-related instructions from her father. For example, Martha's father called and told her to walk to a nearby park, where his friend was having a big party and wanted to buy a sizable order of corn on the cob and raspados for his guests. She called her father to notify him that she was on her way and phoned him again after arriving. Cell phones allow the girls to remain tightly tethered to parental instruction and monitoring.

Gendered Justifications
"Girls Are More Clean than the Guys"
Gendered beliefs that girls sold more than boys came up repeatedly in conversations. Girls were associated with being clean and nonthreatening to customers. According to Katia, "Some people think, 'Oh, she is more clean because she is a girl,' and [when they see] a guy, [they think], 'Oh no.

They say that a lot. . . .'" It was in this light that Katia viewed the family's decision to have her rather than her brother do street vending: it was better for business.

Accordingly, girls are associated with cleanliness, soap, and purity, while boys were associated with dirtiness and dubious hygiene. As Verónica, an eighteen-year-old girl who sold *tejuino* with her father on the side of an isolated highway near a running track, said, "I feel bad for the guys, because they're in the sun too, and they don't sell as much as girls because we see guys as more dirty. They think that girls are more clean than the guys. That's what some of the customers told me before, too. Because they say that the guys don't even clean their hands—they don't wash their hands when they get the money or they [prepare the *tejuino*]. So I think that's why they buy more from the girls." Verónica said, "If I don't come, I don't think that [her father and brothers will] make that much money." Young "virginal girls" and "maternal, nurturing women" are socially constructed as natural purveyors of food. They are seen as clean, and their "natural" service in the kitchen is extended to the public sphere of street vending. . . .

Verónica and Katia's experiences were not isolated. Street vendors were acutely aware of presenting themselves as clean cooks and their work as involving hygienic routines. Street vendors constantly cleaned their stands while customers lingered nearby. They also made sure that their surroundings were clean at all times. Women often used hairnets and plastic gloves. Families with more children had the luxury of assigning one of the children to handle the cash transactions, so that clean hands could remain in contact with the food. Boys or fathers usually had charge of cash transactions, while mothers and daughters prepared food. It was also common to see jugs of water near street-vending stands so that vendors could constantly wash their hands. Bottles of water were also available so that customers could wash their hands.

The street vendors' hygienic performances mattered, but so did their gender. On one occasion, a boy was selling tamales alone from a grocery push-cart. He was modestly dressed in a black cap, black sweatshirt, and blue jeans. Even though his clothes were not new, he looked clean. Like the rest of the vendors, he used plastic gloves when putting the tamales into plastic bags or on plates for the customers. Even though he followed the same routines as the other street vendors, one customer asked him, "Did you make the tamales?" The boy responded, "No, my sister did, but she asked me to come sell them for her. I only sell them." He attempted to reassure the potential customer. The customer ended up not buying the tamales and instead purchased two pupusas from two sisters, sixteen-year-old Linda and fourteen-year-old Susana. While it is possible that this customer's decision to buy pupusas rather than tamales was simply a desire for a particular type of food, the customer may also have been concerned about whether the boy made the tamales and/or was clean enough to sell them.

"Guys Buy More from Girls"

Attractive young girls were a good asset for family businesses. When Katia was fourteen or fifteen and she and her cousin were left alone to tend the fruit stand, they sold more than when her mother or brother was in charge. Katia explained, "You're a girl, and you are growing up, and you know how guys are, *que quieren mirar a las muchachas* [that they want to see the girls]?" She continued, "Guys *les compran más a las muchachas que a* [buy more from girls than they do from] ladies or guys."

Mariana and her teenage sister enjoyed playing games and bantering with male customers. Doing so not only made the time pass quickly but also enabled them to sell more fruit. . . . Customers would often try to pick up Mariana and her sister, encounters that they enjoyed because "*se siente a gusto porque no nos aburrimos allí y así vendemos más* [it feels good because we don't get bored there and we sell more]."

These flirtatious encounters were very frequent and were often initiated by the clients. The encounters were also normal for teenage girls. In small towns throughout Latin America, youth commonly meet at the town plaza, where they chat, laugh, and flirt. While the girls enjoyed what they called *travesuras* (pranks), they also were aware of the dangers they faced. To protect themselves from male customers, they gave false names and claimed to be older.

Parents either were not aware of these flirtatious games or looked the other way. Mariana and her sister said that their father was unaware of these interactions, and if he had seen them talking with young men, "*Pues a lo mejor sí* [*se enoja*] *pero va a pensar que está comprando fruta* [Well, he might (get upset), but he will think that (the customer) is buying fruit]." Other parents were more vigilant. Linda and Susana's mother, for example, reprimanded them and made it clear to the customers that she disapproved of them flirting with or disrespecting her daughters. . . .

Contesting the Gendered Roles

Although street vending takes place in an open space where girls are exposed to many dangers, girls are seen as more apt for these kinds of jobs. While the girls prepared the food at home and later sold it on the street, most of the brothers helped with tasks the girls were unable to do, such as peeling coconut and driving. Mariana frequently woke up early to peel fruit; her sister helped with all the produce, but her brother "would just help peel the coconut." Before Linda and Susana began selling pupusas with their parents at La Cumbrita, they sold the pupusas door-to-door from a basket and shopping cart. Their brother was older and did not accompany them, although, according to Linda, "He would just drive us there. . . . And when we finished, we used to call him. So, he'll be like the driver."

Like Linda, other girls attributed their brothers' failure to do street vending with their parents to the fact that the boys were either too old or too young. The tasks with which the boys helped, such as peeling hard fruit and driving, did not require long workdays. The boys put in less time and effort than the girls.

Some girls also referenced their brothers' lack of skills. For example, when I asked Adriana if her brother helped cut the fruit, she laughed and explained, "*El deja echar más* [*fruta*] *con la cáscara* [he leaves more fruit on the skin he cuts off]." Because he was careless and wasted fruit, he was released from this duty.

Other girls were less amused about their brothers' slacking off and contested the unequal gendered division of labor. Verónica, for example, believed that it was unfair that she worked more than her brothers simply because she was a female: "So then I'm the one [who cleans because] *las mujeres limpian, no los hombres* [women are the ones that clean, not men]. And I get mad, too, and I tell them, 'No, guys could do the same thing. All humans are the same. . . . Guys could clean, too, and everything.' And [my brothers mock me by saying], *'Ay ay muy trabajadora. ¡Cállate!* [Ay, ay, what a hard worker. Shut up!].'" . . .

Other girls, too, were unhappy about the tasks they were assigned or expected to do simply because they were female. In Martha's case, her father rather than her brother reinforced the gendered division of labor at home: "My dad is like old Mexicans, and [he thinks that] guys are not supposed to do anything. . . . Once my brother was ironing his pants, and [my dad] yells at [my sisters and me] and says, 'Why aren't you ironing your brother's pants?'" Martha replied, "He irons his own pants. He doesn't like the way we iron." Martha's father responded, "Well, he's not supposed to iron." Martha challenged the gendered position she had been assigned by her father, labeling him an "old Mexican" for thinking that ironing was a task not suitable for males. . . .

The Third Shift: Burden or Empowerment?

The third shift these girls experienced is tiring, and some of the respondents complained about the workload. Lolita works about twelve hours each Saturday and Sunday with her father and older sister. Her day usually starts at eight o'clock in the morning, as she spends about two hours getting ready, having breakfast, and bagging the peanuts she will sell that day. She starts street vending at eleven o'clock at a park in a neighborhood about twenty minutes away from her home. At the end of the day, usually around eight o'clock in the evening, her father picks her up.

The other girls in this study followed similar schedules, devoting their entire weekends to street vending. Adriana, for example, worked alone selling fruit from ten o'clock in the morning until five o'clock in the evening, while her parents sold at other spots. The family later regrouped at seven o'clock at La Cumbrita, selling CDs and DVDs until midnight.

Even though these girls and their families worked very hard, the girls saw their work positively. Although Lolita found her long work hours "tiring," she added, "I like helping my parents." Many of the respondents echoed these sentiments. Said Monica, "You are doing it because you have to help your parents out, but it's fun at the same time because you have fun seeing different people every day."

While it may appear that girls in this study are constrained, most girls obtained as much benefit from their work as did their families. Some, like Monica, expressed feelings of freedom. According to Gloria, "Every Friday there is something different going on. . . . Before we sold tacos, I was at home Fridays and . . . it would be boring. Like just watching TV and going on the computer and the same things." Unlike her brother, who played soccer, Gloria did not participate in extracurricular activities that would give her a reason to be out of the house; thus, before her family decided to street vend, she was more confined to the home . . .

In addition to experiencing a relief from boredom and more physical freedom from their work, the girls also acquired purchasing power. Those who were paid by their parents liked having the freedom to buy things. . . . These girls also helped invest in their families' businesses. When I asked Adriana what she did with her wages, she said, "*Lo guardo y embebes cuando ellos no tienen [dinero] para comprar fruta les presto [dinero]* [I save it, and sometimes when they don't have (money) to buy fruit, I lend them (money)]." Being able to help their parents financially made the girls feel proud and like they were valuable economic contributors.

In addition to seeing their work as beneficial for their entire family, these girls saw their work as preparation for the future. Katia and others believed that street vending provided them with the skills, strength, and courage to do any other type of work: "Selling fruit, . . . you know how to work—how to be in the sun, how to run from the cops, or whatever. And if you get another job, [it will be] easy. [Selling fruit also teaches you] how to get along with people, because you have to talk to people."

The girls also saw their third shift as a strategy to further their education. Three of the youth attended private schools and recognized that their work helped pay for their education. Carmen and her brothers did not go to private school, but their work helped them pay their tuition at a local California state university. When Carmen was nearing graduation from high school, her parents gave her a choice between helping to street vend or staying at home. She decided to street vend because she knew that going to college would cost money. . . .

While some of the girls complained about their heavy workloads and very full schedules, the majority of them saw the work as opening new opportunities. Street vending made them feel useful and responsible, it ended the boredom that many felt at home, and it offered what the girls perceived as useful socialization experiences for their future. Most important, the girls saw tangible benefits, as their street-vending labor brought more money into the household and thereby allowed their parents to buy them special items—trendy jeans or simply school supplies. On the whole, the girls saw street vending as an empowering experience that opened doors to new possibilities and better life opportunities.

Conclusion

. . . While the girls in this study may appear constrained, restricted, and overburdened, they thought they received as many benefits from their work as did their parents. Parental appreciation and recognition of the girls' contributions filled them with feelings of pride, achievement, and family belonging.

Shedding light on the labor contributions of these Latina adolescent street vendors opens a window for us to see how economically useful girls can transform household dynamics and alter parent-child relations, a topic that merits further research. So much of the research on work and family has been devoted to understanding spousal work-family balance (González de la Rocha 1994; Torres Sarmiento 2002). It is now time to focus on understanding how innovative income earning strategies, particularly in immigrant occupational niches and the informal sector, affect parent child relations.

Moreover, the vast literature on the second generation—the children of immigrants—. . . has focused on the relationship between different modes of cultural assimilation and economic mobility, but it has largely ignored an important facet of reality in many poor and working-class immigrant families: many children work alongside their parents. This study has shown how street vendors in Los Angeles work as part of a family unit. The labor contributions of children—and especially girls—are vital for the family's economic mobility, and complicated gendered beliefs are drawn upon and elaborated to support these practices. Other Latino occupational niches also incorporate children into family work arrangements (for example, suburban maintenance gardening, domestic work, garment work, and agricultural work), and these other immigrant occupational family gender dynamics should be explored.

We have highlighted how Latina adolescent street vendors negotiate triple shifts, the continuities between gendered household divisions of labor and street vending, and the gender belief systems and practices that support these work-family arrangements. Rather than bringing to light yet another instance of women's and girls' oppression, the research suggests better life opportunities for the girls.

NOTE

This research was made possible by partial funding support from the Diversity Placement Research Fellowship in the USC College Office of Graduate Programs.

REFERENCES

Ariès, Philippe. 1962. *Centuries of Childhood: A Social History of Family Life.* New York: Vintage.

Basu, K. 1999. "Child Labor: Cause, Consequence, and Cure, with Remarks on International

Labor Standards." *Journal of Economic Literature* 37:1083–119.

Cross, John, and Alfonso Morales. 2007. "Introduction: Locating Street Markets in the Modern/ Postmodern World." In *Street Entrepreneurs: People, Place, and Politics in Local and Global Perspective*, ed. John Cross and Alfonso Morales, 1–14. New York: Routledge.

Dohan, Daniel. 2003. *The Price of Poverty: Money, Work, and Culture in the Mexican American Barrio*. Berkeley: University of California Press.

Dyrness, Grace R. 2001. *Policy on the Streets: A Handbook for the Establishment of Sidewalk-Vending Programs*. Los Angeles: University of Southern California.

Edmonds, Eric V., and Nina Pavcnik. 2008. "Child Labor in the Global Economy." *Journal of Economic Perspectives* 18:199–220.

Ehrenreich, Barbara, and Arlie Russell Hochschild. 2005. "Global Woman." In *Gender though the Prism of Difference*, ed. Maxine Baca Zinn, Pierrette Hondagneu-Sotelo, and Michael A. Messner, 49–55. 3rd ed. New York: Oxford University Press.

Espiritu, Yen Le. 2001. "'We Don't Sleep around Like White Girls Do': Family, Culture, and Gender in Filipina American Lives." *Signs* 26:415–40.

González de la Rocha, Mercedes. 1994. *The Resources of Poverty: Women and Survival in a Mexican City*. Cambridge, Mass.: Blackwell.

González-López, Gloria. 2003. "De Madres a Hijas: Gendered Lessons on Virginity across Generations." In *Gender and US Immigration: Contemporary Trends*, ed. Pierrette Hondagneu-Sotelo, 217–40. Berkeley: University of California Press.

_____. 2005. *Erotic Journeys: Mexican Immigrants and Their Sex Lives*. Berkeley: University of California Press.

Hamilton, Nora, and Norma S. Chinchilla. 2001. *Seeking Community in a Global City: Guatemalans and Salvadorans in Los Angeles*. Philadelphia: Temple University Press.

Hochschild, Arlie Russell, with Anne Machung. 1989. *The Second Shift: Working Families and the Revolution at Home*. New York: Viking.

Hondagneu-Sotelo, Pierrette. 2001. *Domestica: Immigrant Workers Cleaning and Caring in the Shadows of Affluence*. Berkeley: University of California Press.

Lareau, Annette. 2003. *Unequal Childhoods: Class, Race, and Family Life*. Berkeley: University of California Press.

Muñoz, Lorena. 2008. "'Tamales . . . Elotes . . . Champurrado': The Production of Latino Vending Landscapes

in Los Angeles." PhD diss., University of Southern California.

Oakley, Ann. 1985 (1974). *The Sociology of Housework*. Oxford: Blackwell, 1985.

Ong, Paul, and Veronica Terriquez. 2008. "Can Multiple Pathways Offset Inequalities in the Urban Spatial Structure?" In *Beyond Tracking: Multiple Pathways to College, Career, and Civic Participation*, ed. Jeannie Oakes and Marisa Saunders, 131–52. Cambridge, Mass.: Harvard Education Press.

Orellana, Marjorie. F. 2001. "The Work Kids Do: Mexican and Central American Immigrant Children's Contributions to Households and Schools in California." *Harvard Educational Review* 71:1–21.

Park, Lisa Sun-Hee. 2005. *Consuming Citizenship: Children of Asian Immigrant Entrepreneurs*. Stanford: Stanford University Press.

Pugh, Allison J. 2009. *Longing and Belonging: Parents, Children, and Consumer Culture*. Berkeley: University of California Press.

Smith, Robert Courtney. 2006. *Mexican New York: Transnational Lives of New Immigrants*. Berkeley: University of California Press.

Song, Miri. 1999. *Helping Out: Children's Labor in Ethnic Business*. Philadelphia: Temple University Press.

Suarez-Orozco, Carola, and Marcelo Suarez-Orozco. 1995. *Transformations: Immigration, Family Life, and Achievement Motivation among Latino Adolescents*. Stanford: Stanford University Press.

Thorne, Barrie. 2004. "The Crisis of Care." In *Work-Family Challenges for Low-Income Parents and Their Children*, ed. Nan Crouter and Alan Booth, 149–58. Hillsdale, N.J.: Erlbaum.

Thorne, B., M. F. Orellana, W. S. E. Lam, and A. Chee. 2003. "Raising Children, and Growing Up, across National Borders: Comparative Perspectives on Age, Gender, and Migration." *In Gender and U.S. Immigration: Contemporary Trends*, ed. P. Hondagneu-Sotelo, 241–62. Berkeley: University of California Press.

Torres Sarmiento, Socorro. 2002. *Making Ends Meet: Income-Generating Strategies among Mexican Immigrants*. New York: LFB Scholarly.

Zelizer, Viviana. 1985. *Pricing the Priceless Child: The Changing Social Value of Children*. New York: Basic Books.

_____. 2002. "Kids and Commerce." *Childhood* 4:375–96.

_____. 2005. "The Priceless Child Revisited." In *Studies in Modern Childhood: Society, Agency, and Culture*, ed. Jens Qvortrup, 184–200. London: Palgrave.

Living in a Globalizing World

Keywords: care chain, environmental human rights defenders, extractivism, global factory, international financial institutions, international gendered division of work, neocolonialism, neoliberalism, reproductive work, supply chain

This chapter considers people's experiences of home and family across national borders; the global economic factors that drive migration and displacement, cultural diversity, and homogenization; and the movement of jobs and capital from one nation to another. We emphasize the macro- and global-level structures that shape people's lives. Here, nation is an additional analytical category together with gender, race, class, sexuality, and so on.

LOCATIONS, CIRCUITS, AND FLOWS

We use the imagery of circuits and flows to describe global networks and movements of people, goods, information, work, money, and cultural productions like music and movies. Movement along global pathways is helped or hindered by specific conditions, rules, and assumptions about what should be traded, who should travel, and for what reasons. Notice the direction of these flows. Are they reciprocal? Are they mainly one way? Who and what are travelling in which direction? And why? Major cities constitute activity nodes or hubs in these global networks, including Los Angeles, New York,

Seoul, Tokyo, and Istanbul—locations that provide the context for activities discussed in Readings 21, 22, 35, 41, 43, and 48.

In Reading 36, Gloria Anzaldúa traces historical migrations into North America and the subsequent conquest and settlement of Mexico and the United States by Spanish and British colonizers, respectively. She writes as a mixed-race person, a *mestiza*, located in more than one place and with more than one consciousness. She moves between languages and has learned "to be an Indian in Mexican culture and to be Mexican from an Anglo point of view" (1987, p. 79). The current US-Mexico border was defined in the 1848 Treaty of Guadalupe Hidalgo following the Mexican-American War. This established the Rio Grande as the international boundary and ceded Texas to the United States together with Arizona, California, Nevada, and New Mexico. Referring to this history, Mexican Americans often say: we didn't cross the border; the border crossed us. Anzaldúa describes this 2,000-mile boundary as a place where "the Third World grates against the First and bleeds," (p. 3) and considers the challenges, benefits, and losses involved in geographical and cultural border crossing.

MIGRATIONS AND DISPLACEMENTS

Migration

Historically, the political and economic interests and aspirations of ancient empires, colonial powers, and modern-day states have resulted in huge movements of people, mainly according to the needs and priorities of dominant nations. This includes the transporting of some 12 million enslaved West Africans to the "New World" during the eighteenth and nineteenth centuries, with others taken to the Mediterranean region or across the Indian Ocean. The rise of the United States as a major industrial power, together with weakening economies and political repression in Europe, led to massive European immigration to this country starting in the mid-nineteenth century (see the box feature "A Timeline of US Immigration Laws and Policies" in Chapter 3). After the ending of slavery, Chinese, Filipino, Indian, and Japanese workers were allowed to enter the United States to meet the growing demand for labor. More recent immigration has mainly involved people from Asia and Central America. Some are high-tech employees, but most fill the "3D jobs"—dirty, difficult, and dangerous.

Consider the following migration data for 2017 reported by the United Nations Department of Economic and Social Affairs, Population Division (2017):

- There were an estimated 258 million migrants worldwide, up from 220 million in 2010 and 173 million in 2000.
- Migrants comprised roughly 3 percent of the world population.
- Women accounted for 48 percent of global migrants.
- The largest number of international migrants resided in the United States, followed by Saudi Arabia, Germany, and the Russian Federation.
- The total number of refugees and asylum seekers in 2016 was almost 26 million, mainly hosted by Turkey, Jordan, Palestine, Lebanon, and Pakistan.
- If the total number of migrants were a nation, it would be the fifth most populated country in the world (after China, India, the United States, and Indonesia).

The United Nations distinguishes several types of migrants (see the box feature "Categories of Migrants Recognized by the United Nations"). Personal dreams and decisions, community expectations and pressures, global labor markets, corporate extraction of natural resources, environmental crises, and war and conflict all influence who moves, where they move from and to, the conditions under which they relocate, and the situations they encounter at their destinations. Immigration policies shift in response to economic ups and downs, political support for refugees and asylum seekers, relationships with allied nations, and perceived threats to national security. Overall, tens of millions of people have started new lives in the United States and contributed to the nation's economy and cultural diversity.

Race and class are significant factors in immigration policies, practices, and enforcement. People who hold Australian, Canadian, European, Japanese, and US passports have relative freedom to travel worldwide, especially for short-term visits and vacation trips. By contrast, people from poorer countries, as well as countries identified as "terrorist" or "hostile," need visas and are subject to greater scrutiny at borders.

Currently, immigration is a highly contentious issue in the United States and Europe, with some European countries closing their borders to refugees trying to escape wars, drought, and starvation (see Reading 45). In 2017, President Trump signed executive orders to restrict citizens of seven Muslim-majority countries (Iran, Iraq, Libya,

Key Terms Regarding Migration

Refugees–- People who flee their country due to a "well-founded fear" of persecution based on race, religion, nationality, or membership of a particular social group or political opinion. Refugees are outside of their country of nationality or permanent residence and are unable or unwilling to return because of this fear (Migration Data Portal 2019).

Asylum-seekers—Individuals who have sought international protection and whose claims for refugee status have not yet been determined (Migration Data Portal 2019).

Internally displaced persons (IDPs) —People or groups of people who have been forced or obliged to flee or to leave their homes or places of residence, in order to avoid the effects of armed conflict, situations of generalized violence, violations of human rights or natural or human-made disasters, and who have not crossed an internationally recognized state border (Migration Data Portal 2019).

Mixed migration—A movement in which a number of people are travelling together, using the same routes and means of transport, but for different reasons. They have varying needs and profiles and may include asylum-seekers, refugees, trafficked persons, and unaccompanied/separated children (Migration Data Portal 2019).

Disaster-induced migration— The displacement of people due to a serious disruption of a community or a society involving widespread human, material, economic or environmental losses or impacts, which exceeds the ability of the affected community or society to cope using its own resources (Migration Data Portal 2019).

Human trafficking— The recruitment, transportation, transfer, harboring, or receipt of persons by improper means (such as force, abduction, fraud, or coercion) for an improper purpose including forced labor or sexual exploitation. **Human smuggling** generally involves the consent of the people being smuggled, who may pay large sums of money to be smuggled across international borders. Smuggling becomes trafficking when the element of force or coercion is introduced (National Institute of Justice 2019).

In addition, migrants include foreign students, foreign tourists, diplomats and consular personnel and their employees, contract migrant workers, as well as military personnel, officials and advisors.

Somalia, Sudan, Syria, and Yemen) from entering the United States. Over the past twenty years, the US government has militarized the long border with Mexico in an attempt to stop undocumented people from entering this country. This includes armed guards, infrared night-vision scopes, low-light TV cameras, motion sensors, helicopters, and all-terrain vehicles that patrol the border day and night. In 2018, new immigration guidelines required that children be separated from parents or other adults at the southern border. Due to immense public pressure, these guidelines were suspended after an estimated 2,300 children had been separated from their parents. In Reading 44, Leslie A. Campos discusses the situation of people held in Immigration and Customs Enforcement (ICE) detention centers, and in Reading 57, Deborah Lee describes her faith-based work on behalf of people seeking to cross the US-Mexico border.

Migration Patterns

Migration often originates in the Global South with a northern country as the final destination. People may leave their homes and families in a rural area, move to a city in their country, perhaps to a neighboring country, and finally to their intended destination. Often people try to move to places where they have connections based on national, community, or family ties. In the United States, for example, people from the Middle East, Afghanistan, Bosnia, and Southeast Asia have established communities in Dearborn, Michigan; Fremont, California; Utica, New York; and Minneapolis, Minnesota, respectively.

Contemporary migration patterns are unique in two ways. First, women constitute almost half the world's migrants, often as the primary breadwinners for their families. Many women migrate to Europe, North America, and the Middle East because of the demand for domestic workers, nurses' aides, and home health care workers, as noted in Chapter 7. The crisis of care work in northern countries allows women from impoverished nations like the Philippines, El Salvador, and the Dominican Republic to migrate for these jobs (see, e.g., Boris and Parreñas 2010; Fish 2017; Francisco-Menchavez 2018; Y. Kim 2017). Rhacel Salazar Parreñas (2015) recommends the term **reproductive work**, a broader concept than care work, because it also includes menial, non-relational work—preparing food, doing laundry, cleaning floors—that is mainly done by migrant women and women of color.

Conditions in the sending countries are key factors in migration. For example, in the Philippines, a predominantly agrarian country, over half the population subsists on less than the equivalent of $2 per day. Government policies encourage women and men to seek work abroad. Parreñas (2015) has documented the impact of this macro-level policy on families and communities when mothers work abroad. They have to leave their own children in the care of relatives or neighbors, although they also attempt to parent from afar by cell phone, Facebook, or Skype. Similarly, Indonesia, the country with the world's largest Muslim population, exports women to work in Arab states, such as Jordan, Lebanon, and Saudi Arabia, because Muslim employers prefer Muslim household help. Jacquelyn Litt and Mary Zimmerman (2003) contended that the labor of women from poorer nations "serves as the infrastructure on which **First World** economic expansion depends" (p. 157). In Reading 33, Linda Burnham and Nik Theodore make a similar point in the US context: that reproductive work is the foundation of all other work.

Transnational families that span national borders constitute a second feature of contemporary migration patterns. Such people are bilingual or multilingual and move between cultures, sometimes maintaining a home in two places. This includes migrant workers living in the United States and supporting their families and home communities by sending regular remittances or sponsoring schools or other community projects "back home." It also includes professionals, corporate executives, high-tech workers, and academics, whose families and professional lives straddle national borders.

Although our focus here is on those who move, we note that millions of people are prevented from moving or have their movements monitored and curtailed. Within the United States, for example, it is very difficult for working-class and poor young people of color to move out of urban neighborhoods unless they join the military. Others who are restricted include Arab and Muslim people; Palestinians in Gaza, the West Bank, and Jerusalem; North Koreans; Cubans; and refugees in many war-torn countries. Stringent immigration policies in Europe and North America are intended to stop the movement of poor and needy people, who northern governments do not want to accommodate.

Tourism, Trafficking, and Transnational Adoption and Surrogacy

By contrast, several industries are based on movements of people across national borders. We consider three of them: tourism, trafficking, and transnational adoption and surrogacy. Despite differences, these ventures all include recruiters, procurement agencies, and businesses that deal with government bureaucracies, process paperwork, draw up legal contracts, or provide visas.

Tourism

Many people in the United States want to travel abroad to see new places and meet new people, though such "meetings" usually happen on artificial and unequal terms. In her classic essay "Report from the Bahamas," the late June Jordan (1985) noted sadly the social distance between herself—an African American university professor with leisure time and disposable income—and the Black people staffing the hotel where she stayed. Jamaica Kincaid (1988) wrote a caustic account of what tourists see, what they do not see, and how local people view them on the Caribbean island of Antigua. Attorney and activist Mililani Trask (1992) and Hawai'ian Studies professor Haunani-Kay Trask (1999) pointed to negative effects of tourism on Hawai'ian communities and of the commodified, exoticized version of Hawai'ian culture that is retailed to tourists. Although tourism generates jobs, these are often seasonal and pay low wages. The most profitable businesses geared toward tourists are national and international chains, such as hotels and car rental agencies, which compete with local businesses. Tourism also vies with more sustainable forms of development; consumes scarce resources, including land, water, and food supplies; and leaves local communities to cope with the trash and waste that tourists leave behind.

Trafficking

Researchers and advocates Lora Jo Foo, Gabriela Villareal, and Norma Timbang (2007) defined human trafficking as "the recruitment, harboring, movement, or obtaining of a person by force, fraud, or coercion for the purpose of involuntary servitude, debt bondage, or slavery" (p. 38). A number of factors contribute to the rise in human traffick-ing worldwide: impoverished sending countries, demands for low-wage labor in wealth-ier countries, the availability of electronic communications, and increasingly restrictive immigration laws. People of all genders are trafficked to work in agriculture, fisheries, domestic service, restaurants, hotels, manufacturing, construction, and the sex industry.

Economic policies instituted by the World Bank and International Monetary Fund (IMF), trade agreements between richer and poorer nations, and land grabbing and ex-traction of raw materials by transnational corporations have undermined local econo-mies, reduced social services, and resulted in unemployment, poverty, and starvation in many poorer nations. In addition, religious and political persecution, armed conflict, gang violence, crop failures, environmental disasters, and other hardships are "push" factors that compel people to risk migration. Grace Chang and Kathleen Kim (2007) noted the "coercive nature of most migration" given this reality (p. 327; also see Chang 2013). When faced with responsibilities for their family's survival, people decide to mi-grate, often as a last resort, and despite the risks of fraud, deception, and physical or sexual abuse. Ursula Biemann (2002) noted the complex nature of these illicit networks that are also alternative circuits of survival. Migrants may feel that agents who recruit them are providing a valuable service in helping them to achieve their desire to move to a richer country. According to Chang and Kim (2007), a person may initially participate on the basis of "knowledge and consent." (p. 327) Later, they may "wish to leave the work or particular employment site, yet be held captive by an employer."

Trafficking occurs within a nation or across national borders. Men from Bangla-desh are taken to work in sweatshops in South Korea; women from Russia end up in Israel; people from China and Central America are brought to the United States; men from Turkey are conveyed to France; women from Thailand are taken into Japan; and so on. Traffickers may use complex routes with transit points in a third country. They may shift routes and destinations depending on changes in national laws, immigra-tion policies, and penalties for getting caught. Recruiters may front money for visas, transportation, guidance, and other services so that their clients are indebted to them from the outset.

Trafficking of children, women, and trans people into sex industries has been a focus of news reporting and is significant in Thailand, Cambodia, India, and the Philippines (E. Shih 2007). In the case of the United States, nongovernmental orga-nizations and academic researchers estimate that between one-third and one-half of trafficking occurs in sex-related industries (Chang and Kim 2007). This is in contrast to the US government's conflation of human trafficking with prostitution, which has resulted in the narrow application of the federal Trafficking Victims Protection Act to sex trafficking cases (Chang 2013). Paradoxically, although the United States seeks to clamp down on trafficking, US economic, military, and immigration policies are major factors causing the conditions that lead to it.

Transnational Adoption and Surrogacy

Both of these industries have allowed heterosexual couples, single women, and gay men in northern countries to expand their families. Birth mothers in poorer countries provide babies for adoption depending on their personal circumstances, which are affected by economic conditions, social stigma, or China's one-child policy and cultural preference for sons. Many transnational adoptions to the United States and Europe have involved children from South Korea, Vietnam, Cambodia, Guatemala, and Nicaragua, all countries devastated by wars (see, e.g., Dubinsky 2010; E. Kim 2010; Marre and Briggs 2009; Trenka, Oparah, and Shin 2006). Transnational adoption may be the best option for the birth mother and her baby. However, it also represents a loss to these children's home communities, and some nations have restricted or banned transnational adoptions.

Another option is transnational surrogacy, what France Winddance Twine (2011) called "outsourcing the womb." Intending parents may use their own eggs or sperm, if viable, or purchase this genetic material. Staff in specialized clinics implant fertilized embryos into women contracted to act as surrogates. Laws governing surrogacy vary, and many countries with the technological capacity do not allow it or permit it only on a voluntary basis or only for citizens. For a time, India and Nepal were centers of transnational surrogacy because this service was provided there far more cheaply than in the United States (see, e.g., Deomampo 2016; Pande 2014; Rudrappa 2015). Women who act as commercial surrogates are usually mothers in their thirties. They receive nourishing food and good medical care throughout pregnancy and are closely supervised. More recently, both India and Nepal outlawed commercial surrogacy for foreigners, though some clinics are finding ways around this restriction—for example, by bringing surrogate mothers from Kenya (Rudrappa 2017). This reproductive assembly line relies on reproductive technologies, Internet communications, as well as infertile people's desire for a child and their ability to pay for commercial surrogacy. This practice opens up a range of ethical, legal, political, and practical issues (see, e.g., Danna 2015; K. Davis 2017; Riggs and Due 2018). Opponents argue that it exploits the birth mothers and is tantamount to buying and selling babies. Others counter that like factory work, it provides income for women with few economic opportunities. Feminist geographer Carolin Schurr discusses this business in Reading 38.

CONSUMPTION: GOODS, INFORMATION, AND POPULAR CULTURE

Material Flows

Supermarkets and stores in countries of the **Global North** source products from farms and factories worldwide. In 2018, Walmart, the world's biggest retailer, bought products from thousands of suppliers worldwide and sold to nearly 270 million consumers each week through 11,000 stores in 28 countries, and through online marketing (Walmart 2018). Many North American supermarket chains source fresh produce from Mexico, as described by Deborah Barndt (2008) in her studies of growers, truckers, food processors, and supermarket workers along this food chain.

Companies at the top of global supply chains seek flexibility and the freedom to operate wherever is most beneficial for them. This may result in precarious conditions of employment for those lower down the chain—whether in the **Global South** or low-income citizens of richer countries. Subcontractors in the middle of the chain are pressured for low prices and speedy turnaround. They pass this on to workers in the form of low wages, stressful quotas, and enforced overtime in the rush to fill orders (see Fig. 8.1).

In recent years, transnational corporations have stepped up their efforts to secure access to natural resources. Companies based in the Global North are buying or leasing

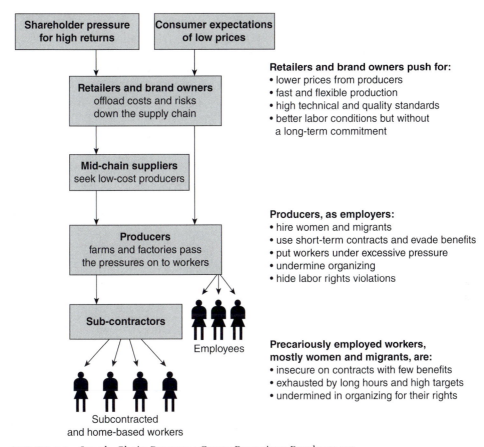

FIGURE 8.1   Supply Chain Pressures Create Precarious Employment

From "Trading Away Our Rights: Women working in global supply chains" is reproduced with the permission of Oxfam, Oxfam House, John Smith Drive, Cowley, Oxford OX4 2JY, UK www.oxfam.org.uk. Oxfam does not necessarily endorse any text or activities that accompany the materials.'

land in Africa, Asia, and Latin America for biofuels, palm oil plantations, ranching, water rights, mining, oil extraction, and solar power generation. This extraction of natural resources, referred to as **extractivism**, is not new but has increased significantly as governments in the Global South, in partnership with local corporations, are selling land or rights to natural resources to foreign companies and investors. Local communities that oppose this, often led by indigenous women, are harshly treated—indeed criminalized—by their governments, as described in Reading 39 (also see, e.g., Cowman 2016; Jenkins 2015). Thus, communities who used to be able to support themselves by farming, forestry, grazing animals, or through local businesses are being displaced and forced to find work elsewhere, which may include migration within their own country or overseas. Women are organizing nationally and regionally to oppose extractivism (see, e.g., WoMin African Gender and Extractives Alliance 2015). In April 2018, women from 13 countries—Bolivia, Brazil, Cambodia, Canada, Colombia, Ecuador, Guatemala, Mexico, Papua New Guinea, Philippines, Peru, South Africa, and Turkey—came together to work together against it (Women Resisting Extractivism 2018).

Information Flows

It is routine to say that we live in an "information age." Increasingly, physical location is immaterial—you can work anywhere as long as you have reliable Internet access. Information workers participate in a fast-paced industry that demands a high degree of flexibility. Work is organized in short-term contracts, and workers are responsible for gaining experience and keeping their skills and contacts up to date. Selling information is very different from selling material goods or services. Information can be sold to multiple buyers and still be retained by the seller; it increases in value the more people are "locked in" to particular products. Although much assembly line work has been outsourced from former industrial centers of the Global North, the design of new products as well as decisions about style, marketing, and finance are retained by company headquarters in the United States, Western Europe, or Japan.

Given the fast, seemingly endless innovation of the information economy, international relations scholar V. Spike Peterson (2003) asked

> whose questions are pursued, whose concerns are silenced . . . whose methods are authorized, whose paradigm is presumed, whose project is funded, whose findings are publicized, whose intellectual property is protected. (p. 139)

She commented that conventional distributions of power are reflected in and reproduced by the information economy. Wikipedia provides one example of this, as pointed out by Mark Graham and Anasuya Sengupta in Reading 40. In 2017, the majority of the world's population had online access, yet "web content remains heavily skewed toward rich, Western countries," a situation that organizations like Whose Knowledge? work to rectify. To understand conditions impacting women in the Global South, people in the Global North need access to accurate information, including accounts by local journalists, academics, and activists that provide policy recommendations and critiques of policies imposed by northern businesses and governments. Relatively few materials are published worldwide or easily available on the Web, which also affected our search for resources for this book.

In Reading 21, Linda Trinh Võ, a professor of Asian American Studies, explores the roles played by young Asian and Asian American women who have managed to insert themselves into what she calls "transnational beauty circuits." Using online communication, especially social media and video-sharing platforms, these "beauty gurus" share information, influence consumers, and promote circle contact lenses and other beauty products and fashions. Manufacturers have sought out these young women for endorsements, product placements, and sponsorships. Võ argues that in this case, cultural transmission is both multifaceted and multidirectional:

> As fashion trendsetters who employ the latest technology, young Asian and Asian American women have found pathways to become pivotal figures of attention and influence, while concurrently being co-opted and marketed by global capital . . .

Cultural Flows

Global cultural flows include mass communications so that US news outlets like CNN and Fox and Britain's BBC are sources of information and opinion worldwide. Al-Jazeera News based in Doha (Qatar) is another example, though smaller in scale.

US-produced music, movies, and TV shows like *Friends, Desperate Housewives*, and *Sex in the City;* reality shows like *Survivor* and *American Idol;* and talk shows featuring Oprah Winfrey or Dr. Phil are distributed worldwide. In many places around the globe, especially metropolitan areas, one can hear the voices of Beyoncé, Christina Aguilera, Mariah Carey, Michael Jackson, and Garth Brooks, as well as artists who were part of earlier US and British pop music scenes, such as the Beatles and "Motown Sound" performers. At the same time, musicians singing in Arabic, Japanese, Korean, and European languages are fusing their respective styles with hip-hop forms that originated in urban, African American youth culture (see, e.g., Condry 2006; Elam and Jackson 2005; Mitchell 2001). Although some commercialized US hip-hop is misogynist and homophobic, the form has been one of resistance, and it has been adopted this way outside the United States.

The direction of flow of globalizing processes reflects the power imbalances among nations and regions. Hollywood-made films and US music dominate global markets. How often do you see titles of films from Chile, China, or Nigeria on the marquee of your local movie theater? Or hear Arabic, French, Japanese, or Korean popular music on your local radio station? The US music industry differentiates various genres, including "world music." What does this term mean? Why is "classical music" in the United States usually taken to mean European classical composers even though all cultures have classical music?

V. Spike Peterson (2003) argued that globalization both homogenizes cultures and also celebrates novelty and the local, although decision-making power over what is selected as valuable is highly concentrated. Some see cultural merging as positive. Critics decry the loss of traditional or locally produced cultural forms and argue that cultural richness and diversity is in danger of becoming flattened into a handful of uniform symbols, representations, and icons. Sociologist George Ritzer (1993) called this "McDonaldization"—meaning standardization. Who controls the flow of cultural productions? Who benefits, who is disadvantaged, and how?

Depictions of US life in TV shows replete with remodeled kitchens, color-coordinated furnishings, lavish meals, and different outfits from scene to scene also generate desires for consumer goods and affluent lifestyles. Regardless of their narratives and plotlines, US movies and TV shows sell the idea of the "America Dream" and notions of US wealth and superiority. They promote dominant beauty standards and help to create a demand for hair straighteners and skin-lightening products, as well as the circle contact lenses discussed in Reading 21. The "B" movies made in the United States that are a staple of TV programming in many nations also sell individualism—with hard, blue-eyed, white masculinity; tough Black gangstas; and long-legged, grasping women in pursuit of greed, money, violence, killing, and sex. How people "read" these media productions depends on their perspectives and values, as discussed in Chapter 2. Audiences may find them appealing or so far removed from local realities and values as to be ridiculous, or they may loathe and despise US popular culture as cultural pollution awash with sleaze, crime, and degradation, what Peterson (2003) called "westoxification" (p. 143).

By contrast, independent projects sustain and celebrate local cultures, adapting them for current times and consciousness. Feminist media projects counter mainstream media stereotypes and provide alternative representations of women's lives, as mentioned in Chapter 2. Examples include Federation of African Media Women, FEMPRESS (Chile), ISIS International Manila, Women's Feature Service (India), and Women's E-news (United States).

age fotostock / Alamy Stock Photo

GLOBAL FACTORIES AND CARE CHAINS

In the past forty to fifty years, electronic communications and air transport have made it increasingly possible for corporations to move work to places where they can pay lower wages, or where there are fewer constraints on their operations. Companies such as Apple, Dell, General Motors, Mattel, Nike, and Playtex (based in the United States); Hyundai, Panasonic, and Sony (based in East Asia); and Nokia, Philips, and Siemens (based in Europe) all have much of their manufacturing work done overseas—for example, in Indonesia, China, Mexico, the Philippines, Guatemala, or Eastern Europe. This organization of work results in inexpensive consumer goods for Australian, European, Japanese, Canadian, and US markets, particularly clothing, toys, household appliances, and electronic equipment.

The global assembly line also includes computer-based services performed by women in the Caribbean, who make hotel reservations for some US and Canadian hotel chains (C. Freeman 2015). Computer support services have been outsourced to India (English speakers) and El Salvador (Spanish speakers). The script readers are "there" and "here" at the same time. Also, we note the **international division of labor** concerning reproductive work, including transnational adoption or surrogacy mentioned earlier, and the recruitment of domestic workers from the Global South for northern nations (see Readings 33 and 38).

The fact that standards of living and wage rates differ widely from country to country means that the process of moving work and workers around the world is likely to continue and to become increasingly complex. In the textile industry, for example, labor costs in 2014 ranged from more than $50 per hour in Switzerland, to less than $5 per hour in Brazil, Tunisia, and Mexico, to less than $1 an hour in Indonesia, Vietnam, Pakistan, and Bangladesh (Werner International 2014).

Note the significance of gender in the global economy and how this intersects with inequalities based on race, ethnicity, and national origin. Roughly 90 percent of the factory workers in "off-shore" production are young women in their late teens and early twenties. Some countries, like the Philippines and China, have established Export Processing Zones, where transnational corporations subcontract work to local companies making products for export. In Mexico, this is done through *maquiladoras*—factories that make goods on contract to "parent" companies mostly based in the United States—located within thirty miles of the border (see, e.g., Fregoso and Bejarano 2010; Peña 1997).

Even in countries like Mexico, with protective labor and environmental laws, these regulations are not often enforced in relation to transnational corporations. Thus, workers experience oppressive working conditions, suffer stress from trying to make the assigned quotas, and contract illnesses from exposure to glues, solvents, and other toxic chemicals, or from lint and dust in the case of textile factories. Women's eyesight deteriorates from hours spent at microscopes. They are subject to sexual harassment by male supervisors and some have been required to undergo pregnancy tests as a condition of employment.

When workers complain and organize to protest these dire conditions, they are often threatened that the plants will close and move elsewhere, and this has happened. For example, when women campaigned for better wages and working conditions, Nike moved some of its production from South Korea to Indonesia and China, pitting workers in one country against those in another, in what has been described as "a race to the bottom."

In Reading 37, sociologist Pun Ngai examines how young Chinese women from rural villages are transformed into an industrial workforce through the imposition of factory discipline. Her ethnographic study explores their desire to leave home and become wage earners even though their work is tedious, repetitive, and low paid. Although this study concerns modern-day China, successive generations of women and men have had to learn to accommodate to factory discipline: meals and bathroom breaks by the clock, work dictated by machines and assembly lines, and forced overtime despite being exhausted. Women in northern England experienced these same pressures in textile mills in the early1800s, as did Irish immigrants in Lowell, Massachusetts, in the 1840s, Mexican women in *maquiladoras* in the 1960s, and now women in Bangladesh and China.

Currently, Chinese workers produce many consumer goods, including cell phones and computer equipment marketed worldwide. Figure 8.2 shows 2010 production costs and profits for the iPhone, produced in China by the Taiwan-based Foxconn Technology Group, a subcontractor for Apple. The iPhone X, introduced in 2017, was priced at $999 in the United States. It cost an estimated $370 in materials to produce. In 2017, Foxconn workers earned $286 per month, with dormitory accommodation provided by the factories, food, and Internet expenses docked directly from their pay (Cuthbertson 2017). The working practices at Foxconn's huge plants in China came under international scrutiny in 2010 after a series of suicides among young women workers due to excessive pressure

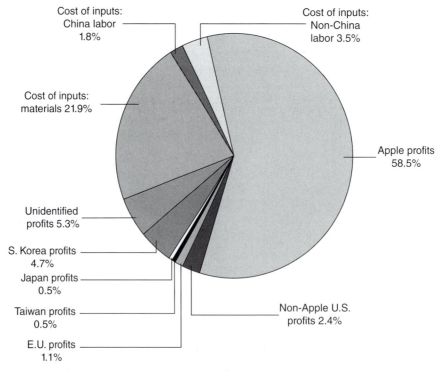

FIGURE 8.2 iPhone Production Costs and Profits, 2010

From Kraemer, Linden, and Dedrick (2011, p. 5). Reproduced here with permission of the authors.

from long working hours, unpaid overtime, and health and safety failings— practices that break Chinese labor laws (Garside 2012). Infractions of labor rights continue at Apple's Chinese suppliers and include forced overtime, chemical hazards, and inadequate safety standards (see, e.g., Chamberlain 2018a; Chan, Pun, and Selden 2016). Samsung, Dell, HP, and Microsoft also contravene workers' rights through the activities of their suppliers in China. In 2018, Amazon admitted that thousands of Chinese workers who made speakers and Kindles were hired and paid illegally (Chamberlain 2018b).

Despite the exploitative conditions, young women have flocked to industrial centers to become wage earners. Their jobs mainly depend on orders from the Global North. Any reduction in demand means that orders are cancelled and workers laid off. As a result, their families eat cheaper food, and some may take girls out of school to help with domestic responsibilities at home. Thus, decisions made by individual consumers and businesses thousands of miles away have a far-reaching impact on people in other locations.

THE INTERNATIONAL FINANCIAL SYSTEM

Rules and agreements that are part of the international economic system are based on **neoliberal** policies that call for the freedom of businesses to operate with minimal interference from governments, international organizations, or labor unions.

Major **international financial institutions** include the World Bank and the IMF, created as part of the Bretton Woods Agreement to rebuild and regulate the international economy following World War II. The World Trade Organization (WTO), established in 1995, adjudicates cases brought by nations regarding restrictions on trade caused by other nations' laws. For instance, the WTO ruled that the US Endangered Species Act, which requires domestic and foreign fishers to catch shrimp by methods that do not kill sea turtles, imposed a limitation on trade that violated WTO rules. In another example, the United States, Canada, and Argentina challenged European Union restrictions on imports of genetically modified foods.

The World Bank and IMF have required nations to make stringent changes to their economies in order to qualify for loans. These are known as Structural Adjustment Programs. The goal is to increase the profitability of corporations on the argument that this will benefit everyone. Required measures include:

- Cutting back government spending on social services.
- Abolishing price controls, particularly on food, fuel, and public transportation.
- Adding new taxes and increasing existing taxes.
- Selling nationalized industries, or at least a majority of the shares, to private corporations, often from outside the country.
- Improving profitability for corporations through wage controls, tax breaks, loans, and credit, or by building ports, better roads, or rail transportation.
- Increasing the output of cash crops for export.

Though not required to do so by the World Bank, successive US administrations have adopted similar policies in favor of corporations, including reductions in taxation for wealthy people, deregulation of air transport, and the privatization of public utilities like water and electricity, parts of the prison industry, and military contracting with private companies.

One of the roles of nation-states is to provide conditions that will allow businesses to operate profitably. Governments may also seek to impose some controls over corporate activities, though this is limited by shared assumptions about the central role of business as well as by their disparate resources. Governments of many small countries have much smaller operating budgets than those of mega-corporations. The logic of economic **globalization** is leading to a borderless world for capital and corporate activities but not for workers or people who migrate for other reasons.

Assumptions and Ideologies

Countries of the Global South are often called developing countries, assuming that they will become industrialized like North America and Western Europe. Positing a continuum from "undeveloped" to "developed" suggests that this process is linear and also the best way for a nation to progress. This continuum masks the fact that so-called developing countries already possess great wealth in terms of people, natural resources, and indigenous knowledge. Indeed, much of the wealth of developed nations has come from poorer ones. Vandana Shiva (1988), a writer on environment and development policy, used the term *devastated* instead of *undeveloped* economies to emphasize this.

Economic growth is often conflated with "progress"—a far more complex concept with social, moral, and intellectual dimensions. This limited view of progress often leads people in a highly material society like the United States to value ourselves primarily in terms of the money we make and the things we own or consume. At a national level, too, it leads to an emphasis on material success and security with support for government policies that facilitate profit making regardless of social costs.

People in dominant positions may justify inequalities among and within nations with reference to ideologies of racism, classism, sexism, and national superiority. Others argue that in principle, inequality is unjust. Some people's freedom and comfort should not be bought at the expense of other people's oppression, degradation, and poverty. More pragmatically, inequality is a source of tension and conflict. On an international level, it is a cause of war; on a national or community level, it leads to alienation, anger, violence, vandalism, and crime. Public health experts Richard Wilkinson and Kate Pickett (2009) present data to show that economic inequality is linked to poorer physical and mental health, violence, and greater rates of imprisonment. In short, they argue, inequalities weaken societies while greater equality makes them stronger.

Legacies of Colonization

Current disparities among nations are often based on older inequalities resulting from colonization. Former British colonies include India, Ghana, Hong Kong, Kenya, Nigeria, and Pakistan. France had colonial possessions in Algeria, Senegal, Togo, and Vietnam. Newer colonial powers have also left their mark, such as the United States in Puerto Rico and the Pacific region, or Japan in what is now South Korea and several countries in Southeast Asia. Although the details varied from one colonial power to another, several factors were central to this process:

- The imposition of legal and political institutions.
- Cultural and spiritual devastation, and replacement of language.
- Changes in social relations, including gender roles, and ethnic and class inequalities.

- Psychological dimensions of ethnocentrism and racism, such as internalized racism and colorism, rooted in white supremacy.
- Distortions of the economy with dependence on a few agricultural products or raw materials.

Colonial powers extracted timber, minerals, and cash crops, which were processed into manufactured goods in colonial centers for consumption there and for export. During the second half of the twentieth century, virtually all colonies gained political independence. However, many have remained tied to their colonizers economically and politically, which has led commentators to characterize the continuing inequalities between richer and poorer countries as **neocolonialism**. In Reading 49, Amina Mama and Margo Okazawa-Rey show how colonial regimes in Africa relied on military force, "deployed along with a formidable array of . . . technologies of violence, thus militarizing the societies they conquered and governed in ways that extended far beyond the barracks, into the very fabric of people's lives."

TRANSNATIONAL ALLIANCES FOR A SECURE AND SUSTAINABLE FUTURE

As this chapter shows, the rules and conditions imposed by corporate and government decision-makers and international financial institutions have led to increasing economic insecurity—even devastation—for many people worldwide. At the same time, increasing cell phone use and Internet access have facilitated international communication among people in an unprecedented manner.

In the Global South, workers' organizations, environmental campaigns, feminist advocates, faith-based groups, and human rights organizations have been demanding better pay and working conditions, along with economic development that is environmentally sound. In the Global North, increased consumer awareness of abusive practices has brought about some changes in wages and working conditions overseas. Organizations are linking across national borders to try to hold corporations accountable for working conditions. Examples of such groups based in north America include China Labor Watch (New York, NY), Global Trade Watch (Washington, DC), the International Labor Rights Forum (Washington, DC), Maquila Solidarity Network (Toronto, Canada), and United Students Against Sweatshops (Washington, DC). US nonprofits like Equal Exchange (West Bridgewater, MA), Global Exchange (San Francisco), Just Coffee (Madison, WI), Pueblo to People (Houston, TX), and Ten Thousand Villages (Akron, PA) support **fair trade** between producers in the Global South and consumers in the Global North. However, addressing consumption—or overconsumption—in the North goes far beyond fair trade and will require fundamental changes in consciousness, priorities, and economic organization, as suggested in Chapter 7.

In the 1960s and 1970s, people active in US social movements made theoretical and practical connections with anti-colonial struggles in South Africa, Vietnam, Cuba, Angola, and Mozambique, as mentioned by the Combahee River Collective in Reading 3. In the twenty-first century, international linkages continue to be crucial because of the impacts of globalization on people's lives regardless of our locations.

QUESTIONS FOR REFLECTION

As you read and discuss this chapter, think about these questions:

1. Why does the globalization of the economy matter to people living in the United States?
2. How is global inequality related to sexism, racism, and national privilege?
3. How do you define wealth, aside from material possessions? List all the ways you are enriched.
4. How do you think about being an ethical consumer? What supports or hinders you in this?
5. How do people in elite positions justify inequalities to others? To themselves? How are the ideologies of nationalism, racial superiority, male superiority, and classism useful here?

FINDING OUT MORE ON THE WEB

1. Study maps on the following sites that show colonial histories and contemporary disparities among nations:

   www-personal.umich.edu/~mejn/cartograms/
   http://en.wikipedia.Org/wiki/Image:World_1898_empires_colonies_territory.png
   http://www.worldmapper.org

2. The following websites have information about alternatives to globalization:

   Association for Women's Rights in Development: https://www.awid.org/
   CorpWatch: www.corpwatch.org
   Global Women's Strike: www.globalwomenstrike.net
   Women's Earth and Climate Action Network: https://wecaninternational.org/
   Women's Environment and Development Organization: https://wedo.org/
   World Social Forum: www.forumsocialmundial.org.br

3. Use your search engine to research organizations concerned with the global sex trade and trafficking such as:

   Coalition Against Trafficking in Women (CATW)
   Global Alliance Against Traffic in Women (GAATW)

TAKING ACTION

1. Interview someone who immigrated to the United States to learn why that person left their home country and how they got to where they are now.
2. Look at the labels in your clothes and on all the products you buy. Where were they made, and how much did workers earn to produce that item? Look up these countries on a map if you don't know where they are.
3. Find out who manufactures the clothing that bears your college's name and whether there are sweatshops in your region.
4. Do you need all you currently own? List everything you need to sustain life. Which items do you need to buy? Which might you make yourself, share, or barter with others?
5. Find a campaign that is tackling a global issue you care about, and participate in it in some way.

36 | THE HOMELAND: AZTLÁN/EL OTRO MÉXICO (1987)

Gloria Anzaldúa (1942–2004) was a Chicana lesbian feminist poet and fiction writer. With Cherríe Moraga, she co-edited the ground-breaking anthology *This Bridge Called My Back: Writings by Radical Women of Color* (1983), winner of the Before Columbus Foundation American Book Award. She taught Chicano Studies, Feminist Studies, and creative writing at various universities. Her other books include *Borderlands: La Frontera—The New Mestiza* (1987) and *This Bridge We Call Home: Radical Visions for Transformation* (edited with AnaLouise Keating, 2002).

El otro México que acá hemos construido
el espacio es lo que ha sido
territorio nacional.
Esté el esfuerzo de todos nuestros hermanos
y latinoamericanos que han sabido
progressar.

—LOS TIGRES DEL NORTE[1]

"The *Aztecas del norte* . . . compose the largest single tribe or nation of Anishinabeg (Indians) found in the United States today. . . . Some call themselves Chicanos and see themselves as people whose true homeland is Aztlán [the US Southwest]."[2]

Wind tugging at my sleeve
feet sinking into the sand
I stand at the edge where earth touches ocean
where the two overlap
a gentle coming together
at other times and places a violent clash.
Across the border in Mexico
   stark silhouette of houses gutted by waves,
    cliffs crumbling into the sea,
     silver waves marbled with spume
      gashing a hole under the border fence.
       Miro el mar atacar
      la cerca en Border Field Park
     con sus buchones de agua,
an Easter Sunday resurrection
of the brown blood in my veins.
Oigo el llorido del mar, el respiro del aire,
   my heart surges to the beat of the sea.

In the gray haze of the sun
   the gulls' shrill cry of hunger,
    the tangy smell of the sea seeping into me.
     I walk through the hole in the fence to
  the other side.
Under my fingers I feel the gritty wire
  rusted by 139 years
   of the salty breath of the sea.
Beneath the iron sky
Mexican children kick their soccer ball across,
run after it, entering the US
  I press my hand to the steel curtain—
  chainlink fence crowned with rolled barbed
  wire—
rippling from the sea where Tijuana touches
San Diego
   unrolling over mountains
    and plains
    and deserts,
this "Tortilla Curtain" turning into *el río Grande*
  flowing down to the flatlands
   of the Magic Valley of South Texas
    its mouth emptying into the Gulf.
1,950-mile-long open wound
   dividing a *pueblo*, a culture,
   running down the length of my body,
    staking fence rods in my flesh,
    splits me splits me
     me raja me raja
    This is my home
    this thin edge of

Source: Excerpted from *Borderlands/La Frontera: The New Mestiza*. © 1987, 1999, 2007, 2012 by Gloria Anzaldúa. Reprinted by permission of Aunt Lute Books. www.auntlute.com.

barbwire.
But the skin of the earth is seamless.
The sea cannot be fenced,
el mar does not stop at borders.
To show the white man what she thought of his
arrogance,
Yemaya blew that wire fence down.
This land was Mexican once,
was Indian always
and is.
And will be again.

Yo soy un puente tendido
del mundo gabacho al del mojado,
lo pasado me estirá pa' 'trás
y lo presente pa' 'delante.
Que la Virgen de Guadalupe me cuide
Ay ay ay, soy mexicana de este lado.

The US-Mexican border *es una herida abierta* where the Third World grates against the First and bleeds. And before a scab forms it hemorrhages again, the lifeblood of two worlds to anyone else-merging to form a third country—a border culture. Borders are set up to define the places that are safe and unsafe, to distinguish *us* from *them*. A border is a dividing line, a narrow strip along a steep edge. A borderland is a vague and undetermined place created by the emotional residue of an unnatural boundary. It is in a constant state of transition. The prohibited and forbidden are its inhabitants. *Los airavesados* live here: the squint-eyed, the perverse, the queer, the troublesome, the mongrel, the mulato, the half-breed, the half-dead; in short, those who cross over, pass over, or go through the confines of the "normal." Gringos in the US Southwest consider the inhabitants of the borderlands transgressors, aliens—whether they possess documents or not, whether they're Chicanos, Indians or Blacks. Do not enter, trespassers will be raped, maimed, strangled, gassed, shot. The only "legitimate" inhabitants are those in power, the whites and those who align themselves with whites. Tension grips the inhabitants of the borderlands like a virus. Ambivalence and unrest reside there and death is no stranger.

In the fields, *la migra*. My aunt saying, "*No corran,* don't run. They'll think you're *del otro lado*." In the confusion, Pedro ran, terrified of being caught. He couldn't speak English, couldn't tell them he was fifth generation American. *Sin papeles*—he did not carry his birth certificate to work in the fields. *La migra* took him away while we watched. *Se lo llevaron*. He tried to smile when he looked back at us, to raise his fist. But I saw the shame pushing his head down, I saw the terrible weight of shame hunch his shoulders. They deported him to Guadalajara by plane. The furthest he'd ever been to Mexico was Reynosa, a small border town opposite Hidalgo, Texas, not far from McAllen. Pedro walked all the way to the Valley. *Se lo llevaron sin un centavo al pobre. Se vino andando desde Guadalajara.*

During the original peopling of the Americas, the first inhabitants migrated across the Bering Straits and walked south across the continent. The oldest evidence of humankind in the US—the Chicanos' ancient Indian ancestors—was found in Texas and has been dated to 35,000 BC[3] In the Southwest United States archeologists have found 20,000-year-old campsites of the Indians who migrated through, or permanently occupied, the Southwest, Aztlán—land of the herons, land of whiteness, the Edenic place of origin of theAzteca.

In 1000 BC, descendants of the original Cochise people migrated into what is now Mexico and Central America and became the direct ancestors of many of the Mexican people. (The Cochise culture of the Southwest is the parent culture of the Aztecs. The Uto-Aztecan languages stemmed from the language of the Cochise people.)[4] The Aztecs (the Nahuatl word for people of Aztlán) left the Southwest in 1168 AD.

Now let us go.
Tihueque, tihueque,
Vámonos, vámonos.
Un pájaro cantó.
Con sus ocho tribus salieron
de la "cueva del origen,"
los aztecas siguieron al dios
Huitzilopochtli.

Huitzilopochtli, the God of War, guided them to the place (that later became Mexico City) where an eagle with a writhing serpent in its beak perched on a cactus. The eagle symbolizes the spirit (as the sun, the father); the serpent symbolizes the soul (as the earth, the mother). Together, they symbolize the struggle between the spiritual/celestial/male and the underworld/earth/feminine. The symbolic sacrifice of the serpent to the "higher" masculine powers indicates that the patriarchal order had already vanquished the feminine and matriarchal order in pre-Columbian America.

At the beginning of the sixteenth century, the Spaniards and Hernán Cortés invaded Mexico and, with the help of tribes that the Aztecs had subjugated, conquered it. Before the Conquest, there were twenty-five million Indian people in Mexico and the Yucatán. Immediately after the Conquest, the Indian population had been reduced to under seven million. By 1650, only one-and-a-half-million pure-blooded Indians remained. The *mestizos* who were genetically equipped to survive small pox, measles, and typhus (Old World diseases to which the natives had no immunity), founded a new hybrid race and inherited Central and South America.[5] *En 1521 nació una nueva raza, el mestizo, el mexicano* (people of mixed Indian and Spanish blood), a race that had never existed before. Chicanos, Mexican-Americans, are the offspring of those first matings.

Our Spanish, Indian, and *mestizo* ancestors explored and settled parts of the US Southwest as early as the sixteenth century. For every gold-hungry *conquistador* and soul-hungry missionary who came north from Mexico, ten to twenty Indians and *mestizos* went along as porters or in other capacities.[6] For the Indians, this constituted a return to the place of origin, Aztlán, thus making Chicanos originally and secondarily indigenous to the Southwest. Indians and *mestizos* from central Mexico intermarried with North American Indians. The continual intermarriage between Mexican and American Indians and Spaniards formed an even greater *mestizaje*.

El destierro/The Lost Land

Entonces corré la sangre
no sabe el indio que hacer,
le van a quitar su tierra,
la tiene que defender,

el indio se cae muerto,
y el afuerino de pie.
Levántate, Manquilef.
Arauco tiene una pena
más negra que su chamal,
ya no son los españoles
los que les hacen llorar,
hoy son los propios chilenos
los que les quitan su pan.
Levántate, Pailahuan.

—Violeta Parra, *"Arauco tiene una pena"*[7]

In the 1800s, Anglos migrated illegally into Texas, which was then part of Mexico, in greater and greater numbers and gradually drove the *tejanos* (native Texans of Mexican descent) from their lands, committing all manner of atrocities against them. Their illegal invasion forced Mexico to fight a war to keep its Texas territory. The Battle of the Alamo, in which the Mexican forces vanquished the whites, became, for the whites, the symbol for the cowardly and villainous character of the Mexicans. It became (and still is) a symbol that legitimized the white imperialist takeover. With the capture of Santa Anna later in 1836, Texas became a republic. *Tejanos* lost their land and, overnight, became the foreigners.

Ya la mitad del terreno
les vendió el traidor Santa Anna,
con lo que se ha hecho muy rica
la nación americana.
¿Qué acaso no se conforman
con el oro de las minas?
Ustedes muy elegantes
y aquí nosotros en ruinas.

—from the Mexican corrido, *"Del peligro de la Intervención"*[8]

In 1846, the US incited Mexico to war. US troops invaded and occupied Mexico, forcing her to give up almost half of her nation, what is now Texas, New Mexico, Arizona, Colorado and California.

With the victory of the US forces over the Mexican in the US-Mexican War, *los norteamericanos* pushed the Texas border down 100 miles, from *el río Nueces* to *el río Grande*. South Texas ceased to be part of the Mexican state of Tamaulipas. Separated from Mexico, the Native Mexican–Texan no longer looked toward Mexico as home; the Southwest became our homeland once more. The border fence that divides the Mexican people was born on February 2, 1848, with the signing of the Treaty of Guadalupe Hidalgo. It left 100,000 Mexican citizens on this side, annexed by conquest along with the land. The land established by the treaty as belonging to Mexicans was soon swindled away from its owners. The treaty was never honored and restitution, to this day, has never been made.

> The justice and benevolence of God
> will forbid that . . . Texas should again
> become a howling wilderness
> trod only by savages, or . . . benighted
> by the ignorance and superstition,
> the anarchy and rapine of Mexican misrule.
> The Anglo-American race are destined
> to be forever the proprietors of
> this land of promise and fulfillment.
> Their laws will govern it,
> their learning will enlighten it,
> their enterprise will improve it.
> Their flocks range its boundless pastures,
> for them its fertile lands will yield . . .
> luxuriant harvests . . .
> The wilderness of Texas has been redeemed
> by Anglo-American blood & enterprise.
>
> —William H. Wharton[9]

The Gringo, locked into the fiction of white superiority, seized complete political power, stripping Indians and Mexicans of their land while their feet were still rooted in it. *Con el destierro y el exilo fuimos desuñados, destroncados, destripados*—we were jerked out by the roots, truncated, disemboweled, dispossessed, and separated from our identity and our history. Many, under the threat of Anglo terrorism, abandoned homes and ranches and went to Mexico. Some stayed and protested. But as the courts, law enforcement officials, and government officials not only ignored their pleas but penalized them for their efforts, *tejanos* had no other recourse but armed retaliation.

After Mexican-American resisters robbed a train in Brownsville, Texas, on October 18, 1915, Anglo vigilante groups began lynching Chicanos. Texas Rangers would take them into the brush and shoot them. One hundred Chicanos were killed in a matter of months, whole families lynched. Seven thousand fled to Mexico, leaving their small ranches and farms. The Anglos, afraid that the *mexicanos*[10] would seek independence from the US, brought in 20,000 army troops to put an end to the social protest movement in South Texas. Race hatred had finally fomented into an all-out war.[11]

> My grandmother lost all her cattle,
> they stole her land.

"Drought hit South Texas," my mother tells me. *"La tierra se puso bien seca y los animales comenzaron a morrirse de se'. Mi papá se murió de un* heart attack *dejando a mamá* pregnant *y con ocho huercos*, with eight kids and one on the way. *Yo fuí la mayor, tenía diez años.* The next year the drought continued *y el ganado* got hoof and mouth. *Se calleron en droves en las pastas y el* brushland, *pansas blancas* ballooning to the skies. *El siguiente año* still no rain. *Mi pobre madre viuda perdió* two-thirds of her *ganado.* A smart *gabacho* lawyer took the land away *mamá* hadn't paid taxes. *No hablaba inglés*, she didn't know how to ask for time to raise the money." My father's mother, Mama Locha, also lost her *terreno.* For a while we got $12.50 a year for the "mineral rights" of six acres of cemetery, all that was left of the ancestral lands. Mama Locha had asked that we bury her there beside her husband. *El cemeterio estaba cercado.* But there was a fence around the cemetery, chained and padlocked by the ranch owners of the surrounding land. We couldn't even get in to visit the graves, much less bury her there. Today, it is still padlocked. The sign reads: "Keep out. Trespassers will be shot."

In the 1930s, after Anglo agribusiness corporations cheated the small Chicano landowners of their land, the corporations hired gangs of *mexicanos* to pull out the brush, chaparral and cactus and to irrigate the desert. The land they toiled over had once belonged to many of them or had been used communally by them. Later the Anglos brought in huge machines and root plows and had the Mexicans scrape the land clean of natural vegetation.

In my childhood I saw the end of dryland farming. I witnessed the land cleared; saw the huge pipes connected to underwater sources sticking up in the air. As children, we'd go fishing in some of those canals when they were full and hunt for snakes in them when they were dry. In the 1950s I saw the land, cut up into thousands of neat rectangles and squares, constantly being irrigated. In the 340-day growth season, the seeds of any kind of fruit or vegetable had only to be stuck in the ground in order to grow. More big land corporations came in and bought up the remaining land.

To make a living my father became a sharecropper. Rio Farms Incorporated loaned him seed money and living expenses. At harvest time, my father repaid the loan and forked over 40% of the earnings. Sometimes we earned less than we owed, but always the corporations fared well. Some had major holdings in vegetable trucking, livestock auctions and cotton gins. Altogether we lived on three successive Rio farms; the second was adjacent to the King Ranch and included a dairy farm; the third was a chicken farm. I remember the white feathers of three thousand Leghorn chickens blanketing the land for acres around. My sister, mother and I cleaned, weighed and packaged eggs. (For years afterwards I couldn't stomach the sight of an egg.) I remember my mother attending some of the meetings sponsored by well-meaning whites from Rio Farms. They talked about good nutrition, health, and held huge barbeques. The only thing salvaged for my family from those years are modern techniques of food canning and a food-stained book they printed made up of recipes from Rio Farms' Mexican women. How proud my mother was to have her recipe for *enchiladas coloradas* in a book.

El cruzar del mojado/Illegal Crossing

. . .

La crisis

Los gringos had not stopped at the border. By the end of the nineteenth century, powerful landowners in Mexico, in partnership with US colonizing companies, had dispossessed millions of Indians of their lands. Currently, Mexico and her eighty million citizens are almost completely dependent on the US market. The Mexican government and wealthy growers are in partnership with such American conglomerates as American Motors, IT&T and DuPont which own factories called *maquiladoras*. One-fourth of all Mexicans work at *maquiladoras*; most are young women. Next to oil, *maquiladoras* are Mexico's second greatest source of US dollars. Working eight to twelve hours a day to wire in backup lights of US autos or solder miniscule wires in TV sets is not the Mexican way. While the women are in the *maquiladoras*, the children are left on their own. Many roam the street, become part of *cholo* gangs. The infusion of the values of the white culture, coupled with the exploitation by that culture, is changing the Mexican way of life.

The devaluation of the *peso* and Mexico's dependency on the US have brought on what the Mexicans call *la crisis*. No *hay trabajo*. Half of the Mexican people are unemployed. In the US a man or woman can make eight times what they can in Mexico. By March, 1987, 1,088 pesos were worth one US dollar. I remember when I was growing up in Texas how we'd cross the border at Reynosa or Progreso to buy sugar or medicines when the dollar was worth eight *pesos* and fifty *centavos*.

La travesía

For many *mexicanos del otro lado*, the choice is to stay in Mexico and starve or move north and live. *Dicen que cada mexicano siempre sueña de la conquista en los brazos de cuatro gringas rubias, la conquista del país poderoso del norte, los Estados Unidos. En cada Chicano y mexicano vive el mito del tesoro territorial perdido.* North Americans call this return to the homeland the silent invasion.

"A la cueva volverán"

—El Puma *en la cancion "Amalia"*

South of the border, called North America's rubbish dump by Chicanos, *mexicanos* congregate in the plazas to talk about the best way to cross. Smugglers, *coyotes, pasadores, enganchadores* approach these people or are sought out by them. *"¿Qué dicen muchachos a echársela de mojado?"*

"Now among the alien gods with weapons of magic am I."

—Navajo protection song, sung when going into battle.[12]

We have a tradition of migration, a tradition of long walks. Today we are witnessing *la migración de los pueblos mexicanos*, the return odyssey to the historical/mythological Aztlán. This time, the traffic is from south to north.

El retorno to the promised land first began with the Indians from the interior of Mexico and the *mestizos* that came with the *conquistadores* in the 1500s. Immigration continued in the next three centuries, and, in this century, it continued with the *braceros* who helped to build our railroads and who picked our fruit. Today thousands of Mexicans are crossing the border legally and illegally; ten million people without documents have returned to the Southwest.

Faceless, nameless, invisible, taunted with "Hey cucaracho" (cockroach). Trembling with fear, yet filled with courage, a courage born of desperation. Barefoot and uneducated, Mexicans with hands like boot soles gather at night by the river where two worlds merge creating what Reagan calls a frontline, a war zone. The convergence has created a shock culture, a border culture, a third country, a closed country.

Without benefit of bridges, the *"mojados"* (wetbacks) float on inflatable rafts across *el río Grande*, or wade or swim across naked, clutching their clothes over their heads. Holding onto the grass, they pull themselves along the banks with a prayer to *Virgen de Guadalupe* on their lips: *Ay virgencita morena, mimadrecita, dame tu bendición.*

The Border Patrol hides behind the local McDonalds on the outskirts of Brownsville, Texas, or some other border town. . . . Hunters in army-green uniforms stalk and track these economic refugees by the powerful nightvision of electronic sensing devices planted in the ground or mounted on Border Patrol vans. Cornered by flashlights, frisked while their arms stretch over their heads, *los mojados* are handcuffed, locked in jeeps, and then kicked back across the border. . . .

Those who make it past the checking points of the Border Patrol find themselves in the midst of 150 years of racism in Chicano *barrios* in the Southwest and in big northern cities. Living in a no-man's-borderland, caught between being treated as criminals and being able to eat, between resistance and deportation, the illegal refugees are some of the poorest and the most exploited of any people in the US. It is illegal for Mexicans to work without green cards. But big farming combines, farm bosses and smugglers who bring them in make money off the "wetbacks'" labor—they don't have to pay federal minimum wages, or ensure adequate housing or sanitary conditions.

The Mexican woman is especially at risk. Often the *coyote* (smuggler) doesn't feed her for days or let her go to the bathroom. Often he rapes her or sells her into prostitution. She cannot call on county or state health or economic resources because she doesn't know English and she fears deportation. American employers are quick to take advantage of her helplessness. She can't go home. She's sold her house, her furniture, borrowed from friends in order to pay the *coyote* who charges her four or five thousand dollars to smuggle her to Chicago. She may work as a live-in maid for white, Chicano or Latino households . . . [o]r work in the garment industry, do hotel work. Isolated and worried about her family back home, afraid of getting caught and deported, living with as many as fifteen people in one room, the *mexicana* suffers serious health problems. *Se enferma de los nervios, de alta presión.*[13]

La mojada, la mujer indocumentada, is doubly threatened in this country. Not only does she have to contend with sexual violence, but like all women, she is prey to a sense of physical helplessness. As a refugee, she leaves the familiar and safe home-ground to venture into unknown and possibly dangerous terrain.

This is her home
    this thin edge of
        barbwire.

NOTES

1. Los Tigres del Norte is a *conjunto* band.
2. Jack D. Forbes, *Aztecas del Norte: The Chicanos of Aztlán* (Greenwich, CT: Fawcett Publications, Premier Books, 1973), 13, 183; Eric R. Wolf, *Sons of Shaking Earth* (Chicago, IL: University of Chicago Press, Phoenix Books, 1959), 32.
3. John R. Chávez, *The Lost Land: The Chicano Images of the Southwest* (Albuquerque, NM: University of New Mexico Press, 1984), 9.
4. Chávez, 9. Besides the Aztecs, the Ute, Gabrillino of California, Pima of Arizona, some Pueblo of New Mexico, Comanche of Texas, Opata of Sonora, Tarahu-mara of Sinaloa and Durango, and the Huichol of Jalisco speak Uto-Aztecan languages and are descended from the Cochise people.
5. Reay Tannahill, *Sex in History* (Briarcliff Manor, NY: Stein and Day/Publishers/Scarborough House, 1980), 308.
6. Chávez, 21.
7. Isabel Parra, *El Libra Major de Violeta Parra* (Madrid, España: Ediciones Michay, S.A., 1985), 156–7.
8. From the Mexican *corrido*, "*Del veligro de la Intervención.*" Vicente T. Mendoza, *El Corrido Mexicano* (México. DF: Fondo De Cultura Económica, 1954), 42.
9. Arnoldo De León, *They Called Them Greasers: Anglo Attitudes Toward Mexicans in Texas, 1821–1900* (Austin, TX: University of Texas Press, 1983), 2–3.
10. The Plan of San Diego, Texas, drawn up on January 6, 1915, called for the independence and segregation of the states bordering Mexico: Texas, New Mexico, Arizona, Colorado, and California. Indians would get their land back, Blacks would get six states from the south and form their own independent republic. Chávez, 79.
11. Jesús Mena, "Violence in the Rio Grande Valley," *Nuestro* (Jan/Feb. 1983), 41–42.
12. From the Navajo "Protection Song" (to be sung upon going into battle). George W. Gronyn, ed., *American Indian Poetry: The Standard Anthology of Songs and Chants* (New York, NY: Liveright, 1934), 97.
13. Margarita B. Melville, "Mexican Women Adapt to Migration," *International Migration Review*, 1978.

37 EXCERPT FROM "MADE IN CHINA" (2005)

Pun Ngai is Professor of Sociology at the University of Hong Kong. She was the first Asian scholar to win the prestigious C. Wright Mills Award, for *Made in China: Women Factory Workers in a Global Workplace* (2005), a book read widely in the United States, Europe, and Asia. Her research interests concern labor and gender, migration, and globalization. She has published in journals in sociology, anthropology, labor studies, China studies, and cultural studies.

. . . Turning a young and rural body into an industrialized and productive laborer, a seemingly universal project of disciplining labor, is the primary task of transnational production when it meets migrant labor in urban China . . .

. . . An often-repeated story in the [Meteor] workplace, made up by Hong Kong businessmen, managers, and technical persons, was that mainland Chinese workers—socialist and rural bodies—were unfit for capitalist production.[1] . . . Because Hong Kong businessmen were very distrustful of mainland workers, rural migrant workers were portrayed as uneducated, "uncivilized," and thus undisciplined in the workplace. There was a general belief that these working bodies were ready to spit on the floor, to leave their work position at will, and even worse, to destroy the production machinery.

. . . Thus the first task of capital was to transform individual undesirable migrants into useful workers, which involved projects of culture and power, both covertly and overtly, that worked on bodies and minds, behaviors and beliefs, gestures and habits, and attitudes and aptitudes. . . .

The Art of Spacing: Positioning on the Line

. . . With twenty to twenty-five workers on assembly lines and fifteen to twenty on quality control (QC) lines, there was a total of ten production assembly lines and four QC lines on the shop floor. Placing a body on the line was the first technique of the disciplinary machine to work on the worker. A cog in a machine, the body was pinned down to its own specific position, functional and productive. . . .

A coworker, Meifang, sat directly across from me on the production line. We had a particular relationship that would not have developed in another place or with other people. My presence as an ethnographer in that particular work position and the demands of production jointly shaped our relationship. Meifang was a fresh hand, hired two days after I arrived. With her rounded face she still looked rustic, and she was timid in expressing herself. At age eighteen she was a fresh junior secondary school graduate from a village in Hunan Province. . . .

We were both placed on . . . a production line of twenty-two workers. We had one foreman, one line leader, and one line assistant. The model produced on the line was an MB201 route-finder, a kind of electronic road map for drivers, produced for a big-name car company in Europe. The product came to our line at nearly the final stage of the production process. We assembled the main board, the liquid crystal display (LCD), and the plastic case around the whole product. With work divided into twelve processes, normally there were two or three people with responsibility for one process. My process was performed by three people: myself, Meifang, and Chinghua. To this day I still believe that Meifang was hired to accelerate the pace on the line because of my slow speed.

. . . Workers were trained as specialists in just one process; only the workers who had been working on the line for more than a year had the opportunity to learn more than one work process. The work process was seldom changed unless a new model required a new arrangement of work positions. In front of every seat there was a layout hung on the shelf that demonstrated meticulously with pictures and graphics each step the worker should follow. The work was minute, specified, and systematic: what the individual could and should do was to follow it with precision, and if one were attentive and disciplined enough, one needed only to mechanically repeat specific bodily movements. . . .

But what the disciplinary machine actually wanted was to produce a body without mind, a mindless body. "I don't need to use my mind anymore. I've been doing the same thing for two years. Things come and go, repeating every second and minute. I can do it with my eyes closed," Damei told me. And because the body was mindless, it was replaceable. Thus the strategy of the production machine, in order to safeguard its power and prevent any possibility of the producing body taking charge, was to ensure that every body be trained to be a mindless body. The Chinese migrant workers, as stated earlier, were always seen as untrustworthy workers who would leave the factory any time they liked. This situation was often exaggerated, but the turnover rate was particularly high during the Chinese New Year period. At Meteor, management estimated that every year at this time more than 20 percent of the workforce would leave for good and never come back. Thus for the producing body to be changeable, it was necessary that it be further individualized. One only took responsibility for one's own duty and only became an expert in one's own position. Everybody was useful, but not crucial; no one individual could know and affect the operation of the whole work. . . .

A Technique of Power: The Assembly Line

If we say the disciplinary spacing of the body results in the individuation and fragmentation of labor power, the assembly line devised in modern industry is a technique of power reuniting individualized

bodies in a concerted action. All ten assembly lines at Meteor were equipped with moving conveyor belts. The moving of the belt was, simply, the movement of power. Like a chain, it coupled an individualized body with a specific position, but at the same time it linked the individuals to form a collective social body devoted to the singular aim of maximizing production.

The operation of the moving belt was not only cooperative and productive but also symbolic. The flashing light set at the head of the belt signaled and dictated the actions of each body and combined individual energies into a collective labor force, thus showing its power to control. The light acted like a conductor directing an orchestra, and each individual act formed part of a symphony. It flashed once every two to two and a half minutes, telling workers on the lines that a new set was being run. It controlled speed, time, and bodily movement. The working body was thus individualized, yet paradoxically not one of the bodies could be individualistic, idiosyncratic, or different. Ultimately it was the collective labor and cooperation of the line that mattered. . . .

Besides the staff in the personnel section, those whom the workers disliked most in the company were the time analysts—all of whom were men. Again and again they came out from the engineering department holding a timing calculator and stood behind the backs of the women workers to measure their time. Male power and female subordination were vividly contrasted. The analysts made suggestions and sent orders, and female bodies would need to catch up to the pace again. The time analysts studied not only the amount of time the work required but also the workers' bodily actions—the gestures and the gaps between bodily movements. No time was wasted; every bodily action had to be accurate and correct. The distance between each body, the distance between the body and the conveyor belt, the height of the chair, and the table and the shelf were all carefully measured and planned. Time and space were all to be used economically; there was to be no waste of surplus bodily actions and no waste of surplus labor force. This was, at least, the dream of the production machine.

On line B, the work of assembling the ROF, the final processing product, was divided into twelve processes. Once a new lot arrived on the line, the time analysts would again measure the work pace. The data they collected would be analyzed by computer to calculate the target for daily production, the speed of the conveyor belt, and the work pace of each individual body. Work speed was reviewed on a weekly basis, which put pressure not only on individuals but also on the line as a whole. Comparisons were made between the lines, and if the gap were too large Mr. Yeung, the chief of the timing analysts section, would personally issue a warning to the workers. The foreperson and the line leader, who were responsible for keeping the line operating, would also share the same pressure. They were assigned to train the workers, keep discipline, and arrange work positions and raw materials. But they also had to keep the line working smoothly by eliminating or controlling human factors such as slow down, sickness, temporary leave to use the washroom, and whatever unpredictable human elements might escape the dictates of the moving line.

We complained every day about the work speed and the unequal arrangement of jobs and time. Although every work process was "scientifically" studied and carefully measured, the simultaneous ordering of a multitude of individualized bodies was not an easy task. Despite the fact that each job was dissected minutely, it was still impossible to keep each work process within a similar amount of time. Some were forced to work faster than others, and some were required to perform more difficult work than others. However, the assembly line simply sped on its way, indifferent to the nature of the work and human differences. Individual bodies were required to accommodate to the line, rather than the line to individual bodies.

Time and time again it was impossible to avoid the units piling up in front of our table. Shutong, who was nicknamed "Fatso" because of her boyish character, sat in front of Meifang and shared the same work process with us. One day she complained: "People can't work at this sort of killing speed. The line should not run so fast. You ought to know that our task requires more time. I am already

killing my body." Bailan, our line leader, quickly came and hushed her. "Don't shout. The line is not under our control." This was true; the running of the line had nothing to do with the workers, not even the line leader or the foreman. As a technique of power, the assembly line was completely autocratic; the movement of the belt had a will of its own once the line was set up by the engineering department. . . .

Speed, Control, and Defiance

Where there was power, there was room for escape, defiance, and transgression. . . . The moving line was set to homogenize the work pace, but the work itself was heterogeneous and variable. . . . Rush orders and frequent changes in production models were characteristic of Meteor because it was a subcontracting factory. So the management had to rely on workers' cooperation and their willingness not only to work overtime but also to finish the work on time. The working women thus held a certain power, albeit interstitial rather than formal, to negotiate their work situation. . . .

Tactics of defiance often targeted work speed. The production machine tried in manifold ways to turn the human body into a working machine, and the *dagongmei* on the line learned very quickly that the moving line was an electric despot, binding their bodies to work as fast as possible for the least amount of money.[2] Fu-hui, the worker stationed in front of me, talked to me one drowsy afternoon: "I dream about the line suddenly stopping for a while. I simply can't take a breath. It drags us to work faster and faster. But the more we work, the more the boss earns. They give the workers a little more, yet they make big money." Class-consciousness was articulated thus in the workplace from time to time, although typically in an individual and passing way. The pressures of the assembly line and the work tensions it produced led the women each day to confront their own exploitation in a very immediate way.

Although the work speed was predetermined, the women nevertheless could exert a certain influence on the pace at certain moments. Sometimes, especially at night, when the work speed was unbearable to overstressed bodies, or when a new speed was set for new products and the workers had not yet gotten used to it, all of the women on the line would suddenly slow down at the same time, demonstrating a silent collective resistance to the line leader and the foreman. Nobody would utter a word but simply let the jobs pile up like hills while someone else was left with empty hands. Thus they let the line alone to run itself, making it like a "paper tiger" (a powerless despot). In response the foreman would say a lot of "good words" to persuade the women to be tolerant and catch up on the work. He would say, "Girls, the more you work, the more bonus you get. So why don't you catch up?" Or, "Have some patience, you are all girls. The more you work, the more you can handle it." But if these "good words" were not heeded and the slowdown persisted, the foreman's only recourse was to report to the supervisor and have the time analysts readjust the pace.

Needless to say, the women would view these moments as victories. They knew the rush seasons were the most appropriate moments to exert their bodily power by simply letting their bodies relax and earn time to breathe. Rush period were the times that the new pace of work and amount of the bonus were often bargained over and fought for. . . . However, once the busy period was over the women's bargaining power was dramatically weakened. The workers knew too well that their bargaining power, although recurrent, was ephemeral. They had to seize the right moment or it would be gone.

Controlling pace was an effective strategy for resisting the overwhelming domination of disciplinary power in the workplace. At Meteor, nonassembly line workers, such as in the bonding room or functional testing room, had more power to "hustle and idle" the work speed according to their own interests. As Hua, foreman of the bonding room, told me one day: "If there is a moody hour, the girls will assemble the components slowly and then pass the work to the next girl slowly. They work as slowly as tortoises. If you force them to do it quicker, they can sometimes make it all wrong and you need to redo it. Or they can all pretend to be ill."

Collective illness was common if the speed were set too fast and the bonus rate was too harsh. The bonus rate was an incentive mechanism that supplemented the fixed hourly rate paid to all of the shop floor workers. Every worker in the workplace knew that the bonus system was designed to induce him or her to work as fast as possible. So when the rate of pay was good, they worked faster; if not, they simply slowed down. . . .

Programming the Work Habit: The Daily Timetable

. . . The usual working day was eleven or twelve hours. If there were a rush order, however, workers were required to stay until 11:00 P.M. or 12 A.M. The nightshift workers started work at 8:00 P.M. and finished at 8:00 A.M. with one rest hour between 3:00 A.M. and 4:00 A.M. Overtime work was considered part of normal working hours, directly violating the Labor Law of 1995 and the Regulation of Labor Contract of Shenzhen Special Economic Zone. These regulating documents address overtime as follows:

1. The working hours of the worker should not be over eight hours per day; the weekly average working hours should not be over forty-four hours.
   - The worker should have one rest day per week.
   - The normal overtime work should not be extended over one hour; for some special reason and with consideration of the worker health condition, the prolonging of working hours should not be over three hours each day.
   - The total overtime work per month should not be over thirty-six hours (Shenzhen Labor Bureau 1995).[3]

No factory in Shenzhen took these regulations seriously, Meteor included. During my time there, half of every month we would be working at night for over three hours. Moreover, although it was called overtime work, the company planned it as normal production.

Daily life was rigorously regulated by the timetable and everybody struggled to live up to the strict schedule. . . . The section following is from my field notes—one of my many attempts to capture a day in the workplace and how the workers struggled to meet the work schedule.

The Sense of Time: 19 January 1995

It was a cold and windy winter day. The sun was still sleeping and the sky was dark, but we had to wake up. The alarms of clocks in my room sounded at 6:30 A.M., some a few seconds faster or slower. Six people, six clocks, and I was definitely sure that with only my own alarm I could never have gotten up. Yunling, Fang, Yue, Huahong, and Mei were my roommates. Yunling slept above me on the upper bunk; she was usually the last one to get up. She murmured in a sleepy voice: "Gosh! What kind of life is this! Wake up at half past six. In winter I thought I'd never experience this kind of bitterness. Only my mum in the village would do it. She's great, getting up to feed us and the pigs." We all laughed and told her it was better to act than talk.

After waking up, we rushed for the toilet, brushed our teeth, washed our faces, and changed our clothes. We had to take turns because there was only one toilet and one washroom. "Hurry up, hurry up"; there was shouting everywhere in the room, but none of the arguing that often occurred in other rooms, especially when someone lost their temper. In our room, the situation was still bearable because we had all learned to keep our patience with one another. Time was pressing and we could not afford to waste a minute, so while someone was using the toilet, others would wash themselves in the washroom, while still others would change their overalls or comb their hair on the bed. Turns were arranged silently and we lived on consent rather than written orders. To make life easier, self-disciplining was nurtured from the moment we woke up.

About 6:45 to 7:00 A.M. we began to leave the dormitory. We could reserve fifteen minutes for breakfast if we could make it to the factory in less than twenty minutes. I often walked with Yunling and Mei, two Cantonese girls from rural Guangdong. Yunling complained of the harsh life in the workplace: "At home, I got up when the sun rose and it was time to be hungry for breakfast. But here, we are all forced to wake up to the alarms." I asked her, "Don't you need to help your mum cook or feed pigs in the morning?" "Sometimes," she replied, "but I was not the one supposed to do so." Yunling had

two elder sisters and one sister-in-law who helped the family do domestic chores and farm work. She was the free hand at home, which was why she was able to do factory work in Shenzhen. . . .

At 7:50 A.M. we had to queue up, enter the factory gate, and punch our timecards. Security guards stood at the big gate carefully checking company permits, which had to be pinned to the chest pocket of one's overalls. Those who forgot to bring the permit would not be allowed in, even if recognized as a company worker by the security guards. There was then no recourse but to go back to the dormitory and find the permit, which would make one late for work and result in a fine and condemnation: five minutes late would be counted as one hour late and wages would be deducted for two hours. . . . Such serious punishment reflected the saying that every minute of labor was crucial to the functioning of the entire production machine.

"Time is money" was the new disciplinary discourse prevailing in the rapidly developed industrialized areas. It was much highlighted in post-socialist China with the rapid growth of global production and the attempts to articulate a global consciousness of speed and money. Work quicker and work harder was the secret to producing wealth and the primary ideology of global capitalism. . . .

With our overalls, caps, and gloves in place and our work tools and materials prepared, the factory clock bell rang at exactly 8:00. The day would start with a ten-minute meeting reporting the output performance and commenting on each line's productivity and quality. After the workers returned to their positions, the light flashed, the line started running, and our morning work began. Music—popular Cantonese songs—was played for fifteen minutes to freshen our minds to work more efficiently. It was said that the workers could work faster in the morning with their energy refreshed by a few hours of sleep, so discipline in the morning was often strict and it was difficult to find a chance to talk or joke. There was a common understanding on the line that the higher management was in a mood to keep things straight in the morning hours. Talk and laughter caught by the foreman or supervisor often was not tolerated. Silence, fast-moving lines, and the speed of time out of control—this was the feel of morning work.

Five minutes before lunch at noon the line would stop and we started to finish up our jobs. Talk immediately mounted and all kinds of noises filled the silence. We had kept quiet for the whole morning, and it seemed that everyone had to talk at once. We were not permitted to leave the shop floor at the same time. Each line took turns to leave because there was only one staircase for all of the shop floor workers. Rushing to eat lunch in fifteen minutes, we would then come back to our seats to take a nap. All of the lights were switched off and the bright workshop turned to a dark world. Because we were exhausted every day, all of us would fall asleep. . . .

At 12:50 P.M., the lights were turned on and we awoke to punch our time cards. At 1:00 the clock bell rang, music was turned on, and the line ran again. Work was repetitive and never-ending. The closed environment, with all of the windows sealed and covered by a plastic curtain, kept the workers from being distracted by the outside world. We could not judge the time by seeing the rising and setting of the sun, nor could we breathe natural air. The workplace air was regulated twenty-four hours a day by the central air conditioning. The temperature was kept at 68°F throughout the year, which was low enough not only to cool the electronic parts but also to wake up drowsy eyes. Talking, gossiping, joking, and secret snacks were sometimes allowed in the afternoon on the condition that they not affect the speed and running of the line. And it seemed that noise and laughter also served as an effective way to keep the workers awake.

What the girls complained about most was not the low wage or harsh workload, but lack of adequate sleep sustained over months and years. An eighteen-year-old worker, Li Peng, told me, "Everyday I can only sleep for five or six hours. It doesn't drive me mad, but makes me like a sleeping pig. Whenever there's a chance. I fall asleep. I can't help but be drowsy." What the girls could do was making an effort to cheer themselves up. Every chance to have fun and share snacks was taken, each little

moment was important to keeping up spirits. Another way of killing drowsiness was to take a short break by going to the washroom. But workers could not leave their work seats unless granted an out-of-position permit by the assistant line leader, and five minutes was the maximum allowed. Workers often complained about the time limit, especially when they were menstruating. Drowsiness was the contagious virus that the disciplinary machine found most difficult to deal with: work pace would slow down and the jobs piled up on the line, and some workers would slip and get hurt by the soldering gun or the molding machine. Small accidents such as hurting a finger often occurred in late afternoon or at night, when workers did not have enough concentration. When somebody suffered more significant bodily pain and was sent to the hospital, the others on the shop floor would suddenly wake up to their work.

By 5:00 P.M. we could all hear our stomachs rumbling and we were hungry for dinner. Work started again at 6:00 P.M. and the time card was punched again. We were then told what time we could end our work that night. If it was at 9:00 we thought we had a lucky day. Normally we stopped work at 10:00, and sometimes the shift extended to 11:00 or 12:00 for a rush production order. Night work was comparatively more relaxed, and the radio was turned on for the duration. The workers listened to the Hong Kong channels, which they found more interesting than the Shenzhen or Guangzhou channels. Chatting about popular film stars and favorite singers helped to pass time quickly; dreaming of the romance provoked by the love songs or stories from the radio helped to kill time in the extreme exhaustion and boredom of night work.

Inspections by the personnel department or higher management in the production department seldom occurred at night. As Fatso explained to me on the line, "The white-collar staff members, with their good fate, need more time to take care of their bodies; they don't have time to inspect us." At 9:00 or 10:00 we stopped for the day and dashed back to the dormitory, queuing up for hot water to bathe. After bathing, we still needed to wash our clothes, and someone with a free hand would cook some snacks because we all felt hungry after working three or four hours after dinner. Eating and talking took another hour. After midnight we all went to bed. . . .

Institutionalizing Everyday Life: The Factory Codes

If the timetable was the heart of the disciplinary power regulating factory life, then the factory regulations were the heart of the timetable. A strict timetable needed a severe prosecutor to enforce it. The modality of power itself was extremely despotic, but it was justified by the nature and massive number of the workers that had to be governed. There were over five hundred workers, and all were from diverse places of origin, spoke different dialects, and had different habits of life and codes of behavior and standards. To order these heterogeneous migrants into one standardized set of behaviors, and mold the confused mind into a well-disciplined psyche, the disciplinary machine needed ingrained techniques of power. It also needed an impartial and equitable legislator machine to set unbiased codes and state clearly how to punish and reward. . . .

New workers were asked to read the factory regulation handbook before they could start work on the shop floor. . . . On the staircase landings and in the canteen, important factory regulations were framed under glass on the wall. . . .

At the landing of the second-floor staircase, every day we could see the following:

PRODUCTION REGULATIONS

1. Workers should do all preparations such as wearing work cap, electronic-prevention belt, gloves, and so forth five minutes before the on-work time. To prevent any dirt on the products, no one is allowed to comb their hair or do anything that may cause dust or dirt. Each violation is fined 2 yuan.
2. All workers should obey the production arrangements of the higher authorities. If anyone has a different opinion, complete the job first before seeking out the authorities.
3. Workers are not allowed to leave work positions or change work position during work time unless approved by the supervisors. If leaving the work position for personal reasons such as going to toilet the worker must apply for a *out-of-position permit*. Each violation is fined 2 yuan.
4. No one will be allowed to leave the factory unless there is a *company exit permit* signed by the affiliated department manager and the personnel department, and examined by the security guard before leaving the factory. Leaving the factory without permission will be seriously punished and each violation is fined 50 yuan.
5. Punching a timecard for others or asking another person to punch a timecard for you is prohibited. The first time of violation will be given serious warning and fined 20 yuan; the second time will be fined 100 yuan and the worker will be dismissed at once.
6. All workers must arrive at work on time. Arriving over five minutes late will be counted as late for one hour, while wages will be deducted at two hours rate.

At the third floor and in the canteen, the following framed rules were on the wall:

DAILY BEHAVIOR REGULATIONS

1. No talking, eating, playing, chasing, or fighting is allowed on the shop floor.
2. No dumping waste and no spitting. Each violation is fined 5 yuan.
3. Receiving or making personal phone calls is not allowed. If discovered, no matter how long the call, the worker will be immediately dismissed and all wages deducted.
4. For stealing factory property the worker will be dismissed at once and fined 50 to 500 yuan. If the case is serious, the offender will be sent to the Public Security Bureau.
5. The normal period of wear for an overall is one year. If one requires a new overall, there should be a reasonable explanation; otherwise, 50 yuan will be deducted from the wage.
6. The normal period of wear for a pair of work shoes is eight months. If there is unreasonable damage, 12 yuan will be deducted from the wage.

. . . These framed codes, of course, did not have a dramatic effect on factory life. We felt their existence only when we were on the verge of violating them or actually violating them. It was possible to find ways around these codes, as there is with any law. No talking, eating, or playing in the workplace was one of the primary regulations. But as I have described above, talking, eating snacks, making jokes, and teasing were all done openly in the late afternoon and on night work. Workers simply could not help but violate the regulation if they were to kill the boredom and drowsiness. Individual defiance like deliberately not performing the job, speaking loudly, making fun of others, or leaving the work seat without waiting for a permit happened from time to time as well. Passing jokes on the line, sometimes overtly, sometimes covertly, could be seen as resistance to the extreme work conditions and as a chance to refresh an empty mind. Sexual innuendoes directed at the male technicians or supervisors were the funniest type of joke on the line. Who forgot to close the zipper of his trousers, or who had a new haircut or wore new clothes were all fodder for assembling jokes. Foremen and line leaders tended to ignore such behavior because they knew that the daily operation of the line could never be guided by factory regulations that were too adamant and relentless. . . . As Bailan, the leader of my line, told me, "It's no use being too harsh. We need to understand the workers' situation and individual problems. I would prefer to ask the worker to leave her seat to wash her face with cold water than to see her yawning all the time. . . . Sometimes I don't prevent them from talking or daydreaming, you know, it is the only way to keep the work moving." . . .

EDITORS' NOTES

1. Pun Ngai chose the name Meteor Electronics Company as a pseudonym for the factory where she did her ethnographic research.
2. The young women working in China's economic processing zones are called *dagongmei*—a new term for a new social identity. Pun Ngai explains that *dagong* "means 'working for the boss' or 'selling labor,' thereby connoting commodification and capitalist exchange of labor for wages" (*Made in China*, p. 120). *Mei* means younger sister: unmarried, female, and signifying a lower status.
3. See Shenzhen Labor Bureau. 1995. *Regulation of labor contract of Shenzhen Special Economic Zone.* Shenzhen: Shenzhen Labor Bureau.

CAROLIN SCHURR

38 THE BABY BUSINESS BOOMS: ECONOMIC GEOGRAPHIES OF ASSISTED REPRODUCTION (2018)

Carolin Schurr is a feminist geographer and currently Assistant Professor of Transcultural Studies, School of Humanities and Social Sciences, University of St. Gallen, Switzerland. A recipient of "The Branco Weiss Fellowship" (2013–2018), her published work focuses on global surrogacy markets, feminist theories of the body, feminist science and technology studies, and geographies of marketization.

1. INTRO: HOW MUCH IS A BABY WORTH?

For 50,000 US$, you can either go through four cycles of in vitro fertilization (IVF) in a US American fertility clinic or 10 IVF cycles in an Ukrainian clinic catering to reproductive tourists, buy yourself the oocytes of an Ivy League egg donor, or travel to Mexico for a surrogate baby gestated by a Mexican surrogate laborer. What this . . . shows is that economic geographies underwrite the global fertility market. The consumption of the same reproductive technologies and services has not only a different cost in different places. Some technologies and services are only legal at certain places; other places restrict the access to certain reproductive technologies to particular populations, denying, for example, single or homosexual people access to IVF treatment, oocyte donation, or surrogacy. Access to assisted reproductive technologies is highly unequal both within and between nation states. In general, wealthier, urban, heterosexual, married, and white(r) people living in the Global North have better access to assisted reproductive technologies than poorer, rural, homo- and transsexual, single, and non-white people in the Global South and the Global East and ethnic minorities in the Global North (Elster, 2005; Jain, 2006; Nachtigall, 2006; Shanley & Asch, 2009). This engenders all kinds of mobilities in which people travel abroad to seek treatment they have no access to or cannot afford in their home country.

While transnational flows and spatial interconnections characterize this fast-growing market, place continues to matter. . . . Fertility specialists in the Global North have higher wages than their colleagues in the Global South and Global East. Postcolonial geographies of beauty shape processes of valuation and price-making in this market. Young, white, Western women with higher education receive up to 100 times more for their oocytes than egg sellers in India, Mexico, Ukraine, or Georgia (Schurr, 2017). Commercial surrogacy—where you contract and pay a woman to gestate your baby—is only legal in a few countries, many of them belonging to the Global East (Müller, 2019) or Global South, where surrogate mothers earn only a fraction of what a Californian surrogate would earn. Just as other kinds of services have been outsourced to low-wage countries to reduce costs within a global commodity chain, reproductive labor is outsourced in global fertility chains to women living in deprived socioeconomic conditions . . . to reduce the price for a baby conceived with the help of a third party. . . .

While in many societies a child is often perceived as "priceless" . . . the rise of the global fertility market since the 1990s has contributed to the increasing commodification of reproductive capacities, bodily tissues, body parts, and ultimately also babies. Parallel to this process, fierce academic and public debates have emerged about whether this . . . commodification is morally and ethically problematic or just another variation of the increasing marketization of everyday life and the body (Dickenson, 2007; Nussbaum, 1998; Parry, 2008;

Source: Carolin Schurr "The Baby Business Booms: Economic Geographies of Assisted Reproduction" *Geography Compass* 12(8), August 2018 (https://doi.org/10.1111/gec3.12395). Reprinted here under Creative Commons license CC-BY 2.0.

Phillips, 2013; Radin, 2001). Given the long history of wet nursing, adoption, and child trafficking, the baby market is nothing new (Rotabi & Bromfield, 2012; Zelizer, 1985). But as economic geographer Bronwyn Parry (2012, p. 215) has argued, "we are witnessing a profound extensification and intensification of trade in human bodies, bodily parts and bodily resources"—including the bodies of babies. Technological development, the rise of cheap air travel, new communication and information technologies, and the accumulation of "biocapital" (Rajan, 2006) have sped up the trade of bodies, body parts, and babies across borders. . . .

The reasons for undergoing IVF treatment, using genetic diagnostic technologies, purchasing gametes, or contracting a surrogate laborer in the global fertility market are diverse. They range from health issues affecting one's abilities to conceive and gestate (Becker, 2000; Thompson, 2005), to infertility issues in response to delayed childbearing (Bühler, 2014; Everywoman, 2013) and social infertility of singles and homosexuals (Nebeling Petersen, 2016; Nebeling Petersen, Kroløkke, & Myong, 2017; Smietana, 2017). Since the birth of the first IVF baby, Louise Brown, in the UK in 1978, reproductive technologies have spread across the globe with infertility treatment now being available in nearly every country of the world (Franklin & Inhorn, 2016; Inhorn & Patrizio, 2015; Rozée & Unisa, 2016). By now, reproductive technologies have become ubiquitous, mundane, and "normal" (Thompson, 2005). In Europe alone, more than half a million of IVF cycles are performed per year (Okhovati, Zare, Zare, Bazrafshan, & Bazrafshan, 2015).

As most of the fertility treatments worldwide take place in private clinics, it has become a booming business with ever more people accessing assisted reproductive technologies of all sorts from IVF, to IVF with donated gametes, genetic testing and screening, and surrogacy (Almeling, 2011; Bratcher Goodwin, 2010; Spar, 2006). It is estimated that the global market of assisted reproductive technology has generated revenues of 22.3 billion US$ in 2015 (Global market insight, 2016) with fertility drugs being a fast-expanding pharmaceutical field (Vertommen, 2017). In short, the baby business booms and has gone global over the last decades. . . .

2. (DE)BORDERING REPRODUCTION: MAKING FERTILE MARKETS FOR INFERTILITY

In the introduction to the special issue "IVF: Global histories," Franklin and Inhorn (2016, p. 2) assert that " the globalization of IVF remains relatively understudied. " They identify the fast changes in this industry and that assisted reproductive technologies are primarily policed by nation-states as the main reasons why it is so challenging to grapple with reproductive technologies as a global form. Despite these difficulties, scholars have started to engage with "the many diverse elements operating on a global scale that make IVF and its associated mobilities a distinct form of global travel in the twenty-first century" (Inhorn, 2016, p. 22). . . . So far, research has focused on the circulation of technoscience (Parry, 2012; Schurr & Verne, 2017), consumers, laborers, fertility experts, body parts involving gametes, frozen embryos, and other biological substances (Bergmann, 2014; Kroløkke, 2014; Parry, Greenhough, Brown, & Dyck, 2015), and systems of administration and business models (Müller & Schurr, 2016). . . .

Beyond analyzing the multiple flows of consumers and laborers, research has started to look at the mobilities of the market itself. The global surrogacy market is an exceptionally well-suited case study to investigate the flexibility, ephemerality, and fluidity of one particular reproductive market and to question the role translocal networks, territoriality, and borders play in the making of this market. The more recent history of the global surrogacy market is characterized by fast changes: In the last 5 years, the major global surrogacy hotspots such as India (Rudrappa, 2016), Thailand (Whittaker, 2016), Nepal (Pink News, 2015), Mexico (Schurr & Perler, 2015), and Cambodia (Bangkok Post, 2016) have all faced comprehensive legislative changes to contract a surrogate, resulting in either a total ban of commercial surrogacy (Thailand, Nepal, and Cambodia) or severe restrictions limiting the legal options to married and heterosexual national citizens (India and Mexico). However, due to the extensive transnational fertility tourism networks, the respective surrogacy industries were quick to undergo a "structural/spatial re-adjustment" (Mitra, 2015, p. 3) by moving their services, and in some cases even their surrogate mothers and IVF labs, to other destinations.

. . . Always already looking for the next business opportunity in face of these fast legislative changes, surrogacy agencies operate at a distance trying to enroll different agents—ranging from IVF clinics to intermediaries who recruit reproductive laborers, lawyers, medical tourism agencies, and so forth— in their networks and to hold these relations stable to guarantee successful surrogacy journeys to their clients. My research reveals that even though the surrogacy agencies have a rather immutable, standardized, and uniform business system in which they circulate the very same templates, contracts, and manuals to their branches in different regions of the world, they are all challenged to adapt their services to these contexts. Local agents and intermediaries play a key role in the medical tourism industry in general (Kaspar & Reddy, 2017; Ormond & Sothern, 2012; Parry et al., 2015) and in facilitating the reterritorialization of surrogacy agencies in new destinations in particular (Parry, 2015b). The shifts and expansion of surrogacy markets takes place within a "networked topography" (Beck, 2012, p. 362) which is not necessarily transnational but rather connects diverse localities and its actors to pursue their commercial interests.

Moreover, even though surrogacy agencies suggest in their promotion material that global surrogacy is an effortless endeavor in a world where borders have dissolved, numerous challenges emerge when it comes to the capacities of different human and non-human agents to cross borders. Gametes and embryos can travel across borders with a special permit and the necessary cryopreservation technology to keep embryos and gametes in good shape in their travels. The resulting baby, however, can often only leave the country when the passport is issued or juridical processes around the legal status of the sans papier baby are settled. The way mobilities are stratified becomes evident when unexpected events happen that shake the usual routines of surrogate markets. For example, when the earthquake in Nepal hit the surrogacy industry . . . "Israeli babies" were flown out of the country, while Indian surrogate workers[1] had to face immense troubles to cross the border by bus in their return travels to India (Mitra, 2015). Whereas borders seem to disappear and vanish for certain actors in the global surrogacy market, they remain impermeable and powerful for others. In short, "inequalities, disjunctures, and obstacles inhibit and even prevent flows of people, technology, and other forms across uneven global terrains" (Inhorn, 2016, p. 24). The gendered, racialized, nationalized, and so forth capacities to move across national borders along with uneven global economic structures result in "stratified forms of reproduction" (Colen, 1995) that characterize the political economy of fertility (Banerjee, 2014; Gerrits, 2018; Ikemoto, 2015; Vertommen, 2016a, 2016b; Weis, 2017).

The story about the surrogacy industry in Nepal seems to re-write postcolonial histories of inequality between the Global North and Global South . . . Bronwyn Parry (2015b), however, cautions against reproducing too simplistic (post-)colonial assumptions in our analysis of the global surrogacy market. Talking about the legislative changes in India, she highlights that the usual spotlight on the Global North–South inequalities consisting of Western intended parents traveling to India to outsource their reproductive labor loses sight of the agency and hegemony of the Indian fertility industry. By now, "it is India's leading IVF specialists who have constructed the most extensive networks of fertility clinics in the developing world building their own 'empires' of commercialized reproductive care in countries from Africa to Thailand and the Gulf states" (Parry, 2015b, pp. 36–37). . . .

Economic geography is well equipped to face the challenge to grapple with the everyday messiness of this market, the way it is constructed along intersecting lines of difference and shaped by multiple processes of bordering and debordering. In particular, two (overlapping) approaches bear great potential for studying the making, expansion, decline, and shifts of surrogacy and fertility markets: geographies of marketization and critical commodity chain analysis. Geographies of marketization study processes of market-making . . . (Berndt & Boeckler, 2012; Boeckler & Berndt, 2013; Çalışkan & Callon, 2010). They are interested in understanding how the transnational arrangements of heterogeneous elements (ranging in the case of fertility markets from lab equipment to medical knowledge, reproductive consumers and laborers, reproductive bodies and body parts, business models, regulations and laws, etc.) organize the circulation of goods across borders. . . . Different national legislations along with price differences between surrogacy packages in different countries that are kept in place due to national border regimes engender transnational mobilities of consumers and the global scope of this market in the first place. At the same time, debordering processes are crucial to facilitate the smooth flow of transnational baby journeys. Borders are shifted across space when transnationally operating surrogacy agencies offer their services in other countries, evading taxes and state control of their medical services in the destination country. This ambivalent play of bordering and debordering is veiled by the work of surrogacy agencies, lawyers, and the consumers themselves.

Critical commodity chain analysis (Bair, Berndt, Boeckler, & Werner, 2013; Bair & Werner, 2011b; Castree, 2004; Werner, 2011, 2016) . . . complements such a marketization perspective by focusing on how processes of inclusion and exclusion shape the making of transnational markets. This approach studies "processes by which regions and actors become disconnected or expulsed from commodity chains that may be incorporating new regions and actors elsewhere" (Bair & Werner, 2011a, p. 989). Looking in particular into how these processes of expulsion affect laborers whose identity is shaped by interlocking categories of social difference, critical commodity chain analysis is a helpful approach to understand how the shifts in global fertility markets affect differently racialized, gendered, nationalized, and classed bodies to different extents. What possibilities do surrogate workers have to continue their reproductive labor when bans are implemented? What strategies

do they employ to offer their labor in neighboring countries and what capacities do they have to cross borders? Who benefits and loses economic opportunities if surrogacy markets shift from one location to another? And who carries the medical, legal, and psychological risks when surrogacy services continued to be offered in legal gray zones? These are questions that such a critical commodity chain approach is apt to analyze and answer.

3. CONTEXT MATTERS! PUTTING REPRODUCTIVE LABOR IN PLACE

Discussions about whether to conceptualize surrogate mothers' and oocyte donors' reproductive service as an altruistic act or a form of labor are currently not only at the heart of scholarly debates (Almeling, 2011; Franklin, 1997; Franklin & Ragoné, 1998; Nahman, 2013; Parry, 2015b; Waldby, 2015; Waldby, Kerridge, Boulos, & Carroll, 2013) but also inform policy making (Rudrappa, 2016; Schurr & Perler, 2015). While countries such as the UK allow only altruistic surrogacy and prohibit any form of financial compensation, in most transnational surrogacy markets, financial compensation plays a key role. In fact, commercialization and altruism intermingle in complex ways in this "affective market" (Schurr & Militz, 2018) according to the context in which the surrogacy arrangement takes place. . . . Unlike US surrogates, who can be rejected from surrogacy programs if they are not financially secure, Teman (2010, p. 23) shows in her study that surrogates in Israel state unapologetically that money is their primary goal in pursuing surrogacy in order to supplement their income to pay off huge debts and provide for their children's basic needs. . . . Surrogate workers in Mexico have deeply incorporated the industry's rhetoric of altruism and gift while openly admitting that economic needs are the main driver to engage in surrogacy (Schurr & Militz, 2018). Siegl (2018) by contrast, shows that Russian surrogates consider any affective involvement into surrogacy process as dangerous and hence prefer to "do it business style." Pande (2009, p. 160, 2014, p. 91) states that metaphors of gift giving are absent from the narratives of Indian surrogates as the surrogates emphasize surrogacy as "majboori" (something we have to do to survive). Parry (2015b), however, points out that affective ties and exchanges of gifts of food, medication, and money characterize the relationship between the Indian surrogates, the recruiting agent who is usually known to the women, and the hospital staff. She concludes "this gifting alters the intrinsic dynamics of this economy ultimately rendering contracts largely moot for surrogates and donors" (Parry, 2015b, p. 36). . . . Framing surrogacy either as an altruistic act or as a new form of labor has important implications not just for the way it is perceived socially but also with regard to the women's rights to reclaim their wage (rather than a non-enforceable compensation) as well as their capacities to fight for their labor rights and working conditions including health and social securities (Cooper & Waldby, 2014; Lewis, 2015, 2017; Pande, 2017; Rudrappa, 2016).

Given the increasing outsourcing of "clinical labor" (Cooper & Waldby, 2014) to countries in the Global South and Global East, discussions have emerged around the exploitative effects of this new baby market on the bodies of women in deprived economic situations in general and women of color in particular who offer their oocytes or gestational capacities in this market (Cooper & Waldby, 2014; Pfeffer, 2011). Ethnographic research has painted a more differentiated picture: Analyzing the racial breakdown of donor pools with regard to the total population of the United States, Daniels and Heidt-Forsyth (2012) show that white Anglo-American donors are clearly overrepresented in US gamete banks . . . They conclude from their analysis that "egg donors continue to reflect the tall and slender stature of class- and race-based standards of Western, idealized feminine beauty" (Daniels & Heidt-Forsyth, 2012, p. 731). Research looking at the racialization of oocyte donors in the context of transnational surrogacy arrangements has come to similar findings (Deomampo, 2016a; Whittaker & Speier, 2010). Western consumers' racial preferences for a white baby influence demand in the global fertility market, "making race a commodity to be selected, acquired and purchased" (Deomampo, 2016b, p. 97). . . . Due to the increased demand for white donors, light-skinned oocyte donors come and often travel from Eastern Europe

(Gunnarsson Payne, 2015; Nahman, 2013; Speier, 2016; Vlasenko, 2015), South Africa (Pande, forthcoming), Spain (Bergmann, 2011; Kroløkke, 2014), and the United States (Martin, 2015) to the destination countries of transnational surrogacy and fertility tourism.

In contrast, sperm is imported mostly from the United States, facing serious competition only from donors from Scandinavia (Kroløkke, 2009; Mohr, 2016). Parry (2015a) has investigated how devices of qualification and singularization have turned US sperm into "America's hottest export" (Jarvis, 2013). She shows how US sperm banks have succeed[ed] to "singularize" their donors by offering extended donor profiles, which package the "pedigree" of each donor—of which skin color is one crucial aspect—in a detailed fashion. Contrary to the assumption that may result from this short overview about the postcolonial desirability of white donors, Almeling (2011, p. 69) reveals that in the United States, Asian American and African American donors are often more highly valued than white donors—resulting in higher compensation rates—as "women of color are perceived as scarce which contributes to their increased value." The latter is an example of the importance of contextualized work to reveal the complex geographies of fertility markets that may—but sometimes also may not—follow the racialized logics of labor markets in particular places.

The racialized geographies of clinical labor are also more complex than often suggested by media when it comes to the gestational surrogates. Jacobson's (2016) recent studies on surrogacy in the United States have shown, for example, that despite early warnings that surrogacy could result in the exploitation of women of color (Corea, 1985), this appears not to be the case in the United States, as surrogacy is "largely the terrain of white women" (Jacobson, 2016, p. 48). Twenty-eight out of the 31 surrogate mothers in Jacobson's sample identified themselves as non-Hispanic Caucasian and none lived below the federal poverty line. . . .

In the last decade, mostly non-white women have catered to the international and national clients . . . in India, Nepal, Thailand, Cambodia, and Laos. Since the increasing regulation and closure of many of the South Asian hotspots after 2015, however, it is mainly white Caucasian women in Ukraine, Georgia, and Russia who carry the global babies to term (Siegl, 2015, 2018; Weis, 2017). Experts estimate that demand for surrogacy alone in Ukraine has increased by 1,000% in the last 2 years (Ponniah, 2018). My own research in Ukraine has revealed that many women are drawn into surrogacy as a result of the rapid fall in living standards in consequence of the deep recession resulting from the ongoing conflict in Eastern Ukraine with Russia.

This last example highlights once more that there is a particular geography to the global surrogacy market in which surrogacy hotspots do not emerge randomly but as a result of wider geopolitical constellations. Bronwyn Parry (2015b, p. 37) makes a case in point for the importance of geography in these debates. She argues that any moral assessment of the exploitative or empowering character of reproductive labor can only be made by studying "the complex lived experiences of clinical labor in situ." Women's reproductive labor in the fertility industry has to be understood within the particular cultural, legal, political, and economic contexts in which their "reproductive biographies" (Perler, 2015) are embedded.

In my view, geography has much to offer to the often rather abstract and apparently universal (feminist) debates around reproductive labor. . . . It is geographers' attempt to pay close attention to the intersectional geographies of labor markets that is helpful for developing a more situated and contextualized analysis of the fertility market. . . .

4. MAKING GEOGRAPHY MATTER IN SOCIAL STUDIES OF ASSISTED REPRODUCTION—MAKING (ASSISTED) REPRODUCTION A MATTER OF ECONOMIC GEOGRAPHY

Most scholars of social studies of assisted reproduction would probably agree . . . that assisted reproductive technologies and their respective markets are deeply entangled with processes of globalization. . . .

While distance and proximity are still often portrayed in Euclidian terms in scholarship looking at transnational reproduction, a relational understanding of space serves to rethink the very spatiality of fertility markets. From such a relational understanding of space, spatial distance is not shaped by the number of kilometers between, for example, intended parents and their surrogate worker but as the product of the interrelations between intended parents and surrogates. These interrelations depend on the use of communication technology to overcome physical distance, the emotional intensity of the interactions, the discursive framing of their relationship (as transactional, friendship, kinship, etc.), and the material conditions of their multiple encounters. . . . In this paper, I have highlighted the importance of ethnographic work in the different localities of the global fertility market. It is only through this ethnographic work in situ that research can recognize the multiplicity and heterogeneity of fertility markets. For me, researching the multiple mobilities and spatial experiences of assisted reproduction is a feminist and postcolonial endeavor, as it allows to counter universal, Western accounts that still dominate media and policy debates.

NOTE

1. Since these women do not officially immigrate to Nepal due to the free border crossover permit for Indian citizens, neither the Indian embassy nor the Nepalese government record their travels (Mitra, 2015).

REFERENCES

Almeling, R. (2011). *Sex cells: The medical market for eggs and sperm*. Berkeley: University of California Press.

Bair, J., Berndt, C., Boeckler, M., & Werner, M. (2013). Dis/articulating producers, markets, and regions: New directions in critical studies of commodity chains. *Environment and Planning A*, 45, 2544–2552.

Bair, J., & Werner, M. (2011a). Commodity chains and the uneven geographies of global capitalism: A disarticulations perspective. *Environment and Planning A*, 43, 988–997.

Bair, J., & Werner, M. (2011b). The place of disarticulations: Global commodity production in La Laguna, Mexico. *Environment and Planning A*, 43, 998–1015.

Banerjee, A. (2014). Race and a transnational reproductive Caste system: Indian transnational surrogacy. *Hypatia*, 29, 113–128.

Bangkok Post (2016). Cambodia bans booming commercial surrogacy industry. *Bangkok Post*, 3 (11), 2016.

Beck, S. (2012). Biomedical mobilities: Transnational lab-benches and other space-effects. In M. Knecht, M. Klotz, & S. Beck (Eds.), *Reproductive technologies as global form: Ethnographies of knowledge, practices and transnational encounters* (pp. 357–374). Frankfurt a. M.: Campus.

Becker, G. (2000). *The elusive embryo how women and men approach new reproductive technologies*. Berkeley: University of California Press.

Bergmann, S. (2011). Fertility tourism: Circumventive routes that enable access to reproductive technologies and substances. *Signs*, 36, 280–289.

Bergmann, S. (2014). *Ausweichrouten der Reproduktion. Biomedizinische Mobiliät und die Praxis der Eizellenspende*. Wiesbaden: Springer VS.

Berndt, C., & Boeckler, M. (2012). Geographies of marketization. In T. Barnes, J. Peck, & E. Sheppard (Eds.), *The new companion to economic geography* (pp. 199–212). Oxford: Wiley-Blackwell.

Boeckler, M., & Berndt, C. (Eds.) (2013). Geographies of circulation and exchange III: The great crisis and marketization 'aftermarkets.' *Progress in Human Geography*, 37, 424–432.

Bratcher Goodwin, M. (Ed.) (2010). *Baby markets. Money and the new politics of creating families*. Cambridge: Cambridge University Press.

Bühler, N. (2014). Ovules vieillissants, mères sans âge? Infertilité féminine et recours au don d'ovocytes en Suisse. *Enfances, Familles, et Générations*, (21), 24–47.

Çalışkan, K., & Callon, M. (2010). Economization, part 2: A research programme for the study of markets. *Economy and Society*, 39,1–32.

Castree, N. (2004). The geographical lives of commodities: Problems of analysis and critique. *Social & Cultural Geography*, 5, 21–35.

Colen, S. (1995). "Like a mother to them": Stratified reproduction and West Indian childcare workers and employers in New York. In F. Ginsburg, & R. Rapp (Eds.), *Conceiving the new world order* (pp. 78–102). Berkeley, CA: University of California Press.

Cooper, M., & Waldby, C. (2014). *Clinical labor: Tissue donors and research subjects in the global bioeconomy*. Durham, NC: Duke University Press.

Corea, G. (1985). *The mother machine: Reproductive technologies from artificial insemination to artificial wombs*. New York: Harper & Row.

Daniels, C. R., & Heidt-Forsyth, E. (2012). Gendered eugenics and the problematic of free market reproductive technologies: Sperm and egg donation in the United States. *Signs*, 37, 719–747.

Deomampo, D. (2016a). Race, nation, and the production of intimacy: Transnational ova donation in India. *Positions: East Asia Cultures Critique*, 24, 303–323.

Deomampo, D. (2016b). *Transnational reproduction: Race, kinship and commercial surrogacy in India*. New York: New York University Press.

Dickenson, D. (2007). *Property in the body: Feminist perspectives*. Cambridge, UK: Cambridge University Press.

Elster, N. R. (2005). ART for the masses? Racial and ethnic inequality in assisted reproductive technologies. *DePaul Journal of Health Care Law*, 9, 719–733.

Everywoman, J. (2013). Cassandra's prophecy: Why we need to tell the women of the future about age-related fertility decline and 'delayed' childbearing. *Reproductive Biomedicine Online*, 27, 4–10.

Franklin, S. (1997). *Embodied progress: A cultural account of assisted conception*. London: Routledge.

Franklin, S., & Inhorn, M. C. (2016). Introduction: Symposium IVF—Global histories. *Reproductive Biomedicine & Society Online*, 2, 1–7.

Franklin, S., & Ragoné, H. (Eds.) (1998). *Reproducing reproduction: Kinship, power, and technological innovation*. Philadelphia: University of Pennsylvania Press.

Gerrits, T. (2018). Reproductive travel to Ghana: Testimonies, transnational relationships and stratified reproduction. *Medical Anthropology*, 37 (2), 131–144. Online first

Global market insight. (2016). Assisted Reproductive Technology (ART) market size by procedure, industry analysis report, regional outlook, application potential, price trends, competitive market share and forecast, 2016–2023. https://www.gminsights.com/segmentation/detail/assisted-reproductive-technology-market.

Gunnarsson Payne, J. (2015). Reproduction in transition: Cross-border egg donation, biodesirability and new reproductive subjectivities on the European fertility market. *Gender, Place & Culture*, 22, 107–122.

Ikemoto, L. C. (2015). Egg freezing, stratified reproduction and the logic of not. *Journal of Law and the Biosciences*, 2, 112–117.

Inhorn, M. C. (2016). Cosmopolitan conceptions in global Dubai? The emiratization of IVF and its consequences. *Reproductive Biomedicine & Society Online*, 2, 24–31.

Inhorn, M., & Patrizio, P. (2015). Infertility around the globe: New thinking on gender, reproductive technologies and global movements in the 21st century. *Human Reproduction Update*, 21, 411–426.

Jacobson, H. (2016). *Labor of love: Gestational surrogacy and the work of making babies*. New Brunswick: Rutgers University Press.

Jain, T. (2006). Socioeconomic and racial disparities among infertility patients seeking care. *Fertility and Sterility*, 85, 876–881.

Jarvis, B. (2013). Come and get it: How sperm became one of America's hottest exports. *The Verge*, 2 (4), 2013.

Kaspar, H., & Reddy, S. (2017). Spaces of connectivity: The formation of medical travel destinations in Delhi National Capital Region (India). *Asia Pacific Viewpoint*, 58, 228–241.

Kr\u00f8lokke, C. (2009). Click a donor: Viking masculinity on the line. *Journal of Consumer Culture*, 9, 7–30.

Krolokke, C. (2014). West is best: Affective assemblages and Spanish oöcytes. *European Journal of Women's Studies*, 21, 57–71.

Lewis, S. (2015, 212). Gestational labor as ground for an affirmative surrogacy politics. In S. Hoffman, & A. Moreno (Eds.), *Intimate economies: Bodies, emotions, and sexualities on the global market* (p. 187). London: Palgrave.

Lewis, S. (2017). Defending intimacy against what? Limits of antisurrogacy feminisms. *Signs*, 43, 97–125.

Martin, L. J. (2015). *Reproductive tourism in the United States: Creating family in the mother country*. New York: Routledge.

Mitra, Sayani (2015). Forces and flows of the market of commercial surrogacy: Expansion of market in and around India (Unpublished workshop manuscript), presented at The ART of reproducing difference: Discussing (in)equality in the context of reproductive travel, University of Bern.

Mohr, S. (2016). Containing sperm—Managing legitimacy: Lust, disgust, and hybridity at Danish sperm banks. *Journal of Contemporary Ethnography*, 45, 319–342.

Müller, Martin (2019). In search of the Global East: Thinking between North and South Geopolitics, in press.

Müller, M., & Schurr, C. (2016). Assemblage thinking and actor-network theory: Conjunctions, disjunctions, cross-fertilizations. *Transactions of the Institute of British Geographers*, 41, 217–229.

Nachtigall, R. D. (2006). International disparities in access to infertility services. *Fertility and Sterility*, 85, 871–875.

Nahman, M. (2013). *Extractions. An ethnography of reproductive tourism*. Basingstoke: Palgrave Macmillan.

Nebeling Petersen, M., Krolokke, C., & Myong, L. (2017). Dad and daddy assemblage: Resuturing the nation through transnational surrogacy, homosexuality, and Norwegian exceptionalism. *GLQ: A Journal of Lesbian and Gay Studies*, 23, 83–112.

Nebeling Petersen, M. (2016). Becoming gay fathers through transnational commercial surrogacy. *Journal of Family Issues*, 39, 693–719.

Nussbaum, M. C. (1998). "Whether from reason or prejudice": Taking money for bodily services. *The Journal of Legal Studies*, 27, 693–723.

Okhovati, M., Zare, M., Zare, F., Bazrafshan, M. S., & Bazrafshan, A. (2015). Trends in global assisted reproductive technologies research: A scientometrics study. *Electronic Physician*, 7, 1597–1601.

Ormond, M., & Sothern, M. (2012). You, too, can be an international medical traveler: Reading medical travel guidebooks. *Health & Place*,18, 935–941.

Pande, A. (2009). Not an "angel," not a "whore": Surrogates as "dirty" workers in India. *Indian Journal of Gender Studies*, 16, 141–173.

Pande, A. (2014). The power of narratives: Negotiating commercial surrogacy in India. In S. Das Gupta, & S. Das Dasgupta (Eds.), *Globalization and transnational surrogacy in India: Outsourcing life* (pp. 87–106). Lanham: Lexington Books.

Pande, A. (2017). Gestational surrogacy in India: New dynamics of reproductive labor. In E. Noronha, & P. D'Cruz (Eds.), *Critical perspectives on work and employment in globalizing India* (pp. 267–282). Singapore: Springer Singapore.

Pande, A. (forthcoming). Cross border repro-flows and the reproduction of white desirability. *Qualitative Sociology*.

Parry, B. (2008). Entangled exchange: Reconceptualizing the characterization and practice of bodily commodification. Geoforum, 39, 1133–1144.

Parry, B. (2012). Economies of bodily commodification. In T. Barnes, J. Peck, & E. S. Sheppard (Eds.), *The Wiley-Blackwell companion to economic geography* (pp. 213–225). Malden: Blackwell.

Parry, B. (2015a). A bull market? Devices of qualification and singularization in the international marketing of US sperm. In B. Parry, B. Greenhough, T.

Brown, & I. Dyck (Eds.), *Bodies across borders: The global circulation of body parts, medical tourists and professionals* (pp. 53–72). Farnham: Ashgate.

Parry, B. (2015b). Narratives of neoliberalism: "Clinical labor" in context. *Medical Humanities*, 41, 32–37.

Parry, B., Greenhough, B., Brown, T., & Dyck, I. (Eds.) (2015). *Bodies across borders: The global circulation of body parts, medical tourists and professionals*. Farnham: Ashgate.

Perler, L. (2015). Im Schatten der Wunschfabrik: Mexikanische Eizellenspenderinnen im Kontext stratifizierter Reproduktion. [Master's thesis]. Berne: University of Berne.

Pfeffer, N. (2011). Eggs-ploiting women: A critical feminist analysis of the different principles in transplant and fertility tourism. *Reproductive Biomedicine Online*, 23, 634–641.

Phillips, A. (2013). *Our bodies, whose property?* Cambridge, MA: Princeton University Press.

Pink News (2015). Nepal surrogacy ban to affect same-sex couples. *Pink News*, 27 (08), 2015.

Ponniah, K. (2018). In search of surrogates, foreign couples descend on Ukraine. *BBC News*, 13 (2), 3018.

Radin, M. J. (2001). *Contested commodities: The trouble with trade in sex, children, body parts, and other things.* Cambridge, Mass: Harvard University Press.

Rajan, K. S. (2006). *Biocapital: The constitution of postgenomic life.* Durham, NC: Duke University Press Books.

Rotabi, K. S., & Bromfield, N. F. (2012). The decline in intercountry adoptions and new practices of global surrogacy. *Affilia*, 27, 129–141.

Rozée, V., & Unisa, S. (Eds.) (2016). *Assisted reproductive technologies in the Global South and North.* London: Routledge.

Rudrappa, S. (2016). Why India's new surrogacy bill is bad for women. *Huffington Post*, 26 (8), 2016.

Schurr, C. (2017). From biopolitics to bioeconomies: The ART of (re-)producing white futures in Mexico's surrogacy market. *Environment and Planning D*, 35, 241–262.

Schurr, C. (forthcoming). Multiple mobilities in Mexico's fertility industry. *Mobilities*.

Schurr, C., & Militz, E. (2018). The affective economy of transnational surrogacy. *Environment and Planning A*, online first, 1–20.

Schurr, C., & Perler, L. (2015). "Trafficked" into a better future? Why Mexico needs to regulate its surrogacy industry (and not ban it). *Open Democracy*. 17 December 2015

Schurr, C., & Verne, J. (2017). Wissenschaft und Technologie im Zentrum der Geographischen Entwicklungsforschung: Science and Technology Studies meets development geographies. *Geographische Zeitschrift*, 105, 125–144.

Shanley, M. L., & Asch, A. (2009). Involuntary childlessness, reproductive technology, and social justice: The medical mask on social illness. *Signs*, 34, 851–874.

Siegl, V. (2015). Märkte der guten Hoffnung. Leihmutterschaft, Arbeit und körperliche Kommodifizierung in Russland. *PROKLA Zeitschrift für kritische Sozialwissenschaft*, 178, 99–115.

Siegl, V. (2018). Aligning the risky body: Commercial surrogacy in Moscow and the emotional labor of "Nastraivatsja." *Tsantsa*, 23.

Smietana, M. (2017). Affective de-commodifying, economic de-kinning: Surrogates' and gay fathers' narratives in US surrogacy. *Sociological Research Online*, 22, 5.

Spar, D. (2006). *The baby business: How money, science, and politics derive the commerce of conception.* Boston: Harvard Business School Press.

Speier, A. (2016). *Fertility holidays: IVF tourism and the reproduction of whiteness.* New York: NYU Press.

Teman, E. (2010). *Birthing a mother. The surrogate body and the pregnant self.* Berkeley: University of California Press.

Thompson, C. (2005). *Making parents: The ontological choreography of reproductive technologies.* Cambridge, MA: The MIT Press.

Vertommen, S. (2016a). Babies from behind the bars: Stratified assisted reproduction in Israel/Palestine. In M. Lie, & N. Lykke (Eds.), *Assisted reproduction across borders: Feminist perspectives on normalizations, disruptions and transmissions* (pp. 207–218). New York: Routledge.

Vertommen, S. (2016b). Towards a political economy of egg cell donations: "Doing it the Israeli way." In C. Kroløkke (Ed.), *Critical kinship studies: Kinship (trans)formed* (pp. 169–184). London: Rowman and Littlefield.

Vertommen, S. (2017). From the pergonal project to Kadimastem: A genealogy of Israel's reproductive-industrial complex. *BioSocieties*, 12, 282–306.

Vlasenko, P. (2015). Desirable bodies/precarious laborers: Ukrainian egg donors in context of transnational fertility. In V. Kantsa, G. Zanini, & L. Papadopoulou (Eds.), *(In)fertile citizens: Anthropological and legal challenges of assisted reproduction technologies* (pp. 197–216). Aegean: In-Fercit.

Waldby, C. (2015). The oocyte market and social egg freezing: From scarcity to singularity. *Journal of Cultural Economy*, 8, 275–291.

Waldby, C., Kerridge, I., Boulos, M., & Carroll, K. (2013). From altruism to monetization: Australian women's ideas about money, ethics and research eggs. *Social Science & Medicine*, 94, 34–42.

Weis, Christina (2017). Reproductive migrations: Surrogacy workers and stratified reproduction in St. Petersburg. [Unpublished PhD thesis]. De Montfort University.

Werner, M. (2011). Coloniality and the contours of global production in the Dominican Republic and Haiti. *Antipode*, 43, 1573–1597.

Werner, M. (2016). *Global displacements: The making of uneven development in the Caribbean*. Oxford: Wiley Blackwell.

Whittaker, A. (2016). From "Mung Ming" to "Baby Gammy": A local history of assisted reproduction in Thailand. *Reproductive Biomedicine & Society Online*, 2, 71–78.

Whittaker, A., & Speier, A. (2010). "Cycling overseas": Care, commodification, and stratification in cross-border reproductive travel. *Medical Anthropology*, 29, 363–383.

Zelizer, V. (1985). *Pricing the priceless child. The changing social value of children*. Princeton, NJ: Princeton University Press.

39 WHEN DEFENDING THE LAND BECOMES A CRIME (2017)

Moira Birss is Communications and Public Affairs Manager at Amazon Watch. Her articles on environmental protection and community-based economies have appeared in *NACLA: Report on the Americas*, *Alternet*, *In These Times*, *The Women's International Perspective*, and *Common Dreams*. She spent two years in Colombia as a Human Rights Observer and served as the US advocacy officer for Peace Brigades International–Colombia.

Berta Cáceres, assassinated in her home [in Honduras] in March 2016, was just one of hundreds of Latin American environmental activists attacked in recent years. At least 577 environmental human rights defenders (EHRDs) were killed in Latin America between 2010 and 2015—more than in any other region. In addition to violence, EHRDs suffer legal threats and harassment, severely impeding their work. Before Cáceres' murder, she faced trumped-up charges due to her opposition to hydroelectric dams on her indigenous community's territory.

Judicial-system harassment attempts to intimidate EHRDs into silence. Such criminalization transforms activism into crime to avoid bloodier tactics that tend to generate greater sympathy and public outcry. It's an effective tool to silence activists, forcing them to devote time, energy, and financial resources to legal defense and also stigmatizing and alienating them from support networks.

Latin America's indigenous peoples are often at the front lines of the conflict in opposition to industrial exploitation of natural resources and

Environmental activist, Berta Cácere

ONU Brasil/Wikimedia Commons (CC-BY 3.0)

Source: Moira Birss, "When Defending the Land Becomes a Crime" Amazon Watch, October 5, 2017. Reprinted with permission of Moira Birss and NACLA. A longer version of this article appeared the Fall 2017 issue of *NACLA Report on the Americas*.

usurpation of traditional land tenure. EHRDs fight to protect the land, water, forests, animals, and the territorial rights of local communities to serve as stewards of those resources. They advocate and organize against large-scale mines, oil drilling, hydro-electric dams, biofuel plantations, cattle ranches, new highways and railways, logging operations, and other types of destructive industrial development.

Nearly every country in the region has ratified International Labor Organization Convention 169, which stipulates that governments consult with indigenous communities that will be affected by proposed projects on their lands and some national laws are even more stringent. Yet, in practice, such projects tend to run roughshod over community rights and interests.

When states prioritize business interests over the rights of their citizens, they tend to see them as obstacles instead of as citizens. . . .

The Legal System as a Weapon Against EHRDs

That Latin American governments readily accommodate powerful economic interests comes as no surprise to Gustavo Castro, a Mexican social-movement leader and the sole eyewitness to Cáceres' murder. In the course of coordinating Latin American anti-mining coalitions, he often sees governments' attempt to streamline foreign investment by modifying local laws including laws guaranteeing freedom of expression. In paving the way for free trade agreements (FTAs), governments have "expanded the concept of expropriation," Castro argues, putting in place rules that abrogate their own sovereignty and the rights of their people in favor of transnational companies.

As Castro explains, the cancellation of a concession can be declared an expropriation and protest a trade impediment if it impedes the flow of goods. To avoid trade disputes, governments outlaw protest and criminalize activism. "It's cheaper for governments to throw some human rights defenders in jail than pay for those million-dollar lawsuits," he says.

The rules imposed by the Peruvian government after the US-Peru FTA and the criminalization of

EHRDs that resulted illustrate Castro's point. In 2008, the Awajún and Wampis, whose ancestral territory spans the Northern Peruvian Amazon, organized massive protests against proposed legislative decrees to make Peruvian law conform to the FTA. These decrees would have allowed companies to exploit Amazonian lands for oil, gas, mining, and logging. Protests continued through 2009, and tensions escalated into a violent confrontation with police officers in Bagua, resulting in 33 deaths.

After the Bagua massacre, 54 protesters were charged with crimes like homicide and rebellion, and the prosecutor sought the most severe penalties possible. As an example of the absurdity of the charges, the president of a national indigenous federation, AIDESEP, faced 35 years to life for "instigation," even though he was in Lima at the time of the confrontation.

In 2016, all defendants (including one who died while on trial) were absolved of all charges. Several of the decrees they had been protesting were also deemed unconstitutional because they had not been written in consultation with indigenous communities.

The bending of government policy to industry's needs is also clear in Ecuador. During his tenure [as president, Rafael] Correa granted numerous mining and oil concessions to foreign companies on indigenous ancestral territories and environmentally sensitive areas like the Amazon rainforest. When EHRDs and indigenous communities protested, they were stigmatized and jailed, and in some cases, their organizations were also shut down.

The case of the Shuar Arutam [people] exemplifies the kinds of targeting of indigenous communities that occurred under the Correa administration.[1] At least 80 more have been indicted protesting the mine, and the National Indigenous Confederation of Ecuador (CONAIE) lists more than 200 people currently criminalized for protest in Ecuador. CONAIE's "Amnesty First" campaign . . . called on the newly-elected president, Lenin Moreno, to pardon these indigenous activists before they would agree to meet with him.

Although Moreno's governing plan states, "Nature is above the economy, [is] invaluable," he has also made clear that he plans to continue the mega-mining projects planned or underway in high-biodiversity areas like the Cordillera del Cóndor. Paradoxically, he also promises to "re-green" the country, using revenues from oil and mining projects.

This double-speak is also evident from states that are home to companies behind many of the resource-exploitation projects being contested by Latin American EHRDs. In 2016, Lolita Chávez was invited to speak before the European Parliament about the companies operating in her region of Guatemala. "But when I spoke about hydroelectric dams, the EU [European Union] wasn't so happy." After all, she explains, our resources also "are sought after by the world powers."

That search for industrial development and natural resource exploitation also involves international financial institutions, both public and private.

The financier of the Peruvian Yanacocha and Conga gold mine projects, which have a long history of criminalizing local opposition, is the International Finance Corporation (IFC), the private lending arm of the World Bank. Like many extractive industry projects in Latin America, these mines, among the largest gold mines in Latin America, are a joint venture between the IFC; an American company, Newmont Mining Corporation; and a Peruvian company, Minas Buenaventura.

In one telling instance, in April 2013, local . . . leaders attended a meeting about the Conga mine organized by the regional governor. Because the location selected by the governor would not accommodate all the community members wishing to participate, the leaders asked the governor to move the meeting to the central plaza. During the meeting, community members made their rejection of the project clear, while the governor defended it. Afterward, the governor filed a criminal complaint against community members for aggravated kidnapping, alleging that he had been forced to participate in the meeting under threat of physical violence. It took nearly four years for the charges to be dismissed. As with cases of hundreds of other protesters and EHRDs facing court

proceedings, a dismissal of charges indicates a political rather than evidentiary basis for the prosecutions.

Stigmatization and Defamation: A Tool to Silence

Often employed together with criminalization campaigns are efforts to stigmatize and defame EHRDs. This strategy is particularly useful when there is a paucity of evidence to support legal claims against EHRDs. If the ERHD is so demonized that she loses community support, defending herself in court becomes more difficult, as does defending herself before the court of public opinion. In many cases, government officials or companies carry out publicity campaigns to incriminate EHRDs before the justice system has examined a case, knowing the media will disseminate the stigmatizing messages.

"When the first charges began to be filed against me," remembered Lolita Chávez in our May 2017 interview, "the media didn't explain that I have the right to prove my innocence but rather assumed that the accusation was truthful." Media amplification increases the emotional toll caused by false accusations. Even if the defender is not found guilty, the reputational damage can be sufficient to severely curtail, or even render impossible, future environmental defense work.

Throughout her defense of K'iche' land rights, Chávez has received multiple death threats, survived an attempt on her life in 2012, been the object of smear campaigns, faced criminalization. "They have accused me of illicit association, of plagiarism and kidnapping, of conspiracy . . . for opposing multinational companies, principally mining and hydroelectric projects," she told me. Over the years, Chávez has had to confront at least 25 legal cases against her, though it is hard to be sure of the exact number, let alone nature, of the legal complaints and charges against her because authorities do not always divulge such information. At times, she has had to file freedom of information requests to learn the details of cases pending against her.

Chávez has also been targeted in a sexualized way, as are many women EHRDs. "As women, we aren't affected by criminalization in the same way as men," Chávez told me. For example, "when they threaten me with going to jail, they tell me that ugly things will happen to me there. They tell me they will rape me, both on the way to the jail and once I am there."

Chávez did not mince words when she spoke of the effects of her criminalization. "To live with false accusations is to live with constant psychological torture," she reported. "It has affected my life, my day-to-day. I began to be seen with all those stigmas attached to me. It's been said that I am a threat to national security. The way I was treated was exhausting and has worn down my social life, my family life, and my economic situation."

To survive both physically and emotionally, Chávez explained, she has formed support networks with other women to provide emotional, spiritual, and organizational assistance. "Creating community is what has helped me."

"We Will Continue Fighting"

Criminalization can, and often does, have a seriously chilling effect on the work of ERHDs across Latin America. But not always.

In northern Chiapas, the arrest of a protest organizer has inspired a movement against the federal government's plans to auction oil concessions in an area that overlaps with Zoque ancestral territory. "The local government arrested her to silence the movement, but by doing so just created more awareness and resistance. . . ." said a local protester.

As Gustavo Castro observed, "At the end of the day resistance is an ethical struggle. It is a struggle we must take up. Resistance is a principle of justice, especially when we see that the people are suffering."

Lolita Chávez agreed. "We are still alive here," she affirmed to me. . . . "For as long as we continue to believe that coexistence with Mother Earth is a responsibility and a lifelong commitment, we will continue fighting. I invite all those who read this article to join with us, to create community with us. This is our hope for life."

EDITORS' NOTE

1. The Shuar Arutam nation is composed of 60 communities of about 6,000 members living in the Condor mountain range along the Ecuador-Peru border. The mountains are home to endemic species of flora and fauna, the headwaters of an important river network, and innumerable waterfalls of great importance to the Shuar people, who are known as the People of the Waterfalls. The Ecuadorian government has sold concessions to part of their territory for an open-pit copper mining project run by the company Explocobres S.A., a subsidiary of the Chinese companies CRCC and Tongling (Mazabanda 2017).

40 WE'RE ALL CONNECTED NOW, SO WHY IS THE INTERNET SO WHITE AND WESTERN? (2017)

Mark Graham is Professor of Internet Geography at the Oxford Internet Institute of the University of Oxford and a faculty fellow at the Alan Turing Institute. His research focuses on digital labor, digital geographies, and inequalities in our digital world.

Anasuya Sengupta is the co-founder and coordinator of Whose Knowledge?—a global, multilingual campaign to center the knowledges of marginalized communities online. She is a feminist advocate, scholar, storyteller, and strategist for communities and organizations in India, the United States, and internationally and an advisor to the Internet Archive and Equality Labs. Published work includes the co-authored volume *Defending Our Dreams: Global Feminist Voices for a New Generation* (2006).

We recently passed a milestone in the history of human connectivity—people online now make up the majority[1] of the world's population. This has largely gone unnoticed, but it is an important moment and not just for statistical reasons.

North American and European Internet users now make up only about a quarter of the world's users. Furthermore, while countries like the US and the UK have almost reached Internet saturation, Africa, Asia and Latin America are home to billions more people who will come online in the next few years.[2]

The networking of humanity is no longer confined to a few economically prosperous parts of the world. For the first time in history, we are creating a truly global and accessible communication network. However, while access to the Internet is quickly being democratized, research by us for the Geonet project at the Oxford Internet Institute[3] shows that web content remains heavily skewed towards rich, Western countries.

All of sub-Saharan Africa combined, despite having 10% of the world's Internet users, registers only 0.7% of the world's domain names[4] (a good proxy for how much web content is produced) and 0.5% of the world's commits (or revisions) to GitHub (a proxy for how much computer code people write and share in a place). France alone produces 5.7 times more GitHub commits and 3.4 times more domain registrations than all the sub-Saharan countries.

The skewed geography and gender of Wikipedia edits is perhaps even more concerning. Research shows[5] that the vast majority of content on Wikipedia written about most African countries is written by (primarily male) editors in Europe or North America. Wikipedia is one of the most used websites in the world and an important data source for countless platforms and services.

So 20% of the world or less shapes our understanding of 80% of the world.[6] This causes an amplification of geographical and gendered biases, including on search engines like Google.[7] If you are using Google to search for local information in Belgium, Canada or Australia, you will be directed to primarily locally produced content. But if you're in Sierra Leone, Pakistan or Indonesia, almost all content is produced by outsiders.

For a Nigerian woman going online, there are hardly any Wikipedia biographies[8] of the women she reads about in a national newspaper. You might speak Mandarin, Bengali or Arabic, all of which are in the top 10 most spoken languages.[9] But there are only 52,000 articles[10] in the Bengali Wikipedia (a language spoken by 237 million people), while the Dutch Wikipedia has nearly

2 million articles[11] for a country whose language is spoken by 28 million people.

In a world riven by stereotypes and discrimination, the Internet should be challenging the biases of our physical world, not deepening them. In fact, the Internet could well serve as a digital space that reflects and produces the richness of our world's multiple forms of knowledge, through a combination of text, voice and visuals. As Google projected a few years ago, the world has nearly 130 million books in at least 480 languages.[12] Yet in a world of nearly 7,000 languages and dialects, that means only about 7% of our languages are in published material.[13] We need to do much more to capture the oral knowledge of our past and present.

So how do we make the Internet look more like the world we live in? Those of us who make up most of the world need to bring our information and knowledge online, and all of us—wherever we are from—need to help make it happen.

A number of individuals, groups and campaigns have been working to make the Internet more diverse and plural. Wikimujeres[14] (and similar initiatives in different languages) work on increasing the number of women's biographies from Latin America on the Spanish Wikipedia. Wiki Loves Africa[15] expands the number of high-quality images from African countries, and Afrocrowd[16] works to create and improve information on black culture and history on Wikipedia. Organizations such as the Association of Progressive Communications[17] focus on women's rights and knowledge in Internet and telecommunications policies.

Whose Knowledge?[18] is a global, multilingual campaign that works with these groups and beyond, to center the histories and knowledge of the majority of the world that is underrepresented on the Internet. For instance, in 2016 when we began, we worked with scholars from the Kumeyaay Native American community of southern California, on the Wikipedia article about the California gold rush,[19] to reflect its deeply negative impact on Native American communities. In April, with our partners in Equality Labs,[20] we held a Wikipedia editing session to include information about the 350 million people of India's Dalit community, and wrote about

inspirations like Grace Banu[21]—the first transgender Dalit person to be admitted to an engineering college in Tamil Nadu. At the same time, we are working with communities such as the Dalit and the Kumeyaay to archive their oral knowledge and histories.

Google[22] and other key mediators of information should have a responsibility to ensure that communities around the world are not flooded with foreign content, and that the Internet begins to resemble the network for billions that it is meant to be. But we—as users—also have a responsibility to question the perspectives presented to us by the Googles and the Wikipedias of the world, and perhaps also to change them: to edit, to create, and to build the Internet we want to see.

NOTES

1. See http://www.internetworldstats.com/stats.htm
2. Ralph Straumann, "World Regions' Access to the Internet," *Geonet*, July 12, 2017, http://geonet.oii.ox.ac.uk/blog/world-regions-access-to-the-internet/
3. Mark Graham, "Towards a Study of Information Geographies: (Im)mutable augmentations and a Mapping of the Geographies of Information," *Geonet*, August 14, 2015, http://geonet.oii.ox.ac.uk/blog/new-paper-towards-a-study-of-information-geographiesimmutable-augmentations-and-a-mapping-of-thegeographies-of-information/
4. Sanaa Ojanperä, Mark Graham, Ralph Straumann, Stefano De Sabatta, and Matthew Zook, "Engagement in the Knowledge Economy: Regional Patterns of Content Creation with a Focus on Sub-Saharan Africa," *Information Technologies and International Development* 13 (2017), http://itidjournal.org/index.php/itid/article/view/1479
5. Mark Graham, "Digging Deeper into the Localness of Participation in Sub-Saharan African Wikipedia Content," *Geonet*, December 16, 2014, http://geonet.oii.ox.ac.uk/blog/digging-deeper-into-the-localness-of-participation-in-sub-saharan-african-wikipedia-content/
6. Mark Graham, Matthew Zook, and Andrew Boulton, "Augmented Reality in Urban Places: Contested Content and the Duplicity of Code," *Transactions of the Institute of British Geographers* 38 (July 2013), 464–479, http://onlinelibrary.wiley.com/doi/10.1111/j.1475-5661.2012.00539.x/abstract

7. Mark Graham, "Digital Hegemonies: The Localness of Search Engine Results," *Geonet*, May 4, 2017, http://geonet.oii.ox.ac.uk/blog/digital-hegemonies-the-localness-of-search-engine-results/

8. Dimitra Kessenides and Max Chafkin, "Is Wikipedia Woke?" *Bloomberg Businessweek*, December 16, 2016, https://www.bloomberg.com/news/features/2016-12-22/how-woke-is-wikipedia-s-editorial-pool

9. See https://stats.wikimedia.org/EN/Sitemap.htm

10. "List of Wikipedieas," *Wikimedia*, https://meta.wikimedia.org/wiki/List_of_Wikipedias

11. Ibid.

12. Joab Jackson, "Google: 129 Million Different Books Have Been Published," *PCWorld*, August 6, 2010, https://www.pcworld.com/article/202803/google_129_million_different_books_have_been_published.html

13. Ibid.

14. See https://meta.wikimedia.org/wiki/Wikimujeres

15. See https://meta.wikimedia.org/wiki/Wiki_Loves_Africa

16. See https://en.wikipedia.org/wiki/AfroCrowd

17. Association for Progressive Communications, "A Feminist Internet," n.d., https://www.apc.org/en/feminist-internet-0

18. See http://whoseknowledge.org/

19. See https://en.wikipedia.org/wiki/California_Gold_Rush#Impact_on_Native_Americans

20. See https://www.equalitylabs.org/

21. "Grace Banu," *Wikipedia*, n.d., https://en.wikipedia.org/wiki/Grace_Banu

22. See https://www.theguardian.com/technology/google

Security and Sustainability

Gender, Crime, and Criminalization

Key concepts: criminalization, decriminalization, incarceration, prison abolition

The number of women and gender nonconforming people who are serving time in US jails and prisons, on probation, or otherwise caught up in the "correctional" system has increased dramatically in the past thirty-five years. **Criminalization** is one of the clearest ways in which gender, race, and class shape people's lives, and students of women's and gender studies should understand the processes whereby they are defined as criminals. Many of us are shielded from this reality because incarcerated people are literally locked away, behind bars, and out of sight. This chapter examines the societal assumptions that justify and reinforce this separation between "inside" and "outside": that these are bad people who must have done something *very wrong* to end up in prison.

FEMALE IN THE CRIMINAL JUSTICE SYSTEM

According to the Sentencing Project (2018), in 2016 more than 102,000 women were held in US jails, many of them awaiting sentencing, and over 111,000 were in prisons, for over 213,000 incarcerated women, with over a million more on probation or parole (p. 1). Historically, researchers and media reporters paid little attention to female offenders because their numbers were small in comparison to males. During the 1990s, however, the rate of growth in women's imprisonment far outstripped that of men's. Why is this? The majority

Photo by Scott Braley. Reprinted with permission.

of female arrests are for minor, nonviolent crimes, such as shoplifting, forging checks, theft, drug use or possession, and so-called "public order" offences that include prostitution. When women commit acts of violence, these are often against abusive spouses or partners (see, e.g., Jacobsen 2008; Rennison 2003; Richie 2012; Stark 2007).

Poverty, unemployment, physical and mental illness, substance abuse, homelessness, police harassment, and a history of physical and sexual abuse often propel women into a revolving cycle inside and outside jails and prisons, as mentioned by Susan Burton and Cari Lynn in Reading 41. Firsthand accounts documenting women's experiences of incarceration mention degrading and harsh prison conditions, humiliating and callous treatment by staff, and women's feelings of guilt, anger, and despair (see, e.g., Díaz-Cotto 2006; P. Johnson 2002; Lamb and the Women of York Correctional Facility 2003, 2007; Lawston and Lucas 2011; Rathbone 2006; Solinger et al. 2010). Over her decades-long imprisonment, the late Marilyn Buck (2004) described how incarcerated women cope with idle time—literally "doing time"—and prison work, which is both a punishment as well as the only way to earn

> a pittance . . . to buy items of personal hygiene, a candy bar . . . any material we might want to use for our own human productivity . . . as well as for telephone calls to our families, children, and friends with whom we desperately seek to maintain some level of attachment. (p. 454)

Buck developed certain routines and habits of mind that helped her to navigate what she called the minefield of prison life, as well as inner resources of patience and forbearance. She commented that women sometimes refuse to cooperate with guards and refuse to do prison work "as an act of resistance" but the price of refusal is often high in terms of increased punishment (p. 454). Stormy Ogden (2006), a member of the Tule River Yokuts, Kashaya Pomo, and Lake County Pomo nations in northern California, pointed out that medicating incarcerated women as a routine practice makes it easier for prison authorities to manage them. She was given Elavil (an antidepressant) and Mellaril (an antipsychotic) while in county jail awaiting sentencing; in prison, she was given Thorazine (an antipsychotic) and chloral hydrate (a sedative), which made her into "one of the 'walking zombies'" (p. 168).

People in Women's Prisons
Ethnic studies professor and prison researcher Julia Sudbury (2011) pointed out that much research and writing on women in prison, including her own earlier work, did not take account of gender fluidity among incarcerated people. Rather, it inadvertently reinforced the gender binary and legitimized the "state's power to determine and police the gender identification of those it imprisons" (p. 171). Recognizing this, she uses the phrase "people in women's prisons" to include trans and gender nonconforming people. In 2016, the US Department of Justice issued new guidelines "prohibiting corrections agencies from placing transgender inmates into men's or women's units solely based on their anatomy at birth" (La Ganga 2016), though it seems that this guideline is not always followed. Moreover, trans people in jails and prisons are disproportionate targets of humiliation and abuse by staff and other inmates (see the box feature "Sexual Abuse of Inmates and Detainees"; Law 2017).

Sexual Abuse of Inmates and Detainees

- Under the Prison Rape Elimination Act jails, prisons, and detention centers are responsible for the safety of every inmate and must make "housing, bed, work, education, and program assignments with the goal of keeping separate those inmates at high risk of being sexually victimized from those at high risk of being sexually abusive" (US Department of Justice 2012, p. 20).

- Routine sexual abuse of women and gender-variant people in jails, prisons, and detention centers by male staff includes insults, harassment, rape, voyeurism in showers and during physical exams, and touching of breasts and genitals during pat-downs and strip searches (K. Brown 2018; Fialho, Cullors, and Martinez 2018).

- Many people in women's prisons have a history of physical and sexual abuse, which makes them more vulnerable to abuse in prison (Buttenweiser 2016).

- A prisoner's sexuality (perceived or actual) or gender expression makes them a target for sexual abuse or for retaliation if they report it (Heidenreich 2011; Just Detention 2012).

- According to Bureau of Justice data released in 2014, 4 percent of females in prison and 3.2 percent in jails reported being sexually assaulted by other inmates or staff during the previous year. For trans inmates, reports were 8 to 10 times higher, at 34.6 percent in prisons and 34 percent in jails (La Ganga 2016).

- Officials may ignore people's complaints or not believe them, and an unknown number of acts of sexual violence go unreported (Lennard 2017).

- Thousands of migrants have said they were sexually abused in the custody of Immigration and Customs Enforcement (ICE) in the past 10 years, according to the US Department of Homeland Security's Office of the Inspector General (Kassie 2018).

- Trans women in immigration detention may be held in men's facilities and sexually assaulted by male detainees and guards—the same kinds of abuses that drove them to flee their home countries in the first place (Human Rights Watch 2016, p.2).

Most people in women's prisons are mothers, many of them single heads of households. Patrice Gaines, who later became a *Washington Post* reporter, was incarcerated on a drug charge. She wrote:

> I stood with my forehead pressed as close as possible to the dark, tinted window of my jail cell. The window was long and narrow, the foot-deep wall that framed it made it impossible to stand close. The thick glass blurred everything outside. I squinted and focused, and I concentrated all my attention on the area where my mother said the family would stand and wave. . . . It would be good to see my grandparents and my mother, but it was my daughter I really wanted to see. My daughter who would be two years old in two months.
>
> A couple of minutes passed, and in that small space of time, I rethought my entire life and how it had come to this absurd moment, when I became a twenty-one-year-old girl in jail on a drug charge, a mother who had to wait for someone to bring my own daughter to glimpse me. I could not rub my hands across her fat, brown cheeks, or plait her curly hair the way I like it. *(Gaines 1994, p. 1)*

In 2018, over 60 percent of women in state prisons had a child under the age of 18 (Sentencing Project 2018, p. 1). African American children are seven times as likely as white children to have an incarcerated parent (Children's Defense Fund 2010, p. H-12). Policy analysts Erika Kates and Paige Ransford (2005) emphasized the criminal justice system's lack of recognition of women's role as mothers and the impacts of incarceration on parenting and family life (also see Arditti 2012). Factors that prevent regular contact between incarcerated mothers and their children include isolated prison locations served by poor or nonexistent public transport, restrictive policies governing visits and phone calls, the removal of infants born to women in prison, speedy termination of child custody for incarcerated women, restrictive welfare policies that make it difficult for families to be reunited, and some women's repeated arrests. The majority of these children live with relatives, primarily grandparents. Despite enormous difficulties, some mothers try a variety of means to care for their children from prison, and children are often *the* motivating factor for women to get their lives back on track, as Gaines (1994) suggested (also see, e.g., Enos 2001; Golden 2005; Solinger et al. 2010).

Some women come to prison pregnant; others become pregnant in prison. Few receive prenatal care, and pregnant prisoners suffer a high rate of miscarriage as a result. Congress has banned the use of federal funds for abortion in prison. Women who can pay for an abortion themselves may be able to get one at a clinic, but they need to convince prison authorities to transport them there. Women who carry their pregnancies to term are often treated inhumanely, denied prompt medical attention, and in some states, still forced to undergo labor and childbirth in shackles (Min 2018).

Access to medical care is a major problem for females in prison. Inadequate staffing leads to long delays, disrupted and poor-quality treatment, and overmedication of prisoners rather than mental health care. What might be considered routine services such as mammograms and Pap smears often entail a long wait. Treatable diseases like asthma, diabetes, sickle cell anemia, and cancer may lead to death or permanent injury due to neglect. Also, trans people may be denied regular access to hormone treatments and other needed medications.

Writer Victoria Law (2009) documented incarcerated women's resistance to prison conditions. These may be small acts of support and kindness that break the dehumanization and alienation of prison life, as well as sharing information or setting up educational resources. Juanita Díaz-Cotto (2006) reported a range of women's efforts to improve their conditions: refusing to return to their cells when ordered, using prison grievance procedures, filing lawsuits, or going on hunger strikes. Stormy Ogden (2006) explained that Native American women are overrepresented in the prison system but are absent from much official data because prisons classify people as white, Black, Hispanic, or "other." Every morning, she would replace "other" with "AI" (American Indian) on the name card outside her cell. Each afternoon she returned to find that prison staff had replaced "AI" with "other." She kept correcting her name card and was punished for this infraction of discipline by losing sixty days of good behavior, but remarked that as an act of self-assertion "it was well worth it" (p. 169).

Race and Class Disparities

Law professor Michelle Alexander (2012) argued that mass incarceration has become normalized in the United States, with more "African American adults . . . under correctional control today . . . than were enslaved in 1850, a decade before the Civil War began" (p. 180). African American women are affected by this in two ways: they are trying to hold their families and communities together while so many Black men are incarcerated, and increasingly, they are in jail or prison themselves.

Incarceration rates vary widely among states, but racial and class disparities have been a steady trend in US law enforcement and a consistent factor in arrests, pretrial treatment, and differential sentencing. In 2016, the incarceration rate for white women was 49 per 100,000 population, compared to 96 for Black women and 67 for Latinas (Sentencing Project 2018, p. 2). White women are more likely to be placed on probation than women of color. Economist Kiaran Honderich (2003) described the channeling of poor women of color into the criminal justice system as a "funnel of injustice" (p. 10) (see Fig. 9.1). Many crimes committed on Native American reservations are classified as

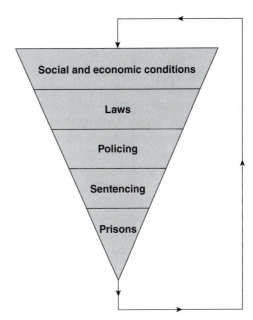

FIGURE 9-1   The Funnel of Injustice
Honderick (2003, p. 10). Reproduced with permission.

federal offenses, which means those convicted must serve their sentences in federal prisons, usually in remote places far from home and hard to get to by public transportation.

Girls in Detention

Race and class disparities also apply to girls. Native American girls are much more likely to be held in detention than white girls or other girls of color. For white girls, the rate is 32 per 100,000. Comparable figures for Native American girls are 134 per 100,000; for African American girls, 110; and for Latinx girls, 44 (Sentencing Project 2018, p. 4). Girls reported that they were mostly arrested for drug and alcohol use and possession, hitting their parents or grandparents, and running away from home or custodial placements (Garcia and Lane 2009). Middle-class girls with similar behavior are more likely to end up in therapy, treatment programs, boarding schools, or private hospitals rather than becoming criminalized.

The number of girls in juvenile detention surged in the 1990s. By 2016, girls accounted for 15 percent of youth in residential placements and 25 percent of teens arrested (Sentencing Project 2018, pp. 4–5). The Girl's Study Group, initiated by the Office of Juvenile Justice and Delinquency Prevention, confirmed that the growing number of girls in juvenile detention was due to policy changes and greater media attention rather than because girls have become more unruly (Zahn et al. 2008). In some areas, running away from home, truancy, scuffling with family members, or repeated discipline problems have been reclassified as crimes. Also, zero-tolerance policies in schools have turned relatively minor offenses that used to be addressed informally—such as misbehavior or a fit of anger—into crimes (Morris 2016; Ritchie 2017a, 2017b). Writer Andrea Ritchie (2017a) cites several cases where young women of color were slammed against the wall, thrown to the floor, and arrested by police officers stationed in their schools for leaving class a few minutes late ("roaming the hallways"), asking for return of a confiscated cell phone ("threatening an officer"), or cursing in the hallway ("disorderly conduct"). Ritchie argues that the presence of law enforcement officers in schools is linked to higher rates of arrest for African American girls, with some as young as age 6 or 7 being handcuffed and taken from school by police.

Many girls in the juvenile justice system have been abused physically, emotionally, or sexually, often from a young age (see, e.g., Chesney-Lind and Pasko 2013, 2004; Chesney-Lind and Irwin 2008). In some cases, their parents are absent due to death, drug use, or incarceration. Sociologist Juanita Díaz-Cotto (2006) found that many Chicanas who ended up in prison were first arrested as juveniles who had become "alienated from their parents and other adults as a result of abuse and neglect" (p. 53). In response, they "confronted their parents angrily at home, cut school, bullied other children, ran away from home, experimented with alcohol and illegal drugs, and/or joined barrio youth gangs" (p. 7). The Sentencing Project (2018) reported that girls are more than 50 percent of youth incarcerated for running away and 38 percent of youth incarcerated for truancy and curfew violations (p. 4). A study of 112 girls in shelter care, juvenile detention, and state correctional facilities asked them to assess the effectiveness of programs they had experienced (Garcia and Lane 2009). They found the programs that helped them to understand their thinking and their anger the most useful, together with counseling for grief and loss and dealing with sexual abuse. They wanted a voice in what happened to them, to work with caring staff and probation officers, and to learn practical life skills that would help them live independently.

Fewer rehabilitation and housing placements exist for girls compared to boys, so girls spend more time in detention awaiting placement. Criminologist Stacy Mallicoat (2012) noted that juvenile facilities are often very poorly equipped to address girls' emotional needs, or their physical and mental health.

Women Political Prisoners

Despite constitutional guarantees of free speech and freedom to organize, political activists may risk arrest and imprisonment. Suffragists were jailed in the early 1900s for peaceful picketing of the White House as part of the decades-long campaign for votes for women, as mentioned in Chapter 1. In January 1917, mainly middle-class, white women organized pickets around the clock. At first, the police ignored them. By June, however, they began to be arrested, and in August, some received thirty- and sixty-day sentences for obstructing traffic. A number of those who were jailed went on hunger strike; they were forcibly fed and threatened with transfer to an insane asylum. These women received disproportionately long sentences and harsh treatment, clearly intended to discourage opposition to government policy. They were released the following year by order of President Wilson, and the Washington, DC, Court of Appeals later ruled that their arrests, convictions, and imprisonment were illegal (Gluck 1976).

Another example concerns activists incarcerated in the 1970s and 1980s, including members of the Puerto Rican Socialist Party, supporters of Native American sovereignty movements, and participants in Black revolutionary movements. Scholar, writer, and activist Angela Davis, for example, was imprisoned for two years on murder, conspiracy, and kidnapping charges—though later acquitted. Silvia Baraldini, Marilyn

Buck, Susan Rosenberg, and Laura Whitehorn, active in the women's movement and the anti–Vietnam War movement, were imprisoned for many years. Marilyn Buck received an eighty-year sentence. She was released in 2010, less than a month before her death from cancer at age 62. In her account of her daily life in prison, she wrote that she worried about becoming "inured to the casual cruelty that prevails. It lures us into becoming the very creatures the prison system advertises us to be. . . . I worry about succumbing, losing my will to resist dehumanization, and ultimately, losing my own sense of who I am as a human being" (Buck n.d., p. 1).

THE NATIONAL CONTEXT: "TOUGH ON CRIME"

Criminalization must be understood in the context of national penal policy and the dramatic expansion of the criminal justice system over the past four decades. Political scientist Marie Gottschalk (2006) noted that the United States has "built a carceral state that is unprecedented among Western countries and in US history," (p. 1). *Washington Post* correspondent Christopher Ingraham (2016) reported that the United States has less than 5 percent of the world's population but nearly 25 percent of the world's prisoners. In 2018, almost 2.3 million people were held in state and federal prisons, local jails, juvenile correctional facilities, and immigration detention (Wagner and Sawyer 2018), with another 4.5 million people on probation or parole (Sawyer and Bertram 2018).

Considering various factors to explain the increased incarceration of African Americans, Alexander (2012) identified the loss of jobs as fundamental:

> In 1954, Black and white youth unemployment rates in America were equal. . . . By 1984, however, the Black unemployment rate had nearly quadrupled, while the white rate had increased only marginally. This was *not* due to a major change in Black values, behavior, or culture; this dramatic shift was the result of deindustrialization, globalization, and technological advancement. Urban factories shut down as our nation transitioned to a service economy. Suddenly African Americans were trapped in jobless ghettos. (p. 218)

She pointed out that the nation could have responded to the economic collapse of inner-city communities in several ways: stimulus packages for businesses, resources for education and job training, and relocation assistance to help people access jobs in other areas. Such interventions would have helped all blue-collar workers, not only African Americans. "All this could have happened, but it didn't," she wrote. "Instead we declared a War on Drugs" (p. 218).

The War on Drugs

The "war on drugs," initiated in the 1980s under the Reagan administration, was largely responsible for the vast increase in incarceration in the United States. Proponents claimed that massive government intervention was necessary to quell the drug epidemic, gang violence, and "narco-terrorism." This resulted in federal and state funding for additional police officers on the streets, more federal law enforcement officers, and construction of new jails and prisons rather than funding for education, job training, drug prevention, or rehabilitation. Mandatory sentencing laws for drug offenses forced judges to send first-time offenders to prison. Moreover, "three-strikes-you're-out" laws in various states required a life sentence for three-time felons. The war on drugs has allowed the police to stop, interrogate, and search anyone for drug investigations, and many commentators have pointed to the racial bias in patterns of arrest and sentencing (Alexander 2012; Gottschalk 2006; P. Johnson 2002). These policies have been pursued aggressively in low-income African American and Latinx neighborhoods despite the fact that white people are the majority of US drug users and sellers. The Children's Defense Fund (2010) maintained that "[a] cradle to prison pipeline, driven by poverty and racial disparities, is becoming the new American apartheid threatening to undermine the hard earned racial and social progress of the last half century" (p. vii). Michelle Alexander (2012) called the racial profiling and incarceration policies that created a permanent racial under-caste "the new Jim Crow." Moreover, mandatory minimum prison sentences appear to have had negligible effect on the drug trade in the United States.

Incarceration as a Business

Incarceration is big business. Prisons and jails employ an estimated 700,000 people nationwide (Alexander 2012, p. 230). Architecture firms design new prisons. Security companies supply equipment. Food distribution companies deliver meals. Other companies provide medical services or employ prison labor. Moreover, prisoners are the ultimate flexible and dependable workforce. They do not have to be paid minimum wage, provided with health benefits or vacation time, or covered by workers' compensation (a tax employers must pay for regular employees), and they cannot unionize. Prisoners are used to fight fires in California. Best Western (the international motel chain) used prisoners to take calls from customers during peak times. Boeing, Microsoft, Nintendo, Starbucks, and Victoria's Secret are just a few of the companies that have used prison labor, and prison-generated products have ended up attached to well-known labels like No Fear, Lee Jeans, and Trinidad Tees. Telephone companies profit from incarceration because family members are not allowed to call prisoners directly; prisoners can only call collect, the most expensive way to make calls. CoreCivic (formerly Corrections Corporation of America) manages many prisons and immigration detention centers across the country and lobbies state and federal politicians to keep up a steady supply of inmates (Herivel and Wright 2007). Borrowing from the term *military-industrial complex* coined by President Dwight Eisenhower, the *prison-industrial complex* refers to a similar mesh of interconnected relationships among private corporations, the public prison system, public investment, and public interests (see, e.g., Herivel and Wright 2007; McShane 2008; Price and Morris 2012).

CRIMINALIZATION AS A POLITICAL PROCESS

Crimes are not fixed, nor decided separately from dominant customs and beliefs. Criminalization is a process whereby people who do not fit societal norms are labeled as criminals and their circumstances and behaviors defined as crimes, as with the increasing criminalization of girls mentioned earlier. Other examples include gender nonconforming people, homeless people, immigrants, and people from "enemy" nations. Ideologies of racism, classism, sexism, heterosexism, and nationalism may be deployed to justify criminalization and mobilize people's support for it.

Definitions and Justifications

Behaviors that were defined as crimes in the past may be **decriminalized** with changes in attitudes. For example, miscegenation laws banning interracial marriage in the United States have been repealed. Homosexuality has been decriminalized. Abortion was made legal, as discussed in Chapter 5. Some states have decriminalized the use of marijuana for medical or recreational purposes.

Rape and domestic violence are now defined as crimes, though this has inadvertently strengthened the power of law enforcement, as argued in Chapter 6. Also, changes in laws or in their interpretation create a host of new offenses, as the following examples show.

States that seek to limit abortion rights, especially those that grant the fetus "legal personhood," have arrested pregnant women, mostly based on suspicion of illegal drug use (Boyd 2004). Thus, women who have miscarried or experienced stillbirth have been arrested for trafficking to the fetus, manslaughter, assault with a deadly weapon, or homicide. Women who use illegal drugs come from diverse backgrounds, but poor women are less protected from state intervention than middle-class and wealthy women. Black women "are ten times more likely to be reported for substance abuse during pregnancy than women of other races" (Warner, 2011, p. 231).

Criminalization is used to assert heteronormativity through police harassment and targeting of trans or genderqueer people (Heidenreich 2011), or by state-imposed bans on gay teachers in public schools, limiting what they can say to students, and banning books said "to promote homosexuality" from school and public libraries. Welfare rules have become more punitive, as mentioned in Chapter 7. Law enforcement officials can access information in welfare files, and states can require drug tests, fingerprints, and photographs from those applying for benefits (Gustafson 2005, 2011). Poor and homeless people—some of them mothers—have become subject to criminalization as cities have passed ordinances that prohibit begging and sleeping in public places.

Politicians and media reports tend to focus on street crime—burglary, auto theft, mugging, murder, and rape committed by strangers—as a vital national issue, even though crime rates for most offenses have steadily decreased over the past decade and the greatest economic losses from crime do not happen on the street. However, high-income criminals who commit fraud and embezzlement—often called "white-collar crime"—are less likely to be incarcerated or to be considered hardened criminals. Dozens of mainly white male corporate executives, financial analysts, and politicians are criticized for conflicts of interest, shady dealing, and the possibility of fraud. Some are investigated; few are convicted.

One last example here concerns people who protest corporate efforts to take over natural resources—for example, in Asia and Latin America, as discussed in Chapter 8. Local communities, often led by indigenous women who oppose the confiscation of their traditional land for palm oil plantations, ranching, mining operations, oil extraction, and the creation of dams, are being criminalized by their governments (see Reading 39; also see Cowman 2016; Jenkins 2015; Okazawa-Rey and JASS 2018). Criminalization of protest is also happening in Europe, Japan, and the United States.

Profiling and Surveillance for "National Security"

National disasters may provide the pretext for criminalizing people from "enemy" groups. The internment of 110,000 people of Japanese ancestry following the bombing of Pearl Harbor by the Japanese military in 1941 was justified on nationalist and racist grounds. This included men, women, children, and babies. Most were US citizens living in West Coast states. They were forced to leave their homes, farms, and businesses and incarcerated in remote prison camps until the end of World War II (see, e.g., Daniels, Taylor, and Kitano 1991; Hirahara and Lindquist 2018; Iwamura 2007; Tateishi 1984; Yoo 2000). Constitutional guarantees regarding "due process of law" were suspended, "and the Government was able to implement this massive program with few questions asked," though there was no evidence that these suspects were in any way "disloyal" to the United States (Takahashi 1998 p. 362).

In a similar move, authorities arrested some 1,200 men, mostly Arabs, after the attacks on the World Trade Center and the Pentagon on September 11, 2001. In November 2002, a "Special Registration" program required males over sixteen years of age, from twenty-five mainly Arab and Muslim countries, to be fingerprinted, photographed, and questioned about terrorism. Several thousand were detained and an unknown number deported, though few, if any, of those arrested were found to have connections to terrorism.

Officials and private citizens committed acts of violence against Arab Americans, South Asians, and "people who look like Muslims," including some women but mainly men. Negative media coverage of Arabs and Arab Americans continues to contribute to a climate of opinion whereby racial profiling, preemptive arrests and detentions, abuse and humiliation of those detained, and suspension of constitutional rights can be justified in the name of "national security" (see, e.g., Alsultany 2012; Bayoumi 2009, 2015; Joseph and D'Harlingue 2007; Nacos and Torres-Reyna 2007). In Reading 43, attorney Diala Shamas describes extensive surveillance of Arab American communities by the New York Police Department following the 9/11 attacks, with severe effects on Muslim students at City University campuses that undermined their ability to study and participate in student life.

Congress increased the government's powers of investigation in the Uniting and Strengthening America by Providing Appropriate Tools Required to Intercept and Obstruct Terrorism Act (USA PATRIOT Act), which became law on October 26, 2001. According to the American Civil Liberties Union (2002), it includes measures that:

- Allow for indefinite detention of noncitizens who are not terrorists on minor visa violations.
- Minimize judicial supervision of federal telephone and Internet surveillance by authorities.
- Expand the government's powers to conduct secret searches.
- Give the Attorney General and the Secretary of State the power to designate domestic groups as terrorist organizations and deport any noncitizens who belong to them.
- Give the FBI access to business records about individuals without having to show evidence of a crime;
- Lead to large-scale investigation of U.S. citizens for "intelligence" purposes.

In addition, the Homeland Security Act of 2002 authorizes the collection of data on individuals and groups from databases that combine personal, governmental, and corporate records, including e-mails and websites viewed. This was justified in terms of the "war on terrorism," but it allows for much broader surveillance and targeting of any individual or group.

Criminalization of Migration

Immigration and Customs Enforcement (ICE) has regularly raided workplaces, homes, and schools in Latinx communities and arrested anyone found without legal documentation. Law professor Nina Rabin (2011) noted that

> [c]ontrary to popular perception, living in the United States without authorization is not a crime . . . crossing the border without proper documentation is a crime, as is re-entering the country without permission after a deportation order. (p. 19)

She argued that "many undocumented immigrants enter the country legally but then overstay their visa or violate its terms" (p. 19).

In the 1990s, a time of relative economic expansion, the federal government authorized an amnesty for undocumented migrants from many nations, recognizing their valuable contribution to the US economy (see Chapter 3). Due to economic recession, shifts in sentiment against immigrants, overt racist attitudes and behavior, and the introduction of harsher federal and state policies against immigrant communities, legal channels for immigration have decreased drastically. In the first decade of this century, the number of people held in ICE detention nearly doubled, from 209,000 in 2001 to 392,000 in 2010 (Detention Watch Network 2011).

At the same time, economic globalization continues to pressure people from poorer nations to migrate for survival, especially those displaced as mentioned previously. Other root causes of immigration include political repression, as well as death threats and demands for extortion payments from gangs (see Chapter 8 and 10). In Reading 44, Leslie Campos describes her work as a paralegal on behalf of immigrant parents who were forcibly separated from their children at the US-Mexico border in May 2018 as part of a government crackdown on migrants from Central America seeking asylum in the United States. The children were sent to shelters across the country while their parents remained in detention centers, not knowing their children's whereabouts for weeks or even longer. In Reading 57, Deborah Lee, an ordained minister with the United Church of Christ, describes her faith-based work on behalf of people in immigration detention.

People in ICE custody are housed in some 300 detention facilities, including centers operated by ICE, facilities managed by private companies, state and county jails under contract with ICE, or facilities run by the Federal Bureau of Prisons. Immigrant, civil rights, and faith-based organizations argue that immigrant families require educational, medical, and legal support, and that detention in closed facilities is both inappropriate and unnecessarily costly (Shah 2012). A factor driving immigration detention is the "bed quota" authorized by Congress that requires ICE to maintain 34,000 immigration beds on a daily basis. According to the National Immigrant Justice Center (2018): "No other law enforcement agency is subject to a statutory quota on the number of individuals to hold in detention." Immigration detention costs over $2 billion a year, or $159 per person per day. This bed quota prevents ICE from developing cheaper alternatives to detention that would allow individuals who pose no risk to public safety to be released while awaiting asylum or immigration hearings.

In Reading 48, Jane Freedman, Zeynep Kivilcim, and Nurcan Özgür Baklacioğlu report on Syrian refugees fleeing war in their homeland and the strains of mass migration on neighboring Middle Eastern countries. Several member nations of the European Union have responded by blocking entry to them. In Reading 45, the Spanish Federation of Feminist Organizations condemns walls and barriers in Europe to keep out refugees and migrants fleeing wars, violence, and environmental disasters.

As the examples in this section show, criminalization is a way of punishing certain groups, and those targeted may change over time, depending on context. In the United States, however, the criminalization of African Americans is a consistent factor (Alexander 2012; Golden 2005). Slavery and Jim Crow segregation are illegal, but low-income African Americans, who are increasingly outside the paid workforce, are controlled and warehoused through mass incarceration. Racial profiling, police shootings, and deaths of Black people in police custody have generated new political organizing to expose and oppose this, as, for example, through the Movement for Black Lives and Say Her Name. Given this reality, Sara Lomax-Reese, the President and CEO of WURD Radio, an African American talk radio station in Pennsylvania, describes her anguish and her parenting strategies as a Black mother of three sons in Reading 32.

INSIDE/OUTSIDE CONNECTIONS

Formerly incarcerated women have been key to establishing supports and services for women in jails and prisons and organizing together with advocates and allies outside the law enforcement system, as shown by A New Way of Life Reentry Project in Los Angeles (see Reading 41; also see, e.g., Law 2009; Lawston and Lucas 2011; Solinger et al. 2010; Women's Prison Association 2009). On their release, formerly incarcerated people have to find housing and a way to survive. They are denied public housing and welfare benefits, and a large number of jobs exclude potential employees with felony records.

Support for People in Women's Prisons

A growing number of organizations support people in women's prisons and those formerly incarcerated. This includes Aid to Inmate Mothers (Montgomery, AL), Chicago Legal Advocacy for Incarcerated Mothers, Families for Justice as Healing (Boston, MA), JusticeWorks Community (Brooklyn, NY), Legal Services for Prisoners with Children (Oakland, CA), Let's Start (St. Louis, MO), Michigan Women's Justice and Clemency Project (Ann Arbor), National Women's Prison Project (Baltimore, MD), Portia Project (Eugene, OR), Power Inside (Baltimore, MD), Women Evolving (Plainfield, VT), WORTH (New York, NY), and Women's Reentry Network (Tucson, AZ). Organizations that support LGBTQI prisoners include Black and Pink (with chapters in many cities), Just Detention International (Los Angeles, CA), and the Sylvia Rivera Law Project (New York, NY). *Women and Prisons: A Site for Resistance* is a Web space for prisoners, those previously incarcerated, activists, students, and teachers that makes visible women's experiences in the criminal justice system (http://womenandprison.org).

Women on the outside are working with prisoners in literacy classes, creative writing, and art projects; providing books (e.g., Books Through Bars, New York, NY; Women's Prison Book Project, Minneapolis, MN); and undertaking theater productions with incarcerated women (e.g., The Medea Project, San Francisco, CA) (Lawston and Lucas 2011). Independent filmmakers have made films to publicize the circumstances of women who killed their abusive partners, such as *Defending Our Lives*, which tells the story of Battered Women Fighting Back! (Framingham Correctional Institution, MA). The Michigan Women's Justice and Clemency Project produced *From One Prison . . .* in collaboration with women at a Michigan prison who are serving life or long-term sentences for killing their batterers.

Another grassroots mobilization is the National Black Mama's Bail Out campaign launched in 2017 by the National Bail Out Collective to provide bail for Black mothers who would otherwise have been separated from their children on Mother's Day 2017. The project emerged from a conversation among millennial activists Charlene Carruthers of Black Youth Project 100 and Mary Hooks and others of Southerners on New Ground (SONG), an organization working in the southern United States for economic and racial justice for LGBTQI people, about a way to address the devastating impacts of incarceration in Black communities:

> We are committed to building a community-based movement to end pretrial detention and ultimately mass incarceration. The Mama's Day action is rooted in the tradition of our enslaved ancestors who went to every length, including harnessing their collective resources, to purchase each other's freedom and keep their families together (Rankin 2018).

Prison Reform, Decriminalization, and Abolition

Given the overwhelmingly punitive nature of the law enforcement system and harsh conditions of incarceration, many legal scholars, researchers, and advocacy organizations argue for substantial changes. Advocates are pressing for health care, drug treatment, and educational, therapeutic, and life skills programs for those incarcerated. The nonprofit Justice Policy Institute has argued for repealing mandatory sentencing, changing drug laws to direct offenders into treatment programs, restructuring sentencing guidelines, and reforming parole practices. Thirty years ago, criminologist Pat Carlen (1989) advocated the supervision of women in noncustodial settings in their communities, where they could remain connected with their children and families and benefit from programs that address their emotional and economic needs. Also, many researchers and advocates challenge the idea that prisons can solve social problems so deeply rooted in racism, poverty, and inequality. They seek to halt prison expansion and redirect resources toward alternative sentencing, crime prevention, and drug treatment programs (see, e.g., Critical Resistance 2005; Magnani and Wray 2006).

The enormous financial costs of mandatory minimum sentences and three-strikes laws have caused some states to reassess those policies and to expand parole and early release programs, to make greater use of electronic surveillance, and to develop alternative sentencing programs. The colossal investment in new jails and prisons has taken a growing proportion of states' resources that could have been invested in other ways (see box feature "Comparable Costs: Education, Drug Treatment, and Imprisonment").

Comparable Costs: Education, Drug Treatment, and Imprisonment

- Prisons and education compete for budget dollars from a state's General Fund. In the last three decades, state and local spending on prisons and jails has increased at triple the rate of funding for public education for preschool through grade 12 (US Department of Education 2016).
- According to the Bureau of Justice Statistics, two-thirds of state prison inmates have not completed high school. Young black men aged 20 to 24 without a high school diploma or equivalent credential have a greater chance of being incarcerated than employed (US Department of Education 2016).
- In 2018, keeping a person in prison was estimated to cost the state of California a record $75,560 per prisoner, or $2,000 more than attending Harvard University per year. New York was the next highest in the country at $69,000 per prisoner (Associated Press 2017).
- Research on the Drug Treatment Alternative-to-Prison Program, started in Brooklyn (NY) in the 1990s,

has shown that participants had lower re-arrest and re-conviction rates compared to those who were incarcerated for similar offenses. Two years after leaving the program, 92 percent of graduates were employed; graduates were 67 percent less likely to be reconvicted than a comparison group who went to prison. These results were achieved at half the average cost of incarceration (Swern 2008).

- Between 1980 and 2000, thirty-eight states and all federal prisons added more African American men to prison populations than to enrollment in state colleges and universities (Justice Policy Institute 2002, Table 6).
- Most African American students in public schools do not read or do math at grade level (Children's Defense Fund 2010, p. G-6). Students in two thousand high schools identified as "dropout factories" account for 46 percent of the nation's Black students and 39 percent of Latino students (p. G-12).

Criminalization is a major source of degradation and insecurity for many women and gender nonconforming people and their families, especially African Americans and Latinxs. As a feminist and ethnic studies professor, Julia Sudbury (2003) has argued that prison is "a fundamentally unjust institution that, like slavery, cannot be reformed" (p. 231). She notes that the idea of prison abolition "challenges the belief that prison works," (p. 231) and that it provides "a critical framework within which proposed legislation, campaigns, and activism can be assessed" (pp. 231-32). Data presented in this chapter give grounds for forging more effective efforts across lines of race, class, sexuality, and gender identity to address the needs of formerly incarcerated women and those currently in custody, as well as to question the nature of the penal system itself.

QUESTIONS FOR REFLECTION

As you read and discuss this chapter, think about these questions:

1. How do you define crime?
2. Where is the jail or prison nearest to where you live or go to school? Who is incarcerated there?
3. When people at your school or in your community commit crimes, how do you think they should be dealt with?
4. Note the official language of "corrections" or the "correctional system." What is being corrected? Why? How? And corrected to what?
5. How do you define security, and for whom? How does incarceration contribute to security at the micro, meso, macro, and global levels?

FINDING OUT MORE ON THE WEB

1. Research organizations cited in this chapter. How are they working to support women and gender nonconforming people in the criminal justice system? Try to find organizations that are active in your city or state.
2. What kinds of professionals are among white-collar criminals? Find out the recent financial and human costs of white-collar crime in the United States. How do the legal consequences for white-collar criminals compare to those for drug offenders? What are the race, class, and gender characteristics of these respective groups?
3. What is the relationship between state spending on the criminal justice system and spending on higher education in your state?

TAKING ACTION

1. Analyze the way the news media report crime, or analyze the portrayal of criminals in popular culture. How are females who have committed crimes portrayed? Pay particular attention to issues of race, class, sexuality, and gender identity.
2. Find out about the daily conditions for people in the jail, prison, or immigrant detention center nearest to you.
3. Find out about activist groups in your area that support people in women's prisons. What can you do on their behalf?
4. The USA PATRIOT Act allows law enforcement agencies access to information on students and to student records. Find out what steps your college or university has taken to provide information under the terms of this act.

41 EXCERPTS FROM "BECOMING MS. BURTON" (2017)

Drawing on her own experiences of incarceration, **Susan Burton** founded A New Way of Life Reentry Project in 1998, a nonprofit organization in Los Angeles that provides housing and other supports to formerly incarcerated women. Nationally known for her advocacy, she was a CNN Top 10 Hero, received the James Irvine Foundation Leadership Award, and has been a fellow of the Open Society Foundation, the Women's Policy Institute, and the California Wellness Foundation.

Cari Lynn is a writer whose work has appeared in *O: The Oprah Magazine*, *The Hollywood Reporter*, *Health*, *Good Housekeeping*, *The Chicago Tribune*, *Huffington Post*, and *The Guardian*. Her books include *Leg the Spread: A Woman's Adventures Inside the Trillion-Dollar Boys' Club of Commodities Trading* (2004) and *The Whistleblower: Sex Trafficking, Military Contractors, and One Woman's Fight for Justice* (co-authored with Kathryn Bolkovac, 2011).

This excerpt originally appeared in slightly different form in the book *Becoming Ms. Burton: From Prison to Recovery to Leading the Fight for Incarcerated Women*.

1.

The women take their first step of freedom at the Greyhound bus station in downtown Los Angeles, around the corner from Skid Row, where America's largest concentration of homeless people live on the sidewalk, the lucky ones in makeshift tents. It's nothing like the freedom you'd dreamed about in your cell. This freedom smells of urine and stale beer. Lingering to check out the new releases are pimps and drug dealers and down-on-their-luck others who may not be intentional predators but who are desperate to find someone to hang on to. Or someone to drag down with them. They all know you are easy prey.

You can almost touch the desperation, the doom in the air. You can feel it on you. On your prison-issue clothes. Everyone recognizes the ill-fitting clothes stitched by inmates: the muumuus with the garish pink and orange and yellow flower pattern; the baseball shirt; the state jeans, so stiff they can nearly stand up on their own—no designer label on the back pocket of these jeans. In order to walk out of prison you had to buy yourself some clothes with the $200 you were given upon release. That money went quickly after you also had to buy your bus ticket, a prison guard watching while you went to the Greyhound window and waiting until you got on that bus and it drove away. . . .

When you step off at the bus station, you have at most $100 left in your pocket, maybe less if you were only granted half your allowed amount, the rest to be doled out to you months later by your parole officer. There's no reason why some people have their gate money withheld. Just like there's no reason to anything in prison. No reason why, on a whim, a guard raids your locker, tearing through your only belongings, dumping your soap powder, and mixing your baby powder into your instant coffee, spoiling both. No reason why some women inmates are assigned to spend their days in a parenting class even if they don't have children, while others must push a mop around for eight cents an hour, and others have to report to fire camp, going through weeks of rigorous physical training to be awarded an orange uniform and delivered to the front lines of a California wildfire for $1 an hour.

There's also no logical reason why federal prisons offer halfway houses to those newly released, but state prisons provide nothing. Four thousand newly released women arrive in Los Angeles County every year to nothing. No reentry programs, no counseling, no services, no assistance. You have no house key, no credit card, no checkbook, no driver's license, no Social Security card, no identification of any sort because anything you were carrying when you were arrested has been destroyed by the state. You're just one woman in the crowd of mostly black and brown faces, one number in the recidivism stats that are decidedly not in your favor.

Like vultures, the pimps circle, eyeing you, assessing you. The drug dealers circle. You know them from the old neighborhood, and they call you by name, offering their brand of a welcome home party. You have little incentive to say no. Ego tells you you're gonna make it by any means necessary. Ego tells you you're a grown woman. But you're scared. How do you calm yourself? How do you connect with something healthy and hopeful when you're surrounded by Skid Row? When you haven't been allowed to make a decision in five, ten, twenty years? When all you want to do is wash prison off you, but you can't, because it's in you. It's seeped into your psyche and into your soul. . . .

The last time I stepped off that bus, I didn't know it would be the last time. Every time I left prison I left saying to myself, *I'm not gonna get caught up again.* Saying to myself, *I'm gonna make a better life. I won't be back.* The prison guard who put me on the bus waved and said, "We got your bed waiting for you. See you soon."

. . . I'd been arrested over and over again for possession of a controlled substance. You'd think someone in the system might have gotten the bright idea that I needed drug treatment, that I needed therapy. But I was never offered help, and I didn't know to ask for it because I didn't know what to ask for. People with my color skin, and who grew up where I did, didn't know concepts like *rehab*. I was always remanded to prison. . . .

2.

. . . I had served six sentences over the past seventeen years and was returning to the same dead-end environment, still not knowing what to do with my feelings, with my life, with myself.

With $100 of gate money in my pocket, I stepped off that Greyhound bus around the corner from Skid Row. Again. No one was there to pick me up. . . .

Mama let me stay in the efficiency behind her house. It was empty but for a daybed and a lamp. . . .

It started with Courvoisier, which seemed fancy and innocent. What was the harm in a nice glass or two of cognac to relax? It soon devolved, and before I knew it, I was caught up all over again, digging in my mother's couch for loose change. It wasn't even a decision, it just happened because there was nothing else that was going to happen.

[My daughter] Toni cut me off from spending time with Ellesse. She was right; I couldn't be a responsible grandmother. Not when two-for-a-dollar cans of beer and crack were my most reliable companions.

. . . Scenes played in my head, incessantly, all pointing to the fact that, throughout my life, my family had little care for my well-being. One night, my oldest brother, Michael, was over, and I confronted him about how he'd treated me when we were kids. He pushed me out of the apartment and locked the door—just as he'd locked me out when I was a little girl. . . .

The next night, my friend Joe and I were sitting in the little efficiency, drinking cheap beer. . . .

"I can't keep on like this, Joe," I confided. "I'm forty-six years old, and my life is a big sum of nothing."

Joe put down his beer and focused on me as if to gauge how serious I was. He always had sad-looking eyes, a sadness I suspected his military-style father had beaten into him. "If you really mean it," Joe said, "I know of a good place you can go." He wrote down the name of a treatment program [the CLARE Foundation]. . . .

3.

To keep moving forward, I knew I had to be honest. But there was something I was hiding, as though it would magically disappear, but I knew it wouldn't.

Before I came to CLARE, I hadn't shown up for meetings with my parole officer—*absconded* was the official term. My next parole meeting was approaching. If I went, I'd be thrown back in prison for parole violations. If I didn't go, I'd be evading getting caught until the day they did catch me, and I'd be incarcerated just the same. I knew I couldn't keep hiding; I had to come forward with the truth, even though that truth could take from me everything I'd been working toward.

When I told Leslie [my AA Sponsor] I needed to see my parole officer and that I was scared, she said she'd drive me. . . . I'd been with the same parole officer—I'll call her Ms. B—the entire time. You'd think we'd have gotten to know each other pretty well by now; yet each time she saw my face for another orientation, she barely blinked. Robotically, she'd go through the motions: reading the conditions of parole, how I wasn't supposed to break any laws, how I was supposed to find a job, and supposed to find housing. She made it all sound like I'd simply walk out the door and, if I wanted it bad enough, all that would magically happen. Ms. B had a way of talking that made me feel put down, as if she needed to remind herself that, although she and I were both black women around the same age and from the same community, she was different. I likened her attitude to how many of the black prison wardens acted—different and apart from you.

Only with some years of distance would I come to understand that they, too, were caught in a system and a culture. Their culture was power. Ms. B had bought in to the idea that punishment was always the answer and was always deserved, that getting tough would solve everything. Most of the country had bought in to this, too. . . .

Ms. B was what the system fed on: someone content to be a gatekeeper. She filled out my paperwork, shrugged her shoulders when I relapsed, and collected her very decent paycheck. How many times had she asked me how I was doing?

"I'm not doing so well," I'd sometimes admit.

"You need to get it together," she'd say, then lead me into the bathroom to watch me pee in a cup. One time, I'd gained weight from inactivity and a lousy diet in prison and I couldn't afford new clothes. Ms. B laughed at me in the bathroom as I struggled to pull my pants over my hips.

Leslie and I sat in the parole building lobby, and I warned her it might be a while. . . .

When Ms. B finally appeared, I watched how, as she noticed Leslie, her face hardened. . . .

I followed Ms. B into her office, and as soon as the door closed, she scowled, "How dare you walk in here and bring that white woman with you."

. . . "I'm sorry," I said. "She's my sponsor. I'm an alcoholic and an addict, and I'm in the program. I couldn't report to you like I was supposed to because I'd been under the influence. But I'm living at the recovery center now. I'm no longer under the grip of drugs and alcohol. It's my responsibility to be honest, and I came here to tell you the truth and turn myself in."

For the first time in all these years, the look of contempt faded from Ms. B's face. She studied me for a long moment.

"Go get your sponsor and bring her in here."

When I returned with Leslie, Ms. B asked her, "Are you going to be responsible for Susan?"

Leslie replied, "No."

Ms. B's head cocked; this wasn't the answer she expected. Leslie said, "Susan's going to be responsible for herself."

I saw the words sinking in as Ms. B looked from her to me. Finally, she said, "Susan, I will give you a pass. But this will be your only pass. You better get it right."

As Leslie drove us back to Santa Monica, we barely said a word. She was digesting the severity of what could have happened. I was still processing what *had* happened, knowing that parole officers weren't in the business of giving passes. Before me was an opening, a first glint, that, this time, it all could be real. This time, my life could change. . . .

After one hundred days at CLARE, I at last felt ready to leave. But I needed a safe place to go. I called my daughter and asked if I could some live with her and Ellesse.

There was silence at the other end of the phone. Toni was thirty-one years old, and we hadn't lived together since she'd been fifteen.

She said, "Let me get back to you."

She'd later tell me her first instinct was that I'd gone crazy. She thought she'd be the last person I'd ever ask. But then it occurred to her: maybe, this time, I was dead serious about keeping myself together.

She broached it with Ellesse. At eleven years old, Ellesse was surprisingly wise to the world, soaking up everything around her, just like her mother did as a little girl.

"We can't say no," Ellesse said. "Grandma's a different person now."

Though she thought it nice that Ellesse believed this, Toni wasn't so sure. She prayed about it. And then she took her jewelry out of the house, counted the VCRs, and prayed some more, before finally calling to tell me okay. . . .

I kept myself busy attending AA meetings at 7 a.m., noon, and 7 p.m. "Why are you always going to meetings?" Ellesse asked, and I explained how important it was to be healthy emotionally and to have a good environment. But the other part was that I was terrified of being alone in the real world, and the meetings felt like a spiritual armor. I was making all new friends, had daily responsibilities, and even felt inspired to give back. I picked up a commitment to conduct a twelve-step program at juvenile hall, where, all those years ago, I'd been taken. . . .

4.

I began to read. In prison, I'd read thrillers and romance novels to escape. Now, I was reading to learn. . . .

The books prompted me to consider other ways to help people. I thought about women like myself, cycling in and out of prison. . . . An idea began to take shape. I envisioned a recovery home for women getting out of prison who, like me, needed a safe, sober place to live.

I talked about the idea with Mitzi, and then with Beverly, who was herself newly out of prison and trying to start over again. She and [my brother] Melvin had gotten back together, and Beverly and I were trying to support each other, going to AA meetings together and holding each other accountable for staying clean. "What if," I posed, "we pooled our money to buy a house? I could live there, and we could take in ten other women whose contributions would cover the mortgage and expenses." . . .

Beverly and Mitzi and I found a house in Watts: a three-bedroom, two-bath bungalow, complete with a lovely yard and a lemon tree, on a residential street lined with trees . . . Though Beverly had more money to put toward the down payment, I would be the one to live in the house with the women. Mitzi didn't have money, but she would cook for everyone . . . There was one problem: none of us had the credit to get a mortgage.

We went to Melvin's son, Lamont, my nephew and Beverly's stepson, and asked if he would sign for us. Lamont had gone straight to work from high school, never having gotten caught up like the rest of us. He had a good job with the Department of Water and Power, was married, and had learned well from Melvin how to be a good father. Only years later, once I had signed for other people, did I fully understand to what lengths Lamont had gone to put up credit for us.

Beverly and I purchased five sets of bunk beds from Ikea, and I asked some men I knew from my twelve-step meeting if they'd help us assemble them. I wasn't used to asking for help, but I discovered that when you're trying to do something good, people want to help. My niece Tamara, Beverly's daughter, and I brainstormed a name to call the recovery home. In the Big Book of Alcoholics Anonymous a line is often repeated about finding a new way of life. We decided A New Way of Life was exactly right. . . .

5.

One day, when I returned home from running errands, Mitzi popped her head out from the kitchen and said, "The court called you."

The court? I didn't have a clue what the court would be calling about. But I knew from personal experience that a call from the court was never good. I ignored it, knowing if they wanted me bad enough I'd be hearing from them again. Five days later a woman named Wanda called. "When are you coming to get me?" she said.

"Where are you?" I asked.

"In county jail. The court released me to you. They tried calling you."

I couldn't believe it. The *court* was releasing someone to the care of A New Way of Life? All those times I went before the court, and now I was a person the court was relying on? Never before had I driven to the county jail with a smile. I had no idea how the court had learned about A New Way of Life, and I never questioned it. I chalked it up to a "God-shot"—what would be the first of many.

Wanda wasn't able to pay our suggested $500 a month toward rent and expenses. But I wasn't about to turn anyone away. Eventually, the county granted Wanda General Relief of $200 a month, which helped, but we still had half a dozen empty beds, and it was becoming clear that covering the mortgage and expenses was going to be much more challenging than we'd thought.

I went to the bus station around the corner from Skid Row. I didn't know who'd be getting off the bus, but I knew that, every day, women released from prison were on it. I showed up there because I wished someone had been there for me. Sometimes I saw a familiar face get off the bus, someone I'd served time with. "I have a house in South LA," I offered. "There's a bed if you'd like it. It's drug and alcohol free. You don't have to go back to the streets if you don't want to."

Some women looked wary and said no. But some said yes.

Still, we had empty beds, and bills to pay.

There was talk in the community that a social services agency called Walden House was looking to contract with local organizations. . . .

Walden House funded $35 per woman per day, to be used for shelter, transportation, and meals. Also, through Walden House, I was granted special clearance to go into the prison system to give presentations about A New Way of Life and recruit future clients.

Prison was the last place I ever wanted to return to. But there I was, in street clothes, walking into the California Institution for Women, knowing I'd be able to walk out. As I passed through the doors into the yard, I felt a rush of emotion. I was here with purpose, in possession of my dignity, my individuality, my own power—all the things that had been stripped from me the last time I stood in this yard. Thoughts of Harriet Tubman and Sojourner

Truth filled my head. In some small way, I hoped my presence and my voice could offer women a way out of the cycle, could help them find their own lasting freedom. . . .

Walden House's drug rehabilitation program, called Forever Free, was held in a trailer. I spoke to the class about my journey and about A New Way of Life, and then asked each person what she wanted to do with her life. I could see the pain all over the women's faces and the fear in their eyes. I could hear their bewilderment about what might be in store for them on the outside. Many said they could only dream of walking back in here to help as I was. . . .

After several months, all ten beds in the house were at last filled. I slept on a cot in the dining room, next to the fax machine. Within the walls of A New of Life, a beautiful community of women helping and supporting each other was blossoming. Together, we were healing. Never again would I feel like it was just me; it was *us*. I watched bonds form, like a family; not without ups and downs, but with support you could count on in a way you couldn't with most people. . . .

I set a schedule for A New Way of Life: 8 a.m., we did a morning meditation together to start each day with positivity and reflection, and to set a personal goal. Then, the women made their own breakfast and completed their assigned household chores. After that, we went our separate ways for the day. I chauffeured women to jobs or to look for a job, to mandated parenting classes, to report to their parole officer, to twelve-step meetings, to social worker appointments, and to courtrooms as they tried to regain custody of their children.

In the evening, Mitzi cooked dinner, and we all ate together, going around the table to hear about each other's day. Maybe, to some, having a cook seemed excessive. But I believed coming home to a meal set a warm foundation for the household and eliminated a worry many of us knew all too well: that we might go to bed hungry.

On weekends we did errands together, like grocery shopping. Some women were eligible for food stamps, though it didn't matter who was or wasn't—everyone contributed what she could. Somehow, we always managed to cobble together enough to cover our bills. . . .

As the months passed, I watched with pride as women made enough strides to begin to transition out of the house. Seeing them go on their own, into their own apartments, some reunited with their children, was victorious. Often they were scared, crying as we hugged goodbye. "Just because you're leaving," I said, "doesn't mean we aren't still here for you." But I knew their fear—in the house there was a cushion of stability, the lights would be on, food would be there. Leaving meant the responsibility was now all on them.

To continue filling the beds as they became available, the women and I wrote to imprisoned women we knew who were approaching the end of their sentences. Our letters said: If you need a safe, sober, women-only environment, call A New Way of Life.

The phone rang. "I got your letter. You said to call."

"Where are you?"

Their voices trembled. "I just got off the bus."

I'd say, "I'll be right there."

As word about A New Way of Life spread, prisoners began writing us. When I was behind bars, I'd written letters to treatment programs asking for help, but I never got any response. Which is why I personally answered every letter we received, even when letters began arriving daily.

"Dear Ms. Burton," they'd write. *Ms. Burton.* It was a title that conveyed a level of respect. It was also, to me, my mother. But here I was, becoming a kind of surrogate mother to others in need—and, in a way, making amends for those years I wasn't the kind of mother my own children deserved. . . .

6.

The more women who came through A New Way of Life, the more I saw the same story played out again and again. I watched women being excluded from public housing; I watched them being denied private housing, unable to rent an apartment when faced with the box indicating a felony conviction. I waded with them through the paperwork and bureaucracy of the LA County Department of Children and Family Services as they tried to reunite with their kids. I saw them, morning after morning, iron their sole business outfit, and then I dropped them off and picked them up from job interview

after job interview, the outcome of rejection almost always the same, despite their capabilities. Capabilities didn't matter; neither did skills, past experience, or aptitude. The sum of everything else was blotted out by a criminal conviction. . . .

For so many years, I, too, had come up against these seemingly insurmountable barriers. But I'd done a good job of convincing myself that my failing was personal, that it was all on my shoulders. Now, a larger picture was emerging: if you got locked up, you get locked out. It didn't matter that you'd paid your debt to society. Nor did it matter how hard you were trying to get your life back together. A criminal history was like a credit card with interest—so what if you paid off the balance, the interest still kept accruing. And accruing and accruing and accruing.

Yet I remained determined. All over the city, I drove women looking for jobs, or tracking copies of their birth certificates, or filing for Social Security cards. With all this running around, gas and upkeep on my old Ford Escort was expensive, and I soon began doling out bus fare. Which led to a bigger issue: I was running out of money.

When Stan from HOP [the Homeless Outreach Program] told me that the First African Methodist Episcopal Church in South Central gave bus tokens, I showed up there right away. But before issuing me tokens, they asked if A New Way of Life was a 501c3.

I paused. "What's a 501c3?"

They explained it was a nonprofit organization, and that they could only issue bus tokens to nonprofits.

I went home and began making phone calls to figure out how to become a nonprofit. Eventually, I found my way to Mr. Malone, who worked with a religious-based recovery home in South LA . . . He knew how to become a 501c3, and he graciously helped me through the application process . . .

During this time, I was invited to speak at CLARE's annual fundraising dinner. I had no idea I'd be speaking to a roomful of some of the biggest power players in Los Angeles. I stood at the podium, looking out over tables of people dressed in the most beautiful clothes. But I was wearing fine clothes too—fine clothes from the CLARE thrift store. I probably had on the discarded dress of somebody sitting in the audience.

I spoke about my past, comparing what life had been like to what my life was now. I expressed gratitude for the help I received. "If there'd been a CLARE in my community," I said, "I could have found intervention and a different outcome sooner." I described my dream of creating a safe place for women getting out of prison, and the creation of A New Way of Life. And I explained how my current goal was to obtain nonprofit status so we could get bus fare for the women's commutes to their jobs.

When I was done, chairs screeched against the floor as people rose to their feet. Never before had I experienced anything like this. *A standing ovation? For me?* In that moment, I flashed back to when I'd first walked through the doors at CLARE, the condition I was in—pain to the point of incapacitation, despair, sorrow, grief, addiction—and how restoration seemed all but impossible. At once, the image seemed both alarmingly stark and like an old, brittle photograph. It was me, and it wasn't. It was where I'd been, and why I was here. . . .

After dinner, a silver-haired man approached me. I didn't know who he was, but he had a commanding presence. He said he wanted to learn more about A New Way of Life and that he'd be in touch.

A few days later, I received a call from the office of Theodore Forstmann, instructing me to make a list of things A New Way of Life needed. I still didn't know anything about this man, but I knew we needed a lot of things. We needed cleaning items and toilet paper and, of course, bus tokens. When Leslie saw the list I was making, she looked me square in the face.

"Susan, ask for what you need."

"We need toilet paper and bus fare," I said.

"You need a washer and dryer," Leslie countered. "You need a van to drive the women around."

"I can't ask for things like that," I balked. "I don't even know this man." And wasn't that the truth—I had no idea Mr. Forstmann was a billionaire, with companies like Gulfstream and Dr Pepper to his name.

"Susan, you need to think big," Leslie said. "He can always say no." Following her advice, I took toilet paper off the list and replaced it with a van.

Even though we didn't have 501c3 status yet, Mr. Forstmann bought us that van. . . .

On the morning of Christmas Eve, 2000, I went to the mailbox and there was the certificate of our federal nonprofit status. I mailed Mr. Forstmann a copy, and he mailed back a $10,000 check with a note that said, "Keep up the good work." . . .

JULIA SUDBURY

42 FROM WOMEN PRISONERS TO PEOPLE IN WOMEN'S PRISONS: CHALLENGING THE GENDER BINARY IN ANTIPRISON WORK (2011)

Julia Sudbury, also Julia Chinyere Oparah, is Provost and Dean of Faculty, and Professor of Ethnic Studies at Mills College, Oakland. Her research interests include African diaspora studies, Black British studies, black feminist theory, and women of color organizing. She co-authored *Black Women and the Maternal Health Care Crisis* (2017); edited *Global Lockdown: Race, Gender, and the Prison-Industrial Complex* (2005); and co-edited *Activist Scholarship: Antiracism, Feminism, and Social Change* (2009) and *Outsiders Within: Writing on Transracial Adoption* (2006). She is a founder of Critical Resistance and of Black Women Birthing Justice.

In October 2007, more than 250 Lesbian Gay Bisexual Transgender Intersex Queer and Questioning (LGBTIQQ) former prisoners, activists, attorneys, and community members came together . . . to generate a national conversation on transgender imprisonment. The conference, Transforming Justice, highlighted the experiences of transgender former prisoners through personal testimonies, written narratives, and photo-diaries. As the transgender former prisoners' lives unfolded on the screen and through personal testimonies, it became clear that the conference was raising important questions for scholars and activists committed to defending the rights of incarcerated women and to ending women's imprisonment.

In this chapter, I first explore some limitations in existing research and activism on "women in prison." I argue that most of this work—and I include my own body of scholarship here—has been complicit with the repression of the gender fluidity and complexity that exist in both men's and women's prisons, jails, and juvenile halls. By examining the experiences of transgender and gender nonconforming prisoners, I demonstrate the violence involved in the production and maintenance of the gender binary in penal regimes. Finally, I aim to develop a new theoretical framework for research

and activism on "women in prison," which makes visible and counters the state's power to define and police gender categories. This *antiracist genderqueer framework* necessarily pays attention to the complex intersections among race, class, gender identity, and sexual orientation that structure the experiences of people in conflict with the law. This approach poses significant challenges to the "business as usual" of feminist research and antiprison activism. I invite readers to consider how their own praxis might need to change in order to engage with the challenges posed by transgender and gender nonconforming prisoners and activists.

My research methodology draws from the insights of feminist action research and participatory action research. This essay is grounded in ten years of activist ethnography in the antiprison movement in the US and Canada. In addition, I have quoted from the testimonies by transgender former prisoners gathered for the Transforming Justice conference. Finally, I interviewed four black transgender antiprison activists. These activists had worked as volunteers and paid staff with the following organizations: Prisoners HIV/AIDS Support Action Network, the Prisoners' Justice Action Committee, and the Prisoners' Justice Day Committee in Canada; Critical Resistance, California Coalition for Women Prisoners, Audre Lorde Project, Prison Moratorium Project, the Trans/Gender Variant in Prison Committee of California Prison Focus, Legal Services for Prisoners with Children, and All of Us or None in the US. By incorporating extracts from testimonies and qualitative interviews, I intend to ground my analysis in the subordinated knowledge produced by marginalized and resisting communities. As Patricia Hill Collins observes, this subordinated knowledge has the potential to reveal new insights that are not available to those who occupy a position of privilege in relation to interlocking systems of oppression (Collins 1990). Those of us—myself included—who conform to societal expectations for gender coherence (between the name, genitalia, self-identity and external presentation for example) may be blind to the violence of gender dualism, even if we ourselves have experienced sexism and homophobia. In order to produce scholarly knowledge that moves beyond the binary gender system, it is essential to start from the lived experience and everyday theorizing of those whose existence it disallows.

Research on "Women In Prison": Two Assumptions

Gender Diversity in Women's Prisons

In this section, I unpack two assumptions that underpin most research (and much activism) on "women in prison." These assumptions form the basis of this work's complicity with the gender binary system. The first is that *all people incarcerated in women's prisons and jails are women*. In the past few years, organizations such as the California Coalition for Women Prisoners (CCWP), Critical Resistance and Justice Now, a nonprofit that provides legal advocacy for people in women's prisons, have shifted the language they use to describe their constituencies. For example, while Justice Now's mission statement refers to ending "violence against women and stop[ping] their imprisonment," materials produced by the organization more recently demonstrate a shift in thinking. In an invitation to a strategy session on gender and prison expansion, "violence against women" was rewritten to read "harm against female-bodied and women-identified people" (Justice Now 2008).

This shift represents a deliberate process of moving from a "women only"–oriented feminist analysis to a broader "gender justice" platform that recognizes a range of experiences of gender oppression. Similarly, these organizations have adopted new language to describe those held in women's prisons. For example, CCWP, which was founded in 1995, now uniformly uses the language "people in women's prisons" rather than "women prisoners," used when it was established.

The new language adopted by these organizations is the outcome of struggle and advocacy by transgender and gender nonconforming activists over the past decade. But the shift is far more than a merely linguistic one. By insisting on using "people in women's prisons," these activists challenge an assumption that has been central to the development of feminist prison studies, feminist criminology, and "women in prison" activism during the past three decades. Previous work by scholars and activists alike assumed that all those labeled by the state as "women" (or female inmates) and thus housed in women's prisons and jails were indeed women. In the context of the women's liberation movement which shaped the formative years of this work, making "women's imprisonment" visible was a radical move that challenged the androcentrism of both criminological research and antiprison activism.

Yet, there were two problems with this approach. First, it ignored the reality of gender fluidity and complexity that actually existed within women's prisons. Second, it legitimated and bolstered the state's power to determine and police the gender identification of those it imprisons, thus stripping transgender and gender nonconforming people in women's prisons of their fundamental right to gender self-determination.

It is interesting to note that researchers have long been aware of and grappled with the diversity of gender identity and sexual orientation that they encountered on entering women's prisons (Hensley and Tewksbury 2002). Some of the earliest and best-known research in this area included extensive attempts to document and understand same-sex relationships inside (Ward and Kassebaum 1965; Giallombardo 1966). From the 1930s onward, researchers met and interviewed prisoners who were in committed relationships inside and referred to their partners as "my man," "my woman," or "my husband" (Selling 1931). Viewed through the lens of heteronormativity and an unquestioned adherence to ascribed gender categories, early researchers viewed these relationships as "pseudo-families" and argued that they were adaptations to life within an unnatural "society of women." Transgender and gender nonconforming prisoners were seen as mimicking the husband in a heterosexual marriage because they were deprived of male contact. These studies were deeply compromised by their classist, heterosexist, and racist bias . . . However, they are evidence that from its inception, research on women's prisons has been confronted with the question of how to theorize the presence of prisoners who do not conform to gender norms. Despite the empirical evidence of gender diversity, researchers have failed to ask gender nonconforming prisoners how they self-identify and have continued to assume a uniformity of gender identity within women's prisons to the present day.

In the past decade, groundbreaking scholars in the field of queer and transgender studies have transformed the way we think about gender. First, they have shown the commonsense notion that there are only two genders to be the outcome of a violent and coercive process of gender policing. That is, the gender binary is not a *given* but a social construction deeply steeped in patriarchal, heteronormative, and racist violence. Second, these scholars have documented the multiplicity of gender identities and the richness of the cultural forms that they have engendered. The work of Judith Halberstam and Bobby Noble in particular has documented a continuum of female and transgendered masculinity encompassing a range of gender identities, from Ags (Aggressives), Studs, and butches to transmen, bois, and FtMs [females-to-males] (Halberstam 1998; Noble 1998). While most of this work has focused on cultural production, particularly literature and performance arts, as the cutting edge of gender expression and resistance, the same diversity of gender expression can be documented inside women's prisons. Indeed, despite their invisibility, gender nonconforming people in prisons and jails are on the

frontline of the battle for gender self-determination in the face of state power and coercion. Rejecting state-imposed gender categorization and acknowledging the gender self-identification of all those in prisons, jails, and juvenile detention is the first step in supporting this struggle.

Women Prisoners in Men's Prisons

The second erroneous assumption underpinning much prison research and activism is that *all women prisoners are in women's prisons*. To early feminist criminologists committed to making visible and ending the unequal treatment of women prisoners, it seemed obvious that their research site would be the women's prison. Yet this apparently self-evident correlation relies upon the erasure of people in men's prison who identify and live as "women" (or "girls") but were categorized at birth as male.

Feminists have had negative and sometimes heated reactions to the suggestion that feminist spaces—and by extension feminist research agendas—should incorporate transwomen. The case of Kimberly Nixon, a transsexual woman who sued Vancouver Rape Relief and Women's Shelter (VRR) when she was denied access to its volunteer program, is exemplary of the polarized and sometimes hostile debate around calls for "trans inclusion" (Chambers 2007). Many feminists were outraged that Nixon inflicted an expensive and protracted court case on a small nonprofit providing support to survivors of rape and domestic violence. In contrast, lawyer and trans advocate Barbara Findlay named Nixon the "Rosa Parks of transwomen," suggesting that the case was only the beginning of a movement for full access to women's spaces by transwomen (Rupp 2007).

The reaction to Nixon should be viewed in the context of the history of the shelter movement and more broadly the women's liberation movement. Feminists can look back three decades to an era when feminist bookstores, women's shelters, and women's studies programs were won only by dedicated struggle. The call for trans inclusion comes at a time when women-only spaces are threatened by neoliberal cutbacks to social welfare, as well as the "postfeminist" generation's lack of commitment to these spaces, leading to closures and mergers of women's bookstores, women's colleges, and women's centers. As women-only spaces disappear, some feminists view demands for inclusion by trans activists as colluding with a wider backlash against feminist autonomous organizing. As such, they often revert to the defensive stance that was necessary in the 1970s when such spaces were under attack by antifeminist men who saw women-only policies as unnecessary and exclusionary. While it is important to contextualize the feminist reaction against trans inclusion, and to honor the difficult choices made by volunteers and community organizers working on the frontline of the feminist movement, we also need to be vigilant about the convergence of arguments in defense of women's spaces and the transphobic defense of "womanhood" against nonnormative femininities.

Feminists who seek to oppose trans inclusion make three main arguments. First, they argue that "born" women have common experiences of surviving sex discrimination and patriarchal violence that are not shared by transwomen, leading to a need for separate and different programs and organizations. Second, and relatedly, they argue that although transwomen may experience gender discrimination, they are relative newcomers to that experience, having been raised with male privilege. In the Nixon case, for example, the Rape Relief collective argued that Nixon could not be an effective helpline volunteer because she "did not share the same life experiences as women born and raised as girls and into womenhood" having been "brought up through a boyhood and lived as a man achieving success as an airline pilot." This argument ultimately prevailed in the Supreme Court [of British Columbia], which in 2003 ruled that VRR did not discriminate and that the organization did indeed have the right to organize "as women only" (Vancouver Rape Relief Society Website). Third, they argue that the presence of "male-bodied" persons in organizations serving vulnerable women may retraumatize women seeking support.

At the Michigan Women's Festival, this argument was actually embraced by transsexual feminists who pushed the landmark women's music and arts festival to relinquish their "Womyn-born-womyn" only admission policy in favor of one that

would allow postoperative transsexuals but deny preop and other transwomen. The distinction was important, they claimed[,] because "male genitals can be so emblematic of male power and sexual dominance that their presence at the festival . . . is inappropriate." By privileging transsexuals who had the resources for surgery, the proposed policy discriminated against low-income transsexuals and transsexuals of color, as well as those who prefer to inhabit a more interstitial gender identity (Koyama 2008).

Whether for or against trans inclusion, those involved in the debate have seldom engaged with the lived experiences of the transgender people who are most likely to encounter state and interpersonal gender violence: low-income transpeople of color (Koyama 2008; Incite! 2008). These experiences make visible the assumptions and misconceptions present in the three arguments outlined above. Testimonies by imprisoned transgender activists at the Transforming Justice Conference demonstrate that transwomen, like "born" women, are subjected to extreme forms of domestic and sexual violence (Lee 2004). However, the former's lack of recognition as "women" exacerbates experiences of violence by placing means of redress and support out of reach. The pathway to prison of Yolanda Gonzalez, a prisoner at the California Medical Facility in Vacaville, was similar to that of many women serving life sentences for defending themselves: "I was convicted of second-degree murder for killing my abusive boyfriend in self-defense." However, her treatment by the criminal justice system was even more punitive: "Although I fit the profile of a 'battered wife' and had been living as a woman for several years, I was not allowed to use this defense because the court system viewed me as male" (Transforming Justice 2007).

Once in prison, the women survived horrifying incidences of rape, violence, and coercion. Nikkas Alamillo-Luchese shared one such experience. Coerced into a sexual relationship with a violent cellmate, she was attacked by him one day: "I woke up bleeding anally . . . It became obvious to me that R. and one of his friends had raped me and stolen my belongings while I was unconscious. The door had been locked, but R. had staff open it to get to me; it was a privilege as a 'pet' of the wing" (Transforming Justice 2007). Nikkas' testimony reminds us that having male genitalia is no determinant of whether one becomes a victim or a perpetrator of sexual violence. After reporting the abuse to a guard who refused to believe her, Nikkas continued to be subjected to sexual assault and physical violence and intimidation. These experiences of gender violence do not necessarily follow an earlier life lived with male privilege . . .

These testimonies reveal that transwomen, especially transwomen of color, experience gender violence and domination in ways that are similar but not identical to born-women. However, they do so without any of the protections that may be associated with gender incoherence. In the context of sex-segregated prisons, this lack of protection means that a prison term may be a sentence to repeated sexual assault and verbal abuse. This suggests that feminist researchers, who have long been dedicated to challenging the unequal treatment and abuse of women in prison, should have a particular incentive to expend their research beyond the born-women-only model. In order to do so, however, we would need to jettison two implicit foundations of feminist criminal justice research. First, that all humans can be divided into two genders, neatly demarcated by differences in genitalia and proven by what is on our birth certificates or government ID. Second, that only women who are assigned to the female gender at birth experience sexual violence and gender oppression. In so doing, we would make visible the complicity between feminist research and the *gender enforcement* activities of the state. The next section examines how the criminal justice system creates and polices the gender binary out of the messy and complex reality of gender fluidity.

Policing the Binary

When scholars enter the prison to carry out research, we enter a site that is overdetermined by the race- and gender-enforcing activities of the state. Yet those activities are most often overlooked, rendered invisible by hegemonic racial and gender ideologies that naturalize what we are presented with: an apparently sex-segregated population of predominantly people of color. Feminists of color have pointed to the socially constructed and performative nature of racialized gender identities. Rather than "being" a Chicana, they argue, we "perform Chicana" through an ongoing series of choices, identifications, and behaviors (Segura 1992). These choices and identifications may be loosely aligned with the gender and racial assignations of our families, communities, and the state, or they may be in direct conflict with them. The criminal justice system is intolerant of such unruly self-determination. Presented with a "motley crew" of racially and culturally syncretic, diversely gendered defendants—Ags and FtMs, top femmes and soft butches, bois and Andros, MtFs [males-to-females], trannies, and genderqueers—the state sets about allocating this transgressive polymorphism into predefined categories (Sharma and Wright 2009). Ags, butches, bois, and FtMs become "female offenders" and are housed in "women's correctional facilities." MtFs and transsexuals become "male offenders" and are sent to "men's" facilities. Mexicanas of Miztec ancestry become white/Hispanic. Black Puerto Rican Tainos become African American. As feminist researchers, we often replicate the violence of this misidentification by adopting the official categorization and ignoring the testimonies of those who challenge the state's power to define and police their racial and gender identification.

Policing the gender binary begins at home where children are pressured to engage in culturally appropriate gendered behavior and play and to wear gender appropriate clothing. For many gender nonconforming young people, the teenage years are when conflicts with parental and school authorities over gender identification become most fraught, as behaviors that were seen as a childhood phase continue into adolescence (Mallon and DeCrescenzo 1985; Human Rights Watch 2001). Conflict in the home over gender identification or sexual orientation often precipitates greater involvement in street life, and in some cases homelessness (Cochran et al. 2002).[1] This in turn leads to involvement in criminalized survival strategies, from sex work to petty theft, as well as drug and alcohol use as coping strategies (Cochran et al. 2002). Transgender and gender-variant young people who leave home because of transphobic violence or verbal abuse are also criminalized through "status offenses," which prohibit running away, truancy, alcohol consumption, or "incorrigibility" (disobeying parents). The construction of these behaviors as offenses puts young people who have been abused or abandoned by parental figures in conflict with the law, often beginning a cycle of policing, appearances in the courts, and institutionalization (Steinhardt 1996). The criminalization of gender nonconforming young people, as with all young people, is racialized. Young people of color are more likely to be stopped by the police and to be sent to criminal court and spend more time in detention (Feld 1999; Office of Juvenile Justice 2002). Thus gender variance in adolescence is most likely to lead to criminalization and institutionalization for young people of color.

While transgender young people face the challenge of age-related poverty, transgender and gender nonconforming adults continue to face poverty due to labor discrimination (San Francisco Bay Guardian 2006).[2] Pushed out of the labor market, many transwomen work in the sex industry as a means of survival and also in order to experience the community and support of other transwomen. Transwomen and men also face insecure housing or homelessness as a result of unstable or underemployment and discrimination by landlords (San Francisco Bay Guardian 2006). The intersection of racial and transgender discrimination in the labor and housing markets creates a highly vulnerable positionality, which is exacerbated by the role of law enforcement.

The dangers of gender variance are most visible in police mistreatment of transgender people of color. An investigation of police abuse and misconduct against LGBT people by Amnesty International documented widespread identity-based abuse related to sexual orientation, gender identity, race, age, and economic status. The report concluded: "Law enforcement officers profile LGBT individuals, in particular gender-variant individuals and LGBT individuals of color, as criminal in a number of different contexts, and selectively enforce laws relating to 'morals regulations,' bars and social gatherings, demonstrations and 'quality of life'"

(Amnesty International 2005; Incite! 2008). This criminalization of nonnormative gender identity, in a context of intersecting systems of oppression, leads to extremely high rates of incarceration for transpeople of color. While national statistics are not available, a survey of 515 transgender people in San Francisco found that 64 percent of the MtF respondents and 29 percent of FtM respondents had been incarcerated (SF Department of Public Health 1999; Minter and Daley 2003).[3] The cumulative effects of parental and school intolerance and abuse, housing and labor discrimination, criminalization and law enforcement–targeting produce the *racialized (trans)gender entrapment* of transgender and gender nonconforming people of color (Richie 1995).[4] This process channels transgender and gender nonconforming youth and adults into juvenile halls, jails, and prisons where gender policing is experienced at a heightened level.

Gender Enforcement behind the Walls

Those of us who fit relatively comfortably within the normative limits of the binary gender system often fail to understand the coercive force that is necessary for its continuation. Feminists have long noted that, far from a biologically given identity determined at birth, *gender*, like *race*, is a "very demanding verb" (Trent 1997; Butler 1990). Criminologists have demonstrated the ways in which prison regimes are gendered, often seeking to induce particularly gendered behaviors as a means of reforming "unruly women" (Dobash et al. 1986; Howe 1994; Faith 1993). Yet this insight has infrequently led to interrogations of [the] role of the prison in (re)producing the binary gender system itself. The neat division of prison populations into two genders is achieved at the expense of transgender and gender nonconforming prisoners who are policed and punished because of the threat they pose to the gendered order of the penal system.

The violence of gender policing is psychological, emotional, physical, and sexual. Transgender and gender nonconforming people are assigned to a juvenile hall, prison, or jail based on their "legal" gender identity as given on their birth certificate. As such, their self-definitions and lived experiences of gender are ignored in favor of a classification based on their genitalia. In an interview, antiprison activist Bakari called attention to the mismatch between the penal system and the lived experience of living outside the binary: "You have male and female prisons. I ain't male or female, so which one do I get to go to? And you're housed according to your genitalia, which to me does not connote gender."

On entering California Institute for Women [CIW], Bakari was forced to give up street attire of boxers, baggy jeans, and a long shirt and to put on "feminine" clothing. Bakari saw this as an attempt by prison authorities to assert their power by policing gender expression: "How they control you and mandate you to this gender binary is if you're in a women's facility you must wear whatever society says is for women . . . At CIW when I first got there, I had on boxers; they took them, said they were contraband . . . Then they make you wear panties and a mumu, an old lady housedress." Some guards use the misalignment between a transgender prisoner's self-identity and appearance and his or her government classification as a basis for psychological abuse, for example by calling transwomen "he" or "Sir." Another interviewee, Nathaniel, explained the psychological impact of this type of discrimination:

> [F]or trans people, depression and suicide, you can have really high risk factors for that when you're consistently being denied for who you are. When people take away your opportunity to have self-determination which happens in many ways in prison, but can be so detrimental when you're a trans woman and you're put in a men's prison, and you're denied your hormones and you're denied being called the name that you chose and you're being called "he" all the time.

Assignation by genitalia rather than self-identity is particularly devastating for transsexual prisoners. Since many transsexuals do not chose or cannot afford gender reassignment surgery, prisoners who may have had hormone treatment and "top surgery" (to remove breasts) will be assigned to an institution according to a gender assignation based on one part of their body, which does not match the rest of their physical and emotional experience. This means that a prisoner who lives and works as a woman, and is known by friends and family as a woman, will be placed in a men's prison. Yolanda Gonzalez shared this experience:

> Being a transgender woman with fully-developed breasts upon entering prison, proved to be a nightmare for me. While I was still in the orientation, I had a Facility Captain . . . tell me that I was not going to be allowed onto the general population mainline due to my having breasts. And that due to feminine appearance, I would be in extreme danger of sexual attack, and/or being raped by other prisoners. Just my presence in the general population would jeopardize the safety and security of the prison. (Transforming Justice 2007)

Studies of rape in men's prisons indicate that the creation of an environment of hypermasculine control and dominance contributes to the high rates of sexual assault against feminine, young, and new prisoners (Sabo, Kupers, and London 2001). Rape and sexual exploitation are sometimes encouraged by guards, who provide access and impunity as a means of controlling social hierarchies and maintaining order (Lee 2008).

In addition to the initial victimization of physical or sexual assault, transgender prisoners experience secondary victimization when they report abuses that are ignored or disbelieved. When Nikkas reported multiple violent sexual assaults: "The officer went and told R. that I had reported him. R. assaulted and raped me the next day . . . I didn't report the incidents again because a correctional staff member told me that if I filed a formal report, I would be sent to Administrative Segregation (the "hole") automatically and there would have to be an investigation for making 'false allegations'" (*Transforming Justice* 2007). In the context of a penal system that is based on a rigid and definitive gender division, transgender prisoners are most frequently viewed as a threat to the "security" and "order" of the prison. Their victimization or potential victimization is therefore seen as an indication of disorder rooted in the presence of the transgender person, rather than a human rights violation rooted in the violence of the gender binary system and devaluing of those who do not conform to it. Having identified transgender prisoners as a problem to the smooth functioning of the prison, administrators see removal of the prisoner from general population as the solution. As a result, transgender prisoners are often placed in "protective" housing. This may be a cell block or pod reserved for those considered vulnerable to abuse, or it may be administrative segregation (National Center for Lesbian Rights). Also known as the "hole," administrative segregation is where prisoners viewed as disruptive or violent are sent for punishment and "correction." Transgender prisoners locked in administrative segregation are denied many of the privileges available to other prisoners, including access to work, recreation, education, and association with others. Segregation is therefore experienced by transgender prisoners as another form of punishment for gender nonconformity.

Toward an Antiracist, Genderqueer Antiprison Agenda

What would it take to develop an agenda for feminist research that is in solidarity with transgender and gender nonconforming people in both men's and women's prisons? This final section seeks to develop a new theoretical framework for feminist antiprison activist research that makes visible and counters the state's power to define and police gender categories. I outline five principles that might be applied to a wide range of research projects. First, while feminist researchers, in particular women of color, have demonstrated the importance of applying an intersectional lens to research on prisons, actively engaging the complex articulations of race, class, gender, and sexuality (Richie 1995; Díaz-Cotto 2006; Sudbury 2006; Ross 1998), we need to expand our understanding of intersectionality to include the impact of gender identity (Demmons 2007). This does not simply mean adding gender identity to the "shopping list" of oppressions. Rather, it means a rigorous theoretical interrogation of the ways that gender policing and the punishment of gender nonconformity structure racialized and class-based experiences of imprisonment.

Second, our research practice needs to recognize the gender complexity and fluidity of human beings warehoused in prisons. Rather than adopting an unquestioning stance toward state-generated gender categorizations, we should adopt a gender self-determination model. This would require us to question how people in prison self-identify, rather than assuming that we can read the person's gender from the prison in which he or she is incarcerated. This also means recognizing the ways in which gender expression and identity are racially and culturally specific. Researchers would therefore need to familiarize ourselves with common gender terminology and identities adopted within different racialized communities.

Third, and relatedly, we need to acknowledge the existence of female masculinity and gender nonconformity in women's prisons. Shifting our language from "women in prison" to "people in women's prisons" is a starting point, but it is certainly not enough. Future research could examine and challenge the psychological and physical abuse of gender nonconforming prisoners in women's prisons, including prison policies that mandate inappropriate clothing or further criminalize prisoners seen as "masculine" or "aggressive." Or it might explore the role of transgender and gender nonconforming people in and released from women's prisons in building a movement to abolish prisons. Our work can also rectify the history of research by women that exoticizes and stigmatizes nonnormative gender and sexual identities in women's prisons.

Fourth, we need to adopt a more expansive conceptualization of womanhood. If, as demonstrated in the testimonies in this chapter, femininity does not depend on genitalia at birth or in the present moment, then our solidarities with women prisoners would need to reach beyond the women's prison. By including the experiences of transwomen in our analyses of women in prison, we expand our understanding of the role of the criminal justice system in policing gender roles for all women. The lives of transwomen make the social construction of gender visible and force us to examine the ways in which gender is policed by the state. As such, their lives can serve as an entryway for feminist interrogations of gendered state violence. Our research can also serve to promote alliances and heal the wounds between feminist and transgender movements, by demonstrating that imprisoned trans- and born-women share an interest in and commitments to gender justice and antiviolence work.

Finally, our research agenda should be informed by the subordinated knowledges of transgender and gender nonconforming communities and antiprison activists. This means learning from and working with antiprison organizations that have shifted toward a transgender solidarity model, as well as transgender and LGBT organizations that are taking up questions of transgender criminalization and human rights abuses in prison. By rooting future research in the priorities that emerge from antiprison and transgender activism, we make amends for the history of complicity between feminist research and violent gender policing by the state. We also create more nuanced and complex work that addresses the concerns of those working for change at the grassroots. I call this approach an "antiracist genderqueer antiprison framework" to signal a feminist praxis that actively challenges the state's power to define and police gender while simultaneously challenging the racialized build-up of the prison-industrial complex. As we explore ways to apply this framework to our research and activism, we can draw on the wisdom and experience of transgender and gender nonconforming activists and prisoners of color. Their refusal to be silenced is the starting point for what may become a paradigm shift in feminist antiprison work.

NOTES

1. A study of 375 homeless adolescents found that LGBT youth were more likely to leave home than their heterosexual counterparts, due to physical abuse, alcohol use in the home, and conflicts over sexual orientation.

2. For example, a survey of 194 transgender people living or working in San Francisco found that nearly 60 percent were living in poverty, 40 percent did not have a bank account, only 25 percent were working full time, and 9 percent had no source of income. While discrimination in housing and employment against transgender people is outlawed in 21 states and District of Columbia, low-income and marginalized-housed transgender people have little access to such legal protections.

3. Of transgender people surveyed, 10 percent self-identified as homeless, and another 31 percent were living in unstable situations. Nearly 27 percent reported experiencing housing discrimination.

4. I am refining a concept coined by Beth Richie.

REFERENCES

Amnesty International USA. 2005. *Stonewalled: Police Abuse and Misconduct Against Lesbian, Gay and Transgender People in the U.S.* Amnesty International USA, 4. http://www.amnesty.org/en/library/asset/AMR51/122/2005/en/dom AMR511222005en.pdf (accessed October 30, 2008).

Butler, Judith. 1990. *Gender Trouble: Feminism and the Subversion of Identity.* New York: Routledge.

Chambers, Lori. 2007. "Unprincipled Exclusions: Feminist Theory, Transgender Jurisprudence and Kimberly Nixon," *Canadian Journal of Women and the Law* 19 (2): 305–34.

Cochran, Bryan N., et al. 2002. "Challenges Faced by Homeless Sexual Minorities: Comparison of Gay, Lesbian, Bisexual and Transgender Homeless Adolescents with Their Heterosexual Counterparts." *American Journal of Public Health* 92 (5):773–77.

Collins, Patricia Hill. 1990. *Black Feminist Thought: Knowledge, Consciousness, and the Politics of Empowerment.* Boston: Unwin Hyman.

Demmons, Shawnna. Spring/Summer 2007. "Race, Class and Transgender." *The Fire Inside* 35.

Díaz-Cotto, Juanita. 2006. *Chicana Lives and Criminal Justice.* Austin: University of Texas Press.

Dobash, R. Emerson, Russell P. Dobash, and Sue Gutteridge. 1986. *The Imprisonment of Women.* New York: Routledge.

Faith, Karlene. 1993. *Unruly Women: The Politics of Confinement and Resistance.* Vancouver: Press Gang.

Feld, Barry C. 1999. *Bad Kids: Race and the Transformation of the Juvenile Court.* New York: Oxford University Press.

Giallombardo, Rose. 1966. *Society of Women: A Study of a Women's Prison.* New. York: John Wiley.

Halberstam, Judith. 1998. *Female Masculinity.* Durham, NC: Duke University Press.

Hensley, Christopher, and Richard Tewksbury. "Inmate-to-Inmate Prison Sexuality: A Review of Empirical Studies." *Trauma Violence and Abuse* 3 (2002): 226–43.

Howe, Adrian. 1994. *Punish and Critique: Towards a Feminist Analysis of Penality.* London: Routledge.

Human Rights Watch. 2001. *Hatred in the Hallways: Violence and Discrimination against Lesbian, Gay, Bisexual, and Transgender Students in U.S. Schools, 2001.* http://www. hrw.org/reports/2001/uslgbt/toc.htm (accessed October 31, 2008.)

Incite! Women of Color against Violence. 2008. *Law Enforcement Violence against Women of Color and Trans People of Color: A Critical Intersection of Gender Violence and State Violence.* Redmond, WA: Incite! Women of Color against Violence.

Justice Now. 3 March 2008. Personal email communication.

Koyama, Emi. "Whose Feminism Is It Anyway? The Unspoken Racism of the Trans Inclusion Debate." http://eminism.org/readings/pdf-rdg/whose-feminism.pdf (accessed October 28, 2008).

Lee, Alexander L. Summer 2004. "Gendered Crime and Punishment: Strategies to Protect Transgender, Gender Variant, and Intersex People in America's Prisons." *GIC TIP Journal.* 4–16.

——. 2008. "Prickly Coalitions: Moving Prison Abolition Forward." Ed. CR10 Publications Collective. *Abolition Now! Ten Years of Struggle and Strategy against the Prison Industrial Complex.* Oakland: AK.

Mallon, Gerald P., and Teresa DeCrescenzo. 1985. "Transgender Children and Youth: A Child Welfare Practice Perspective." *Child Welfare* 2: 215–41.

Minter, Shannon, and Christopher Daley. 2003. *Trans Realities: A Legal Needs Assessment of San Francisco's Transgender Communities.* San Francisco: National Center for Lesbian Rights and Transgender Law Center. 26–27. http://www.transgenderlawcenter.org/tranny/pdfs/Trans%20Realities%20Final%20Final.pdf (accessed October 31, 2008).

National Center for Lesbian Rights. Undated. Rights of Transgender Prisoners. http://www.nclrights.org/site/DocServer/tgprisoners.pdf?docID=1285 (accessed October 31, 2008).

Noble, Bobby J. 1998. *Masculinities without Men.* Vancouver: University of British Columbia Press.

Office of Juvenile Justice and Delinquency Prevention. 2002. *Disproportionate Minority Confinement, 2002 Update.* Washington, DC: US Department of Justice. http://www.ncjrs.gov/pdffiles1/ojjdp/201240.pdf (accessed October 30, 2008).

Richie, Beth. 1995. *Compelled to Crime: The Gender Entrapment of Battered Black Women,* New York: Routledge.

Ross, Luanna. 1998. *Inventing the Savage: The Social Construction of Native American Criminality.* Austin: University of Texas Press.

Rupp, Shannon. 3 February 2007. "Transsexual Loses Battle with Women's Shelter." *The Tyee.* http://the-tyee.ca/News/2007/02/03/Nixon/ (accessed October 31, 2008).

Sabo, Don, Terry Kupers and Willie London. 2001. *Prison Masculinities.* Philadelphia: Temple University Press.

San Francisco Bay Guardian and Transgender Law Center, 2006, *Good Jobs Now! A Snapshot of the Economic Health of San Francisco's Transgender Communities, 2006,* http://www.transgenderlawcenter.org/pdf/Good%20Jobs%20NOW%20report.pdf (accessed October 31, 2008).

San Francisco Department of Public Health. 1999. *The Transgender Community Health Project, 1999.* http://hivinsite.ucsf.edu/InSite?page=cftg-02-02#S5.1X (accessed November 6, 2008).

Segura, Denise. 1992. "Chicanas in White Collar Jobs: 'You Have to Prove Yourself More.'" *Sociological Perspectives* 35:163–82.

Selling, L. 1931. "The Pseudo-family." *American Journal of Sociology* 37: 247–53.

Sharma, Nandita, and Cynthia Wright. 2009. "Organizing the Motley Crew and Challenging the Security of National States." In *Activist Scholarship: Antiracism, Feminism and Social Change,* ed. Julia Sudbury and Margo Okazawa-Rey. Boulder, CO: Paradigm.

Steinhart, David J. Winter 1996. "Status Offenses." *The Future of Children, the Juvenile Court.* 6 (3): 86–99.

——. 2006. *Global Lockdown: Race, Gender and the Prison-Industrial Complex.* New York: Routledge.

Transforming Justice. 2007. "Letters from Trans and Gender Non-Conforming Activists in Prison." *Transforming Justice Program Book.* 8. Available online: http://www.transformingjustice.org/100907.tjprogrambook.pdf (accessed October 31, 2008).

Trent, Judy Scales. 1997. "Notes of a White Black Woman." In *Critical White Studies: Looking Behind the Mirror.* ed. Richard Delgado and Jean Stafancic. Philadelphia: Temple University Press.

Vancouver Rape Relief Society. "Chronology of Events in Kimberly Nixon vs. Vancouver Rape Relief Society." http://www.rapereliefshelter.bc.ca/issues/knixon_chronology.html (accessed October 28, 2008).

Ward, D., and G. Kassebaum. 1965. *Women's Prisons: Sex and Social Structure.* New York: Aldine.

DIALA SHAMAS

43 LIVING IN HOUSES WITHOUT WALLS: MUSLIM YOUTH IN NEW YORK CITY IN THE AFTERMATH OF 9/11 (2018)

Diala Shamas is a staff attorney at the Center for Constitutional Rights (CCR; New York, NY), where she works on challenging government and law enforcement abuses perpetrated under the guise of national security, both in the United States and abroad. Prior to joining the CCR, she was Clinical Supervising Attorney and Lecturer in Law at the International Human Rights and Conflict Resolution Clinic, and Senior Staff Attorney supervising the CLEAR (Creating Law Enforcement Accountability & Responsibility) project at City University of New York School of Law.

> I felt like I was living in a house without walls.
>
> —MOHAMMAD ELSHINAWY[1]

. . . In the immediate aftermath of September 11, the New York City Police Department (NYPD) aimed to set itself apart on the national landscape, seeking to become the leading local law enforcement agency in counterterrorism efforts. . . . A central pillar to this response was the targeting of New York City's large, diverse, and overwhelmingly immigrant Muslim American population for surveillance. Thanks to documents that have been leaked to the public, we can now read about the details of an elaborate, secret surveillance program that mapped, monitored, and analyzed American Muslim daily life throughout New York City, and surrounding areas. . . .

The details of the NYPD's surveillance program have spurred a range of criticisms: Investigative reporters and scholars have debunked the notion that such suspicionless surveillance was effective. Even the then-chief of the NYPD Intelligence Division, Lieutenant Paul Galati, admitted during sworn testimony in 2012 that in the six years of his tenure, the unit tasked with much of this surveillance—the Demographics Unit—had not yielded a single criminal lead. Legal challenges were brought in federal courts raising constitutional and other arguments against many aspects of these practices.[2] Among the responses of supporters of surveillance was that these practices were "harmless," and that only those who had something to hide should have something to fear. Yet as any observer of totalitarian regimes knows, surveillance in and of itself, without more, has a transformative effect on its target. . . .

This chapter moves beyond the arguments—all of them important and meritorious—that focus on the ineffectiveness and the illegality of the City's surveillance practices, and toward paying attention to the harms of surveillance. In 2011, understanding the consequences of surveillance on its targets—and the need to respond to the allegation of harmlessness—spurred my colleagues at the Creating Law Enforcement Accountability & Responsibility (CLEAR) project, a clinical project based out of City University of New York (CUNY) School of Law, our students and I to undertake a series of interviews in New York City. We set out to identify the experiences of those whose daily speech, religious practice, friendships, clothing, and behavior were put under the lens of the state. In identifying interviewees as well as verifying our findings, we drew on our organization's community-based partnerships.[3] We conducted fifty-seven semistructured interviews with Muslim religious figures, students, youth, business owners, and professionals. In particular, we reached out to individuals who frequented many of the mosques, student groups, or [who] lived in neighborhoods that had been featured in the NYPD's documents.

The result was a fifty-four-page report entitled *Mapping Muslims: NYPD Spying and Its Impact on American Muslims.*[4] . . . Our findings . . . showed how surveillance chilled constitutionally protected rights—curtailing religious practice, censoring speech, and stunting political organizing. We also found that surveillance severed the trust that should exist between the police department and the communities it is charged with protecting. Finally, the report documented the stigmatizing effect that government surveillance has on the targeted communities—labeling entire communities as "suspect communities."

Of our interviews, those with New York City's Muslim youth—college-age students whose entire political awakening was in a post-9/11 world—were the most jarring . . . Capitalizing on our presence at a CUNY campus and our deep community ties, we were able to hear, in great detail and greater confidence, so many of these students' deepest fears and understanding of their place as New Yorkers. In the following pages, I draw heavily on the interviews and other research that we gathered as part of the *Mapping Muslims* effort, and update them with more recent developments.

Five years since the public revelations, a reflection on the impacts of the NYPD surveillance program remains timely and is unfortunately not just backward looking. Surveillance is increasingly accepted as a post-9/11 reality. . . . Although New York City's experience with surveillance may be more acute than other American cities, it is certainly not aberrant. The federal government, as well as other local police departments, have engaged in similar broad-based surveillance and targeting of Muslim populations. . . .

Background on the NYPD's Surveillance Practices

In 2001, the NYPD established a secret section within its Intelligence Division (later renamed "Intelligence Bureau"), tasked with mapping and spying on the residential, social, and business landscape of American Muslims.[5] The unit, called the Demographics Unit—which was subsequently renamed "Zone Assessment Unit"—focused explicitly on twenty-eight listed "ancestries of interest," all populations from Muslim-majority countries, along with "American Black Muslims." The details of the program were revealed in August 2011, through a series of news reports by the Associated Press based on a trove of leaked NYPD documents. While the reports were surprising in their detail and depth, the fact of surveillance was not a surprise to those who had been its targets. Some degree of covert surveillance had been known—whether it was through the public revelations of some informants' identities, or frequently encountered suspicious behavior. Overt surveillance has also been a regular part of Muslim American life, particularly since the attacks of September 11, 2001: Individuals are regularly approached by local or federal law enforcement for questioning, such as questioning at borders, by immigration officials. A range of federal programs that disproportionately and overwhelmingly affect American Muslims also work as a way to track or question them. These include overbroad terrorism databases that can affect immigration or travel.

The NYPD, however, implemented an acute, local, and intimate version of these national surveillance programs. It sent undercover officers, who were allegedly called "rakers," into identified neighborhoods to identify what the documents described as "hot spots": restaurants, cafes, Muslim student associations, halal shops, and hookah bars. The NYPD boasted that it was able to recruit a force from diverse backgrounds, thus sending police officers who could blend in to the communities they watched.[6]

The department launched various "initiatives," named after the targeted group: The "Moroccan initiative" mapped businesses that were assumed to be Moroccan, many of which were in Astoria, Queens. The "Egyptian initiative" did the same with Egyptian businesses and went as far as New Jersey. Officers were instructed to "listen to neighborhood gossip" and get an overall "feel for the community." They were instructed to visit schools and interact with business owners and patrons to "gauge sentiment."[7]

Looking through the documents, it is clear that the common thread across all targets is their Muslim identity. In fact, in the "Syrian Locations of Concern" report, the document was clear that the effort excluded the sizable Syrian Jewish population and focused on the "smaller Muslim community."[8] This targeting of the Muslim faith was based on a theory of Muslim "radicalization" that the NYPD championed and that has similar purchase at the federal level, despite having been shown to be deeply flawed. The radicalization theory purports to identify a trajectory through which an individual becomes a terrorist. According to this theory, the NYPD would take special interest in signs of Muslim religiosity, including individuals who self-identified as [strictly orthodox or] "salafi," student groups who hosted certain types of speakers, and noted religious behavior. NYPD agents documented how many times a day Muslim students prayed during a university whitewater rafting trip, which Egyptian businesses shut their doors for daily prayers, which restaurants played Al-Jazeera, and which Newark businesses sold halal products and alcohol.

Muslims were only the latest targets of a long history of NYPD surveillance: Race and dissent-based surveillance has a long lineage in the NYPD. Police surveillance of dissident and minority groups can be traced as far back as the NYPD's "Italian Squad," founded in 1904 to monitor the practices and activities of the city's Italian immigrants. The NYPD also had an "anarchist squad," which focused on anarchists and labor activists. The NYPD's surveillance of political activists of various kinds—communists, anarchists, labor activists, and civil rights activists—continued through the 1930s and the 1960s, and included the Bureau of Special Services (BOSS). BOSS notoriously focused its investigations on dissident groups and individuals, including the NAACP, the American Civil Liberties Union, the Fifth Avenue Peace Parade Committee, and the Lower East Side Mobilization for Peace Action, compiling detailed profiles of organizations and individuals. Yet the NYPD's Demographics Unit represents the most prominent instance of targeting of an entire religious group for special monitoring.

The NYPD's Special Focus on College Campuses

The NYPD Intelligence Division identified thirty-one Muslim Student Associations (MSAs) in the New York area, and its officers zeroed in on seven that it listed as "of concern": Baruch College, Hunter College, La Guardia Community College, City College, Brooklyn College, St. John's University, and Queens College. Significantly, all but one (St. John's University) of these were part of the CUNY system, public schools that draw from New York's lower-income communities. Students at these campuses are often the first in their families to attend college and come from working-class or immigrant backgrounds. Among the student populations of New York's schools, they represent the least politically connected and privileged. But they are also the schools that recruit most locally, educating generations of New Yorkers.

The leaked NYPD documents suggest that these particular MSAs were targeted for a range of reasons . . . Yahoo student groups, email listservs, and blogs were monitored "as a daily routine."[9] The documents noted which speakers the students were hosting for an event, the speakers' backgrounds, political beliefs, and even the names of students who posted events online.[10]

More troublingly, the Intelligence Division sent undercover police officers and informants into MSAs and other youth groups. At City College, the NYPD dispatched an undercover [agent] to attend a whitewater rafting trip to upstate New York with students. In the notes from that trip, he reported that the students prayed at least four times a day.[11] At Brooklyn College, an undercover officer who went by "Mel" befriended the young women who were active members of the Muslim Students Association, attending their wedding parties and study groups.[12] Another informant was paid to befriend a group of Muslim students and their friends who had started a charity.[13]

Our interviews also confirmed what we learned through the press: The NYPD regularly sought to recruit students to become informants. One college student recalled a visit he received from two NYPD detectives shortly after he and his family had emigrated from Malaysia. The detectives wanted him to surf the Internet and monitor certain websites. He recalled the odd questions they put to him: "What do you think of the Shi'a? Do you think they are real Muslims? What would you do if a white American girl came to you and asked for intercourse?" After he repeatedly refused to meet with them, they eventually left him alone—until several months later, when he enrolled at a CUNY school:

> This time, they offered me 400 or 500 dollars a month, they said "all your work would require would be sitting in front of your computer and look at what people are doing." . . . Within four meetings I moved from being a suspect to someone they wanted to pay.
>
> —Jamal*, 23, CUNY student

Another young woman we interviewed recounted how when she was sixteen, she got a call from the principal's office at her public school. The principal told her that the NYPD had asked her to come in for questioning. She had assumed that it was in response to her complaints about someone who had been stalking her. However, once there, she found that the officers were more interested in her and her friends' online activities. A few weeks later, the same NYPD officers that she spoke to at her school came to her home while her parents were away. They searched through her belongings and her computer and ultimately offered her work as an informant. She described how at the time, this was a very enticing offer, in particular as she was poor and living with her parents:

> [The detective] said the department can provide you with a place, a job if that's what you're looking for, an apartment, we can give you your freedom.
>
> —Grace*, 23, Queens resident

Grace then articulated a sentiment that was common across MSA students—even though they had not yet obtained the leaked internal NYPD documents, or known the extent of the programs. They and their peers' experiences made it seem inevitable that they were constantly surrounded by informants:

> Everyone is being asked to spy, and I know it myself they must have been threatened or bribed to spy. Nobody would just do it voluntarily. And they probably get people in trouble. I know this because they tried to bribe me.
>
> —Grace*, 23, Queens resident

. . .Thus, students—who already faced surveillance in their neighborhoods, in their home setting, and in their mosques—were also experiencing this surveillance perhaps most intensively on their campuses.

Chilling Religious Practice and Study

. . . We found, perhaps unsurprisingly, that surveillance of Muslims' quotidian activities has created a pervasive climate of fear and suspicion, in particular on college campuses.

Perhaps the most obvious area of impact was the impact of surveillance on students' religious life and expression. The NYPD's spotlight on how individuals practiced their faith, their degree of religiosity and their places of worship disrupted Muslims' ability to practice freely. Interviewees, no matter how young, showed an acute awareness of the direct badge of suspicion accorded to religious practice:

> It's as if the law says: the more Muslim you are, the more trouble you can be, so decrease your Islam.
>
> —Sari*, 19, Brooklyn College

> I can't grow my beard, I'll get in trouble. I can't dress like this, I can't talk like that . . . It's stressful.
>
> —Kaled Refat, 24, New Jersey resident . . .

Within heterogeneous Muslim communities, this resulted in the suppression of certain practices of Islam more than others, with the more conservative individuals bearing the brunt of the burden. Younger interviewees described how parents warned them about appearing "too Muslim" or forbade them from attending Muslim student group events or wearing traditional Muslim clothing. One Queens College student who wears the *niqab*, or face veil, noted that her mother asked her to stop wearing all black because she worried her dress would make her a target for surveillance, whereas her mother was not as concerned about her brother because "he doesn't necessarily 'look Muslim.'"

Many students we interviewed also discussed fear of discussing important religious concepts. For example, the word *jihad*, a central concept in Islam, translates from Arabic as "to strive" or "to struggle." The term is used as a term denoting an effort, endeavor, or struggle to improve one's own religious practice. Yet it has prominently been reduced, often by the press and in other public debates, to only refer to a violent struggle. It is a concept and term that calls for debate, explanation, and elaboration. The negative attention brought to the term has placed it at the center of law enforcement interest. As a result, many students we interviewed described avoiding using the term altogether. . . .

> We don't use the word jihad. Sometimes speakers will steer away from that word, or make extra effort to explain it more, explain exactly what we mean, so that nobody can misinterpret or get the wrong idea, especially in larger gatherings.
>
> —Amira,* 22, Sunday school teacher

> I don't talk about the concept of jihad. But anytime someone asks that question, my first reaction is to deflect that question to someone else who can answer without me having to talk about it. Because of the known things that happen when you talk about jihad, it's one of those words that can trigger automatic surveillance.
>
> —Jawad Rasul, 25, CUNY student

Impact on Campus Life

Another key finding was how surveillance has a chilling effect on freedom of speech and expression on campuses. Our interviews showed that college students became afraid to discuss matters that were deemed overtly political, including civil rights issues or international affairs. Surveillance has interfered in how and whether they make the

meaningful friendships that are typically developed in college and that might last a lifetime. Professors described this chilling of student life as "devastating" to the student experience in and out of the classroom. College, for most, is when students begin to experiment with their political identities, their beliefs, self-expression, and opinions. They test out their voices, and they become involved in causes that may result in fundamental shifts in their life and career choices. They learn how to lead, how to navigate institutions, and how to be citizens. The post-9/11 climate of surveillance and close scrutiny has deterred scores of American Muslims from developing their leadership skills and mobilizing for social causes. The long-term effects of these phenomena on these students and their communities have yet to be fully seen or understood.

It is perhaps the sense of community and belonging that is the first casualty during what is an already fraught college experience. This is particularly the case for those exploring new identities, including those who converted to Islam during college.

> I was very naive at one point. I converted to Islam. At first I thought all Muslims were great people and you could trust them all. And then someone said hey, you should know about all these things (referring to informants) . . .
>
> —Hassan*, 20, board member of a CUNY MSA . . .

Chilled Student Activism

. . . The stifling and self-censorship of both routine and political speech have especially dire consequences for college students as political activism, student organizing and academic pursuits are derailed during the most formative years of a young person's life. Students have found themselves unable to organize effectively or even to respond to news of surveillance, often times directly linking their silencing to the knowledge of NYPD surveillance.

> The [NYPD's] MSA documents say we are becoming more political, we want to avoid that.
>
> —Jamal*, 23, CUNY student

At the Muslim Student Organization it's a given that you don't touch a sensitive topic.

—Jawad Rasul, 25, CUNY student

We don't bring up politics aside from humanitarian causes like natural disasters, and then we just remind others to pray for others.

—Samia*, 21, CUNY student[14]

Interviewees noted steering clear from conversations relating to foreign policy, civil rights and activism, and even surveillance. This same fear deterred mobilization around Muslim civil-rights issues on campus and quelled demands for police accountability. Surveillance, in this way, ensured more surveillance as it created a space void of calls for accountability.

. . . This silencing effect is exacerbated by the vulnerability or lack of privilege that students on CUNY campuses feel. They couldn't rely on connected parents or well-resourced schools to protect them. As one longtime CUNY faculty member told us:

CUNY students are so grateful to be in CUNY in the first place. They don't want to rock the boat. The last thing they want to do is anything that would endanger their chances of getting an education.[15]

Faculty and student government bodies were vociferous in their condemnation of the news of spying. They made several calls on the CUNY system to provide better protection to its students and demanded guarantees of nonrepetition.[16] Such university involvement continues to this day, Brooklyn College's student-run paper still regularly reporting on the fallout of the NYPD's surveillance program.[17] However, only the NYPD could ultimately provide that certainty.

In addition to muting themselves on campus, students reported withdrawing from engaging with their non-Muslim classmates and colleagues. One of the major components of the mission of any Muslim Student Association is to engage non-Muslims on their campus and to increase the Muslim community's visibility.[18] Students worried that wide press coverage announcing that the NYPD had infiltrated Muslim student groups with the hope of finding radicals or criminals would damage their outreach efforts. Several interviewees noted feeling that many on campus did not want to associate with the MSA or its active members.

For college students, typically aged between seventeen and twenty-two, the prospect of dealing with surveillance by a police department, infiltration of events and extracurricular activities by informants, and the potentially devastating academic, professional, and personal repercussions can be overwhelming. . . . We found that the NYPD's surveillance of students chilled First Amendment activity in what is perhaps the single most important formative and expressive space for any American youth: the college campus.

Responding to the News

With the first round of press reports unveiling the NYPD's infiltration of seven MSAs in the CUNY system, MSA leaders were hesitant to speak out. Tensions were high on the various campuses, as the college students deliberated how to respond to the national headlines publicizing that the NYPD considers them to be potentially dangerous. Although many members of CUNY faculties and student governments spoke out in solidarity with the Muslim student groups, the official administrations were less quick to condemn covert NYPD activities on their campuses. . . .

Some MSAs limited their response to inviting local attorneys and civil rights organizations such as CLEAR to facilitate "Know Your Rights" workshops. Yet even holding these events was sometimes controversial. On one campus, a student leader told us that his group opted to not record these events despite their normal policy of doing so, in order to protect the students. Several students noted a general hesitation to address surveillance on their campus. Interviewees also noted that, as a matter of policy, many MSA boards refrained from hosting "political" conversations and events. They reasoned that where their group was already under surveillance, such conversations would be recorded and misconstrued, and, if their group was not under surveillance, political conversations by a Muslim group would trigger surveillance or have the group identified as "extremist." Student groups were cognizant of the unwarranted attention controversial discussions might attract from peers.

Chilled Academic Expression

Our research found . . . that surveillance of Muslims' political opinions had devastating effects on classroom dynamics, and stunted students' personal and academic growth. Discussions, debates, exchanges, political and theoretical experimentation, and even role-playing and posturing are critical aspects of a healthy educational environment. Several of the students we interviewed described self-censoring classroom comments . . . Yet others noted a concern that other classmates or professors would misinterpret their views, given the ambient discourse on young, overtly political Muslims.

One college student noted that she would check with her friend who worked at a Muslim civil-rights organization ahead of submitting her papers for school, or even ahead of choosing her paper topics. She was advised to write freely, while also keeping in mind that her papers might be shared with the police department. One of the students who was on the whitewater rafting trip that was infiltrated by an NYPD undercover told us:

Colleges are a place where these discussions are supposed to happen so people can learn from each other. We're losing out.

—Jawad Rasul, 25, CUNY student

Similar observations played out for how student groups chose their speakers and their events. For example, they refrained from inviting speakers that would be deemed to be "salafi" to their campus events. Such a concern was not unfounded: in its policy paper "Radicalization in the West," the NYPD explicitly identified certain routine American Muslim behaviors as suspicious and broadly characterized these behaviors as Salafi. The NYPD then claimed that anyone who participates in these Salafi behaviors might be exhibiting indicators of "radicalization." The conflation between religious ideology, religious practice, and indicators of potential criminal activity was not lost on the students we spoke with:

We try to position ourselves by thinking whether the NYPD is going to think the speaker is Salafi, or whether the person has training from Saudi, that might give us unwanted attention from the NYPD.

—Jamal*, 23, CUNY student

Two students we spoke with, both active members of their MSAs, reported switching their majors from political science . . . after becoming concerned about law enforcement scrutiny of "political" young Muslim males.

Jeanne Theoharis noticed a retreat from non-professional degrees, even as secondary concentrations, among her Muslim students at Brooklyn College. In largely immigrant communities where social and familial pressures are to direct oneself toward professional degrees—business administration, accounting, engineering, or medicine—a secondary concentration or extracurricular activities have always been a way for students to explore their passions or their interests in other directions.

These impacts aren't limited to the Muslim students. Their peers, their teachers, and the intellectual community as a whole suffer when diverse views are stifled. Professors noted that students are concerned about speaking in class, or general reticence or anxiety around certain discussions, in particular those deemed "political."

Israel/Palestine and Muslim youth culture are the two topics where you feel the air goes out of the room. Students get anxious. The conversation is uncomfortable, the atmosphere changes in the room.

—Carla Bellamy, Professor, Baruch College

Poisoned College Experiences

MSA offices and prayer rooms are intended to be safe spaces for Muslim students to come together, support each other and talk freely about issues affecting their community. This need is especially important on CUNY campuses with large student bodies spread out over urban campuses, or where the resources devoted to extracurricular activities might be slimmer. Infiltration of MSAs by undercover police officers and informants is a blow to the groups' core function. On some campuses, interviewees noted drops in attendance at MSA events in the immediate aftermath of the Associated Press reports.

> [The upperclassmen] told us we encourage you to have free speech and political conversations, just not inside the MSA room. Because we don't want an informant to be here to catch one of your lines or crazy rants and you would get in trouble. I don't want to go to the MSA room because I'm worried that someone will report what I'm saying. . . . The MSA felt more awkward for everyone. No one was talking about it but we knew there was a problem, we were just scared to say something.
>
> —Fatima*, 19, CUNY student

At Brooklyn College, the college paper reported that following the Associated Press stories about on-campus surveillance, the annual "Islam Awareness Week" events were significantly less well attended than previous years, and that speakers requested not to be identified by name or have their photographs taken.

Though the feelings of suspicion toward others are corrosive to any community, students' youth and the fragility of their nascent social ties make it particularly destructive in the college setting. . . . Students we spoke with were ever cognizant that an undercover officer or informant might be among them. Several students noted that either a sudden surge or a sudden drop in someone's MSA activity would make them suspicious of that person.

> It made me feel hostile to other MSA members. I didn't know who to trust anymore.
>
> —Fatima*, 19, CUNY student-S>

> Our students are convinced that there must be spies or undercover agents. . . . We have a huge student body, it's impossible to know everyone. They also note that many students have financial concerns, and are thus likely to be pressured to become informants.
>
> —Jamal*, 23, CUNY student

Because of this atmosphere, students observed that their MSA is not able to fulfill its role as a support group or as a safe space to discuss the very issues that are silencing them. One interviewee was a young man who had the NYPD come to his home to question him about his political opinions and who had, as a result, withdrawn from all public events. He described the atmosphere when he finally mustered the courage to attend an MSA event after a long absence. He said that "people were looking at [him] funny because they hadn't seen [him] before" and may have thought he was an informant.

The suspicion and mistrust that surveillance breeds also stifled opportunities for reaching out across student groups and communities, including for support:

> Even to bring all the MSAs in one room, we're not going to trust them. From one MSA to another, you'll need to establish trust. Where do you start doing that? A CUNY-wide Know-Your-Rights event would be great, but because of the lack of trust anything more than that would be difficult. We would be wondering who is writing what down, what meaning would be imposed on the words, who would come and knock on their doors next.
>
> —Samia*, 21, CUNY student

> I don't want to be sitting at a roundtable, I'll just be wondering whether someone will be secretly taking notes and sending it God knows where. They would write "that girl thinks this."—then whose door are they going to knock on?
>
> —Inas*, 20, CUNY student

The Intimacy of Betrayal via Informant

As students learned that their classmates or friends had been undercover officers or informants, an atmosphere of mistrust settled in. . . . The force of betrayal is significantly more powerful than other forms of monitoring, no matter how intrusive they might be. . . . On campuses, the intensity of the friendship bonds and relationships made this aspect all the more devastating.

One nineteen-year-old student who was caught on a marijuana possession charge was "turned" into an informant and infiltrated a number of different college-age circles around New York City. Eventually, he "outed" himself on Facebook, shocking many of the students whom he had befriended and on whom he was spying. One of the students he befriended, who eventually became a plaintiff in a lawsuit against the NYPD, told us:

> I met him (the informant) through the MSA's Facebook connections. He had told me he wanted to become a better person and to strengthen his faith. So I took him in, introduced him to all of my friends, got him involved in our extracurricular activities. I would wake him up for prayer every morning. He even slept over at my house, and I let him in even though he smelled of marijuana but I tried to look past it because I knew he was new to Islam. When I was texted the news (that he was an informant), the shock caused me to drop my phone. It took me 24 hours to get myself together and to respond, everyone on Facebook was waiting to hear what I would say, because I'm the one who introduced him to them.
>
> —Asad Dandia, 19, CUNY student

Perhaps the most striking illustration of the intimacy of this betrayal occurred after our research and report were concluded. In 2016, a group of young alumnae at Brooklyn College learned that their friend and confidante from their college years was actually an NYPD undercover officer all along. The undercover agent, a woman who went by the name of "Mel," posed as a recent convert to Islam with Turkish origins. She befriended them, attended bridal showers, visited their homes, and became an integral part of their college experience. This information was not obtained through leaked documents—rather, her identity was revealed after the students recognized her in press reports about a prosecution of two young women on terrorism related charges. The NYPD has confirmed that they had deployed an informant to infiltrate Brooklyn College's Muslim student group for a year, not yielding any investigations.[19]

And yet, as we were interviewing Brooklyn College students, some of the very same women who had befriended her had spoken with my colleagues and me about their concerns about informants, even describing, in vague and secretive terms, this specific young woman. As we listened to them, the students were struggling to balance their concerns about a woman they described as having odd behavior and asking intrusive and invasive questions, with their desire to abide by what they believe to be their faith-based obligation to not engage in gossip. . . . Jeanne Theoharis, a professor at Brooklyn College who became an important resource for her students . . . wrote:

> Mel wormed her way into their friendships, their trips to Coney Island, their picnics and jokes. She even became a bridesmaid in one woman's wedding. She inquired about their politics and mimicked their religious practices. Claiming she'd been raised in a secular Muslim Turkish family but now wanted to embrace Islam, she recited the Shahada, a declaration of Muslim faith, at the first meeting many students remember her attending, and later spent dozens of hours "praying" next to them. She participated in clubs on campus, joined numerous listservs, and invited students to go with her to events around the city.[20]

The story of these young women at Brooklyn College has been well documented thanks to an unlikely alignment of facts with the official "outing" of Mel, a group of brave and outspoken students, support from engaged faculty, and thoughtful journalists and documentarians who also sought to tell their story. . . .

The Stratifying, Stigmatizing Role of Surveillance

> They say "don't you go to Queens College? Isn't that where all the terrorists are?" They saw it on the news that they were spying on us.
>
> If they [weren't] already monitoring me, now that I'm in the MSA at Queens College, I'm definitely monitored.
>
> —Sameera*, 19, CUNY student

Debates about the merits of surveillance put a primacy on the loss of privacy—and that is certainly a concern here, especially to the student who suddenly finds out that what she thought were her private conversations with a friend were actually being recorded. Such privacy harms are primarily experienced at the individual, interpersonal level. However, the state's betrayal also presents communal harms. . . .

Some have posited that the difference between the surveillance practices of a liberal democracy and those of a totalitarian regime is not so much in the techniques used, but in the scope of their reach and who they target.[21] A totalitarian regime subjects its entire population to surveillance, whereas in a liberal democracy, invasive techniques are limited to politically marginalized groups. Policy decisions around matters relating to counterterrorism surveillance are often discussed as striking a balance between security and privacy, or security and liberty. "On the one hand, it is creepy, Orwellian, and corrosive of civil liberties. On the other hand, it keeps us and our children safe."[22] The problem with this fallacy is that groups that are usually not involved in decision-making around what balance to strike disproportionately shoulder the costs. In other words, it is an easier cost to accept if it is not one that is being directly experienced. The other problem with this framing is the assumption that surveillance yields safety, when it has not been shown to do so—certainly not in the context of the NYPD's surveillance program.

There is also something about the spying being at the hands of a local police department as opposed to the federal government that increases the stratifying effects of surveillance. The NYPD is tasked with protecting New Yorkers. By associating itself with deception and covert activity, some of the most vulnerable segments of New York's immigrant communities are essentially deprived of the protections of their local police department. Variants of this argument have been recognized in the context of immigration enforcement, as immigrant-rights advocates and police departments alike have recognized the harms of enlisting local police departments to do the work of federal immigration enforcement agencies. In that context, many local police departments (including the NYPD) have declined participating in immigration enforcement. A similar analysis has yet to be developed in the context of the NYPD's surveillance program. However, the unique harms that flow from police surveillance were certainly identified by the young people we interviewed:

> Now that it's the NYPD it's a lot closer to home. It's more local. You don't know how to differentiate between the two. . . . Usually, police officers, you ask them for directions, they're around on campus. Now, how am I supposed to differentiate between the NYPD and the FBI? People don't understand how different it is that a local law enforcement agency is doing this.
>
> —Fareeda*, 21, Brooklyn College student

Conclusion

In March 2017, after years of community organizing and accompanying litigation, the NYPD reached a settlement in two lawsuits challenging the legality of its surveillance program. The terms of the settlement established a number of reforms to the police department's rules that aim to limit the police department's ability to engage in suspicionless surveillance, and increase oversight of the NYPD's intelligence division. While these are important changes, the longer-term impacts of NYPD surveillance, in particular of Muslim students, are yet to be fully seen. A generation of American Muslim youth has adjusted how they go about their studies, partake in extracurricular activities, choose their professions, engage with their classmates, and develop their social roles and relationships. Our report observed that the isolationism that comes with being a member of a "spied on" community means that Muslim students are getting a fundamentally different and less rewarding college experience compared to their non-Muslim peers. That has long term and immeasurable impacts on the city's social fabric and institutions. . . .

NOTES

1. The quotation from Mohammad Elshinawy is taken from in-court testimony delivered on April 19, 2016, speaking in support of a joint settlement reached in two separate lawsuits: *Raza et al. v. City of New York et al.*, No. 13-cv-3448 (March 20, 2017, E.D.N.Y.), and *Handschu v. Special Services Division*, 71-cv-2203 (March 13, 2017, S.D.N.Y).

2. *Raza v. City of New York; Handschu v. Special Services Division; Hassan v. City of New York* (Third Circuit, Oct. 13, 2015). The author and my colleagues at CLEAR were counsel for plaintiffs in *Raza v. City of New York*.

3. The overwhelming majority of our interviewees opted for anonymity, some on the further condition that we not disclose even generic information about them, including their class year, college, or country of origin. To honor these concerns, we used aliases for those interviewees who requested to remain anonymous. In addition, we have scrubbed details that might identify a particular mosque or Muslim students' association to respect the privacy of other members whom we have not necessarily interviewed but whose interests are implicated in the representation of their community or sentiments.

4. Shamas, Diala, and Nermeen Arastu. *Mapping Muslims: NYPD Spying and Its Impact on American Muslims*. New York: CLEAR, MACLC, AALDEF, 2013. Available at https://goo.gl/jxyXcy.

5. Many of the documents that were leaked to the press are available on the Associated Press website, as part of a series of Pulitzer Prize–winning reporting: https://goo.gl/LaAh2L.

6. *Handschu v. Special Services Division*, Deposition of Galati, 68–69.

7. Shamas and Arastu, 2013, 10.

8. New York Police Department Intelligence Division, Syrian Locations of Concern, https://goo.gl/EqkzsX.

9. New York City Police Department, Weekly MSA Report (2006).

10. Ibid.

11. Chris Hawley, "NYPD Monitored Muslim Students All over Northeast," *Associated Press*, February 18, 2012.

12. Jeanne Theoharis, "'I Feel like a Despised Insect': Coming of Age under Surveillance in New York," *The Intercept*, February 18, 2016.

13. Asad Dandia, "My Life under NYPD Surveillance: A Brooklyn Student and Charity Leader on Fear and Mistrust," *American Civil Liberties Union*, June 18, 2013.

14. Shamas and Arastu, 2013, 41.

15. Ibid., 42.

16. Zainab Iqbal, "Two Years Later, Brooklyn College Looks Back on NYPD's Surveillance of Muslims," *The Excelsior*, November 8, 2017.

17. Ahmed Aly, "Professors Explain Surveillance on Campus and First Amendment Rights," *The Kingsman*, February 28, 2017.

18. Shamas and Arastu, 2013, 43.

19. Aviva Stahl, "Brooklyn College Students: NYPD Illegally Spied on Us & Lied about It," *The Gothamist*, January 5, 2016.

20. Jeanne Theoharis, "I Feel like a Despised Insect."

21. Hewitt, Steve. *Snitch! A History of the Modern Intelligence Informer*. New York: Continuum, 2010, 120

22. Richards, Neil. "The Dangers of Surveillance." *Harvard Law Review* 126 (2013): 1934–1965.

LESLIE A. CAMPOS

44   UNEXPECTED BORDERS (2018)

Leslie A. Campos was born to Salvadorean immigrant parents and raised in Houston, Texas. She majored in Government at Hamilton College (Clinton, NY), with a focus on politics, migration, and social identity in the Americas. After graduating in 2017, Leslie returned to Houston, where she works as a paralegal with Kids in Need of Defense, Inc. (KIND), an organization that tries to ensure children do not go through the immigration court process without legal representation. She hopes to attend law school one day to further her knowledge of how to bring justice to immigrant communities in the United States.

Between May 5 and June 9, 2018, 2,342 children were separated from 2,206 parents at the US-Mexico border. No flyer or announcement was made to traveling families that they would be separated on arrival. While there are never guarantees, migrants rely on the idea that if they make it to the border they will be released to reside in this country, even if they are held in detention for a while. Those on the journey had no idea about these new barriers for families and children.

In July 2018, I went to Harlingen (Texas) for a week to work as a paralegal with KIND attorneys and other pro-bono attorneys who were trying to help detained parents reunite with their children. Due to the sensitive nature of this work, I cannot disclose details of a specific family's experience. However, my brief time in Harlingen gave me insights that I want to share to help others understand the terrible feeling of being separated from your loved ones in this way, probably incomprehensible to most people. In this article I draw on recordings that I made that week (sections in italics) and explain my experience in the context of immigration policy and practice.

Port Isabel Detention Center (PIDC) in Los Fresnos (Texas) is what it sounds like: a jail-like detention center. Detained adults are forced to give up their street clothes for blue shirts and pants. Guards mainly speak to them in English although some speak in other languages in hushed tones or when absolutely necessary. Those detained

have been caught attempting to cross the border without acceptable documentation. People wait—sometimes with no legal representation—for a federal judge to determine whether they will be deported, to their home country or another country, or allowed to stay here to fight their cases in immigration court.

In May 2018, a large number of the adults in PIDC were parents who had been separated from their children after crossing the border—either through a formal "port of entry" or by crossing the Rio Grande. Children were sent to "shelters" around the country, while their parents remained in detention centers. Parents would not know their children's whereabouts for days, weeks, or even longer.

I got in on a Saturday night in July and was immediately thrown into things by the KIND support staff, who had already been there a week. Before they left the next day, they gave me some guidance—thankfully!—and invited me to go with them to the border, only thirty minutes away. I was curious to see what it was like. I'm from Texas but there are some things I don't see living in Houston, even though we're only eight hours away.

I hadn't been to the border since high school. Going into Brownsville felt like I was in Costa Rica or Chile—places where I'd spent some time while in college. It was very interesting to see how, early on, the US and Mexico would blend together geographically. Brownsville is right on the border. The port of entry, where US Immigration

Source: Leslie A. Campos, written for this volume.

and Customs Enforcement (ICE) operates, is right there. But it was still odd to see it in person. Families and individuals travel miles from their home countries, sometimes walking long distances, to reach this place that looked like an ordinary Latin American town. I wondered, "Am I in the US or have I made it into Mexico?" In fact we almost drove into the port of entry ourselves. If it weren't for the wall, the signs, or border patrol, you wouldn't even notice that you were crossing an international boundary. It's been said many times, but humans construct borders.

We got out of the car. A wall defines large portions of the border. At Brownsville it stretches away for miles. Behind the wall I could see the bridge that leads into Mexico: one way in, one way out. The line of people waiting to enter Mexico was short and quick. People were crossing with shopping bags, making their weekend trip to purchase items that they can't find in the United States. The line to enter the US, however, was a different story. I couldn't tell how far back it extended. All I could see were faces peering through the solid gate that kept them one step away from entering this country.

I could also see the Rio Grande. The river flowed calm and peaceful. However, I couldn't help but think about the hundreds of lives lost to deadly currents over the last decades, people who had traveled through one or more countries, who had made it so close to their longed-for destination. Seeing the border made me remember anew why I was sent to Harlingen that week: to help those who had survived the treacherous river and who were now attempting to survive unexpected heartbreak.

Unaccompanied Minors

For years, children under the age of 18 have arrived at this border on their own or without a parent or legal guardian. Children flee their home countries due to threats of violence and as victims of harm, abuse, slave-like servitude, lack of protection, and so on. Under US law they are defined as "unaccompanied minors" in recognition of their vulnerability, and to protect them better.

So, when an unaccompanied minor arrives in the United States they are not processed in the same way as adults. Take "Rosa" as a hypothetical example. She is an eleven-year-old girl fleeing El Salvador where she was a victim of child labor at the hands of

some of her family members. She decided to flee to the United States because her mother lives in New York. Indeed, Rosa's mother had left El Salvador to try to provide a better life for Rosa. Without consulting her mother (who did not know about the abuse Rosa had endured), Rosa fled to the United States, traveling through Guatemala and Mexico on her own. She was very scared but nurtured the larger hope that she would be with her mother again. Once Rosa arrived at the border she crossed the Rio Grande and was detained almost immediately by US Customs and Border Patrol (CBP) officers. Because she had no documentation giving her legal right to be in this country, she was taken into CBP custody and transferred to an Office of Refugee Resettlement (ORR) facility in Miami (Florida).

ORR falls under the Department of Health and Human Services and assists unaccompanied minors "who enter the United States from other countries without an adult guardian."[1] Children like Rosa are placed in an ORR shelter while they wait to be released to a parent or other eligible adult. ORR staff work with each child to transition to a new home in this country. Release from the shelter may take days or months, depending on who the child hopes to live with after they leave the ORR facility. Currently, the average length of stay in an ORR facility is 75 days. While the children wait to be released, they make friends with each other and take grade school classes taught by teachers employed by ORR.

In Rosa's case, her mother would need to verify that she is biologically related to Rosa through a birth certificate, other identification, and possibly even a DNA test. ORR may require a house visit and evaluation to confirm that Rosa will receive adequate support after she is released from the shelter. Children who want to be released to the care of a distant relative or someone who is not a relative may have to stay in the shelter for longer while ORR verifies that this person is an appropriate caretaker and that the child will not be at risk of homelessness or trafficking.

Most unaccompanied minors do not expect to have to go through the ORR process. Nevertheless, they have an idea of who they hope to live with after leaving the facility. Due to changes in the Trump administration's policy and practices during the "Zero Tolerance" period, even children who made the journey with their parent(s) or adult guardian were classified as unaccompanied minors. They were labeled "alone" only seconds after letting go of their parent's hand, not knowing where they would be taken or when, where, and who they would be released to.

My work week started on Sunday night. I began to organize the red folders that the KIND attorneys would take with them into PIDC. The folders contained documents that attorneys would use to understand the cases of the many parents who'd been separated from their children: Why did the parents decide to come to the US? Do they know where their children are? Have they been able to communicate with their children? And so on.

On Monday, I introduced myself briefly to the team I'd be working with. News kept changing. I'd already missed two meals due to new developments. Later, I recorded some of my observations from the day. One, a lot of parents were being released from PIDC, which was both good and bad. Good, because they didn't have to be in detention and it seemed that they wouldn't be deported. But the challenge continues to reunite these parents with their children. Two, we heard of an incident from a detained parent, in which a mother was told that she'd be reunited with her child. The child would be brought to PIDC. The mother was taken to the place where her child would to be waiting for her. There was a child present but it was not the woman's child. We were not able to verify this report—maybe a rumor. It sounded like yet another mistake in this crisis: a mother expecting to see her child and a child expecting to see their mother only to result in further heartbreak for both of them. Three, some parents have been released with their children but we didn't know under what circumstances or where they were released. Four, there was another rumor that children were being brought to PIDC and held in an unknown location nearby, but with no clear purpose.

Things changed day by day, and the week brought more unexpected events. There were so many questions but fewer answers.

Family Detention
In 2014, the Obama administration began to open or renovate facilities to detain immigrants without documentation. Mothers and children were sent to two family detention centers in Texas: Karnes Residential Center in Karnes City, and South Texas Family Residential Center in Dilley. Together they have capacity for 3,200 women and children.[2]

Prior to family separation, women and children would almost always have their immigration cases heard together before the same judge. Even though they were held in detention, at least mothers and children faced that intimidating process together. Mothers could watch out for their children, knowing their exact location in the facility at all times. Children could run to their parent's side when feeling scared. This changed with the new policy.

Family Separation
Let's take the Chocon family as another hypothetical example. The Chocons—two parents with their son and daughter—fled Guatemala, their country of origin, as a result of racial and ethnic persecution due to their indigenous identity as K'iche' people. Let's say they left Guatemala in mid-April 2018 and arrived at the US-Mexico border 13 days later. They crossed the border via the Rio Grande and walked for a few minutes before being surrounded by CBP. Border patrol officers took them to the *hielera*—nicknamed by immigrants as the cooler—a location with low indoor temperatures, where recent migrants were processed before being transferred to a (family or adult) detention center or ORR shelter.

The Chocon family was told that they would be in the *hielera* for one night, before being transferred. At around 11 pm, an officer told the parents that they needed to take the children to bathe before sleeping. Without knowing what would happen, the parents gave consent for their children to be taken to another part of the building. They waited all night but the children were not returned. Feeling frantic, these parents found that they were not the only ones with missing children. After several parents asked questions, CBP officials told them that all their children had been moved to locations unknown even to them. As the Chocon parents attempted to process this information and their own distress, they were quickly moved out of the *hielera* and into an adult detention facility.

On my fourth day, some of the attorneys went to observe immigration court hearings, where detained people have their cases and credible fear interviews (CFIs)[3] reviewed by an immigration judge. The court closest to PIDC is in Harlingen, a forty-minute drive from the detention center. The attorneys returned with detailed accounts that were almost unbelievable.

Fathers and mothers wept in front of the judges, begging to be reunited with their children. Some parents were suffering so much emotionally that they hardly knew where they were or what was happening. One indigenous woman requested an interpreter as she did not think she could express herself fully or describe her experiences in Spanish, as this was not her first language. However, the judge proceeded to hold the hearing with a Spanish-language interpreter. The mother answered his questions as best she could. At the end of the hearing he said, "Well, it seems like you were able to express yourself." What a slap in the face!

Another woman seemed to be in both emotional and physical pain. She kept telling the judge, "I don't think I can go through with this [hearing]. I don't feel well. I feel ill." The judge didn't pause the hearing or reschedule it for another date. He proceeded to hear her case and only acknowledged her discomfort afterwards, instructing officers to take her to a DHS [Department of Health Services] health facility.[4]

I didn't witness this in person due to my workload. I was partly glad not to see this handling of "justice" despite people's emotional reactions to these traumatic events. I felt strongly that our justice system was being thrown out the window for the sake of God knows what. Solo Dios conoce sus corazones. Racism, politics. I can't say what it is completely but I know it isn't humanity.

On June 20, 2018, President Trump signed an executive order stating: "It is also the policy of this Administration to maintain family unity, including by detaining alien families together where appropriate and consistent with law and available resources."[5] Although CBP was being ordered to keep families together when possible, this did not mean that already-separated parents and children would be immediately reunited. Months later,

some families were still separated. Detained parents were coerced into signing documents that they did not understand. Some signed after being told that if they did so they would be quickly reunited with their children. Others signed because they were told that if they refused they would never see their children again. As a result, parents signed documents agreeing to be deported without their children, waiving their right for their cases to be heard before a judge, or other actions that affected their chances of seeing their children again.

Because of this, family separation is not over. Some parents have been deported while their children remain in ORR shelters.[6] In other cases children have been released from the shelters into the custody of close or distant family members while their parents remain detained. And even if families are reunited, there may still be emotional borders (or distance) between parents and children as they deal with the trauma caused by this government-imposed separation.

KIND still focuses on helping unaccompanied minors but we have also continued our work in helping separated families, some who are still detained and others who have already been released. Meeting with families who experienced this separation is sometimes difficult. I notice the clients' distress (especially the parents), but I try to provide what support I can. This topic brings up a lot of stress. I know this not from asking parents or children, but from my personal experience.

My time in Harlingen was short-lived. I worked fourteen-hour days, with just enough time to squeeze in meals. Every day started with unexpected challenges, and every night ended with a new list of goals that would be abandoned when the sun rose. If I think about it too much, I start to cry because I cannot contemplate the stress and pain these families endured. And I only lived this for one week. There are thousands (THOUSANDS!) of children and parents who have to live with what this country has done to them. I write this not to replace their voices with mine but hoping that when they are ready to speak, there is a foundation of understanding and open minds ready to hear them and to fight with them.

NOTES

1. Office of Refugee Resettlement: https://www.acf.hhs.
gov/orr/about/what-we-do

2. American Immigration Lawyers Association,
Cara Family Detention Project: https://www.aila.
org/practice/pro-bono/find-your-opportunity/
cara-family-detention-pro-bono-project

3. Credible Fear Interviews (CFIs) are initial screenings
that adults (and children—if they are accompanied
by an adult) are required to take in order to be considered for asylum based on previous or future persecution. Individuals receive either a "positive" or
"negative" result on their interview conducted by a
US Citizenship and Immigration Services asylum
officer.

4. CNN: https://www.cnn.com/2018/07/24/politics/
exclusive-audio-separated-parents-in-court/index.
html

5. Executive Orders Affording Congress the Opportunity to Address Family Separation: https://www.
whitehouse.gov/presidential-actions/affording-
congress-opportunity-address-family-separation/

6. *New York Times*: https://www.nytimes.com/2018/
09/01/world/americas/immigrant-families-separation-
border.html

45 · WALLS AND ENCLOSURES: THIS IS NOT THE EUROPE IN WHICH WE WANT TO LIVE (2016)

Founded in 1978, the **Spanish Federation of Feminist Organizations** has campaigned for the right to divorce, free abortion, equal employment opportunities, equal distribution of domestic labor, and against gender-based violence. A Spanish-language version of this manifesto was first posted to their website, at http://www.feministas.org.

> To be able to be where we want is the original sign of being free, whereas the limitations of such freedom have been since time immemorial the prelude of slavery.
> We cannot choose with whom we live in the world.
>
> —HANNAH ARENDT

Barbed wires, walls, and enclosures are multiplying in Europe. The roads taken by fleeing migrants, both women and men, are turning into roads of war, and are filled with mines, metaphorical and real. We are also seeing chilling symbolic elements like the numbers drawn on migrants' arms and the welcoming of refugees in the concentration camps of Buchenwald. The routes of exodus are changing. Right now, we are seeing an overland route in the Balkans, although the journeys and deaths on the sea still continue. Some fugitives are dying, electrocuted, in Calais as they try to climb the net that blocks the entrance to the United Kingdom. Other people are seriously injured in the border fences in Ceuta and Melilla.

Together with many other networks of women, we believe it is necessary to highlight a different kind of immigration policy, another type of reception.

1. The international community has the duty to guarantee safe travel routes for every asylum applicant. This duty must be carried out with special care by humanitarian organizations controlling women's status at refugee camps, for instance the camps in Libya, as well as in other places where women suffer from violence.

2. Every immigrant should be guaranteed asylum, including the so-called "economic immigrants," who risk their lives as they flee unbearable conditions. These unbearable conditions include the unsustainable effects of climate change as well as the negative effects of Western and neocolonialist powers (desertification, drought, land grabbing, resource hoarding, price increase of raw materials . . .).

3. There are no "clandestine people," just people avoiding hunger and war, with no intention of hiding. This language distortion is unacceptable.

4. Following the "safe cities" example, promoted by the Mayor of Barcelona, Ada Colau, it is necessary to guarantee refugees a dignified reception, welcoming them to be a part of communities without segregating them into isolated camps where they would forever remain "foreigners."

Women and men who are seeking refuge enter our societies and become part of our realities. Their bodies could be our bodies. Their children could be our children. We could be the ones feeling the same coldness, the same fear, the same hunger.

Source: Reprinted here with permission of Spanish Federation of Feminist Organizations.

What does it mean, then, for us to be European citizens? What do borders represent to us in connection with the right to live? "Primum vivere": it is the challenge many women initiated at the conference in Paestum. A Europe full of penitentiary logic and borders is not the place where we want to live.

We are aware that behind the rejection of immigrants lies the rejection of what is different. This rejection is founded in patriarchal ideology that has created hierarchies among human beings, defining one's superiority in relation to another: white-black, north-south, and above all masculine-feminine . . . In the world of politics only a few seem to understand what is at stake: the deep and unstoppable metamorphosis that immigrants are carrying out, a change that will transform thoughts, practices, rules of coexistence. It is all about overcoming fear and the rejection of what is different . . . Women know very well what this means.

Keeping in mind Hannah Arendt's simple but beautiful words regarding freedom and the right to relocate, we have to take an evolutionary leap in our civilization. Changes made by globalization, especially in the realm of communication, have made it impossible and unacceptable to maintain those barriers and borders that divide humanity into those who have the right to live and those who don't.

Ancient and new powers are trying to keep the system of domination alive by strengthening the tools of patriarchy—weapons, wars, borders—against a fleeing "continent" (almost 60 million people) that is trying to move forward. In contrast, it is increasingly evident that we need to construct an understanding of citizenship that considers the real material conditions of life that are common to all people on this planet. It is also essential to recognize our individual and collective differences as sources of enrichment. This is not an easy path. It requires care. But it is necessary to begin. Women's ways of thinking and their experience can effectively contribute to this project, because historically our gender has learned to confront being ignored and excluded.

Finally, we believe that it is necessary to learn to reflect deeply so that we can overcome the barriers set by patriarchal norms. Such patriarchal barriers are still based on a concept of citizenship that forms an identity by belonging to an "exclusive" nation. Every day we witness the consequences of this patriarchal structure, as the meaning of Europe itself disintegrates.

NOTE

1. Federación Estatal de Organizaciones Feministas, "Manifiesto: Murallas y recintos: no es la Europa en la que queremos vivir," Feb. 26, 2016. Translated by Madeleine Brink and Violeta Martinez Morones.

Gender, Militarism, War, and Peace

Keywords: demilitarization, militarism, militarization, militarized masculinity, postcolonial wars

In the United States, most people grow up with pride in this country, its wealth, its power, and its dominant position in the world. We learn the Pledge of Allegiance, a sense of patriotism, and that "our way of life" is worth fighting and perhaps dying for. The United States is number one in the world in terms of military technology, exports, and expenditure. It accounts for 36 percent of world military spending, equal to the next seven nations combined (McCarthy 2017). Congress authorized $717 billion for fiscal year 2019 (US Department of Defense 2018). This covers current and past military operations, including the upkeep of over four hundred bases and installations at home and one thousand more abroad; the development and maintenance of weapons; pensions for retired service personnel and veterans benefits; and interest on the national debt attributable to military spending (Werner 2018).

Companies with household names like Westinghouse, Boeing, and General Electric research and produce weapons systems and military aircraft. War movies are a film industry staple. The Army has its own video game, *America's Army*, which is also a recruitment tool (www.americasarmy.com). Many aspects of everyday life have become militarized (Enloe 2004), with, for example, flyovers of military jets during the Superbowl; the popularity of

Nick Tomecek/Northwest Florida Daily News via AP

war toys and military-inspired vehicles such as the Ford Bronco, Jeep, Humvee, Mercedes-Benz G-Class, and Toyota Land Cruiser; universities' Defense Department research contracts; and "boot camp" fitness programs offered by many physical fitness centers around the country. High-fashion designers promote the "military look" and camouflage chic. Backpacks, cell phone covers, baby clothes, and condoms all come in "camo." What other examples of everyday **militarism** can you think of?

The military is a central institution, culturally, politically, and economically. It shapes people's notions of patriotism, heroism, honor, duty, adventure, and citizenship. This has been more explicit since the attacks on the World Trade Center and Pentagon on September 11, 2001, a point we return to later.

WOMEN IN THE US MILITARY

Having women in the US military in significant numbers is a relatively new phenomenon. In 1972, near the end of the Vietnam War, females were only 1.2 percent of service personnel. The following year, after much debate, Congress ended the draft for men, though males are still required to register for "selective service" when they turn age 18. Many left the services as soon as they could, which caused a "manpower" shortfall that has been made up by recruiting women.

The Office of the Under Secretary of Defense, Personnel, and Readiness (OUSDPR) reports on military demographics each year. In 2016, women made up 15.5 percent of enlisted service members and 18 percent of officers, who need a college degree to join (OUSDPR 2016, Figs. 18 and 20). Women were 19.1 percent of Air Force enlisted personnel. Figures for other services were as follows: Navy, 18.9 percent; Army, 14.1 percent; and Marines, 8.2 percent (OUSDPR 2016, p. 67). Females were 20.6 percent of Air Force officers. Comparable data for the other services were as follows: Navy, 18.4 percent; Army, 18.4 percent; and Marines, 7.5 percent (OUSDPR 2016, Fig. 20). Black women make up 31 percent of enlisted women, although they are only 15 percent of the civilian population aged 18 to 44. Asian women are underrepresented compared to their numbers in the overall population. Latinas are somewhat underrepresented at 17 percent of enlisted women, compared to 18 percent in the population (OUSDPR 2016, p. 67). More women officers are white than women of color.

In the military, as in the civilian job market, most enlisted women do "women's work," including support and administration (25 percent), medical care (15 percent), service and supply (14 percent), and communications and intelligence (10 percent) (OUSDPR 2016, Fig. 33). As part of the process of accommodating women, all service branches have designed uniforms, including for pregnant soldiers, and specified detailed rules for hairstyles, nails, and makeup.

People join the military for many reasons. For some, it is a career choice or a patriotic decision. For others, the military offers opportunities not available to them in civilian society: jobs with better pay, lifelong medical insurance, pensions and other benefits, as well as the chance for education, travel, and escape from crisis-torn inner cities or economically depressed towns and rural areas. As argued in Chapter 7, the US labor market has changed markedly over the past forty years through automation and the movement of jobs overseas. In addition, government funding for education and social services has been cut back, but the military budget has been maintained at high levels. Over 80 percent of military women interviewed in 2011 joined because they wanted to serve the country and receive education benefits. More women than men said they joined because jobs were hard to find (42 percent of women compared to 25 percent of men) (Patten and Parker 2011).

Returning women veterans face similar challenges in adjusting to civilian life as reported by male soldiers (Patten and Parker 2011). Fully half said they experienced strains in family and social relations, and 42 percent said that they suffered from posttraumatic stress disorder (PTSD). However, 97 percent felt proud of their service. Recognizing that many women veterans are not adequately cared for by Veterans Administration programs, the Service Women's Action Network (SWAN) was founded in 2007 to support women veterans, especially women of color, and to offer alternative options in the many-layered process of healing and transitioning back to civilian life.

Women's presence creates various contradictions for militaries, as women threaten the manliness of war and the very nature of militarism as male. Two examples are the deployment of mothers and women in combat.

Soldier Mothers

In 1991, significant numbers of US military women were deployed for the Persian Gulf War. As they hugged their children goodbye, news reports portrayed them as professional soldiers as well as mothers. Commentators noted the change in social attitudes this represented, and some questioned whether war was the right place for mothers. Military men and women are more likely to be married than their civilian counterparts, and they marry at younger ages. The military's mission and absolute priority at all times is "readiness" for war, but with dual-military couples in the services, the Department of Defense has made a Family Care Plan mandatory for parents of dependent children. This must name a short-term and long-term caregiver, detail financial and practical arrangements, and designate a guardian in the event of a parent's death or incapacity. If a child care plan falls through, deployment may be deferred until this is resolved, and commanders have the option to terminate service if the service member cannot piece together adequate child care arrangements.

Women in Combat

With the increased participation of women, the question of whether they should be able to train for combat roles exposed a range of stereotypical attitudes on the part of military commanders, Pentagon planners, and members of Congress, depending on the degree to which they thought of combat as male. Many argued that women are not physically strong enough, are too emotional, and lack discipline or stamina. They would be bad for men's morale, it was said, and would disrupt fighting units because men would be distracted if a female buddy was hurt or captured. In practice, women have confounded many of these stereotypes by their professionalism, skills, focus, endurance, strength, and loyalty to the services.

Defining combat in modern warfare is not as simple as it might seem. Communications and supply, for example, once defined as noncombat areas, are both likely targets of attack. During the Iraq War, "traditional front lines were virtually obliterated, and women were tasked to fill lethal combat roles more routinely than in any conflict in US history" according to *Chicago Tribune* reporter Kirsten Scharnberg (2005). She described a mission just south of Baghdad where

> a young soldier jumped into the gunner's turret of an armored Humvee and took control of the menacing .50-caliber machine gun. She was 19 years old, weighed barely 100 pounds and had a blond ponytail hanging out from under her Kevlar helmet.
>
> "This is what is different about this war," Lt. Col. Richard Rael, commander of the 515th Corps Support Battalion, said of the scene at the time. "Women are fighting it. Women under my command have confirmed kills. These little wisps of things are stronger than anyone could ever imagine and taking on more than most Americans could ever know."

Such realities led to changes in laws and regulations that had kept women out of combat assignments. By 2008, close to 90 percent of military jobs were open to women: to fly helicopters and fighter jets, work on combat ships, or command military police units. In 2010, the Navy allowed women to work on submarines. In January 2016, the Department of Defense opened all military occupations to women as long as they meet the required standards. These changes offer the possibility of greater career advancement for women, as senior positions often require combat experience. But note Julie Pulley's views in Reading 46. As a former paratrooper and Army captain who was deployed in Afghanistan and South Korea, she weighs in on the gender integration debate by warning that opening formerly restricted military occupations may not serve women well.

Seeing an advantage in deploying women, in 2010 the Marine Corps established a new Female Engagement Team (FET) in the war in Afghanistan to engage with Afghan women, provide supplies to local schools, organize women's discussions, and seek out information concerning local conditions. Second Lieutenant Melanie Piedra said that the FETs are seen as a "third gender": Afghan men recognize that they have power and responsibility "on the same level as a male. Yet, FETs are still viewed as females, allowing the teams to have access . . . to Afghan females" (NATO News 2011).

MILITARISM AS A SYSTEM

Because so many people in the United States have family members or friends who have served in the military, it may be difficult to separate these personal connections—and feelings of love and respect—from militarism as an institution. At the macro and global levels, we see militarism as a system of investments, institutions, values, and practices that take their meaning and value from war. This includes everyday cultural assumptions, political attitudes, and economic investments that are bigger than any specific war or what militaries do. Militarism continues even without overt conflicts. It is the mycelium, invisible underground, out of which wars spring up.

At the global level, militarism is the accepted way for nations to resolve disputes, even if reluctantly or as a last resort. The realist paradigm in international relations, which dominates political, military, and academic thinking about security, assumes "a hostile international environment" in which "sovereign, self-interested states" seek their own security through maintaining a balance of political and military power among them (Tickner 2001, p. 38). On this view, war is always a possibility, and "states must rely on their own power and capabilities . . . to enhance their national security" (Tickner 2001, p. 38). Hence, nations train and equip militaries and authorize them to engage in warfare. In some countries, there are more soldiers than doctors, and it is easier to get guns than a decent-paying job. Moreover, the sale and distribution of weapons is a major international business, whether AK-47s or high-tech weapons systems, as mentioned in Chapter 8.

Militarism, Patriarchy, and Masculinity

Several readings included earlier in this book are useful in thinking about relationships among militarism, patriarchy, and masculinity. For example, Allan G. Johnson argued that patriarchy is a system whose core values are control and domination (Reading 7). And V. Spike Peterson showed how modern states rely on the fusion of (heterosexist) masculinism, nationalism, and militarism (Reading 19).

Psychologist Stephen Ducat (2004) argued that in most patriarchal cultures, "the most important thing about being a man is *not being a woman*" (p. 6) and emphasized men's need to avoid "the wimp factor," especially in public life. As the US president is commander-in-chief of the armed forces, in the 2016 presidential election Hillary Clinton and Donald Trump both sought to present themselves as tough candidates who would not be "soft on defense." Political scientist Cynthia Enloe (1990, 1993) introduced the concept of **militarized masculinity**, a constructed ideal of manhood that involves physical strength, emotional detachment, the capacity for violence and killing, and an appearance of invulnerability. From basic training onward, military preparations break down civilian individuality and construct disciplined soldiers regardless of gender, race, or class.

Peterson remarks that in modern states, homosexuals and women have been excluded from militaries. For many years, the Pentagon considered homosexuality incompatible with military service, and regulations precluded lesbians and gay men from serving openly despite their presence as officers and enlisted personnel (see, e.g., Scott and Stanley 1994; Webber 1993). In 1993, the Clinton administration introduced the "Don't Ask, Don't Tell" rule regarding LGBTQI service members. Reports of antigay harassment—including verbal abuse, beatings, death threats, and apparent killings—more than doubled in the late 1990s, even though military policy expressly forbade it (Richter 2000). Between 1998 and 2003, 6,300 people were discharged, including linguists, nuclear warfare experts, and those in other job specialties that require years of training and expertise (Fouhy 2004). Women, who were 15 percent of active duty personnel, constituted 30 percent of those discharged. The Army was responsible for 41 percent of discharges, although it was down on its recruitment targets at the time and had imposed a "stop loss" order to prevent soldiers from retiring or leaving if they were deployed to Iraq or Afghanistan. The repeal of "Don't Ask, Don't Tell" in 2010 can be attributed to shifts in military culture, personnel shortages in a time of war, and the concerted efforts of service members, their allies, and organizations such as Gay, Lesbian, and Bisexual Vets of America; the National Gay and Lesbian Task Force; and Service-members Legal Defense Network. In June 2016, the Pentagon lifted the ban on trans people serving openly, as is the case in Australia, Canada, Israel, and the United Kingdom. A year later, President Trump opposed this policy. Legal challenges to this ban are still in process (Human Rights Campaign 2018a).

Peterson contends that the discourse around these exclusions and political and legal challenges to them show how deeply heterosexist assumptions underpin military masculinity. Army veteran and political scientist Jean Grossholtz (1998) pointed to the contradiction implicit in this situation: the military is based on male bonding, yet homosexuality was banned. Indeed, Peterson argues that "the military affords men a relatively unique opportunity to experience intimacy and interdependence, especially with men, in ways that heterosexist identities and divisions of labor otherwise constrain."

As a way of keeping up the morale of their troops, military commanders have long tolerated, and sometimes actively encouraged, women to live outside military encampments to support and sexually service the men. Governments may organize this, as in World War II when an estimated 400,000 "comfort women" from 13 countries were forced to provide sexual services for the Japanese Imperial Army (see, e.g., Hicks 1997; Kim-Gibson 1999; Soh 2008; Norma 2016). Similarly, US officials have made arrangements with their counterparts in the Philippines, Japan, Thailand, and South Korea to allow women to "entertain" US troops in bars and clubs (see, e.g., Enloe 2000; Moon 1997; Sturdevant and Stoltzfus 1992). Cynthia Enloe (1990, 1993) has emphasized male officials' shared assumptions about male soldiers' sexuality as in need of regular release. Such officials make a distinction between so-called "bad women" who are to be available to US servicemen and "good women" who are to be protected from the predatory sexuality attributed to military men. Racist and sexist assumptions about Asian women—as exotic, accommodating, and sexually compliant—are an integral part of this system, both held by individual soldiers and at the institutional level. Also, we note the incidence of sexual violence perpetrated by some US troops against their colleagues, both women and men. The US military has had a "zero tolerance" policy for some years, but this has not stopped apparently routine abuse.

In Readings 47 and 49, the authors show the routine nature of gender-based violence in war and in the aftermath of wars, perpetrated by combatants and noncombatants. In Reading 49, Amina Mama and Margo Okazawa-Rey discuss the many ways women survived brutal wars in West Africa, including fluid and situational relationships with men from state militaries or armed militias, whether as military "wives" or engaging in transactional sex.

Rape is used as a weapon of war, a strategic and systematic way to dishonor and attack enemy men that involves a complex intertwining of gender and race/ethnicity (see, e.g., Leatherman 2011; Peterson and Runyan 1993; Tétreault 1997). In the 1990s, soldiers conducted systematic rapes in the Balkans (see, e.g., Kesic 2000; Walsh 2000) and Rwanda (see, e.g., Newbury and Baldwin 2001; Rehn and Sirleaf 2002), with the goal of impregnating enemy women as part of a strategy of "ethnic cleansing." In the 2000s, this continued in the Darfur region of Sudan (Lacey 2004) and in the Democratic Republic of the Congo (Whitman 2010).

Militarism and Histories of Colonization

Colonial histories are deeply implicated in militarism and in contemporary conflicts. In Reading 49, Amina Mama and Margo Okazawa-Rey discuss the ruthlessness of British, French, and Belgian colonial regimes in various African countries, and the long-term impacts of this on modern states. In Reading 48, the authors focus on the situation of refugees fleeing war and devastation in Syria and seeking safety in surrounding countries, especially Turkey, Lebanon, and Egypt. For centuries, these nations were part of the Ottoman Empire centered on Constantinople (now Istanbul). Western European powers carved up the Ottoman Empire during World War I. Based on their imperialist interests, Britain and France drew lines on a map to demarcate new nations, such as Syria and Iraq. Contemporary wars in the Middle East are complex, but their colonial histories and the promises, lies, and betrayals of Western European powers should not be overlooked.

The United States also relied on militarism on this continent and abroad in establishing itself as a state. US troops fought indigenous nations and forced their displacement from traditional lands in order to impose European settlement. In the nineteenth century, the Mexican-American War (1846–1848) and Spanish-American War (1898) vastly expanded US territory. This included Texas, California, Arizona, Nevada, and New Mexico, as mentioned by Gloria Anzaldúa in Reading 36, and former Spanish colonies (Cuba, Puerto Rico, Guam, and the Philippines), which all came under US rule. A more recent example includes twentieth-century US involvement—selling arms, providing financial support, or training military leaders—in conflicts in Central America, especially in Nicaragua, El Salvador, Guatemala, and Honduras.

Root causes of contemporary displacement and migration include colonial military policies, wars, gang violence, and military priorities in many nations. In Reading 48, the authors note that European governments refer to the huge numbers of people fleeing war in Syria as a "crisis," in which the causes of migration are "out of their hands." These governments focus on a humanitarian emergency rather than acknowledge their failure to find political solutions, or the historical role of some European states in creating the conditions that have led to war. By contrast, in Reading 45 the Spanish Federation of Feminist Organizations presents a declaration that condemns the walls—literal and metaphorical—built to keep refugees and migrants out of Europe.

Militarization as a Process

As well as thinking of militarism as a system, it is also important to understand **militarization** as a process. Anthropologist Catherine Lutz (2002) maintains that militarization

> involves an intensification of the labor and resources allocated to military purposes, including the shaping of other institutions in synchrony with military goals. Militarization is simultaneously a discursive process, involving a shift in general societal beliefs and values in ways necessary to legitimate the use of force, the organization of large standing armies and their leaders, and the higher taxes or tribute used to pay for them. Militarization is intimately connected to the less visible deformation of human potentials into the hierarchies of race, class, gender, and sexuality, and to the shaping of national histories in ways that glorify and legitimate military action. (p. 5)

Militarization happens through the accumulation of thousands of routine decisions taken by elected officials, their advisors and aides, voters, government administrators, news editors, scientists, investors, and corporate employees and executives. Societies vary in how militarized they are, and within any particular society, the degree of militarization may change over time.

As mentioned earlier, the United States has become more overtly militarized since the attacks of 9/11. This includes the creation of the US Department of Homeland Security, ramped up airport security measures, an expanded Border Patrol, and increasing militarization of the US-Mexico border. Starting in the 1990s, Congress created a military-transfer program whereby local police departments can receive surplus equipment no longer needed on battlefields overseas, including machine guns, night-vision equipment, and armored vehicles (Apuzzo 2014). Private security forces operate in malls and schools. Gradually, these changes have come to seem normal so that people become accustomed to increasing degrees of militarization.

Because nation-states authorize armies, police, and other security agencies, their use of force, even killing, is sanctioned as legitimate. In some contexts, such as the wars in West Africa, non-state actors like militias and private security firms are part of the militarization of these nations. In Reading 49, Mama and Okazawa-Rey note the importance of economic resources like oil, diamonds, and rubber in driving militarization. Also, coltan, used in cell phones, laptops and other electronics, is mined in various African countries, including conflict zones. Another factor concerns disaster militarism. In Reading 48, the authors show that the involvement of US troops as first responders to environmental disasters in the Asia-Pacific region has been used as a justification for increasing US militarization of the region.

When nations move in the direction of increased militarization, their decision-making processes become more centralized or autocratic. This may involve greater use of secrecy, presidential edicts, surveillance, arbitrary arrests, military courts, the "disappearance" of "suspects," or the shut-down of elected decision-making bodies. It may lead to outlawing opposition groups; closing down community newspapers, radio stations, and presses; and banning books. It includes the demonization of enemy groups or peoples. Governments may jettison citizens' rights to organize, to lawful assembly, or to free speech—moves which they justify as necessary for national security. Militarization requires and serves to enforce greater social and cultural conformity, leading Zorica Mršević, a professor of human rights law, to comment: "The opposite of war is not peace—it is creativity" (Mršević 2000, 41).

IMPACTS OF WAR AND MILITARISM

Living through war and armed conflict is an extreme experience, often with long-lasting impacts. Obvious effects on human beings include being killed, whether as combatants—mainly younger men—or as civilians—mainly women, children, and elders; the trauma of experiencing or witnessing rape, torture, and destruction; physical and mental injuries and disabilities; attempting to survive the chaos of everyday life; and the trauma of being forced to flee from home. Currently, an unprecedented 65.6 million people are displaced, both internally and externally, by war and violence (UNHCR 2017). The proportion of war victims who are civilians has leapt from 5 percent after World War I to over 90 percent of casualties these days.

Vulnerability and Agency

People are vulnerable in war situations as civilians or combatants, and also due to age, race/ethnicity, gender, sexuality, and national origin, depending on context. Reading 48 presents data regarding Syrian refugees fleeing war in their country. A majority of them are women; some are LGBTQI people who may not reveal their gender identity or sexual orientation for fear of violence. The authors also mention young single male refugees who are often considered those least in need of support. In this context they may be considered a security threat: Will they commit acts of violence? Or their manliness may be questioned: Why are they not fighting? These authors note that the "ongoing war in Syria has led to the forced migration of nearly seven million people." The sheer scale of these numbers is overwhelming to the refugees themselves, to relief agencies, and to the resources of neighboring nations.

In Reading 49, Amina Mama and Margo Okazawa-Rey give a harrowing account of women's efforts to survive wars in their homelands: Liberia, Nigeria, and Sierra Leone. The authors describe women's relationships to these wars: as mothers who cope with devastation of their homes and livelihoods, as combatants or supporters of armed factions, and as participants in women's peace organizing. Despite the appalling circumstances women face, these authors point out that women are not just victims. Perforce, many women have taken on new roles and responsibilities and developed new skills and leadership. They used their community connections and links to women's trading associations, as well as their own skills, resourcefulness, and courage, to try to survive the wars and support their families. Mama and Okazawa-Rey distinguish between tactical and strategic agency, where "tactical agency refers to the individual negotiations of survival that occur even in the context of extreme disempowerment or overwhelmingly negative options." Strategic agency is evident in the collective mobilizations they cite. Among Syrian refugees, too, women have had to depart from traditional roles within the home in order to support themselves and their families. For many, it may be difficult to return to their old roles in the aftermath of conflict. Peterson argued that women may be agents, not just victims of military systems: supporting their men/nation, participating in militarization, and increasingly, taking up arms. To be effective, however, in hypermasculinized arenas, she argued, women must support and reinforce heteronormative/masculinist strategies, including the devaluation and destruction of "others." Some US women who fought in Iraq commented that the physical and mental challenges of serving in a war zone and engaging in combat gave them a sense of agency and accomplishment (see, e.g., Benedict 2009; Blair 2011; Bowden and Cain 2008; Crow 2012; Holmstedt 2007; F. Williams 2005).

War changes soldiers: leaving home, following orders, witnessing brutality, and also committing atrocities. Combatants, who are mainly men, experience brutalization as they learn to dehumanize others so as to be able to torture, rape, or kill. Psychologist Robert Jay Lifton (2005) contends that war trauma greatly affects those in combat, particularly those who kill. The wider system of militarism also shapes everyday culture, impacts human and environmental health, and diverts resources that could be used to promote everyday security.

The Militarization of Everyday Culture

War toys, video games, war movies, and TV shows all teach children what it means to be a "real man." Everyday dynamics of dehumanization link sexualized violence committed by family members, acquaintances, or strangers and state violence perpetrated by police officers, prison guards, immigration officers, and soldiers. The stress of war leads to increased violence against women who absorb the aggression and fear of men returning from training or from battle—whether as wives or girlfriends or as women who sexually service soldiers.

Environmental Impacts of War and Preparations for War

Militarism and wars impact the environment and human health. Examples include the atomic bombing of Hiroshima and Nagasaki in 1945, the use of the defoliant "Agent Orange" in the Vietnam War, the burning of oil fields and use of depleted uranium in the 1991 Persian Gulf War, and the blanket bombing of Kosovo, Afghanistan, Iraq, and Syria. Landmines make large areas a long-term danger, especially to children. War and routine military training damage crops and agricultural land. Fuels, oils, solvents, and heavy metals used in the maintenance and repair of armored vehicles, ships, and planes contaminate land, water, and the ocean. Land used for bombing training is pulverized to dust and rubble.

Civilians and soldiers are affected by toxic contamination. The radioactive legacy of nuclear tests conducted in the Pacific by the United States, Britain, and France from 1946 to 1958 continues to wreak havoc on the health of Marshall Islands people and others in Micronesia affected by the fallout. In the years following the explosions, many women miscarried. Others gave birth to stillborn babies or to "jellyfish" babies without heads, limbs, or skeletons. Since then, survivors and their descendants have developed many forms of cancer, as have US troops present in the area at the time, who were ordered to watch and celebrate the tests as a high point of scientific achievement. The spraying of defoliants in Vietnam affected Vietnamese people and also US veterans who were exposed to it.

Diverting Resources Needed for Everyday Security

Resources committed to war and militarism could be redirected. Changing budget priorities would allow nations to provide decent housing, health care, and education for their people; provide renewable energy; clean up environmental contamination; and counter the effects of climate change. In human terms, militaries take capable young people from their home communities, often depriving those communities of young people's energy and potential leadership. In industrialized countries, a significant number of scientists, technologists, and researchers spend their lives working on military-related projects, especially weapons research and robotics.

Healing from War

A growing literature has established the complex nature of the interrelated psychological, economic, political, legal, and spiritual processes involved in healing and rebuilding after the upheavals, atrocities, and trauma of war (see, e.g., Barsalou 2005; Cane 2002; Meintjes, Pillay, and Turshen 2001; Simonovic 2004; Stover and Weinstein 2004; Theidon 2007).

Recovery and rebuilding are needed at all levels. At the micro level, this involves healing from physical and emotional wounds and applying resources—skills, time, connections, money, care, persistence, and imagination—to rebuild people's homes and livelihoods. At the meso level, communities may focus on repairing damaged buildings, clearing land, planting trees, mending water systems, providing health care, and fostering community renewal through art, music, video, or radio shows. At the macro level, this means upholding the rule of law and international human rights standards, holding governments and combatants accountable for the commitments they made in peace agreements, and supporting candidates for local and national office who will facilitate healing and rebuilding, including the adoption of national budget priorities that support sustainable development.

Ideally, these undertakings will reinforce each other, but even under favorable circumstances, healing and rebuilding take time and great dedication. Individuals, groups, and nations also need to be willing to recognize and take responsibility for their part in the conflict. This may involve a sincere apology, redress, and reparations. Some US veterans have sought to make amends to Vietnamese people, for example, by planting trees and helping to support communities affected by Agent Orange. In 2016, Iraq War veterans supported Standing Rock communities against the Dakota Access Pipeline (DAPL). In a ceremony of reconciliation, they knelt before indigenous elders and apologized for US wars against their people (see, e.g., Joseph 2016; Van Gelder 2016). Such individual or group efforts provide experiences of forgiveness and reconciliation. These are important in themselves and also because they show what is involved in doing this at a larger scale.

REDEFINING SECURITY

National security discourse focuses on *states* and assumes that military security makes the state secure. At the same time, large groups of people within a state could be destitute; disrespected; violated on account of their race, gender, gender identity, or sexuality; or be exposed to damaging chemical pollutants. Although continually invoked in political discourse, feminist geographer Joni Seager (1993) noted that national security "is a vague and constantly shifting concept" (p. 38) that can be defined according to context and the political needs of the day.

By contrast, a human security paradigm focuses on *people*. The UN Development Program (1994) identified four basic requirements for human security:

- The environment in which we live must be able to sustain human and natural life.
- People's basic survival needs for food, clothing, shelter, health care, and education must be met.
- People's fundamental human dignity, agency, and cultural identities must be honored.
- People and the natural environment must be protected from avoidable harm.

Feminist organizations like PeaceWomen Across the Globe took up a broad definition of human security in recognizing one thousand women from over 150 countries for their peace-making work, which included:

- Alleviating poverty.
- Maintaining a healthy environment.
- Addressing structural violence and discrimination based on gender, race, ethnicity, class, sexuality, ability, or culture.
- Changing priorities in government spending away from military budgets and toward social needs.
- Ensuring universal and equitable access to resources.
- Promoting conflict resolution and mediation.
- Enhancing health and education policies and practices.
- Promoting gun control.
- Caring for survivors of armed conflicts, promoting reconciliation and healing, and contributing to peaceful reconstruction and demilitarization of the society.

This organization nominated one thousand women for the Nobel Peace Prize in 2005 and also created a record of their work. Choosing a thousand women was symbolic—a way of saying that one cannot make peace alone. Although the group did not win the prestigious prize, the documentation of their work continues to spread knowledge of their wide-ranging efforts (Vieceli 2005; also see Cockburn 2007; Porter 2007).

Women's Peace Organizing

In Reading 1, Paula Gunn Allen mentions centuries-old practices that gave Native American women policy-making power in the Iroquois Confederation, especially the power to decide matters of peace and war. Currently, there is no nation-state where women have such power, though as shown by the 1,000 Women project, women on all continents are making steps toward demilitarization, and women's peace movements are active in many countries (see, e.g., Cachola et al. 2010; Chedelin and Eliatamby 2011; Cockburn 2007, 2012; de Alwis 2001; Fisher 1999; Swerdlow 1993; Vincent 2016).

In the nineteenth century, US women's opposition to militarism and war had roots in Quaker beliefs and in suffrage and temperance movements (see, e.g., Alonso 1993; Plastas 2011; Washburn 1993). Julia Ward Howe, author of the Civil War song "The

Battle Hymn of the Republic," was involved in the suffrage movement as a way to organize women for peace. In 1873, she initiated Mothers' Day for Peace on June 2, a day to honor mothers, who, she felt, best understood the suffering caused by war. Howe's "Mother's Day Proclamation," written in 1870 and reprinted here as Reading 50, calls on women to oppose war. Women's peace festivals were organized in several US cities with women speakers who opposed war and military training in schools. The Philadelphia Peace Society was still organizing in this way as late as 1909 (Alonso 1993).

DO YOU HAVE A FEMALE *ACTION FIGURE* THAT SPEAKS OUT AGAINST *DISCRIMINATION AND WAR!?*

By Bulbul. Reproduced with permission.

In 1915, over one thousand women from twelve countries, "cutting across national enmities," participated in a Congress of Women in The Hague (Netherlands), calling for an end to World War I (Bussey and Tims, 1980, p. 18). Women's delegations met with heads of state in fourteen nations and sought to influence press and public opinion (Foster 1989). A second Congress at the end of the war established the Women's International League for Peace and Freedom (WILPF), which is still active in forty-seven countries today with international offices at the United Nations in New York and Geneva (Switzerland).

The United Nations provided a tool for women's involvement in peace-making in 2000 when the Security Council adopted Resolution 1325 on women, peace, and security. This resolution addressed the disproportionate impact of armed conflict on women. It recognized the undervalued contributions that women make to conflict prevention, conflict resolution, and peace building, and it stressed the importance of women's equal and full participation in peace negotiations. Although not binding on governments, Resolution 1325 set a new standard of inclusiveness and gender sensitivity in peace negotiations and provided leverage for women's efforts to influence policy in postconflict reconstruction (Lynes and Torry 2005).

Since the attacks of September 11, 2001, and the Bush administration's immediate decision to take military action, many people have questioned whether militarism can provide everyday human security or even national security. In the United States, Families for Peaceful Tomorrows came together soon after 9/11, declaring, "Our Grief is Not a Cry for War." Military Families Speak Out formed in 2002 to oppose the war against Iraq. Gold Star Families for Peace came to prominence in the summer of 2005, when Cindy Sheehan and others who had lost sons in the Iraq War camped outside the Bush family ranch in Crawford, Texas, asking the president to explain why their sons had been killed. The war on terrorism generated new feminist debate, research, and analysis (see, e.g., Riley, Mohanty, and Pratt 2008; Sjoberg and Via 2010; Sutton, Morgen, and Novkov 2008) and new energy for organizations like WILPF (Boston, MA), Women's Action for New Directions (WAND; Arlington, MA), Women in Black (New York and other cities), and Women Against Military Madness (Minneapolis, MN). It gave rise to new groups, including Code Pink (Washington, DC, and other cities). The Women of Color Resource Center (Oakland, CA) created a fashion show, "Fashion Resistance to Militarism," in 2005 as a popular way to highlight and critique the militarization of daily life, and other groups have staged similar shows (Ahn and Kirk 2009; Enloe 2007, chap. 6).

Demilitarization as a Process

Just as militarization moves a society in the direction of greater militarism, so demilitarization reverses this (Enloe 2000a). In this discussion, we emphasize demilitarization—of cultures, political systems, and economic investments—as a step-by-step process rather than peace as a static condition.

Demilitarization of Culture

This involves rethinking service, heroism, and adventure in ways that provide opportunities for individuals to stretch, grow, and gain respect while serving communities in the United States or elsewhere. It means learning about the power of behind-the-scenes efforts of diplomats and negotiators in working out agreements between groups or nations. It means not wearing camo as a fashion statement and finding another name for fitness programs that does not rely on military ideas of strength. It requires disentangling masculinity, heteronormativity, and militarism. What other examples can you think of that would contribute toward the demilitarization of culture?

Demilitarization of Political Systems

This includes changing definitions of security from military security to everyday security centered on respect for people and the planet, as mentioned earlier. It involves new notions of political strength based on nurturing the whole society, helping to provide for nations that have been impoverished, designating adequate resources for disaster relief, and protecting people from avoidable harm. It means changing police protocols and addressing the root causes of migration. It means an end to oppositional politics but working together to create the best conditions for all. What else can you think of?

Demilitarization of Economic Investments

This will involve investing in renewable energy sources, providing for food security, and working for economic justice in a world of finite resources. It means stopping the sale of weapons for profit, reducing military budgets, and directing tax money to provide for people's needs. What else would you put on this list?

Demilitarization and Feminist Thinking

This chapter covers heavy material. Militarism's central distortion is that organized state violence is essential for providing security. On the contrary, feminists, environmental activists, and indigenous people working for sovereignty and self-determination have shown that militarism creates insecurity for subjugated peoples, for many within dominant nations, and for the planet. Militarism also renders those of us in dominant nations as participants or complicit in other people's vulnerability and oppression. Conflicts and wars tear apart connections among people, as well as between people and the land that sustains us. We believe that feminists and students of women's and gender studies must include militarism in our theorizing and consider how our knowledge and perspectives can contribute to demilitarization: nurturing and remaking ties among people, re-humanizing those who have been defined as enemies, and healing the devastation caused by war and preparations for war.

QUESTIONS FOR REFLECTION

As you read and discuss this chapter, think about these questions:

1. What do you know about war and peace? What are your sources of information?
2. What is your idea of security at all levels of analysis? How do you know when you are secure?
3. What can you do to improve your sense of safety/security in different settings?
4. Based on your reading of this chapter, how well do you think militarism contributes to human security as defined by the UN Development Program?
5. How can individuals and nations resolve conflict without violence?

FINDING OUT MORE ON THE WEB

1. Compare the proportion of the federal budget that is spent on education, social services, health, and foreign aid with that spent on the military. How much does your state contribute to military spending? How much do you contribute? Use the following websites:
   National Priorities Project: www.nationalpriorities.org
   War Resisters League: www.warresisters.org/resources/pie-chart-flyers-where-your-income-tax-money-really-goes
2. Find out more about the experiences of US military women:
   nextgenmilspouse: http://nextgenmilspouse.com/
   Service Women's Action Network: www.servicewomen.org
   Women in the Military: www.military.com/topics/women-military
3. Find out more about the countries mentioned in this chapter and women's organizations working for demilitarization in those countries.

TAKING ACTION

1. Has any member of your family served in the US or any national military. How did they serve? Are any of your family members war survivors? Bearing in mind that this may be a difficult topic for them to talk about, try to find out more about their experiences or thoughts and opinions on war and militarism.
2. Think about how you usually resolve conflicts or serious differences of opinion with your family, friends, teachers, or employers. What are the dynamics involved in each case? Do you cave in without expressing your opinion? Do you insist that you are right, regardless? Does violence play a part in this process? If so, why? What, if anything, do you want to do differently about resolving conflicts in the future?

3. List alternatives to military service that would improve people's security at the micro, meso, macro, and global levels.
4. Keep a personal log for a week of the ways that militarism affects your life on a daily basis. Watch what makes you feel proud, what you find moving—are any of these things linked to the militarization of our culture?
5. Analyze the representation of armed conflict and war in the news media or popular culture. Compare various US news reports with those from other nations.

JULIE PULLEY

46 THE TRUTH ABOUT THE MILITARY GENDER INTEGRATION DEBATE (2016)

A graduate of the US Military Academy at West Point, **Julie Pulley** is a former Army captain who served in Afghanistan and South Korea.

Unprecedented change is underway in our military. But as a former woman paratrooper who supported both the 82nd Airborne Division in Afghanistan and the 2nd Infantry Division in South Korea, I am concerned that Americans are only hearing one side of the military gender integration debate.

I hope that CNN's military town hall meeting on Wednesday night will show that these concerns—shared by so many who have served the country—are being addressed.

Back in January, Secretary of Defense Ash Carter opened all military jobs to women. The following month, lawmakers in the House of Representatives introduced the "Draft America's Daughters Act of 2016"[1] proposing extension of Selective Service registration and conscription requirements to women between the ages of 18 and 26. In June, the legislation passed the Senate.[2]

Many who advocated opening all combat occupations declare women should be subject to the draft. They assume women will only serve in support roles unless able to prove via physical strength test ability to fill more physically demanding combat occupations. But such testing would allow capable people to intentionally avoid difficult, high-mortality assignments. Simply put, reserving all the support jobs for women constitutes unequal treatment, and drafted men aren't likely to accept women occupying an unfair share of low-risk jobs.

Some allege the Draft America's Daughters Act is reprisal for gender integration. However, not requiring women's draft registration when they are now permitted to serve in every capacity is sexist. As Sen. John McCain wrote in a statement,[3] "It is the logical conclusion of the decision to open combat positions to women."

Yet while Sen. McCain's statement is true, the implication[4] that all military leadership supports the notion of women joining the infantry is untrue. Last year, for example, then–Marine Corps Commandant Gen. Joseph Dunford recommended[5] that infantry jobs remain closed to women, based on findings of the Marine Corps' yearlong gender integration study.

Some in favor of military gender equality argue the draft should be abolished. After all, it hasn't been used for 42 years. But a half a century passed between the federal draft for the Civil War and draft registration for World War I. *The Washington Post* quoted Director of the Selective Service Lawrence G. Romo as saying: "You can never say never. We are a deterrent. We want to make sure our adversaries understand that if we had an extreme national emergency, we would have the draft."[6]

It's a good point. So why not force women to register for the draft? For one thing, both the Army[7] and the Marine Corps[8] reported women were between two and six times more likely than their male peers to suffer training injuries. Research from both Israel[9] and the United Kingdom indicate considerable injury inequity as well, with the UK noting that "in general, women have smaller hearts, about 30% less muscle, slighter skeletal structure and wider pelvic bones . . . "[10]

These findings are significant in light of individual infantrymen[11] load weights topping 127 pounds.[12] Armor soldiers handle rounds weighing over 50 pounds[13] and must accomplish physically demanding duties such as "breaking track."[14]

Another flawed assumption made by gender integration supporters is listed in the 2015 Army Gender Integration Study. It reads, "Women who enter formerly closed units and MOSs [Military Occupational Specialty] will be volunteers."[15]

This assumption is erroneous not only in the aforementioned draft scenario, but also in peacetime. Numerous examples exist of men routinely forced into these same units either permanently or temporarily when vacancies are not willingly chosen. Cadets typically are not assigned a specific occupation until after they are contractually obligated to service.

In 1999, at West Point, a number of men were forced into permanent infantry assignments. Every year, per Army Regulation 614-100,[16] men are branch-detailed from their chosen branches into the infantry. In 2010, for instance, over 300 male officers were branch-detailed infantry for a period of three years.[17] Again, by this point in their career, cadets are committed to service and can't simply decline assignment. If treated equally, women officers should expect to be involuntarily assigned at an equal proportion to branches such as infantry just as their male counterparts are presently.

Enlisted women aren't safe, either. Women who enlist into formerly restricted occupations should not expect to simply transfer to another job should they find their initial selection too strenuous. The military currently prefers to remediate those who can't meet physical standards. An infantry soldier unable to keep pace can't just drop out of the infantry. The military enforces officer obligations and enlistment contracts because initial job training is expensive—over $30,000 for enlisted occupational training, according to an Army estimate[18] obtained by the Center for Military Readiness.

This is especially alarming in light of last month's Associated Press report of aggressive recruiting of women high school athletes by the Marines.[19] Disturbing, also, is the Army Gender Integration Study's proposed mitigation control: "Reclassify or take administrative action against Soldiers who fail to meet specified physical standards of their MOS. Administrative action includes possible separation from the Army."

Those champions of change would have Americans believe that the majority of servicewomen wanted formerly out-of-reach opportunities. In fact, 92.5% of 30,000 Army women responding to a 2013 Army survey weren't interested.[20] Three years later, the survey data seems to be holding true.

The *Army Times* reported last month that Sergeant Major of the Army Dan Dailey said there are not enough female NCOs and officers looking to transfer to combat arms jobs.[21] A similar scenario is playing out in the Marine Corps, where, according an August *Marine Corps Times* report, no women are enrolled or slated to attend the Infantry Officer Course.[22]

Most reasonable people support equal opportunity for women. Often, they are women themselves, or are men with mothers, sisters, daughters, or wives. But once in a while, the push for equality has unforeseen and unpleasant consequences. In the case of opening restricted military occupations, American women are now vulnerable to involuntary military service that will without question subject them to unequal danger and suffering.

NOTES

1. See https://www.congress.gov/bill/114th-congress /house-bill/4478/text
2. Jennifer Steinhauer, "Senate Votes to Require Women to Register for Draft," *New York Times*, June 14, 2016, http://www.nytimes.com/2016/06/15/ us/politics/congress-women-military-draft.html
3. Niels Lesniewski, "John McCain Joints Call to Register Women for the Draft," *Roll Call*, February 10, 2016, http://www.rollcall.com/news/home/john-mccain-joins-call-to-register-women-for-the-draft
4. Steinhauer, "Senate Votes."
5. Lolita C. Baldor, "Officials: Marine Commandant Recommends Women Be Banned from Some Combat Jobs," *Marine Corps Times*, September 18, 2015, https://www.marinecorpstimes.com/story/ military/2015/09/18/officials-marine-

commandant-recommends-women-banned-some-combat-job/72421888/

6. Tine Griego, "American May Never Have a Draft Again. But We're Still Punishing Low-Income Men for not Registering," *The Washington Post*, October 16, 2014, https://www.washingtonpost.com/news/storyline/wp/2014/10/16/america-may-never-have-a-draft-again-but-were-still-punishing-low-income-men-for-not-registering/

7. US Army Institute of Public Health, "IET Injury Surveillance: Entry-Level AIT at Forts Sill and Benning," May 12, 2015, http://cmrlink.org/data/sites/85/CMRDocuments/M-1IETInjurySurveillanceBates1-25-24JUL15.pdf

8. Eyder Peralta, "Marine Corps Study: All-Male Combat Units Performed Better than Mixed Units," *NPR.org*, September 10, 2015, http://www.npr.org/sections/thetwo-way/2015/09/10/439190586/marine-corps-study-finds-all-male-combat-units-faster-than-mixed-units

9. Aharon S. Finestone, et al., "Evaluation of the Performance of Females as Light Infantry Soldiers," *BioMed Research International*, 2014, https://www.hindawi.com/journals/bmri/2014/572953/

10. "Women in Ground Close Combat (GCC) Review Paper," December 1, 2014, https://www.gov.uk/government/uploads/system/uploads/attachment_data/file/389575/20141218_WGCC_Findings_Paper_Final.pdf

11. See https://www.youtube.com/watch?v=PAGosGhqa10

12. http://www.natick.army.mil/about/pao/2004/04-03.htm

13. See https://www.orbitalatk.com/defense-systems/armament-systems/120mm/

14. See https://www.youtube.com/watch?v=rbFh8lY_z5U

15. http://www.defense.gov/Portals/1/Documents/wisr-studies/Army%20-%20Gender%20Integration%20Study3.pdf

16. http://armypubs.army.mil/Search/ePubsSearch/ePubsSearchForm.aspx

17. See http://www.usma.edu/orcen/siteassets/sitepages/tech%20reports/final%20tech%20report%20officer%20flow%20model%20(16%20aug%2011).pdf

18. See http://cmrlink.org/data/sites/85/CMRDocuments/Tab_2.pdf

19. http://bigstory.ap.org/article/6cf42f913b5849928c344a312f87b0a2/marines-turn-high-school-girls-sports-teams-recruits

20. Lolita C. Baldor, "Few Army Women Want Combat Jobs, Study Finds," *USA Today*, February 25, 2014, http://www.usatoday.com/story/news/nation/2014/02/25/army-women-combat/5811505/

21. Michelle Tan, "SMA: Army Needs Female Soldiers to Step Up for Combat Jobs," *Army Times*, August 1, 2016, https://www.armytimes.com/story/military/2016/08/01/sma-army-needs-female-soldiers-step-up-combat-jobs/87931290/

22. Jeff Schogol, "Female Marine Can't Complete Infantry Office Course: No More Women Now Enrolled," *Marine Corps Times*, August 12, 2016, https://www.marinecorpstimes.com/story/military/2016/08/12/female-marine-cant-complete-infantry-officer-course-no-more-women-now-enrolled

ANNIE ISABEL FUKUSHIMA, AYANO GINOZA, MICHIKO HASE, GWYN KIRK, DEBORAH LEE, AND TAEVA SHEFLER

47   DISASTER MILITARISM: RETHINKING US RELIEF IN THE ASIA-PACIFIC (2014)

Annie Isabel Fukushima, Ayano Ginoza, Michiko Hase, Gwyn Kirk, Deborah Lee, and **Taeva Shefler** wrote this article as members of Women for Genuine Security, a US-based group that is part of the International Women's Network Against Militarism.

March 11 marks the third anniversary of the 9.0-magnitude earthquake that shook northeastern Japan in 2011, triggering a tsunami in a dual disaster that killed more than 16,000 people. The earthquake and tsunami caused the worst nuclear disaster in history with three meltdowns at the Fukushima Daiichi Nuclear Power Plant. Three years after the catastrophe, 136,000 people from Fukushima prefecture are still displaced, and numerous disaster-related deaths have resulted from stress-related illnesses and suicide. Because of the nuclear meltdown, highly radioactive material continues to leak into the ocean[1], presenting numerous technical challenges with no solution yet in sight. This environmental contamination, which has impacted residents, workers, and military personnel responders, will have a global effect. Lessons learned from Chernobyl suggest that all this is only the tip of the iceberg.[2]

"The Great East Japan Earthquake" is just one of several massive disasters in the Asia-Pacific this past decade. The 2004 Indian Ocean tsunami took the lives of 230,000 people in 14 countries. Most recently, Typhoon Haiyan (Yolanda) ripped through Samar and Leyte in the Philippines, causing 6,000 deaths last November. The Philippines has witnessed several other devastating typhoons, including Ketsana (Ondoy) in 2009 and Bopha (Pablo) in 2012. A rising pattern of intense storms and disasters in the Asia-Pacific region has led to the death and displacement of thousands of people and the destruction of essential urban and rural infrastructure such as roads, bridges, schools, health centers, and workplaces.

Paralleling these disasters has been the disaster response of the US military. According to this "disaster militarism"—which is a pattern of rhetoric, beliefs, and practices—the military should be the primary responder to large-scale disasters. Disaster militarism is not only reflected in the deployment of troops but also in media discourse that naturalizes and calls for military action in times of environmental catastrophes.

Justifying US Military Presence

Military Humanitarian Assistance and Disaster Relief (HADR) operations, such as Operation Damayan in the Philippines in 2013 and Operation Tomodachi (Friend) in Japan in 2011, have showcased the US military's "helpfulness," legitimized its presence, and softened its image. Charles-Antoine Hofmann and Laura Hudson, researching this topic for the British Red Cross, note several factors driving the growing military interest in responding to disasters. Assisting relief efforts, they observed, can improve the military's image and provide training opportunities. It is also a way for the military to diversify its role when armed forces face budget cuts.

Disaster relief has also become part of the justification for increased US troop deployments in the Asia-Pacific region—even as the new military basing component of the "Pacific Pivot" has met with strong opposition in Okinawa, Japan[,] and Jeju, South Korea. This massive permanent presence in the Asia-Pacific region has enabled the US military to be the "first and fastest" to respond to sudden calamity. The Pacific Command boasts 330,000 personnel (one-fifth of all US forces), 180 ships, and 2,000 aircraft in an area that spans half the earth's surface and is home to half the earth's population.[3]

Disaster relief is not the military's primary mission, role, or area of expertise. Nevertheless, disaster response missions facilitate military expansion and dominance. Yoshiyuki Uehara, the vice-governor of Okinawa at the time of the earthquake and tsunami, has opposed the plan to construct a new offshore US Marine base on the island. "I hope we stop glorifying Operation Tomodachi," he warned. "Our gratitude [for US military assistance after the earthquake and tsunami] and US military base problems are separate issues." The core of Operation Tomodachi was Joint Task Force 519 from the United States Pacific Command. Arguably, the response to disaster was a perfect opportunity for the United States to demonstrate to China that an immediate US-Japan joint military operation was possible.

The United States spent $80 million for this operation. Less than three weeks after the Fukushima disaster, Japan promised to increase its Host Nation Support from three to five years and to pay 188 million yen annually for US military facilities in the country.[4] The US government used the rhetoric of disaster militarism to justify Japan's dependence on US military forces and the high concentration of US bases in tiny Okinawa. The *Okinawa Times* argued that this was a clear "political exploitation of the earthquake disaster."

This was not the first time that disaster relief was used to further larger geopolitical and military goals. The rapid mobilization of assistance using military capabilities from the United States, Japan, India, and Australia in the wake of the 2004 Indian Ocean tsunami "set the ball rolling for a four-way security dialogue a few years later," former Australian diplomat Rory Medcalf has argued.[5] Just weeks after Typhoon Haiyan, meanwhile, the Philippine

and U.S. governments were touting relief efforts as justification for the need for a new long-term agreement for greater bilateral military cooperation and an increased US military presence in the Philippines (the Philippine constitution currently bans permanent troops and bases). Washington has used disaster militarism as additional leverage to pressure the Philippine government to accept a mutual defense agreement.[6]

The race to provide relief for political leverage is not limited to the United States. China offered its 14,000-ton floating military hospital, the *Peace Ark*, for Haiyan relief efforts—its first humanitarian response operation. Japan also sent military forces to the Philippines for relief work, in cooperation with the US military, a political effort by the current Japanese government to secure a greater military role overseas.

The Contradictions of Disaster Militarism

The conflation of military power and disaster relief is highly problematic. It is not cost-effective, efficient, or transparent.[7] Military operations exhaust limited budgets for humanitarian assistance, rehabilitation, and reconstruction activities. Confusion about the military's role as soldiers or relief providers can lead to suspicion and fear, and some people may not access relief as a result. According to the Department of Defense, the Pacific Command offers not only aid to countries in the region dealing with disasters, but also "forms of advice and assistance, training, satellite imagery or intelligence, surveillance, and reconnaissance support." More troops on the ground offer greater opportunities for the gathering of intelligence. Revelations that a CIA-funded fake vaccination program in Pakistan was used to find and kill Osama bin Laden provide another example of co-mingling humanitarian relief and military operations, rightly contributing to civilian confusion, public distrust, and questions of transparency and accountability.[8]

Disaster militarism does not address the underlying causes for the increasing number of intense storms and natural disasters. Nor can disaster militarism be separated from the US military's record as a the "worst polluter on the planet" for its "uninhibited use of fossil fuels, massive creation of greenhouse gases, and extensive release of radioactive and chemical contaminants into the air, water, and soil," as a recent Project Censored story detailed.[9] In times of disaster, the US military positions itself as a "savior" and attempts to obscure its role as a major contributor to the rise of climate disasters.

There is certainly an urgent need for disaster preparedness, with trained emergency personnel in local communities as well as international teams. The first responders in disasters are families, neighbors, community groups, professional organizations, churches, international humanitarian organizations, and governments. Resources should go to these local institutions to strengthen their capacity to respond to disasters and continue the work when emergency teams have all gone home. Padayon sa Pag-laum (Hope After Haiyan or WEDPRO) and other local Philippine organizations focus their relief efforts on the needs of the most vulnerable sectors of society, especially women and children. Their longer-term goal is to co-create solutions for a more resilient, more sustainable, and more inclusive future for the communities affected by the typhoon.

Nor should we wait for climate disasters to hit before we respond. Long-term and sustained resources should be made available ahead of time, especially to countries like the Philippines that experience typhoons on a regular basis. This would make for greater local independence in allocating relief resources.

It would also lessen dependency on military operations. World military expenditure totaled a massive $1.75 trillion in 2012, with the United States and its allies responsible for the vast majority.[10] These expenditures, which have made disaster militarism such a prominent feature of humanitarian relief operations, have not created more security for individuals, nations, or the planet. The alternative approach, human security, requires a physical environment that can support life; guarantees people's material needs for livelihood, food, and shelter; and protects people and the environment from avoidable harm. To minimize the impact of climate disasters—and reduce the contributing factors to the uptick in hurricanes, typhoons, and big storms—the disaster militarism model must give way to the human security model as soon as possible.

NOTES

1. Oskin, B. 2017. Japan earthquake and tsunami of 2011: Facts and information. *Live Science.* At https://www.livescience.com/39110-japan-2011-earthquake-tsunami-facts.html

2. Sturdee, S. 2016. Lessons of Chernobyl disaster, 30 years on. *Phys.Org.* At https://phys.org/news/2016-04-lessons-chernobyl-disaster-years.html

3. United States Pacific Command, Fact Sheet. At https://www.pacom.mil/Portals/55/Documents/pdf/USPACOM%20FACT%20SHEET%20v3.pdf

4. Cronk, T. M. 2015. U.S., Japan agree to host-nation support for U.S. troops. *DoD News,* At https://dod.defense.gov/News/Article/Article/637009/us-japan-agree-to-host-nation-support-for-us-troops/

5. Medcalf, R. 2013. Typhoon Haiyan and the geopolitics of disaster relief. *The Interpreter.* At https://www.lowyinstitute.org/the-interpreter/typhoon-haiyan-and-geopolitics-disaster-relief

6. Romero, A. 2014. 6th round of talks on US troops presence in Phl to resume. *Philippine Star.* At https://www.philstar.com/headlines/2014/03/04/1297089/6th-round-talks-us-troops-presence-phl-resume

7. Poole, L. 2013. Counting the cost of humanitarian aid delivered through the military. *Global Humanitarian Assistance.* At https://www.unocha.org/sites/dms/Documents/130301_Counting_the_cost_of_humanitarian_aid_delivered_through_the_mil.pdf

8. Swain, F. 2011. CIA fake vaccination program used in hunt for Osama bin Laden could cost lives. *The Telegraph.* At https://www.telegraph.co.uk/news/science/8646547/CIA-fake-vaccination-programme-used-in-hunt-for-Osama-bin-Laden-could-cost-lives.html

9. *Project Censored.* 2010. US department of Defense is the worst polluter on the planet. At https://www.projectcensored.org/2-us-department-of-defense-is-the-worst-polluter-on-the-planet/?doing_wp_cron=1560369161.4991579055786132812500

10. Stockholm International Peace Research Institute. 2013. At https://www.sipri.org/media/press-release/2013/world-military-spending-falls-china-russias-spending-rises-says-sipri

JANE FREEDMAN, ZEYNEP KIVILCIM, AND NURCAN ÖZGÜR BAKLACIOĞLU

48 GENDER, MIGRATION AND EXILE (2017)

Jane Freedman is a professor of politics at the Université Paris 8, France, and a research at the Centre de Recherches Sociologiques et Politiques de Paris. Her research focuses on gender, conflict, and migration. Recent publications include *Gendering the International Asylum and Refugee Debate* (2015) and *Gender, Violence and Politics in the Democratic Republic of Congo* (2015).

Zeynep Kivilcim is an associate professor of public international law at Istanbul University. Her work includes critical and gendered analysis regarding the legal status of Syrian refugees living in Turkey and field research with Syrian women and LGBTI urban refugees.

Nurcan Özgür Baklacioğlu is an associate professor of international relations at Istanbul University. Her work includes research on international migration in the Balkans, among African women in Konya (Turkey), and Syrian women and LGBTI refugees in Istanbul.

The ongoing war in Syria has led to the forced migration of nearly seven million people. With little hope for any immediate end to the war in Syria, and with the continuation of other conflicts and violence in countries such as Iraq and Afghanistan, the question of refugees has become one of the most pressing regional and global issues of current times. The majority of Syrian refugees are located in neighboring countries including Turkey (with over 2.5 million registered Syrian refugees), Lebanon (over one million Syrian refugees), Jordan, Iraq and Egypt.[1] This massive displacement clearly poses serious questions for the host countries, as well as for the human rights and security of the refugees themselves. There have been many reports of violence against Syrian refugees, both inside and outside of refugee camps, as well as exploitation in the labor market, gender-based violence, forced marriages etc. Although the majority of refugees have stayed in neighboring countries, many have also tried to reach the European Union, leading to what European political leaders as well as the media have described as a refugee "crisis," with thousands of refugees drowning in their attempts to reach Europe and others suffering violence and insecurity on their routes and on arrival in the destination country.

Conflict, Violence and Gender in Syria: Regional Responses

The Syrian refugee crisis has had massive impacts in a region where there are already a large number of refugees from Palestine and Iraq. Access to resources, food, health care and education are a major problem both for internally displaced people (IDP) and refugees, and increasingly for refugees' host countries (Zetter and Ruaudel, 2014). A Regional Response Plan (RRP) has been put in place by the Office of the United Nations High Commissioner for Refugees (UNHCR) to coordinate the efforts of various UN agencies and nongovernmental organizations (NGOs) in response to the crisis, but the scale of displacement, and the pre-existing political and economic tensions in the regions, have limited the efficacy of this response. As Zetter and Ruaudel explain: "The overall picture, then, is one of chronic vulnerability which is both deepening and becoming more entrenched" (Zetter and Ruaudel, 2014: 7). Refugees who are not registered with UNHCR, or who have lost their registration status and have thus become irregular residents in neighboring countries, are particularly marginalized and vulnerable. Women with irregular status are increasingly vulnerable to sexual and gender-based violence as they cannot rely on the local authorities for protection.

Source: From: *A Gendered Approach to the Syrian Refugee Crisis*, edited by Jane Freedman, Zeynep Kivilcim, and Nurcan Özgür Baklacioğlu (New York: Routledge, 2017). Reproduced by permission of Taylor & Francis Books UK.

© Roberto Scandola/123RF

Turkey, Jordan and Lebanon allowed Syrian refugees to cross into their territories during the first years of the Syrian war. However, since 2014 the governments of these countries have gradually closed the formal and informal border crossing points, built walls at their frontiers and strengthened border control with military actions that target refugees. They also introduced legal barriers to Syrian refugees by imposing visa requirements or legislation that exclude new refugees from the legal right to legal stay. In December 2014 Lebanon closed its borders to refugees fleeing Syria's civil war with exceptions for "humanitarian reasons." And in 2015 the Lebanese government announced new restrictions on Syrians entering Lebanon, requiring all refugees to apply for visas before entering (Amnesty International, 2015). Jordan allowed Syrians to enter its country through all of its informal border crossings in the east and the west, although it refused entry to many single Syrian men and to Palestinian refugees from Syria. Since May 2014 several border closures, restrictions on informal border crossings and . . . cases that hinder Syrians crossing into Jordan have been reported (Amnesty International, 2015). In addition, in January 2016 the Turkish government terminated the Syria–Turkey Visa Waiver Agreement that was allowing Syrian nationals to cross into Turkey without visa requirements. It is reported that since early 2015 Turkey has closed its land borders to Syrians (Human Rights Watch, 2015, 2016; Amnesty International, 2016). Turkey has also decided to physically hinder the crossings by constructing a 550-mile concrete wall along its border with Syria; half of this wall was completed by May 2016.

Women make up the majority of those displaced by the Syrian conflict, but the exact figures are not known. The United Nations Population Fund (UNFPA) reports that about 78 percent of those displaced are women and children (UNFPA, 2014), but this figure is problematic as it mixes together women and children in a manner which has been widely criticized by many feminist scholars (Enloe, 1993). As with other refugee situations, there is a lack of accurate sex-disaggregated data on Syrian IDPs and refugees. This is partly due to the very difficult and complicated circumstances surrounding data collection, particularly on IDPs within Syria. But, as has also been reported, during the initial stages of registration in several countries, data was collected by a conversation with the presumed head of household who was often a man (Women's Refugee Commission, 2014). In the Zaatari refugee camp in Jordan, it was also reported that data gathering and passing of information was organized through a structure of "street leaders" who were mostly men. Thus women were excluded from the flow of data gathering and information sharing. The lack of accurate sex-disaggregated data clearly hampers efforts to put in place programs which respond to the needs of male and female refugees.

The number of lesbian, gay, bisexual, trans- and intersex (LGBTI) among Syrian refugees is not known, particularly as many fear revealing their gender identity or sexual orientation. However, it is clear that LGBTI have been specifically targeted for violence in Syria and that because of this targeting by all sides in the conflict many LGBTI people flee Syria and seek refuge in other countries. LGBTI refugees may be considered more vulnerable than other refugees as they may not have access to the same emotional and financial support networks. They face persecution from host countries' citizens as well as from other members of the refugee community, and confront many barriers while accessing basic services. The informal networks that provide support to Syrian refugees in the neighboring countries that host them often fail to include individuals from the LGBTI community.

Studies on the conditions of refugees in various camps in neighboring countries have shown that familiar problems regarding gender equality and women's rights are occurring within these camps. Although the UNHCR and various other international organizations and NGOs have pledged to take gendered needs seriously in their provisions for Syrian refugees, in practice these needs are still not being fully addressed. For example, one study by the Women's Refugee Commission (WRC) found that: "Certain populations receive less attention and less access to programs, including the elderly, women and girls living outside the camps, people with disabilities and sexual minorities" (Women's Refugee Commission, 2014: 1). . . .

Several reports have highlighted increasing intimate partner and domestic violence against displaced women, which comes in addition to the sexual and gender-based violence that many of these women have faced in the conflict and during their flight. The WRC's report on refugee camps in Jordan recounts that:

> Intimate partner and domestic violence in homes, particularly targeting women and girls, is becoming more common, while challenges for reporting remain, especially in the case of sexual violence. This kind of violence may be aggravated by the fact that households are socially isolated, suffering from tremendous financial stress and lack of privacy due to overcrowding, which all contribute to increasing tensions that sometimes lead to violence, often perpetrated by a male head of household. (Women's Refugee Commission, 2014: 12)

Some research has shown that women have relativized this type of violence in an attempt to show empathy with the situation of men who have lost their traditional gender roles. This may be one of the reasons why such violence is under-reported.

Women have also expressed the fear that if they report violence their husbands will send them back to Syria (Masterson, 2012). Charles and Denman suggest that these fears are supported by structural aspects that "create the intersectionality of violence that is produced through individual acts and institutes." They explain that in pre-conflict Syria, married women were not allowed to travel outside of the country without their husband's permission. "This law now feeds into the patriarchal control and fear for women of being sent back by their husbands" (Charles and Denman, 2013: 105). For these reasons, many women do not report violence and, even if they do wish to report it, there are few services for support or trauma counseling. The situation may be even worse for women who are living outside the refugee camps. In an assessment of urban refugees in Jordan, it was shown that nearly half of female-headed households had no income and were dependent on donations (Usta and Masterson, 2013). These women face harassment, including offers of transactional sex and marriage (Sami et al., 2013). The Turkish Prime Ministry Disaster and Emergency Management Authority (AFAD), one of main institutions dealing with Syrian refugees in Turkey, indicates that almost one-third of Syrian refugee households in Turkey are headed by women or children.[2] AFAD reports that 80 percent of out-camp female Syrian refugees live in extreme poverty; they claim that they do not have a sufficient amount of food for the next week.[3]

Many of the women and girls who have been forcibly displaced have also been victims of rape and sexual violence. A report for the Women Under Siege Project recounts that "rape has been reportedly used widely as a tool of control, intimidation, and humiliation throughout the conflict. And its effects, while not always fatal, are creating a nation of traumatized survivors" (Wolfe, 2013: 1). . . . Clearly it is very difficult, or virtually impossible, to obtain accurate data on levels of sexual violence in the Syrian conflict because of the problems in accessing and reporting on the conflict, and also because victims of such violence often do not report for fear of stigma and marginalization. However, these reports tend to support the idea that sexual violence is a huge problem in this conflict. . . . One

researcher who visited Syrian refugees in Lebanon to assess their health needs reports that:

> Here, there are no viable comprehensive medical options for survivors of rape. Considered taboo and seen as a family issue, rape survivors are left with nowhere to go to seek clinical care. Life-saving treatments to prevent HIV, unwanted pregnancy, or sexually transmitted infections require immediate action, such as the limited window of 72h for HIV post-exposure prophylaxis. This lack of access to care has emerged as a humanitarian crisis all of its own. (Ouyang, 2013: 2165)

A further threat to the security of young women and girls is posed by the practice of early or forced marriage which, reports have shown, is common in Syrian refugee camps across the region. The reasons for this . . . are complex. For some families it provides a form of security for their daughters in that they believe marriage will protect them from sexual violence and assault from other men. Marrying their daughters can be seen as a way of protecting their family honor, and girls who have been victims of rape or sexual violence inside Syria may be married after they become refugees in order to save the family honor. For other parents who do not believe that they will live long enough to protect their daughters, marriage is a way of making sure that the daughter will be provided for after the death of her parents (Charles and Denman, 2013).

For other families, marrying their daughters is a way of generating income in a situation where they have no other access to resources. The forced marriage may take place within refugee communities or with men from outside the refugee community in the host country. The "marriage" is often an informal marriage, with no real legal status, sometimes amounting to little more than forced prostitution. As one report recounts:

> In Jordan, hundreds of Syrian females have been affected by an informal trade that has sprung up since the start of the war in Syria, where men use "agents" to source Syrian refugees for sex. Often this is done under the guise of "marriage." (Sherlock and Malouf, cited in Jessen, 2013)

Another report describes how young Syrian women in Turkish border towns are marrying older men out of desperation and fear for their future. As most of these women do not have legal status in Turkey the marriages are not legally registered, thus leaving women without any protection or any rights if the couple separate, or if the husband dies (Letsch, 2014). One of the problems in dealing with this issue is that it is sometimes assumed that the practice of early marriage is a cultural practice that has been imported by the refugees from their rural communities in Syria. This assumption that certain forms of violence against women are "cultural" practices which cannot or should not be questioned, rather than the products of particular economic, social and political contexts, means that the practices in question are not properly addressed by those organizing interventions to protect refugees.

The legal measures relative to early, forced and polygamous marriages are developed within the immigration legislation of European countries for dealing with the practice of these marriages among refugee and migrant communities. The approach adopted is characterized by the conception of a "clash" between Western and non-Western cultures and victimization of "imperiled Muslim women"' by [their] own backward culture (Razack, 2004: 135–150). Feminist scholarship has criticized this approach and highlighted the fact that forced, early or polygamous marriages are based on imbalances concerning gender and sexuality rather than simply being a reflection of culture (Dauvergne and Millbank, 2010: 57–67). Feminist authors point out that the answer lies in the commitment to ensure women's sexual and social agency (Razack, 2004: 162) and demonstrate that otherwise legal measures for the prevention and prohibition of forced and polygamous marriages create profound negative consequences for the immigrant women they purport to protect (Eichenberger, 2012: 1085 and 1110).

The Syrian refugee crisis also highlights another gendered dimension of displacement and forced migration which is sometimes overlooked, namely, the vulnerability of young men to forced recruitment, and the difficulties that these young men may face in fleeing forced recruitment and being recognized as refugees. In March 2012 the Syrian Government banned all men between the ages of eighteen and forty-two from traveling outside of the country without prior authorization (Davis et al., 2014). This ban has not prevented men from fleeing, but when they do flee they may find it harder to find protection because they are viewed as a threat by other governments. Some neighboring countries have imposed intermittent bans on the entry of young Syrian men, especially when they are not accompanied by family. "This discrimination against men traveling alone derives from the premise that single men and boys visibly detached from a family unit pose a threat to security, whereas men who function as fathers, sons, brothers and/or husbands do not" (Davis et al., 2014). This type of gendered perception may serve to increase the vulnerability of these single men, who are forced to become illegal residents in the host country and who, in addition, may find themselves last on the list for humanitarian aid, behind those deemed more "vulnerable" by the international organizations and aid agencies. Single men may not be allocated housing in refugee camps, as they are not seen as a priority, which further increases their insecurity. As Carpenter has argued in relation to other conflict situations, this false dichotomy between men as "combatants" and women as "civilians" merely acts to reinforce gender inequalities and can lead to increasing insecurities for men as well as women (Carpenter, 2005, 2006). In order to respond to the protection needs of both men and women, such dichotomous representations need to be overcome and the complexity of the situation of all refugees and IDPs needs to be recognized.

Just as men's vulnerability in some circumstances should be acknowledged, so too should women's active role and their agency in protecting and providing for families and communities displaced by the conflict. Within Syria there are few international NGOs who are physically present on the ground and able to distribute aid to the millions of displaced people. Because of this absence, women have frequently become active in distributing emergency assistance, food and medicine (Haddad, 2014). Many women IDPs have also found themselves as heads of household, and have thus had to depart from their traditional roles within the home and come out of the house to look for food and engage in activities that generate income and resources for their family and dependents. This change in roles has had a real impact on women's lives and for some it seems that it will be very difficult to return to previous gender roles and patterns when the conflict ends. As one woman interviewed by Haddad says, the conflict has "turned everything on its head." She continues: "I can never go back to doing what I did before; I can never be so meek and ordinary" (quoted in Haddad, 2014: 46).

The Refugee "Crisis" in Europe

In 2015 over one million refugees[4] arrived in Europe, seeking protection from armed conflict and violence in Syria and other countries of origin. As the EU had previously made it more and more difficult to arrive in Europe across a land border, the majority of these migrants arrived by sea and many lost their lives in the process. The huge numbers of arrivals on the coasts of Italy, and principally, of Greece, has led the EU to label this a migration "crisis." The influx of migrants from 2015 onwards is not the first time that European leaders have labeled migration as a crisis, and indeed, the term "crisis" was already employed in 2011 when migration increased following the "Arab Spring" uprisings (Jeandesboz and Pallister-Wilkins, 2014). The use of the term "crisis" may seem banal, but we would argue that this labeling is serving a powerful political and symbolic purpose and, as Edelman has argued, signals a claim that this situation is "different from the political and social issues we routinely confront" and that it came about for reasons outside of the control of political leaders (Edelman, 1977: 44). In the current situation, EU leaders have repeatedly stressed the unprecedented nature of the flows of refugees trying to reach the EU, and the way that the causes of migration are "out of their hands." They have invoked crisis to justify exceptional measures such as the closing of borders or mass return of migrants to Turkey, which can be seen as contrary to international and European law.

This crisis labeling has served to reinforce an ongoing process of securitization of migration to the EU, and at the same time to raise calls and pressure for a humanitarian (rather than a mainly political) response to the migration. In fact, we could argue that the labeling of the current migration flows as a "crisis" has served the interests of political leaders in EU member states and EU institutions by diverting attention away from their failures to find any real political solutions to this problem and focusing attention on the humanitarian emergency of migration and the increasingly insecure, dangerous and insanitary conditions in which migrants are living (and dying) in their attempts to reach the EU. . . .

The current European migration "crisis" is not new and has not developed out of nowhere. It is the culmination and combination of, on the one hand, the growing restriction of legal channels of migration to Europe and securitization of European borders (de Haas, 2007; Lutterbeck, 2009) and, on the other hand, huge instability and conflict in certain areas of the Middle East and Africa, in particular Syria, which are causing more and more desperate people to flee their countries and seek protection in Europe. While some European leaders have been quick to point to the existence of trafficking and smuggling gangs as the cause of the increased numbers of migrants attempting to cross the Aegean and Mediterranean, it can in fact be argued that these traffickers and smugglers are only gaining more work as the regular and safer routes to Europe are progressively blocked, leading migrants to take riskier journeys and to pay more to do so. As EU countries have increasingly tried to restrict entry through more regular means, and have closed down previous routes of "irregular" migration, migrants who are trying to reach Europe have been forced to find new and more perilous routes. As Lutterbeck points out: "Plugging one hole in the EU perimeter quickly leads to enhanced pressure on other parts of its external borders" (Lutterbeck, 2009: 123).

Migration, in particular "illegal" or irregular migration, has been constructed as a security issue in Europe for many years with migrants portrayed as posing an economic threat—a threat to European social cohesion and European "values" and, more recently, a terrorist threat. This supposed security threat has justified the use of increasingly drastic measures to limit migration and has led to attempts to create regional policies and frameworks for migration control. Within this context of securitization, migration control has become one of the strategic priorities of the EU's external relations and European policy-makers have shown increasing concern with trying to stem flows of migrants across the Mediterranean and, more recently, the Aegean.

In the early and mid-2000s the major concern of European policy-makers was migrants arriving across the Mediterranean from sub-Saharan Africa and landing in the Canary Islands, Sicily or Malta. Already back in 2007 the European Commission argued in a strategy paper that it was vital to deal with migratory pressures in the Mediterranean, pointing out that: "The events in Lampedusa, Ceuta and Melilla, the Canary Islands or in the Maltese and Greek waters concretely illustrate the increasing migratory pressure from Africa which the EU is confronted with" (European Commission, 2007).

The outbreak of conflict in Syria has magnified migratory pressures as millions of Syrians have been displaced beyond their own borders and are trying to reach the EU. Faced with the scale of the refugee population in Syria and its neighboring countries, there have been many criticisms of the EU's failure to do enough to support neighboring states and to offer protection to those seeking to reach Europe (Fargues and Fandrich, 2012). As the numbers arriving increase, more and more EU member states are closing their borders and refusing to take any further refugees, while attempts at regional resettlement agreements have been largely unsuccessful. Migrants are also arriving in large numbers from other areas where conflict is ongoing such as Afghanistan, Iraq, Iran, Somalia and Eritrea. On 23 April 2015 the European Council held a special meeting in response to the crisis situation in the Mediterranean during which they acknowledged that the situation has become a "tragedy" and promised to take measures including strengthening the EU's presence at sea, fighting against traffickers, preventing illegal migration flows and reinforcing international solidarity and responsibility.[5] The EU's approach has been heavily criticized, however, by human rights groups and migrant support groups because of its focus on repression of trafficking and prevention of illegal migration rather than on protecting the rights and lives of migrants who are desperate to reach Europe (Giuffre and Costello, 2015). In principle, a plan has been agreed under which each EU state should resettle a certain number of Syrian refugees, but this plan has met with a negative response from some of the Eastern European member states, and even where member states have agreed to the plan

the numbers actually resettled so far have been minimal. The failure of the EU to agree on and implement regional plans or policies for facilitating the legal migration of refugees and organizing resettlement has increased the insecurities and dangers of refugees' journeys—insecurities which may take specific forms for women. . . .

All of these developments in EU policy seem to demonstrate a failure to engage with how best to ensure the security and protection of refugees fleeing conflict, and a prioritization of the EU's perceived security and political interests through increasing investment in border control. The impacts of the security politics on refugees and the ways in which they have affected individuals have been under-explored. More specifically, there have been few studies which address the gendered impacts of these policies. This book hopes to redress this balance somewhat by considering how the experiences of individual refugees—women, men, LGBTI people—have been affected by these policy decisions, and how their security has been threatened by attempts to close EU borders.

Gender and Forced Migration

Gender was for a long time invisible in academic research on forced migration and refugees. Indra, for example, describes the way in which in early academic research on refugees gender was either not mentioned at all or else was considered as "just another variable like age or occupation. . . Women's issues were still not well-publicized 'refugee problems,' and so little academic research on women was produced" (Indra, 1989). This situation has changed in the last twenty years or so with the emergence of a much greater body of research that considers gender as a primary factor of analysis. This research has led to studies of the operation of gender in conflicts that create refugees and in refugee camps (Indra, 1999; Hyndman, 2000, 2004; Giles et al., 2003; Giles and Hyndman, 2004); these studies combine with feminist investigations in international relations (Enloe, 1989, 1993, 2000; Whitworth, 1997; Baines, 2004) to provide us with insights into the experiences of gender among refugees and the internally displaced, and into the ways in which international organizations such as the UNHCR have sought to respond to the needs of "refugee women" and refugee LGBTI. These studies tend to show that while the UNHCR and other international organizations and NGOs have adopted gender mainstreaming as a policy commitment, in practice gender issues are often still ignored. Other studies have examined the ways in which gender issues may or may not be integrated into the 1951 Refugee Convention and its application in various states, and thus how those claiming protection on the basis of gender-related persecutions they have suffered may or may not be protected (Spijkerboer, 2000, 2013; Crawley, 2001; Freedman, 2008, 2010, 2015; Arbel et al., 2014). Although there has been progress in recognizing some forms of gender-related persecution under national asylum laws, women and LGBTI asylum seekers still face specific obstacles in obtaining protection as refugees.

NOTES

1. For . . . figures on Syrian refugees see UNHCR, Syrian Regional Refugee Response, http://data.unhcr.org/syrianrefugees/regional.php.
2. Prime Ministry Disaster and Emergency Management Authority, "Syrian Women in Turkey 2014," Ankara.
3. Ibid.
4. There has been much debate among politicians and in the media as to whether people entering (or attempting to enter) Europe in the current "crisis" should be referred to as migrants or as refugees. While some argue that they cannot be correctly called refugees as they have not as yet obtained official refugee status from the UNHCR or from one of the EU member states, others point to the fact that they have been forced to flee from their home countries because of conflict and persecution, and are thus de facto refugees.
5. European Council Statement, 23 April 2015, www.consilium.europa.eu/en/press/press-releases/2015/04/23-special-euco-statement.

REFERENCES

Amnesty International (2015) *The Global Refugee Crisis: A Conspiracy of Neglect.* Available at www.amnestyusa.org/sites/default/files/p4575_global_refugee_crisis_syria.pdf.

Amnesty International (2016) "Turkey: Illegal Mass Returns of Syrian Refugees Expose Fatal Flaws in EU-Turkey Deal." Available at www.amnesty.org/en/press-releases/2016/04/turkey-illegal-mass-returns-of-syrian-refugees-expose-fatal-flaws-in-eu-turkey-deal/.

Arbel, E., Dauvergne, C. and Millbank, J. (eds) (2014) *Gender in Refugee Law: From the Margins to the Centre,* Abingdon, UK: Routledge.

Baines, E. (2004) *Vulnerable Bodies: Gender, the UN and the Global Refugee Crisis,* Alder-shot, UK: Ashgate.

Carpenter, C. (2005) *Innocent Women and Children: Gender Norms and the Protection of Civilians,* Alder-shot, UK: Ashgate.

Carpenter, C. (2006) "Recognizing Gender-Based Violence Against Civilian Men and Boys in Conflict Situations," *Security Dialogue,* 37(1): 83–103.

Charles, L. and Denman, K. (2013) "Syrian and Palestinian Refugees in Lebanon: The Plight of Women and Children," *Journal of International Women's Studies,* 14(5): 95–111.

Crawley, H. (2001), *Refugees and Gender: Law and Process,* Bristol, UK: Jordan Publishing.

Dauvergne, C. and Millbank, J. (2010) "Forced Marriage as a Harm in Domestic and International Law," *Modern Law Review,* 73: 57–88.

Davis, R., Taylor, A. and Murphy, E. (2014) "Gender, Conscription and Protection and the War in Syria," *Forced Migration Review,* 47: 35–39.

de Haas, H. (2007) "The Myth of Invasion: Irregular Migration from West Africa to the Maghreb and the European Union," International Migration Institute, University of Oxford.

Edelman, M. (1977) *Constructing the Political Spectacle,* Chicago, IL: University of Chicago Press.

Eichenberger, S.L. (2012) "When for Better is for Worse: Immigration Law's Gendered Impact on Foreign Polygamous Marriage," *Duke Law Journal,* 61: 1067–1110.

Enloe, C. (1989) *Bananas, Beaches and Bases: Making Feminist Sense of International Politics,* Berkeley, CA: University of California Press.

Enloe, C. (1993) *The Morning After: Sexual Politics at the End of the Cold War,* Berkeley, CA: University of California Press.

Enloe, C. (2000) *Maneuvers: The International Politics of Militarizing Women's Lives,* Berkeley, CA: University of California Press.

European Commission (2007) "Strategy Paper for the Thematic Program of Cooperation with Third Countries in the Areas of Migration and Asylum," European Commission, Brussels.

Fargues, P. and Fandrich, C. (2012) *The European Response to the Syrian Refugee Crisis: What Next?* Florence: European University Institute.

Freedman, J. (2008) "Women's Right to Asylum: Protecting the Rights of Female Asylum Seekers in Europe?," *Human Rights Review*, 9(4): 413–433.

Freedman, J. (2010) "Mainstreaming Gender in Refugee Protection," *Cambridge Review of International Affairs*, 23(4): 589–607.

Freedman, J. (2015) *Gendering the International Asylum and Refugee Debate*, 2nd edn, Basingstoke, UK: Palgrave Macmillan.

Giles, W. and Hyndman, J. (eds) (2004) *Sites of Violence: Gender and Conflict Zones*, Berkeley, CA: University of California Press.

Giles, W.M., Kora, M., Kneževi, D. and Papi, Z. (2003), *Feminists under Fire: Exchanges across War Zones*, Toronto: Between the Lines.

Giuffre, M. and Costello, C. (2015) "'Tragedy' and Responsibility in the Mediterranean," *openDemocracy*, 27 April 2015. Available at www.opendemocracy.net/can-europe-make-it/mariagiulia-giuffr%C3%A9-cathryn-costello/crocodile-tears-tragedy-and-responsibility-i.

Haddad, Z. (2014) "How the Crisis is Altering Women's Roles in Syria," *Forced Migration Review*, 47: 46–50.

Human Rights Watch (2015) "Turkey: Syrians Pushed Back at the Border: Closures Force Dangerous Crossings with Smugglers." Available at www.hrw.org/news/2015/11/23/turkey-syrians-pushed-back-border

Human Rights Watch (2016) "Turkey: Open Border to Displaced Syrians Shelled by Government: No Escape for Thousands Fleeing Attacks on Border Camps." Available at www.hrw.org/news/2016/04/20/turkey-open-border-displaced-syrians-shelled-government.

Hyndman, J. (2000) *Managing Displacement: Refugees and the Politics of Humanitarianism*, Minneapolis, MN: University of Minnesota Press.

Hyndman, J. (2004) "Refugee Camps as Conflict Zones: The Politics of Gender," in W. Giles and J. Hyndman (eds), *Sites of Violence: Gender and Conflict Zones*, Berkeley, CA: University of California Press, 193–213.

Indra, D.M. (1989) "Ethnic Human Rights and Feminist Theory: Gender Implications for Refugee Studies and Practice," *Journal of Refugee Studies* 2(2): 221–242.

Indra, D.M. (1999) *Engendering Forced Migration: Theory and Practice*, New York and Oxford: Berghahn.

Jeandesboz, J. and Pallister-Wilkins, P. (2014) "Crisis, Enforcement and Control at the EU Borders," in A. Lindley (ed.), *Crisis and Migration:* *Critical Perspectives*, London and New York: Routledge, 115–135.

Jessen, A. (2013) "The Government of Turkey and Syrian Refugees: A Gender Assessment of Humanitarian Assistance Programming," Georgetown Institute for Women, Peace and Security, Washington, DC.

Letsch, C. (2014) "Syria's Refugees: Fears of Abuse Grow as Turkish Men Snap up Wives," *The Guardian*, 8 September 2014.

Lutterbeck, D. (2009) "From Blame Game to Cooperation: Coping with the 'Migration Crisis' in the Central Mediterranean," *Border Politics*, 2009: 36–39.

Masterson, A.R. (2012) *Assessment of Reproductive Health and Gender-Based Violence among Displaced Syrian Women in Lebanon*, Beirut: UNFPA.

Ouyang, H. (2013) "Syrian Refugees and Sexual Violence," *The Lancet*, 381: 2165–2166.

Razack, S. (2004) "Imperiled Muslim Women, Dangerous Muslim Men and Civilized Europeans: Legal and Social Responses to Forced Marriages," *Feminist Legal Studies* 12: 129–174.

Sami, S., Williams, H., Krause, S., Onyango, M., Burton, A. and Tomczyk, B. (2013) "Responding to the Syrian Crisis: The Needs of Women and Girls," *The Lancet*, 383: 1179–1181.

Spijkerboer, T. (2000) *Gender and Refugee Status*, Aldershot, UK: Ashgate.

Spijkerboer, T. (2013) *Fleeing Homophobia: Sexual Orientation, Gender Identity and Asylum*, New York and London: Routledge.

UNFPA (2014) "Women and Girls in the Syria Crisis," UNFPA, Amman.

Usta, J. and Masterson, A.R. (2013) "Assessment of Reproductive Health and Gender-Based Violence among Displaced Syrian Women in Lebanon," Geneva: UNHCR.

Whitworth, S. (1997) *Feminism and International Relations: Towards a Political Economy of Gender in Interstate and Non-Governmental Institutions*, Basingstoke, UK: Palgrave Macmillan.

Wolfe, L. (2013) "Syria has a Massive Rape Crisis," Women Under Siege Project, New York, 3 April 2013.

Women's Refugee Commission (2014) "Unpacking Gender: The Humanitarian Response to the Syrian Refugee Crisis in Jordan," Women's Refugee Commission, New York.

Zetter, R. and Ruaudel, H. (2014) "Development and Protection Challenges of the Syrian Refugee Crisis," *Forced Migration Review*, 47: 6–11.

MILITARISM, CONFLICT AND WOMEN'S ACTIVISM IN THE GLOBAL ERA: CHALLENGES AND PROSPECTS FOR WOMEN IN THREE WEST AFRICAN CONTEXTS (2012)

Amina Mama is Professor of Gender, Sexuality, and Women's Studies at the University of California-Davis. She led the establishment of the University of Cape Town's African Gender Institute as a continental resource for transformative scholarship bringing together feminist theory and activism (1999–2009). She is a founding editor of the journal *Feminist Africa*, has published widely, and is committed to strengthening activism and activist research in African contexts.

Margo Okazawa-Rey is Barbara Lee Distinguished Chair in Women's Leadership and Visiting Professor of Women, Gender, and Sexuality Studies and of Public Policy at Mills College, Oakland, California. Also, she is Professor Emerita at San Francisco State University. Recent publications are "No Freedom without Connections: Envisioning Sustainable Feminist Solidarities" (2018) in *Feminist Freedom Warriors*, and *Between a Rock and Hard Place: Southeast Asian Women Confront Extractivism, Militarism, and Religious Fundamentalisms* (2018).

The real security need for Africans is not military security but social security, security against poverty, ignorance, anxiety and fear, disease and famine, against arbitrary power and exploitation; security against those things which render democracy improbable in Africa.

(AKE, 2000: 147)

Historical Context: How Militarism Has Underdeveloped Africa[1]

Africa's modern history is deeply marked by the history of colonization, a project that relied directly and indirectly on the military superiority of the colonizers. The military might of imperial and colonial armies was buttressed by a far-reaching array of technologies of governance, from brutal forced labor and taxation systems to sophisticated psychological and cultural strategies. These strategies worked together to create complex tapestries of consent and coercion, terrorizing local populations and orchestrating complicity (see, e.g., Lazreg (2009) on Algeria during French colonialism;

Elkins (2005) on British colonialism in Kenya; Hochschild (1999) on the Belgian occupation of the Congo; and Mamdani (2001) on Rwanda). These examples illustrate how colonial regimes relied on military force, deployed along with a formidable array of political, economic and cultural technologies of violence, thus militarizing the societies they conquered and governed in ways that extended far beyond the barracks, into the very fabric of peoples' lives. . . .

During the first decades of independence (1950s–1990s), which overlap with the Cold War era, Africa was caught up in the politics of East versus West. Both sides provided massive military assistance driven by their strategic interests (Schroeder and Lamb, 2006). Throughout the 1990s, in one estimate, the US sold over $1.5 billion worth of weaponry to Africa, with many of the top buyers—Liberia, Somalia, Sudan and the Democratic Republic of the Congo (DRC)—holding the dubious distinction of violence, instability and economic collapse (Hartung and Moix, 2000). It is ironic that some of the Western governments expressing support for development and democratization, such as

Britain, France and particularly the US, have been implicated in providing military support to some of the region's most dictatorial regimes. As Hartung and Moix note:

> From 1991–1995, the US provided military assistance to 50 countries in Africa, 94 percent of the nations on the continent. Between 1991–1998, US weapons and training deliveries to Africa totaled more than $227 million. Because many of the recipient countries remain some of the world's poorest, the US government provided around $87 million in foreign military financing loans to cover the costs, increasing the debt burden that is already suffocating the continent. These loans, accrued while corrupt dictators were serving as US clients, have further contributed to the economic hardships of these nations by saddling them with unproductive military debt. (Hartung and Moix, 2000) . . .

Although the amount of money spent on arming the continent is relatively small compared with other regions, the consequences and devastation caused are incalculable. The political consequence has been that much of the continent emerged from colonial rule to remain imbued with a patriarchal militarist logic that is authoritarian and anti-democratic. The plethora of conflicts that have taken place in postcolonial Africa and the high political, economic and cultural costs of military rule provide good grounds for arguing that African militarism has generated more insecurity than security, often terrorizing rather than protecting local populations, dominating the political sphere, blurring the boundaries between civilian and military, and thereby undermining all non-military forms of political and institutional authority and accountability. More broadly, militarism is conceptualized as an extreme variant of patriarchy, a gendered regime characterized by discourses and practices that subordinate and oppress women, as well as non-dominant men, reinforcing hierarchies of class, gender, race and ethnicity, and in some contexts caste, religion and location. Lutz describes the ways in which militarism becomes embedded and normalized in a society and highlights its broader, socially divisive effects:

> [T]he contradictory and tense social process in which civil society organizes itself for the production of violence . . . This process involves an intensification of the labor and resources allocated to military purposes, including the shaping of other institutions in synchrony with military goals. Militarization is simultaneously a discursive process, involving a shift in general societal beliefs and values in ways necessary to legitimate the use of force, the organization of large standing armies and their leaders, and the higher taxes or tribute used to pay for them. Militarization is intimately connected to the less visible deformation of human potentials into the hierarchies of race, class, gender, and sexuality, and to the shaping of national histories in ways that glorify and legitimate military action. (Lutz, 2002: 5)

. . . In seeking to address militarism as a gendered and gendering phenomenon, feminist scholars have critically engaged with its more enduring cultural, ideological, political and economic aspects, as well as the gendered nature of military institutions. A key argument pursued in this article is that these more enduring and gendered features precede the explicit emergence of military regimes and conflicts, and persist long after "peace" has been officially declared. . . . The fact is that male-dominated security institutions and military forces dominate the post-conflict policy landscape, with clear implications for women's prospects. In addition to national armies and various rebel forces, the West African region has seen the involvement of the Economic Community of West Africa's Monitoring Group (ECOMOG) forces, the United Nation's peacekeeping forces and a plethora of foreign military advisors. The question is whether conventional security-centered strategies can actually lead to demilitarization or to genuine security. There is now evidence that, for all the good that they may do in vanquishing local military forces involved in conflicts, the very forces deployed to quell unrest and secure conflict areas become participants in the war economy. They are also implicated in abusing and exploiting women in ways that resemble the actions of the forces they are mandated to control (Higate and Henry, 2004; Defeis, 2008). . . .

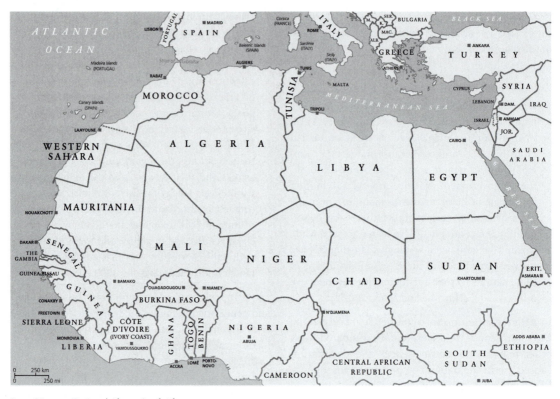

Peter Hermes Furian / Alamy Stock Photo

Conceptualizing Postcolonial Militarism in Africa

In this section, we review some key contributions to the theorization of postcolonial militarism in Africa—as manifest in many undemocratic regimes and armed conflicts. Mkandawire (2009) examines the rebel movements that have been the major actors in Africa's postcolonial conflicts, identifying failures of the political system to manage social pluralism, and failed decolonization processes as key sources of conflict, along with the effects of two decades of economic crisis worsened by globalized neoliberal economic policies, particularly externally imposed structural adjustment programs. He argues that these have put extreme pressure on the body politic by exacerbating the gaps between the *nouveau riche* political class and the impoverished majorities, creating a strong sense of relative deprivation and giving rise to intense contestations over the spoils of the nation state, most of which differ

profoundly from the anti-colonial liberation wars that preceded independence. According to Mkandawire, the armed forces are often made up of horizontally dispersed, roving bands that operate at great cost to the communities they pass through, acting more as predators than as the liberators they sometimes claim to be. The modes of violence used to pursue their objectives include attacking and terrorizing civilian populations who are considered part of the problem. To this we would add the horrific sexual violence—the widespread and systematic rape and assault of women and girls—along with mutilation and massacre of civilians. . . .

Although international relations theorist Mary Kaldor's (1999) work does not focus on Africa, her depiction identifies several features of the kinds of wars we explore in this article.[2] Kaldor suggests that the end of the Cold War marked, in essence, the end of the old state-centered warfare, which we argue includes imperialist, colonial and national liberation wars. She proposes that "new wars" differ from their state-centered precursors with respect to the manner of military organization, as well as in the economic and cultural features of wars. Kaldor emphasizes the profound changes in how armed forces are organized and conflicts are fought, attributing these to the technological developments in information, communication and transportation that have led to "increasing interconnectedness, the shrinking of distance and time." She observes that the protagonists in "new wars" are not conventional armies, but rather decentralized networks of state and non-state actors such as paramilitaries that include charismatic leaders, multinational corporations, warlords, terrorist cells, zealous volunteers, organized criminal groups, units of regular forces, mercenaries, private military contractors or other security service providers. These include the various transnational actors who appear in places where the authority of the state has weakened and the financing of war has become dispersed:

> Because these networks flourish in states where systems of taxation have collapsed and where little new wealth is being created, and where the wars destroy physical infrastructure, cut off trade and create a climate of insecurity that prohibits investment, they have to seek alternative, exploitative forms of financing. They raise money through loot and plunder, through illegal trading in drugs, illegal immigrants, cigarettes and alcohol, through "taxing" humanitarian assistance, through support from sympathetic states and through remittances from members of the networks. All of these types of economic activity are predatory and depend on an atmosphere of insecurity. Indeed, the new wars can be described as a central source of the globalized informal economy—the transnational criminal and semi-legal economy that represents the underside of globalization.[3] . . .

Militarism and war, in Africa and other regions, are also essential features of the globalized political economy. As many have convincingly argued, militarism and capitalism are inextricably linked (e.g.[,] Kirk and Okazawa-Rey, 2000; Staples, 2000; Enloe, 2007). Federici observes that "war is on the global agenda precisely because the new phase of

capitalist expansionism requires the destruction of any economic activity not subordinated to the logic of accumulation, and this is necessarily a violent process" (quoted in Mohanty, 2011: 77). Extraction of oil in Nigeria, diamonds in Sierra Leone and rubber in Liberia has fueled armed conflicts of unspeakable dimensions (Okonta and Douglas, 2001; Leavitt, 2005; Smillie, 2010). . . .

Peterson (2008) cogently delineates three main economic modes that specifically characterize war economies: coping, combat and criminal. We explore how each of these may be differently gendered through our consideration of women's livelihoods. Peterson identifies a "coping economy" as the first to emerge in situations of conflict . . . In relation to Africa, the coping economy may well be considered as a basic feature of long-term economic crises. Economic crises have preceded conflicts and are seen to increase the likelihood of violent outbreaks. It is the most obviously feminized aspect of the economy, as the work of finding and providing food, care and nurture of children and elders, as well as the men who fight, falls even more heavily to the women in crisis situations. . . . As we show in the next section, things become a great deal worse for women when their peacetime pursuit of farming, trading food and service provisioning are disrupted and made perilous, and when they are dislocated en masse, and thus forced to find new ways of sustaining their families and communities. In militarized and war-torn zones, women's livelihoods are altered, sometimes drastically and with enduring effects on their lives . . .

Peterson's "combat economy" coexists with the coping economy, but is somewhat more specific to preparation and execution of war, being run by combatants who directly supply and fund fighters and insurgent activities. This male-dominated fraternity is locally and transnationally networked. Moreover, she defines the "criminal economy" as opportunistic, run by profit-seeking entrepreneurs who take full advantage of economic deregulation and the collapse of the state to pursue their profitable businesses, in ruthless, free-market bliss. They include gunrunners, conflict entrepreneurs, traffickers of people and goods including sex traffickers, and money launderers—in short, all those who supply the combatants and other actors to make profit from conflict.

The feature of the "new wars" thesis that we find least compelling is the assertion that new wars are more identity based than their predecessors, on the basis that they are more about "identity-based claims to power" than the territorially based, geopolitical objectives of old. Depicting this as something new seems to neglect the central role of identity politics in conventional wars. . . . From a feminist perspective, it is clear that identities—typically heteronormative and ethnicized masculinities—have always been key to militarization, the creation of security apparatuses, war preparedness and war-making, something that Kaldor overlooks in her claim for the distinctiveness of "new wars."

Given the colonial experience referred to above and despite the fact they exhibit aspects of Kaldor's characterization of "new wars," we assert that the various manifestations of conflict in postcolonial Africa cannot really be considered new. . . . [M]any of Africa's conflicts have roots in the history of colonialism and manifest colonial-era dynamics of class, race, ethnicity and other social pluralities, all of which are gendered and augmented by militarism. Hence, we agree with other writers on the region's conflicts who refer to them as postcolonial conflicts, thus emphasizing the political and economic continuities with colonialism (Nhema and Zeleza, 2009). As feminists, we add a serious consideration of women's gender and positionality to this in our discussion of the three cases we consider below. In the remainder of this article, we develop these ideas through a discussion of the various ways in which women were involved in the secessionist civil war in Nigeria (1966–1970) and compare this to the more recent conflicts in Sierra Leone (1991–2002) and Liberia (1989–2003). We explore women's economic and military involvement, and how the manner in which they have organized across ethnic, religious and national borders in the pursuit of peace and security has changed between the time of the Nigerian war and the present.

Nigeria

The Nigerian civil war was one of the earliest of Africa's postcolonial conflicts. What began as a military coup soon turned into a bloody secessionist struggle that cost over a million lives and resulted in massive destruction and disruptions felt across the entire nation. Peace was declared in 1969, long before the existence of transitional justice mechanisms such as the International Criminal Court and truth and reconciliation commissions. Peace was not built so much as declared under the victorious Federal Government's slogan "No Victors, No Vanquished." However, the war was followed by over three decades of military rule . . .

. . . Uchendu (2007) offers the first substantive gendered research of the civil war era. Her investigation focuses on the Anioma region, located in today's Delta State, in the oil-rich Niger Delta. Although the Anioma area was not included in the secessionist demarcation of the Biafra Republic, the Biafran forces occupied it as they headed for the capital Lagos. It then became the site of bitter battles between the Biafran secessionist forces and the Federal forces until it was re-captured and occupied by the government forces for twenty months of the thirty-month conflict, with profound consequences for women's lives. It was the site of the notorious Asaba Massacre, on 7 October 1997, when Federal forces shot and killed over 500 Asaba men, after they had taken control of the area (Oputa Commission, 2002). Interviews with survivors conducted four decades later confirm that women were subjected to widespread killing, rape and harassment. Thousands fled and lived in the bush for weeks or even months. Those who did not flee into the forests found themselves living with fear of the Federal troops throughout the military occupation (Uchendu, 2007).

Combat

The Nigerian military has remained an exclusively masculine domain since its establishment in colonial times. The exclusion of women meant that there were no women fighters on the Federal side during the war. . . . Uchendu's interviews indicate that the few who fought on the Biafran side did so out of commitment to the cause, often after witnessing the killing of close kin or the destruction of their communities. Others followed family members. They were expected to perform support and servicing roles for the male soldiers, and very few received military training. As a result, there are only isolated examples of individual women becoming platoon leaders and being allowed to carry guns. Mostly, they simply were not recognized:

> Biafran army officers did not recognize [women's] zeal for service and did not treat them in the same manner as they did the regular soldiers. [U]nlike the soldiers the female militia members were not on the Biafran payroll and if found taking part in combat could be disarmed and sent back to the camp. (Uchendu, 2007: 122)

Women serving as self-appointed spies and volunteers were often able to elude capture and enjoy greater mobility than men, so both armies began to use them for high-risk intelligence work. . . .

Livelihoods

The war situation severely disrupted the farming and trading activities that constituted the major forms of livelihood, discussed here in relation to the concept of a coping economy, introduced above. Many thousands were dislocated and, as men either fled or were killed, women assumed many of the responsibilities previously held by men and adapted them as needed. Those who remained in their home areas survived by farming and trading across the lines at great risk, and by finding ways of coexisting with occupying forces. For women farmers, journeying to and from farms became extremely hazardous, leading them to adopt a strategy of traveling with caution and always in groups, covering their bodies and disguising themselves as old or disabled to avoid unwanted attention. Women learned to grow faster-yielding crops and to hide their produce from the soldiers. Those who lived by hiding in the bush learned to forage, to scavenge from abandoned villages and to beg from those they encountered in their wandering. Women who had never farmed learned to catch fish and small animals, or learned how to farm from others. They devised ways of preparing unfamiliar foods found in the bush or on abandoned farms, while women on the coasts learned to boil sea water to extract salt . . .

Trading was profoundly affected by the economic blockade the Federal forces imposed to sever supply lines to the East. Some local trading was able to continue, as this supplied the occupying forces with food and commodities. Many women also engaged in the dangerous business of illicit trading with communities on the other side of the lines, regularly changing the multiple land routes they used to avoid military skirmishes and evade detection by Federal forces. Long distances were covered, both on foot and by canoe, and young girls were often relied on to carry the loads to and from trading points. . . .

Women who stayed in the towns also survived in various ways. Some managed eating-houses and bars, brewed and distilled local gin, or provided indigenous medicinal and herbal remedies to the soldiers. As the war dragged on, a growing number of local women entered into liaisons with Federal soldiers, with some casting their lot as "companions" to soldiers until the end of the war, despite the social stigma. According to Uchendu (2007), many of these offered advantages to the women involved, such as enabling them to access basic necessities, and provided a degree of protection from other soldiers, enabling greater freedom of movement. In a few cases, women procured other women for sexual services for Federal soldiers. An uncounted number of women and girls were raped by Federal soldiers during the conquest. Women's continued vulnerability to sexual aggression during occupation led mothers to keep their adolescent daughters hidden indoors, but even mature women were not safe.

This limited available evidence confirms the emergence of a heavily feminized coping economy in which women traded across the frontlines and provided supplies and services to military forces on either side of the lines, often at great risk to themselves. Although stories abound of women becoming big contractors, locally referred to as *cash madams*, and making fortunes as a result of the war economy, there is little evidence to support this, although analyses of the post-war-era military rule confirm the emergence of [a] militarized elite who continued to amass wealth and power (Diamond et al., 1997; Mama, 1998, 1999; Adekanye, 1999). From the 1970s onwards, the oil economy was to prove extremely lucrative for this ruling minority, while the majority communities, especially those in the Niger Delta, have remained impoverished and have become increasingly militarized (Okonta and Douglas, 2001).

Women's Activism

There is little evidence that women engaged in organized peace activism during the Nigerian civil war. It is hard to ascertain whether this reflects the actuality, or merely the lack of gender studies during this period. The post-war period saw women mobilizing independently, and later joining forces with other pro-democracy movements to protest against military rule (Mba, 1982). By the 1990s, the movement for women in politics had grown, as women's political summits were held across the nation, calling for politics to be rid of violence and corruption, and launching a nationwide political agenda for Nigerian women (Gender and Action Development, 1996).

Sierra Leone

Sierra Leone's trajectory over a decade (1991–2002) of bloody conflict provides a second example of a postcolonial war. Here the conflict ensued after an extended period of military rule and economic instability, but it was started by an externally supported rebel movement, instigated and supported by the Liberian warlord Charles Taylor, and backed by Libyan government. The Revolutionary United Front (RUF) rebels, led by former Sierra Leone Army Corporal Foday Sankoh, entered Sierra Leone from Liberia in March 1991 in an attempted coup (Fanthorpe, 2003; Abdullah, 2004; Gberie, 2005).... Initially made up of a combination of Libyan-trained fighters and seasoned soldiers from Charles Taylor's army, the National Patriotic Front of Liberia, the RUF swelled its ranks by attracting large numbers of illiterate, unemployed and alienated men with few prospects for a better future in the poverty-stricken Sierra Leonean economy. Whatever ideological rhetoric Sankoh might have articulated in the beginning, it very rapidly degenerated into a bloody quest marked by unprecedented brutality . . as different parties battled to secure the lucrative diamond reserves that would sustain both the RUF and the Charles Taylor government through their connections to the international markets. This focus also led the poorly trained and underpaid soldiers of the national army to defect in increasing numbers as the situation deteriorated, complicated by other major militia formations that emerged later during the civil war (Abdullah, 2004). . . .

Combat

The conflict was massively destructive and notorious for the terror tactics—amputations, hangings, burnings and extraordinary levels of sexual violence—used to intimidate rural communities. . . . [B]y 1999 approximately 2 million people, nearly half the 4.5 million population, were displaced, either internally or as refugees in Guinea and Liberia. Overall, an estimated 50,000–75,000 people were killed and as many as 250,000 girls and women had been raped. The war involved Guinea and Cote d'Ivoire in addition to Liberia and Sierra Leone, as roving bands roamed across borders, and civilians fled from one camp to another trying to escape the violence. . .

The RUF rebels engaged in widespread conscription of children and women. Estimates suggest that 25–50 percent of the fighters were women and girls (McKay and Mazurana, 2004; MacKenzie, 2009), dramatically more than in the Nigerian war. Government forces negatively affected by the deteriorating situation and falling salaries also became a source of the violence against civilians, using and abusing women.

To what extent did women elect to become fighters? Researchers found that the vast majority of women and girls in all the fighting forces reported "abduction" or "forced recruitment" following raids and destruction of their communities.[4] Some women were involved in ceremonies and rituals, serving [as] spiritual leaders, medics, herbalists, spies and cooks, as well as frontline fighters and commanders. According to Mazurana and Carlson, among the girls 44 percent received military and weapons training from their commanders or captor "husbands," while many served as cooks (70 percent), porters (68 percent), carers for the sick and wounded (62 percent), "wives" (60 percent), food producers (44 percent), messengers between camps (40 percent), spies (22 percent), communication technicians (18 percent) and workers in diamond mines (14 percent).[5] Although many of these roles were fluid and situational, some women preferred the status of fighters, because it allowed them to protect themselves, to have access to food and other benefits, and to gain greater opportunities to escape than the captives. Within the RUF, child-wives were often left in command of the compounds, where they could exercise substantial authority, deciding who would fight, carrying out reconnaissance and raids for food and loot, selecting and sending troops and spies and generally supporting and advising their commander-husbands. They had their own weapons, and were often provided with personal bodyguards, usually groups of other girls and boys charged with their security. They commanded the Small Boys Units and Small Girls Units carrying out scouting and food-raiding, but some were also involved in brutal killings and mutilations. Surrogate "families" were formed in many of the camps, and it was through these that food and favor were distributed. Girls seeking protection from gang rape are reported to have tried to establish liaisons with commanders and boys. However, the vulnerability of even the most powerful of these girls and women persisted, as those who fell from favor were easily disposed of (Denov and Maclure, 2006; Coulter, 2009).

When ECOMOG peacekeepers arrived and attacked Freetown in March 1997 to retrieve it from the RUF/AFRC regime and restore President Kabbah, they too carried out widespread violations of desperate women and girls, at times coercing them into spying on enemy camps, a practice that led the RUF to target them for torture and murder during their attacks (Coulter, 2009).

Livelihoods

It is clear from the above discussion that participation in the various military and rebel forces became a significant livelihood option for women in Sierra Leone. Women who did not become fighters faced challenges very similar to those described above in relation to the Nigerian civil war, complicated by the multiplicity of military forces. As in the Nigerian civil war, women came to rely on farming and trading within and across borders under hazardous and unstable conditions. Sierra Leone also included mining areas that utilized forced labor in the arduous extraction of diamonds. Women traders played an important economic role, and organized to defend their interests, as illustrated by the fact that in 1996, right in the middle of the war, one group officially formed the Sierra Leone Market Women Association, to resist the discrimination they faced from their male colleagues (Solomon, 2005). During this time, some market women were filling the economic vacuum left by severely devastated infrastructure by engaging in high-risk trading. They smuggled goods across the Guinea–Sierra Leone border by collaborating with and bribing border police and customs officials, and they traded with various armed forces. Their entrepreneurship was based on complicated relationships with sets of cross-border and ethnic business partners that demanded extraordinary strategizing:

> Market women profiteers were also engaged in a thriving trade with rebels. Foodstuffs and petrol were smuggled from "safe" stores in Freetown to rebel-held areas in the provinces, on board trailers or big trucks, and sold to rebel commanders. In turn, they were either paid in cash (Leones or Dollars) or in kind, including jewelry, gold or diamonds. Back in Freetown, market women either sold their diamonds to Lebanese diamond dealers or smuggled the gems across the border to Guinea where they fetched higher prices enabling them to buy more foodstuffs. (Solomon, 2005: 10)

However, many women met their deaths in road accidents or ambushes, and sometimes their own customers would organize for them to be pursued after their business was ostensibly completed. The economic impact of the war worsened as the country faced UN sanctions placed in 1997.

In short, Sierra Leonean women and girls were drawn into all aspects of the war, in ways that exploited pre-war gender inequalities, worsening them sharply in ways that typify the coping economy. There is not much evidence that they were afforded any significant role in a criminal economy that was dominated by warlords engaged in diamond trafficking and weapons and drug trafficking. The poor social and material situation of thousands of girls, now women, many of whom bore children, remains a pressing problem to date. The information available suggests that women were being re-marginalized in the heavily gendered and narrowly prescribed DDR [demobilization, disarmament and reconstruction] process, despite the courageous roles they . . . played surviving, enabling the survival of others and brokering the eventual cessation of fighting (MARWOPNET/Isis-WICCE, 2009).

Women's Activism

Despite the appalling situation they endured, women from all classes and ethnic groups, and across borders, mobilized extensively to facilitate the ending of the war and build peace. Among the best-known examples are the Mano River Women's Peace Network (MARWOPNET), the Women's Movement for Peace, the Sierra Leone Women's Forum, the Network of Women Ministers and Parliamentarians, and the Sierra Leone Women's Movement for Peace. The various strategies they used included behind-the-scenes lobbying of warlords and political leaders, as well as organizing public rallies, demonstrations, and the provision of peace-making-related services such as civilian electoral education and training. As early as 1996, a delegation of women's groups led by Women Organized for a Morally Enlightened Nation pressured the military government to hold democratic elections. However, when the elections that brought President Kabbah to power were held, only five women were on the victorious party's list of sixty-eight candidates. In 1999, women played a leading role in the negotiations that led to the signing of the 1999 Lomé Peace Accord. Their insistence on inclusion of the RUF in a power-sharing arrangement was probably crucial to the deal, even though it was to be another three years before the end of the war was finally declared. The involvement of women in the Lomé process is reflected in several articles that called for attention to the victimization of women in the plans for rehabilitation and reconstruction.[6]

Liberia

Liberia has the dubious distinction of being the only nation in Africa founded by the USA. Like the British colony of Freetown in Sierra Leone, Monrovia was settled in 1816 by mixed-race free offspring of white slave-owners and former African slaves with the support of the American Colonization Society. After gaining independence from the Society in 1847, the Americo-Liberians constituted themselves as the elite, formed The True Whig Party, and monopolized power from independence until 1980. Liberian scholar Abayomi Karnga noted early in the twentieth century that:

> [T]he status divisions among the Liberians eventually evolved into a hierarchical caste system with four distinct orders. At the top were the Americo-Liberian officials, consisting largely of light-complexioned people of mixed Black and white ancestry [also known as "Mulattos"]. They were followed by darker skinned Americo-Liberians, consisting mostly of laborers and small farmers. Then came the recaptives [also known as "Congos"], the Africans who had been rescued by the US Navy while aboard US-bound slave ships and brought to Liberia. At the bottom of the hierarchy were the indigenous African Liberians. (Cited in Dennis, 2006: 1)

The subordinated indigenous African majority were not granted citizenship until 1904 and otherwise disenfranchised, and most have remained poor and marginalized.

The 1980 military coup led by Samuel Doe effectively destroyed the century-and-a-half-long oligarchic regime, as he was able to capitalize on the hostilities generated by the political, economic and social inequalities between the Americo-Liberians and the African Liberians. Doe's installation as the country's leader, first through the coup and later fraudulent national elections, did not effect the kinds of changes promised. Rather, he carried out his own reign of terror by introducing a form of ethnocide against indigenous ethnic groups other than his own, the Khran, and effectively created ethnic divisions, upon which Charles Taylor would rely in his assent to power (Pugel, 2007).

The civil war began when Charles Taylor with his forces entered Liberia from neighboring Cote d'Ivoire in 1989 and continued until 1996, only for fighting to resume from 1997 to 2003. As many as 250,000 Liberians lost their lives, and approximately one-third (800,000) of the 2.5 million population were displaced internally, became refugees in neighboring countries such as Ghana, or both.[7] Central government effectively ceased to function, and by 1995 seven major armed factions controlled the people and resources in the various regions (Dennis, 2006).

The Liberian conflict was also prolonged and catastrophic. The level of carnage and its spillover in the form of refugee camps in the neighboring countries, combined with the refusal of Liberia's traditional patron the USA to intervene, prompted ECOWAS (The Economic Community of West African States) to take action in 1990. ECOMOG troops became part of the conflict by allying themselves to various factions and joining in the looting and pillaging. Nonetheless, Nigerian government intervention eventually succeeded in bringing about peace and led to the Abuja II Peace Agreement being implemented in 1997.

ECOWAS and the international community hastily "resolved" matters. As a result of this haste, disarmament was not carried out, and Charles Taylor, the leading warlord in the conflict, was elected to power after running as the sole candidate in an election that could hardly be regarded as credible. He soon reneged on the agreement, taking absolute control, and ignoring the commitment to restructuring to bring about better ethnic representation, with the result that a second phase of war took place between 1997 and 2003. A new rebel formation, Liberians United for Reconstruction and Democracy (LURD), launched a military offensive against the Taylor regime from military outposts in neighboring Guinea. LURD gained control of large swathes of the North Liberia and, after being joined by the rebel Movement for Democracy in Liberia (MODEL) that had started from the southeast of the country, Taylor lost control of all but the capital Monrovia. The final onslaught took place in summer 2003, during which thousands of Liberians were killed on the streets and injured, and the population was further threatened by the collapse of food supplies and all services.

The conflict ravaged communities and led to widespread destruction and pervasive militarization including proliferation of small arms in the hands of the population. Post-conflict Liberia had the largest UN peacekeeping mission in the world (until the devastation of Haiti required a larger number), with approximately 10,000 uniformed personnel and another 2,000 non-uniformed ones making up United Nations Mission in Liberia.[8] On the basis of various reports gathered by

the International Rescue Committee, an estimated three-quarters of Liberian women between ages of 15–49 living in refugee camps in Sierra Leone were subjected to various forms of violence including random acts of sexual assault, mass rape, sexual slavery and exploitation that took place regardless of whether women remained in their communities or became displaced (cited in Omanyondo, 2005).

Combat

Estimates put the number of women fighters in Liberia at somewhere between 20 and 40 percent, with MODEL showing the highest proportion of women (Pugel, 2007). Here too there is evidence that most of the women in the armed groups were coerced into joining after experiences of trauma and gang rape (Isis-WICCE, 2008).[9] According to findings from a United Nations Development Program–sponsored study of ex-combatants participating in the DDR process, women combatants "served more in logistical roles than their male counterparts and were less likely to be injured while participating as an active member" (Pugel, 2007: 7). Occasional, sensationalized media reports portray women fighters as "worse than men" and "even crueler than men." However, it may well be that perceptions are exaggerated because women's violent behavior transgresses gender norms. The most well-known example is LURD's woman commander referred to as "Black Diamond[,]" who gained notoriety in the world media in 2003.[10] A victim of vicious gang rape in her teenage years, Colonel Black Diamond's unflinching aggressiveness clearly challenged Western stereotypes of women as victims. In fact, she headed the Women's Auxiliary Corps and commanded a group of young girls who played a major role in LURD's merciless final advance on Monrovia.

Both Utas (2005) and Fuest (2008) emphasize that women engage in multiple liaisons with men in their efforts to seek protection and survive. Most of those who acquired the status of fighters appear to have done so through their liaisons with male fighters. Their situation can be contrasted with that of girls and women who did not have the protection of guns or men, and therefore remained far more vulnerable. At the bottom of the war hierarchy were women prisoners, kept under horrendous conditions of confinement and multiply raped at the will of their captors, a great many of whom did not survive to tell of their experience.

Livelihoods

Traditionally, Liberian ruling society has been highly patriarchal, with the clear male domination of political, public and economic life complicated by ethnic and class factors. For example, Americo-Liberian women have been privileged socially, often being favored over African Liberian men, although remaining subordinate to Americo-Liberian men.

The few available sources on women's experience of the conflict years indicate a fluidity of roles similar to that described for Sierra Leone. Utas (2005) carried out an informative biographical study of a woman referred to as "Binta." He uses her example to challenge the assumptions of women as victims that have tended to prevail, observing that she displays a degree of "tactic agency," a term borrowed from Alcinda Honwana's (2007) groundbreaking study of child soldiers in Mozambique. Tactic agency is defined as a limited-level agency, somewhere between agency and victimhood. To illustrate, he details the complex social navigation that Binta engages in as she moves through the various locations and situations in which she finds herself during the course of the war: mistress, girlfriend, prisoner, multiple-rape victim, refugee, fighter and trader (Utas, 2005). He describes her actions—"girlfriending" and participating in the "loving business"[—]as motivated by multiple considerations that go beyond mere survival (Utas, 2005: 408). It seems that many of the women who survived the conflict in Liberia, not unlike those in Sierra Leone and in Nigeria four decades earlier, did so by navigating extremely hazardous environments and playing multiple roles that include engaging in transactional sexual relations with boyfriends and being co-wives, commanders, peacekeepers and humanitarian agency staff. The fact that some of these livelihood strategies are about more than mere survival blurs the boundary between the coping economy and the combat economy as women clearly move between the two,

in ways that display limited agency rather than passivity or victimhood.

Prior to the war, structural inequalities kept all but a small elite of Liberian women at the base of the formal economy, heavily reliant on farming, informal trading and other entrepreneurial activities that drew on extensive socio-economic networks. Also prior to the war, a growing proportion of urban women were acquiring land and property, and choosing to remain as heads of their own households, to take fuller advantage of economic opportunities (Fuest, 2008). The war years saw women take on many of the roles previously carried out by men, with reports of women making bricks, building and roofing houses, clearing farms, and trading. However, this was largely due to the high casuality rates and departure of men from the communities, rather than to a fundamental shift in gender relations and values. Indeed, the diminished options facing women in a war economy increased the involvement of women in sex work, and were thus likely to have worked against the emergence of a more equitable relation between the genders. . . .

Women's Activism

The Liberian conflict wrought devastation on the lives of many thousands of women, but it also provoked women to organize. Indeed, many of the women's groups that now exist were formed expressly to agitate for an end to the war, prevailing upon warlords and political leaders, in concerted actions all over Liberia, as well as in Nigeria and Ghana where the peace processes were hosted. Women's activism during the civil war was marked by two phases, reflecting the two phases of the war. During the early years of the war (1989–1996), a Monrovia-based group, Concerned Women of Liberia, made contact with women in territories held by warring factions and encouraged mediation, prayer and conflict-resolution techniques that drew on old traditions and new methods. The Christian Health Association of Liberia, comprising women health workers, provided support to refugee women, while the Abused Women and Girls program alongside lawyers from the Association of Female Lawyers of Liberia worked to provide support for women who had been raped. Numerous other women's groups, such as Women in Action for Liberia, and mixed groups with women in leadership, such as Special Emergency Life Food Program, maintained communication across community lines, distributed food and cared for the elderly and refugees in short, supporting affected communities in multiple ways.

The formation of the Liberian Women's Initiative (LWI) during the latter part of this period has been described as the "turning point" because it was "a movement not simply an organization or a coalition of organizations" that brought together a broader cross-section of women of Liberia, and hence becoming a more inclusive and stronger peace movement. The LWI went door to door, took to the streets and mobilized diverse groups of Liberian women, and, although not invited to the table, their work influenced the 1997 Abuja Peace Accord (AWPSG [African Women and Peace Support Committee], 2004: 17). . . .

The later years of the war (2000–2003) saw a second round of mobilization in which the Women's Peace Network (WIPNET), sometimes described as the "second generation" (AWPSG, 2004), steered the movement. They along with Women in Peace and Security Network-Africa and other partners responded to the prolonged crisis of 2003 by organizing more aggressively, setting off mass protests by thousands of women who wore white t-shirts and held sit-ins on the streets for many weeks. They were eventually able to present a petition for peace to President Taylor. Once the peace talks were in progress, WIPNET mobilized protests and advocacy to ensure the success of the talks. When the talks continued for weeks with no sign of a settlement, a large group blockaded the protagonists in their hotel to prevail upon the Nigerian and Ghanaian hosts to insist on progress. The women's sustained activism and its escalation during the peace talks, Charles Taylor's indictment for war crimes by the International Criminal Court during the talks, and the final major assault on Monrovia launched by LURD and MODEL together appear to have persuaded Taylor to accept asylum in Nigeria. The warring factions signed the peace agreement, and the war officially ended.

Discussion and Implications

Compelling theorizations regarding the dramatic changes that conflict has wrought on women's lives and livelihoods in all three contexts combine attention to material and to cultural features of conflict. Thus, Peterson's conceptualization of the "coping economy" is helpful because it invokes women's culturally ascribed roles in the care economy, transposing these onto the idea of the war economy. We have shown that women in all three countries have also been involved in the combat economy as fighters, commanders, heads of Small Girls Units, as well as the more conventional subordinate roles as porters, intelligence gathers, food providers, spies and "wives." To the extent that individual women moved beyond the survivalism characteristic of the coping economy, it was as beneficiaries of the combat economy, although through their highly precarious relations with powerful male combatants and whatever protection this could afford them. There is little evidence of women being significantly involved in the more lucrative and often illicit criminal economy. The profits of war, accrued through international networks trafficking in weapons, drugs and other commodities key to the war, remained dominated by male warlords and commanders. The fluidity of women's livelihood strategies and the role of sexuality and gender dynamics that are both economic and cultural are worth further study. . . .

The concept of a gendered war economy is thus analytically productive, but does not adequately attend to aspects that we have identified as key features of women's lives in militarized contexts. . . . The particular subjugation of women as sexual commodities is evident in both the war economy and the militarized culture of misogyny in which rape, trafficking, imprisonment and torture reach new extremes, affecting countless women and girls. Even these become normalized everyday occurrences that persist long after the cessation of hostilities. Yet there is evidence of immense courage, as women pursue limited options in a daily struggle to support their dependents, even where this requires them to rely on using their own bodies to negotiate their survival.

Women are far from passive . . . The material discussed here points to women's capacity for both tactical and strategic agency, where tactical agency refers to the individual negotiations of survival that occur even in the context of extreme disempowerment or overwhelmingly negative options. It sits in contrast to the more strategic forms of agency that are evident in the collective mobilization of Liberian and Sierra Leonean women into peace activism.

Overall, it is apparent that all the war situations discussed here bequeath immense political and social development challenges, many of which marginalize and subordinate women, and many of which have so far eluded policymakers. It highlights the need to consider the gendered economic and cultural distortions that precede and accompany violent conflict, as it is clear that these do not simply wither away once the fighting has stopped. . . . [T]he global rise of economic neoliberal policies that diminish regulation and constrain government services has facilitated the informal and illegal networks and systems of the criminal economy to gain ground . . . Today—in the context of continuing neoliberal globalization—it remains easier for illicit networks to proliferate and harder for states to control them. The power of the state is significantly diminished with regard to reconstruction and rehabilitation, as illustrated by the role of security corporations in post-conflict SSR [security sector reform] . . . The growing role of private corporations in the security sector poses new challenges to feminist movements seeking demilitarization. In all three countries, women's movements are more accustomed to lobbying publicly accountable state institutions than to taking action against corporations, yet it is clear that the state, even if it builds a new national army and police force that are under its command, no longer exercises the political or economic sovereignty that might once have been assumed. This suggests the need for women's movements to develop new strategies and methodologies. So far, these have included greater degrees of transnational networking, and taking international governance arenas much more seriously than before, but a great more needs to be done to strengthen women's capacities for new modes of activism in the West African sub-region.

Peace and Post-Conflict Prospects: When and What are "Peace" and "Post"?

We agree with those who argue that "war" and "peace" are not two discrete, opposite conditions and circumstances (Cockburn and Zarkov, 2002; Coulter, 2009). Rather, there are continuities that endure and become more or less visible, more or less salient, during different times and in various ways. Especially for women, the boundary between conflict and post-conflict is not so clearly demarcated. . . .

In the West African countries discussed, there are several important continuities between colonial and contemporary militarism, and these inform our preference for conceptualizing contemporary conflicts as postcolonial, rather than as "new" wars. These continuities include the following:

1. High civilian casualties, and extensive destruction and seizure of property, both reminiscent of the colonial punitive expeditions.
2. Misogynistic, militarized sexualities enacted through sexual violence, coercion and abuse with enduring effects on social and cultural fabric.
3. Local cultures and value systems replaced with a culture of violence that relies on gendered and ethnicized violence against dehumanized "others." Captives are often subject to torture and mutilation, and coerced into joining the perpetuation of violence and humiliation against others. The orchestration of collaboration was also a feature in the colonial contexts cited above.
4. The colonial capitalist economy of loot and plunder has evolved into today's late capitalist extraction of mineral wealth and other natural resources. Conflicts in former colonies discussed here have been facilitated and fueled by equally ruthless quests for oil (Nigeria), diamonds (Sierra Leone), rubber (Liberia) and other natural resources for sale on international markets. In colonial and contemporary contexts, transnational capitalist interests rely on tacit or overt state support, including legitimizing the use of modern-day private security contractors

alongside elite military and civilian collaborators. The externalized nature of corporate interests is given visual form in the brightly lit high-security compounds complete with exclusive facilities for largely foreign staff, bearing a strong resemblance to state military bases.

5. Establishment of a parallel criminal economy, with transactions between male-dominated international networks and cabals that connect across private and corporate interests.

By establishing these features as continuities and applying a feminist analysis, it is possible to recognize, as Coulter (2009: 8) suggests, the "significance of structural violence, long term oppression, and impoverishment" in the production of conflict and militarism. Thus, in essence, the prevailing notion of "peace" and "post-conflict" does not take adequate account of the multiple dimensions of insecurity characterizing women's lives.

Feminist Redefinition of Security: Whose Security?

Finally, our analysis underlines the importance of redefining security (Peterson, 1992; Tickner, 1992; Steans, 1998; Enloe, 2000; Olonisakin, 2007; Sjoberg, 2009).[11] Although feminist perspectives could provide the basis for potentially more transformative approaches to gender and security, their uptake in policy has been somewhat limited. At present, the key UN resolutions remain focused on adding women to security reform (UNSCR 1325), or on limited constructions of women as victims of male violence (UNSCR 1820, UNSCR 1888). . . . Militarized notions of security promise protection yet rely on institutionalizing fear and violence at all levels of society, thus creating and sustaining profound insecurity, especially among women. . . .

As numerous activists and scholars have long observed, insecurity characterizes the lives of women in Africa in many ways, key among which are women's exclusion from political arenas, denial of the exercise of full citizenship and the exploitation and invisibilization of their economic roles. All of these are significantly worsened by outbreaks of conflict. Restoring women to the unequal preconflict situation will not be a sufficient strategy, given the realities of gender inequality and injustice before. . . .

We take genuine security as being based on a respect for human life as a foundational principle of politics and economics. As such, it requires a comprehensive process of demilitarization, rather than mere reform of the security sector. The gender dynamics of militarism discussed here indicate that demilitarization will require no less than the transformation of the patriarchal gender relations. One effective way of achieving this is to strengthen women's movements in militarized zones. Feminist critical analysis applied to consideration of diverse examples offers valuable insights that can contribute to strengthening solidarities against global militarism. As Mohanty (2011) states, "an alternative vision of connectivity and solidarity requires building ethical, cross-border feminist solidarities that confront neoliberal militarization globally' (ibid.: 83). We remain compelled by the exciting possibilities for transnational feminist praxis in the global struggle for demilitarization and democratization.

NOTES

1. Walter Rodney's (1972) classic text was entitled "How Europe Underdeveloped Africa."
2. Kaldor, M. (2001) "Beyond militarism, arms races and arms control," Prepared for Nobel Peace Prize Centennial, available on SSRC website, http:// essays.ssrc.org/sept11/essays/kaldor.htm, last accessed June 2011.
3. Kaldor, M. (2001) "Beyond militarism, arms races and arms control," Prepared for Nobel Peace Prize Centennial, available on SSRC website, http:// essays.ssrc.org/sept11/essays/kaldor.htm, last accessed June 2011.
4. See Coulter (2009) and Mazurana, D. and Carlson, K. (2004) "From combat to community: women and girls of Sierra Leone," Women's International League for Peace and Freedom, http:// www.peacewomen.org/resources/Sierra_Leone/ sierraleoneindex.html, last accessed June 2009.
5. Mazurana, D. and Carlson, K. (2004) "From combat to community: women and girls of Sierra Leone," Women's International League for Peace

and Freedom, 12, http://www.peacewomen.org/resources/Sierra_Leone/sierraleoneindex.html, last accessed June 2009.

6. Lomé Peace Accord (1999), http://www.sierra-leone.org/lomeaccord.html, last accessed August 2011.

7. UNHCR (2006) *Refugees by the Numbers*, 2006 Edition, http://www.unher.org/basics/BASICS/3b028097c.html#Refugees, last accessed June 2011.

8. United Nations Security Council (2011) *Twenty-third progress report of the Secretary-General on the United Nations Mission in Liberia*, http://www.un.org/ga/search/view_doc.asp?symbol=S/2011/497, last accessed September 2011.

9. Amnesty International (2008) "Liberia: A Flawed Process that Discriminates Against Women and Girls," http://www.amnesty.org/en/library/info/AFR34/004/2008/en, last accessed June 2009.

10. See http://news.bbc.co.uk/2/hi/africa/3181529.stm and http://www.girlswithguns.org/news/news0008.htm.

11. Also see Clarke, Y. (2009) "Security sector reform in Africa: a lost opportunity to deconstruct militarized masculinities?" *Feminist Africa 10*, http://www.feministafrica.org, accessed June 2011.

REFERENCES

Abdullah, I. (2004) editor, *Between Democracy and Terror: The Sierra Leone Civil War*, Dakar: CODESRIA.

Adekanye, J.B. (1999) *The Retired Military as Emergent Power Factors in Nigeria*, Ibadan: Heineman.

African Women and Peace Support Committee (2004) *Liberian Women Peacemakers: Fighting for the Right to Be Seen, Heard, and Counted*, Trenton, NJ/Asmara, Eritrea: Africa World Press.

Ake, C. (2000) *The Feasibility of Democracy in Nigeria*, Dakar: CODESRIA.

Cockburn, C. and Zarkov, D. (2002) editors, *Postwar Moment: Militaries, Masculinities and International Peacekeeping*, London: Lawrence & Wishart.

Coulter, C. (2009) *Bush Wives and Girl Soldiers: Women's Lives through War and Peace in Sierra Leone*, Ithaca, NY: Cornell University Press.

Defeis, E.F. (2008) 'U.N. peacekeepers and sexual abuse and exploitation: an end to impunity' *Washington University Global Studies Law Review*, Vol. 7, No. 2: 185–214.

Dennis, P. (2006) *A Brief History of Liberia*, New York: The International Center for Transitional Justice.

Denov, M. and Maclure, P. (2006) 'Engaging the voices of girls in the aftermath of Sierra Leone's conflict: experiences and perspectives in a culture of violence' *Anthropologica*, Vol. 48, No. 1: 73–85.

Diamond, L., Kirk-Green, A. and Oyediran, O. (1997) editors, *Transition without End: Nigerian Politics and Civil Society under Babangida*, Boulder, CO/London: Lynne Rienner.

Elkins, C. (2005) *Imperial Reckoning: The Untold Story of Britain's Gulag in Kenya*, New York: Owl Books.

Enloe, C. (2000) *Maneuvers: The International Politics of Militarizing Women's Lives*, Berkeley, CA: University of California Press.

Enloe, C. (2007) *Globalization and Militarism: Feminists Make the Link*. Lanham, MD: Rowman & Littlefield.

Fanthorpe, R. (2003) *Humanitarian Aid in Post-war Sierra Leone: The Politics of Moral Economy*, London: Overseas Development Institute.

Fuest, V. (2008) '"This is the time to get in front": changing roles and opportunities for women in Liberia' *African Affairs*, Vol. 107, No. 427: 201–226.

Gberie, L. (2005) *A Dirty War in West Africa: The RUF and the Destruction of Sierra Leone*, Bloomington, IN: Indiana University Press.

Gender and Development Action (1996) *Report of the One-day Meeting of Nigerian Women on Women Democracy and Governance*. Lagos: Author.

Hartung, W.D. and Moix, B. (2000) *Deadly Legacy: U.S. Arms to Africa and the Congo War*, New York: World Policy Institute.

Higate, P. and Henry, M. (2004) 'Engendering (in)security in peace support operations' *Security Dialogue*, Vol. 35, No. 4: 481–498.

Hochschild, A. (1999) *King Leopold's Ghost: A Story of Greed, Terror, and Heroism in Colonial Africa*, New York: Mariner Books.

Honwana, A. (2007) *Child Soldiers in Africa: The Ethnography of Political Violence*, Philadelphia, PA: University of Pennsylvania Press.

Isis-WICCE (2008) *A Situation Analysis of the Women Survivors of the 1989–2003 Armed Conflict in Liberia*, Kampala: Isis-WICCE.

Kaldor, M. (1999) *New and Old Wars: Organized Violence in a Global Era*, Oxford: Blackwell.

Kirk, G. and Okazawa-Rey, M. (2000) editors, 'Neoliberalism, militarism, and armed conflict: an introduction' *Social Justice*, Vol. 27, No. 4: 1–17.

Lazreg, M. (2009) *Torture in the Twilight of Empire: From Algiers to Baghdad*, Princeton, NJ: Princeton University Press.

Leavitt, J. (2005) *The Evolution of Deadly Conflict in Liberia: From 'Paternaltarianism' to State Collapse*, Durham, NC: Carolina Academic Press.

Lutz, C. (2002) *Homefront: A Military City and the American 20th Century*, Boston, MA: Beacon Press.

MacKenzie, M. (2009) "Securitization and desecuritization: female soldiers and the reconstruction of women in post-conflict Sierra Leone" *Security Studies*, Vol. 18, No. 2: 241–261.

Mama, A. (1998) "Khaki in the family: gender discourses and militarism in Nigeria" *African Studies Review*, Vol. 41, No. 2: 1–18.

Mama, A. (1999) "Dissenting daughters? Gender politics and civil society in a militarized state" *CODESRIA Bulletin/Bulletin du CODESRIA*, No. 3/4: 29–36.

Mamdani, M. (2001) *When Victims Become Killers: Colonialism, Nativism and the Genocide in Rwanda*, Princeton, NJ: Princeton University Press.

MARWOPNET/Isis-WICCE (2009) *Sierra Leonean Women and Girls Experience of the Post Conflict Reconstruction Process*, Final Report, MARWOPNET/Isis-WICCE Documentation Project 2007–2009, Freetown, Sierra Leone.

Mba, N. (1982) *Nigerian Women Mobilized: Women's Political Activity in Southern Nigeria, 1900–1965*, Berkeley, CA: University of California Institute of Internaitonal Studies.

McKay, S. and Mazurana, D. (2004) *Where are the Girls? Girls in Fighting Forces in Northern Uganda, Sierra Leone and Mozambique: Their Lives during and after War*, Ottawa: IDRC.

Mkandawire, T. (2009) "The terrible toll of postcolonial rebel movements: towards an explanation" in Nhema, A. and Zeleza, P.T. (2009) editors, *The Roots of African Conflicts: The Causes and the Costs*, Athens, OH: Ohio University Press/Oxford: James Currey co-publishers.

Mohanty, C.T. (2011) "Imperial democracies, militarized zones, feminist engagements" *Economic & Political Weekly*, Vol. xlvi, No. 13: 76–84.

Nhema, A., and Zeleza, P.T. (2009) editors, *The Roots of African Conflicts: The Causes and the Costs*, Athens, OH: Ohio University Press/Oxford: James Currey co-publishers.

Okonta, I. and Douglas, O. (2001) *Where Vultures Feast: Shell, Human Rights and Oil*, San Francisco, CA: Sierra Club Books.

Olonisakin, F. (2007) "Pan-African approaches to civilian control and defense of democracy" in Ghebali, V.-Y. and Lambert, A. (2007) editors, *Democratic Governance of the Security Sector beyond the OSCE Region: Regional Approaches in Africa and the Americas*, Geneva: DCAF.

Omanyondo, M.-C. (2005) *SGBV and Health Facility Needs Assessment (Lofa, Nimba, Grand Gedeh And Grand Bassa Counties) Liberia*. Report for the World Health Organization (WHO). Monrovia: WHO.

Oputa Commission (2002) *HRVIC Report: Conclusions and Recommendations*, Abuja: Human Rights Violations Investigation Commission.

Peterson, V.S. (1992) editor, *Gendered States: Feminist (Re)visions of International Relations Theory*, Boulder, CO: Lynne Rienner.

Peterson, V.S. (2008) "'New wars' and gendered economies" *Feminist Review*, Issue 88: 7–20.

Pugel, J. (2007) *What the Fighters Say: A Survey of Ex-combatants in Liberia February–March 2006*, New York: UNDP.

Rodney, W. (1972) *How Europe Underdeveloped Africa*, London: Bogle L'Ouverture.

Schroeder, M. and Lamb, G. (2006) "The illicit arms trade in Africa: a global enterprise" *African Analyst*, Third Quarter, No. 1: 69–78.

Sjoberg, L. (2009) *Gender and International Security: Feminist Perspectives*, New York: Routledge.

Smillie, I. (2010) *Blood on the Stone: Greed, Corruption and War in the Global Diamond Trade*, New York: Anchor Books.

Solomon, C. (2005) "The role of women in economic transformation: the market women of Sierra Leone" Paper presented at the Transformation of War Economies—Expert's Conference at Plymouth, UK, 16–19 June 2005.

Staples, S. (2000) "The relationship between globalization and militarism and capitalism" *Social Justice*, Vol. 27, No. 4: 18–22.

Steans, J. (1998) *Gender and International Relations: An Introduction*, New Brunswick, NJ: Rutgers University Press.

Tickner, J.A. (1992) *Gender in International Relations: Feminist Perspectives on Security in a Global Economy*, New York: Columbia University Press.

Uchendu, E. (2007) *Women and Conflict in the Nigerian Civil War*, Trenton, NJ: Africa World Press.

Utas, M. (2005) "Victimcy, girlfriending, soldiering: tactic agency in a young woman's social navigation of Liberian war zone" *Anthropology Quarterly*, Vol. 78, No. 2: 403–430.

50 MOTHER'S DAY PROCLAMATION (1870)

Julia Ward Howe (1819–1910) is known for her Civil War poem, *The Battle Hymn of the Republic*, championing freedom for all men and women. She published poems, plays, and travel books and played a prominent role in several women's suffrage organizations. She saw the devastation of the Civil War through her work with widows and orphans on both sides, and called for women to oppose war in all its forms.

Arise then . . . women of this day!
Arise, all women who have hearts!
Whether your baptism be of water or of tears!
Say firmly:
"We will not have questions answered by irrelevant agencies,
Our husbands will not come to us, reeking with carnage,
For caresses and applause.
Our sons shall not be taken from us to unlearn
All that we have been able to teach them of charity, mercy and patience.
We, the women of one country,
Will be too tender of those of another country
To allow our sons to be trained to injure theirs."
From the voice of a devastated Earth a voice goes up with
Our own. It says: "Disarm! Disarm!
The sword of murder is not the balance of justice."
Blood does not wipe out dishonor,
Nor violence indicate possession.
As men have often forsaken the plough and the anvil
At the summons of war,

Let women now leave all that may be left of home
For a great and earnest day of counsel.
Let them meet first, as women, to bewail and commemorate the dead.
Let them solemnly take counsel with each other as to the means
Whereby the great human family can live in peace . . .
Each bearing after his own time the sacred impress, not of Caesar,
But of God—
In the name of womanhood and humanity, I earnestly ask
That a general congress of women without limit of nationality,
May be appointed and held at someplace deemed most convenient
And the earliest period consistent with its objects,
To promote the alliance of the different nationalities,
The amicable settlement of international questions,
The great and general interests of peace.

Source: Julia Ward Howe, "Mother's Day Proclamation" (1870)

CHAPTER 11

Gender and Environment

The Body, the First Environment
Food and Water
Population, Resources, and Climate Change
Gender Perspectives on Environmental Issues
Creating a Sustainable Future
    Questions for Reflection
    Finding Out More on the Web
    Taking Action
Readings

Keywords: agroecology, biocapacity, ecofeminism, ecological foot-print, environmental justice, overshoot, environmental racism, food security, precautionary principle, sustainability

Place and environment are fundamental in people's lives, whether we live in a leafy suburb, a recently gentrified or poor urban neighborhood, or on a farm, ranch, or reservation. Urban neighborhoods change over time so that a formerly Polish American or Italian American community may now be home to Vietnamese immigrants or gentrified by more affluent people. In general, middle-class and upper-middle-class neighborhoods have better school buildings; more sports facilities, doctors' offices, and banks; more open space; and a wider range of stores, cafés, and restaurants than low-income neighborhoods. They are also farther from factories, oil refineries, power plants, sawmills, stockyards, railway terminals, highways, garbage dumps, waste incin-erators, and other sources of pollution, bad smells, and noise.

This chapter is concerned with interconnections among social, economic, and en-vironmental issues, as well as with gendered theorizing and activism for a more sus-tainable future. Environmental issues are experienced at the micro and meso levels but, like other topics in this book, also have macro- and global-level dimensions.

THE BODY, THE FIRST ENVIRONMENT

People often think of the environment as "out there"—a beautiful place to hike at weekends perhaps, or somewhere to be avoided as full of bugs and creepy crawlies. But it is much more intimate than that. The edge between inside and outside is not the skin; it is deep inside our bodies, in the fleshy interiors of our guts, lungs, cells, and membranes. We take inside everything we eat, drink, and breathe.

Thus, many people ingest a daily diet of chemical residues: from pesticides, car exhausts, waste dumps, oil refineries, incinerators, and power plants, for example. Chemicals are widespread in cleaning materials and beauty products. Also, people who work in computer manufacturing, chicken processing, the dairy industry, nail salons, and housecleaning—many of them working-class women—are exposed to chemicals on the job. Women's bodies may become what some have termed "unhealthy environments" for their babies (Kettel 1996). Firms have tried to keep women of childbearing age out of the most noxious industrial processes—which are often the highest paid—or insist that they are sterilized, lest women sue them later for fetal damage (see, e.g., Gonen 2003; D. Stone 2000). Environmental contamination impacts men, too, an egregious example being the deadly herbicide "Agent Orange," used in the Vietnam War (Reno 2016). Dioxin contained in this defoliant has affected the health of US veterans, Vietnamese people, and those who live near US factories that produce it (Ornstein, Fresques, and Hixenbaugh 2016).

In Reading 51, biologist Sandra Steingraber argues that infants and children are particularly vulnerable to environmental toxins due to their small body weight and because their bodies are still developing. In the excerpt reprinted here, she discusses the effects of lead on fetal brain development, a delicate and complex process, and describes efforts in the United States to ban lead from paints and gasoline. Mothers who have been exposed to toxins like lead, DDT, PCBs, dioxin, mercury, benzene, arsenic, or flame retardants may pass traces of these substances to their babies through the placenta or breast milk. Nevertheless, Steingraber (2001) stresses that breastfeeding is still the best way to nurture infants, as it is uniquely suited to their growth and development. An ingredients label would read: 4 percent fat; vitamins A, C, E, and K; lactose; essential minerals; growth hormones; proteins; enzymes; and antibodies (F. Williams 2005).

Those most affected by poor physical environments in the United States are women and children, particularly in communities of color. Twenty years after the publication of *Toxic Wastes and Race in the United States* (Lee 1987), an updated study showed that "racial disparities in the distribution of hazardous wastes are greater than previously reported" (Bullard et al. 2007, p. x). The theory of **environmental racism** and the movement for **environmental justice** grew out of this reality, based on the conviction that all citizens have a right to healthy living and working conditions.

Steingraber maintains that environmental policies and regulations do not protect people's health adequately. Moreover, the legal system requires victims to show specific harm caused by a particular facility or practice in order to claim legal remedies. This is an onerous standard of proof because it may take months or even years for hazardous effects to show; also people may be exposed to several sources of toxins at the same time. The onus is on victims to prove that specific products or activities harmed them, not on corporations to prove that what they do is safe. Many environmentalists argue for the **precautionary principle,** defined as follows:

> When an activity raises threats of harm to human health or the environment, precautionary measures should be taken even if some cause and effect relationships are not fully established scientifically. In this context the proponent of an activity, rather than the public, should bear the burden of proof. (Rachel's Environment and Health Weekly 1998, p. 1)

Or as the French philosopher Voltaire succinctly put it, "In ignorance, abstain" (quoted in Reading 51).

FOOD AND WATER

Clean water and wholesome food are cornerstones of health. Given the gendered division of household labor, women bear the major responsibility for providing food for their families: making menus, grocery shopping, cooking, preparing school lunches, and so on. Women are the majority of subsistence farmers in rural Africa and Asia, and are responsible for fetching water for their households, often walking long distances to do so. They are involved in preparing and selling foods at informal markets in many countries, including in the United States (see Reading 35). Also, women are prominent among community gardeners who produce food for local use, including Latinx and Asian immigrants who continue the gardening traditions of their homelands (Mares and Peña 2010). In rural areas, women may be farmers; others cultivate garden plots, planting, harvesting, and processing fruits and vegetables for home use. Some know the woods or backcountry areas in great detail, as ethnobotanists, and gather herbs for medicinal purposes (see, e.g., Holmes 2016; Perrone, Stockel, and Krueger 1989). People are tending community gardens in many places around the United States. In cities like Milwaukee and Detroit, they have flourished, partly because corporate and government investors have abandoned impoverished inner-city neighborhoods. As well as gender, race is a salient factor here. Will Allen, founder and CEO of Growing Power (based in Milwaukee and Chicago), sees urban farming as helping to heal "a painful rift in African American history between its agricultural past and its urban present" and notes the importance of defining farming as something "entrepreneurial and black-owned rather than . . . associated with sharecropping and slavery" as in the past (W. Allen 2012, 206).

Women work in the food industry, typically in low-waged work. Also, they are at the forefront of grassroots efforts to improve access to healthy food as consumers, growers, organizers, researchers, and policy-makers (see, e.g., Allen and Sachs 2007; Bollinger 2007; Costa 2010; Sachs et al. 2016). We see this as connected to gendered roles, and the fact that many women in science are involved in environmental sciences. Although there is a rich feminist literature on body politics, as mentioned in Chapter 5, substantial gaps remain in feminist theorizing about the food system, as well as a lack of attention to gender by agriculturalists.

The Food Industry

US consumers have become accustomed to even-sized fruits and vegetables selected as much for their shelf life and ability to withstand being transported over long distances as for their flavor or nutritional value. Many North American supermarket chains source fresh produce from Mexico, as described by Deborah Barndt (2008) in her studies of growers, truckers, food processors, and supermarket workers along this food chain. Fruits are imported from countries in the southern hemisphere, like Chile and New Zealand, where summer coincides with the northern winter so that we can eat apples year-round. Tea, coffee, and tropical fruits are imported from countries of the Global South, where they take land, water, and people's labor from subsistence farming. These cash crops earn hard currency; in addition, agricultural exports are required under World Bank and International Monetary Fund structural adjustment programs to increase market profitability, as mentioned in Chapter 8.

The food industry is a for-profit business, and one that is increasingly dominated by a few transnational corporations like Monsanto and Cargill. Agribusiness methods require chemical pesticides and fertilizers and focus on monoculture—large fields of one crop, such as soybeans or corn. Research shows that chemically dependent agriculture is not sustainable over the long term as it results in declining yields and impoverished soils (see, e.g., Kimbrell 2002; Kremen, Iles, and Bacon 2012; Pimentel et al. 2005). Monoculture makes plants more vulnerable to pests and diseases that can wipe out a whole crop. Industrialized food production provides relatively "cheap" food in the United States because the government subsidizes agribusiness under the Farm Bill. But this food is not cheap if the prices of fuel and transportation, and costs to the environment and people's health, are included.

Another hazard of industrial food production in the United States is pesticide poisoning of farm workers, many of them from Mexico or Mexican Americans. Among an estimated two million agricultural workers, physicians diagnose from ten thousand to twenty thousand pesticide poisonings a year (National Institute for Occupational Safety and Health 2012). Consumers may choose to buy organically grown produce, although this is more expensive. It is beneficial for individuals, but it does not improve conditions for farmworkers who need a secure livelihood as well as a sound work environment.

Food Security

In the United States, access to nourishing food is linked to race and class. Low-income neighborhoods lack supermarkets that carry a full range of fresh produce, as mentioned in Chapter 5 (also see, e.g., Gonzalez 2008; Shaffer and Gottlieb 2007). More fast-food restaurants are found in low-income compared to middle-class neighborhoods, and fast food is offered at a much lower price compared to more healthy options. Government food stamps and the Women, Infants, and Children (WIC) Program provide limited support to buy certain foods. Local government agencies and nonprofit organizations run food pantries and food banks, and these are well used, especially toward the end of the month. In 2018, 13 percent of US households were food insecure at some time during the year, meaning that they were unable to provide adequate food for one or more household members (US Department of Agriculture 2018).

Despite the existence of hunger in the United States and many other countries, food is not scarce, as argued decades ago by Frances Moore Lappé and Joseph Collins (1998), founders of Food First: Institute for Food and Development Policy. Indeed, food is wasted every day. Hunger is caused by social, political, and economic factors rather than by insufficient food production. These include low wages, limited access to affordable food, difficulties and expense of getting food from farmers to customers, dislocation of people from land and agricultural livelihoods, and cuts in state subsidies for food under structural adjustment programs (see, e.g., McMichael 2009; Food and Agriculture Organization 2011; Rosset 2011).

Trade agreements also affect the availability and price of food. In 2008, a new phase of the North American Free Trade Agreement (NAFTA) came into effect, opening up the Mexican market for low-priced imports of US-grown corn, which undercut Mexican corn production. Further, the development of biofuel has sent corn prices skyrocketing as corporations buy up stocks of corn for fuel and take them out of the food supply. As mentioned in Chapter 8, corporate extraction of natural resources in the Global South has displaced people, especially indigenous communities, who were able to support themselves by farming, forestry, or grazing animals (see Reading 39; also see, e.g., Cowman 2016; Jenkins 2015; Women Resisting Extractivism 2018; *WoMin African Gender and Extractives Alliance 2015*). People in many poorer countries regularly protest food shortages or high prices—sparked by droughts, crop failures, increased oil costs, and competition from cash crops and biofuels. The growing world population, estimated to reach over nine billion by 2050, means that there is a need for increased food production, but food justice requires that food is considered a basic human right and that people are able to feed themselves by hunting, gathering, fishing, farming, gardening, or buying food at affordable prices.

Although much scientific literature supports industrialized farming as highly productive, biologist Jules Pretty (2009) contends that it is possible to feed nine billion people or more with sustainable agriculture. And agroecological farming systems have many environmental benefits beyond yields (Kremen and Miles 2012). They conserve biodiversity, enhance natural pest control, increase pollination, improve soil quality, use water and energy more efficiently, reduce the potential for global warming, and increase resilience of farming systems to extreme weather conditions—now a key issue worldwide.

Consumer demand may influence production methods. For example, more food is produced according to organic practices, though in the United States, this designation is overly broad and inadequate. Eating steak may be considered a sign of affluence, but commercial beef production has enormous environmental costs. It takes 5,100 gallons of water to produce one pound of beef, compared to 174 gallons of water for one pound of wheat (Hiller et al. 2005). In Reading 53, sociology professor Michelle R. Loyd-Paige describes her decision to "eat like a vegan" on health grounds, and also to bring her eating habits into line with her ideas of social justice and equitable distribution of the earth's resources. She argues:

> The conditions under which many feed animals are raised are inhumane. . . . Animals are a part of creation, just as humans. Treating them so callously is symptomatic of a general disregard for anything our culture defines as inferior and expendable.

She adds that this "is reminiscent of how people of color were treated." In choosing a mainly plant-based diet, Loyd-Paige asks, "Why do we commit so much of our land and water resources to growing grain to feed animals when we could grow grain that is a healthier source of protein" for people? Opinion is mixed about the role of animals in sustainable farming systems, depending on context, though recent research shows that cutting down forests for ranching is a factor intensifying climate change (Carrington 2018).

Safeguarding Water

Water is essential for all living things. There are no alternatives; we die without it. Most of the earth's surface is composed of water, but almost all of it is saltwater or frozen in glaciers. Less than 1 percent is freshwater that could be available for human use. Water has long been assumed to be part of the Commons—the wealth of natural resources available to all to fulfill our basic needs. Access to adequate supplies of uncontaminated water has become a major issue worldwide, exacerbated by the fact that increasingly, water supplies are owned and managed by transnational corporations. Again, structural adjustment programs are implicated as indebted countries are pressured by international financial institutions to allow the privatization of public water supplies. Two French companies, Veolia Environnement and Suez Environnement, and the British conglomerates Biwater and Thames have water operations in Europe, Africa, the Middle East, and the Americas. Coca-Cola (Dasani) and Pepsi (Aquafina) make enormous profits from bottled water, widely consumed in the Global North as well as by elite and middle-class people in the Global South. Bottled water is marketed as pristine. In the United States, it may be no safer than tap water. City water supplies are regulated by the US Environmental Protection Agency and must be tested several times a day for contaminants. The US Food and Drug Administration regulates bottled water, which is considered a food and is not subject to such stringent testing (Barrett 2011).

People in many parts of the world—including India, Latin America, Europe, and the United States—oppose corporate control of water. Local communities have sued Coca-Cola, Nestlé, and Pepsi for excessive use of water supplies. A case in Plachimada (southern India), for example, led to a series of court rulings against Coca-Cola. The company closed down its operations, though without compensating local communities for their losses (see Reading 55). Note that it takes 25 liters of water to manufacture 1 liter of Coca-Cola—and 250 liters of water to irrigate the sugar cane that sweetens it (Glantz 2007).

In the United States, the city of Flint, Michigan, switched its source of water from Detroit to the Flint River in 2014 as a cost-cutting measure. Residents, a majority of them African American, immediately noticed a foul smell and discoloration in the water flowing through their taps, although officials assured them it was safe for drinking and bathing. Strong community and national pressure forced the city to provide water filters and bottled water for residents. Independent research and class action lawsuits followed and pushed the city to change its water testing and treatment protocols, though many people continue to question how effective this is in view of earlier official unresponsiveness and cover-ups (see, e.g., Jacobson 2018; Sanburn 2017).

A second US example of water activism concerns the Standing Rock Lakota people. Together with thousands of Native Americans from various parts of the country and non-indigenous allies, they opposed Energy Transfer Partners' drilling of the Dakota Access Pipeline under Lake Oahe in the Missouri River in 2016. Indigenous communities, with strong women's leadership, stood firm for many weeks—calling for divestment from dirty energy, recognition of indigenous peoples rights, and the protection of water—in the face of increasingly militarized police tactics (see, e.g., Arasim and Lake 2016; Devault 2016). The completed pipeline now links shale oilfields in North Dakota to an oil terminal in Illinois.

POPULATION, RESOURCES, AND CLIMATE CHANGE

In 2018, the world's population topped 7.6 billion, though as Betsy Hartmann and Elizabeth Barajas-Román point out in Reading 52, the rate of population growth has slowed. In some industrialized countries like Japan and South Korea, population is actually declining. These authors show how arguments for population control have been linked to concerns over climate change, immigration, and national security. For example, anti-immigration groups have used environmental arguments to oppose immigration into the United States on the grounds that additional people will overburden the country's resource base. Typically, such arguments are cast in terms of "overpopulation" in the Global South rather than on high levels of consumption in the Global North.

Overpopulation, Overconsumption, or Both?

Hartmann and Barajas-Román argue that a simplistic emphasis on numbers masks the vast inequities in resource consumption among and within nations. Not only is consumption unequal, but the planet's **biocapacity** is in deficit also. This refers to Earth's ability to generate renewable resources and to absorb wastes. This went into deficit in 1969, and the shortfall has grown steadily since then. The Global Footprint Network calculates "Earth Overshoot Day," the date each year when people's demand for ecological resources exceeds what the planet can regenerate in that year. In 2018 "Earth Overshoot Day" was calculated to be August 1, meaning that we needed 1.7 Earths to consume resources and generate waste at current levels (Global Footprint Network 2019). Continual expansion ignores the fact that we live on one finite planet. Moreover, ecological relationships are circular, as with the water cycle, the oxygen cycle, and the decaying of organic matter that fertilizes soil to support new growth. Thus, there is an inherent contradiction between the linear expansionism of capitalist economies and long-term ecological sustainability.

Science, Gender, and Climate Change

Potentially catastrophic changes in climate are underway due to increased carbon emissions that affect the entire planet. This includes the melting of glaciers and ice caps, rising sea levels, warmer sea temperatures, changing weather patterns, and greater extremes of weather, such as droughts and heavy storms.

In Reading 51, Sandra Steingraber comments on the role of scientific evidence in the decision to ban lead paint and leaded gasoline in the United States. The lead industry fought hard to avoid this for many years after scientists and policy-makers understood the damaging impacts of lead on fetal development and children's health. Steingraber notes, "[D]ecades were wasted in denials, obfuscations, deflections of responsibility, counter-accusations, intimidation of scientists, and attempts to tranquilize a legitimate public concern." Now a similar process is at work regarding climate change. Some US elected representatives still debate whether this is really happening and, if so, whether it is caused by human activity, despite an international consensus on this issue among scientists for more than a decade (Oreskes 2004).

In Reading 52, Betsy Hartmann and Elizabeth Barajas-Román argue that some US and international organizations are avoiding the reality of climate change by urging population control, as if population growth is the cause of high carbon emissions. They oppose this logic as it blames the world's poorest people, who, although they have higher birthrates, are the least responsible for global warming due to their very low levels of consumption.

Recognizing the high US carbon footprint and disproportionate consumption of resources relative to population, environmentalists urge us to use less electricity, recycle reusable materials, take public transportation, reduce plane travel, eat less meat, and simplify our lifestyles. Important as these recommendations are, such micro- and meso-level efforts cannot keep up with the scale and pace of global warming, the most difficult environmental challenge facing humankind. In the United States, for example, macro-level factors affecting climate change include the development of low-density suburbs, zoning laws separating homes and workplaces, and inadequate public transportation so that many people have to drive on a regular basis unless meaningful alternatives are made available. Solutions require macro- and global-level agreements within and among nations to make drastic and rapid cuts in greenhouse-gas emissions.

Feminist researchers point to gendered effects of climate crises like hurricanes, typhoons, and heavy flooding. From New Orleans and New York to Bangladesh and the Philippines, women are responsible for feeding their families and keeping them safe, including elderly parents and young children—the most vulnerable family members, who may not be able to evacuate their homes or flee rising flood waters. After a disaster, women clean up the mud and debris, which may be contaminated by broken sewers or dead animals, and put what is left of their shattered homes to rights (see, e.g., Castañeda and Gammage 2011; Intergovernmental Panel on Climate Change 2007; Nagel 2016; Ransby 2006). In Reading 54, journalist Whitney Eulich describes community recovery efforts in the aftermath of Hurricane Maria in Puerto Rico, many of them organized by older women.

Environmental researchers see overconsumption and climate change as rooted in unsustainable lifestyles in rich nations and among elites of poorer nations. Geraldine Terry (2009) pointed out that climate change discourse has been dominated by natural science approaches focused on technical solutions and complex computer modeling, work mainly done by male researchers. She argued that "rather than seeking technical and economic 'fixes,' we need to move away from consumerism as a way of life and reject globalization in its current, big-business driven form, in order to avert environmental disaster" (p. 9).

Generally, gender analysis and the gendered effects of climate change are left out of climate debate at the international level (see, e.g., Detraz 2017; Wheeling 2016). If women are mentioned in official policy documents, they are considered victims of climate change rather than people who can contribute to solutions. Political scientist Nicole Detraz (2017) argues that feminist approaches to climate change sit at the intersection of gender justice, environmental sustainability, and human security. Indeed, women on all continents are applying their knowledge of local environments, farming practices, and consumption patterns to find ways to survive the current effects of climate change. Because of their grounded daily experience, they are well placed to make policy and to train others in this matter (see, e.g., Aguilar, Granat, and Owren 2015; Diep 2015; Wheeling 2016; Women Engage for a Common Future 2016).

GENDER PERSPECTIVES ON ENVIRONMENTAL ISSUES

Many women worldwide are working on environmental issues, especially at a grass-roots level, caring for families and communities in their roles as daughters, wives, and mothers. In the United States, women of color and low-income white women are active in hundreds of local environmental justice organizations (see, e.g., Adamson, Evans, and Stein 2002; Barry 2012; Bell 2013; LaDuke 1999; Sze 2004). They have been persistent in searching for explanations for environmental illnesses or tracing likely sources of pollution affecting their neighborhoods (see, e.g., Gibbs 1995, 1998; T. Kaplan 1997; Krauss 1993). Officials and reporters have ridiculed them as "hysterical housewives" and trivialized their research as emotional and unscholarly. By contrast, women's health advocate Lin Nelson (1990) honored this work as "kitchen table science." Examples include the Asia Pacific Environmental Network (Oakland, CA), the Mothers of East Los Angeles, the Newtown Florist Club (Gainesville, GA), and West Harlem Environmental Action (New York, NY). Women organizing in Flint, Michigan, and in South Dakota are also part of these efforts.

In October 1991, women made up 60 percent of participants at the First National People of Color Environmental Leadership Summit. A decade later, women were credited as the major organizers of the Second Environmental Justice Summit, and several were honored for their life work in this area (Bullard 2002). Many women in the environmental justice movement ground their activism in experiences of race and class rather than gender so that their work is not identified as feminist "in the sense of being strategically oriented toward improving gender relations" (Allen and Sachs 2007, p. 1), a pointed echoed by Christina Holmes in her study of Chicana environmentalism (2016).

By contrast, **ecofeminists** have emphasized connections between patriarchy and environmental destruction (see, e.g., Griffin 1978; Merchant 1980). Vandana Shiva (1988) noted that in the Western model of development, *sources*, living things that can reproduce life, including forests, seeds, and women's bodies, are turned into *resources* to be objectified, controlled, and used. A central point in ecofeminist thought involves the concept of dualism, where various attributes are defined as oppositions: culture/nature, mind/body, male/female, civilized/primitive, sacred/profane, subject/object, self/other. Philosopher Val Plumwood (1993) argued that these dualisms are mutually reinforcing and should be thought of as an interlocking set. In each pair, one side is valued over the other. Culture, mind, male, and civilized, for example, are valued over nature, body, female, and primitive, respectively, which are thought of as "other" and inferior. Plumwood saw dualism as the logic of hierarchical systems like colonialism, racism, sexism, and militarism that rely on otherness and inferiority to justify superiority and domination. Ecofeminists have included **speciesism** as an analytical category akin to sexism and racism, and have argued for the liberation of animals as part of ecofeminist theory and practice (see, e.g., C. Adams 1999; Gaard 1993, 2011).

Given the vital importance of environmental matters, it is critical that more feminists engage with these issues. We argue that intersectional feminist thinking makes it possible to link women's liberation, antiracist principles and practices, and economic justice as integral to environmental justice and sustainability (see, e.g., Hawthorne 2002; Kirk 1997, 1998; Mies and Shiva 1993).

CREATING A SUSTAINABLE FUTURE

Creating a sustainable future will require fundamental changes in industry and agribusiness, as well as in economic priorities and operations. Such changes will also entail redefinitions of wealth. This is not a philosophy of denial or a romanticization of poverty, though it does involve a fundamental **paradigm shift,** or change of worldview, especially in nations like the United States that are dominated by material consumption and wealth. A broader notion of wealth includes everything that has the potential to enrich a person or a community, such as health, physical energy and strength, safety and security, time, skills, talents, wisdom, creativity, love, community support, a connection to one's history and cultural heritage, and a sense of belonging.

Defining Sustainability

The term *sustainability* has become commonplace but means different things to different people. For corporate economists, it means sustained economic growth that will yield ongoing profits; for ecologists, it involves the maintenance of natural systems—wetlands, forests, wilderness, air and water quality; for environmentalists, it means using renewable resources and generating low or non-accumulating levels of pollution (Pearce, Markandya, and Barbier 1990).

Giovannna Di Chiro (2009) argued that sustainability must incorporate everything needed to reproduce daily life. This **social reproduction** includes biological reproduction, socializing and educating children, training workers, and caring for all members of society, as well as "the ability to produce healthy food, clean water, decent shelter, clothing and health care" (p. 2). Taking care of children and other family members should be everyone's responsibility, including governments and corporations. Sociologist Mary Mellor (1992) showed that caring work is geared to biological time. Children need feeding when they are hungry; sick people need care regardless of what time of day it is; gardens need planting in the right season. She argued that "women's responsibility for biological time means that men have been able to create a public world that largely ignores it," a world "no longer rooted in the physical reality of human existence" (pp. 258–259). Vandana Shiva (2005) maintained that a sustainable economy puts people and nature at the center, rather than the market system, as mentioned in Chapter 7. Also, Shiva (2002a) argued for **relocalization** so that "what can be grown and produced locally should be used locally" rather than exported, and further, that "relocalization everywhere—in the South and in the North—would conserve resources, generate meaningful work, fulfill basic needs and strengthen democracy" (p. 249), all factors in sustainability.

Projects and Models for a Sustainable Future

Projects that intertwine ecological, economic, and cultural development are key to a sustainable future. Examples in the United States include Tierra Wools (Los Ojos, NM), where a workers' cooperative produces high-quality, handwoven rugs and clothing, as well as organically raised lamb from their sheep (see, e.g., Peña 1999; Pulido 1996; Sargent et al. 1991); the Women's Intercultural Center (Anthony, NM), established to address the needs of local women, mainly Mexican Americans, through classes in economic self-sufficiency, personal empowerment, organic gardening (Holmes 2016); and the White Earth Land Recovery Project (Callaway, MN), which harvests wild rice, maple sugar, berries, and birch bark using indigenous, sustainable practices (LaDuke 1993, 1999). Urban examples include Sustainable South Bronx; urban farming projects in Detroit, Milwaukee, Oakland, and other cities (see, e.g., W. Allen 2012; Boggs and Kurashige 2012); and the Dudley Street Neighborhood Initiative, Boston, which entailed major environmental cleanup and the development of affordable housing for a low-income, multicultural community (see, e.g., Layzer 2006; Tulloss 1996). Of the many examples outside the United States, we note the projects and mobilizations against extractivism and for gender justice mentioned above (also see Readings 39 and 55), and the Greenbelt Movement, founded in Kenya in 1977 by the late Nobel Laureate Wangari Maathai, in response to deforestation and drought. Women have planted millions of trees in Kenya and other parts of Africa under its auspices (Maathai 2003, 2010). The Women's Rural Assembly is a coalition of Southern African organizations that focus on the care of land, life, and seeds.

Feminist Thinking for a Sustainable Future

Writers in this chapter argue for a future in which human life and the life of the natural world must be valued and sustained. The widespread and profoundly serious nature of environmental devastation means that environmental issues have great potential to bring people together across lines of race, class, and gender, as well as transnationally. As Betsy Hartmann and Elizabeth Barajas-Román and other writers in this chapter demonstrate, this will need sound feminist analyses and practices to link issues and peoples.

QUESTIONS FOR REFLECTION

As you read and discuss this chapter, think about these questions:

1. What does the environment mean to you?
2. Who grew and prepared the food you eat, and under what circumstances?
3. How far are you from farming, both in geographical distance and in generations of your family?
4. What is your relationship to animals and plants? To water?
5. What would you like your parents' generation to leave to you? What does the older generation owe you, if anything? What do you want to leave to your children? What do you owe them?

FINDING OUT MORE ON THE WEB

1. Find out about pollution in your community at http://scorecard.goodguide.com/. Find the safety assessment of ingredients in personal care products at https://www. ewg.org/skindeep/

2. What are the theoretical frameworks and organizing practices of these environmental organizations? Who is their constituency?

    Center on Race, Poverty and the Environment: https://crpe-ej.org/en/

    Center for Health, Environment, and Justice: http://chej.org/

    Committee on Women, Population, and the Environment: temp-cwpe.gaiahost. net/resources/environment

    Global Women's Water Initiative: https://www.globalwomenswater.org/

    Indigenous Environmental Network: www.ienearth.org

    Pesticide Action Network: www.panna.org

    Student Environmental Action Coalition: www.seac.org

    Women's Earth Alliance: www.womensearthalliance.org

    Women's Environment and Development Organization: https://wedo.org/

3. Use resources developed by the Global Footprint Network to compare the biocapacity and ecological footprint of different nations: http://data.footprintnetwork.org/#/

TAKING ACTION

1. Write your personal environmental history—the places where you have lived and that have nurtured you. Use the theoretical lenses outlined in this book to analyze and reflect on your experiences.

2. Identify plants, birds, and animals; sources of food and water; sewage; and trash disposal for your campus or community.

3. Find out what happened to the Native American people who lived where you live now. How did they support themselves? Where and how are they living now? If there are few or no Native American people where you live why is that?

4. Find out about sustainability efforts on your campus or in your community. What are the theoretical lenses shaping those efforts? How can you help/participate?

5. Create and plan an activity concerning the environment that would bring people together across lines of gender, race, class, and nationality.

51 ROSE MOON (2001)

Biologist **Sandra Steingraber** is an award-winning science writer, teacher, cancer survivor, and expert on environmental links between cancer and human health. Her books include *Living Downstream: An Ecologist Looks at Cancer and the Environment* (1997); *Having Faith: An Ecologist's Journey to Motherhood* (2001); and *Compendium of Scientific, Medical, and Media Findings Demonstrating Risks and Harms of Fracking.* (2010) She is Distinguished Visiting Scholar at Ithaca College, New York.

In *Having Faith*, Sandra Steingraber names the months of her pregnancy according to traditional names given to each month's full moon in the agricultural calendar. Rose moon is the sixth month. At the end of a semester as visiting professors in Illinois, Steingraber and her husband drive back to their home in Somerville, near Boston. This excerpt refers to their conversations and to Steingraber's ongoing research into fetal development.

. . . In its narration of life in the womb, the popular literature waxes eloquent over a completely different set of milestones than do the academic texts to which I'm more accustomed. The textbooks devote most of their pages to the complicated early events of organogenesis, with all their origami-like precision. The writing perks up again at the end with the avalanche of hormonal changes that triggers labor and delivery. But the discussion of fetal changes during the second and third trimesters is swift and almost dismissive: growth of body parts, fat deposition, refinement of features. . . .

By contrast, the popular media pass swiftly over the treacherous early months—except to mention morning sickness and symptoms of imminent miscarriage—and hit their rhetorical stride during the months of mid- and late pregnancy. These periodicals dote lovingly on such achievements as growth of the eyebrows (well developed by month six!), the secretion of waxy *vernix* (protects the skin from chapping), and the growth of *lanugo* (fine downy hair that holds the vernix in place). What mother-to-be can resist these endearing details, this special language, which resembles the vocabulary of a Catholic Mass? ("Vernix" is Latin for varnish, "lanugo," for wool). From the popular books, I learn that a six-month-old fetus is about thirteen inches long and weighs a little more than a pound. I learn that the top of my uterus has risen above my belly button and that the fetus, now pressed directly against the wall of the uterus, is affected by the womb's various squeezings. . . .

What the popular books and magazines do not talk much about are environmental issues. Even the March of Dimes publication, *Mama*, which is devoted to the prevention of birth defects, does not mention solvents or pesticides or toxic waste sites or Minamata or Vietnam. There is some kind of disconnect between what we know scientifically and what is presented to pregnant women seeking knowledge about prenatal life. At first, I assumed the silence around environmental threats to pregnancy might be explained by the emerging nature of the evidence. Perhaps the writers of public educational materials choose to present only the dangers for which the data are iron-clad and longstanding. All the books and periodicals include a standard discussion of rubella, for example, and urge pregnant smokers to quit.

But the more I read, the more I realize that scientific certainty is not a consistent criterion by which reproductive dangers are presented to pregnant mothers. For example, pregnant women are urged to drink no alcohol. The guidebooks and magazines are unanimous about this. While fetal alcohol syndrome is a well-described and incontrovertible phenomenon . . . no one knows if an occasional glass of wine is harmful. Nevertheless, caution dictates—and again I wholeheartedly agree—that in the absence of information to the contrary, one should assume no safe threshold level. One of the pregnancy books in my collection, *Life Before Birth*, even quotes Voltaire on this issue: "In ignorance, abstain."

Yet this same principle is not applied to nitrates in tap water. Here we assume we *can* set safe thresholds—in this case ten parts per million—even though these thresholds have never been established for fetuses and even though almost nothing is known about transplacental transfer of nitrates or about how nitrate-inactivated hemoglobin in the mother's blood might interfere with oxygen delivery to the fetus. What's more, we allow 4.5 million Americans to drink water with nitrate levels above this arbitrary limit. Four and a half million people surely includes a lot of pregnant women. We also presume we can set safe limits on pesticide residues, solvents, and chlorination byproducts in drinking water—and yet none of these thresholds has ever been demonstrated to protect against fetal damage. In fact, plenty of evidence exists to the contrary. When it comes to environmental hazards, not only do we dispense with the principle of "In ignorance, abstain," we fail to inform pregnant women that the hazards even exist. . . .

The more I read, the more contradictions I see. A recent scientific report summarizing the reproductive effects of chemical contaminants in food reaches a strong conclusion: "The evidence is overwhelming: certain persistent toxic substances impair intellectual capacity, change behavior . . . and compromise reproductive capacity. The people most at risk are children, pregnant women, women of childbearing age. . . . Particularly at risk are developing embryos and nursing infants."

By comparison one of the most popular guidebooks to pregnancy opens a discussion of this same topic with a complaint about that kind of bad news:

"Reports of hazardous chemicals in just about every item in the American diet are enough to scare the appetite out of anyone. . . . Don't be fanatic. Though trying to avoid theoretical hazards in food is a commendable goal, making your life stressful in order to do so is not."

Of course, the don't-worry-be-happy approach does not apply to smoking and drinking; the authors take a very stern, absolutist position on these topics.

I look over at my [husband] who's been singing louder and louder.

"Hey, Jeff?"

"Mmm."

"I'm trying to figure something out."

"What's that?" He turns down the radio.

"Not a single one of these pregnancy magazines encourages mothers to find out what the Toxics Release Inventory shows for their own communities."

"You did it though, right?"

"Yeah, I looked it up on the Internet."

"And?"

"And McLean County is one of the top counties in Illinois for airborne releases of reproductive poisons."

I detail for him the results of my research. The biggest emissions of fetal toxicants are hexane from the soybean processing plant and toluene from the auto plant. My list also includes glycol ethers and xylene. All are solvents.

"Jesus," says Jeff.

"I also found out that the university uses six different pesticides on their grounds and fields. So I looked up their toxicology profiles. Two of them are known to cause birth defects in animals." . . .

"So what are you trying to figure out?"

"Two things. One, why is there is no public conversation about environmental threats to pregnancy?"

"What's the other thing?"

I quote Voltaire: "In ignorance, abstain." "Why does abstinence in the face of uncertainty apply only to individual behavior? Why doesn't it apply equally to industry or agriculture?"

"Okay, let me think for a minute." Jeff turns the radio back on. And then turns it off again. "I think the questions overlap. Pregnancy and motherhood are private. We still act like pregnant women are not part of the public world. Their bodies look strange. They seem vulnerable. You are not supposed to upset them. If something is scary or stressful, you shouldn't talk about it."

"But pregnant women are constantly being told what to do. No coffee. No alcohol. No sushi. Stay away from cat feces."

"That's still private. Industry and agriculture are political, public. They exist outside one's own body, outside one's own house. You can't do something immediately about them within the time period of a pregnancy. So it seems unmanageable."

"It's pregnant women who have to live with the consequences of public decisions. We're the ones who will be raising the damaged children. If we don't talk about these things because it's too upsetting, how will it ever change?" . . .

Back in our Somerville neighborhood, with its views of Bunker Hill and low-lying, wealthier Cambridge, I forget the expanses of Illinois. Up in our third-floor apartment in this most densely populated city in North America (or so claims the Somerville newspaper on a regular basis), Jeff and I spend a few days bumping into each other and reacquainting ourselves with car alarms and Indian take-out food. In the evenings, we sit out on the balcony and wait for an ocean breeze. The neighbor who shares the balcony with us has planted morning glories and tomatoes, which are already twining up the latticework. In the mornings, I walk the dog to the park, sharing the sidewalk with caravans of strollers pushed by pouty teenagers and muttering grandmothers. I never noticed how many babies lived in my neighborhood. Up and down the block, rhododendrons are blooming in tiny cement yards, and vines of purple wisteria wrap the porches of shingled triple-deckers. Underwear flaps on a hundred clotheslines. From the park's old locust trees hang panicles of fragrant white flowers. It is Somerville's finest season.

With the public library only two blocks away, I resume my research. What interests me now is the sine qua non of pregnancy's sixth month: fetal brain development.

Trying to understand the embryological anatomy of the vertebrate brain nearly unhinged me two decades ago. It was some of the most difficult biology I had ever encountered—and the most beautiful. It was like watching a rose bloom in speeded-up time. Or like spelunking in an uncharted cave. My embryology professor, Dr. Bruce Criley, used to drill us by flashing slides of fetal brain sections on a huge screen while we sat in the darkened lab trying to keep our bearings. "Okay, where are we now?" he would demand, whacking a pointer against an unfamiliar structure. Prosencephalon, rhombencephalon, mesencephalon—ancient-sounding names identified rooms in a continuously morphing cavern.

Both the brain and the spinal cord are made up of the same three layers. The brain then adds a fourth layer when cells migrate from the inside out to form the cortex. It's what happens during and after this migration that is so dazzlingly disorienting. Indeed, in order to explain it all, the language of human brain development borrows its vocabulary from botany, architecture, and geography. There are lumens, islands, aqueducts, and isthmuses. There are ventricles, commissures, and hemispheres. There are roofs and floors, pyramids and pouches. There are furrows called sulci and elevations called gyri. Structures are said to balloon, undulate, condense, fuse, and swell. They pass by, flatten, overgrow, and bury each other. They turn, grow downward, turn again, grow upward.

Some structures are formed from tissues derived from two completely different locations. The pituitary gland, for example, is at the place where an upgrowth from a valley near the mouth meets a downgrowth from the forebrain. Meanwhile, the twelve cranial nerves go forth like apostles to make contact with the far-flung, newly developing eyes, ears, tongue, nose, etc. It was all enough to make us mild-mannered, high-achieving biology majors reel with panic. It also was enough to make us feel, once the lights went on again, that we had just emerged from a secret temple, the likes of which we had never seen before.

On a microscopic scale, the story is a bit simpler—although this may only be because we know so little about what actually goes on at the cellular level. All embryological structures are created through migration. But brain cells travel like spiders, trailing silken threads as they go.

There are two kinds of threads: dendrites and axons. Dendrites are fine and short. They receive messages from other nearby cells. Axons are ropy and long. They send out messages, often over great distances. Of the two, axons develop first. They grow out from the body of the brain cell along a specific pathway and in a specific direction. In this they are guided by proteins called cell adhesion molecules. The dendrites are spun out later. In fact, the peak period of dendrite growth doesn't even begin until late in the third trimester, and it continues until at least a year after birth.

Despite these differences, axons and dendrites have a lot in common. Both types of fibers branch after they elongate so that connections can be made with many other cells. These connecting points—the synapses—continue to increase in number throughout the first two years of life. Both axons and dendrites transmit messages by sending electrochemical signals down their lengths. Sometimes, these signals can also fly between fibers. But in most cases, in order to continue a message from one nerve cell to the next, chemicals have to diffuse across the synaptic space. These are the neurotransmitters, with their roll call of familiar names: acetylcholine, dopamine, serotonin.

Fetal brain mysteries abound. Chief among them is the role of the neuroglia, whose name means nerve glue. These are brain cells that do not themselves conduct messages but that apparently exert control over the cells that do. They are far more than glue. In some cases they act as coaches to the neurons' athletes—wrapping their axons in ace-bandage layers of fat and thereby speeding the passage of electricity. They also appear to alter the neurons' diets, for example, by modulating the amount of glucose available. And they provide signals and pathways for migration. In this last capacity, they work in tandem with early-migrating neurons. That is to say, the brain cells that are the first to make the journey to the cortex provide essential cues—along with those of the neuroglia— that help later migrants find their way. But no one knows exactly how these trails are blazed, maps are drawn, and bread crumbs scattered.

Once you understand how the embryonic brain unfolds, chamber after hidden chamber, and how its webs of electricity all get connected up, you can easily see why neurological poisons have such profound effects in utero. Exposures that produce only transient effects in adult brains can lay waste to fetal ones. This happens through a variety of pathways. Neurotoxins can impede synapse formation, disrupt the release of neurotransmitters, or strip off the fatty layers wound around the axons. Neurotoxins can also slow the outward-bound trekking of migrating fetal brain cells. Because the earliest-maturing brain cells erect a kind of scaffolding to help their younger siblings find their way, a single exposure at the onset of migration can irretrievably alter the brain's architecture. A fetus also lacks the efficient detoxification systems that already-born human beings carry around within their livers, kidneys, and lungs. And, until they are six months old, fetuses and infants lack a blood-brain barrier, which prevents many blood-borne toxins from entering the brain's gray matter.

As if all this weren't enough, fetal brains are made even more vulnerable by lack of fat in the fetal body. The brain is 50 percent fat by dry weight, and after birth, body fat competes with the brain in attracting fat-soluble toxic chemicals. But throughout most of pregnancy, the fetus is lean, plumping up only during the last month or so. In fetuses, toxic chemicals that are fat-soluble—and many of them are—do not have other fat depots in which to be sequestered, and so they have disproportionately greater effects on the brains of fetuses than on the brains of the rest of us.

More than half of the top twenty chemicals reported in the 1997 Toxics Release Inventory are known or suspected neurotoxins. These include solvents, heavy metals, and pesticides. And yet our understanding of brain-damaging chemicals is vague and fragmentary. Part of the problem is that animal testing is of limited use in trying to figure out how a human baby might be affected by exposure to a particular neurotoxin. Humans are born at a much earlier stage of fetal brain development than, for example, monkeys. Rhesus monkeys' brains are closer to their final form when the monkeys are born, and the young are upright and walking before they are two months old, whereas the average age of human walking is thirteen months. Certain structures within rodent brains, on the other hand, are less well developed at birth than ours. For example, cells in the human hippocampus, the seat of memory, are finished being produced at the time of birth, whereas in rodents, they are not formed until well into postnatal life. These kinds of differences between species mean that extrapolating from animal studies to humans is tricky. The windows of vulnerability are different. And obviously, conducting controlled experiments on human embryos and fetuses is not permissible.

Unhappily, plenty of human fetuses have been exposed to brain-damaging chemicals anyway—not through controlled experiments but through unintended exposures. There is much we can learn by studying their various deficits. However, this kind of research did not begin in earnest until the last few decades. According to the old thinking, either a chemical killed the fetus or it didn't. Either a chemical could produce an obvious structural deformity like anencephaly (no brain) or it couldn't. Not until the 1960s and '70s did fetal toxicologists recognize that certain low-level exposures can elicit functional abnormalities in the brain. That is, the brain *looks* fine—it has all the necessary structures—but it doesn't *act* fine. Once researchers tested children who had had low-level exposures to toxicants on cognitive and motor performance, subtle problems became apparent. The same was true for animals. As soon as laboratory testing of neurotoxicants was expanded to include not just birth defects but also behavioral problems (learning, memory, reaction time, the ability to run a maze), myriad other problems became evident. In both cases, researchers began to see that toxicants can affect brain functioning at much lower levels of exposure than they had previously imagined.

Unfortunately, this epiphany in brain research happened long after the establishment of environmental regulations governing toxic chemicals. Many of these regulations are based on pre–World War II assumptions about neurological development, not on the findings of recent studies. When it comes to fetal neurotoxicants, instead of following the admonition "In ignorance, abstain," we adhere to the principle "In ignorance and disregarding emerging science, proceed recklessly."

The sixth month of pregnancy is a joyful one. My round belly elicits smiles and happy comments from postal workers, dog walkers, and fellow subway riders, who compete to be the first to surrender a seat to me.

Meanwhile, the random fetal movements of last month have evolved into a predictable and reassuring choreography. And as the weeks go by, I begin to notice something else about the baby's movements: they are often generated *in response* to something that I do. When I take a warm bath, she begins to squirm and shimmy, as if she were bathing as well. When I curl up to Jeff at night, my belly pressing against his back, she kicks—with enough force that Jeff can feel it, too. If I roll over in bed, she sometimes rolls over. If police cars or fire trucks suddenly blare down the sheet, she becomes very still, and I know I won't hear much from her for a while. I pat my belly and try to comfort her. "It's okay, baby; it's just a siren." In these moments, I realize that I am beginning to perceive her as a sentient being—as a child—and myself more and more as her mother. . . .

A commonly held belief is that natural substances are less toxic to the human body than synthetic ones. Like a lot of folk biology, this idea is both true and misleading at the same time. It all depends on what you mean by "natural."

Consider lead, the element that occupies square number eighty-two in the periodic chart. It is indeed present in the earth's crust. But lead is not really part of nature in the sense that it has no function in the world of living organisms. While abundant in the geological world, it does not naturally inhabit the ecological one. A normal blood lead level in a human being—or any other animal—should be zero. And even in the inanimate world of rocks, the soft, dense, silvery substance we know as lead cannot really be said to exist. Elemental lead has to be roasted and smelted out of other minerals. In this sense, a lead fishing weight is as much a synthetic creation as polyester, plastic wrap, or DDT.

There is no doubt that lead is a remarkable material. Its Latin name *plumbum* (abbreviated Pb by chemists) hints at its usefulness. Think plumbing. Essentially uncorrodible, it has long been used to line water pipes. For the same reason, it has found a place in roofing. Lead salts make excellent pigments, thus lead paint. Tetraethyl lead stops engine knocking, thus leaded gasoline. Lead also has handy electrical properties. Its largest use now is in the manufacture of lead-acid storage batteries, especially the ones used in cars.

Lead is also a formidable destroyer of human brains. This property has been recognized for at least 2,000 years. Once called plumbism, lead poisoning causes capillaries in the brain to erode, resulting in hemorrhage and swelling. Its symptoms include irritability, abdominal spasms, headache, confusion, palsy, and the formation of a black line across the gums. Prenatal transfer of lead across the placenta is also old news. In 1911, women working in the white-lead factories of Newcastle noticed that pregnancy cured plumbism. They were right: by passing lead on to their fetuses, workers lowered their own body burdens and thereby alleviated their symptoms of lead poisoning. Of course, most of their babies died. We now know that lead, once it gains entry into the adult female body, settles into bones and teeth. During the sixth month of pregnancy, when the fetal skeleton hardens, placental hormones free up calcium from the mother's bones and direct it through the placenta. Whatever stores of lead lay in the bones are also mobilized and follow calcium into the fetal body. In this way, a developing baby receives from its mother *her* lifetime lead exposure.

Our understanding about lead's toxicity changed radically in the 1940s. Before then, victims of acute lead poisoning who escaped death were presumed to enjoy a complete recovery. But soon a few observant physicians began to notice that child survivors often suffered from persistent nervous disorders and were failing in school. In the 1960s, behavioral changes were noted in experimental animals exposed to low doses of lead. Then, in the early 1970s, children living near a lead smelter in El Paso, Texas, were found to have lower IQ scores than children living farther away. By the 1980s, studies from around the world documented problems in lead-exposed children who had never exhibited any physical symptoms of acute poisoning. These included short attention spans, aggression, poor language skills, hyperactivity, and delinquency. We now know that lead can decrease mental acuity at levels one-sixth those required to trigger physical symptoms. The new thinking is that no safe threshold exists for lead exposure in children or fetuses.

Fetal neurologists have also shed new light on the various ways by which lead wrecks brain development. At levels far lower than required to swell the brain, lead alters the flow of calcium in the synapses, thereby altering neurotransmitter activity. It also prevents dendrites from branching, and it interferes with the wrapping of fat around axons. But it doesn't stop there. Lead affects the adhesion molecules that guide the growth of these axons, thereby altering the architecture of the entire electrical web. It also poisons the energy-generating organelles (mitochondria) within the neuronal bodies and so lowers overall brain metabolism. In laboratory rats, lead inhibits a receptor known to play a key role in learning and memory. The adult brain can fend off some of these problems, thanks both to its blood-brain barrier and to an ability to bind lead to protein and so keep it away from the mitochondria. Fetal brains lack these defenses. This is why early lead exposures have life-changing consequences.

On its surface, the story of lead seems like a story of science triumphing over ignorance. Lead paint was banned in the United States in 1977, the year I graduated from high school, and leaded gas was phased out soon after, finally banned in 1990. With paint and gasoline as the two biggest sources of human lead exposure, the decisions to prohibit—and not just regulate—these products is a shining victory for public health. In their wake, the average blood lead levels in American children have fallen dramatically—75 percent between 1976 and 1991.

But there is another story about lead, told by historians and toxicologists who fought long and hard to banish lead from the human economy. It's a story about the willful suppression of science by industry. It's a story that helps explain why one in twenty American children still suffers from lead poisoning in spite of everything we know. It helps explain why lead, never outlawed for use in cosmetics, can still be found in some lipsticks and hair dyes. And it helps explain why the soil in my neighborhood in Somerville is so full of lead that we are still advised not to grow vegetables in our gardens.

Consider lead paint. Its production was halted in this country in the late 1970s. But in 1925, an international covenant had already banned lead-based paints for interior use in much of the rest of the world. This agreement acknowledged that lead was a neurotoxin and that lead paint in the homes produced lead dust, which is easily ingested when crawling babies put their hands in their mouths or chew on toys. But the United States was not a signatory to this agreement. In fact, the same industry trade group that prevented the United States from adopting the covenant also succeeded in blocking restrictions on lead in plumbing. The lead industry—which owned at least one paint company outright—treated the emerging science on low-level lead poisoning as a public relations problem, dismissing objective research as "anti-lead propaganda."

As has been meticulously documented by two public health historians, Gerald Markowitz and David Rosner, the manufacturers of lead pigments went on the offensive after the 1925 agreement. They reassured the American public that lead fears were unfounded. They even promoted lead paint for use in schools and hospitals. Most wickedly, they employed images of children in advertising. The most famous of these was the Dutch Boy, a cartoon character dreamed up by the National Lead Company. With his requisite haircut, overalls, and wooden shoes, the little Dutch Boy cheerfully sloshed buckets of paint labeled "white lead" in ad campaigns throughout the midcentury. The implicit message was that lead paint was safe for children to handle. . . .

The industry also fought labeling requirements that would warn buyers not to use lead paint on children's toys, furniture, or rooms. Many a nursery was painted with lead by pregnant women eagerly awaiting the birth of their babies. Those

questioning the safety of such practices were repeatedly reassured by Lead Industry Associates that a link between lead paint exposure and mental deficiencies has never been proved. And up until the 1970s, this was true—in no small part because the lead industry was the main source of funding for university research on the health effects of lead. Researchers with other opinions and other funding sources were condemned as hysterical and sometimes threatened with legal action. Only when the US government became a major funder of lead research did the case against lead begin to mount.

When the truth eventually became undeniable, the industry shifted tactics. Instead of denying lead's powers to damage children's brains, it blamed inner-city poverty and unscrupulous landlords who, the argument went, had allowed paint to peel in their tenement buildings. And the neglected children living there, with nothing better to do, ate it. At one point, recalls a leading toxicologist deeply involved in the lead wars, an industry representative actually suggested that the problem was not that eating lead paint chips made children stupid but rather that stupid children ate paint. All these arguments finally collapsed under the weight of emerging scientific evidence. But decades were wasted in denials, obfuscations, deflections of responsibility, counter-accusations, intimidation of scientists, and attempts to tranquilize a legitimate public concern. The result is that any home built and painted before 1978 probably contains lead paint, and all children and pregnant women living in such buildings continue to face risks from it. And since I live in a century-old building listed on Somerville's historical registry, I am now such a woman. It is a problem that continues to vex landlords and homeowners alike, as removing the lead is expensive and is itself a health menace. It is a problem that could have been solved in 1925.

Now consider leaded gas. In 1922, General Motors discovered that adding lead to gasoline helped alleviate its tendency to "knock," to burn explosively under high compression. Solving this problem meant that automobile engines could be made bigger, and cars could go faster. Ethanol, which can be distilled from corn, also worked well as an antiknock additive but could not be patented and was therefore not as profitable to the oil companies. In 1923 leaded gas went on sale for the first time. This development immediately attracted the attention of public health officials, who raised urgent questions about the effects of broadcasting lead-laced fumes into public air space. At about the same time, serious health problems began afflicting refinery workers whose jobs involved formulating the lead additive. Several died and many others suffered hallucinations. The tetraethyl lead building at one plant was even nicknamed the House of Butterflies because so many employees who worked in it saw imaginary insects crawling on their bodies.

Then a remarkable thing happened. In 1925, a meeting was convened by the US Surgeon General to address the issue of lead dust. And a moratorium was declared. The sale of leaded gas was banned on the grounds that it might well pose a public health menace. It was a perfect expression of the principle "In ignorance, abstain"—what is now popularly called the precautionary principle. Unfortunately for us all, the moratorium did not hold. After the prohibition took effect, the lead industry funded a quick study that showed no problems with lead exposure. Over the objection that lead was a slow, cumulative poison and that such a study could not possibly reveal the kind of human damage researchers were worried about, the ban was subsequently lifted. The production of leaded gas resumed.

It continued for almost seventy years. By the time it was banned again, this time for good, more than 15.4 billion pounds of lead dust had been released into the environment. Much of this has sifted down into the topsoil. As a metal, lead is not biodegradable and is considered absolutely persistent. In other words, it is not going away anytime soon. It is tracked into homes on the bottoms of shoes. It is absorbed from soil into plant roots. This is why, in high-traffic urban areas such as my neighborhood in Somerville, we cannot grow and eat carrots.

The irony of our gardening situation is that lead in gasoline was finally removed on the basis of a landmark 1979 study showing significant IQ changes among first- and second-graders in response to environmental lead exposures. And the children investigated lived here in Somerville.

Should you ever find yourself in Boston, you may wish to pay a visit to the Old North Church in the North End. It's the one-if-by-land-two-if-by-sea church made famous by Paul Revere. If you go, take a look at the pale violet walls inside the sanctuary. Jeff painted them. Well, he and a crew of men that he supervised. Restoration work and decorative painting are specialties of his; these skills have helped to fund a lot of art projects over the years and paid a lot of rent. Elegant old homes up and down Beacon Hill and on Cambridge's Brattle Street contain his handiwork, as do buildings at Harvard University. Jeff is more at ease with a paintbrush and a sander in his hands than anyone else I have ever met, which is one reason (among others) I fell in love with him.

Now we lie awake on a summery night, reggae drifting into the window from the street below, and discuss whether or not he should continue this work. His blood lead levels are more than double that of the average American male. One physician actually congratulated him for this. Given that his line of work puts him in direct contact with old, lead-based paint, she expected they would be much higher. Jeff is very careful. But even when he changes clothes at the job site and leaves his work pants out on our fire escape, he still comes home covered in dust and paint. He's paying the price for reckless decisions made three generations ago.

But we would like to ensure that our daughter doesn't. Almost nothing is known about how lead exposures in fathers affect their unborn children. "Lower lead levels have not been well studied for their possible effects on the male reproductive system or on pregnancy in the partners of exposed males."

In ignorance, abstain. But can we afford to? With a baby coming? In the end, we decide that Jeff should fold his business. And as soon as the baby is crawling, we'll move out of our apartment. We know there is lead paint under the many layers of latex—our landlord has confirmed it—and we know that painting over lead paint is not considered a safe method of containment. We also know that our neighbors around the corner discovered very high lead levels in the soil in their back yard. Nevertheless, a home lead detector kit has revealed no lead on the surface of our interior walls, in the cupboards, or in the dusty corners behind the radiators. For now, we'll stay put. . . .

"Don't grow our own root vegetables. Quit a job I like. How come we're always the ones that have to do the abstaining?" Jeff wants to know.

And that is my question exactly. . . .

NOTES

p. 498. Quotation by Voltaire: P. W. Nathanielsz, *Life Before Birth: The Challenges of Fetal Development* (New York: W. H. Freeman, 1996), p. 158. The literal translation of the original quotation is "Abstain from an action if in doubt as to whether it is right or not" (from "Le Philosophe Ignorant," in *Mélanges de Voltaire* [Paris: Bibliothèque de la Pléiade, Librairie Gallimard, 1961], p. 920). Thanks to Dr. James Matthews, a French scholar, of Illinois Wesleyan University for tracking down the original source.

p. 498. Standards for nitrates in drinking water not shown safe for fetuses: Committee on Environmental Health, American Academy of Pediatrics, *Handbook of Pediatric Environmental Health* (Elk Grove Village, Ill.: AAP, 1999), p. 164; National Research Council, *Nitrate and Nitrite in Drinking Water* (Washington, DC: National Academy Press, 1995), p. 2.

p. 498. 4.5 million Americans drink water with elevated nitrate levels: AAP, *Handbook of Pediatric Environmental Health*, p. 164.

p. 498. Quote from scientific report: International Joint Commission, *Ninth Biennial Report on Great Lakes Water Quality* (Ottawa, Ont.: International Joint Commission, 1998), p. 10.

p. 498. Quote from popular guidebook: A. Eisenberg et al., *What to Expect When You're Expecting* (New York: Workman, 1996), pp. 129–32.

p. 498. Toxic releases in McLean County: Data on toxic emissions are measured and sent by the industries in question to the US Environmental Protection Agency (www.scorecard.org).

p. 498. University's use of pesticides: According to the director of the grounds crew, pesticides used in 1999 include mecoprop and bromoxynil. As of 2001 they are no longer used. Thanks to my student, Sarah Perry, for investigating this issue.

p. 498. 34 million pounds of reproductive toxicants released in Illinois in 1997: Toxics Release Inventory (www.scorecard.org).

p. 499. Description of fetal brain development, gross anatomy: B. M. Carlson, *Human Embryology and Developmental Biology*, 2d ed. (St. Louis: Mosby, 1999) pp. 208–48; England, *Life Before Birth*, pp. 51–70.

p. 499. Description of fetal brain development, cellular anatomy: D. Bellinger and H. L. Needleman, "The Neurotoxicity of Prenatal Exposure to Lead: Kinetics, Mechanisms, and Expressions," in H. L. Needleman and D. Bellinger, eds., *Prenatal Exposure to Toxicants: Developmental Consequences* (Baltimore: Johns Hopkins University Press, 1994), pp. 89–111; Carlson, *Human Embryology*, pp. 208–48; England, *Life Before Birth*, pp. 51–70; Victor Friedrich, "Wiring of the Growing Brain," presentation at the conference Environmental Issues on Children: Brain, Development, and Behavior, New York Academy of Medicine, New York City, 24 May 1999; Nathanielsz, *Life Before Birth*, pp. 38–42; T. Schettler et al., *In Harm's Way: Toxic Threats to Child Development* (Cambridge: Greater Boston Physicians for Social Responsibility, 2000), pp. 23–28.

p. 500. Neuroglia modulate available glucose: Nathanielsz, *Life Before Birth*, p. 16.

p. 500. Later brain cells follow early-migrating neurons: K. Suzuki and P. M. Martin, "Neurotoxicants and the Developing Brain," in G. J. Harry, ed., *Developmental Neurotoxicology* (Boca Raton: CRC Press, 1994), pp. 9–32.

p. 500. Mechanisms of fetal neurotoxicity: G. J. Harry, "Introduction to Developmental Neurotoxicology," in Harry, *Developmental Neurotoxicology*, pp. 1–7.

p. 500. More than half of TRI chemicals are neurotoxins: US releases of neurotoxins into air, water, wells, and landfills totaled 1.2 billion pounds in 1997. These chemicals include heavy metals such as lead and mercury as well as methanol, ammonia, manganese compounds, chlorine, styrene, glycol ethers, and a variety of solvents, such as toluene and xylene (Schettler, *In Harm's Way*, pp. 103–5).

p. 500-501. Interspecific differences in brain development: E. M. Faustman et al., "Mechanisms Underlying Children's Susceptibility to Environmental Toxicants," *EHP 108* (2000, sup. 1): 13–21; P. M. Rodier, "Comparative Postnatal Neurologic Development," in Needleman and Bellinger, *Prenatal Exposure to Toxicants*, pp. 3–23.

p. 501. When testing expanded to include behavior: Harry, "Introduction to Developmental Neurotoxicology"; H. L. Needleman and P. J. Landrigan, *Raising Children Toxic Free: How to Keep Your Child Safe from Lead, Asbestos, Pesticides and Other Environmental*

Hazards (New York: Farrar Straus & Giroux, 1994), pp. 11–15.

p. **502. Historical awareness of lead poisoning:** Bellinger and Needleman, "The Neurotoxicity of Prenatal Exposure to Lead: Kinetics, Mechanisms, and Expressions"; Suzuki and Martin, "Neurotoxicants and the Developing Brain."

p. **502. Lead's migration into fetal body:** Bellinger and Needleman, "The Neurotoxicity of Prenatal Exposure to Lead."

p. **502. Awareness in the 1940s:** AAP, *Handbook of Pediatric Environmental Health*, pp. 131–43; H. L. Needleman, "Childhood Lead Poisoning: The Promise and Abandonment of Primary Prevention," *Am. J. of Public Health* 88(1998): 1871–77; Needleman and Landrigan, *Raising Children Toxic Free*, pp. 11–15.

p. **502. Lowering of IQs in El Paso:** Described in Needleman and Landrigan, *Raising Children Toxic Free*, pp. 11–15.

p. **502. Studies from around the world:** AAP, *Handbook of Pediatric Environmental Health*, pp. 131–43.

p. **502. Lead levels required to affect mental acuity:** Suzuki and Martin, "Neurotoxicants and the Developing Brain."

p. **502. Mechanisms by which lead wrecks brain development:** Bellinger and Needleman, "The Neurotoxicity of Prenatal Exposure to Lead"; M. K. Nihei et al., "N-Methyl-D-Aspartate Receptor Subunit Changes Are Associated with Lead-Induced Deficits of Long-Term Potentiation and Spatial Learning," *Neuroscience* 99(2000): 233–42; Suzuki and Martin, "Neurotoxicants and the Developing Brain."

p. **502. Vulnerability of fetus to lead:** The elderly are also at risk. As bone demineralizes with age, blood lead levels can rise. In seniors, even slight elevations can have adverse cognitive effects (Bernard Weiss, University of Rochester, personal communication).

p. **502. Life-changing consequences:** New research suggests that these consequences include a propensity to violent behavior, as well as a lowered IQ. See, for example, R. Nevin, "How Lead Exposure Relates to Temporal Changes in I.Q., Violent Crime, and Unwed Pregnancy," *Environmental Research* 83(2000): 1–22.

p. **502. Public health triumph of lead bans:** AAP, *Handbook of Pediatric Environmental Health*, pp. 131–43.

p. **502. 75 percent decline:** Nevin, "How Lead Exposure Relates to Temporal Changes."

p. **503. One in twenty children:** G. Markowitz and D. Rosner, "'Cater to the Children': The Role of the Lead Industry in a Public Health Tragedy, 1900–1955," *Am. J. of Public Health*, 90 (2000): 36–46.

p. **503. Lead not outlawed in cosmetics:** T. Schettler et al., *Generations at Risk: Reproductive Health and the Environment* (Cambridge: MIT Press, 1999), p. 273.

p. **503. Lead paint:** Markowitz and Rosner, "'Cater to the Children'"; E. K. Silbergeld, "Protection of the Public Interest, Allegations of Scientific Misconduct, and the Needleman Case," *Am. J. of Public Health* 85(1995): 165–66; Schettler et al., *Generations at Risk*, pp. 52–57.

p. **503. A leading toxicologist remembers:** Herbert Needleman, "Environmental Neurotoxins and Attention Deficit Disorder," presentation at the conference Environmental Issues on Children: Brain, Development, and Behavior, New York Academy of Medicine, New York, N.Y., 24 May 1999.

p. **503. Leaded gas:** J. L. Kitman, "The Secret History of Lead," *The Nation* 270(20 March 2000): 11–41; Needleman, "Childhood Lead Poisoning"; H. L. Needleman, "Clamped in a Straitjacket: The Insertion of Lead into Gasoline," *Environmental Research* 74(1997): 95–103; D. Rosner and G. Markowitz, "A 'Gift of God'?: The Public Health Controversy over Leaded Gasoline During the 1920s," *Am. J. of Public Health* 75(1985): 344–52; Silbergeld, "Protection of the Public Interest."

p. **504. 1979 study of Somerville children:** Needleman, J. Palca, "Lead Researcher Confronts Accusers in Public Hearing," *Science* 256(1992): 437–38.

p. **504. Quote on lower lead levels in men:** Schettler et al., *Generations at Risk*, p. 57.

BETSY HARTMANN AND ELIZABETH BARAJAS-ROMÁN

52 REPRODUCTIVE JUSTICE, NOT POPULATION CONTROL: BREAKING THE WRONG LINKS AND MAKING THE RIGHT ONES IN THE MOVEMENT FOR CLIMATE JUSTICE (2009)

Betsy Hartmann writes fiction and nonfiction about important global challenges. Her books include *The America Syndrome: Apocalypse, War, and Our Call to Greatness* (2017); *Reproductive Rights and Wrongs: The Global Politics of Population Control* (1995, 2016), and as co-editor, *Making Threats: Biofears and Environmental Anxieties* (2005).

Elizabeth Barajas-Román is CEO of the Solidago Foundation (Northampton, MA). She has been a leader in progressive movements for more than 20 years, including advocating for the health and rights of immigrant women and their families.

Climate change is clearly one of the most urgent environmental, economic and social issues of our time. . . . This paper argues that we are presently witnessing the development of a population/immigration/national security nexus in the climate change arena. This . . . poses a serious threat to the advancement of climate justice both nationally and internationally. To counter this threat and to strengthen the climate justice movement, we need to clearly articulate an alternative vision based on progressive linkages between reproductive, environmental and climate justice.

Wrong Links: Population/Immigration/National Security

The past year [2009] has witnessed escalating rhetoric from mainstream population and environment organizations about how population growth is a major cause of global warming. For example, the Washington, DC–based Population-Health-Environment Policy and Practice Group, a coalition of key NGOs and the US Agency for International Development, recently issued a fact sheet on Human Population Growth and Greenhouse Gas Emissions. It argues that population growth threatens to offset progress in emission reductions and investments in family planning and reproductive health should be a key part of strategies to address climate change.[1]

There are a number of . . . problems with this approach. For one, it doesn't make demographic sense. Today most countries in the world are already moving to a smaller family size. While world population is projected to increase from 6.7 billion today to 9.2 billion in 2050, the rate of growth has slowed considerably. The average number of children per woman in the Global South is now 2.75, and the UN predicts this figure will drop to 2.05 by 2050. The future trend is towards population stabilization.[2]

Moreover, per capita carbon emission rates are low in countries where birth rates remain relatively high, as in sub-Saharan Africa. From 1950–2000, the entire continent of Africa was responsible for only 2.5 percent of greenhouse gas emissions. In Kenya the average per capita carbon emission in 2002 was 0.3 tons, compared to 20 in the US. Rapidly industrializing countries such as China will account for a higher percentage of emissions in the future, but it will be a long time before their accumulated emissions reach the level of today's

Source: Reprinted with permission of Betsy Hartmann.

Reproduced with permission of Stephanie McMillan.

already industrialized nations.[3] China already has a negative birth rate; the most effective approach to emissions reduction there is clearly investment in conservation, green technologies and alternative energy. Worldwide, reducing the population of cars makes a lot more sense than trying to drive down already decreasing birth rates.

Focusing on population growth as a major cause of climate change places the blame on the world's poorest people who are the least responsible for global warming and lets rich countries, corporations and consumers off the hook. It obscures the difference between survival and luxury emissions. It is part of a long tradition of eugenic environmentalism in which environmental and economic resource scarcities are attributed to "too many people"—usually meaning too many people of color—and not to highly inequitable and environmentally damaging capitalist processes of production and consumption.[4] . . .

Arguably, current rhetoric on population and climate change is based less on reality than on the decision of population and environment groups to hitch their horse to the global warming bandwagon. This strategy is seen as a way to build

political support for international family planning. . . . Though understandable, this strategy is shortsighted. In trying to counter one segment of the Right, namely the anti-abortion movement, population and environment groups play into the hands of conservative anti-immigrant and national security forces that deploy overpopulation fears to further repressive agendas.

In the greening of hate, anti-immigrant groups masquerading as liberal environmentalists argue that immigrants are overpopulating the US and causing everything from urban sprawl to traffic jams to water scarcity. For example, the headline of a recent ad in the *New York Times* by right-wing anti-immigrant groups reads, "Population, Immigration and the Foreseeable Limits of America's Capacity: A Conundrum of Epic Proportions for the Progressive Thinker."[5] Now they are adding climate change to the mix. In August 2008, the Center for Immigration Studies released a report blaming immigrants for rising carbon emissions and suggesting they remain in their home countries where they consume less energy. The message is that reducing immigration is a far more effective way to address global warming than investing in conservation and renewable energies[6] . . .

In the national security arena, narratives about climate conflict and climate refugees build on racialized fears of overpopulation in the Global South and encourage anti-immigrant sentiment. A 2003 Pentagon-sponsored study of the potential impacts of abrupt climate change paints a grim scenario of poor, starving, overpopulated communities overshooting the reduced carrying capacity of their lands, engaging in violent conflict over scarce resources, and storming en masse towards Western borders.[7] Such narratives provide a rationale for further militarization of immigration enforcement and the expansion of US military intervention, especially into Africa. Unfortunately, this kind of reasoning is not limited to national security and intelligence reports. A recent article on global warming and sea-level rise in Bangladesh in the Natural Resources Defense Council's *onEarth* magazine depicts millions of destitute Bangladeshi environmental refugees as potential Islamic terrorists.[8]

This is not to argue that climate change won't displace large numbers of people—it well could in many places. But to portray those people as a dark, dangerous, overpopulated mass of violent migrants instead of human beings with human rights is deeply problematic. During Hurricane Katrina, the media whipped up the same kind of fears about African Americans in New Orleans, with devastating effects on rescue, relief and recovery efforts. . . .

By normalizing the idea that population growth is a major cause of global warming and giving it a liberal, feminist gloss, mainstream population and environment organizations make these kinds of stereotypes more palatable to the general public and contribute to generating a negative climate of fear. They also reduce reproductive rights to an instrumental means to an end, rather than ends worthy of pursuit in and of themselves. Meanwhile, they obscure the real causes of the climate crisis, hindering action on realistic economic and political solutions. . . .

Right Links: Reproductive Justice/ Environmental Justice/Climate Justice

Developed and advanced by women of color activists, the concept of reproductive justice strongly condemns population control, noting its long history of targeting the fertility of oppressed communities. At the same time it includes support for full access to safe, voluntary birth control, abortion and reproductive health services. But reproductive justice goes far beyond the need for adequate services. According to Asian Communities for Reproductive Justice (ACRJ), reproductive justice "will be achieved when women and girls have the economic, social and political power and resources to make healthy decisions about our bodies, sexuality and reproduction for ourselves, our families and our communities in all areas of our lives."[9] Reproductive justice refers not only to biological reproduction but to social reproduction.

Feminist scholar Giovanna Di Chiro argues that the concept of social reproduction is crucial to understanding the possibilities for linking struggles for women's rights and environmental justice. "Social reproduction is the intersecting complex of political-economic, socio-cultural, and material-environmental processes required to maintain everyday life and to sustain human cultures and communities on a daily basis and intergenerationally."[10] Whether or not individuals and communities can fulfill their basic needs and sustain themselves depends critically on the extent of race, class and gender inequalities in access to resources and power. Unlike the population framework with its focus on numbers, social reproduction focuses on social, economic and political *systems*. It helps us to look more deeply at the underlying power dynamics that determine who lives and who dies, who is healthy and who is sick, whose environment is polluted and whose is clean, who is responsible for global warming and who suffers most from its consequences.

Looking through this lens leads to a much more liberatory understanding of the convergences of reproductive and climate politics. It encourages us to consider:

Connections between the Local and the Global

Some of the same powerful forces that drive environmental injustice at the local level contribute to climate change on the global level. While marginalized communities all over the world experience environmental injustices at the hands of powerful corporate and political actors, their experiences and concerns are diverse. Local battles against environmental injustice include coal mining towns in rural Appalachia, indigenous communities of the Arctic and Subarctic, the oil fields of Nigeria and the oil refineries of the Gulf Coast. The task of confronting global climate change challenges us to build alliances, coalitions, and political solidarity across borders and among a wide range of communities. The global nature of climate change means our struggles are not in isolation from one another.

Environmental Dimensions of Health

Communities subjected to environmental racism experience daily exposure to cancer-causing chemicals and other toxins that cause respiratory, reproductive, and skin disorders. Women experience this toxic burden twofold. They often must shoulder their own health concerns while taking on the role of caring for others in the community who have been harmed, particularly children and the elderly. Women are also physiologically more susceptible to the health effects of a number of common pollutants which can build up and be stored for long periods of time in the fatty tissue of their breasts. Women may then pass on concentrated doses of toxins to their infants during breastfeeding. Women have spearheaded many of the battles against environmental injustice. This stems largely from their roles as caretakers of their families and the fact that they are more often in a position to bear direct witness to the health impacts of toxic infrastructure on their community. The dialogue on climate change must open space for these women to contribute their knowledge and voice their concerns.

Food Security

Climate-related scarcities of food and other natural resources such as water and firewood are likely to create burdens that fall disproportionately on poor people, especially women and girls whose domestic responsibilities include the management of these resources. In some families and communities, gendered food hierarchies in the household can put women at greater risk of malnutrition in times of crisis.[11] Achieving food security for all people should be a high priority in national and international responses to climate change. This means challenging present corporate food systems that appropriate land from peasant producers (many of whom are women) for large-scale luxury export crop production; engage in environmentally unsustainable mono-cropping and chemical-intensive agriculture; and draw down water supplies through inappropriate irrigation technologies. It also means opposing the transformation of lands that grow food crops into plantations of commercial biofuels.

The Failure of Corporate Solutions to Climate Change

In the international arena, corporate needs outweigh human needs when it comes to official climate change agreements. Ironically, a number of the mechanisms put in place by the Kyoto Protocol are not only doing little to reduce carbon emissions, but are increasing poor people's vulnerability. Carbon trading schemes allow corporate energy guzzlers to maintain high levels of emissions if they invest in carbon sequestration projects in the Global South. Many of these projects are huge monoculture tree plantations (also corporately owned) that reduce biodiversity and take over lands and forests from indigenous peoples, preventing women from collecting plants and firewood. These projects effectively shut the door on small-scale, non-corporate solutions such as systems that encourage local control of existing forests and improvements in their ability to sequester carbon and produce sustainable fuelwood supplies for community needs.

The Nature of Disaster Response

Early warning systems and disaster management schemes often neglect the needs of poor women and communities of color. In the US Hurricane Katrina illustrated how race, class and gender intersect in shaping who is most at risk during a disaster and who has the right to return afterwards. Activists should work together to press for more socially just and effective disaster responses, including those that take into account women's increased vulnerability to sexual and domestic violence and their need for safe reproductive health services in periods of dislocation. For strategic reasons, the US military presently wants to expand its role in disaster response in the US and globally. We need to resist this development and insist that publicly accountable civilian institutions be strengthened to cope with climate-related natural disasters.

Saying No to Nuclear Power

The reproductive health effects of the release of radiation and toxic chemicals are a powerful reason to oppose the expansion of nuclear power as a solution to climate change. Plutonium, the most dangerous byproduct of nuclear energy, crosses the placenta in the developing embryo and can cause birth defects. Plutonium affects male reproductive health as well. Stored in the testicles, it can cause mutations in reproductive genes, increased incidence of genetic disease in future generations, and testicular cancer. . . . A resurgence of nuclear power would also bring increased uranium mining on indigenous lands, with consequent environmental pollution and negative health impacts. Nuclear power threatens both biological and social reproduction.

Immigrant and Refugee Rights

In the US reproductive justice advocates have been some of the most vocal supporters of immigrant rights and effective organizers in immigrant communities. They point out how policies restricting immigration and blocking access to social services prevent immigrant women from getting the reproductive and basic health care they need[12] . . . This support of immigrant and refugee rights helps counter the negative scapegoating of immigrants by the population/immigration/national security nexus. Climate justice must include immigrant rights high on the agenda. In the event that people are displaced by global warming, we need to ensure that they are welcomed—not further traumatized and stigmatized.

Ending Militarism

Militarism in all its forms . . . is one of the most powerful obstacles to the achievement of reproductive, environmental and climate justice. Ending militarism is a point where our struggles can and should converge, where there are multiple overlaps. The list is long: Military toxins damage the environment and harm reproductive health. Militarism increases violence against women, racism and anti-immigration activity. Militarism robs resources from other social and environmental needs. War destroys ecosystems, livelihoods, and health and sanitation infrastructure; it is the biggest threat of all to sustainable social reproduction.

Militarism also stands in the way of effective solutions to climate change. Not only is the US military a major emitter of greenhouse gases—it burns the same amount of fossil fuel every day as the entire nation of Sweden—but it spends up to 30 percent of its annual budget on military actions to secure oil and gas reserves around the world. Imagine if those funds flowed instead to the development of renewable energy, green technologies, and programs to ensure that low-income people are not

adversely affected by the transition to a new energy regime. Meanwhile, military research into controlling the climate poses a potentially grave danger to the environment.[13] . . .

Conclusion: Toward a Holistic Politics

While addressing climate change is clearly an urgent priority, a failure to consider how it is connected to a host of other social and environmental justice issues could lead to narrow technocratic proposals that take some steps to reduce carbon emissions but none to reduce inequality. With the escalating rhetoric about overpopulation and climate conflict and refugees, we could also witness a resurgence of population control programs and the increased militarization of the climate policy arena. This could dangerously shrink the space for open democratic participation and debate. Contextualizing climate change, and locating it within a progressive nexus of related concerns, is a way to challenge these developments and build a broader and more powerful movement for climate justice. . . .

NOTES

1. Population-Health-Environment-Policy and Practice Group, *Human Population Growth and Greenhouse Gas Emissions*, January 2008. The members of this coalition are Conservation International, National Audubon Society, Population Action International, Population Reference Bureau, Sierra Club, US Agency for International Development, Woodrow Wilson Center, World Wildlife Fund, and Worldwatch Institute.
2. UN Population Division, *World Population Prospects: The 2006 Revision (Highlights)*, accessed at http://www.un.org/esa/population/publications/wpp2006WPP2006_Highlights_rev.pdf on 5 January 2009.
3. Kirsten Dow and Thomas E. Downing. *The Atlas of Climate Change.* (University of California Press, 2007): 40–41, 96, 100.
4. For a history of population control, see Matthew Connelly, *Fatal Misconception: The Struggle to Control World Population.* (Harvard University Press, 2008). On the link between eugenics and

environmentalism, see Alexandra Minna Stern. *Eugenic Nation: Faults and Frontiers of Better Breeding in Modern America.* (University of California Press, 2005).

5. *The New York Times*, 12 October 2008 (Page 33). Sponsors of the ad are the American Immigration Control Foundation, Californians for Population Stabilization, FAIR, Numbers USA and Social Contract Press.

6. Leon Kolankiewicz and Stephen A. Camarota. *Immigration to the United States and Worldwide Greenhouse Gas Emissions.* (Center for Immigration Studies, 2008). Accessed at http://www.cis.org/GreenhouseGasEmissions on 2 January 2009. For a critique, see Angela Kelley, "Voodoo Science Blames Climate Change on Immigrants," 18 August 2008, accessed at http://www.alternet.org/story/95493/ on 30 December 2008.

7. Peter Schwartz and Doug Randall. *An Abrupt Climate Change Scenario and its Implications for United States National Security.* 2003. Accessed at http://www.gbn.com/GBNDocumentDisplayServlet.srv?aid=26231&url=/UploadDocumentDisplay-Servlet.srv?id=28566 on 5 January 2009.

8. George Black, "The Gathering Storm: What Happens When Global Warming Turns Millions of Destitute Muslims into Environmental Refugees?" *onEarth*, Summer 2008: 22–37.

9. Asian Communities for Reproductive Justice, *A New Vision for Advancing our Movement for Reproductive Health, Reproductive Rights and Reproductive Justice*, accessed at http://www.sistersong.net/documents/ACRJ_Reproductive_Justice_Paper.pdf on 7 January 2009. [Also] see Jael Silliman, Marlene Gerber Fried, Loretta Ross, and Elena R. Gutiérrez. *Undivided Rights: Women of Color Organize for Reproductive Justice* (South End Press, 2004).

10. Giovanna Di Chiro, "Living Environmentalisms: Coalition Politics, Social Reproduction, and Environmental Justice," *Environmental Politics* 17 (April 2008): 281.

11. For more on gender and climate change, see Irene Dankelman, *Gender, Climate Change and Human Security*, Women's Environment and Development Organization (May 2008), accessed at http://www.wedo.org/files/HSN%20Study%20Final%20May%2020,%202008. pdf on 7 January 2009.

12. See Reading 23 in this volume.

13. On military consumption of oil, see Nick Turse, "The Military-Petroleum Complex," *Foreign Poiicy in Focus*, 24 March 2008, accessed at http://www.fpif.org/fpiftxt/5097/ on 7 January 2009; on military costs of securing oil supplies, see Anita Danes, *The Military Cost of Securing Energy*, National Priorities Project (October 2008), accessed at http://www.nationalpriorities.org/auxiliary/energy_security/full_report.pdf on 7 January 2009; on military schemes of climate control, James R. Fleming, "The Climate Engineers," *The Wilson Quarterly* (Spring 2007), accessed at http://www.wilsoncenter.org/index. cfm?fuseaction=wq.essay&essay_id=231274 on 7 January 2009.

MICHELLE R. LOYD-PAIGE

53 THINKING AND EATING AT THE SAME TIME: REFLECTIONS OF A SISTAH VEGAN (2010)

Michelle R. Loyd-Paige is Professor of Sociology and Executive Associate to the President for Diversity and Inclusion at Calvin College, Grand Rapids, Michigan. Her research interests include Christian responses to racism and organizational change within higher education. She serves as associate pastor at Angel Community Church (Muskegon, MI).

It was the Saturday after Thanksgiving in 2005. I was out shopping at the local mall when my husband called and asked me if I would pick up a six-piece chicken-wing snack for him on my way home because he was tired of the turkey leftovers. Soon after his call, I found myself at a fast-food chicken restaurant. I was standing in line trying to remember what type of sauce he said he wanted—*Was it the hot barbeque, the honey mustard, or the teriyaki? Was that with or without ranch dressing?*—when, from out of nowhere, I began wondering what happened to the rest of the bodies of the three chickens it took to create this snack for my husband that I was about to so casually order. Almost immediately, other questions popped into my head: *Just how many other people would stand in this same line in this restaurant to order chicken wings today? And how many other fast-food chicken restaurants are experiencing an increase in business today because people are out shopping and they are tired of leftover turkey from Thanksgiving? Just how many chickens were being grown so my husband, and three hundred million other Americans, could have chicken wings anytime they wanted—not to mention in the world?*

Little did I know that my questions about chicken wings on that day would lead to a radical change in the way I eat. Believe me, it's not that I have some great love for chickens as a part of God's creation and think that they should have the same sacred status as cows in India or humans in every part of the world. My thinking and eating habits changed as a result of what I call a *kairos* moment. *Kairos* is an ancient Greek word meaning the "right or opportune moment."[1] In my faith tradition it also means "the appointed time in the purpose of God." At this appointed time, four previously unassociated thoughts—the content of a lecture I had just presented four days prior on the global inequities in food distribution; a vague recollection of a statement from PETA [People for the Ethical Treatment of Animals] about the cruelties associated with chicken production; the remembrance of how surprisingly good I felt physically while on a forty-day spiritually motivated fast from meat and dairy at the beginning of the year; and my own desire to live an authentic life—yanked me into an uncomfortable realization that, when it came to food consumption, I was not living according to my beliefs.

I did purchase the chicken-wing snack for my husband, but with that sales transaction I began earnestly thinking about what I ate. I became conscious that what I ate was not merely a combination of taste preference, convenience, and cultural heritage. Before that moment in the chicken restaurant, I had given very little thought to how the food I enjoyed got to my table, and I certainly

Source: "Thinking and Eating at the Same Time" is reprinted from *Sistah Vegan: Black Female Vegans Speak on Food, Identity, Health, and Society*, edited by A. Breeze Harper, pp. 1-7. (New York: Lantern Books, 2010). Reprinted here with permission of Michelle Loyd-Paige and Lantern Books.

didn't think I was hurting anything or anyone. I am a socially aware college professor who challenges her students to think about how their social (and predominantly white) privilege supports the inequities that position people of color on the fault lines of life AND how their privilege allows them to be unconcerned about issues they do not think pertain to them. *How could I be guilty of the offense with which I indicted my students?*

As a middle-class citizen of the United States, I had been exercising status privilege every time I went to the grocery store or picked up a takeout dinner on my way home from work or shopping. It's a privilege to be able to eat what I want without ever having to think about how the food gets to my table. As I exercise this privilege, I am unconsciously participating in patterns of indifference and oppression. *I was guilty of the offense with which I indicted my students!* And here was truth in a Styrofoam box, which held six whole chicken wings covered in hot barbeque sauce with a side of ranch dressing. The truth is that no matter how good a person I was, my eating habits were contrary to what I believed. All of my actions either contribute to patterns of social inequities or to the solutions to the ills of our society. All social inequities are linked. Comprehensive systemic change will happen only if we are aware of these connections and work to bring an end to all inequalities—not just our favorites or the ones that most directly affect our part of the universe. No one is on the sidelines; by our actions or inactions, by our caring or our indifference, we are either part of the problem or part of the solution. I was beginning to see my lifestyle as it really was: a part of the problem and not part of the solution.

Not liking what I saw, I made a conscious decision to change my eating habits so that they would more closely represent my thinking on issues of social justice, the equitable use and distribution of global resources, and the health-diet-survival connection for African Americans. Since my *kairos* moment in a chicken fast-food restaurant, I have chosen to eat like a vegan and have changed my shopping habits. I now buy fair trade tea and chocolate, and when possible, I purchase fresh and organic produce from local farmers. I do have a few

nonvegan-friendly clothing items hanging in my closet from before my transformation, but none of my post-transformation clothing purchases contain animal skins or animal products.

My initiation into veganism actually occurred eleven months before that *kairos* moment in the fast-food chicken restaurant. I usually spend the first weekend of a new year on a personal spiritual retreat. In January 2005, I also participated in a month of fasting from meat, dairy, and sugar, facilitated by my church. The fast was voluntary and was supposed to *detoxify* the mind, body, and spirit. My church called it a "Daniel Fast." With the exception of the sugar restriction, the diet fit the vegan way of eating—soybean products became the mainstay of family and church dinners. (I'm sure the local health-food store was wondering what was going on with *all* these Black people buying up everything soy during that month.)

Twenty of us stuck with the fast for the entire month without slipping back into old eating habits. We all saw improvements in our health. Not unexpectedly, we lost weight; I lost ten pounds. But to my surprise, by the end of the month I was also experiencing fewer hot flashes (associated with approaching menopause) and was sleeping better at night. However, as soon as the fast was over, I added poultry, dairy, and sugar products back into my diet. Red meat was no longer on the menu in my home because it was giving my daughter headaches and my husband had been told to change his diet in order to lower his cholesterol levels. A month after reintroducing these foods to my diet, the hot flashes began to return. Several months after the reintroduction of meat and dairy, right around the time of the chicken-restaurant moment, the hot flashes were becoming so bothersome that I actually began to think seriously about hormone replacement therapy. I spoke to my doctor, and he suggested that I first consider adding the soy back into my diet.

I now credit the end of my hot flashes to the elimination of all meat and dairy from my diet, the eating of organic produce (when possible), and the daily consumption of soy. January 2005 marked the beginning of my understanding of how food affects the functioning of my body. It was

November 2005 that marked the beginning of my understanding of how the food I ate contributed to social inequalities, and it marked my transformation to eating like a vegan; in late November I began thinking and eating at the same time.

Thinking about what I was eating led me on a search for the answer to the question I had raised to myself about chicken consumption in the US. I discovered that in 2005 the total number of broilers—chickens raised for their meat—produced in the US for the year was 8.87 billion.[2] "Each week, Pilgrim's Pride (the number-two poultry producer) turns about 30 million chickens into nuggets, wings, drumsticks, and sundry other parts." According to the National Chicken Council, "American consumers are eating an unprecedented 81 pounds of chicken per person this year . . . and plan to purchase more in the months to come."[3] The US appetite for chicken has grown steadily since 1970 when the per-person average was 37 pounds.[4] Americans eat more chicken than beef (69 pounds) and pork (52 pounds). The amount of meat in a typical American diet far exceeds the daily allowances suggested by the US Department of Agriculture's food pyramid.[5]

The sheer number of feed animals necessary to satisfy the American diet is staggering. In order to keep costs low and production high, animals and chickens are routinely crowded into small pens or cages, mutilated, and drugged with antibiotics and growth hormones. Crowded and stressful conditions have been associated with feed animals and chickens becoming ill. Because chickens in such conditions will turn on each other, chickens are de-beaked so they will not kill each other. Feed animals that do not grow fast enough or are too old or sick are sometimes killed and ground into animal feed. Cows, who are by nature herbivores, are routinely fed a protein mixture prepared from ground cows.[6] Laying chicks who are the wrong sex are discarded in garbage bags—sometimes still living.[7] The conditions under which many feed animals are raised are inhumane. While humankind may have been granted dominion over animals,[8] I don't believe we were also given the right to be cruel, brutal, and heartless in our treatment of them. Animals are a part of creation, just as humans. Treating

them so callously is symptomatic of a general disregard for anything our culture defines as inferior and expendable.

In the US, how we treat food animals is reminiscent of how people of color were treated. Andrea Smith made such a connection with Native women and children and animals in her book *Conquest*:

> Native people often view their identities as inseparable from the rest of creation, and hence, creation requires care and respect, but colonizers viewed Indian identity as inseparably linked to animal and plant life, and deserving of destruction and mutilation. This equation between animals and Native people continues.[9]

Smith's statement was in the context of discussing the US government's practices of medical experimentation on Native inhabitants in reservations. African Americans have also been used as human guinea pigs for some of our government's medical experiments: The Tuskegee syphilis studies are a well-known example. Africans were brought to this country in mass numbers as slaves. They were chained together and kept in the cramped holds of ships as they crossed the Atlantic. In order to justify the brutality of slavery, the oppressors deemed Africans as less-than-human and undeserving of decent housing, education, food, health care, justice, or respect. African women who were enslaved were often used as breeders for a new crop of slaves. It was not uncommon for Africans who were too sick, too old, or too rebellious to be killed if it was thought cheaper to replace them than to keep them. Prized animals were often treated better than slaves.

Seeing a connection between the treatment of feed animals, laying chickens, and people of color is a rather recent phenomenon for me. Two years ago, I wouldn't have believed there was such a connection. Today, I know better. The connection becomes clear with a careful reading of our history and an understanding of the true nature of food production in the United States. The connection, however, is also observable by a thorough analysis of today's headlines and an informed critique of social policy and community life. Understanding the connection strengthens my resolve to continue eating like a vegan. Choosing to eat this way is a reminder to myself and a demonstration to those around me that all of creation is worthy of respect and humane treatment, even chickens.

At the time I raised my questions about chicken consumption, I was simply curious about how many chickens Americans ate. As I searched to satisfy my curiosity of that day, I have changed from wondering about numbers of chickens to the costs of the American diet. *What are the health-related costs to the lives of people eating a typical American diet? Why does it cost more to eat healthy? Why is it "unusual" to have a meal without meat? Why do feed animals need so many growth hormones and antibiotics in their feed? What do these animal growth hormones and antibiotics do in our human bodies? Why do we commit so much of our land and water resources to growing feed for animals when we could grow grain that is a healthier source of protein? Can we really afford to not know where our food comes from and how it is produced?* I am convinced that eating a meat-based diet—not to mention dairy products, eggs, and fish—is not only hazardous to food animals and harmful to the land, but, more important to me, perilous to the health of my people.

The top five leading causes of death among African Americans are: heart disease, cancer, cerebrovascular disease, accidents, and diabetes.[10] Currently, 27 percent of deaths in the Black US population are from heart disease, and the death rate from diabetes for Blacks is twice that of whites.[11] . . .

. . . The traditional African American diet is loaded with deep-fried chicken; meats are smothered in cream-based gravies; vegetables are slow-cooked with pork and pork fat until the color of the vegetables is no longer bright; and desserts are loaded with butter and cream. Soul Food (a.k.a. Southern home-cooking or comfort food) is often jokingly referred to as a "heart-attack on plate."

For African Americans, however, it's no laughing matter. We are literally killing ourselves and decreasing our quality of life by the way we eat. Of the leading causes of death for African Americans, all but one, accidents, have a connection to diet and lifestyle. Heart disease, obesity, and diabetes do not have to be such a prominent part of the African American experience. Switching to an all-plant or nearly all-plant diet is one of the most effective ways to stop the progress of heart disease,[12] reversing the tendency to obesity, and controlling the onset of diabetes.

Every now and then my husband will ask me, "How long are you going to eat like this?" He used to ask because he and the rest of my immediate family thought that I wasn't going to get enough protein in my diet. Through my sharing of nutrition facts with them, they no longer think that eating like a vegan is unhealthy—strange for a Black person, perhaps, but not unhealthy. In fact, my husband has switched to soy butter and eats several meatless meals a week with me. My mother has also declared that a vegan restaurant I introduced her to is now one of her favorites and has dined there several times without me. Now when my husband asks, "How long are you going to eat like this?" it's because he has noticed that I no longer have hot flashes and he wants me to stay hot-flash-free, because "if momma is happy, everybody is happy." Although he appreciates the improvement in my comfort level and disposition, he and I are reminded of just how challenging it can be to maintain this lifestyle every time we try to go out for dinner, attend a birthday party, or go to a church potluck.

I'm the only vegan in my household. I think I'm the only Black female in all of western Michigan who eats like a vegan; if I'm not, it sure seems like it. There are no true vegan restaurants within ninety miles of our home. The closest vegetarian restaurant is forty-eight miles away, in a trendy, white, college-student side of town. When we do go out to eat (which is not very often) I usually opt for a salad without meat or cheese. Family holiday dinners, church potlucks, and birthday parties call for several different strategies. There's the "I'll be happy to bring something" so I can be sure that there's at least one item I can eat; there's the "Really, I am full. I just ate, all I want is a glass of water" so I don't have to explain to sistah sistah why I'm not eating her prized chicken salad; and then there are the times when I feel up to being an educator and I share with people why I no longer eat meat.

How long will I continue to eat like this? I can't see returning to eating meat, eggs, or dairy products, even with the inconveniences associated with eating out, dinner parties, church potlucks, family holiday dinners, and birthday parties. I am healthier now. I know too much now. I am committed to living an authentic life and to working for the elimination of all forms of injustice. I am now thinking and eating at the same time. There is no turning back.

NOTES

1. Retrieved from en.wikipedia.org/wiki/Kairos.
2. National Agricultural Statistical Service, USDA, Washington DC. Retrieved from www.slate.com/id/2112698.
3. Retrieved from www.spcnetwork.com/mii/2000/000508.htm.
4. Ibid.
5. Marilyn Hughes Gaston and Gayle Porter, *Prime Time: The African American Woman's Guide to Midlife Health and Wellness* (New York: One World Press, 2001), p. 174.
6. Erik Marcus, *Vegan: New Ethics of Eating* (Ithaca, NY: McBooks Press, 2001).
7. Ibid.
8. Genesis 1:26 (Living Bible) reads, "Then God said, 'Let us make a man—someone like ourselves, to be the master of all life upon the earth and in the skies and in the seas.'" Many people interpret this passage of scripture as God's mandate for humans to dominate animals.
9. Andrea Smith, *Conquest: Sexual Violence and American Indian Genocide* (Cambridge, Mass.: South End Press, 2005), p. 117.
10. American Cancer Society, *Cancer Facts and Figures for African Americans 2005–2006* (Atlanta: author, 2005), p. 1.
11. Ibid.
12. Marcus, *Vegan: New Ethics of Eating*, p. 4.

WHITNEY EULICH

54 — MONTHS AFTER HURRICANE MARIA, PUERTO RICANS TAKE RECOVERY INTO THEIR OWN HANDS (2018)

Whitney Eulich is the Latin America editor for the *Christian Science Monitor* and also curates the Latin America Monitor Blog. She has lived in Venezuela and worked in Colombia and Guatemala as an oral historian and radio journalist. Her reporting has aired on NPR programs including *Latino USA* and PBS's *The NewsHour* (online). She has conducted trainings for radio reporters and worked in disaster management after Hurricanes Katrina and Rita.

Gloria Cotto stands in an abandoned elementary school in [Las Carolinas] in central Puerto Rico, stirring a giant silver pot of beans. It's 7:30 a.m., and the blue flame of the donated gas stove is the brightest light in the room since the country plunged into darkness six months ago. . . .

Cotto and a core group of volunteers have been filling this former public-school cafeteria with donated food and home-cooked meals three days a week since Nov. 6 [2017], joining hundreds of volunteers across the island who are heroically helping communities survive after an unprecedented natural disaster and epic power outage. Without them, hundreds in this town would go hungry.

The winds of hurricanes Irma and Maria felled trees, cut off water supplies, and pulled the plug on the island's power last September [2017]. Tens of thousands of families are still without electricity, requiring them to adapt to a situation everyone believed would be temporary but has proved to be a punishing new normal. That means studying by candlelight; using generators for things once taken for granted, such as keeping medications cold or chilling fresh meat; and coping with family separations that have accelerated in the aftermath of the tragedy. . . .

"It wasn't long before we realized if we wanted to see a response, it would have to come from us," says Carmen Texidor, a retired health-center administrator who helped launch the community kitchen here. In many communities—particularly rural, mountainous ones—neighbors like [Ms.] Cotto and Ms. Texidor have turned to one another, sharing resources informally and launching Centers of Mutual Support (CAMs for their initials in Spanish), of which there are about a dozen across the island. They're cooking food en masse . . . for neighbors without functioning kitchens, delivering meals to the bedridden and elderly, installing water filtration stations by riverbanks, and fostering a sense of purpose in a situation where many feel forgotten and left behind.

The community mobilization that has come out of Puerto Rico's one-two punch of natural disasters is, in part, a reflection of the struggling economic state of the island. Puerto Rico filed for the equivalent of federal bankruptcy protection in May 2017, owing more than $100 billion in debt and unfunded pensions. Maria transformed the already dire economic situation into a humanitarian crisis. But for those involved in the efforts to help families and neighborhoods help themselves, this is a chance to instill a sense of leadership—and push Puerto Rico in a new direction [See the box feature "Puerto Rico's Colonial Past and Present"].

Puerto Rico's Colonial Past and Present

In 1493, Christopher Columbus claimed Puerto Rico for Spain from the indigenous Taino people, and the islands remained under Spanish rule for just over 400 years.

In 1898, following the Spanish-American War, the Treaty of Paris transferred former Spanish colonies—Puerto Rico, Cuba, Guam, and the Philippines—to US control. Puerto Rico became an unincorporated US territory. Puerto Ricans were granted US citizenship in 1917 but have no voting representative in Congress.

From Spanish colonial times, Puerto Rico produced sugar, tobacco, and coffee for export. This continued under US rule, but the extractive economy could not support the population. Throughout the twentieth century, many people left for the US mainland, especially New York City, trying to escape poverty.

Starting in 1955, trials of birth control pills were tested on poor Puerto Rican women before release on the US market at much lower dosages (Simón 2016). At least one-third of Puerto Rican mothers aged 20 to 49 were sterilized, ten times more than in the United States (Krase 2014).

In 1976, to spur industrial development, new regulations exempted US companies operating in Puerto Rico from paying taxes on income or capital gains. Successive governments relied on loans to offset this reduction in tax revenue (Whitney 2017). Starting in 1996, these regulations were phased out, which meant that US companies cut or reduced their operations in Puerto Rico.

Together these factors led to a downward spiral of layoffs, out-migration, budget cuts for social services and education, and dismissal of public employees. In 2015, the governor announced that Puerto Rico's debt was unpayable (Oliver-Didier 2017).

In 2016, Congress passed the Puerto Rico Oversight, Management, and Economic Stability Act (PROMESA), which created a control board to decide financial policy for Puerto Rico.

As of 2017, 44.4 percent of residents of Puerto Rico lived below the federal poverty line (US Census Bureau 2017).

Source: Gwyn Kirk and Margo Okazawa-Rey

"When we started the CAM, we didn't see it as temporary relief," says Giovanni Roberto, a community leader in nearby Caguas. "Our analysis was that Maria wasn't the crisis. The storm just exposed the need for structural change. This is our opportunity."

Volunteers—mostly retired women—trickle onto the school grounds throughout the morning on a recent Monday. Donning aprons and plastic gloves, they can see exactly where their help is needed, and they jump in: stirring pots, chopping meat and vegetables, organizing carry-out containers, and sweeping the floors.

Charito Arroyo pulls partially frozen chicken breasts out of a large white cooler and starts unwrapping them. She travels to a nearby town and buys the frozen meat and other ingredients the night before most meals. "Have you seen our fridge?" she asks a visitor, pointing to a plastic cooler.

Ms. Arroyo lives in a nearby town but grew up in Las Carolinas. The community of about 500 people, 40 minutes south of the Puerto Rican capital of San Juan, is dotted with homes that cling to steep, lush hillsides or sit along washed-out riverbanks. Most of the houses are one-story concrete structures, but many have second floors jerry-built out of wood.

It is the wooden additions that were most damaged by the hurricanes' lethal winds and rain. Some obliterated homes are already overgrown with twisting vines. Elsewhere, driveways are filled with water-damaged furniture waiting to be removed.

Arroyo's mother, who lives in Las Carolinas, had to travel to her daughter's house for the first three months after the hurricanes to take showers. Other local residents bathed and washed their clothes in the river that runs through town.

In November, two area residents, Texidor and Rosario Gonzalez, hopped the fence surrounding the local elementary school, which had been closed in the spring because of declining enrollment. They were looking for a place—any place—that had survived and could be used as a staging center. Soon, children as young as 12 and retirees in their 80s came together to scrub floors and remove debris in the low-slung building, transforming the school's abandoned cafeteria into a community kitchen.

"Everything was unlocked. The doors just opened," says Cotto, who worked at the school for nearly three decades. Like most people in the community, Cotto doesn't have access to a working stove or refrigerator at home since she has no electricity. Her roof leaks.

"It was the center of our community," says Cotto of the school, as she rummages through a storage room in search of more jambalaya seasoning. "You either went to school here or sent your children here. When it closed, we lost something . . . that brought us together."

Others quickly chipped in to help. A local chef who cooked at the San Juan airport left Puerto Rico for Orlando, Fla., after the storm. He donated his knives, pots, pans, and a stove. Churches and mosques started showing up with donated food, and members of the Puerto Rican diaspora have sent money so the CAM can purchase meat and other necessities to keep their neighbors fed.

Meals here were provided free of charge until March 5, when the CAM started asking diners to donate $1 if they planned to take extra food. A sign at the entryway offers other options: "Trade: food, work, money. Thank you."

Today, the building serves as more than just an emergency canteen. One former classroom is filled with donated clothing and home goods. Locals stage weekend dance classes and storytelling events or hold workshops to teach residents how to make their own mosquito repellent. Volunteers are painting another room bright yellow to cover the water stains on the walls. It will serve as an acupuncture center, run by trained volunteers on the weekend.

"You'll see how beautiful this will be. It will motivate people," says Teresa Pinto Gonzalez, a volunteer who decided it needed the makeover and bought the paint. "People's homes are damaged, and it's one hard thing after another. It's important to see something cared for."

Yet the CAM does more than provide food and give people a social outlet. It has helped residents feel that they are part of something bigger than themselves.

"Helping gives me purpose," says Texidor. Her home wasn't badly damaged in the storms, but she watched as neighbors moved away and others struggled to maintain their health. "The work is therapeutic for me."

About a five-minute drive over the undulating roads of Las Carolinas, Maria Ortiz points to where her son's home used to sit. Signs of his former life are evident in the rubble: A framed painting of three musicians hangs lopsidedly near a blown-away wall. A lone angel magnet sticks to the abandoned refrigerator.

"I lost my family," Ms. Ortiz . . . says. Her loved ones lived through the storm, but her children have fled to the mainland United States.

"I got really depressed," Ortiz says. She came to eat at the CAM one afternoon and was invited to come back and help cook.

"I didn't want to be imprisoned in my home anymore," she says. "Cooking for the community became a mental refuge for me. I realized I have to do more than survive if I want to build a better future."

Most of the volunteers here are women. . . . Across the country, women have played a vital part in trying to help Puerto Rico revive.

"Many women are leading, organizing, and participating in these spaces," says Mr. Roberto, the community leader in Caguas. "In Puerto Rico we talk about youth [leadership], but we don't value older women. . . . I believe this movement is making us recognize" their key role in the island's communities.

It's also a reflection of the depopulation and demographic shifts that have been taking place in Puerto Rico for years. An estimated 80,000 people were leaving the country each year in search of more opportunity before the hurricanes. Now those numbers are expected to swell to several hundred thousand annually for the foreseeable future.

At the same time, the island's population of 3.3 million is increasingly skewing older. The neighborhood association president in Las Carolinas estimates that more than 60 percent of local residents are over the age of 60—and dependent on government assistance.

Still, the people who have stayed have forged a bond in hardship. "It's like a funeral: After suffering the tragedy, we were brought together emotionally," says Jose Enrique Algare, a 70-something volunteer at the CAM. "I see my neighbors in a new way. We are sharing as if we are all family."

On this day, the team is preparing a special meal in hopes that "Los Gringos" will swing by to eat with them. That's the term used lovingly to describe the electricity workers who have traveled from all over the mainland US to repair power lines and towers in Puerto Rico. The electricity trucks pulled into town over the weekend.

No one's power has been restored yet—it could still take months—but the community is buzzing with excitement. Two mothers leaving a nearby Head Start center with their toddlers stop to cheer when a truck from upstate New York whizzes by. The workers honk and wave like celebrities . . .

The island was entirely without power following Maria.

By February, nearly half a million families were still living in the dark. As of March 9, some 145,000 people were waiting to get back on the grid. That includes the entire community of Las Carolinas. Even when power is restored, outages are common: On April 20 the entire island was plunged into darkness for a day after a transmission line went down.

"The magnitude of destruction to the Puerto Rican power grid is beyond anything we've ever seen in the United States," says Col. Jason Kirk, the US Army Corps of Engineers commander for the power restoration task force in Puerto Rico. Part of the problem was the 155-mile-per-hour winds that tore across the island. But poorly maintained infrastructure—combined with the mountainous terrain in rural areas, which has made access difficult, as well as the need for large amounts of replacement materials—has added to the severity of the restoration challenge.

Utility crews focused first on municipal areas with large populations. Now they are finally reaching rural towns. In some cases, the terrain is so difficult that crews are using helicopters to string power lines from pole to pole.

"These are first-pass efforts," Kirk says of what is still considered "emergency" power repairs, half a year after the hurricanes hit. A lot of the fixes, in other words, are temporary. The priority is simply to get people plugged in. Then, says Kirk, it will be up to the Federal Emergency Management Agency;

Puerto Rico's power utility, PREPA; and the Puerto Rican government to design what the permanent grid will look like in the future.

While local residents are aware of the challenges utility workers face, that doesn't make living without power any easier. Many are paying $20 to $30 a day for gas to fuel their generators. In the town of Mariana, on the east coast of the island, one family painted the street in front of their home to read "SOS Water Food." A poster hangs from their balcony decrying the expense of running a few key electronics through a generator: "1/2 a year without light we can't manage more $$$."

"I can barely talk about this," says Nelida Colon, sobbing as she motions toward the sign. "My husband and I have $900 a month in Social Security, and we're running out of money" paying for a generator. "The government isn't here. There's no work. It's like we don't exist, like our town's not on the map."

The CAM in her community recently installed a water purification system in the river near her home, and Ms. Colon visits their community kitchen for meals periodically as well.

"I never thought it would be this way," she says. "But at least my neighbors are organizing."

At 11:30 a.m. four volunteers hop into a black minivan at the CAM in Las Carolinas. The back of the car is loaded with crates of hot soup and containers brimming with rice and chicken. The team cruises through the steep, curving streets of the neighborhood with both sliding doors open. They're the hunger SWAT team: speedy, prepared, and full of energy. Texidor, the driver, honks periodically, signaling to neighbors that her team is on its way.

At each delivery, women jump out of the van wearing plastic gloves and carry food to the homes of the nearly 100 bedridden or elderly people in this small community. Sometimes, Texidor starts driving ahead, leaving a volunteer to grab the next delivery while the van is still moving. Some of the houses they pass have blue tarps draped over roofs and orange netting acting as fencing.

After several deliveries, the team hits a snag: No one's home. Carmen Broges, one of the volunteers, calls out *"Buenas!"* as she walks down the steep driveway. "Lunch! Good afternoon!" she tries again, this time knocking and peeking through a back window. Just when she's about to give up, a car pulls in, and an older man helps his wife, dressed in a flowing nightgown, slippers, and hot-pink socks, out of the car.

"Oh thank you, thank you," he says, when he sees Ms. Broges. She helps the couple walk the rest of the steep path into their dark home. "What would we do without you?" the man asks.

The US has been no stranger to natural disasters over the past 15 years. From hurricane Katrina, Superstorm Sandy, and more recently, Hurricane Harvey, relief officials have been absorbing lessons for future prevention of and response to storm damage.

But the economic situation in Puerto Rico is so dire that it has exacerbated the hurricanes' effects, making both emergency relief and long-term planning more difficult. The poor are becoming poorer. Jobs are becoming even more scarce.

"The biggest thing right now is the urgency of how Congress and the White House will address [Maria and Irma damage] down the road," says Raúl Santiago-Bartolomei, a project manager at the leading Puerto Rican think tank, the Center for a New Economy.

Puerto Rico has elected government officials (with no representation in Congress) but is limited in how it can spend or borrow by a fiscal control group appointed under President Barack Obama. The board is meant to help the island climb out of its economic crisis.

"If you compare this with New Orleans or [Superstorm] Sandy, there's less emphasis on long-term recovery," says Mr. Santiago. "Who will implement long-term goals here? Who will refine those goals? The control board wants to be more proactive, but they don't really govern or implement solutions."

As a result, he says, the situation is pushing citizens to develop their own answers locally. His only concern is how this will work in the aggregate. "Not all communities have access to the same resources," he says. "There are many solutions that aren't scalable right now. What does that look like for Puerto Rico in the long term?"

One vision might lie in the town of Adjuntas, a 70-mile twisting and turning drive from Las Carolinas.

Back in 1980, Adjuntas was at risk of becoming a site for open-pit mining. The community joined forces to fight the development, organizing protests and creating a center for community support known as Casa Pueblo. Once Adjuntas successfully won its battle, the community-run organization had to decide what was next.

"Do we evolve, or do we disappear?" recalls Casa Pueblo co-founder Alexis Massol González, sitting at a long wooden table inside the bustling community center. Outside, music students sit on the porch of a solar-powered radio station. Volunteers give visitors cups of coffee brewed from beans cultivated by the community group.

After Maria, Casa Pueblo became a center for educating about solar power across the island. Locally, it reached out to some of the most vulnerable families, providing solar-powered fridges for those with urgent medical needs and solar lamps to anyone who requested one. As the months rolled on without power, neighbors started asking for more information about installing solar panels on their homes. A barbershop downtown now runs entirely on solar power.

"So many groups have emerged after Maria, focusing on education, on feeding their neighbors, on helping their communities survive," says Mr. Massol. "These new groups, they're not running out of ideas. There's long-term work ahead of them. It's fundamental for Puerto Rico."

The volunteers at the cafeteria in Las Carolinas are thinking about what's next, too. Once the lights are flipped back on, the question is whether people simply retreat to their former lifestyles.

"We won't stop feeding the elderly and the sick, now that we know who they are," says Arroyo.

Inside the cafeteria, the volunteers are cleaning up after serving roughly 200 meals that day. Kids start arriving after school, picking up brooms to help with the cleanup.

"My hope is that when people come through the CAM, they leave and see their community in a new light," says Texidor. "We're breaking the stereotype of always taking and receiving. We're doing it ourselves. And that's why, when the light finally returns, our work won't end. What we've created will only shine brighter."

VANDANA SHIVA

55 BUILDING WATER DEMOCRACY: PEOPLE'S VICTORY AGAINST COCA-COLA IN PLACHIMADA (2004)

Vandana Shiva directs the Research Foundation for Science, Technology, and Natural Resource Policy in Dehra Dun, India, where she is also involved in Navdanya, a movement for biodiversity conservation and farmers' rights. An award-winning activist and writer, she is a recipient of the Right Livelihood Award (an alternative to the Nobel Prize). Her many books include *Staying Alive: Women, Ecology and Development* (1988); *Water Wars: Privatization, Pollution, and Profit* (2002); *Earth Democracy: Justice, Sustainability and Peace* (2005); and *Making Peace with the Earth* (2013).

Two years ago, Adivasi[1] women in a small hamlet, Plachimada, in Palghat, Kerala, started a movement against Coca-Cola. Today, the Coca-Cola plant in Plachimada has been shut down. The victory of the Plachimada movement is a major step in reversing corporate hijacking of our precious water resources. It provides both inspiration and lessons for building water democracy in other parts of India and in the rest of the world.

The Coca-Cola plant in Plachimada was commissioned in March 2000 to produce 1,224,000 bottles of Coca-Cola, Fanta, Sprite, Limca, Thums Up, Kinley Soda, and Maaza. The Panchayat[2] was issued a conditional license for installing a motor for drawing water. However, the company started to illegally extract millions of liters of clean water from more than six bore wells installed by it using electric pumps in order to manufacture millions of bottles of soft drink.

According to the local people, Coca-Cola was extracting 1.5 million liters per day. The water level started to fall, going from 150 feet to 500 feet. Not only did Coca-Cola "steal" the water of the local community, it also polluted what was left. The company is also pumping wastewater into dry bore wells within the company premises for disposing of solid waste.

Earlier it was depositing the waste material outside the company premises, and during the rainy season it spread into paddy fields, canals, and wells, causing serious health hazards.

As a result of this, 260 bore wells which were provided by public authorities for drinking water and agriculture facilities have become dry. Complaints were also being received from tribals and farmers that storage of water and sources of water were being adversely affected by indiscriminate installation of bore wells for tapping ground water, leading to serious consequences for crop cultivation in the area on which residents of the Panchayat depend for their living: e.g., maintenance of traditional drinking water sources, preservation of ponds and water tanks, maintenance of waterways and canals, and shortage of drinking water. When the Panchayat asked for details, the company failed to comply.

The Panchayat therefore served a show cause notice and cancelled the license. Coca-Cola tried to bribe the Panchayat President A. Krishnan with Rs. 300 million, but he refused to be corrupted and coopted. In 2003, the district medical officer informed the people of Plachimada their water was unfit for drinking.

The women already knew their water was toxic. Instead of drawing water from the wells in their homes they had to walk miles. Coca-Cola had created a water scarcity in a water-abundant region. And the women of Plachimada were not going to

Source: Vandana Shiva "Building Water Democracy: People's Victory Against Coca-Cola in Plachimada" (2004)

Latuff 2009

allow this "hydropiracy." They started a "dharna" (sit-in) at the gates of Coca-Cola. On Earth Day 2003, they invited me to celebrate one year of their agitation.

On 21st September, 2003, a huge rally was organized to give an ultimatum to Coca-Cola. On 21st and 22nd of January, 2004, a World Water Conference brought global activists like Jose Bove and Maude Barlow to Plachimada to support the local activists.

A movement started by local Adivasi women had unleashed a national and global wave of people's energy in their support. On 17th February, 2004, the Kerala Chief Minister, under pressure of the growing movement and the aggravation of the water crisis because of a drought, ordered closure of the Coke plant. The victory of the movement in Plachimada was the result of creating broad alliances and using multiple strategies.

The rainbow alliances, beginning with the local women and activists like Veloor Swaminthan, Convenor of the anti–Coca-Cola task force in Plachimada, grew to include the local Gram Panchayat and its members Girija Devi, Geetha Mohandas, Sheeba Radhakrishnan, Aruchamy K, Sivakam, Subbayyan, MK Arumugham, K Varathara, A Krishnan, President, K Parthan, Presitha Mohandas, M Shanmugham, G Ponnukkuttam, N Chellankutty, C Murughan.

The local Panchayat used its constitutional rights to serve notice to Coca-Cola. The Perumatty Panchayat also filed a public interest litigation in the Kerala High Court against Coca-Cola.

The courts supported the women's demands. In an order given on 16th December, 2003, Justice Balakrishnana Nair ordered Coca-Cola to stop pirating Plachimada's water. As the Honorable Justice stated:

The Public Trust Doctrine primarily rests on the principle that certain resources like air, sea waters and the forests have such a great importance to the people as a whole that it would be wholly unjustified to make them a subject of private ownership. The said resources being a gift of nature, they should be made freely available to everyone irrespective of the status in life. The doctrine enjoins upon the government to protect the resources for the enjoyment of the general public rather than to permit their use for private ownership or commercial purpose. . . .

Our legal system—based on English common law—includes the public trust doctrine as part of its jurisprudence. The State is the trustee of all natural resources, which are by nature meant for public use and enjoyment. Public at large is the beneficiary of the seashore, running waters, airs, forests and ecologically fragile lands. The State as a trustee is under a legal duty to protect the natural resources. These resources meant for public use cannot be converted into private ownership. . . .

In view of the above authoritative statement of the Honorable Supreme Court, it can be safely concluded that underground water belongs to the public. The State and its instrumentalities should act as trustees of this great wealth. The State has got a duty to protect ground water against excessive exploitation and the inaction of the State in this regard is tantamount to infringement of the right to life of the people, guaranteed under Article 21 of the Constitution of India.

The Apex Court has repeatedly held that the right to clean air and unpolluted water forms part of the right to life under Article 21 of the Constitution. So, even in the absence of any law governing ground water, I am of the view that the Panchayat and the State are bound to protect ground water from excessive exploitation. In other words, the ground water, under the land of the 2nd respondent, does not belong to it.

Even assuming the experts' opinion that the present level of consumption by the 2nd respondent is harmless, the same should not be permitted for the following reasons:

The underground water belongs to the general public and the 2nd respondent has no right to claim a huge share of it and the Government have no power to allow a private party to extract such a huge quantity of ground water, which is a property, held by it in trust.

If the 2nd respondent is permitted to draw such a huge quantity of ground water, then similar claims of the other landowners will also have to be allowed. The same will result in drying up of the underground aqua-reservoirs.

Accordingly, the following directions are issued:

The 2nd respondent shall stop ground water for its use after one month from today.

The Panchayat and the State shall ensure that the 2nd respondent does not extract any ground water after the said time limit. This time is granted to enable the 2nd respondent to find out alternative sources of water.

The alliance grew to include people like Veerandra Kumar of Mathrubhumi and me. And we mobilized our networks to offer our full support to the local movement. The January conference was co-organized with the local Panchayat. It brought on one platform every political party, and the leader of the opposition V.S. Achuthanandan who kept up the pressure in the Kerala Assembly to translate the Court decision into Executive action.

The literary movement provided leadership through Dr. Sukumar Azhikode. And global support came in the presence of Jose Bove, Maude Barlow, European Parliamentarians and activists from across the world. The women's protest, the heart and soul of the movement, got support through legal action, parliamentary action and

scientific research. This pluralism and diversity in support of local action was the secret of the victory of people against Coke in Plachimada.

This is the strength of our multiplicities and complementarities; we have to mobilize in other parts of India where Coke and Pepsi are mining and stealing people's water resources. The Plachimada Declaration issued at the World Water conference of 21st–23rd January, 2004, states:

Plachimada Declaration

Water is the basis of life; it is the gift of nature; it belongs to all living beings on earth.

Water is not a private property. It is a common resource for the sustenance of all.

Water is the fundamental right of man. It has to be conserved. Protected and managed. It is our fundamental obligation to prevent water scarcity and pollution and to preserve it for generations.

Water is not a commodity. We should resist all criminal attempts to marketize, privatize and corporatize water. Only through these means we can ensure the fundamental and inalienable right to water for the people all over the world.

The Water Policy should be formulated on the basis of this outlook.

The right to conserve, use and manage water is fully vested with the local community. This is the very basis of water democracy. Any attempt to reduce or deny this right is a crime.

The production and marketing of the poisonous products of the Coca-Cola, Pepsi Cola corporates lead to total destruction and pollution and it also endangers the very existence of local communities.

The resistance that has come up in Plachimada, Pududdery and in various parts of the world is the symbol of our valiant struggle against the devilish corporate gangs who pirate our water.

We, who are in the battlefield in full solidarity with the Adivasis who have put up resistance against the tortures of the horrid commercial forces in Plachimada, exhort the people all over the world to boycott the products of Coca-Cola and Pepsi Cola.

Coca-Cola—Pepsi Cola: "Quit India."[3]

EDITORS' NOTES

1. *Adivasi* means "original inhabitants" in Sanskrit, or indigenous people, who have a distinct identity and culture. They have been marginalized within India, often brutally, starting with the British colonial administration, which opened up Adivasi areas for timber and developed these lands as estates. Adivasis continue to struggle for autonomy, control over resources, and restoration of traditional rights. Access to land is a major issue for Adivasis of Kerala.

2. *Panchayat* is the local community in tribal areas, recognized under the 1996 Provision of the Panchayats Act as the highest form of authority in matters of culture, resources, and conflict resolution. Village communities retained the power to approve or reject development plans and programs (Shiva 2002b).

3. In July 2017, *The Hindu* reported that Coca-Cola had made a submission before the Supreme Court that it had no intention of restarting operations at its contentious facility in Kerala, thus bringing the prolonged legal battle between the company and tribal people in Plachimada to a close (see https://www.thehindu.com/sci-tech/energy-and-environment/water-wars-plachimada-vs-coca-cola/article19284658.ece). However, the well waters are still unusable, villagers have not received compensation for their losses, and did not have adequate water supplies (Govind 2016).

Activism and Change

Creating Change

Theories, Visions, and Actions

Keywords: gender gap, identity-based politics, multiple positionality, transnational feminisms, United Nations standards

Major social movements—for labor rights, the civil rights of people of color, women's liberation, disability rights, and LGBTQI rights—have made gains in the United States over past decades. The data presented in this book also show currently contested issues for people of all genders, including immigration, sexuality, reproductive justice, economic security, affordable health care, freedom from violence, and respect for all people. Gains have been made but also eroded, as conservative politicians, aided by religious leaders and media personalities, have organized to limit or reverse them.

In this last chapter we consider how change happens, whether this is in one's own life and community or the wider world. The suggestions for action presented in other chapters are also relevant here.

Knowing what matters to you is an important start in taking charge of your life. This involves examining your experience, as suggested in the questions we have included in each chapter; otherwise, you will be absent from your system of knowledge. Abra Fortune Chernik provides an excellent example of this in Reading 56, where she reflects on her struggle with an eating disorder. Moving beyond her personal experience, she asks "why society would reward my starvation and encourage my vanishing." She explores psychological, sociological, and feminist theories to answer this question, which help her to change her earlier beliefs about herself and what mattered to her. Other writers in this collection start by examining their own lives and also go beyond micro-level accounts: Dorothy Alison (Reading 11), Melanie Kaye/Kantrowitz (Reading 12), Eli Clare (Reading 13), Daisy Hernández (Reading 16), Aurora Levins Morales (Reading 26), and Michelle R. Loyd-Paige (Reading 53). In Reading 57 Deborah Lee, who is an ordained minister with the United Church of Christ, writes about her faith as a tool for social change. She comments: "Once I discovered that it was possible to be both religious and political, a whole world opened up. This was a world that did not accept a false divide between the spiritual and political realms of life but saw them as interwoven."

HOW DOES SOCIAL CHANGE HAPPEN?

The process of creating social change requires a combination of theoretical insights and understandings, visions of alternatives, and action: using your head, heart, and hands together.

Using the Head: Theories for Social Change

As we pointed out in Chapter 2, doing something about an issue requires us to have a theory or explanation for it. The theory we create affects what we think ought to be done. As editors, our theoretical ideas and assumptions run through this book—sometimes explicit, sometimes implicit—and we summarize them here:

- A social constructionist perspective allows people to see how social and political forces shape our lives and our sense of ourselves. Thus, situations and structures are not necessarily fixed for all time but are changeable under the right circumstances.
- How a problem is defined and framed will affect how we think about it, where we look for probable causes, ideas about what ought to be done, and who is likely to become involved in working to change things.
- It is necessary to analyze social situations at micro, meso, macro, and global levels and to understand how these levels affect one another. Strategies for change need to address all levels.
- Using an intersectional framework and the concept of social location enables us to see similarities, differences, and contradictions in our lives and the lives of others.
- Many elected officials, organizations, and movements are working on the issues discussed in this book.
- Efforts to create equal opportunities for people of all genders and equal access to current institutions have made a difference, but by themselves, they cannot achieve a secure and sustainable world because these are not the goals of most institutions.

Using the Heart: Visions for Social Change

Vision is the second ingredient needed for social change—some idea of a different way of doing things, a different future. Otherwise, as the saying goes, "If you don't know where you're headed, any road will take you there."

Vision is about drawing on what we value and daring to think big. The many demands of our busy lives leave most people with little time or opportunity to envision alternatives. In school and college, students are rarely asked to think deeply about their hopes and dreams for a more truly human world in which to live. Much of what we do day-to-day is not guided by our own visions but is in reaction to the expectations of others and external pressures we face. Social issues, too, are framed in reactive and negative terms. People talk about "antiracism," for instance, not about what they want in a just, multiracial, multicultural society.

Some people scorn this process as time wasting and unrealistic. Our ideas are often limited to what we know, which makes it difficult to break out of our cramped habits of thought. Envisioning something different also means ignoring the voice inside your head that says: "You're too idealistic! This will never work! Who do you think you are? You'll never do it." And worst of all: "This is just how things are. It's human nature."

Go ahead. Envision your blossoming sexuality, the intimate relationship of your dreams, the caring and inclusive LGBTQI community, the reproductive justice app, the community play/read/care program for elders and children, the female taxi service, or whatever. Imagine a school, workplace, and community where everyone is deeply respected and valued simply for who they are. Visualize any one of these in as much detail as you can. Share your vision with others who you think will be sympathetic to it, and imagine even more possibilities together. This is where you're headed. Now all you need is to create the road. The projects we mention throughout this book, like this book itself, all started as somebody's dream.

Using the Hands: Action for Social Change

The third requirement for change is action. In Chapter 2, we mentioned philosopher Alan Rosenberg's (1988) distinction between *knowing* and *understanding*. Rosenberg maintained that understanding compels us to action, even though we may not initially want to change our habitual ways of thinking and being. When you understand something, he said, you

> find that [your] world becomes a different world and that [you] must generate a new way to be in the new world. Since each person's way of being in the world is relatively fixed—and serves as protection against the anxieties of the unknown—integration is extremely hard. To give up a world in which one's life makes sense means undergoing great loss. Yet without the readiness to risk that loss we cannot hope to pursue understanding. (p. 382)

never give up

© Jacky Fleming

Thinking back over this course, how has your understanding of gendered lives deepened? Are there things you want to do differently in your life as a result? Look back at how you defined feminism at the beginning. What have you learned?

Here, we suggest several ways to try to implement your visions. Some will be more appropriate than others depending on goals and theoretical perspectives.

Some of these activities may be difficult if you have many other commitments. You may be taking classes, working long hours, even supporting your family, concentrating on finishing college, getting a job, paying off school loans—or all of these. Progressive social change is a long-term project; there will be plenty to do after you graduate.

- Think about how you want to live your beliefs and ideals. Also, think of yourself as someone with something valuable to say, someone who can take the initiative and start something.
- Express your ideas: talk to others; write 'zines, leaflets, speeches, or letters to news editors and elected representatives; put up flyers or posters; organize a film series; perform poems, paint murals, dance, or sing your ideas.
- Spend your time and money where these resources will uphold your values and beliefs.
- Support women's organizations, LGBTQI groups, antiracist organizations, or environmental groups by letting them know you appreciate their work, and by letting others know these groups exist. Attend their events, donate money or something the group needs, volunteer your time, propose ideas for projects, or work as an intern for college credit.
- Decide to step up. In your family, you may want to stop others from telling sexist or racist jokes or to develop different relationships. At school, you may want to set up study groups, point out gaps in the curriculum or college services, or challenge racism or sexual harassment.
- Take back the old Nike slogan: Just Do It! Depending on the setting, this may mean interrupting; keeping silent; joining with women, queer, or trans people to walk together at night; defending women's health services; or participating in demonstrations and rallies, vigils and boycotts.
- Get together with others, and use the lenses presented in this book to analyze an issue of shared concern. Based on your analysis, work out how you can tackle it together.
- Learn more about local and national issues, and let your city, state, and congressional representatives know your opinions. Use your vote to help elect progressive candidates. Support them if they get into office, and hold them accountable to their election promises.
- Learn more about international networks and organizations working on topics that concern you. Consider participating in an international meeting if you can, and bring back the knowledge you gain to your organizing work at home.

A range of factors help us in taking action: frustration and anger at inequalities and injustices, a sense of hope and conviction that our and others' lives can be better, as well as reliable allies, well-thought-out strategies, and encouragement from parents, friends, classmates, or teachers.

Evaluating Activism, Refining Theory

Through action, theories and visions are tested, sharpened, and refined to create even more useful theories and more dynamic visions. Interventions may not always work; that is, a chosen course of action may not achieve your original goals. Maybe you had inadequate understandings of the issue, inappropriate strategies, or poor follow through. Perhaps you needed more people for a particular strategy to be effective. Possibly the group did not work together well enough, or people you thought were allies did not come through when needed, or the timing was wrong. The other major reason, of course, is that the opposition—whether this is your uncle, your boss, the university administration, the city school board, another political party, or the US Congress—was simply more powerful.

It is disheartening to feel that an action has failed, but do not give up. Action *always* accomplishes something, and in this sense, it always works. At the very least, activism that does not meet your goals teaches you something. What may seem like mistakes are valuable lessons about what you are up against, and how to be more effective in the future. This is what we called socially lived theorizing in Chapter 2. Always evaluate an activity or event, both personally and with your group. If it worked as you hoped, why was that? If it did not work, what will you do differently next time, and why? How might you even re-think what you were trying to change?

Personal blocks to activism may include practical factors like not having enough time or energy or needing to focus on schoolwork, a paid job, or some other aspect of life. Emotional blocks include guilt—a paralyzing feeling that keeps us stuck—and cynicism—frustrated idealism that has turned hopeless and bitter. Anger can be a high-octane fuel if you channel it in a constructive direction. Overextending yourself is not a sign of commitment to your ideals, and trying to do more than you can is one sure way to burn out quickly. Note that activism for progressive social change is not the same as simply being anti-authoritarian. It is strategic, and it needs patience, humor, creativity, resources, an ability to work with others, and a willingness to listen and to be reflective as you refine your ideas and your visions.

IDENTITIES AND IDENTITY-BASED POLITICS

Several contributors to this book write about identity. They describe coming to terms with who they are, and recognizing the complexities of their contradictory positions or their difficulties in breaking silence surrounding taboo thoughts and feelings. They also comment that coming to new understandings about themselves and being able to speak from a place of self-knowledge is very empowering.

Identity politics is, literally, a politics that puts identity at the center, based on gender, age, race, ethnicity, dis/ability, sexual orientation, nationality, or some other social category. It involves the assumption that this particular characteristic is important in the lives of a specific group: queers, Asian Americans, or seniors, for example. Identity politics is concerned with wider opportunities—greater visibility and recognition, equality, justice, even liberation—for us and our group. Our authority in speaking out comes from a common ground of experience that allows a group to say "we." This is the foundation for student organizations, community groups, national networks, and major social movements. Thus, identity can be an effective springboard for action.

At the same time, by itself, identity politics is limited. Groups tend to keep to themselves, focused on their issues and concerns, sometimes competing with each other for recognition and resources. Often there is an assumption of sameness, of basic characteristics and experiences that make one an authentic member, which may be truer for some members than for others. The language of identity politics gives voice to discrimination and oppression but does not encourage us to think about identity in a more complex way, as a mix of privilege and disadvantage. As noted in Chapter 3, salient aspects of identity may vary significantly depending on context. For instance, an African American graduate student who is about to receive her PhD may be highly respected by her teachers and peers, yet a white man walking past her in the street may only see her skin color and insult her because she is Black.

The related idea of **multiple positionality** helps us to see how different identity groups fit together in the wider society. Again, context is crucial. In US public discourse about immigration, for example, white people may fear being "overrun" by Latinxs or Asians, even if they do not say this explicitly. When the context shifts to a discussion of peoples of color, however, Asian Americans become the "model minority," the standard against which Latinxs or African Americans are compared unfavorably. Understanding how we are privileged as well as disadvantaged allows people to focus on the circumstances and concerns of our own group as well as make connections to other groups. This point is crucial in building alliances with others, and we return to it later. For now, we make a distinction between a narrower identity politics, discussed above, and **identity-based politics**, which has a strong identity component and also a broader view that enables people to make connections to other groups and issues. In this book, the Combahee River Collective (Reading 3), Deborah Lee (Reading 57) and Patricia St. Onge (Reading 58) all exemplify this approach, as do organizations founded by Loretta Ross (Reading 23), Anasuya Sengupta (Reading 40), and Susan Burton (Reading 41).

ELECTORAL POLITICS AND POLITICAL INFLUENCE

Women's political participation includes active membership in a wide range of organizations at local, state, and national levels, as mentioned throughout this book, and also in faith-based groups, community associations, parent-teacher associations, and labor unions. Anthropologist Leith Mullings (1997) pointed to women's transformational work—volunteering in community organizations and professional groups—in discussing Black women's lives. More recently, journalist Eisa Nefertari Ulen (2018) emphasized Black women's commitment to serving their communities, providing role models, and helping to grow leadership, although these involvements are not always recognized or given credit. Several articles in this collection are concerned with organizing (see Readings 9, 27, 29, 33, 54, and 57).

Political scientists interested in political influence tend to focus on formal arenas of power, especially the US Congress, where there are relatively few women. As a result, women's political participation outside of government has been seriously underestimated. Many of the organizations and projects we mention in this book record people's stories, undertake research, organize campaigns, and work to create a climate of opinion that will benefit oppressed people, whether women, queers, trans people, those who are incarcerated, and so on. Through websites, blogs, podcasts, and social media, they coordinate counterdiscourses to oppose sexist, racist, homophobic, and transphobic opinion and behavior in the public sphere. In the polarized political environment following the tight 2016 US presidential election, thousands of people, many wearing knitted pink "pussy hats," joined in vibrant Women's Marches in January 2017. Since then, opposition to government policies has continued, especially with regard to immigration, the environment, reproductive rights, and voting rights.

In Reading 59, Louise Burke shows the power of a social media campaign as the #MeToo movement, originated some years earlier by Tarana Burke, went viral overnight in October 2017. Allegations of sexual harassment and assault against Hollywood film producer Harvey Weinstein were the flashpoint that sparked the #MeToo and #TimesUp movements. These linked millions of women worldwide, often through established networks. Similarly, the fatal shooting of Michael Brown by a white police officer in Ferguson, Missouri, in 2014 was the catalyst for #Black Lives Matter, initiated by Patrisse Cullors, Alicia Garza, and Opal Tometi. This generated a broad **coalition** for racial and economic justice, the Movement for Black Lives (https://policy.m4bl. org/). Such flashpoints stimulate public awareness and new mobilizations, but these are often based on existing activist networks, personal connections, and "decades of quiet, painstaking groundwork" (Solnit 2018).

Running for Office

Some women who want to make political change set their sights on elected office—whether this is the school board, city council, state legislature, or the US Congress. A majority (58 percent) of people polled in 2016 thought that the United States would

A WOMAN'S PLACE IS IN THE HOUSE.

Mike Luckovich Editorial Cartoon used with the permission of Mike Luckovich and Creators Syndicate.
All rights reserved.

be better off with more women in public office. However, support for this view varied according to party affiliation. More than three quarters (77 percent) of Democrats agreed, but only 37 percent of Republicans—including only 42 percent of Republican women (Cooperman and Deckman 2016). Those who support women candidates often argue that a critical mass of elected women is needed to pass legislation to ensure better opportunities for women.

In 2018, women were 25.4 percent of state legislators nationwide; of those, 1,875 women, or 24.3 percent, were women of color (Center for American Women and Politics [CAWP] 2018a, 2018b, 2018c). The proportion of women in state legislatures has increased steadily from 5 percent in 1971, with high numbers of African American women now serving as state legislators in southern states: 62 percent in Alabama, 50 percent in Mississippi, 49 percent in Georgia, and 36 percent in Louisiana (Higher Heights, CAWP, and Eagleton Institute 2018, p. 7). At the Congressional level, starting January 2019, women hold a record number of seats: 23 of 100 seats in the Senate (17 Democrats and 6 Republicans) and 102 (23 percent) of the 435 seats in the House of Representatives (89 Democrats and 13 Republicans) (CAWP 2018d). This includes 43 women of color (22 Black women, 12 Latinas, 6 Asia/Pacific Islanders, 2 Native Americans, and 1 woman of Middle Eastern/North African ancestry). Numbers of women in Congress have increased from 5.6 percent in 1990, though the United States was 103rd out of 193 nations before the 2018 mid-term elections, with far fewer women in national office than many other countries (Table 12.1). In 2017, at least nine trans people were elected to state and local offices in several states across the country (Sopelsa 2017). In 2018, LGBTQI candidates ran for office in all 50 states, a first in US history (Victory Fund 2018).

Together with male allies in Congress, women elected officials and their staff have worked to pass the Family and Medical Leave Act, the Violence Against Women Act, and Title IX of the 1972 Education Act, which requires schools and colleges that receive federal funding to provide equal opportunities for students regardless of gender (see the box feature "Title IX"). They have also supported reproductive rights, health services, improvements in wage rates, the opening of combat roles to women, and so on. In interviews conducted by the Center for American Women in Politics, many Congresswomen observed that women must

> work harder to prove they belong, and they struggle to be heard on all issues and in all congressional spaces. They still are too often evaluated on style over substance and face greater challenges than men in meeting the conflicting demands of work and family. (Dittmar et al. 2017, p. 8)

Sociologist Margaret Andersen (2000) noted limitations for women who wanted to run for political office: voter and media prejudice against women candidates, lack of support from party leaders, lack of extensive political networks, and lack of money. Organizations like Emily's List, the Fund for a Feminist Majority, Higher Heights, and the National Women's Political Caucus are working to overcome these limitations (see, e.g., Dittmar 2015; Lawless and Fox 2010; Woods 2000). Political scientists Danny Hayes and Jennifer L. Lawless (2016) reassessed the significance of gender differences in their analysis of the 2010 and 2014 (mid-term) US House elections. They found that male and female candidates communicated similar messages, received similar coverage

Title IX

Title IX ("Title Nine") of the 1972 Education Act, signed into law by President Nixon, requires educational institutions that receive federal funding to provide equal opportunities for male and female students in academics, athletics, financial assistance, and resources like student health and housing. Title IX is a key reason that women have made gains in higher education. In sports, a college must meet one of three standards to comply with the law. It must have roughly the same proportion of women among its varsity athletes as it has in its undergraduate student body; it must have a "history and continuing practice" of expanding opportunities for women; or it must demonstrate that it is "fully and effectively accommodating the interests and abilities" of its women students (Suggs 2002, p. 39).

Detractors argued that increased resources for women would result in fewer opportunities for men, and some athletics departments achieved parity by cutting resources for male students rather than increasing those

for women. Several Ivy League and state universities have been forced into compliance as women sued them for discrimination. In March 2005, the Supreme Court held that retaliation against those who come forward to report discrimination must be prohibited, for effective enforcement of Title IX.

Sexual assault on campus is a factor in guaranteeing female and gender nonconforming students equal access to education. Governments have provided guidelines on this to schools and colleges that receive federal funding. In November 2018, the Department of Education announced new guidelines that "narrow the definition of sexual harassment and increase protections for students accused of misconduct" (Associated Press 2018). Know Your Title IX (https://actionnetwork.org/forms/join-the-ix-campus-action-network) is a student organization to help students address gender-based violence on college campuses.

in the local press, and had similar evaluations from voters in their districts. These researchers concluded that the declining novelty of women in politics together with polarization between the two major parties left little space for a candidate's gender to influence campaigns.

At the highest level, electoral politics is ruthlessly competitive and constrained by the need to raise huge campaign funds. Most women who consider elected office want to solve problems, and many do not want to embroil themselves in what they see as a "dirty" business. In addition, a US Supreme Court ruling that "the government may not ban political spending by corporations in candidate elections" has allowed a more explicit corporate role in politics (Liptak 2010). Corporations have long been considered "persons" under the US Constitution and entitled to First Amendment rights to free speech. Critics argued that the effect of this decision would be to further distort the electoral process and drown out the voices of ordinary citizens in Washington.

Gendered Voting Patterns

More women are registered voters than men. In 2016, there were 83.8 million women registered, compared to 73.8 million men (Dittmar 2018). Moreover, women vote at higher rates than men across all racial groups, a pattern that has held since 1980 (CAWP 2017, Table 1). In November 2016, 63.3 percent of female voters went to the polls, compared to 59.3 percent of male voters. A higher proportion of younger women have voted in the last twenty years compared to younger men. For older voters, this pattern is reversed, with more men voting than women (CAWP 2017, p. 2). Also, a clear **gender gap** in party identification has been evident since the early 1980s; larger proportions of women than men are Democrats (Dittmar 2014). More women support a comprehensive national health care system, government funding for social programs, gun control, workplace equity, reproductive freedom, LGBTQI rights, and an end to wars. Consistently, African American women are the most progressive group. In the 2016 Presidential election, for example, African American women voted for Hillary Clinton in large numbers compared to white women (see the box feature "Voting for President, 2016"). Voting patterns were similar in the 2018 mid-term election, with 49 percent of white women voting for Republican candidates and 49 percent voting for Democrats—though the Democratic share was higher (59 percent) for college-educated women. As in 2016, Black voters supported Democrats (92 percent of Black women and 88 percent of Black men). A larger number of young people voted in 2018, with 67 percent of voters aged 18 to 29 voting Democrat (Tyson 2018). Professor of Women's, Gender, and Sexuality Studies Treva Lindsey (2018) pointed out that among women voters, "white women voters continue to be the weakest link" in supporting a progressive agenda and argued that "progressive white female voters must continue to work in their communities to move more white women to the left".

Voting for President, 2016

	for Trump	for Clinton
Numbers	62,985,106	65,853,625
Electoral College	304	227
% Voters		
All men	53	41
All women	42	54
White voters	58	37
White women	53	43
Black voters	8	88
Hispanic	29	65
Asian	29	65
Income <$50,000	41	52
$50,000+	49	47
No high school diploma	51	45
Rural voters	62	34
Suburban voters	50	45
Urban areas	35	59
Age:		
18–29	37	55
30–44	42	50
45–64	53	44
65+	53	45

Source: BBC News (2016; based on Edison Research for the National Election Pool) and *New York Times* (2017). Totals do not add up to 100 percent because there were other candidates, and some voters did not answer every question.

ALLIANCES FOR CHALLENGING TIMES

Effective alliances are necessary for long-term political efforts, as well as coalition work where people stand together on a specific issue regardless of other differences. We see alliances across lines of difference as both a means and an end: they provide a process for moving toward, and also the experience of cross-cultural connections. The many inequalities among women, mentioned throughout this book, often separate us and make it difficult to work together effectively. Those with power over us know this and exploit differences to pit one group against another. Think about examples you know where this is happening.

Some Principles for Alliance Building

Alliances may be personal, campuswide, citywide, national, or transnational in scope. Regardless of scale, some basic principles apply:

- Know who you are, what matters to you, and what are your non-negotiables. Know your strengths and what you bring to a partnership or project.
- Decide whether you want to be allies with a particular person or group. What are their values? What are they interested in doing in terms of creating social change? Are they open to the alliance? What is the purpose for coming together? Are you coming together as equals? Or in solidarity with another group?
- Check out the person or the group as the acquaintance grows. Are they who they say they are? Judge them by their track record and what actually happens, not by your fears, hopes, or expectations based on previous experiences.
- Commit yourself to the process of communication rather than being overly attached to a specific position. Listen, talk, and listen more. Communication may be through conversations, reading, seeing films, attending events, or learning about one another's communities. Work together on projects and support one another's projects. Go into one another's settings as guests, observers, or participants.
- Share your history. Talk about what has happened to you and to the people of your group.
- Be patient. Wanting to understand, to hear more, to stay connected requires patience from the inside. Allow one another room to explore ideas, make mistakes, or be tentative. Hold judgment until you understand what's going on.
- Be honest and authentic, and ask for authenticity from others. If this is not possible, what is the alliance worth?
- Keep the process "clean." Call one another on bad things if they happen. Don't try to disentangle difficulties when it is impossible to do so meaningfully, but don't use externals (too late, too tired, too busy, too many items on the agenda) to avoid this.
- Be open to being called on your mistakes, admitting when you're wrong, even if it is embarrassing or makes you feel vulnerable. Tell the other person when their opinions and experiences give you new insights and help you to see things differently.
- Do some people in the group take up a lot of time talking about their own concerns? Are they aware of it? How does privilege based on gender, race, class,

nation, sexuality, dis/ability, age, culture, or language play out in this relationship or alliance? Can you talk about it openly?

- What is the "culture" of your group or alliance? What kinds of meetings do you have? What is your decision-making style? If you eat together, what kind of food do you serve? What kind of music do you listen to? Where do you meet? What do you do when you are together? Does everyone in the group feel comfortable with these cultural aspects?
- Work out the boundaries of your responsibilities to one another. What do you want to do by and for yourself? What do you need others to help with? When? How?
- Look for the common ground. What are the perspectives, experiences, and insights we share?
- Especially for people of privilege, know when to "step back" and when to "step up."

Overcoming Obstacles to Effective Alliances

Many sincere and committed attempts at building alliances have been thwarted, despite the best of intentions. Be aware of several common impediments to creating effective alliances, including the following beliefs and behaviors, which can apply at micro, meso, macro, and global levels of interaction and analysis:

- *Internalized Oppression.* This is a learned mindset of subservience and inferiority in oppressed peoples. It includes the acceptance of labels, prejudices, and perceptions promoted by the dominant society. Specific behaviors include self-hatred and dislike, disrespect for, or even hatred of others of the same group.
- *Internalized Domination.* This is a mindset of entitlement and superiority among members of dominant groups. Always speaking first in discussions, being unconscious of the large amount of physical and social space one takes up, and automatically assuming leadership roles are some of its manifestations.
- *Operating from a Politics of Scarcity.* This results from a deeply held, sometimes unconscious, belief that there is not enough of anything—material things as well as nonmaterial things like power, respect, popularity, friendship, time—and, more important, that however much there is, it will not be shared equally. In this view, inequality is simply a given that cannot be changed. It also justifies individualism and competition.
- *Subscribing to a Hierarchy of Oppression.* This involves the placement of one oppressed group in relation to another so that one group's experiences of discrimination, prejudice, and disadvantage are deemed to be worse or better than another's. Sometimes called the "Oppression Olympics."
- *Not Knowing One Another's History.* Ignorance about other people's backgrounds often results in drawing incorrect conclusions about their experiences. This prevents us from recognizing the diversity of people's experiences and can hide the ways our experiences are both different and similar.

Keeping different groups separate, and at odds with each other, is a colonizing strategy to maintain dominance. In Reading 58, Patricia St. Onge, who is of Haudenosaunee descent and a mother of mixed-race children, discusses connections between contemporary struggles of the Standing Rock Sioux people and the Movement for Black Lives. She points to the histories of Native American and African American people in this country, based on white supremacy perpetrated by settlers, although those in dominant positions do not necessarily see these two groups in the same way. St. Onge notes that many people "romanticize Indigenous people and lifeways in much the same way that we demonize Blackness." She acknowledges that both communities have resisted dehumanization "[i]n all the ways they could" and invites Indigenous and Black Peoples to come together as relatives, across this imposed divide. In general, overcoming the obstacles mentioned here will need thoughtful interventions and honest conversations to help keep alliances robust and healthy.

Transnational Women's Organizing

Alliances are central to social change movements in the United States and other nations. Historian Bonnie Anderson (2000) found that in the mid-nineteenth century, feminists from Britain, France, Germany, Italy, Sweden, and the United States shared ideas and tactics through letters, personal visits, and published writings. Nowadays feminist work across national boundaries, facilitated by e-mail, conference calls, and air travel, involves many coordinated campaigns and activities, as with struggles against extractivism in Latin America (see Reading 39) and militarism in Africa (see Reading 49), as well as support for immigrants in Western Europe (see Reading 45) and Syrian refugees (see Reading 47). In Reading 60, three established international feminist organizations combine their perspectives on the need for a just economy to support people worldwide. The points they make recap issues discussed in this book: the need for community knowledge, agroecology, reclaiming the commons, and challenges to the growth model of economics that cannot sustain people or the planet.

Many women's organizations around the world, particularly outside the United States, view the United Nations, headquartered in New York, as a potential ally in their struggles for women's rights. The United Nations was established after World War II and focuses on relations among nations. The chief deliberative body, the UN General Assembly, comprises 193 member nations, but the much smaller Security Council is the center of power and is dominated by five permanent members: China, France, the Russian Federation, the United Kingdom, and the United States.

The United Nations has introduced recommendations and standards for national laws and policies, including the Sustainable Development Goals (see the box feature 2030 UN Agenda for Sustainable Development). These exemplify the constructive nature of UN efforts to generate an alternative discourse to current global trends, a discourse that is both hopeful and human centered. However, achieving these goals will require significant change in prevailing economic and political priorities. Another example is the UN Convention on the Elimination of All Forms of Discrimination against Women (CEDAW), adopted by the UN General Assembly in 1979. Since then, women from many nations have pressured their government to implement CEDAW recommendations to advance women's status in that society. Other examples are the International Covenant on Economic, Social, and Cultural Rights; the Convention on the Rights of the Child; and the Convention on the Elimination of All Forms of Racial Discrimination. Individual governments must ratify UN conventions and resolutions for them to become national law and policy. Even if governments do not ratify them—and the

2030 UN Agenda for Sustainable Development

The 2030 Agenda for Sustainable Development, adopted by all United Nations member states in 2015, provides a blueprint for peace and prosperity for people and the planet, and includes the following Sustainable Development Goals:

1. No Poverty
2. Zero Hunger
3. Good Health and Well-being
4. Quality Education
5. Gender Equality
6. Clean Water and Sanitation
7. Affordable and Clean Energy

8. Decent Work and Economic Growth
9. Industry, Innovation and Infrastructure
10. Reduced Inequalities
11. Sustainable Cities and Communities
12. Responsible Consumption and Production
13. Climate Action
14. Life below Water
15. Life on Land
16. Peace, Justice and Strong Institutions
17. Partnerships for the Goals

Source: UN Sustainable Development Goals: Knowledge Platform. n.d.

United States has not ratified several UN conventions, including CEDAW—they may be useful for activists in their attempts to hold governments to **United Nations standards** and to show what other nations have pledged to do for women and girls.

Even though women are elected to national parliaments, as shown in Table 12.1, government priorities and resources may not support women. Thus, women's organizations may turn to the United Nations if their own government's policies toward women are weak or inadequate. Their governments may be dominated by wealthy elites, tightly aligned with business or military interests, or unable or unwilling to stop violence imposed by militias, often described as "non-state actors" (see Reading 49). The Universal Declaration of Human Rights, the UN's foundational document, and its organizational structure assume equality among nations, which is not current reality. Some feminists question whether it is meaningful to talk of universal human rights and how women can be protected in cases where cultural values and practices violate their rights and dignity. Nonetheless, conferences and hearings organized under UN auspices provide one avenue for international feminist networking, consolidating shared understandings, and generating solidarity (see, e.g., Antrobus 2004; Miles 2013; Moghadam 2005).

Chandra Talpade Mohanty (2003c) embraces **transnational feminism** but warns against organizing efforts that reproduce power dynamics and inequalities among feminists that parallel those in the wider world. She calls for ethical and caring "noncolonized" dialogue across differences, divisions, and conflicts, as mentioned in Chapter 2. From their different social locations, women define what Mohanty called "common contexts of struggle." This requires knowledge and political awareness, as well as determination, creativity, trust, and considerable patience to tackle, let alone surmount, structural inequalities between women from richer and poorer nations. Inequalities include the fact that some women may not have reliable Internet access, few fundraising opportunities, unequal purchasing power of local currencies, and difficulties in securing visas for international travel to attend meetings in the Global North. In addition, interpretation and translation services must be provided to include women who do not speak a common language.

TABLE 12.1   Women's Representation in National Legislatures (a sample)

COUNTRY	% WOMEN IN LOWER OR SINGLE HOUSE
Rwanda	61.3
Cuba	53.2
Bolivia	53.1
Costa Rica	45.6
Sweden	43.6
South Africa	42.7
Mozambique	39.6
Spain	39.1
Ethiopia	38.8
Denmark	37.4
Netherlands	36.0
Uganda	34.3
United Kingdom	32.0
Zimbabwe	31.5
Germany	30.7
Angola	30.5
Philippines	29.5
Poland	28.0
Canada	27.0
Vietnam	26.7
China	24.9
Bulgaria	23.8
Chile	22.6
Ireland	22.5
Venezuela	22.2
Kenya	21.8
Pakistan	20.6
Uruguay	20.2
United States of America	19.6
Greece	18.7
Colombia	18.1
Turkey	17.4
Republic of South Korea	17.0
Latvia	16.0
India	11.8
Japan	10.1
Liberia	9.9
Mali	8.8
Iran (Islamic Republic of)	5.9
Thailand	4.8
Kuwait	3.1
Haiti	2.5
Yemen	0.0

Source: Inter-Parliamentary Union. Women in National Parliaments (1 September 2018) http://archive.ipu.org/wmn-e/classif.htm

Next Steps for Feminist Movements

Given that corporations control more and more of the world and that women's rights are under serious attack in the United States and many other countries, people of all genders need to work together to address interconnected issues: economic survival, reproductive rights, all forms of violence (including state violence), respect for people's integrity, and so on. The challenge for the future is to maintain and expand this work: by sustaining progressive projects and organizations, running for office, voting, influencing public opinion, and putting out visions of freedom, genuine security, and sustainability.

In the United States, there is much accumulated experience and insight about how to work on multi-issue politics, generated over the years. As we build on the foundations laid by others, we come to the work of social change with contemporary expectations, hopes, and consciousness. Some things mentioned in this book were not possible ten or twenty years ago. Understandings of gender have changed profoundly. Young people learn about the importance of intersectional thinking at an earlier age. Technological changes have provided new tools as part of changing material conditions. In Reading 60, transnational feminist writers offer an invitation: "Now is the time to imagine futures free from oppression, injustice, war and violence, and to develop concrete strategies for people and the planet based on our shared humanity." The project of human development has been in process for a very long time. It is our challenge to take the next steps in this effort. How can we settle for anything less?

> Activism is not issue-specific.
> It's a moral posture that, steady state, propels you forward, from one hard hour to
> the next.
> Believing that you can do something to make things better, you do
> Something, rather than nothing.
> You assume responsibility for the privilege of your abilities.
> You do whatever you can.
> You reach beyond yourself in your imagination, and in your wish for
> Understanding, and for change.
> You admit the limitations of individual perspectives.
> You trust somebody else.
> You do not turn away. (June Jordan 1999, p. 17)

QUESTIONS FOR REFLECTION

As you read and discuss this chapter, think about these questions:

1. Think about an important change you have made in your life: in your beliefs, habits, or behavior. How did you do this? Who or what helped you to do so?
2. What are your assumptions about how people and societies change? What do you think needs changing, if anything? How is knowledge related to social change?
3. Have you tried to establish and maintain an intimate relationship, friendship, or working partnership with someone from a background very different to your own? What did you learn from that experience?

4. If you have had such a relationship, why did you become involved? Was this a good enough reason? Why or why not? If you never have, why not?
5. What do you know about the history of your family and the various groups you are a part of? What do you know about other groups? How does knowing this history help, and how does not knowing it hinder you in making alliances across lines of difference? How can you learn what you don't know?
6. Have you been involved in an activist project or electoral politics? If so, what was your experience like? If you have not, why not?
7. What is your vision of a secure and sustainable personal relationship? Community? Society? World?
8. Assuming you had time, energy, resources, and support, what kind of project or organization would you create to help make change for women, queer, trans and gender nonconforming people? What do you think this would need to be effective?
9. Even if you don't have the time, energy, or resources and support you'd like to have, which cause would you be willing to shift your priorities for?

FINDING OUT MORE ON THE WEB

1. Research the work of women's organizations mentioned in this chapter. What are their strategies and visions?
2. Research the history and activities of a current or past social movement that interests you. This can include movements across the political spectrum and working primarily in the United States or outside this country. How do those activists frame the issue/problem they are addressing? What is their theoretical foundation? Do they name specific constituencies and allies? If so, who are they? If international, what could US-based activists and organizers learn from these groups?

TAKING ACTION

1. List all the ways you are an activist. Review the suggestions for taking action at the end of each chapter. Commit to continuing to involve yourself in issues that matter to you.
2. Think about how aspects of your identity can help you to make alliances with others. Support campus or community groups that are working together on an issue of shared concern.
3. Where do your elected officials (at city, state, and national levels) stand on issues that concern you? What is their voting record on these issues? Write to thank them for supporting issues you care about (if they do), or urge them to change their positions. Present them with information from your course materials or other sources to make a strong case.

56   THE BODY POLITIC (1995)

Abra Fortune Chernik, a teacher and writer of essays, plays, and screenplays, is based in Chapel Hill, North Carolina. She established the Chernik Group in 1999 following graduate school. This is a tutoring practice to help high school students reach their potential, and has now expanded to offer services online.

My body possesses solidness and curve, like the ocean. My weight mingles with Earth's pull, drawing me onto the sand. I have not always sent waves into the world. I flew off once, for five years, and swirled madly like a cracking brown leaf in the salty autumn wind. I wafted, dried out, apathetic.

I had no weight in the world during my years of anorexia. Curled up inside my thinness, a refugee in a cocoon of hunger, I lost the capacity to care about myself or others. I starved my body and twitched in place as those around me danced in the energy of shared existence and progressed in their lives. When I graduated from college crowned with academic honors, professors praised my potential. I wanted only to vanish.

It took three months of hospitalization and two years of outpatient psychotherapy for me to learn to nourish myself and to live in a body that expresses strength and honesty in its shape. I accepted my right and my obligation to take up room with my figure, voice and spirit. I remembered how to tumble forward and touch the world that holds me. I chose the ocean as my guide.

Who disputes the ocean's fullness?

Growing up in New York City, I did not care about the feminist movement. Although I attended an all-girls high school, we read mostly male authors and studied the history of men. Embracing mainstream culture without question, I learned about womanhood from fashion magazines, Madison Avenue and Hollywood. I dismissed feminist alternatives as foreign and offensive, swathed as

they were in stereotypes that threatened my adolescent need for conformity.

Puberty hit late; I did not complain. I enjoyed living in the lanky body of a tall child and insisted on the title of "girl." If anyone referred to me as a "young woman," I would cry out, horrified, "Do not call me the W word!" But at sixteen years old, I could no longer deny my fate. My stomach and breasts rounded. Curly black hair sprouted in the most embarrassing places. Hips swelled from a once-flat plane. Interpreting maturation as an unacceptable lapse into fleshiness, I resolved to eradicate the physical symptoms of my impending womanhood.

Magazine articles, television commercials, lunchroom conversation, gymnastics coaches and write-ups on models had saturated me with diet savvy. Once I decided to lose weight, I quickly turned expert. I dropped hot chocolate from my regular breakfast order at the Skyline Diner. I replaced lunches of peanut butter and Marshmallow Fluff sandwiches with small platters of cottage cheese and cantaloupe. I eliminated dinner altogether and blunted my appetite with Tab, Camel Lights, and Carefree bubble gum. When furious craving overwhelmed my resolve and I swallowed an extra something, I would flee to the nearest bathroom to purge my mistake.

Within three months, I had returned my body to its preadolescent proportions and had manipulated my monthly period into drying up. Over the next five years, I devoted my life to losing my weight.

Source: Reprinted with permission of Hachette Books Group from *Listen Up: Voices from the Next Feminist Generation*, edited by Barbara Findlen (Seattle: Seal Press, a member of Perseus Books, 1995); permission conveyed through Copyright Clearence Center, Inc.

I came to resent the body in which I lived, the body that threatened to develop, the body whose hunger I despised but could not extinguish. If I neglected a workout or added a pound or ate a bite too many, I would stare in the mirror and drown myself in a tidal wave of criticism. Hatred of my body generalized to hatred of myself as a person, and self-referential labels such as "pig," "failure" and "glutton" allowed me to believe that I deserved punishment. My self-hatred became fuel for the self-mutilating behaviors of the eating disorder.

As my body shrank, so did my world. I starved away my power and vision, my energy and inclinations. Obsessed with dieting, I allowed relationships, passions and identity to wither. I pulled back from the world, off of the beach, out of the sand. The waves of my existence ceased to roll beyond the inside of my skin.

And society applauded my shrinking. Pound after pound the applause continued, like the pounding ocean outside the door of my beach house.

The word "anorexia" literally means "loss of appetite." But as an anorexic, I felt hunger thrashing inside my body. I denied my appetite, ignored it, but never lost it. Sometimes the pangs twisted so sharply, I feared they would consume the meat of my heart. On desperate nights I rose in a flannel nightgown and allowed myself to eat an unplanned something.

No matter how much I ate, I could not soothe the pangs. Standing in the kitchen at midnight, spotlighted by the blue-white light of the open refrigerator, I would frantically feed my neglected appetite: the Chinese food I had not touched at dinner; ice cream and whipped cream; microwaved bread; cereal and chocolate milk; doughnuts and bananas. Then, solid sadness inside my gut, swelling agitation, a too-big meal I would not digest. In the bathroom I would rip off my shirt, tie up my hair, and prepare to execute the desperate ritual, again. I would ram the back of my throat with a toothbrush handle, crying, impatient, until the food rushed up. I would vomit until the toilet filled and I emptied, until I forgave myself, until I felt ready to try my life again. Standing up from my position over the toilet, wiping my mouth, I would believe that I

was safe. Looking in the mirror through puffy eyes in a tumescent face, I would promise to take care of myself. Kept awake by the fast, confused beating of my heart and the ache in my chest, I would swear I did not miss the world outside. Lost within myself, I almost died.

By the time I entered the hospital, a mess of protruding bones defined my body, and the bones of my emaciated life rattled me crazy. I carried a pillow around because it hurt to sit down, and I shivered with cold in sultry July. Clumps of brittle hair clogged the drain when I showered, and blackened eyes appeared to sink into my head. My vision of reality wrinkled and my disposition turned mercurial as I slipped into starvation psychosis, a condition associated with severe malnutrition. People told me that I resembled a concentration camp prisoner, a chemotherapy patient, a famine victim or a fashion model.

In the hospital, I examined my eating disorder under the lenses of various therapies. I dissected my childhood, my family structure, my intimate relationships, my belief systems. I participated in experiential therapies of movement, art and psychodrama. I learned to use words instead of eating patterns to communicate my feelings. And still I refused to gain more than a minimal amount of weight.

I felt powerful as an anorexic. Controlling my body yielded an illusion of control over my life; I received incessant praise for my figure despite my sickly mien, and my frailty manipulated family and friends into protecting me from conflict. I had reduced my world to a plate of steamed carrots, and over this tiny kingdom I proudly crowned myself queen.

I sat cross-legged on my hospital bed for nearly two months before I earned an afternoon pass to go to the mall with my mother. The privilege came just in time; I felt unbearably large and desperately wanted a new outfit under which to hide gained weight. At the mall, I searched for two hours before finally discovering, in the maternity section at Macy's, a shirt large enough to cover what I perceived as my enormous body.

With an hour left on my pass, I spotted a sign on a shop window: "Body Fat Testing, $3.00." I suggested to my mother that we split up for ten minutes; she headed to Barnes & Noble, and I snuck into the fitness store.

I sat down in front of a machine hooked up to a computer, and a burly young body builder fired questions at me:

"Age?"

"Twenty-one."

"Height?"

"Five nine."

"Weight?"

"Ninety-nine."

The young man punched my statistics into his keyboard and pinched my arm with clippers wired to the testing machine. In a moment, the computer spit out my results. "Only ten percent body fat! Unbelievably healthy. The average for a woman your age is twenty-five percent. Fantastic! You're this week's blue ribbon winner."

I stared at him in disbelief. *Winner? Healthy? Fantastic?* I glanced around at the other customers in the store, some of whom had congregated to watch my testing, and I felt embarrassed by his praise. And then I felt furious. Furious at this man and at the society that programmed him for their ignorant approbation of my illness and my suffering.

"I am dying of anorexia," I whispered. "Don't congratulate me."

I spent my remaining month in the hospital supplementing psychotherapy with an independent examination of eating disorders from a social and political point of view. I needed to understand why society would reward my starvation and encourage my vanishing. In the bathroom, a mirror on the open door behind me reflected my backside in a mirror over the sink. Vertebrae poked at my skin, ribs hung like wings over chiseled hip bones, the two sides of my buttocks did not touch. I had not seen this view of myself before.

In writing, I recorded instances in which my eating disorder had tangled the progress of my life and thwarted my relationships. I filled three and a half Mead marble notebooks. Five years' worth of: *I wouldn't sit with Daddy when he was alone in the hospital because I needed to go jogging; I told Derek not to visit me because I couldn't throw up when he was there; I almost failed my comprehensive exams because I was so hungry; I spent my year at Oxford with my head in the* *toilet bowl; I wouldn't eat the dinner my friends cooked me for my nineteenth birthday because I knew they had used oil in the recipe; I told my family not to come to my college graduation because I didn't want to miss a day at the gym or have to eat a restaurant meal.* And on and on for hundreds of pages.

This honest account of my life dissolved the illusion of anorexic power. I saw myself naked in the truth of my pain, my loneliness, my obsessions, my craziness, my selfishness, my defeat. I also recognized the social and political implications of consuming myself with the trivialities of calories and weight. At college, I had watched as classmates involved themselves in extracurricular clubs, volunteer work, politics and applications for jobs and graduate schools. Obsessed with exercising and exhausted by starvation, I did not even consider joining in such pursuits. Despite my love of writing and painting and literature, despite ranking at the top of my class, I wanted only to teach aerobics. Despite my adolescent days as a loud-mouthed, rambunctious class leader, I had grown into a silent, hungry young woman.

And society preferred me this way: hungry, fragile, crazy. *Winner! Healthy! Fantastic!* I began reading feminist literature to further understand the disempowerment of women in our culture. I digested the connection between a nation of starving, self-obsessed women and the continued success of the patriarchy. I also cultivated an awareness of alternative models of womanhood. In the stillness of the hospital library, new voices in my life rose from printed pages to echo my rage and provide the conception of my feminist consciousness.

I had been willing to accept self-sabotage, but now I refused to sacrifice myself to a society that profited from my pain. I finally understood that my eating disorder symbolized more than "personal psychodynamic trauma." Gazing in the mirror at my emaciated body, I observed a woman held up by her culture as the physical ideal because she was starving, self-obsessed and powerless, a woman called beautiful because she threatened no one except herself. Despite my intelligence, my education, and my supposed Manhattan sophistication, I had believed all of the lies; I had almost given my life in order to achieve the sickly impotence that this culture aggressively links with female happiness, love and success. And everything I had to offer to the world, every tumbling wave, every thought and every passion, nearly died inside me.

As long as society resists female power, fashion will call healthy women physically flawed. As long as society accepts the physical, sexual and economic abuse of women, popular culture will prefer women who resemble little girls. Sitting in the hospital the summer after my college graduation, I grasped the absurdity of a nation of adult women dying to grow small.

Armed with this insight, I loosened the grip of the starvation disease on my body. I determined to re-create myself based on an image of a woman warrior. I remembered my ocean, and I took my first bite.

Gaining weight and getting my head out of the toilet bowl was the most political act I have ever committed.

I left the hospital and returned home to Fire Island. Living at the shore in those wintry days of my new life, I wrapped myself in feminism as I hunted seashells and role models. I wanted to feel proud of my womanhood. I longed to accept and honor my body's fullness.

During the process of my healing, I had hoped that I would be able to skip the memory of anorexia like a cold pebble into the dark winter sea. I had dreamed that in relinquishing my obsessive chase after a smaller body, I would be able to come home to rejoin those whom I had left in order to starve, rejoin them to live together as healthy, powerful women. But as my body has grown full, I have sensed a hollowness in the lives of women all around me that I had not noticed when I myself stood hollow. I have made it home only to find myself alone.

Out in the world again, I hear the furious thumping dance of body hatred echoing every place I go. Friends who once appeared wonderfully carefree in ordering late-night french fries turn out not to eat breakfast or lunch. Smart, talented, creative women talk about dieting and overeating and hating the beach because they look terrible in bathing suits. Famous women give interviews insulting their bodies and bragging about bicycling twenty-four miles the day they gave birth.

I had looked forward to rejoining society after my years of anorexic exile. Ironically, in order to preserve my health, my recovery has included the development of a consciousness that actively challenges the images and ideas that define this culture. Walking down Madison Avenue and passing emaciated women, I say to myself, *those women are sick*. When smacked with a diet commercial, I remind myself, *I don't do that anymore*. I decline invitations to movies that feature anorexic actors, I will not participate in discussions about dieting, and I refuse to shop in stores that cater to women with eating-disordered figures.

Though I am critical of diet culture, I find it nearly impossible to escape. Eating disorders have woven their way into the fabric of my society. On television, in print, on food packaging, in casual conversation and in windows of clothing stores populated by ridiculously gaunt mannequins, messages to lose my weight and control my appetite challenge my recovered fullness. Finally at home in my body, I recognize myself as an island in a sea of eating disorder, a sea populated predominantly by young women.

A perversion of nature by society has resulted in a phenomenon whereby women feel safer when starving than when eating. Losing our weight boosts self-esteem, while nourishing our bodies evokes feelings of self-doubt and self-loathing.

When our bodies take up more space than a size eight (as most of our bodies do), we say, *too big*. When our appetites demand more than a Lean Cuisine, we say, *too much*. When we want a piece of a friend's birthday cake, we say, *too bad*. Don't eat too much, don't talk too loudly, don't take up too much space, don't take from the world. Be pleasant or crazy, but don't seem hungry. Remember, a new study shows that men prefer women who eat salad for dinner over women who eat burgers and fries.

So we keep on shrinking, starving away our wildness, our power, our truth.

Hiding our curves under long T-shirts at the beach, sitting silently and fidgeting while others eat dessert, sneaking back into the kitchen late at night to binge and hating ourselves the next day, skipping breakfast, existing on diet soda and cigarettes, adding up calories and subtracting everything else.

We accept what is horribly wrong in our lives and fight what is beautiful and right.

Over the past three years, feminism has taught me to honor the fullness of my womanhood and the solidness of the body that hosts my life. In feminist circles I have found mentors, strong women who live with power, passion and purpose. And yet, even in groups of feminists, my love and acceptance of my body remains unusual.

Eating disorders affect us all on both a personal and a political level. The majority of my peers—including my feminist peers—still measure their beauty against anorexic ideals. Even among feminists, body hatred and chronic dieting continue to consume lives. Friends of anorexics beg them to please start eating; then these friends go home and continue their own diets. Who can deny that the millions of young women caught in the net of disordered eating will frustrate the potential of the next wave of feminism?

Sometimes my empathy dissolves into frustration and rage at our situation. For the first time in history, young women have the opportunity to create a world in our image. But many of us concentrate instead on re-creating the shape of our thighs.

As young feminists, we must place unconditional acceptance of our bodies at the top of our political agenda. We must claim our bodies as our own to love and honor in their infinite shapes and sizes. Fat, thin, soft, hard, puckered, smooth, our bodies are our homes. By nourishing our bodies, we care for and love ourselves on the most basic level. When we deny ourselves physical food, we go hungry emotionally, psychologically, spiritually and politically. We must challenge ourselves to eat and digest, and allow society to call us too big. We will understand their message to mean too powerful.

Time goes by quickly. One day we will blink and open our eyes as old women. If we spend all our energy keeping our bodies small, what will we have to show for our lives when we reach the end? I hope we have more than a group of fashionably skinny figures.

57 FAITH AS A TOOL FOR SOCIAL CHANGE (2018)

Deborah Lee is an ordained minister with the United Church of Christ and serves as the Executive Director of the Interfaith Movement for Human Integrity, an organization that connects people of faith to the work of social justice. Rev. Lee has worked at the intersection of faith and social justice for over twenty-five years in popular education, community organizing, and advocacy, connecting issues of race, gender, economic justice, anti-militarism, LGBTQ inclusion and immigrant rights.

"When you're an immigrant, you don't need people to tell you that you don't belong, you feel like that every minute of the day," said my mom, who came to this country in 1966 escaping the violence and turmoil in Indonesia at that time. Her first lonely months in northeastern Ohio were made more tolerable by certain "angels" she met at critical and opportune moments. On one occasion, she had no place to stay, no way to move her belongings, and knew hardly anyone to ask for help. She wandered into a church and the organist ended up helping her find a rooming house and eventually a job. Another time, she walked by a church when a man with a booming voice shouted, "Welcome!" "Who, me?" she thought, looking around. It was the first time anyone had ever said "Welcome" to her as a newcomer and a foreigner. It made such an impression that she still tells this story fifty years later. When people think about faith, they don't often think of these small powerful gestures. They think of religious history, ancient stories, dogma and beliefs. But to my mother, these daily practices of faith and kindness were life-saving actions, which symbolized to her that God was with her on her journey.

For my family church was our extended family as our real relatives were far away in Indonesia and Hong Kong. Church was a big part of our lives socially and theologically. The Christianity I was exposed to then was the scary kind, where I feared being sentenced to a tormented afterlife if I didn't believe and follow the rules. But the vivid stories of

Jesus's life made a big impression on me—the miracles, healings, encounters with unusual characters, friends and enemies. I got baptized and committed myself to follow Jesus, but by the time I went away to college I was struggling with many contradictions in Christian faith and practice.

One of these was gender. I had a basic understanding of 1980's feminism that said it was wrong to discriminate on the basis of gender. So how could I rationalize being part of a church and biblical tradition that subordinated women? Women were not allowed to be pastors or preach from the pulpit. They seemed to be valued only for teaching Sunday School to small children and organizing church potlucks. Another concern I had was the emphasis on people's souls going to heaven rather than caring what they were dealing with today. The response to the homelessness of children and families was shockingly passive: we could pray about it, save their souls, and rely on God's will to fix the situation. It seemed grossly inadequate and not what Jesus would do.

I enrolled in a big state university and witnessed political activism for the first time. For every problem there seemed to be a group of people trying to do something about it: feeding the hungry, saving the planet, making campuses safer for women, challenging racism, ending wars. There were hundreds of actions and solutions that seemed far more effective than prayer. It was heartening to know that change could be affected and human suffering addressed in so many ways. The Christianity I grew

Source: Deborah Lee, written for this volume.

up with drew a hard line between faith and politics. I thought I had to choose. So I chose politics as it seemed to be making more of a difference. It wasn't until I encountered a whole breed of faith-inspired and religious people like me engaged in activism, that I realized faith and politics can co-exist and be a powerful tool for social change.

Once I discovered that it was possible to be both religious and political, a whole world opened up. This was a world that did not accept a false divide between the spiritual and political realms of life but saw them as interwoven. These people viewed human beings as having both spiritual and material needs like jobs, health care, education, housing, and racial and gender justice. They cared about the whole person. They saw political action as an extension of their spiritual beliefs and practices, just as important as prayer and piety. They brought the values, songs, and tone of faith to their political actions. I met Christians from El Salvador who had worked with Archbishop Oscar Romero. He was assassinated for calling for an end to the US-backed civil war in that country, which took the lives of tens of thousands of Salvadorans and caused over a million refugees to flee. I met people in the Philippines and South Korea engaging in anti-dictatorial struggles as people of faith, sometimes at risk of their lives. These deeply spiritual activists were not just engaging in acts of charity, but were seriously challenging structural power and oppression. They did not separate or hide their religion. Instead, their faith sustained them in the hard work of creating social change and helped advance their struggles for freedom and justice.

Of course, the engagement of religious folks in activism is not always an easy fit. Many secular activists are suspicious of or turned off by religious people. And with good reason. Christianity, in particular, has been an instrument of harm and domination, contributing to colonialism, the doctrine of Manifest Destiny, and the genocide of indigenous nations. It has been used to justify slavery, misogyny, homophobia, white supremacy, and Christian dominance. Christian activists in the US have to be willing to acknowledge the harm and transgressions caused by our religion. It is a painful process, but failure to address foundational lies and to

accept this truth will prevent us from facing other lies that continue to diminish and divide people.

It is important to see the oppressive elements of one's own religious tradition clearly and critically. But this doesn't contradict the fact that many people have found liberation, healing and meaning from their faith, and we need to understand and hold up this complexity. In African American communities, for example, religion may have been imposed by the dominant group, yet some adopted it and used it as a liberatory force for emancipation from that very same oppressor. We should recognize that faith has been a force for survival, resilience and the resistance of African American communities in the face of historic and modern-day systemic dehumanization. Also, for many immigrant communities, faith and culture are a vital source of spiritual sustenance and meaning as people navigate the realities of living in the United States. Faith congregations provide community, networks for resources and jobs, and a place for people to express their needs, offer their gifts and their leadership, which are sometimes unrecognized in the outside world. Faith matters to people, especially those at the margins, who have very little else to rely on.

In 2006, I became an ordained minister. Nationwide, the number of female pastors in Christian protestant churches is 10 percent, a small proportion, but a number that has doubled in the past 10 years.[1] In some protestant denominations, like mine, it is up to 25 percent, but others like the Southern Baptists and the Roman Catholic Church continue to disallow female ordination. As a minister, I have sought to practice my faith in ways that are relevant to the political and social challenges in the world. In our organization, the Interfaith Movement for Human Integrity,[2] we call this faith-rooted organizing, a method of community organizing or change-making that is shaped and guided by spiritual values.[3] We see ourselves as part of the long, but sometimes not widely known strand of liberatory faith that exists in all religious traditions. The spiritual practices of First Nation indigenous communities, for instance, embody a holistic approach that combines ceremony with direct action to protect sacred land and assert self-determination as seen at Standing Rock and in indigenous movements to protect land and water. Engaged Buddhism couples social action with meditation and mindfulness. Thich Nhat Hanh, a Vietnamese Buddhist monk, began this approach in Vietnam during wartime, wanting to address violence, war, and environmental, political, and economic suffering, as part of Buddhist spiritual practice. Hindu and Jain philosophies influenced Gandhi's theories and practices of nonviolence. Judaism has a long tradition of addressing social justice issues, summed up in the phrase "tikkun olam"—repairing the world. Rabbi Abraham Joshua Heschel, a leading Jewish theologian active in the US civil rights movement famously said, "When I marched with Rev. Martin Luther King Jr. in Selma, I felt my legs were praying." Within Christianity, liberation theology provided a religious foundation to address the crushing poverty and inequalities in Latin American countries in the 1950's–60's, and has inspired the involvement of people of faith in wider social and revolutionary struggles. Also, this liberation theology inspired many other theologies of liberation, such as Black theology and feminist theology that address racial or gender oppression. In Islam, contemporary organizations like Muslims for Progressive Values provide educational and theological resources for Muslims with a liberal or progressive Islamic worldview that affirms gender equality and LGBTQI inclusion. The Muslim organization MPower Change sees itself as continuing the 120-year history of Muslims engaged in US political life.

As an activist pastor my work looks different from that of a traditional minister. Instead of preaching on Sunday mornings, mostly I preside over interfaith prayer services in the street: outside prisons, immigration detention centers, courthouses, City Hall, the State Capitol, and the Pentagon. I have learned to feel and invoke the Spirit in the midst of traffic and sidewalk bustle. Together with all kinds of people—those of faith and no-faith, documented and undocumented, housed and unhoused, rich and poor—we do all the things one would do in a religious ritual only out in public: We sing, chant, and pray with those who need a prayer of solidarity and encouragement. We march, advocate, and sometimes get arrested. We practice inclusion and beloved community. We leave feeling inspired and hopeful, perhaps with new ideas about how next to intervene in pressing social problems.

As an interfaith organization we have created sacred spaces and brought spiritual practices into the streets as part of innovative public prayer and protest that shines a light on the injustices of our nation's treatment of immigrants. We bring our street liturgies and the power of truth to confront systems of injustice and to sustain the spirit and hope of those struggling for a life of respect and dignity. In this work, we have held Passover seders outside the detention facility, a Ramadan fast for justice, and a Christmas Posada with recent immigrants re-enacting their own perilous migration stories. During Christian Holy Week, before Easter, we conduct a public footwashing ritual in front of the Immigration Customs and Enforcement (ICE) office, to honor the dignity and lives of immigrants, to wash the feet of those wearing ankle monitoring bracelets and facing deportation.

For International Women's Day 2018, at a public gathering at the San Francisco Comfort Women Memorial, we offered this prayer for women migrants as part of a ceremony to honor and remember many women affected by systemic state-sponsored violence[4]:

> "We honor women today who are facing the hard reality of forced migration.
> Forced by the lack of jobs, hiring discrimination against women over 30, failed government policies to ensure dignified work and decent wages at factories sewing t-shirts and teddy bears.
> Forced by contamination of lands by international mining, and land evictions to grow export crops.
> Unable to feed their children, pay their school fees, buy shoes, their only option is to seek work elsewhere—the big city—or the next rich country which will pay 10 times what they would earn in a day at home.
> Forced to migrate because of violence . . . from intimate partners, or strangers who target trans, lesbian, gay and women's bodies, or hired assassins who try to intimidate them to keep quiet, not to protest, to move on. Violence rooted in governments which fail to prosecute gender-motivated killings. Their only option is to migrate for lack of justice and a place to breathe free.

We honor all women today who are on the journey. . . leaving in the middle of the night . . . following the stars . . . bringing one child with them, leaving other children behind. Knowing that they will lose things on the way. Things carried . . . things lost . . . things that will carry them through.

We marvel and wonder how women somehow manage to parent from afar . . . through guilt and Skype . . . Or on the journey, through the desert, in the bottoms of cars and big rigs, being chased by helicopters. . . Being separated on the journey, lost, or in freezing detention centers that give only 4 ounces of milk and half a sandwich. . . "Mami, I'm cold. I'm hungry. I'm scared."

We decry the systematic way that women's bodies and women's lives have been put in harm's way because of laws and policies that have made migration illegal. Migration, which is as old as our ancient ancestors from Africa who moved in search of food and freedom. Now people are on the run from border patrol, electronic sensors, helicopters, high security systems, and drones. Migration, which comes from our animal ancestors, the birds and the butterflies, is now met by a 30-foot high concrete wall.

Making migration illegal, makes migration more dangerous:

- Between 60 and 80 percent of female migrants traveling through Mexico are raped along the way. Policies and appropriations approved in the halls of Congress have made sexual violence against women's bodies part of the "ticket" to freedom.

Making migration illegal, makes migration more profitable:

- to organized crime, which extorts, robs, kidnaps, rapes and traffics;
- to Mexican state police and immigration agents which extort, rob, kidnap, rape and traffic; and
- to US border patrol, border contractors, lobbyists, prison guards and the growing private prison industry which profit off women's bodies through prolonged detention and deportation.

As Mujeres Unidas y Activas states: "Deportation is Violence Against Women."

We honor migrant women who despite all the violent obstacles and barriers
Nonviolently resist. . . by coming anyway.
By moving their bodies across those borders in search of life, work, and freedom.
Who say: It was for my children. . . for their future . . . so I could live. . . .no price was too great.
We honor and lift up:

- The two Guatemalan teenagers who came forward to sue US Border Patrol officers for raping them during their detainment.
- The 22 detained immigrant mothers who led a 16-day hunger strike for better conditions and called for their families' release after over a year in detention.
- The 39 women in the Richmond West County Detention Facility who boldly created a petition to condemn poor conditions—racial abuse, excessive lockdown in their cells for 23 hours a day, limited access to bathrooms, phone calls, and human dignity.
- The tens of thousands of women who are holding their families together while their menfolk are in immigration detention and prison.

We honor those who fight for the right to migrate with dignity. For the end of immigration detention. For the end of deportations and the right to stay.
For those who say: There is another way— tearing down walls, lifting up justice.
For "The immigrant who resides with you shall be to you as one of your citizens; you shall love them as yourself. . . for you were once immigrants . . . " (Leviticus 19:33–34)

I believe that faith communities are a significant part of social movements. They bring unique gifts: powerful symbols, cultural resonance, moral authority, and creative and spiritual practices to sustain a movement. I realize that not everyone is comfortable with or interested in religion or spirituality. In fact, in the US, an increasing percentage of people identify as non-religious: atheist, agnostic or "nothing in particular."[5] Thirty-five percent of Millennials and roughly 23 percent of the adult population categorize themselves this way. This is prompting many of us in the religious community to rethink what we mean by "religious" or "spiritual" and to frame this more broadly.

For me, faith and spirituality mean reflecting on the following questions: What does it mean to be human? What is a just society? How do I live authentically? What is my relationship and responsibility to others? How do I walk in this world? What meaning do I make of my life?

At root, spirituality is about relationship and connection. Capitalism, violence, racism, and sexism have undermined and destroyed our fundamental sense of relatedness. We are increasingly fearful and separated from each other, as well as separated from our natural environment and the earth. This breeds alienation, hopelessness, and a crisis of meaning although we, as humans, long for meaning, belonging and connection. Faith or spirituality can help remind us of our relatedness, and what it means to be human even amidst fear, fragmentation, and cynicism. Spirituality can help us strengthen our love, empathy and responsibility for the world we inhabit and will pass on to the next generation. I have hope that faith, spirituality, or whatever we may call it in the future, will make a difference in making change to support our collective life and our survival as a human family on this planet.

NOTES

1. See Hartford Institute for Religious Research: http://hirr.hartsem.edu/research/quick_question3.html
2. See http://www.im4humanintegrity.org/
3. See *Faith Rooted Organizing: Mobilizing the Church in Service to the World* by Alexia Salvatierra and Peter Heltzel. Intervarsity Press, 2014.
4. See https://www.youtube.com/watch?v=E2-OeXLezw0&feature=youtu.be
5. Pew Research Center, "A closer look at America's religious 'nones'." May 13, 2015.
http://www.pewresearch.org/fact-tank/2015/05/13/a-closer-look-at-americas-rapidly-growing-religious-nones/

58   TWO PEOPLES, ONE FIRE (2016)

Patricia St. Onge, of Haudenosaunee descent, is the founder of Seven Generations Consulting and Coaching. A grandmother of six, she is adjunct faculty at Pacific School of Religion and Mills College and is a board member of the Highlander Research and Education Center. She is part of a growing community, Nafsi ya Jamii (The Soul Community) in East Oakland, hosting a retreat center and farm.

I'm Haudenosaunee (Mohawk) and French Canadian, adopted Cheyenne River Lakota. My daughters are all that and African American. Between us, my partner and I have ten grown children (six daughters and their spouses); straight and queer, Black, Indigenous, Chicano and white. I'm a member of Idle No More SF Bay, and part of a circle of Indigenous grandmothers. I sit on the edge of the Movement for Black Lives as a mother, loving and supporting my grown children, some of whom are fully immersed.

My daughter Karissa shared a Facebook post that expressed frustration about the outpouring of support for Standing Rock that looks different from the support for BLM. I understand the frustration. I also know that we romanticize Indigenous people and lifeways in much the same way that we demonize Blackness.

The post led to a rich discussion about the connections between Standing Rock water protectors and the Movement for Black Lives. I know there are delegations of BLM folks who've been to Standing Rock to stand in solidarity. There's an intuitive sense that the two are interconnected. I have some thoughts about how to put language around it.

There's something about this moment that feels like a phase shift. I think of a historical phase shift as akin to that split second when water turns to steam. If you don't know how evaporation works, it can easily seem spontaneous, even magical. We *do know* how evaporation works. Heat has to be applied to the water; it simmers, and then boils for some time before it actually turns to steam.

The heat that led to this national phase shift got turned on at the moment of contact; when Europeans landed here. As soon as the Nations already here saw that the colonizers' intentions were to take everything they wanted, without recognizing they were meeting their relatives, there emerged a culture of resistance. A spark was lit. Across the waters of our Mother, Earth, another spark was lit when the Westerners landed in Africa. As people on both continents were captured, enslaved, murdered, raped, the spark in each land grew.

In our time, Black Lives Matter, and the Movement for Black Lives turned the spark once again into a blazing fire. They heated the water, past its long, long simmer. They turned it to a rolling boil. When Standing Rock Sioux Tribe and neighboring Lakota Nations saw the black snake of the prophecies materialize in the form of the Dakota Access Pipeline (DAPL), they were lit by the fires that had been rekindled by the Movement for Black Lives. The two flames live in the hearts and minds and spirits in both communities. Like my children, they both live in many bodies as well. There's no need for "Oppression Olympics" here. Black people and Indians come from the same fire.

There's a long history of that fire burning, sometimes blazing, other times just barely a spark. Looking back on first contact with settlers on both continents, when it was clear that neither People could be fully subjugated in their own homelands, Gambians, Ghanaians, Sierra Leonians, by their own names for themselves, were shipped over to this continent uprooted and stripped of the

Source: Author.

capacity to speak their Native languages. Children were sold away from their families. The spark of language and ceremony was kept, barely alive, by the ancestors who were praying for and thinking about the generations to come. In all the ways they could, they resisted dehumanization.

Here on this continent, in neighboring communities, the spark grew; also in secret, as ceremonies were outlawed. Children were extracted from families, sent to boarding schools, or adopted out. Still, the spark grew; sometimes rising to flames bright enough to light the hearts of those who had lost touch with who they really were.

Then, the poisons would come; hoses, dogs, bullets, crack and alcohol; tools of oppression meant to steal the souls of those on whom they were unleashed. But, because of the spark of resistance, the poison water, while it had some effect on its intended targets, splashed back and deadened the souls of those who were pouring it out.

When the Pope and the Monarchs sent Europeans, who were just finished devastating the Moors (Muslims) via the Crusades, out to "discover" "new" lands, they sent them with what they saw as God's mandate to claim any land they found for the monarchy. God was on their side as proclaimed in the Doctrine of Discovery. Armed with that sense of purpose, there was no room in their hearts and minds for curiosity. They expected to meet no humans along the way. So, they didn't see any; instead they saw property. From this lack of imagination, the inability to see the relatives who stood in front of them, grew the need to see everything and everyone as a commodity. The land had no sovereignty. It became real estate. The water wasn't a relative, it was a "thing" to extract, exploit and destroy. This is the legacy of the settler world view. Yet, as all that happened, and continues today, the spark of the flames of resistance continues to grow. The descendants of those colonized and those enslaved can find courage and strength in the legacy of the fire. Some of the descendants of the colonizers are waking up to their legacy too.

My invitation is that we, Indigenous and Black Peoples, find the courage in our legacies, and come together as relatives, to continue to come back to the fire. Together, as we liberate the land, the water, the air, and all our relatives (four legged, swimmers, flying ones, standing ones, etc.), we will find our collective liberation.

In that space of liberation, may we unleash our imaginations to build on the legacy of resistance. As the Hopi say, we are the ones we've been waiting for.

LOUISE BURKE

59 THE #METOO SHOCKWAVE: HOW THE MOVEMENT HAS REVERBERATED AROUND THE WORLD (2018)

Louise Burke is Assistant Foreign News Editor at The Daily Telegraph, a British national daily newspaper.

In Naomi Alderman's novel *The Power*, girls around the world suddenly and mysteriously gain the ability to electrocute people. At first governments think they can contain it, but soon the relationship between men and women begins to shift rapidly. A global revolution follows in which women, now physically dominant, topple patriarchal institutions like dominoes.

Five days before Alderman's book was published in the USA, the *New York Times* reported allegations of sexual harassment and assault against film producer Harvey Weinstein. Five days after it was published, the hashtag #MeToo went viral. And two months after that, *Time* magazine named "the silence breakers," women who spoke out about abuse, assault and rape, as its "person of the year." A global revolution has indeed begun—though where it is going nobody yet knows.

From its origins in the US, the impact of the movement spread rapidly, with millions of women around the world sharing their own stories of rape, assault and harassment in the workplace. Most cases will never meet the public eye in the way the Weinstein scandal did, with its rota of famous faces coming forward day after day to deliver lurid and disturbing details of the director's alleged predatory behavior. But a glance at local media reports reveals that almost every country in the world has had its own #MeToo moment: From Britain's Westminster scandal to "Australia's Weinstein" Don Burke and journalist Shiori Ito's unprecedented public discussion about her alleged rapist in Japan.

The phrase "Me Too" was first used by activist Tarana Burke 10 years ago in a grassroots campaign to reach underprivileged girls dealing with sexual abuse. But it became an overnight phenomenon after actress Alyssa Milano encouraged victims of sexual abuse to tweet #MeToo as a way to show the world a "sense of the magnitude of the problem" following the Weinstein scandal. By the time she woke up the next day, thousands had responded. Within weeks it was more than a million.

As a viral campaign, part of the success of #MeToo was to do with how deeply personal it felt. Within days our social media feeds were flooded with friends and family members adding their stories. "Of course, me too," a friend added simply on Facebook, neatly summarizing the depressing inevitability that she too had experienced sexual harassment. The women mostly exchanged familiar stories and knowing looks. Surprise was the domain of men: "I knew it happened, but I had no idea it was *this* bad" was a common sentiment.

In Spain it became #YoTambien, in France it became #BalanceTonPorc, roughly translated as "expose your pig"; in Italy #quellavoltache ("That Time When"). In Israel, a Hebrew phrase translated as "Us Too." In China, where Facebook is blocked, posts appeared briefly on local social media channels before being ripped down by censors.

In Japan, journalist Shiori Ito did "the unthinkable" when she appeared before television cameras in May 2017 to publicly accuse a prominent correspondent of rape. At the time she only used her first name, but in late October, amid the explosion of #MeToo confessions, she revealed her full identity and published a book about her experience. In an article for *Politico*[1] she wrote that it is taboo to even use the word "rape" in Japan and it is often changed to "violated" or "tricked." "My coming forward made national news and shocked the public," she wrote. "The backlash hit me hard. I was vilified on social media and received hate messages and emails and calls from unknown numbers. I was called a "slut" and "prostitute" and told I should 'be dead'." But Ito believed she had no other choice. She said #MeToo has provided an opening in the Japanese media to discuss sexual harassment and assault.

Meanwhile in Australia, television personality Don Burke, a household name from his long-running gardening program *Burke's Backyard*, was about to be exposed by allegations of bullying and harassment of women who worked with him over two decades. Among them was eight-time Olympic gold medalist Susie O'Neill, who claimed Burke compared her genitals to a painting of a flower by her husband. "Is your c**t as big as that?", she said he asked her during a visit to her Brisbane home ahead of the 2000 Olympics.

Burke has denied all allegations of sexual harassment, but admitted he "might have terrified a few people" because he was a tough taskmaster.

Allegations against Burke came to light after journalist Tracey Spicer, inspired by #MeToo, put a call out on social media for women who had experienced sexual harassment in the Australian media. The response was so great (she terms it "a tsunami of injustice") that she worked with the country's media union to set up a kind of triage service for the hundreds of replies she received, directing people towards counselling, legal and police support, before hearing their stories. Before the dust could settle on the Burke allegations, *Neighbours* actor Craig McLachlan was also accused of sexual misconduct by multiple women who worked with him on the Australian Rocky Horror show (allegations he denies and plans to fight).

"Globalization, connectivity and the women's rights movement have created the perfect storm," Spicer told the *Telegraph*. "Women are able to share their experiences, from Sydney to Suffolk. "Suddenly, we realize we're not alone. And our experiences are being believed. For the first time, men are understanding what women have suffered for centuries."

The Australian cases have been highly organized, with senior journalists and several media organizations directing investigations and filtering and verifying the information. But they highlight a common theme emerging around the world—the way in which women are now using social media to network and share information about sexual harassment, usually under the radar, before coming forward as a united front against repeat offenders.

Spicer said online networks had "changed everything. "Almost all of the whistleblowers who've approached me do so via Twitter (direct message) or Facebook (private message) before a phone or email conversation," she said. "Our personal devices are such an intimate part of our lives, these women feel comfortable using social mediums—at any time of the day or night—to share details about these experiences. And it's easy to connect with other alleged victims. For example, in the Don Burke case, the first whistleblower was able to easily connect me with two women in the US."

In some cases, the method used to gather this information has been less controlled, throwing up ethical questions which have fed into a growing backlash against the #MeToo movement. The Westminster dossier, a spreadsheet filled with the names of 40 MPs and ministers accused of various forms of misconduct, was criticized for containing unverified accusations. A similar style of crowd-sourced document was used by University of California graduate student Raya Sarkar to gather accusations against more than 50 academics in India and the US. In both instances, feminists have been split over the methods used. Some argue that such extreme methods risk damaging the credibility of women's legitimate demands to be heard. Others argue that they are excusable when the existing systems have acted to protect predators, rather than victims.

Numerous prominent women, mostly from an older generation than the majority of the first wave of #MeToo Hollywood accusers, have accused the movement of becoming puritanical. Actress Catherine Deneuve was among 99 French women who signed a letter in *Le Monde* arguing that the campaign had gone too far and was fueled by a "hatred of men,"[2] highlighting a fundamental debate among French women about the type of feminism the country identifies with—feminine sexuality as a source of power vs. a source of oppression. Meanwhile Germaine Greer, never one to shy from controversy . . . described #MeToo as "whingeing," lamenting that "in the old days" women would "slap down" men who harassed them.

But the backlash has done little to stem the progression of the debate, which has now widened beyond discussion of more explicit cases of assault and harassment to a conversation about the thorny issues surrounding consent. This was driven in part by Kristen Roupenian's fictional story, "Cat Person," published by the *New Yorker*, and an account of a woman's date with comedian Aziz Ansari, which turned into "the worst night of my life."

While long-overdue conversations like this are highly publicized in the West, perhaps the greatest measurable impact of #MeToo has been in its arrival in countries where ideology or religious doctrine have traditionally hampered open conversations about sexual assault. Countries like China, where a university professor has been sacked—and another was investigated—over allegations from students via Sina Weibo, China's Twitter. Or conservative Indonesia, where a woman defied police inaction by obtaining and sharing CCTV footage of her own assault, resulting in an arrest.

There is a recurring image in *The Power* which helps us understand all this. Alderman uses the spreading, forking, tree-like shape of lightning—and which lightning strikes lave on skin or wood—as a metaphor to describe social change. It starts at the bottom, with millions of individual people suddenly realizing that the rules have shifted, that they can do something. Their behavior filters up and up until the whole of society turns upside down.

What remains to seen is where all of this disruption leads to in the long term. Will women across the world see significant change, or will it be reserved for the privileged few? Will some be punished for their attempt to rise up, like those in Alderman's book who were blinded in an attempt to suppress their new-found power? Or will they be ignored and quietly silenced? One thing is for certain: The #MeToo movement has exposed an epidemic of sexual assault and harassment across every corner of the world and unbottled a collective fury which can no longer be contained. Any notion that it is a short-lived Western fad can safely be dismissed.

NOTES

1. Shiori Ito, "Saying #MeToo in Japan," *Politico*, January 2, 2018, https://www.politico.eu/article/metoo-sexual-assault-women-rights-japan/.
2. Our Foreign Staff, "'Feminist' Catherine Deneuve Apologizes to Sex Assault Victims," *The Telegraph*, January 15, 2018, https://www.telegraph.co.uk/news/2018/01/15/feminist-deneuve-apologises-sex-assault-victims/.

EDITORS' NOTE

1. The original publication includes a timeline, "The spreading ripples of the #MeToo movement: How it happened," which amplifies this article. See https://www.telegraph.co.uk/news/world/metoo-shockwave/

60 FEMINIST PROPOSITIONS FOR A JUST ECONOMY: TIME FOR CREATIVE IMAGINATIONS (2016)

The **Association for Women's Rights in Development** (https://www.awid.org), **Center for Women's Global Leadership** (https://cwgl.rutgers.edu), and **African Women's Development and Communications Network** (https://femnet.org) are international feminist organizations committed to gender equality, sustainable development, social justice, and women's human rights.

Close your eyes and imagine the global economic systems of your dreams. One in which feminist theory and practice are integrated and concepts like market, growth, and profit are replaced with solidarity, sharing of resources and collective well-being.

What Needs to Change?

The neoliberal model driving the global economy has consistently demonstrated its inability to address the root causes of poverty, inequalities, and exclusion. In fact, it has contributed to the creation and exacerbation of these injustices.

In the current context, there are many obstacles but five major documented threats[1] to the struggle towards feminist just economies have been identified:

1. Growing financialization of the world economy.
2. Harmful trade agreements.
3. Unprecedented scale of threat to ecosystems and biodiversity.
4. Accelerating commodification of land and resource grabbing.
5. Entrenched patriarchal foundations that structure the capitalist system.

These threats challenge feminists to re-think our frameworks and strategies and to renew and reactivate our commitment to movement building with others for a just economy.

Where to Start

We are not starting from zero, nor are we alone in this attempt to dream that another world is possible. Different experiences have been advanced, or exist in practice, within diverse communities challenging and resisting the mainstream market and growth-based economic systems.

A joint online project[2] by Association for Women's Rights in Development (AWID), the Center for Women's Global Leadership[3] (CWGL), and the African Women's Development and Communication Network[4] (FEMNET) offers a space to share, document, analyze, critique and improve some of these propositions for a feminist economic justice agenda.

As feminists struggling for gender, peace, economic, social and environmental justice, we know there is no single recipe for creating an alternative economic system, but rather that an array of possibilities can, and are, making change happen. The opportunities are as diverse as our movements and the communities in which we live and struggle.

The Propositions

What if the value of goods and services was determined by communities that depend on them and not by profit logic and companies? What if human relationship, generation of goodwill, and attention to nurturing the whole society, and not just one's immediate self, were the norm?

Source: This article was originally published by the Association for Women's Rights in Development (AWID).

Solidarity Economy

A solidarity economy framework[5] proposes just that. Proponents have been experimenting, resisting and co-existing for years with the capitalist system in the forms of cooperatives and other associations. Experiences of a solidarity economy have huge potential, but should not be romanticized. It is essential to actively identify and pushback against capitalism, patriarchal norms, sexism, racism, classism and other sources of discrimination and oppression that could be reproduced within this framework.

Community Knowledge to Build Just Futures

Community knowledge[6] is at risk of being erased from practice, commodified and colonized. Despite this, communities continue to make huge contributions to integrate production and reproduction as inseparable processes of the economy. For example the concept of Buen Vivir (living well), a concept adapted from Andean Indigenous peoples' knowledge, is about collective achievement based on harmonic and balanced relations among human beings and all living beings, in reciprocity and complementarity.

There have been important criticisms, from a feminist perspective, of the binary interpretations of gender that leave little space for a deeper discussion on heteropatriarchy. Nevertheless, one of the main contributions of centralizing the principle of Buen Vivir to political, economic and social frameworks, is that equality is no longer the paradigm of individual rights, but the transformation of society as a whole.

Agroecology and Food Sovereignty

Agroecology and food sovereignty[7] propose a break with the hegemonic rural development model, based on large landed estates and single-crop plantations, which use technologies harmful to the environment. Instead, they involve rural people, particularly women, building on local priorities and knowledge. Reflection on socially constructed gender roles are also important to advance the emancipatory potential of agroecology as an alternative means of food production.

Reclaiming the Commons

The concept of the commons rests on the cultural practice of sharing livelihood spaces and resources (including the resources of knowledge, heritage, culture, virtual spaces, and even climate) as nature's gift, for the common good, and for the sustainability of the common. Experiences that aim to reclaim the commons[8] seek to restore the legitimate rights of communities to these common resources. Patriarchy is reinforced when women and other oppressed genders are denied access and control of these resources. A feminist perspective towards the commons acknowledges women and other oppressed gender roles, and provides equal opportunities for decision-making, seeing all as equal claimants to these resources.

Challenging the economic growth model

Contesting the premise that a country's economy must always "grow or die," de-growth propositions[9] aim to shift towards a lower, sustainable, level of production and consumption. In essence, shrinking the economic system to leave more space for human cooperation and ecosystems. Looking at this proposal through a feminist lens, there is potential within de-growth to devalue capital driven activities that fuel the current model of economic growth. Instead to redefine and re-validate unpaid and paid, care and market labor, to overcome traditional gender stereotypes, and the prevailing wage gaps and income inequalities that devalue care work.

Some of the important critiques to this proposal come from Southern perspectives. Not everyone can afford de-growth—countries on the periphery are still overcoming colonialism, building and adapting sustainable production models, and many still lack access to basic needs such as water, food, healthcare and education, to enter in a de-growth mode.

An Invitation to Co-create Across Movements

Feminist propositions for a just economy are critical to create dents in the system and draw lessons for transformative systemic change. Now is the time to imagine futures free from oppression, injustice, war and violence, and to develop concrete strategies for people and the planet based on our shared humanity. . . .

As Arundhati Roy said, "Another world is not only possible, she is on her way. On a quiet day, I can hear her breathing."

NOTES

1. AWID, "5 Major Threats," http://www.awid.org/5-major-threats.
2. AWID, "Where Does the Project Come From?" http://www.awid.org/where-does-project-come.
3. See http://www.cwgl.rutgers.edu/.
4. See http://femnet.co/.
5. AWID, "Solidarity Economy," http://www.awid.org/solidarity-economy.
6. AWID, "Community Knowledge to Build Just Futures," http://www.awid.org/community-knowledge-build-just-futures.
7. AWID, "Agroecology and Food Sovereignty," http://www.awid.org/agroecology-and-food-sovereignty.
8. AWID, "Reclaiming the Commons," http://www.awid.org/reclaiming-commons.
9. AWID, "Challenging the Economic Growth Model," http://www.awid.org/challenging-economic-growth-model.

GLOSSARY

AGEISM Attitudes, actions, and institutional practices that subordinate elderly persons on the basis of their age.

ANTI-ARABISM Attitudes, actions, and institutional practices that subordinate Arabs and Arab Americans.

ANTI-SEMITISM Attitudes, actions, and institutional practices that subordinate Jewish people. (Note: the term *Semite* is used also to refer to some Arabs.)

ASSIMILATION The process by which a minority group adopts the customs, values, and attitudes of the dominant culture

BIOCAPACITY The Earth's ability to generate renewable resources and to absorb wastes.

BIOLOGICAL DETERMINISM A general theory holding that a group's biological or genetic makeup shapes its social, political, and economic destiny. This view is used to justify women's subordination or the subordination of peoples of color on the argument that they are biologically or genetically different from, and usually inferior to, men or white people, respectively.

CAPITALISM An economic system in which most of the capital—property, raw materials, and the means of production (including people's labor)—and goods produced are owned or controlled by individuals or groups—capitalists. The goal of all production is to maximize profit-making. Also referred to as *free market system*.

CISGENDER People whose gender identity is the same as they were assigned at birth.

CLASSISM Attitudes, actions, and institutional practices that subordinate working-class and poor people on the basis of their economic condition.

COALITION Usually a short-term collaboration of organizations in which the strategy is to stand together to achieve specific goals around a particular issue, regardless of other differences among the organizations.

COMMODIFICATION The process of turning people into things, or commodities, for sale; an example is the commodification of women's bodies through advertising and media representations. Sometimes, a cultural group's sacred objects, such as Native American people's dreamcatchers, are also commodified and sold.

COMPARABLE WORTH A method of evaluating jobs that are traditionally defined as men's work or women's work—in terms of the knowledge and skills required for a particular job, the mental demands or decision-making involved, the accountability or degree of supervision involved; and working conditions, such as how physically safe the job is—so as to eliminate inequities in pay based on gender.

CRIMINALIZATION The processes whereby people who do not fit dominant societal norms are labeled as criminals. Their circumstances and behaviors are defined as crimes, such as mothers with HIV/AIDS, homeless people, immigrants, and gender nonconforming people. The opposite process is decriminalization.

CULTURAL APPROPRIATION Taking possession of specific aspects of another group's culture in a gratuitous, inauthentic way, as happens, for example, when white people wear their hair in "dreads" or when non-indigenous people use indigenous people's names and symbols or adopt indigenous people's spiritual practices without being taught by indigenous practitioners. A particularly egregious form of cultural appropriation involves using another group's culture to make money. This is routine in the tourist industry, for example.

CULTURAL CAPITAL   A form of power and advantage where an attribute that society values, like thinness or professional contacts, can be cultivated and exchanged for other forms of power.

DISCRIMINATION   Differential treatment against less powerful groups (e.g., women, seniors, or people of color) by those in positions of dominance.

DOMINANT CULTURE   the values, symbols, language, and interests of the people in power in this society.

ECOFEMINISM   A philosophy that links the domination of women with the domination of nature.

ENVIRONMENTAL JUSTICE   A philosophy and movement based on the belief that all citizens have a right to healthy living and working conditions.

ENVIRONMENTAL RACISM   The strong correlation between the distribution of environmental pollution and race in the United States.

EPISTEMOLOGY   A theory about knowledge, including its sources, structure, validity, and limits. This includes who can know, under what circumstances, as well as the researchers' values and choices about how to carry out their inquiries.

EXTRACTIVISM   The process whereby corporations extract natural resources like oil, timber, or minerals, often from countries of the Global South, whose governments sell land or rights to natural resources to foreign companies and investors.

EUGENICS   The belief that the human race can be "improved" through selective breeding; linked to racism and able-bodyism or attitudes, actions, and institutional practices that subordinate people with disabilities.

FAIR TRADE   This includes paying a fair wage in a local context; providing equal opportunities, especially for disadvantaged people; engaging in environmentally sustainable practices; providing healthy and safe working conditions; and being open to public accountability. Even with fair trade, however, producers of export crops like coffee depend on the vagaries of the international coffee market, which makes them vulnerable to fluctuations in price and demand.

FEMINIZATION OF POVERTY   Women and children constitute the majority of poor people in the United States and throughout the world, a result of structural inequalities and discriminatory policies.

FIRST-WAVE FEMINISM   Organizations and projects undertaken by suffragists and women's rights advocates from the 1830s to the 1920s.

FIRST WORLD   Countries grouped together according to political alliances and economic status: Western Europe, Japan, Australia. New Zealand, Canada, and the United States. This is often contrasted with *Third World*, which includes most of Asia, Latin America, Africa, and the Caribbean.

GENDER BINARY   The belief that there are two separate genders, male and female.

GENDER EXPRESSION   The ways people choose to show their **gender identity**—for example, through clothing, hairstyle, makeup, and body language, as well as their name and preferred pronouns.

GENDER GAP   A significant difference between the perspectives, political attitudes, and voting patterns based on gender.

GENDER IDENTITY   An individual's sense of identity as male, female, gender neutral, gender nonconforming, genderqueer, gender variant, or trans.

GENDER ROLES   The roles and behaviors considered culturally appropriate for women or men.

GENDER SOCIALIZATION   The process of learning the attitudes and behaviors that are considered culturally appropriate for boys or girls.

GENDERED DIVISION OF LABOR   A division of duties between men and women under which women have the main responsibility for home and nurturing and men are mainly active in the public sphere. Also referred to as **gender roles.**

GLASS CEILING   An unseen barrier to women's promotion to senior positions in the workplace. Women can see the senior positions in their company or field, but few women reach them because of negative attitudes toward senior women and low perceptions of their abilities and training. This barrier may also be based on race/ethnicity.

GLOBALIZATION   Contemporary form of cultural and economic integration facilitated by electronic media, international financial institutions, trade agreements, and national immigration policies.

GLOBAL LEVEL   A term used to describe and analyze the connections among people, institutions, and issues as viewed from a worldwide perspective.

GLOBAL NORTH   A term used to refer to economically developed countries like Western Europe, Japan, Canada, and the United States, as well as Australia and New Zealand, which are not in the north geographically. The Global North has a quarter of the world's population but controls four-fifths of the income earned anywhere in the world.

GLOBAL SOUTH A term used to refer to Africa, Latin America, the Caribbean, and developing countries in Asia; their histories of colonization; and their current impoverished status with low living standards. The Global South has three-quarters of the world's population and access to one-fifth of world income. The *South within the North* refers to poor people and areas within rich countries.

HATE CRIME A crime motivated by the perpetrator's prejudice against the victim's actual or perceived race, sexual orientation, or gender identity.

HETERONORMATIVITY Portrayal of the institution of heterosexuality, its norms and practices, as natural and inevitable; also "compulsory heterosexuality" (Rich 1986a).

HETEROPATRIARCHY A term that combines heterosexuality as a central institution of patriarchal societies, where many aspects of daily life—marriage, family arrangements, work, and law—are organized along heteropatriarchal lines.

HETEROSEXISM Attitudes, actions, and institutional practices that subordinate people on the basis of their gay, lesbian, bisexual, or queer orientation and identification.

IDENTITY-BASED POLITICS Activism and politics that have a strong identity component but also a broader view that enables people to make connections to other groups and issues.

IDENTITY POLITICS Activism and politics that put identity at the center. This usually involves the assumption that a particular characteristic, such as race, ethnicity, or sexual orientation, is the most important in the lives of group members and that the group is not differentiated according to other characteristics in a significant way.

IDEOLOGY Ideas, attitudes, and values that represent the interests of a group of people. The dominant ideology comprises the ideas, attitudes, and values that represent the interests of the dominant group(s). The ideological role of the idealized two-parent family, for example, is to devalue other family forms.

IMPERIALISM The process of domination of one nation over other nations that are deemed inferior for the purpose of exploiting their human and natural resources to consolidate its power and wealth. An empire is able to draw resources from many nations and to use their institutions and territory in its interests. Examples include the Roman empire, the British empire, and the current US empire.

INTERNALIZED OPPRESSION Attitudes and behavior of some oppressed people that reflect the negative, harmful, stereotypical beliefs of the dominant group directed at them. An example of internalized sexism is the view of some women that they and other women are inferior to men, which causes them to adopt attitudes and behaviors that reinforce the subordination of women.

INTERNATIONAL DIVISION OF LABOR A division of work between rich and poor countries under which low-waged workers in the Global South do assembly, manufacturing, and office work on contract to companies based in the Global North. The *international gendered division of labor* focuses on the gender of the workers involved.

INTERNATIONAL FINANCIAL INSTITUTIONS These include the World Bank, the International Monetary Fund (IMF), and the World Trade Organization (WTO), which were created to coordinate the world economy.

INTERSECTIONALITY An integrative perspective that shows how gender, class, nation, sexuality, religion, and other social categories interconnect to affect the lives of individuals and groups and social, economic, and political phenomena at community, societal, and global levels.

LIBERAL FEMINISM A philosophy that sees the oppression of women as a denial of equal rights, representation, and access to opportunities.

LIBERALISM A political theory about individual rights, freedom, choice, and privacy with roots in seventeenth-century European ideas (e.g., the writings of political philosopher John Locke).

MACRO LEVEL A term used to analyze the relationships among issues, individuals, and groups as viewed from a national institutional perspective like education or law, for example.

MARGINALITY The situation in which a person has a deep connection to more than one culture, community, or social group but is not completely able to identify with or be accepted by that group as an insider. For example, bisexual, mixed-race/mixed-culture, trans, and immigrant people have connections with different groups. They may find themselves caught between two or more social worlds and also able to bridge differences among people from those groups.

MATRIX OF OPPRESSION, PRIVILEGE, AND RESISTANCE The interconnections among various forms of power based on gender, race, class, nation, and so on. These social attributes can be sources of privilege or disadvantage. Negative ascriptions and experiences may be the source of people's resistance to oppression.

MEDIA LITERACY The ability to analyze and evaluate media content and messages and to make informed decisions as users and producers of information and media.

MEDICALIZATION The process of turning life processes, like pregnancy, childbirth, or menopause, into medical issues. Thus, menopause becomes an illness to be treated by medical professionals with formal educational qualifications and accreditation. By the same token, experienced midwives are considered unqualified because they lack these credentials.

MESO LEVEL A term used to analyze the relationships among issues, individuals, and groups as viewed from a community, or local, perspective.

MICRO LEVEL A term used to analyze the connections among people and issues as seen from a personal or individual perspective.

MILITARISM A system and worldview based on the objectification of "others" as enemies, a culture that prepares for, invests in, and celebrates war and killing. This worldview operates through specific political, economic, and military institutions, investments, and actions.

MILITARIZATION The processes whereby a society moves towards greater acceptance of militarism, for example, in popular culture, public policy, economic investments, technological development, recruitment into the armed services, and so on. The opposite is demilitarization.

MILITARIZED MASCULINITY A masculinity constructed to support militarism, with an emphasis on heroism, physical strength, lack of emotion, and appearance of invulnerability (Enloe 1990,1993).

MISOGYNIST Woman-hating attitudes and behavior.

MULTIPLE POSITIONALITY The various ways a person is situated or positioned in terms of gender, race, class, sexuality, age, ability, national origin, etc. Also see **social location**.

NEOCOLONIALISM Economic, political, and cultural domination by which a nation maintains or extends its control and influence over other nations, creating new forms of colonialism.

NEOLIBERAL/NEOLIBERALISM Economic philosophy and policies that call for the freedom of business to operate with minimal interference from governments, international organizations, or labor unions. Basic tenets include the rule of the market, free trade, economic deregulation, privatization of government-owned industries, reduction of social welfare spending, and belief in individual responsibility rather than valuing community and the public good. Termed "neo" liberal because it calls for a revival of the free-market philosophy that prevailed in the United States through the 1800s and early 1900s prior to the enhanced role of government that gained legitimacy during the Great Depression (1930s) and the "War on Poverty" and other "Great Society" programs of the 1960s.

OBJECTIFICATION Attitudes and behaviors by which people are treated as if they were "things." One example is the objectification of women through advertising images.

OBJECTIVITY A form of understanding in which knowledge and meaning are believed to come from outside oneself and are presumably not affected by personal opinion or bias.

OPPRESSION Prejudice and discrimination directed toward whole social groups and promoted by the ideologies and practices of all social institutions. The critical elements differentiating oppression from simple prejudice and discrimination are that it is a group phenomenon and that institutional power and authority are used to support prejudices and enforce discriminatory behaviors in systematic ways. Everyone is socialized to participate in oppressive practices, either as direct and indirect perpetrators or passive beneficiaries or—as with some oppressed peoples—by directing discriminatory behaviors at members of one's own group or another group deemed inferior. Also see **internalized oppression.**

ORIENTALISM A Western view that defines Eastern or Oriental people in terms of cultural or religious essences that are assumed to be fixed and unchanging.

PARADIGM SHIFT A complete change in one's view of the world.

PATRIARCHY A family, social group, or society in which men hold power and are dominant figures. Patriarchal power in the United States plays out in the family, the economy, the media, religion, law, and electoral politics.

POWER The ability to influence others, whether through persuasion, charisma, law, political activism, or coercion. Power operates informally and through formal institutions and at all levels (micro, meso, macro, and global).

PRECAUTIONARY PRINCIPLE The view that when an activity raises threats of harm to human health or the environment, precautionary measures should be taken even if some cause-and-effect relationships are not fully established scientifically. Those proposing the activity should bear the burden of proof rather than the public.

PREJUDICE A closed-minded prejudging of a person or group as negative or inferior, even without personal knowledge of that person or group and often contrary to reason or facts; unreasonable, unfair, and hostile attitudes toward people.

PRIVILEGE Benefits and power from institutional inequalities. Individuals and groups may be privileged without realizing, recognizing, or even wanting it.

PRODUCTIVE ECONOMY Characterized by monetary exchanges through trade, the organization of work, distribution and marketing of goods, contracts, negotiation of wages and salaries, and so forth.

QUEER A term used to describe nonheterosexual sexual orientation in a general, even ambiguous way that emphasizes sexual fluidity. It can include all who oppose and challenge **heteronormativity** and sexual binaries. As a verb, "queering" refers to reading a story, TV show, movie, performance, or historical text in ways that question its assumptions and make new interpretations.

RACISM Racial prejudices and discrimination that are supported by institutional power and authority. In the United States, racism is based on the ideology of white (European) superiority and is used to the advantage of white people and the disadvantage of peoples of color.

RADICAL FEMINISM A philosophy that sees the oppression of women in terms of patriarchy, a system of male power and authority, especially manifested in sexuality, personal relationships, and the family and carried into the male-dominated world of work, government, religion, media, and law.

RELATIVISM The view that all "authentic" experience is equally valid and cannot be challenged by others. For example, white supremacist views of Ku Klux Klan members are seen to be equally as valid as those held by antiracist activists. There are no external standards or principles by which to judge people's attitudes and behaviors.

RELOCALIZATION A development strategy based on the local production of food, energy and goods,

in order to increase community energy security, to strengthen local economies, and to improve environmental conditions and social equity.

REPRODUCTIVE ECONOMY This refers to domestic labor, including biological and social reproduction, mainly done by women, to maintain daily life, raise children, care for elders, and so on. It is often considered unproductive because it is unwaged, but it is fundamental to the ability to do waged work. Also see **social reproduction.**

REPRODUCTIVE JUSTICE A perspective that links health and reproductive rights to broader issues of social and economic justice. It offers a view of wellness for individuals, communities, and the wider society based on the eradication of inequality, oppression, and injustice.

REPRODUCTIVE WORK Includes the physical and emotional work of raising children, maintaining a family, housekeeping, preparing food, doing laundry, cleaning floors, and so on.

SECOND SHIFT Responsibilities for household chores and child care mostly by women who also work outside the home.

SECOND-WAVE FEMINISM Feminist projects and organizations from the late 1960s to the mid-1980s that campaigned for women's equality in all spheres of life and, in some cases, that argued for a complete transformation of patriarchal, capitalist structures. Also see **liberal feminism, radical feminism**, and **socialist feminism**.

SEXISM Attitudes, actions, and institutional practices that subordinate individuals because of their gender.

SITUATED KNOWLEDGE Knowledge and ways of knowing that are specific to particular historical and cultural contexts and life experiences. Also see **standpoint theory**.

SOCIAL CONSTRUCTIONISM The view that concepts such as gender, race, and sexual orientation are not biological or innate but are defined by human beings and can vary, depending on cultural and historical contexts. On this view, for example, heterosexuality is something learned—a social construction—not innate. The "normalcy" of heterosexuality is systematically transmitted, and appropriate attitudes and behaviors are learned through childhood socialization, life experiences, and reinforced through institutional norms, policies, and law.

SOCIAL INSTITUTIONS Institutions such as the family, education, mass media, organized religion, law, and government.

SOCIAL LOCATION The social features of one's identity incorporating individual, community, societal, and global factors, such as gender, class, ability, sexual orientation, age, and so on. Also see **multiple positionality**.

SOCIAL REPRODUCTION Everything needed to reproduce everyday life, much of which is unpaid work done by women. Also see **reproductive work**.

SOCIALIST Someone who believes that work should be organized for the collective benefit of workers rather than the profit of managers and corporate owners, and that the state should provide for human needs.

SOCIALIST FEMINISM A view that sees the oppression of women in terms of their subordinate positions in a system defined as both patriarchal and capitalist.

SOLIDARITY ECONOMY Ideas and practices that challenge the economic growth model and put people and nature, rather than the market system, at the center of a sustainable economy. This may include democratically controlled worker cooperatives, food sovereignty projects, local currencies, community bartering schemes, and reclaiming control of common resources.

SPECIESISM Attitudes, actions, and institutional practices that subordinate nonhuman species; usually used in discussions of environmental and ecological issues.

STANDPOINT THEORY The view that different social and historical situations give rise to very different group and individual experiences and theories about those experiences. Standpoint shapes a group's view of the world and what they may or may not be able to comprehend about it. Also see **situated knowledge**.

STATE Government institutions, authority, and control. This includes the machinery of electoral politics, law-making, government agencies that execute law and policy, law enforcement agencies, the prison system, and the military.

STATE VIOLENCE Violence committed by state employees (e.g., police officers, Border Patrol, or prison guards) as part of their work, as well as the violence of oppressive legal and political systems.

STICKY FLOOR Structural limitations for women in low-paid, low-status jobs that block them from moving up. Also see **glass ceiling**.

SUBJECTIVITY A form of understanding in which knowledge and meaning are grounded in people's lived experiences; also, being the subject rather than an object of theorizing. Historically powerless groups have been treated as objects of "objective" knowledge production, so feminist assertions of subjectivity are also assertions of objectified groups' claims to the subject position (that of actor and agent of action) and their ability to create knowledge.

SUBJUGATED KNOWLEDGE Knowledge generated from positions of subordination.

THEORETICAL FRAMEWORK A perspective that allows one to analyze the causes and implications of a particular issue, rather than simply describing it.

THEORY An explanation of how things are and why they are the way they are; a theory is based on a set of assumptions, has a perspective, and serves a purpose.

THIRD-WAVE FEMINISTS Feminists active in the 1990s, often younger women, who emphasized personal voice and multiple identities, intersectionality, ambiguity, and contradictions.

TRANS(GENDER) People whose gender identity is not the same as they were assigned at birth.

TRANSNATIONAL Relationships, organizations, or movements that connect individuals or groups across national boundaries. These boundaries are not erased but are greatly reduced as barriers. Emphasis is on activities that transcend national boundaries, such as transnational corporations or transnational feminist organizing.

TRANSNATIONAL FEMINISM Feminism that links scholars and activists from different locations in "non-colonized" dialogue across differences. This includes a commitment to avoid reproducing inequalities among feminists that parallel those among nations.

TRANSPHOBIA Fear, disgust, loathing, revulsion, or mistrust of transgender people. Expressed as a phobia or aversion, this term does not refer directly to systems of prejudice and discrimination supported by institutional power and authority as, for example, with terms like *sexism* or *racism*.

UNITED NATIONS STANDARDS Recommendations and standards for national laws and policies such as the Convention on the Elimination of All Forms of Discrimination against Women (CEDAW); the International Covenant on Economic, Social, and Cultural Rights; the Convention on the Rights of the Child; and the Convention on the Elimination of All Forms of Racial Discrimination.

XENOPHOBIA Fear and dislike of or prejudice against people from other countries.

REFERENCES

AAUW. 2018. *The simple truth about the gender pay gap.* Washington, DC: AAUW. Accessed on August 17, 2018, at https://www.aauw.org/aauw_check/pdf_download/show_pdf.php?file=The-Simple-Truth

Abdil, A. 2018. *Fathering from the margins: An intimate examination of Black fatherhood.* New York: Columbia University Press.

Abramovitz, M. 1996. *Regulating the lives of women.* Rev. ed. Boston: South End Press.

Adair, V. 2004. Reclaiming the promise of higher education: Poor single mothers in academe. *On Campus with Women* 33(3–4), Spring/Summer.

——, and S. Dahlberg. 2003. *Reclaiming class: Women, poverty, and the promise of higher education in America.* Philadelphia: Temple University Press.

Adams, C. J. 1999. *The sexual politics of meat: A feminist-vegetarian critical theory.* 10th anniversary ed. New York: Continuum.

Adamson, J., M. M. Evans, and R. Stein, eds. 2002. *The environmental justice reader: Politics, poetics and pedagogy.* Tucson: Arizona University Press.

Agosín, M., ed. 2001. *Women, gender, and human rights: A global perspective.* New Brunswick, NJ: Rutgers University Press.

Aguilar, L., M. Granat, and C. Owren. (2015). *Roots for the future: The landscape and way forward on gender and climate change.* Washington, DC: IUCN and GGCA. Accessed on October 18, 2018, at https://wedo.org/wp-content/uploads/2015/12/Roots-for-the-future-final-1.pdf

Agyeman, J., and A. H. Alkon, eds. 2011. *Cultivating food justice: Race, class and sustainability.* Cambridge, MA: MIT Press.

Ahn, C., and G. Kirk. 2005. Why war is all the rage. *San Francisco Chronicle*, May 29, p. D5.

Alcoff, L. M. 2013. Feminists we love: Chandra Talpade Mohanty. *The Feminist Wire*, October 4. Accessed on October 12, 2018, at https://thefeministwire.com/2013/10/feminists-we-love-chandra-mohanty/

Alexander, M. 2012. *The new Jim Crow: Mass incarceration in the age of colorblindness.* Rev. ed. New York: New Press.

Allard, J., C. Davidson, and J. Matthaei, eds. 2008. *Solidarity economy: Building alternatives for people and the planet.* Chicago: ChangeMaker Publications.

Allen, P. G. 1986. *The sacred hoop: Recovering the feminine in American Indian traditions.* Boston: Beacon Press.

Allen, P., and C. Sachs. 1991. The social side of sustainability: Class, gender and race. *Science as Culture* 2(pt. 4, no. 13).

Allen, P., and C. Sachs. 2007. Women and Food Chains: The gendered politics of food, *International Journal of Sociology of Food and Agriculture* 15(1): 1–23.

Allen, W. 2012. *The good food revolution: Growing healthy food, people, and communities.* New York: Gotham Books.

Alonso, H. H. 1993. *Peace as a women's issue: A history of the US movement for world peace and women's rights.* Syracuse, NY: Syracuse University Press.

Alsultany, E. 2012. *Arabs and Muslims in the media: Race and representation after 9/11.* New York: New York University Press.

American Civil Liberties Union. 2002. *The USA Patriot Act.* Accessed online at http://www.aclu.org

American Heritage Dictionary. 1993. 3rd ed. Boston: Houghton Mifflin.

American Psychiatric Association. 2013. *Diagnostic and statistical manual of mental disorders.* 5th ed. Washington, DC: American Psychiatric Association.

——. 2018. *What is gender dysphoria?* Accessed on November 23, 2018, at https://www.psychiatry.org/patients-families/gender-dysphoria/what-is-gender-dysphoria

American Psychological Association. 2016. *Stress in America: The impact of discrimination.* Accessed on November 20, 2018, at https://www.apa.org/news/press/releases/stress/2015/impact-of-discrimination.pdf

Andersen, M. 2000. Women, power and politics. In *Thinking about women: Sociological perspectives on sex and gender,* 5th ed., pp. 290–322. Boston: Allyn and Bacon.

Anderson, B. 2000. *Joyous greetings: The first international women's movement. 1830–60.* New York: Oxford University Press.

Andre, J. 1988. Stereotypes: Conceptual and normative considerations. In *Racism and sexism: An integrated study,* ed. P. S. Rothenberg. New York: St. Martin's Press.

Antrobus, P. 2004. *The global women's movement: Origins, issues and strategies.* New York: Zed Books.

Anzaldúa, G. 1987. *Borderlands/La Frontera: The new mestiza.* San Francisco: Spinsters/Aunt Lute.

——. 2002. Now let us shift . . . the path of conocimiento . . . inner work, and public acts. In *This bridge we call home,* ed. G. Anzaldúa and A. Keating, pp. 540–78. New York: Routledge.

Applewhite, A. 2016. *This chair rocks: A manifesto against ageism.* New York: Celadon Books.

Apuzzo, M. 2014. War gear flows to police departments. *New York Times,* June 8. Accessed on October 23, 2018, at http://www.nytimes.com/2014/06/09/us/war-gear-flows-to-police-departments.html?_r=0

Arasim, E., and O. O. Lake. 2016. 15 Indigenous women on the frontlines of the Dakota Access Pipeline Resistance. *Women's Earth and Climate Action Network, October 29.* Accessed on October 18, 2018, at https://www.ecowatch.com/indigenous-women-dakota-access-pipeline-2069613663.html

Arcana, J. 1994. Abortion is a motherhood issue. In *Mother journeys: Feminists write about mothering,* ed. M. Reddy, M. Roth, and A. Sheldon, pp. 159–63. Minneapolis: Spinsters Ink.

——. 2005. *What if your mother.* Goshen, CT: Chicory Blue Press.

Arditti, J. A. 2012. *Parental incarceration and the family: Psychological and social effects of imprisonment on children, parents, and caregivers.* New York: New York University Press.

Associated Press. 2017. At $75,560, housing a prisoner in California now costs more than a year at Harvard. *Los Angeles Times,* June 4. Accessed on October 29, 2018, at http://www.latimes.com/local/lanow/la-me-prison-costs-20170604-htmlstory.html

——. 2018. Betsy DeVos to alter sexual misconduct guidelines to bolster rights of accused. *Guardian,* November 16. Accessed on November 23, 2018, at https://www.theguardian.com/education/2018/nov/16/betsy-devos-us-education-secretary-college-sexual-misconduct

Astor, M. 2017. Violence against transgender people is on the rise, advocates say. *New York Times.* November 9. Accessed online at https://www.nytimes.com/2017/11/09/us/transgender-women-killed.html

Audre Lorde Project. 2017. Statement: Do not militarize our mourning; Orlando and the ongoing tragedy against LGBTSTGNC POC. In *Feminist Manifestos: A global documentary reader,* ed. P. A. Weiss, pp. 666–67. New York: New York University Press.

Azuma, A. 2007. Food access in Central and South Los Angeles: Mapping injustice, agenda for action. Urban and Environmental Policy Institute, Occidental College. Accessed online at http://www.uepi.oxy.edu

Bailey, M., P. Kandaswamy, and M. U. Richardson. 2004. Is gay marriage racist? In *That's revolting: Queer strategies for resisting assimilation,* ed. M. B. Sycamore. Brooklyn: Soft Skull Press.

Baldwin, J. 1984. On being white and other lies. *Essence* (April): 90-92.

Barndt, D. 2008. *Tangled routes: Women, work and globalization on the tomato trail.* 2nd ed. Lanham, MD: Rowman and Littlefield.

Barnes, R. J. D. 2016. *Raising the race: Black career women redefine marriage, motherhood, and community.* New Brunswick: Rutgers University Press.

Barrett, M. 2011. Bottled water regulation: Regulated less than tap water. *Natural Society Newsletter,* November 16. Accessed on October 16, 2018, at http://naturalsociety.com/bottled-water-regulation-regulated-less-than-tap-water/

Barry, J. 2012. *Standing our ground: Women, environmental justice, and the fight to end mountaintop removal.* Athens: Ohio University Press.

Barsalou, J. 2005. *Trauma and transitional justice in divided societies.* Special Report No. 135. Washington, DC: United States Institute for Peace.

Bass, E., and L. Davis. 1988. *The courage to heal.* New York: Harper & Row.

Basu, A. 2016. *Women's movements in the global era: The power of local feminisms.* 2nd ed. New York: Routledge.

Bayoumi, M. 2009. *How does it feel to be a problem? Being young and Arab in American.* New York: Penguin Books.

——. 2015. *This Muslim American life: Dispatches from the war on terror.* New York: New York University Press.

Baxandall, R., and L. Gordon, eds. 2000. *Dear sisters: Dispatches from the women's liberation movement.* New York: Basic Books.

BBC News. 2016. *Reality check: Who voted for Donald Trump?* November 9. Accessed on October 19, 2018, at https://www.bbc.com/news/election-us-2016-37922587

Beasley, M., and D. Thomas. 1994. Violence as a human rights issue. In *The public nature of private violence: The discovery of domestic abuse,* ed. M. A. Fineman and R. Mykitiuk, pp. 323–46. New York: Routledge.

Beauboeuf-Lafontant, T. 2007. "You have to show strength": An exploration of gender, race, and depression. *Gender and Society* 21(1): 28–51.

——. 2009. *Behind the mask of the strong black woman: Voice and the embodiment of a costly performance.* Philadelphia: Temple University Press.

Belkin, L. 2007. The feminine critique. *New York Times,* November 1. Accessed online at http://www.nytimes.com/2007/11/01/fashion/01WORK.html?pagewanted=2&_r=l&ei=5070&en=91feaf95fabced83&ex=1194580800

Bell, S. E. 2013. *Our roots run deep as ironweed: Appalachian women and the fight for environmental justice.* Urbana, IL: University of Illinois Press.

Benard, C., and E. Schlaffer. 1997. "The man in the street": Why he harasses. In *Feminist frontiers IV,* ed. L. Richardson, V. Taylor, and N. Whittier, pp. 395–98. New York: McGraw-Hill.

Benedict, H. 2009. *The lonely soldier: The private war of women serving in Iraq.* Boston: Beacon Press.

Berger, M. T., and C. Radeloff. 2011. *Transforming scholarship: Why women's and gender studies students are changing themselves and the world.* New York: Routledge.

Bernstein, R., and S. C. Silberman, eds. 1996. *Generation Q.* Los Angeles: Alyson.

Biemann, U. 2002. Remotely Sensed: A topography of the global sex trade, *Feminist Review,* 70: 75-88.

Bisexual Resource Center. 2019. Welcome home. Accessed on March 14, 2019, at https://biresource.org

Black Women's Health Project. 1995. *Reproductive health and African American women. Issue brief.* Washington, DC: Black Women's Health Project.

Blair, J. 2011. *Hesitation kills: A female officer's combat experience in Iraq.* Lanham, MD: Rowman and Littlefield.

Blauner, R. 1972. *Racial oppression in America.* New York: Harper & Row.

Bleier, R. 1984. *Science and gender: A critique of biology and its theories on women.* New York: Pergamon Press.

Bloom, S., J. Miller, J. Warner, and P. Winkler, eds. 1994. *Hidden casualties: Environmental, health and political consequences of the Persian Gulf War.* Berkeley, CA: North Atlantic Books.

Boggs, G. L. . 2012. *The next American revolution: Sustainable activism for the twenty-first century.* Expanded ed. Berkeley: University of California Press.

Bollinger, H. 2007. *Women of the harvest: Inspiring stories of contemporary farmers.* Osceola, WI: Voyageur Press.

Bordo, S. 1993. *Unbearable weight: Feminism, Western culture, and the body.* Berkeley: University of California Press.

Boris, E. 2010. Feminism's histories. In K. A. Laughlin et al. Is it time to jump ship? *Feminist Formations* 22(1): 90–97.

——, and J. Klein. 2012. *Caring for America: Home health workers in the shadow of the welfare state.* New York: Oxford University Press.

——, and R. S. Parreñas, eds. 2010. *Intimate labors: Cultures, technologies, and the politics of care.* Palo Alto: Stanford University Press.

Boston Women's Health Book Collective. 2011. *Our Bodies, Ourselves.* New York: Simon and Schuster.

Boswell, J. 1994. *Same-sex unions in premodern Europe.* New York: Villard Books.

Bounegru, L., J. Gray, T. Venturini, and M. Mauri. 2017. *A field guide to fake news.* Public Data Lab. Available at https://fakenews.publicdatalab.org/

Bowden, L., and S. Cain. 2008. *Powder: Writing by women in the ranks from Vietnam to Iraq.* Tucson, AZ: Kore Press.

Boyd, S. C. 2004. *From witches to crack moms: Women, drug law, and policy.* Durham, NC: Carolina Academic Press.

Boylan, J. F. 2003. *She's not there: A life in two genders.* New York: Broadway Books.

Boynton, C. W. 2018. Alias Jane. *Ms. Magazine,* Fall, pp. 38–43.

Bradt, S. 2010. "One-drop" rule persists. *The Harvard Gazette,* December 9. Accessed on August 2, 2018, at https://news.harvard.edu/gazette/story/2010/12/one-drop-rule-persists/

Breastcancer.org. 2018. *US breast cancer statistics.* Accessed on October 31, 2018, at https://www.breastcancer.org/symptoms/understand_bc/statistics

Breeden, A., and E. Peltier. 2018. Response to French letter denouncing #MeToo shows a sharp divide. *New York Times,* January 12. Accessed on November 5, 2018, at https://www.nytimes.com/2018/01/12/world/europe/france-sexual-harassment.html

Brennan, S., J. Winklepleck, and G. MacNee. 1994. *The resourceful woman.* Detroit: Visible Ink.

Brettschneider, M. 2006. *The family flamboyant: Race politics, queer families, Jewish lives.* Albany: State University of New York Press.

Brown, K. 2018. Women in prison are still waiting for their Me Too moment. *Huffington Post,* April 11. Accessed on October 29, 2018, at https://www.huffingtonpost.com/entry/opinion-brown-me-too-women-prisons_us_5ac28e1de4b00fa46f854abf

Brown, T. M. 2011. *Raising Brooklyn: Nannies, childcare and Caribbeans creating communities.* New York: New York University Press.

Brownell, K. D., and K. B. Horgen. 2004. *Food fight: The inside story of the food industry, America's obesity crisis, and what we can do about it.* Chicago: Contemporary Books.

Brownmiller, S. 1975. *Against our will: Men, women, and rape.* New York: Simon & Schuster.

Brumberg, J. J. 1997. *The body project: An intimate history of American girls.* New York: Random House.

Bryant, S. L. 2013. The beauty ideal: The effects of European standards of beauty on Black women. *Columbia Social Work Review* IV: 80–91. Accessed on October 30, 2018, at https://cswr.columbia.edu/article/the-beauty-ideal-the-effects-of-european-standards-of-beauty-on-black-women/

Buck, M. 2004. Women in prison and work. *Feminist Studies* 30(2): 451–55.

——,. n.d. *Prison Life: A day.* Accessed at http://womenandprison.org/prison-industrial-complex/category/political_prisoners/

Bullard, R. D. 2002. Crowning women of color and the real story behind the 2002 EJ Summit. Accessed online at http://www.ejrc.cau.edu/SummCrowning04.html

——, P. Mohai, R. Saha, and B. Wright. 2007. *Toxic waste and race at twenty 1987–2007: Grassroots struggles to dismantle environmental racism in the United States.* Cleveland, OH: United Church of Christ.

Bunch, C. 1987. *Passionate politics: Essays 1968–1986.* New York: St. Martin's Press.

——. 2018. *Vienna + 25.* Center for Women's Global Leadership. Accessed on November 24, 2018, at https://globalfeministjourneys.com/2018/06/charlotte-bunch-vienna-25/

——, and R. Carillo. 1991. *Gender violence: A human rights and development issue.* New Brunswick, NJ: Center for Women's Global Leadership, Rutgers University.

——, and N. Reilly. 1994. *Demanding accountability: The global campaign and Vienna Tribunal for women's human rights.* New Jersey: Center for Women's Global Leadership, Rutgers University; New York: UNIFEM.

Burnham, Linda. 2001. *The wellspring of Black feminist theory.* Oakland: Women of Color Resource Center. Available at http://www.coloredgirls.org

Bush, M. E. L. 2004. *Breaking the code of good intentions: Everyday forms of whiteness.* Lanham, MD: Rowman and Littlefield.

Bussey, G. and M. Tims. 1980.*Pioneers for peace: Women's International League for Peace and Freedom 1915-1965.* London: WILPF British Section.

Butler, J. 1990. *Gender trouble: Feminism and the subversion of identity.* New York: Routledge, Chapman, & Hall.

Buttenweiser, S. 2016. *Women's incarceration: Frequent starting point is childhood abuse,* Women's Media Center. March 22. Accessed on April 8, 2019 at http://www.womensmediacenter.com/news-features/womens-incarceration-frequent-starting-point-is-childhood-abuse

Cachola, E.-R., G. Kirk, L. Natividad, and M. R. Pumarejo. 2010. Women working across borders for peace and genuine security. *Peace Review: A Journal of Social Justice* 22(2): 164–70.

Calasanti, T. M., and K. F. Slevin, eds. 2006. *Age matters: Realigning feminist thinking.* New York: Taylor and Francis.

Cane, P. M. 2002. *Trauma healing and transformation.* Santa Cruz, CA: Capacitar International.

Cantor, D., B. Fisher, S. Chibnall, R. Townsend, et al. 2015. *Report on the AAU Campus Climate Survey on Sexual Assault and Sexual Misconduct,*

September 21. Association of American Universities (AAU).Accessed on April 2, 2019, at https://www.aau.edu/sites/default/files/%40%20Files/Climate%20Survey/AAU_Campus_Climate_Survey_12_14_15.pdf

Caplan, P., ed. 1987. *The cultural construction of sexuality.* London: Tavistock.

Carlen, P. 1989. Feminist jurisprudence, or women-wise penology. *Probation Journal* 36(3): 110–14.

Carpenter, Z. 2014. The police violence we aren't talking about. *The Nation,* August 27. Accessed on November 25, 2018, at https://www.thenation.com/article/police-violence-we-arent-talking-about/

Carrington, D. 2018. Avoiding meat and dairy is "single biggest way" to reduce your impact on Earth. *Guardian,* May 31. Accessed on October 18, 2018, at https://www.theguardian.com/environment/2018/may/31/avoiding-meat-and-dairy-is-single-biggest-way-to-reduce-your-impact-on-earth?CMP=share_btn_link

Casselman, A. 2016. *Injustice in Indian Country: Jurisdiction, American law and sexual violence against Native women.* New York: Peter Lang Publishing.

Castañeda, I., and S. Gammage. 2011. Gender, global crises, and climate change. In *Harvesting feminist knowledge for public policy: Rebuilding progress,* ed. D. Jain and D. Elson, pp. 170–99. Thousand Oaks, CA: SAGE.

Catalyst. 2010. Fortune 500 women executive officers and top earners, Accessed online at http://www.catalyst.org/publication/459/2010-catalyst-census-fortune-500-women-executive-officers-and-top-earners

Cavin, S. 1985. *Lesbian origins.* San Francisco: Ism Press.

Center for American Women and Politics. 2018a. Facts: Women in the US Congress 2018. Accessed on October 21, 2018, at http://www.cawp.rutgers.edu/women-us-congress-2018

——. 2018b. Facts: Women in state legislatures 2018. Accessed on October 21, 2018, at http://www.cawp.rutgers.edu/women-state-legislature-2018

——. 2018c. Facts on women of color in elected office. Accessed on October 21, 2018, at http://www.cawp.rutgers.edu/fact-sheets-women-color

——. 2018d. Results: Women candidates in the 2018 elections. Accessed on November 25, 2018, at http://www.cawp.rutgers.edu/sites/default/files/resources/results_release_5bletterhead5d_1.pdf

Center on Institutions and Governance. n.d. *State violence.* University of California-Berkeley. Accessed on November 25, 2018, at https://igov.berkeley.edu/node/529

Centers for Disease Control and Prevention. 2015. *New findings from CDC survey suggest too few schools teach prevention of HIV, STDs, pregnancy.* Accessed on March 28, 2019 at https://www.cdc.gov/nchhstp/newsroom/2015/nhpc-press-release-schools-teaching-prevention.html

——. 2017. *Findings from the National Intimate Partner and Sexual Violence Survey, 2010–2012 state report.* Washington, DC: US Department of Justice, Office of Justice Programs.

——. 2018a. *HIV among women.* Accessed on October 31, 2018, at https://www.cdc.gov/hiv/group/gender/women/index.html

——. 2018b. *Infant mortality.* Accessed on October 31, 2018, at https://www.cdc.gov/reproductivehealth/MaternalInfantHealth/InfantMortality.htm

——. 2018c. *New CDC analysis shows steep and sustained increases in STDs in recent years.* Accessed on October 31, 2018, at https://www.cdc.gov/nchhstp/newsroom/2018/press-release-2018-std-prevention-conference.html

Chamberlain, G. 2018a. "Metal particles splash into eyes": Study claims iPhone workers face toxic risks. *Guardian,* January 16. Accessed on October 15, 2018, at https://www.theguardian.com/global-development/2018/jan/16/workers-making-iphones-in-china-exposed-to-toxic-hazards-report-says-apple-catcher-technology?CMP=share_btn_link

——. 2018b. Workers not paid legally by Amazon contractor in China. *Guardian,* June 9. Accessed on October 15, 2018, at https://www.theguardian.com/technology/2018/jun/09/amazon-contractor-foxconn-pay-workers-illegally?CMP=share_btn_link

Chan, J., P. Ngai, and M. Selden. 2016. Dying for an iPhone: The lives of Chinese workers. *China Dialogue,* April 15. Accessed on September 22, 2018, at https://www.chinadialogue.net/article/show/single/en/8826-Dying-for-an-iPhone-the-lives-of-Chinese-workers

Chang, G. 2013. This is what trafficking looks like. In *Immigrant women workers in the neoliberal age,* ed. N. Flores-González, A. R. Guevara, M. Toro-Morn, and G. Chang, pp. 56–77. Urbana: University of Illinois Press.

——, and K. Kim. 2007. Reconceptualizing approaches to human trafficking: New directions and perspectives from the field(s). *Stanford Journal of Civil Rights and Civil Liberties* III(2): 317–44.

Chateauvert, M. 2013. *Sex workers unite: A history of the movement from Stonewall to SlutWalk.* Boston: Beacon Press.

Chedelin, S. I., and M. Eliatamby. 2011. *Women waging war and peace: International perspectives of women's roles in conflict and post-conflict reconstruction.* London: Bloomsbury Press.

Chesler, P. 1972. *Women and madness.* New York: Avon.

Chesney-Lind, M., and K. Irwin. 2008. *Beyond bad girls: Gender, violence and hype.* New York: Routledge.

——, and L. Pasko. 2004. *The female offender: Girls, women and crime.* 2nd ed. Thousand Oaks, CA: Sage.

——, eds. 2013. *Girls, women and crime: Selected readings.* Thousand Oaks, CA: Sage. Second edn.

Children's Defense Fund. 2010. The state of America's children. Accessed online at http://www.childrens defense.org/child-research-data-publications/data/state-of-americas-children.pdf

——. 2017. Child poverty in America 2016: National analysis. Accessed on September 5, 2018, at https://www.childrensdefense.org/wp-content/uploads/2018/06/child-poverty-in-america-2016.pdf

Chodorow, N. 1978. *Reproduction and mothering: Psychoanalysis and the sociology of gender.* Berkeley: University of California Press.

Cisneros, S. 1996. Guadalupe the Sex Goddess. In *Goddess of the Americas: Writings on the Virgin of Guadalupe,* edited by Ana Castillo. New York: Riverhead Books. pp.

Clare, E. 2009. *Exile and pride: Disability, queerness and liberation.* Cambridge, MA: South End Press.

——. 2013. Body shame, body pride: Lessons from the disability rights movement. In *The transgender studies reader 2,* ed. S. Stryker and A. Z. Aizura, pp. 261–65. New York: Routledge.

——. 2017. *Brilliant imperfection: Grappling with cure.* Durham, NC: Duke University Press.

Cockburn, C. 2007. *From where we stand: War, women's activism and feminist analysis.* London: Zed Press.

——. 2012. Antimilitarism: Political and gender dynamics of peace movements. London: Palgrave McMillan.

Cofer, J. O. 1993. The story of my body. In *The Latin deli: Prose and poetry.* Athens: University of Georgia Press.

Cohn, J. 2018. #WOMENAGAINSTFEMINISM: Towards a phenomenology of incoherence. In *Emergent feminisms: Complicating a postfeminist media culture,* ed. J. Keller and M. E. Ryan, pp. 176–192. New York: Routledge.

Cole, J., and B. Guy-Sheftall. 2003. *Gender talk: The struggle for women's equality in African American communities.* New York: Ballantine.

Coleman, P. 2017. The political is personal: A critique of what popular culture teaches about consent (and how to fix it). In *Ask: Building consent culture,* ed. K. Stryker, pp. 25–30. Portland, OR: Thorntree Press.

Collins, C., and J. Hoxie. 2017. *Billionaire bonanza: The Forbes 400 and the rest of us.* Washington, DC: Institute for Policy Studies. Accessed on September 5, 2018, at https://inequality.org/wp-content/uploads/2017/11/BILLIONAIRE-BONANZA-2017-Embargoed.pdf

Collins, L. 2008. Pixel perfect: Pascal Dangin's virtual reality. *The New Yorker.* May 12. Accessed online at http://www.newyorker.com/reporting/2008/05/12/080512fa_fact_collins

Collins, P. H. 1990. *Black feminist thought: Knowledge, consciousness, and the politics of empowerment.* Boston: Unwin Hyman.

——. 1997. Comment on Hekman's "Truth and method: feminist standpoint revisited": Where's the power? *Signs: Journal of Women in Culture and Society* 22(2): 375–81.

——. 2004. *Black sexual politics: African Americans, gender, and the new racism.* New York: Routledge.

Condry, I. 2006. *Hip-hop Japan: Rap and the paths of cultural globalization.* Durham: Duke University Press.

Cooper, B. C. 2017. SlutWalks vs. Ho Strolls. In *The CRUNK feminist collection,* ed. B. C. Cooper, S. M. Morris, and R. M. Boylorn, pp. 51–54. New York: The Feminist Press at the City University of New York.

Cooperman, R., and M. Deckman 2016. Republican women poised to play a key role as messengers in 115th Congress. *Footnotes: CAWP Blog,* December 22. Accessed on October 21, 2018, at http://www.cawp.rutgers.edu/footnotes/search?search_value=cooperman

Costa, T. 2010. *Farmer Jane: Women changing the way we eat.* Layton, UT: Gibbs Smith.

Cowman, S. 2016. The Fight against mining in Peru. *Women Across Frontiers.* March, Issue 3. Accessed online at https://wafmag.org/2016/02/the-fight-against-mining-in-peru/

Cox, T. 1999. *Hot sex: How to do it.* New York: Bantam Books.

Crenshaw, K. 1993. The marginalization of sexual violence against Black women. Speech to the National Coalition Against Sexual Assault, 1993 Conference, Chicago. Accessed online at http://www.ncasa.org/marginalization.html

Critical Resistance. 2005. *Instead of prisons: A handbook for abolitionists.* Oakland, CA: AK Press.

Crittenden, A. 2001. *The price of motherhood Why the most important job in the world is still the least valued* (New York: Metropolitan Books).

Crow, T. 2012. *Eyes right: Confessions from a woman Marine.* Lincoln: University of Nebraska Press.

Cruickshank, M. 2013. *Learning to be old: Gender, culture and aging.* 3rd ed. Lanham, MD: Rowman and Littlefield.

Currans, E. 2107. *Marching dykes, liberated sluts and concerned mothers: Women transforming public space.* Urbana: University of Illinois Press.

Cuthbertson, A. 2017. iPhone X release: The human cost of Apple's most expensive iPhone ever. *Newsweek.* November 3. Accessed on September 2, 2018, at https://www.newsweek.com/iphone-x-release-human-cost-apples-most-expensive-ever-iphone-699901iP

Cutler-Seeber, A. 2018. *Trans* lives in the United States: Challenges of transition and beyond.* New York: Routledge.

Daniels, R., S. C. Taylor, and H. H. L. Kitano, eds. 1991. *Japanese Americans from relocation to redress.* Seattle: University of Washington Press.

Danna, D. 2015. *Contract children: Questioning surrogacy.* Stuttgart, Germany: *ibidem* Press.

Danquah, M. 1998. *Willow weep for me: A Black women's journey through depression.* New York: W. W. Norton.

das Dasgupta, S., and S. DasGupta. 1996. Public face, private space: Asian Indian women and sexuality. In *"Bad girls"/"good girls": Women, sex, and power in the nineties,* ed. N. Bauer Maglin and D. Perry, pp. 226–43. New Brunswick, NJ: Rutgers University Press.

Davis, Angela. 2000. The color of violence against women. *Colorlines,* October 10. Accessed online at https://www.colorlines.com/articles/color-violence-against-women

Davis, Antoinette. 2008. Interpersonal and physical dating violence among teens. *The National Council on Crime and Delinquency Focus.* Accessed online at http://www.nccd-crc.org/nccd/pubs/2008_focus_teen_dating_violence.pdf

Davis, D. 2009. *Genetic dilemmas: Reproductive technology, parental choices, and children's futures.* New York: Oxford University Press.

Davis, K. 2007. *The making of* Our Bodies, Ourselves: *How feminist knowledge travels across borders.* Durham, NC: Duke University Press.

Davis, M., ed. 2017. *Babies for sale: Transnational surrogacy, human rights and the politics of reproduction.* London: Zed Books.

Daly, F. Y. 1994. Perspectives of Native American women on race and gender. In *Challenging racism and sexism: Alternatives to genetic explanations,* eds. E. Tobach and B. Rosoff. City University of New York: Feminist Press.

de Alwis, M. 2001. Ambivalent Maternalisms: Cursing as public protest in Sri Lanka. In *The Aftermath: Women in post-war reconstruction,* eds. S. Meintjes, A. Pillay and M. Turshen, pp. 210-224. London and New York: Zed Books.

Deech, R., and A. Smajdor. 2007. *From IVF to immortality: Controversy in the era of reproductive technology.* New York: Oxford University Press.

Deer, S. 2015. *The beginning and end of rape: Confronting sexual violence in Native America.* Minneapolis: University of Minnesota Press.

Deerinwater, J. 2018. Our pride: Honoring and recognizing our two spirit past and present. *Rewire News,* June 5. Accessed on November 5, 2018, at https://rewire.news/article/2018/06/05/pride-honoring-recognizing-two-spirit-past-present/

D'Emilio, J. 1984. Capitalism and gay identity. In *Powers of desire: The politics of sexuality,* ed. A. Snitow et al., pp. 100–13. New York: Monthly Review Press.

Deomampo, D. 2016. *Transnational reproduction: Race, kinship, and commercial surrogacy in India.* New York: New York University Press.

Detention Watch Network. 2011. Securely insecure: The real costs, consequences and human face of immigration detention. Accessed online at http://www.detentionwatchnetwork.org/sites/detentionwatchnetwork.org/files/1.14.11_Fact%20Sheet%20FINAL_0.pdf

Detraz, N. 2017. *Gender and the environment.* Cambridge, UK: Polity Press.

DeVault, K. 2016. Four ways to look at Standing Rock: An indigenous perspective. *Yes! Magazine,* November 22. Accessed on October 18, 2018, at http://www.yesmagazine.org/planet/four-ways-to-look-at-standing-rock-an-indigenous-perspective-20161122

Diamond, L. M. 2008. *Sexual fluidity: Understanding women's love and desire.* Cambridge. MA: Harvard University Press.

Di Chiro, G. 2009. Sustaining everyday life: Bringing together environmental, climate and reproductive justice. *Climate Change Series, no. 58.* Population and Development Program. Available at http://popdev.hampshire.edu/projects/dt/58

Dicker, R., and A. Piepmeier, eds. 2003. *Catching a wave: Reclaiming feminism for the 21st century.* Boston: Northeastern University Press.

Diep, F. 2015. Four ways climate change affects women more than men. *Pacific Standard*, September 30. Accessed on October 18, 2018, at https://psmag.com/news/climate-change-impacts-women

Digby, T., ed. 1998. *Men doing feminism*. New York: Routledge.

Dines, G. 2010. *PornLand: How pornography has hijacked our sexuality*. Boston: Beacon Press.

Dinnerstein, D. 1976. *Sexual arrangements and the human malaise*. New York: Harper & Row.

Díaz-Cotto, J. 2006. *Chicana lives and criminal justice: Voices from el barrio*. Austin: University of Texas Press.

Dittmar, K. 2014. *The gender gap: Gender differences in vote choice and political orientations*. July 15. Accessed on March 30, 2019, at https://www.cawp.rutgers.edu/sites/default/files/resources/closer-look_gender-gap-07-15-14.pdf

——. 2015. *Navigating gendered terrain: Stereotypes and strategy in political campaigns*. Philadelphia: Temple University Press.

——. 2018. *The gender gap in voting: Setting the record straight*. July 3. Accessed on March 30, 2019 at https://www.cawp.rutgers.edu/footnotes/gender-gap-voting-setting-record-straight

——, K. Sanbonmatsu, S. J. Carroll, D. Walsh, and C. Wineinger. 2017. *Representation matters: Women in the US Congress*. New Brunswick, NJ: Center for American Women and Politics, Eagleton Institute of Politics, Rutgers University. Accessed on October 21, 2018, at http://www.cawp.rutgers.edu/sites/default/files/resources/representationmatters.pdf

Donovan, M. K., 2018. Self-managed medication abortion: Expanding the available options for US abortion care. *Guttmacher Policy Review*, October 17. Accessed on October 31, 2018, at https://www.guttmacher.org/gpr/2018/10/self-managed-medication-abortion-expanding-available-options-us-abortion-care

Douglas, S. 2010. *Enlightened sexism: The seductive message that feminism's work is done*. New York: Henry Holt.

Duberman M. B., M. Vicinus, and G. Chauncey Jr. 1989. *Hidden from history: Reclaiming the gay and lesbian past*. New York: New American Library.

Dubinsky, K. 2010. *Babies without borders: Adoption and migration across the Americas*. New York: New York University Press.

Ducat, S. J. 2004. *The wimp factor: Gender gaps, holy wars, and the politics of anxious masculinity*. Boston: Beacon Press.

Duff, K. 1993. *The alchemy of illness*. New York: Pantheon.

Duffy, Mignon. 2011. *Making care count: A century of gender, race and paid care work*. New Brunswick, NJ: Rutgers University Press.

Dujon, D., and A. Withorn, eds. 1996. *For crying out loud: Women's poverty in the United States*. Boston: South End Press.

Dunbar-Ortiz, R. 2014. *An indigenous people's history of the United States*. Boston: Beacon Press.

Duran, J. 1998. *Philosophies of science/feminist theories*. Boulder, CO: Westview Press.

Dworkin, A. 1993. *Letters from a war zone*. Chicago: Chicago Review Press.

Edison, L. T., and D. Notkin. 1994. *Women en large: Images of fat nudes*. San Francisco: Books in Focus.

Edmond, C. 2017. These rich countries have high levels of child poverty. *World Economic Forum*. Accessed on September 5, 2018, at https://www.weforum.org/agenda/2017/06/these-rich-countries-have-high-levels-of-child-poverty/

Ehrenreich, B., and D. English. 2010. *Witches, midwives, and nurses: A history of women healers*, 2nd ed. Old Westbury, NY: Feminist Press.

Eisenstein, Z. R. 1981. *The radical future of liberal feminism*. New York: Longman.

Eisler, R. 2012. Economics as if caring matters. *Challenge*, March/April. Accessed on September 15, 2018, at http://rianeeisler.com/wp-content/uploads/2014/06/Economics-as-if-Caring-Matters.pdf

Elam, H., and K. Jackson, eds. 2005. *Black cultural traffic: Crossroads in global performance and popular culture*. Ann Arbor: University of Michigan Press.

Elliott, L. 2018. Inequality gap widens as 42 people hold same wealth as 3.7bn poorest. *Guardian*, January 21. Accessed on September 5, 2018, at https://www.theguardian.com/inequality/2018/jan/22/inequality-gap-widens-as-42-people-hold-same-wealth-as-37bn-poorest?CMP=share_btn_link

Eng, D., and A. Y. Hom, eds. 1998. *Q & A: Queer in Asian America*. Philadelphia: Temple University Press.

Enloe, C. 1983. *Does khaki become you? The militarization of women's lives*. Boston: South End Press.

——. 1990. *Bananas, beaches and bases: Making feminist sense of international politics*. Berkeley: University of California Press.

——. 1993. *The morning after: Sexual politics at the end of the cold war*. Berkeley: University of California Press.

——. 2000. *Maneuvers: The international politics of militarizing women's lives*. Berkeley: University of California Press.

——. 2004. Sneak Attack: The militarization of US culture. In *The Curious Feminist: Searching for women in a new age of empire*. Berkeley: University of California Press. pp. 145-147.

——. 2007. *Globalization and militarism: feminists make the links*. Lanham, MD: Rowman and Littlefield.

Enos, S. 2001. *Mothering from the inside: Parenting in a women's prison*. Albany: State University of New York Press.

Ensler, E. 1998. *The vagina monologues*. New York: Villard/Random House.

Evans, K. Bell, and N. K. Burton, eds. 2017. *Black women's mental health: Balancing strength and vulnerability*. Albany: State University of New York Press.

Ewing, B., D. Moore, S. Goldfinger, A. Oursler, A. Reed, and M. Wackernagel. 2010. *The ecological footprint atlas*. Oakland, CA: Global Footprint Network.

Faderman, L. 1981. *Surpassing the love of men: Romantic friendship and love between women from the Renaissance to the present*. New York: William Morrow.

Family Equality Council. 2011. LGBT families: Facts at a glance. Accessed online at http://action.familyequality.org/site/DocServer/AllChildrenMatterFacts Final10192011.pdf?docID=2404

Fausto-Sterling, A. 2000. The five sexes, revisited. *The Sciences*, July/August 40(4): 18. Accessed online at http://www.neiu.edu/lsfuller/5sexesrevisited.htm

Federici, S. 2012. *Revolution at point zero: Housework, reproduction, and feminist struggle*. Oakland, CA: PM Press.

Feinberg, L. 1996. *Transgender warriors: Making history from Joan of Arc to RuPaul*. Boston: Beacon Press.

——. 1998. *Trans liberation: Beyond pink or blue*. Boston: Beacon Press.

Feminist Anti-Censorship Task Force. 1992. *Caught looking: Feminism, pornography, and censorship*. East Haven, CT: Long River Books.

Fernando, S. 2010. *Mental health, race and culture*. 3rd ed. New York: Palgrave Macmillan.

Fialho, C., P. Cullors, and L. Martinez. 2018. If you want to end sexual violence start with prisons, *The Hill*, December 21. Accessed on October 29, 2018, at https://thehill.com/opinion/civil-rights/365897-if-you-want-to-end-sexual-violence-start-with-prisons

Fisher, J. 1999. *Mothers of the Disappeared*. Boston: South End Press.

Findlen, B., ed. 1995. *Listen up: Voices from the next feminist generation*. Seattle, WA: Seal Press.

Finger, A. 1990. *Past due: A story of disability, pregnancy, and birth*. Seattle, WA: Seal Press.

Firestone, S. 1970. *The dialectics of sex: The case for feminist revolution*. New York: Morrow.

Fish, J. N. 2017. *Domestic workers of the world unite! A global movement for dignity and human rights*. New York: New York University Press.

Flood. A. 2017. Fifty Shades sequel tops bestseller lists but whips up little enthusiasm. *Guardian*, December 7. Accessed on November 5, 2018, at https://www.theguardian.com/books/2017/dec/07/fifty-shades-sequel-darker-tops-bestseller-lists-sales-el-james

Flores-González, N., A. R. Guevara, M. Toro-Morn, and G. Chang. 2013. *Immigrant women workers in the neoliberal age*. Urbana: University of Illinois Press.

Folbre, N. 2006. Measuring care: Gender, empowerment, and the care economy, *Journal of Human Development* 7(2): 183–99.

——., ed. 2012. *For love and money: Care provision in the United States*. New York: Russell Sage Foundation.

Foo, L. J., G. Villareal, and N. Timbang. 2007. The Trafficking of Asian Women. In *Asian American women: Issues, concerns, and responsive human and civil rights advocacy*, ed. L. J. Foo. 2nd ed. New York: National Asian American Women's Forum, iUniverse.

Food and Agriculture Organization. 2011. The state of food insecurity in the world, Accessed online at http://www.fao.org/docrep/014/i2330e/i2381e00.pdf

Foster, C. 1989. *Women for all seasons: The story of W.I.L.P.F.* Athens: University of Georgia Press.

Foucault, M. 1980. *Power/knowledge: Selected interviews and other writings 1972–1977*, ed. Colin Gordon. New York: Pantheon.

Fouhy, B. 2004. Gay, patriotic and banished. *San Francisco Examiner*, June 21, p. 1.

Fox, K., and J. Diehm. 2017. #MeToo's global moment: The anatomy of a viral campaign. *CNN*, November 9. Accessed online at https://www.cnn.com/2017/11/09/world/metoo-hashtag-global-movement/index.html

Francisco-Menchavez, V. 2018. *The labor of care: Filipina migrants and transnational families in the digital age*. Urbana: University of Illinois Press.

Frankenberg, R. 1993. *White women, race matters: The social construction of whiteness*. Minneapolis: University of Minnesota Press.

Free, L. E. 2015. *Suffrage reconstructed: Gender, race, and voting rights in the Civil War era*. Ithaca, NY: Cornell University Press.

Freedman, E. 2013. *Redefining rape: Sexual violence in the era of suffrage and segregation.* Cambridge, MA: Harvard University Press.

Freeman, C. 2015. Designing women: Corporate discipline and Barbados's off-shore pink-collar sector. In *The gender, culture and power reader,* ed. D. L. Hodgson, pp. 315–22. New York: Oxford University Press.

Fregoso, R.-L., and C. Bejarano, eds. 2010. *Terrorizing women: Feminicide in the Americas.* Durham, NC: Duke University Press.

Freire, P. 1989. *Pedagogy of the oppressed.* New York: Continuum.

Friedan, B. 1963. *The feminine mystique.* New York: W. W. Norton.

Friedman, J., and J. Valenti. 2008. *Yes means yes! Visions of female sexual power and a world without rape.* Berkeley, CA: Seal Press.

Fryar, C. D., M. D. Carroll, and C. L. Ogden. 2016. *Prevalence of overweight, obesity and extreme obesity among adults aged 20 and over: United States 1960–1962 through 2013–2014.* National Center for Health Statistics. Accessed on October 30, 2018, at https://www.cdc.gov/nchs/data/hestat/obesity_adult_13_14/obesity_adult_13_14.htm

Frye, M. 1992. *Willful virgin: Essays in feminism 1976–1992.* Freedom, CA: The Crossing Press.

Fuchs, L. 1990. The reaction of Black Americans to immigration. In *Immigration reconsidered,* ed. V. Yans-McLaughlin. New York: Oxford University Press.

Gaard, G., ed. 1993. *Ecofeminism: Women, animals, nature.* Philadelphia: Temple University Press.

——. 2011. Ecofeminism revisited: Rejecting essentialism and re-placing species in a materialist feminist environmentalism, *Feminist Formations* 22(3): 26–53.

Gage, S., L. Richards, and H. Wilmot. 2002. *Queer.* New York: Thunder's Mouth Press.

Gaines, P. 1994. *Laughing in the dark: From colored girl to woman of color—A journey from prison to power.* New York: Anchor Books.

Garcia, C. A., and J. Lane. 2009. What a girl wants, what a girl needs. Findings from a gender-specific focus group study. *Crime and Delinquency,* doi: 10.1177/0011128709331790

Garcia. L. 2012. *Respect yourself, protect yourself: Latina girls and sexual identity.* New York: New York University Press.

Garland-Thomson, R. 2002. Integrating Disability, Transforming Feminist Theory, *NWSA Journal,* Vol. 14, no. 3, pp. 1-32.

Garside, J. 2012. Apple's factories in China are breaking employment laws, audit finds. *Guardian,* March 29. Accessed online at http://www.guardian.co.uk/technology/2012/mar/30/apple-factories-china-foxconn-audit

Gay, R. 2014. *Bad feminist: Essays.* New York: Harper Collins.

Geller, J. 2001. *Here comes the bride: Women, weddings, and the marriage mystique.* New York: Four Walls Eight Windows.

Gibbs, L. 1995. *Dying from dioxin: A citizens' guide to reclaiming our health and rebuilding democracy.* Boston: South End Press.

——. 1998. *Love canal: The story continues.* Gabriola Island, BC: New Society.

Gill, R. 2014. Postfeminist sexual culture. In *The Routledge companion to media and gender,* eds. C. Carter, L. Steiner, and L. McLaughlin. New York: Routledge, pp. 589-599.

Gilman, C. P. 2000. *The yellow wallpaper and other writings.* New York: Modern Library.

Gilpin, L. 2016. Why Native American women still have the highest rates of rape and assault. *High Country News,* June 7. Accessed on November 26, 2018, at https://www.hcn.org/articles/tribal-affairs-why-native-american-women-still-have-the-highest-rates-of-rape-and-assault

Glantz, A. 2007. Coke faces new charges in India, including "greenwashing." *One World,* June 7. Available at http://us.oneworld.net/section/us/current

Global Footprint Network. 2019. Earth overshoot day: Media backgrounder. Accessed on April 4, 2019 at https://www.overshootday.org/newsroom/media-backgrounder/

Gluck, S. 1976. *From parlor to prison: Five American suffragists talk about their lives.* New York: Vintage Books.

Gold, J., and S. Villari, eds. 2000. *Just sex: Students rewrite the rules on sex, violence, activism, and equality.* Lanham, MD: Rowman and Littlefield.

Gold, S. S. 2011. *Food: The good girl's drug. How to stop using food to control your feelings.* New York: Berkley Books.

Golden, R. 2005. *War on the family: Mothers in prison and the families they leave behind.* New York: Routledge.

Gonen, J. S. 2003. *Litigation as lobbying: Reproductive hazards and interest aggregation.* Columbus: Ohio State University Press.

Gonzalez, D. 2008. The lost supermarket: A breed in need of replenishment. *New York Times,* May 5.

Accessed online at http://www.nytimes.com/ 2008/05/05/nyregion/05citywide.html?_r=1& oref=slogin

Gordon, L. 1988. *Heroes of their own lives: The politics and history of family violence, Boston 1880–1960.* New York: Viking.

——. 1997. Killing in self-defense. *The Nation*, March 24, pp. 25–28.

Gore, A. 2004. *The essential* Hip Mama: *Writing from the cutting edge of parenting.* Seattle, WA: Seal Press.

Gottfried, J., and E. Shearer. 2016. News use across social media platforms 2016. Pew Research Center, Journalism and Media. Accessed on September 18, 2018, at http://www.journalism.org/2016/05/26/ news-use-across-social-media-platforms-2016/

Gottlieb, R., and A. Joshi. 2010. *Food justice.* Cambridge: Massachusetts Institute of Technology.

Gottschalk, M. 2006. *The prison and the gallows: The politics of mass incarceration in America.* New York: Cambridge University Press.

Government Accountability Office. 2004. Defense of Marriage Act: Update to prior report. GAO-04-353R, January 23. US Government Accountability Office. Accessed on November 21, 2018, at https://www.gao.gov/products/GAO-04-353R

Govind, B. 2016. Plachimada: Still waiting for justice and compensation. *Mathrubhumi*, March 22. Accessed on October 16, 2018, at https://english.mathrubhumi.com/news/kerala/plachimada-still-waiting-for-justice-and-compensation-english-news-1.945359

Grahn, J. 1984. *Another mother tongue: Gay words, gay worlds.* Boston: Beacon Press.

Green, E., K. Benner, and R. Pear. 2018. "Transgender" could be defined out of existence under Trump administration. *New York Times*, October 21. Accessed on November 20, 2018, at https://www.nytimes.com/2018/10/21/us/politics/transgender-trump-administration-sex-definition.html

Griffin, S. 1971. Rape: The all-American crime. *Ramparts* 10(3): 26–35.

——. 1978. *Woman and nature: The roaring inside her.* San Francisco: Harper Colophon.

Grossholtz, J. 1998. The search for peace and justice: Notes toward an autobiography. In *Women's Lives: Multicultural perspectives.* 1st ed. New York: McGraw-Hill.

Guerino, P., P. M. Harrison, and W. J. Sabol. 2011. Prisoners in 2010. Bureau of Justice Statistics. Accessed online at http://bjs.gov/index.cfm?ty=pbdetail&iid=2230

Gullette, M. M. 2004. *Aged by culture.* Chicago: University of Chicago Press.

——. 2011. *Agewise: Fighting the new ageism in America.* Chicago: University of Chicago Press.

Gurr, B. 2015. *Reproductive justice: The politics of health care for Native American women.* New Brunswick, NJ: Rutgers University Press.

Gustafson, K. 2005. *To punish the poor: Criminalizing trends in the welfare system.* Oakland: Women of Color Resource Center.

——. 2011. *Cheating welfare: Public assistance and the criminalization of poverty.* New York: New York University Press.

Guthman, J. 2011. *Weighing in: Obesity, food justice, and the limits of capitalism.* Berkeley: University of California Press.

Guttmacher Institute. 2014. Data center. Accessed on October 31, 2018, at https://data.guttmacher.org/states/table?state=US&topics=58+59&dataset=data

——. 2018a. *Improvements in contraceptive use continue to drive declines in pregnancy among US adolescents.* August 30. Accessed on October 31, 2018, at https://www.guttmacher.org/search/site?f%5B0%5D=bundle%3Anews_release

——. 2018b. *Induced abortion in the United States, fact sheet.* January. Accessed on October 31, 2018, at https://www.guttmacher.org/fact-sheet/induced-abortion-united-states

Guy-Sheftall, B., ed. 1995. *Words of fire: An anthology of African American feminist thought.* New York: The New Press.

Halberstam, J. 1998. *Female masculinity.* Durham, NC: Duke University Press.

——. 2005. *In a queer time and place.* New York: New York University Press.

Hall, K. Q., 2011. *Feminist disability studies.* Bloomington: Indiana University Press.

Hall, S. 1980. Encoding/decoding. In *Culture, media, language*, eds. S. Hall, D. Hobson, A Lowe, and P. Willis. London: Unwin Hyman, pp. 117-127.

Harding, S. 1987. *Feminism and methodology: Social science issues.* Bloomington: University of Indiana Press.

——. 1998. *Is science multicultural? Postcolonialisms, feminisms, and epistemologies.* Bloomington: Indiana University Press.

Harman, B. 1996. Happy ending. In *"Women in the trees": US women's short stories about battering and resistance, 1839–1994*, ed. S. Koppelman, pp. 286–90. Boston: Beacon Press.

Hartmann, H. 2012. *Can boomer women afford to retire?* Washington, DC: Institute for Women's

Policy Research. Accessed online at http://www.iwpr.org/publications/pubs/can-boomer-women-afford-to-retire

Hartsock, N. 1983. *Money, sex, and power: Toward a feminist historical materialism*. New York: Longman.

Hawthorne, S. 2002. *Wild politics: Feminism, globalization, bio/diversity*. Melbourne, Australia: Spinifex.

Hayes, D., and J. L. Lawless. 2016. *Women on the run: Gender, media, and political campaigns in a polarized era*. New York: Cambridge University Press.

Hayes, J., and H. Hartmann. 2011. *Women and men living on the edge: Economic insecurity after the Great Recession*. Washington DC: Institute for Women's Policy Research, Rockefeller Survey of Economic Insecurity. Accessed on September 18 2018, at https://iwpr.org/publications/women-and-men-living-on-the-edge-economic-insecurity-after-the-great-recession/

Healey, S. 1997. Confronting ageism: A MUST for mental health. In *In our own words: Readings on the psychology of women and gender*, ed. M. Crawford and R. Unger, pp. 368–76. New York: McGraw-Hill.

Heidenreich, L. 2011. Transgender women, sexual violence, and the rule of law: An argument in favor of restorative and transformative justice. In *Razor wire women*, ed. J. M. Lawston and A. E. Lucas. Albany: State University of New York Press.

Heise, L., J. Pitanguy, and A. Germain. 1994. *Violence against women: The hidden health burden*. World Bank Discussion Papers #255. Washington, DC: The World Bank.

Hemmings, C. 2002. *Bisexual spaces: A geography of sexuality and gender*. New York: Routledge.

Hennessy, R., and C. Ingraham, eds. 1997. *Materialist feminism: A reader in class, difference, and women's lives*. New York: Routledge.

Herivel, T., and P. Wright, eds. 2007. *Prison profiteers. Who makes money from mass incarceration*. New York: New Press.

Herman, J. 1992. *Trauma and recovery*. New York: Basic Books.

Hernández, A. 1975. *Equal Opportunity Commission and the women's movement (1965–1975)*. Unpublished paper for the Symposium on the Tenth Anniversary of the US EEOC, sponsored by Rutgers University Law School, November 28–29.

——. 2002. *In pursuit of equality: The ups and downs in the struggle for inclusion*. Available from Aileen C. Hernández Associates, 81847th Ave., San Francisco, CA 94121.

Hernandez, D. 2017. The Case against "Latinx." *Los Angeles Times*, December 17. Accessed on August 26, 2018, at http://www.latimes.com/opinion/op-ed/la-oe-hernandez-the-case-against-latinx-20171217-story.html#

Hicks, G. 1997. *The comfort women: Japan's brutal regime of enforced prostitution in the Second World War*. New York: W. W. Norton.

Higher Heights, Center for American Women and Politics, and Eagleton Institute. 2018. *The Chisholm effect: Black women in American politics 2018*. New Brunswick, NJ: Center for American Women and Politics. Accessed on October 21, 2018, at http://www.cawp.rutgers.edu/sites/default/files/resources/chisholm_effect_black_women_in_politics.pdf

Hiller, L., L. Gates, N. Munger, N. Douttiel, E. Ehrlich-Walsh, and M. Zepernick. 2005. *Save the water: A curriculum study guide*. Philadelphia: Women's International League for Peace and Freedom.

Hirahara, N., and H. C. Lindquist. 2018. *Life after Manzanar*. Berkeley, CA: Heyday Books.

History Project. 1998. *Improper Bostonians: Lesbian and gay history from the Puritans to Playland*. Boston: Beacon Press.

Hite, S. 1994. *Women as revolutionary agents of change: The Hite Report and beyond*. Madison: University of Wisconsin Press.

Hochschild, A. R. 1989. *The second shift: Working parents and the revolution at home*. New York: Viking.

Holmes, C. 2016. *Ecological borderlands: Body, nature, and spirit in Chicana feminism*. Urbana: University of Illinois Pres.

Holmstedt, K. 2007. *Band of sisters: American women at war in Iraq*. Mechanicsburg, PA: Stackpole Books.

Hondagneu-Sotelo, P. 2001. *Doméstica: Immigrant workers cleaning and caring in the shadows of affluence*. Berkeley: University of California Press.

Honderich, K. 2003. *The real cost of prison for women and their children*. Washington, DC: The Real Cost of Prisons Project/The Sentencing Project.

hooks, b. 1984. Feminist movement to end violence. In *Feminist theory: From margin to center*, ed. b. hooks, pp. 117–31. Boston: South End Press.

——. 1994. Seduced by violence no more. In *Outlaw culture: Resisting representations*, ed. b. hooks, pp. 109–13. New York: Routledge.

——. 2000. *Feminism is for everybody: Passionate politics*. Cambridge, MA: South End Press.

Howey, N., and E. Samuels, eds. 2000. *Out of the ordinary: Essays on growing up with gay, lesbian, and transgender parents*. New York: St. Martin's Press.

Human Rights Campaign. 2018. *Violence against the transgender community in 2018*. Accessed online at https://www.hrc.org/resources/violence-against-the-transgender-community-in-2017

Human Rights Watch. 2016. *"Do you see how much I'm suffering here?" Abuse against transgender women in US immigration detention*. New York: Human Rights Watch.

Ingraham, Chrys. 2004. *Thinking straight: The power, promise, and paradox of heterosexuality*. New York: Routledge.

Ingraham, Christopher. 2016. The states that spend more money on prisoners than on college students. *Washington Post*, July 7. Accessed on October 28, 2018, at https://www.washingtonpost.com/news/wonk/wp/2016/07/07/the-states-that-spend-more-money-on-prisoners-than-college-students/?noredirect=on&utm_term=.c526aac45fad

Institute for Women's Policy Research. 2011. Social Security helps older women, especially Black women and Latinas, stay out of poverty. Accessed online at http://www.iwpr.org/press-room/press-releases/new-research-social-security-helps-older-women-especially-black-women-and-latinas-stay-out-of-poverty

Intergovernmental Panel on Climate Change. 2007. Fourth Assessment Report: Climate Change Synthesis Report. Accessed on May 12, 2012, at http://www.ipcc.ch/publications_and_data/ar4/syr/en/contents.html

Iwamura, J. M. 2007. Critical faith: Japanese Americans and the birth of a new civil religion. *American Quarterly* 59(3): 937–68.

Jacob, K. 2002. *Our choices, our lives: Unapologetic writings on abortion*. Minneapolis, MN: Writers Advantage.

Jacobsen, C. 2008. Creative politics and women's criminalization in the United States. *Signs: Journal of Women in Culture and Society* 33(2).

Jacobson, L. 2018. Is Michelle Wolf right that Flint still doesn't have clean water? *PunditFact*, May 1. Accessed on October 16, 2018, at https://www.politifact.com/punditfact/statements/2018/may/01/michelle-wolf/michelle-wolf-right-flint-still-doesnt-have-clean-/

Jefferis, J. L. 2011. *Armed for life: The Army of God and anti-abortion terror in the United States*. Santa Barbara, CA: Praeger.

Jeffreys, S. 2003. *Unpacking Queer Politics: A lesbian feminist perspective*. Cambridge, UK: Polity Press.

Jenkins, K. 2015. Women's everyday resilience in opposing large-scale mining. *OXFAM Policy and Practice Blog*, December 17. Accessed on October 18, 2018, at https://policy-practice.oxfam.org.uk/blog/2015/12/womens-everyday-resilience-in-opposing-large-scale-mining

Johnson, A. G. 2005. *The gender knot: Unraveling our patriarchal legacy*. Philadelphia: Temple University Press.

Johnson, M. L. 2002. *Jane sexes it up: True confessions of feminist desire*. New York: Four Walls, Eight Windows.

Johnson, P. C. 2002. *Inner lives: Voices of African American women in prison*. New York: New York University Press.

Jones, R. K., and J. Jerman. 2017. Abortion incidence and service availability in the United States, 2014. *Perspectives on Sexual and Reproductive Health* 49(1): 17–27. Accessed on October 31, 2018, at https://www.guttmacher.org/journals/psrh/2017/01/abortion-incidence-and-service-availability-united-states-2014

Jong, E. 1998. Ally McBeal and *Time* magazine can't keep the good women down. *New York Observer*, July 13, p. 19.

Jordan, J. 1985. Report from the Bahamas. In *On call: Political essays*. Boston: South End Press.

——. 1992. A new politics of sexuality. In *Technical difficulties: African American notes on the state of the union*. New York: Pantheon Books.

——. 1999. Breast cancer; Still here. *The Progressive*, vol. 63, no.2, February, pp. 17-18.

Joseph, A. 2016. Wes Clark Jr. at Standing Rock. *Salon*, December 5. Accessed on October 24, 2018, at http://www.salon.com/2016/12/05/wes-clark-jr-at-standing-rock-generals-activist-son-heads-to-n-d-driven-by-spiritual-fire-and-ready-to-be-killed/

Joseph, S. and B. D'Harlingue. 2007. Media Representations and the Criminalization of Arab Americans and Muslim Americans. In *Women's Lives: Multicultural Perspectives*. 4th ed. eds. G. Kirk and M. Okazawa-Rey, pp. 464-468. New York: McGraw-Hill.

Just Detention. 2012. Vulnerable inmates. Accessed online at http://www.justdetention.org/en/vulnerable.aspx

Justice Policy Institute. 2002. *Cell blocks or classrooms?* Washington, DC: Justice Policy Institute. Accessed online at http://www.justicepolicy.org/article.php?id=3

Kadi, J. 1996. *Thinking class: Sketches from a cultural worker.* Boston: South End Press.

Kafer, A. 2013. *Feminist queer crip.* Bloomington: Indiana University Press.

Kamen, P. 2000. *Her way: Young women make the sexual revolution.* New York: New York University Press.

Kaplan, T. 1997. *Crazy for democracy: Women in grassroots movements.* New York: Routledge.

Kassie, E. 2018. Sexual assault inside ICE detention: 2 survivors tell their stories. *New York Times*, July 17. Accessed on October 29, 2018, at https://www.nytimes.com/2018/07/17/us/sexual-assault-ice-detention-survivor-stories.html

Kastrup, M. 2016. The impact of racism and discrimination on mental health of refugees and asylum seekers. *European Psychiatry,* Vol. 33, pp. S43–S43.

Kates, E., and P. Ransford, with C. Cardozo. 2005. *Women in prison in Massachusetts: Maintaining family connections—A research report.* Boston: Center for Women in Politics and Public Policy, McCormack Graduate School of Public Policy, University of Massachusetts.

Katz, J. N. 1995. *The invention of heterosexuality.* New York: Plume.

Katz Rothman, B. 1986. *Tentative pregnancy: Prenatal diagnosis and the future of motherhood.* New York: Viking.

Kaufman, M., and M. Kimmel. 2011. *The guy's guide to feminism.* Emeryville, CA: Seal Press.

——, C. Silverberg, and F. Odette. 2003. *The ultimate guide to sex and disability: For all of us with disabilities, chronic pain and illness.* San Francisco: Cleis Press.

Kaysen, S. 1994. *Girl interrupted.* New York: Vintage Books.

Kellner, D., and J. Share. 2005. Toward critical media literacy: Core concepts, debates, organizations, and policy. *Discourse: Studies in the Cultural Politics of Education* 26(3): 369–86.

Kempadoo, K., and J. Doezema, eds. 1998. *Global sex workers: Rights, resistance and redefinition.* New York: Routledge.

Kerr, J., ed. 1993. *Ours by right: Women's rights as human rights.* London: Zed Books.

Kesic, V. 2000. From reverence to rape: An anthropology of ethnic and genderized violence. In *Frontline feminisms: Women, war, and resistance,* ed. M. Waller and J. Rycenga. New York: Garland Publishing.

Kettel, B. 1996. Women, health and the environment. *Social Science Medicine* 42(10): 1367–79.

Kilbourne, J. 1999. *Deadly persuasion: Why women and girls must fight the addictive power of advertising.* New York: Free Press.

Kim, E. 2010. *Adopted territory: Transnational Korean adoptees and the politics of belonging.* Durham, NC: Duke University Press.

Kim, M. 2006. Alternative interventions to violence: Creative interventions. *The International Journal of Narrative Therapy and Community Work.* no. 4, pp. 45–52. Accessed online at http://www.creative-interventions.org/wp-content/uploads/2012/06/Alternative-interventions-Narrative-Therapy.pdf

Kim, Y. 2017. *Childcare workers, global migration and digital media.* New York: Routledge.

Kim-Gibson, D. S. 1999. *Silence broken: Korean comfort women.* Parkersburg, IA: Mid Prairie Books.

Kimbrell, A., ed. 2002. *Fatal harvest: The tragedy of industrial agriculture.* Washington, DC: Island Press.

Kimmel, M. 2000. *The gendered society.* New York: Oxford University Press.

——, and M. Messner. 1998. *Men's lives.* 3rd ed. Boston: Allyn & Bacon.

Kincaid, J. 1988. *A small place.* New York: Penguin/Plume.

King, Y. 1993. The other body. *Ms. Magazine,* March/April, pp. 72–75.

Kingo, A. G. 2018. This calculator tells you exactly how much money you lose when you stay home with your kids. *Working Mother,* October 11. Accessed on November 21, 2018, at https://www.workingmother.com/this-calculator-tells-you-exactly-how-much-money-you-lose-when-you-stay-home-with-your-kids

Kinser, A, 2010. *Motherhood and feminism.* Emeryville, CA: Seal Press.

Kirk, G. 1997. Standing on solid ground: Towards a materialist ecological feminism. In *Materialist feminism: A reader in class, difference, and women's lives,* ed. R. Hennessy and C. Ingraham, pp. 345–63. New York: Routledge.

——. 1998. Ecofeminism and Chicano environmental struggles: Bridges across gender and race. In *Chicano culture, ecology, politics: Subversive kin,* ed. D. G. Peña, pp. 177–200. Tucson: University of Arizona Press.

Klein, R. 2017. *Surrogacy: A human right's violation.* North Geelong, Australia: Spinifex Press.

Koedt, A. 1973. The myth of the vaginal orgasm. In *Radical feminism,* ed. A. Koedt, E. Levine, and A. Rapone. New York: Times Books.

Kohl, H. 1992. *From archetype to zeitgeist: Powerful ideas for powerful thinking.* Boston: Little Brown.

Kolmar, W. K., and F. Bartowski. 2010. *Feminist theory: A reader.* 3rd ed. New York: McGraw-Hill.

Koppleman, S., ed. 2004. *"Women in the trees": US Women's short stories about battering and resistance, 1839–2000.* New York: Feminist Press at CUNY.

Krase, K. 2012. History of forced sterilization and current US abuses. *Our Bodies Ourselves.* Accessed on October 5, 2018, at https://www.ourbodies-ourselves.org/book-excerpts/health-article/forced-sterilization/

Krauss, C. 1993. Blue-collar women and toxic-waste protests: The process of politicization. In *Toxic struggles: The theory and practice of environmental justice,* ed. R. Hofrichter, pp. 107–17. Philadelphia and Gabriola Island, BC: New Society.

Kremen, C., A. Iles, and C. Bacon. 2012. Diversified farming systems: An agro-ecological, systems-based alternative to modern industrial agriculture, *Ecology and Society,* 17 (4): 44.

——, and A. Miles. 2012. Ecosystem services and diversified farming systems: Analysis of costs, benefits and tradeoffs for food production, resilience and biodiversity, *Ecology and Society,*17 (4): 40.

Kristjansson, M. 2014a. Fashion's "forgotten woman": How fat bodies queer fashion and consumption. In *Queering fat embodiment,* ed. C. Pausé, J. Wykes, and S. Murray, pp. 131–146. Burlington, VT: Ashgate Publishing.

——. 2014b. How Fat Bodies Queer Fashion. *Bitch Media.* July 25. Accessed online at https://www.bitchmedia.org/post/how-fat-bodies-queer-fashion

La Ganga, M. 2016. US prohibits imprisoning transgender inmates in cells based on birth anatomy. *Guardian.* March 24. Accessed on October 29, 2018, at https://www.theguardian.com/us-news/2016/mar/24/transgender-prison-gender-identity-anatomy-doj-rules?CMP=share_btn_link

Labaton, V., and D. Lundy Martin, eds. 2004. *The fire this time: Young activists and the new feminism.* New York: Anchor/Random House.

Lacey, M. 2004. Amnesty says Sudan militias use rape as a weapon. *New York Times,* July 19. Accessed on April 20, 2012, at http://www.nytimes.com/2004/07/19/world/amnesty-says-sudan-militias-use-rape-as-weapon.html

LaDuke, W. 1993. A society based on conquest cannot be sustained: Native peoples and the environmental crisis. In *Toxic struggles: The theory and practice of environmental justice,* ed. R. Hofrichter. Philadelphia and Gabriola Island, BC: New Society.

——. 1999. *All our relations: Native struggles for land and life.* Cambridge, MA: South End Press.

Lagarde y de los Ríos, M. 2010. Feminist keys for understanding feminicide: Theoretical, political and legal constructions. In *Terrorizing women: Feminicide in the Americas,* ed. R.-L. Fregoso and C. Bejarano, pp. xi–xxvi. Durham, NC: Duke University Press.

Lamb, W., and the Women of York Correctional Facility. 2003. *Couldn't keep it to myself: Testimony from our imprisoned sisters.* New York: ReganBooks.

——, ed. 2007. *I'll fly away: Further testimonies from the women of York Prison.* New York: HarperCollins.

Lamm, N. 1995. It's a big, fat revolution. In *Listen up: Voices from the next feminist generation,* ed. B. Findlen, pp. 85–94. Seattle, WA: Seal Press.

Lancaster, R. N., and M. di Leonardo, eds. 1997. *The gender/sexuality reader: Culture, history, political economy.* New York: Routledge.

Lappé, F. M., , Collins, J., Rosset, P., and Esparza, L. 1998. *World hunger: Twelve myths.* New York: Grove Press.

Lasch, C. 1977. *Haven in a heartless world: The family besieged.* New York: Basic Books.

Laughlin, K. A., J. Gallaher, D. S. Cobble, E. Boris, P. Nadasen, S. Gilmore, and L. Zarnow. 2010. Is it time to jump ship? Historians rethink the waves metaphor. *Feminist Formations* 22(1): 76–135.

Law, V. 2009. *Resistance behind bars: The struggles of incarcerated women.* Oakland, CA: PM Press.

——. 2017. Trapped in a transphobic hell: Ky Peterson and the trials of trans people in prison. *Truthout,* September 15. Accessed on October 29, 2018, at https://truthout.org/articles/trapped-in-a-transphobic-hell-ky-peterson-and-the-trials-of-trans-people-in-prison/

Lawless, J. L., and R. Fox. 2010. *It still takes a candidate: Why women don't run for office.* New York: Cambridge University Press.

Lawrence, E., and J. Ringrose. 2018. @NoToFeminism, #FeministsAreUgly, and misandry memes: How social media feminist humor is calling out antifeminism. In *Emergent feminisms: Complicating a postfeminist media culture,* ed. J. Keller and M. E. Ryan, pp. 211–232. New York: Routledge.

Lawston, J. M., and A. E. Lucas, eds. 2011. *Razor wire women: Prisoners, activists, scholars, and artists.* Albany: State University of New York Press.

Layzer, J. A. 2006 Community activism and environmental justice: The Dudley Street Neighborhood Initiative. In *The environmental case: Translating values into policy.* 2nd ed. Washington, DC: CQ Pres.

Le Monde. 2018. Full translation of French anti-#MeToo manifesto signed by Catherine Deneuve. January 10, translated by WorldCrunch. Accessed on November 5, 2018, at https://www.worldcrunch.com/opinion-analysis/full-translation-of-french-anti-metoo-manifesto-signed-by-catherine-deneuve

Leatherman, J. 2011. *Sexual violence and armed conflict.* Boston: Polity Press.

Lee, C. 1987. *Toxic wastes and race in the United States.* New York: New York Commission for Racial Justice United Church of Christ.

Lennard, N. 2017. Will the prison rape epidemic ever have its Weinstein moment? *The Intercept,* Nov. 21. Accessed on April 8, 2019 at https://theintercept.com/2017/11/21/prison-rape-sexual-assault-violence/

Leong, R., ed. 1996. *Asian American sexualities: Dimensions of the gay and lesbian experience.* New York: Routledge.

Levin, Sam. 2017. Google segregates women into lower paying jobs, stifling careers lawsuit says. *Guardian,* September 14, Accessed on October 16, 2018, at https://www.theguardian.com/technology/2017/sep/14/google-women-promotions-lower-paying-jobs-lawsuit?

Levy, A. 2005. *Female chauvinist pigs: Women and the rise of raunch culture.* New York: Free Press.

Lifton, R.J. 2005. *Home from the war: Learning from Vietnam veterans.* New York: Other Press. Revised edition.

Lindsey, T. B. 2018. The betrayal of white women voters: In pivotal state races they still backed the GOP. *Vox,* November 9. Accessed on November 21, 2018, at https://www.vox.com/first-person/2018/11/9/18075390/election-2018-midterms-white-women-voters

Liptak. A. 2010. Justices, 5-4, reject corporate spending limit. *New York Times,* January 21. Accessed online at http://www.nytimes.com/2010/01/22/us/politics/22scotus.html?pagewanted=all

Litt, J. S., and M. K. Zimmerman. 2003. Global perspectives on gender and carework: An introduction. *Gender and Society* 17(2): 156–65.

Lopez, A. P. 2018. The X in Latinx is a wound, not a trend. *Efniks,* September 18. Accessed on September 20, 2018, at http://efniks.com/the-deep-dive-pages/2018/9/11/the-x-in-latinx-is-a-wound-not-a-trend

Lorber, J. 1991. Dismantling Noah's ark. In *The social construction of gender,* ed. J. Lorber and S. A. Farrell. Thousand Oaks, CA: SAGE Publications, pp. 355–69

Lorber, J., and S. A. Farrell, eds. 1991. *The social construction of gender.* Thousand Oaks, CA: SAGE Publications.

Lublin, N. 1998. *Pandora's box: Feminism confronts reproductive technology.* Lanham, MD: Rowman and Littlefield.

Luebke, B. F., and M. E. Reilly. 1995. *Women's studies graduates: The first generation.* New York: Teachers College Press.

Lutz, C. 2004. Living room terrorists. *Women's Review of Books* 21(5): 17–18.

Lynes, K., and G. Torry. 2005. *From local to global: Making peace work for women. Security Council Resolution 1325 five years on.* New York: NGO Working Group on Peace and Security.

Maathai, W. 2003. *The Greenbelt Movement: Sharing the approach and the experience.* New York: Lantern Books.

———. 2010. *Replenishing the Earth: Spiritual values for healing ourselves and the world.* New York: Doubleday.

Macdonald, C. L. 2010. *Shadow mothers: Nannies, au pairs, and the micropolitics of mothering.* Berkeley: University of California Press.

Macharia, Sarah. 2015. *Who makes the news? Global Media Monitoring Project 2015.* London and Toronto: World Association for Christian Communication.

Mackinnon, C. 1991. From practice to theory, or what is a white woman anyway? *Yale Journal of Law and Feminism* 4(13–22): 1281–328.

Magnani, L., and H. L. Wray. 2006. *Beyond prisons: A new interfaith paradigm for our failed prison system.* Minneapolis: Fortress Press.

Mahdavi, P. 2018. How #MeToo became a global movement. *Foreign Affairs,* March 6. Accessed online at https://www.foreignaffairs.com/articles/2018-03-06/how-metoo-became-global-movement

Maher, F. A., and M. K. T. Tétreault. 1994. *The feminist classroom.* New York: Basic Books.

Mallicoat, S. L. 2012. *Women and crime: A text/reader.* Los Angeles: Sage.

Mantilla, K. 2015. *Gendertrolling: How misogyny went viral.* Santa Barbara, CA: Praeger/ABC-CLIO.

Mares, T. M., and D. G. Peña. 2010. Urban agriculture in the making of insurgent spaces in Los Angeles and Seattle. In *Insurgent public space: Guerrilla urbanism and the remaking of contemporary cities*, ed. J. Hou (pp. 241–254). New York: Routledge.

Markle, G. 2008. "Can women have sex like a man?": Sexual scripts in *Sex and the City. Sexuality and Culture* 12: 45–57.

Marre, D., and L. Briggs, eds. 2009. *International adoption: Global inequalities and the circulation of children*. New York: New York University Press.

Martin, C. E. 2007. *Perfect girls, starving daughters: The frightening new normalcy of hating your body*. New York: Simon and Schuster.

Martinson, K., and J. Strawn. 2003. *Built to last: Why skills matter for long-run success in welfare reform*. Washington, DC: Center for Law and Social Policy.

Marx, F. 2002. Grassroots to graduation: Low-income women accessing higher education. In *Final Report: Evaluation of the Women in Community Development Program, Women's Institute for Housing and Economic Development*. Boston: Center for Research on Women, Wellesley College.

Mason, M. G. 2004. *Working against odds: Stories of disabled women's work lives*. Boston: Northeastern University Press.

Mazabanda, C. 2017. The People of the Waterfalls Threatened by Mining. *Amazon Watch*, May 5. Accessed on October 5, 2018, at https://amazonwatch.org/news/2017/0505-the-people-of-the-waterfalls-threatened-by-mining

McCarthy, N. 2017. The top 15 countries for military expenditure in 2016. *Forbes*, April 24. Accessed on October 22, 2018, at https://www.forbes.com/sites/niallmccarthy/2017/04/24/the-top-15-countries-for-military-expenditure-in-2016-infographic/#251edeee43f3

McConnaughy, C. M., 2013. *The woman suffrage movement in America: A reassessment*. New York: Cambridge University Press.

McMichael, P. 2009. A food regime analysis of the "world food crisis." *Agriculture and Human Values* 26(4): 281–95.

McShane, M. 2008. *Prisons in America*. New York: LFB Scholarly Publishing.

Media Matters. 2015. Limbaugh: Feminism was established so as to allow unattractive women access to the mainstream of pop culture. Accessed on August 26, 2018, at https://www.mediamatters.org/video/2015/09/11/limbaugh-feminism-was-established-so-as-to-allo/205504

Meintjes, S., A. Pillay, and M. Turshen, eds. 2001. *The aftermath: Women in post-war reconstruction*. London and New York: Zed Books.

Mellor, M. 1992. *Breaking the boundaries: Towards a feminist green socialism*. London: Virago Press.

Merchant, C. 1980. *The death of nature: Ecology and the scientific revolution*. San Francisco: Harper & Row.

Mies, M., and V. Shiva, eds. 1993. *Ecofeminism*. London: Zed Books.

Migration Data Portal. 2019. *Types of migrations: Definitions*. Berlin, Germany. Accessed on April 11, 2019 at https://migrationdataportal.org/themes/forced-migration-or-displacement#definitions

Milan, T., and K. K. Milan. 2016. A queer vision of love and marriage. *TEDWomen*, October. Accessed on November 13, 2018, at https://www.ted.com/talks/tiq_milan_and_kim_katrin_milan_a_queer_vision_of_love_and_marriage/transcript

Miles, A., ed. 2013. *Women in a globalizing world: Transforming equality, development, diversity and peace*. Toronto: Inanna Publications.

Millett, Kate. 1990. *The loony bin trip*. New York: Simon & Schuster.

Min, L. 2018. These are the states that still allow female inmates to be shackled during childbirth. *The Cut*, March 28. Accessed on October 29, 2018, at https://www.thecut.com/2018/03/these-states-still-allow-shackling-inmates-during-childbirth.html

Mishel, L., and J. Schieder. 2017. *CEO pay remains high relative to the pay of typical workers and high wage-earners*. Washington, DC: Economic Policy Institute. Accessed on September 5, 2018, at https://www.epi.org/files/pdf/130354.pdf

Mitchell, T., ed. 2001. *Global noise: Rap and hip hop outside the USA*. Middletown, CT: Wesleyan University Press.

Moghadam, V. M. 2005. *Globalizing women: Transnational feminist networks*. Baltimore, MD: Johns Hopkins University Press.

Mohanty, C. T. 2003a. *Feminism without borders: Decolonizing theory, practicing solidarity*. Durham, NC: Duke University Press.

——. 2003b. Genealogies of community, home, and nation, In *Feminism without borders: Decolonizing theory, practicing solidarity*. Durham, NC: Duke University Press, pp. 124-136.

——. 2003c. Under Western eyes revisited: Feminist solidarity though anticapitalist struggles. In *Feminism without borders: Decolonizing theory, practicing solidarity.* Durham, NC: Duke University Press, pp. 221-251.

Molina-Guzmán, I. 2010. Disciplining J. Lo: Booty politics in the tabloid news. In *Dangerous curves: Latina bodies in the media,* pp. 51–86. New York: New York University Press.

Moniz, T., ed. 2016. *Rad families: A celebration.* Oakland: PM Press.

——, and J. A. Smith, eds. 2011. *Rad dad: Dispatches from the frontiers of fatherhood.* Oakland: PM Press.

Moraga, C. 1997. *Waiting in the wings: Portrait of a queer motherhood.* Ithaca, NY: Firebrand.

——, and G. Anzaldua. 1981. *This bridge called my back: Writings by radical women of color.* New York: Kitchen Table/Women of Color Press.

Morris, M. W. 2016. *Pushout: The criminalization of Black girls in schools.* New York: The New Press.

Morrone, L. 2009. *Overcoming overeating: It's not what you eat, it's what's eating you!* Eugene, OR: Harvest House.

Mršević, Z. 2000. The Opposite of War is Not Peace—It is Creativity. In *Frontline Feminisms: Women, war, and resistance,* eds. M. R. Waller and J. Rycenga pp. 41-55. New York: Garland.

Mullings, L. 1997. *On our own terms: Race, class, and gender in the lives of African American women.* New York: Routledge.

Mulvey, L. 1975. Visual pleasure and narrative cinema, *Screen* 16: 3. Accessed on November 20, 2018, at https://academic.oup.com/screen/article-abstract /16/3/6/1603296?redirectedFrom=fulltext

Muscio, I. 1999. *Cunt: A declaration of independence.* Seattle, WA: Seal Press.

Nacos, B. L., and O. Torres-Reyna. 2007. *Fueling our fears: Stereotyping, media coverage, and public opinion of Muslim Americans.* Lanham, MD: Rowman and Littlefield.

Nadasen, P. 2005. *Welfare warriors: The welfare rights movement in the United States.* New York: Routledge.

Nagel, Jill. 1997. *Whores and other feminists.* New York: Routledge.

Nagel, Joane. 2016. *Gender and climate change: Impacts, science, policy.* New York: Routledge.

Naples, N., and M. Desai. 2002. *Women's activism and globalization: Linking local struggles and transnational politics.* New York: Routledge.

National Immigrant Justice Center. 2018. *Detention bed quota.* Accessed on October 30, 2018, at https://www.immigrantjustice.org/eliminate-detention-bed-quota

National Institute for Occupational Safety and Health. 2012. A story of impact. Accessed online at http://www.cdc.gov/niosh/docs/2012-108/pdfs/2012-108.pdf

National Institute of Justice. 2019. *Human Trafficking.* US Department of Justice. Accessed on April 11, 2019 at https://www.nij.gov/topics/crime/human-trafficking/pages/welcome.aspx

NATO News. 2011. Engaging women on the frontline. July 18. Accessed online at http://www.nato.int/cps/en/natolive/news_76542.htm

Nelson, L. 1990. The place of women in polluted places. In *Reweaving the world: The emergence of ecofeminism,* ed. I. Diamond and G. Orenstein. San Francisco: Sierra Club Books.

Nestle, J., C. Howell, and R. Wilchins. 2002. *Genderqueer: Voices from beyond the sexual binary.* Los Angeles: Alyson.

New York Times. 2017. Presidential Election Results: Donald J. Trump Wins. August 9. Accessed on October 19, 2018, at https://www.nytimes.com/elections/2016/results/president

Newbury, C., and H. Baldwin. 2001. Confronting the aftermath of conflict: Women's organizations in post-genocide Rwanda. In *Women and civil war: Impact, organizations, and action,* ed. K. Kumar. Boulder, CO: Lynne Reinner.

Nimoy, L. 2007. *The full body project.* Brooklyn, NY: Five Ties.

Nisenson, A. 2017. Faculty rights in the classroom. *Academe* 103(5). Accessed on November 24, 2018, at https://www.aaup.org/issue/september-october-2017?link_id=3&can_id=6f3e24f3522b354fe20db71b80645594&source=email-faculty-in-the-crosshairs&email_referrer=email_232672&email_subject=faculty-in-the-crosshairs

Noble, S. U. 2018. *Algorithms of oppression: How search engines reinforce racism.* New York: New York University Press.

Norma, C. 2016. *The Japanese comfort women and sexual slavery during the China and Pacific wars.* London: Bloomsbury Academic.

Notte, J. 2017. Sex and love when you hate yourself and don't have your shit together. In *Ask: Building consent culture,* ed. K. Stryker, pp. 9-14. Portland, OR: Thorntree Press.

Office of the Under Secretary of Defense, Personnel and Readiness. 2016. *Population Representation in the Military Services: FY 2016 Summary Report.* Accessed on October 24, 2018, at https://www.cna.org/pop-rep/2016/summary/summary.pdf

Ogden, S. 2006. Pomo woman, ex-prisoner, speaks out. In *The color of violence*, ed. Incite! Women of Color Against Violence, pp. 164–169. Cambridge, MA: South End Press.

Okazawa-Rey, M. and JASS (Just Associates). 2018. *Between a rock and a hard place: Women, power, and change in South-East Asia.* Accessed at https://justassociates.org/sites/justassociates.org/files/jass_sea_report_jan_2019_e-version.pdf

Oliver-Didier, O. 2017. The invisibility of poverty in Puerto Rico, *Counterpunch*, December 11. Accessed on October 8 at https://www.counterpunch.org/2017/12/11/the-invisibility-of-poverty-in-puerto-rico/

Olson, R. 2008. *This is who I am: Our beauty is all shapes and sizes.* New York: Artisan/Workman.

Omolade, B. 1983. Hearts of darkness. In *Powers of desire*, eds. A. Snitow, C. Stansell, and S. Thompson. New York: Monthly Review Press.

——. 1986. *It's a family affair: The real lives of Black single mothers.* New York: Kitchen Table: Women of Color Press.

Oparah, J. C., and A. D. Bonaparte, eds. 2015. *Birthing justice: Black women, pregnancy, and childbirth.* Boulder, CO: Paradigm Publishers.

——, H. Arega, D. Hudson, L. Jones, and T. Oseguera. 2017. *Battling over birth: Black women and the maternal health care crisis.* Amarillo, TX: Praeclarus Press.

O'Reilly, A, 2006. *Rocking the cradle: Thoughts on feminism, motherhood, and the possibility of empowered mothering.* Toronto, ON: Demeter Press.

——, ed. 2010. *Twenty-first century motherhood: Experience, identity, policy, agency.* New York: Columbia University Press.

Ornstein, C., H. Fresques, and M. Hixenbaugh. 2016. The children of Agent Orange. *Pro Publica*, December 16. Accessed on October 16, 2018, at https://www.propublica.org/article/the-children-of-agent-orange

Oreskes, N. 2004. The scientific consensus on climate change. *Science* 36(3): 1686.

Orleck, A. 2005. *Storming Caesar's Palace: How black mothers fought their own war on poverty.* Boston: Beacon Press.

Pagonis, P. 2015. Nine damaging lies doctors told me when I was growing up intersex. *Everyday Feminism*, December 3. Accessed on October 30, 2018, at https://everydayfeminism.com/2015/12/lies-from-doctors-intersex/

Pande, A. 2014. *Wombs in labor: Transnational commercial surrogacy in India.* NY: Columbia University Press.

Parks, S. 2010. *Fierce angels: The strong black woman in American life and culture.* New York: Random House.

Parreñas, R. S. 2015. *Servants of globalization: Migration and domestic work.* 2nd ed. Stanford: Stanford University Press.

Patten, E., and K. Parker. 2011. Women in the US military: Growing share, distinctive profile. Pew Research Center. Accessed online at http://www.pewsocialtrends.org/2011/12/22/women-in-the-u-s-military-growing-share-distinctive-profile/

Patrick, K., and S. D. Heydermann. 2018. Union membership is critical for equal pay: Fact sheet. Washington, DC: National Women's Law Center. Accessed on September 5, 2018, at https://nwlc-ciw49tixgw5lbab.stackpathdns.com/wp-content/uploads/2016/02/Union-Membership-is-Critical-for-Equal-Pay-2018.pdf

Pearce, D., A. Markandya, and E. B. Barbier. 1990. *Blueprint for a green economy.* London: Earthscan.

Peña, D. 1997. *The terror of the machine: Technology, work, gender, and ecology of the US-Mexico border.* Austin: University of Texas Press.

——. 1999. Cultural landscapes and biodiversity: The ethnoecology of an Upper Rio Grande watershed commons. In *Ethnoecology: Situated knowledge/located lives*, ed. V. D. Nazarea. Tucson: University of Arizona Press.

Penny, L. 2017. Foreword. In *Ask: Building consent culture*, ed. K. Stryker, pp. vii–x. Portland, OR: Thorntree Press.

Perrone, B., H. H. Stockel, and V. Krueger. 1989. *Medicine women, curanderas, and women doctors.* Norman: University of Oklahoma Press.

Peterson, V. S. 2003. *A critical rewriting of global political economy: Integrating reproductive, productive, and virtual economies.* New York: Routledge.

——, and A. S. Runyan. 1993. *Global gender issues.* Boulder, CO: Westview Press.

Peterson's. 2018. *Resources for college student survivors of sexual assault.* Accessed on March 28, 2019, at https://www.petersons.com/blog/resources-for-college-student-survivors-of-sexual-assault/

Piepmeier, A. 2013. The inadequacy of "choice": Disability and what's wrong with feminist framings of reproduction. *Feminist Studies* 39(1): 159–86.

Pimentel, D., P. Hepperly, J. Hanson, D. Douds, and R. Seidel. 2005. Environmental, energetic, and economic comparisons of organic and conventional farming systems. *Bioscience* 55(7), 573–82.

Plastas, M. 2011. *A band of noble women: Racial politics in the women's peace movement.* Syracuse, NY: Syracuse University Press.

Plath, S. 1971. *The bell jar.* New York: Harper and Row.

Plumwood, V. 1993. *Feminism and the mastery of nature.* New York: Routledge.

Poo, A.-J., with A. Conrad. 2015. *The age of dignity: Preparing for the elder boom in a changing America.* New York: The New Press.

Porter, E. 2007. *Peacebuilding: Women's international perspectives.* Routledge: New York.

Pratt, M. B. 1984. Identity: Skin blood heart. In *Yours in struggle: Three feminist perspectives on anti-Semitism and racism*, E. Bulkin, M. B. Pratt, and B. Smith, pp. 9–63. Brooklyn, NY: Long Haul Press.

Pretty, J. 2009. Can ecological agriculture feed nine billion people? *Monthly Review*, November, pp. 46–58.

Price, B. E., and J. C. Morris, eds. 2012. *Prison privatization: The many facets of a controversial industry.* Santa Barbara, CA: Praeger.

Prilleltensky, O. 2003. A ramp to motherhood: The experience of mothers with physical disabilities. *Sexuality and Disability*, 21: 21–47.

Pulido, L. 1996. *Environmentalism: and economic justice: Two Chicano struggles in the Southwest.* Tucson: University of Arizona Press.

Quart, A. 2018. Go fund yourself: Crowd funding is now an essential part of America's safety net. *Guardian*, May 7. Accessed on September 5, 2018, at https://www.theguardian.com/us-news/2018/may/07/gofundme-crowdfunding-essential-america-safety-net

Queen, C., with S. Rednour. 2015. *The sex and pleasure book: Good vibrations guide to great sex for everyone.* Berkeley, CA: Good Vibrations.

Rabin, N. 2011. *Disappearing parents: A report on immigration enforcement and the child welfare system.* Tucson, AZ: Southwest Institute for Research on Women and Bacon Immigration Law and Policy Program, University of Arizona. Accessed online at http://http://www.detentionwatchnetwork.org/sites/detentionwatchnetwork.org/files/06.09.2011_DisappearingParents.pdf

Rachel's Environment and Health Weekly. 1998. *The precautionary principle.* February 19, p. 1. Available at http://www.monitor.net/rachel/r586.html

Radical Women. 2001. *The radical women manifesto: Socialist feminism theory, program, and organizational structure.* Seattle, WA: Red Letter Press.

Ragone, H., and F. W. Twine, eds. 2000. *Ideologies and technologies of motherhood: Race, class, sexuality and nationalism.* New York: Routledge.

Ramirez, T. L., and Z. Blay. 2016. Why people are using the term "Latinx". *Huffington Post*, July 5. Accessed on August 26, 2018, at https://www.huffingtonpost.com/entry/why-people-are-using-the-term-latinx_us_57753328e4b0cc0fa136a159

Rankin, K. 2018. National Black Mama's Bail Out Seeks to Reunite Families for Mother's Day, *Colorlines*, May 7. Accessed on April 2, 2019, at https://www.colorlines.com/articles/national-black-mamas-bail-out-seeks-reunite-families-mothers-day

Ransby, B. 2006. Katrina, Black women, and the deadly discourse on Black poverty in America. *Du Bois Review* 3(1): 215–22.

Rathbone, C. 2006. *A world apart: Women, prison, and life behind bars.* New York: Random House.

Raymond, D. 2003. Popular culture and queer representation. In *Gender, race, and class in media: A text-reader*, ed. Gail Dines and Jean M. Humez, pp. 98–110. Thousand Oaks, CA: Sage.

Reaves, S., J. B. Hitchon, S.-Y. Park, and G. W. Yun. 2004. If looks could kill: Digital manipulation of fashion models. *Journal of Mass Media Ethics* 19(1): 56–71.

Reese, E. 2005. *Backlash against welfare mothers: Past and present.* Berkeley: University of California Press.

Rehn, E., and E. J. Sirleaf. 2002. *Women, war, peace: The independent experts' assessment.* New York: UNIFEM.

Reichard, R. 2015a. Mexico's indigenous "muxes" challenge the gender binary in a major way. *Latina*, December 18. Accessed on September 3, 2018, at http://www.latina.com/lifestyle/our-issues/mexico-muxes-gender

———. 2015b. Why we say Latinx: Trans & gender nonconforming people explain. *Latina*, August 29. Accessed on September 3, 2018, at http://www.latina.com/lifestyle/our-issues/why-we-say-latinx-trans-gender-non-conforming-people-explain

Reis, E. 2011. Young women's eggs: Elite and ordinary. *Biopolitical Times*, September 15. Accessed on October 31, 2018, at https://www.geneticsandsociety.org/article/young-womens-eggs-elite-and-ordinary

———. 2018. The Trump administration wants to define a person's sex at birth. It's just not that simple. *Time*, October 23. Accessed on November 20, 2018, at http://time.com/5432006/trump-administration-transgender-definition-intersex-gender-sex/

Rennison, C. M. 2002. *Rape and sexual assault: Reporting to police and medical attention, 1992–2000.* Bureau of Justice.

Rennison, C. M. 2003. *Intimate partner violence, 1993–2001*. Bureau of Justice Statistics, Crime Data Brief. Washington, DC: US Department of Justice.

Reno. J. 2016. The lingering health effects of Agent Orange. *Healthline*, May 19. Accessed on October 16, 2018, at https://www.healthline.com/health-news/lingering-health-effects-of-agent-orange#1

Rich, A. 1986a. Compulsory heterosexuality and lesbian existence. In *Blood, bread, and poetry*. New York: W. W. Norton.

——. 1986b. *Of woman born: Motherhood as experience and institution*. 10th anniversary ed. New York: W. W. Norton.

——. 1986c. Notes towards a politics of location. In *Blood, bread, and poetry*, pp. 210–31. New York: W. W. Norton.

Richie, B. 2012. *Arrested justice: Black women, violence, and America's prison nation*. New York: New York University Press.

Richter, P. 2000. Armed forces find "disturbing" level of gay harassment. Los *Angeles Times*, March 25, p. A1.

Riggs, D., and C. Due. 2018. *A critical approach to surrogacy: Reproductive desires and demands*. New York: Routledge.

Riley, R., C. T. Mohanty, and M. B. Pratt, eds. 2008. *Feminism and war: Confronting US imperialism*. New York: Zed Books.

Riley, S. J. 2002. The Black Beauty Myth. In *Colonize this! Young women of color on today's feminism*, edited by D. Hernàndez and B. Rehman. Emeryville: Seal Press, pp. 357-369.

Rios, C. 2018. Moving on to Plan C. *Ms. Magazine*, Summer, p. 12.

Risman, B. J. 2018. *Where the millennials will take us: A new generation wrestles with the gender structure*. New York: Oxford University Press.

Ritchie, A. 2017a. How black women's bodies are violated as soon as they enter school. *Guardian*, August 16. Accessed on October 30, 2018, at https://www.theguardian.com/us-news/2017/aug/16/black-women-violated-us-policing-racial-profiling

——. 2017b. *Invisible no more: Police violence against Black women and women of color*. Boston: Beacon Press.

Ritzer, G. 1993. The *McDonaldization of society: An investigation into the changing character of contemporary social life*. Thousand Oaks, CA: Pine Forge Press.

Robb, A. 2010. Not a lone wolf. *Ms. Magazine*, 20(2), pp. 26–31.

Roberts, D. 1997. *Killing the Black body: Race, reproduction, and the meaning of liberty*. New York: Pantheon.

Rodríguez, J. M. 2003. *Queer latinidad: Identity practices, discursive spaces*. New York: New York University Press.

Roediger, D. R. 1991. *The wages of whiteness: Race and the making of the American working class*. New York: Verso.

Rosay, A. B. 2016. Violence against American Indian and Alaska Native Women and Men. *National Institute of Justice Journal* no. 277. Office of Justice Programs. Accessed on November 26, 2018, at https://nij.gov/journals/277/Pages/violence-against-american-indians-alaska-natives.aspx

Rose, T. 2003. *Longing to tell: Black women talk about sexuality and intimacy*. New York: Farrar, Straus & Giroux.

Rosenberg, A. 1988. The crisis in knowing and understanding the Holocaust. In *Echoes from the Holocaust: Philosophical reflections on a dark time*, ed. A. Rosenberg and G. E. Meyers. Philadelphia: Temple University Press.

Ross, L. J. 1993. African-American women and abortion: 1800–1970. In *Theorizing black feminisms: The visionary pragmatism of black women*, ed. S. M. James and A. P. A. Busia, pp. 141–59. New York: Routledge.

Rosset, P. 2011. Preventing hunger: Change economic policy. *Nature* 479 (73/74): 472–73.

Roth, B. 2003. *Separate roads to feminism: Black, Chicana and white feminist movements in America's second wave*. New York: Cambridge University Press.

Rothblum, E., and S. Solovay, eds. 2009. *The fat studies reader*. New York: New York University Press.

Rousso, H. 2013. *Don't call me inspirational: A disabled feminist talks back*. Philadelphia: Temple University Press.

Rudrappa, S. 2015. *Discounted life: The price of global surrogacy in India*. New York: New York University Press.

——. 2017. India outlawed commercial surrogacy—Clinics are finding loopholes. *The Conversation*. October 23. Accessed on October 15, 2018, at https://theconversation.com/india-outlawed-commercial-surrogacy-clinics-are-finding-loopholes-81784

Russell, D. 1995. *Women, madness, and medicine*. Cambridge, UK: Polity Press.

Russell, D. E. H. 1975. *The politics of rape: The victim's perspective*. New York: Stein and Day.

Sachs, C., M. E. Barbercheck, K. J. Brasier, N. E. Kiernan, and A. R. Terman. 2016. *The rise of women farmers and sustainable agriculture*. Iowa City, IA: University of Iowa Press.

Said, E. 1979. *Orientalism*. New York: Vintage Books.

Sanburn, J. 2017. Flint's water crisis still isn't over: Here's where things stand a year later. *Time*, January 18. Accessed on October 16, 2018, at http://time.com/4634937/flint-water-crisis-criminal-charges-bottled-water/

Sandberg, S. 2013. *Lean in: Women, work and the will to lead*. New York: Knopf.

Sanger, M. 1920. *Women and the new race*. New York: Brentano's.

Santos, A. F. 1992. Gathering the dust: The bases issue in the Philippines. In *Let the good times roll: Prostitution and the US military in Asia*, ed. S. Sturdevant and B. Stoltzfus, pp. 32–44. New York: The New Press

Sarah, R. 2006. *Single mom seeking: Playdates, blind dates, and other dispatches from the dating world*. Emeryville, CA: Seal Press.

Sargent, F. O., P. Lusk, J. Rivera and M. Varela. 1991. *Rural environmental planning for sustainable communities*. Washington, DC: Island Press.

Sawyer, W., and W. Bertram. 2018. New reports show probation is down, but still a major driver of incarceration. *Prison Policy Initiative*, April 26. Accessed on October 28, 2018, at https://www.prisonpolicy.org/blog/2018/04/26/probation_update-2/

Saxton, M. 1995. Reproductive rights: A disability rights issue. *Sojourner*, July.

Scharnberg, K. 2005. Female GIs hard hit by war syndrome. *Chicago Tribune*, March 24.

Schmidt, J. 2016. Being "like a woman": Fa'afāfine and Samoan masculinity. *Asia Pacific Journal of Anthropology* 17(304): 287–304.

Schneir, M. 1994. *Feminism: The essential historical writings*. New York: Vintage Books.

Schreiber, K. 2016. Why transgender people experience more mental health issues. *Psychology Today*, December 6. Accessed on November 20, 2018, at https://www.psychologytoday.com/us/blog/the-truth-about-exercise-addiction/201612/why-transgender-people-experience-more-mental-health

Schur, L. 2004. Is there still a "double handicap"? Economic, social and political disparities experienced by women with disabilities. In *Gendering disability*, ed. B. G. Smith and B. Hutchison, pp. 253–71. New Brunswick: Rutgers University Press.

Schwartz, P. 1994. *Love between equals: How peer marriage really works*. New York: Free Press.

Scott, J. W. 1993. The evidence of experience. In *The lesbian and gay studies reader*, ed. H. Abelove, M. A. Barale and D. M. Halperin, pp. 397–415. New York: Routledge.

Scott, W. J., and S. C. Stanley. 1994. *Gays and lesbians in the military: Issues, concerns, and contrasts*. Hawthorne, NY: Aldine de Gruyter.

Seager, J. 1993. *Earth follies: Coming to feminist terms with the global environmental crisis*. New York: Routledge.

Secwepcul'ecw Assembly. 2017. What are man camps? Accessed on November 24, 2018, at https://www.secwepemculecw.org/no-mans-camp

Sedensky, M. 2015 Hundreds of officers lose licenses over sex misconduct. Associated Press, October 31. Accessed on November 25, 2018, at https://apnews.com/fd1d4d05e561462a85abe50e7eaed4ec

Segrest, M. 1994. *Memoir of a race traitor*. Boston: South End Press.

Sentencing Project. 2018. *Fact Sheet: Incarcerated women and girls, 1980–2016*. Accessed on October 28, 2018, at https://www.sentencingproject.org/wp-content/uploads/2016/02/Incarcerated-Women-and-Girls-1980-2016.pdf?eType=EmailBlastContent&eId=12d509dd-a247-4f77-a4f8-6d0fdbe0cd6e

Serano, J. 2007. Skirt chasers: Why the media depicts the trans revolution in lipstick and heels. In *Whipping Girl: A transsexual women on sexism and the scapegoating of femininity*. Emeryville, CA: Seal Press. pp. 35-52.

——. 2008. Why nice guys finish last. In *Yes means yes! Visions of female sexual power and a world without rape*, ed. J. Friedman and J. Valenti, pp. 227–240. Berkeley, CA: Seal Press.

——. 2013. *Excluded: Making feminist and queer movements more inclusive*. Berkeley, CA: Seal Press.

Shaffer, A., and R. Gottlieb. 2007. Filling in "food deserts." *Los Angeles Times*, November 5. Accessed online at http://www.latimes.com/news/opinion/la-oe-gottlieb5nov05,0,7040113.story?coll=la-opinion-rightrail

Shah, S. 2012. Family detention center halted in Texas. *Detention Watch Network*, February 8. Accessed online at http://detentionwatch-network.wordpress.com/2012/02/08/family-detention-centers-halted-in-texas/

Shanley, M., ed. 2004. *Just marriage*. New York: Oxford University Press.

Shannonhouse, R. 2003. *Out of her mind: Women writing on madness*, Expanded ed. New York: Modern Library.

She, P., and G. A. Livermore. 2006. *Long-term poverty and disability among working-age adults*. Washington, DC: Cornell University Institute for Policy Research.

Shepherd, T. 2014. Gendering the commodity audience in social media. In *The Routledge companion to media and gender,* ed. C. Carter, L. Steiner, and L. McLaughlin, pp. 157–167. New York: Routledge.

Shih, E. 2007. Spirits in traffic: Transient community formation in opposition to forced victimization. In *Shout out: Women of color respond to violence*, ed. M, Ochoa and B. K. Ige, pp. 86–100. Emeryville, CA: Seal Press.

Shiva, V. 1988. *Staying alive: Women, ecology and development*. London: Zed Books.

——. 2002a. Relocalization not globalization. In *Rethinking globalization: Teaching for justice in an unjust world*, ed. B. Bigelow and B. Peterson, pp. 248–49. Milwaukee, WI: Rethinking Schools.

——. 2002b. *Water wars: Privatization, pollution, and profit*. Cambridge, MA: South End Press.

——. 2005. *Earth democracy: justice, sustainability, and peace*. Cambridge, MA: South End Press.

Showalter, E. 1987. *The female malady: Women, madness, and English culture, 1830–1980*. London: Virago.

Sidel, R. 1996. *Keeping women and children last: America's war on the poor*. New York: Penguin Books.

Silliman, J. M. G. Fried, L. Ross, and E. R. Gutiérrez. 2004. *Undivided rights: Women of color organize for reproductive justice*. Cambridge, MA: South End Press.

Simón, Y. 2016. Revisiting the dark history of birth control testing in Puerto Rico. *Remezcla*, November 4. Accessed on October 7, 2018, at http://remezcla.com/culture/birth-control-testing-puerto-rico/

Simonovic, I. 2004. Attitudes and types of reaction toward past war crimes and human rights abuses. *Yale Journal of International Law* 29(2): 343–62.

Sinozich, S., and L. Langton. 2014. *Rape and sexual assault victimization among college-age females, 1995–2013*. Office of Justice Programs, Bureau of Justice Statistics Special Report. Washington, DC: US Department of Justice.

Sirimanne, S. 2009. *The gender perspectives of the financial crisis*. For United Nations Commission on the Status of Women, 2009. Accessed online at http://www.un.org/womenwatch/daw/csw/csw53/panels/financial_crisis/Sirimanne.formatted.pdf

Sjoberg, L., and S. Via, eds. 2010. *Gender, war, and militarism: Feminist perspectives*. Santa Barbara, CA: Praeger Security International.

Skover, S. 2012. *The continuous appetite: Understanding your cravings, ending your overeating!* Bloomington, IN: Balboa Press.

Slater, L. 1998. *Prozac diary*. New York: Random House.

Smith, A. 1999. Sexual Violence and American Indian Genocide, *Journal of Religion and Abuse*, Vol 1. No. 2: 31-52.

——. 2005a. Beyond pro-choice versus pro-life: Women of color and reproductive justice. *NWSA Journal* 17(1): 119–40.

——. 2005b. *Conquest: Sexual violence and American Indian genocide*. Cambridge, MA: South End Press.

Smith, B. 1998. *The truth that never hurts: Writings on race, gender, freedom*. New Brunswick, NJ: Rutgers University Press.

Smith, B. G., and B. Hutchison, eds. 2004. *Gendering disability*. New Brunswick, NJ: Rutgers University Press.

Smith, S. 2005. *Women and socialism: Essays on women's liberation*. Chicago: Haymarket Books.

Soh, C. S. 2008. *The comfort women: Sexual violence and postcolonial memory in Korea and Japan*. Chicago: Chicago University Press.

Solinger, R. 2000. *Wake up little Susie: Single pregnancy and race before Roe v. Wade*. New York: Routledge.

——, P. C. Johnson, M. L. Raimon, T. Reynolds, and R. C. Tapia, eds. 2010. *Interrupted life: Experiences of incarcerated women in the United States*. Berkeley: University of California Press.

Solnit, R. 2018. Feminists have slowly shifted power: There's no going back. *Guardian*, March 8. Accessed on October 21, 2018, at https://www.theguardian.com/commentisfree/2018/mar/08/feminists-power-metoo-timesup-rebecca-solnit?CMP=share_btn_link

Sopelsa, B. 2017. Meet 2017's newly elected transgender officials. *NBC News*, December 28. Accessed on November 25, 2018, at https://www.nbcnews.com/feature/nbc-out/meet-2017-s-newly-elected-transgender-officials-n832826

Springer, K. 2005. *Living for the revolution: Black feminist organizing, 1968–1980*. Durham, NC: Duke University Press.

St. Paige, E. 1999. *Zaftig: The case for curves*. Seattle, WA: Darling and Co.

Stacey, C. 2011. *The caring self: The work experiences of home care aides*. Ithaca, NY: Cornell University Press/ILR Press.

Stacey, Jackie. 1993. Untangling feminist theory. In *Thinking feminist: Key concepts in women's studies*, ed. D. Richardson and V. Robinson, pp. 49–73. New York: Guilford Press.

Stacey, Judith. 1996. *In the name of the family: Rethinking values in the postmodern age*. Boston: Beacon Press.

Stark, E. 2007. *Coercive control: The entrapment of women in personal life*. New York: Oxford University Press.

Statista. 2017. Gross domestic product (GDP) ranking by country 2017. Accessed on April 13, 2019 at https://www.statista.com/statistics/268173/countries-with-the-largest-gross-domestic-product-gdp/

Stein, A. 2018. *Unbound: Transgender men and the remaking of identity*. New York: Pantheon Books.

Steinem, G. 1983. *Outrageous acts and everyday rebellions*. New York: Holt, Rinehart, & Winston.

Steingraber, S. 2001. *Having faith: An ecologist's journey to motherhood*. Cambridge, MA: Perseus.

Stewart, N. A. 2007. Transform the world: What you can do with a degree in women's studies, *Ms. Magazine*, Spring, pp. 65–66.

Stoller, E. P., and R. C. Gibson, eds. 1994. *Worlds of difference: Inequality in the aging experience*. Thousand Oaks, CA: Pine Forge.

Stone, D. 2000. Fetal risks, women's rights: Showdown at Johnson Controls. *The American Prospect*, December 4. Accessed online at http://prospect.org/article/fetal-risks-womens-rights-showdown-johnson-controls

Stotzer, R. 2009. Violence against transgender people: A review of United States data. *Aggression and Violent Behavior* 14(3): 170–79. Accessed online at https://www.sciencedirect.com/science/article/pii/S1359178909000202?via%3Dihub

Stover, E., and H. Weinstein, eds. 2004. *My neighbor, my enemy: Justice and community in the aftermath of mass atrocity*. Cambridge, UK: Cambridge University Press.

Stryker, K. ed. 2017. *Ask: Building consent culture*. Portland, OR: Thorntree Press.

Stryker, S. 2008. *Transgender history*. Emeryville, CA: Seal Press.

Sturdevant, S., and B. Stoltzfus. 1992. *Let the good times roll: Prostitution and the US military in Asia*. New York: New Press.

Sudbury, J. 2003. Women of color, globalization and the politics of incarceration. In *The criminal justice system and women: Offenders prisoners, victims, and workers*, 3rd ed., ed. B. R. Price and N. J. Sokoloff, pp. 219–234. New York: McGraw-Hill.

——. 2011. From women prisoners to people in women's prisons: Challenging the gender binary in antiprison work. In *Razor wire women*, ed. J. M. Lawston and Ashley E. Lucas. Albany: State University of New York Press.

Suggs, W. 2002. Title IX at 30. *The Chronicle of Higher Education*, June 21, pp. A38–41.

Sutton, B., S. Morgen, and J. Novkov, eds. 2008. *Security disarmed: Critical perspectives on gender, race, and militarization*. New Brunswick, NJ: Rutgers University Press.

Swerdlow, A. 1993. *Women strike for peace: Traditional motherhood and radical politics in the 1960s*. Chicago: University of Chicago Press.

Swern, A. J. 2008. *Drug treatment alternative-to-prison, seventeenth annual report*. Kings County District Attorney's Office. Available at http://www.BrooklynDA.org

Sze, J. 2004. Gender, asthma politics, and urban environmental justice activism. In *New perspectives on environmental justice Gender, sexuality, and activism*. ed. R. Stein. pp, 177-190. New Brunswick, NJ: Rutgers University Press.

Takahashi, R. 1998. US concentration camps and exclusion policies. In *Women's lives: Multicultural perspectives*, ed. G. Kirk and M. Okazawa-Rey, pp. 362–68. Mountain View, CA: Mayfield.

Takaki, R. 1987. *Strangers from a different shore: Perspectives on race and ethnicity in America*. New York: Oxford University Press.

Tanenbaum, L. 2000. *Growing up female with a bad reputation*. New York: HarperCollins.

——. 2015. *I am not a slut. Slut shaming in the age of the internet*. New York: Harper Perennial.

Tarrant, S., ed. 2007. *Men speak out: Views on gender, sex and power*. New York: Routledge.

Tateishi, J. 1984. *And justice for all: An oral history of the Japanese American detention camps*. New York: Random House.

Taylor, S. 2017. *Beasts of burden: Animal and disability liberation*. New York: The New Press.

Teaching Tolerance. 2018. *Reading against the grain*. Accessed on August 27, 2018, at https://www.tolerance.org/classroom-resources/teaching-strategies/close-and-critical-reading/reading-against-the-grain

Teays, W., and L. Purdy. 2001. *Bioethics, justice, and health care*. Belmont, CA: Wadsworth.

Teich, N. M. 2012. *Transgender 101: A simple guide to a complex issue*. New York: Columbia University Press.

Tenenbein, S. 1998. Power, beauty, and dykes. In *Looking queer*, ed. D. Atkins, pp. 155–60. Binghamton, NY: Harrington Park Press.

Terry, G. 2009. No climate justice without gender justice: An overview of the issues, *Gender and Development* 17(1): 5–18.

Tetlow, T. 2009. Discriminatory acquittal. *William & Mary Bill of Rights Journal* 18(1): 75–129. Accessed online at http://scholarship.law.wm.edu/wmborj/vol18/iss1/4

Tétreault, M. A. 1997. Accountability or justice? Rape as a war crime. In *Feminist frontiers IV*, ed. L. Richardson, V. Taylor, and N. Whittier, pp. 427–39. New York: McGraw-Hill.

Theidon, K. 2007. Gender in transition: Common sense, women, and war. *Journal of Human Rights*, 6: 453–478. Accessed on October 25, 2018, at http://wcfia.harvard.edu/publications/gender-transition-common-sense-women-and-war

Thielking, M. 2015. Sky-high C-section rates don't translate to better birth outcomes. *STAT*, December 1. Accessed on October 31, 2018, at https://www.statnews.com/2015/12/01/cesarean-section-childbirth/

Thompson, B. 2002. Multiracial Feminism: Recasting the Chronology of Second Wave Feminism, *Feminist Studies*, 28(2): 337-360.

Thompson, C., and M. Wiggins, eds. 2002. *The human cost of food: Farmworkers' lives, labor and advocacy*. Austin: University of Texas Press.

Tickner, J. A. 2001. *Gendering world politics: Issues and approaches in the post-Cold War era*. New York: Columbia University Press.

Toosi, M., and T. L. Morisi. 2017. Women in the workforce before, during, and after the Great Recession. US Bureau of Labor Statistics. Accessed on September 3, 2018, at https://www.bls.gov/spotlight/2017/women-in-the-workforce-before-during-and-after-the-great-recession/pdf/women-in-the-workforce-before-during-and-after-the-great-recession.pdf

Traister, R. 2016. *All the single ladies: Unmarried women and the rise of an independent nation*. New York: Simon and Schuster.

Trask, H.-K. 1999. *From a native daughter: Colonialism and sovereignty in Hawaii*. Honolulu: University of Hawaii Press.

Trask, M. 1992. Native Hawaiian historical and cultural perspectives on environmental justice. *Race, Poverty and the Environment* 3(1).

Trenka, J. J., J. C. Oparah, and S. Y. Shin, eds. 2006. *Outsiders within: Writing on transracial adoption*. Cambridge, MA: South End Press.

Trujillo, C., ed. 1991. *Chicana lesbians: The girls our mothers warned us about*. Berkeley, CA: Third Women Press.

Tuana, N., ed. 1989. *Feminism and science*. Bloomington: Indiana University Press.

Tucker, J., and A. K. Matsui. 2018. *Today's a reminder of how important social security is to women*. Washington, DC: National Women's Law Center. Accessed on September 5, 2018, at https://nwlc.org/blog/todays-a-reminder-of-how-important-social-security-is-to-women/

Tuloss, J. K. 1996. Transforming urban regimes—A grassroots approach to comprehensive community development: The Dudley Street Neighborhood Initiative. Accessed on May 18, 2012, at http://comm-rg.wisc.edu/papers98/tulloss.htm

Twine, F. W. 2011. *Outsourcing the womb: Race, class and gestational surrogacy in a global market*. New York: Routledge.

Tyson, A. 2018. The 2018 midterm vote: Divisions by race, gender, education. *Pew Research Center*, November 9. Accessed on November 21, 2018, at http://www.pewresearch.org/fact-tank/2018/11/08/the-2018-midterm-vote-divisions-by-race-gender-education/

Ulen, E. N. 2018. Building on a deep organizing history, Black women are reshaping the electoral landscape. *Truthout*. February 10. Accessed on October 21, 2018, at https://truthout.org/articles/building-on-a-deep-organizing-history-black-women-are-reshaping-the-electoral-landscape/

UN Department of Economic and Social Affairs, Population Division. 2017. *International Migration Report 2017: Highlights* (ST/ESA/SER.A/404). Accessed on September 20, 2018, at http://www.un.org/en/development/desa/population/migration/publications/migrationreport/docs/MigrationReport2017_Highlights.pdf

UN Development Program. 1994. *Human Development Report 1994*. New York: Oxford University Press. Accessed on March 29, 2019 at http://hdr.undp.org/sites/default/files/reports/255/hdr_1994_en_complete_nostats.pdf

UN General Assembly Resolution. 2015. *Convention on the Rights of Persons with Disabilities and the Optional Protocol Thereto*. 70/145. December 17. Accessed on November 18 at http://undocs.org/A/RES/70/145

UN Sustainable Development Goals: Knowledge Platform. n.d. Accessed on April 19, 2019 at https://sustainabledevelopment.un.org/sdgs

UNESCO, 2018. *Media and information literacy.* Accessed August 1, 2018, at http://www.unesco.org/new/en/communication-and-information/media-development/media-literacy/mil-as-composite-concept/

UNHCR, 2017. *War, violence, persecution push displacement to new unprecedented high.* Accessed on June 19, 2018, at http://www.unhcr.org/en-us/news/press/2017/6/5943ec594/war-violence-persecution-push-displacement-new-unprecedented-high.html

University of Maryland. 2007. J-school administrators overwhelmingly white and male, survey finds. Press release, August 14. Accessed online at http://www.journalism.umd.edu/newrel/07newsrel/jmcsurvey07.html

US Bureau of Labor Statistics. 2018a. *American time use survey, 2017.* Accessed on September 4, 2018, at https://www.bls.gov/news.release/pdf/atus.pdf

——. 2018b. *Employment characteristics of families, 2017.* Accessed on September 3, 2018, at https://www.bls.gov/news.release/famee.nr0.htm

——. 2018c. *Labor force statistics from the current population survey: Household data annual averages.* Accessed on September 4, 2018, at https://www.bls.gov/cps/cpsaat11.htm

US Census Bureau. 2017. *Quick facts, Puerto Rico.* Accessed on October 7, 2018, at https://www.census.gov/quickfacts/pr

——. 2018. *Current population survey: Highlights of women's earnings in 2017.* Report 1075. Accessed on August 29, 2018, at https://www.bls.gov/opub/reports/womens-earnings/2017/pdf/home.pdf

US Department of Agriculture 2018. *Current population survey food security supplement.* Accessed on August 4, 2018, at https://www.ers.usda.gov/webdocs/DataFiles/50764/techdoc2017.pdf?v=0

US Department of Defense 2018. *FY 2019 defense budget.* Accessed on November 23, 2018, at https://dod.defense.gov/News/SpecialReports/Budget2019.aspx

US Department of Education. 2016. *Report: Increases in spending on corrections far outplace education.* July 7. Accessed on October 30, 2018, at https://www.ed.gov/news/press-releases/report-increases-spending-corrections-far-outpace-education

US Department of Health and Human Services. 2016. *Trends in teen pregnancy and childbearing.* Office of Adolescent Health. Accessed on October 31, 2018, at https://www.hhs.gov/ash/oah/adolescent-development/reproductive-health-and-teen-pregnancy/teen-pregnancy-and-childbearing/trends/index.html

——. 2018. *2018 Poverty Guidelines.* Office of the Assistant Secretary for Planning and Evaluation. Accessed on April 9, 2019 at https://aspe.hhs.gov/2018-poverty-guidelines

US Department of Justice. 2012. *Prison rape elimination acts, prisons and jail standards.* 28 CFR Part 115, Docket No. OAG-131, RIN 1105-AB34, May 17. Accessed on October 29, 2018, at https://www.prearesourcecenter.org/sites/default/files/content/prisonsandjailsfinalstandards_0.pdf

Van Gelder, S. 2016. Why I kneeled before Standing Rock elders and asked for forgiveness. *Yes! Magazine,* December 16. Accessed on October 24, 2018, at http://www.yesmagazine.org/people-power/why-i-kneeled-before-standing-rock-elders-and-asked-for-forgiveness-20161221

Vance, C., ed. 1984. *Pleasure and danger: Exploring female sexuality.* Boston: Routledge and Kegan Paul.

Victory Fund. 2018. *For the first time in US history, LGBTQ candidates ran for office in every state this cycle.* Accessed on November 25, 2018, at https://victoryfund.org/news/for-the-first-time-in-u-s-history-lgbtq-candidates-ran-for-office-in-every-state-this-cycle/

Vieceli, A., ed. 2005. *1000 Peacewomen across the globe.* Zurich: Scalo.

Vincent, R. M., ed. 2016. *When we are bold: Women who turn our upsidedown world right.* Ottawa, ON: Art and Literature Mapalé & Publishing, Inc.

Volkan, V. D. 2017. *Immigrants and refugees: Trauma, perennial mourning, prejudice, and border psychology.* New York: Routledge. Accessed on November 24, 2018, at https://ebookcentral.proquest.com/lib/sfsu/detail.action?docID=4771367

Wade-Gayles, G. 1993. *Pushed back to strength: A Black woman's journey home.* Boston: Beacon Press.

Wagner, P., and W. Sawyer. 2018. Mass incarceration: The whole pie. *Prison Policy Initiative,* March 14. Accessed on October 28, 2018, at https://www.prisonpolicy.org/reports/pie2018.html

Walmart. 2018. Walmart: About Us. Accessed on August 20, 2018, at https://corporate.walmart.com/our-story

Walsh, M. 2000. *Aftermath: The impact of conflict on women in Bosnia and Herzegovina.* Working Paper

No. 302. Washington, DC: Center for Development Information and Evaluation, US Agency for International Development. Accessed on April 19, 2012, at http://pdf.usaid.gov/pdf_docs/PNACJ322.pdf

Walters, S. D. 1996. From here to queer: Radical feminism, postmodernism, and the lesbian menace (or, why can't a woman be more like a fag?). *Signs: Journal of Women in Culture and Society* 21(4): 830–69.

Waring, M. 1988. *If women counted: A new feminist economics.* New York: Harper & Row.

Warner, M. 1999. *The trouble with normal: Sex, politics and the ethics of queer life.* New York: The Free Press.

Warner, S. 2011. Restorytive justice: Theater as a redressive mechanism for incarcerated women. In *Razor wire women*, ed. J. M. Lawston and A. E Lucas. Albany, NY: State University of New York Press.

Washburn, P. 1993. Women and the peace movement In *Women and the use of military force*, ed. R. Howes and M. Stevenson, pp. 135–48. Boulder, CO: Lynne Rienner.

Waters, M. C. 1996. Optional ethnicities: For whites only? In *Origins and destinies: Immigration, race, and ethnicity in America*, ed. S. Pedraza and R. G. Rumbaut, pp. 444–454. Belmont, CA: Wadsworth Press.

Webber, W. S. 1993. *Lesbians in the military speak out.* Northboro, MA: Madwoman Press.

Weeks, J. 2010. *Sexuality.* New York: Routledge.

Weiss, E. 2018. *The woman's hour: The great fight to win the vote.* New York: Viking.

Werner, B. 2018. Pentagon to start FY 2019 with defense spending bill signed into law. *USNI News*, September 28. Accessed on October 22, 2018, at https://news.usni.org/2018/09/28/36944

Werner International. 2104. *Textile industry labor cost.* Accessed on August 20, 2018, at http://www.werner-newtwist.com/en/newsl-vol-011/index.htm

Wheeling, K. 2016. How women are going from climate victims to climate leaders. *Pacific Standard*, November 22. Accessed on October 18, 2018, at https://psmag.com/news/how-women-are-going-from-climate-victims-to-climate-leaders#.6ms6bd5tz

Whisnant, R., and C. Stark. 2004. *Not for sale: Feminists resisting prostitution and pornography.* North Melbourne, Australia: Spinifex.

White, E. 2002. *Fast girls: Teenage tribes and the myth of the slut.* New York: Penguin.

White, L. 2016. White power and the performance of assimilation: Lincoln Institute and Carlisle Indian School. In *Carlisle Indian Industrial School: Indigenous histories, memories, and reclamations*, ed. J. Fear-Segal and S. D. Rose. Lincoln: University of Nebraska Press.

Whitman, S. 2010. Sexual violence, coltan and the Democratic Republic of Congo. In *Critical environmental security: Rethinking the links between natural resources and political violence*, ed. M. A. Schnurr and L. A. Swatuk. Halifax, NS: Dafhousie University, Center for Foreign Policy Studies.

Whitney, W. T. 2017. Colonialist assault on PR and the prospects for independence. *Counterpunch.* March 17. Accessed on October 7, 2018, at https://www.counterpunch.org/2017/03/17/colonialist-assault-on-puerto-rico-and-the-prospects-for-independence/

Wilkerson, A. 2011. Disability, sex radicalism, and political agency. In *Feminist disability studies*, ed. Kim Q. Hall, pp. 193–217. Bloomington: Indiana University Press.

Wilkinson, R., and K. Pickett. 2009. *The spirit level: Why greater equality makes societies stronger.* New York: Bloomsbury Press.

Williams, F. 2005. Toxic breast milk? *New York Times Magazine*, January 9.

Williams, J. 2000. *Unbending gender: Why family and work conflict and what to do about it.* New York: Oxford University Press.

Wilson, A. 2019. United becomes first airline to introduce non-binary gender option on bookings. *Guardian*, March 27. Accessed on March 30, 2019 at https://www.theguardian.com/travel/2019/mar/27/united-becomes-first-airline-to-introduce-non-binary-gender-option-on-bookings?CMP=share_btn_link

Wilson, M. 1993. *Crossing the boundary: Black women survive incest.* Seattle, WA: Seal Press.

Winterich, J. A. 2007. Review of "Age matters" edited by T. M. Calasanti and K. F. Slevin. *Gender and Society* 21(5): 783–86.

Withorn, A. 1999. Temp work: "A devil's bargain" for women. *Sojourner: The Women's Forum*, October, p. 9.

Wittig, M. 1978. *The straight mind.* Boston: Beacon Press.

Woelfle-Erskine, C., J. O. Cole, L. Allen, and A. Danger. 2007. *Dam nation: Dispatches from the water underground.* Brooklyn, NY: Soft Skull Press.

Wolf, N. 2009. *The beauty myth: How images of beauty are used against women.* Reprinted ed. New York: Harper Collins.

Women Engage for a Common Future. 2016. *Gender just climate solutions.* Accessed on October 18, 2018, at http://womengenderclimate.org/gender-just-climate-solutions/

Women Resisting Extractivism. 2018. *Declaration.* Accessed on October 18, 2018, at http://femmesen-resistance.cdhal.org/en/declaration/

Women's Bureau. 2016. *Working mothers issue brief.* US Department of Labor. Accessed on September 4, 2018, at https://www.dol.gov/wb/resources/WB_WorkingMothers_508_FinalJune13.pdf

Women's Foundation. 2002. *Failing to make ends meet: The economic status of women in California.* San Francisco: The Women's Foundation.

Women's Prison Association. 2009. *Women's voices: Advocacy by criminal justice involved women.* Accessed online at http://66.29.139.159/pdf/Womens Voices March 2009.pdf

WoMin African Gender and Extractives Alliance, 2015. *African women united against destructive resource extraction.* Accessed on October 18, 2018, at http://ecosocialisthorizons.com/2015/10/african-women-unite-against-destructive-resource-extraction/

Wong, C. M. 2018. Arkansas has been offering a non-binary gender option on state IDs for years. *Huffington Post*, Oct. 17. Accessed on March 30, 2019 at https://www.huffpost.com/entry/arkansas-gender-neutral-state-id-option_n_5bc79f75e4b0d38b5874a669

Woods, H. 2000. *Stepping up to power: The political journey of American women.* Boulder, CO: Westview Press.

World Health Organization. 1946. *Preamble to the constitution of the World Health Organization*, adopted by the International Health Conference, New York, June 19–22.

——. 2017. *Violence against women.* Accessed on November 25, 2018, at http://www.who.int/news-room/fact-sheets/detail/violence-against-women

——. 2018. *Children: reducing mortality.* Accessed on October 31, 2018, at http://www.who.int/news-room/fact-sheets/detail/children-reducing-mortality

Yancey, A. K., J. Leslie, and E. K. Abel. 2006. Obesity at the crossroads: Feminist and public health perspectives. *Signs: Journal of Women in Culture and Society* 31(2): 425–43.

Yates, E. 2016. Disability and sex are not mutually exclusive. *Guardian*, October 15. Accessed on November 2, 2018, at https://www.theguardian.com/lifeandstyle/2016/oct/15/disability-and-sex-are-not-mutually-exclusive?CMP=share_btn_link

Yeung, B. 2018. *In a day's work: The fight to end sexual violence against America's most vulnerable workers.* New York: The New Press.

Yoo, D. K. 2000. *Growing up Nisei: Race, generation and culture among Japanese Americans of California, 1924–1949.* Urbana-Champagne: University of Illinois Press.

Zahn, M. A., S. R. Hawkins, J. Chiancone, and A. Whitworth. 2008. *The Girls Study Group: Charting the way to delinquency prevention for girls.* Office of Juvenile Justice and Delinquency Prevention, Accessed online at http://www.ncjrs.gov/pdffiles1/ojjdp/223434.pdf

NAME INDEX

SUBJECT INDEX

The letter *b* following a page locator indicates a word bolded in the text, the letter *f* indicates a figure.

ABOUT THE AUTHORS

Photo Courtesy of Jerry Yoon

Gwyn Kirk has taught courses in women's and gender studies, environmental studies, political science, and sociology at several US academic institutions. She shared the Jane Watson Irwin Chair in Women's Studies at Hamilton College with Margo Okazawa-Rey (1999–2001), received a Rockefeller Fellowship in Women's and Gender Studies at the University of Hawaii (2002), and was a Visiting Scholar at the Women's Leadership Institute, Mills College (2001–2003).

Her articles on feminism, ecology, militarism, and transnational feminist organizing have appeared in various anthologies and journals, including *Asia-Pacific Journal, Berkeley Women's Law Journal, Feminist Formations, Foreign Policy in Focus, Frontiers, Peace Review*, and *Social Justice*. Recent publications include "Unsettling Debates: Women and Peace Making," a special issue of *Social Justice*, guest edited with Suzy Kim and M. Brinton Lykes (2019). Other publications are *Greenham Women Everywhere: Dreams, Ideas, and Actions from the Women's Peace Movement* (1983), co-authored with Alice Cook and translated into French and Japanese, and *Urban Planning in a Capitalist Society* (1980, reissued 2018). As an editor, she has contributed to materials published by Asian Communities for Reproductive Justice, California Wellness Foundation, Dasi Hamkke Center, and Women's Center for Legal Aid and Counseling.

Gwyn Kirk is a founding member of the International Women's Network Against Militarism, started in 1997 by scholars and activists concerned about the negative effects of US military operations on local communities, and a founder member of Women for Genuine Security, the US-based partner in this Network. She co-directed the 2012 documentary, *Living Along the Fenceline*. She is a member of the Comfort Women Justice Coalition, and has served on the Steering Committee of Women Cross DMZ (2015-2019), the Board of Agape Foundation (2007-2010), and the Board of WAND Education Fund (2000-2006), She holds a PhD in sociology from the London School of Economics.

Margo Okazawa-Rey is Barbara Lee Distinguished Chair in Women's Leadership and Visiting Professor of Women, Gender, and Sexuality Studies and of Public Policy at Mills College (2018–2020). Also, she is Professor Emerita of Social Work at San Francisco State University. Her primary areas of research and activism for over twenty years have been militarism, armed conflict, and violence against women, examined intersectionally. She has engaged with feminist activists and scholars in East Asia, English-speaking West Africa, and Palestine regarding these issues.

Her publications include "'Nation-izing' Coalition and Solidarity Politics for US Anti-militarist Feminists," *Social Justice*, Special issue on Women and Peace Making (2019); "Liberal Arts Colleges Partnering with Highlander Research and Education Center: Intergenerational Learning for Student Campus Activism and Personal Transformation," *Feminist Formations*, Special Issue on Feminist Social Justice Pedagogy (2018); "No Freedom without Connections: Envisioning Sustainable Feminist Solidarities," in *Feminist Freedom Warriors: Genealogies, Justice, Politics, and Hope* (2018); *Between a Rock and Hard Place: Southeast Asian Women Confront Extractivism, Militarism, and Religious Fundamentalisms* (2018); "A 'Nation-ized' Intersectional Analysis: The Politics of Possibility for Student Life," *New Directions for Student Services*, Special Issue on Enacting Intersectionality (2017, Spring); "Critical Ethnic Studies and Gender Studies: Education for Justice, Transformation, and Progressive Social Change," in *The Race Controversy in American Education* (2015); and with Chinyere Oparah (Julia Sudbury), *Activist Scholarship: Anti-racism, Feminism, and Social Change* (2009).

Margo Okazawa-Rey is a founding member of the International Women's Network Against Militarism. She serves on the International Boards of Du Re Bang in Uijongbu (South Korea) and PeaceWomen Across the Globe in Bern (Switzerland), and is a member of the Board of Highlander Research and Education Center in New Market (Tennessee). She received her doctorate from the Harvard Graduate School of Education.